Fodor's 27th Edition

The South

The Guide
for All Budgets

Completely
Updated

Where to Stay, Eat,
and Explore

On and Off
the Beaten Path

When to Go,
What to Pack

Maps, Travel Tips,
and Web Sites

Fodor's Travel Publications • New York, Toronto, London, Sydney, Auckland
www.fodors.com

Fodor's The South

EDITOR: Nuha E. Ansari

Editorial Contributors: Carissa Bluestone, Gene Bourg, Andrew Collins, Robert Flemming, Hollis Gillespie, Paul A. Greenberg, Linda Peal Herbst, Satu Hummasti, Mary Sue Lawrence, Michelle Roberts Matthews, Diane Mehta, Emmanuelle Morgen, Michaela Morrissey, Martha Lucia Rodríguez, Lisa H. Towle

Editorial Production: David Downing

Maps: David Lindroth, *cartographer*; Rebecca Baer, *map editor*

Design: Fabrizio La Rocca, *creative director*; Guido Caroti, *art director*; Jolie Novak, *senior picture editor*; Melanie Marin, *photo editor*

Cover Design: Pentagram

Production/Manufacturing: Yexenia Markland

Cover Photograph: Peter Guttman (Roan Mountain, Blue Ridge Mountains)

Copyright

Important Tip

Although all prices, opening times, and other details in this book are based on information supplied to us at press time, changes occur all the time in the travel world, and Fodor's cannot accept responsibility for facts that become outdated or for inadvertent errors or omissions. So **always confirm information when it matters,** especially if you're making a detour to visit a specific place.

Special Sales

Fodor's Travel Publications are available at special discounts for bulk purchases for sales promotions or premiums. Special editions, including personalized covers, excerpts of existing guides, and corporate imprints, can be created in large quantities for special needs. For more information, contact your local bookseller or write to Special Markets, Fodor's Travel Publications, 1745 Broadway, New York, NY 10019. Inquiries from Canada should be directed to your local Canadian bookseller or sent to Random House of Canada, Ltd., Marketing Department, 2775 Matheson Boulevard East, Mississauga, Ontario L4W 4P7. Inquiries from the United Kingdom should be sent to Fodor's Travel Publications, 20 Vauxhall Bridge Road, London SW1V 2SA, England.

PRINTED IN THE UNITED STATES OF AMERICA

10 9 8 7 6 5 4 3 2 1

CONTENTS

Maps

ON THE ROAD WITH FODOR'S

A trip takes you out of yourself. Concerns of life at home completely disappear, driven away by more immediate thoughts—about, say, what marvels will beguile the next day, or where you'll have dinner. That's where Fodor's comes in. We make sure that you know all your options, so that you don't miss something that's around the next bend just because you didn't know it was there. Mindful that the best memories of your trip might have nothing to do with what you came to the South to see, we guide you to sights large and small all over the region. You might set out to bar-hop on Bourbon Street, but back at home you find yourself unable to forget shuddering through a tour of a French Quarter graveyard and learning to *fais-do-do* in an Uptown music club. With Fodor's at your side, serendipitous discoveries are never far away.

About Our Writers

Our success in showing you every corner of the South is a credit to our extraordinary writers. Although there's no substitute for travel advice from a good friend who knows your style, our contributors are the next best thing—the kind of people you would poll for travel advice if you knew them.

Born to a Creole-Acadian mother with an affinity for cooking, **Gene Bourg** maintains an acute interest in the unique cuisines of New Orleans. "Eating Out" columnist for the *Times-Picayune* from 1985 to 1994, he is currently a freelance food writer and host of *News You Can Eat,* a weekly program on New Orleans radio station WBYU. He adds his insight to our New Orleans dining reviews.

Andy Collins, a former resident of Atlanta, has authored more than a dozen guidebooks, including *Fodor's Gay Guide to the USA.* He updated the Smart Travel Tips chapter. He also writes a syndicated weekly newspaper column and has contributed to *Travel & Leisure* and *The Holland Herald.*

Robert Fleming is a Wilmington-based freelance writer. A transplanted New Jersey native, he quickly discovered the splendor of his adopted state, from the Smokies to the Outer Banks. In addition to updating the North Carolina chapter, Rob has been a regular contributor for Fodor's and has had travel-related articles published in regional periodicals.

Hollis Gillespie was born in Southern California but moved to Atlanta in 1989 and almost immediately swapped her Valley Girl accent for a Southern drawl. A prolific travel writer and foreign-language interpreter, she writes a weekly humor column called "Mood Swings" for *Creative Loafing,* Atlanta's alternative newsweekly.

Mississippi updater **Linda Peal Herbst** is a native Mississippian, and has written extensively about her home state for publications including the Oxford American magazine and Outside magazine. She lives in Oxford, Mississippi.

South Carolina's **Mary Sue Lawrence** is a freelance writer and editor whose features on travel, entertainment, health, and business have appeared in national and British magazines. She is a South Carolina native and a proud descendant of General William Moultrie. She lives in downtown Charleston, and is a frequent Fodor's contributor.

Louisiana updater **Michaela Morrissey,** is a New Orleans-based freelance writer and graphic designer who writes and edits interviews and features for local and national publications.

Alabama updater **Michelle Roberts Matthews** is a Mobile native and lifelong resident of the South. As editor of Mobile Bay Monthly and Coast magazines, she has written numerous features on food, travel, books, homes, and people.

Journalist **Martha Lucia Rodríguez** lives in Nashville. She is a keen traveler and an accomplished hiker, and has written lifestyle and travel articles for numerous publications. She updated the Tennessee chapter in this book.

You can rest assured that you're in good hands—and that no property mentioned in the book has paid to be included. Each has been selected strictly on its merits, as the best of its type in its price range.

How to Use This Book

Up front is Smart Travel Tips A to Z, arranged alphabetically by topic and loaded with tips, Web sites, and contact information. Destination: The South helps get you in the mood for your trip. The Books and Movies section suggests enriching reading and viewing. Subsequent chapters in The South are arranged regionally. All city chapters begin with exploring information, with a section for each neighborhood (each recommending a good tour and listing sights alphabetically). All regional chapters are divided geographically; within each area, towns are covered in logical geographical order, and attractive stretches of road between them are indicated by the designation En Route. To help you decide what you'll have time to visit, all chapters begin with our writers' favorite itineraries. (Mix itineraries from several chapters, and you can put together a really exceptional trip.) The A to Z section that ends every chapter lists additional resources.

Icons and Symbols

★ Our special recommendations
✕ Restaurant
🏠 Lodging establishment
✕🏠 Lodging establishment whose restaurant warrants a special trip
⚘ Campgrounds
☺ Good for kids (rubber duckie)
☞ Sends you to another section of the guide for more information
✉ Address
☎ Telephone number
🕓 Opening and closing times
💰 Admission prices (those we give apply to adults; substantially reduced fees are almost always available for children, students, and senior citizens)

Numbers in white and black circles ③ ❸ that appear on the maps, in the margins, and within the tours correspond to one another.

For hotels, you can assume that all rooms have private baths, phones, TVs, and air-conditioning unless otherwise noted and that all hotels operate on the European Plan (with no meals) if we don't specify another meal plan. We always list a property's facilities but not whether you'll be charged extra to use them, so when pricing accommodations, do ask what's included. For restaurants, it's always a good idea to book ahead; we mention reservations only when they're essential or not accepted. All restaurants we list are open daily for lunch and dinner unless stated otherwise; dress is mentioned only when men are required to wear a jacket or a jacket and tie. Look for an overview of local dining-out habits in Smart Travel Tips A to Z and in the Pleasures and Pastimes section that follows each chapter introduction.

Don't Forget to Write

Your experiences—positive and negative—matter to us. If we have missed or misstated something, we want to hear about it. We follow up on all suggestions. Contact the South editor at editors@fodors. com or c/o Fodor's at 1745 Broadway, New York, New York 10019. And have a fabulous trip!

Karen Cure

Karen Cure
Editorial Director

The South

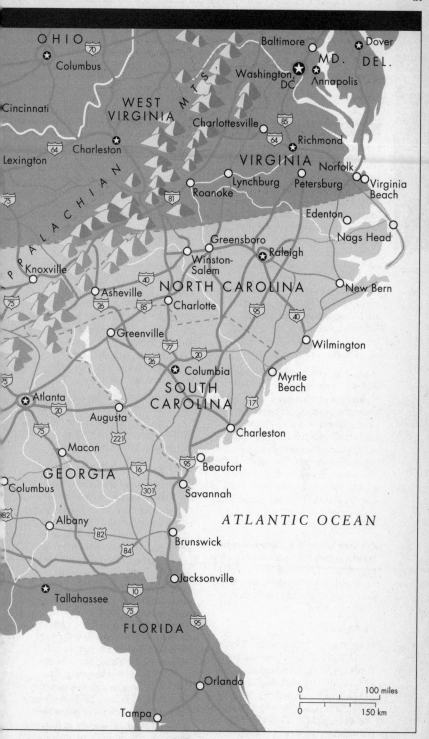

SMART TRAVEL TIPS A TO Z

AIR TRAVEL

BOOKING

Price is just one factor to consider when booking a flight: frequency of service and even a carrier's safety record are often just as important. Major airlines offer the greatest number of departures. Smaller airlines—including regional and no-frills airlines—usually have a limited number of flights daily. On the other hand, so-called low-cost airlines usually are cheaper, and their fares impose fewer restrictions, such as advance-purchase requirements. Safety-wise, low-cost carriers as a group have a good history—about equal to that of major carriers.

When you book **look for nonstop flights** and **remember that "direct" flights stop at least once.** Try to avoid connecting flights, which require a change of plane. Two airlines may operate a connecting flight jointly, so ask if your airline operates every segment of the trip; you may find that the carrier you prefer flies you only part of the way. To find more booking tips and to check prices and make on-line flight reservations, log on to www.fodors.com.

Ask your airline if it offers electronic ticketing, which eliminates all or most paperwork. There's no ticket to pick up or misplace. You go directly to the gate and give the agent your confirmation number.

CARRIERS

➤ MAJOR AIRLINES: **America West** (☎ 800/235–9292). **American** (☎ 800/433–7300). **Continental** (☎ 800/525–0280). **Delta** (☎ 800/221–1212). **Northwest Airlines** (☎ 800/225–2525). **TWA** (☎ 800/221–2000). **United** (☎ 800/241–6522). **US Airways** (☎ 800/428–4322).

For further information on airports and airlines serving the South, see individual state chapters.

➤ SMALLER AIRLINES: **Air Canada** (☎ 800/776–3000). **AirTran** (☎ 770/994–8258 or 800/825–8538). **American Eagle** (☎ 800/433–7300). **America West** (☎ 800/235–9292). **ASA/Delta Connection** (☎ 800/221–1212). **Atlantic Southeast** (☎ 800/221–1212 or 800/282–3424). **ComAir** (☎ 800/221–1212). **Continental Express** (☎ 800/525–0280). **Kiwi** (☎ 800/538–5494). **Markair** (☎ 800/521–9854). **Midway** (☎ 888/226–4392). **Midwest Express** (☎ 800/452–2022). **Northwest Airlink** (☎ 800/225–2525). **Southwest Airlines** (☎ 800/435–9792). **TWA Express** (☎ 800/221–2000). **Western Pacific** (☎ 800/930–3030).

➤ FROM THE U.K.: **American** (☎ 0345/789789), **British Airways** (☎ 0345/222111), and **Delta** (☎ 0800/414767) have direct service to a number of cities in the South.

CHECK-IN AND BOARDING

Always **ask your carrier about its check-in policy.** Plan to arrive at the airport about two hours before your scheduled departure time for domestic flights and 2½ to 3 hours before international flights. Assuming that not everyone with a ticket will show up, airlines routinely overbook planes. When everyone does, airlines ask for volunteers to give up their seats. In return, these volunteers usually get a certificate for a free flight and are rebooked on the next flight out. If there are not enough volunteers, the airline must choose who will be denied boarding. The first to get bumped are passengers who checked in late and those flying on discounted tickets, so **get to the gate and check in as early as possible,** especially during peak periods.

Always **bring a government-issued photo I.D. to the airport;** even when it's not required, a passport is best.

CUTTING COSTS

The least expensive airfares to the South are priced for round-trip travel and must usually be purchased in advance. Airlines generally allow you to change your return date for a fee; most low-fare tickets, however, are nonrefundable. It's smart to **call a number of airlines,** and when you are quoted a good price, **book it on the spot**—the same fare may not be available the next day. Always **check different routings** and look into using alternative airports. Also, price off-peak flights, which may be significantly less expensive than others. Travel agents, especially low-fare specialists (☞ Discounts & Deals, *below*), are helpful.

When flying within the United States, **plan to stay over a Saturday night** and **travel during the middle of the week** to get the lowest fare. These low fares are usually priced for round-trip travel and are nonrefundable. You can, however, change your return date for a fee ($75 on most major airlines).

Consolidators are another good source. They buy tickets for scheduled international flights at reduced rates from the airlines, then sell them at prices that beat the best fare available directly from the airlines. Sometimes you can even get your money back if you need to return the ticket. Carefully read the fine print detailing penalties for changes and cancellations, purchase the ticket with a credit card, and **confirm your consolidator reservation with the airline.**

➤ CONSOLIDATORS: **Cheap Tickets** (☎ 800/377–1000 or 888/922–8849, WEB www.cheaptickets.com). **Discount Airline Ticket Service** (☎ 800/576–1600). **Unitravel** (☎ 800/325–2222, WEB www.unitravel.com). **Up & Away Travel** (☎ 212/889–2345). **World Travel Network** (☎ 800/409–6753).

ENJOYING THE FLIGHT

State your seat preference when purchasing your ticket, and then repeat it when you confirm and when you check in. For more legroom, you can request one of the few emergency-aisle seats at check-in, if you are capable of lifting at least 50 pounds—a Federal Aviation Administration requirement of passengers in these seats. Seats behind a bulkhead also offer more legroom, but they don't have under-seat storage. Don't sit in the row in front of the emergency aisle or in front of a bulkhead, where seats may not recline.

If you have dietary concerns, **ask for special meals when booking.** These can be vegetarian, low-cholesterol, or kosher, for example. It's a good idea to pack some healthful snacks and a small (plastic) bottle of water in your carry-on bag. On long flights, try to maintain a normal routine, to help fight jet lag. At night, **get some sleep.** By day, **eat light meals, drink water** (not alcohol), and **move around the cabin** to stretch your legs. For additional jet-lag tips consult *Fodor's FYI: Travel Fit & Healthy* (available at bookstores everywhere).

Smoking policies vary from carrier to carrier. Many airlines prohibit smoking on all of their international flights; others allow smoking only on certain routes or certain departures. Ask your carrier about its policy.

FLYING TIMES

Flying time to Atlanta is 2½ hours from New York, 2 hours from Chicago, 4½ hours from Los Angeles, 2 hours from Dallas, and 9 hours from London. New Orleans is about 75 minutes southwest of Atlanta by plane, Jackson an hour west, Memphis 75 minutes northwest, Nashville an hour northwest, Knoxville an hour north, Charlotte an hour northeast, Raleigh 75 minutes northeast, Wilmington an hour and 45 minutes east, and Charleston, Hilton Head, and Savannah an hour east–southeast.

HOW TO COMPLAIN

If your baggage goes astray or your flight goes awry, complain right away. Most carriers require that you **file a claim immediately.** The Aviation Consumer Protection Division of the Department of Transportation publishes *Fly-Rights,* which discusses airlines and consumer issues and is available on-line. At PassengerRights. com, a Web site, you can compose a letter of complaint and distribute it electronically.

➤ AIRLINE COMPLAINTS: **Aviation Consumer Protection Division** (✉ U.S. Department of Transportation, Room 4107, C-75, Washington, DC 20590, ☎ 202/366–2220, WEB www. dot.gov/airconsumer). **Federal Aviation Administration Consumer Hotline** (☎ 800/322–7873).

RECONFIRMING

Check the status of your flight before you leave for the airport. You can do this on your carrier's Web site, by linking to a flight-status checker (many Web booking services offer these), or by calling your carrier or travel agent.

AIRPORTS

For information on airports serving the South, see the A to Z sections at the end of each regional section in the individual state chapters.

BIKE TRAVEL

Most of the South is great terrain for biking, in particular South Louisiana, the Mississippi Delta, coastal Georgia, South Carolina, and North Carolina, where hills are few and the scenery remarkable. You'll find a number of extensive, in many cases marked, bike routes throughout North Carolina's Outer Banks, along southern Louisiana's Great River Road, around Savannah and Georgia's coastal islands, and throughout greater Charleston and coastal South Carolina's Low Country. There are dozens of local bike clubs in the South. To reach one of these groups, which generally welcome visitors and can provide detailed advice on local routes and rental shops, contact the local tourist boards, many of which also distribute bike-trail maps.

BIKES IN FLIGHT

Most airlines accommodate bikes as luggage, provided they are dismantled and boxed; check with individual airlines about packing requirements. Airlines sell bike boxes, which are often free at bike shops, for about $15 (bike bags start at $100). International travelers often can substitute a bike for a piece of checked luggage at no charge; otherwise, the cost is

about $100. Domestic and Canadian airlines charge $40–$80 each way.

BUS TRAVEL

Regional bus service, provided by Greyhound, is abundant throughout the South. It's a handy and affordable means of getting around; however, this style of travel prevents the sort of spontaneity and freedom to explore that you're afforded if traveling by car. Still, if it's a simple matter of getting from one city to another and you've got a bit of time on your hands, consider this option. Remember that buses sometimes make frequent stops, which may delay you but may also provide you the chance to see parts of the region you might not otherwise.

Within most large Southern cities, it's possible to use municipal bus service to get around town, but relatively few nonlocals go this route—bus schedules and routes take a bit of learning, and many Southern cities sprawl to a degree that sightseeing this way is impractical. *See* the A to Z sections within regional chapters for specific information on municipal buses.

CUTTING COSTS

Greyhound offers the **Ameripass,** which allows unlimited travel in the United States within any 7-, 10-, 15-, 30-, 45-, or 60-day period ($199–$549, depending on length of the pass), and the similar International Ameripass (for non-U.S. residents only), which offers the same 7- to 60-day passes for $135–$494. Greyhound also has senior-citizen, children's, and student discounts.

FARES AND SCHEDULES

Approximate standard sample fares (based on 14-day advance purchase—prices can be 10% to 50% higher otherwise), times, and routes (note that times vary greatly, depending on the number of stops): Atlanta to New Orleans, 9–11 hours, $45 one-way; Memphis to New Orleans, 9–10 hours, $49 one-way; Lafayette to Mobile, 5–6 hours, $50 one-way; and Raleigh to Savannah, 6–9 hours, $71 one-way.

➤ BUS INFORMATION: **Greyhound** (☎ 800/231–2222, WEB www.greyhound. com).

BUSINESS HOURS

Hours differ little in the South from other parts of the United States. Banks are usually open weekdays from 9 to 3 and some Saturday mornings, the post office from 8 to 5 weekdays and often on Saturday morning. Shops in urban and suburban areas, particularly in indoor and strip malls, typically open at 9 or 10 daily and stay open until anywhere from 6 PM to 10 PM on weekdays and Saturday, and until 5 or 6 on Sunday. Hours vary greatly, so call ahead when in doubt.

On major highways and in densely populated areas you'll usually find at least one or two supermarkets, drugstores, and gas stations open 24 hours, and in a few big cities and also some college towns you'll find a smattering of all-night fast-food restaurants (Waffle House is especially popular in the South among the 24/7 chain eateries), diners, and coffeehouses. In Atlanta a handful of nightclubs are open 24 hours on weekends, and in New Orleans bars are permitted to remain open and serve booze around the clock.

MUSEUMS AND SIGHTS

Most major museums and attractions in big cities are open daily or six days a week (with Monday being the most likely day of closing). Hours are often shorter on Saturdays and Sundays. The South also has scads of smaller museums—historical societies, small art galleries, highly specialized collections—that open only a few days a week, and sometimes by appointment only during the winter or slow season.

PHARMACIES

Smaller local pharmacies tend to close at 6 or 7 PM, have abbreviated Saturday hours, and often don't open on Sundays. That's where the big chain stores (Rite Aid, Walgreens, Kroger supermarkets) come in handy; most are open late if not 24 hours.

CAMERAS
AND PHOTOGRAPHY

The *Kodak Guide to Shooting Great Travel Pictures* (available at bookstores everywhere) is loaded with tips.

➤ PHOTO HELP: Kodak Information Center (☎ 800/242–2424, WEB www.kodak.com).

EQUIPMENT PRECAUTIONS

Don't pack film and equipment in checked luggage, where it is much more susceptible to damage. X-ray machines used to view checked luggage are becoming much more powerful and therefore are much more likely to ruin your film. Try to **ask for hand inspection of film,** especially if your film is 800 speed or higher, as it can become cloudy after successive exposures to airport X-ray machines, and **keep videotapes and computer disks away from metal detectors.** Always **keep film, tape, and computer disks out of the sun.** Carry an extra supply of batteries, and **be prepared to turn on your camera, camcorder, or laptop** to prove to airport security personnel that the device is real.

CAR RENTAL

Rates vary from city to city, generally being lowest in destinations with busy airports, where there's the greatest competition. Below is a range of actual sample rates, for both economy and luxury car rentals, quoted by the most popular agencies in three major Southern cities (note that unlimited mileage is nearly always included):

In Atlanta, daily rates range from about $37 to $52 for an economy car to $76 to $100 for a luxury car; weekly rates range from $190 to $285 for economy to $390 to $530 for luxury. Atlanta has an additional 7% sales tax, and at the airport location an 11% "concession recoupment fee" and a 3% airport excise tax are added on.

In Raleigh, daily rates range from about $28 to $44 for an economy car to $66 to $88 for a luxury car; weekly rates range from $140 to $205 for economy to $350 to $440 for luxury. Raleigh has an additional 8% sales tax and a 5% local transportation tax, and at the airport location there's also a 10% "concession recoupment fee."

In New Orleans, daily rates range from about $35–$44 for an economy car to $60–$90 for a luxury car; weekly rates range from $175–$230 for economy to $320–$415 for luxury. Additionally, in New Orleans there's an 8.75% sales tax, a 3% local transportation tax, and at the airport location there's also the 10% "concession recoupment fee."

Remember to **reserve a car well in advance of your expected arrival.**

➤ MAJOR AGENCIES: **Alamo** (☎ 800/327–9633; 020/8759–6200 in the U.K.; WEB www.alamo.com). **Avis** (☎ 800/331–1212; 800/879–2847 in Canada; 02/9353–9000 in Australia; 09/526–2847 in New Zealand; 0870/606–0100 in the U.K.; WEB www.avis.com). **Budget** (☎ 800/527–0700; 0870/156–5656 in the U.K.; WEB www.budget.com). **Dollar** (☎ 800/800–4000; 0124/622–0111 in the U.K., where it's affiliated with Sixt; 02/9223–1444 in Australia; WEB www.dollar.com). **Hertz** (☎ 800/654–3131; 800/263–0600 in Canada; 020/8897–2072 in the U.K.; 02/9669–2444 in Australia; 09/256–8690 in New Zealand; WEB www.hertz.com). **National Car Rental** (☎ 800/227–7368; 020/8680–4800 in the U.K.; WEB www.nationalcar.com).

CUTTING COSTS

To get the best deal, **book through a travel agent who is willing to shop around.** When pricing cars, **ask about the location of the rental lot.** Some off-airport locations offer lower rates, and their lots are only minutes from the terminal via complimentary shuttle. Also ask whether certain frequent-flyer, AAA, corporate, or other such promotions are accepted and whether the rates might be lower the day before or after you had originally intended to travel. In some cases you'll find that the same agency offers a region's cheapest luxury car rates but priciest economy cars, or that the cheapest agency in one city may have high rates in another. It pays to check around. Think carefully about how much and where you'll be using the car before choosing among economy, compact, standard, luxury, or premium; it may be worth the extra few dollars per day for a more substantial vehicle if you're traveling long distances, driving up into the mountains or over rugged terrain, traveling with more than a couple of passengers, or using the car extensively.

Remember to ask about required deposits, cancellation penalties, and drop-off charges if you're planning to pick up the car in one city and leave it in another.

Also **ask your travel agent about a company's customer-service record.** How has the company responded to late plane arrivals and vehicle mishaps? Are there often lines at the rental counter? If you're traveling during a holiday period, does a confirmed reservation guarantee you a car?

INSURANCE

When driving a rented car you are generally responsible for any damage to or loss of the vehicle. You may also be liable for any property damage or personal injury that you may cause while driving. Before you rent, see what coverage you already have under the terms of your personal auto-insurance policy and credit cards.

For about $15 to $20 a day, rental companies sell protection, known as a collision- or loss-damage waiver (CDW or LDW), that eliminates your liability for damage to the car; it's always optional and should never be automatically added to your bill. In most states you don't need a CDW if you have personal auto insurance or other liability insurance. However, **make sure you have enough coverage to pay for the car.** If you do not have auto insurance or an umbrella policy that covers damage to third parties, purchasing liability insurance and a CDW or LDW is highly recommended.

REQUIREMENTS AND RESTRICTIONS

Most agencies won't rent to you if you're under the age of 21.

SURCHARGES

Before you pick up a car in one city and leave it in another, **ask about drop-off charges or one-way service fees,** which can be substantial. Note, too, that some rental agencies charge extra if you return the car before the time specified in your contract. To avoid a hefty refueling fee, **fill the tank just before you turn in the car,** but be aware that gas stations near the rental outlet may overcharge. It's almost never a deal to buy the tank of gas in the car when you rent it; the understanding is that you'll return it empty, but some fuel usually remains. Surcharges may apply if you're under 25. You'll pay extra for child seats (about $6 a day), which are compulsory for children under five, and for additional drivers (about $5 per day).

CAR TRAVEL

A car is your most practical and economical means of traveling around the South, the only exception being a trip centered primarily in New Orleans, where you can get by with a combination of public transportation and cabs. In Atlanta a car works best because businesses and attractions tend to be far apart and mass-transit coverage spotty. Savannah, Charleston, Myrtle Beach, Nashville, Memphis, and Asheville can be explored fairly easily on foot or by using public transit and cabs, but a car is helpful to reach many of the most intriguing museums, parks, restaurants, and lodgings nearby. You really need a car to get around cities such as Birmingham, Lafayette, Mobile, Raleigh, Durham, Charlotte, and most others.

Although you'll make the best time traveling along the South's extensive network of interstate highways, keep in mind that U.S. and state highways offer some delightful scenery and the opportunity to stumble upon funky roadside diners, leafy state parks, and historic town squares. Although the South is rural, it's still densely populated, so you'll rarely drive for more than 20 or 30 mi—even on local roads—without passing roadside services, such as gas stations, restaurants, and ATMs.

Among the most scenic highways in the South, consider the following: the **Natchez Trace,** from Natchez, Mississippi, to just south of Nashville, Tennessee; **U.S. 78** from Memphis, Tennessee, across northern Mississippi and Alabama to near Augusta, Georgia; the **Great River Road** through southern Louisiana's Cajun Country; **U.S. 61** from New Orleans north through the Mississippi Delta to Memphis; **U.S. 441, 321, 25, 19,** 74, and 64 through the Smoky Mountains of eastern Tennessee and western North Carolina; **U.S. 17** from Brunswick, Georgia, along the coast through South Carolina and North Carolina; and the **Blue Ridge Parkway** from the eastern fringes of the Smoky Mountains through western North Carolina into Virginia.

Here are some common distances and approximate travel times between Southern destinations: Atlanta to New Orleans is 475 mi and about 6½ hours; Nashville to Mobile is 450 mi and 6 hours; Memphis to Raleigh is 750 mi and 10 hours; Nags Head and the Outer Banks of North Carolina to Savannah is 515 mi and 7½ hours; Lake Charles (LA) to the North Carolina/Virginia border on I-95 is 1,150 mi and 15 hours; and Birmingham to Charleston is 465 mi and a little more than six hours.

RULES OF THE ROAD

State lawmakers now set speed limits, even for federal interstate highways. Limits vary from state to state and from rural to urban areas, so **check posted speeds frequently.** The South is laced with busy interstate highways, where speed limits typically reach 65 mph, and gas is cheaper on average in these states than elsewhere in the country.

Always **strap children under age into approved child-safety seats.**

CHILDREN IN THE SOUTH

Most of the South is ideal for travel with kids. It's an enjoyable part of the country for family road trips, and it's also relatively affordable—you'll have no problem finding inexpensive kid-friendly hotels and family-style restaurants. Just keep in mind that a number of fine, antiques-filled bed-and-breakfasts and inns punctuate the landscape, and these places are less suitable for kids—many flat-out refuse to accommodate children. Also, some of the quieter and more rural parts of the region—although exuding history—lack child-oriented attractions.

Favorite destinations for family vacations in the South include Cajun Country around Lafayette, the Gulf

Coast from Mississippi to Alabama, the Atlantic seaboard from Georgia through the Carolinas (especially Myrtle Beach and the Outer Banks), Opryland and the country-music sites in Nashville, the outstanding zoo in Atlanta, the space and rocket center in Huntsville, Mud Island and the Civil Rights Museum in Memphis, and the many lively attractions strung throughout the Smoky Mountains from Chattanooga and Knoxville east to Asheville. You might guess that upscale historic cities such as Charleston and Savannah cater primarily to adults, but these towns also have plenty of museums and attractions geared toward children, as does New Orleans, although parts of the French Quarter are inappropriate—especially at night—for youth.

If you are renting a car, don't forget to **arrange for a car seat** when you reserve. For general advice about traveling with children, consult *Fodor's FYI: Travel with Your Baby* (available in bookstores everywhere).

FLYING

If your children are two or older, **ask about children's airfares.** As a general rule, infants under two not occupying a seat fly at greatly reduced fares or even for free.

Experts agree that it's a good idea to use safety seats aloft for children weighing less than 40 pounds. Airlines set their own policies: U.S. carriers usually require that the child be ticketed, even if he or she is young enough to ride free, since the seats must be strapped into regular seats. Do **check your airline's policy about using safety seats during takeoff and landing.** Safety seats are not allowed everywhere in the plane, so get your seat assignments as early as possible.

When reserving, **request children's meals or a freestanding bassinet** (not available at all airlines) if you need them. But note that bulkhead seats, where you must sit to use the bassinet, may lack an overhead bin or storage space on the floor.

GROUP TRAVEL

When planning to take your kids on a tour, look for companies that specialize in family travel.

➤ FAMILY-FRIENDLY TOUR OPERATORS: **Families Welcome!** (✉ 92 N. Main St., Ashland, OR 97520, ☎ 541/482–6121 or 800/326–0724, FAX 541/482–0660).

LODGING

Most hotels in the South allow children under a certain age to stay in their parents' room at no extra charge, but others charge for them as extra adults; be sure to **find out the cutoff age for children's discounts.**

SIGHTS AND ATTRACTIONS

Places that are especially appealing to children are indicated by a rubber-duckie icon (🦆) in the margin.

CONSUMER PROTECTION

Whether you're shopping for gifts or purchasing travel services, **pay with a major credit card** whenever possible, so you can cancel payment or get reimbursed if there's a problem (and you can provide documentation). If you're doing business with a particular company for the first time, **contact your local Better Business Bureau and the attorney general's offices** in your state and (for U.S. businesses) the company's home state as well. Have any complaints been filed? Finally, if you're buying a package or tour, always **consider travel insurance** that includes default coverage (☞ Insurance, *below*).

➤ BBBs: **Council of Better Business Bureaus** (✉ 4200 Wilson Blvd., Suite 800, Arlington, VA 22203, ☎ 703/276–0100, FAX 703/525–8277, WEB www.bbb.org).

CUSTOMS AND DUTIES

IN AUSTRALIA

Australian residents who are 18 or older may bring home A$400 worth of souvenirs and gifts (including jewelry), 250 cigarettes or 250 grams of tobacco, and 1,125 ml of alcohol (including wine, beer, and spirits). Residents under 18 may bring back A$200 worth of goods. Prohibited items include meat products. Seeds, plants, and fruits need to be declared upon arrival.

➤ INFORMATION: **Australian Customs Service** (Regional Director, ✉ Box 8, Sydney, NSW 2001, ☎ 02/9213–

2000, FAX 02/9213–4000, WEB www.customs.gov.au).

IN CANADA

Canadian residents who have been out of Canada for at least seven days may bring in C$750 worth of goods duty-free. If you've been away fewer than seven days but more than 48 hours, the duty-free allowance drops to C$200; if your trip lasts 24 to 48 hours, the allowance is C$50. You may not pool allowances with family members. Goods claimed under the C$750 exemption may follow you by mail; those claimed under the lesser exemptions must accompany you. Alcohol and tobacco products may be included in the seven-day and 48-hour exemptions but not in the 24-hour exemption. If you meet the age requirements of the province or territory through which you reenter Canada, you may bring in, duty-free, 1.5 liters of wine or 1.14 liters (40 imperial ounces) of liquor or 24 12-ounce cans or bottles of beer or ale. If you are 19 or older you may bring in, duty-free, 200 cigarettes and 50 cigars. Check ahead of time with the Canada Customs and Revenue Agency or the Department of Agriculture for policies regarding meat products, seeds, plants, and fruits.

You may send an unlimited number of gifts (only one gift per recipient, however) worth up to C$60 each duty-free to Canada. Label the package UNSOLICITED GIFT—VALUE UNDER $60. Alcohol and tobacco are excluded.

➤ INFORMATION: **Canada Customs and Revenue Agency** (✉ 2265 St. Laurent Blvd. S, Ottawa, Ontario K1G 4K3, ☎ 204/983–3500; 506/636–5064; 800/461–9999 in Canada, WEB www.ccra-adrc.gc.ca).

IN NEW ZEALAND

All homeward-bound residents may bring back NZ$700 worth of souvenirs and gifts; passengers may not pool their allowances, and children can claim only the concession on goods intended for their own use. For those 17 or older, the duty-free allowance also includes 4.5 liters of wine or beer; one 1,125-ml bottle of spirits; and either 200 cigarettes, 250 grams of tobacco, 50 cigars, or a

combination of the three up to 250 grams. Meat products, seeds, plants, and fruits must be declared upon arrival to the Agricultural Services Department.

➤ INFORMATION: **New Zealand Customs** (✉ Head Office, The Customhouse, 17–21 Whitmore St., Box 2218, Wellington, ☎ 09/300–5399, WEB www.customs.govt.nz).

IN THE U.K.

From countries outside the European Union, including the United States, you may bring home, duty-free, 200 cigarettes or 50 cigars; 1 liter of spirits or 2 liters of fortified or sparkling wine or liqueurs; 2 liters of still table wine; 60 ml of perfume; 250 ml of toilet water; plus £145 worth of other goods, including gifts and souvenirs. Prohibited items include meat products, seeds, plants, and fruits.

➤ INFORMATION: **HM Customs and Excise** (✉ St. Christopher House, Southwark, London SE1 OTE, ☎ 020/7928–3344, WEB www.hmce.gov.uk).

DINING

Although certain ingredients and preparations are common in Southern cooking, the genre as a whole varies greatly not only from state to state but also from county to county. Nevertheless, in the South you'll often find restaurants serving black-eyed peas, catfish, chitlins (fried tripe), corn on the cob, crab claws, coleslaw, crawfish, fried chicken, hush puppies, fried green tomatoes, grits, collard greens, chicken-fried steak, raw and fried shellfish (especially oysters and shrimp), and desserts infused with pecans, peaches, peanuts, caramelized bananas, or sweet potatoes.

More specific regional influences include similar but distinct Creole and Cajun cuisines of southern Louisiana, the soul food served in many African-American households, the coastal recipes of the Low Country in the Carolinas, and—of course—barbecue. However, the preparation of this latter delicacy differs tremendously, depending on whether you're in the Mississippi Delta, central Tennessee, the pine flats of North Carolina, or some other part of the South. Depending on where you are, you might find it prepared with shredded pork in a tomato-vinegar-based sauce, or perhaps with a mustard-based sauce and chicken or beef. The South's myriad culinary disciplines intermingle and influence one another, but Southern foodies are quite careful to recognize—and preserve—the localized distinctions among them.

A number of fast-food chain eateries are based in the South. These include the Krispy Kreme doughnut chain (Winston-Salem, North Carolina), Shoney's (Nashville, Tennessee), Cracker Barrel (Lebanon, Tennessee), Waffle House (Atlanta), Hardee's (Greenville, North Carolina), Popeye's (New Orleans), and Chick-fil-A (Atlanta). Indeed, Southerners take their fast food seriously, and you'll find that many branches of these chain restaurants offer not only simple, quick sustenance but also a colorful, aromatic, and more than likely fattening glimpse into regional identities.

You'll also likely to encounter hearty and filling, if at times greasy, cuisine at most of the affordable luncheonettes, diners, and family-style eateries that proliferate in rural, suburban, and urban areas. Over the past couple of decades, most Southern cities—especially boomtowns such as Atlanta, Charleston, New Orleans, Savannah, and Charlotte—have partaken of the nation's culinary revolution. In these parts you'll discover regional ingredients and time-honored recipes running head-on with inventive twists and foods and styles borrowed from myriad faraway places, from Latin America to the Mediterranean. Chefs who dabble in such creative practices often dub their fare "New Southern" or a term along these lines. It's no gimmick. Some of America's finest culinary talents operate restaurants in the South, in big cities, of course, but also in a surprising number of tiny, off-the-beaten-path hamlets.

The restaurants we list are the cream of the crop in each price category. Properties indicated by a ✕🏠 are lodging establishments whose restaurant warrants a special trip.

In general, when you order a regular coffee, you get coffee with milk and sugar. Iced tea is usually served sweetened.

RESERVATIONS AND DRESS

Reservations are always a good idea; we mention them only when they're essential or not accepted. Book as far ahead as you can, and reconfirm as soon as you arrive. (Large parties should always call ahead to check the reservations policy.) We mention dress only when men are required to wear a jacket or a jacket and tie.

DISABILITIES AND ACCESSIBILITY

The South ranks on a par with the rest of America in its accessibility for people with disabilities or special needs. A drawback is the abundance of historic accommodations, restaurants, and attractions with narrow staircases, doorways, and small rooms that fail to conform to the Americans with Disabilities Act's (ADA) guidelines. Increasingly, however, businesses throughout the South—especially those in densely populated areas—are changing to improve accessibility.

LODGING

Despite the Americans with Disabilities Act, the definition of accessibility seems to differ from hotel to hotel. Some properties may be accessible by ADA standards for people with mobility problems but not for people with hearing or vision impairments, for example.

If you have mobility problems, ask for the lowest floor on which accessible services are offered. If you have a hearing impairment, check whether the hotel has devices to alert you visually to the ring of the telephone, knock at the door, and a fire/emergency alarm. Some hotels provide these devices without charge. Discuss your needs with hotel personnel if this equipment isn't available, so that a staff member can personally alert you in the event of an emergency.

If you're bringing a guide dog, get authorization ahead of time and write down the name of the person you spoke with.

RESERVATIONS

When discussing accessibility with an operator or reservations agent, **ask hard questions.** Are there any stairs, inside *or* out? Are there grab bars next to the toilet *and* in the shower/tub? How wide is the doorway to the room? To the bathroom? For the most extensive facilities meeting the latest legal specifications, **opt for newer accommodations.** If you reserve through a toll-free number, consider also calling the hotel's local number to confirm the information from the central reservations office. Get confirmation in writing when you can.

➤ COMPLAINTS: **Aviation Consumer Protection Division** (☞ Air Travel, *above*) for airline-related problems. **Departmental Office of Civil Rights** (for general inquiries, ⊠ U.S. Department of Transportation, S-30, 400 7th St. SW, Room 10215, Washington, DC 20590, ☎ 202/366–4648, FAX 202/366–9371, WEB www.dot.gov/ost/docr/index.htm). **Disability Rights Section** (⊠ U.S. Department of Justice, Civil Rights Division, Box 66738, Washington, DC 20035-6738, ☎ 202/514–0301 or 800/514–0301, for ADA inquiries; WEB www.usdoj.gov/crt/ada/adahom1.htm).

TRAVEL AGENCIES

In the United States, the Americans with Disabilities Act requires that travel firms serve the needs of all travelers. Some agencies specialize in working with people with disabilities.

➤ TRAVELERS WITH MOBILITY PROBLEMS: **Access Adventures** (⊠ 206 Chestnut Ridge Rd., Scottsville, NY 14624, ☎ 716/889–9096), run by a former physical-rehabilitation counselor. **Accessible Vans of America** (⊠ 9 Spielman Rd., Fairfield, NJ 07004, ☎ 877/282–8267; 888/282–8267 reservations, FAX 973/808–9713, WEB www.accessiblevans.com). **CareVacations** (⊠ No. 5, 5110–50 Ave., Leduc, Alberta T9E 6V4, Canada, ☎ 780/986–6404 or 877/478–7827, FAX 780/986–8332, WEB www.carevacations.com), for group tours and cruise vacations. **Flying Wheels Travel** (⊠ 143 W. Bridge St., Box 382, Owatonna, MN 55060, ☎ 507/451–5005 or 800/535–6790, FAX 507/451–1685, WEB www.flyingwheelstravel.com).

DISCOUNTS AND DEALS

Be a smart shopper and **compare all your options** before making decisions. A plane ticket bought with a promotional coupon from travel clubs, coupon books, and direct-mail offers or purchased on the Internet may not be cheaper than the least expensive fare from a discount ticket agency. And always keep in mind that what you get is just as important as what you save.

CREDIT-CARD BENEFITS

When you use your credit card to make travel purchases, you may get free travel-accident insurance, collision-damage insurance, and medical or legal assistance, depending on the card and the bank that issued it. American Express, MasterCard, and Visa provide one or more of these services, so **get a copy of your credit card's travel-benefits policy.** If you are a member of an auto club, always **ask hotel and car-rental reservations agents about auto-club discounts.** Some clubs offer additional discounts on tours, cruises, and admission to attractions.

DISCOUNT RESERVATIONS

To save money, **look into discount reservations services** with Web sites and toll-free numbers, which use their buying power to get a better price on hotels, airline tickets, even car rentals. When booking a room, always **call the hotel's local toll-free number** (if one is available) rather than the central reservations number—you'll often get a better price. Always ask about special packages or corporate rates.

➤ AIRLINE TICKETS: ☎ **800/AIR–4LESS.**

➤ HOTEL ROOMS: **Accommodations Express** (☎ 800/444–7666, WEB www.accommodationsexpress.com). **Central Reservation Service** (CRS; ☎ 800/548–3311, WEB www.roomconnection.net). **Hotel Reservations Network** (☎ 800/964–6835, WEB www.hoteldiscount.com). **Quikbook** (☎ 800/789–9887, WEB www.quikbook.com). **RMC Travel** (☎ 800/245–5738, WEB www.rmcwebtravel.com). **Steigenberger Reservation Service** (☎ 800/223–

5652, WEB www.srs-worldhotels.
com). **Turbotrip.com** (☎ 800/473–
7829, WEB www.turbotrip.com).

PACKAGE DEALS

Don't confuse packages with guided
tours. When you buy a package, you
travel on your own, just as though
you had planned the trip yourself.
Fly/drive packages, which combine
airfare and car rental, are often a
good deal.

GAY AND LESBIAN TRAVEL

Attitudes about gays and lesbians
tend toward disapproving, if intoler-
ant, in parts of the South, especially
outside urban areas. On the whole,
however, despite a reputation for
conservative-minded residents, this
part of the country is not any more
hostile or dangerous for lesbians and
gays—traveling solo or together—
than the rest of the United States. It's
prudent, however, to show an awareness of your surroundings and exercise a degree of discretion whenever
you're venturing into unfamiliar
territory.

As for lesbian and gay resources, there
are several major newspapers serving
the community throughout the South,
including *Southern Voice,* in Atlanta,
and *Impact* and *Ambush,* in New
Orleans, plus a host of smaller local
papers in Memphis, Nashville, Birmingham, and in the Carolinas. The
gay nightlife and social scenes in New
Orleans and Atlanta rival those of
virtually any comparably sized cities
in North America, and you'll also find
thriving gay communities of varying
sizes in Savannah, Charlotte,
Charleston, Raleigh/Durham,
Nashville, Memphis, Birmingham,
and Columbia. With a much lower
profile than most cities with gay
populations, Asheville is something of
a well-kept secret, with sizable
women's and gay communities and a
high number of gay-friendly businesses and accommodations.

For details about the gay and lesbian
scene, consult *Fodor's Gay Guide to
the USA* (available in bookstores
everywhere). The book provides
information on the gay scenes in
Asheville, Atlanta, Birmingham,
Charleston, Charlotte, Memphis,

Mississippi's Gulf Coast, Mobile,
Nashville, New Orleans, Oxford
(MS), Raleigh–Durham, and Savan-
nah.

➤ GAY- AND LESBIAN-FRIENDLY TRAVEL
AGENCIES: **Different Roads Travel**
(✉ 8383 Wilshire Blvd., Suite 902,
Beverly Hills, CA 90211, ☎ 323/
651–5557 or 800/429–8747, FAX 323/
651–3678). **Kennedy Travel** (✉ 314
Jericho Turnpike, Floral Park, NY
11001, ☎ 516/352–4888 or 800/
237–7433, FAX 516/354–8849,
WEB www.kennedytravel.com). **Now,
Voyager** (✉ 4406 18th St., San Francisco, CA 94114, ☎ 415/626–1169
or 800/255–6951, FAX 415/626–8626,
WEB www.nowvoyager.com). **Skylink
Travel and Tour** (✉ 1006 Mendocino
Ave., Santa Rosa, CA 95401, ☎ 707/
546–9888 or 800/225–5759, FAX 707/
546–9891, WEB www.skylinktravel.
com), serving lesbian travelers.

GUIDEBOOKS

Plan well and you won't be sorry.
Guidebooks are excellent tools—and
you can take them with you. You may
want to check out *Fodor's Road
Guide USA: Georgia, North Carolina, South Carolina,* which has
comprehensive restaurant, hotel, and
attractions listings for driving vacations. The color-photo-illustrated
*Compass American Guides: New
Orleans, Compass American Guides:
Georgia, Compass American Guides:
North Carolina,* and *Compass American Guides: South Carolina* are
thorough on culture and history and
available at on-line retailers and
bookstores everywhere.

HEALTH

There are relatively few health issues
specific to the South. Hospitals are as
common and medical care as profi-
cient as elsewhere in the United
States.

PESTS AND OTHER HAZARDS

In coastal regions, especially along the
Atlantic seaboard, swimmers and
boaters should be respectful of the at-
times powerful surf. Adhere to posted
riptide warnings, and to be perfectly
safe, stick with areas that have lifeguards. Summers can be exceptionally
hot and humid throughout much of
the South—wear light-color, loose-

fitting, practical clothing during the summer months, drink plenty of fluids (and bring along bottled water on hikes, boat trips, and bike rides), and stay indoors during the hottest times of the day.

Mosquitoes, seasonal black flies, and just about every other flitting and annoying insect known to North America proliferates in the humid and often lush Southern states. Exercise common precautions and wear lotions or sprays that keep away such pests.

Although you might associate Lyme disease with New England, where it was first well documented, this relatively common and potentially dangerous disease strikes frequently in the South, too. Lyme disease is spread by bites from infinitesimal deer ticks. Symptoms, unfortunately, vary considerably from victim to victim, and one common problem is delayed diagnosis—the longer you go without treating this problem, the more severe its effects.

Most victims show a red-ring-shape rash around the bite from the deer tick, somewhat resembling a little bull's eye and appearing from a week to many weeks after the incident. Flulike symptoms often follow—fever, achy joints, swelling, and if left untreated for more than a couple of months, chronic arthritis may set in.

Unfortunately, testing for Lyme disease is a sketchy business at best, as no definitive method has yet been developed. Doctors typically rely on a series of blood tests and even more often on observation of various symptoms.

When spending time in areas **where tick infestation is a problem, wear long-sleeve clothing** and slacks, tuck your pant legs into your boots and/or socks, **apply tick and insect repellent generously,** and check yourself carefully for signs of ticks or bites. It's a good idea to don light-color clothing, as you'll have an easier time sighting ticks, which are dark. Remember that the more commonly found wood ticks do not carry the disease, and that deer ticks are extremely small—about the size of a pinhead.

HOLIDAYS

Major national holidays include New Year's Day (Jan. 1); Martin Luther King, Jr., Day (3rd Mon. in Jan.); Presidents' Day (3rd Mon. in Feb.); Memorial Day (last Mon. in May); Independence Day (July 4); Labor Day (1st Mon. in Sept.); Thanksgiving Day (4th Thurs. in Nov.); Christmas Eve and Christmas Day (Dec. 24 and 25); and New Year's Eve (Dec. 31).

INSURANCE

The most useful travel-insurance plan is a comprehensive policy that includes coverage for trip cancellation and interruption, default, trip delay, and medical expenses (with a waiver for preexisting conditions).

Without insurance you will lose all or most of your money if you cancel your trip, regardless of the reason. Default insurance covers you if your tour operator, airline, or cruise line goes out of business. Trip-delay covers expenses that arise because of bad weather or mechanical delays. Study the fine print when comparing policies.

U.K. residents can buy a travel-insurance policy valid for most vacations taken during the year in which it's purchased (but check preexisting-condition coverage).

Always **buy travel policies directly from the insurance company**; if you buy them from a cruise line, airline, or tour operator that goes out of business you probably will not be covered for the agency or operator's default, a major risk. Before making any purchase, **review your existing health and home-owner's policies** to find what they cover away from home.

➤ TRAVEL INSURERS: In the U.S.: **Access America** (✉ 6600 W. Broad St., Richmond, VA 23230, ☎ 800/284–8300, ℻ 804/673–1491 or 800/346–9265, WEB www.etravelprotection.com). **Travel Guard International** (✉ 1145 Clark St., Stevens Point, WI 54481, ☎ 800/826–1300; 715/345–0505 international callers, ℻ 800/955–8785, WEB www.travelguard.com).

FOR INTERNATIONAL TRAVELERS

For information on customs restrictions, *see* Customs & Duties, *above.*

CAR RENTAL

When picking up a rental car, non-U. S. residents need a reservation voucher for any prepaid reservations that were made in the traveler's home country, a passport, a driver's license, and a travel policy that covers each driver.

CAR TRAVEL

In the South gasoline costs anywhere from $.90 to $1.50 a gallon. Stations are plentiful. Most stay open late (24 hours along large highways and in big cities), except in rural areas, where Sunday hours are limited and where you may drive long stretches without a refueling opportunity. Highways are well paved. Interstate highways—limited-access, multilane highways whose numbers are prefixed by "I–"—are the fastest routes. Interstates with three-digit numbers encircle urban areas, which may have other limited-access expressways, freeways, and parkways as well. Tolls may be levied on limited-access highways. So-called U.S. highways and state highways are not necessarily limited-access but may have several lanes.

Along larger highways, roadside stops with rest rooms, fast-food restaurants, and sundries stores are well spaced. State police and tow trucks patrol major highways and lend assistance. If your car breaks down on an interstate, pull onto the shoulder and wait for help, or have your passengers wait while you walk to an emergency phone. If you carry a cell phone, dial *55, noting your location on the small green roadside mileage markers.

Driving in the United States is on the right. Do **obey speed limits** posted along roads and highways. Watch for lower limits in small towns and on back roads. Most states require front-seat passengers to wear seat belts. Always **strap children under age 3 into approved child-safety seats.** *See* individual state chapters' A to Z sections for specific information. On weekdays between 6 and 10 AM and again between 4 and 7 PM **expect heavy traffic,** especially in big cities such as Atlanta, New Orleans, and Charlotte. To encourage car pooling, some freeways have special lanes for so-called high-occupancy vehicles (HOV)—cars carrying more than one passenger.

Bookstores, gas stations, convenience stores, and rest stops sell maps (about $3) and multiregion road atlases (about $10).

CONSULATES AND EMBASSIES

➤ AUSTRALIA: **Australian Embassy** (1601 Massachusetts Ave. NW, Washington, DC 20036, ☎ 202/797–3000).

➤ CANADA: **Canadian Embassy** (501 Pennsylvania Ave. NW, Washington, DC 20001, ☎ 202/682–1740).

➤ NEW ZEALAND: **New Zealand Embassy** (37 Observatory Circle NW, Washington, DC 20008, ☎ 202/328–4800).

➤ UNITED KINGDOM: **British Embassy** (19 Observatory Circle NW, Washington, DC 20008, ☎ 202/588–7800).

CURRENCY

The dollar is the basic unit of U.S. currency. It has 100 cents. Coins include the copper penny (1¢); the silvery nickel (5¢), dime (10¢), quarter (25¢), and half-dollar (50¢); and the golden $1 coin, replacing a now-rare silver dollar. Bills are denominated $1, $5, $10, $20, $50, and $100, all green and identical in size; designs vary. The exchange rate at press time was US$1.45 per British pound, US$.64 per Canadian dollar, US$.54 per Australian dollar, and US$.45 per New Zealand dollar.

ELECTRICITY

The U.S. standard is AC, 110 volts/60 cycles. Plugs have two flat pins set parallel to each other.

EMERGENCIES

For police, fire, or ambulance, **dial 911** (0 in rural areas).

INSURANCE

Britons and Australians need extra medical coverage when traveling overseas.

➤ INSURANCE INFORMATION: In the U. K.: **Association of British Insurers** (⊠ 51 Gresham St., London EC2V 7HQ, ☎ 020/7600–3333, FAX 020/7696–8999, WEB www.abi.org.uk). In Australia: **Insurance Council of Australia** (⊠ Level 3, 56 Pitt St., Sydney, NSW 2000, ☎ 02/9253–5100, FAX 02/9253–5111, WEB www.ica.com.au). In Canada: **RBC Insurance** (⊠ 6880 Financial Dr., Mississauga, Ontario L5N 7Y5, ☎ 905/816–2400 or 800/668–4342, FAX 905/813–4704, WEB www.rbcinsurance.com). In New Zealand: **Insurance Council of New Zealand** (⊠ Level 7, 111–115 Customhouse Quay, Box 474, Wellington, ☎ 04/472–5230, FAX 04/473–3011, WEB www.icnz.org.nz).

MAIL AND SHIPPING

You can buy stamps and aerograms and send letters and parcels in post offices. Stamp-dispensing machines can occasionally be found in airports, bus and train stations, office buildings, drugstores, and the like. You can also deposit mail in the stout, dark blue, steel bins at strategic locations everywhere and in the mail chutes of large buildings; pickup schedules are posted.

For mail sent within the United States, you need a 37¢ stamp for first-class letters weighing up to 1 ounce (23¢ for each additional ounce) and 23¢ for domestic postcards. For overseas mail, you pay 80¢ for 1-ounce airmail letters, 70¢ for airmail postcards, and 35¢ for surface-rate postcards. For Canada and Mexico you need a 60¢ stamp for a 1-ounce letter and 50¢ for a postcard. For 70¢ you can buy an aerogram—a single sheet of lightweight blue paper that folds into its own envelope, stamped for overseas airmail.

To receive mail on the road, have it sent c/o General Delivery at your destination's main post office (use the correct five-digit ZIP code). You must pick up mail in person within 30 days and show a driver's license or passport.

PASSPORTS AND VISAS

When traveling internationally, **carry your passport** even if you don't need one (it's always the best form of I.D.) and **make two photocopies of the data page** (one for someone at home and another for you, carried separately from your passport). If you lose your passport, promptly call the nearest embassy or consulate and the local police.

Visitor visas are not necessary for Canadian citizens, or for citizens of Australia and the United Kingdom who are staying fewer than 90 days.

➤ AUSTRALIAN CITIZENS: **Australian State Passport Office** (☎ 131–232, WEB www.dfat.gov.au/passports). **United States Consulate General** (⊠ MLC Centre, 19–29 Martin Pl., 59th floor, Sydney, NSW 2000, ☎ 1902/941–641 visa-inquiry line, WEB www.usis-australia.gov/consular/visas.html).

➤ CANADIAN CITIZENS: **Passport Office** (☎ 819/994–3500; 800/567–6868 in Canada).

➤ NEW ZEALAND CITIZENS: **New Zealand Passport Office** (☎ 04/494–0700; 04/474–8100 for application procedures, WEB www.passports.govt.nz). **Embassy of the United States** (⊠ 29 Fitzherbert Terr., Thorndon, Wellington, ☎ 04/462–6000, WEB usembassy.state.gov/wellington). **United States Consulate General** (⊠ Citibank Center, 3rd floor, 23 Customs St. E, Auckland, ☎ 09/303–2724, WEB www.usembassy.state.gov/wellington).

➤ U.K. CITIZENS: **London Passport Office** (☎ 0870/521–0410, WEB www.ukpa.gov.uk), for application procedures and emergency passports. **U.S. Consulate General** (⊠ Queen's House, 14 Queen St., Belfast BTI 6E2, Northern Ireland). **U.S. Embassy Visa Branch** (⊠ 5 Upper Grosvenor St., London W1A 2JB); send a self-addressed, stamped envelope. **U.S. Embassy Visa Information Line** (☎ 09068/200–290 or 020/7355–3335, WEB www.usembassy.org.uk).

TELEPHONES

All U.S. telephone numbers consist of a three-digit area code and a seven-digit local number. Within many local calling areas, dial only the seven-digit number; but in larger cities or regions with more than one area code (such as Atlanta and Charlotte), dial "1" then all 10 digits for both local and long-distance calls. To call between area-code regions, dial "1" then all 10 digits; the same goes for calls to numbers prefixed by "800," "888," "877," and "866"—all toll free. For calls to numbers preceded by "900" you must pay—usually dearly.

For international calls, dial "011" followed by the country code and the local number. For help, dial "0" and ask for an overseas operator. The country code is 61 for Australia, 64 for New Zealand, 44 for the United Kingdom. Calling Canada is the same as calling within the United States. Most local phone books list country codes and U.S. area codes. The country code for the United States is 1.

For operator assistance, dial "0." To obtain someone's phone number, call directory assistance, 555–1212 or occasionally 411 (free at some public phones). To have the person you're calling foot the bill, phone collect; dial "0" instead of "1" before the 10-digit number.

At pay phones, instructions are usually posted. Usually you insert coins in a slot (25¢–50¢ for local calls) and wait for a steady tone before dialing. When you call long-distance, the operator will tell you how much to insert; prepaid phone cards, widely available in various denominations, are easier and usually much more cost-effective. Follow the instructions on the back of the card.

LODGING

With the exception of Atlanta, New Orleans, Savannah, and Charleston, most lodging rates in the South fall below the national average. All major chains are well represented in this part of the country, both in cities and suburbs, and interstates are lined with inexpensive to moderate chains. It's not uncommon to find clean but extremely basic discount chains offering double rooms for as little as $25 to $30 nightly along the busiest highways.

In cities and some large towns you might want to forgo the usual cookie-cutter modern hotel in favor of a historic property—there are dozens of fine old hotels throughout the South, many of them fully restored and quite a few offering better rates than chain

properties that may have comparable amenities but nowhere near the ambience.

Rates can vary a great deal seasonally. Gulf and Atlantic coastal regions as well as the Smoky Mountains tend to have significantly higher rates in summer, and New Orleans peaks in fall and spring (especially during Mardi Gras). Many Southern cities, including New Orleans, drop their rates a bit during the extremely hot summer months, when vacationers are more likely to flock to the mountains or the sea.

Assume that hotels operate on the **European Plan** (EP, with no meals) unless we specify that they use the **Continental Plan** (CP, with a Continental breakfast), **Breakfast Plan** (BP, with a full breakfast), **Modified American Plan** (MAP, with breakfast and dinner), or the **Full American Plan** (FAP, with all meals).

APARTMENT AND VILLA [OR HOUSE] RENTALS

If you want a home base that's roomy enough for a family and comes with cooking facilities, **consider a furnished rental.** These can save you money, especially if you're traveling with a group. Home-exchange directories sometimes list rentals as well as exchanges.

➤ INTERNATIONAL AGENTS: **Hideaways International** (✉ 767 Islington St., Portsmouth, NH 03801, ☎ 603/430–4433 or 800/843–4433, FAX 603/430–4444, WEB www.hideaways.com; membership $129). **Vacation Home Rentals Worldwide** (✉ 235 Kensington Ave., Norwood, NJ 07648, ☎ 201/767–9393 or 800/633–3284, FAX 201/767–5510, WEB www.vhrww.com).

BED AND BREAKFASTS AND INNS

Historic bed-and-breakfasts and inns are found in just about every region in the South, including in quite a few former plantation houses and lavish Southern estates. In many rural or less touristy areas, B&Bs offer an affordable and homey alternative to chain properties, but in tourism-dependent destinations you can expect to pay about the same or more for a historic inn as for a full-service hotel. Many of the South's finest restaurants are also found in country inns. Although many B&Bs and smaller establishments offer a low-key, homey experience without TVs or numerous amenities, the scene has changed greatly in recent years, especially in cities and upscale resort areas, where many such properties now attempt to cater to business and luxury leisure travelers with in-room data ports, voice mail, whirlpool tubs, and VCRs. In keeping with the South's fondness for filling meals, quite a few inns and B&Bs serve substantial full breakfasts—the kind that may keep your appetite in check for the better part of the day.

CAMPING

The South is popular both for RVing and tent camping, with facilities found throughout the region, especially in state and national parks, and extensively throughout the Atlantic and Gulf coasts.

HOME EXCHANGES

If you would like to exchange your home for someone else's, **join a home-exchange organization,** which will send you its updated listings of available exchanges for a year and will include your own listing in at least one of them. It's up to you to make specific arrangements.

➤ EXCHANGE CLUBS: **HomeLink International** (✉ Box 47747, Tampa, FL 33647, ☎ 813/975–9825 or 800/638–3841, ℻ 813/910–8144, 𝖶𝖤𝖡 www.homelink.org; $106 per year). **Intervac U.S.** (✉ Box 590504, San Francisco, CA 94159, ☎ 800/756–4663, ℻ 415/435–7440, 𝖶𝖤𝖡 www.intervacus.com; $93 yearly fee includes one catalog and on-line access).

HOSTELS

No matter what your age, you can **save on lodging costs by staying at hostels.** In some 4,500 locations in more than 70 countries around the world, Hostelling International (HI), the umbrella group for a number of national youth-hostel associations, offers single-sex, dorm-style beds and, at many hostels, rooms for couples and family accommodations. Membership in any HI national hostel

association, open to travelers of all ages, allows you to stay in HI-affiliated hostels at member rates; one-year membership is about $25 for adults (C$35 for a two-year minimum membership in Canada, £12.50 in the U.K., A$52 in Australia, and NZ$40 in New Zealand); hostels run about $10–$25 per night. Members have priority if the hostel is full; they're also eligible for discounts around the world, even on rail and bus travel in some countries.

➤ ORGANIZATIONS: **Hostelling International—American Youth Hostels** (✉ 733 15th St. NW, Suite 840, Washington, DC 20005, ☎ 202/783–6161, ℻ 202/783–6171, 𝖶𝖤𝖡 www.hiayh.org). **Hostelling International—Canada** (✉ 400–205 Catherine St., Ottawa, Ontario K2P 1C3, ☎ 613/237–7884; 800/663–5777 in Canada, ℻ 613/237–7868, 𝖶𝖤𝖡 www.hihostels.ca). **Youth Hostel Association of England and Wales** (✉ Trevelyan House, 8 St. Stephen's Hill, St. Albans, Hertfordshire AL1 2DY, U.K., ☎ 0870/8708808, ℻ 01727/844126, 𝖶𝖤𝖡 www.yha.org.uk). **Youth Hostel Association Australia** (✉ 10 Mallett St., Camperdown, NSW 2050, ☎ 02/9565–1699, ℻ 02/9565–1325, 𝖶𝖤𝖡 www.yha.com.au). **Youth Hostels Association of New Zealand** (✉ Level 3, 193 Cashel St., Box 436, Christchurch, ☎ 03/379–9970, ℻ 03/365–4476, 𝖶𝖤𝖡 www.yha.org.nz).

HOTELS

Most hotels will hold your reservation until 6 PM; **call ahead if you plan to arrive late.** Hotels will be more willing to hold a late reservation if you reserve with a credit-card number.

All hotels listed have private bath unless otherwise noted.

➤ TOLL-FREE NUMBERS: **Adam's Mark** (☎ 800/444–2326, 𝖶𝖤𝖡 www.adamsmark.com). **Baymont Inns** (☎ 800/428–3438, 𝖶𝖤𝖡 www.baymontinns.com). **Best Western** (☎ 800/528–1234, 𝖶𝖤𝖡 www.bestwestern.com). **Choice** (☎ 800/221–2222, 𝖶𝖤𝖡 www.choicehotels.com). **Clarion** (☎ 800/252–7466, 𝖶𝖤𝖡 www.clarionhotel.com). **Colony Resorts** (☎ 800/777–1700). **Comfort Inn** (☎ 800/228–5150, 𝖶𝖤𝖡 www.comfortinn.com).

Days Inn (☎ 800/325–2525, WEB www.daysinn.com). **Doubletree and Red Lion Hotels** (☎ 800/222–8733, WEB www.doubletree.com). **Embassy Suites** (☎ 800/362–2779, WEB www. embassysuites.com). **Fairfield Inn** (☎ 800/228–2800, WEB www. marriott.com). **Four Seasons** (☎ 800/332–3442, WEB www.fourseasons. com). **Hilton** (☎ 800/445–8667, WEB www.hilton.com). **Holiday Inn** (☎ 800/465–4329, WEB www.basshotels. com). **Howard Johnson** (☎ 800/654–4656, WEB www.hojo.com). **Hyatt Hotels & Resorts** (☎ 800/233–1234, WEB www.hyatt.com). **Inter-Continental** (☎ 800/327–0200, WEB www. interconti.com). **La Quinta** (☎ 800/531–5900, WEB www.laquinta.com). **Le Meridien** (☎ 800/543–4300, WEB www.lemeridien-hotels.com). **Marriott** (☎ 800/228–9290, WEB www. marriott.com). **Omni** (☎ 800/843–6664, WEB www.omnihotels.com). **Quality Inn** (☎ 800/228–5151, WEB www.qualityinn.com). **Radisson** (☎ 800/333–3333, WEB www.radisson. com). **Ramada** (☎ 800/228–2828; 800/854–7854 international reservations, WEB www.ramada.com or www. ramadahotels.com). **Renaissance Hotels & Resorts** (☎ 800/468–3571, WEB www.renaissancehotels.com). **Ritz-Carlton** (☎ 800/241–3333, WEB www.ritzcarlton.com). **Sheraton** (☎ 800/325–3535, WEB www.starwood. com/sheraton). **Sleep Inn** (☎ 800/753–3746, WEB www.sleepinn.com). **Westin Hotels & Resorts** (☎ 800/228–3000, WEB www.starwood. com/westin). **Wyndham Hotels & Resorts** (☎ 800/822–4200, WEB www.wyndham.com).

MOTELS

➤ TOLL-FREE NUMBERS: **Budget Hosts Inns** (☎ 800/283–4678). **Econo Lodge** (☎ 800/553–2666). **Friendship Inns** (☎ 800/453–4511). **Motel 6** (☎ 800/466–8356). **Rodeway** (☎ 800/228–2000). **Super 8** (☎ 800/848–8888).

MEDIA

NEWSPAPERS AND MAGAZINES

There's no major regional newspaper that serves the South, but the *Atlanta Journal and Constitution* and New Orleans's *Times-Picayune* rank among the most influential dailies in the region; just about every city with a population of greater than 40,000 or 50,000 also publishes its own daily paper. Most major cities have very good alternative newsweeklies with useful Web sites and copious information on area dining, arts, and sightseeing—these are usually free and found in restaurants, coffeehouses, bookstores, tourism offices, hotel lobbies, and some nightclubs. Of particular note is Atlanta's *Creative Loafing,* which has separate editions for a number of additional Southern cities and regions, including Charlotte and Raleigh–Durham, where it's called *Spectator,* and Greenville, South Carolina. Visit its Web site (www.cln.com) to find links to each of these editions, as well as to other useful alternative newsweeklies in Athens (GA), Augusta (GA), Columbia (SC), Asheville, Charleston, Greensboro/Winston-Salem, Myrtle Beach, Savannah, and Wilmington (NC).

Monthly *Southern Living* magazine gives a nice sense of travel, food, and lifestyle issues relevant to the region. And local lifestyle magazines—including *Atlanta, Louisiana Life, New Orleans, Charlotte's Best,* and *Memphis*—offer colorful stories and dining and entertainment coverage.

RADIO AND TELEVISION

All the major television and radio networks are well represented throughout the South, and Ted Turner's omnipresent CNN empire is based in Atlanta.

MONEY MATTERS

As with most of the United States, credit and debit cards are accepted at the vast majority of shops, restaurants, and accommodations in the South. Common exceptions include a handful of small, independent stores and also B&Bs in more rural areas. Banks—as well as convenience stores, groceries, and even nightclubs—with ATMs are easy to find in just about every community.

The cost of living and traveling throughout most of the South is either slightly lower or comparable to that of most of the United States and is significantly cheaper than in many urban areas such as metropolitan San Francisco, New York, and Chicago. Although the cost of living remains fairly low in most parts of the South, travel-related costs (such as dining, lodging, museums, and transportation) have become increasingly steep in Nashville, New Orleans, and Atlanta over the years and can also be dear in resort communities throughout Georgia and the Carolinas.

Prices throughout this guide are given for adults. Substantially reduced fees are almost always available for children, students, and senior citizens. For information on taxes, *see* Taxes, *below*.

ATMS

➤ ATM LOCATIONS: **Cirrus** (☎ 800/424–7787). **Plus** (☎ 800/843–7587) for locations in the United States and Canada, or visit your local bank.

CREDIT AND DEBIT CARDS

Throughout this guide, the following abbreviations are used: **AE**, American Express; **D**, Discover; **DC**, Diners Club; **MC**, MasterCard; and **V**, Visa.

NATIONAL AND STATE PARKS

National and state parks abound in the South and offer a broad range of visitor facilities, including campgrounds, picnic grounds, hiking trails, boating, and ranger programs. State forests are usually somewhat less developed. For more information on any of these, contact the state tourism offices or parks departments (☞ Contacts and Resources, at the end of each state chapter).

Look into discount passes to save money on park entrance fees. The National Parks Pass ($50) gets you and your companions free admission to all parks for one year. (Camping and parking are extra.) A percentage of the proceeds from sales of the pass will fund National Parks projects. Both the Golden Age Passport ($10), for those 62 and older, and the Golden Access Passport (free), for travelers with disabilities, entitle holders to free entry to all national parks, plus 50% off fees for the use of many park facilities and services. You must show proof of age and of U.S.

citizenship or permanent residency (such as a U.S. passport, driver's license, or birth certificate) and, if requesting Golden Access, proof of disability. The Golden Age and Golden Access passes are available at all national parks wherever entrance fees are charged. The National Parks Pass is available by mail or through the Internet.

➤ PASSES BY MAIL: **National Park Service** (✉ National Park Service/Department of Interior, 1849 C St. NW, Washington, DC 20240, ☎ 202/208–4747, WEB www.nps.gov). **National Parks Pass** (✉ 27540 Ave. Mentry, Valencia, CA 91355, ☎ 888/467–2757 or 888/467–2757, WEB www.nationalparks.org).

NATIONAL PARKS OF THE SOUTH

This part of the country contains a number of well-visited national parks, monuments, seashores, and forests. Probably the most famous is the swath of the Appalachians that comprises the 800-acre Great Smoky Mountains National Park—the park straddles the eastern Tennessee and western North Carolina borders and contains some 16 peaks higher than 6,000 ft. Hiking, camping, and boating are among the park visitors' favorite activities.

At the other extreme, at least vertically speaking, are the several national parks that lie along the Atlantic coastline, as well as the Gulf Islands National Seashore, a 150-mi long chain of islands that stretches from the coast of Mississippi to Pensacola, Florida. In coastal Alabama birdwatchers flock to Bon Secour National Wildlife Refuge; the same is true at Louisiana's Sabine National Wildlife Refuge. The top Atlantic shore parks are Pea Island National Wildlife Refuge and Cape Hatteras and Cape Lookout national seashores, in North Carolina; Cumberland Island National Seashore, Fort Pulaski and Fort Frederica national monuments, and Okefenokee National Wildlife Refuge, in Georgia; and Fort Sumter National Monument, in South Carolina.

OUTDOORS AND SPORTS

With daytime temperatures rarely dipping below freezing and a plethora of waterways, mountains, forests, and swamps, the South makes for an ideal destination among outdoors enthusiasts. Fans of pro and college sports will also find the South rife with live athletic events and Southerners to be among the most passionate and knowledgeable of sports enthusiasts.

PARTICIPANT SPORTS AND RECREATION

It's tough to come up with an outdoor activity that isn't celebrated somewhere in this part of the country, but fishing, golf, and tennis lead in popularity among most vacationers. These pastimes are widespread and covered in detail within specific state chapters of this book, but bear in mind a few key destinations for certain sporting endeavors: **Golfers** will find an entire community of world-class courses in the Pinehurst region of North Carolina, the Hilton Head and Myrtle Beach regions of South Carolina, and the coastal islands off Georgia. These areas also have plenty to offer in the way of **tennis.** In the inland Appalachian regions, from the Carolinas to Tennessee, you'll find many excellent mountain courses.

Fishing diehards find plenty of freshwater action in every state in the South, with stocked lakes and rivers at many state and municipal parks. Deep-sea and surf fishing prevail (including crabbing and shrimping) all along the Atlantic seaboard and the Gulf Coast; you'll find that charter- and guided-fishing operators abound in these parts.

Other activities with a strong following in the South include bicycling, boating and rafting, bowling, camping and hiking, hang gliding, and hunting.

SPECTATOR SPORTS

Several Southern cities have major pro sports teams. In **baseball** check out the Atlanta Braves; **basketball** fans cheer on the Atlanta Hawks and Charlotte Hornets; for **football** there are the Atlanta Falcons, Carolina Panthers, New Orleans Saints, and Tennessee Titans; and **hockey** fans watch the Atlanta Thrashers and Carolina Hurricanes. Just about every Southern city has at least one minorleague sports franchise, including baseball, and these are among the most enjoyable teams to watch. College sports are, in some cases, equally or even more popular than pro events, with basketball and football especially well regarded in the South. Among the most popular **college basketball** programs are those of Duke (North Carolina), LSU (Louisiana), North Carolina, North Carolina State, Tennessee, and Vanderbilt (Tennessee), to name a few. Hugely successful **college football** programs include Alabama, East Carolina, Georgia, Georgia Tech, Mississippi State, Southern Mississippi, Tennessee, and Wake Forest (North Carolina). Other major sporting events in the South include numerous pro **golf** tournaments, highlighted by the Masters in Augusta, Georgia, and the women's LPGA AFLAC Champions in Mobile, Alabama. A smattering of world **tennis** tournaments are held in the South, and **auto-racing** fans will find NASCAR events staged throughout the region.

PACKING

There was a time, not too long ago, when any traveler planning to enjoy fine dining or the cushy confines of a luxury hotel in the South had to pack semiformal attire. As with the rest of the country, however, restaurants or hotel lobbies that require or even appreciate men dressed in jackets and ties and women in dresses have nearly disappeared. With a few formal exceptions, most of them in New Orleans and Atlanta, smart but casual attire works fine wherever you go.

Much of the South has hot, humid summers and sunny, mild winters. For colder months, pack a lightweight coat, slacks, and sweaters; you'll need heavier clothing in the more northerly states, where cold, damp weather prevails and snow is not unusual. Keeping summer's humidity in mind, **pack absorbent natural fabrics that breathe;** bring an umbrella, but leave the plastic raincoat at home. You'll want a jacket or sweater for summer evenings and for too-cool air-conditioning. And **don't forget insect repellent.**

In your carry-on luggage, **pack an extra pair of eyeglasses or contact lenses and enough of any medication** you take to last the entire trip. You may also ask your doctor to write a spare prescription using the drug's generic name, since brand names may vary from country to country. In luggage to be checked, **never pack prescription drugs or valuables.** And don't forget to carry with you the addresses of offices that handle refunds of lost traveler's checks. Check *Fodor's How to Pack* (available in bookstores everywhere) for more tips.

To avoid customs and security delays, carry medications in their original packaging. Don't pack any sharp objects in your carry-on luggage, including knives of any size or material, scissors, manicure tools, and corkscrews, or anything else that might arouse suspicion.

CHECKING LUGGAGE

You are allowed one carry-on bag and one personal article, such as a purse or a laptop computer. Make sure that everything you carry aboard will fit under your seat or in the overhead bin. Get to the gate early, so you can board as soon as possible, before the overhead bins fill up.

If you are flying internationally, note that baggage allowances may be determined not by piece but by weight—generally 88 pounds (40 kilograms) in first class, 66 pounds (30 kilograms) in business class, and 44 pounds (20 kilograms) in economy.

Airline liability for baggage is limited to $2,500 per person on flights within the United States. On international flights it amounts to $9.07 per pound or $20 per kilogram for checked baggage (roughly $640 per 70-pound bag) and $400 per passenger for unchecked baggage. You can buy additional coverage at check-in for about $10 per $1,000 of coverage, but it excludes a rather extensive list of items, shown on your airline ticket.

Before departure, **itemize your bags' contents** and their worth, and label the bags with your name, address, and phone number. (If you use your home address, cover it so potential thieves can't see it readily.) Inside each bag, **pack a copy of your itinerary.** At check-in, **make sure that each bag is correctly tagged** with the destination airport's three-letter code. If your bags arrive damaged or fail to arrive at all, file a written report with the airline before leaving the airport.

SAFETY

At the risk of generalizing, Southerners are more often willing to offer assistance or at least a friendly word of advice or direction than many other Americans. Those old clichés you might have heard about the South's remarkable sense of hospitality hold uniformly true in most places. Still, economic disparity and poverty, which are prevalent both in urban and rural areas all over the South, can breed crime. In certain tourist-dependent destinations, you should be wary of suspicious-looking figures, and you should never leave valuables in your car or in unsecured places.

About the only Southern destination of note with a truly infamous reputation for crime, including an unfortunate degree of murder and assault, is New Orleans, which has cleaned up a great deal in recent years but is still a place where you should always walk with your head up and an eye open for potential trouble. Your most prudent approach, here and in other cities, is to avoid venturing out alone and to rely on cabs when getting around at night.

SENIOR-CITIZEN TRAVEL

To qualify for age-related discounts, **mention your senior-citizen status up front** when booking hotel reservations (not when checking out) and before you're seated in restaurants (not when paying the bill). Be sure to have identification on hand. When renting a car, ask about promotional car-rental discounts, which can be cheaper than senior-citizen rates.

➤ EDUCATIONAL PROGRAMS: **Elderhostel** (✉ 11 Ave. de Lafayette, Boston, MA 02111-1746, ☎ 877/426–8056,

FAX 877/426–2166, WEB www.
elderhostel.org). **Interhostel** (✉
University of New Hampshire, 6
Garrison Ave., Durham, NH 03824,
☎ 603/862–1147 or 800/733–9753,
FAX 603/862–1113, WEB www.learn.
unh.edu).

STUDENT TRAVEL

➤ I.D.s AND SERVICES: **Council Travel**
(CIEE; ✉ 205 E. 42nd St., 15th floor,
New York, NY 10017, ☎ 212/822–
2700 or 888/268–6245, FAX 212/822–
2699, WEB www.counciltravel.com).
Travel Cuts (✉ 187 College St.,
Toronto, Ontario M5T 1P7, Canada,
☎ 416/979–2406; 800/667–2887 in
Canada, FAX 416/979–0956, WEB
www.travelcuts.com).

➤ STUDENT TOURS: **Contiki Holidays**
(✉ 300 Plaza Alicante, Suite 900,
Garden Grove, CA 92840, ☎ 714/
740–0808 or 800/266–8454, FAX
714/740–2034).

TAXES

Sales taxes in the South are as follows:
Alabama, Georgia, and Louisiana,
4%; North Carolina, 4.5%; Mississippi, 7%; South Carolina, 5%; and
Tennessee, 6%. Most municipalities
also levy a lodging tax (from which
small inns with only a few rooms are
usually exempt, but rules vary regionally), and in some cases a restaurant
tax. The hotel taxes in the South can
be rather steep, greater than 10% in
Georgia, Tennessee, and many counties in North Carolina.

TELEPHONES

AREA AND COUNTRY CODES

Some cities are served by multiple
area codes; in these places it's often
necessary to dial the full 10-digit
number (including area code), sometimes preceded by "1," even when
placing local calls (if in doubt, dial
"0" when you arrive to check with an
operator, or ask your hotel's front
desk). Note that several area codes
were added to the region in 2001–
2002; 980 and 803 are the area codes
in Charlotte, North Carolina; 984
and 919 in the Raleigh-Durham area;
and 470, 678, 404, and 770 are the
area codes in metropolitan Atlanta.
Also, 478 replaced 912 in parts of 23
Georgia counties, including Macon
and Milledgeville; 229 replaced 912

in 38 counties in southwestern Georgia, including Albany, Valdosta,
Tifton, and Thomasville; 985 replaced 504 in parts of several
Louisiana parishes, including the
Houma/Thibodaux area, South
Lafourche, the North Shore, and the
river parishes; 251 replaced 334 in
parts of several southwestern Alabama counties, including Mobile and
the communities along the Gulf shore;
and 731 replaced 901 in all of western Tennessee (Fayette, Shelby, and
Tipton counties) except for
metropolitan Memphis.

CREDIT-CARD CALLS

To get a credit card, **contact your
long-distance telephone carrier,** such
as AT&T, MCI, or Sprint.

DIRECTORY AND OPERATOR
INFORMATION

For assistance from an operator, dial
"0." To find out a telephone number,
call directory assistance, 555–1212 in
every locality. There's usually a small
charge for this call, up to about 75¢.

LONG-DISTANCE CALLS

Competitive long-distance carriers
make calling within the United States
relatively convenient and let you
avoid hotel surcharges. By dialing an
"800" number, you can get connected
to the long-distance company of your
choice.

If you want to charge a long-distance
call to the person you're calling, you
can call collect by dialing "0" instead
of "1" before the 10-digit number,
and an operator will come on the line
to assist you (the party you're calling,
however, has the right to refuse the
call). It's far less costly, however, to
purchase a long-distance phone
card—these are available in a wide
range of denominations from convenience stores, gas stations, and newsstands and offer rates competitive
with those set by most major long-
distance carriers.

➤ LONG-DISTANCE CARRIERS: **AT&T**
(☎ 800/225–5288). **MCI** (☎ 800/
888–8000). **Sprint** (☎ 800/366–
2255).

TIME

Georgia, the Carolinas, and eastern
Tennessee fall in the Eastern Standard

time zone (EST), three hours ahead of California, the same as New York and Florida. Western Tennessee, Alabama, Mississippi, and Louisiana fall in the Central Standard time zone (CST), the same as Chicago and Dallas.

TIPPING

At restaurants, a 15%–20% tip is standard for waiters, depending on the level of service provided. The same goes for taxi drivers, bartenders, and hairdressers. Coat-check operators usually expect $1; bellhops and porters should get 50¢ to $1 per bag; hotel maids should get about $1 per day of your stay—$2 in upscale hotels. A concierge typically receives a tip of $5 to $10, with an additional gratuity for special services or favors. On package tours, conductors and drivers usually get $10 per day from the group as a whole; check whether this has already been figured into your cost. For local sightseeing tours, you may individually tip the driver-guide $1 if he or she has been helpful or informative. Ushers in theaters do not expect tips.

TOURS AND PACKAGES

Because everything is prearranged on a prepackaged tour or independent vacation, you spend less time planning—and often get it all at a good price.

BOOKING WITH AN AGENT

Travel agents are excellent resources. But it's a good idea to collect brochures from several agencies, as some agents' suggestions may be influenced by relationships with tour and package firms that reward them for volume sales. If you have a special interest, **find an agent with expertise in that area**; the American Society of Travel Agents (ASTA; ☞ Travel Agencies, *below*) has a database of specialists worldwide.

Make sure your travel agent knows the accommodations and other services of the place being recommended. Ask about the hotel's location, room size, beds, and whether it has a pool, room service, or programs for children, if you care about these. Has your agent been there in person or sent others whom you can contact?

Do some homework on your own, too: local tourism boards can provide information about lesser-known and small-niche operators, some of which may sell only direct.

BUYER BEWARE

Each year consumers are stranded or lose their money when tour operators—even large ones with excellent reputations—go out of business. So **check out the operator.** Ask several travel agents about its reputation, and try to **book with a company that has a consumer-protection program.** (Look for information in the company's brochure.) In the United States, members of the National Tour Association and the United States Tour Operators Association are required to set aside funds to cover your payments and travel arrangements in the event that the company defaults. It's also a good idea to choose a company that participates in the American Society of Travel Agents' Tour Operator Program (TOP); ASTA will act as mediator in any disputes between you and your tour operator.

Remember that the more your package or tour includes, the better you can predict the ultimate cost of your vacation. Make sure you know exactly what is covered, and **beware of hidden costs.** Are taxes, tips, and transfers included? Entertainment and excursions? These can add up.

➤ TOUR-OPERATOR RECOMMENDATIONS: **American Society of Travel Agents** (☞ Travel Agencies, *below*). **National Tour Association** (NTA; ✉ 546 E. Main St., Lexington, KY 40508, ☎ 859/226–4444 or 800/682–8886, WEB www.ntaonline.com). **United States Tour Operators Association** (USTOA; ✉ 275 Madison Ave., Suite 2014, New York, NY 10016, ☎ 212/599–6599 or 800/468–7862, FAX 212/599–6744, WEB www.ustoa.com).

TRAIN TRAVEL

Amtrak has a number of routes that pass through the South; however, many regions are not served by train, and those cities that do have service usually have only one or two arrivals and departures each day. Major cities served in the South include Atlanta,

Georgia; Biloxi, Mississippi; Birmingham, Alabama; Charleston, South Carolina; Charlotte, North Carolina; Columbia, South Carolina; Durham, North Carolina; Greenville, South Carolina; Hilton Head, South Carolina; Jackson, Mississippi; Memphis, Tennessee; Mobile, Alabama; Lafayette, Louisiana; New Orleans, Louisiana; Raleigh, North Carolina; Savannah, Georgia; and Winston-Salem, North Carolina. In addition, a number of additional cities—including Nashville, Tennessee, and Myrtle Beach, South Carolina—are handled by Amtrak connecting services (depending on the route, these services may be provided by train, bus, or van).

CUTTING COSTS

Amtrak offers a **North America rail pass** that gives you unlimited travel within the United States and Canada within any 30-day period ($674 peak, $475 off-peak), and several kinds of **USA Rail passes** (for non-U.S. residents only) offering unlimited travel for 15 to 30 days. Amtrak also has senior-citizen, children's, disability, and student discounts, as well as occasional deals that allow a second or third accompanying passenger to travel for half price or even free. The **Amtrak Vacations** program customizes entire vacations, including hotels, car rentals, and tours.

FARES AND SCHEDULES

Here are a few sample fares (these are regular fares; discount or special fares may be lower), times, and routes: Atlanta to New Orleans, 11 hours, $83 one-way; Memphis to New Orleans, 10 hours, $61 one-way; Lafayette to Mobile, 10 hours, $54 one-way; and Raleigh to Savannah, eight hours, $83 one-way.

➤ TRAIN INFORMATION: **Amtrak** (☎ 800/872–7245, WEB www.amtrak.com).

TRANSPORTATION TO AND AROUND THE SOUTH

Although a car is your best bet for getting around the South, it's worth considering a few other strategies for convenient and economical travel.

If you're planning to spend more than several days and visit more than a

couple of cities, you might consider driving your own car rather than flying in and renting one—especially if you live anywhere within 500 mi of the region (i.e., the mid-Atlantic states, the Midwest, the lower Plains states, and Texas) and you're traveling with three or more in your group. Even if you have to spend a night at a motel on your way there and back, you'll save a considerable amount of money on airfare and car rentals this way. If, however, you lease your car rather than own it outright, you might factor in the number of miles you're planning to burn up before deciding which strategy works best. And, of course, if time is tight, flying is your best bet.

If coming by plane, plan to fly in to one of the South's major airports, to which fares tend to be considerably lower than to smaller regional facilities. For example, the sheer competition and wealth of connections at Atlanta's busy Hartsfield Airport makes it an excellent choice—car-rental rates here are also highly competitive, and Atlanta is less than 500 mi from virtually every town in the South and within 300 mi of Savannah, Charleston, Charlotte, Asheville, Knoxville, Nashville, Birmingham, and Montgomery. Charlotte-Douglas International Airport, in North Carolina, is probably the second-most central airport geographically. Less central but also with a wide range of connections and generally reasonable fares are the airports in New Orleans, Memphis, and Nashville.

It's difficult to find direct flights to most of the additional airports in the South, especially if flying from outside the region. However, within the South, check to see what airfares are between some smaller cities—very often airlines offer specials between popular shorter routes such as Atlanta to New Orleans, Atlanta to Savannah, Charlotte to Hilton Head, and so forth.

If you're trying to save money, you have a fair amount of time, and you're interested in taking in the landscape without having to drive, consider getting around via bus—Greyhound has frequent and regular service to virtually every city in the

South. Some routes, near the coastal areas and over the mountainous interior section, can be quite breathtaking. And if you book at least a couple of days ahead, you'll find the rates quite reasonable. A bit less practical is relying on Amtrak, as coverage within the South is a bit spotty, and round-trip fares are sometimes quite a bit higher than comparable bus fares—occasionally even more than corresponding airfares. However, if you are planning a one-way or multisegment trip through the South, you'll likely find that train travel offers a better value with more flexibility and fewer restrictions than attempting such an endeavor by plane. And you'd generally find the ride more comfortable and pleasant by train than by bus.

TRAVEL AGENCIES

A good travel agent puts your needs first. Look for an agency that has been in business at least five years, emphasizes customer service, and has someone on staff who specializes in your destination. In addition, **make sure the agency belongs to a professional trade organization.** The American Society of Travel Agents (ASTA)—the largest and most influential in the field with more than 24,000 members in some 140 countries—maintains and enforces a strict code of ethics and will step in to help mediate any agent-client disputes involving ASTA members if necessary. ASTA (whose motto is "Without a travel agent, you're on your own") also maintains a Web site that includes a directory of agents. (If a travel agency is also acting as your tour operator, see Buyer Beware in Tours & Packages, above.)

➤ LOCAL AGENT REFERRALS: American Society of Travel Agents (ASTA; ⊠ 1101 King St., Suite 200, Alexandria, VA 22314, ☎ 800/965–2782 24-hr hot line, FAX 703/739–3268, WEB www.astanet.com). Association of British Travel Agents (⊠ 68–71 Newman St., London W1T 3AH, ☎ 020/7637–2444, FAX 020/7637–0713, WEB www.abtanet.com). Association of Canadian Travel Agents (⊠ 130 Albert St., Suite 1705, Ottawa, Ontario K1P 5G4, ☎ 613/237–3657, FAX 613/237–7052, WEB www.

acta.net). **Australian Federation of Travel Agents** (⊠ Level 3, 309 Pitt St., Sydney, NSW 2000, ☎ 02/9264–3299, FAX 02/9264–1085, WEB www.afta.com.au). **Travel Agents' Association of New Zealand** (⊠ Level 5, Tourism and Travel House, 79 Boulcott St., Box 1888, Wellington 10033, ☎ 04/499–0104, FAX 04/499–0827, WEB www.taanz.org.nz).

VISITOR INFORMATION

For general information and brochures before you go, contact the state tourism bureaus.

➤ STATE TOURISM BUREAUS: **Alabama Bureau of Tourism and Travel** (⊠ 401 Adams Ave., Montgomery, AL 36104, ☎ 334/242–4413 or 800/252–2262, FAX 334/242–4554). **Georgia Department of Industry, Trade and Tourism** (⊠ 285 Peachtree Center Ave., N.E. Marquis Tower II, Suite 1100, Atlanta, GA 30303, ☎ 404/656–3553 or 800/847–4842, FAX 404/651–9462). **Louisiana Office of Tourism** (⊠ Box 94291, Baton Rouge, LA 70804-9291, ☎ 225/342–8119 or 800/677–4082, FAX 225/342–8390). **Mississippi Division of Tourism** (⊠ Box 849, Jackson, MS 39205, ☎ 601/359–3297 or 800/927–6378, FAX 601/359–5757). **North Carolina Travel and Tourism Division** (⊠ 301 N. Wilmington St., Raleigh, NC 27601, ☎ 919/715–5900 or 800/847–4862, FAX 919/733–2616). **South Carolina Department of Parks, Recreation, and Tourism** (⊠ 1205 Pendleton St., Suite 106, Columbia, SC 29201, ☎ 803/734–0122 or 888/727–6453, FAX 803/734–0138). **Tennessee Department of Tourist Development** (⊠ 320 6th Ave. N, Rachel Jackson Bldg., 5th floor, Nashville, TN 37243, ☎ 615/741–2159 or 800/836–6200, FAX 615/741–7225).

WEB SITES

Do check out the World Wide Web when planning your trip. You'll find everything from weather forecasts to virtual tours of famous cities. Be sure to **visit Fodors.com** (www.fodors.com), a complete travel-planning site. You can research prices and book plane tickets, hotel rooms, rental cars, vacation packages, and more. In addition, you can post your pressing questions in the Travel Talk section.

Other planning tools include a currency converter and weather reports, and there are loads of links to travel resources.

For more information specifically on the South, take a look at the sites listed below.

➤ ALABAMA: www.touralabama. org (Alabama Bureau of Tourism and Travel); www.bcvb.org (Birmingham Convention and Visitors Bureau); www.mobile.org (Mobile Convention and Visitors Corp.); www. montgomerychamber.com (Montgomery Area Chamber of Commerce CVB).

➤ GEORGIA: www.georgia.org (Georgia Department of Industry, Trade and Tourism); www.atlanta. net (Atlanta Convention and Visitors Bureau); www.bgivb.com (Brunswick and the Golden Isles of Georgia Visitors Bureau); www.savcvb.com (Savannah Area Convention and Visitors Bureau).

➤ LOUISIANA: www.louisianatravel. com (Louisiana Office of Tourism); www.lafayettetravel.com (Lafayette Convention and Visitors Commission); www.neworleanscvb.com (New Orleans Metropolitan Convention and Visitors Bureau).

➤ MISSISSIPPI: www.mississippi.org (Mississippi Division of Tourism); www.visitjackson.com (Jackson Convention and Visitors Bureau); www.gulfcoast.org (Mississippi's Gulf Coast); www.tupelo.net (Tupelo Convention and Visitors Bureau).

➤ NORTH CAROLINA: www. visitnc.com (North Carolina Tourism Division); www.ashevillechamber.org (Asheville Convention and Visitors Bureau); www.cape-fear.nc.us (Cape Fear Coast and Wilmington Convention and Visitors Bureau); www. charlottecvb.org (Charlotte Convention and Visitors Bureau); www. durham-nc.com (Durham Convention and Visitors Bureau); www. raleighcvb.org (Greater Raleigh Convention and Visitors Bureau); www.wscvb.com (Winston-Salem Convention and Visitors Bureau).

➤ SOUTH CAROLINA: www. discoversouthcarolina.com (South Carolina Department of Parks, Recreation, and Tourism); www. charlestoncvb.com (Charleston Convention and Visitors Bureau); www. columbiasc.net (Columbia Metro Convention and Visitors Bureau); www.hiltonheadisland.org (Hilton Head Island Chamber of Commerce); www.myrtlebeachlive.com (Myrtle Beach Area Chamber of Commerce).

➤ TENNESSEE: www.tourism.state. tn.us (Tennessee Department of Tourist Development); www. chattanoogacvb.com (Chattanooga Area Convention and Visitors Bureau); www.knoxville.org (Knoxville Convention and Visitors Bureau); www.memphistravel.com (Memphis Convention and Visitors Bureau); www.nashvillecvb.com (Nashville Convention and Visitors Bureau).

WHEN TO GO

Spring is probably the most attractive season in this part of the United States. Throughout the region cherry blossoms are followed by azaleas, dogwood, and camellias from April into May and by apple blossoms in May. Summer can be hot and humid in many areas, but temperatures will be cooler along the coasts or in the mountains. Folk, crafts, art, and music festivals tend to take place in summer, as do sports events. State and local fairs are held mainly in August and September, though there are a few in early July and into October. Fall can be a delight, with spectacular foliage, particularly in the mountains. The region is large and conditions vary; see the individual state chapters for more information.

CLIMATE

In winter, temperatures generally average in the low 40s inland, in the 60s by the shore. Summer temperatures, modified by mountains in some areas, by water in others, range from the high 70s to the mid-80s, now and then the low 90s.

The following are average daily maximum and minimum temperatures for key Southern cities.

BIRMINGHAM, ALABAMA

Jan.	56F	13C	May	82F	28C	Sept.	86F	30C
	35	2		58	14		63	17
Feb.	58F	14C	June	89F	32C	Oct.	77F	25C
	37	3		66	19		51	11
Mar.	65F	18C	July	90F	32C	Nov.	64F	18C
	42	6		69	21		40	4
Apr.	74F	23C	Aug.	90F	32C	Dec.	56F	13C
	50	10		65	20		35	2

ATLANTA, GEORGIA

Jan.	52F	11C	May	79F	26C	Sept.	83F	28C
	36	2		61	16		65	18
Feb.	54F	12C	June	86F	30C	Oct.	72F	22C
	38	3		67	19		54	12
Mar.	63F	17C	July	88F	31C	Nov.	61F	16C
	43	6		70	21		43	6
Apr.	72F	22C	Aug.	86F	30C	Dec.	52F	11C
	52	11		70	21		38	3

NEW ORLEANS, LOUISIANA

Jan.	63F	17C	May	83F	28C	Sept.	86F	30C
	47	8		68	20		74	23
Feb.	65F	18C	June	88F	31C	Oct.	79F	26C
	50	10		74	23		65	18
Mar.	72F	22C	July	90F	32C	Nov.	70F	21C
	56	13		76	24		56	13
Apr.	77F	25C	Aug.	90F	32C	Dec.	65F	18C
	61	16		76	24		49	9

JACKSON, MISSISSIPPI

Jan.	59F	15C	May	85F	29C	Sept.	88F	31C
	38	3		63	17		65	18
Feb.	63F	17C	June	92F	33C	Oct.	81F	27C
	41	5		70	21		54	12
Mar.	68F	20C	July	94F	34C	Nov.	67F	19C
	47	8		72	22		43	6
Apr.	76F	24C	Aug.	94F	34C	Dec.	61F	16C
	54	12		70	21		40	4

RALEIGH, NORTH CAROLINA

Jan.	50F	10C	May	78F	26C	Sept.	81F	27C
	29	− 2		55	13		60	16
Feb.	52F	11C	June	85F	29C	Oct.	71F	22C
	30	− 1		62	17		47	8
Mar.	61F	16C	July	88F	31C	Nov.	61F	16C
	37	3		67	19		38	3
Apr.	72F	22C	Aug.	87F	31C	Dec.	52F	11C
	46	8		66	18		30	− 1

CHARLESTON, SOUTH CAROLINA

Jan.	59F	15C	May	81F	27C	Sept.	84F	29C
	41	6		64	18		69	21
Feb.	60F	16C	June	86F	30C	Oct.	76F	24C
	43	7		71	22		59	15
Mar.	66F	19C	July	88F	31C	Nov.	67F	19C
	49	9		74	23		49	9
Apr.	73F	23C	Aug.	88F	31C	Dec.	59F	11C
	56	13		73	23		42	6

NASHVILLE, TENNESSEE

Jan.	46F	8C	May	79F	26C	Sept.	83F	28C
	28	− 2		57	14		61	16
Feb.	51F	11C	June	87F	31C	Oct.	72F	22C
	30	− 1		65	18		48	9
Mar.	60F	16C	July	90F	32C	Nov.	59F	15C
	38	3		69	21		32	3
Apr.	71F	22C	Aug.	89F	32C	Dec.	50F	10C
	48	9		68	20		31	− 1

➤ FORECASTS: **Weather Channel Connection** (☎ 900/932–8437), 95¢ per minute from a Touch-Tone phone.

FESTIVALS AND SEASONAL EVENTS

Starting with Mardi Gras in New Orleans and ending with Christmas in Natchez, Mississippi, the Southern states hold a wide variety of festivals and special events throughout the year. Call local or state visitor information offices for further information.

➤ JANUARY: The year begins with two major **college football competitions**, the Senior Bowl in Mobile, Alabama, and the Sugar Bowl, played in New Orleans. In South Carolina, Orangeburg invites the country's finest coon dogs to compete in the **Grand American Coon Hunt**. Regional **runners race** in the Savannah Marathon and Half Marathon in Savannah, Georgia, and the Charlotte Observer Marathon and Runners' Expo in Charlotte, North Carolina. **Martin Luther King Jr. Week** is celebrated in Atlanta. The **New Orleans Classical Music Festival** takes place late in the month.

➤ FEBRUARY: The big event of the month is **Mardi Gras** in New Orleans—the South's biggest parade and party; the week is also celebrated in Mobile and Fairhope, Alabama, and Biloxi and Natchez, Mississippi. **Black History Month** is observed throughout the South, with special events at Tuskegee University in

Tuskegee, Alabama, and the W. C. Handy home in Florence, Alabama. Wilmington stages the **North Carolina Jazz Festival**. In Jackson, Mississippi, the **Dixie National Livestock Show** runs most of the month in conjunction with the **Dixie National Rodeo** and the **Dixie National Western Festival**.

➤ MARCH: The Old South comes alive: **Antebellum mansion and garden tours** are given in Natchez, Port Gibson, Vicksburg, and Columbus, Mississippi, and in Charleston and Beaufort, South Carolina. A **Revolutionary War battle** is reenacted on the anniversary of the Battle of Guilford Courthouse in Greensboro, North Carolina. The Grand VIllage of the Natchez Indians in Mississippi hosts the **Natchez Pow-Wow**. Spring is celebrated with a Cherry Blossom Festival in Macon, Georgia; the Festival of Flowers, in Mobile, Alabama; the Fairhope Arts and Crafts Festival in Fairhope, Alabama; the Spring Flower Show in Montgomery, Alabama; Springfest, on Hilton Head Island, South Carolina; and the Great Smoky Arts and Crafts Community Spring Show in Gatlinburg, Tennessee. **St. Patrick's Day** in Savannah is one of the nation's largest celebrations of the day. New Orleans celebrates its **Tennessee Williams/New Orleans Literary Festival**. In Aiken, South Carolina, horse racing's **Triple Crown** includes Thoroughbred trials, harness races, and steeplechases. Fairhope, on Mobile Bay in Alabama, hosts a large weekend **Arts and Crafts Festival.**

➤ APRIL: In Alabama a **Civil War reenactment** draws thousands to Selma in late April. Eufaula, Alabama, stages its annual **Pilgrimage and Antiques Show.** The **Festival International de la Louisiane** in Lafayette, Louisiana, celebrates Cajun Country with several days of music, food, and crafts. **Spring festivals** abound, including dogwood festivals in Atlanta, Georgia; Fayetteville, North Carolina; and Knoxville, Tennessee. Also consider the Okefenokee Spring Fling, in Waycross, Georgia; the Strawberry Festival in Ponchatoula, Louisiana; the Festival of Flowers, at the Biltmore Estate in Asheville, North Carolina; and the Spring Wildflower Pilgrimage, in Gatlinburg, Tennessee. **Fish and shellfish lovers** should take note of the World Catfish Festival in Belzoni, Mississippi; the self-described World's Biggest Fish Fry, in Paris, Tennessee; and the Louisiana Crawfish Festival in St. Bernard, Louisiana. The **World Grits Festival** is held in St. George, South Carolina. **Music festivals** include the New Orleans Jazz and Heritage Festival and, in Wilkesboro, North Carolina, the Merle Watson Memorial Festival, featuring Doc Watson's renowned bluegrass picking. The **Masters Golf Tournament** in Augusta, Georgia, attracts top pros and thousands of spectators. More than 40,000 people participate in the **Cooper River Bridge Run and Walk,** in Charleston.

➤ MAY: Festivals take to the air this month with the **Alabama Jubilee Hot Air Balloon Classic,** in Decatur. The annual **Hang Gliding Spectacular** is in Nags Head, North Carolina. Over Memorial Day weekend Greenville, South Carolina, hosts **Freedom Weekend Aloft,** the second-largest balloon rally in the country. **Memphis in May** is a monthlong salute to the city that includes the Beale Street Music Festival, the World Championship Barbecue Cooking Contest, the Memphis in May Triathlon, and the Great Southern Food Festival. **Spoleto Festival USA,** in Charleston, South Carolina, is one of the world's biggest arts festivals. **Piccolo Spoleto,** which runs concurrently with the Spoleto Festival, showcases local and regional talent. Mississippi hosts **two music festivals,** the Atwood Music Festival, in Monticello, and the Jimmie Rodgers Country Music Festival, in Meridian. In South Carolina Beaufort's **Gullah Festival** highlights the fine arts, customs, language, and dress of Lowcountry African-Americans.

➤ JUNE: June is **food month** in Louisiana, with the Okra Festival in Kenner, the Jambalaya Festival in Gonzales, the Great French Market Tomato Festival, in New Orleans, the Louisiana Blueberry Festival, in Mansfield, the Feliciana Peach Festival, in Clinton, and the famed Louisiana Catfish Festival, in Des Allemands. Alabama hosts the **Gehart Chamber Music Festival,** in Guntersville, as well as the annual **Blessing of the Fleet** and a seafood festival in Bayou La Batre, south of Mobile. Georgiana, Alabama, pays tribute to country music's legendary **Hank Williams Sr.** on the first Saturday in June. Also in Alabama, the **City Stages music festival** rocks the city of Birmingham with dozens of bands performing on stages throughout the downtown area. The nine-day juried **Arts Festival of Atlanta** is held downtown in Centennial Olympic Park and celebrates performing and visual arts. Mississippi hosts Biloxi's colorful **Black Heritage and Culture Juneteenth Celebration.** June is the time for Durham, North Carolina's renowned **American Dance Festival.** Summer gets under way at the **Sun Fun Festival** on Myrtle Beach's Grand Strand on the South Carolina coast. The outdoor **Summer Lights Music City Festival** is held in Nashville during the first weekend in June. The **International Country Music Fan Fair** takes place in the second week of June. **Carnival Memphis,** a music festival and local society event, is a city highlight. Chattanooga's **Riverbend Festival** showcases music from rock to blues for nine days.

➤ JULY: **Independence Day** celebrations are annual traditions around the South. **Deep-sea fishing rodeos** take place at both Dauphin Island, Alabama, and Gulfport, Mississippi; the latter is one of the largest fishing contests in the South. **Cajun Bastille Day** is celebrated in Baton Rouge for three days. Both Franklinton, Louisiana, and Mize, Mississippi, host **watermelon festivals.** In North Carolina clog and figure dancing are part of the **Shindig-on-the-Green,** in Asheville. The annual **Highland Games & Gathering of the Scottish Clans** is held on Grandfather Mountain near Linville, North Carolina.

➤ AUGUST: The **Elvis International Tribute Week** in Memphis attracts the King's fans from around the globe. The **Georgia Mountain Fair,** a mountain crafts and music extravaganza, is held in Hiawasse. North Carolina holds an **apple festival** in Hendersonville. The **Louisiana Shrimp and Petroleum Festival** is in Morgan City. August **music festivals** include the Beach Music Festival, on Jekyll Island, Georgia, and the annual Mountain Dance and Folk Festival, in Asheville, North Carolina. For four days in mid-August, the **Highway 127 Corridor Sale** (☎ 800/327–3945) lures shoppers along 450 mi of road, including sections in Tennessee and Alabama, to a mammoth outdoor sale and community festivals.

➤ SEPTEMBER: Truly a **festival month,** September welcomes local events throughout the South. In **Alabama** Greensboro stages the Alabama Catfish Festival, and Tuscumbia holds Harvest Jam at the Alabama Music Hall of Fame. In **Georgia** Stone Mountain Park is the site of both the Yellow Daisy Festival, celebrating both the flower and area arts and crafts, and the Highland Games, with events and foods in honor of the South's Scottish heritage. In **Louisiana** some of the best festivals are the Zydeco Music Festival in Plaisance, the Frog Festival, in Rayne, Festival Acadiens, in Lafayette, and the Louisiana Sugar Cane Festival, in New Iberia. In **Mississippi** Columbus has the Possum Town Pig Fest, Indianola the Indian Bayou Arts and Crafts Festival, Biloxi the Seafood Festival, and Greenville the Delta Blues Festival. The annual **Woolly Worm Festival** takes place in Banner

Elk, North Carolina. The **Candlelight Tour of Houses and Gardens** is held in Charleston during this month and October. The **Tennessee State Fair** is held annually in the fairgrounds of Nashville, with rides and attractions, as well as displays and competitions of floral, agricultural, and bovine beauty. The **National Storytelling Festival** captivates audiences over a weekend in historic Jonesborough, Tennessee.

➤ OCTOBER: Autumn brings more **celebrations of food,** including Alabama's National Shrimp Festival, in Gulf Shores; the National Peanut Festival, in Dothan; and the Chitlin' Jamboree, in Clio. The **Big Pig Jig,** in Vienna, Georgia, celebrates the glories of authentic Southern barbecue. A barbecue and parade of pigs guarantee fun at the **Lexington Barbecue Festival,** in North Carolina. Gulf Shores, in Alabama, hosts the annual **Orange Beach Fishing Rodeo.** The **South Carolina State Fair** is a Columbia highlight. Allart, Tennessee, hosts the two-day **Great Pumpkin Festival,** with contests, crafts, and gospel singing. **Oktoberfest** is celebrated in Helen, Georgia, in Myrtle Beach and Walhalla, South Carolina, and in Memphis and Clarkville, Tennessee. The "ghost capital of the world"—Georgetown, South Carolina—stages a ghost tour. In Mississippi the **Scottish Highland Games** are held in Biloxi. Natchez, Mississippi, stages the **Fall Pilgrimage,** highlighted by the prestigious Antiques Forum. In Canton, Mississippi, the **Canton Flea Market** features antiques and objets d'art on the Courthouse Square. During the last week of October, Oneonta, Alabama, holds its annual **Covered Bridge Festival.**

➤ NOVEMBER: **Thanksgiving** celebrations take place all over: The Creek Indian Thanksgiving Day Homecoming and Pow-Wow is held in Poarch, Alabama, and the Richland Pumpkin Festival is held in Richland, Mississippi. **Christmas preparations** include mistletoe markets in Albany, Georgia, and Jackson, Mississippi. Autumn **food festivals** include the Taste of Montgomery, in Montgomery, Alabama, and the pecan festivals in

Theodore, Alabama, and Colfax, Louisiana. The Catfish Festival takes place in Society Hill, South Carolina, and the Chitlin' Strut in Salley, South Carolina.

➤ DECEMBER: **Christmas** is celebrated all over the South, with events in almost every city. Highlights include Creole Christmas in the French Quarter of New Orleans and Old Salem Christmas, which re-creates a Moravian Christmas in Winston-Salem, North Carolina. Tennessee holiday events of note are Christmas in the City in Knoxville, Smoky Mountain Christmas in Gatlinburg, and Nashville's Trees of Christmas. The annual Festival of Trees in Atlanta highlights specially decorated trees, and Savannah glows with candlelight tours of the Historic District. The **Festival of Lights** in Natchitoches, Louisiana, begins the first weekend of the month and continues through December. **New Year's** events include the Peach Bowl, played in Atlanta; the AXA/Equitable Liberty Bowl, played in Memphis; and the First Night Charlotte festival, held on the Town Square in Charlotte, North Carolina.

1 DESTINATION: THE SOUTH

Southern Culture(s)

Books & Videos

What's Where

Pleasures and Pastimes

Fodor's Choice

Great Itineraries

SOUTHERN CULTURE(S)

TO TRAVEL THE SOUTH is to be over-whelmed by its variety. People who study such things for a living report that the region is home to one-third of the nation's people and, depending on who's doing the counting, as much as a quarter of its territory. They also say that its speech patterns are more diverse than those in other parts of the country, that it has given the nation much of its music, and that it abounds with mountains (the highest in the East), water (including one-half of the contiguous U.S. coastline), caves (spelunkers find heaven under earth), plant life (think Spanish moss, Southern magnolia, Venus flytrap, and the leafy, ubiquitous perennial, kudzu), formal gardens (at 2,500 acres, Georgia's Calloway Gardens is one of the country's biggest), golf courses (about half of the professional tournaments in the United States take place on premier Southern courses), barbecue (how best to prepare pork—dressed with vinegar and red pepper, a tomato sauce, or a sweet mustard-based sauce—leads to vehement disagreements and tasty annual cook-offs), and corn bread (in South Carolina alone there are more than 100 words for different kinds of corn bread).

And, yes, there are also splendiferous plantations—Oak Alley and Rosedown in Louisiana, and Drayton Hall in South Carolina, to name just a few. There are paddle-wheel steamboats and Civil War sites, including Vicksburg National Military Park, considered the best-preserved battlefield in the United States. The first city museum built in America was the Charleston Museum (1773); it has relocated to more modern quarters. The South has civil rights museums in Memphis and Birmingham, and in Montgomery the First White House of the Confederacy. In stark contrast to the past stand monuments to the present and to the most powerful economy in the country. There are the tall skyscrapers of Charlotte, the nation's second-largest financial center; the World of Coca-Cola museum in Atlanta, headquarters for the company that makes the best-selling soft drink; and the U.S. Space and Rocket Center in Huntsville, Alabama, home to the Redstone Arsenal, a missile research facility.

The South's is a mosaic culture, past and present glued together by a sense of place. Mississippi's Eudora Welty wrote: "Southerners feel passionately about Place. Not simply in the historical or philosophical connotation of the word, but in the sensory thing, the experienced world of sight and sound and smell, in its earth and water and sky and in its seasons."

There's that, and then there's the legend. "One of the main ways the South is different from the rest of the country is that it's more thickly overlaid with mythologies, all these competing mythologies," lamented poet James Applewhite. The myths about Southern lives and character began in the colonial period and haven't slowed. It's gotten to the point, noted Southern comic writer William Price Fox, that "no lie, the average Yankee knows about as much about the South as a hog knows about the Lord's plan for salvation." There was the new Eden idealism, followed by a romanticized moonlight-and-magnolias South, followed by the benighted South, followed by talk of the Sun Belt and yet another New South (a speech in 1886 by Henry Grady, editor of the Atlanta *Constitution,* first popularized the phrase). The fact is, each complex and contradictory myth contains some truth, and native Southerners, with the aid of Hollywood and prime time, have helped reinforce stereotypes and clichés.

Still, social scientists and other astute observers of the culture have documented some interesting regional differences. Helpfulness and delightfully old-fashioned chivalry do indeed appear to be Southern traits. They found that smiling among middle-class people on the street was most common in Atlanta, Memphis, and Nashville, and that five of the six top cities for behaviors such as picking up an "accidentally" dropped pen and making change were Southern. When a damsel was in distress, two-thirds of Georgia men stopped to help, whereas only a third of non-Southerners responded. Meanwhile, in *Southerners: Portrait of a People,* North Carolinian and CBS correspondent Charles Kuralt wrote, "By contrast with the Yankee, the Southerner never uses one word when 10 or 20 will do."

Sometimes, such as when the supernatural is involved, no words are needed. Hoodoo (conjuring), or voodoo, as pronounced by whites, came to Louisiana with slaves and free blacks after the Haitian revolution in the early 19th century. An underground religion, it was practiced with intensity, and apparently still is—by blacks and whites alike. Addressing the subject's past and present is the New Orleans Historic Voodoo Museum. The *Wall Street Journal* has reported that A. Schwab's department store in Memphis sells 21 tons of hoodoo supplies annually. Voodoo, of course, was one of the themes in John Berendt's true-life thriller *Midnight in the Garden of Good and Evil.* Set in Savannah, a city whose principal role has been as leader in the effort to preserve the South's past, the book has given rise to a cottage industry—tours of haunts such as Bonaventure Cemetery. The Myrtles plantation in St. Francisville, Louisiana, has been called the most haunted house in America. And rumor has it that William Faulkner ("The past is never dead. It's not even past") heard ghostly piano music and footsteps at Rowan Oak, his Oxford, Mississippi, home.

T HIS IS ALL A PART OF FOLKLIFE whose traditions, with roots in Anglo-American, African-American, ethnic, and Native American cultures, are intimately tied to the region. Ensuring the continuation of tradition is the purpose of many of the plethora of festivals held throughout the South every year. People will lay aside their work for a day to pay homage to a slice of life, the old times: festivals celebrate everything from azaleas, bluegrass, collards, and crawfish to mules, storytelling, Scottish clans, yams, and woolly worms. It is to the South's credit that down-home cultural gatherings exist side by side, sometimes literally, with events that reflect an urbane sophistication, such as the American Dance Festival, held every summer in Durham, North Carolina, at Duke University. It has presented more than 400 premieres, including many works it commissioned. Each June in South Carolina, thousands head to Charleston for the Spoleto Festival's big-name outpouring of drama, Dixie-nurtured jazz, dance, and classical music.

Here's a key to one of the doors that leads to the heart of the South: don't be afraid to stray from the major thoroughfares, for off the beaten paths—sometimes not too far off—are real jewels. Want to see antebellum homes? Then roam through Eufaula, Alabama; it's chock-full of them. Want to see folk art being created? Head for the small towns of the High Country of North Carolina.

Travel along the coast of the Carolinas and Georgia during the summer months, and you will hear the strains of beach music, sanctified oldies such as "Under the Boardwalk," made famous by the Drifters. The focal point of this music is a dance ritual, the shag, immortalized in the Pat Conroy novel *Beach Music.* Now the state dance of South Carolina, the ever-evolving shag—no relation to the shag of the Northeast in the 1940s—has been described as a more refined cousin of the jitterbug and a kind of cooled-down lindy hop. Shagging classes are offered year-round in cities such as Raleigh, and the dance has its own contests and festivals. The Society of Stranders (from the Grand Strand, the nickname for South Carolina's northeast coastal area) meets each year in North Myrtle Beach; thousands of people gather for several days of festivities, and all skill levels are welcome.

If you'd rather just listen, then Macon and the Georgia Music Hall of Fame is the place to pass the day. From Georgia has come an amazing array of music industry leaders and artists. To name a few: gospel's Thomas Dorsey and R&B's Ma Rainey and Ray Charles, soul's Isaac Hayes, alternative rock's R.E.M., and urban contemporary's Babyface and Toni Braxton. Macon itself is where Little Richard and Otis Redding grew up, Lena Horne lived as a child, and James Brown began his career.

The $6 million shrine, filled with memorabilia lent or donated by artists or their relatives, is divided according to musical styles. Scattered throughout are listening stations. Settle back, focus on the variety of stories set to melody, and you will understand what soul and gospel singer Al Green meant when he said of the South,

"All I can say is that there's a sweetness here . . . that makes sweet music. . . . If I had to tell somebody who had never been to the South, who had never heard of soul music, what it was, I'd just have to tell him that it's music from the heart, from the pulse, from the innermost feeling. . . . That's the South."

— Lisa H. Towle

BOOKS & VIDEOS

Before your trip you may want to read some books or watch some movies about the South. The region has its own language, rich in metaphor and rooted in Elizabethan speech, and it has given rise to a substantial literary heritage: novels, drama, and poetry, as well as short stories and songs. Its authors have won Nobel prizes (William Faulkner, from Mississippi) and many a Pulitzer, among them Georgia-born Caroline Miller for fiction (*Lamb in His Bosom,* 1934). You can choose from works by Eudora Welty, Tennessee Williams, Walker Percy, Reynolds Price, Pat Conroy, and Flannery O'Connor, to name just a few. Charles Frazier's 1997 novel, *Cold Mountain,* about the journeys of a Confederate soldier in western North Carolina, won a National Book Award. The South has produced writers of popular fiction as varied as Margaret Mitchell (*Gone With the Wind*), Anne Rivers Siddons, Anne Rice, and John Grisham. Although it's not authored by a Southerner, John Berendt's nonfiction *Midnight in the Garden of Good and Evil* is a tale of modern-day mayhem in Savannah.

The other element important in Southern culture is the region's passion for history, defined as both personal, family history and regional history. To see the importance of the Civil War period, view Ken Burns's nine-episode PBS television documentary *The Civil War.* Shelby Foote's three-volume history, *The Civil War,* is excellent, as is James McPherson's one-volume *Battle Cry of Freedom,* another history of the war. *Confederates in the Attic,* by Tony Hurwitz, discusses the appeal of Civil War reenactments.

The classic treatise on the culture of the South is W. J. Cash's groundbreaking *The Mind of the South,* published more than 50 years ago. The *Oxford Book of the American South,* edited by Edward L. Ayers and Bradley C. Mittendorf, is an outstanding collection of Southern writing about the region from the 18th century to the present.

For a clear picture of classic Southern architecture, look at Mills B. Lane's series *The Architecture of the Old South,* from his Beehive Press. Each book is devoted to a single state and has black-and-white photographs. The definitive book on Southern food is sociologist John Egerton's *Southern Cooking: On the Road, at Home, and in History,* a veritable treatise on Southern culture that includes many fine recipes.

Alfred Uhry's *Driving Miss Daisy,* a Pulitzer Prize–winning play and award-winning film, portrays an aspect of relationships between races and religions in the South. The novel (and film) *To Kill a Mockingbird,* by Alabama writer Harper Lee, portrays the good and the ugly in race relations in Southern society. Black Southern writers, of both fiction and nonfiction, now get the recognition they deserve. Although well-known author Alice Walker now lives in San Francisco, she is originally from Eaton, Georgia; Walker made her mark with the book *The Color Purple,* later a film.

The most important resource for Southern culture produced in recent years is the work of the Center for Southern Culture at the University of Mississippi in Oxford. Its single-volume *Encyclopedia of Southern Culture* serves as a guide to all matters Southern.

WHAT'S WHERE

Alabama

From sites where Native Americans lived for 8,000 years before the arrival of European settlers, to forts occupied during French colonial settlement in the 1700s and the American Revolution in the 1800s, to antebellum mansions that survived the Civil War, Alabama is a state loaded with history. It also brims with natural beauty—wooded hills and vast caves in the northeast, expansive lakes and broad rivers in the interior, and snow-white beaches along the Gulf Coast—within an easy drive of thriving cities such as Birmingham, Montgomery, and Mobile.

Georgia

Georgia is notable for its contrasting landscapes and varied cities and towns, each reflecting its own special Southern charm. The northern part of the state has the Appalachian Mountains and their waterfalls; Dahlonega, the site of an early gold rush; and Alpine Helen, a re-created Bavarian village in the Blue Ridge Mountains. Also in the north is Atlanta, a fast-growing city that serves as a banking center; and Macon, an antebellum town with thousands of cherry trees. If you drive some five hours southeast from Atlanta, you'll reach Savannah, which has the nation's largest historic district, filled with restored colonial and 19th-century buildings. From Savannah, the state's 100-mi Atlantic coast runs south to the Florida border. Along this stretch is a string of lush, subtropical barrier islands, the Golden Isles, which include the elegant seaside communities of Jekyll, Sea, and St. Simons islands. Farther south is Cumberland Island National Seashore, a sanctuary of marshes, beaches, forests, lakes, and ponds. Much of southern Georgia consists of gator-infested swampland, including the mysterious rivers and lakes of the Okefenokee.

Louisiana

Louisiana is a state divided, both physically and philosophically, around midstate in Alexandria. North Louisiana, with its rolling hills and piney woods, is strongly Southern in flavor and appeal, whereas flatter, marshy South Louisiana is considered Cajun Country, with sharp differences in food, music, and even language. Riverboats ply the mighty Mississippi and antebellum homes line the wayside in both regions, but it's New Orleans, home of the famous Mardi Gras festivities, great music, and fine restaurants, that garners the lion's share of attention, drawing most visitors to South Louisiana.

Mississippi

Filled with Civil War battlegrounds and slightly partisan tales of ancestors who fought valiantly for the Confederacy, Mississippi has some of the best-preserved examples of antebellum architecture in the South. The Natchez Trace, a beautiful string of magnolias and hilltop vistas, cuts across the heart of Dixie, passing through Tupelo (Elvis Presley's birthplace), Jackson (the capital), and antebellum Natchez. The mighty Mississippi provides the natural western border of the state, winding slowly through the Delta past the port towns of Greenville and Vicksburg. The Gulf Coast offers gambling, sun, sand, fishing, and general lazing, and in the north of the state, Oxford, a sophisticated courthouse town, still vibrates with the words of William Faulkner, Eudora Welty, and Tennessee Williams.

North Carolina

Historic sights and natural wonders abound in North Carolina, from Old Salem, where the 1700s spring to life in modern-day Winston-Salem, to the Great Smoky and Blue Ridge mountains in the west, where waterfalls cascade over high cliffs into gorges thick with evergreens. On the Cape Hatteras and Cape Lookout national seashores, tides wash over the wooden skeletons of ancient shipwrecks, and lighthouses stand as they have for 200 years. Here, too, you'll find sophisticated cities such as Charlotte and Raleigh, world-class golf in the Pinehurst Sandhills, and the rich soil of the gently rolling Piedmont, which has supported generations of farmers and potters alike.

South Carolina

South Carolina's scenic Lowcountry shoreline is punctuated by the lively port city of Charleston, decked out with fine museums (several in restored antebellum homes) and anchored by the recreational resorts of Myrtle Beach and Hilton Head at either end of the coast. The state capital, Columbia, is set in the fertile interior, and the Blue Ridge Mountains form the western border of the state. Also to the west are the rolling fields of Thoroughbred Country, noted for top racehorses and sprawling mansions, and Upcountry, at the state's northwestern tip, with incredible mountain scenery and white-water rafting.

Tennessee

Among Tennessee's dominating characteristics is its geography. Bordered by the Great Smoky Mountains on the east and the Mississippi River on the west, the state offers breathtaking scenery. Carved by rivers and mountains into three vertical regions, the state spans more than 500 mi east–west but only about 115 mi north–south. Here are forests, fields, and streams for the nature lover, outlet malls for the die-hard shopper, and an array of amusements for the whole family. Memphis and Nashville are musts for music lovers, and Chattanooga has attractions that range from a world-class aquarium to nearby Chickamauga/Chattanooga National Military Park.

PLEASURES AND PASTIMES

Dining

Southern dining comes in a variety of flavors: you can choose down-home cookin' like Mama used to make, with plenty of country ham, corn bread, and fried catfish, or you can savor the refined creations of brash young chefs who use fresh local ingredients in inventive new ways. You'll find both styles of cooking in Atlanta and many other Southern cities. In Louisiana, try Creole food, with its French influences, and hearty, heavily seasoned Cajun dishes. South Carolina's Lowcountry cooking highlights such specialties as she-crab soup, stuffed oysters, and pecan pie. And don't forget to sample the local barbecue, with seasonings that vary from state to state, or the fine seafood available at casual waterfront eateries or elegant dining rooms all along the coast. Your culinary explorations won't end with Southern cuisines, though. The increasing sophistication of the South has spurred the growth of restaurants that offer everything from good French and Italian fare to Thai and Tex-Mex.

History

On and off the beaten path, the South is rich in history. The lives of Native Americans, the area's first inhabitants, can be studied in such sites as Moundville Archaeological Park in Alabama and the Museum of the Cherokee Indian in Cherokee, North Carolina. You'll find evidence of early French settlers in New Orleans and Mobile, and Old Salem in Winston-Salem re-creates the world of Moravian immigrants. Colonial history comes alive

at Revolutionary War sites, whether at Kings Mountain National Military Park in Upcountry South Carolina or at Guilford Courthouse National Military Park near Greensboro, North Carolina. Throughout the South you can visit plantation houses or walk through historic districts in cities such as Savannah that stand as testimony to the antebellum era. The Civil War is commemorated on the great battlefields of Chickamauga, Shiloh, Vicksburg, and many others, but studying a Civil War monument in a town square can also take you to the heart of that wrenching conflict. In a later era, the South was the birthplace of the civil rights movement, and its landmarks and memorials stand proudly across the region, from the Ebenezer Baptist Church in Atlanta to the Civil Rights Memorial in Montgomery.

Music

Many people would say that the South is inseparable from music, and no visit here would be complete without taking in some performances and exploring the area's music museums. New Orleans, the birthplace of jazz, has plenty of choices, and in South Louisiana you can dance to the beat of Cajun music. The Mississippi Delta and Memphis gave birth to the blues, and on Beale Street and at museums or shrines such as Elvis's Graceland, you can trace the fortunes of the blues and rock and roll. Nashville, with the Grand Ole Opry, is the place for country music, but there's plenty of blues and rock, too. Myrtle Beach in South Carolina has a large number of country venues as well. For fine bluegrass, you can head to the mountains of western North Carolina. But whether you're in Atlanta or Asheville, clubs and an abundance of musical festivals celebrate a full range of sounds. Classical music isn't neglected, either: Spoleto Festival USA in Charleston is just one showcase, and many cities have fine orchestras and chamber groups.

Outdoor Activities and Sports

Name your sport, and you'll discover superb places to pursue it throughout the South. This is a golfer's paradise, from the courses of the Robert Trent Jones Golf Trail in Alabama to the resorts of North Carolina's Pinehills. Boaters can explore the lakes of South Carolina's Heartland or travel the Intracoastal Waterway, and rivers provide thrilling white-water rafting and excellent flat-water canoeing in every state. All this water holds challenges for anglers, whether in fresh water or out on the ocean. The region's mountains, from the Blue Ridge to the Great Smokies, have well-marked hiking trails, including the Appalachian Trail, to help you get away from it all. And if beaches are your passion, take your pick: the white sands of the Gulf Coast, the windswept shores of Cape Hatteras National Seashore in North Carolina, the bustling resorts at Myrtle Beach in South Carolina, or Georgia's lush barrier islands, known as the Golden Isles.

FODOR'S CHOICE

No two people will agree on what makes a perfect vacation, but it's fun and helpful to know what others think. We hope you'll have a chance to experience some of Fodor's Choices yourself in the South. For detailed information about each entry, refer to the appropriate chapter.

Special Moments

Birmingham Civil Rights Institute, Alabama. Observing the multimedia exhibits covering the movement from the 1920s to today, you can't help but reflect on the civil rights struggle through the years.

Okefenokee National Wildlife Refuge, southeastern Georgia. Savor nature at its most primeval as alligators and frogs bellow their respective mating calls in spring.

Martin Luther King Jr. Center, Atlanta, Georgia. The eternal flame burning at Martin Luther King Jr.'s tomb in front of the downtown center inspires reflection.

Historic District, Savannah, Georgia. Architecture buffs will have a field day strolling by the hundreds of restored buildings within a 2½-square-mi area.

Pirate's Alley, New Orleans, Louisiana. Romance comes alive in this section of town, redolent of old New Orleans, especially when viewed through the early morning mists.

French Quarter, New Orleans, Louisiana. From the deck of a riverboat, colors and shapes draw the eye to this section of the shoreline.

Elvis's birthplace, Tupelo, Mississippi. You'll understand how meager and humble were the beginnings of the King of Rock and Roll when you step into this tiny, two-room cabin.

Plantation dinner, Monmouth, Mississippi. Diners step back 150 years in time to experience the graciousness and grandeur of a formal soiree at this beautiful plantation in Natchez.

Old Salem, Winston-Salem, North Carolina. A 1700s village of brick-and-wood structures peopled by tradesmen and gentlewomen in period costume provides a slice of living history.

Cape Hatteras National Seashore, North Carolina. Stretching from Oregon Inlet to Ocracoke Island, this scenic coastline is dotted with beach communities, historic lifesaving stations, wildlife refuges, and beaches cluttered only by wild sea oats.

Cypress Gardens, South Carolina. A boat tour among the spring blossoms reflecting in the black waters of the gardens is a visual dazzler.

Viewing the Great Smokies from Lookout Tower at Clingmans Dome, East Tennessee. Here you'll see forested mountains capped by a gray haze of clouds as the early morning mists melt into midday. The drive up is more difficult in the morning mists, but those mists impart the true Smokies feel.

Dining

Voyagers, Orange Beach, Alabama. The airy two-level dining room of the Perdido Beach Resort is one of the most elegant restaurants on Alabama's Gulf Coast. $$$

Highlands Bar and Grill, Birmingham, Alabama. Owner-chef Frank Stitt, an Alabama native, unites the comfort foods of the American South with those of southern France in his restaurant. $$$–$$$$

Bacchanalia, Atlanta, Georgia. Mediterranean cuisine with Asian influences is served in a new, stunning location that matches its exquisite menu. $$$–$$$$

The 1838 Langston House at Henderson Village, Perry, Georgia. You'll dine on French-based fare made with local ingredients and interpretations of regional dishes in a restored early 19th-century Greek Revival house outside Macon. $$$

Elizabeth on 37th, Savannah, Georgia. In an elegant turn-of-the-century mansion in the city's Victorian district, the emphasis is on seafood enhanced by delicate sauces. *$$$*

Mrs. Wilkes Dining Room, Savannah, Georgia. Expect long lines waiting to devour the reasonably priced, well-prepared Southern food, served family style at big tables. *$*

Commander's Palace. New Orleans's gastronomic heritage and celebratory spirit are perfectly captured in the creatively prepared Creole dishes served in a stately Garden Distric mansion. *$$$–$$$$*

Lafitte's Landing, Donaldsonville, Louisiana. Celebrity chef John Folse (of PBS fame) serves his regional fare in this upscale Acadian cottage. *$$$–$$$$*

Joe's "Dreyfus Store," Livonia, Louisiana. The old general store is still outfitted with polished-wood cabinets and other period memorabilia, an interesting, relaxed setting for the South Louisiana cuisine featured here. *$$–$$$*

Café des Amis, Beaux Bridge, Louisiana. Cajun and Creole seafood specialties are served in this little Acadian cottage, whose walls are decorated with paintings and folk art by local artists. *$*

Nick's, Jackson, Mississippi. As any local who comes here to dine on the tasty seafood will tell you, no visit to Jackson is complete without a meal here. *$$–$$$$*

City Grocery, Oxford, Mississippi. Attentive service and inventive Southern cuisine are your reward for visiting this trendy bistro. *$$–$$$*

Gabrielle's at Richmond Hill, Asheville, North Carolina. The fabulous dinners at this Victorian inn are not to be missed—held by some to be the most imaginative (wild boar sausage and grilled antelope medallions) and delicious food in the state. *$$$$*

Second Empire, Raleigh, North Carolina. Elegance and epicurean innovation are the bywords at this renovated Victorian-era mansion just blocks from the capital building. *$$$$*

Lamplighter, Charlotte, North Carolina. Fine contemporary cuisine served in the softly lighted interior of an old Dilworth home is the hallmark of this favorite. *$$$–$$$$*

Woodlands Inn, Summerville, South Carolina. The restaurant at this luxurious inn continues to be the most sophisticated in the Charleston area. *$$$–$$$$*

Collectors Cafe, Myrtle Beach, South Carolina. This pleasantly arty spot includes a gallery, so you can shop after you try the barbecued duck or veal-stuffed ravioli. *$$–$$$*

Magnolias, Charleston, South Carolina. Lots of Lowcountry dishes and a magnolia theme infuse this refurbished warehouse with Southern charm. *$$–$$$*

Chez Philippe, Memphis, Tennessee. The art deco setting is incredible, and the sophisticated French food lives up to the surroundings. *$$$$*

212 Market, Chattanooga, Tennessee. Light, healthful cuisine—poached salmon in ginger-lime sauce or vegetable terrine—is served in a colorful, contemporary setting. *$$*

Burning Bush Restaurant, Gatlinburg, Tennessee. The atmosphere is colonial, the menu Continental at this pleaser. *$*

Lodging

The Tutwiler, Birmingham, Alabama. Marble floors, chandeliers, and period reproduction furnishings are fitting touches in this elegant National Historic Landmark. *$$$$*

Marriott's Grand Hotel, Point Clear, Alabama. For more than 150 years the Grand—in an enviable spot on Mobile Bay—has offered guests personal service and comfortable elegance. *$$$–$$$$*

Perdido Beach Resort, Orange Beach, Alabama. Fantastic views, a splendid beach location, and lovely Mediterranean style set this one apart. *$$$–$$$$*

Malaga Inn, Mobile, Alabama. Two antiques-furnished town houses built by a wealthy landowner in 1862 house this romantic retreat. *$$–$$$*

Ritz-Carlton, Buckhead, Atlanta, Georgia. The Ritz's signature 18th- and 19th-century furnishings grace this discreetly elegant gem close to Lenox Mall and Phipps Plaza shopping. *$$$$*

Kehoe House, Savannah, Georgia. Elegance, refinement, and Victorian opulence make a stay at this bed-and-breakfast inn a grand experience in every way. $$$–$$$$

Henderson Village, Perry, Georgia. An elegant, rustic cluster of farmhouses with a fine restaurant, it's the perfect base for your visit to Macon. $$$

Jekyll Island Club Hotel, Jekyll Island, Georgia. This former private winter hunting retreat for the wealthy now has luxurious guest rooms for the public and an excellent restaurant. $$$

Windsor Court Hotel, New Orleans, Louisiana. The Windsor embodies elegance with its fine service and luxurious furnishings. $$$$

Lloyd Hall Plantation, Cheneyville, Louisiana. A quiet country retreat features surprisingly upscale accommodations furnished in grand 19th-century Louisiana antiques. $$–$$$

Butler Greenwood, St. Francisville, Louisiana. Seven individually decorated cottages, each with hot tub and kitchenette, dot the tree-shaded acreage of a historic 18th-century mansion. $$

Cedar Grove, Vicksburg, Mississippi. Civil War cannonballs are still visible in the walls of this enormous 1840s mansion set near the river in Vicksburg. $$–$$$$

Millsaps-Buie House, Jackson, Mississippi. This 1888 Queen Anne Victorian, complete with turret and columned porch, is a lovely bed-and-breakfast furnished with antiques. $$–$$$$

Fearrington House, Chapel Hill, North Carolina. This French-style country inn was once a working farm and looks like an English country village. You'll get top-notch service in a genteel atmosphere. $$$$

Grove Park Inn, Asheville, North Carolina. The city's premier resort, Grove Park Inn has Arts and Crafts furnishings. It has been the haunt of guests such as Thomas Edison and F. Scott Fitzgerald since its opening in 1913. $$$$

First Colony Inn, Nags Head, North Carolina. Four-poster beds, English antiques, and whirlpool tubs lend an air of romance to this inn by the ocean, reminiscent of the beach hotels of years past. $$$–$$$$

Charleston Place, Charleston, South Carolina. The upscale address for Charleston, this full-service hotel is conveniently located in the historic district. $$$$

Kingston Plantation, Myrtle Beach, South Carolina. This self-contained resort, loaded with facilities such as a spa and a marina, has a great location on a broad beach well removed from the bustle of the pavilion area. $$$–$$$$

Westin Resort, Hilton Head Island, South Carolina. Top of the line for Hilton Head, the Westin concentrates on luxury and service. $$$–$$$$

Opryland Hotel, Nashville, Tennessee. Top flight and massive, this resort hotel includes a waterfall and indoor gardens. $$$$

Peabody Hotel, Memphis, Tennessee. Legendary in the Delta, this grande dame was a locale for movie scenes in *The Firm*. Observing the Peabody ducks on parade is a unique part of the experience. $$$$

Buckhorn Inn, Gatlinburg, Tennessee. This unassuming country inn set on 40 secluded acres has been a celebrity hideaway for decades. $$$–$$$$

Nightlife

Blind Willie's, Atlanta, Georgia. This is one of the country's best blues venues. Only first-rate, nationally famous musicians get the nod.

Dancing at Mulate's, Breaux Bridge, Louisiana. Devote at least one night to the foot-stompin' fun at Mulate's.

New Orleans funk at Tipitina's, New Orleans, Louisiana. This music blends R&B and Afro-Caribbean rhythms to create a sound entirely unique to New Orleans. This is the music the locals prefer.

Traditional jazz at Preservation Hall, New Orleans, Louisiana. When most people think of the New Orleans sound, traditional jazz comes to mind, and there's no better showcase than Preservation Hall.

The blues on Beale Street, Memphis, Tennessee. Whether you're at B. B. King's Blues Club or the Rum Boogie, savor the atmosphere of this legendary street.

GREAT ITINERARIES

The following recommended itineraries, arranged by both theme and area, are offered as a guide to planning individual travel.

Prominent Sites of African-American History

Alabama Tour

5 to 7 days. Alabama's historic civil rights sites provide a close look at the long struggle for racial equality.

1 day. In Mobile see the antebellum State Street A.M.E. (African Methodist Episcopal) Zion Church and the St. Louis Street Missionary Baptist Church, two of four black congregations established in Alabama prior to 1865. Check out the black heritage display at Fort Condé and the National African-American Archives and Museum.

2 or 3 days. Travel to Montgomery and visit the Civil Rights Memorial and Dexter Avenue King Memorial Baptist Church, considered by many to be the birthplace of the civil rights movement. Then move on to Selma and see the Edmund Pettus Bridge, famous during the 1960s for clashes between civil rights marchers and police. Near the bridge, don't miss the National Voting Rights Museum. Make an excursion east from Montgomery to the Tuskegee Institute National Historic Site, which consists of Booker T. Washington's home, the Oaks; the George Washington Carver Museum; and Tuskegee University.

1 or 2 days. From Montgomery go north to Birmingham and visit its Civil Rights district, the centerpiece of which is the Birmingham Civil Rights Institute. A few blocks south is the Alabama Jazz Hall of Fame, where jazz greats with Alabama ties are spotlighted. Among those honored is Erskine Hawkins, who wrote "Tuxedo Junction." Next, take in the Alabama Sports Hall of Fame, which pays tribute to many of the state's great African-American athletes.

1 day. Travel north to Decatur and visit the Old Courthouse, noted for the 1933 retrial of the Scottsboro Boys. Northwest is Florence, site of the W. C. Handy Home and Museum.

Information: Chapter 2.

Tennessee and Mississippi Tour

4 or 5 days. For a glimpse of African-American life in the Deep South, visit the cotton country of the Mississippi Delta.

1 day. Begin in Memphis with a stop at the National Civil Rights Museum, on the site of Martin Luther King Jr.'s 1968 assassination. After this, you can walk through the shops and blues clubs in the Beale Street Historic District. About 45 mi northeast is Henning, hometown of the late Alex Haley and the setting for his novel *Roots.* Chapter 8.

1 or 2 days. Next stop is Jackson, to get an overview of the civil rights movement's history in Mississippi. See the Old Capitol Historical Museum and Eudora Welty Library, which houses a number of exhibits on writers from the South. Chapter 5.

2 days. Head to Oxford and the Ole Miss campus, where an African-American was first graduated in 1963; see the Center for the Study of Southern Culture, which focuses on Southern music and folklore. Then go 62 mi southwest to Clarksdale and tour the Delta Blues Museum, which honors famous blues musicians. Chapter 5.

Lowcountry Tour

2 days. Blacks and whites in South Carolina's Lowcountry have always lived side by side, though, as evidenced by the 1739 Stono Plantation Rebellion and the 1822 Denmark Vesey plot to take over Charleston, not always peaceably. This distrust also motivated blacks to develop a lilting dialect called Gullah to communicate exclusively with one another. Historic sites in the Lowcountry recall this unique black experience.

The **African-American Trail,** outlined in a brochure put out by South Carolina Parks, Recreation and Tourism, highlights African and African-American sites in three Lowcountry counties. Divided into two parts—the Coastal Trail, which winds along the coast, and the Folkways & Communities Trail, which travels through rural and urban centers—the trail familiarizes visitors with the lifestyle, culture, and achievements of enslaved Africans and African-Americans in the counties of Charleston, Dorchester, and Colleton.

1 day. In Charleston, begin with a walking tour of Cabbage Row, home of Du-Bose Heyward and setting for his novel *Porgy.* Then see the Emanuel A.M.E. Church—the place of worship of the South's oldest A.M.E. congregation. Also here is the Old Exchange and Provost Dungeon, site of the city's busiest slave market. The Avery Research Center in the historic district has an archives and museum that document the heritage of Low-country blacks.

1 day. Travel on to the Beaufort area, where you'll see the Penn Center Historic District and York W. Bailey Cultural Museum on St. Helena Island. This community center consists of 17 buildings on the campus of a school that was established in 1862 for freed slaves. Also in Beaufort County is Daufuskie Island, until recently inhabited exclusively by descendants of slaves.

Information: Chapter 7.

Prominent Civil War Sites

The Southeastern Tour

7 to 9 days. South Carolina seceded from the Union on December 20, 1860, and the first shot of the war was fired the following April. The following itinerary takes in the major sites and sights in South Carolina, Georgia, and Alabama.

1 day. Visit the Fort Sumter National Monument in Charleston. On April 12, 1861, Confederate general P. G. T. Beauregard ordered the first shot fired, and the bloody four-year struggle began. Charleston in Chapter 7.

2 or 3 days. From Charleston, drive the 300 mi south to Atlanta to see the Eternal Flame of the Confederacy, and visit the Cyclorama, depicting the 1864 Battle of Atlanta. Explore 3,200-acre Stone Mountain Park, where there's a Confederate Memorial carved into the mountain—the world's largest monument. Atlanta in Chapter 3.

2 days. 160 mi southwest of Atlanta lies Montgomery, the Cradle of the Confederacy. Visit the state capitol, which was the site of the first capital of the Confederacy, and the First White House of the Confederacy, which was occupied by President Jefferson Davis and his family. Chapter 2.

2 or 3 days. From Montgomery head southwest toward Mobile. Next stop is Fort Morgan, about 20 mi from Gulf Shores. A museum in Fort Morgan describes the dramatic 1864 Battle of Mobile Bay, during which Admiral David Farragut shouted, "Damn the torpedoes! Full speed ahead!" Chapter 2.

The South Central Tour

8 to 10 days. The long, colorful trek through Mississippi, Louisiana, and Tennessee offers Civil War–history buffs a wealth of well-preserved battle sites.

2 or 3 days. From Mobile, head west toward New Orleans (146 mi). Overlooking the Gulf of Mexico between Gulfport and Biloxi, Mississippi, is Beauvoir, the home of Confederate president Jefferson Davis. At the Louisiana–Mississippi border, turn off to Baton Rouge (bypassing New Orleans, which fell to the Union in 1862) and then north to the Port Hudson State Commemorative Area, a 650-acre area on the site where, in 1863, 6,800 Confederates held off between 30,000 and 40,000 Federals from May 23 till July 9. Continue north to Vicksburg, the Mississippi River city that withstood Grant's siege for 47 days and nights before falling in July 1863, a Northern victory that was a major turning point in the war. Here you can visit the Vicksburg National Military Park. Baton Rouge in Chapter 4 and Vicksburg in Chapter 5.

3 days. From Vicksburg make the 242-mi trip to Jackson; then head north to Memphis. Another 100 mi east is Shiloh National Military Park and Cemetery, commemorating those who died in the April 1862 battle, one of the bloodiest of the Civil War. Jackson in Chapter 5 and Memphis in Chapter 8.

3 or 4 days. Head south to Chattanooga. See the Battles for Chattanooga Museum and Point Park and visit the eight locations of the Chickamauga-Chattanooga National Military Park, whose headquarters is 10 mi south of the city. This is one of the nation's largest and oldest national military parks. Chattanooga in Chapter 8.

2 ALABAMA

From the Civil War to civil rights, Alabama
has weathered the upheavals in Southern
society. Steeped in history, rich in culture
and tradition, and possessing a wealth of
natural beauty from forested mountains to
sugar-white Gulf Coast beaches, the Cotton
State provides myriad opportunities to enjoy
life in the heart of Dixie among the friendly,
welcoming people who call it home.

Updated by
Michelle
Roberts
Matthews

ALABAMA IS A STATE OF SURPRISES. Visitors marvel at its physical beauty: the rocky, wooded hills and vast caves of the northeast; the expansive lakes and broad rivers of the interior; and the white beaches of the Gulf Coast. Venturing off the interstates, you'll find something unexpected at almost every turn—a cascading waterfall or showy stand of wildflowers, an archaeological excavation or colonial fort, or perhaps one of Alabama's 13 covered bridges.

Alabama has had its share of accomplished sons and daughters. Father of the Blues William Christopher Handy, son of a Methodist minister descended from slaves, was born in Florence in 1873. A teacher, bandleader, and author, Handy is best remembered for such songs as "Memphis Blues" and "St. Louis Blues." In nearby Tuscumbia, the tiny frame cottage where Helen Keller overcame her loss of hearing and sight sits as a monument to her inspirational life. Farther south, Tuskegee Institute, founded in 1881 by the distinguished black educator Booker T. Washington, was where the young botanist George Washington Carver headed the agricultural department and did his seminal work in plant derivatives and crop diversification. And in Monroeville, Harper Lee grew up to tell the tale of Atticus Finch, his children Scout and Jem, and their odd neighbor Boo Radley, in her Pulitzer Prize–winning novel *To Kill a Mockingbird*.

History and Southern tradition are around every bend of the road, whether you follow the path of Civil War soldiers or that of civil rights marchers. Many sections of the state have preserved the elegant antebellum homes so typical of the 19th century, yet the cities have an eye on the future. Huntsville hosts the high-tech Space and Rocket Center, where the Saturn rocket was designed. Birmingham, the state's largest city, is a major medical center. The new and progressive blend nicely with the old and historic—Montgomery's modern state government buildings stand just one block from the First White House of the Confederacy. As part of Mobile's yearlong 300th birthday celebration in 2002, Mayor Mike Dow and the city council broke ground for the Retirement Systems of Alabama Tower, the state's largest skyscraper, which will rise downtown next to the long-abandoned but soon-to-be-renovated Battle House Hotel.

Pleasures and Pastimes

Beaches

Some people find it difficult to believe that a state filled with mountains also has beaches. Yet those who discover the coast will find pure white sand, outstanding seafood restaurants, amusement parks, and golf courses. In Bon Secour National Wildlife Refuge, you can hike an undisturbed pocket of coastline. Fishing boats, which are especially abundant in Orange Beach, are available for half- or full-day charters. Whether you visit Alabama's beaches to take in the sun or to fish and hike, you won't be disappointed.

Dining

From the fresh seafood served along the coast to the traditional Southern comfort food found inland to the upscale nouveau Southern cuisine that helps define the state's cosmopolitan cities, there's something for every taste in Alabama. An abundance of catfish farms throughout the state ensures an ample supply of fresh fried catfish, usually served with a hearty helping of hush puppies (deep-fried cornmeal dumplings). All over the state, you'll find heated discussions regarding which are

Alabama

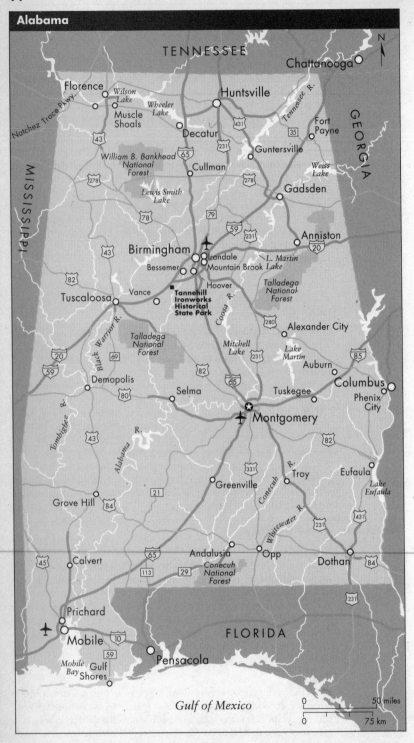

TENNESSEE

Chattanooga

GEORGIA

Florence
Wilson Lake
Muscle Shoals
Wheeler Lake
Huntsville
Fort Payne
Natchez Trace Pkwy.
43
Decatur
231
65
35
431
Guntersville
Tennessee R.

MISSISSIPPI

William B. Bankhead National Forest
278
Cullman
278
Gadsden
Weiss Lake

Lewis Smith Lake
78
79
59
231
Anniston
20

43
Birmingham
Irondale
Mountain Brook
L. Martin Lake
Bessemer
Hoover
Talladega National Forest
82
Vance
Tannehill Ironworks Historical State Park
Coosa R.
280
Alexander City
85

Tuscaloosa
Talladega National Forest
69
Black Warrior R.
82
Mitchell Lake
231
Lake Martin
Auburn
Columbus

20
59
Demopolis
80
Selma
65
Tuskegee
Phenix City

Tombigbee R.
43
Alabama R.
Montgomery
82
Eufaula
Lake Eufaula

21
Grove Hill
84
Greenville
331
Conecuh R.
Troy
Whitewater R.
231
431

45
Calvert
65
113
29
Andalusia
Conecuh National Forest
Opp
Dothan
84
231

Prichard
Mobile
10
Mobile Bay
59
Gulf Shores
Pensacola

FLORIDA

Gulf of Mexico

50 miles
0
0   75 km

the best barbecue joints. And even in the fanciest restaurants, no meal is complete without the ubiquitous "sweet tea."

CATEGORY	COST*
$$$$	over $26
$$$	$18–$26
$$	$10–$18
$	under $10

per person for a main course at dinner, or at lunch if no dinner is served, excluding 8% sales tax

Golf

Golf in Alabama is a popular pastime and can be played year-round, with spring and fall the ideal times. The state's wide-ranging topography offers various levels of hilly courses in the north and central parts of the state, fanning out to the flatland of the plains of south-central and lower Alabama. Greens fees are more reasonable than in Florida or Georgia, particularly at the eight locations of the public Robert Trent Jones Golf Trail, which spans the state.

Lodging

Lodging around Alabama falls into several categories. There's a growing trend toward country inns and bed-and-breakfasts in many of the rural northern counties, whereas the cities are a pleasant blend of remodeled older hotels and modern business complexes. Along the coast, full-service resorts with their own golf courses provide a relaxing stay with a spectacular view of the Gulf of Mexico.

CATEGORY	COST*
$$$$	over $210
$$$	$140–$210
$$	$70–$140
$	under $70

All prices are for a standard double room, excluding 4%–5% tax (depending on the county).

Spring Pilgrimage

Each spring a number of Alabama towns, among them Selma and Eufaula, hold "pilgrimages"—tours of historic homes (including many private residences not otherwise open to the public), mansions, plantations, churches, gardens, and even cemeteries. Hosts and hostesses, often dressed in period costume, greet you and tell tales of life in bygone days. It's a lovely time to visit, with the gardens decked out in dogwoods, azaleas, and magnolias. Candlelight tours add a romantic touch.

Exploring Alabama

With the Appalachian Mountains stretching into the center of the state, Alabama has two very different types of terrain. The northern part of the state is quite mountainous, the southern part fairly flat and covered with extensive pine forests. Each is filled with outdoor recreational areas, historic sites, and plenty of chances to sample a touch of Southern tradition and culture. The small towns and back roads of Alabama are often a throwback to earlier, less hectic times, when people knew their neighbors.

Great Itineraries

You could easily spend a month touring the state, but three to five days in each area can provide a good sampling of Alabama life. If you have 10 days, you can cross from the mountains to the shore.

IF YOU HAVE 3 DAYS

You'll find historic sites mixed in with plenty of Southern culture on a short visit to Montgomery and Birmingham. In ⊞ **Montgomery,** you can stand on the steps of the Alabama State Capitol where Jefferson Davis took the oath of office as president of the Confederacy and look out at the Dexter Avenue King Memorial Baptist Church where Dr. Martin Luther King Jr. preached a hundred years later. Country music fans can trace the life of Hank Williams Sr. from his boyhood home in **Georgiana,** 60 mi south of Montgomery, to his final resting place at Montgomery's Oakwood Cemetery. Ninety minutes north via I–65 is the state's largest city, ⊞ **Birmingham.** Here you will find diverse sites, including the Birmingham Civil Rights Institute, Birmingham Museum of Art, Birmingham Zoo, and the Alabama Sports Hall of Fame. Outside the city, Tannehill Ironworks Historical State Park is laced with hiking trails and steeped in Civil War history.

IF YOU HAVE 5 DAYS

You can spend two days seeing the sights of ⊞ **Birmingham,** then take a trip along the Tennessee River basin. You could begin along Alabama's portion of the Natchez Trace near the Mississippi border, then stop at ⊞ **The Shoals** (the quad cities of Tuscumbia, Sheffield, Muscle Shoals, and Florence) to visit Helen Keller's birthplace at Ivy Green, the Alabama Music Hall of Fame, and the W. C. Handy Home. Moving eastward, plan a day at ⊞ **Huntsville**'s U.S. Space and Rocket Center, and EarlyWorks, a living-history center featuring Alabama Constitution Village. For your final day, venture farther eastward; stay near beautiful Lake Guntersville State Park in ⊞ **Guntersville** or in peaceful ⊞ **Mentone,** near the Georgia border.

Another five-day option is to explore Alabama's Gulf Coast, where you'll have to resist the temptation to do nothing more than sun yourself and sample seafood. Either ⊞ **Gulf Shores** or ⊞ **Orange Beach** is good for overnights on your first three days. You can have fun at Waterville USA (a water park) or hike in Bon Secour National Wildlife Refuge. Another day's option is to explore Gulf State Park. You can charter a deep-sea fishing boat for a day or just a sailboat. If outlet shopping appeals, head for the Riviera Centre, just north of Foley. On your fourth day (if you're willing to leave the beach), drive 50 mi north to ⊞ **Mobile,** exploring Fort Morgan en route. In Mobile, Fort Condé, the USS *Alabama,* the Gulf Coast Exploreum and IMAX Dome Theater, the Museum of Mobile, and the Oakleigh Garden Historic District will occupy you, but save at least a half day for the spectacular Bellingrath Gardens and Home, in nearby **Theodore.**

IF YOU HAVE 10 DAYS

In 10 days you can travel across Alabama from The Shoals to the seashore. Begin in the northwest in ⊞ **The Shoals,** visiting the homes of Helen Keller and W. C. Handy. Spend the next day exploring ⊞ **Decatur**'s historic districts and Point Mallard Park or Wheeler Wildlife Refuge. On your third day, visit ⊞ **Huntsville**'s U.S. Space and Rocket Center and EarlyWorks living-history museum. Spend your fourth day relaxing at Lake Guntersville State Park, overnighting in ⊞ **Guntersville.** The next day wind your way south to **Childersburg** and DeSoto Caverns Park before heading to ⊞ **Birmingham.** Spend the sixth day exploring the city; the following morning, proceed southwest to ⊞ **Tuscaloosa,** where you can visit the Paul W. "Bear" Bryant Museum and the Warner Collection. At nearby Moundville Archaeological Park, native life has been preserved. On the eighth day, drive south into what was plantation country, stopping to see the old homes in **Demopolis** before going to ⊞ **Selma,** with its Civil War and civil rights heritage.

On the ninth day start early as you head south on I–65 for ⊡ **Mobile,** detouring along the way to see ⊡ **Monroeville,** hometown of *To Kill a Mockingbird* author Harper Lee. Once you reach the coast and Mobile, you can tour historic Fort Condé or the battleship USS *Alabama.* You may want to visit Bellingrath Gardens and Home in **Theodore** or drive south to the beaches of the ⊡ **Gulf Coast,** stopping en route in charming ⊡ **Fairhope,** on Mobile Bay's Eastern Shore.

When to Tour Alabama

Although the state is a year-round haven, be advised that sometimes the summer heat and humidity can be a bit overpowering, especially for those not used to it. The summer is, however, prime time for going to the beach and deep-sea fishing. The offshore breezes along the Gulf Coast help keep you comfortable.

Spring, when the azaleas are in full bloom, is perhaps the most beautiful time of all, and late spring is perfect for the wildflowers of northern Alabama along the Tennessee River basin and atop Lookout Mountain near Mentone. Fall visitors will find almost summerlike conditions along the coast until November. It may be a little cool at night, but the warm sunny days are ideal for strolling along the sand dunes.

Winters, although not severe, do get a touch cold at times, but normally the temperatures moderate quickly. Golf is played year-round, but wintertime golfers and bird-watchers might need a sweater or jacket to ward off the chill.

BIRMINGHAM AND NORTH ALABAMA

Huntsville, The Shoals, Tuscaloosa

From the Tennessee border south to Birmingham and Tuscaloosa, you'll find verdant hills, parks, natural beauty, and history all competing for your attention.

Numbers in the margin correspond to points of interest on the Birmingham and North Alabama maps.

Birmingham

90 mi north of Montgomery.

Birmingham, set in a valley below the foothills of the Appalachians, first blossomed around the coal mines and the iron industry in the late 1800s. Its rapid growth earned it a nickname: the Magic City. Today the largest employer here is the University of Alabama at Birmingham, with its highly regarded medical center. In the 1960s, the city was a center for civil rights activity; Dr. Martin Luther King Jr. was jailed here for fighting racial inequality. By the 1990s, a diverse, progressive Birmingham had reconciled its turbulent history, the evidence of which is displayed in the museums, churches, and landmarks that make up the city's Civil Rights District. Less densely populated than Atlanta to the east, Birmingham is a comfortably sprawling, easily navigable city with a growing reputation for sophisticated shopping and dining.

★ ❶ Alabama has long been noted for its excellence in sports, and the **Alabama Sports Hall of Fame,** adjacent to the Convention Complex, displays memorabilia of such Alabama heroes as coach Paul "Bear" Bryant, Jesse Owens, Willie Mays, Billy Williams, and Hank Aaron. ✉ *2150 Civic Center Blvd., Downtown,* ☎ *205/323–6665,* WEB *www. alasports.org.* ▦ *$5.* ◷ *Mon.–Sat. 9–5, Sun. 1–5.*

18

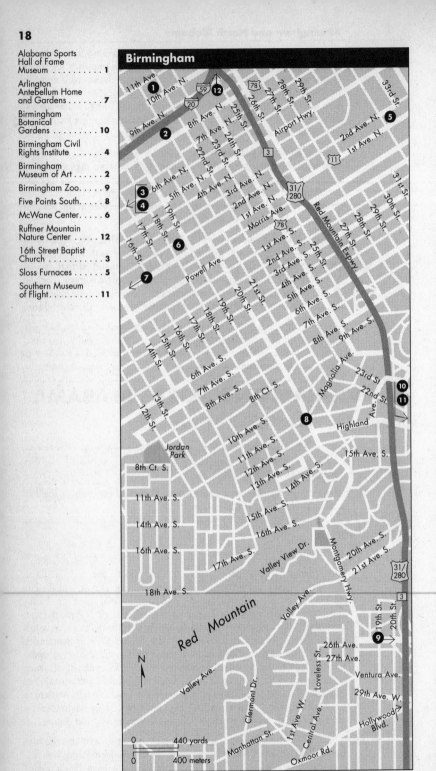

② The **Birmingham Museum of Art,** with a multilevel sculpture garden, has one of the world's largest collections of Wedgwood, the largest collection of contemporary Chinese paintings outside the People's Republic of China, and some extraordinary examples of Western American art, plus Italian Renaissance and pre-Columbian art. ⊠ *2000 8th Ave. N, Downtown,* ☎ *205/254–2565,* WEB *www.artsbma.org.* 🎫 *Free.* ⊙ *Tues.–Sat. 10–5, Sun. noon–5.*

③ The **16th Street Baptist Church** was the site of one of the saddest and most memorable occurrences of the civil rights movement. On the morning of September 15, 1963, a bomb exploded, killing four young black girls who were attending Sunday school in the basement. A plaque erected to their memory bears this legend: MAY MEN LEARN TO REPLACE BITTERNESS AND VIOLENCE WITH LOVE AND UNDERSTANDING. The event was again the subject of national attention in May 2002, when former Ku Klux Klansman Bobby Frank Cherry was convicted of first-degree murder for his role in the bombing. ⊠ *1530 16th St., Downtown,* ☎ *205/251–9402.* 🎫 *$2 for tour.* ⊙ *Tues.–Fri. 10–4, Sat. by appointment.*

★ **④** The **Birmingham Civil Rights Institute** traces the roots of the civil rights movement from the late 1800s through the troubled 1960s, showing its effect on the present day via exhibits, multimedia presentations, music, and storytelling. ⊠ *520 16th St. N, Downtown,* ☎ *205/328–9696,* WEB *www.bcri.bham.al.us.* 🎫 *$5.* ⊙ *Tues.–Sat. 10–5, Sun. 1–5.*

The **Alabama Jazz Hall of Fame,** two blocks from the Civil Rights Institute, has photos and memorabilia of the state's jazz greats, including Nat "King" Cole, Duke Ellington, and Lionel Hampton. ⊠ *1631 4th Ave. N, Downtown,* ☎ *205/254–2720,* WEB *www.jazzhall.com.* 🎫 *Free.* ⊙ *Tues.–Sat. 10–5, Sun. 1–5.*

⑤ **Sloss Furnaces,** a National Historic Landmark, is a massive, 32-acre ironworks that from 1882 to 1971 produced pig iron from ore dug from the hills surrounding Birmingham. Retired blast-furnace workers sometimes conduct tours of the plant. At other times tours are self-guided. The site is also a design center for metal-art sculptors. ⊠ *20 32nd St. N, off 1st Ave. N, Downtown,* ☎ *205/324–1911,* WEB *www.slossfurnaces.com.* 🎫 *Free.* ⊙ *Tues.–Sat. 10–4, Sun. noon–4.*

⑥ The **McWane Center** is a hands-on science learning center with an IMAX theater for large-screen movies. It's meant for kids, but adults will love it as well. ⊠ *200 19th St. N, Downtown,* ☎ *205/558–2000 or 877/462–9263,* WEB *www.mcwane.org.* 🎫 *$7.50 for museum, $7.50 for IMAX, $13 for both; parking $2.* ⊙ *Sept.–May, weekdays 9–5, Sat. 10–6, Sun. 1–5; June–Aug., Mon.–Sat. 10–6, Sun. 1–6.*

⑦ **Arlington Antebellum Home and Gardens** is Birmingham's only remaining antebellum mansion (the city was not founded until after the Civil War). It was used as a headquarters by Union general James H. Wilson in March 1865 as he and his troops swept south through Alabama to Selma, destroying iron furnaces along the way. Today the classic Greek Revival structure houses Civil War memorabilia and some prime examples of 19th-century furniture. ⊠ *331 Cotton Ave. SW, West Birmingham,* ☎ *205/780–5656,* WEB *www.ci.bham.al.us/arlington.* 🎫 *$3.* ⊙ *Tues.–Sat. 10–4, Sun. 1–4.*

⑧ The revitalized **Five Points South** historic district (⊠ around 20th St., Magnolia Ave., and 11th Ave. S, Southside), just south of downtown, has quaint shops and trendy restaurants. The neighborhood, named for the landmark circle where five streets converge, was one of Birmingham's first streetcar suburbs. Its various architectural styles include Spanish baroque, as seen in the **Highlands United Methodist Church** (⊠ 1045 20th St. S, Southside), and art deco.

★ ⏱ ❾ The wooded **Birmingham Zoo** is home to some 700 exotic and endangered animals representing 202 species from around the world. Don't miss the white rhinoceroses, elephants, gorillas, giraffes, and llamas in outdoor exhibits; reptiles, tropical birds, and snow leopards are indoors. ⊠ 2630 Cahaba Rd., Mountain Brook, ☎ 205/879–0408, WEB www.birminghamzoo.com. ☞ $5. ☉ Daily 9–5, with extended summer hrs.

❿ Under a great glass dome at the **Birmingham Botanical Gardens,** waterfalls cascade into pools with plants of every shade of green and flowers of every color imaginable. Outside, a quiet Japanese garden has small bridges over bubbling brooks and an authentic tea house. Wear your best walking shoes: the gardens are as extensive as they are beautiful. The gardens are adjacent to the Birmingham Zoo. ⊠ 2612 Lane Park Rd., Mountain Brook, ☎ 205/414–3900, WEB www.bbgardens.org. ☞ Free. ☉ Daily sunrise–sunset.

⓫ The **Southern Museum of Flight,** near the airport, has the Alabama Aviation Hall of Fame, the first Delta Air Lines plane, and World War II training planes. In addition to housing artifacts, this museum specializes in painstakingly renovating old aircraft. ⊠ 4343 73rd St. N, East Birmingham, ☎ 205/833–8226. ☞ $3. ☉ Tues.–Sat. 9:30–4:30, Sun. 1–4:30.

⓬ The **Ruffner Mountain Nature Center** has 10 mi of well-marked nature trails and a wildflower garden. Bird-watchers can spot migratory birds and resident red-tailed hawks. ⊠ 1214 81st St. S (about 8 mi east of downtown via Exit 132 at 1st Ave. N from I–59), East Birmingham, ☎ 205/833–8264, WEB www.ruffnermountain.org. ☞ Free. ☉ Tues.–Sat. 9–5, Sun. 1–5.

⏱ Highlights of **VisionLand,** a 35-acre theme park, are Celebration City, with games and thrill rides, and Steel Waters, a 7-acre water park. Special attractions include the Rampage, a wooden roller coaster, and Sky Wheel, a 106-ft-tall Ferris wheel. The park is 16 mi southwest of Birmingham. ⊠ I–20/59, Exit 108, Bessemer, ☎ 205/481–4750, WEB www.visionlandpark.com. ☞ $25, parking $4. ☉ Late May–late Aug., daily 10–10 (closing time may vary); late Aug.–Oct., weekends 10–10 (closing time may vary).

OFF THE
BEATEN PATH

MERCEDES-BENZ VISITOR CENTER – This center, some 30 mi west of Birmingham, is the first of its kind outside Germany. A museum contains historic Mercedes vehicles and offers a multimedia look at the past, present, and future of automotive technology. The adjacent factory produces M-Class sport-utility vehicles. ⊠ Exit 89, off I–20/59, Vance, ☎ 888/286–8762 or 205/507–2252, WEB www.bamabenz.com. ☞ Free; $5 for factory tour. ☉ Weekdays 9–5; 1st Sat. of each month, 10–3; factory tours weekdays 9, 9:15, 11, 11:15, 1, and 1:15.

TANNEHILL IRONWORKS HISTORICAL STATE PARK – Built around reconstructed ironworks and blast furnaces that produced munitions for the Confederacy, the park has an Iron and Steel Museum, crafts demonstrations from March through November, a pioneer farm, a country store, and a minitrain ride. There are also hiking trails, fishing spots, a campground, and horseback riding tours. ⊠ Exit 100 off I–59 (about 30 mi west of Birmingham), ☎ 205/477–5711, WEB www.tannehill.org. ☞ $2. ☉ Daily 7–sunset; museum weekdays 9–5, weekends 10–5.

Dining and Lodging

$$$–$$$$ ✕ **Arman's at ParkLane.** In a former grocery store in Birmingham's elite English Village enclave, Arman's is elegant and open, with expansive hardwood floors, a raised seating area, and picture windows. Chef Chris Dupont's menu changes daily, but it might include organic salmon stuffed with crabmeat, roasted tomatoes, and potato gnocchi, all wrapped in prosciutto. The wine list includes more than 200 bottles. ✉ *2117 Cahaba Rd., Mountain Brook,* ☎ *205/871–5551. Reservations essential. AE, DC, MC, V. Closed Sun., Mon. No lunch.*

$$$–$$$$ ✕ **Highlands Bar and Grill.** Owner-chef Frank Stitt continues to achieve
★   national acclaim with his innovative cooking that combines his love of "two Souths"—the rural Southern fare of his childhood and the rustic cuisine of southern France. The dining room is reminiscent of a French bistro with vintage posters and butter-yellow walls. The menu may include pork rillettes with foie gras and spicy coleslaw; grilled grouper and Provençale pepper sauté with Niçoise olives; and roast Carolina quail and pork tenderloin with creamy grits, blackstrap molasses, and mustard greens. ✉ *2011 11th Ave. S, Southside,* ☎ *205/939–1400. Reservations essential. AE, MC, V. Closed Sun.–Mon. No lunch.*

$$$–$$$$ ✕ **Hot and Hot Fish Club.** The unusual name of this upscale eatery can be traced to owner-chef Christopher Hastings's great-great-grandfather's gentlemen's club of the same name. Hastings and his wife, Idie, the general manager, have decorated their West Coast–style restaurant with funky local artwork, including handmade bowls and serving plates. The menu changes nightly but may include seared tuna with Asian vegetable slaw, and pork and beans with collard greens and cracklin' corn bread. The chocolate soufflé with crème anglaise is the perfect way to end the evening. ✉ *2180 11th Court S., Southside,* ☎ *205/ 933–5974. AE, MC, V. Closed Sun., Mon. No lunch.*

$$$ ✕ **Bottega.** Celebrated chef Frank Stitt's second restaurant is housed in an early 20th-century limestone building with high ceilings, warm walnut paneling, and a gleaming copper bar. A mezzanine overlooks the main dining room. The Italian-Mediterranean menu changes nightly to incorporate the freshest ingredients. One well-liked Stitt creation is lobster served with penne pasta and a saffron tomato sauce with garlic, chilies, and orange zest. ✉ *2240 Highland Ave., Southside,* ☎ *205/ 939–1000. Reservations essential. AE, MC, V. Closed Sun. No lunch.*

$–$$ ✕ **Fish Market Restaurant.** Reasonable prices and consistent quality have made this restaurant a local favorite. A wide variety of fresh fish is served here, from the West Indies salad (with lump crabmeat) and seafood gumbo to blackened redfish, fried scallops, and raw oysters. Chef George Sarris is at his best with grilled seafood prepared Greek style. Fishnets, lobster traps, and carved-wood fish decorate the walls. You can buy fresh fish, shrimp, oysters, and crab at the adjacent market. ✉ *611 21st St. S, Southside,* ☎ *205/322–3330. Reservations not accepted. AE, D, MC, V. Closed Sun.*

$–$$ ✕ **Nabeel's Cafe and Market.** Scattered tables and high-back booths
★   give this eatery the feel of a neighborhood spot you might find somewhere in the Mediterranean. Greek-born John Krontiras, his Italian-born wife, Ottavia, and their son, Anthony, prepare that region's foods with artistry, whether it's an eggplant casserole, spinach-and-feta croissant, or spinach pie. Next door, Nabeel's Cafe Capri serves coffee drinks and pastries. ✉ *1706 Oxmoor Rd., Homewood,* ☎ *205/879–9292. AE, MC, V. Closed Sun.*

$–$$ ✕ **Silvertron Café.** Since 1986 owner-chef Alan Potts has been creating outstanding dishes with ingredients such as Black Angus beef, chicken, pasta, and orange roughy. A specialty is the chicken salad with almonds. The casual dining room has walls covered with photos of early Birmingham. Save room for a Bailey's brownie, but ask for two spoons:

only the brave can eat this one alone. ⊠ *3813 Clairmont Ave., Southside,* ☎ *205/591–3707. AE, DC, MC, V.*

$ ✕ **Irondale Café.** This homey little restaurant was the inspiration for the café in Fannie Flagg's *Fried Green Tomatoes at the Whistle Stop Café.* Of course, fried green tomatoes are available, along with dozens of other fresh vegetables, several entrées, and a handful of desserts—all served cafeteria style. Unlike the tiny café in the book and movie, this now-sprawling restaurant has five dining rooms, the largest of which features photos and memorabilia of interest to fans of Flagg, whose aunt ran the café from 1932 until 1972. ⊠ *1906 1st Ave. N, Irondale (7 mi east of Birmingham),* ☎ *205/956–5258. No credit cards. Closed Sat. No dinner Sun.–Tues.*

$$$–$$$$ 🏨 **Wynfrey Hotel.** The posh Wynfrey rises 15 stories above the sprawl-
★   ing Riverchase Galleria mall. An Italian marble floor, Oriental rug, Chippendale furniture, fresh flowers, a brass escalator, and a dramatic mural of the Birmingham skyline set a formal tone in the lobby. Spacious guest rooms have thick floral comforters and 25-inch TVs equipped with Internet access. There's a 24-hour business center and Spa Japonika for those who would prefer to unwind. ⊠ *U.S. 31, 1000 Riverchase Galleria, Hoover 35244,* ☎ *205/987–1600 or 800/996–3739,* 𝔽𝔸𝕏 *205/988–4597,* 𝚆𝙴𝙱 *www.wynfrey.com. 310 rooms, 19 suites. Restaurant, café, room service, in-room data ports, in-room fax, cable TV with movies and video games, pool, health club, hot tub, lounge, laundry service, business services; no-smoking rooms. AE, D, DC, MC, V.*

$$–$$$ 🏨 **Crowne Plaza Birmingham–The Redmont.** Thanks to a $3 million renovation in 2001, the city's oldest hotel, dating from 1925, has modern conveniences as well as an art deco lobby and lounge that retain a sense of the past. Rooms have contemporary furnishings and high-speed Internet connections. A free shuttle serves the airport and nearby attractions such as the McWane Center and Five Points South. The property is one block from the financial district and four blocks from I-59. ⊠ *2101 5th Ave. N, Downtown 35203,* ☎ *205/324–2101,* 𝔽𝔸𝕏 *205/324–0610,* 𝚆𝙴𝙱 *www.sixcontinenthotels.com. 114 rooms, 11 suites. Restaurant, room service, in-room data ports, cable TV with movies and video games, gym, bar, lobby lounge, laundry service, business services, airport shuttle; no-smoking rooms. AE, D, DC, MC, V.*

$$–$$$ 🏨 **Sheraton Birmingham Hotel.** This deluxe hotel, with a curved glass and concrete facade, is connected by a skywalk to the Birmingham-Jefferson Convention Complex. A 17-story atrium overlooks public areas. The spacious contemporary rooms are decorated in bright colors and include irons, coffeemakers, and large desks. ⊠ *2101 Richard Arrington Jr. Blvd., Downtown 35203,* ☎ *205/324–5000 or 800/325–3535,* 𝔽𝔸𝕏 *205/307–3045,* 𝚆𝙴𝙱 *www.sheraton.com/birmingham. 770 rooms, 51 suites. 2 restaurants, café, room service, cable TV, indoor pool, health club, sauna, bar, 2 lounges, laundry service, business services; no-smoking rooms. AE, D, DC, MC, V.*

$$–$$$ 🏨 **Sheraton Birmingham South.** On the southern edge of Birmingham, this hotel overlooks the Colonnade shopping center and is just a mile from the Summit shopping center. Rooms are filled with traditional furniture including armoires and sofas. ⊠ *8 Perimeter Dr., Inverness 35243,* ☎ *205/967–2700 or 800/567–6647,* 𝔽𝔸𝕏 *205/972–8603,* 𝚆𝙴𝙱 *www.starwood.com. 205 rooms, 2 suites. Restaurant, room service, in-room data ports, cable TV with movies, pool, gym, 2 lounges, laundry service, business services, meeting rooms, airport shuttle; no-smoking rooms. AE, D, DC, MC, V.*

$$–$$$ 🏨 **The Tutwiler.** A National Historic Landmark, the Tutwiler was built
★   in 1913 as luxury apartments and converted into a hotel in 1986. The elegant lobby has marble floors, chandeliers, brass banisters, antiques,

and lots of flowers. Rooms have period reproduction furnishings, including armoires and high-back chairs, plus velour love seats. ⊠ *2021 Park Pl., Downtown 35203,* ☎ *205/322–2100 or 800/845–1787,* FAX *205/325–1183,* WEB *www.wyndham.com. 95 rooms, 52 suites. Restaurant, room service, in-room data ports, cable TV with movies, health club, pub, laundry service; no-smoking rooms. AE, D, DC, MC, V.*

$$ 🏨 **Mountain Brook Inn.** This spacious, comfortable hotel at the foot of Red Mountain has an eight-story glass exterior, a marble lobby, and bilevel suites with spiral staircases. Although the hotel doesn't have a gym, you can use a nearby health club for free. Several upscale restaurants and boutique shops are within easy walking distance. ⊠ *2800 U.S. 280, Mountain Brook 35223,* ☎ *205/870–3100 or 800/523–7771,* FAX *205/414–2128,* WEB *www.mountainbrookinn.com. 170 rooms. Restaurant, room service, some in-room data ports, minibars, cable TV with movies and video games, pool, bar, laundry service, business services, airport shuttle; no-smoking rooms. AE, D, DC, MC, V.*

$$ 🏨 **Pickwick Hotel.** Part of the Five Points South area, the eight-story Pickwick was built in 1931 as an office building and converted in 1986 to a bed-and-breakfast hotel. Rooms are art deco style, with pink walls, green carpets, and elegant reproduction period furnishings. Afternoon tea is served Monday through Thursday from 3 to 5; wine and cheese from 5 to 7; both are complimentary. Use of a nearby health club and shuttle transportation to the airport and nearby attractions are also free. ⊠ *1023 20th St. S, Southside 35205,* ☎ *205/933–9555 or 800/255–7304,* FAX *205/933–6918,* WEB *www.pickwickhotel.com. 35 rooms, 28 suites. Dining room, room service, some kitchens, some minibars, cable TV, lounge, laundry service, airport shuttle; no-smoking rooms. AE, DC, MC, V. CP.*

$$ 🏨 **Radisson Hotel Birmingham.** This 14-story hotel is near the University Medical Center and Five Points South. The lobby has a marble floor, crystal chandeliers, and a piano lounge. Rooms are contemporary and comfortable. ⊠ *808 20th St. S, Southside 35205,* ☎ *205/933–9000 or 800/333–3333,* FAX *205/933–0920,* WEB *www.radisson.com. 287 rooms, 11 suites. Restaurant, room service, in-room data ports, cable TV, pool, gym, sauna, steam room, piano bar, laundry service, business services, airport shuttle; no-smoking rooms. AE, D, DC, MC, V.*

$–$$ 🏨 **Ramada Inn Airport.** This property, three minutes from the airport, has a lobby with a crystal chandelier, plants, sofas, and high-back upholstered chairs. Rooms are done in green and tan and with framed reproductions of Italian sites such as Pompeii. Executive Level rooms have three phones, marble baths, king-size beds, and 25-inch televisions. ⊠ *5216 Airport Hwy., East Birmingham 35212,* ☎ *205/591–7900 or 800/767–2426,* FAX *205/592–6476,* WEB *www.ramada.com. 186 rooms, 7 suites. Restaurant, in-room data ports, cable TV, pool, gym, hot tub, bar, laundry service, business services, meeting rooms, airport shuttle; no-smoking rooms. AE, D, DC, MC, V.*

Nightlife and the Arts

For an up-to-date listing of happenings in the arts, get the current issue of *Birmingham* magazine on the newsstand. For ticket information contact the **Greater Birmingham Convention and Visitors Bureau** (☎ 205/458–8000 or 800/458–8085, WEB www.birminghamal.org).

THE ARTS

The **Alabama Ballet** (☎ 205/322–4300, WEB www.alabamaballet.org) performs periodically at the Convention Complex from September through April. **Opera Birmingham** (⊠ Alabama Theatre, 1817 3rd Ave. N, Downtown, ☎ 205/322–6737) presents two or three major productions each season, September through May.

The **Birmingham-Jefferson Convention Complex and Arena** (✉ 2100 Richard Arrington Jr. Blvd. N, Downtown, ☎ 205/458–8400)—a seven-block complex with an exhibition hall, a theater, a concert hall, a conference center, a hotel, and the Arena—presents touring Broadway shows, major rock concerts, and exhibitions. The **Terrific New Theatre** (✉ 2821 2nd Ave. S, Lakeview District, ☎ 205/328–0868) hosts touring drama groups. The **Birmingham Children's Theater** (☎ 205/458–8181, WEB www.bct123.org), one of the nation's largest professional children's theatrical groups, performs for children from September through May at the Convention Complex.

Concerts, from rock to country to classical, are held at the **Convention Complex Arena** (✉ 2100 Richard Arrington Jr. Blvd. N, Downtown, ☎ 205/458–8400). The covered amphitheater at **Sloss Furnaces** (✉ 1st Ave. N and 32nd St., Downtown, ☎ 205/324–1911) hosts music concerts and seasonal civic festivals. National acts perform under the stars at **Oak Mountain Amphitheater** (✉ U.S. 119 off I–65, Pelham, ☎ 205/985–0703). Theatrical productions and music concerts are among the performances at the restored, 1927 **Alabama Theatre for the Performing Arts** (✉ 1817 3rd Ave. N, Downtown, ☎ 205/252–2262). The summer film series brings classics back to the big screen.

Each spring, Birmingham celebrates the culture, economic development, education, art, and music of a foreign country (South Africa was highlighted in 2002) at its **Birmingham International Festival** (☎ 205/252–7652, WEB www.bifsalutes.org). Performances and exhibits are staged at various locations throughout the city, though the Civic Center is usually the hub, and the festival culminates in a three-day street fair downtown. In May the city hosts a music festival, **City Stages** (☎ 205/251–1272, WEB www.citystages.org), where concerts are held on 15 stages and performance areas in and around downtown's Linn Park.

NIGHTLIFE

The Comedy Club at the Stardome Theater (✉ 1818 Data Dr., Hoover, ☎ 205/444–0008) showcases nationally known and up-and-coming comedians nightly except Monday. **Park Place Lounge** (✉ Sheraton Perimeter, U.S. 280 at I–459, Inverness, ☎ 205/972–8606 or 205/967–2700) spins dance tunes nightly. Music lovers frequent the **22nd Street Jazz Café and Brewery** (✉ 710 22nd St. S, Southside, ☎ 205/252–0407). College crowds and the mostly under-30 set flock to **Five Points South Music Hall** (✉ 1016 20th St. S, Southside, ☎ 205/322–2263) to catch local and national bands.

Outdoor Activities and Sports
BASEBALL

The **Birmingham Barons,** a Chicago White Sox affiliate in the Southern League, play at Hoover Metropolitan Stadium (✉ 100 Ben Chapman Dr., Hoover, ☎ 205/988–3200), off AL 150.

CANOEING

South of Birmingham, beginner and intermediate canoeing can be found on the Cahaba River; **Limestone Park Canoe Rental** (✉ Rte. 139, Brierfield ☎ 205/926–9672) can supply you with everything you need for a trip. **Bulldog Bend Canoe Park** (✉ Bulldog Bend Rd., Brierfield, ☎ 205/926–7382) rents canoeing equipment and inner tubes seven days a week for trips on the Cahaba River.

FISHING

Excellent largemouth and spotted bass fishing can be found about 30 mi east of Birmingham, on the Coosa River, at **Logan Martin Lake** (✉ I–20 east, near Pell City). There's fine fishing for crappie or bass at the lakes in **Oak Mountain State Park** (✉ I–65 south, Exit 247 onto Cahaba Valley Pkwy., Pelham, ☎ 205/620–2520).

In the Birmingham area, the Robert Trent Jones Golf Trail continues with the 18-hole, par-72 **Oxmoor Valley** (✉ 100 Sunbelt Pkwy., Homewood, ☎ 205/942–1177). The 18-hole, par-72 course in **Oak Mountain State Park** (✉ I–65 south, Exit 247 onto Cahaba Valley Pkwy., Pelham, ☎ 205/620–2522), just south of Birmingham, is both scenic and challenging.

Oak Mountain State Park (✉ I–65 south, Exit 247 onto Cahaba Valley Pkwy., Pelham, ☎ 205/620–2522) is laced with trails for hiking or jogging. Joggers favor the quiet streets in and around the city's **Five Points South** (✉ around 20th St., Magnolia Ave., and 11th Ave. S, Southside).

Shopping

Hanna Antiques (✉ 2424 7th Ave. S, Southside, ☎ 205/323–6036) is an antiques mall with European, English, American, and country items.

Mountain Brook Village (✉ Cahaba Rd., Mountain Brook), a small shopping area tucked away in the hollows of Birmingham's ritziest neighborhood, has a number of specialty shops. **Riverchase Galleria** (✉ I–459 and U.S. 31, Hoover, ☎ 205/985–3039, WEB www.riverchasegalleria.com) is one of the largest shopping malls in the Southeast. Its two levels contain more than 200 stores, including Rich's, JCPenney, McRae's, Sears, and Parisian department stores, plus Banana Republic and Ann Taylor. **The Summit** (✉ I–459 and U.S. 280, Inverness, ☎ 205/967–0111, WEB www.thesummitonline.com), one of Birmingham's newest malls, is a one-level shopping center with easy access to Neiman Marcus and Parisian department stores, upscale stores such as Restoration Hardware, Williams-Sonoma, and Eddie Bauer, and several restaurants. **Colonial Brookwood Village** (✉ 780 Brookwood Village, between U.S. 280 and U.S. 31S, Mountain Brook/Homewood, ☎ 205/871–0406) offers valet parking and is adorned with skylights and stone floors. The mall is anchored by Rich's and McRae's and has 75 specialty stores, including some with upscale merchandise. There's also a food court.

OFF THE
BEATEN PATH

ONEONTA – This rural community 35 mi north of Birmingham on Route 75 has three charming old wooden covered bridges. They're especially charming when the fall foliage brings the Blount County countryside into play as a backdrop. In late October Oneonta hosts its annual Covered Bridge Festival—four days of entertainment, arts and crafts, and special tours to see the bridges and colorful leaves. For information contact the Blount County–Oneonta Chamber of Commerce (✉ 227 2nd Ave. E, Oneonta 35121, ☎ 205/274–2153, WEB www.coveredbridge.org).

Cullman

50 mi north of Birmingham on I–65.

Besides an unusual collection of miniature buildings, this town in the heart of an agricultural area in the mountain lakes district has the charming **Cullman County Museum** (✉ 211 2nd Ave. N, ☎ 256/739–1258, WEB www.cullman.com/museum; ✉ $2). Exhibits tell the story of the city's founding in 1873 by a German immigrant.

North Alabama

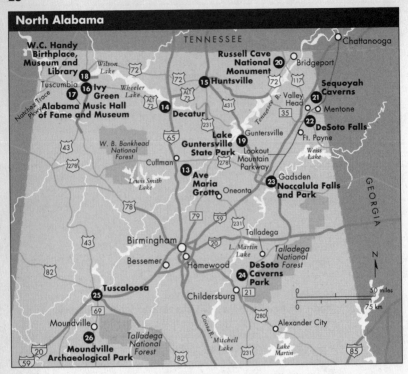

13 At **Ave Maria Grotto**, on the grounds of St. Bernard Abbey, you'll see 125 miniature churches, buildings, and shrines, painstakingly created in imitation of originals found in the United States and Europe by a Benedictine monk over the course of 50 years. Brother Joseph Zoettl had never been to most of these places, but through books and pictures the monk created amazingly accurate copies of such structures as the Vatican in Rome and Notre-Dame in Paris. The miniatures are constructed from materials ranging from semiprecious stones to soup cans and building blocks. They are set in a 4-acre landscaped garden. ✉ *1600 St. Bernard Dr. SE,* ☎ *256/734–4110,* ⒲⒠⒝ *www.avemariagrotto. com.* ▨ *$5.* ◷ *Daily 7–5.*

Dining and Lodging

$$–$$$$ ✗ **All Steak.** This locally owned restaurant, with a parking deck entrance, has kept diners happy for more than 65 years. The menu includes steak, chicken, fish, fresh vegetables, and home-cooked cakes and pies. Tasty orange rolls are a mainstay. ✉ *314 2nd Ave. SW,* ☎ *256/734–4322. MC, V.*

$–$$ 🏨 **The Main Street Inn.** Innkeepers Tom and Linda Murphree turned this 1890 Victorian home into a comfortable B&B in 2000. Each of the four guest rooms has a roomy private bath, quilts on the beds, and hardwood floors. The front porch is a favorite gathering spot. ✉ *201 Main Ave. NW, 35055,* ☎ *256/739–3043 or 888/412–3043,* ⒲⒠⒝ *www. themainstreetinn.com. 4 rooms. Cable TV, meeting room; no kids under 12, no smoking. AE, D, MC, V. BP.*

Decatur

14 *30 mi north of Cullman on I–65 and U.S. 31, 80 mi north of Birmingham.*

Some of Decatur's appeal comes from its two historic districts, Old Decatur and New Albany, which hold the state's largest concentration of

Victorian homes. The **Decatur Convention and Visitors Bureau** (☎ 256/350–2028 or 800/524–6181, WEB www.decaturcvb.org) can provide information about the districts, local festivals, and shopping along downtown's historic Bank Street, where you can find art galleries, specialty shops, and antiques. The town is on Wheeler Lake, formed by a Tennessee Valley Authority (TVA) dam downstream, and has become a center for recreation in the mountain lakes region.

☾ **Point Mallard Park** is a 750-acre spread with an aquatic park that includes a swimming pool, wave pool, and water slide; an indoor ice-skating rink; an 18-hole championship golf course; miniature golf; a duck pond; campgrounds; and a 4-mi hiking and biking trail. ⊠ *1800 Point Mallard Dr.,* ☎ *256/350–3000 or 800/669–9283,* WEB *www. pointmallardpark.com.* ☞ *$12.* ☉ *Aquatic park, mid-May–Labor Day, Tues. and Thurs. 10–9, Wed. and Fri.–Mon. 10–6; ice complex, daily hrs vary; golf course, Tue.–Sun. 7–6, Mon. noon–6; park grounds, daily dawn–dusk.*

★ **Wheeler National Wildlife Refuge** is a haven for more than 300 species of waterfowl and other birds. This is a wintering waterfowl refuge, so don't expect to see many ducks in summer. Late afternoons are the best viewing time. You can sit in a building overlooking the lake and watch thousands of ducks and geese; special one-way glass and spotting scopes allow viewing without disturbing the birds. Shaded walking trails provide a pleasant stroll through 34,500 acres of natural beauty. The visitor center has outstanding exhibits. ⊠ *AL 67, 2 mi west of I–65,* ☎ *256/350–6639.* ☞ *Free.* ☉ *Oct.–Feb., daily 10–5; Mar.–Sept., Wed.–Sun. 10–5.*

Dining and Lodging

$$–$$$ ✗ **Simp McGhee's.** This seafood restaurant in an early 1900s general-
★ store building in Old Decatur is named after a riverboat captain who was a close friend of Kate Lackner, a turn-of-the-20th-century madam. The pub-style bar is original, the ceiling is pressed tin, and the old red-oak floor is stained dark. The upstairs dining room, with white linen tablecloths, is more formal than downstairs. The filé gumbo is popular, but the house specialty is the Pontchartrain: fresh fish of the day topped with shrimp and crabmeat, in a butter and wine sauce and served on a bed of wild rice. ⊠ *725 Bank St.,* ☎ *256/353–6284. AE, D, DC, MC, V.* ☉ *Closed Sun. No lunch Sat.*

$ ✗ **Big Bob Gibson's Bar-B-Q.** In response to friends who envied the tempt-
★ ing smells rising from his backyard cooking, "Big" Bob Gibson opened his first restaurant in 1925. Big Bob's is now overseen by grandson Don McLemore; some staff have been with the eatery for years. Meats—tender, moist, and smoked—are doused in the aptly named "championship red sauce," which has won numerous state and national awards. Chicken and turkey are served with Big Bob's secret white sauce. Save room for a slice of made-from-scratch pie—chocolate, coconut, and lemon icebox are the favorites. ⊠ *1715 6th Ave. SE,* ☎ *256/350–6969. AE, D, DC, MC, V.*

$–$$ ▥ **Country Inns and Suites.** In historic Old Decatur, this three-story hotel has an elegant lobby with marble floors and a fireplace, courtyards, and spacious two-room suites. Each suite comes with a sofa and swivel rocker, two televisions, and a kitchenette. ⊠ *807 Bank St. NE 35601,* ☎ *256/355–6800 or 800/456–4000,* FAX *256/350–0965,* WEB *www.countryinns.com. 110 suites. Dining room, in-room data ports, kitchenettes, microwaves, cable TV, pool, hot tub, sauna, laundry facilities, airport shuttle. AE, D, DC, MC, V. CP*

Huntsville

⑮ *90 mi north of Birmingham via I–65.*

The largest town in North Alabama, Huntsville is best known for the center that helped produce a rocket that took astronauts to the moon. Yet the Rocket City has a clutch of other attractions, including golf courses, historic homes, and museums.

✋ ★ At the **U.S. Space and Rocket Center,** a NASA research facility, you can learn the fascinating story of space exploration and experience some of the training that real astronauts must undergo. The center offers a bus tour of the NASA labs and shuttle test sites; hands-on exhibits in the museum; space travel simulators; the IMAX Spacedome Theater, with large-format films photographed in space; and an outdoor park filled with spacecraft, including a full-size model of a space shuttle. The admission includes the museum, film, and NASA tour. ⊠ *1 Tranquility Base,* ☎ *256/837–3400 or 800/637–7223,* WEB *www.spacecamp.com.* 🎟 *$16.95.* ☼ *Daily 9–5.*

✋ The **EarlyWorks Museum Complex** is a hands-on history center comprising four properties: **Alabama Constitution Village** is the site of Alabama's 1819 Constitutional Convention. Craftspeople in period dress demonstrate skills here such as woodworking, printing, cooking, and weaving. At the **EarlyWorks Children's Museum** you can hear stories from a talking tree, build a house at an interactive architectural exhibit, and examine a 46-ft keelboat. The circa 1848 **Humphreys-Rodgers House**—saved from demolition and moved to its current location—holds period furnishings and hosts special exhibits on the decorative arts. A few blocks from the village, the **Historic Huntsville Depot,** built in 1860, offers a glimpse of railroad life in the mid-19th century. Free, guided walking tours of Huntsville's Twickenham Historic District, with its many antebellum homes, start here every Saturday at 10 AM. ⊠ *404 Madison St.,* ☎ *800/678–1819 or 256/564–8100,* WEB *www.earlyworks.com.* 🎟 *$14.* ☼ *Constitution Village and Historic Huntsville Depot, Tues.–Sat. 9–5; Children's Museum, Mon.–Sat. 9–5; Humphreys-Rodgers House, hrs vary.*

The **Huntsville Museum of Art,** in Big Spring International Park, has seven galleries that host traveling exhibitions in addition to the museum's substantial 2,300-piece permanent collection of American, especially Southern, art. ⊠ *300 Church St. S,* ☎ *800/786–9095 or 256/535–4350,* WEB *www.hsvmuseum.org.* 🎟 *$5.* ☼ *Sun. 1–5, Tues.–Wed., Fri.–Sat. 10–5, Thurs. 10–9.*

Gardening enthusiasts will enjoy walking among the dogwoods, ferns, wildflowers, and other flora and fauna at the **Huntsville-Madison County Botanical Garden,** close to the U.S. Space and Rocket Center. ⊠ *4747 Bob Wallace Ave.,* ☎ *256/830–4447,* WEB *www.hsvbg.org.* 🎟 *$6.* ☼ *Nov.–Mar., Mon.–Sat. 9–5, Sun. 1–5; Apr.–Oct., Mon.–Sat. 9–6:30, Sun. 1–6:30.*

Dining and Lodging

$–$$ ★ ✗ **Greenbrier Restaurant.** This rustic eatery in Madison was built by hand in 1952 by the owner, Jack Webb. Good catfish, ribs, and chicken served in generous portions have kept it a local favorite. The chicken is served with a special white barbecue sauce. Add tasty coleslaw and hot hush puppies, and you'll know why people drive long distances to eat here. ⊠ *27028 Old Hwy. 20, Madison (8 mi west of Huntsville, 2 mi off I–565),* ☎ *256/351–1800. AE, D, MC, V.*

$–$$ 🏨 **Hilton Huntsville.** Claiming a prize location in town, the Hilton is within walking distance of the historic district and museums, and

TEE TIME: ALABAMA'S ROBERT TRENT JONES GOLF TRAIL

ALABAMA DOESN'T HAVE MUCH in the way of golf history, unlike Georgia, its neighbor to the east, which spawned golfing great Bobby Jones. Jones built the acclaimed Augusta National Golf Course and founded the Masters tournament, which captures the golfing world's undivided attention each April. But another Jones, the legendary and prolific golf architect Robert Trent Jones Sr., a namesake of, but no relation to, Bobby Jones, has placed Alabama golf on the map in the past decade with a series of scenic, challenging public golf courses spanning the state.

The **Robert Trent Jones Golf Trail** comprises eight locations with 378 holes of golf stretching more than 100 mi through bucolic scenery. Jones, whose long, storied career includes designing more than 500 courses, took on the ambitious project as an octogenarian in the late 1980s and met with rave reviews. Unlike most resort courses where you are routed through a developer's concocted maze of condos and town houses, only indigenous pines, oaks, rivers, streams, and lakes surround the Golf Trail courses. And more good news for golfers: wherever you are in Alabama, chances are you're not too far from one of the trail stops in Huntsville, Anniston/Gadsden, Birmingham, Montgomery, Greenville, Auburn, Dothan, Mobile, or Point Clear.

Courses on the trail are often described as challenging—a euphemism for just plain hard. It's recommended that you leave the championship tees to the pros, and move up one set of tees from your normal location, particularly for shorter hitters. Golf carts on the trail have global positioning systems (GPS), providing yardage measurements on a small computer screen and limited information about the course. Purchasing a yardage book with suggestions on how to play each hole is a good idea. Tee shots that don't find the fairway are often severely punished by a forest, a splash in a lake or creek, or a difficult hillside lie. There are no breaks once you get to the green either, as almost every hole on the trail features gigantic undulating greens.

The three south-central Alabama locations make an excellent and convenient trip, with terrain much hillier than you might expect. **Capitol Hill** in Prattville, northwest of Montgomery, is the grandest course with the most layouts. There are three championship, 18-hole courses starting out from a fantastic clubhouse built with a view of downtown Montgomery. **Cambrian Ridge** in Greenville, about an hour south of Montgomery, is also one not to miss. Three challenging nines wind around the clubhouse, situated on the highest point in Butler County. Cambrian Ridge's Sherling Nine is stunningly serene and beautiful, particularly holes three through seven, which border placid, tree-lined Lake Sherling. Its Canyon Nine runs through an old deer-hunting site, starting off dramatically, with a 501-yard par 4 that plays 200 ft straight downhill. The parallel finishing holes for both the Sherling and Canyon nines play uphill past unique geologic weathered brown boulders in a gully separating the two fairways. **Grand National** in Opelika, near Auburn University, has two excellent championship courses that play along the banks of Lake Saughahatche. The Lakes Course at Grand National has hosted the NCAA Golf Championships and is a regular stop on the professional Buy.com Tour Championship. The latest acquisition on the Trail is the lush **Lakewood Golf Club** at Marriott's Grand Hotel in Point Clear, with two 18-hole courses paralleling beautiful Mobile Bay.

These state-owned golf courses are much more economical than comparable lush resort courses of the Southeast, with greens fees ranging from as little as $35 to the peak rate of $65 in springtime at the busier tracks. The courses also are well managed, and the pace of play is steady, even in peak times in April. The only way you can go wrong here is to hit poor shots. Otherwise, Alabama can hold its head up high, knowing that there's more than one destination in the South worthy of a golfer's attention.

— Sam Starnes

many rooms overlook either Big Spring International Park or the Von Braun Convention Center. The lobby has lovely Oriental rugs, antique chairs and tables, and a grand piano, which provides entertainment most evenings. The spacious rooms are decorated in neutral tones with standard hotel furnishings. ⊠ *401 Williams Ave., 35801,* ☎ *256/ 533–1400,* FAX *256/534–7787,* WEB *www.hilton.com. 268 rooms, 9 suites. Restaurant, room service, in-room data ports, minibars, cable TV, pool, gym, hot tub, bar, laundry service, business services, meeting rooms; no-smoking rooms. AE, D, DC, MC, V.*

Outdoor Activities and Sports

GOLF

The three golf courses at **Hampton Cove** (⊠ 450 Old Hwy. 431S, Owens Cross Rd., ☎ 256/551–1818), 12 mi from Huntsville, are part of the Robert Trent Jones Golf Trail. All have 18 holes; two are par 72, and the third is par 54.

The Shoals

70 mi west of Huntsville.

The adjoining quad cities of Tuscumbia, Florence, Sheffield, and Muscle Shoals are known throughout Alabama simply as The Shoals. Spreading out on both sides of the Tennessee River basin, The Shoals is an attractive area rich in culture and history. Nearby Wilson Dam, begun in 1918 as a power supply center for munitions plants in World War I, later became the cornerstone of the Tennessee Valley Authority (TVA). This government agency, created in 1933, is involved with the integrated development of the region; its dams and reservoirs have greatly affected the economics of the area, providing both business and recreational opportunities.

★ ⑯ **Ivy Green** is the childhood home of Helen Keller, born in Tuscumbia in 1880. At the carriage house, behind the simple white frame main house, Annie Sullivan taught young Helen the meaning of language. The annual **Helen Keller Festival** (☎ 256/383–0783 or 800/344–0783), held the third weekend in June, celebrates her life with arts and crafts, concerts, and performances of her inspirational story *The Miracle Worker,* which is staged on the grounds Friday and Saturday nights at 8:15 during June and July; on performance nights, the grounds open at 7 so that ticket holders can tour the house (no extra charge). ⊠ *300 W. North Commons, Tuscumbia,* ☎ *256/383–4066,* WEB *www. helenkellerbirthplace.org.* ☞ *$5; The Miracle Worker $5–$8.* ⊙ *Mon.– Sat. 8:30–4, Sun. 1–4.*

★ ⑰ At the **Alabama Music Hall of Fame and Museum,** you can wander through the history of Alabama's musical heritage and see the original contracts of Elvis Presley's deal with Sun Records, the actual touring bus of the country-music band Alabama, and exhibits on the likes of Hank Williams, Lionel Richie, and Nat "King" Cole. The annual September **Concert Series** festival draws performers and fans from across the country. ⊠ *U.S. 72W, Tuscumbia,* ☎ *256/381–4417 or 800/ 239–2643,* WEB *www.alamhof.org.* ☞ *$6.* ⊙ *Mon.–Sat. 9–5, Sun. 1–5.*

⑱ The **W. C. Handy Birthplace, Museum and Library** includes the cabin where the internationally acclaimed Father of the Blues was born. Handy (1873–1958), a mainly self-taught songwriter and bandleader, was one of the first to write down the blues. The cabin is furnished with items typical of the period when he grew up. Much of his memorabilia has been preserved in the museum. Here you'll see his piano and famous golden trumpet, and testimonials to his genius by such con-

temporaries as George Gershwin and Louis Armstrong. The annual
W. C. Handy Music Festival (☎ 256/766–7642), held during the first
week in August, draws thousands. ✉ *620 W. College St., Florence,* ☎
256/760–6434. ☞ *$2.* ☉ *Tues.–Sat. 10–4.*

Dining and Lodging

$$–$$$$ ★ ✗ **Dale's Restaurant.** Dine in comfort as red-jacketed waiters serve flame-grilled steaks seasoned with Dale's famous marinade. Chicken and seafood dishes round out the menu. ✉ *1001 Mitchell Blvd., Florence,* ☎ *256/766–4961. AE, DC, MC, V.* ☉ *Closed Sun. No lunch.*

$$–$$$$ ✗ **Renaissance Grille.** You can watch the sun set from a vantage point 350 ft above the Tennessee River basin at this casual restaurant atop the Renaissance Tower. Choose from a traditional American menu of fine steaks, chicken, seafood, or pasta dishes. ✉ *1 Hightower Pl., Florence,* ☎ *256/718–0092. AE, D, DC, MC, V.*

$$–$$$ ✗ **Louisiana "The Restaurant."** New Orleans's French Quarter influences the long menu here. Seafood, like shrimp and crawfish, can be fried, served in cream sauce, or wrapped in crepes. There are also grilled steaks, veal, lamb, chicken, and a Sunday creole brunch. ✉ *1311 6th St., Muscle Shoals,* ☎ *256/386–0801. AE, D, DC, MC, V.* ☉ *Closed Mon.*

$$ 🏨 **Joe Wheeler State Park Lodge.** This three-story fieldstone-and-redwood lodge, at the center of a 3,400-acre state park, slopes down a hill, giving every room a view of Wheeler Lake. All rooms have balconies; suites have living rooms and tiny kitchenettes. Boats are available for trips on the lake, countless hiking trails lead to secluded spots and picnic areas, and redwood walkways connect the guest rooms with the pool area. Nearby are small, rustic brick or wood cabins, which are no-frills but comfortable. ✉ *U.S. 72, near Rogersville (between Athens and Florence), 4401 McLean Dr., Rogersville 35652,* ☎ *256/247–5461 or 800/544–5639,* FAX *256/247–5471,* WEB *www.joewheelerstatepark.com. 69 rooms, 6 suites, 24 cabins. Restaurant, 18-hole golf course, 4 tennis courts, pool; no-smoking rooms, no phones in some rooms, no TV in some rooms. AE, MC, V.*

$–$$ ★ 🏨 **Holiday Inn–The Shoals.** Serving both Florence and Sheffield, this motel has a courteous staff and spacious rooms with traditional motel furniture. A songwriters' showcase is hosted in the lounge on Thursday evening. ✉ *4900 Hatch Blvd., Sheffield 35660,* ☎ *256/381–4710,* FAX *256/381–4710 Ext. 403,* WEB *www.sixcontinenthotels.com. 201 rooms, 3 suites. Restaurant, in-room data ports, some microwaves, some refrigerators, cable TV, pool, gym, hot tub, lounge, laundry facilities, laundry service. AE, D, MC, V.*

Guntersville

40 mi southeast of Huntsville via U.S. 431.

The town of Guntersville, a TVA port, attracts vacationers with its parks and Lake Guntersville. The lake, with 949 mi of winding shoreline and 69,000 acres of water, was created by the Guntersville Lock and Dam. Eight public launch areas and eight full-service marinas make it ideal for all types of boating and fishing. You can rent everything from fishing boats to houseboats here. Watch for bald eagles in January.

★ ⑲ **Lake Guntersville State Park** lies along the southern bank of the Tennessee River just east of Guntersville and in the shadow of Sand Mountain. The natural beauty combines with a wealth of outdoor recreational opportunities, such as golf, hiking, camping, and world-class bass fishing, to make the park one of Alabama's most popular destinations. ✉ *7966 AL 227,* ☎ *256/571–5444.* ☞ *Free.*

Dining and Lodging

$–$$ ✕🏨 **Lake Guntersville State Park Lodge.** People come here for the natural surroundings; the lodge itself is a fairly standard motel-type accommodation with simple furnishings. Rooms on the bluff side have balconies with great views of the lake and forest. There are also lakefront two-bedroom cottages, which are as modern and plain as the lodge rooms but have a sitting room and kitchen. The A-frame chalets have living rooms and two bedrooms. The Chandelier Dining Room ($–$$$) overlooks the gigantic man-made lake and offers thick steaks, chicken, and seafood. Fried mushrooms and fried zucchini are tasty starters. ⊠ *1155 Lodge Dr., 35976,* ☎ *256/571–5440 or 800/548–4553. 94 rooms, 6 suites, 18 chalets, 16 cottages. Restaurant, coffee shop, in-room data ports, cable TV, 18-hole golf course, 2 tennis courts, pool, sauna, boating, fishing, laundry facilities; no-smoking rooms. AE, MC, V.*

Bridgeport

65 mi east of Huntsville via U.S. 72.

⑳ Seven miles outside Bridgeport is a cave with evidence of prehistoric settlement in the area. **Russell Cave National Monument,** an archaeological site, was occupied by Native Americans' prehistoric ancestors 10,000 years before the arrival of European settlers. You can tour the cave shelter—the entrance to more than 7 mi of cavernous passages—and view museum exhibits of prehistoric artifacts and a Native American burial ground. There are also tool demonstrations, a video program, a nature trail, and picnic grounds. ⊠ *3729 County Rd. 98,* ☎ *256/ 495–2672,* 🌐 *www.nps.gov/ruca.* 🎟 *Free.* ☉ *Daily 8–4:30.*

Valley Head

25 mi southeast of Bridgeport on AL 117 to AL 11, 115 mi northeast of Birmingham via I–59.

Near the Georgia state line, this small town is a pleasant hideaway.

㉑ A half-mile guided tour through the **Sequoyah Caverns,** in Sand Mountain, brings you past rock formations mirrored in lakes. In the 1930s, dances were held in the largest room, now called the Ballroom. Outside, there's a picnic area, a small zoo, hiking trails, and a campground with a swimming pool and playground. ⊠ *1438 County Road 731,* ☎ *256/635–0024 or 800/843–5098.* 🎟 *$7.* ☉ *Mar.–Nov., daily 8:30– 5; Dec.–Feb., weekends 8:30–5. Campgrounds open year-round.*

$$–$$$ 🏨 **Winston Place Bed and Breakfast.** At the foot of Lookout Mountain, 2 mi from downtown Mentone, this 1831 Georgian-style antebellum home with two wraparound porches is a popular place for weddings—with good reason. The six guest rooms are sumptuously furnished, with gleaming hardwood floors, and each has a private bath and doors leading to one of the porches. ⊠ *353 Railroad St., 35989,* ☎ *256/635–6381 or 888/494–6786. 6 rooms, 1 cottage. Cable TV, some in-room VCRs, video game room, business services; no room phones, no smoking. AE, D, MC, V. BP.*

Mentone

2 mi east of Valley Head on AL 117, 117 mi northeast of Birmingham via I–59.

Mentone, whose name means "musical valley spring," has narrow, twisting streets filled with shops, restaurants, and crafts studios, many in historic buildings.

Dining and Lodging

$–$$ ✕ **Log Cabin Deli.** This early 1800s original pine-log cabin was once
★ used as a Native American fur-trading post. Dine on the open front
porch, the screened back porch, or in the main dining room, with its
great rock fireplace. The hand-cut cedar tables and rough wooden floors
complete the rustic effect. Everything here is home-cooked, and the deli
has become famous for its soups, hefty sandwiches (just try to finish
the cabin roast beef special), country ham, and Southern-style vegetables. Desserts are a big hit; try the hot-fudge nut cake with ice cream.
⊠ *AL 117,* ☎ *256/634–4560. No credit cards.* ☉ *Closed Mon.*

Fort Payne

15 mi south of Mentone via I–59, 100 mi northeast of Birmingham.

Fort Payne, known as the "sock capital of the world" because of the
huge number of socks produced here, offers a pleasantly slow-paced
lifestyle. The **Depot Museum** (⊠ 105 5th St. NE, ☎ 256/845–5714)
has artifacts from local history. The **Alabama Museum** (⊠ 101 Glenn
Blvd. SW, ☎ 256/845–1646, WEB www.thealabamaband.com) and fan
club headquarters is dedicated to the music group Alabama.

㉒ **DeSoto Falls,** a 120-ft waterfall, is a mesmerizing attraction in 5,000-
acre **DeSoto State Park,** 8 mi northeast of Fort Payne. Unsupervised
swimming is allowed in DeSoto Lake, and the park has a supervised
pool, plus a picnic area and campgrounds. **Little River Canyon,** one
of the deepest canyons east of the Rocky Mountains, is just outside
the park's boundary. The scenery is breathtaking at this 600-ft-deep
and 16-mi-wide canyon. ⊠ *DeSoto State Park, County Rd. 89,* ☎ *256/*
845–0051 or 800/252–7275. ☞ *Free; picnicking $1 per person.* ☉ *Daily*
7–dusk.

Gadsden

35 mi south of Fort Payne via I–59, 63 mi northeast of Birmingham.

At the southern end of Lookout Mountain, Gadsden has an impressive waterfall. **Lookout Mountain Parkway,** a scenic 100-mi drive that
ends in Chattanooga, also begins here (☎ 256/549–0351 for information). In mid-May the town hosts **Riverfest** (☎ 256/543–3472 for
information), a three-day family-oriented event with good music and
several blocks of food and arts and crafts. You can ride the Coosa River
on the **Alabama Princess** riverboat (☎ 256/549–1111).

☝ **㉓** **Noccalula Falls and Park** is a 100-acre woodland area with a 90-ft waterfall, miniature golf, minitrain rides, a small zoo, a botanical garden,
a covered bridge, and a 1776 pioneer homestead—four log cabins
were moved here from the backwoods of Tennessee. There are also campgrounds and picnic areas. ⊠ *1500 Noccalula Rd.,* ☎ *256/549–4663.*
☞ *Homestead and garden $1.50; train ride $1.* ☉ *Daily 8–sunset.*

Talladega

40 mi south of Gadsden on AL 21.

Talladega's diverse attractions include a NASCAR racing track, a racing hall of fame, and a nearby national forest. The town's **Silk Stock-
ing Historic District** has homes built mainly from 1885 to 1915 for
leading citizens such as textile merchants, lawyers, and doctors (whose
wives could afford to wear the silk stockings that gave the district its
name). The buildings range from simple cottages to elaborate Queen
Anne homes. Call the Talladega Area Chamber of Commerce (☎ 256/
362–9075) for information on a walking tour.

Near the Talladega Superspeedway, the **International Motorsports Hall of Fame** (✉ 3198 Speedway Blvd., ☎ 256/362–5002, WEB www.motorsportshalloffame.com, 🎫 $8) has more than 100 racing vehicles and memorabilia.

Considered by many to have the state's best hiking terrain, the trails of a nearby unit of the **Talladega National Forest** (☎ 256/362–2909 for district ranger) wind through the southernmost extension of the Appalachian Mountains. You'll discover scenic overlooks, hardwood trees, lakes, and mountain streams.

Outdoor Activities and Sports

The **Talladega Superspeedway** (✉ 3366 Speedway Blvd., ☎ 256/362–2261, WEB www.talladegasuperspeedway.com) hosts two major NASCAR races each year, in April and October, drawing hundreds of thousands of racing fans to this small town.

Childersburg

72 mi southwest of Gadsden via U.S. 411/231, 40 mi southeast of Birmingham via U.S. 280.

Years before frontier settlers arrived here in the early 19th century, the area was a sacred Native American capital called Coosa. The town has evolved into a lumber and farming community, but visitors know it best for its caverns.

🖐 ㉔ **DeSoto Caverns Park** is the site of a 2,000-year-old Native American burial ground. These vast onyx caves were rediscovered in 1540 by Hernando DeSoto and later served as a Confederate gunpowder mining center and a Prohibition speakeasy. Curious formations of stalagmites and stalactites allow the imagination free rein. Part of your cave tour includes a sound, laser, light, and water show in the largest cave, which is more than 12 stories high. A campground and picnic grove, gemstone mining, a water-fight maze, and other activities provide plenty of diversions. ✉ 5181 DeSoto Caverns Pkwy., ☎ 256/378–7252 or 800/933–2283. 🎫 $10.95; FunPac ticket (includes tour, maze, and gemstone mining) $13.75. ☉ Mon.–Sat. 9–5, Sun. 12:30–5; extended hrs spring and summer.

Tuscaloosa

㉕ *50 mi west of Birmingham via I–20/I–59.*

Thanks to the teams of the University of Alabama, this city's leading export may well be football, but its wealth of cultural offerings cannot be overlooked.

The **Paul W. "Bear" Bryant Museum** follows the University of Alabama's 100-year tradition of football preeminence. The museum has many of Coach Bryant's personal belongings, as well as those of others who have laid the foundation for the University of Alabama football program. ✉ 300 Paul W. Bryant Dr., ☎ 205/348–4668, WEB www.museums.ua.edu/bryant. 🎫 $2. ☉ Daily 9–4.

★ The **Warner Collection,** displayed in two locations and comprising several hundred paintings as well as dozens of artifacts and sculptures, is quite possibly the nation's largest private collection of American painting. The Asian-style, beautifully landscaped **Gulf States Paper Corporation headquarters** (✉ 1400 River Rd. NE, ☎ 205/553–6200; 🎫 Free) houses works by such artists as Wyeths, Albert Bierstadt, Frederic

Remington, Thomas Cole, and George Catlin. It's open Saturday from 10 to 4 and Sunday from 1 to 4. Tours are on weekdays at 5:30 and 6:30. A short drive away is the even more impressive collection in the exquisitely furnished **Mildred Warner House** (⊠ 1925 8th St., ☎ 205/ 345–4062; ≣ Free), a log cabin built in 1822 (with an 1835 brick addition). William Aiken Walker's revealing Southern folk paintings, which depict 19th-century African-American life, are enough to make a visit worthwhile. There are works by such painters as Winslow Homer, John Singer Sargent, Childe Hassam, Georgia O'Keeffe, and James A. M. Whistler. The house is open Saturday and Sunday from 1 to 5; tours are given on the hour.

History and architecture aficionados can take a tour with the **Tuscaloosa County Preservation Society,** at the Battle-Friedman House (⊠ 1010 Greensboro Ave., ☎ 205/758–2238 or 205/758–6138, WEB www. historictuscaloosa.org).

Dining

$$$–$$$$ ✕ **The Globe.** Ten minutes from downtown Tuscaloosa, across the Black Warrior River, you'll find the town of Northport and the big barnlike structure that once housed a dry goods store. Two actors have turned it into an adventurous dining establishment. Named after Shakespeare's first theater, the restaurant has a long English tavern–style bar in one of the two dining rooms; giant line drawings of scenes from Shakespeare's plays adorn the walls. The international menu includes such entrées as pan-sautéed orange roughy, vegetarian quesadillas, Thai emerald curry, and broiled tilapia. The only thing that's typically Southern is the friendly service. ⊠ *430 Main Ave., Northport,* ☎ *205/ 391–0949. Reservations not accepted. AE, D, MC, V. Closed Sun.– Mon.*

Nightlife and the Arts

As a college town at least an hour away from the nearest major city, Tuscaloosa offers an abundance of bars and clubs that, of course, cater mostly to college crowds. Most are concentrated in an area known as "the Strip" along University Boulevard. **Jupiter Bar and Grill** (⊠ 1307 University Blvd., ☎ 205/248–6611) has attracted some national rock bands. At **Dionysus** (⊠ 2310 University Blvd., ☎ 205/345– 6638) the scene is more sedate and sophisticated.

Classical music lovers may want to stop in to hear the estimable **Tuscaloosa Symphony Orchestra** (⊠ Battle-Friedman House, 1010 Greensboro Ave., ☎ 205/752–5515). Crafts collectors enjoy October's outstanding **Kentuck Festival of the Arts** (☎ 205/758–1257), in nearby Northport, a town that has attracted many artists.

Moundville

14 mi south of Tuscaloosa on U.S. 69.

➋ Near Moundville is a site that illuminates the lives of the area's prehistoric residents. **Moundville Archaeological Park** contains a number of artifacts that can be traced to the prehistoric forefathers of local Seminole, Creek, and Cherokee Native Americans. On the grounds are 20 earthen temple mounds (the largest of which supports a reconstructed Native American temple), an archaeological museum, a reconstructed native village, a nature trail leading to the Black Warrior River, picnic areas, and a campground. ⊠ *AL 69S,* ☎ *205/371–2572.* ≣ *$4.* ⊙ *Museum daily 9–5, park daily 8–8.*

Birmingham and North Alabama A to Z

AIR TRAVEL
CARRIERS

Birmingham and Huntsville international airports are served by American, ComAir, Continental, Delta, Northwest/KLM, Southwest, and US Airways. Northwest Alabama Regional Airport is served by Northwest.
➤ AIRLINES AND CONTACTS: For airline contacts, *see* Air Travel *in* Smart Travel Tips A to Z.

AIRPORTS AND TRANSFERS

Birmingham International Airport is less than 3 mi from downtown. Taxi fare to most hotels is about $10 for one passenger, $5 for each additional passenger. Many hotels provide limousine service from the airport by prior arrangement. If you're traveling by car, follow the clearly marked signs downtown. Huntsville International Airport, at Exit 7, is off I–565, and Northwest Alabama Regional Airport is on T. Ed Campbell Drive in Muscle Shoals.
➤ AIRPORT INFORMATION: **Birmingham International Airport** (☎ 205/595–0533, WEB www.bhamintlairport.com). **Huntsville International Airport** (☎ 256/772–9395, WEB www.hsvairport.org). **Northwest Alabama Regional Airport** (☎ 256/381–2869, WEB www.flytheshoals.com).

BUS TRAVEL

Greyhound serves Birmingham, Huntsville, Decatur, and Florence. The Metro Area Express (MAX) serves Birmingham. Buses require exact change—$1 fare, 25¢ transfer—and run only on weekdays, 6–6.
➤ BUS INFORMATION: **Greyhound** (19th Ave. North and Park Place, Birmingham, ☎ 800/231–2222, WEB www.greyhound.com). **Metro Area Express** (☎ 205/521–0101).

CAR TRAVEL

I–59 goes northeast from Birmingham to Chattanooga, southwest to Tuscaloosa, and on into Mississippi. I–20 runs east to Anniston and Atlanta. I–65 goes north to Decatur and Nashville and south to Montgomery and Mobile. U.S. 72 and Alternate U.S. 72 run east–west across the northern part of the state and connect Florence, Tuscumbia, Decatur, and Huntsville.

EMERGENCIES

University Hospital has the all-night emergency room closest to downtown Birmingham. The CVS Pharmacy in Red Mountain Plaza is open 24 hours.
➤ CONTACTS: **Ambulance, police** (☎ 911). **CVS Pharmacy** (✉ 48 Green Springs Hwy., ☎ 205/942–1629). **University Hospital** (✉ 619 S. 19th St., ☎ 205/934–6500).

MEDIA
RADIO

AM: WERC 960, talk; WDJC 1260, Christian.

FM: WBHM 90.3, public; 94.5, soft rock; WZZK 104.7, country; WODL 106.9, oldies; WRAX 107.7, modern rock.

TAXIS

Birmingham's Yellow Cab charges $1.75 plus $1.20 for each additional mile.
➤ TAXI COMPANIES: **Yellow Cab** (☎ 205/252–1131).

TOURS

The Greater Birmingham Convention and Visitors Bureau (☞ Visitor Information, *below*) has free brochures for self-guided tours of the downtown and Five Points South areas.

TRAIN TRAVEL

The only Amtrak station in central Alabama is on Morris Avenue in downtown Birmingham. Trains run daily.

➤ TRAIN INFORMATION: **Amtrak** (☎ 205/324–3033 or 800/872–7245, WEB www.amtrak.com).

VISITOR INFORMATION

➤ TOURIST INFORMATION: **Birmingham Convention and Visitors Bureau** (⊠ 2200 9th Ave. N, 35203, ☎ 205/458–8000 or 800/458–8085, WEB www.birminghamal.org). **Cullman Area Chamber of Commerce** (⊠ 211 2nd Ave. NE, 35056, ☎ 256/734–0454, WEB www.cullman.com). **Decatur Convention and Visitors Bureau** (⊠ 719 6th Ave. SE, 35602, ☎ 256/350–2028 or 800/524–6181, WEB www.decaturcvb.org). **Huntsville Convention and Visitors Bureau** (⊠ 700 Monroe St., 35801, ☎ 256/533–5723 or 800/772–2348, WEB www.huntsville.org). **Tuscaloosa Convention and Visitors Bureau** (⊠ 1305 Greensboro Ave., 35401, ☎ 205/391–9200 or 800/538–8696, WEB www.tcvb.org).

MONTGOMERY AND CENTRAL ALABAMA

Selma, Demopolis, Tuskegee

The flatlands of Alabama's central section, called the Black Belt region for its rich, fertile soil, provide the stage for stories of life on a Southern plantation in a different century, the Civil War, and the civil rights movement. Montgomery is a good base for exploring this region's Old South plantations, historic sites, and big fishing lakes.

Numbers in the margin correspond to points of interest on the Downtown Montgomery and Central and South Alabama maps.

Montgomery

From the days when the Civil War was the national preoccupation to another era when civil rights dominated the headlines, Montgomery has been in the forefront of Southern life. Today Montgomery is the epitome of a progressive Southern business city. New hotels and restaurants spring up frequently, along with skyscraper office complexes. Still, many historic homes and buildings remain. Alabama's capital city is rich in its past and strives to become richer in its future.

★ ㉗ The **Alabama State Capitol** was built in 1851 and briefly (for a few months in 1861) served as the first capitol for the Confederate States of America. On the front portico, a bronze star marks the spot where Jefferson Davis stood to take the oath of office as president of the Confederacy. There is an amazing piece of interior design: the stairway curling up the sides of the circular hallway is freestanding, without visible support. The state's rich history has been caught by an artist's brush in great, colorful murals. In the large House chamber and smaller Senate chamber, there are fireplaces with black Egyptian marble mantel pieces. ⊠ *600 Dexter Ave., at Bainbridge St.,* ☎ *334/242–3935,* WEB *www.preserveala.org.* ▣ *Free.* ☉ *Weekdays 9–5, Sat. 9–4.*

38

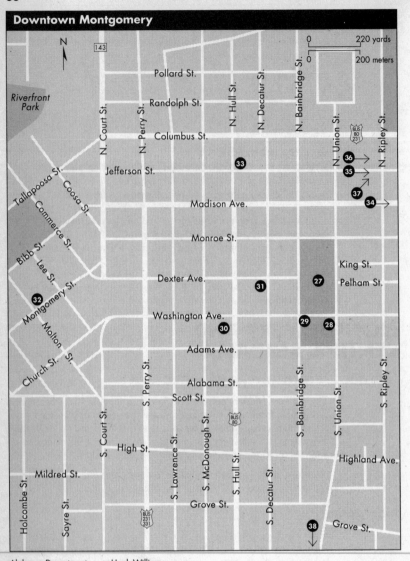

Downtown Montgomery

28 Built in 1840, the **First White House of the Confederacy** was occupied by Jefferson Davis and his family while the Confederacy was being organized. Today it contains many of their possessions, plus other artifacts of the Civil War period. The house is across the street from the State Capitol. ⊠ *644 Washington Ave.,* ☎ *334/242–1861.* ⊟ *Free.* ☉ *Tours weekdays 8–4:30. Closed weekends.*

29 The **Alabama Department of Archives and History** houses the first state-funded archives in the United States as well as galleries with artifacts documenting the state's past, with an emphasis on 19th-century Alabama. ⊠ *624 Washington Ave.,* ☎ *334/242–4363,* WEB *www.archives. state.al.us.* ⊟ *Free.* ☉ *Weekdays 8–5, Sat. 9–5. Reference room closed Mon.*

★ **30** On the grounds of the Southern Poverty Law Center, the **Civil Rights Memorial** has water flowing over a table that bears the names of 40 people who gave their lives for racial equality. On a wall behind this, over which water also flows, is a biblical quote used in a speech by Dr. Martin Luther King Jr.: UNTIL JUSTICE ROLLS DOWN LIKE WATERS AND RIGHTEOUSNESS LIKE A MIGHTY STREAM. The sculptor, Maya Lin, also created the Vietnam Veterans Memorial in Washington, D.C. ⊠ *400 Washington Ave.,* ☎ *334/264–0286.* ⊟ *Free.* ☉ *24 hrs.* WEB *www.splcenter.org.*

31 The **Dexter Avenue King Memorial Baptist Church** is where Dr. Martin Luther King Jr. began his career as a minister in 1955. From the church he directed the Montgomery bus boycott, which began after Rosa Parks was arrested for refusing to give up her seat to a white man. The church's sanctuary and the basement Sunday-school rooms are open to visitors. A mural covering one basement wall depicts people and events associated with Dr. King and the civil rights movement. ⊠ *454 Dexter Ave.,* ☎ *334/263–3970,* WEB *www.dexterkingmemorial.org.* ⊟ *Free.* ☉ *Tours Mon.–Thurs. at 10 and 2, Fri. at 10.*

32 Troy State University Montgomery's **Rosa Parks Library and Museum** (⊠ 251 Montgomery St., ☎ 334/241–8661, WEB www.tsum. edu/museum; ⊟ $5) was built on the site where Parks refused to give up her seat on a city bus, sparking the 381-day Montgomery bus boycott that resulted in the U.S. Supreme Court decision in 1956 to desegregate the nation's public transportation system. The museum holds artifacts—including a replica of the bus—and documents from that era of history.

33 **Old Alabama Town,** about six blocks northwest of the capitol between Madison Avenue and Columbus Street, consists of 40 restored houses, barns, stores, and other structures built between 1818 and circa 1920. The **Loeb Reception Center** has a self-guided cassette walking tour that covers the 10 house museums clustered in the Living Block. Volunteers give tours of the Italianate **Ordeman Townhouse** (⊠ 230 N. Hull St.), and its restored outbuildings and gardens. The Working Block, just off Columbus Street on the district's north side, includes a gristmill, blacksmith shop, the **Cotton Gin and Cotton Museum,** the **Haigler Plantation Office,** and the **Rose-Morris Craft Center.** ⊠ *Loeb Reception Center, 301 Columbus St.,* ☎ *334/240–4500 or 888/240–1850,* WEB *www. oldalabamatown.com.* ⊟ *Self-guided tour $7.* ☉ *Mon.–Sat. 9–3.*

34 Alabama's oldest fine arts museum, the **Montgomery Museum of Fine Arts** has an impressive facility in the Wynton M. Blount Cultural Park, near the Alabama Shakespeare Festival Theatre. Highlights are works by Southern artists; ARTWORKS, a hands-on gallery for children and adults; a permanent gallery exhibiting the Blount, Inc., Corporate Collection of American Art; and a gift shop, auditorium, and print gallery, as well as galleries for changing exhibitions. You can eat lunch in Cafe

M. ⊠ *1 Museum Dr.,* ☎ *334/244–5700,* WEB *www.mmfa.org.* 🎟 *Free.* ☉ *Tues.–Wed. and Fri.–Sat. 10–5, Thurs. 10–9, Sun. noon–5.*

🦢 **③⑤** The 40-acre **Montgomery Zoo** is home to 800 animals from five continents. Dining, a gift shop, and a train ride are offered as well. Don't miss the bald eagles, black bears, and monkey island. ⊠ *2301 Coliseum Pkwy.,* ☎ *334/240–4900.* 🎟 *$4.50.* ☉ *Daily 9–5.*

③⑥ The **Hank Williams Memorial** tombstone marks the burial place of one of Alabama's own, country-music singer and songwriter Hank Williams; after his untimely death at age 29 on New Year's Day 1953, he was brought here for one of the city's grandest funerals. It was held at City Hall, with top country stars delivering eulogies and singing sad songs. The memorial depicts him, along with sheet music from his most popular songs, including "Your Cheatin' Heart." ⊠ *Oakwood Cemetery Annex, 1305 Upper Wetumpka Rd.,* ☎ *334/264–4938.* ☉ *Sunrise–sunset.*

③⑦ **Jasmine Hill Gardens and Outdoor Museum,** atop a wooded hill, are 20 acres of beautiful gardens with reproductions of Greek sculptures and of the ruins of the Temple of Hera. The visitor center is a replica of the original temple facade as it once stood intact on Mt. Olympus. ⊠ *3001 Jasmine Hill Rd.,* ☎ *334/567–6463.* 🎟 *$5.* ☉ *Tues.–Sun. 9–5.*

③⑧ The **F. Scott and Zelda Fitzgerald Museum** displays belongings of the colorful couple in their former home. Zelda Fitzgerald grew up in the area, and some of her artwork hangs at Montgomery's Museum of Fine Arts. Her husband, F. Scott, is famous for novels including *The Great Gatsby* and *Tender Is the Night.* A 25-minute video on their life in Montgomery is shown. ⊠ *919 Felder Ave.,* ☎ *334/264–4222.* 🎟 *$1.* ☉ *Wed.–Fri. 10–2, weekends 1–5, and by appointment.*

Dining and Lodging

$$–$$$$ ✕ **Vintage Year.** Owner/chef Judy Martin's innovative menu makes this
★ Cloverdale restaurant one of Montgomery's best. She insists on only the freshest snapper, tuna, shrimp, salmon, and other fish, as well as lamb and duck, and prepares them with an assortment of fresh herbs. The bar is a favorite neighborhood meeting place. ⊠ *405 Cloverdale Rd.,* ☎ *334/264–8463. Reservations essential. AE, MC, V. Closed Sun.–Mon. No lunch.*

$$$ ✕ **Sahara Restaurant.** Joe and Mike Deep's Sahara has been one of Montgomery's favorite traditional Southern restaurants since 1952. Linen tablecloths and uniformed servers add to the charm. Fresh snapper, grouper, and scampi are broiled to taste, and succulent steaks are grilled over coals. The seafood gumbo is a specialty. ⊠ *511 E. Edgemont Ave., Cloverdale,* ☎ *334/262–1215. AE, D, DC, MC, V. Closed Sun.*

$–$$$ ✕ **Jubilee Seafood Company.** In a very pleasant small café, Bud Skinner cooks some of the finest and freshest seafood dishes in town, such as snapper prepared in several different ways, soft-shell crabs, crab claws, and other delicacies. For a real treat, try the barbecued shrimp, which are marinated in a secret red sauce, wrapped in bacon, and charbroiled. Bud also has a tasty West Indies salad with marinated crab. ⊠ *1057 Woodley Rd., Cloverdale Plaza,* ☎ *334/262–6224. Reservations not accepted. AE, MC, V. Closed Sun.–Mon. No lunch.*

$–$$ ✕ **Corsino's.** Serving Montgomery since 1954, family-run Corsino's is
★ one of the city's most popular restaurants. The noontime crowd gathers daily from state government offices and downtown businesses to enjoy some of the South's finest pasta dishes. You can also choose a savory, foot-long Italian sandwich served on hot, homemade Italian bread, or a hand-tossed New York–style pizza. The restaurant isn't fancy,

just comfortable and friendly. ⊠ *911 S. Court St.,* ☎ *334/263–9752. Reservations not accepted. No credit cards. Closed weekends.*

$ ✕ **Chris' Hot Dogs.** A Montgomery tradition since opening as a hot dog
★ stand in 1917, this eatery has booths and an old-fashioned lunch counter with stools. The famous sauce combines chili peppers, onions, and herbs to give the hot dogs a one-of-a-kind flavor. Try the hot dog with "kitchen chili," a heavy, hot chili of beans and onions that you eat with a knife and fork. ⊠ *138 Dexter Ave.,* ☎ *334/265–6850. Reservations not accepted. No credit cards. Closed Sun.*

$ **Martin's Restaurant.** Martin's—a Montgomery institution since 1940—
is plain but comfortable, with friendly servers dishing out generous helpings of home-cooked fresh vegetables, Southern fried chicken, and delicious pan-fried catfish fresh from Alabama ponds. The corn-bread muffins literally melt in your mouth. ⊠ *1796 Carter Hill Rd.,* ☎ *334/ 265–1767. No credit cards. Closed Sat.*

$$ 🏨 **Embassy Suites Hotel.** This all-suites high-rise hotel between the Civic
★ Center and the old railroad station pampers travelers with all the comforts of home: sprawling rooms that include TVs and phones in the bedrooms as well as the den area, plus kitchenettes. A spectacular atrium lobby filled with plants resembles a tropical rain forest. Glass elevators give you a bird's-eye view. Rates include a full breakfast. ⊠ *300 Tallapoosa St., 36104,* ☎ *334/269–5055,* FAX *334/269–0360,* WEB *www. jqhhotels.com. 237 suites. Restaurant, in-room data ports, kitchenettes, microwaves, refrigerators, cable TV, indoor pool, health club, hot tub, sauna, steam room, lounge, laundry service, concierge, business services, meeting rooms, airport shuttle. AE, D, DC, MC, V. BP.*

$$ 🏨 **GuestHouse International Hotels and Suites.** Elvis Presley once slept
here, but you're more likely to run into legislators and businesspeople than rock stars. The Civic Center is two blocks away. The hotel's atrium lobby has a waterfall, palm trees, and wrought-iron sofa sets that establish a New Orleans theme. ⊠ *120 Madison Ave., 36104,* ☎ *334/264–2231 or 800/214–8378,* FAX *334/263–3179,* WEB *www. guesthouseintl.com. 153 rooms, 19 suites. Restaurant, in-room data ports, some microwaves, some refrigerators, cable TV, pool, gym, lounge, laundry facilities, business services, meeting rooms, some pets allowed; no-smoking rooms. AE, D, DC, MC, V.*

$$ 🏨 **Red Bluff Cottage.** This bright, cheerful home in the heart of downtown overlooks the Alabama River plain. There's a raised porch that lets you survey the view, and a gazebo on the grounds. Each of the four guest rooms—all on the ground floor—is decorated with antique furniture and wall hangings, and each has a private bath. One has an adjacent children's room. The library has a common TV, movies, and lots of books. ⊠ *551 Clay St., Box 1026, 36101,* ☎ *334/264–0056 or 800/ 551–2529,* FAX *334/263–3054,* WEB *www.redbluffcottage.com. 4 rooms. In-room data ports, library, recreation room; no room TVs, no smoking. AE, D, MC, V. BP*

$–$$ 🏨 **La Quinta Inn.** This affordable, two-story, adobe-style inn is just off
I–85, less than a mile from the Alabama Shakespeare Festival. Rooms are contemporary, decorated in light earth tones. ⊠ *1280 East Blvd., 36117-2231,* ☎ *334/271–1620,* FAX *334/244–7919,* WEB *www.laquinta. com. 130 rooms. In-room data ports, cable TV, pool, laundry facilities, some pets allowed. AE, D, DC, MC, V. CP.*

The Arts

The **Montgomery Symphony Orchestra** (☎ 334/240–4004) performs at the **Davis Theatre for the Performing Arts** (⊠ 251 Montgomery St., ☎ 334/241–9567).Shakespearean plays, modern drama, and musicals are performed on two stages at the **Alabama Shakespeare Festival** (☎ 334/271–5353 or 800/841–4273, WEB www.asf.net) in the **Carolyn**

Blount Theatre (⌷ 1 Festival Dr.) in the Wynton Blount Cultural Park on the east side of Montgomery. The festival's season runs from November through September; tickets cost $21–$30. While you're there, take time to smell the roses—and other flowers and herbs planted in the **Shakespeare Garden.**

Montgomery's **Civic Center** (⌷ 300 Bibb St., ☎ 334/241–2100) hosts music concerts. At the campus theater of **Auburn University at Montgomery** (⌷ 7300 University Dr., ☎ 334/244–3632), student actors perform drama and comedy. Foreign and independent film buffs will enjoy Cloverdale's nonprofit **Capri Theatre** (⌷ 1045 E. Fairview Ave., ☎ 334/262–4858, WEB www.capritheatre.org), the city's first neighborhood theater, built in 1941, and now its only independent cinema.

Outdoor Activities and Sports
DOG RACING
Greyhound races are held at **VictoryLand** (☎ 334/269–6087 or 800/688–2946, WEB www.victoryland.com) about 20 mi east of Montgomery, just off I–85N in Shorter. There are racing and pari-mutuel betting every night but Sunday and several matinees during the week. Thoroughbred and greyhound events are also simulcast on race days. No one under 19 is admitted.

GOLF
Montgomery is home to **Lagoon Park** (⌷ 2855 Lagoon Park Dr., ☎ 334/271–7000), a very flat 18-hole, par-72 course with some water hazards and trees, consistently rated by *Golf Digest* as one of the top 50 public courses in the United States. **River Run** (⌷ AL 5, ☎ 334/271–2811) has 36 holes, a pro shop, and putting greens. **Kolomi** (⌷ 800 Dozier Rd., ☎ 334/279–6686) is an 18-hole, par-72 course adjacent to the Tallapoosa River.

MINIATURE GOLF
Funtasia (⌷ 5761 Atlanta Hwy., ☎ 334/277–4653) takes golfers on a safari through and around a man-made mountain, complete with large model elephants and other animals, and a cave.

Shopping
ANTIQUES
Herron House (⌷ 7834 Troy Hwy., ☎ 334/265–2063), Montgomery's oldest antiques shop, specializes in garden statuary as well as 18th- and 19th-century European furniture and accessories. **Bodiford's Antiques** (⌷ 919 Hampton St., ☎ 334/265–4220) has a mishmash of general antiques, including furniture and accessories.

MALLS
In addition to its anchor stores—Sears, Parisian, and Dillard's—**Eastdale Mall** (⌷ Eastern Bypass at Atlanta Hwy., ☎ 334/277–7359) has specialty stores, restaurants, an eight-screen cinema complex, and an ice-skating rink. **Montgomery Mall** (⌷ 2925-A Montgomery Mall, at South Blvd. and McGehee Ave., ☎ 334/281–0242) is anchored by JCPenney, Parisian, and Dillard's and has a food court.

Selma

39 *45 mi west of Montgomery via U.S. 80.*

Selma has played major roles in both Civil War and civil rights history. With the Confederacy's second-largest arsenal and foundry, Selma was a target of Union attack in 1865. Almost 100 years after that fighting—Alabama's only major inland Civil War battle—Selma came again to the forefront on March 21, 1965, as the stage of "Bloody Sunday." Civil rights protesters seeking to draw attention to the voting rights issue set

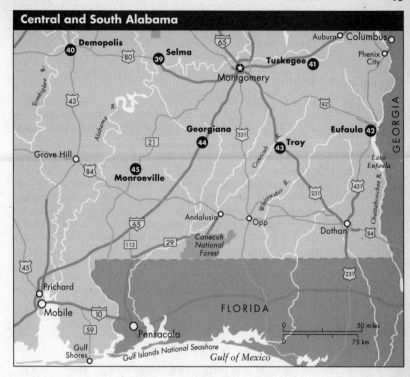

Central and South Alabama

out on a 50-mi march to Montgomery, where they intended to present their plight to lawmakers. At Edmund Pettus Bridge, marchers were beaten by state troopers with billy clubs as photographers captured the atrocities. The several hundred protesters on that failed march tried again three weeks later. Joined by some 20,000 supporters and led by civil rights leader Dr. Martin Luther King Jr., they accomplished a carefully guarded march to Montgomery, which resulted ultimately in the passing of the nation's Voting Rights Act. The path of that walk is a national All-American Road and an official National Trail, and the city honors the event the first weekend in March at the annual Bridge Crossing Jubilee festival.

Among the many sites worth visiting are **Old Town,** the largest historic district in the state, with more than 1,200 buildings, including the Greek Revival **Sturdivant Hall,** and **Martin Luther King Jr. Street,** a historic walking tour. You can pick up self-guided tour pamphlets at the **Selma-Dallas County Chamber of Commerce** (⊠ 513 Lauderdale St., ☎ 334/875–7241 or 800/457–3562, WEB www.selmaalabama. com) or print them out from the Web site. The **National Voting Rights Museum and Institute** (⊠ 1012 Water Ave., ☎ 334/418–0800) presents documents, photographs, and other exhibits that offer evidence of the important role of voting rights in the civil rights struggle.

Memorabilia at the **Old Depot Museum** (⊠ 4 Martin Luther King Jr. St., ☎ 334/874–2197) offers a glimpse of life in Selma from 1820 through the 21st century. The **Smitherman Historic Building** (⊠ 109 Union St., ☎ 334/874–2174) is an antebellum structure that houses the Art Lewis Civil War Collection.

In mid-March a **Historic Selma Pilgrimage and Antique Show** (☎ 800/457–3562) takes visitors through several antebellum homes, museums, and churches. In late April, one of the largest biannual **Civil War reenactments** (☎ 800/457–3562) in the nation draws thousands to the site of the Battle of Selma, on the Alabama River. The **Visitor Information Center** (✉ 2207 Broad St., ☎ 334/875–7485) has information about the city and its events such as the Tale Tellin' Festival and the Riverfront Market, held in October.

Dining and Lodging

$–$$ ✕ **Major Grumbles.** Named for a true Southern character—a self-appointed "major" in the Civil War—Major Grumbles is in a circa-1830s former cotton warehouse. Old photos of Selma decorate the walls. The restaurant is known for its marinated, char-grilled chicken breast. ✉ 1 Grumbles Alley, ☎ 334/872–2006. AE, DC, MC, V. Closed Sun.

$–$$ ✕🏨 **St. James Hotel.** Parlors here bustled with wealthy cotton planters, merchants, and politicians in the 1830s. Later that century, outlaws Jesse and Frank James were guests. One of the few remaining antebellum riverfront hotels in the country, the completely restored St. James has a lobby outfitted with antiques and rooms with 1800s plantation reproductions; suites have fireplaces and hot tubs. This is downtown Selma's only full-service hotel, and the adjacent St. James Place anchors the Water Avenue Historic District. ✉ 1200 Water Ave., 36701, ☎ 334/872–3234 or 888/264–6788, FAX 334/872–0332. 38 rooms, 4 suites. Restaurant, cable TV, lounge, laundry service, business services; no-smoking rooms. AE, D, DC, MC, V.

Demopolis

40   40 mi west of Selma via U.S. 80.

Demopolis takes great pride in its Southern heritage. Take time to ride past antebellum homes and 18th-century buildings in the historic downtown area. The 10,000-acre Demopolis Lake offers fishing, boating, swimming, picnicking, and campgrounds. For details contact the **Demopolis Area Chamber of Commerce** (✉ 102 E. Washington St., ☎ 334/289–0270, WEB www.demopolischamber.com), open weekdays 8:30–5. You can also pick up brochures anytime at the **information center** (☎ 334/289–5772) at the Best Western Hotel on U.S. 80.

★   **Gaineswood,** built between 1843 and 1861, is a fine Greek Revival mansion. The house has been extensively restored, down to reproductions of the original French wallpapers. It contains the original furnishings, such as carved four-poster beds and a flutina—a one-of-a-kind musical instrument invented by the original owner (who also designed Gaineswood itself). Interior architectural elements include elaborate columns and pilasters; friezes and medallions of wood, plaster, cast iron, and leather; and ceiling-dome window lanterns. ✉ 805 S. Cedar Ave., ☎ 334/289–4846. 🎟 $5. ☉ Mon.–Sat. 9–5, Sun. 1–5.

Bluff Hall, on a chalky cliff above the Tombigbee River, was built in 1832 as a Federal-style house and remodeled in the Greek Revival style several years later. It has a columned front portico, a huge double parlor with Corinthian columns, and Empire and Victorian furnishings donated by friends and descendants of the original owner. Also on display is a collection of period clothing. ✉ 405 N. Commissioners Ave., ☎ 334/289–9644. 🎟 $5. ☉ Jan.–Feb., Tues.–Sat. 10–4, Sun. 2–4; Mar.–Dec., Tues.–Sat. 10–5, Sun. 2–5.

Tuskegee

41   35 mi east of Montgomery via U.S. 80.

In addition to being the home of the historic Tuskegee Institute, Tuskegee has some antebellum houses and is near **Tuskegee National**

Forest (☎ 334/727–2652), with fishing spots, hiking trails, and a replica of the childhood home of Booker T. Washington.

The **Tuskegee Institute National Historic Site** includes the school founded by educator Booker T. Washington in 1881, one of America's first black universities; the institute's Victorian buildings, many designed and constructed by students; and Washington's actual redbrick Victorian home, **the Oaks.** The **George Washington Carver Museum** on the campus includes Carver's original laboratory and a historical study of the Tuskegee Institute. An agricultural chemist, Carver helped improve agricultural practices and also discovered hundreds of uses for the peanut, sweet potato, and soybean. A walking tour of the Historic Campus District originates at the Carver Museum. ⊠ *On Tuskegee College campus, off Old Montgomery Rd.,* ☎ *334/727–3200,* WEB *www.nps. gov/tuin.* ☞ *Free.* ⊙ *Daily 9–5.*

Eufaula

❷ *90 mi east of Montgomery on U.S. 82.*

Eufaula is a town rich in Southern tradition and antebellum homes; it's also near a national wildlife refuge and has great fishing areas. During the **Eufaula Spring Pilgrimage** (☎ 334/687–3793) in early April, you can take daytime and candlelight tours through some of the homes, built between 1834 and 1911. There are also garden tours and antiques shows.

Shorter Mansion, a white-columned house built in 1884, is a fine example of neoclassical architecture and a showplace of the Seth Lore–Irwinton Historic District. Inside, a museum honors the six former governors of Alabama who were Barbour County natives. ⊠ *340 N. Eufaula Ave.,* ☎ *334/687–3793.* ☞ *$3.* ⊙ *Mon.–Sat. 9–4, Sun. 1–4.*

Fendall Hall, one of the great 19th-century Italianate-style houses surviving in Alabama, has deep overhanging eaves, a hip roof topped with a cupola, and a long, wraparound porch. ⊠ *917 W. Barbour St.,* ☎ *334/687–8469.* ☞ *$4.* ⊙ *Mon.–Sat. 10–4.*

Outdoor Activities and Sports

Lake Eufaula is one of the best bass lakes in the country, with 8- to 10-pound largemouth bass caught with regularity. **Lakepoint State Park Resort** (⊠ U.S. 431N, ☎ 334/687–6676), north of town, has six lighted tennis courts and an 18-hole, par-72 golf course.

Troy

❸ *50 mi south of Montgomery on U.S. 231.*

This town is home to Troy State University and a fine pioneer museum. The **Pike Pioneer Museum** complex has more than 14,000 artifacts of the pioneer period—clothing, furniture, farm implements—plus spinning and weaving demonstrations. Don't miss the turn-of-the-century schoolhouse, log house, well-stocked general store, and 1883 steam logging locomotive. Special events—such as fall and spring Pioneer Days, and the Jean Lake Festival—take place throughout the year. Folklife artisans appear the first Saturday of the month from April through December. A picnic area is adjacent to the amphitheater. ⊠ *248 U.S. 231N,* ☎ *334/566–3597.* ☞ *$3.* ⊙ *Mon.–Sat. 9–5, Sun. 1–5.*

Georgiana

❹ *60 mi south of Montgomery on I–65.*

The small, rural community of Georgiana was the birthplace of one of country music's greatest performers—Hank Williams Sr. (1923–1953).

★ The city of Georgiana has established the **Hank Williams Sr. Boyhood Home and Museum,** and fans from around the world have donated Hank Williams memorabilia to fill the house to the brim. Rocking chairs line the large wraparound porch, so you can relax as you listen to the songs of this country-music legend. Many of Williams's personal items are on display, along with an excellent collection of photographs. On the first Saturday in June, Georgiana comes alive for the **Hank Williams Sr. Festival,** as fans and performers pay tribute to their idol. The music goes on long into the night. ⊠ *127 Rose St.,* ☎ *334/376–2396.* ⊡ *$3.* ☉ *Mon.–Sat. 10–5, Sun. 1–5.*

Monroeville

⑮ Monroeville's most famous daughter, Harper Lee, won a Pulitzer Prize for her novel *To Kill a Mockingbird,* which incorporates many of her childhood remembrances of the town—and her friendship with novelist Truman Capote—in the 1930s. The local Monroeville Players offer the hottest theater tickets around with their amateur productions of a two-act play based on the book. Tickets for the May event sell out soon after they go on sale in March. The play is staged at the **Old Courthouse Museum** (⊠ 32 N. Alabama Ave., ☎ 251/575–7433, WEB www.tokillamockingbird.com), the model for the famous trial scene, on the town square. The museum is open year-round; a self-guided tour is available.

In celebration of its status as the "literary capital of Alabama" (proclaimed by the Legislature in 1997), Monroeville hosts Alabama Southern Community College's annual **Alabama Writers' Symposium** (☎ 251/575–3156), a three-day literary festival, each May.

Montgomery and Central Alabama A to Z

AIR TRAVEL
CARRIERS
Montgomery Regional Airport at Dannelly Field is served by Atlantic Southeast Airlines/Delta, Northwest Airlink, and US Airways Express (☞ Air Travel *in* Smart Travel Tips A to Z for telephone numbers).

AIRPORTS
Montgomery Regional Airport is 6 mi southwest of downtown. Taxis are available, though many hotels provide transportation from the airport by prior arrangement. To drive downtown from the airport, turn north onto I–65, follow signs to I–85, and take the first exit, Court Street. To drive to the airport from downtown, take Exit 167 off I–65 to U.S. 80W and go 3 mi to airport entrance.
➤ AIRPORT INFORMATION: **Montgomery Regional Airport** (☎ 334/281–5040, WEB www.montgomeryairport.org).

BUS TRAVEL
Montgomery has Demand and Response Transit (DART) buses that run by reservation from 5 AM to 9:30 PM. Exact change is required for the $1.50 fare.
➤ BUS INFORMATION: **DART** (☎ 334/262–7321). **Greyhound** (⊠ 950 W. South Blvd., Montgomery, ☎ 334/286–0953 or 800/231–2222).

CAR TRAVEL
I–65 runs north to Birmingham and south to Mobile. I–85 begins in Montgomery and runs northeast to Atlanta. U.S. 80 runs west past the airport to Selma. U.S. 80 cuts east–west across the state, connecting Demopolis, Selma, Montgomery, and Tuskegee. U.S. 82 runs east–west through Montgomery and Eufaula.

EMERGENCIES

For medical emergencies, contact the Montgomery Baptist Medical Center. Rite Aid in Montgomery is open daily from 8 AM to midnight.

➤ CONTACTS: **Ambulance, police** (☎ 911). **Montgomery Baptist Medical Center** (✉ 2105 E. South Blvd., ☎ 334/288–2100). **Rite Aid** (✉ Capitol Plaza Shopping Center, South Bypass, Montgomery, ☎ 334/281–1312).

MEDIA

RADIO

AM: WACV 1170, talk; WXVI 1600, jazz.

FM: WAPR 88.3, NPR; WLWI 92.3, country; WXFX 95.1, rock; WBAM 98.9, pop; WZHT 105.7, soul.

OUTDOORS AND SPORTS

GOLF

Several sections of Alabama's Robert Trent Jones Golf Trail are in this region: the Grand National course at Auburn/Opelika; Capitol Hill, at Prattville; Highland Oaks, at Dothan; and Cambrian Ridge, at Greenville (considered by many golfers to be the most spectacular on the trail). The four sites offer 11 courses; fees run $54–$64.

➤ CONTACTS: **Cambrian Ridge** (✉ 101 Sunbelt Pkwy., ☎ 334/382–9787). **Capitol Hill** (✉ 2600 Constitution Ave., ☎ 334/285–1114). **Grand National** (✉ 3000 Sunbelt Pkwy., ☎ 205/749–9042). **Highland Oaks** (✉ 704 Royal Pkwy., ☎ 334/712–2820). **Robert Trent Jones Golf Trail reservations and information** (☎ 800/949–4444, WEB www.rtjgolf.com).

TAXIS

Taxis in Montgomery charge $1.75 for the first ⅙ mi, $1.20 for each additional mile. Try Yellow Cab.

➤ TAXI COMPANIES: **Yellow Cab** (☎ 334/262–5225).

TOURS

Landmark Tours and Whirlwind Tours offer van and bus tours of area sights.

➤ FEES AND SCHEDULES: **Landmark Tours** (☎ 334/262–4044). **Whirlwind Tours** (☎ 334/272–5940).

TRAIN TRAVEL

The nearest Amtrak service to Montgomery and central Alabama is in Birmingham. Montgomery has a Thruway Intermodal Transit Terminal offering bus service to the Amtrak station in Atlanta, which is about 150 mi, or 2½ hours, northeast.

➤ TRAIN INFORMATION: **Amtrak** (☎ 800/872–7245, WEB www.amtrak.com). **Thruway Intermodal Transit Terminal** (☎ 800/872–7245).

VISITOR INFORMATION

➤ TOURIST INFORMATION: **Eufaula/Barbour County Chamber of Commerce** (✉ 102 N. Orange Ave., Eufaula 36027, ☎ 334/687–6664 or 800/524–7529, WEB www.eufaula-barbourchamber.com). **Montgomery Visitors Center** (✉ 300 Water St., 36104, ☎ 334/262–0013 or 800/240–9452, WEB www.visitingmontgomery.com). **Selma–Dallas County Chamber of Commerce** (✉ 513 Lauderdale St., ☎ 334/875–7244 or 800/457–3562, WEB www.selmaalabama.com).

MOBILE AND THE GULF COAST

Mobile, which celebrated its 300th birthday in 2002, is the state's oldest city and one of its most graceful. A springtime explosion of azaleas beneath Spanish moss–draped oak canopies gives Mobile the name

Azalea City. During the third weekend in March, the Azalea Trail Festival brings the Azalea Trail Run, which attracts world-class athletes
to the city, and the Festival of Flowers, a spectacular garden and flower
show in the campus of Spring Hill College. Just a short drive west of
Mobile, Bellingrath Gardens is a not-to-be-missed public garden that's
especially sensational in the spring.

Mobilians boast that Mardi Gras began here, long before New Orleans
ever celebrated Fat Tuesday, and today the city celebrates the pre-Lenten
season, usually in February, with parades and merrymaking day and
night. In March the two-day Historic Mobile Homes Tour showcases
the city's architecture, which includes Federal-style town houses, creole cottages, and antebellum plantation homes. In fall BayFest—a
music festival covering several downtown blocks—rocks Mobile the
first weekend in October.

The area of the Gulf Coast around Gulf Shores, to the south of Mobile, encompasses about 50 mi of pure white-sand beach, including a
former peninsula called Pleasure Island and Dauphin Island to the west.
Though hotels and condominiums take up a good deal of the beachfront, some of it remains public. Here you'll find small-town Southern beach life, with excellent deep-sea fishing as well as freshwater fishing
in the bays and bayous, water sports of all types, and world-class golf.

Those with more time might explore the eastern shore of Mobile Bay—
Spanish Fort, Daphne, and Fairhope—where, sometime between June
and September, locals and tourists eagerly await the mythical phe-
nomenon known as a Jubilee. During a Jubilee the bay's bounty—fish,
crabs, shrimp, and more—scramble for shore and into the waiting nets
of those who have usually stumbled out of bed in the middle of the
night, awakened by their neighbors' excited cries. At Point Clear, south
of Fairhope, is the bayside Marriott's Grand Hotel, host since the
mid-19th century to wealthy vacationers.

*Numbers in the margin correspond to numbers on the Mobile and the
Gulf Coast map.*

Mobile

46 *170 mi southwest of Montgomery on I–65.*

Fort Condé was the name given by the French in 1711 to the site known
today as Mobile; around it blossomed the first white settlement in what
is now Alabama. For eight years it was the capital of the French colonial empire, and it remained under French control until 1763, long after
the capital had moved to New Orleans.

Mobile, a busy international port, is noted for its tree-lined boulevards
fanning westward from the riverfront. In the heart of busy downtown
is Bienville Square, a park with an ornate cast-iron fountain and shaded
by centuries-old live oaks. One of the city's main thoroughfares,
Dauphin Street, has many thriving restaurants, bars, and shops.

In the center of town, **Fort Condé** survives as a reminder of the city's
beginnings, thanks to a reconstruction (one-third of the original size)
that preserved it when its remains were discovered—150 years after the
fort was destroyed—during the building of the I–10 interchange. A portion of the fort, originally built in 1724–35, houses the **visitor center**
for the city, as well as a museum. Among the many brochures at the
center are ones outlining excellent walking tours of the city's historic
districts, including De Tonti Square, Church Street East, and Dauphin
Street. ⊠ *150 S. Royal St.,* ☎ *251/434-7304.* ⌨ *Free.* ☉ *Daily 8–5.*

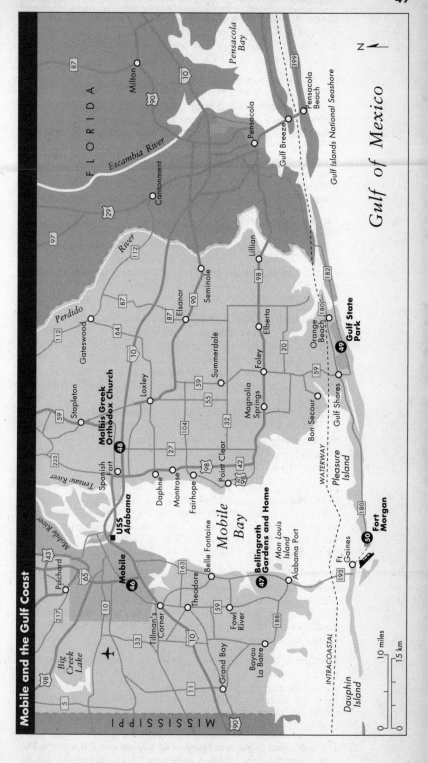

Mobile and the Gulf Coast

49

The **Condé-Charlotte Museum House,** next to Fort Condé, was built in 1822–24 as Mobile's first official jail and contains rooms furnished in the style from different periods of the city's history. ✉ *104 Theatre St.,* ☎ *251/432–4722,* 🎟 *$3.* 🕒 *Tues.–Sat. 10–4.*

The **Mobile Museum of Art** reopened in late 2002 after undergoing a $15 million expansion and renovation, tripling its former space. In addition to its impressive permanent collection of some 6,000 pieces of mostly American art, the museum hosts traveling exhibits and organized "Picturing French Style: 300 Years of Art and Fashion" in homage to the city's French roots to coincide with its grand opening and Mobile's tercentenary. A branch gallery, **Mobile Museum of Art Downtown** (✉ 300 Dauphin St., ☎ 251/208–5200), is near Cathedral Park. ✉ *Langan Park, 4850 Museum Dr.,* ☎ *251/208–5200,* WEB *www. mobilemuseumofart.com.* 🎟 *$6.* 🕒 *Mon.–Sat. 10–5, Sun. 1–5.*

The **Museum of Mobile,** in the former Southern Market/Old City Hall building next to the Gulf Coast Exploreum, has interactive exhibits that tell Mobile's history from the founding of the French settlement of Fort Louis de la Mobile to Mobile Bay's involvement in the Civil War to the most notorious hurricanes in the past century. ✉ *111 S. Royal St.,* ☎ *251/208–7569,* WEB *www.museumofmobile.com.* 🎟 *$5.* 🕒 *Mon.– Sat. 9–6, Sun. 1–5.*

The **Oakleigh Garden Historic District** begins 1 mi southwest of Fort Condé; signs lead to **Oakleigh,** an antebellum Greek Revival mansion with a stairway circling under ancient live oaks to a small portico. The high-ceilinged half-timber house was built between 1833 and 1838 and is typical of the most expensive dwellings of its day. Fine period furniture, portraits, silver, jewelry, kitchen implements, toys, and more are displayed. Next door is the **Cox-Deasy House,** a raised creole cottage built in 1850 that is a more typical middle-class home. Members of the Historic Mobile Preservation Society conduct tours of Oakleigh and the Cox-Deasy House. ✉ *350 Oakleigh Pl.,* ☎ *251/432–1281.* 🎟 *$5 for both homes.* 🕒 *Mon.–Sat. 10–4. Guided tours every ½ hr, last tour begins at 3:30.*

In the DeTonti Square Historic District, the Italianate **Richards–DAR House Museum,** built in 1860, holds magnificent period furnishings. Note the white lace ironwork outside the brick townhouse. The Daughters of the American Revolution administer this welcoming museum, which serves tea and cookies. ✉ *256 N. Joachim St.,* ☎ *251/434–7320,* 🎟 *$4.* 🕒 *Tues.–Sat. 10–4, Sun. 1–4.*

Several of Mobile's churches figure prominently in African-American history. The **State Street A.M.E. Zion Church** (✉ 502 State St., ☎ 251/ 432–3965) is one of the oldest and most striking African Methodist Episcopal Zion churches in town. The **St. Louis Street Missionary Baptist Church** (✉ 108 N. Dearborn St., ☎ 251/438–3823) hosted the conference that established Selma University.

The modest **National African-American Archives and Museum** holds portraits and biographies of well-known African-Americans. There is also a collection of carvings and artifacts, including Mardi Gras costumes, documents, and books. ✉ *564 Dr. Martin Luther King Jr. Ave.,* ☎ *251/433–8511.* 🎟 *Donations accepted.* 🕒 *Tues.–Fri. 9–noon and 1–4; weekends by appointment.*

🕲 The **Gulf Coast Exploreum Museum of Science and IMAX Dome Theater,** across from the Mobile Convention Center downtown, is a science museum with a very popular Hands On Hall, where kids of all ages can have fun while learning through interactive exhibits. Films in the state-of-the-art IMAX Dome Theater change every few months. Parking is at a premium in this area, but is available in the parking lot across from Fort Conde off Royal Street. ⊠ *65 Government St.,* ☎ *251/208–6883 or 877/625–4386,* WEB *www.exploreum.net.* ☒ *Exhibits $6; IMAX theater $6; both $11.* ☉ *Mon.–Thurs. 9–5, Fri. 9–9, Sat. 10–9, Sun. noon–5. Open Thurs. until 8 Memorial Day–Labor Day.*

The **USS Alabama** is anchored in Mobile Bay just east of downtown Mobile off I–10. Public subscription saved the mighty gray battleship from being scrapped ignominiously after her heroic World War II service, which ranged from Scapa Flow to the South Pacific. A tour of the ship gives a fascinating look into the life of a 2,500-member crew. Anchored next to the battleship is the submarine USS *Drum,* another active battle weapon during World War II, also open to visitors. Other exhibits in the 100-acre **Battleship Memorial Park** include a B-52 bomber called *Calamity Jane* and a P-51 Mustang fighter plane. ⊠ *2703 Battleship Pkwy. (U.S. 90),* ☎ *251/433–2703 or 800/426–4929,* WEB *www.ussalabama.com.* ☒ *$10; parking $2.* ☉ *Apr.–Sept., daily 8–6, Oct.–Mar., daily 8–4.*

OFF THE BEATEN PATH ☙ | **ESTUARIUM AT THE DAUPHIN ISLAND SEA LAB –** This facility on Dauphin Island, a 17-mi-long barrier island about 40 mi south of Mobile, spotlights the ecosystems of the Mobile Bay estuary, including the Mobile-Tensaw River Delta, Mobile Bay, the barrier islands, and the Gulf of Mexico. Outside, the Living Marsh Boardwalk has signs explaining the natural history of the state's marshes. Indoors, there are displays, interactive exhibits, a 9,000-gallon aquarium simulating the underwater environment of Mobile Bay, and a 16,000-gallon tank with sea life from the Gulf of Mexico. ⊠ *101 Bienville Blvd. Take I–10 to Exit 17A, then Rte. 193S to Dauphin Island; turn left at the water tower and proceed 2.2 mi,* ☎ *251/861–7500,* WEB *www.disl.org.* ☒ *$6.* ☉ *Sept.–Feb., Mon.–Sat. 9–5, Sun. 1–5; Mar.–Aug., Mon.–Sat. 9–6, Sun. 12–6.*

Dining and Lodging

$$–$$$ ✕ **Gus's Azalea Manor Restaurant and Courtyard.** In a former storefront on Dauphin Street downtown, Gus's has an airy bar with a colorful mural and a street view. The lush courtyard behind the restaurant is a great place to dine alfresco on cool nights. Greek chef Gus Ravanos's menu highlights pastas, seafood, steaks, and chicken. ⊠ *751 Dauphin St.,* ☎ *251/433–4877. AE, D, DC, MC, V. Closed Sun.*

$$–$$$ ✕ **Justine's at the Pillars.** When chef Matt Shipp acquired the Pillars, one of Mobile's most beloved fine-dining landmarks, the city breathed a collective sigh of relief, knowing the restaurant would be in good hands. Shipp, a Mobile native who trained in kitchens from New York to New Orleans, earned his local reputation at his Justine's Courtyard and Carriageway downtown. With Justine's at the Pillars, housed in a midtown mansion, he's continuing the tradition of excellent service and the finest in steaks and seafood, but adding his own Gulf Coast favorites such as turtle soup, and shrimp and grits. Sunday brunch with champagne and live jazz provides a quintessential Mobile experience. ⊠ *1757 Government St.,* ☎ *251/471–3411. AE, D, DC, MC, V. No lunch.*

$$–$$$ ✕ **Loretta's.** At a colorful corner just a block off Dauphin Street, Loretta's has its own dramatic flair. Hidden behind a wall of glass covered in creeping fig, this restaurant flaunts its unique style with gleaming silver palm trees and whimsical, mismatched salt and pepper shakers. In the kitchen, owner/chef Christopher Hunter adds creative nuances to Southern favorites, such as sausage-stuffed pork chop and

pan-seared sashimi tuna steak. ⊠ *19 S. Conception St.,* ☎ *251/432–2200. AE, D, DC, MC, V. Closed Mon. No dinner Tues. and Sun.*

$$–$$$ ✕ **Roussos Restaurant.** With a nautical look created by lots of fishnets and scenes of ships at sea, Roussos serves seafood fried, broiled, or served Greek style (with a blend of spices and oils). Steaks and chicken also are available. The appetizers are big favorites—especially the baked oysters and seafood gumbo. ⊠ *166 S. Royal St.,* ☎ *251/433–3322. AE, D, DC, MC, V. Closed Sun.*

$–$$ ✕ **Dew Drop Inn.** Mobile's oldest restaurant, the no-frills Dew Drop
★ Inn is also one of the city's most popular places to meet and eat. The menu's most popular item is the "world famous" Dew Drop Inn hot dog, which goes well with homemade onion rings or thick-cut steak fries. Daily specials include down-home favorites such as fried chicken or catfish, accompanied by perfectly seasoned vegetables. ⊠ *1808 Old Shell Rd.,* ☎ *251/473–7872. Reservations not accepted. MC, V. Closed Sun. No dinner Sat.*

$$–$$$ ✕⌂ **Adam's Mark Mobile.** This 28-story riverfront hotel, completely renovated in 2002, is connected to the Mobile Convention Center by a covered skywalk. The large guest rooms have floor-to-ceiling windows with views of downtown Mobile or Mobile Bay, and standard chain hotel–style furniture. The Riverview Cafe and Grill specializes in Gulf Coast seafood; lighter fare and live entertainment are offered six nights a week in the Tiffany Rose Restaurant. ⊠ *64 S. Water St., 36602,* ☎ *251/438–4000,* ⅏ *251/415–3060,* ⓦ *www.adamsmark. com. 375 rooms, 12 suites. 2 restaurants, room service, in-room data ports, minibars, cable TV, pool, health club, hot tub, sauna, bar, dry cleaning, laundry service, concierge, business services, meeting rooms; no-smoking rooms. AE, D, DC, MC, V.*

$$–$$$ ⌂ **Malaga Inn.** A delightful, romantic getaway, the Malaga comprises
★ two townhouses built by a wealthy landowner in 1862. The lobby is furnished with 19th-century antiques and opens onto a landscaped central courtyard with a fountain. The rooms are large, airy, and furnished with antiques. The Malaga is on a quiet street downtown, within walking distance of the Museum of Mobile and the Gulf Coast Exploreum. ⊠ *359 Church St., 36602,* ☎ *251/438–4701 or 800/235–1586,* ⅏ *334/438–4701,* ⓦ *www.malagainn.com. 35 rooms, 3 suites. Cable TV, pool, lounge, business services. AE, D, MC, V.*

$$ ⌂ **Radisson Admiral Semmes Hotel.** This restored 1940 hotel in the historic district is a favorite with local politicians. It's also popular with party goers, particularly during Mardi Gras, because of its excellent location directly on the parade route. The spacious, high-ceilinged rooms have a burgundy-and-green color scheme and are furnished in Queen Anne and Chippendale styles. ⊠ *251 Government St., 36602,* ☎ *251/432–8000,* ⅏ *251/405–5942,* ⓦ *www.radisson.com/mobileal. 148 rooms, 22 suites. Restaurant, pool, bar, business services. AE, D, DC, MC, V.*

Nightlife and the Arts

The **Joe Jefferson Players** (☎ 251/471–1534), an amateur group started more than 50 years ago, performs plays and musicals at the Joe Jefferson Playhouse (⊠ 11 S. Carlen St.). The 1927 **Saenger Theater** (6 S. Joachim St., ☎ 251/433–2787, ⓦ www.mobilesaenger. com) hosts orchestras and touring companies. The **Mobile Civic Center** (⊠ 401 Civic Center Dr., ☎ 251/434–7381) presents theater groups, orchestras, and concerts of all kinds. The **Mitchell Center** at the University of South Alabama (⊠ Old Shell Rd., ☎ 251/460–6101), home to the university's Jaguars basketball team, hosts concerts and other special events throughout the year. In the lobby the spectacular restored 1940s Waterman Globe, 12 ft in diameter, rotates with the Earth's axis.

Near the Mobile Museum of Art, the Playhouse in the Park's **Pixie Players** (Langan Park, ☎ 251/344–1537) is a children's theater company that puts on five shows annually.

Much of Mobile's nightlife centers around downtown's former commercial district, **Dauphin Street,** which today has a number of restaurants and nightspots spread out over several blocks. Mobilians have taken to calling the area LoDa, short for Lower Dauphin. Occupying the space of a former pharmacy in the 1906 Van Antwerp Building, **Drayton Place** (⌧ 101 Dauphin St., ☎ 251/432–7438) offers a vast selection of imported beers at its oversize bar (the former druggist's counter), as well as Creole-inspired cuisine for lunch, dinner, or Sunday jazz brunch. In the back, there's a billiards room; bands play jazz on Thursday through Saturday nights. **Monsoon's** (⌧ 210 Dauphin St., ☎ 334/433–3500) is one of several almost indistinguishable bars that host local bands as well as a few national ones, drawing crowds of 20-somethings on Friday and Saturday nights. In midtown Mobile, the **Double Olive** (⌧ 2033 Airport Blvd., ☎ 251/450–5001) is an artsy, urbane martini bar that draws hip crowds.

Outdoor Activities and Sports
DOG RACING
At the **Mobile Greyhound Park** (⌧ Theodore-Dawes Rd. at Exit 13 off I–10W, ☎ 251/653–5000, WEB www.mobilegreyhoundpark.com), about 10 mi from Mobile, there is pari-mutuel betting and a restaurant overlooking the finish line. The track offers simulcasts. The minimum age for admission is 18.

BASEBALL
The **Mobile BayBears,** the AA affiliate of the San Diego Padres, play baseball from April through October at "the Hank"—Hank Aaron Stadium (⌧ 755 Bolling Brothers Blvd., just off I–65 at the Government Blvd. exit, ☎ 251/479–2327), named for the baseball legend and Mobile native.

GOLF
Magnolia Grove (⌧ 7000 Lamplighter Dr., ☎ 251/645–0075 or 800/949–4444), part of the Robert Trent Jones Golf Trail, has 54 holes of championship golf: two par-72 courses and an 18-hole, par-54 (each hole is par 3) course that is anything but easy. The 18-hole, par-72 **Azalea City Golf Club** (⌧ 1000 Gaillard Dr., ☎ 251/342–4221) is operated by the city of Mobile. **TimberCreek** (⌧ 9650 TimberCreek Blvd., ☎ 251/621–9900), in Daphne, has 27 holes and is par 72. **Rock Creek** (⌧ 140 Clubhouse Dr., ☎ 251/928–4223), in Fairhope, on the eastern shore of Mobile Bay, has 18 holes and is par 72.

NATURE-WATCHING
Wildland Expeditions, led by Captain Gene Burrell and his son, Tony, on the *Gator Bait,* explores the Mobile-Tensaw Delta on two-hour trips that leave from Chickasaw (just north of Mobile). You'll get close-up views of plants and animals, especially alligators and nesting osprey. ☎ *251/460–8206.* ⌧ *$20.*

Shopping
Most shopping in Mobile is in malls and shopping centers in the suburban areas. Stores are generally open Monday–Saturday 10–9, Sunday 1–6. Sales tax is 9%.

ANTIQUES
Antiques buffs love Mobile because it offers more than 25 individual shops and malls that specialize in antiques. In the Loop area of midtown (where Government Street, Airport Boulevard, and Dauphin Is-

land Parkway converge), several shops are within walking distance. The **Red Barn Antique Mall** (⊠ 418 Dauphin Island Pkwy., ☎ 251/473–9227) has at least 15 shops with antiques, from glassware and books to furniture. The **Cotton City Antique Mall** (⊠ 2012 Airport Blvd., ☎ 251/479–9747) offers 12,000 square ft of antique furniture, vintage linens, clocks, and more. **Yellow House Antiques** (⊠ 1902 Government St., ☎ 251/476–7382) is an upscale shop with 18th- and 19th-century English, Continental, and American furniture and accessories. The seemingly endless **Antiques at the Loop** (⊠ 2100 Airport Blvd., ☎ 251/476–0309) has lamps, stained glass, furnishings, and garden accessories.

MALLS

Colonial Mall Bel Air (⊠ Airport Blvd. and I–65, ☎ 251/478–1893) has 175 stores, including JCPenney, Parisian, Target, Dillard's, and Sears. Directly across the street, **Springdale Mall** (⊠ Airport Blvd. and I–65, ☎ 251/479–9871), anchored by Dillard's and McRae's, has more than 100 stores, including Best Buy, Linens and Things, and Barnes and Noble.

Theodore

20 mi south of Mobile.

★ ㊼   One of the most popular gardens in the South is near the town of Theodore. **Bellingrath Gardens and Home** is famous for its magnificent azaleas, which are part of 65 acres of gardens set amid a 905-acre semitropical landscape. Show time for the azaleas is late February through mid-March, when some 250,000 plantings of 200 different species are ablaze with color. But Bellingrath is a year-round wonder, with 2,500 rosebushes blooming in summer, 60,000 chrysanthemum plants cascading in the fall, and red fields of poinsettias brightening the winter. At the annual Magic Christmas in Lights event, holiday decorations in the gardens light up the night throughout December. Countless species and flowering plants spring up along Fowl River, a stream, and a lake populated by ducks and swans. Guides can assist you, but a free map lets you plan your own strolls along flagstone paths and across charming bridges. In April and October, large numbers of migratory birds drop by.

Coca-Cola bottling pioneer Walter D. Bellingrath began the nucleus of the gardens in 1917, when he and his wife bought a large tract of land to use as a fishing camp. But their travels prompted them to create, instead, a garden rivaling some they had seen in Europe, and before long they opened it to the public. Today the brick home they built is open to visitors and has a fine collection of antiques, including the world's largest display of Boehm porcelain birds. One-hour **boat cruises** on Fowl River aboard the *Southern Belle* leave from the dock next to the Bellingrath Home at regular intervals. ⊠ *12401 Bellingrath Rd.,* ☎ *251/973–2217 or 800/247–8420,* WEB *www.bellingrath.org.* ⊟ *Gardens $8.50; gardens and home $15.75; value pack (gardens, home, and cruise) $20.* ☉ *Gardens daily 8–sunset; home opens daily at 9 with closings varying by season.*

Malbis

10 mi east of Mobile on U.S. 90 via I–10.

Malbis is the outgrowth of a development begun in 1906 by Jason Malbis, a Greek immigrant and former monk who bought tracts of land and established a cannery, bakery, farm, and power plant; today it includes portions of a residential golf community, TimberCreek, as well as the residential development known as Historic Malbis Plantation.

48 The **Malbis Greek Orthodox Church** is a replica of a beautiful Byzantine church in Athens, Greece. It was built in 1965 as a memorial to the faith of Jason Malbis, founder of the community. The marble for the interior was imported from the same quarries that provided stone for the Parthenon, and a master painter was brought over from Greece to paint murals on the walls and the 75-ft dome of the rotunda. The stained-glass windows are stunning. ✉ *29300 County Rte. 27,* ☎ *251/626–3050.* 🎟 *Free.* ☉ *Tours daily 9–noon and 2–5.*

Fairhope and Point Clear

12 mi south of Malbis on U.S. 98A.

Clinging to the eastern shore of Mobile Bay, the quiet towns of Fairhope and Point Clear have restored clapboard houses with wide porches overlooking the bay and live oak trees cloaked with Spanish moss. Fairhope was settled around 1900 by a group of Midwesterners, who established it as a utopian single-tax community (the system is still in use). Today Fairhope's streets are lined with seasonal flowers year-round—even the trash receptacles double as planters—and the downtown area has antiques shops, funky stores, art galleries, and B&Bs, making it a relaxing weekend escape. The Fairhope Municipal Pier, the centerpiece of town, offers fishing, boating, and marine services. Fairhope's Arts and Crafts Festival, held each March, is a large juried show that draws more than 200 exhibitors for a weekend.

Point Clear's incomparable Grand Hotel, operating since 1847, is a leading resort destination hidden away among million-dollar bayside estates. A walk along the hotel's boardwalk provides a glimpse of the summer homes that line Mobile Bay.

Dining and Lodging

$$$–$$$$ ✗ **The Fairhope Inn and Restaurant.** Owner/chef Tyler Kean's restaurant, inside a B&B, is fast becoming "the" place to dine in Fairhope. Elegant yet not stuffy, the small dining room extends onto an enclosed porch that overlooks a lush private courtyard. Kean's menu changes seasonally but may include pan-roasted grouper with asparagus and morel mushrooms in a red-wine sauce served over grits. Sunday brunch is quite popular. ✉ *63 S. Church St.,* ☎ *251/928–6226. AE, D, DC, MC, V. Closed Mon. No lunch Sat.*

$–$$ ✗ **Lulu's Sunset Grill.** With a famous brother lending celebrity status, and an enviable location on scenic Weeks Bay, Lucy Buffett—Jimmy's sister—couldn't miss with her laid-back restaurant. Fortunately, the food is as good as the atmosphere. Start with the black-eyed-pea dip on crackers, and don't miss the blackened grouper po'boy topped with fried green tomato slices. ✉ *11525 U.S. 98,* ☎ *251/990–9907. Reservations not accepted. AE, D, MC, V. Closed Mon.*

$$$–$$$$ 🏨 **Marriott's Grand Hotel Resort and Golf Club.** Nestled amid 550 acres
★   of beautifully landscaped grounds on Mobile Bay, the Grand has been a cherished landmark since 1847 and is one of the South's premier resorts. The octagonal, two-story cypress-paneled and -beamed lobby serves as the hub for several wings. Its large three-sided fireplace, armchairs, and porcelain display evoke a casual elegance that is echoed in the half-moon dining room overlooking the bay. In 2002, the resort underwent a $30 million renovation and expansion, adding a water park with fountains and geysers, a beach with a boat launch, a European spa, and contemporary suites. The resort's Lakewood Golf Club is the southernmost link in the Robert Trent Jones Golf Trail. ✉ *1 Grand Blvd., just off Scenic 98, or 98A, Point Clear 36564,* ☎ *251/928–9201 or 800/544–9933,* 📠 *251/928–1149,* 🌐 *www.marriottgrand.com. 400 rooms, 30 suites. 6 restaurants, room service, in-room data ports,*

*minibars, refrigerators, cable TV, some in-room VCRs, 2 18-hole golf
courses, 8 tennis courts, 2 pools, hot tub, sauna, spa, horseback riding, beach, boating, fishing, bicycles, lounge, baby-sitting, children's
programs (5–12), playground, laundry facilities, laundry service, business services, meeting rooms; no-smoking rooms. AE, D, DC, MC, V.*

$$–$$$ 🏨 **Bay Breeze Bed & Breakfast.** A winding white-shell driveway leads
through a camellia and azalea garden to this stucco-and-wood B&B
owned by Bill and Becky Jones. The property, which was Becky's
childhood home, fronts Mobile Bay not far from downtown Fairhope
and has a 462-ft-long pier for fishing, crabbing, sunbathing, or just relaxing (sometimes breakfast is served at the end of the pier). Bedrooms in the main house have wood floors, brass queen-size beds, and
antique furnishings. The cottage suites are light and spacious. ⊠ 742
*S. Mobile St., Box 526, Fairhope 36533, ☎ 251/928–8976 or 866/928–
8976, FAX 251/928–0360. 3 rooms, 2 cottages. Fans, some kitchenettes,
cable TV, fishing, bicycles, recreation room; no kids under 18, no
smoking. AE, MC, V. BP.*

Magnolia Springs

10 mi east of Fairhope on U.S. 98.

Sleepy Magnolia Springs, between Fairhope and Foley, is one of the
last places in the country where mail is still delivered by boat to homes
along the Magnolia River.

Dining and Lodging

$$–$$$ ✗ **Jesse's Restaurant.** In the town's former post office, this charming
café and gourmet grocery draws visitors from miles around with its
lovely location and New Orleans-inspired menu. Favorite dishes include barbecue shrimp served over grits, lightly fried soft-shell crabs,
and whole roasted baby flounder. Take the scenic route back to U.S.
98 via Oak Street. ⊠ *14770 Oak St., ☎ 251/965–3827. Reservations
not accepted. AE, MC, V. Closed Sun.*

$$–$$$ 🏨 **Magnolia Springs Bed and Breakfast.** David Worthington fulfilled
his lifelong dream when he spotted this diamond in the rough and turned
the 100-year-old former inn into a homey, inviting B&B. Nestled
among live oaks and just across the street from a boat launch on Magnolia River, this B&B is a great spot to relax and unwind—you can
start on the wide front porch. Guest rooms have wood paneling and
country-style furnishings, and Worthington provides fresh flowers
every day. ⊠ *14469 Oak St., ☎ 800/965–7321 or 251/965–7321,* WEB
*www.magnoliasprings.com. 5 rooms. In-room data ports, cable TV;
no smoking. AE, D, MC, V.*

The Gulf Coast

50 mi south of Mobile via U.S. 90E and AL 59.

With sugary white sand and gentle warm water, the Gulf Coast is by
far one of the state's greatest attractions. The cooling offshore breezes
provide a nice respite from the hot, humid temperatures found around
Alabama in summer. Although the Gulf Shores beach area has plenty
of concessions and is usually crowded, those seeking isolated beach walks
need only venture a couple of miles west. To the east of Gulf Shores is
Orange Beach, a heavily developed coastal strip between the Gulf of
Mexico and Perdido Bay, with its peaceful bayous and creeks.

OFF THE   **BURRIS FARM MARKET –** For a true sampling of Baldwin County's agricul-
BEATEN PATH   tural heritage, stop in at this sprawling family-owned market selling local
                produce—much of it grown on the Burris family farm. In spring you can

pick your own strawberries. Besides fresh fruit and vegetables, you'll find homemade relishes, pickles, and dressings. Burris Bakery, an air-conditioned area at the rear, will tempt you with freshly baked breads, pies, and cookies. ⊠ *Hwy. 59, Loxley (from I–10, take I–59 south 3 mi to Loxley),* ☎ *251/964–6464.* 🖃 *Free.* ☉ *Feb.–Dec., daily 8–6.*

★ ㊾   **Gulf State Park** (⊠ 20115 AL 135, Gulf Shores, ☎ 251/948–7275, 800/544–4853, or 800/252–7275) covers more than 6,000 acres. Along with 2½ mi of pure white beaches and glimmering dunes, the park has two freshwater lakes with fishing, plus biking, hiking, and jogging trails through pine forests. Near the large beach pavilion, a concrete fishing pier juts about 800 ft into the Gulf. There is also a gulf-front resort lodge and convention center, 468 campsites, and 21 cottages, plus tennis courts and a golf course.

The 6,200 acres of the **Bon Secour National Wildlife Refuge** (⊠ AL 180W, ☎ 251/540–7720) are home to native and migratory birds and a number of endangered species, including the loggerhead sea turtle. You can hike or swim at some of the five units of the refuge.

☉   **Waterville USA,** set on 17 acres, has a wave pool with 3-ft waves, eight exciting water slides, and a lazy river ride around the park. For younger children there are gentler rides in a supervised play area. The adjacent amusement park has a 36-hole miniature golf course, a video-game arcade, and an amusement park with roller coaster, motion simulator, NASCAR go-karts, kiddie area, laser tag, and ride ejection seat—all priced per ride or game. ⊠ *906 Gulf Shores Pkwy. (AL 59), Gulf Shores,* ☎ *251/948–2106,* 𝚆𝙴𝙱 *www.watervilleusa.com.* 🖃 *$21.* ☉ *Water park, Memorial Day–Labor Day, daily 10–6; amusement park, daily 10–6.*

❺⓿   **Fort Morgan** was built in the early 1800s to guard the entrance to Mobile Bay. The fort saw fiery action during the Battle of Mobile Bay in 1864: Confederate torpedoes sank the ironclad *Tecumseh,* after Union admiral David Farragut gave his famous command: "Damn the torpedoes! Full speed ahead!" The original outer walls still stand; outside, a museum chronicles the fort's history and displays artifacts from Indian days through World War II, with an emphasis on the Civil War. ⊠ *51 Hwy. 180W, Gulf Shores,* ☎ *251/540–7125.* 🖃 *$3.* ☉ *Weekdays 8–5, weekends 9–5.*

Dining and Lodging

$$–$$$$ ✕ **Bayside Grill.** For fine dining overlooking the back bays that channel to the Gulf, you can't beat this choice. Seafood is the New Orleans–born chef's specialty, but you will also find pasta, steak, salads, and chicken, all served in large portions. The restaurant also offers a spectacular Sunday brunch. ⊠ *27842 Canal Rd., Orange Beach,* ☎ *251/981–4899. AE, D, DC, MC, V.*

$$–$$$$ ✕ **Voyagers.** Roses and art deco touches set the tone for this airy, elegant dining room. Two-level seating allows beach or poolside views from every table. Renowned chef Gerhard Brill creates dishes such as trout with roasted pecans in creole meunière sauce and soft-shell crab topped with creole *choron* (a hollandaise sauce). Finish up with a fried apple beignet with French vanilla sauce or crepe soufflé praline. Service is deft, and there's an extensive wine selection. ⊠ *Perdido Beach Resort, 27200 Perdido Beach Blvd., Orange Beach,* ☎ *251/981–9811. Reservations essential. AE, D, DC, MC, V. Closed Mon.–Tues. No lunch.*

$–$$$ ✕ **Mikee's.** The food at this popular, no-nonsense seafood restaurant in the heart of Gulf Shores will be worth the inevitable wait. There's no view—it's a couple of blocks north of the beach—but while you wait, you can check out the photos of the owners' biggest catches among the other local memorabilia decorating the walls. The menu offers all-you-can-eat fried shrimp, steamed shrimp, barbecue shrimp, fried crab claws, and fried oysters, as well as po'boy sandwiches on New Orleans–style French bread. ⊠ *1st Ave. N and 2nd Ave. E,* ☎ *251/948–6452. Reservations not accepted. AE, D, DC, MC, V.*

$$$–$$$$ ★ ⊞ **Perdido Beach Resort.** The eight- and nine-story towers of this resort are Mediterranean stucco and red tile. The lobby is tiled in terracotta and decorated with a brass sculpture of gulls in flight and mosaics by Venetian artists. Rooms are furnished in comfortable coastal style, and all have a beach view and balcony. ⊠ *27200 Perdido Beach Blvd., Box 400, Orange Beach 36561,* ☎ *251/981–9811 or 800/634–8001,* FAX *251/981–5670,* WEB *www.perdidobeachresort.com. 333 rooms, 12 suites. Restaurant, cable TV with movies, 4 tennis courts, indoor-outdoor pool, health club, 2 hot tubs, beach, bar, lobby lounge, lounge, laundry service, meeting rooms; no-smoking rooms. AE, D, DC, MC, V.*

$$–$$$$ ★ ⊞ **Gulf Shores Plantation.** This 320-acre family resort, 12 mi west of Gulf Shores, faces the Gulf and has several condominium complexes as well as two-story duplex cottages that can accommodate up to 33 people. Recreational activities abound, yet the remote location allows for peace and quiet. Located next door, Kiva Dunes Golf Course is consistently ranked among the state's best by magazines such as *Golf Digest* and *Golf.* ⊠ *AL 180W, Box 1299, Gulf Shores 36547,* ☎ *251/540–5000 or 800/554–0344,* FAX *251/540–6055,* WEB *www.gulfshoresplantation.com. 524 units. Café, kitchens, microwaves, refrigerators, cable TV, some in-room VCRs, 8 tennis courts, 7 pools (1 indoor), exercise equipment, hot tub, sauna, steam room, beach, horseshoes, shuffleboard, volleyball, lounge, recreation room, shop, laundry facilities; no-smoking rooms. AE, MC, V.*

$$–$$$ ⊞ **Lighthouse Resort Motel.** This complex of five two- to four-story buildings, surrounded by brightly colored exotic flowers, is set on a 680-ft private beach. The waterfront rooms have private balconies and contemporary furniture; some units have kitchens. ⊠ *455 E. Beach Blvd., Box 233, Gulf Shores 36547,* ☎ *251/948–6188,* FAX *251/948–6100,* WEB *www.lighthouseresortmotel.com. 200 rooms. Some kitchens, some kitchenettes, some refrigerators, cable TV, 3 pools (1 indoor), 2 hot tubs, beach, laundry facilities; no-smoking rooms. AE, D, DC, MC, V.*

$$ ⊞ **Original Romar House.** This unassuming beach cottage is filled with surprises—from the Caribbean-style upstairs sitting area to the Purple Parrot Bar to the art-deco-style guest rooms, each with a private bath. ⊠ *23500 Perdido Beach Blvd., Orange Beach 36561,* ☎ *251/981–6156 or 800/487–6627,* FAX *251/974–1163. 6 rooms. Cable TV, hot tub, beach, bicycles, bar; no kids under 12, no smoking. AE, MC, V. BP.*

Nightlife and the Arts

On the Alabama–Florida line is the sprawling **Flora-Bama Lounge** (⊠ Perdido Key Dr., Pensacola, FL, ☎ 251/980–5118 or 251/980–5119, WEB www.florabama.com), home of the annual Interstate Mullet Toss. It's open 11 AM–2:30 AM, and the bar brings in live bands nightly. There's outdoor seating in summer.

Outdoor Activities and Sports

BIKING

Gulf State Park (⊠ 20115 AL 135, Gulf Shores, ☎ 251/948–7275) has biking trails through pine forests and rents bicycles. **Island Recreation Services** (⊠ 360 E. Beach Blvd., Gulf Shores, ☎ 251/948–7334) rents bikes and water-sports equipment.

FISHING

Freshwater and saltwater fishing in the Gulf area are excellent. Lovely **Gulf State Park** (⊠ 20115 AL 135, ☎ 251/948–7275), in Gulf Shores, has fishing from an 825-ft pier and rents flat-bottom boats for lake fishing. Deep-sea fishing from charter boats is very popular, but not a good idea if you tend to become seasick.

In Gulf Shores, you can sign on board the **Moreno Queen** (☎ 251/981–8499 or 251/317–4850) or one of many other charter boats for a full- or half-day fishing expedition. For a brochure on Orange Beach's offerings, call the **Alabama Gulf Coast Convention & Visitors Bureau** (☎ 800/745–7263). Catches from deep-sea expeditions include king mackerel, amberjack, tuna, white marlin, blue marlin, grouper, bonito, sailfish, and red snapper.

GOLF

Coastal Alabama has developed into one of the nicest golfing destinations in the Southeast. More courses are opening, and the names of their architects read like a who's who of the golfing world—Robert Trent Jones Sr., Arnold Palmer, and Jerry Pate, to name just a few. With winter temperatures averaging in the 60°F range and pleasant breezes, the area has become a true year-round-fun spot. Prices for all the courses range from about $35 to $70 for greens fees and a cart.

The spectacular 18-hole, par-72 **Kiva Dunes** course adjacent to Gulf Shores Plantation Resort (✉ 12 mi west of Gulf Shores on AL 180, ☎ 251/540–7000, WEB www.kivadunes-golf.com), designed by Jerry Pate, combines oceanfront dunes golf with Scottish-style links golf. The **Craft Farms** complex, off AL 59 just north of Gulf Shores (✉ 3840 Cotton Creek Blvd., ☎ 251/968–7500 or 800/327–2657, WEB www.craftfarms.com), has three 18-hole, par-72 courses: the Arnold Palmer–designed course at Cotton Creek; the Larry Nelson–designed Woodlands course; and Cypress Bend. About 12 mi north of Gulf Shores in Foley, the **Glenlakes Golf Club** (✉ 9530 Clubhouse Dr., ☎ 251/955–1220 or 800/435–5253, WEB www.glenlakesgolf.com), a course designed by Bruce Devlin, has 18 challenging holes that play par-72 over 7,000 yards and another nine holes that play par-35 stretching 3,100 yards. The 18-hole, par-72 course at **Gulf State Park** (✉ 20115 AL 135, ☎ 251/948–7275), in Gulf Shores, is one of the area's oldest but most scenic and best-maintained courses along the coast.

HORSEBACK RIDING

Sea Horse Stables (✉ off Hwy. 59, Foley, ☎ 251/971–7433) offers guided trail rides.

SAILING AND WATER SPORTS

The **T. J. Spithre** is a 53-ft catamaran (☎ 251/981–9706 for Island Sailing Center) that can be rented with a captain. The **Daedalus** (☎ 251/986–7018) is a sailboat available for cruises in Gulf Shores. **Caribiana** (☎ 251/981–4442 or 888/203–4883) offers private, customized tours of the Perdido Bay area and its sand islands. Up to six people are accommodated aboard a 23-ft sea skiff.

Fun Marina (☎ 251/980–5122), in Orange Beach, offers parasailing and rents Jet Skis, pontoon boats, and 16-ft bay-fishing boats. In Gulf Shores, **Island Recreation Services** (✉ 360 E. Beach Blvd., ☎ 251/948–7334) rents Jet Skis, bikes, body boards, surfboards, and sailboats.

Shopping

The 120 outlet stores in the **Riviera Centre**, 8 mi north of Gulf Shores, offer savings of up to 75% off regular retail prices. Stores include Danskin, Calvin Klein, Liz Claiborne, Bose, Coach, Bass Shoes, and Pfaltzgraff. ✉ AL 59S, Foley, ☎ 251/943–8888 or 800/523–6873, WEB www.shoprivieracentre.com. ☺ Mon.–Sat. 9–9, Sun. 10–6. Hrs vary Jan.–Feb.

Mobile and the Gulf Coast A to Z

AIR TRAVEL

CARRIERS

The Mobile Regional Airport at Bates Field is served by Delta, Northwest Airlink, Continental Express, and US Airways. Pensacola Regional Airport (☞ *below*) is served by AirTran, Continental, Delta, Northwest Airlink, and US Airways.

➤ AIRLINES AND CONTACTS: For airline telephone numbers, *see* Air Travel *in* Smart Travel Tips A to Z.

AIRPORTS

The Mobile Regional Airport is about 10 mi west of I–65. Pensacola Regional Airport is some 40 mi east of Gulf Shores in Florida.

➤ AIRPORT INFORMATION: **Mobile Regional Airport** (✉ 8400 Airport Blvd., ☎ 251/633–0313, WEB www.mobairport.com). **Pensacola Regional Airport** (✉ 2430 Airport Blvd., ☎ 850/435–1746, WEB www.flypensacola.com).

BUS TRAVEL

Greyhound has stations in Mobile and in Pensacola, Florida.

➤ BUS INFORMATION: **Greyhound** (✉ 2545 Government Blvd., Mobile, ☎ 800/231–2222 or 251/478–6089; ✉ 505 W. Burgess Rd., Pensacola, FL, ☎ 800/231–2222 or 904/476–4800; WEB www.greyhound.com).

CAR TRAVEL

I–10 travels east from Mobile into Florida through Pensacola, west into Mississippi. I–65 slices Alabama in half vertically, passing through Birmingham and Montgomery and ending at Mobile. Gulf Shores is connected with Mobile via I–10 and AL 59; AL 180 and 182 are the main beach routes. The most practical way to get around this area is by car.

EMERGENCIES

The University of South Alabama Hospital, in Mobile, offers 24-hour medical care in its emergency room.

➤ CONTACTS: **Ambulance, police** (☎ 911). **University of South Alabama Hospital** (✉ 2451 Fillingim St., ☎ 251/471–7000).

MEDIA

RADIO

In Mobile, AM: WNTM 710, talk; WGOK 900, gospel and jazz; WKSJ 1270, country.

FM: WZEW 92.1, modern rock; WKSJ 94.5, country; WABB 97.5, contemporary rock; WMXC 99.9, soft rock; WWRO 100.7, oldies.

TOURS

Gray Line Tours, in Mobile, has excellent 1- to 3½-hour trolley or motorcoach tours, departing from Fort Condé daily, to Mobile's historic points of interest, as well as to Bellingrath Gardens and the USS *Alabama*. Memorable Mobile Tours, Inc. conducts customized guided tours of Mobile and Eastern Shore area attractions.

➤ FEES AND SCHEDULES: **Gray Line Tours** (☎ 251/432–2229 or 800/338–5597, WEB www.grayline.com). **Memorable Mobile Tours, Inc.** (☎ 251/344–8687 or 800/441–1146).

TRAIN TRAVEL

Amtrak service on the *Sunset Limited* links Mobile with both the East and West coasts. Westbound trains run Monday, Wednesday, and Saturday; eastbound trains run Sunday, Tuesday, and Thursday.

➤ TRAIN INFORMATION: **Amtrak** (☎ 800/872–7245, WEB www.amtrak. com).

VISITOR INFORMATION

Call the Mobile Convention & Visitors Corporationfor general information on the area. You can visit Fort Condé, which has the official welcome center for Mobile.

➤ TOURIST INFORMATION: **Alabama Gulf Coast Convention & Visitors Bureau** (✉ 23658 Perdido Beach Blvd., Orange Beach 36561, ☎ 251/ 968–7511 or 800/745–7263, WEB www.gulfshores.com). **Fort Condé** (✉ 150 S. Royal St., ☎ 251/434–7304). **Mobile Convention & Visitors Corporation** (☎ 251/208–2000 or 800/566–2453, WEB www. mobile.org).

ALABAMA A TO Z

AIRPORTS

Major airports are Birmingham International Airport, Montgomery Regional Airport, Huntsville International Airport, and Mobile Regional Airport. Many visitors to the Gulf Coast find it convenient to fly into the Pensacola Regional Airport, an hour east in Florida, or the Gulfport-Biloxi Regional Airport, an hour west in Mississippi.

➤ AIRPORT INFORMATION: **Birmingham International Airport** (☎ 205/ 599–0500, WEB www.bhamintlairport.com). **Montgomery Regional Airport** (☎ 334/281–5040, WEB www.montgomeryairport.org). **Gulfport-Biloxi Regional Airport** (☎ 228/863–5953, WEB www.gulfcoast. org/gpt). **Huntsville International Airport** (☎ 256/772–9395, WEB www. hsvairport.org). **Mobile Regional Airport** (☎ 251/633–0313, WEB www. mobairport.com). **Pensacola Regional Airport** (☎ 850/435–1746, WEB www.flypensacola.com).

BUS TRAVEL

Greyhound has service to the major cities—Birmingham, Huntsville, Mobile, and Montgomery—with intermediate stops at many of Alabama's smaller cities. Check for scheduled stops.

➤ BUS INFORMATION: **Greyhound** (☎ 800/231–2222, WEB www. greyhound.com).

CAR TRAVEL

Surrounded by Mississippi, Georgia, Tennessee, Florida, and the Gulf of Mexico, Alabama is accessible by a number of interstates. I–10 cuts across the southern tip of the state, providing a direct route from Mississippi on the west and the Florida Panhandle on the east. From Atlanta, I–85 takes you to the central part of the state; I–20 takes you to Birmingham and points in North Alabama. The main north–south routes are I–65 coming down from Nashville and I–59 from the Chattanooga area. U.S. 80 cuts east–west across the state, connecting Demopolis, Selma, Montgomery, and Tuskegee. U.S. 82 runs northwest to southeast from Tuscaloosa through Montgomery and Eufaula.

Some sample mileages are as follows: Birmingham to Huntsville, 95 mi; Birmingham to Mobile, 253 mi; Birmingham to Montgomery, 90 mi; Birmingham to Gulf Shores, 274 mi; Birmingham to Tuscaloosa, 57 mi.

RULES OF THE ROAD

In Alabama, you can turn right during a red light unless otherwise noted by street signs. The speed limit on interstate highways is 70 mph in most places.

EMERGENCIES

In towns and cities, dial 911 for police, fire, and ambulance assistance.

LODGING

BED AND BREAKFASTS

Use a B&B brochure available from the Alabama Bureau of Tourism and Travel (☞ Visitor Information, *below*) to make reservations at individual B&Bs.

OUTDOORS AND SPORTS

FISHING

Residents and nonresidents 16 or over need a valid fishing license to fish in Alabama; for information call the Alabama Department of Conservation and Natural Resources.

➤ CONTACTS: **Alabama Department of Conservation and Natural Resources** (☎ 251/242–3826).

GOLF

Some of Alabama's most scenic and challenging courses are part of the Robert Trent Jones Golf Trail, 18 courses spread out among eight locations around the state, providing 378 holes of challenging golf (*see also* Up-Close: Tee Time, *above*). There's also good golf in Alabama's state parks. Greens fees with cart range from $35 to $65.

➤ CONTACTS: **Robert Trent Jones Golf Trail information and reservations** (☎ 800/949–4444, WEB www.rtjgolf.com). **State parks golf information** (☎ 800/252–7275).

STATE PARKS

Alabama's 24 state parks offer plenty of recreational activities and accommodations. Choose among resort lodges, hotels, campgrounds, chalets, and cabins, both modern and rustic. Several parks have marinas, golf courses, and tennis facilities. Contact Alabama State Parks for reservations or information.

➤ CONTACTS: **Alabama State Parks** (✉ 64 N. Union St., Folsom Administrative Bldg., Suite 547, Montgomery 36130, ☎ 800/252–7275, WEB www.alapark.com).

TRAIN TRAVEL

Amtrak has daily service to Birmingham. Service into Mobile is on Sunday, Tuesday, and Thursday. East–west routes are serviced by Amtrak's *Sunset Limited* across the southern part of the state; north–south travelers board the *Crescent* from New York and Washington or New Orleans.

Montgomery has a Thruway Intermodal Transit Terminal offering bus service to Amtrak service in Atlanta.

➤ TRAIN INFORMATION: **Amtrak** (☎ 800/872–7245, WEB www.amtrak.com). **Thruway Intermodal Transit Terminal** (☎ 800/872–7245).

VISITOR INFORMATION

Alabama Bureau of Tourism and Travel welcome centers can be found on I–59 near Valley Head; I–59 at Cuba; I–65 at Elkmont; I–10 north of Seminole; I–10 at Grand Bay; I–20 east of Heflin; I–85 at Lanett; and U.S. 231 south of Dothan. Call the Alabama Bureau of Tourism and Travel for a free copy of "Alabama's Black Heritage," a 56-page guide to African-American culture that includes hundreds of sites.

➤ TOURIST INFORMATION: **Alabama Bureau of Tourism and Travel** (✉ 401 Adams Ave., Montgomery 36104, ☎ 334/242–4169 or 800/252–2262, WEB www.touralabama.org).

3 GEORGIA

Geographically speaking, Georgia is the largest state east of the Mississippi River. Its varied terrain ranges from the foothills of the Appalachian Mountains, in the north, to the great coastal plain that stretches from the state's center toward the shore to the beaches of the Golden Isles and the Okefenokee National Wildlife Refuge, in the southeast. From progressive Atlanta to antebellum Macon and colonial Savannah, each of Georgia's cities and towns has a unique charm.

Updated by
Hollis Gillespie

F ROM THE AIR, and during spring, the sight of Georgia might mislead you into believing the entire state is hidden under trees, or at least under the ubiquitous kudzu vines, which blanket everything if not vigilantly kept at bay. This might give the landscape a deceptively monotonous appearance, but this is just superficial. Of course, anything worth exploring is worth delving beneath its surface. With Georgia you don't even have to delve that far because from the ground it's immediately apparent that the multiedged Peach State is anything but monotonous.

Its landscape encompasses the hazy blue foothills of the Appalachian Mountains, in the north, the coastal plain, which connects the heartland to the unspoiled beaches of the Atlantic, and the mysterious black-water swamps of the state's southern end. Most people travel its interstate highways (I–75, I–85, I–95, and I–16), but the adventurous traveler who decides to explore the state's byways will be rewarded with pristine vistas and detours through charming towns.

Within the landscape lies a rich diversity of unusual flora, including mountain laurels, rhododendrons, azaleas, and camellias. Spanish moss drapes live oak trees in the southern and coastal areas, and flat fields of white puffy cotton line the horizon through the middle of the state. Known for its peaches, Georgia is also proud of its apples, and the fruit trees' soft blooms create splendid sights in spring. Hiking in the north Georgia mountains could reveal their wealth of deer charging through the forest. Along the coast alligators, egrets, and herons take curiosity-seekers in stride.

As varied as its landscape, Georgia's citizens reflect the diversity of early settlers, Native American peoples, and, to this day, a constant stream of new arrivals from all parts of the globe. During the 18th century not only English and Scottish immigrants but also Jewish settlers, both Sephardic and Ashkenazic, and German religious refugees (the Salzburgers) arrived to take up positions of importance and prominence in the Georgia colony. Africans and Native peoples—chiefly Cherokee and Creek—added their cultural spice to the mix, creating a state that is richer in ethnic character than is often recognized. Irish immigrants arriving throughout the 19th century and Greeks, Middle Easterners, and Asians during the late 19th and early 20th centuries contributed to the state's diversity. Georgians speak with accents that vary from the classic, slightly nasal mountain "twang" to the distinctive, soft coastal lilt of upper-crust Savannahians.

Georgia's towns each define in their own way that famous Southern charm of fable and film. Bustling Atlanta, the state capital since the Civil War ended in 1865, has been compared with Margaret Mitchell's heroine, Scarlett O'Hara, the classic Steel Magnolia: gentle in form but brash and tough in substance. Colonial Savannah, with the nation's largest historic district, lures all sorts to its 21 cobblestone squares, giant parterre gardens, waterfront gift shops, jazz bars, and parks. Dahlonega, site of the nation's early gold rush in 1828, is a typical example of the small Georgia town, with its central square dominated by a county courthouse. Macon, full of flowering Japanese cherry trees and images of both the antebellum and Victorian South, celebrates its heritage as the home of poet and flutist Sidney Lanier. A few small towns are named for glittering foreign capitals that they resemble not in the slightest: Vienna (pronounced vy-*en*-ah), Madrid (may-*drid*), Rome, Athens, Cairo (*cay*-row), and so forth.

Georgia's 100-mi coast runs from the mouth of the Savannah River south to the mouth of the St. Marys River. The seaside resort communities blend Southern elegance with a casual sensibility. St. Simons Island, about 70 mi south of Savannah, attracts a laid-back crowd of anglers, beachgoers, golfers, and tennis players. On nearby Jekyll Island, the lavish lifestyle of America's early 19th-century rich and famous is still evident in their stately Victorian "cottages." Cumberland Island's protected forests and miles of sandy coastline, the rustically beautiful Sapelo Island, the isolated solitude of Little St. Simons Island, and the dark waters of the Okefenokee are favorite haunts of nature lovers.

Other historical riches include 1,000-year-old Native American homesites and burial mounds, antebellum mansions, war heroes' memorials, and intriguing monuments built by eccentric folk artists and obsessive gardeners. Georgia's many state parks have superb facilities for white-water rafting, canoeing, fishing, golf, and tennis, and nature trails wind through mountain forests delicately laced with wild rhododendrons, dogwoods, and azaleas.

Pleasures and Pastimes

Dining

Dining in Georgia has its ups and downs. Areas that have attracted substantial tourism have respectable to downright outstanding restaurants. Others lag far behind, with their best offerings chain restaurants or the local barbecue joint.

Atlanta sets the culinary pace, of course, with cutting-edge fare from outstanding chefs. Dress in Atlanta—and elsewhere in the state—is casual unless otherwise noted. Classic meat-and-threes—diners serving a meat entrée with three side dishes—abound throughout Georgia. On the byways of Georgia, barbecue stands and restaurants still cook the whole pig, serving customers its meat pulled off the bone for sandwiches or its tender ribs, both bathed in tangy sauce. Brunswick stew, a hunter's stew that traditionally contained the day's catch, is the standard accompaniment. Some of these places are full-fledged restaurants; others have no place to sit at all. If you're off the beaten path, these establishments offer your best chance for decent food.

CATEGORY	COST*
$$$$	over $30
$$$	$20–$30
$$	$10–$20
$	under $10

*per person for a main course at dinner

Historic Sites

You may want to plan your trip with Georgia's historic sites in mind. From the moment you enter the state along the interstate highways, brown markers with white lettering alert you to the locations of the state's principal historical sights along those routes. Georgia's towns constitute a special glimpse into the past. Savannah, founded in 1733, can be viewed from carriage or bus via specialty tours, by private car, or on foot; it's an excellent walking city. Augusta, founded in 1736, has a fine Riverwalk, a restored downtown, and the 19th- and 20th-century houses of Olde Town and Summerville. Macon, founded in 1823, is known for its wealth of fine antebellum and Victorian mansions that may be viewed by private car or on specialty tours. You'll find more than a fair share of battlefields to explore, including the dark woods and open fields of Chickamauga, and unusual historic sites such as New Echota, the lost capital of the Cherokee Nation.

Georgia

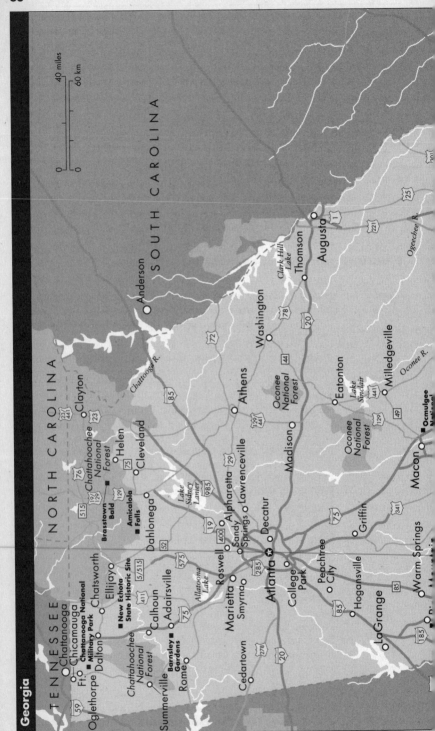

TENNESSEE

NORTH CAROLINA

SOUTH CAROLINA

Chattanooga

Ft. Oglethorpe
Chicamauga National Military Park

Dalton

Chatsworth

Ellijay

Chatahoochee National Forest

New Echota State Historic Site

Summerville

Barnsley Gardens

Rome

Calhoun

Adairsville

Cedartown

Allatoona Lake

Marietta

Smyrna

Roswell

Sandy Springs

Atlanta

Decatur

College Park

Peachtree City

Hogansville

LaGrange

Warm Springs

Brasstown Bald

Amicalola Falls

Dahlonega

Cleveland

Helen

Chattahoochee National Forest

Clayton

Lake Sidney Lanier

Alpharetta

Lawrenceville

Griffin

Madison

Athens

Washington

Anderson

Thomson

Augusta

Ogeechee R.

Oconee National Forest

Oconee National Forest

Eatonton

Lake Sinclair

Milledgeville

Oconee R.

Macon

Ocmulgee National

Clark Hill Lake

Chattooga R.

40 miles

60 km

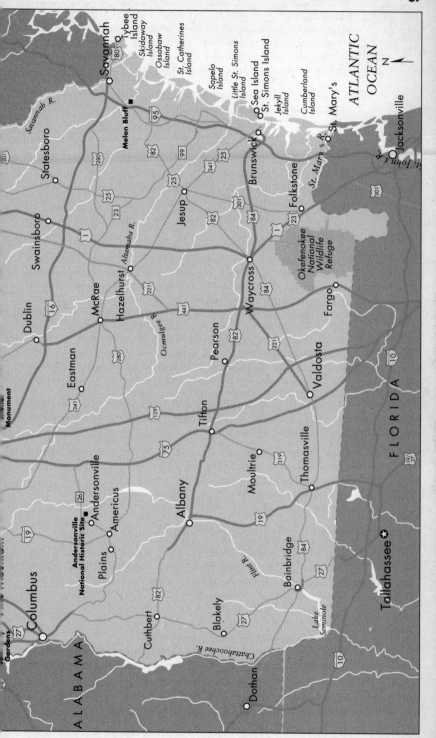

Lodging

Most national and some international hotel and motel chains have establishments in Georgia. Bed-and-breakfast inns abound throughout the state, some providing exquisite lodging, others perfunctory but usually comfortable accommodations. Campsites are marked along the interstate highways, and the state has a fine network of parks, some of which offer campsites and overnight facilities. Always telephone ahead to B&Bs and campsites for reservations, as these are popular accommodations.

CATEGORY	ATLANTA AND SAVANNAH*	OTHER AREAS*
$$$$	over $240	over $175
$$$	$170–$240	$125–$175
$$	$100–$170	$75–$125
$	under $100	under $75

All prices are for a standard double room, excluding 13% tax and service.

Nightlife

No night in Georgia need ever be boring. Clubs, music venues, theater, film, symphony, and comedy revues all make nightlife hum. Blues and jazz, country and western, gospel, and rock and roll are all part of this region's—and Georgia's—homegrown musical tradition. Local composers and performers who made their marks on the national music scene include Savannah's Johnny Mercer; Macon's Otis Redding and the Allman Brothers; and Augusta's James Brown, the godfather of soul. Macon's Little Richard and Albany's Ray Charles still perform. Local groups that have gained national and international fame include R.E.M. and the B-52's, from Athens; Indigo Girls, from Decatur; and Black Crowes, from Marietta. In country-and-western music, Travis Tritt started out in Marietta and Trisha Yearwood in Monticello. To hear rising new stars, not to mention the cadre of reigning hip-hop royalty with roots in Georgia, call local radio stations for information about venues.

In the classical department, opera diva Jessye Norman is from Augusta, and violinist Robert McDuffie is from Macon. The state abounds in symphony orchestras, chamber groups, and classical and jazz ensembles, many of which perform on college campuses. For details contact a local college campus or consult the local newspaper.

Theater is vital not only in Atlanta but also throughout the state, which was the first home of thespians Joanne Woodward (Thomasville), Julia and Eric Roberts (Smyrna), Holly Hunter (Conyers), Melvin Douglas (Macon), Pernell Roberts (Waycross), and playwright Alfred Uhry (Atlanta). If you can catch a performance of *Swamp Gravy,* by residents of Colquitt, Georgia, or *Reach of Song,* based on the poetry of mountain poet Byron Herbert Reece, you'll enjoy traditional local subject matter and music.

Outdoor Activities and Sports

For the sports enthusiast Georgia has a full plate of activities—fishing, camping, golf and tennis, sailing and rowing. There's also a beloved baseball team, the Atlanta Braves. Hiking abounds: at the Chattahoochee Nature Center, outside Atlanta, you can see birds and other woodland animals in their natural habitat while hiking through 124 acres of lush forests and wetlands. Another outdoor favorite is Stone Mountain Park and its Walk Up Trail, an atmospheric jaunt up the west side of the mountain culminating in a rigorous 825-ft climb to the peak. It's well worth the challenge, as the ensuing panoramic view of Atlanta is stunning.

Exploring Georgia

Georgia has several distinct touring areas; the state is large, and you'd need more than a week to hit even some of the highlights. The foothills of the Appalachian Mountains run from west to east in north Georgia, making this a popular destination for tourists, especially in spring and fall. Atlanta alone warrants serious exploration. The coast offers plenty for the history aficionado; it's a good place to start if you have just a few days. From Savannah, Georgia's oldest city, to Augusta, its third oldest, colonial and Civil War history awaits at every turn. It's in east Georgia where you'll see most of the columned antebellum homes that people have come to expect. The coastal islands have fine beaches and nature-focused expeditions. The best spot for would-be naturalists, of course, is the Okefenokee Natural Wildlife Refuge. Southwest Georgia, with its pastoral agricultural towns, numerous options for antiquing, and the bustling river city of Columbus, makes an agreeable weekend adventure.

Great Itineraries

IF YOU HAVE 3 DAYS

Explore the coast to get a true taste of what early Georgia was all about. Spend a day and night in ⊞ **Augusta,** being sure to visit Meadow Garden, home of George Walton, youngest signer (at age 26) of the Declaration of Independence. Exhibits at the Morris Museum of Southern Art range from luminous 19th-century landscapes to folk art and the challenging abstracts of Augusta native Jasper Johns. Give the remaining two days over to an exploration of ⊞ **Savannah.** Stay at a B&B (be sure to make reservations, especially for weekends) and tour some of the city's fine restored homes. Spend some time along Riverfront Plaza, enjoying the waterfront, dining in restaurants, and just plain kicking back. Other must-see sights include the 1815 Isaiah Davenport House and the Colonial Park Cemetery, the final resting place for some of America's founders.

IF YOU HAVE 7 DAYS

Add a three-day trip to ⊞ **Atlanta** to the above itinerary, using the final extra day to partake of the recreations and resorts of ⊞ **Jekyll Island,** along the coast. In Atlanta history enthusiasts will want to visit the Atlanta History Center and its gardens, touring its two house museums. A fine small museum, the African-American Panoramic Experience, chronicles the history of blacks in America. In Grant Park, the Atlanta Cyclorama contains a truly huge painting of the 1864 Battle of Atlanta. The Chattahoochee National Recreational Area is a great spot for joggers, walkers, hikers, and nature lovers. At Stone Mountain Park you can see the Confederate Memorial (the world's largest sculpture), two Civil War museums, and the Road to Tara Museum.

IF YOU HAVE 10 DAYS

Follow the seven-day itinerary. Then take a run up to the north Georgia mountains, visiting **Clayton,** with its many art and antiques shops; ⊞ **Dahlonega,** where you can pan for gold in "them thar hills"; and **Chickamauga,** site of one of the Civil War's most important conflicts. The north Georgia mountains are glorious from spring through fall. Then turn south back through Atlanta and visit the heart of the state, taking in ⊞ **Macon,** with its antebellum and Victorian homes and museums.

When to Tour Georgia

Spring is the best time to visit, although autumn, especially beginning in early October, when the hardwoods change color, is another glorious season. Spring in middle Georgia is splendid, with azaleas and other flowers in full bloom. Many garden and historic home tours are scheduled at this time. And in Savannah you can tour some of the most spectacular of the city's private gardens.

ATLANTA

Though steeped in history, Atlanta nevertheless remains a comparatively new city by East Coast standards, having been founded only in 1837 as the end of the Western & Atlantic railroad line (it was first named Marthasville in honor of the then-governor's daughter, nicknamed Terminus for its rail location, and then changed soon after to Atlanta, the feminine of Atlantic—as in the railroad). Today the fast-growing city remains a transportation hub, not just for the country but for the world: Hartsfield Atlanta International Airport is one of the nation's busiest in daily passenger flights. Direct flights to Europe, South America, and Asia have made metro Atlanta easily accessible to the more than 1,000 international businesses that operate here and the more than 50 countries that have representation in the city through consulates, trade offices, and chambers of commerce. The city has emerged as a banking center and is the world headquarters for such Fortune 500 companies as CNN, Coca-Cola, Delta Airlines, Holiday Inn Worldwide, and United Parcel Service.

Atlanta's character has evolved from a mix of peoples: transplanted Northerners and those from elsewhere account for more than half the population and have undeniably affected the mood and character of the city. Irish immigrants had a major role in the city's early history, along with Germans and Austrians; the Hungarian-born Rich brothers founded Atlanta's principal department store. And the immigrants keep coming. In the past two decades Atlanta has seen spirited growth in its Asian and Latin-American communities. Related restaurants, shops, and institutions have become part of the city's texture.

For more than four decades Atlanta has been linked to the civil rights movement. Among the many accomplishments of which Atlanta's African-American community is proud is the Nobel Peace Prize that Martin Luther King Jr. won in 1964. Dr. King's widow, Coretta Scott King, continues to operate the King Center, which she founded after her husband's assassination in 1968. In 1972 Andrew Young was elected the first black congressman from the South since Reconstruction. After serving as ambassador to the United Nations during President Jimmy Carter's administration, Young was elected mayor of Atlanta. Since his term ended in the early '90s, Young has kept busy being co-chairman of the Atlanta Committee for the Olympic Games, chairman of the Metro Atlanta Chamber of Commerce, and president of the National Council of Churches.

The traditional South—which in romantic versions consists of lacy moss dangling from tree limbs; thick, sugary Southern drawls; a leisurely pace; and luxurious antebellum mansions—rarely reveals itself here. Even before the Civil War, the columned house was a rarity—and prior to the construction boom of the 1850s, houses of any kind were rare. The frenetic pace of rebuilding that characterized the period after the Civil War continues unabated. Still viewed by die-hard Southerners as the heart of the Old Confederacy, Atlanta has become the best example of the New South, a fast-paced modern city proud of its heritage.

In the past two decades Atlanta has experienced unprecedented growth—the official city population remains steady, at about 420,000, but the metro population has grown in the past decade by nearly 40%, from 2.9 million to 4.1 million people. A good measure of this growth is the ever-changing downtown skyline, along with skyscrapers constructed in the Midtown, Buckhead, and outer perimeter (fringing I–285) business districts. Since the late 1970s dozens of dazzling skyscrapers designed by such luminaries as Philip Johnson, I. M. Pei, and Marcel Breuer have reshaped the city's profile. Residents, however, are less likely to measure the city's growth by skyscrapers than by increasing traffic jams, crowds, higher prices, and the ever-burgeoning subdivisions that continue to push urban sprawl farther and farther into surrounding rural areas. The core of Atlanta revolves around five counties. The city of Atlanta is primarily in Fulton and DeKalb counties, with its southern end and the airport in Clayton County. Outside I–285, Cobb and Gwinnett counties, to the northwest and northeast, respectively, are experiencing much of Atlanta's population increase.

Atlanta's lack of a grid system confuses many drivers, even locals. Some streets change their names along the same stretch of road, including the city's most famous thoroughfare, Peachtree Street, which follows a mountain ridge from downtown to suburban Norcross, outside I–285N: it becomes Peachtree Road after crossing I–85 and then splits into Peachtree Industrial Boulevard beyond the Buckhead neighborhood and the original Peachtree Road, which heads into Chamblee. Adding to the confusion, more than 60 other streets in the metropolitan area use the word *Peachtree* in their names. Before setting out anywhere, get the complete street address of your destination, including landmarks, cross streets, or other guideposts, as street numbers and even street signs often are difficult to find.

Downtown Atlanta

Downtown Atlanta clusters around the hub known as Five Points. Here you'll find the MARTA station that intersects the north–south and east–west transit lines. On the surface Five Points is formed by the intersection of Peachtree Street with Marietta, Broad, and Forsyth streets.

Numbers in the text correspond to numbers in the margin and on the Downtown Atlanta and Sweet Auburn map.

A Good Walk

This walk branches in three directions, which are most efficiently managed by taking MARTA trains to get quickly from one spot to the next. The valiant will, of course, prefer to go it on foot. Begin at **Woodruff Park** ①, and then proceed north on Peachtree Street, noting Atlanta's **Flatiron Building** ② on the west side of Peachtree and the **Candler Building** ③ on the east side of the street. Nearby on Peachtree Street at John Wesley Dobbs Avenue is the modern **Georgia-Pacific Center** ④, and across from it are **Margaret Mitchell Park** ⑤ and the **Atlanta-Fulton Public Library** ⑥. Continuing north up Peachtree Street, note the sprawling **Peachtree Center** ⑦ complex, which includes the small but worthwhile **Atlanta International Museum of Art and Design** ⑧. Walk east on Baker Street one block to Courtland Street; head north on Courtland until you reach Ralph McGill Boulevard, and go one block east to the corner of Piedmont Road. Here you'll find an open-air folk art exhibition known as the **Folk Art Park** ⑨.

Return to Peachtree Center and take the subway one stop to the **Five Points MARTA station** ⑩, from which you can walk north on Peachtree Street to the **William-Oliver Building** ⑪. (From Folk Art Park you can also follow Ralph McGill Boulevard west to Peachtree and retrace your steps south to the William-Oliver Building.) From here go east on Edgewood Avenue, and just ahead you'll see the **Hurt Building** ⑫, a rare Atlanta example of Chicago-style architecture. Around the corner on

Marietta Street at Broad Street is the handsome **Bank of America Building** ⑬, and nearby is the **Statue of Henry Grady** ⑭, right across from the building now housing the newspaper he founded, the *Atlanta Journal-Constitution* ⑮. At Marietta Street and Techwood Drive, **Centennial Olympic Park** ⑯ hosts concerts and special events. Adjacent to the park is **CNN Center** ⑰, which you may tour (by reservation). At the rear of the center is the **Georgia Dome** ⑱.

At the CNN Center/Georgia Dome station, take MARTA one station to the Five Points station and exit at the sign for **Underground Atlanta** ⑲. After taking a rest and a restorative snack in its food court, wander the maze of subterranean streets here and leave through the Central Avenue exit of Underground Atlanta, bearing slightly south toward the **Georgia Railroad Freight Depot** ⑳. Across the plaza from the depot is the **World of Coca-Cola Pavilion** ㉑, with fun memorabilia on display. Across Martin Luther King Jr. Drive at Central Avenue is the historic **Shrine of the Immaculate Conception** ㉒, one of many historic churches still operating in downtown. Just south of the shrine are the neo-Gothic **City Hall** ㉓, with a modern addition housing a permanent art collection, which is on Mitchell Street, and the Renaissance-style **Georgia State Capitol** ㉔, on Washington Street.

TIMING

This walk requires at least a day, assuming you don't spend much time at any one location. If you plan to walk at a more leisurely pace, finish the first day at the Folk Art Park, and allow another half day for the rest of the walk. If you plan tours of CNN Center, the Georgia Dome, and World of Coca-Cola, you'll need an additional half day. If you tour these sights at length, it will probably take two full days to cover the territory. The terrain is fairly level and not too taxing.

Sights to See

OFF THE BEATEN PATH

ATLANTA CYCLORAMA & CIVIL WAR MUSEUM – In Grant Park (named for a New England–born Confederate colonel, not the U.S. president), you'll find a huge circular painting, completed by a team of expert European panorama artists shortly after the Civil War, depicting the 1864 Battle of Atlanta. The museum has one of the best Civil War bookstores anywhere. To reach the Cyclorama by car, take I–20 east to Exit 59A, turn right onto Boulevard, and then take a right at the next traffic light into Grant Park; follow signs to the Cyclorama. ✉ *Grant Park, 800 Cherokee Ave., Grant Park*, ☎ *404/658-7625*, WEB *www.webguide. com/cyclorama.html.* ☜ *$5.* ⊙ *June–early Sept., daily 9:30–5:30; early Sept.–May, daily 9:30–4:30.*

❻ **Atlanta-Fulton Public Library.** The Marcel Breuer–designed building houses, on its fourth floor, a large collection of *Gone With the Wind* memorabilia and newspapers from most major cities in the United States and elsewhere. ✉ *1 Margaret Mitchell Sq., Downtown*, ☎ *404/730-1700.* ⊙ *Mon. and Fri.–Sat. 9–6, Tues.–Thurs. 9–8, Sun. 2–6.*

★ ❽ **Atlanta International Museum of Art and Design.** In the Peachtree Center in the Marriott Marquis Two Tower, this museum mounts major international exhibitions covering such subjects as textiles, puzzles, boxes, masks, and baskets. Exhibits focus on arts and crafts, design, and culture from around the globe. ✉ *285 Peachtree Center Ave., Downtown*, ☎ *404/688-2467*, WEB *www.atlantainternationalmuseum. org.* ☜ *Free.* ⊙ *Weekdays 11–5.*

⑮ *Atlanta Journal-Constitution.* The building containing the business offices and printing plant for the city's—and the state's—dominant newspaper has a lobby that displays front-page news of historic events, an old printing press, and photographs of famous former employees. ⊠ *72 Marietta St., Downtown,* ☎ *404/614–2688.* ☉ *Tours have been postponed indefinitely; call for information.*

⓭ Bank of America Building. Originally a Chicago-style edifice known as the Empire Building, this handsome 1901 classic was designed by Atlanta architect Phillip Trammel Shutze. In 1929 Shutze refashioned the first three floors, bestowing on them a decidedly Renaissance look. This is one of the city's first steel-frame structures, and at 14 stories one of its tallest, but during the renovation Shutze resheathed the base with masonry. ⊠ *35 Broad St., Downtown.*

❸ Candler Building. Asa G. Candler, founder of the Coca-Cola Company, engaged the local firm of Murphy and Stewart to design this splendid terra-cotta and marble building in 1906. The ornate bronze and marble lobby shouldn't be missed. ⊠ *84 Peachtree St., Downtown* ☉ *Daily 9–5.*

⓰ Centennial Olympic Park. This 21-acre urban landscape, the largest urban park to be developed in this country in more than two decades, was the central venue for the 1996 Summer Olympics. The park's Fountain of Rings (the world's largest using the Olympic symbol) centers a court of 24 flags, each of them representing the Olympic Games as well as the host countries of the modern Games. The seating in the fountain amphitheater allows you to enjoy the water and music spectacle (five tunes are programmed and timed to coincide with water displays). The park has a 6-acre great lawn and pathways formed by commemorative brick paving stones. ⊠ *Marietta St. and Techwood Dr., Downtown,* ☎ *404/223–4412; 404/222–7275 for information,* WEB *www. centennialpark.com.* ☉ *Daily 7* AM*–11* PM.

㉓ City Hall. When the 14-story neo-Gothic building, designed by Atlanta architect G. Lloyd Preacher, was erected in 1929, critics dubbed it the Painted Lady of Mitchell Street. The newer wing, with its five-story glass atrium and beautiful marble entryway, houses a splendid permanent collection of art. ⊠ *68 Mitchell St., Downtown,* ☎ *404/330–6000,* WEB *www.ci.atlanta.ga.us.* ☉ *Weekdays 8:30–5.*

⓱ CNN Center. The home of Ted Turner's Cable News Network occupies all 14 floors of this dramatic structure on the edge of downtown. The 45-minute CNN studio tour begins with a ride up the world's longest escalator to an eighth-floor exhibit about Turner's global broadcasting empire. Tours are not open to children under age 6. ⊠ *1 CNN Center, Downtown,* ☎ *404/827–2300,* WEB *www.cnn.com/studiotour. Reservations required 48 hrs in advance held with credit card.* ☏ *50-min tour $8.* ☉ *Daily 9–5.*

⓾ Five Points MARTA Station. Even if you're driving everywhere, it's worth visiting the busiest public-transit rail station in the city, bustling with people and pushcart vendors. It also has its own entrance to underground Atlanta, via a tunnel below Peachtree Street. On the practical side, this MARTA station serves Underground Atlanta and nearby Woodruff Park, Georgia State University, and numerous businesses; the station is at the crossroads of MARTA's east–west and north–south lines. Stand on the corner of Peachtree and Alabama streets, outside the station, and notice the old-fashioned gas streetlight, with its historic marker proclaiming it the **Eternal Flame of the Confederacy.** ⊠ *Peachtree and Alabama Sts., Downtown.*

❷ Flatiron Building. The English-American Building, as it was originally known, was designed by Bradford Gilbert. Similar to the famous New York City Flatiron Building, built in the early 1900s, this one dates from

1897 and is the city's oldest high-rise. ⊠ *74 Peachtree St., Downtown.*
🕑 *Weekdays 8:15–5:30.*

❾ Folk Art Park. Revitalizing an ignored part of the city, the park pays
homage to an important American art form by gathering works that
reflect the diverse styles of American (especially Southern) folk art. Works
by more than a dozen artists are on display, among them Harold Rit-
tenberry, Howard Finster, and Eddie Owens Martin. Martin's brightly
painted totems and snake-top walls replicate portions of *Pasaquan* (the
legendary visionary environment that Martin created at his farm near
Columbus, Georgia). ⊠ *Ralph McGill Blvd. at Courtland St., Baker
St., and Piedmont Ave., Midtown.*

⑱ Georgia Dome. This arena accommodates 71,500 spectators with good
visibility from every seat; it's the site of Atlanta Falcons football games,
major rock concerts, conventions, and trade shows. The white, plum,
and turquoise 1 million-square-ft facility is crowned with the world's
largest cable-supported oval, giving the roof a circus-tent top. ⊠ *1 Georgia Dome Dr., Downtown,* ☎ *404/223–8687,* 🕸 *www.gadome.com.*
🎫 *Tour $2 (groups of 15 or more only).* 🕑 *Tours daily every hr 10–4.*

❹ Georgia-Pacific Center. The towering, 52-story structure occupies the
site of the old Loew's Grand Theatre, where *Gone With the Wind* premiered in 1939. From certain angles the red-marble high-rise appears
to be flat against the sky. The **High Museum of Art Folk Art and Photography Galleries** is inside. ⊠ *133 Peachtree St., at John Wesley
Dobbs Ave., Downtown Museum:* ⊠ *Georgia-Pacific Center, 133
Peachtree St. NE, gallery entrance on 30 John Wesley Dobbs Ave., Sweet
Auburn,* ☎ *404/577–6940 for information line,* 🕸 *www.high.org.* 🎫
Free. 🕑 *Mon.–Sat. 10–5, first Thurs. of every month 10–8.*

⑳ Georgia Railroad Freight Depot. After downtown's oldest extant building was constructed in 1869 to replace the one torched by Sherman's
troops in 1864, it burned again in 1935 and was rebuilt in its present
form. It is now used by several downtown companies as a banquet hall
and for special events. It may be viewed only by appointment. ⊠ *65
Martin Luther King Jr. Dr., Downtown,* ☎ *404/656–3850.*

★ ㉔ Georgia State Capitol. A Renaissance-style edifice, the capitol was
dedicated on July 4, 1889. The gold leaf on its dome was mined in nearby
Dahlonega. Inside, the **Georgia Capitol Museum** houses exhibits on
the history of the capitol building. On the grounds, state historical markers commemorate the 1864 Battle of Atlanta, which destroyed 90%
of the city. Statues memorialize a 19th-century Georgia governor and
his wife (Joseph and Elizabeth Brown), a Confederate general (John
B. Gordon), and a former senator (Richard B. Russell). Former governor and president Jimmy Carter is depicted with his sleeves rolled
up, a man at work. ⊠ *Capitol Sq., Downtown,* ☎ *404/656–2844,* 🕸
www.sos.state.ga.us/museum. 🕑 *Guided tours weekdays at 10, 11, 1,
and 2 (during legislative session, Jan.–Mar., the first 2 tours operate
at 9:30 and 10:30).*

OFF THE
BEATEN PATH
HAMMONDS HOUSE GALLERIES AND RESOURCE CENTER – Dr. Otis Thrash
Hammonds donated his handsome Eastlake Victorian house and his fine
collection of Victorian furniture and paintings to the city of Atlanta as an
art gallery and resource center. The permanent and visiting exhibitions
are devoted chiefly to work by African-American artists, although art from
anywhere in the African-influenced world can be a focus. ⊠ *503 Peeples
St., West End,* ☎ *404/752–8730,* 🕸 www.hammmondshouse.org. 🎫
$2. 🕑 *Tues.–Fri. 10–6, weekends 1–5.*

HERNDON HOME – Alonzo Herndon emerged from slavery and founded both a chain of successful barbershops and the **Atlanta Life Insurance Company.** He traveled extensively and influenced the cultural life around Atlanta's traditionally black colleges. Alonzo's son, Norris, created a foundation to preserve the handsome beaux arts home as a museum and heritage center. ⊠ *587 University Pl., near Morris Brown College, West End,* ☎ *404/581–9813,* WEB *www.theherndonhome.org.* 🖫 *$5.* ☉ *Tues.–Sat. 10–4; tours every hr.*

⓬ Hurt Building. Named for Atlanta developer Joel Hurt, this restored 1913 Chicago-style high-rise, with its intricate grillwork and sweeping marble staircase, has a lower level of shops and art galleries. The excellent City Grill restaurant is at the top of the sweeping staircase. ⊠ *50 Hurt Plaza, Downtown.*

❺ Margaret Mitchell Park. A cascading waterfall and columned sculpture are highlights of this park named for Atlanta's most famous author, whose masterpiece and only novel is *Gone With the Wind.* ⊠ *Margaret Mitchell Sq., Midtown.*

❼ Peachtree Center. John Portman designed this skyscraper complex, built between 1960 and 1992, which contains shops, offices, and restaurants. Across the street, connected to Peachtree Center by skywalks, is the massive **Atlanta Market Center.** Two additional Portman creations, the **Atlanta Marriott Marquis** and the **Hyatt Regency Hotel,** are also connected to the center by skywalks. A MARTA stop is available at Peachtree Center. ⊠ *225 Peachtree St., Downtown,* ☎ *404/654–1255,* WEB *www.peachtreecenter.com.*

㉒ Shrine of the Immaculate Conception. During the Battle of Atlanta, Thomas O'Reilly, the church's pastor, persuaded Union forces to spare his church and several others around the city. That 1848 structure was then replaced by this much grander building, whose cornerstone was laid in 1869. O'Reilly, a native of Ireland, was interred in the basement of the church. The church was nearly lost to fire in 1982 but has been exquisitely restored. The vestibule is always open, allowing you to view the interior, or you may contact the rectory for an appointment. ⊠ *48 Martin Luther King Jr. Dr., at Central Ave., Downtown,* ☎ *404/521–1866.* ☉ *Weekdays 8:30–5, Sat. 9–7, Sun. 7–3.*

⓮ Statue of Henry Grady. New York artist Alexander Doyle's bronze sculpture honors the post–Civil War editor of the *Atlanta Constitution* and early advocate of the so-called New South. Much about Grady is reminiscent of Ted Turner, the contemporary Atlanta media mogul. The memorial was raised in 1891, after Grady's untimely death at age 39. ⊠ *Marietta and Forsyth Sts., Downtown.*

⓳ Underground Atlanta. This six-block entertainment and shopping district, dotted with historic markers, was created from the web of underground brick streets, ornamental building facades, and tunnels that fell into disuse in 1929, when the city built viaducts over the train tracks. Merchants then moved their storefronts to the new viaduct level, leaving the original street level for storage. Today it houses restaurants, clubs, art galleries, shopping emporiums, and a food court, making it a good stop on a walking tour. ⊠ *50 Upper Alabama St., Downtown,* ☎ *404/523–2311,* WEB *www.underatl.com.*

⓫ William-Oliver Building. Walk through the lobby of this art deco gem and admire the ceiling mural, brass grills, and elevator doors. Formerly an office building, it has been renovated for luxury downtown residences and won a prestigious award for historic preservation from the Atlanta Urban Design Commission. ⊠ *32 Peachtree St., Downtown.*

❶ Woodruff Park. Named for the city's great philanthropist Robert W. Woodruff, the late Coca-Cola magnate, the triangular park fills during lunchtime on weekdays with executives, street preachers, politicians, Georgia State University students, and homeless people. ⊠ *Bordered by Pryor, Houston, and Peachtree Sts., Downtown.*

↻ **㉑ World of Coca-Cola Pavilion.** At this three-story, $15 million special-exhibit facility, you can sip samples of 38 Coca-Cola Company products from around the world and study memorabilia from more than a century's worth of corporate archives. Everything Coca-Cola, the gift shop, sells everything from refrigerator magnets to evening bags. ⊠ *55 Martin Luther King Jr. Dr., Downtown,* ☎ *404/676–5151,* WEB *www. woccatlanta.com.* ☑ *$6.* ☉ *June–Aug., Mon.–Sat. 9–6, Sun. 11–6; Sept.–May, Mon.–Sat. 9–5, Sun. noon–6.*

OFF THE   **ZOO ATLANTA** – This zoo has nearly 1,000 animals living in naturalistic
BEATEN PATH   habitats, such as the Ford African Rain Forest, Flamingo Lagoon, Masai
               Mara (re-created plains of Kenya), and Sumatran Tiger exhibits. Sibling
               gorillas Kudzoo and Olympia are always hits. Don't miss the popular
               Chinese panda exhibit, consisting of two precocious bears named Yang
               Yang and Lun Lun. To reach the zoo by car, take I–20 east to Exit 59A,
               turn right on Boulevard, then right again at the next light into Grant
               Park. Follow signs to the zoo. ⊠ *Grant Park, 800 Cherokee Ave., Grant
               Park,* ☎ *404/624–5600,* WEB *www.zooatlanta.org.* ☑ *$16.* ☉ *Daily
               9:30–4:30.*

Sweet Auburn

Between 1890 and 1930 the historic Sweet Auburn district was Atlanta's most active and prosperous center of black business, entertainment, and political life. Following the Depression, the area went into an economic decline that lasted until the 1980s, when the residential area where civil rights leader Rev. Martin Luther King Jr. was born, raised, and later returned to live was declared a National Historic District.

Numbers in the text correspond to numbers in the margin and on the Downtown Atlanta and Sweet Auburn map.

A Good Walk

Start your walk in the Martin Luther King Jr. National Historic District, the heart of Sweet Auburn, where you can get a sense of what the civil rights movement and its principal leader were all about. First visit the **Martin Luther King Jr. Birth Home** ㉕, on Auburn Avenue, and on the next block west, the **Martin Luther King Jr. Center for Nonviolent Social Change** ㉖, where Dr. King is entombed. Next stop at the nearby **Ebenezer Baptist Church** ㉗, where Dr. King preached along with his grandfather, father, and brother. Proceed a few blocks west near the I–75/85 overpass to enjoy the **John Wesley Dobbs Plaza** ㉘, a good place to take a breather. The **Odd Fellows Building** ㉙, on the other side of Auburn Avenue just after you walk under the expressway, is a handsome structure not to be missed. At this point, go south on Bell Street and walk one block to Edgewood Avenue to visit the **Sweet Auburn Curb Market** ㉚. Walk three blocks west on Edgewood Avenue, and you'll reach the **Baptist Student Center** ㉛, a fine example of Victorian architecture. Returning north to Auburn Avenue, you'll see the **Atlanta Daily World Building** ㉜ and next to it the **African-American Panoramic Experience (APEX)** ㉝. Continue down Auburn Avenue just a few steps and enter the lobby of the **Atlanta Life Insurance Company** ㉞ to view its fabulous art collection. Now, proceed across the street and finish your walk with a stop at the **Auburn Avenue Research Library on African-American Culture and History** ㉟.

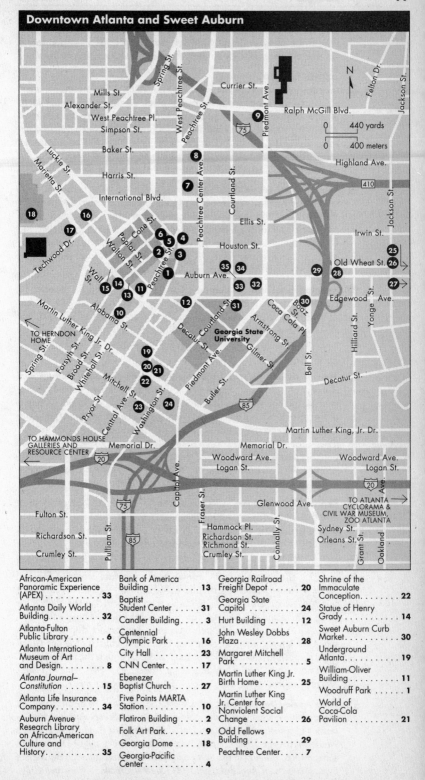

Downtown Atlanta and Sweet Auburn

TIMING

This is a leisurely walk along level sidewalks, with shops and historic sites along the way. If you stop for tours, you'll fill an entire day. If you simply stroll and look, the walk should take an hour or two.

Sights to See

★ ㉝ **African-American Panoramic Experience (APEX).** The museum's quarterly exhibits chronicle the history of black people in America. Videos illustrate the history of Sweet Auburn, the name bestowed on Auburn Avenue by businessman John Wesley Dobbs, who fostered business development for African-Americans on this street. ⊠ *135 Auburn Ave., Sweet Auburn,* ☎ *404/521–2739,* WEB *www.apexmuseum.org.* 🎫 *$3.* ☉ *June–Aug., Tues.–Sat. 10–5, Sun. 1–5; Sept.–May, Tues.–Sat. 10–5.*

㉜ **Atlanta Daily World Building.** This simple two-story brick building, banded with a white frieze of lion's heads, was constructed in the early 1900s; since 1945 it has housed one of the nation's oldest black newspapers (is no longer a daily, however). Alexis Reeves, publisher and CEO, is the granddaughter of William A. Scott II, who founded the paper as a weekly in 1928. ⊠ *145 Auburn Ave., Sweet Auburn,* ☎ *404/659–1110,* WEB *www.atlantadailyworld.com.*

㉞ **Atlanta Life Insurance Company.** The landmark enterprise founded by Alonzo Herndon, a former slave, was in modest quarters at 148 Auburn Avenue until the modern complex at No. 100 was opened in 1980. The lobby holds an exhibition of art by black artists from the United States and Africa. ⊠ *100 Auburn Ave., Sweet Auburn,* ☎ *404/659–2100.* ☉ *Weekdays 8–5.*

㉟ **Auburn Avenue Research Library on African-American Culture and History.** This unit is an extension of the **Atlanta-Fulton Public Library** system, and houses a noncirculating library with about 35,000 volumes devoted to African-American subjects. Special exhibits, programs, and tours are free to the public. The archives division contains art and artifacts, ephemera, oral histories, pamphlets, prints, rare periodicals, rare books, manuscript collections, photographs, and memorabilia. ⊠ *101 Auburn Ave., Sweet Auburn,* ☎ *404/730–4001,* WEB *http://aarl.af.public.lib.ga.us.* ☉ *Mon.–Thurs. 10–8, Fri.–Sun. noon–6.*

㉛ **Baptist Student Center.** Adjacent to the Georgia State University campus, this restored Victorian building once contained the Coca-Cola Company's first bottling plant. ⊠ *125 Edgewood Ave., Sweet Auburn,* ☎ *404/659–8726,* WEB *www.gsu.edu/~wwwbsu.*

㉗ **Ebenezer Baptist Church.** A Gothic Revival–style building completed in 1922, the church became known as the spiritual center of the civil rights movement after Martin Luther King Jr. won the Nobel Peace Prize in 1964. Members of the King family have preached at the church for three generations; Dr. King's funeral was held here. The grand building has just been restored extensively to its appearance during the '60s, when Dr. King preached inside it. A tour of the church includes an audiotape outlining the history of the building, though the congregation itself now occupies the building across the street. ⊠ *407 Auburn Ave., Sweet Auburn,* ☎ *404/688–7263.* 🎫 *Free.* ☉ *Tours weekdays 9–5.*

㉘ **John Wesley Dobbs Plaza.** John Wesley Dobbs was an important civic leader whose legacy includes coining the name *Sweet Auburn* for Atlanta's black business and residential neighborhood. The plaza, which was built for the 1996 Olympic Games, has a life mask of Dobbs himself; children playing in the plaza may view the street through the mask's eyes. ⊠ *Auburn Ave. adjacent to I–75/85 overpass, Sweet Auburn.*

★ ㉕ **Martin Luther King Jr. Birth Home.** This modest Queen Anne–style historic home is managed by the National Park Service, which also has a visitor center across the street from the Martin Luther King Jr. Center for Nonviolent Social Change. The visitor center contains a multimedia exhibit focused on the civil rights movement and Dr. King's role in it. To sign up for tours, go to the **fire station** (⊠ 39 Boulevard, Sweet Auburn). ⊠ *501 Auburn Ave., Sweet Auburn,* ☎ *404/331–6922,* WEB *www.thekingcenter.org.* ⊡ *Free.* ☉ *Daily guided ½-hr tours every hr 10–5.*

㉖ **Martin Luther King Jr. Center for Nonviolent Social Change.** The Martin Luther King Jr. National Historic District occupies several blocks on Auburn Avenue, a few blocks east of Peachtree Street in the black business and residential community of Sweet Auburn. The neighborhood is the birthplace of Martin Luther King Jr., who was born here in 1929. After Dr. King's assassination in 1968, his widow, Coretta Scott King, established the center, which exhibits personal items, such as King's Nobel Peace Prize, Bible, and tape recorder, along with memorabilia and photos chronicling the civil rights movement. In the courtyard in front of Freedom Hall, on a circular brick pad in the middle of the rectangular Meditation Pool, is Dr. King's white-marble tomb; the inscription reads; FREE AT LAST! Nearby, an eternal flame burns. A chapel of all faiths sits at one end of the reflecting pool. ⊠ *449 Auburn Ave., Sweet Auburn,* ☎ *404/524–1956,* WEB *www.thekingcenter.org.* ☉ *Daily 9–5.*

㉙ **Odd Fellows Building.** The Georgia Chapter of the Grand United Order of Odd Fellows was a trade and social organization for African-Americans. In 1912 the membership erected this handsome Romanesque Revival–style building housing meeting rooms, a theater, commercial spaces, and a community center. African-featured terra-cotta figures adorn the splendid entrance. Now handsomely restored, the building houses offices. ⊠ *250 Auburn Ave., Sweet Auburn.*

㉚ **Sweet Auburn Curb Market.** The market, an institution on Edgewood Avenue since 1923, sells vegetables, fish, flowers, prepared foods, and meat. Individual stalls are operated by separate owners, making this a true public market. Don't miss the splendid totemic sculptures by young Atlanta artist Carl Joe Williams. The pieces were placed as part of Atlanta's Olympic art program. ⊠ *209 Edgewood Ave., Sweet Auburn,* ☎ *404/659–1665.* ☉ *Mon.–Thurs. 8–6, Fri.–Sat. 8–7.*

Midtown

Just north of downtown lies this thriving area, a hippie hangout in the late '60s and '70s and now housing a large segment of the city's gay population, along with young families, young professionals, artists, and musicians. Formerly in decline, Midtown has evolved into one of the city's most interesting and sought-after neighborhoods. Confirming its other facet as one of the city's most burgeoning business centers, its gleaming office towers now define a skyline that nearly rivals that of downtown, and the renovated mansions and bungalows in its residential section have made it a city showcase.

Numbers in the text correspond to numbers in the margin and on the Atlanta Neighborhoods map.

A Good Drive

From downtown take Piedmont Avenue about a half mile to **SciTrek** ㊱, a science museum all ages will enjoy. Turn left from Piedmont Avenue onto Ponce de Leon Avenue and drive two blocks to Peachtree Street; then turn right and find the 1929 **Fox Theatre** ㊲ and, across the street, the **Georgian Terrace** ㊳, a luxury suites hotel. From Peachtree Street circle around the block, turning right onto 3rd Street to Juniper Street; then turn right on Juniper Street, continue two blocks, and turn right onto North Avenue. Turn right again onto Peachtree Street to view the **Bank of America Plaza Tower** ㊴. Continuing up Peachtree Street to Peachtree Place (one block south of 10th Street), you'll find the **Margaret Mitchell House** ㊵, the restored building where the Pulitzer Prize–winning author lived while completing *Gone With the Wind*. Across the street to the north is the new home of the **Federal Reserve Bank** ㊶. Walk west two blocks on 10th Street, then turn right onto West Peachtree Street, and continue north to its intersection with 14th Street, where you'll see Philip Johnson's distinctive One Atlantic Center. Turn left onto 18th Street to reach the **Center for Puppetry Arts** ㊷. Take 18th Street east back to Peachtree Street, turn left, and continue on to the **Woodruff Arts Center** ㊸, which includes the modern structure of the **High Museum of Art** ㊹. From this point travel two blocks north on Peachtree Street to **Rhodes Memorial Hall** ㊺. From here take Beverly Road east off Peachtree Street for about a quarter mile to Montgomery Ferry Drive; turn a quick dogleg left, then right, continuing on Beverly to Park Lane, and then turn right onto Park Lane and drive about a quarter mile to where it intersects the Prado. Here, these two streets dead-end onto Piedmont Avenue, where you'll enter the **Atlanta Botanical Garden** ㊻, which adjoins **Piedmont Park** ㊼, bounded by Piedmont Avenue, 10th Street, and Westminster Drive.

TIMING

This drive is best accomplished between midmorning (about 9:30) and midafternoon (3:30) to avoid rush-hour traffic. Give yourself between four and five hours to visit all the sights. Each place has parking no more than a few steps away, and often it's free.

Sights to See

㊻ **Atlanta Botanical Garden.** Occupying 30 acres inside Piedmont Park, the grounds contain 15 acres of display gardens, including a serene Japanese garden, a 15-acre hardwood forest with walking trails, and the Fuqua Conservatory, which has unusual and threatened flora from tropical and desert climates. A permanent Fuqua Conservatory exhibit of tiny, brightly colored poison-dart frogs is popular, especially with children. ⊠ *1345 Piedmont Ave., at the Prado, Midtown,* ☎ *404/876–5859.* WEB *www.atlantabotanicalgarden.org.* ⊡ *$10; free Thurs. after 3.* ⊙ *Mar.–Sept., Tues.–Sun. 9–7; Oct.–Feb., Tues.–Sun. 9–6.*

㊴ **Bank of America Plaza Tower.** Built in 1992, the skyscraper has a graceful birdcage roof easily visible from the interstate; it's the South's tallest building, at 1,023 ft. The elegant marble central lobby is worth a glimpse. ⊠ *600 Peachtree St., Midtown.*

★ ㊷ **Center for Puppetry Arts.** At this interactive museum you can see puppets from around the world and attend puppet-making workshops. Elaborate performances, which include original dramatic works and classics adapted for the museum theater, are presented by professional puppeteers—youngsters and adults alike are spellbound. In particular, the popular Christmas performances of *The Velveteen Rabbit* and *The Shoemaker and the Elf* are truly magical experiences. ⊠ *1404 Spring St., at 18th St., Midtown,* ☎ *404/873–3391,* WEB *www.puppet.org.* ⊡ *$5; special exhibits and programs extra.* ⊙ *Mon.–Sat. 9–5, Sun. 11–5.*

㊶ **Federal Reserve Bank.** Don't miss this grand, recently renovated monetary museum whose exhibits explain the story of money as a medium of exchange and the history of the U.S. banking system. Items displayed include rare coins, uncut sheets of money, and a gold bar. There are a

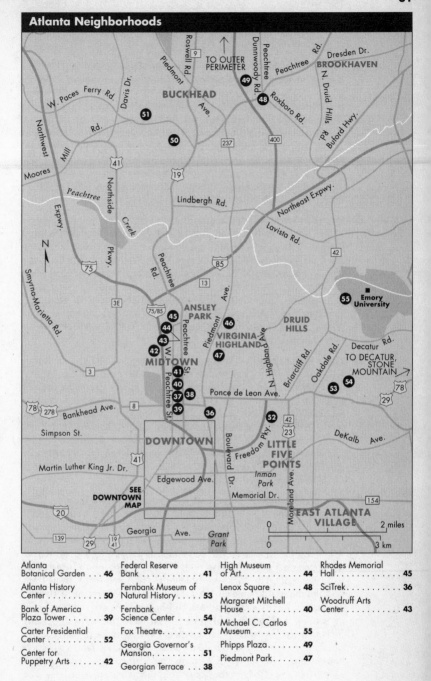

Atlanta Neighborhoods

Atlanta Botanical Garden . . . **46**	Federal Reserve Bank **41**	High Museum of Art **44**	Rhodes Memorial Hall **45**
Atlanta History Center **50**	Fernbank Museum of Natural History **53**	Lenox Square **48**	SciTrek **36**
Bank of America Plaza Tower **39**	Fernbank Science Center **54**	Margaret Mitchell House **40**	Woodruff Arts Center **43**
Carter Presidential Center **52**	Fox Theatre **37**	Michael C. Carlos Museum **55**	
Center for Puppetry Arts **42**	Georgia Governor's Mansion. **51**	Phipps Plaza **49**	
	Georgian Terrace . . . **38**	Piedmont Park **47**	

tour and a video, *The Fed Today.* ✉ *1000 Peachtree St., Midtown,* ☎ *404/498–8764 or 800/498–8318,* WEB *www.frbatlanta.org.* ☉ *Weekdays 9–4.*

37 **Fox Theatre.** One of a dwindling number of vintage movie palaces in the nation, the Fox was built in 1929 in a fabulous Moorish-Egyptian style to be the headquarters of the Shriners Club. The interior's crowning glory is its skylike ceiling—complete with clouds and stars above Alhambra-like minarets. Threatened by demolition in the 1970s, the Fox was saved from the wrecker's ball by concerted civic action and is still a prime venue for musicals, rock concerts, dance performances, and film festivals. ✉ *660 Peachtree St., Midtown,* ☎ *404/881–2100; 404/876–2041 for Atlanta Preservation Center,* WEB *www.foxtheatre. org.* 🎫 *Tour, conducted by Atlanta Preservation Center, $10.* ☉ *Tours Mon., Wed., and Thurs. at 10, Sat. at 10 and 11.*

38 **Georgian Terrace.** Originally built in 1911 as a fine beaux arts–style hotel, the Georgian Terrace, designed by William L. Stoddart, housed the stars of the film *Gone With the Wind* when it premiered at the nearby Loew's Theater (now demolished) in 1939. President Calvin Coolidge also slept here. Stars of the Metropolitan Opera stayed at the hotel when the Met used to make its annual trek to Atlanta, and according to locals, Enrico Caruso routinely serenaded passersby from its balconies. Renovated with style and historic sensitivity, the building is now a luxury hotel. ✉ *459 Peachtree St., Midtown,* ☎ *404/897–1991,* WEB *www. thegeorgianterrace.com.*

44 **High Museum of Art.** The permanent holdings of this high-tech museum built in 1983 focus on American decorative arts and African art. The Uhry Print Collection contains works by French impressionists and other European artists. In 1991 the American Institute of Architects listed the sleek structure, designed by Richard Meier, among the 10 best works of American architecture of the decade. ✉ *Woodruff Arts Center, 1280 Peachtree St., MARTA Arts Center station, Midtown,* ☎ *404/ 733–4444 recorded information,* WEB *www.high.org.* 🎫 *$8 (varies for special events).* ☉ *Tues.–Sat. 10–5, Sun. noon–5 (hrs often extended for special exhibits).*

40 **Margaret Mitchell House.** Although the author of *Gone With the Wind* detested the turn-of-the-20th-century house (she called it "the dump") where she lived when she wrote her masterpiece, determined volunteers got backing to restore the house and open it to the public. To many Atlantans, the Margaret Mitchell House is a lightning rod, symbolizing the conflict between promoting the city's heritage and respecting its varied roots. The house has been gutted by arsonists twice, in 1995 and '96, the second time within days of a major restoration. Although Mitchell is the city's most famous author, her fame derived from writing a book that includes stereotypes of African-Americans that many find offensive. Yet others point out that before her tragically early death, Mitchell secretly helped to fund medical school scholarships to Morehouse College for scores of African-American college students. Both supporters and critics of the house hold their views passionately. The visitor center exhibits photographs, archival material, and personal possessions, including her original typewriter. ✉ *990 Peachtree St., at Peachtree Pl., Midtown,* ☎ *404/249–7015,* WEB *www.gwtw.org.* 🎫 *$12.* ☉ *Daily 9:30–5.*

47 **Piedmont Park.** The city's outdoor recreation center, this park is a major venue for special events. Tennis courts, a swimming pool, and paths for walking, jogging, and rollerblading are part of the attraction, but many retreat to the park's great lawn for picnics with a smashing view of the Midtown skyline. Each April the park hosts the popular Dogwood Festival. ⊠ *Piedmont Ave. between 10th St. and the Prado, Midtown.*

45 **Rhodes Memorial Hall.** Headquarters of the **Georgia Trust for Historic Preservation,** this former residence is one of the finest works of Atlanta architect Willis F. Denny II. Built at the northern edge of the city in 1904 for Amos Giles Rhodes, the wealthy founder of a Southern furniture chain, the hall has stained-glass windows that depict the heroes of the Confederacy. ⊠ *1516 Peachtree St., Midtown,* ☎ *404/881–9980,* WEB *www.georgiatrust.org/rhodes.html.* ⊡ *$5.* ⊙ *Weekdays 11–4, Sun. noon–3.*

★ ☕ **36** **SciTrek.** The Science and Technology Museum of Atlanta covers 96,000 square ft and has rotating exhibitions and daily science demonstrations at the Coca-Cola Science Show Theater. About 150 hands-on exhibits occupy four environments: *Simple Machines; Light, Color, and Perception; Electricity and Magnetism;* and *Kidspace,* for children ages 2–7. The Information Petting Zoo exhibits "cybercritters." ⊠ *395 Piedmont Ave., Midtown,* ☎ *404/522–5500,* WEB *www.scitrek.org.* ⊡ *$7.50.* ⊙ *Mon.–Sat. 10–5, Sun. noon–5.*

43 **Woodruff Arts Center.** The center houses the world-renowned **Atlanta Symphony Orchestra,** the **High Museum of Art,** the **Alliance Theatre,** and the **14th Street Playhouse,** which includes several repertory companies. Both theaters present contemporary dramas, classics, and frequent world premieres. ⊠ *1280 Peachtree St., Midtown,* ☎ *404/733–4200,* WEB *www.woodruffcenter.org.*

Buckhead

Atlanta's sprawl doesn't lend itself to walking between major neighborhoods, so take a car or MARTA to reach Buckhead. Many of Atlanta's trendy restaurants, music clubs, chic shops, and hip art galleries are concentrated in this neighborhood. Finding a parking spot on the weekends and at night can be a real headache, and waits of two hours or more are common in the hottest restaurants.

Numbers in the text correspond to numbers in the margin and on the Atlanta Neighborhoods map.

A Good Drive

Begin this drive at the intersection of two splendid shopping malls. The older and larger of the two is **Lenox Square** ㊽. Across the street you'll find the elegant shops of **Phipps Plaza** ㊾. Leaving Phipps Plaza, exit onto Peachtree Road and turn right (south), traveling about ⅓ mi to West Paces Ferry Road. Turn right and proceed to the **Atlanta History Center** ㊿. Leaving the center, head back to West Paces Ferry Road and then turn left, driving about ½ mi to reach the **Georgia Governor's Mansion** ㊿.

From Buckhead a 4-mi drive north along Peachtree-Dunwoody Road takes you by some of the city's most impressive residential dwellings and leads you straight to the popular **Perimeter Mall,** a sprawling "shop-opolis" bolstered with nearby megastores and home-designer outlets. Its location is at the northern crest of I–285, the freeway circling the city in an approximate 10-mi radius, thus delineating the inner and outer perimeters of metro Atlanta. Loosely speaking, the Perimeter area, which is most heavily focused along this northern section of I–285, has become one of the nation's fastest-growing "edge cities," complete with hundreds of trendy restaurants, office towers, mostly business-oriented hotels, and condo and housing subdivisions galore.

TIMING

Simply driving the distance around the five sights, looking briefly at each one, will consume, generally, no more than 30 minutes. Allot several hours if you want to shop or tour the Atlanta History Center and Georgia Governor's Mansion. And give yourself at least another two hours if you wish to explore the Perimeter area north of Buckhead—a section that's plagued by heavy traffic much of the time.

Sights to See

★ ❺⓪ **Atlanta History Center.** The museum highlights materials native to Georgia, with a floor of heart pine and polished Stone Mountain granite. Displays are provocative, juxtaposing *Gone With the Wind* romanticism with the grim reality of Ku Klux Klan racism. Also on the 33-acre site are the elegant 1928 **Swan House**; the **Tullie Smith Farm,** with a two-story plantation plain house (1840s); and **McElreath Hall,** an exhibition space for artifacts from Atlanta's history. ⊠ *130 W. Paces Ferry Rd., Buckhead,* ☎ *404/814–4000,* WEB *www.atlantahistorycenter. com.* ⌨ *$12.* ☉ *Mon.–Sat. 10–5:30, Sun. noon–5:30.*

❺① **Georgia Governor's Mansion.** Built in 1967, this 24,000-square-ft Greek Revival mansion contains 30 rooms and sits on 18 acres originally belonging to the Robert Maddox family (no relation to Georgia governor Lester Maddox, who was its first occupant). Federal-period antiques fill the public rooms. ⊠ *391 W. Paces Ferry Rd., Buckhead,* ☎ *404/261–1858.* ☉ *Free guided tours Tues.–Thurs. 10–11:30.*

❹⑧ **Lenox Square.** Local shoppers come for the more than 250 stores and several good restaurants at this mall. ⊠ *3393 Peachtree Rd., Buckhead,* ☎ *404/233–6767,* WEB *www.shopsimon.com.*

❹⑨ **Phipps Plaza.** The mall is one of Atlanta's premier shopping areas, with upscale chain stores, specialty shops, and restaurants. It also includes a 14-screen movie theater. ⊠ *3500 Peachtree Rd., Buckhead,* ☎ *404/ 262–0992 or 800/810–7700,* WEB *www.shopsimon.com.*

Virginia-Highland and the Emory Area

Restaurants and art galleries are the backbone of Virginia-Highland/Morningside, northeast of Midtown. Like Midtown, this residential area was down-at-the-heels only 25 years ago. Reclaimed by writers, artists, and a few visionary developers, Virginia-Highland (and its bordering Morningside neighborhood, to the north) today offers intriguing shopping and delightful walking. Nightlife hums here as well. To the east, the Emory University area is studded with envious mansions and expansive landscaping.

Numbers in the text correspond to numbers in the margin and on the Atlanta Neighborhoods map.

A Good Drive

This tour meanders through some residential areas, such as Druid Hills, the location for the film *Driving Miss Daisy,* by local playwright Alfred Uhry. The neighborhood was designed by the firm of Frederick Law Olmsted, which also designed New York's Central Park. Begin at the **Carter Presidential Center** ❺②, the central attraction in a subneighborhood called Poncey Highlands, because it lies south of Ponce de Leon Avenue and south of Virginia-Highland. The former president's center is bounded by Freedom Parkway, which splits and encircles the facility. To reach it from downtown, drive on Ralph McGill Boulevard about 1 mi east of I–75/85 (Exit 248C) to where the boulevard intersects with Freedom Parkway.

From the center take a left, drive only one short block on Highland Avenue to Ponce de Leon Avenue, and turn right (east), continuing for 1 mi to Clifton Road; next, take a left onto Clifton Road and almost immediately enter the driveway for the **Fernbank Museum of Natural History** ⑤. On the east end of this extensive forest and recreational-educational preserve lies **Fernbank Science Center** ⑤. Nearby on Emory University's campus visit the **Michael C. Carlos Museum** ⑤, an exquisite contemporary structure.

TIMING

You can drive this tour in about 15 minutes without stops. If you spend a few hours at each sight, it can easily take a full day.

Sights to See

★ ☺ ⑤ **Carter Presidential Center.** This complex occupies the site where Union general William T. Sherman orchestrated the Battle of Atlanta (1864). The museum and archives detail the political career of former president Jimmy Carter. The center itself, which is not open to the public, focuses on conflict resolution and human rights issues. It sponsors foreign-affairs conferences and projects on such matters as the world food supply. Outside, the Japanese-style garden is a serene spot to unwind. ⊠ *1 Copenhill Ave., Virginia-Highland,* ☎ *404/331–3942,* WEB *www.cartercenter.org.* 🎫 *$5.* ☉ *Mon.–Sat. 9–4:45, Sun. noon–4:45.*

☺ ⑤ **Fernbank Museum of Natural History.** The largest natural history museum south of the Smithsonian Institution in Washington, D.C., holds a permanent exhibit, *A Walk Through Time in Georgia.* You can meander through 15 galleries to explore the earth's natural history. The museum's IMAX theater shows films about the natural world. The café, with an exquisite view overlooking the forest, serves great food. ⊠ *767 Clifton Rd., Emory,* ☎ *404/370–0960; 404/370–0019 IMAX; 404/370–0850 for directions hot line,* WEB *www.fernbank.edu/museum/.* 🎫 *Museum $12, IMAX $10, combination ticket $17.* ☉ *Museum Mon.–Sat. 10–5, Sun. noon–5; IMAX Mon.–Thurs. 10–5, Fri. 6:30 PM–10 PM, Sat. 10–5, Sun. noon–5.*

☺ ⑤ **Fernbank Science Center.** The museum focuses on geology, space exploration, and ecology; it's best for younger children. Special seasonal programs for children under 5, priced at 50¢, are offered weekends at 1:30 from October through November, from early December through the first week of January, from the end of January to March 15, and during the summer. ⊠ *156 Heaton Park Dr., Emory,* ☎ *404/378–4311,* WEB *http://fsc.fernbank.edu/.* 🎫 *Museum free, planetarium shows $2.* ☉ *Mon. 8:30–5, Tues.–Fri. 8:30 AM–10 PM, Sat. 10–5, Sun. 1–5; planetarium shows Tues.–Fri. at 3:30 and 8, weekends at 3:30.*

★ ☺ ⑤ **Michael C. Carlos Museum.** Housing a permanent collection of more than 16,000 objects, this excellent museum designed by renowned American architect Michael Graves exhibits artifacts from Egypt, Greece, Rome, the Near East, the Americas, and Africa. European and American prints and drawings cover the Middle Ages through the 20th century. The gift shop has rare art books, jewelry, and art-focused items for children. The museum's Caffé Antico is a good lunch spot. ⊠ *Emory University, 571 S. Kilgo St., Emory,* ☎ *404/727–4282,* WEB *http://carlos.emory.edu/.* 🎫 *Suggested donation $5.* ☉ *Tues.–Wed. 10–5, Thurs. 10–9, Fri.–Sat. 10–5, Sun. noon–5.*

OFF THE BEATEN PATH | **INMAN PARK AND LITTLE FIVE POINTS –** Since this once grand neighborhood—about 4 mi east of downtown—was laid out by famous developer Joel Hurt in 1889, the area has faded and flourished a number of times, which explains the vast gaps in opulence evident by examining much of the architecture here. Huge, ornate Victorian mansions sit next to humble shotgun shacks. But no matter the exact address or style of home—be it modest or massive—all of Inman Park now commands considerable cachet among all types, from young families to empty nesters to gays and lesbians. Here you'll also find the delightfully countercultural Little Five Points section, ground zero for Atlanta funk. Though many of the storefronts here where Moreland, Euclid, and McLendon avenues intersect defy description, all are delightful. Check out the fascinating but almost scary **Urban Tribe Tattoo and Piercing Studio** (⊠ 1131 Euclid Ave., Inman Park, ☎ 404/659–6344). There's a plethora of colorful vintage-clothing stores here, including **Clothing Warehouse** (⊠ 420 Moreland Ave., Inman Park, ☎ 404/524–5074). In a former garage, **Groovy Girls Clothing Exchange** (⊠ 211 Moreland Ave., Inman Park, ☎ 404/659–3669) is a wonderland of edgy fashion pieces from the past.

Other Area Attractions

Atlanta's suburbs have excellent entertainment options. It is essential to drive to these venues, so plan your visits with Atlanta's notorious rush hours in mind.

★ **Château Élan.** A 16th-century-style French château has Georgia's best-known winery, ensconced in 2,400 rolling acres about an hour north of downtown Atlanta. Château Élan is also a complete resort: European luxury blends with Southern hospitality at the 274-room inn and spa with private villas, golf courses, and an equestrian center. ⊠ *100 Rue Charlemagne, Braselton I–85 to GA 211, Exit 126 (Chestnut Mountain/Winder),* ☎ *770/932–0900 or 800/233–9463,* FAX *770/271–6005,* WEB *www.chateauelan.com.* ☜ *Winery tours and tastings free.* ☉ *Wine market daily 10–9. Tours weekdays at 11, 12:30, 2, 3:30; Sat. hourly 11–5; Sun. noon–4.*

☾ **Chattahoochee Nature Center.** Birds and animals in their natural habitats may be seen from nature trails and a boardwalk winding through 124 acres of woodlands and wetlands. A gift shop, indoor exhibits, birds-of-prey aviaries, and a picnic area are on the property. Naturalist guides accompany evening canoe floats from May through August. ⊠ *9135 Willeo Rd., Roswell,* ☎ *770/992–2055,* WEB *www.chattnaturecenter.com.* ☜ *$3.* ☉ *Mon.–Sat. 9–5, Sun. noon–5.*

★ **Decatur Historical Courthouse.** Known as the Old Courthouse on the Square, this charming building was constructed in 1823 and now houses the DeKalb Welcome Center. One reason to visit this historical site is its location—it's right in the center of delightful Decatur Square, a quaint town quad with a sophisticated artistic feel, teeming with interesting specialty shops and delectable coffeehouses and cafés. Lively downtown Decatur is one of metro Atlanta's favorite spots for sidewalk-strolling and window-shopping. ⊠ *101 E. Court Sq., Decatur, Ponce de Leon Ave. east 8 mi to Decatur Sq. at Clairmont Ave.,* ☎ *404/373–1088,* FAX *404/373–8287,* WEB *www.dekalbhistory.org.* ☉ *Weekdays 9–4.*

Kennesaw Mountain National Battlefield. A must for Civil War buffs, this 2,884-acre park with 16 mi of hiking trails was the site of several crucial battles in June 1864. The visitor center contains a small museum with exhibits of Civil War weapons, uniforms, and other items recovered from the battlefield. A 10-minute slide presentation explains the battles. ⊠ *Old U.S. 41 and Stilesboro Rd. (look for signs on I–75N), Kennesaw,* ☎ *770/427–4686,* WEB *www.nps.gov/kemo.* ☜ *Free.* ☉ *Daily 7:30–dusk.*

🐣 **Six Flags over Georgia.** Atlanta's major theme park, with eight sections, heart-stopping roller coasters, and water rides (best saved for last to prevent being damp all day), is a child's ideal playground. The Georgia Scorcher, a roller coaster that you ride standing up, moves at 54 mph. The park also has well-staged musical revues, concerts by top-name artists, and other performances. Take MARTA's west line to the Hightower station and then the Six Flags bus. ✉ *I–20W at 7561 Six Flags Pkwy., Austell,* ☎ *770/739–3400,* WEB *www.sixflags.com.* ✉ *All-inclusive 1-day pass $39.99, parking $9 or $12 (depending on the lot).* ☉ *June–Aug., daily 10 AM–11 PM; Mar.–May and Sept.–Oct., weekends from 10, closing times vary.*

🐣 **Stone Mountain Park.** This 3,200-acre state park 15 mi east of Atlanta has the largest exposed granite outcropping on earth. The Confederate Memorial on the north face of the 825-ft-high domed mountain is the world's largest sculpture, measuring 90 ft by 190 ft. The park has a skylift to the mountaintop, a steam locomotive ride around the mountain's base, an antebellum plantation, a swimming beach, a campground, a hotel, a resort, a wildlife preserve, restaurants, and two Civil War museums. Summer nights are capped with a laser light show, and annual events such as the Yellow Daisy Festival and the Scottish Highland Games are popular in the fall. ✉ *U.S. 78E (Stone Mountain Pkwy.), Stone Mountain,* ☎ *770/498–5600,* WEB *www.stonemountainpark.com.* ✉ *Per car $7; annual pass $30; day pass to all attractions $13.91 for GA residents, $17.12 for out-of-state visitors; additional fees for special events.* ☉ *Daily 6 AM–midnight.*

OFF THE BEATEN PATH

EAST ATLANTA VILLAGE – This earthy outpost of edgy-cool shops and restaurants evolved when a cadre of proprietors with dreams much bigger than their bank accounts spurned the high rents of fancier parts of town and set up businesses in this then-blighted but beautiful ruin of a neighborhood 4 mi southeast of downtown. Soon artists and trendoids began soaking up the ensuing creative atmosphere, and like attracted like. Years later East Atlanta, which is centered at Flat Shoals and Glenwood avenues, just southeast of Moreland Avenue at I-20, now ranks among the hippest neighborhoods in metro Atlanta. The majestic homes have almost all been renovated, and what remains unrestored seems simply to romanticize the area's hint of "fashionable" danger. The coffeehouse Sacred Grounds (✉ 508 Flat Shoals Ave., East Atlanta, ☎ 404/524–4779) is the credited cornerstone for the new wave of jazzy businesses here. Check out the delightfully funky gift shop Traders (✉ 485 Flat Shoals Ave., East Atlanta, ☎ 404/522–3006). And stop by Space Tribe (✉ 490 Flat Shoals Ave., East Atlanta, ☎ 404/688–0780), where the funkadelic inventory is out of this world.

Dining

Atlanta has sophisticated kitchens run by world-class chefs, myriad ethnic restaurants, and classic Southern establishments serving such regional favorites as fried chicken, Brunswick stew, fried catfish, and hush puppies. There's no shortage of urban chic in the dining scene, but traditional Southern fare—including Cajun and creole, country-style and plantation cuisine, coastal and mountain dishes—continues to thrive.

The local taste for things sweet and fried holds true for restaurants serving traditional Southern food. Tea in the South comes iced and sweet; if you want hot tea, specify hot. Desserts in the region are legendary. Catch the flavor of the South at breakfast and lunch in modest establishments that serve only these meals. Reserve evenings for culinary exploration, including some of the new restaurants that present traditional

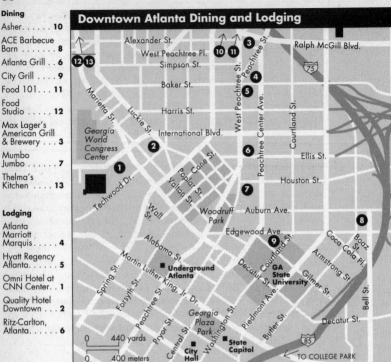

ingredients and dishes in fresh ways. The influx of Asian immigrants makes Atlanta the perfect city to sample Thai, Vietnamese, Japanese, and authentic Chinese cuisines.

Downtown

$$$$ ✕ **City Grill.** It's the poshest power-lunch spot in Atlanta and has made
★ the most of its grand location in the elegantly renovated historic Hurt Building. Dinners are prix fixe, and an impressive wine list accompanies the equally impressive menu. ⊠ *50 Hurt Plaza, Downtown,* ☎ *404/524–2489. AE, D, DC, MC, V. Closed Sun. No lunch Sat.*

$$–$$$$ ✕ **Atlanta Grill.** With an outdoor veranda overlooking Peachtree Street, this restaurant in the Ritz-Carlton, Atlanta, has taken dining in the hotel from formal to casual. Chef Peter Zampaglione focuses on regional Southern ingredients and specializes in grilled seafood and game. Savor such Southern culinary artworks as molasses-grilled pork tenderloin and dry-rubbed Carolina chicken. ⊠ *181 Peachtree St., Downtown,* ☎ *404/221–6550. AE, D, DC, MC, V.*

$$–$$$$ ✕ **Food Studio.** No less stylish for being a piece of a former plow fac-
★ tory, the restaurant gleams with high-tech and industrial touches. From the same group that made South City Kitchen a success, the Studio is known for innovative American food—but has added a few more traditional dishes, such as the braised beef short ribs with maple-soy glazed carrots. Desserts range from the parfaitlike frozen lemon-basil bombe to mango mousse. ⊠ *887 W. Marietta St., Studio K-102, King Plow Arts Center, Downtown,* ☎ *404/815–6677. Reservations essential. AE, DC, MC, V. No lunch weekends.*

$$–$$$ ✕ **Mumbo Jumbo.** After you pass both the long bar that skirts the left
★ side of the establishment and the posh clientele, you'll approach sleek young staffers who will conduct you to your table. The menu emphasizes game in cool weather, fish and shellfish in summer, and regional ingredients and locally grown produce year-round. Tempting dishes in-

SOUTHERN FLAVORS

GEORGIA IS AN EXCELLENT PLACE to sample Southern food. In Atlanta and Savannah you'll find restaurants that serve the finest traditional cuisine, as well as more innovative cooking. Remember that Southern food varies widely across the region and even within states. Nothing reflects this more than barbecue, and few culinary differences produce as many passionate opinions. Taste as you travel, and add to the debate.

Locals in Georgia and Mississippi generally prefer tomato-based sauces on ribs or chopped meat—but variations abound. In North Carolina barbecue is chopped pork piled on a bun with hand-cut coleslaw on top. Sauces range from vinegar and pepper (and little else) to Lexington style, with some tomato in the mix. And North Carolinians serve hush puppies (deep-fried ball-shape cornmeal fritters) with barbecue, which, for them, does not generally include ribs. For the rest of the South, the hush puppy is reserved for fried fish, whether fin or shell.

In South Carolina mustard-based barbecue sauces are widely savored, whether on chopped meat or on ribs. In eastern Alabama (and the Florida Panhandle), you'll find a unique white sauce for barbecue. Memphis-style 'cue is famous for its dry rub, although there is also a "wet" style, in which the same spices, moistened, are rubbed on the ribs. In parts of Tennessee, barbecued mutton is traditional.

Prior to the Depression, there were two sorts of cooking in the South—country food and the elegant plantation fare drawn from French and English models. More recent country cooking blends European, African, and Native American styles and has come to be the defining Southern cuisine in most people's minds.

But in the past many an elegant table was set with European-based dishes, especially along the coasts.

Gumbo, the spicy soup that is so clearly from this region, is a more apt metaphor for the South's demographics than the term *melting pot* because the word *gumbo* reflects all that comes to the Southern table (and to Southern culture) from its people. The term is African, from *ngombo*, which meant "okra" in that part of the world. And what would gumbo be without okra? But gumbo is also French: a proper gumbo is based on a *roux*, a sauté of fat and flour cooked to the color of peanut butter. The cook might sauté vegetables for a gumbo, making a kind of *sofrito*, a legacy from the Spanish settlers in the lower part of Louisiana. Using sassafras or filé powder to thicken gumbo is a legacy of Southern Native Americans.

One defining ingredient in Southern cooking is corn—another Native American legacy. Parch the corn with lye, which swells the grains, and you get hominy. Grind the corn, white or yellow, and you have grits. Sift the grits, and you have cornmeal for making corn bread, fluffy spoon bread, corn pone, hoecakes, hush puppies, johnnycake (or Native American "journey" cake). Ferment the grain, and you get corn whiskey, also known as white lightning or moonshine (and arguably like Southern grappa).

When traveling in Georgia and the rest of the South, you'll find the area's diversity on its tables. Many of the region's chefs use the traditional ingredients to craft "new" Southern dishes as a way of restoring that sense of elegant dining to the region's cuisine. Others wouldn't get near that sort of style, preferring to do the original dishes proud. Take your pick: either way you'll dine divinely.

clude braised hen-of-the-woods mushrooms with roasted tomatoes and caramelized garlic; braised rabbit legs with goat-cheese macaroni; and sautéed halibut with fennel salad and smoked-eel butter. ⊠ *89 Park Pl., Downtown,* ☎ *404/523–0330. Reservations essential. AE, D, DC, MC, V. No lunch weekends.*

$–$$ ✕ **ACE Barbecue Barn.** Delicious ribs and chopped rib tips, baked chicken and dressing, and sweet-potato pie are the draws at this slightly worn down-home restaurant. It's near the Martin Luther King Jr. Center. ⊠ *30 Bell St. NE, Sweet Auburn,* ☎ *404/659–6630. No credit cards. Closed Tues.*

$–$$ ✕ **Max Lager's American Grill & Brewery.** Line up a tasting of the house brews—the pale ale and brown ale are tops—and then order the Gulf Coast gumbo, the "Maximum" T-bone (an 18-ounce steak), or one of the popular specialty pizzas. This lively brewpub near the city's major high-rise buildings is hopping after business hours. The pub has its own root and ginger beers, which are brewed here. ⊠ *320 Peachtree St., Downtown,* ☎ *404/525–4400. AE, D, DC, MC, V.*

$ ✕ **Thelma's Kitchen.** After losing her original location to the Centennial Olympic Park, Thelma Grundy moved her operation down the road to the street level of the somewhat renovated Roxy Hotel. Brighter, spiffier, and more cheerful than the earlier spot, it has okra pancakes, fried catfish, "cold" slaw, and macaroni and cheese, all of which are among the best in town. Thelma's desserts are stellar. ⊠ *768 Marietta St. NW, Downtown,* ☎ *404/688–5855. Reservations not accepted. No credit cards. Closed weekends. No dinner.*

Midtown

$$$–$$$$ ✕ **The Abbey.** Established in 1968, the restaurant is housed in a for-
★ mer church. Stained-glass windows and celestial music played by a harpist in the former choir loft reinforce the headiness. Dishes range from the dramatic Pommery mustard–crusted veal chop to the tandoori-seared tuna. Finish your meal with sweet abandon: the white chocolate–and-roasted banana napoleon is worth losing control over. ⊠ *163 Ponce de Leon Ave., Midtown,* ☎ *404/876–8532. Reservations essential. AE, D, DC, MC, V. No lunch.*

$$$–$$$$ ✕ **Park 75.** It's a swank place and is considered a prominent jewel in
★ Atlanta's culinary crown. Chef Kevin Hickey has created a sumptuous menu, with offerings that include smoked Copper River salmon and baby-chicken stew. Delightfully, it's possible to reserve a table in the middle of the kitchen and observe the master at work while sampling a constant steam of delicacies. ⊠ *75 14th St., Four Seasons Hotel, Midtown,* ☎ *404/253–3840. AE, D, MC, V. No dinner Sun.*

$$$ ✕ **Terra di Siena.** Siena native Ricardo Campinoti imported his love of Tuscany when he opened this fine, upscale Italian bistro, in the same building as the breathtaking Fox Theatre. Entrées include a creative collection of traditional Tuscan dishes, often accented with Southern-style cooking techniques (turning out such dishes as sautéed shrimp with puree of local peas). ⊠ *654 Peachtree St., Midtown,* ☎ *404/885–7505. Reservations essential. AE, MC, V. Closed Mon. No lunch Sat.*

$$–$$$ ✕ **Sotto Sotto.** Atlanta's hot spot close to downtown is an adventurous take on Italian cuisine. The former commercial space hops with young, hip patrons dining on grilled scallops with white beans and truffle oil, tortelli with roasted eggplant and walnuts, spaghetti with sun-dried mullet roe, and utterly perfect *panna cotta* (a custard of cooked cream). ⊠ *313 N. Highland Ave., Inman Park,* ☎ *404/523–6678. Reservations essential. AE, MC, V. No lunch.*

$$–$$$ ✕ **South City Kitchen.** The culinary traditions of South Carolina's Low-country inspire the cooking at this cheerful restaurant. The spare, art-filled interior attracts a hip crowd. This is the place to get fried green

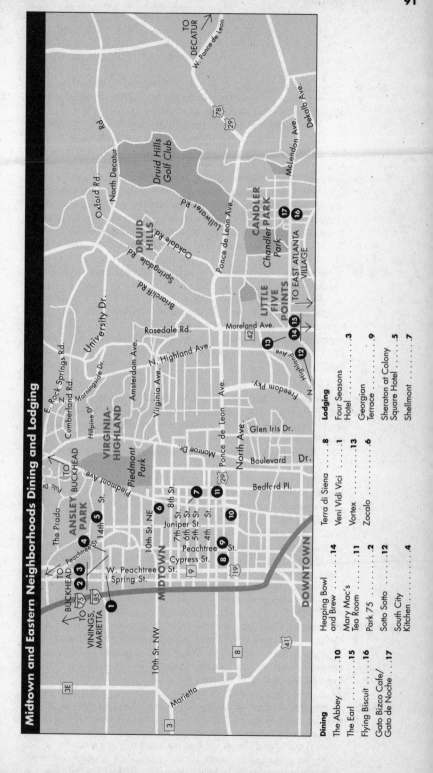

Midtown and Eastern Neighborhoods Dining and Lodging

Dining

The Abbey 10
The Earl 15
Flying Biscuit 16
Gato Bizco Cafe/
Gato de Noche ...17
Heaping Bowl
and Brew 14
Mary Mac's
Tea Room 11
Park 75 2
Sotto Sotto 12
South City
Kitchen 4
Terra di Siena 8
Veni Vidi Vici 1
Vortex 13
Zocalo 6

Lodging

Four Seasons
Hotel 3
Georgian
Terrace 9
Sheraton at Colony
Square Hotel 5
Shellmont 7

tomatoes with goat cheese, she-crab soup, or buttermilk fried chicken. The chef prepares catfish in many intriguing ways. Crab hash, served with poached eggs and chive hollandaise, is a classic. Do not skip the chocolate pecan pie. ⊠ *1144 Crescent Ave., Midtown,* ☎ *404/873–7358. AE, MC, V.*

$$–$$$ ✕ **Veni Vidi Vici.** Gleaming woods, contemporary styling, and an out-
★ door boccie court and dining patio create the perfect place for an indulgent Italian meal. Start with *piatti piccoli* (savory appetizers), then try one of the following: beef tenderloin, rack of lamb, or the excellent osso buco. Gnocchi with Gorgonzola is another favorite, or order one of the fragrant rotisserie meats. ⊠ *41 14th St., Midtown,* ☎ *404/875–8424. AE, D, DC, MC, V. No lunch weekends.*

$$ ✕ **Zocalo.** Come to this inviting open-air patio restaurant—warmed
★ in the frigid winter months by giant heaters—if you want some of the best Mexican food in town. Spicy *chipotle*-pepper shrimp and creamy *poblano*-pepper soup are delicious proof of the chef's culinary prowess. The bar has an excellent selection of epicurean tequilas. ⊠ *187 10th St., Midtown,* ☎ *404/249–7576. Reservations not accepted. AE, D, MC, V.*

$–$$ ✕ **Mary Mac's Tea Room.** Local celebrities and ordinary folk line up for the country-fried steak, fried chicken, and fresh vegetables. Here, in the Southern tradition, lunch is called "dinner," and the evening meal is referred to as "supper." Waitresses will call you "honey" and pat your arm to assure you that everything's all right. It's a great way to experience Southern food and hospitality all at once. ⊠ *224 Ponce de Leon Ave., Midtown,* ☎ *404/876–1800. No credit cards. No dinner Sun.*

Buckhead

$$$$ ✕ **Dining Room, The Ritz-Carlton, Buckhead.** If you like the style of an old gentlemen's club, you'll appreciate this elegant, restrained room, with formal hunt scenes on the walls, romantic lighting, and generously spaced tables. Chef Bruno Menarch ensures a delectable daily assortment of creative options on the prix-fixe menu. Specialties have included veal loin with lemongrass, tomato confit, and chanterelle mushrooms. ⊠ *3434 Peachtree Rd., Buckhead,* ☎ *404/237–2700. Reservations essential. Jacket and tie. AE, D, DC, MC, V. Closed Sun. No lunch.*

$$$$ ✕ **Seeger's.** Celebrated chef Guenter Seeger, formerly at the Dining
★ Room in the Ritz-Carlton, presides over this sophisticated, sleek place. Some find it a bit noisy, but after the first fragrant, flavorful bite you'll forget about the volume. The smoked salmon with horseradish cream and the grilled squab are outstanding. Local inspirations include sweet-onion tarts with pecan sauce. Your prix-fixe options are a vegetable menu and, in season, an entire menu based on truffles. ⊠ *111 W. Paces Ferry Rd., Buckhead,* ☎ *404/846–9779. Reservations essential. Jacket required. AE, D, DC, MC, V. Closed Sun. No lunch.*

$$$–$$$$ ✕ **Morton's.** This Chicago transplant sticks to quintessential steakhouse
★ classics: filet Oskar, a filet mignon topped with lump crab meat, fresh asparagus, and béarnaise sauce; and fillet Diane, which is topped with sautéed mushrooms and a demiglace sauce. Morton's is in the Peachtree Lenox building. ⊠ *3379 Peachtree Rd., Buckhead,* ☎ *404/816–6535. AE, D, MC, V. No dinner Sun.*

$$–$$$ ✕ **Aria.** Here, chef Gerry Klaskala is known for making masterful en-
★ trées of rustic heartiness that also appeal to the epicurean palate. His signature talent is best captured by his love of "slow foods"—braises, stews, steaks, and chops cooked over a roll-top French grill. This makes for very weighty plates, but still Klaskala lovingly flavors every ounce. For example, pork shoulder is presented with a delicious balsamic reduction and Gorgonzola polenta. Don't miss renowned

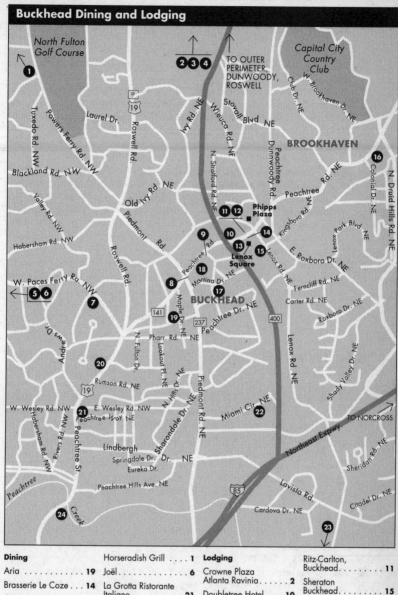

Buckhead Dining and Lodging

Dining

Aria **19**

Brasserie Le Coze . . . **14**

Canoe **5**

Colonnade
Restaurant **23**

Dining Room,
The Ritz-Carlton,
Buckhead **12**

Eclipse di Luna **22**

Horseradish Grill **1**

Joël **6**

La Grotta Ristorante
Italiano **21**

Meritage **17**

Morton's **9**

Oh...Maria! **8**

Seeger's **7**

Toulouse **24**

Vino! **20**

Lodging

Crowne Plaza
Atlanta Ravinia **2**

Doubletree Hotel . . . **10**

Embassy Suites
Hotel **18**

Holiday Inn Select
Atlanta Perimeter **4**

Ritz-Carlton,
Buckhead **11**

Sheraton
Buckhead **15**

Sierra Suites Atlanta
Brookhaven **16**

Swissôtel **13**

W Atlanta **3**

pastry chef Kathryn King's mouthwatering dessert menu, including Valrhona chocolate cream pie with Drambuie sauce. ⊠ *490 E. Paces Ferry Rd., Buckhead,* ☎ *404/233–7673. Reservations essential. Jacket and tie. AE, D, DC, MC, V. Closed Sun. No lunch.*

$$–$$$ ✕ **Brasserie Le Coze.** This bistro draws raves from critics and foodies
★ alike. Shoppers stream into this glowing, wood-paneled space with comfortable banquettes, and once they try the comforting bistro-style fare, they forget they're in a mall. Traditional dishes include coq au vin, and seared codfish in a white-bean stew. *Vacherin* (meringue rings placed on a pastry base) filled with ice cream is one of many extravagant desserts. ⊠ *3393 Peachtree Rd., Lenox Sq., near Neiman Marcus, Buckhead,* ☎ *404/266–1440. AE, DC, MC, V. Closed Sun.*

$$–$$$ ✕ **Canoe.** This popular spot on the banks of the Chattahoochee River
★ brims with appreciative patrons nearly all day. In nice weather the outdoor dining spaces allow the best view of the river. The restaurant has built a national reputation based on such dishes as herb-crusted grouper with roasted sweet-corn succotash, oak-roasted duck breast, and slow-roasted Carolina rabbit. Sunday brunch is superb. ⊠ *4199 Paces Ferry Rd. NW, Buckhead,* ☎ *770/432–2663. AE, D, DC, MC, V.*

$$–$$$ ✕ **Horseradish Grill.** Once a red horse barn, this establishment is now
★ painted gray with white trim and has arched windows across the front that brighten the space. It may be a little noisy, but it's a must for authentic, if upscale, Southern dishes. The menu changes seasonally, with entrées ranging from autumn venison stew to "crispy-spit" roasted duck. ⊠ *4320 Powers Ferry Rd., Buckhead,* ☎ *404/255–7277. AE, D, DC, MC, V.*

$$–$$$ ✕ **Joël.** Chef Joël Antunes, former executive chef at the heralded Din-
★ ing Room in the Ritz Carlton Buckhead, spices up this chic French brasserie with Mediterranean and Asian influences. Signature entrées include roast lobster with fried vermicelli, snow peas, and Thai sauce; braised beef ribs with tamarind and rutabaga; and sea bass with tomato lasagna and tapenade. ⊠ *3290 Northside Pkwy., Berkeley Park,* ☎ *404/233–3500. Reservations essential. AE, DC, MC, V. Closed Sun.–Mon.*

$$–$$$ ✕ **La Grotta Ristorante Italiano.** Overlook the location in the ground level of a posh condominium—though the burgundy-and-cream interior is elegant—and know that this is an expertly managed dining room. Old northern Italian favorites are the core of the menu. Savor prosciutto with grilled pears and mascarpone cheese, then try the potato-and-herb gnocchi tossed in a crayfish cream sauce. ⊠ *2637 Peachtree Rd., Buckhead,* ☎ *404/231–1368. Reservations essential. AE, D, DC, MC, V. Closed Sun. No lunch.*

$$–$$$ ✕ **Meritage.** In this snazzy space you'll find a serious menu of contemporary American food, prepared with tremendous care. Of note is pumpkin seed–encrusted sea scallops, crab-stuffed salmon wrapped in rice paper, and roasted quail stuffed with white truffles. A lengthy dessert list includes similarly elaborate creations. ⊠ *3125 Piedmont Rd., Buckhead,* ☎ *404/231–6700. AE, D, DC, MC, V. Closed Sun. No lunch.*

$$–$$$ ✕ **Vino!** The Mediterranean colors here impart warmth and intimacy, which is perfect for enjoying tapas and the good selection of wines by the glass (and you also can eat a full meal). Tapas ($5–$6) are traditional; among the best are shaved fennel with citrus and olive oil, and Spanish serrano ham (similar to prosciutto). ⊠ *2900 Peachtree Rd., Buckhead,* ☎ *404/816–0511. AE, DC, MC, V. Closed Sun.*

$–$$$ ✕ **Oh . . . Maria!** It's touted as Atlanta's premiere upscale Mexican eatery,
★ so don't expect to find plastic baskets of chips on your table. This gorgeously decorated restaurant makes good on its mission to introduce the South to sumptuous Mexican haute cuisine, with such offerings as lobster sautéed in regional herbs topped with chipotle-pecan salsa and

red mole poblano. ⊠ *3167 Peachtree Rd., Buckhead,* ☎ *404/261–2032. AE, D, DC, MC, V.*

$$ ✕ **Toulouse.** Open spaces enclosed by warm, rough-brick walls characterize this attractive room. The food is inspired—in theory—by the cooking of southwestern France, but in execution it clearly draws on some American influences. The country potato soup is a perfect cold-weather meal. Especially wonderful are the roast chicken, duck confit with blueberry vinaigrette, and crème brûlée. ⊠ *2293B Peachtree Rd., Peachtree Walk, Buckhead,* ☎ *404/351–9533. AE, DC, MC, V. No lunch.*

$–$$ ✕ **Colonnade Restaurant.** For traditional Southern food—oyster stew, ham steak, and turkey and dressing—insiders head here, an Atlanta institution since 1927. The interior, with patterned carpeting, is a classic version of a 1950s restaurant. ⊠ *1879 Cheshire Bridge Rd., Buckhead,* ☎ *404/874–5642. Reservations not accepted. No credit cards.*

$ ✕ **Eclipse di Luna.** This hot spot has captured the fancy of twen-
★ tysomethings, who flock here on weekends. Lunch is sandwiches and salads, and evening fare is tapas ($3) and wine by the glass. *Patatas bravas* (potatoes with olive oil and spicy sauce), tender braised chicken with saffron and garlic, and flan will take you to Castile. The restaurant is tucked at the very end of Miami Circle, a to-the-trade-only design center. ⊠ *764 Miami Circle, Buckhead,* ☎ *404/846–0449. AE, DC, MC, V. Closed Mon.*

Inman Park, Candler Park, and East Atlanta Village

$–$$ ✕ **The Earl.** A scrappy yet delightful addition to the East Atlanta bar scene, the Earl offers a hearty menu of classic pub food, as well as a few entrées that are more innovative. Don't let the comically eclectic interior fool you: the food is surprisingly substantial and well prepared, considering the no-nonsense digs. There's a casual stage in the corner, too—this one of the city's favorite rock venues. ⊠ *488 Flat Shoals Ave., East Atlanta Village, East Atlanta,* ☎ *404/522–3950. AE, MC, V.*

$–$$ ✕ **Flying Biscuit.** There's an hour-long wait on weekends for the big,
★ fluffy biscuits. Other huge hits at this garage sale–decorated spot include egg dishes, turkey sausage, and bean cakes with tomatillo salsa, as well as a side item called Pudge, a dense mound of mashed potatoes and rosemary. Note that the formerly all-day breakfast café now serves dinner, too. ⊠ *1655 McLendon Ave., Candler Park,* ☎ *404/687–8888. Reservations not accepted. AE, D, MC, V.*

$–$$ ✕ **Gato Bizco Cafe/Gato de Noche.** It's weird but it works. This pocket of a café is actually two restaurants in one. By day it's the popular breakfast-and-lunch joint Gato Bizco, where people line up for fabulous omelets or hearty midday fare. Then Wednesday–Saturday evenings the place transforms into Gato de Noche, a culinary incubator for chef Mike Geier's whimsical creations. Try fresh salmon cakes with papaya salsa or a coconut red-curry rice bowl with fresh garden vegetables. At either time you're in for a treat. ⊠ *1660 McClendon Ave., Candler Park,* ☎ *404/371–0889. AE, MC, V. Closed Mon.–Tues. No dinner Sun.*

$–$$ ✕ **Heaping Bowl and Brew.** Trendoids and scenesters from all over town are devoted to this eatery in ultrahip East Atlanta Village. Meals come in big bowls, be it noodles, seared salmon, mashed potatoes, or southwestern-style chicken. Specials often depend on what's growing fresh in the garden that day. ⊠ *469 Flat Shoals Ave., East Atlanta Village, East Atlanta,* ☎ *404/523–8030. AE, D, MC, V.*

$–$$ ✕ **Vortex.** Talk about a funky design: you enter this restaurant through
★ the mouth of a massive, spiral-eyed skull. The restaurant's motto, printed on waitstaff T-shirts, is IT'S NEVER TOO LATE TO START WASTING YOUR LIFE. But beyond the shenanigans are tasty delights, particularly the hefty burgers. A little-known perk is the bar's amazingly extensive

selection of top-shelf liquor, consistently voted "Best in Atlanta" by the city's namesake magazine. ✉ *438 Moreland Ave., Little Five Points,* ☎ *404/688–1828. AE, MC, V.*

Metro Atlanta

$$$$ ✕ **Asher.** This swank spot serves up a creative prix fixe menu from which diners may opt for such delicacies as grilled rack of venison with African squash purée and lobster wrapped in Savoy cabbage with white truffle oil. The dining room, an inviting alcove filled with unique antiques, is one reason why those in the know consider it one of the most romantic restaurants in the metro area. ✉ *1085 Canton St., Roswell (21 mi north of Atlanta),* ☎ *770/650–9398. AE, D, MC, V. No lunch.*

$–$$$$ ✕ **Hi Life Kitchen & Cocktails.** This hip restaurant 20 mi northeast of downtown Atlanta presents an eclectic menu of American favorites, but devotees swear by the Lobster Menu, a heaping plate of lobster prepared three ways—chilled, steamed, and roasted. The meal ends with the dessert of the day. The design is trendy upscale, with light-wood and wrought-iron accents. ✉ *3380 Holcomb Bridge Rd., Norcross,* ☎ *770/409–0101. AE, MC, V. No lunch weekends.*

$$–$$$ ✕ **The Crab House.** Get your seafood fix here. The menu lists a dizzying variety of fish, along with lobster, crab, and other shell-dressed creatures prepared any number of inventive ways. The seafood-and-salad bar is popular, thanks to its selection of fresh crab, shelled shrimp, Louisiana crawfish, and freshly shucked oysters. For all this, you'll have to drive to Marietta, a suburb 21 mi northwest of Atlanta. ✉ *2175 Cobb Pkwy., Marietta (20 mi northwest of Atlanta),* ☎ *770/955–2722. AE, D, DC, MC, V.*

$$–$$$ ✕ **Lickskillet Farm.** Although the name of this elegantly rustic farmhouse, which General Sherman once used as a hospital, has a name that suggests greasy-spoon down-home cooking, the chefs at Lickskillet run a serious—and commendable—kitchen. Sample such exquisite entrées as pan-flashed salmon, apple-wood-smoked pork chops, and smoked sea scallops. For starters, don't miss the roasted, stuffed Vidalia onion, made from a classic family recipe. ✉ *1380 Old Roswell Rd., Roswell (20 mi north of Atlanta),* ☎ *770/475–6484. AE, D, DC, MC, V. No lunch Sat. and Mon.*

$$–$$$ ✕ **Oscar's.** This friendly, upscale bistro continues to wow both locals and big-city types who don't mind venturing 10 mi south of downtown. Behind the prosaic facade of a former pawn shop, you'll discover a dazzling interior of peppermint-stripe lights, mod tableware, and light-wood furnishings. The inventive menu includes intriguing appetizers—lobster-and-cabbage pockets with shiitake mushrooms and crab-and-avocado *tian* (a Provençal-style gratin). For a main course try the Georgia stuffed trout with Swiss cardoons and melted tomatoes. ✉ *3725 Main St., College Park,* ☎ *404/766–9688. AE, MC, V.*

$$ ✕ **Cafe Alsace.** This tiny culinary enclave in historic downtown Decatur serves estimable (and affordable) French food accented with German touches. Take the tasty spaetzle dishes, created around homemade Alsatian noodles: in the *au saumon* version, the noodles are baked with salmon chunks, garlic, basil, and cheese—and that alone is worth a visit. ✉ *121 E. Ponce de Leon Ave., Decatur (6 mi east of Atlanta),* ☎ *404/373–5622. AE, D, MC, V. Closed Mon. No lunch Sat.*

$$ ✕ **Food 101.** It was a smash hit as soon as it opened, and no wonder, given the gut-filling comfort food—stuffed pork chop with mashed potatoes, gravy, and string beans; and turkey with stuffing, giblet gravy, and cranberry sauce. Wine drinkers especially love this place for its selection of 50 American wines by the glass. ✉ *4969 Roswell Rd., #200, Sandy Springs (6 mi north of Atlanta),* ☎ *404/497–9700. AE, MC, V. No lunch weekends.*

$$ ✕ **Villa Christina.** Look no farther for elegant Italian food with a twist. You enter down a lighted path resplendent with gardens, a waterfall, and a stone bridge. Once inside, you'll see that the dining room doubles as an art gallery, with two murals depicting a glorious Tuscan landscape. From the kitchen comes seared wild striped sea bass on a bed of spinach, and grilled Tuscan veal chops with a sweet-onion brûlée of Parma ham; and the house specialty, Christina's seafood cioppino, a medley of succulent shellfish swimming in a saffron-tomato stew. ✉ *4000 Perimeter Summit Blvd., Dunwoody (14 mi north of Atlanta),* ☎ *404/303–0133. AE, D, DC, MC, V. Closed Sun. No lunch Sat.*

$–$$ ✕ **El Mexica Gourmet.** The owners of El Mexica insist that by sampling the authentic fare from their kitchen you'll learn quickly that Mexican cuisine is not all tacos and enchiladas—though if that's what you're up for, you'll find plenty of that here, too. Alongside those Mexican staples dig into specialties like *carne tampiquena* (charbroiled steak smothered with sautéed onions and peppers) and red snapper Veracruz (panfried with a fresh tomato sauce). ✉ *11060 Alpharetta Hwy., Suite 172 (behind Applebee's), Roswell (20 mi north of Atlanta),* ☎ *770/ 594–8674. AE, MC, V.*

$–$$ ✕ **Watershed.** Indigo Girl Emily Saliers and three of her friends
★ launched this casual restaurant–cum–gift shop. Chef Scott Peacock makes the planet's best shrimp salad, homemade flat bread, chicken salad with white truffles, homemade pimento cheese with sharp cheddar and egg, and lusty desserts—any and all are worth the trip. Consider the Georgia pecan tart with a scrumptious shortbread crust. Also an *enoteca* (wine bar), Watershed sells wine both retail in bottles and by the glass at the comfy bar. When she's not in the recording studio, Saliers makes a fine sommelier and loves to talk about wine. ✉ *406 W. Ponce de Leon Ave., Decatur (6 mi north of Atlanta),* ☎ *404/378–4900. AE, MC, V.*

Lodging

One of America's most popular convention destinations, Atlanta offers plenty of variety in terms of lodgings. More than 76,000 rooms are in metro Atlanta, with about 12,000 downtown, close to the Georgia World Congress Center, Atlanta Civic Center, Atlanta Merchandise Mart, and Omni Coliseum. Other clusters are in Buckhead, in the north I–285 perimeter, and around Hartsfield Atlanta International Airport.

Downtown

$$$–$$$$ 🏨 **Omni Hotel at CNN Center.** The hotel is adjacent to the home of Ted Turner's Cable News Network. The lobby combines traditional and modern accents, with marble floors, Oriental rugs, and exotic floral and plant arrangements. Rooms have large windows and contemporary-style furniture, including a sofa. Guests have access to the Downtown Athletic Club and two small meeting rooms. ✉ *100 CNN Center (by Omni MARTA), Downtown 30305,* ☎ *404/659–0000 or 800/843– 6664,* FAX *404/525–5050,* WEB *www.omnihotels.com. 470 rooms, 15 suites. 2 restaurants, lobby lounge, business services, parking (fee). AE, D, DC, MC, V.*

$$$–$$$$ 🏨 **Ritz-Carlton, Atlanta.** Traditional afternoon tea—served in the inti-
★ mate, sunken lobby beneath an 18th-century chandelier—sets the mood. Notice the 17th-century Flemish tapestry when you enter from Peachtree Street. Some of the most luxurious guest rooms are decorated with marble writing tables, plump sofas, four-poster beds, and white-marble bathrooms. The Atlanta Grill is one of downtown's few outdoor dining spots. ✉ *181 Peachtree St. (opposite Peachtree Center MARTA), Downtown 30303,* ☎ *404/659–0400 or 800/241–3333,*

FAX *404/688–0400,* WEB *www.ritzcarlton.com. 441 rooms, 13 suites. Restaurant, bar, laundry service, business services, parking (fee). AE, D, DC, MC, V.*

\$\$–\$\$\$\$ 🏨 **Atlanta Marriott Marquis.** Immense and coolly contemporary, the building seems to go up forever as you stand under the lobby's huge fabric sculpture that hangs from the skylighted roof 47 stories above. Guest rooms, which open onto this atrium, are decorated in dark greens and neutral shades. Major suites have live plants and fresh flowers; two suites have grand pianos and ornamental fireplaces. ✉ *265 Peachtree Center Ave., Downtown 30303,* ☎ *404/521–0000 or 800/932–2198,* FAX *404/586–6299,* WEB *www.marriott.com. 1,675 rooms, 69 suites. 4 restaurants, indoor-outdoor pool, health club, 2 bars, business services, meeting rooms, parking (fee). AE, D, DC, MC, V.*

\$\$–\$\$\$\$ 🏨 **Hyatt Regency Atlanta.** This was John Portman's first atrium-centered building, and it became the model for his other hotels, including the San Francisco Embarcadero and the Atlanta Marriott Marquis. The blue-bubble top stands out against the Atlanta skyline. Expect the careful service and quality facilities typical of Hyatt hotels. Constructed in 1967, it was the first major hotel to be built downtown since the 1920s. From the exterior the most notable feature is the space-age blue dome crowning the structure, which houses a revolving cocktail lounge. Inside is a spectacular 22-story skylighted atrium, a John Portman trademark, which encompasses a massive aviary and another cocktail lounge beneath a stunning suspended canopy. The exposed glass elevators zipping up and down the length of the atrium are also a Portman trademark. ✉ *265 Peachtree St. (connected by skywalk to Peachtree Center), Downtown 30303,* ☎ *404/577–1234 or 800/233–1234,* FAX *404/588–4137,* WEB *www.hyatt.com. 1,206 rooms, 58 suites. 4 restaurants, pool, health club, bar, business services, parking (fee). AE, D, DC, MC, V.*

\$–\$\$ 🏨 **Quality Hotel Downtown.** This quiet, older downtown hotel, two blocks off Peachtree Street, has a marble lobby with sofas and a grand piano, with paid entertainment. Modest-size rooms are decorated in teal and navy. It's priced reasonably for its location and thus has become popular during conventions due to its proximity to the World Congress Center and the show marts; prices go up when conventions are in town. ✉ *89 Luckie St., Downtown 30303,* ☎ *404/524–7991 or 888/729–7705,* FAX *404/524–0672,* WEB *www.qualityinn.com. 75 rooms. Pool, parking (fee). AE, D, DC, MC, V.*

Midtown

\$\$\$–\$\$\$\$ 🏨 **Four Seasons Hotel.** From the lobby a sweeping staircase leads up to a refined but welcoming bar and to Park 75, the hotel's American-chic dining establishment. Rose-hue marble creates a warm feeling in the public spaces and lounges. Amenities abound throughout—marble bathrooms with extra-large soaking tubs, pale lemon or celadon color schemes, and polished brass chandeliers—and let's not forget their famously comfortable mattresses (Julia Roberts declared on Oprah that her favorite place to relax is in a Four Seasons bed). The hotel prides itself on its immensely courteous staff—a phone call to reception is considered scandalous if it exceeds two rings before it's answered. Stewards and other staff members are on hand—sightlessly—'til the moment you need their help. ✉ *75 14th St., Midtown 30309,* ☎ *404/881–9898 or 800/819–5053,* FAX *404/873–4692,* WEB *www.fourseasons.com. 226 rooms, 18 suites. Restaurant, pool, health club, spa, bar, high-speed Internet, business services, meeting rooms, parking (fee). AE, D, DC, MC, V.*

\$\$–\$\$\$\$ 🏨 **Georgian Terrace.** Spend a night where Enrico Caruso and the Metropolitan Opera stars once lodged. This fine 1911 hotel, across the street from the Fox Theatre, is on the National Register of Historic

Places. From its beginning it has housed the rich and famous, but it fell into disrepair for a few decades—and now has undergone a restoration, with an added matching tower. The lobby is sleek and plush, and breathtaking terraces traverse the exterior, making it one of the most popular wedding-reception venues in the city. All units are suites with balconies (and washer-dryers); they are pastel and plush, providing competent if not luxurious comfort. ⊠ *659 Peachtree St., Midtown 30308,* ☎ *404/897–1991 or 800/651–2316,* FAX *404/724–0642,* WEB *www. thegeorgianterrace.com. 326 suites. Restaurant, kitchens, kitchenettes, pool, health club, convention center, meeting rooms, parking (fee). AE, D, DC, MC, V.*

$$$　🏨 **Sheraton at Colony Square Hotel.** Theatricality and opulence are epitomized by the moodily lighted lobby with overhanging balconies, live piano music, and fresh flowers. Rooms are modern, with muted tones; those on higher floors have city views. The hotel is two blocks from MARTA's Arts Center station and two blocks from the Woodruff Arts Center and the High Museum of Art; it anchors the Colony Square complex of office, residential, and retail buildings. ⊠ *188 14th St., Midtown 30361,* ☎ *404/892–6000 or 800/422–7895,* FAX *404/872– 9192,* WEB *www.starwood.com. 467 rooms, 32 suites. Restaurant, pool, lobby lounge, meeting rooms, parking (fee). AE, D, DC, MC, V.*

INNS AND GUEST HOUSES

$$–$$$$　🏨 **Shellmont.** The house, on the National Register of Historic Places, was named for the shell motif that adorns it. It was designed in 1891 by Massachusetts-born, Atlanta-reared architect Walter T. Downing and has antique stained, leaded, and beveled glass, enhanced by artfully carved woodwork and charming hand-painted stencils. Guest rooms have American-made Victorian-style antiques and CD players. ⊠ *821 Piedmont Ave., Midtown 30306,* ☎ *404/872–9290 or 404/872–5379,* WEB *www.shellmont.com. 5 rooms, 2 suites, 1 carriage house. AE, D, DC, MC, V. BP.*

Buckhead and Outer Perimeter

$$$–$$$$　🏨 **Crowne Plaza Atlanta Ravinia.** You can't beat the convenience—it anchors Atlanta's Perimeter Center and is near several Fortune 500 companies, so it's perfect for convention-center attendees. It's a 10- to 20-minute trip north of Buckhead and downtown, but you don't need to travel far for shopping and other excitement because there is plenty of upscale shopping and dining nearby. All rooms are furnished opulently and have hair dryers and upscale bath amenities. ⊠ *4435 Ashford-Dunwoody Rd., Dunwoody 30346,* ☎ *770/395–7700 or 800/227–6963,* FAX *770/392–9503,* WEB *www.crowneplazaravinia.com. 459 rooms, 36 suites. 3 restaurants, tennis court, indoor pool, gym, hot tub, lounge, Internet, laundry service, free parking. AE, D, DC, MC, V.*

$$$–$$$$　🏨 **Ritz-Carlton, Buckhead.** Decorated with 18th- and 19th-century ★ antiques and art, this is an elegant gem of a hotel. The richly paneled Lobby Lounge is a respite for shoppers from nearby Lenox Square mall and Phipps Plaza; afternoon tea or cocktails are popular here. The Dining Room is one of the city's finest restaurants; don't pass up the Wine Bar, either—the lounge hosts informative wine tastings, which both novices and aficionados attend. The spacious rooms are furnished with traditional reproductions and have luxurious white-marble baths. ⊠ *3434 Peachtree Rd., Buckhead 30326,* ☎ *404/237–2700 or 800/ 241–3333,* FAX *404/239–0078,* WEB *www.ritzcarlton.com. 524 rooms, 29 suites. 3 restaurants, pool, health club, hot tub, bar, parking (fee). AE, D, DC, MC, V.*

$$$–$$$$　🏨 **Swissôtel.** Sleek and efficient, this stunner has a chic, modern glass and white-tile exterior with curved walls and Biedermeier-style interiors. Convenient to Lenox Square mall, a prime shopping and dining

destination, the hotel is popular with business travelers. The restaurant, the Palm, is noted for its steaks. ⊠ *3391 Peachtree Rd., Buckhead 30326,* ☎ *404/365–0065 or 800/253–1397,* ℻ *404/365–8787,* 🖳 *www. swissotel.com. 349 rooms, 16 suites. Restaurant, pool, spa, gym, health club, bar, business services, parking (fee). AE, D, DC, MC, V.*

$$–$$$ 🏨 **Sheraton Buckhead.** This modern, eight-floor hotel has the advantage of being right across from the Lenox Square mall (Shangri-la to Georgians). Rooms have contemporary furnishings; some have a desk and chair, others sofas. All are equipped with amenities, such as hair dryers, coffeemakers, and irons with ironing boards. ⊠ *3405 Lenox Rd., Buckhead 30326,* ☎ *404/261–9250 or 888/625–5144,* ℻ *404/ 848–7391,* 🖳 *www.starwood.com. 355 rooms, 7 suites. Restaurant, pool, bar, parking (fee). AE, D, DC, MC, V.*

$$–$$$ 🏨 **W Atlanta.** An ultrachic member of the W hotel chain, this Perimeter property makes good on its promise to pamper business travelers. Guest rooms are sweepingly large, with oversize wet bars and all the comforts of home (assuming your home is a dazzling showcase of impeccable taste). In your room you'll find a lush terry robe and a coffeemaker complete with the hotel's own brand of specialty coffee. Baths are outfitted with high-end-salon shampoos, conditioners, and soaps. ⊠ *111 Perimeter Center W, Dunwoody 30346,* ☎ *770/396–6800 or 888/625– 5144,* ℻ *770/394–4805,* 🖳 *www.starwood.com/whotels. 252 rooms, 23 suites. Restaurant, pool, gym, hot tub, sauna, lounge, Internet, free parking. AE, D, DC, MC, V.*

$–$$$ 🏨 **Embassy Suites Hotel.** Just blocks from the Phipps Plaza and Lenox Square malls, this modern high-rise offers different kinds of suites— from deluxe presidential (with wet bars) to more basic sleeping- and sitting-room combinations. All rooms open to a 16-story sunlighted atrium towering above the lobby. Rates include afternoon cocktails. ⊠ *3285 Peachtree Rd., Buckhead 30305,* ☎ *404/261–7733 or 800/ 362–2779,* ℻ *404/261–6857,* 🖳 *www.embassysuites.com. 317 suites. Restaurant, indoor pool, gym, parking (fee). AE, D, DC, MC, V. BP.*

$$ 🏨 **Doubletree Hotel.** If the complimentary fresh-baked chocolate-chip cookies that welcome you don't convince you to stay here, maybe the spacious rooms and reasonable rates—given the excellent location— will. The hotel offers complimentary transportation within 2 mi of the hotel and is adjacent to the Buckhead MARTA station. ⊠ *3342 Peachtree Rd., Buckhead 30326,* ☎ *404/231–1234 or 800/222–8733,* ℻ *404/231–5236,* 🖳 *www.doubletree.com. 222 rooms, 8 suites. Restaurant, health club, free parking. AE, D, DC, MC, V.*

$–$$ 🏨 **Holiday Inn Select Atlanta Perimeter.** If frills come second to comfort and familiarity, consider this hotel—which generally caters to the briefcase set—with a superb location in the Perimeter business district. Rooms are reliably appointed with coffeemakers, hair dryers, and work desks. ⊠ *4386 Chamblee-Dunwoody Rd., Dunwoody 30341,* ☎ *770/457–6363 or 800/465–4329,* ℻ *770/936–9592,* 🖳 *www. hiselect.com/atl-perimeter. 250 rooms, 2 suites. Restaurant, pool, gym, lounge, laundry service, free parking. AE, D, DC, MC, V.*

$–$$ 🏨 **Sierra Suites Atlanta Brookhaven.** The feel is modern southwestern—rife with pastel Indian prints—at this comfortable hotel, just 1 mi north of Lenox Square. Cream-and-green color schemes decorate the one-bedroom studio suites with kitchenettes (no ovens). ⊠ *3967 Peachtree Rd., Brookhaven 30319,* ☎ *404/237–9100 or 800/474–3772,* ℻ *404/237–0055,* 🖳 *www.sierrasuites.com. 92 suites. Pool, gym, laundry service. AE, D, DC, MC, V.*

Nightlife and the Arts

The Arts

For the most complete schedule of cultural events, check the *Atlanta Journal-Constitution*'s Friday "Weekend Preview" and Saturday "Leisure" sections. Also available for cultural and entertainment listings is the city's lively and free alternative newsweekly, *Creative Loafing.*

Tickets for the Fox Theatre, Atlanta Civic Center, and other locations are handled by **TicketMaster** (☎ 404/249–6400 or 800/326–4000). **Ticket-X-Press, Inc.** (☎ 404/231–5888) is a good ticket outlet.

CONCERTS

The **Atlanta Symphony Orchestra (ASO),** now under the musical direction of Robert Spano, is now more than a half century old, with 14 Grammy awards to its credit. It performs the fall–spring subscription series in the 1,800-seat Symphony Hall at **Woodruff Arts Center** (✉ 1280 Peachtree St., Midtown, ☎ 404/733–5000). In summer the orchestra regularly plays with big-name popular and country artists in Chastain Park's **outdoor amphitheater** (✉ 4469 Stella Dr., Chastain Park, ☎ 404/733–4800).

Emory University (✉ N. Decatur Rd. at Clifton Rd., Emory, ☎ 404/727–6187, FAX 404/727–6421), an idyllic suburban campus, has four venues where both internationally renowned guest artists and faculty and student groups perform. Expect quality music from various ensembles, including woodwind, brass, jazz, and vocal.

Georgia State University (✉ Art and Music Bldg., Peachtree Center Ave. and Gilmer St., Downtown, ☎ 404/651–4636 or 404/651–3676), with the entrance on Gilmer Street and free parking at the corner of Edgewood and Peachtree Center avenues, sponsors many concerts (about 80%) that are free and open to the public. Performances by faculty, student, and local groups and guest artists focus on jazz and classical. There are also performances at the **Rialto Center for the Performing Arts** (✉ 80 Forsyth St., ☎ 404/651–4727, WEB www.rialtocenter.org), an old movie theater the university turned into a performance venue.

DANCE

The **Atlanta Ballet** (✉ 1400 W. Peachtree St., Midtown, ☎ 404/873–5811), founded in 1929, is the country's oldest continuously operating ballet company. Thanks to artistic director John McFall—who has choreographed such dance greats as Mikhail Baryshnikov and Cynthia Gregory—it has been internationally recognized for its productions of classical and contemporary works. Performances are usually at the Fox Theatre but sometimes take place elsewhere. Artistic director John McFall, only the third in the company's history, brings a constant stream of innovative ideas and vision to the group.

FESTIVALS

The **Atlanta Jazz Festival,** held Memorial Day weekend, gathers the best local, national, and international musicians to give mostly free concerts at Atlanta's Piedmont Park. For information contact the **Atlanta Bureau of Cultural Affairs** (☎ 404/817–6815, FAX 404/817–6827).

The **Montreux/Atlanta International Music Festival** began in 1988, when Atlanta joined with Montreux, Switzerland, to cohost a music festival featuring jazz, blues, gospel, reggae, and classical. The festival typically starts during Labor Day weekend, with performances in Piedmont Park (free) and Chastain Park (expensive). For information contact the **Atlanta Bureau of Cultural Affairs** (☎ 404/817–6815, FAX 404/817–6827).

The **Atlanta Opera** (✉ 728 W. Peachtree St., Midtown, ☎ 404/881–8801 or 800/356–7372) usually mounts four main-stage productions each year from spring through fall at the Fox Theatre. Major roles are performed by national and international guest artists, while the chorus and orchestra come from the local community. Call **TicketMaster** (☎ 404/817–8700) for information.

PERFORMANCE VENUES

Atlanta Civic Center (✉ 395 Piedmont Ave., Midtown, ☎ 404/523–6275) presents touring Broadway musicals, pop music, and dance concerts.

Fox Theatre (✉ 660 Peachtree St., Midtown, ☎ 404/881–2100), a dramatic faux-Moorish theater, is the principal venue for touring Broadway shows and national productions, as well as the home of the Atlanta Opera and the Atlanta Ballet.

Georgia Tech Center for the Performing Arts (✉ 349 FerstDr., Georgia Tech, ☎ 404/894–9600), at the Georgia Institute of Technology, offers performances that run the gamut, from classical to jazz, from dance to theater. The highly regarded student-operated theater, DramaTech, is in the James E. Dull Theatre. There's ample free parking.

Rialto Center for the Performing Arts (✉ 80 Forsyth St., Downtown, ☎ 404/651–4727), developed by Georgia State University in a beautifully renovated and restructured former movie theater, shows film, theater, and dance, as well as musical performances by local and international performers.

Spivey Hall (campus: ✉ 5900 N. Lee St., Morrow, ☎ 770/961–3683) is a gleaming, modern, acoustically magnificent performance center at Clayton College and State University, 15 mi south of Atlanta in Morrow. The hall is considered one of the country's finest concert venues. Internationally renowned musicians perform everything from chamber music to jazz.

Variety Playhouse (✉ 1099 Euclid Ave., Inman Park, ☎ 404/524–7354), a former movie theater, is one of the cultural anchors of the hip Little Five Pointsneighborhood. Its denizens don't don fancy frocks to listen to rock, bluegrass and country, blues, reggae, folk, jazz, and pop.

Woodruff Arts Center (✉ 1280 Peachtree St., Midtown, ☎ 404/733–4200) houses the Alliance Theatre and the Atlanta Symphony Orchestra.

THEATER

Check local newspaper listings for information on the outstanding companies in Atlanta and its suburbs.

Actor's Express (✉ 887 W. Marietta St., Downtown, ☎ 404/607–7469), an acclaimed theater group, presents an eclectic selection of classic and cutting-edge productions in the 150-seat theater of the **King Plow Arts Center** (✉ 887 W. Marietta St., ☎ 404/885–9933, WEB www.kingplow.com), a stylish artists' complex hailed by local critics as a showplace of industrial chic. For an evening of dining and theater, plan dinner at the Food Studio, at the King Plow Arts Center.

Alliance Theatre (✉ 1280 Peachtree St., Midtown, ☎ 404/733–4200), Atlanta's premier professional theater, presents everything, from Shakespeare to the latest Broadway and off-Broadway shows from New York, in the Woodruff Arts Center.

☾ **Atlanta Shakespeare Tavern** (✉ 499 Peachtree St., Midtown, ☎ 404/874–5299) produces plays by the Bard and his peers, as well as by contemporary dramatists. Performances vary in quality but are always fun. The Elizabethan-style playhouse is a tavern, so alcohol and pub-style food are available. It also houses the Kaleidoscope Children's Theater (same phone), which presents classics, such as *The New Adventures of the Three Musketeers,* on most weekends during the day.

14th Street Playhouse (✉ 175 14th St., Midtown, ☎ 404/733–4750 or 404/733–4754) is part of the Woodruff Arts Center. The house has three theaters, a 400-seat main stage, a 200-seat second stage, and an 90-seat third stage, which are rented for special productions. There is no resident company. Musicals, plays, and sometimes opera are presented.

Horizon Theatre Co. (✉ 1083 Austin Ave., Little Five Points, Inman Park, ☎ 404/584–7450) is a professional troupe that was established in 1983; it produces premieres of provocative and entertaining contemporary plays in its 185-seat theater.

Nightlife

The pursuit of entertainment—from Midtown to Buckhead—is known as the "Peachtree shuffle." Atlanta's vibrant nightlife includes everything from coffeehouses to sports bars, from country line dancing to high-energy dance clubs. Atlanta has long been known for having more bars than churches, and in the South that's an oddity.

Most bars and clubs are open seven nights, until 2 AM–4 AM. Those with live entertainment usually charge a cover.

ACOUSTIC

Eddie's Attic (✉ 515B N. McDonough St., Decatur, ☎ 404/377–4976) is a good spot for catching local and some national acoustic, folk, pop, and country-music acts. It has a full bar and restaurant and is right near the Decatur MARTA station. Covers range from $6 to $12.

BARS

The **Beluga Martini Bar** (✉ 3115 Piedmont Rd., Buckhead, ☎ 404/ 869–1090) has caviar, smoked salmon, champagne by the glass, and other light fare in an intimate, comfortable space with live music.

For Irish fun, food, beer, and music (both live and on CD), head to **Irish Bred Pub & Grill** (✉ 94 Upper Pryor St., Downtown, ☎ 404/524– 5722). The food ranges from *boxty* (potato pancakes with savory fillings) to Irish stew made with lamb, cottage pie, and whiskey trifle.

Limerick Junction (✉ 822 N. Highland Ave., Virginia-Highland, ☎ 404/ 874–7147), a lively Irish pub, showcases singers from the large Atlanta community that ably render traditional Irish music, as well as performers from the Old Sod itself. It has a rollicking, good-time feeling about it. Parking is dreadful, so consider a cab. A small cover may be charged.

Manuel's Tavern (✉ 602 N. Highland Ave., Virginia-Highland, ☎ 404/ 525–3447) is a neighborhood saloon where families, politicians, writers, students, and professionals gather to brainstorm and partake of the tavern's menu of pleasantly upscale pub food. When the Atlanta Braves play, the crowd gathers around the wide-screen TVs.

To make it through the door at **Tongue & Groove** (✉ 3055 Peachtree Rd., Buckhead, ☎ 404/261–2325), you must dress up—long dresses for ladies and jackets for men. Live music—sometimes rock, sometimes salsa—alternates with recorded tunes. The light-fare menu is as chic as the sense of style here. Covers range from $5 to $10, depending on the program.

Vortex (✉ 898 Peachtree St., Midtown, ☎ 404/875–1667) has a friendly style, knowledgeable bartenders, live bands, and hearty pub fare, making it a local favorite.

COMEDY

The **Punchline** (⌧ 280 Hilderbrand Dr., Balconies Shopping Center, Sandy Springs, ☎ 404/252–5233), Atlanta's oldest comedy club, books major national acts. The small club is popular, so you need a reservation. Cover charges vary and can be upward of $20 for some acts, but it's usually worth it.

COUNTRY

Buckboard Country Music Showcase (⌧ 2080 Cobb Pkwy., Windy Hill, ☎ 770/955–7340), a 425-seat house, has a large dance floor, pool tables, and two full bars; it serves food of the hamburgers, nachos, and chicken fingers variety. The house band is the Buckboard Bandits, and Nashville-based bands play on Thursday night. The cover charge is $5–$10.

The 44,000-square-ft **Cowboys Concert Hall** (⌧ 1750 N. Roberts Rd., Kennesaw, ☎ 770/426–5006) attracts national talent twice monthly on Friday. On Wednesday, Thursday, Friday, and Sunday, line-dancing classes and couple-dancing lessons are taught. The cover is $5, unless an unusually high-profile act is slated.

GAY AND LESBIAN

Backstreet (⌧ 845 Peachtree St., Midtown, ☎ 404/873–1986), though it draws men and women of all affinities, has been Midtown's mainstay gay club for nearly two decades. Downstairs is the dance floor with recorded music, and upstairs is Charlie Brown's Cabaret, with female impersonators. As the club is open 24 hours, membership is required; quarterly memberships cost $10, entitling cardholders to free admission Sunday through Thursday and $5 covers Friday and Saturday.

JAZZ AND BLUES

Blind Willie's (⌧ 828 N. Highland Ave., Virginia-Highland, ☎ 404/873–2583) showcases New Orleans– and Chicago-style blues that sends crowds into a frenzy. The name honors Blind Willie McTell, a native of Thomson, Georgia, whose original compositions include "Statesboro Blues," made popular by the Macon, Georgia–based Allman Brothers. Cajun and zydeco are also on the agenda from time to time. Cover charges run in the $10 range.

Dante's Down the Hatch (⌧ 3380 Peachtree Rd., Buckhead, ☎ 404/266–1600) is popular for its music and sultry sensibility. Regular entertainers include the Paul Mitchell Trio, which conjures silky-smooth jazz in the "hold" of a make-believe sailing ship.

Fuzzy's Place (⌧ 2015 N. Druid Hills Rd., Druid Hills, ☎ 404/321–6166), a crowded and smoke-filled neighborhood bar, begins the day by serving lunch to the denizens of nearby office buildings. By night it's a restaurant with a surprisingly sophisticated menu, sports bar, and blues room. The finest local talent holds forth on the stage, including the venerable Francine Reed, one of Atlanta's favorite entertainers. There's usually no cover.

Sambuca Jazz Cafe (⌧ 3102 Piedmont Rd., Buckhead, ☎ 404/237–5299), with decent dining, a lively bar, and good live jazz, attracts a trendy young set.

Whiskers (⌧ 8371 Roswell Rd., in a shopping center at Northridge Rd., Sandy Springs, ☎ 770/992–7445) hosts blues and rock groups, with some of the best local talent. There's no cover.

ROCK

Masquerade (⌧ 695 North Ave., Poncey-Highland, ☎ 404/577–8178) is a grunge hangout with music, from disco to techno, from industrial rock to swing. Basic bar food is available. The mix of people reflects the club's three separate spaces, dubbed Heaven, Hell, and Purgatory. The cover is $2–$10.

Smith's Olde Bar (⊠ 1578 Piedmont Ave., Ansley Park, ☎ 404/875-1522) schedules different kinds of talent, both local and regional, in its acoustically fine performance space. Food is available in the downstairs restaurant. Covers vary depending on the act but are usually $5–$10.

Star Community Bar (⊠ 437 Moreland Ave., Inman Park, ☎ 404/681-9018) is highly recommended for those who enjoy garage bands and rockabilly. Bands are featured almost nightly, with covers varying depending on the act. The bar is fully equipped, with an all-Elvis jukebox and an Elvis shrine that must be seen to be believed.

Outdoor Activities and Sports

Participant Sports

At almost any time of the year, in parks, private clubs, and neighborhoods throughout the city, you'll find Atlantans pursuing everything from tennis to soccer to rollerblading. **Atlanta Sports & Fitness** magazine (☎ 404/843–2257), available free at many health clubs and sports and outdoors stores, is a good link to Atlanta's athletic community. Pick up **Georgia Athlete** at gyms and sports stores if you need a guide to individual sporting events.

BIKING AND ROLLERBLADING

Piedmont Park (⊠ Piedmont Ave. between 10th St. and the Prado, Piedmont Park) is closed to traffic and is popular for rollerblading and other recreational activities. **Skate Escape** (⊠ 1086 Piedmont Ave., across from the park, Midtown, ☎ 404/892–1292) rents bikes and skates.

GOLF

Golf is enormously popular here, as the large number of courses attest. The only public course within sight of downtown Atlanta is the **Bobby Jones Golf Course** (⊠ 384 Woodward Way, Buckhead, ☎ 404/355–1009), named after the famed golfer and Atlanta native and occupying a portion of the site of the Battle of Peachtree Creek. Despite having some of the city's worst fairways and greens, the immensely popular 18-hole, par-71 course is always crowded. At Chastain Park, the 18-hole, par-71 **North Fulton Golf Course** (⊠ 216 W. Wieuca Rd., Sandy Springs, ☎ 404/255–0723) has one of the best layouts and lies within the I–285 perimeter.

Stone Mountain Park (⊠ U.S. 78, Stone Mountain, ☎ 770/498–5715) has two courses. Stonemont, an 18-hole, par-72 course with several challenging and scenic holes, is the better of the two. The other course, Lakemont, is also 18-hole, par 72.

JOGGING AND RUNNING

Chattahoochee National Recreation Area contains different parcels of land that lie in 16 separate units spread along the banks of the Chattahoochee River, much of which has been protected from development. The area is crisscrossed by 70 mi of trails. ⊠ 1978 Island Ford Pkwy., Roswell, ☎ 770/399–8070. ☉ Daily 7–7.

TENNIS

Bitsy Grant Tennis Center (⊠ 2125 Northside Dr., Buckhead, ☎ 404/609–7193), named for one of Atlanta's best-known players, is the area's best public facility, with 13 clay courts (6 of which are lighted) and 10 lighted hard courts. Charges are $2 per person per hour for the hard courts during the day and $2.50 at night (courts close around

10 PM), $3–$3.50 for the clay courts, which close around 7 PM. The clubhouse closes at 8 PM.

Piedmont Park, Atlanta's most popular park, has 12 lighted hard courts. Access the tennis center from Park Drive off Monroe Drive; even though the sign says DO NOT ENTER, the security guard will show you the parking lot. Courts are always open, but personnel keep specific hours. Costs are $1.50 per person per hour before 6 PM and $1.75 after 6. ⊠ *Piedmont Ave. between 10th St. and the Prado, Midtown.* ☎ FAX *404/853–3461.* ☉ *Weekdays 9–9, weekends 9:30–6.*

Spectator Sports

BASEBALL

Major League Baseball's best overall team the past decade, the **Atlanta Braves** (⊠ Turner Field, I–75/85, Exit 246 [Fulton St.]; I–20, westbound Exit 58A [Capitol Ave.], eastbound Exit 56B [Windsor St./Spring St.], Downtown, ☎ 404/522–7630) play in Turner Field, formerly the Olympic Stadium.

BASKETBALL

The **Atlanta Hawks** (⊠ Philips Arena, 1 CNN Center, Downtown, ☎ 404/827–3800) had a proud Olympics moment in '96 when then-coach Lenny Wilkens was selected to head the U.S. Olympic men's basketball team in Atlanta.

FOOTBALL

The **Atlanta Falcons** (⊠ Georgia Dome, 1 Georgia Dome Dr., Downtown, ☎ 404/223–9200, WEB www.atlantafalcons.com), currently under coach Dan Reeves, have made the playoffs seven times in their history.

HOCKEY

The National Hockey League's young **Atlanta Thrashers** (⊠ Philips Arena, 1 CNN Center, Downtown, ☎ 404/827–5300, WEB www.atlantathrashers.com) debuted during the 1999–2000 season. Named for the state bird, the brown thrasher, the team is backed by Atlanta's sports and media mogul Ted Turner.

Shopping

Atlanta's department stores, specialty shops, large enclosed malls, and antiques markets draw shoppers from across the Southeast. Most stores are open Monday–Saturday 10–9, Sunday noon–6. Many downtown stores close Sunday. Sales tax is 7% in the city of Atlanta and Fulton County and 6%–7% in the suburbs.

Shopping Centers

Brookwood Square (⊠ 2140 Peachtree Rd., Buckhead) is an arrangement of unusual shops, including the Vespermann Gallery and the Piano Gallery, Atlanta's Steinway dealership.

Buckhead, a village with many specialty shops and strip malls, is no minor shopping destination. At Peachtree Plaza, at the intersection of Peachtree Road and Mathieson Drive, you'll find Beverly Bremer's Silver Shop, devoted to fine antique silver, and Irish Crystal Co., offering fine cut glass and linens. Down Maple Drive off Peachtree Road you'll find Yesteryear, dealing in antique books, next to the Atlanta Guitar Center. Boutiques and gift shops, and some fine restaurants, line Grandview Avenue (off Peachtree Road), and another similar collection runs down East Shadowlawn Avenue. East Village Square (Buckhead Avenue and Bolling Way) has art galleries and restaurants. Across from Lenox Square, the Around Lenox Shopping Center includes Tower Records–Video–Books. Andrews Square, on East Andrews

Drive, is a good conglomeration of shops, eateries, nightspots, and galleries. Next to it, Cates Center has similar stores.

Lenox Square mall (⊠ 3393 Peachtree Rd., Buckhead, ☎ 404/233–6767, WEB www.shopsimon.com), one of Atlanta's oldest and most popular shopping centers, has branches of Neiman Marcus, Rich's (the regional department store), Crate & Barrel, and Macy's looming next to specialty shops such as Geode (fine art jewelry) and Mori (luggage and travel gifts). You'll do better at one of the several good restaurants here—even for a quick meal—than at the food court.

Peachtree Center Mall (⊠ 231 Peachtree St., ☎ 404/524–3787) does steady business. Stores here are chiefly specialty shops, such as International Records and Tapes, the Architectural Book Center, and the Atlanta International Museum gift shop.

Perimeter Mall (⊠ 4400 Ashford-Dunwoody Rd., Dunwoody), known for upscale family shopping, has Nordstrom, the High Museum of Art Gift Shop, Gap Kids, and the Nature Company, as well as branches of Rich's, Sears Roebuck, and JCPenney, and a good food court.

Phipps Plaza (⊠ 3500 Peachtree Rd., Buckhead, ☎ 404/262–0992 or 800/810–7700, WEB www.shopsimon.com) has branches of Tiffany & Co., Saks Fifth Avenue, Birmingham-based Parisian, Lord & Taylor, and Abercrombie & Fitch alongside such shops as Skippy Musket (unique jewelry, collectibles, and decorative items for the home).

Underground (⊠ 50 Upper Alabama St., Downtown, ☎ 404/523–2311) has galleries, such as African Pride, with objets d'art from Africa; specialty shops, including Hats Under Atlanta; and Habersham Vineyard & Winery, a tasting room for Georgia wines. The classic chicory-laced New Orleans coffee and beignets at Café du Monde are the perfect way to refuel.

Outlets

The interstate highways leading to Atlanta have discount malls similar to those found throughout the country. Worth noting is the huge cluster around both sides of Exit 149 off I–85, 60 mi north of the city. Also, the **North Georgia Premium Outlets** mall (⊠ 800 Rte. 400, at Dawson Forest Rd., Dawsonville, ☎ 706/216–3609) is worth the 45 minutes it takes to get there from Atlanta's northern perimeter. This shopping center has more than 140 stores, including Williams-Sonoma for cookware; OshKosh B'gosh, a clothing store for children; Music for a Song, dealing in discount CDs and tapes; Stone Mountain Handbags, specializing in quality leather goods; and numerous designer outlet shops not found in most malls.

Specialty Shops

ANTIQUES

Buckhead has several antiques shops, most of them along or near Peachtree Road; expect rare goods and high prices here. Venture into Virginia-Highland and the city's suburban towns to find all sorts of treasures.

Bennett Street (⊠ 116 Bennett St., Buckhead, ☎ 404/352–4430, WEB www.buckhead.org/bennettstreet) has art galleries, including Out of the Woods; antiques shops, such as Kelim; and a good restaurant, **Fratelli di Napoli** (⊠ 2101B Tula St., Buckhead, ☎ 404/351–1533), making it easy to spend an entire day here. The Stalls on Bennett Street is a good antiques market.

Chamblee Antique Row, at Peachtree Road and Broad Street in the suburban town of Chamblee just north of Buckhead and about 10 mi north of downtown, is a browser's delight. For information contact the Chamblee Antique Dealers Association (☎ 770/458–1614, WEB www. antiquerow.com).

Little Five Points (✉ Moreland and Euclid Aves., Inman Park) attracts "junking" addicts, who find happiness in Atlanta's version of Greenwich Village, characterized by vintage clothing stores, art galleries, used-record and -book shops, and some stores that defy description.

Miami Circle, off Piedmont Road, is an upscale enclave for antiques and decorative arts lovers. Drop in for a snack at Eclipse di Luna (✉ Miami Circle, Buckhead, ☎ 404/846–0449).

Stone Mountain Village (✉ Main St., Stone Mountain, ☎ 770/879–4971 for visitor center) is a 19th-century village beside a railroad track at the foot of Stone Mountain. Storefronts are exquisitely decorated at holiday time. Shops of note include **Stone Mountain Handbags Factory Store** (☎ 770/498–1316), which sells designer bags, such as Coach and Dooney & Bourke, at discount prices. **Stone Mountain General Store** (☎ 770/469–9331) is a quaint outpost offering bulk items, handmade crafts, and nickel candy. The village is 17 mi from downtown. For a quick snack have a coffee milkshake at **Continental Park Café** (✉ 941 Main St., Stone Mountain, ☎ 770/413–6448).

2300 Peachtree Road is one of Buckhead's most stylish complexes—it has more than 25 antiques shops, art galleries, and enough home furnishing stores to fill multiple mansions (✉ just north of Midtown, near Peachtree Memorial Dr. intersection, Buckhead).

Virginia-Highland is one of the city's gentrified areas, full of art galleries, restaurants, fashionable boutiques, antiques shops, and bookstores. Atlanta designer **Bill Hallman** (✉ 792 N. Highland Ave., Virginia-Highland, ☎ 404/876–6055) showcases his own designs at his eponymous boutique. There's lots of memorabilia from **20th Century Antiques** (✉ 1044 N. Highland Ave., Virginia-Highland, ☎ 404/892–2065).

ART GALLERIES

The city bursts with art galleries—some well established, others new, some conservative, others cutting edge. For more information on the Atlanta art gallery scene, including openings and location maps, consult *Museums & Galleries* (☎ 770/992–7808), a magazine distributed free at welcome centers and select area galleries.

Fay Gold Gallery (✉ 247 Buckhead Ave., East Village Sq., Buckhead, ☎ 404/233–3843) displays works by nationally renowned contemporary artists. **Jackson Fine Art Gallery** (✉ 3115 E. Shadowlawn Ave., Buckhead, ☎ 404/233–3739) exhibits fine art photography. **Modern Primitive** (✉ 1393 N. Highland Ave., Virginia-Highland, ☎ 404/892–0556) has a fascinating assembly of folk and visionary art from around the state and the region. **Marcia Wood Gallery** (✉ 1831 Peachtree St., Buckhead, ☎ 404/351–5709) shows exquisite original paintings by such notable artists as Daniel Troppy and Ruth Laxson. **Vespermann Gallery** (✉ 2140 Peachtree Rd., Brookwood Sq., Buckhead, ☎ 404/350–9698) has lovely handblown glass objects.

BOOKS

Chapter 11 (✉ 6237 Roswell Rd., Sandy Springs, ☎ 404/256–5518) is a great place to find recently published titles at good prices. **Yesteryear** (✉ 3201 Maple Dr., Buckhead, ☎ 404/237–0163) is the destination of choice for antiquarians. Its strengths include military history, Georgiana, and old cookbooks.

FOOD

DeKalb Farmers Market (✉ 3000 E. Ponce de Leon Ave., Decatur, ☎ 404/377–6400) has 175,000 square ft of exotic fruits, cheeses, seafood, sausages, breads, and delicacies from around the world. The cafeteria-style buffet, with a selection of earthy and delicious hot foods and salads, alone is worth the trip. **East 48th St. Market** (✉ 2462 Jett Ferry Rd., at Mt. Vernon Rd., Williams at Dunwoody Shopping Center, Dunwoody, ☎ 770/392–1499) sells Italian deli meats, fabulous breads, cheeses, and Italian prepared foods. Shop at **Eatzi's Market & Bakery** (✉ 3221 Peachtree Rd., Buckhead, ☎ 404/237–2266) for prepared foods, imported cheeses, great breads, and fine wines. The healthwise can take comfort at **Whole Foods Market** (✉ 2111 Briarcliff Rd., Druid Hills, ☎ 404/634–7800), with a dizzying amount of additive- and pesticide-free foods and baked goods.

Atlanta A to Z

To research prices, get advice from other travelers, and book travel arrangements, visit www.fodors.com.

AIR TRAVEL TO AND FROM ATLANTA
CARRIERS

Atlanta is served by AirTran, America West, American, Atlantic Southeast Airlines, Continental, Delta, GP Express, Markair, Midwest Express, National, Northwest, TWA, United, and US Airways, as well as many international carriers.

AIRPORTS AND TRANSFERS
Hartsfield Atlanta International Airport is 13 mi south of downtown.
➤ AIRPORT INFORMATION: **Hartsfield Atlanta International Airport** (✉ 6000 N. Terminal Pkwy., Hapeville, ☎ 404/530–6600, WEB www.atlanta-airport.com).

AIRPORT TRANSFER

Atlanta Airport Shuttle operates vans every quarter hour between 7 AM and 11 PM daily. The downtown trip, $14 one-way, $22 round-trip, takes about 20 minutes and stops at major hotels. Vans also go to the Buckhead/Lenox area: $20 one-way, $30 round-trip.

If your luggage is light, take MARTA (Metropolitan Atlanta Rapid Transit Authority) high-speed trains between the airport and downtown and other locations. Trains operate 5 AM–1 AM weekdays and 6 AM–12:30 AM weekends. The trip downtown takes about 15 minutes to the Five Points station, and the fare is $1.75.

From the airport to downtown the taxi fare is $22 for one person, $26 for two, and $30 for three or more, including tax. From the airport to Buckhead, the fare is $35 for one, $36 for two, and $39 for three or more. With a reasonable advance reservation, Carey-Executive Limousine will provide 24-hour service. Buckhead Safety Cab and Checker Cab offer 24-hour service.
➤ TAXIS AND SHUTTLES: **Airport Shuttle Bus** (☎ 770/932–9127). **Atlanta Airport Shuttle** (☎ 404/766–5312). **Buckhead Safety Cab** (☎ 404/233–1152). **Carey-Executive Limousine** (☎ 404/223–2000). **Checker Cab** (☎ 404/351–1111). **MARTA** (☎ 404/848–4711).

BUS TRAVEL TO AND FROM ATLANTA
Greyhound Bus Lines provides transportation to downtown Atlanta. Amtrak operates its Thru-Way bus service daily from Birmingham and Mobile, Alabama, to Atlanta's Brookwood station. Another bus goes daily from the station to Macon.

➤ BUS INFORMATION: **Amtrak** (✉ 1688 Peachtree St., Buckhead, ☎ 404/
881–3060 or 800/872–7245, WEB www.amtrak.com). **Greyhound Bus
Lines** (✉ 232 Forsyth St., Downtown, ☎ 404/584–1731 or 800/231–
2222, WEB www.greyhound.com).

BUS TRAVEL WITHIN ATLANTA

The Metropolitan Atlanta Rapid Transit Authority (MARTA), with a
fleet of about 700 buses, operates 150 routes covering 1,500 mi. The
fare is $1.75, and exact change is required. Weekly and monthly Trans-
Cards give you a slight discount. Service is very limited outside the perimeter set by I–285, except for a few areas in Clayton, DeKalb, and Fulton
counties.

➤ BUS INFORMATION: **Metropolitan Atlanta Rapid Transit Authority**
(☎ 404/848–4711).

CAR TRAVEL

The city is encircled by I–285. Three interstates—I–85, running northeast–southwest from Virginia to Alabama; I–75, north–south from Michi-
gan to Florida; and I–20, east–west from South Carolina to Texas—also
crisscross Atlanta.

TRAFFIC

Some refer to Atlanta as the Los Angeles of the South, because driving is virtually the only way to get to most parts of the city. Although
the congestion hasn't quite caught up to L.A.'s, Atlantans have grown
accustomed to frequent delays at rush hour—the morning and late-afternoon commuting periods seem to get longer every year. Beware: the
South as a whole may be laid-back, but Atlanta drivers are not; they
tend to drive faster than drivers in other Southern cities.

EMERGENCIES

For 24-hour emergency rooms contact Georgia Baptist Medical Center, Grady Memorial Hospital, Northside Hospital, and Piedmont
Hospital.

➤ EMERGENCY SERVICES: **Ambulance, police** (☎ 911).

➤ HOSPITALS: **Georgia Baptist Medical Center** (✉ 303 Parkway Dr.,
Downtown, ☎ 404/265–4000). **Grady Memorial Hospital** (✉ 80 Butler St., Downtown, ☎ 404/616–4307). **Northside Hospital** (✉ 1000
Johnson Ferry Rd., Dunwoody, ☎ 404/851–8000). **Piedmont Hospital** (✉ 1968 Peachtree Rd., Buckhead, ☎ 404/605–5000).

➤ 24-HOUR PHARMACIES: **CVS** (✉ 1943 Peachtree Rd., Buckhead, ☎
404/351–7629; ✉ 1554 N. Decatur Rd., Emory, ☎ 404/373–4192;
✉ 2350 Cheshire Bridge Rd., Buckhead, ☎ 404/486–7289).

LODGING

BED AND BREAKFASTS

Bed & Breakfast Online can provide detailed cyber-brochures on inns
in Atlanta and the surrounding Georgia territory.

➤ RESERVATION INFORMATION: **Bed & Breakfast Online** (✉ Box 829,
Madison, TN 37116, WEB www.bbonline.com/ga, ☎ 615/868–1946).

SUBWAY TRAVEL

MARTA has clean and safe rapid-rail subway trains with somewhat limited routes that link downtown with many major landmarks. The system's two main lines cross at the Five Points station downtown. TransCards
and information on public transportation are available at Rides Stores,
open weekdays 7–7 and Saturday 8:30–5; Rides Stores are at the airport, Five Points station, the headquarters building by Lindbergh station, and Lenox station. You can also buy TransCards at Kroger and
Publix groceries. Obtain free transfers, needed for some bus routes, by
pressing a button on the subway turnstile or requesting one from the driver.

FARES AND SCHEDULES
Trains run 5 AM–1 AM, and large parking lots (free) are at most stations beyond downtown. Tokens ($1.75 each) can be bought from machines outside each station.
➤ SUBWAY INFORMATION: **MARTA** (☎ 404/848–4711, WEB www.itsmarta.com).

TAXIS
Taxi service in Atlanta can be uneven. Drivers often lack correct change, so be prepared either to charge your fare (many accept credit cards) or insist that the driver obtain change. Drivers can also appear as befuddled as you may be by Atlanta's notoriously winding and hilly streets, so if your destination is something other than a major hotel or popular sight, come with directions.

Taxi fares start at $2 on entry, $1.75 for the first mile, with 25¢ for each additional ¼ mi, $1 per extra passenger, and $18 per hour of waiting time. Within the Downtown Convention Zone a flat rate of $6 for one person plus $1 per additional passenger will be charged for any destination. Buckhead Safety Cab and Checker Cab offer 24-hour service.
➤ TAXI COMPANIES: **Buckhead Safety Cab** (☎ 404/233–1152). **Checker Cab** (☎ 404/351–1111).

TOURS
BUS TOURS
Gray Line of Atlanta has tours of downtown, Midtown, Buckhead, the King Center, and sometimes Stone Mountain.
➤ FEES AND SCHEDULES: **Gray Line of Atlanta** (☎ 770/449–1806 or 800/593–1818, FAX 770/249–9397, WEB www.americancoachlines.com/Grayline.htm).

WALKING TOURS
The Atlanta Preservation Center offers several walking tours of historic areas and neighborhoods for $10 each; tours usually last from one to two hours. Especially noteworthy are tours of Sweet Auburn, the neighborhood associated with Martin Luther King Jr. and other leaders of Atlanta's African-American community; Druid Hills, the verdant, genteel neighborhood where *Driving Miss Daisy* was filmed; and the Fox Theatre, the elaborate 1920s picture palace.
➤ FEES AND SCHEDULES: **Atlanta Preservation Center** (☎ 404/876–2041; 404/876–2040 for tour hot line, WEB www.preserveatlanta.com).

TRAIN TRAVEL
Amtrak operates the *Crescent* train, with daily service to Atlanta's Brookwood station from New York; Philadelphia; Washington, D.C.; Baltimore; Charlotte, North Carolina; and Greenville, South Carolina. It also goes daily from New Orleans to New York through Atlanta.
➤ TRAIN INFORMATION: **Amtrak** (✉ 1688 Peachtree St., Buckhead, ☎ 404/881–3060 or 800/872–7245, WEB www.amtrak.com).

VISITOR INFORMATION
The Atlanta Convention & Visitors Bureau (ACVB) has information on Atlanta and the outlying area. The ACVB has several visitor information centers in Atlanta: Hartsfield Atlanta International Airport, in the atrium of the main ticketing terminal; Underground Atlanta; Georgia World Congress Center; and Lenox Square mall.
➤ TOURIST INFORMATION: **Atlanta Convention & Visitors Bureau** (✉ 233 Peachtree St., Suite 2000, Downtown 30303, ☎ 404/222–6688 or 800/285–2682, www.atlanta.net; ✉ Underground Atlanta, 65 Upper Alabama St., Downtown; Georgia World Congress Center, 285 Inter-

national Blvd., Downtown, ☎ 404/223–4000, ᵂᴱᴮ www.gwcc.com; ⊠ Lenox Mall, 3393 Peachtree Rd., Buckhead; ᵂᴱᴮ www.shopsimon. com).

SAVANNAH

The very sound of the name *Savannah* conjures up misty images of mint juleps, handsome mansions, and a somewhat decadent city moving at a lazy Southern pace. It's hard even to say "Savannah" without drawling. Well, brace yourself. The mint juleps are there all right, along with the moss and the mansions and the easygoing pace, but this Southern belle rings with surprises. Take, for example, St. Patrick's Day: Savannah has a St. Patrick's Day celebration second only to New York's. The greening of Savannah began in 1812, and everybody in town talks a blue (green) streak about St. Patrick's Day. Everything turns green on March 17, including scrambled eggs and grits.

Savannah's modern history began on February 12, 1733, when English general James Edward Oglethorpe and 120 colonists arrived at Yamacraw Bluff on the Savannah River to found the 13th and last colony in the New World. As the port city grew, people from England and Ireland, Scottish Highlanders, French Huguenots, Germans, Austrian Salzburgers, Sephardic and Ashkenazic Jews, Moravians, Italians, Swiss, Welsh, and Greeks all arrived to create what could be called a rich gumbo.

In 1793 Eli Whitney of Connecticut, who was tutoring on a plantation near Savannah, invented a mechanized means of "ginning" seeds from cotton bolls. Cotton soon became king, and Savannah, already a busy seaport, flourished under its reign. Waterfront warehouses were filled with "white gold," and brokers trading in the Savannah Cotton Exchange set world prices. The white gold brought in solid gold, and fine mansions were built in the prospering city.

In 1864 Savannahians surrendered their city to Union general Sherman rather than see it torched. Later, following World War I and the decline of the cotton market, the city's economy virtually collapsed, and its historic buildings languished for more than 30 years. Elegant mansions were razed or allowed to decay, and cobwebs replaced cotton in the dilapidated riverfront warehouses.

In 1955 Savannah's spirits rose again. News that the exquisite Isaiah Davenport House (⊠ 324 E. State St.) was to be destroyed prompted seven outraged ladies to raise money to buy the house. They saved it the day before the wrecking ball was to swing. Thus was born the Historic Savannah Foundation, the organization responsible for the restoration of downtown Savannah, where more than 1,000 restored buildings form the 2½-square-mi Historic District, the nation's largest. Many of these buildings are open to the public during the annual tour of homes, and today Savannah is one of the country's top 10 cities for walking tours.

John Berendt's wildly popular *Midnight in the Garden of Good and Evil* has lured many people to Savannah since the book's publication in 1994. A nonfiction account of a notorious 1980s shooting, the book brings to life such Savannah sites as Monterey Square, Mercer House, and Bonaventure Cemetery. Clint Eastwood's film adaptation, only loosely based on the book, was neither a box-office nor a critical success, but the public's interest in Savannah has remained intense—to the consternation of old-timers who find the story's characters less than savory and the nosy Northerners a nuisance. Other Savannahians have rolled out the welcome mat, while still others have hiked prices, profiting from the tourist dollars.

Georgia's founder, General James Oglethorpe, laid out the city on a perfect grid. The Historic District is neatly hemmed in by the Savannah River, Gaston Street, East Street, and Martin Luther King Jr. Boulevard. Streets are arrow-straight, public squares of varying sizes are tucked into the grid at precise intervals, and each block is sliced in half by narrow, often unpaved streets. Bull Street, anchored on the north by City Hall and the south by Forsyth Park, charges down the center of the grid and lunges around the five public squares that stand in its way.

Numbers in the text correspond to numbers in the margin and on the Savannah Historic District map.

The Historic District

A Good Walk and Drive

You can cover historic Savannah on foot, but to save time and energy, you might want to drive part of this tour. Start at the **Savannah Visitors Center** ⑤⑥, on Martin Luther King Jr. Boulevard. In the same building, the **Savannah History Museum** ⑤⑦ is an ideal introduction to the city's history. There is public parking next to the center and museum.

Exit the parking lot and turn left (north), walking or driving two short and one very long blocks on Martin Luther King Jr. Boulevard to the **Scarborough House** ⑤⑧, which contains the Ships of the Sea Museum. Cross Martin Luther King Jr. Boulevard and continue two blocks east on West Congress Street, past Franklin Square to **City Market** ⑤⑨. Skirting around Franklin Square north on Montgomery Street, go two blocks to West Bay Street and turn right.

From this point continue east on West Bay Street four blocks to Bull Street. On your left you'll see **City Hall** ⑥⓪. Continue east along West Bay Street (which now becomes East Bay Street) to **Factors Walk** ⑥①, which lies south of River Street and the Savannah River. If you're driving, leave your car here to continue on foot (be sure to choose long-term parking, as the short-term meters are monitored vigilantly). Step down from Factors Walk toward the river and visit **Riverfront Plaza** ⑥②, which is best seen on foot.

At this point, if you're driving, you'll probably want to get back in your car to continue the tour. Return to East Bay Street and head west two long blocks back to Bull Street. Walk four blocks south on Bull Street to **Wright Square** ⑥③; then turn right (west) and go two blocks to Telfair Square, where you can stop at the **Telfair Mansion and Art Museum** ⑥④. Stroll around Telfair Square and then continue east on West York Street back toward Wright Square, and turn right on Bull Street, heading two blocks south to the **Juliette Gordon Low Birthplace/Girl Scout National Center** ⑥⑤. Two more short blocks south from the Low House on Bull Street, and you'll reach **Chippewa Square** ⑥⑥. Continue south on Bull Street to the Gothic Revival **Green-Meldrim House** ⑥⑦. Next, walk four blocks south on Bull Street to **Monterey Square** ⑥⑧. Proceed two blocks farther south from Monterey Square to **Forsyth Park** ⑥⑨, the divide between East and West Gaston streets.

From the park walk east on East Gaston Street and go one block to Abercorn Street; then turn left (north) on Abercorn Street to Calhoun Square and note the **Wesley Monumental Church** ⑦⓪. Continue north on Abercorn four blocks to Lafayette Square and view the **Andrew Low House** ⑦①. Northeast of Lafayette Square looms the **Cathedral of St. John the Baptist** ⑦②, on East Harris Street. Two blocks north, at the inter-

114

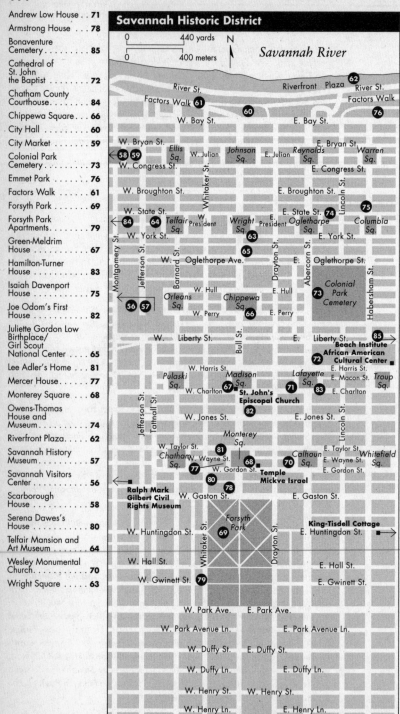

Savannah Historic District

section of Abercorn and East Oglethorpe streets, is the huge **Colonial Park Cemetery** ⑦. Proceeding two blocks north on Abercorn Street from the cemetery takes you to Oglethorpe Square; across from the square is the **Owens-Thomas House and Museum** ⑦. From the house walk east on East President Street two blocks to Columbia Square. Northwest of the square on East State Street stands the **Isaiah Davenport House** ⑦. From here continue north up Habersham Street to **Emmet Park** ⑦, a splendid park to relax in at the end of your tour.

TIMING

This is a long but comfortable walk, as Savannah has no taxing hills. Allow a full day to see everything along this route, especially if you plan to read all the historic markers and explore the sights thoroughly, stopping for tours. Driving around the squares can be slow—but you can drive the entire route in two hours, a pace that allows for some stopping along the way. Allow extra time if you want to linger in Riverfront Plaza for a half hour or so.

Sights to See

❼❶ Andrew Low House. This residence was built in 1848 for Andrew Low, a native of Scotland and one of Savannah's merchant princes. The home later belonged to his son William, who married Juliette Gordon. After her husband's death, she founded the Girl Scouts in this house on March 12, 1912. The house has 19th-century antiques, stunning silver, and some of the finest ornamental ironwork in Savannah. ⊠ *329 Abercorn St., Historic District,* ☎ *912/233–6854,* WEB *www.andrewlow. com.* ⊡ *$7.* ⊙ *Mon.–Wed. and Fri.–Sat. 10:30–3:30, Sun. noon–3:30.*

Beach Institute African-American Cultural Center. It's in the building that housed the first school for African-American children in Savannah, established after emancipation (1867). The center exhibits works by African-American artists from the Savannah area and around the country. ⊠ *502 E. Harris St., Historic District,* ☎ *912/234–8000,* WEB *www.kingtisdell.org/beach.* ⊡ *$3.50.* ⊙ *Tues.–Sat. noon–5.*

❼❷ Cathedral of St. John the Baptist. Soaring over the city, the French Gothic–style cathedral, with pointed arches and free-flowing traceries, is the seat of the diocese of Savannah. It was founded in 1799 by the first French colonists to arrive in Savannah. Fire destroyed the early structures; the present cathedral dates from 1874. ⊠ *222 E. Harris St., Historic District,* ☎ *912/233–4709.* ⊙ *Weekdays 9–5.*

❻❻ Chippewa Square. Daniel Chester French's imposing bronze statue of General James Edward Oglethorpe, founder of Savannah and Georgia, anchors the square. Also note the **Savannah Theatre,** on Bull Street, which claims to be the oldest continuously operated theater site in North America. ⊠ *Bull St. between Hull and Perry Sts., Historic District.*

❻❶ City Hall. Built in 1905 on the site of the Old City Exchange (1799–1904), this imposing structure anchors Bay Street. Notice the bench commemorating Oglethorpe's landing on February 12, 1733. ⊠ *1 Bay St., Historic District,* ☎ *912/651–6410.* ⊙ *Weekdays 8–5.*

❺❾ City Market. Alas, the original 1870s City Market was razed years ago to make way for a dreary-looking parking garage. Next to the garage you'll find this popular pedestrians-only area that encompasses galleries, nightclubs, restaurants, and shops. ⊠ *Between Franklin Sq. and Johnson Sq. on W. St. Julian St., Historic District.*

★ **❼❸ Colonial Park Cemetery.** The park is the final resting place for Savannahians who died between 1750 and 1853. You may want to stroll the shaded pathways and read some of the old tombstone inscriptions. There are several historical plaques, one of which marks the grave of Button

Gwinnett, a signer of the Declaration of Independence. ⊠ *Oglethorpe and Abercorn Sts., Historic District.*

Columbia Square. When Savannah was a walled city (1757–90), Bethesda Gate (one of six) was here. The square was laid out in 1799. ⊠ *Habersham St. between E. State and E. York Sts., Historic District.*

76 **Emmet Park.** The lovely tree-shaded park is named for Robert Emmet, a late-18th-century Irish patriot and orator. ⊠ *Borders E. Bay St., Historic District.*

61 **Factors Walk.** A network of iron walkways connects Bay Street with the multistory buildings that rise up from the river level, and iron stairways descend from Bay Street to Factors Walk. Cobblestone ramps lead pedestrians down to River Street (these are serious cobblestones, so wear comfortable shoes). ⊠ *Bay St. to Factors Walk, Historic District.*

69 **Forsyth Park.** The park forms the southern border of Bull Street. On its 20 acres it has a glorious white fountain dating to 1858, Confederate and Spanish-American War memorials, and the Fragrant Garden for the Blind, a project of Savannah garden clubs. There are tennis courts and a tree-shaded jogging path. Outdoor plays and concerts often take place here. At the northwest corner of the park, in **Hodgson Hall,** a 19th-century Italianate–Greek Revival building, you'll find the **Georgia Historical Society,** which shows selections from its collection of artifacts and manuscripts. ⊠ *501 Whitaker St., Historic District,* ☎ *912/ 651-2128,* WEB *www.georgiahistory.com.* ☼ *Tues.–Sat. 10–5.*

★ **67** **Green-Meldrim House.** Designed by New York architect John Norris and built in 1850 for cotton merchant Charles Green, this Gothic Revival mansion cost $90,000 to build—a princely sum back then. The house was bought in 1892 by Judge Peter Meldrim, whose heirs sold it to **St. John's Episcopal Church** to use as a parish house. General Sherman lived here after taking the city in 1864. Sitting on **Madison Square,** the house has such Gothic features as a crenellated roof, oriels, and an external gallery with filigree ironwork. Inside are mantels of Carrara marble, carved black-walnut woodwork, and doorknobs and hinges of either silver plate or porcelain. ⊠ *1 W. Macon St., Historic District,* ☎ *912/233–3845.* ☞ *$5.* ☼ *Tues., Thurs., and Fri. 10–4, Sat. 10–1. Closed last 2 wks of Jan. and 2 wks before Easter.*

★ **75** **Isaiah Davenport House.** The proposed demolition of this historic Savannah structure galvanized the city's residents into action to save their treasured buildings. Semicircular stairs with wrought-iron trim lead to the recessed doorway of the redbrick federal mansion that master builder Isaiah Davenport built for himself between 1815 and 1820. Three dormered windows poke through the sloping roof of the stately house, and the interior has polished hardwood floors, fine woodwork and plasterwork, and a soaring elliptical staircase. Furnishings, from the 1820s, are Hepplewhite, Chippendale, and Sheraton. ⊠ *324 E. State St., Historic District,* ☎ *912/236–8097,* WEB *www.davenportsavga.com.* ☞ *$7.* ☼ *Mon.–Sat. 10–4, Sun. 1–4.*

Johnson Square. The oldest of James Oglethorpe's original 24 squares was laid out in 1733 and named for South Carolina governor Robert Johnson. A monument marks the grave of Nathanael Greene, a hero of the Revolutionary War. The square was once a popular gathering place: Savannahians came here to welcome President Monroe in 1819, to greet the Marquis de Lafayette in 1825, and to cheer for Georgia's secession in 1861. ⊠ *Bull St. between Bryan and Congress Sts., Historic District.*

⑥⑤ **Juliette Gordon Low Birthplace/Girl Scout National Center.** This majestic Regency town house, attributed to William Jay (built 1818–21), was designated in 1965 as Savannah's first National Historic Landmark. "Daisy" Low, founder of the Girl Scouts, was born here in 1860, and the house is now owned and operated by the Girl Scouts of America. Mrs. Low's paintings and other artwork are on display in the house, restored to the style of 1886, the year of Mrs. Low's marriage. ⊠ *142 Bull St., Historic District,* ☎ *912/233–4501,* WEB *www. girlscouts.org/birthplace.* ⊞ *$8.* ☉ *Mon.–Tues. and Thurs.–Sat. 10– 4, Sun. 12:30–4:30.*

OFF THE BEATEN PATH **KING-TISDELL COTTAGE –** Tucked behind a picket fence is this museum dedicated to the preservation of African-American history and culture. The Negro Heritage Trail Tour visits this little Victorian house. Broad steps lead to a porch, and dormer windows pop up through a steep roof. The interior is furnished to resemble a middle-class African-American coastal home of the 1890s. To reach the cottage by car, go east on East Bay Street to Price Street and turn south (right) on this street; continue for about 30 blocks to East Huntington Street and take a left (east). The building is in the middle of the block. ⊠ *514 E. Huntington St., Historic District,* ☎ *912/234–8000,* WEB *www.kingtisdell.org.* ⊞ *$3.50.* ☉ *By appointment.*

Lafayette Square. Named for the Marquis de Lafayette, the square contains a graceful three-tier fountain donated by the Georgia chapter of the Colonial Dames of America. ⊠ *Abercorn St. between E. Harris and E. Charlton Sts., Historic District.*

Madison Square. A statue on the square, laid out in 1839 and named for President James Madison, depicts Sergeant William Jasper hoisting a flag and is a tribute to his bravery during the Siege of Savannah. Though mortally wounded, Jasper rescued the colors of his regiment in the assault on the British lines. ⊠ *Bull St. between W. Harris and W. Charlton Sts., Historic District.*

⑥⑧ **Monterey Square.** Commemorating the victory of General Zachary Taylor's forces in Monterrey, Mexico, in 1846, this is the fifth and southernmost of Bull Street's squares. A monument honors General Casimir Pulaski, the Polish nobleman who lost his life in the Siege of Savannah during the Revolutionary War. Also on the square is Temple Mickve Israel. ⊠ *Bull St. between Taylor and Gordon Sts., Historic District.*

★ ⑦④ **Owens-Thomas House and Museum.** English architect William Jay's first Regency mansion in Savannah is the city's finest example of that architectural style. Built in 1816–19, the English house was constructed mostly with local materials. Of particular note are the curving walls of the house, Greek-inspired ornamental molding, half-moon arches, stained-glass panels, and Duncan Phyfe furniture. In 1825 the Marquis de Lafayette bade a two-hour au revoir from a wrought-iron balcony to a crowd below. ⊠ *124 Abercorn St., Historic District,* ☎ *912/233–9743,* WEB *www.telfair. org.* ⊞ *$8.* ☉ *Mon. noon–5, Tues.–Sat. 10–5, Sun. 1–5.*

OFF THE BEATEN PATH **RALPH MARK GILBERT CIVIL RIGHTS MUSEUM –** In Savannah's Historic District, this history museum has a series of 15 exhibits on segregation, from emancipation through the civil rights movement. The role of black and white Savannahians in ending segregation in their city is detailed in these exhibits, largely derived from archival photographs. The museum also has touring exhibits. ⊠ *460 Martin Luther King Jr. Blvd., Historic District,* ☎ *912/231–8900,* FAX *912/234–2577.* ⊞ *$4.* ☉ *Mon.–Sat. 9–5.*

Reynolds Square. John Wesley, who preached in Savannah and wrote the first English hymnal in the city in 1736, is remembered here. A monument to the founder of the Methodist Church is shaded by greenery and surrounded by park benches. The **Olde Pink House** (⊠ 23 Abercorn St., Historic District), built in 1771, is one of the oldest buildings in town. Now a restaurant, the porticoed pink-stucco Georgian mansion has been a private home, a bank, and headquarters for a Yankee general during the Civil War. ⊠ *Abercorn St. between E. Bryant and E. Congress Sts., Historic District.*

62 Riverfront Plaza. Here you can watch a parade of freighters and pugnose tugs; youngsters can play in the tugboat-shape sandboxes. River Street is the main venue for many of the city's celebrations, including the First Saturday festivals, when flea marketers, artists, and artisans display their wares and musicians entertain the crowds. ⊠ *River St. between Abercorn and Barnard St., Historic District.*

57 Savannah History Museum. This museum in a restored railway station is an excellent introduction to the city. Exhibits range from old locomotives to a tribute to Savannah-born songwriter Johnny Mercer. On top of the **site of the Siege of Savannah,** it marks the spot where in 1779 the colonial forces, led by Polish count Casimir Pulaski, laid siege to Savannah in an attempt to retake the city from the redcoats. They were beaten back, and Pulaski was killed while leading a cavalry charge against the British. The dead lie underneath the building. ⊠ *303 Martin Luther King Jr. Blvd., Historic District,* ☎ *912/238–1779,* WEB *www.chsgeorgia. org/historymuseum.cfm.* ⊡ *$4.* ☉ *Daily 9–5.*

56 Savannah Visitors Center. Come here for free maps and brochures, friendly advice, and an audiovisual overview of the city. The starting point for a number of guided tours, the center is in a big 1860 red-brick building with high ceilings and sweeping arches. It was the old Central of Georgia railway station. The parking lot is a good spot to leave your car while you explore the nearby Historic District. ⊠ *301 Martin Luther King Jr. Blvd., Historic District,* ☎ *912/944–0455,* WEB *www.savannahvisit.com.* ☉ *Weekdays 8:30–5, weekends 9–5.*

58 Scarborough House. This exuberant Greek Revival mansion, built during the 1819 cotton boom for Savannah merchant prince William Scarborough, was designed by English architect William Jay. Scarborough was a major investor in the steamship *Savannah.* The house has a Doric portico capped by one of Jay's characteristic half-moon windows. Four massive Doric columns form a peristyle in the atrium entrance hall. Inside is the **Ships of the Sea Museum,** with displays of ship models, including steamships, a nuclear-powered ship (the *Savannah*), China clippers with their sails unfurled, and Columbus's vessels. ⊠ *41 Martin Luther King Jr. Blvd., Historic District,* ☎ *912/232–1511,* WEB *www.shipsofthesea.org.* ⊡ *$5.* ☉ *Tues.–Sun. 10–5.*

64 Telfair Mansion and Art Museum. The oldest public art museum in the Southeast was designed by William Jay in 1819 for Alexander Telfair and sits across the street from **Telfair Square.** Within its marble rooms are American, French, and Dutch impressionist paintings; German tonalist paintings; a large collection of works by Kahlil Gibran; plaster casts of the Elgin Marbles, the Venus de Milo, and the Laocoön, among other classical sculptures; and some of the Telfair family furnishings, including a Duncan Phyfe sideboard and Savannah-made silver. ⊠ *121 Barnard St., Historic District,* ☎ *912/232–1177,* WEB *www.telfair.org.* ⊡ *$8, free Sun.* ☉ *Mon. noon–5, Tues.–Sat. 10–5, Sun. 1–5.*

Temple Mickve Israel. A Gothic Revival synagogue on Monterey Square houses the third-oldest Jewish congregation in the United States; its founding members settled in town five months after the establishment of Savannah in 1733. The synagogue's collection includes documents and letters (some from George Washington, James Madison, and Thomas Jefferson) pertaining to early Jewish life in Savannah and Georgia. ⊠ *20 E. Gordon St., Historic District,* ☎ *912/233–1547,* WEB *www.mickveisrael.org.* ◷ *Weekdays 10–noon and 2–4.*

70 **Wesley Monumental Church.** This Gothic Revival–style church memorializing the founders of Methodism is patterned after Queen's Kerk in Amsterdam. Noted for its magnificent stained-glass windows, the church celebrated a century of service in 1968. ⊠ *429 Abercorn St., Historic District,* ☎ *912/232–0191.* ◷ *By appointment only.*

63 **Wright Square.** Named for James Wright, Georgia's last colonial governor, the square has an elaborate monument in its center that honors William Washington Gordon, founder of the Central of Georgia Railroad. A slab of granite from Stone Mountain adorns the grave of Tomo-Chi-Chi, the Yamacraw chief who befriended General Oglethorpe and the colonists. ⊠ *Bull St. between W. State and W. York Sts., Historic District.*

Midnight in the Garden of Good and Evil

Town gossips can give you the best introduction to a city, and as author John Berendt discovered, Savannah's not short on them. In his 1994 best-seller, *Midnight in the Garden of Good and Evil,* Berendt shares the juiciest of tales imparted to him during the eight years he spent here wining and dining with Savannah's high society and dancing with her Grand Empress, drag queen the Lady Chablis, among others. By the time he left, there had been a scandalous homicide and several trials: the wealthy Jim Williams was accused of killing his assistant and sometime lover, Danny Hansford.

Before you set out, find a copy of the book, pour yourself a cool drink, and enter an eccentric world of cutthroat killers and society backstabbers, voodoo witches, and garden-club ladies. Then head over to the Historic District to follow the characters' steps. By the end of this walking tour, you'll be hard-pressed to find the line between Berendt's creative nonfiction and Savannah's reality. Note: unless otherwise indicated, the sights on this tour are not open to the public.

A Good Walk

Begin at the southwest corner of Monterey Square, site of the **Mercer House** ⑦, whose construction was begun by songwriter Johnny Mercer's great-grandfather just before the Civil War. Two blocks south on Bull Street is the **Armstrong House** ⑱, an earlier residence of Jim Williams, the main character in the book. Walk south through Forsyth Park to the corner of Park Avenue and Whitaker Street. The **Forsyth Park Apartments** ⑲, where author John Berendt lived, are on the southwest corner of Forsyth Park. Then turn back north through the park. At the midpoint of the park's northern edge, turn north up Bull Street in the direction of Monterey Square. Turn left on West Gordon Street off Bull Street and walk toward the corner of West Gordon Street and Whitaker Street, where you'll reach **Serena Dawes's House** ⑳. Next, cross West Gordon Street, walk north on Bull Street in front of Mercer House, cross Wayne Street, and you'll find that the first house on the left facing Bull Street at Wayne Street is **Lee Adler's Home** ㉑, which sits across from Monterey Square's northwest corner. Continue walking north on Bull Street and take a right (east) on East Jones Street. **Joe Odom's first house** ㉒ is the third house on the left before Drayton Street.

Continue on East Jones Street to Abercorn Street and turn left (north), walking two blocks on Abercorn Street to East Charlton Street and the **Hamilton-Turner House** ⑧, now a B&B inn. Then swing around Lafayette Square to East Harris Street, and take it about six blocks west to Pulaski Square at Barnard Street; turn right (north) on Barnard Street through Orleans Square and continue north to Telfair Square. On foot, you may elect to head west down West York Street to find the **Chatham County Courthouse** ⑧, scene of all those trials, two blocks away. Finally, take either Whitaker Street or Abercorn Street south to Victory Drive and turn left. Go through Thunderbolt to Whatley Avenue, and turn left again. Whatley Avenue leads directly to Bonaventure Road, which curves in both directions; bear left, and on your right about a quarter mile up the road is **Bonaventure Cemetery** ⑧.

TIMING
Allow a leisurely two hours to walk the main points of the tour, plus another hour to visit the cemetery.

Sights to See

❼⑧ **Armstrong House.** Antiques dealer Jim Williams lived and worked in this residence before purchasing the Mercer House. On a late-afternoon walk past the mansion, Berendt met Mr. Simon Glover, an 86-year-old singer and porter for the law firm of Bouhan, Williams, and Levy, occupants of the building. Glover confided that he earned a weekly $10 for walking the deceased dogs of a former partner of the firm up and down Bull Street. Baffled? So was the author. Behind the house's cast-iron gates are the offices of Frank Siler, Jim Williams's attorney, who doubles as keeper of Uga, the Georgia Bulldog mascot. ✉ *447 Bull St., Historic District.*

❽⑤ **Bonaventure Cemetery.** A cemetery east of downtown is the final resting place for Danny Hansford. The haunting female tombstone figure from the book's cover has been removed to protect surrounding graves from sightseers. Now you can view the figure at the Telfair Mansion. ✉ *330 Bonaventure Rd., Eastside,* ☎ *912/651–6843.*

❽④ **Chatham County Courthouse.** The courthouse was the scene of three of Williams's murder trials, which took place over the course of about eight years. An underground tunnel leads from the courthouse to the jail where Williams was held in a cell that was modified to allow him to conduct his antiques business. ✉ *133 Montgomery St., Historic District.*

❼⑨ **Forsyth Park Apartments.** Here was Berendt's second home in Savannah; from his fourth-floor rooms he pieced together the majority of the book. While parking his newly acquired 1973 Pontiac Grand Prix outside these apartments, Berendt met the Lady Chablis coming out of her nearby doctor's office, freshly feminine from a new round of hormone shots. ✉ *Whitaker and Gwinnett Sts., Historic District.*

❽③ **Hamilton-Turner House.** After one too many of Joe Odom's deals went sour, Mandy Nichols, his fourth fiancée-in-waiting, left him and took over his third residence, a Second Empire–style mansion dating from 1873. Mandy filled it with 17th- and 18th-century antiques and transformed it into a successful museum through which she led tour groups. The elegant towering hulk is at the southeast corner of Lafayette Square. The house was sold in the late '90s and has since become the elegant Hamilton-Turner Inn. ✉ *330 Abercorn St., Historic District.*

❽② **Joe Odom's first house.** At this stucco town house, Odom, a combination tax lawyer, real-estate broker, and piano player, hosted a 24-hour stream of visitors. The author met Odom through Mandy Nichols, a former Miss Big Beautiful Woman, who stopped by to borrow ice one time after the power had been cut off, a frequent occurrence. ⊠ *16 E. Jones St., Historic District.*

㉛ Lee Adler's Home. Just north of the Mercer House, in half of the double town house facing West Wayne Street, Lee Adler, the adversary of Jim Williams, runs his business of restoring historic Savannah properties. Adler's howling dogs drove Williams to his pipe organ, where he churned out a deafening version of César Franck's *Pièce Heroïque.* Later, Adler stuck reelection signs in his front lawn, showing his support for the district attorney who prosecuted Williams three times before he was finally found not guilty. ⊠ *425 Bull St., Historic District.*

㉗ Mercer House. This redbrick Italianate mansion on the southwest corner of Monterey Square became Jim Williams's Taj Mahal; here he ran a world-class antiques dealership and held *the* Christmas party of the season; here also Danny Hansford, his sometime house partner, succumbed to gunshot wounds. Williams himself died here of a heart attack in 1990, near the very spot where Hansford fell. Today his sister lives quietly among the remnants of his Fabergé collection and his Joshua Reynolds paintings, in rooms lighted by Waterford crystal chandeliers. ⊠ *429 Bull St., Historic District.*

㉚ Serena Dawes's House. Near the intersection of West Gordon and Bull streets, this house was owned by Helen Driscoll, also known as Serena Dawes. A high-profile beauty in the 1930s and '40s, she married into a Pennsylvania steel family. After her husband accidentally and fatally shot himself in the head, she retired here, in her hometown. Dawes, Berendt writes, "spent most of her day in bed, holding court, drinking martinis and pink ladies, playing with her white toy poodle, Lulu." Chief among Serena's gentlemen callers was Luther Driggers, rumored to possess a poison strong enough to wipe out the entire city. ⊠ *17 W. Gordon St., Historic District.*

Other Area Attractions

Old Fort Jackson. About 2 mi east of Broad Street via President Street, you'll see a sign for the fort, which is 3 mi from the city. Purchased in 1808 by the federal government, this is the oldest standing fort in Georgia. It was garrisoned in 1812 and was the Confederate headquarters of the river batteries. The brick edifice is surrounded by a tidal moat, and there are 13 exhibit areas. Battle reenactments, blacksmithing demonstrations, and programs of 19th-century music are among the fort's activities for tour groups. ⊠ *1 Ft. Jackson Rd., Fort Jackson,* ☎ *912/232–3945,* WEB *www.chsgeorgia.org/fortjackson.cfm.* ⊠ *$3.50.* ☉ *Daily 9–5.*

★ ☾ Fort Pulaski National Monument. Named for Casimir Pulaski, a Polish count and Revolutionary War hero, this must-see sight for Civil War buffs was built on Cockspur Island between 1829 and 1847. Robert E. Lee's first assignment after graduating from West Point was as an engineer here. During the Civil War the fort fell, on April 11, 1862, after a mere 30 hours of bombardment by newfangled rifled cannons. The restored fortification, operated by the National Park Service, has moats, drawbridges, massive ramparts, and towering walls. The park has trails and picnic areas. It's 14 mi east of downtown Savannah; you'll see the entrance on your left just before U.S. 80 reaches Tybee Island. ⊠ *U.S. 80, Fort Pulaski,* ☎ *912/786–5787,* WEB *www.nps.gov/fopu.* ⊠ *$3.* ☉ *Daily 9–5.*

Melon Bluff. On a centuries-old 3,000-acre plantation that has been in one family since 1735, Melon Bluff includes a nature center and facilities for canoeing, kayaking, bird-watching, hiking, and other outdoor activities. You can camp here or stay at one of the three B&B inns ($$–$$$): Palmyra Plantation, an 1850s cottage; the Ripley Farmhouse, a classic rural house with a tin-covered roof; and an old barn, renovated to contain nine guest rooms. From Melon Bluff you can visit nearby **Seabrook Village,** a small but growing cluster of rural buildings from an African-American historic community; **Old Sunbury,** whose port made it a viable competitor to Savannah until the Revolutionary War ended its heyday; **Fort Morris,** which protected Savannah during the revolution; and **Midway,** an 18th-century village with a house museum and period cemetery. To reach Melon Bluff, take I–95 south from Savannah (about 30 mi) to Exit 76 (Midway/Sunbury), turn left, and go east for 3 mi. The other sites mentioned here are all within a short drive. ⊠ *2999 Islands Hwy., Midway,* ☎ *912/884–5779 or 888/246–8188,* FAX *912/884–3046,* WEB *www.melonbluff.com.*

Mighty Eighth Air Force Heritage Museum. The famous World War II squadron the Mighty Eighth Air Force was formed in Savannah in January 1942 and shipped out to the United Kingdom. Flying Royal Air Force aircraft, the Mighty Eighth became the largest air force of the period, with some 200,000 combat crew personnel. Many lost their lives during raids on enemy factories or were interned as prisoners of war. Exhibits begin with the prelude to World War II and the rise of Adolf Hitler and continue through Desert Storm. ⊠ *175 Bourne Ave. (I–95, Exit 102, to U.S. 80), Pooler (14 mi west of Savannah),* ☎ *912/ 748–8888,* WEB *www.mightyeighth.org.* ⌦ *$8.* ☉ *Daily 9–5.*

♻ **Skidaway Marine Science Complex.** On the grounds of the former Modena Plantation, Skidaway has a 14-panel, 12,000-gallon aquarium with marine and plant life of the continental shelf. Other exhibits highlight coastal archaeology and fossils of the Georgia coast. Nature trails overlook marsh and water. ⊠ *30 Ocean Science Circle, Skidaway Island (8 mi south of Savannah),* ☎ *912/598–2496.* ⌦ *$2.* ☉ *Weekdays 9–4, Sat. noon–5.*

Tybee Island. *Tybee* is an Indian word meaning "salt." The Yamacraw Indians came to this island in the Atlantic Ocean to hunt and fish, and legend has it that pirates buried their treasure here. The island is about 5 mi long and 2 mi wide, with seafood restaurants, chain motels, condos, and shops—most of which sprang up during the 1950s and haven't changed much since. The entire expanse of white sand is divided into a number of public beaches, where you can shell and crab, charter fishing boats, and swim. It's 18 mi east of Savannah; take Victory Drive (U.S. 80), sometimes called Tybee Road, onto the island. On your way here stop by Fort Jackson and Fort Pulaski National Monument. Nearby, the misnamed Little Tybee Island, actually larger than Tybee Island, is entirely undeveloped. Contact **Tybee Island Convention and Visitors Bureau** (⊠ Box 491, Tybee Island 31328, ☎ 800/868–2322, WEB www.tybeevisit.com).

Dining

Savannah has excellent seafood restaurants, though locals also have a passion for spicy barbecued meats. The Historic District yields culinary treasures, especially along River Street. Several of the city's restaurants—such as Elizabeth on 37th, 45 South, the Olde Pink House, and Sapphire Grill—have been beacons that have drawn members of the culinary upper crust to the region for decades. From there they explored and discovered that such divine dining isn't isolated to Savannah's Historic District, as nearby Thunderbolt, Skidaway, Tybee, and Wilmington islands also have a collection of remarkable restaurants.

$$$–$$$$ ✕ **Elizabeth on 37th.** Regional specialties are the hallmark at this ac-
    ★   claimed restaurant that goes so far as to credit local produce suppli-
               ers on its menu. Chef Elizabeth Terry manages to make dishes such as
               Maryland crab cakes and a plate of roasted shiitake and oyster mush-
               rooms sit comfortably beside Southern-fried grits and country ham.
               The extravagant Savannah cream cake is the way to finish your meal
               in this elegant turn-of-the-20th-century mansion with hardwood floors
               and spacious rooms. ⊠ *105 E. 37th St., Victorian District,* ☎ *912/
               236–5547. Reservations essential. AE, D, DC, MC, V. No lunch.*

$$$–$$$$ ✕ **45 South.** This popular Southside eatery is small and stylish, with
    ★   a contemporary mauve-and-green interior. The game-heavy menu often
               includes a confit of tender rabbit with morels and mashed potatoes.
               ⊠ *20 E. Broad St., Victorian District,* ☎ *912/233–1881. Reservations
               essential. AE, D, DC, MC, V. Closed Sun. No lunch.*

$$–$$$ ✕ **Belford's Steak and Seafood.** In the heart of City Market, Belford's
               is great for Sunday brunch, when so many of the downtown venues
               are closed. A complimentary glass of sparkling wine arrives at your
               table when you place your order. Brunch entrées include egg dishes,
               such as smoked salmon Florentine and crab frittatas. The lunch and
               dinner menus focus on seafood, including Georgia pecan grouper and
               Lowcountry shrimp and grits. ⊠ *315 W. St. Julian St., Historic Dis-
               trict,* ☎ *912/233–2626. AE, D, DC, MC, V.*

$$–$$$ ✕ **Bistro Savannah.** High ceilings, burnished heart-pine floors, and gray-
    ★   brick walls lined with local art contribute to the bistro-ish qualities of
               this spot by City Market. The menu has such specialties as seared beef
               tenderloin with shiitakes, scallions, corn pancakes and horseradish sauce,
               and shrimp and *tasso* (seasoned cured pork) on stone-ground grits. An-
               other treat is the crispy roasted duck. ⊠ *309 W. Congress St., Historic
               District,* ☎ *912/233–6266. AE, MC, V. No lunch.*

$$–$$$ ✕ **Cafe@Main.** This upscale but easygoing restaurant offers a com-
               pendium of Continental and regional American dishes, such as pork
               tenderloin with mashed potatoes and fresh green beans, and potato-
               onion-crusted grouper. Also of note is the wine list, with an unusually
               extensive selection of by-the-glass offerings. ⊠ *1 W. Broughton St., His-
               toric District,* ☎ *912/447–5979. AE, MC, V.*

$$–$$$ ✕ **Georges' of Tybee.** From the proprietors of the North Beach Grill
               came Tybee's first fine restaurant. The warmly lighted interior, with its
               inviting dining room, with a lovely stone fireplace and dark rose-painted
               walls, is a fine place to spend a romantic evening. Duck liver and frisée
               salad, and Thai-barbecued Muscovy duck breast are popular. Lobster,
               crab, and four-cheese ravioli with carrots, snow peas, and arugula, in
               a saffron-cream sauce, is also outstanding. ⊠ *1105 E. U.S. 80, Tybee
               Island,* ☎ *912/786–9730. AE, MC, V. Closed Mon. No lunch.*

$$–$$$ ✕ **Il Pasticcio.** Sicilian Pino Venetico turned this former department store
    ★   into his dream restaurant—a bistro-style place gleaming with steel, glass,
               and tile, and a lively, hip, young crowd to populate it. The menu
               changes frequently, but fresh pastas and sauces are a constant. Don't
               miss the second-floor art gallery. Excellent desserts, including a supe-
               rior tiramisu, make this one worth seeking out. ⊠ *2 E. Broughton St.,
               Historic District,* ☎ *912/231–8888. AE, D, DC, MC, V. No lunch.*

$$–$$$ ✕ **Olde Pink House.** The brick Georgian mansion was built in 1771
               for James Habersham, one of the wealthiest Americans of his time. One
               of Savannah's oldest buildings, the tavern has original Georgia pine
               floors, Venetian chandeliers, and 18th-century English antiques. The
               she-crab soup is a light but flavorful version of this Lowcountry spe-
               cialty. Regional ingredients find their way into many of the dishes, in-
               cluding the black grouper stuffed with blue crab and served with a Vidalia
               onion sauce. ⊠ *23 Abercorn St., Historic District,* ☎ *912/232–4286.
               AE, MC, V. No lunch.*

124

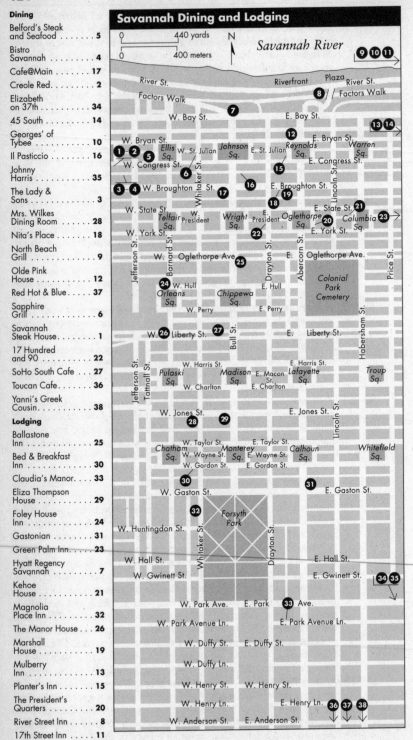

Savannah Dining and Lodging

$$–$$$ ✕ **Sapphire Grill.** Savannah's young and restless pack this trendy haunt
★   nightly. Chef Chris Nason focuses his seasonal menus on local ingredients, such as Georgia white shrimp, crab, and fish. Vegetarians will
delight in his elegant vegetable presentations—perhaps including
roasted sweet onions, spicy peppers, wild mushrooms, or roasted shallots. Chocoholics: get the remarkably delicious, intensely potent chocolate flan. ⊠ *110 W. Congress St., Historic District,* ☎ *912/443–9962.*
Reservations essential. AE, D, DC, MC, V. No lunch.

$$–$$$ ✕ **Savannah Steak House.** This art-filled, dashing restaurant with a
striking collage on its ceiling has made an impressive splash in Savannah dining circles. The menu offers a tremendously varied number of
inventive delicacies. Traditionalists might stick with the hefty rib-eye
steak, but if you're game for something more exotic, consider "wild"
entrées like ostrich fillet, wild-boar chili, and antelope medallions. ⊠
423 W. Congress St., Historic District, ☎ *912/232–0092. AE, MC, V.*
Closed Sun.

$$–$$$ ✕ **17 Hundred and 90.** Chef Deborah Noelk keeps a creative kitchen
★   in this restaurant—in a rustic structure dating to the 13th colony and
tucked in among ancient oaks dripping with Spanish moss. The restaurant is in Savannah's oldest inn of the same name. Entrées include pan-
seared veal medallions with artichoke hearts and capers in a lemon butter;
roasted half duckling with a port wine lingonberry sauce; and local
shrimp stuffed with scallops and crabmeat and served with a lemon
beurre blanc sauce. There is a ghost story to go with dinner, so make
sure the waiter fills you in. ⊠ *307 E. Presidents St., Historic District,*
☎ *912/231–8888. AE, D, DC, MC, V. No lunch weekends.*

$$–$$$ ✕ **The Lady & Sons.** Expect to take your place in line, along with lo-
cals, here. Everyone patiently waits to attack the buffet, which is
stocked for both lunch and dinner with such specials as moist, crispy
fried chicken; the best baked spaghetti in the South; green beans cooked
with ham and potatoes; tender, sweet creamed corn; and homemade
lemonade. The interior of this 1870s-era building, painted pale pink
with faux ivy tendrils draped along its perimeter, is bright, cheerful,
and busy. Owner Paula H. Deen's book, *The Lady & Sons: Savannah*
Country Cookbook, includes recipes for the most popular dishes. ⊠
311 W. Congress St., Historic District, ☎ *912/233–2600. AE, D, MC,*
V. No dinner Sun.

$$ ✕ **Johnny Harris.** What started as a small roadside stand in 1924 has
grown into one of the city's mainstays, with a menu that includes steaks,
fried chicken, seafood, and meats spiced with the restaurant's famous
tomato-and-mustard sauce. The lamb barbecue is a treat, and their sauces
are now so famous that they bottle them for take-home and shipping.
There's live music Friday and Saturday night, except on the first Sat-
urday night of the month, when there's dancing. ⊠ *1651 E. Victory*
Dr., Eastside, ☎ *912/354–7810. AE, D, DC, MC, V. Closed Sun.*

$$ ✕ **Mrs. Wilkes Dining Room.** Folks line up for a culinary orgy of fine
★   Southern food, served family style at big tables. For breakfast there are
eggs, sausage, piping hot biscuits, and grits. At lunch try fried or roast
chicken, collard greens, okra, mashed potatoes, and corn bread. ⊠ *107*
W. Jones St., Historic District, ☎ *912/232–5997. Reservations not ac-*
cepted. No credit cards. Closed Jan. and weekends. No dinner.

$$ ✕ **North Beach Grill.** The tiny kitchen of this casual beachfront locale
serves up a taste of the Caribbean. The jerk-rubbed fish tacos with fruit
salsa—which you'll be hard-pressed to find prepared right in the South—
are wonderful. Also expect to be tempted by the grilled okra and by
the sea bass topped with caramelized onions with cilantro-lime beurre
blanc. You can come in a swimsuit for lunch, but throw on something
casual for dinner. ⊠ *41A Meddin Dr., Tybee Island,* ☎ *912/786–9003.*
Reservations not accepted. D, MC, V. Closed weekdays Dec.–Jan.

$–$$ ✕ **Nita's Place.** Juanita Dixon has a reputation for perfectly prepar-
★ ing down-home Southern cooking at this renowned steam-table operation, which remains authentic (despite now being housed in a more
polished-looking space than its original location). People flock here for
salmon patties, baked chicken, perfectly cooked okra, outstanding
squash casserole, and homemade desserts. The fresh vegetables and other
side dishes alone are worth the trip, if only for the sheer number (11)
from which to choose: rutabagas, fried corn, string beans, potato
salad, collard greens, sautéed spinach, black-eyed peas, macaroni and
cheese, fried sweet potatoes, baked sweet potatoes, and Nita's famous
squash casserole. ✉ *129 E. Broughton St., Historic District,* ☎ *912/
238–8233. Reservations not accepted. MC, V. Closed Sun. No dinner
Mon.–Thurs.*

$–$$ ✕ **Red Hot & Blue.** Their motto is: "Best Barbecue You'll Ever Have
★ in a Building that Hasn't Already Been Condemned!" With such specialties as pulled-pig spare ribs, pork spare ribs, beef brisket, smoked
chicken, and smoked sausage, all meticulously smoked over hickory
wood for a long time, this place may be worth the drive to the Southside for barbecue aficionados, even if it is a chain location. ✉ *11108
Abercorn St., Southside,* ☎ *912/961–7422. Reservations not accepted.
MC, V.*

$–$$ ✕ **SoHo South Cafe.** This is not your normal soup-and-salad pit stop—
it's a soup-and-salad pit stop for epicureans. The tuna salad in your
tuna-salad sandwich will be made to order—from the café's own
recipe, no less—and the smoked ham and Brie on a baguette is enough
to make your taste buds swoon. The soups are also fittingly fabulous.
✉ *12 W. Liberty St., Historic District,* ☎ *912/233–1633. MC, V.
Closed Sun. Dinner served 6–9:30 Fri.–Sat. only.*

$–$$ ✕ **Toucan Cafe.** This colorful café has food to satisfy every kind of eater—
the menu is sympathetic to vegetarian tastes but doesn't leave meat eaters
out in the cold. Offerings include Indian veggie *samosas* with curried
broccoli, Jamaican jerk chicken, and rib-eye steaks. ✉ *531 Stephen-
son Ave., Southside,* ☎ *912/352–2233. AE, D, MC, V. Closed Sun.*

$–$$ ✕ **Yanni's Greek Cuisine.** A gregarious waitstaff serves a wonderful,
★ authentic Greek cuisine in this Southside eatery with walls emblazoned by murals of Mediterranean seaside panoramas. Menu items include Grecian shrimp kebabs with feta, garlic, onions and tomatoes,
as well as salmon sautéed in a creamy white-wine and dill sauce. There
is plenty of pork, beef, and chicken to choose from as well, all prepared with finesse. ✉ *11211 Abercorn Expressway, Southside,* ☎
912/925–6814. AE, D, MC, V. Closed Sun.

$ ✕ **Creole Red.** This jaunty little no-frills storefront café is patronized
with great enthusiasm by locals. Everybody seems to love the delicious
and inexpensive Louisiana specialties, from fresh crawfish étouffée to
deviled crabs, served with warmth and aplomb by the friendly proprietor
and staff. ✉ *409 W. Congress St., Historic District,* ☎ *912/234–6690.
MC, V.*

Lodging

Although Savannah has its share of chain hotels and motels, the city's
most distinctive lodgings are the more than two dozen historic inns,
guest houses, and B&Bs gracing the Historic District.

If the term *historic inn* brings to mind images of roughing it in shabby-
genteel mansions with antiquated plumbing, you're in for a surprise.
Most of these inns are in mansions with the requisite high ceilings, spacious rooms, and ornate carved millwork. And most do have canopy,
four-poster, or Victorian brass beds. But amid all the antique surroundings, there is modern luxury: enormous baths, many with

whirlpools or hot tubs; film libraries for in-room VCRs; and turndown service with a chocolate, a praline, even a discreet brandy on your nightstand. Continental breakfast and afternoon refreshments are often included in the rate. Prices have risen since the filming of *Midnight in the Garden of Good and Evil*. Special seasons and holidays, such as St. Patrick's Day, push prices up a bit as well. On the other hand, weekdays and the off-season can yield excellent bargains.

Inns and Guest Houses

$$$$
★
🏠 **Gastonian.** Guest rooms at this inn, built in 1868, have working fireplaces and antiques from the Georgian and Regency periods; most also have whirlpool tubs or Japanese soak tubs. The Caracalla Suite is named for the oversize whirlpool tub built in front of the fireplace. At breakfast you'll find such specialty items as ginger pancakes. Afternoon tea, evening cordials, and complimentary wine are other treats. ⊠ *220 E. Gaston St., Historic District 31401,* ☎ *912/232–2869 or 800/322–6603,* 𝖥𝖠𝖷 *912/232–0710,* 𝖶𝖤𝖡 *www.gastonian.com. 14 rooms, 3 suites. Internet. AE, D, MC, V. BP.*

$$$–$$$$
★
🏠 **Ballastone Inn.** This sumptuous inn occupies an 1838 mansion that once served as a bordello. Rooms are handsomely furnished, with luxurious linens on canopy beds, antiques and fine reproductions, and a collection of original framed prints from *Harper's* scattered throughout. On the garden level rooms are small and cozy, with exposed brick walls, beam ceilings, and, in some cases, windows at eye level with the lush courtyard. Most rooms have working gas fireplaces, and three have whirlpool tubs. Afternoon tea and free passes to a nearby health club are included. ⊠ *14 E. Oglethorpe Ave., Historic District 31401,* ☎ *912/236–1484 or 800/822–4553,* 𝖥𝖠𝖷 *912/236–4626,* 𝖶𝖤𝖡 *www.ballastone. com. 14 rooms, 3 suites. In-room VCRs, bicycles. AE, MC, V. BP.*

$$$–$$$$
🏠 **Eliza Thompson House.** Eliza Thompson was a socially prominent widow when she built her fine town house around 1847; today the lovely Victorian edifice remains one of the oldest B&Bs in Savannah. The lovingly weathered exterior still retains the majestic beauty of its stately heyday, when regal homes were all the rage. A peaceful garden courtyard provides a quiet respite where you can read or simply breathe in the floral scents. The rooms are lavishly decorated, with marble baths and rare antiques, boasting walls painted in deep primaries, such as forest green or pencil yellow—which provide stunning backdrops for the plush bedding and other designer accents. Continental breakfast and complimentary afternoon wine and cheese are served in the parlor or on the patio, with its fine patio, the latter of which has a fine Ivan Bailey sculpture. ⊠ *5 W. Jones St., Historic District 31401,* ☎ *912/236–3620 or 800/348–9378,* 𝖥𝖠𝖷 *912/238–1920,* 𝖶𝖤𝖡 *www. elizathompsonhouse.com. 25 rooms. MC, V. BP.*

$$$–$$$$
★
🏠 **Foley House Inn.** Two town houses, built 50 years apart, form this elegant inn. Proprietor Phillip Jenkins often entertains during the evening wine-and-dessert service—he plays lively numbers on the baby grand piano in the parlor. Most rooms have antiques and reproductions; five rooms have whirlpool tubs. A carriage house to the rear of the property has less expensive rooms. ⊠ *14 W. Hull St., Historic District 31401,* ☎ *912/232–6622 or 800/647–3708,* 𝖥𝖠𝖷 *912/231–1218,* 𝖶𝖤𝖡 *www.foleyinn.com. 17 rooms, 2 suites. In-room VCRs. AE, MC, V. BP.*

$$$–$$$$
🏠 **Kehoe House.** A fabulously appointed 1890s B&B, the Victorian Kehoe House has brass-and-marble chandeliers, a courtyard garden, and a music room. On the main floor a double parlor holds two fireplaces and sweeps the eye upward with its 14-ft ceilings. Turndown service is included. Rates include access to the Downtown Athletic Club. ⊠ *123 Habersham St., Historic District 31401,* ☎ *912/232–1020 or*

800/820–1020, FAX *912/231–0208,* WEB *www.kehoehouse.com. 13 rooms, 2 suites. Meeting room. AE, D, DC, MC, V. BP.*

$$–$$$$ 🏨 **Magnolia Place Inn.** Looking out directly across breathtaking Forsyth
★   Park, this opulent 1878 inn dazzles. There are regal antiques, prints, and
           porcelain from around the world—you'd expect one of Savannah's
           wealthy old cotton merchants to occupy such a mansion. Many rooms
           have Jacuzzis and fireplaces. With expansive verandas, lush terraces, and
           soaring ceilings, the Magnolia Place Inn typifies Savannah's golden era.
           ✉ *503 Whitaker St., Historic District 31401,* ☎ *912/236–7674 or 800/
           238–7674,* FAX *912/231–1218,* WEB *www.magnoliaplaceinn.com. 13 rooms,
           3 suites, 2 town houses. In-room VCRs, Internet. AE, MC, V. BP.*

$$–$$$ 🏨 **Claudia's Manor.** Proprietors Claudia and Larry Collins create a
           warm and inviting feeling in this sweeping Spanish Mediterranean home
           in the southern reaches of the city's Historic District, just a half mile south
           of Forsyth Park. Some of the accommodations in this turn-of-the-20th-
           century house have themed decors—one has African furnishings, and an-
           other is a homage to the East. Each of the large suites has a pair of
           queen-size beds. ✉ *101 E. 35th St., Historic District 31401,* ☎ *912/233–
           2379 or 800/773–8177,* FAX *912/238–5919,* WEB *www.claudiasmanor.com.
           4 rooms, 3 suites. AE, DC, MC, V. Internet, business services, meeting
           room. BP.*

$$–$$$ 🏨 **The Manor House.** Built for the Lewis Byrd family in the 1830s, this
★   majestic historic structure (it's the city's oldest building south of Lib-
           erty Street) once housed Union officers during General Sherman's Civil
           War march to the sea. All rooms are suites with a master bedroom and
           a separate cozy sitting area, and each has been decorated with a de-
           lightful individuality. Some even come complete with fireplace and
           kitchen. The Manor House also oversees three additional properties
           off-site from the main inn: a gorgeous, antiques-filled loft suite on Fac-
           tors Walk overlooking the historic Savannah waterfront; a large his-
           toric town house complete with formal dining room on Broughton Street;
           and a magnificent, two-bedroom oceanfront town house with two
           sprawling private decks on Tybee Island. ✉ *201 W. Liberty St., His-
           toric District 31401,* ☎ *912/233–9597 or 800/462–3595,* WEB *www.
           manorhouse-savannah.com. 8 suites. In-room VCRs, some whirlpool
           baths. AE, D, DC, MC, V. BP.*

$$–$$$ 🏨 **The President's Quarters.** You'll be impressed even before you enter
★   this lovely inn, which has an exterior courtyard so beautiful and invit-
           ing it has become a popular wedding-reception spot. Each room in this
           classic Savannah inn, fashioned out of a pair of meticulously restored
           1860s town houses, is named for an American president. Some rooms
           have four-poster beds, working fireplaces, and private balconies. Ex-
           pect to be greeted with wine and fruit, and a complimentary afternoon
           tea will tempt you with sweet cakes. Turndown service includes a glass
           of port or sherry. There are also rooms in an adjacent town house. ✉
           225 E. President St., Historic District 31401, ☎ *912/233–1600 or 800/
           233–1776,* FAX *912/238–0849,* WEB *www.presidentsquarters.com. 11
           rooms, 8 suites. Some hot tubs. D, DC, MC, V. BP.*

$–$$ 🏨 **Bed & Breakfast Inn.** So called, the owner claims, because it was
           the first such property to open in Savannah more than 20 years ago,
           the inn is a restored 1853 federal-style row house on historic Gordon
           Row near Chatham Square. The courtyard garden is a lovely cluster
           of potted tropical flowers surrounding an inviting koi pond. A sweep-
           ing renovation has added private baths to all the rooms but managed
           to keep many elements of the original charm, such as beamed ceilings
           and exposed-brick walls; only the Garden Suite has a full kitchen. Af-
           ternoon pastries, lemonade, coffee, and tea are served. ✉ *117 W. Gor-
           don St., Historic District 31401,* ☎ *912/238–0518,* FAX *912/233–2537,*
           WEB *www.savannahbnb.com. 15 rooms. AE, D, DC, MC, V. BP.*

$–$$ 🏠 **Green Palm Inn.** This inn is quite a pleasing little discovery. Origi-
★   nally built in 1897 but renovated top to bottom by owners Jack Moore
         and Rick Ellison, it's now a B&B. The elegant furnishings, meant to
         reflect a minimized subtropical aesthetic, were inspired by Savannah's
         British colonial heritage; some rooms have fireplaces. A separate cot-
         tage has two bedrooms, a fireplace, and a lush garden with a marble
         wading pool. ⊠ *548 E. President St., Historic District 31401,* ☎ *912/
         447–8901 or 888/606–9510,* FAX *912/236–4626,* WEB *www.greenpalminn.
         com. 5 suites, 1 cottage. Fans, cable TV. AE, MC, V. BP.*

$–$$ 🏠 **17th Street Inn.** The deck of this 1920 inn, which is adorned with
         plants, palms, and swings, is a gathering place where you can chat, sip
         wine, and enjoy breakfast both with other guests and your hosts: Susie
         Morris and her spouse, Stuart Liles. Steps from the beach, the inn has
         two-story porches and brightly colored rooms, each with a double iron
         bed. ⊠ *12 17th St., Box 114, Tybee Island 31328,* ☎ *912/786–0607
         or 888/909–0607,* FAX *912/786–0601,* WEB *www.tybeeinn.com. 8 rooms,
         1 condo. Kitchenettes. D, MC, V. CP.*

Hotels and Motels

$$$–$$$$ 🏠 **Hyatt Regency Savannah.** When this riverfront hotel was built in
         1981, preservationists opposed the construction of the seven-story
         modern structure in the Historic District. The main architectural fea-
         tures are the towering atrium and glass elevators. Rooms have mod-
         ern furnishings, marble baths, and balconies overlooking either the atrium
         or the Savannah River. MD's Lounge is the ideal spot to have a drink
         and watch the river traffic drift by. Windows, the hotel's restaurant,
         serves a great Sunday buffet. ⊠ *2 W. Bay St., Historic District 31401,*
         ☎ *912/238–1234 or 800/233–1234,* FAX *912/944–3673,* WEB *www.
         savannah-online.com/hyatt. 325 rooms, 22 suites. Restaurant, bar, in-
         door pool, health club, lounge, business services, meeting rooms. AE,
         D, MC, V.*

$$$ 🏠 **Mulberry Inn.** This Holiday Inn–managed property is ensconced in
★   an 1860s livery stable that later became a cotton warehouse and then
         a Coca-Cola bottling plant. Gleaming heart-pine floors and antiques,
         including a handsome English grandfather clock and an exquisitely
         carved Victorian mantel, make it unique. Deluxe-grade rooms, as ex-
         pected, have extras; the 24 suites have living rooms and wet bars. The
         café is a notch nicer than most other Holiday Inn restaurants. An ex-
         ecutive wing, at the back of the hotel, is geared to business travelers.
         ⊠ *601 E. Bay St., Historic District 31401,* ☎ *912/238–1200 or 800/
         465–4329,* FAX *912/236–2184,* WEB *www.savannahhotel.com. 145 rooms,
         24 suites. Restaurant, bar, café, some in-room VCRs, some microwaves,
         some refrigerators, outdoor pool, outdoor hot tub, Internet, meeting
         room. AE, D, DC, MC, V.*

$$$ 🏠 **Planters Inn.** Formerly the John Wesley Hotel, this inn is housed in
★   a structure built in 1812, and though it retains the regal tone of that
         golden age, it still offers all the intimate comforts you would expect from
         an upscale inn. The inn's 60 guest rooms are all decorated in the finest
         fabrics and Baker furnishings (a '20s design style named for the Dutch
         immigrant cabinetmaker). According to lore, a (good) ghost inhabits
         the hotel, floating through the hallways and rearranging skewed paint-
         ings hanging in the hallway. ⊠ *29 Abercorn St., Historic District 31401,*
         ☎ *912/232–5678,* FAX *912/236–2184,* WEB *www.plantersinnsavannah.
         com. 60 rooms. Cable TV, hot tubs. AE, D, DC, MC, V.*

$$–$$$ 🏠 **Marshall House.** This restored hotel, with original pine floors,
         woodwork, and bricks, caters to business travelers while providing the
         intimacy of a B&B. Different spaces reflect different parts of Savan-
         nah's history, from its founding to the Civil War. Artwork is mostly
         by local artists. You can listen to live jazz on weekends in the hotel
         lounge. Café M specializes in local cuisine, such as Southern pot-au-

feu, a seafood-rich Lowcountry dish with okra and greens, and Georgia smoked quail. Guests get free passes to a downtown health club. ⊠ *123 E. Broughton St., Historic District 31401,* ☎ *912/644–7896 or 800/589–6304,* FAX *912/234–3334,* WEB *www.marshallhouse.com. 65 rooms, 3 suites. Restaurant, lounge, meeting room. AE, D, MC, V.*

$$–$$$ 📷 **River Street Inn.** The interior of this 1817 converted warehouse is so lavish that it's hard to believe the five-story building once stood vacant in a state of disrepair. Today the 86 guest rooms are filled with antiques and reproductions from the era of King Cotton. One floor has charming souvenir and gift shops and a New Orleans–style restaurant. ⊠ *115 E. River St., Historic District 31401,* ☎ *912/234–6400 or 800/678–8946,* FAX *912/234–1478,* WEB *www.riverstreetinn.com. 86 rooms. 2 restaurants, 3 bars, shops, billiards, business services, meeting rooms. AE, D, DC, MC, V. BP.*

Nightlife and the Arts

Savannah's nightlife reflects the city's laid-back personality. Some clubs have live reggae, hard rock, and other contemporary music, but most stick to traditional blues, jazz, and piano-bar vocalists. After-dark merrymakers usually head for watering holes on Riverfront Plaza or the south side.

Bars and Nightclubs

The **Bar Bar** (⊠ 219 W. St. Julian St., Historic District, ☎ 912/231–1910), a neighborhood hangout, has pool tables, games, and a varied beer selection. Once a month at **Club One Jefferson** (⊠ 1 Jefferson St., Historic District, ☎ 912/232–0200), a gay bar, the Lady Chablis bumps and grinds her way down the catwalk, lip-synching disco tunes in a shimmer of sequin and satin gowns; the cover is $5. **Kevin Barry's Irish Pub** (⊠ 114 W. River St., Historic District, ☎ 912/233–9626) has a friendly vibe, a full menu until 1 AM, and traditional Irish music from Wednesday to Sunday; it's *the* place to be on St. Patrick's Day. The rest of the year there's a mix of tourists and locals of all ages. Go to **M.D.'s Lounge** (⊠ 2 W. Bay St., Historic District, ☎ 912/238–1234) if you have a classy nightcap in mind. The bar is literally perched above the Savannah River and surrounded by windows big enough to be glass walls. **Stogies** (⊠ 112 W. Congress St., Historic District, ☎ 912/233–4277) has its own humidor where patrons buy expensive cigars. It's a fun spot if you can take the smoke.

Coffeehouses

Thanks to a substantial student population, the city has sprouted coffeehouses as if they were spring flowers. **Christy's Espresso Delights** (⊠ 7400 Abercorn St., Highland Park, ☎ 912/356–3566) is a full-service espresso café with a wonderful selection of fine desserts and a light-lunch menu. The **Express** (⊠ 39 Barnard St., Historic District, ☎ 912/233–4683) is a warm, unassuming bakery and café that serves specialty coffees along with decadent desserts and tasty snacks. **Gallery Espresso** (⊠ 6 E. Liberty St., Historic District, ☎ 912/233–5348) is a combined coffee haunt and art enclave, with gallery shows; it stays open late.

Jazz and Blues Clubs

Bayou Café and Blues Bar (⊠ 14 N. Abercorn St., at River St., Historic District, ☎ 912/233–6414) has acoustic music during the week and the Bayou Blues Band on the weekend. The food is Cajun. **Cafe Loco** (⊠ 1 Old Hwy. 80, Tybee Island, ☎ 912/786–7810), a few miles outside Savannah, showcases local blues and acoustics acts. You can rollick with Emma Kelly, the undisputed "Lady of 6,000 Songs," at **Hard Hearted Hannah's East** (⊠ 20 E. Broad St., Historic District, ☎ 912/233–2225) Tuesday through Saturday.

Outdoor Activities and Sports

Boating

At the **Bull River Yacht Club Marina** (⊠ 8005 Old Tybee Rd., Tybee Island, ☎ 912/897–7300), you can arrange a dolphin tour, a deep-sea fishing expedition, or a jaunt through the coastal islands. **Lake Mayer Park** (⊠ Montgomery Crossroads Rd. and Sallie Mood Dr., Cresthill, ☎ 912/652–6780) has paddleboats, sailing, canoeing, and an in-line skating and hockey facility. **Saltwater Charters** (⊠ 111 Wickersham Dr., Skidaway Island, ☎ 912/598–1814) provides packages ranging from two-hour sightseeing tours to 13-hour deep-sea fishing expeditions. Water taxis to the coastal islands are also available. Public boat ramps are found at **Bell's on the River** (⊠ 12500 Apache Ave., off Abercorn St., Windward, ☎ 912/920–1113), on the Forest River. **Savannah Islands Expressway** (⊠ adjacent to Frank W. Spencer Park, Skidaway Island, ☎ 912/231–8222) offers boat ramps on the Wilmington River. **Savannah Marina** (⊠ Thunderbolt) provides ramps on the Wilmington River.

Golf

Bacon Park (⊠ 1 Shorty Cooper Dr., Southside, ☎ 912/354–2625), a public course with 27 holes, is par 72 for 18 holes and has a lighted driving range. **Henderson Golf Club** (⊠ 1 Al Henderson Dr., at I–95, Exit 94 to Rte. 204, Southside, ☎ 912/920–4653) is an 18-hole, par-71 course about 15 mi from downtown Savannah. The **Mary Calder Golf Course** (⊠ W. Lathrop Ave., West Chatham, ☎ 912/238–7100) is par 35 for its 9 holes.

Jogging and Running

Savannah's low-lying coastal terrain makes it an ideal place for joggers. **Forsyth Park** (⊠ Bull St. between Whitaker and Drayton Sts., Historic District) is a flat, pleasant place to walk, jog, or run. **Tybee Island** has a white-sand beach that is hard packed and relatively debris free, making it a favorite with runners. For suburban jogging trails head for **Daffin Park** (⊠ 1500 E. Victory Dr., Edgemere), with level sidewalks available during daylight hours. **Lake Mayer Park** (⊠ Montgomery Crossroads Rd. and Sallie Mood Dr., Southside) has 1½ mi of level asphalt available 24 hours a day.

Tennis

Bacon Park (⊠ 6262 Skidaway Rd., Southside, ☎ 912/351–3850) has 16 lighted asphalt courts. Fees are $2.50 an hour per person. **Forsyth Park** (⊠ Drayton St. and Park Ave., Historic District, ☎ 912/652–6780) contains four lighted courts available until about 10 PM; there is no charge to use them. **Lake Mayer Park** (⊠ Montgomery Crossroads Rd. and Sallie Mood Dr., Southside, ☎ 912/652–6780) has eight asphalt lighted courts available at no charge and open 8 AM–10 PM (until 11 PM May–September).

Shopping

Find your own Lowcountry treasures among a bevy of handcrafted wares—handmade quilts and baskets; wreaths made from Chinese tallow trees and Spanish moss; preserves, jams, and jellies. The favorite Savannah snack, and a popular gift item, is the benne wafer. It's about the size of a quarter and comes in different flavors. Savannah has a wide collection of colorful businesses—revitalization is no longer a goal but an accomplishment. Antiques malls and junk emporiums beckon you with their colorful storefronts and eclectic offerings, as do the many specialty shops and bookstores clustered along the moss-embossed streets.

Shopping Districts

City Market (⊠ W. St. Julian St. between Ellis and Franklin Sqs., Historic District) has sidewalk cafés, jazz haunts, shops, and art galleries. **Riverfront Plaza/River Street** (⊠ Historic District) is nine blocks of shops in renovated waterfront warehouses where you can find everything from popcorn to pottery.

Specialty Shops

ANTIQUES

Alexandra's Antique Gallery (⊠ 320 W. Broughton St., Historic District, ☎ 912/233–3999) is a four-level extravaganza of items from kitsch to fine antiques. **Arthur Smith Antiques** (⊠ 402 Bull St., Historic District, ☎ 912/236–9701) has four floors showcasing 18th- and 19th-century European furniture, porcelain, rugs, and paintings.

ART GALLERIES

Compass Prints, Inc./Ray Ellis Gallery (⊠ 205 W. Congress St., Historic District, ☎ 912/234–3537) sells original artwork, prints, and books by internationally acclaimed artist Ray Ellis. **Gallery Espresso** (⊠ 6 E. Liberty St., Historic District, ☎ 912/233–5348) has a new show every two weeks focusing on work by local artists. A true coffeehouse, it stays open until the wee hours. **Gallery 209** (⊠ 209 E. River St., Historic District, ☎ 912/236–4583) is a co-op gallery, with paintings, watercolors, pottery, jewelry, batik, stained glass, weavings, and sculptures by local artists. **Off the Wall** (⊠ 206 W. Broughton St., Historic District, ☎ 912/233–8840) exhibits artists from everywhere, including Savannah. **Jack Leigh Gallery** (⊠ 132 E. Oglethorpe Ave., Historic District, ☎ 912/234–6449) displays the work of Jack Leigh, whose photograph of Bonaventure Cemetery graces the cover of *Midnight in the Garden of Good and Evil.*

Savannah College of Art and Design (⊠ 516 Abercorn St., Historic District, ☎ 912/525–5200), a private art college, has restored at least 40 historic buildings in the city, including 12 galleries. Work by faculty and students is often for sale, and touring exhibitions are frequently in the on-campus galleries. Stop by Exhibit A, Pinnacle Gallery, and the West Bank Gallery, and ask about other student galleries. Garden for the Arts has an amphitheater and shows performance art.

BENNE WAFERS

Byrd Cookie Company & Gourmet Marketplace (⊠ 6700 Waters Ave., Highland Park, ☎ 912/355–1716), founded in 1924, is the best place to get the popular cookies that are also sold in numerous gift shops around town.

BOOKS

For regional to general Southern subjects and Americana, visit the **Book Lady** (⊠ 17 W. York St., Historic District, ☎ 912/233–3628), in a 200-year-old house for more than two decades. The shop also has an on-line search service. **E. Shaver Booksellers** (⊠ 326 Bull St., Historic District, ☎ 912/234–7257) is the source for 17th- and 18th-century maps and new books on regional subjects; the shop occupies 12 rooms. **V. & J. Duncan** (⊠ 12 E. Taylor St., Historic District, ☎ 912/232–0338) specializes in antique maps, prints, and books.

COUNTRY CRAFTS

Charlotte's Corner (⊠ 1 W. Liberty St., Historic District, ☎ 912/233–8061) carries expensive and moderately priced Savannah souvenirs, children's clothes and toys, and beachwear.

Savannah A to Z

To research prices, get advice from other travelers, and book travel arrangements, visit www.fodors.com.

AIR TRAVEL TO AND FROM SAVANNAH
CARRIERS
Savannah is served by AirTran Airways, ASA, Comair, Continental Express, Delta, United Express, and US Airways/Express for domestic flights.

AIRPORTS AND TRANSFERS
Savannah International Airport is 18 mi west of downtown. Despite the name, international flights are nonexistent. The foreign trade zone, a locus for importing, constitutes the "international" aspect.
➤ AIRPORT INFORMATION: **Savannah International Airport** (✉ 400 Airways Ave., West Chatham, ☎ 912/964–0514, WEB www.savannahairport.com).

AIRPORT TRANSFER
Vans operated by McCall's Limousine Service leave the airport daily for downtown locations. The trip takes 15 minutes, and the one-way fare is $16 for one-way, $30 round-trip for one person; the two-person rate is $11 per person one-way, $22 per person round-trip. Routes can include other destinations in addition to downtown. Advance reservation is required.

Taxi service is an easy way to get from the airport to downtown; try AAA Adam Cab Incorporated and Yellow Cab Company; the one-way fare is about $20, plus $5 for each addition person. By car take I–95 south to I–16 east into downtown Savannah.
➤ TAXIS AND SHUTTLES: **AAA Adam Cab Incorporated** (☎ 912/927–7466). **McCall's Limousine Service** (☎ 912/966–5364). **Yellow Cab Company** (☎ 912/236–1133).

BUS TRAVEL TO AND FROM SAVANNAH
➤ BUS INFORMATION: **Greyhound/Trailways** (✉ 610 W. Oglethorpe Ave., Downtown, ☎ 912/233–8186 or 800/231–2222).

BUS TRAVEL WITHIN SAVANNAH
Chatham Area Transit (CAT) operates buses in Savannah and Chatham County Monday through Saturday from 6 AM to 11 PM, Sunday from 9 to 7. Some lines may stop running earlier or may not run on Sunday. The CAT Shuttle operates throughout the Historic District; the cost is 75¢ one-way. Buses require 75¢ in exact change.
➤ BUS INFORMATION: **Chatham Area Transit** (☎ 912/233–5767, WEB www.catchacat.org).

CAR TRAVEL
I–95 slices north–south along the eastern seaboard, intersecting 10 mi west of town with east–west I–16, which dead-ends in downtown Savannah. U.S. 17, the Coastal Highway, also runs north–south through town. U.S. 80, which connects the Atlantic to the Pacific, is another east–west route through Savannah.

EMERGENCIES
Candler Hospital and Memorial Health University Medical Center are the area hospitals with 24-hour emergency rooms.
➤ EMERGENCY SERVICES: **Ambulance, police** (☎ 911).
➤ HOSPITALS: **Candler Hospital** (✉ 5353 Reynolds St., Kensington Park, ☎ 912/692–6000). **Memorial Health University Medical Center** (✉ 4700 Waters Ave., Fairfield, ☎ 912/350–8000).

➤ 24-HOUR PHARMACIES: **CVS Pharmacy** (✉ Medical Arts Shopping Center, 4725 Waters Ave., Fairfield, ☎ 912/355–7111).

LODGING

Bed & Breakfast Online can provide detailed cyber-brochures on inns in Atlanta as well as the surrounding area.
➤ RESERVATION INFORMATION: **Bed & Breakfast Online** (✉ Box 829, Madison, TN 37116, WEB www.bbonline.com/ga, ☎ 615/868–1946).

TAXIS

AAA Adam Cab Co. is a reliable 24-hour taxi service. Calling ahead for reservations could yield a flat rate. Taxis start at 60¢ and cost $1.20 for each mile. Yellow Cab Company is another dependable taxi service; it has comparable rates.
➤ TAXI COMPANIES: **AAA Adam Cab Co.** (☎ 912/927–7466). **Yellow Cab Company** (☎ 912/236–1133).

TOURS

HISTORIC DISTRICT TOURS

Beach Institute African-American Cultural Center is headquarters for the Negro Heritage Trail Tour. A knowledgeable guide traces the city's more than 250 years of black history. Tours, which begin at the Savannah Visitors Center, are at 1 and 3 and cost $15.

Carriage Tours of Savannah takes you through the Historic District by day or by night at a 19th-century clip-clop pace, with coachmen spinning tales and telling ghost stories along the way. A romantic evening tour in a private carriage costs $65 ($85 on Friday and Saturday evenings), and although champagne can no longer be included, you may bring whatever refreshments you wish; regular tours are a more modest $17 per person.

Garden Club of Savannah runs spring tours of private gardens tucked behind old brick walls and wrought-iron gates. It costs $20 and finishes with tea at the Green-Meldrim House.

Old Town Trolley Tours has narrated 90-minute tours traversing the Historic District. Trolleys stop at 13 designated stops every half hour daily 9–4:30; you can hop on and off as you please. The cost is $18–$22.
➤ FEES AND SCHEDULES: **Beach Institute African-American Cultural Center** (☎ 912/234–8000). **Carriage Tours of Savannah** (☎ 912/236–6756). **Garden Club of Savannah** (☎ 912/238–0248). **Old Town Trolley Tours** (☎ 912/233–0083).

SPECIAL-INTEREST TOURS

Gray Line conducts a four-hour tour to Isle of Hope and the Lowcountry, including Thunderbolt (a shrimping community) and Wormsloe Plantation Site. Options include walking tours, minibus tours, and trolley tours. The cost is $17–$22.

Historic Savannah Foundation, a preservation organization, leads tours of the Historic District and the Lowcountry. Preservation, *Midnight in the Garden of Good and Evil,* the Golden Isles, group, and private tours also are available. In addition, the foundation leads specialty excursions to the fishing village of Thunderbolt; the Isle of Hope, with its stately mansions lining Bluff Drive; the much-photographed Bonaventure Cemetery, on the banks of the Wilmington River; and Wormsloe Plantation Site, with its mile-long avenue of arching oaks. Fees for the specialty tours start at $75 per hour, with a two-hour minimum for a private group of up to five people.

Square Routes provides customized strolls and private driving tours that wend through the Historic District and other parts of the Low-country. In-town tours focus on the city's architecture and gardens, and specialized tours include the *Midnight in the Garden of Good and Evil* walk. Tours usually last two hours and start at $35 per person, with a minimum of two people per tour.

➤ FEES AND SCHEDULES: **Gray Line** (☎ 912/234–8687 or 800/426–2318). **Historic Savannah Foundation** (☎ 912/234–4088 or 800/627–5030). **Square Routes** (☎ 912/232–6866 or 800/868–6867).

WALKING TOURS

Much of the downtown Historic District can easily be explored on foot. Its grid shape makes getting around a breeze, and you'll find any number of places to stop and rest.

A Ghost Talk Ghost Walk tour should send chills down your spine during an easy 1-mi jaunt through the old colonial city. Tours, lasting an hour and a half, leave from the middle of Reynolds Square, at the John Wesley Memorial. Call for dates, times, and reservations; the cost is $10.

Savannah-by-Foot's Creepy Crawl Haunted Pub Tour is a favorite. It seems there are so many ghosts in Savannah they're actually divided into subcategories. On this tour, charismatic guide and storyteller Greg Proffit specializes in those ghosts that haunt taverns only, regaling you with tales from secret subbasements discovered to house skeletal remains, possessed gum-ball machines, and animated water faucets. Tours traditionally depart from the Six Pence Pub, where a ghost named Larry likes to fling open the bathroom doors, but routes are open to customizing, so call for departure times and locations; the cost is $15.

➤ FEES AND SCHEDULES: **A Ghost Talk Ghost Walk Tour** (✉ Reynolds Sq., Congress and Abercorn Sts., Historic District, ☎ 912/233–3896). **Savannah-By-Foot's Creepy Crawl Haunted Pub Tour** (☎ 912/398–3833). **Six Pence Pub** (✉ 245 Bull St., Historic District).

TRAIN TRAVEL

Amtrak has regular service along the eastern seaboard, with daily stops in Savannah. The Amtrak station is 4 mi southwest of downtown. Cab fare into the city is $7–$10, depending on the number of passengers.

➤ TRAIN INFORMATION: **Amtrak** (✉ 2611 Seaboard Coastline Dr., Telfair Junction, ☎ 912/234–2611 or 800/872–7245, WEB www.amtrak.com).

VISITOR INFORMATION

➤ TOURIST INFORMATION: **Savannah Area Convention & Visitors Bureau** (✉ 101 E. Bay St., Historic District 31401, ☎ 912/644–6401 or 877/728–2662, FAX 912/944–0468, WEB www.savcvb.com).

THE COASTAL ISLES AND THE OKEFENOKEE

Jekyll, St. Simons, and Sea Islands

The coastal isles are a string of lush, subtropical barrier islands meandering lazily down Georgia's Atlantic coast from Savannah to the Florida border. The islands have a long history of human habitation; Native American relics have been found here that date from about 2500 BC. The four designated Golden Isles—Little St. Simons Island, Sea Island, St. Simons Island, and Jekyll Island—are great vacation spots. The best way to appreciate the barrier islands' rare ecology is to visit Sapelo and Cumberland islands—part of Georgia's coastal isles—or to take a guided tour.

Each coastal isle has a distinct personality, shaped by its history and ecology. All the Golden Isles but Little St. Simons are connected to the mainland by bridges in the vicinity of Brunswick; these are the only coastal isles accessible by automobile. Little St. Simons Island, a privately owned retreat with guest accommodations, is reached by a launch from St. Simons. Sapelo Island is accessible by ferry from the visitor center just north of Darien (on the mainland). The Cumberland Island National Seashore is reached by ferry from St. Marys. About 60 mi inland is the Okefenokee National Wildlife Refuge, which has a character all its own.

Lodging prices quoted here may be much lower during nonpeak seasons, and specials are often available during the week in high season. All Georgia beaches are in the public domain.

Numbers in the margin correspond to points of interest on the Coastal Isles map.

Sapelo Island

86 *8 mi east of Darien.*

In Sapelo's fields you might find chips of Guale Indian pottery dating as far back as 2000 BC and shards of Spanish ceramics from the 16th century. On the northern end, remains of the Chocolate Plantation recall the island's French heritage and role during the plantation days of the 19th century. Today researchers occupy the southern sector of the island, studying ecology at the Sapelo Island National Estuarine Research Reserve and evaluating the marshland at the Marine Institute. The organizations' studies are instrumental in preserving Sapelo's delicate ecosystem and others like it throughout the world.

You can explore many historical periods and natural environments here, but facilities on the island are limited for the most part to drinking fountains and rest rooms. Bring insect repellent, especially in summer, and leave your pets at home.

Start your visit at the **Sapelo Island Visitors Center** (✉ Rte. 1, Box 1500, Darien 31305, ☎ 912/437–3224; 912/485–2300 for group tours; 912/485–2299 for camping reservations, WEB www.gacoast.com/navigator/sapelo.html). To get here from downtown Darien, go north on Route 99 for 8 mi, following signs for the Sapelo Island National Estuarine Research Reserve. At the visitors center you'll see an exhibition on the island's history, culture, and ecology. Here you can purchase a ticket good for a round-trip ferry ride and bus tour of the island. The sights that make up the bus tour vary depending on the day of the week but always included are the marsh, the sand dune ecosystem, and the wildlife management area. On Saturday the tour includes the 80-ft **Sapelo Lighthouse,** built in 1820, a symbol of the cotton and lumber industry once based out of Darien's port. To see the island's **Reynolds Mansion,** schedule your tour for Wednesday. Reservations are required for tours. If you wish to stay overnight on Sapelo, you can either camp or choose from several B&B inns. If you stay overnight (and only if you do), you may visit the beach and, on a tour, the **Hog Hammock Community,** the few remaining sites on the south Atlantic coast where ethnic African-American culture has been preserved. Hog Hammock's 65 residents are descendants of slaves who worked the is-

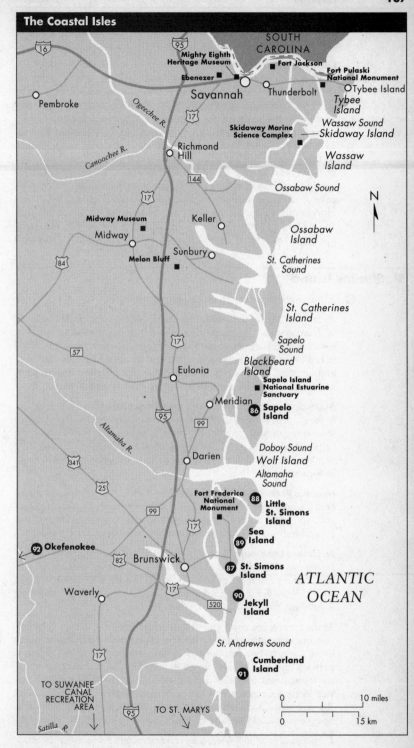

The Coastal Isles

land's plantations during the 19th century. You can rent a bicycle at
your hotel if you want to tour the area, but you cannot bring a bicycle on the ferry.

Dining and Lodging

$-$$ ✕ **Mudcat Charlie's.** It's plastic forks and plates all the way at this ca-
sual eatery. Local seafood—crab stew, fried oysters, and shrimp—is the
specialty. The steaks, burgers, and pork chops are good, too. Peach and
apple pies are made on the premises. It's between Brunswick and
Darien on U.S. 17, 8 mi from Sapelo Island. ✉ *250 Ricefield Way,* ☎
912/261–0055. AE, D, DC, MC, V.

$$ ⌂ **Open Gates.** Fine antiques fill the public spaces and guest rooms of
this comfortable white-frame Victorian house, which dates from 1876.
Breakfast specialties include fresh fig preserves, plantation (puffed) pan-
cakes, and hunter's casserole (a baked egg strata). Innkeeper Carolyn
Hodges offers guided tours of the Altamaha River. ✉ *Vernon Sq., Box
1526, Darien 31305,* ☎ *912/437–6985,* ℻ *912/882–9427,* 🌐 *www.
opengatesbnb.com. 4 rooms, 2 with bath. Pool, library. No credit
cards. BP.*

St. Simons Island

❽⑦   *22 mi south of Darien, 6 mi south of Brunswick.*

As large as Manhattan, with more than 14,000 year-round residents,
St. Simons is the Golden Isles' most complete resort destination. For-
tunately, all this development has not spoiled the natural beauty of the
island's regal live oaks, beaches, and salt marshes. Here you can swim
and sun, golf, bike, hike, go fishing, horseback ride, tour historic sites,
and feast on fresh local seafood at more than 50 restaurants.

Many sights and activities are in the **village** area along Mallory Street
at the more developed south end of the island, where you'll find shops,
several restaurants, pubs, and a popular public pier. For $10 a quaint
"trolley" takes you on a 1½-hour guided tour of the island, leaving from
near the pier several times a day in high season; tours run less frequently
in winter.

☾   **Neptune Park** (✉ 550 Beachview Dr., ☎ 912/638–2393), on the is-
land's south end, has picnic tables, a children's play park, miniature
golf, and beach access. A swimming pool ($3 per person), with show-
ers and rest rooms, is open each summer in the **Neptune Park Casino.**

St. Simons Lighthouse, a beacon since 1872, is virtually the symbol of
St. Simons. The **Museum of Coastal History,** in the lightkeeper's cot-
tage, has a permanent exhibit of coastal history. ✉ *101 12th St.,* ☎
912/638–4666, 🌐 *www.saintsimonslighthouse.org.* ☜ *$4, including
lighthouse.* ☾ *Mon.–Sat. 10–5, Sun. 1:30–5.*

At the burgeoning north end of the island there's a marina, a golf club,
and a housing development, as well as **Fort Frederica National Monu-
ment,** the ruins of a fort built by English troops in the mid-1730s as a
bulwark against a Spanish invasion from Florida. Around the fort are
the foundations of homes and shops. Start at the **National Park Ser-
vice Visitors Center,** which has a film and displays. ✉ *Off Frederica
Rd. just past Christ Episcopal Church,* ☎ *912/638–3639,* 🌐 *www.
nps.gov/fofr.* ☜ *$4 per car.* ☾ *Daily 8–5.*

Consecrated in 1886 following an earlier structure's desecration by Union
troops, the white-frame Gothic-style **Christ Episcopal Church** is sur-
rounded by live oaks, dogwoods, and azaleas. The interior has beau-
tiful stained-glass windows. ✉ *6329 Frederica Rd.,* ☎ *912/638–8683.*
☜ *Donations suggested.*

Dining and Lodging

$$–$$$$ ✕ **Georgia Sea Grill.** This tiny and very popular place presents eclectic dishes, with fresh local seafood the house specialty. Standouts include tender shrimp au gratin, as well as fresh seafood prepared five different ways. Nightly specials are prepared personally by the chef–owners. ✉ *310B Mallory St.,* ☎ *912/638–1197. D, MC, V. Closed Mon. May–Sept.; Sun.–Mon. Oct.–Apr. No lunch.*

$$–$$$ ✕ **CARGO Portside Grill.** Don't miss this superb seaside pub, a short drive across the bridge in the small city of Brunswick. The menu reads like a foodie's wish list, with succulent coastal and cross-coastal fare from many ports. All of it is creatively presented by owner–chef Alix Kanegy, formerly of Atlanta's Indigo Coastal Grill. Specials have included pasta Veracruz with grilled chicken, smoked tomatoes, poblano peppers, and caramelized onions in a chipotle cream sauce; in season, soft-shell crab is often on the menu. ✉ *1423 Newcastle St., Brunswick,* ☎ *912/267–7330. MC, V. Closed Sun.–Mon.*

$$–$$$ ✕ **Redfern Café.** A popular spot with locals, the Redfern has up to six specials nightly in addition to the regular menu. Fried oysters in a light cornmeal coating, shrimp and crab bisque with corn fritters, and the crab cakes are specialties. ✉ *200 Redfern Village,* ☎ *912/634–1344. Reservations essential. MC, V. Closed Sun.*

$–$$$ ✕ **P. G. Archibald's.** In the village this lively restaurant and nightclub has a "bayou Victorian" style, with lots of antiques and memorabilia. The menu highlights seafood as well as basic steak and chicken dishes, plus oysters prepared 15 ways. Blue-crab soup is a local favorite, and the huge seafood platter could easily feed two. Open late, the restaurant also presents live entertainment Thursday through Saturday. ✉ *440 King's Way,* ☎ *912/638–3030. AE, DC, MC, V.*

$ ✕ **Rafters Blues Club, Restaurant and Raw Bar.** If you're looking for cheap, great food and a raucous good time, this place serves it up by the boatload. Revelers sit at long wooden-plank picnic tables and heartily partake in the offerings of both the prodigious bar and the equally generous kitchen. The restaurant serves ocean fare prepared in interesting ways—a seafood burrito, for example. Rafters is open late and presents live entertainment Wednesday through Saturday. ✉ *315½ Mallory St.,* ☎ *912/634–9755. AE, D, MC, V. Closed Sun.*

$$$$ 🏨 **The Lodge at Sea Island Golf Club.** This small but opulent lodge has assumed its place among the coast's most exclusive accommodations. Dashingly decorated rooms and suites all have water or golf-course views, and you can expect to be pampered by 24-hour butler service. You can also choose from among four stellar restaurants for dining. The lodge serves as the clubhouse for the Sea Island Golf Club (although this whole complex lies on St. Simons Island, so don't let the title disorient you) and encompasses a trophy room, locker rooms, and the Sea Island Golf Learning Center. ✉ *St. Simons Island 31522,* ☎ *912/638–3611 or 866/465–3563,* WEB *www.golflodge.com. 40 rooms, 2 suites. 4 restaurants, bar, in-room VCRs, 2 18-hole golf courses, tennis court, pool, health club, hot tub, lounge, Internet, meeting room. AE, D, DC, MC, V.*

$$$ 🏨 **King and Prince Beach and Golf Resort.** Most people who visit feel it's worth the expense to get a room with easy beach access at this cushy retreat. Guest rooms are spacious, and villas have two or three bedrooms. The villas are owned by private individuals, so the total number available for rent varies from time to time. ✉ *201 Arnold Rd., Box 20798, 31522,* ☎ *912/638–3631 or 800/342–0212,* FAX *912/634–1720,* WEB *www.kingandprince.com. 148 rooms, 10 suites, 43 villas. 2 restaurants, bar, golf privileges, 2 tennis courts, 1 indoor and 4 outdoor pools, 3 hot tubs, bicycles, lounge, Internet. AE, D, MC, V.*

$$ 🏨 **Holiday Inn Express.** With brightly decorated rooms at great prices, this nonsmoking facility is an excellent midprice option. The six King

Executive rooms have sofas and desks. ⊠ *Plantation Village, 299 Main St., 31522,* ☎ *912/634–2175 or 800/787–4666,* ℻ *912/634–2174. 60 rooms. Cable TV, pool, bicycles, laundry service, meeting room. AE, D, MC, V.*

$–$$ ⛳ **Sea Palms Golf and Tennis Resort.** Given this resort's emphasis on golf and tennis, it's an ideal milieu if you're the sports-minded type. Rooms have balconies overlooking the golf course, and they are large— so large they're touted as the biggest standard guest rooms in the Golden Isles. The furnishings are somewhat unimaginative, however. This is a contemporary complex with fully furnished villas (suites), most with kitchens, nestled on an 800-acre site. Guests also enjoy beach club privileges. ⊠ *5445 Frederica Rd., 31522,* ☎ *912/638–3351 or 800/841–6268,* ℻ *912/634–8029,* ⓦⒺⒷ *www.seapalms.com. 149 rooms, 26 suites. 2 restaurants, bar, 27-hole golf course, 3 tennis courts, 2 pools, health club, bicycles, volleyball, children's programs, convention center. AE, DC, MC, V.*

RENTALS

For St. Simons condo and cottage rentals, contact **Golden Isles Realty** (⊠ 330 Mallory St., 31522, ☎ 912/638–8623 or 800/337–3106, ℻ 912/638–6925). **Trupp-Hodnett Enterprises** (⊠ 520 Ocean Blvd., 31522, ☎ 912/638–5450 or 800/627–6850, ℻ 912/638–2983) provides boat rentals.

Little St. Simons Island

88 *10–15 mins by ferry from the Hampton River Club Marina on St. Simons Island.*

Six miles long, 2–3 mi wide, and skirted by Atlantic beaches and salt marshes teeming with birds and wildlife, this privately owned resort is custom-made for *Robinson Crusoe*–style getaways. The island's only development is a rustic but comfortable guest compound. Guided tours, horseback rides, canoe trips, fly-fishing lessons, and other extras can be arranged, some for no additional charge. Inquire about the advisability of bringing children, as there are some limitations. In summer day tours can be arranged.

The island's forests and marshes are inhabited by deer, armadillos, horses, raccoons, gators, otters, and more than 200 species of birds. As a guest you're free to walk the 6 mi of undisturbed beaches, swim in the mild surf, fish from the dock, and seine (you and others take a net, walk into the ocean, and drag the net back to shore) for shrimp and crabs in the marshes. There are also horses to ride, nature walks with experts, and other island explorations via boat or the back of the hotel's pickup truck. From June through September up to 10 nonguests per day may visit the island by reservation; the $75 cost includes the ferry to the island, an island tour by truck, lunch at the lodge, and a beach walk. Contact the Lodge on Little St. Simons Island for more information.

Dining and Lodging

$$$$ ✕⛳ **Lodge on Little St. Simons Island.** A recent winner of *Condé Nast Traveler*'s "Best Small Hotel in North America" title, this gorgeous resort cites full capacity at a mere 30 guests. Meals are included—platters are heaped with fresh fish, homemade breads, and pies. You also get complimentary drinks during cocktail hour. Transportation from St. Simons Island, transportation on the island, and interpretive guides are also provided. ⊠ *Box 21078, 31522,* ☎ *912/638–7472 or 888/733–5774,* ℻ *912/634–1811,* ⓦⒺⒷ *www.littlestsimonsisland.com. 14 rooms, 1 suite. Restaurant, pool, beach, boating, fishing, bicycles, horseback riding. AE, D, MC, V. FAP.*

Sea Island

89   *5 mi northeast of St. Simons Island.*

Separated from St. Simons Island by a narrow waterway and a good many steps on the social ladder, Sea Island has been the domain of the well-heeled and the Cloister Hotel since 1928. There is no entrance gate, and nonguests are free to admire the beautifully planted grounds and to drive past the mansions lining Sea Island Drive. The owners of the 180 or so private cottages and villas treat the hotel like a country club, and their tenants may use the hotel's facilities. For rentals contact **Sea Island Cottage Rentals** (⊠ Box 30351, 31561, ☎ 912/638–5112 or 800/732–4752, FAX 912/638–5824).

Lodging

$$$$ 🏨 **The Cloister.** The Cloister undeniably lives up to its celebrity status as a grand coastal resort. You can get a spacious, comfortably appointed room or suite in the Spanish Mediterranean–style hotel—designed by Florida architect Addison Mizner—or in the property's later-built Ocean Houses, which offer 56 dramatic suites connected by lavish house parlors with fireplaces and staffed bars. The state-of-the-art spa at the Cloister is in a beautiful building all its own. You also get access to the nearby Sea Island Golf Course. ⊠ *Sea Island 31561,* ☎ *912/638–3611 or 800/732–4752,* FAX *912/638–5823,* WEB *www.cloister.com. 274 rooms, 32 suites. 4 restaurants, bar, cable TV, 3 18-hole golf courses, 18 tennis courts, 2 pools, health club, spa, bicycles, 2 lounges, children's programs, business services, airport shuttle. AE, D, DC, MC, V. FAP.*

Jekyll Island

90   *18 mi south of St. Simons Island, 90 mi south of Savannah.*

For 56 winters, between 1886 and 1942, America's rich and famous faithfully came south to Jekyll Island. Through the Gilded Age, the Great War, as World War I was originally known, the Roaring '20s, and the Great Depression, Vanderbilts and Rockefellers, Morgans and Astors, Macys, Pulitzers, and Goodyears shuttered their 5th Avenue castles and retreated to the serenity of their wild Georgia island. Here they built elegant "cottages," played golf and tennis, and socialized. Early in World War II the millionaires departed for the last time. In 1947 the state of Georgia purchased the entire island for the bargain price of $675,000.

Jekyll Island is still a 7½-mi playground but is no longer restricted to the rich and famous. The golf, tennis, fishing, biking, and jogging, the water park, and the picnic grounds are open to all. One side of the island is lined by nearly 10 mi of hard-packed Atlantic beaches; the other, by the Intracoastal Waterway and picturesque salt marshes. Deer and wild turkeys inhabit interior forests of pine, magnolia, and moss-veiled live oaks. Egrets, pelicans, herons, and sandpipers skim the gentle surf. Jekyll's clean, mostly uncommercialized public beaches are free and open year-round. Bathhouses with rest rooms, changing areas, and showers are open at regular intervals along the beach. Beachwear, suntan lotion, rafts, snacks, and drinks are available at the **Jekyll Shopping Center,** facing the beach at Beachview Drive.

The **Jekyll Island Museum Visitor Center** gives tram tours of the Jekyll Island National Historic Landmark District. Tours originate at the museum's visitor center on Stable Road and include several millionaires' residences in the 240-acre historic district. Faith Chapel, illuminated by Tiffany stained-glass windows, is open for meditation daily 2–4. ⊠ *381 Riverview Dr., I–95, Exit 29,* ☎ *912/635–2762 or 800/841–6586,* FAX *912/635–4004.* 🎫 *$10.* ☉ *Daily 9–5, tours daily 10–3.*

Dining and Lodging

$$$ ✕ **Grand Dining Room.** In the Jekyll Island Club Hotel, the dining room
★   sparkles with silver and crystal. The cuisine reflects the elegance of the
private hunting club that flourished from the late 19th century to the
World War II era and which brought a fine chef and staff in from New
York's Delmonico's. Enjoy the blue-crab cakes, grilled pork with Vi-
dalia onion, and local seafood. The restaurant has its own label pinot
noir and chardonnay, made by Mountain View Vineyards. ✉ *371
Riverview Dr.,* ☎ *912/635–2600. Reservations essential. AE, D, DC,
MC, V.*

$$ ✕ **Courtyard at Crane.** This notable addition to the island's restaurant
scene offers alfresco dining in the courtyard of Crane Cottage, part of
the Jekyll Island Club Hotel. The menu focuses on creative salads and
entrées inspired by the world-famous kitchens of the Napa/Sonoma Valley wine country. You might sample the Mediterranean platter of
grilled vegetables, imported olives, and fresh mozzarella with *crostini*;
or a lobster-salad croissant with avocado, red onion, apple-wood-
smoked bacon, tomato, and alfalfa sprouts. ✉ *371 Riverview Dr., Jekyll
Island Club Hotel,* ☎ *912/635–2600. AE, D, DC, MC, V. Closed Sun.*

$$ ✕ **SeaJay's Waterfront Cafe & Pub.** Convivial and festive, with a
swamp-shack style, this tavern serves delicious—and inexpensive—
seafood, including a crab chowder that locals love. This is also the home
of a wildly popular shrimp-boil buffet: a Lowcountry all-you-can-eat
feast of local shrimp, corn on the cob, smoked sausage, and new pota-
toes served in a pot. ✉ *Jekyll Harbor Marina,* ☎ *912/635–3200. AE,
MC, V.*

$$$–$$$$ ☷ **Jekyll Island Club Hotel.** This sprawling 1886 resort, the focal point
★   of which is a four-story clubhouse—with couches and a fireplace—has
wraparound verandas and Queen Anne–style towers and turrets. Guest
rooms, suites, apartments, and cottages are custom-decorated with ma-
hogany beds, armoires, and plush sofas and chairs. Two beautifully
restored former "millionaires' cottages"—the Crane Cottage and the
Cherokee Cottage—add 23 elegant guest rooms to this gracefully
groomed compound. Note the B&B packages—they're a great deal.
✉ *371 Riverview Dr., 31527,* ☎ *912/635–2600 or 800/535–9547,* 𝔽𝔸𝕏
912/635–2818, 𝕎𝔼𝔹 *www.jekyllclub.com. 139 rooms, 15 suites. 3
restaurants, bar, cable TV, 13 tennis courts, pool, beach, bicycles, cro-
quet, lounge, Internet, meeting room. AE, D, DC, MC, V.*

$$–$$$$ ☷ **Beachview Club.** They literally raised the roof on an old motel to
★   build this luxury lodging. Stucco walls are painted light yellow, and
big old oak trees shade the grounds. Efficiencies have either one king-
or two queen-size beds, a desk, and a kitchenette. All rooms either are
on the oceanfront or have at least a partial ocean view from the balcony, and some rooms are equipped with a hot tub and gas fireplace.
The interior design reflects an understated island theme. An attempt
to target the corporate crowd has proven effective, and the unique meeting room in the Bell Tower accommodates up to 35 people for business events. Higher-end suites have full kitchens. ✉ *721 N. Beachview
Dr., 31527,* ☎ *912/635–2256 or 800/299–2228,* 𝔽𝔸𝕏 *912/635–3770,*
𝕎𝔼𝔹 *www.beachviewclub.com. 21 efficiencies, 7 suites. Restaurant,
bar, some kitchenettes, microwaves, pool, hot tub, Internet, meeting
room. AE, D, DC, MC, V.*

$$–$$$ ☷ **Holiday Inn Beach Resort.** Amid natural dunes and oaks in a secluded
oceanfront location, this hotel has a private beach. Each room has a
balcony, but none has an ocean view (though it's a short walk away).
The boardwalk out to the beach meanders through a lovely regional
landscape, thick with palm trees and other native flora. ✉ *200 S.
Beachview Dr., 31527,* ☎ *912/635–3311 or 800/753–5955,* 𝔽𝔸𝕏 *912/
635–2901,* 𝕎𝔼𝔹 *www.sixcontinentshotels.com. 198 rooms. Restaurant,*

bar, 2 tennis courts, pool, health club, bicycles, lobby lounge, playground. AE, D, DC, MC, V.

$–$$ ⊞ **Jekyll Inn.** This popular oceanfront spread's 15 verdant acres space the buildings generously apart. Popular with families, the inn accommodates children under 17 free when they stay with parents or grandparents. Packages include summer family-focused arrangements and romantic getaways. The Italian restaurant offers basic, hearty fare. ⊠ *975 N. Beachview Dr., 31527,* ☎ *912/635–2531 or 800/431–5190,* ⒻⒶⓍ *912/635–2332,* ⓌⒺⒷ *www.jekyllinn.com. 188 rooms, 66 villas. Restaurant, 2 bars, refrigerators, pool, volleyball, lobby lounge, playground, children's programs, laundry service, meeting room. AE, D, DC, MC, V.*

RENTALS

Jekyll's more than 200 rental cottages and condos are handled by **Jekyll Realty** (⊠ Box 13096, 31527, ☎ 912/635–3301 or 888/333–5055, ⒻⒶⓍ 912/635–3303). **Parker-Kaufman Realty** (⊠ Box 13126, 31527, ☎ 912/635–2512 or 888/453–5955, ⒻⒶⓍ 912/635–2190) is a small outfit that provides cottage and condo rental information.

Outdoor Activities and Sports

GOLF

The **Jekyll Island Golf Club** (⊠ 322 Capt. Wylly Rd., ☎ 912/635–2368) has 63 holes, including three 18-hole, par-72 courses, and a clubhouse. Greens fees are $35, good all day, and carts are $14.50 per person per course. There's also a 9-hole, par-36 course, the **Historic Oceanside Nine** (⊠ N. Beachview Dr., ☎ 912/635–2170), where the millionaires used to play. Greens fees are $21, and carts are $7.25 for every 9 holes.

NATURE CENTER

Ⓒ The **Coastal Encounters Nature Center** runs summer programs for children and families on the ecology of the coastal islands. Programs and excursions are individually priced. At the center are exhibits about the fauna of the region. ⊠ *100 S. Riverview Dr.,* ☎ *912/635–9102,* ⓌⒺⒷ *http://coastalgeorgia.com/coastalencounters.* ▨ *Donation.* ☉ *Mon.–Sat. 9–5.*

TENNIS

The **Jekyll Island Tennis Center** (⊠ 400 Capt. Wylly Rd., ☎ 912/635–3154) has 13 clay courts, with seven lighted for nighttime play; it hosts eight USTA-sanctioned tournaments throughout the year. Costs are $14 per hour daily 9–6 and $16 per hour for lighted courts (available until 10 PM); reservations for lighted courts are required and must be made prior to 6 PM the day of play.

WATER PARK

Ⓒ **Summer Waves,** an 11-acre water park, has an 18,000-square-ft wave pool, water slides, a children's activity pool with two slides, and a circular river for tubing and rafting. You are not permitted to bring your own equipment. ⊠ *210 S. Riverview Dr.,* ☎ *912/635–2074,* ⓌⒺⒷ *www. summerwaves.com.* ▨ *$14.95.* ☉ *Late May–early Sept. (and some additional weekends in early May and late Sept.), Sun.–Fri. 10–6, Sat. 10–8 (hrs vary at beginning and end of season).*

Cumberland Island

➒ *47 mi south of Jekyll Island, 115 mi south of Savannah to St. Marys via I–95, 45 mins by ferry from St. Marys.*

The largest, most southerly, and most accessible of Georgia's primitive coastal islands is Cumberland Island, a 16- by 3-mi sanctuary of marshes, dunes, beaches, forests, lakes and ponds, estuaries, and inlets. Waterways are homes for gators, sea turtles, otters, snowy egrets, great blue herons, ibises, wood storks, and more than 300 other species of birds. In the forests are armadillos, wild horses, deer, raccoons, and an assortment of reptiles.

After the ancient Guale Indians came 16th-century Spanish missionaries, 18th-century English soldiers, and 19th-century planters. During the 1880s the Thomas Carnegie family (he was the brother of industrialist Andrew) of Pittsburgh built several lavish homes here, but the island remained largely as nature created it. In the early 1970s the federal government established the **Cumberland Island National Seashore** and opened this natural treasure to the public. There is no transportation on the island itself, and the only public access to the island is via the *Cumberland Queen,* a reservations-only, 146-passenger ferry based near the National Park Service Information Center at St. Marys. Ferry bookings are heavy in summer, but cancellations and no-shows often make last-minute space available. Reservations may be made up to 11 months in advance.

From the park-service docks at the island's south end, you can follow wooded nature trails, swim and sun on 18 mi of undeveloped beaches, go fishing and bird-watching, and view the ruins of Thomas Carnegie's great estate, **Dungeness.** You can also join history and nature walks led by park-service rangers. Bear in mind that summers are hot and humid and that you must bring everything you need, including your own food, soft drinks, sunscreen, and a reliable insect repellent. ⊠ *Cumberland Island National Seashore, Box 806, 31558,* ☎ *912/882–4335,* FAX *912/673–7747,* WEB *www.nps.gov/cuis.* ✉ *Round-trip ferry $12, day pass $4, annual pass $20.* ☉ *Mid-May–Sept., ferry departure from St. Marys daily at 9 and 11:45, from Cumberland Mar.–Nov., Wed.–Sat. at 10:15, 2:45, and 4:45, Sun.–Tues. at 10:15 and 4:45. No ferry service Dec.–Feb. Tues.–Wed.*

Dining and Lodging

ISLAND

$$$$ ╳🆔 **Greyfield Inn.** Cumberland Island's only accommodations are in a turn-of-the-20th-century Carnegie family home. Greyfield's public areas are filled with family mementos, furnishings, and portraits (you may feel as though you've stepped into one of Agatha Christie's mysterious Cornwall manors). Prices include all meals, transportation, tours led by a naturalist, and bike rentals. ⊠ *8 N. 2nd St., Box 900, Fernandina Beach, FL 32035,* ☎ *904/261–6408,* FAX *904/321–0666,* WEB *www.greyfieldinn.com. 13 rooms, 4 suites. Restaurant, bar, bicycle rentals. AE, D, MC, V. FAP.*

$ 🛖 **Camping.** The island has three primitive camping sites in a National Wilderness Area. Reservations are required for all camping at these sites, and the rate is $2 per person per day. To reach the sites (Hickory Hill, Yankee Paradise, and Brickhill Bluff), start north of Sea Camp dock and then hike (with all equipment) from 4 to 10 mi. Equipment must include rope to suspend provisions from trees for critter control. Non-wilderness Stafford Beach is good for novice backpackers. A half mile from the dock, with rest rooms and showers adjacent to campsites, Sea Camp is the ideal spot for first-time campers ($4 per person per day). Also available are 16 campsites that can accommodate a maximum of 60 persons. Reservations are required (recommended at least two months in advance), no pets or fires are allowed, and a seven-day stay is the limit. Bring all required equipment. The beach is just beyond the dunes. To make a reservation, contact the Cumberland Island National Seashore.

MAINLAND

$$ ✕ **Greek Mediterranean Grill.** It's a block from the St. Marys River, but the sky-blue murals and Greek proprietors make it seem more like the Mediterranean than the South. Traditional Greek dishes, such as *pastitsio* (pasta and ground beef baked with cinnamon and white cream sauce) and moussaka, are the mainstay. ✉ *122 Osborne St., St. Marys,* ☎ *912/576–2000. No credit cards.*

$$–$$$ 🏠 **Spencer House Inn.** This comfortable Victorian inn dates from 1872 and is named for the sea captain who built it as a hotel. Some rooms have expansive balconies that overlook the neatly tended grounds; others have antique claw-foot bathtubs. Innkeepers Mike and Mary Neff reside here and will prepare picnic lunches if you ask. The inn makes a perfect base for a tour of historic St. Marys and the waterfront and is convenient to the *Cumberland Queen* ferry. ✉ *200 Osborne St., St. Marys 31558,* ☎ *912/882–1872,* FAX *912/882–9427,* WEB *www.spencerhouseinn. com. 13 rooms, 1 suite. No room phones, no room TVs. AE, D, MC, V. BP.*

Okefenokee National Wildlife Refuge

65 mi southwest of Brunswick, 42 mi west of St. Marys.

★ 92   Covering 730 square mi of southeastern Georgia and spilling over into northeastern Florida, the **Okefenokee,** with its mysterious rivers and lakes, bristles with seen and unseen life. Scientists agree that the Okefenokee, the largest intact freshwater wetlands in the contiguous United States, is not duplicated anywhere else on earth. The impenetrable Pinhook Swamp, to the south, part of the same ecosystem, adds another 100 square mi. If the term *swamp* denotes a dark, dank place, the Okefenokee is never that. Instead, it is a vast peat bog with numerous and varied landscapes, including aquatic prairies, towering virgin cypress, sandy pine islands, and lush subtropical hammocks. During the last Ice Age 10,000 years ago, it was part of the ocean flow. Peat began building up 7,000 years ago atop a mound of clay, now 120 ft above sea level. Two rivers, the St. Marys and the Suwanee, flow out of the refuge, and it provides at least a part-time habitat for myriad species of birds, mammals, reptiles, amphibians, and fish.

As you travel by canoe or speedboat among the water lilies and the great stands of live oaks and cypress, be on the lookout for, among many others, alligators, otters, bobcats, raccoons, opossums, white-tailed deer, turtles, bald eagles, red-tailed hawks, egrets, muskrats, herons, cranes, and red-cockaded woodpeckers. The black bears tend to be more reclusive.

The Seminole people, in their migrations south toward Florida's Everglades, once took refuge in the Okefenokee. The last Native Americans to occupy the area, they were evicted by the army and Georgia's militia in the 1830s. When the Okefenokee acquired its present status of federal preserve (1937), the white homesteaders living on its fringe were forced out.

Noting the many floating islands, the Seminole named this unique combination of land and water "Land of the Quivering Earth." If you have the rare fortune to walk one of these bogs, you will find the earth does indeed quiver, rather like fruit gelatin in a bowl.

The Okefenokee Swamp Park, 8 mi south of Waycross, is a nonprofit development. The northern entrance to the refuge is here. There are two other gateways to the swamp: an eastern entrance at the U.S. Fish and Wildlife Service headquarters in the Suwanee Canal Recreation Area, near Folkston; and a western entrance at Stephen C. Foster State Park, outside the town of Fargo. You may take an overnight canoeing-camping trip into the interior, but the Okefenokee is a wildlife refuge and designated national wilderness, not a park. Access is restricted by permit. The best way to see the Okefenokee up close is to take a day trip at one of the three gateways. Plan your visit between September and April to avoid the biting insects that emerge in May, especially in the dense interior.

South of Waycross, via U.S. 1, **Okefenokee Swamp Park** has orientation programs, exhibits, a 1½-mi nature trail, observation areas, wilderness walkways, an outdoor museum of pioneer life, and boat tours into the swamp that reveal its unique ecology. A boardwalk and 90-ft tower are excellent places to glimpse cruising gators and birds. You may arrange for guided boat tours at an additional cost. A 1½-mi train tour passes by a Seminole village and stops at Pioneer Island, a re-created pioneer homestead, for a 30-minute walking tour. ⊠ *5700 Swamp Park Rd., Waycross 31501,* ☎ *912/283–0583,* FAX *912/283–0023,* WEB *www.okefenokee.com.* ☞ *$10, plus $4–$8 extra for boat-tour packages.* ☉ *Daily 8–5.*

Stephen C. Foster State Park, 18 mi northeast of Fargo via Route 177, is an 80-acre island park within the Okefenokee National Wildlife Refuge. The park encompasses a large cypress-and-black-gum forest, a majestic backdrop for one of the thickest growths of vegetation in the southeastern United States. Park naturalists leading boat tours will spill out a wealth of Okefenokee lore while you observe alligators, birds, and native trees and plants. You may also take a self-guided excursion in rental canoes and a motorized flat-bottom boat. Campsites and cabins are available. ⊠ *Rte. 1, Box 131, Fargo 31631,* ☎ *912/637–5274.* ☞ *$5 per vehicle to National Wildlife Refuge.*

Suwanee Canal Recreation Area, 8 mi southwest of Folkston via Route 121, is administered by the U.S. Fish and Wildlife Service. Stop first at the visitor center, with exhibits on the Okefenokee's flora and fauna. A boardwalk takes you over the water to a 50-ft observation tower. The concession has equipment rentals and daily food service; you may sign up here for one- or two-hour guided boat tours. Hikers, bicyclists, and private motor vehicles are welcome on the Swamp Island Drive; several interpretive walking trails may be taken along the way. Picnicking is allowed. Wilderness canoeing and camping in the Okefenokee's interior are by reserved permit only (for which a fee is charged). Permits are hard to get, especially in cool weather. Call refuge headquarters (☎ 912/496–3331) when it opens at 7 AM *exactly* two months in advance of your desired starting date. Guided overnight canoe trips can be arranged by refuge concessionaire Carl E. Glenn Jr. ⊠ *Rte. 2, Box 3325, Folkston 31537,* ☎ *912/496–7156;* ⊠ *Refuge headquarters: Rte. 2, Box 3330, Folkston 31537,* ☎ *912/496–7836.* ☞ *$5 per car; 1-hr tours $11; 2-hr tours $19.* ☉ *Refuge Mar.–Sept. 10, daily 6:30 AM–7:30 PM; Sept. 11–Feb., daily 8–6.*

Lodging

$$–$$$ 🏠 **The Inn at Folkston.** This craftsman-style inn, just 7 mi from the refuge, has a huge front veranda and four working gas-log fireplaces. Guest rooms are individually decorated. The romantic Lighthouse Room, for example, has a king-size bed and screened-in porch with a fireplace. The Garden Room woos romantics with a whirlpool tub, and the Oriental Room has an Asian theme. ⊠ *509 W. Main St., Folkston 31537,* ☎ *912/496–6256 or 888/509–6246,* WEB *www.innatfolkston.com. 4 rooms. Hot tub, library. AE, MC, V. BP.*

$ ⚠ **Laura S. Walker State Park.** Named for a Waycross teacher who championed conservation, the park, 9 mi northeast of Okefenokee Swamp Park, has campsites with electrical and water hookups. Be sure to pick up food and supplies on the way to the park. Boating and skiing are permitted on the 120-acre lake, and there's an 18-hole championship golf course. Rustic cabins cost $21.40 per night, plus $2 parking. ⊠ *5500 Laura Walker Rd., Waycross 31503,* ☎ *912/287–4900 or 800/864–7275. 44 campsites. Picnic area, pool, fishing, playground.*

$ ⚠ **Stephen C. Foster State Park.** The park has two-room furnished cottages, each capable of sleeping eight, and campsites with water, electricity, rest rooms, and showers. Because of roaming wildlife and poachers and because of the park's location inside the refuge, the gates close between sunset and sunrise. If you're staying overnight, stop for groceries before you get here. Cottages cost $66–$86 per night, depending on the season. ⊠ *Fargo 31631,* ☎ *912/637–5274 or 800/864–7275. 66 campsites.*

The Coastal Isles and the Okefenokee A to Z

To research prices, get advice from other travelers, and book travel arrangements, visit www.fodors.com.

AIR TRAVEL
CARRIERS
Glynco Jetport is served by Delta affiliate Atlantic Southeast Airlines (ASA), with flights from Atlanta.
➤ AIRLINES AND CONTACTS: **Atlantic Southeast Airlines** (☎ 800/282–3424).

AIRPORTS
The coastal isles are served by Glynco Jetport, 6 mi north of Brunswick near the coastal isles.
➤ AIRPORT INFORMATION: **Glynco Jetport** (⊠ 500 Connole St., ☎ 912/265–2070, 800/235–0859, WEB www.glynncountyairports.com).

BOAT AND FERRY TRAVEL
Cumberland Island and Little St. Simons are accessible only by ferry or private launch. You also can get to Sapelo Island by ferry.

BUS TRAVEL
Greyhound Bus Lines serves Savannah, Brunswick, and Waycross.
➤ BUS INFORMATION: **Greyhound Bus Lines** (☎ 800/231–2222, WEB www.greyhound.com).

CAR TRAVEL
From Brunswick take the Jekyll Island Causeway ($2 per car) to Jekyll Island and the Torras Causeway to St. Simons and Sea Island. You can get by without a car on Jekyll Island and Sea Island, but you'll need one on St. Simons. You cannot bring a car to Cumberland Island or Little St. Simons.

VISITOR INFORMATION
The Brunswick and the Golden Isles Visitors Center provides helpful information on all of the Golden Isles. Reservations are centralized through the Georgia State Parks department (Reservation Resource).
➤ TOURIST INFORMATION: **Brunswick and the Golden Isles Visitors Center** (⊠ 2000 Glynn Ave., Brunswick 31520, ☎ 912/264–5337 or 800/933–2627, WEB www.bgivb.com). **Georgia State Parks** (☎ 800/864–7275 for reservations; 770/398–7275 within metro Atlanta; 404/656–3530 for general park information; WEB www.gastateparks.org).

ATHENS TO MACON TO AUGUSTA

If it's traces of the old South you crave, you'll want to take in Georgia's Antebellum Trail, a former stagecoach route that is now a highway, U.S. 441. It is dotted with small towns, like Madison, Eatonton, and Milledgeville, saturated in historic architecture: you'll find an abundance of white-columned mansions, shaded verandas, and magnolia gardens reminiscent of pre–Civil War days. Try to plan a visit in April or October, when these towns host community tours of their homes and gardens.

Begin in Athens—with its historic homes, thriving music, and entertainment scene, and the University of Georgia—following the Antebellum Trail south to Macon. A visit to Washington and Augusta necessitates a side trip east along U.S. 78 and I–20, but both are well worth the detour, as they are steeped in history and tradition.

Athens

70 mi east of Atlanta via I–85 north to Rte. 316.

Athens, an artistic jewel of the American South, is known as a breeding ground for such famed rock groups as the B-52's and R.E.M. Because of this distinction, creative types from all over the country flock to its trendy streets in hopes of becoming, or catching a glimpse of, the next big act to take the world by storm. At the center of this artistic melee is the University of Georgia (UGA). With more than 28,000 students, UGA is an influential ingredient in the Athens mix, giving the quaint but compact city a distinct flavor that falls somewhere between a misty Southern enclave, a rollicking college town, and a smoky, jazz club–studded alleyway. It truly is a fascinating blend of Mayberry R.F.D. and MTV. The effect is as irresistible as it is authentic.

Although the streets bustle at night with students taking in the coffeehouse and concert life, Athens's quieter side also flourishes. The streets are lined with many gorgeous old homes, some of which are open to the public. Most prominent among them is the **Athens Welcome Center** (⊠ 280 E. Dougherty St., ☎ 706/353–1820, WEB www.visitathensga.com), in the town's oldest surviving residence, the 1820 Church-Waddel-Brumby House. Athens has several splendid Greek Revival buildings, including the **university chapel**, on campus, built in 1832. The **university president's house** (⊠ 570 Prince Ave.), on campus, was built in the late 1850s. The **Taylor-Grady House** (⊠ 634 Prince Ave.) was constructed in 1844. The 1844 **Franklin House** (⊠ 480 E. Broad St.) has been restored and reopened as an office building.

Just outside the Athens city limits is the **State Botanical Gardens of Georgia,** a tranquil, 313-acre wonderland of aromatic gardens and woodland paths. It has a massive conservatory overlooking the International Garden that functions as a welcome foyer and houses an art gallery, gift shop, and café. ⊠ 2450 S. Milledge Ave., off U.S. 129/441, ☎ 706/542–1244, WEB www.uga.edu/botgarden. ☜ Free. ☉ Grounds Apr.–Sept., weekdays 8–8; Oct.–Mar., weekdays 8–6. Visitor center Tues.–Sat. 9–4:30, Sun. 11:30–4:30.

Dining and Lodging

$–$$$ ✕ **Last Resort Grill.** This is a pleasant place to unwind—especially with the restaurant's cheery sidewalk café section. The cuisine is a cross between Tex-Mex and California, with items such as salmon and black-bean quesadillas, and grilled shiitake mushrooms and feta cheese tossed with pasta. ⊠ 174 W. Clayton St., ☎ 706/549–0810. AE, D, MC, V.

$$ ✗ **Harry Bissett's.** Get primed to taste the offerings at one of the best restaurants in Athens, where you can expect sumptuous Cajun recipes straight from the streets of New Orleans. Nosh on oysters on the half shell at the raw bar while waiting for a table (if it's the weekend, expect to wait a while). Popular main dishes include amberjack Thibodaux (broiled fresh fillet smothered in crawfish étouffée) and chicken Rochambeau (a terrine of chicken breast, béarnaise sauce, shaved ham, and wine sauce). ⊠ *279 E. Broad St.,* ☎ *706/353–7065. AE, D, MC, V. No lunch Mon.*

$ ✗ **Weaver D's Fine Foods.** Besides serving some of the best soul food in Athens-Clarke County, this place represents a piece of musical history: R.E.M. was so inspired by Weaver D's service motto, "Automatic for the People," that the band named its 1992 album after it. The cooks specialize in hearty home-style meals—fish and chicken, barbecued pork, meat loaf, and steak with gravy. All entrées come with vegetables picked fresh from the garden. ⊠ *1016 E. Broad St.,* ☎ *706/353–7797. No credit cards.*

$$–$$$ ⊞ **Magnolia Terrace.** This B&B is housed in a 1912 mansion right in the middle of the historic district. Each room is decorated with a mishmash of antiques. The rooms are warmly appointed with individual care, favoring rich, stately hues, such as burnt orange and velvet red. Some are carpeted with intricate Persian rugs, and others have large claw-foot tubs. Many have working fireplaces. ⊠ *288 Hill St., 30601,* ☎ *706/548–3860,* FAX *706/369–3439,* WEB *www.magnoliaterrace.com. 8 rooms, 1 suite. AE, D, MC, V. BP.*

$$ ⊞ **Nicholson House.** This 19th-century house, on 6 acres of an 18th-century land grant originally deeded to William Few, one of Georgia's two signers of the U.S. Constitution, literally is a two-over-two log house. Later additions and changes hide this original structure beneath a 1947 colonial revival exterior. The inn has a wide front veranda with rocking chairs. Rooms are decorated in rich colors, and furnishings are a mix of antiques and good reproductions. ⊠ *6295 Jefferson Rd., 30607,* ☎ *706/353–2200,* FAX *706/353–7799,* WEB *www.bbonline.com/ga/nicholson. 7 rooms, 2 suites. AE, D, MC, V. BP.*

$ ⊞ **Best Western Colonial Inn.** Just a half mile from the UGA campus, it's a favorite among relatives who come to attend graduation. Don't expect to be blown away by the architectural design, as the hotel building itself, like the rooms it offers, is basic. Rooms, however, are still quite comfortable, with thick flowery bedspreads; each room comes equipped with a coffeemaker. Excellent freshly baked cookies are offered every afternoon. Directly across the street is the Varsity Drive-In, where hungry students feast on smothered hot dogs and heaps of fries. ⊠ *170 N. Milledge Ave., 30607,* ☎ *706/546–7311 or 800/528–1234,* FAX *706/546–7959,* WEB *www.bestwestern.com. 69 rooms. Some microwaves, some refrigerators, pool. AE, D, DC, MC, V.*

Nightlife and the Arts

THE ARTS

The **Classic Center** (⊠ 300 N. Thomas St., ☎ 706/357–4444) puts on a splendid variety of plays and other theatrical performances. The ultramod **Georgia Theater** (⊠ 215 N. Lumpkin St., ☎ 706/549–9918) doubles as a movie house and concert hall, showcasing edgy cinema and booking local bands. **UGA's Performing Arts Center** (⊠ South Campus on River Rd., ☎ 706/542–4400) routinely has world-class music recitals—by the Atlanta Symphony Orchestra, for example—and modern dance shows.

NIGHTLIFE

For boisterous rockabilly tunes check out **Bumpers** (⊠ 1720 Commerce Dr., ☎ 706/369–7625). The **40 Watt Club** (⊠ 285 W. Washington St.,

☎ 706/549–7871) has been the launching pad of numerous well-known rock groups, such as R.E.M. In the '30s and '40s famed jazz greats such as Bessie Smith and Cab Calloway regularly performed at the **Morton Theatre** (✉ 195 W. Washington St., ☎ 706/613–3770), listed on the National Register of Historic Places; it is now a performing arts center, presenting musicals, concerts, and modern dance.

Madison

30 mi south of Athens via U.S. 129/441, 60 mi east of Atlanta via I–20.

Directly south of Athens you'll find this small treasure of a town—filled with plenty of restaurants and irresistible antiques shops and gift boutiques. Here you'll also get to see some well-preserved examples of antebellum and Victorian architecture, a treat because so few buildings in Atlanta escaped the torches of the Union troops. Madison's homes are well preserved largely because of a curious stroke of luck: when General Sherman burned a path through Georgia during the Civil War, he left Madison intact because of his friendship with U.S. senator Joshua Hill, a Madison resident and Union sympathizer. That's how Madison earned the moniker "the town that Sherman refused to burn." Hill's former home (not open to the public) is now one of Madison's most cherished mansions.

The **Madison-Morgan Cultural Center,** housed in an early 20th-century schoolhouse built in Romanesque Revival style, has tools and furniture from the late 19th century and a restored classroom of the period, plus information and printed guides on the Joshua Hill house and other historic sites in town. ✉ 434 S. Main St., ☎ 706/342–4743, WEB *www.morgan. public.lib.ga.us/madmorg.* ➿ *$3.* ☉ *Tues.–Sat. 10–5, Sun. 2–5.*

At **Heritage Hall** (✉ 277 S. Main St., ☎ 706/342–9627) you can take a guided tour of a preserved 1833 Greek Revival home and learn about aspects of antebellum highbrow society life.

Dining and Lodging

$–$$ ✕ **Yesterday Cafe.** The brick walls of this former pharmacy are lined with archival black-and-white photographs. Patrons come from counties far away to delight in the traditional but updated Southern fare: country-fried steak with mashed red-skin potatoes, fresh vegetables, and buttermilk pie from an old recipe. The full Southern breakfast, served Tuesday through Sunday, is outstanding. ✉ *120 Fairplay St., Rutledge (10 mi west of Madison),* ☎ *706/557–9337. AE, MC, V. No dinner Sun.–Wed.*

$$–$$$ ▦ **The Farmhouse Inn.** This inn is on a farm that has been in Melinda Hartney's family for generations. Rooms have private entrances (from the outside); the rooms are off a common area where everyone enjoys breakfast and late-afternoon gatherings. Over the barn is an apartment suite. The inn is 6 mi east of Madison. ✉ *1051 Meadow La., 30650,* ☎ *706/342–7933,* WEB *www.thefarmhouseinn.com. 5 rooms, 1 suite. AE, MC, V. BP.*

Eatonton

22 mi south of Madison on U.S. 129/441.

Right in the middle of the Antebellum Trail, Eatonton is a historical trove of houses that still retain the rare Southern antebellum architecture that survived Sherman's torches. But this is not the only thing for which this idyllic town is so proud. Take a look at the courthouse lawn, it's not your imagination—that really is a giant statue of a rabbit. This small town is the birthplace of celebrated novelist Joel Chandler Harris of Br'er Rabbit and Uncle Remus fame. The **Uncle Remus Museum,** built from authentic slave cabins, houses countless carvings, paintings, and other artwork depicting the characters made famous by the imaginative author. It's on the grounds of a park. ⊠ *Turner Park, U.S. 441,* ☎ *706/485–6856.* ⊴ *50¢.* ⊙ *Wed.–Mon. 10–5. Closed Tues.*

The **Eatonton-Putnam Chamber of Commerce** (⊠ 105 Sumter St., ☎ 706/485–7701) provides printed maps detailing landmarks from the upbringing of Eatonton native Alice Walker, who won the Pulitzer Prize for her novel *The Color Purple.* It also has information on the many fine examples of antebellum architecture in Eatonton, including descriptions and photographs of the town's prize antebellum mansions, and a walking tour of Victorian antebellum homes.

Lodging

$$ ⊞ **Crockett House.** With its aromatic gardens, majestic wraparound porch, and in-room fireplaces, this B&B nestled in a restored 1895 Victorian home is perfect for a romantic getaway. Make sure to get a room with an old-fashioned claw-foot bathtub. All rooms have working fireplaces. ⊠ *671 Madison Rd., 31024,* ☎ *706/485–2248,* ⱲⱭ *www. bbonline/ga/crocketthouse. 5 rooms. AE, MC, V. BP.*

Milledgeville

20 mi south of Eatonton on U.S. 441.

Locals believe ghosts haunt what remains of the antebellum homes in Milledgeville. Laid out as the state capital of Georgia in 1803 (a title it held until Atlanta assumed the role in 1868), the town was not as fortunate as Madison in escaping being torched during the Civil War. Sherman's troops stormed through with a vengeance after the general heard hardship stories from Union soldiers who had escaped from a prisoner-of-war camp in nearby Andersonville. The 1838 Greek Revival **Old Governor's Mansion** became Sherman's headquarters during the war. His soldiers are said to have tossed government documents out of the windows and fueled their fires with Confederate money. Guided tours of the building, now a museum home, are given daily. ⊠ *120 S. Clark St.,* ☎ *478/453–4545.* ⊴ *$5.* ⊙ *Mon.–Sat. 10–4, Sun. 2–4.*

On West Hancock Street is the Georgia College and State University campus. One of its most famous students was prolific Southern novelist and short-story writer Flannery O'Connor, author of such acclaimed novels as *Wise Blood* and *The Violent Bear It Away.* O'Connor did most of her writing at the family farm, Andalusia, just north of Milledgeville on U.S. 441. The **Flannery O'Connor Room,** inside the **Ina Russell Library,** has many of the author's handwritten manuscripts on display. It also contains O'Connor's typewriter and some of her furniture. ⊠ *231 W. Hancock St.,* ☎ *478/445–4047.* ⊴ *Free.* ⊙ *Weekdays 9–4.*

Dining

$–$$ ✕ **Brewers Downtown Café.** Pocketed nicely in a historic building, this warmly decorated restaurant specializes in Californian/Mediterranean fare with such entrées as braised mussels and steak prepared Tuscanstyle. ⊠ *138 W. Hancock St.,* ☎ *478/452–5966. AE, D, MC, V. Closed Sun.*

Macon

32 mi southwest of Milledgeville via U.S. 441 to Rte. 49, 85 mi southeast of Atlanta via I–75.

At the state's geographic center, Macon, founded in 1823, has more than 100,000 flowering cherry trees, which it celebrates each March with a knockout festival. Its antebellum and Victorian homes are among the state's best preserved.

★ Among the city's many sites is the **Georgia Music Hall of Fame,** appropriately located in Macon as a tribute to the city's extensive contribution to American music. The museum pays tribute to the Georgians who have helped to define America's musical culture. Among the honorees are Ray Charles, James Brown, the Allman Brothers Band, Chet Atkins, R.E.M., and the B-52's. Exhibits also celebrate classical musicians including Robert Shaw, the late director emeritus of the Atlanta Symphony Orchestra; opera singers Jessye Norman and James Melton; and violinist Robert McDuffie. ⊠ *200 Martin Luther King Jr. Blvd.,* ☎ *478/750–8555,* WEB *www.gamusichall.com.* 🖃 *$8.* ⊙ *Mon.–Sat. 9–5, Sun. 1–5.*

Ⓒ The **Georgia Sports Hall of Fame,** with its old-style ticket booths, has the look and feel of an old ballpark. Exhibits honor sports at all levels, from prep and college teams to professional. ⊠ *301 Cherry St.,* ☎ *478/752–1585,* WEB *www.gshf.org.* 🖃 *$6.* ⊙ *Mon.–Sat. 9–5, Sun. 1–5.*

★ The unique **Hay House,** designed by the New York firm T. Thomas & Son, is a virtual study in fine Italianate architecture prior to the Civil War. The marvelous stained-glass windows and many technological advances, including indoor plumbing, make a tour worthwhile. ⊠ *934 Georgia Ave.,* ☎ *478/742–8155,* WEB *www.georgiatrust.org/hay.html.* 🖃 *$6.* ⊙ *Mon.–Sat. 10–5, Sun. 1–5.*

African-American entrepreneur Charles H. Douglass built the **Douglass Theatre** in 1921. Great American musicians have performed here, among them Bessie Smith, Ma Rainey, Cab Calloway, Duke Ellington, and locals Little Richard and Otis Redding. It is currently a venue for movies, plays, and other performances. You can take a guided tour of the building. ⊠ *355 Martin Luther King Jr. Blvd.,* ☎ *478/742–2000,* WEB *www.douglasstheatre.org.* 🖃 *$2.* ⊙ *Tues.–Sat. 9–5.*

Ⓒ The **Macon Museum of Arts and Sciences and Mark Smith Planetarium** displays everything from a whale skeleton to fine art. Discovery House, an interactive exhibit for children, is modeled after an artist's garret. ⊠ *4182 Forsyth Rd.,* ☎ *478/477–3232,* WEB *www.masmacon.com.* 🖃 *$7.* ⊙ *Mon.–Thurs. and Sat. 9–5, Fri. 9–9, Sun. 1–5.*

Just 3 mi east of downtown, the **Ocmulgee National Monument,** a significant archaeological site, was occupied for more than 10,000 years and was at its peak under the Mississippian peoples who lived here between AD 900 and AD 1100. There are a reconstructed earth lodge and displays of pottery, effigies, and jewelry of copper and shells discovered in the burial mound. ⊠ *1207 Emery Hwy. (take U.S. 80 east),* ☎ *478/752–8257,* WEB *www.nps.gov/ocmu.* 🖃 *Free.* ⊙ *Daily 9–5.*

The **Tubman African American Museum** honors the former slave who led more than 300 people to freedom as one of the conductors of the Underground Railroad. A mural depicts several centuries of black culture. The museum also has an African artifacts gallery. ⊠ *340 Walnut St.,* ☎ *478/743–8544,* WEB *www.tubmanmuseum.com.* 🖃 *$3.* ⊙ *Mon.–Sat. 9–5, Sun. 2–5.*

OFF THE   **MUSEUM OF AVIATION** – This museum at Robins Air Force Base has an
BEATEN PATH   extraordinary collection of 90 vintage aircraft including a MiG, an SR-71 (Blackbird), a U-2, and assorted other flying machines from past campaigns. From Macon take I–75 south to Exit 146 (Centerville/

Warner Robins), and turn left onto Watson Boulevard, 7 mi to Route 247/U.S. 129, then right for 2 mi. ⊠ *Rte. 247/U.S. 129 at Russell Pkwy., Warner Robins, 20 mi south of Macon,* ☎ *478/926–6870,* WEB *www.museumofaviation.org.* 🎞 *Free; film $2.* ☉ *Daily 9–5.*

Dining and Lodging

$$ ✕ **Naple's on Forsyth.** This romantic enclave serves Italian food inspired by the Southern region of the country. Specials include homemade pastas, pungent pestos, and spaghetti *al scoglio,* which is a virtual seafood stew over linguine. The restaurant is quite romantic, and conversation is kept to a pleasant murmur. ⊠ *4524 Forsyth Rd.,* ☎ *478/471–7017. AE, DC, MC, V. Closed Sun. No lunch Sat.*

$$$–$$$$ ✕🏨 **Henderson Village.** At this resort, 38 mi south of Macon, you'll
★   find stunning 19th- and early 20th-century Southern homes clustered around a green. Guest rooms have a rustic-style elegance, with fine antiques and access to inviting wraparound porches; suites are even nicer, with fireplaces and whirlpool tubs. Buttermilk-yellow walls add warmth to the fine 1838 Langston House restaurant, which is perfect for a meal of Southern-style turbot and pan-seared beef fillet. ⊠ *125 S. Langston Circle, Perry 31069,* ☎ *478/988–8696 or 888/615–9722,* FAX *912/988–9009,* WEB *www.hendersonvillage.com. 19 rooms, 5 suites. Restaurant, bar, in-room VCRs, pool, hot tub, hiking, horseback riding, fishing, library, meeting rooms. AE, MC, V. BP.*

$$$–$$$$ 🏨 **1842 Inn.** With its grand white-pillared front porch and period antiques, this inn offers a true taste of antebellum grandeur, and it's easy to see why this place is considered to be one of America's top inns. The rooms have an aristocratic flair, with plush coverlets and embroidered pillows. There are also loveseats, ornate window stoops, and tile fireplaces, as well as period antiques and heirloom-quality accessories. In the morning you can eat breakfast in your room, in one of the parlors, or in the gorgeous courtyard. It's within an easy walk of downtown and the historic district. ⊠ *353 College St., 31201,* ☎ *800/336–1842,* ☎ FAX *478/741–1842,* WEB *www.the1842inn.com. 21 rooms, 1 guest house. Cable TV, laundry services, hot tub, Internet. AE, DC, MC, V. BP.*

Washington

38 mi east of Athens via U.S. 78, 100 mi east of Atlanta via I–20 to Exit 154, 100 mi northeast of Macon via U.S. 129 to I–20 to Rte. 47.

Washington, the first city chartered in honor of the country's first president, is a living museum of Southern culture. Brick buildings, some of which date to the American Revolution, line the lively downtown area, which bustles with people visiting shops, cafés, and antiques shops. Residents live and work downtown, giving Washington a little-city appeal that distinguishes it from most other small Southern towns. The Confederate treasury was moved here from Richmond in 1865, and soon afterward the half-million dollars in gold vanished. This mysterious event has been the inspiration for many a treasure hunt, as many like to believe the gold is still buried somewhere in Wilkes County.

The **Washington Historical Museum** (⊠ 308 E. Robert Toombs Ave., ☎ 706/678–2105, WEB www.ohwy.com/ga/w/washismu.htm) houses a collection of Civil War relics, including the camp chest of Jefferson Davis. The **Robert Toombs House** (⊠ 216 E. Robert Toombs Ave., ☎ 706/678–2226) is furnished with 19th-century antiques, some of which are the personal items of the former U.S. senator for which it is named, who served as secretary of state for the Confederacy during part of the Civil War.

Be sure to stop by historic **Callaway Plantation,** 4 mi west of downtown. Here, at a site dating to 1785, you can experience the closest thing to an operating plantation. Among a cluster of buildings on the estate you'll find a blacksmith's house, schoolhouse, and weaving house. An ancient family cemetery is also fun to explore. During the second week of both April and October the estate comes alive with Civil War reenactments and activities such as butter-churning and quilting demonstrations. ⊠ *U.S. 78,* ☎ *706/678-7060,* WEB *www.ohwy. com/ga/c/calplant.htm.* ⌨ *$4.* ☉ *Tues.–Sat. 10–5, Sun. 2–5.*

Dining and Lodging

$–$$ ✕ **Another Thyme Café.** This eating establishment has at least three things going for it: homemade breads and desserts (including pecan pie), location (right on the square in downtown Washington), and excellent salads and sandwiches (try the grilled vegetables on focaccia). Dinner runs slightly more upscale but stays regional with fried green tomatoes, sweet-potato chips, and fried seafood. ⊠ *5 E. Public Sq.,* ☎ *706/ 678–1672. AE, D, MC, V. Closed Sun. No dinner Sun.–Thurs.*

$$ 🏠 **Maynard's Manor.** Expect to be greeted with a pleasant wine-and-cheese service. Fireplaces in the main house warm the public spaces of this 1820 classic revival structure. You might find it fun to join the others who gather in the library and parlor for conversation and light refreshments. The day begins with coffee, tea, and juice in the main hall at 7 AM, followed by a full breakfast in the morning rooms. In the evening there's a dessert service conducted in the parlor, where a buffet of homemade sweets beckons. The proprietors make sure you return to turned-down bedding once you retire to your room for the evening, one of the little touches of luxury in which this inn takes pride. ⊠ *219 E. Robert Toombs Ave., 30673,* ☎ *706/678–4303,* WEB *www.kudcom. com/maynard. 6 rooms, 1 suite. Library, lounge. MC, V. BP.*

Augusta

55 mi east of Washington via U.S. 78 and I–20, 150 mi east of Atlanta via I–20, 70 mi southwest of Columbia, SC, via I–20.

Although Augusta escaped the ravages of Union troops during the Civil War, nature itself was not so kind. On a crossing of the Savannah River, the town was flooded many times before modern-day city planning redirected the water into a collection of small lakes and creeks. Now the current is so mild that citizens gather to send bathtub toys downstream every year in the annual Rubber Duck Race.

Augusta is Georgia's third-oldest city, founded in 1736 by James Edward Oglethorpe, who founded Savannah in 1733. The city was named for Augusta, Princess of Wales, wife of Frederick Louis, Prince of Wales. Augusta served as Georgia's capital from 1785 to 1795. The well-maintained paths of **Riverwalk** (between 5th and 10th streets) curve along the Savannah River and are the perfect place for a leisurely stroll. **Olde Town,** lying along Telfair and Greene streets, is a restored neighborhood of Victorian homes. The 1845 tree-lined **Augusta Canal** is another pleasant place for a walk. Many antebellum and Victorian homes of interest are spread throughout the city.

Meadow Garden was the home of George Walton, one of Georgia's three signers of the Declaration of Independence and, at age 26, its youngest signer. It has been documented as Augusta's oldest extant residence. ⊠ *1320 Independence Dr.,* ☎ *706/724–4174,* WEB *www. downtownaugusta.com/meadowgarden.* ⌨ *$3.* ☉ *Weekdays 10–4, weekends by appointment.*

The **Morris Museum of Southern Art** has a splendid collection of Southern art, from early landscapes, antebellum portraits, and Civil War art, through neo-impressionism and modern contemporary art. ⊠ *Riverfront Center, 1 10th St., 2nd floor,* ☎ *706/724–7501,* WEB *www.themorris.org.* 🖾 *$3, free on Sun.* ☉ *Tues.–Sat. 10–5, Sun. noon–5.*

🧒 Children love the National Science Center's **Fort Discovery,** an interactive museum with a moonwalk simulator, a bike on square wheels, a hot-air balloon, and a little car propelled by magnets. ⊠ *1 7th St.,* ☎ *706/821–0200 or 800/325–5445,* WEB *www.nationalsciencecenter.org/fortdiscovery.* 🖾 *$8.* ☉ *Mon.–Sat. 10–5, Sun. noon–5.*

Dining and Lodging

$$–$$$$ ✕ **La Maison on Telfair.** Augusta's finest restaurant, operated by chef–owner Heinz Sowinski, presents a classic menu of game, sweetbreads, and, with a nod to the chef's heritage, Wiener schnitzel. The experience is enhanced by the quiet and elegant style here. ⊠ *404 Telfair St.,* ☎ *706/722–4805. AE, D, DC, MC, V. Closed Sun. No lunch.*

$$–$$$ 🏨 **Partridge Inn.** A National Trust Historic hotel, this restored inn sits at the gateway to Summerville, a hilltop neighborhood of summer homes dating to 1800. There's a splendid view of downtown Augusta from the roof. Rooms are elegant, and have double-line cordless phones and high-speed Internet lines. The hotel's exterior has 12 common balconies and a breathtaking upper veranda accented with shaded architectural porticos over wood-plank flooring, creating a truly lustrous reprieve for a quick coffee and newspaper read. There's also videoconferencing for those who can't bear to be out of sight of their business partners. ⊠ *2110 Walton Way, 30904,* ☎ *706/737–8888 or 800/476–6888,* FAX *706/731–0826,* WEB *www.partridgeinn.com. 133 rooms, 26 suites. Restaurant, bar, some kitchens, pool, gym, lounge, rooftop concierge floor, Internet, meeting room. AE, D, DC, MC, V. BP.*

Spectator Sports

In early April Augusta hosts the much-celebrated annual **Masters Tournament** (WEB www.masters.org), one of pro golf's most distinguished events. Tickets for actual tournament play are not available to the general public, but you can try to get tickets for one of the practice rounds earlier in the week—which, for golf addicts, is still hugely entertaining. Tickets are awarded on a lottery basis; write to the Masters Tournament Practice Rounds office (⊠ Box 2047, Augusta, GA 30903) by July 15 of the year preceding the tournament.

Athens to Macon to Augusta A to Z

To research prices, get advice from other travelers, and book travel arrangements, visit www.fodors.com.

AIR TRAVEL
CARRIERS
Atlantic Southeast Airlines (ASA), Delta, and US Airways all serve the Athens, Macon, and Augusta area.

AIRPORTS
Athens Ben Epps Airport is served by US Airways. Augusta Regional Airport is served by Delta, ASA, and US Airways Express. Middle Georgia Regional Airport is served by Atlantic Southeast Airlines.
➤ AIRPORT INFORMATION: **Athens Ben Epps Airport** (⊠ 1010 Ben Epps Dr., ☎ 706/613–3420, WEB www.athensairport.net). **Augusta Regional Airport** (⊠ 1501 Aviation Way, ☎ 706/798–3236). **Middle Georgia Regional Airport** (⊠ 1000 Terminal Dr., Rte. 247 at I–75, ☎ 478/788–3760).

BUS TRAVEL

Greyhound Bus Lines serves Athens, Augusta, Macon, Madison, Milledgeville, and Washington.

➤ BUS INFORMATION: **Greyhound Bus Lines** (☎ 800/231–2222, WEB www.greyhound.com).

CAR TRAVEL

U.S. 441, known as the Antebellum Trail, runs north–south, merging with U.S. 129 for a stretch and connecting Athens, Madison, Eatonton, and Milledgeville. Macon is on Route 49, which splits from U.S. 441 at Milledgeville. Washington lies at the intersection of U.S. 78, running east from Athens to Thomson, and Route 44, running south to Eatonton. I–20 runs east from Atlanta to Augusta, which is about 93 mi east of U.S. 441.

EMERGENCIES

➤ EMERGENCY SERVICES: **Ambulance, police** (☎ 911).

➤ HOSPITALS: **Doctors Hospital** (⊠ 3651 Wheeler Rd., Augusta, ☎ 706/651–3232). **Medical Center** (⊠ 1199 Prince Ave., Athens, ☎ 706/549–9977). **Macon Northside Hospital** (⊠ 400 Charter Blvd., Macon, ☎ 478/757–8200).

➤ 24-HOUR PHARMACIES: **CVS** (⊠ 1271 Gray Hwy., Macon, ☎ 478/743–6979 or 912/743–8936).

LODGING

BED AND BREAKFASTS

Bed & Breakfast Online can provide detailed cyber-brochures on inns in Atlanta and surrounding areas.

➤ RESERVATION INFORMATION: **Bed & Breakfast Online** (⊠ Box 829, Madison, TN 37116, WEB www.bbonline.com/ga, ☎ 615/868–1946).

TAXIS

Augusta Cab Company provides transportation throughout Augusta-Richmond County. There is a $1.75 initial charge, plus $1.50 per mile.

Your Cab Company is a reliable, 24-hour taxi service in Athens. Rates, based on a grid of designated area zones, start at $3. The fare to downtown from the airport costs $6.

➤ TAXI COMPANIES: **Augusta Cab Company** (☎ 706/724–3543). **Your Cab Company** (☎ 706/546–5844).

TOURS

The Augusta Cotton Exchange conducts free tours of its historic brick building, with exhibits from its past as an arbiter of cotton prices. It also has Saturday van tours throughout the historic district of Augusta; the fee is $10 per person.

Classic City Tours conducts daily walking tours starting from the steps of the Athens Welcome Center at 2 PM. The 1½-hour tour takes participants through the city's antebellum neighborhoods. The fee is $10 per person ($8 per person for groups of 10 or more).

➤ TOUR OPERATORS: **Augusta Cotton Exchange** (☎ 706/724–4067). **Classic City Tours** (☎ 706/208–8687).

VISITOR INFORMATION

Georgia Welcome Center provides maps and brochures about prominent historical and recreational sites around the state.

➤ TOURIST INFORMATION: **Athens Convention and Visitors Bureau** (⊠ 300 N. Thomas St., 30601, ☎ 706/357–4430 or 800/653–0603, FAX 706/549–5636, WEB www.visitathensga.com). **Eatonton-Putnam Chamber of Commerce** (⊠ 105 Sumter St., Eatonton 31024, ☎ 706/485–7701, WEB www.eatonton.com). **Georgia Welcome Center** (⊠ Box

211090, Martinez 30917, ☎ 706/737–1446). **Macon-Bibb County Convention and Visitors Bureau** (⊠ 200 Cherry St., 31201, ☎ 478/743–3401 or 800/768–3401, WEB www.maconga.org). **Madison/Morgan County Chamber of Commerce** (⊠ 115 E. Jefferson St., Madison 30605, ☎ 706/342–4454, WEB www.madisonga.org). **Milledgeville Convention and Visitors Bureau** (⊠ 200 W. Hancock St., 31061, ☎ 478/452–4687, WEB www.milledgevillecvb.com). **Washington-Wilkes Chamber of Commerce** (⊠ 104 E. Liberty St., Box 661, Washington 30673, ☎ 706/678–2013, WEB www.washingtonga.org).

NORTH GEORGIA

As an antidote to the congestion of city life, nothing beats the clear skies, cascading waterfalls, and tranquil town squares of north Georgia. Within a half-day's drive from Atlanta, you'll find yourself in the middle of a refreshing cluster of old Southern towns and nature sites that pepper the northern region of the state—the heart of Appalachia.

In Dahlonega, Helen, and Clayton, north and northeast of Atlanta, you'll find shops selling handmade quilts, folk-art pottery, antiques, and loads of Grandma's chowchow in gingham-capped mason jars. These towns also offer plenty of activities—you can descend into a gold mine, explore a re-created Alpine village, or go apple picking. To the northwest are two of Georgia's most important historic sites: New Echota State Historic Site and Chickamauga and Chattanooga National Military Park. And whether your preference is rustic or romantic, there are plenty of B&Bs and campgrounds to accommodate you.

Dahlonega

65 mi north of Atlanta via Rte. 400/U.S. 19.

Hoards of fortune seekers stormed the town of Dahlonega (named after the Cherokee word for "precious yellow metal") in the early 1800s after the discovery of gold in the hills nearby, but by 1849 miners were starting to seek riches elsewhere. In fact, the famous call "There's gold in them thar hills!" originated as an enticement to miners in the Georgia mountains to keep their minds away from the lure of the gold rush out West. It worked for a while, but government price fixing eventually made gold mining unprofitable, and by the early 1920s Dahlonega's mining operations had halted completely.

Many former mining settlements became ghost towns but not Dahlonega. Today it thrives as a rustic country outpost with an irresistible town square rife with country stores, art galleries, coffeehouses, gem shops, old small-town businesses, and even a sophisticated restaurant or two. The gold mines are still here but are open mainly for show. **Consolidated Gold Mine** gives guided tours. You enter the mine, which has been reconstructed for safety, pass through a breathtaking stone passage, and then begin a descent down 120 ft into the mine's depths to gaze at the geological wonders. Guides expound on historical mining techniques and tools, such as the "widowmaker," a drill that kicks up mining dust and that caused disease in many miners. You'll also be invited to pan for gold prospector style, from a long wooden sluice. ⊠ *185 Consolidated Rd.,* ☎ *706/864–8473,* WEB *www.consolidatedgoldmine.com.* ☞ *$10.* ☉ *Daily 10–5.*

The **Gold Museum,** in the present-day courthouse on the square, has coins, tools, and a 5½-ounce nugget. The building is the oldest in north Georgia, and if you look closely at the bricks that form the building's foundation, you'll notice a sprinkling of gold dust in their formation. (A U.S. Mint operated in this modest boomtown from 1838 to 1861—it closed and was later destroyed by fire, but the foundation remained intact.) Along with the exhibits, the museum shows a short film celebrating the region's history through interviews with Appalachian old-timers. ⊠ *Public Sq.*, ☎ *706/864–2257*, WEB *www.dahlonega.org/museum/goldmuseum.html.* 🎟 *$2.50.* ☉ *Mon.–Sat. 9–5, Sun. 10–5.*

OFF THE
BEATEN PATH
AMICALOLA FALLS – Rushing waters will tumble your troubles away in no time. This is the highest waterfall east of the Mississippi, with waters plunging an eye-popping 729 ft through a cluster of seven cascades. The surrounding state park is dotted with scenic campsites and cottages strategically situated near a network of nature trails, picnic sites, and fishing streams. ⊠ *Off Rte. 52, 18 mi west of Dahlonega,* ☎ *706/ 265–8888,* WEB *www.ngeorgia.com/parks/amicalola.html.* 🎟 *Parking $2.* ☉ *Daily 7 AM–10 PM.*

Dining and Lodging

$$–$$$ ✕ **Renée's Café & Wine Bar.** This fine yet casual restaurant in a 19th-century restored residence lies within walking distance of the village square. The contemporary cuisine has regional and Mediterranean accents, such as crawfish tails with spinach tortellini and Gorgonzola Alfredo sauce. Upstairs, patient patrons wait for their tables in a warmly lighted bar or attend one of the monthly wine tastings. ⊠ *135 N. Chestatee St.,* ☎ *706/864–6829. AE, MC, V. No lunch.*

$–$$ ✕ **Smith House.** One of the most popular dining destinations in the north Georgia mountains, Smith House has all-you-can-eat family-style meals that'll have the tables groaning under the weight of the heaping plates. Potatoes, fried chicken, peas, cobbler—you name a Southern dish, and it's probably offered here. ⊠ *84 S. Chestatee St.,* ☎ *706/864–2348,* WEB *www.smithhouse.com. AE, D, MC, V. Closed Mon.*

$$ 🛏 **Blueberry Inn & Gardens.** The inn, which crowns the crest of a low hill, takes its name from the wild blueberries growing on its 55 acres. Porch rocking chairs welcome you at the end of a busy day of touring. Gracious hosts Phyllis and Harry Charnley have built a structure reminiscent of a 1920s farmhouse. Rooms are decorated with antiques and family pieces. On the grounds are mountain laurel, oaks, and dogwoods, along with flowering plants of all kinds. ⊠ *400 Blueberry Hill, 30533,* ☎ *706/219–4024 or 877/219–4024,* FAX *706/219–4793,* WEB *www.blueberryinnandgardens.com. 12 rooms. MC, V. BP.*

$$ 🛏 **Worley Homestead.** This pristine B&B occupies an 1845 mansion with two garden courtyards. Everyone sits family style at the large, formally set dining room table; breakfast includes caramelized French toast, casseroles, ham, sausage, and cheese grits. Often on weekend evenings the proprietors arrange a wine table with cheese and crackers in the entry foyer. Rooms are beautifully furnished. The B&B is right at the southern tip of the Appalachian Trail, and near the entrance to Chattanooga National Forest. ⊠ *410 W. Main St., 30533,* ☎ *706/864–7002,* WEB *www.bbonline.com/ga/worley. 7 rooms. MC, V. BP.*

Outdoor Activities and Sports

Appalachian Outfitters (⊠ 1236 Golden Ave. [Box 793], Dahlonega 30533, ☎ 800/426–7177, 800/426–7117, WEB www.appoutga.com) provides equipment and maps for self-guided canoeing and kayaking expeditions on the Chestatee River. River trails begin at its outpost in town and extend to Route 400.

Shopping

Golden Memories Antiques (⊠ 121 S. Public Sq., ☎ 706/864–7222) has an impressive number of local rocks and minerals and Coca-Cola collectibles for sale. **Amber Rose Quilts** (⊠ 10 S. Chestatee St., ☎ 706/ 864–5326) carries a splendid selection of hand-stitched quilts. **Quigley's**

Antiques and Books (⊠ 170-B N. Public Sq., ☎ 706/864–0161) sells used and rare books, Blue Ridge china, vintage trunks, and old toys.

Helen

13 mi northest of Atlanta via I-985 and U.S. 129

When Helen was founded at the turn of the 20th century, it was a simple little lumber outpost. By the 1960s it was in danger of turning into a ghost town because of a logging bust. Local business leaders came up with a plan to save the town: they transformed the tiny village of 300 into a virtual theme town, and "Alpine Helen" was born. Today businesses along Helen's central streets sport a distinctive German facade, giving you the impression that you've stumbled on a Bavarian vista in the middle of Appalachia. (There's also a scattering of Swiss, Belgian, Danish, Dutch, and Scandinavian facades.) Everywhere you look are beer halls, steepled roofs, flowering window boxes, and billboards written in Renaissance script. As phony as it all is, the effect is contagious and makes you feel as if you've walked into a fairy tale.

The entrance to the village is particularly picturesque, with a narrow bridge traversing a pretty section of the Chattahoochee River. Along Main Street are a multitude of patio cafés lushly shaded by trees. A network of cobblestone walkways and plazas spans a thicket of bakeries and little shops selling Bavarian-theme souvenirs. Costumed shop workers add to the charade. A faux castle that can't be missed is the **Castle Inn,** long considered a gateway of sorts to this manufactured Bavarian oasis in the middle of the Georgia mountains. ⊠ *8590 Main St.,* ☎ *706/878–3140, 877/878–3140,* WEB *www.castleinn-helen.com.*

OFF THE BEATEN PATH | **BRASSTOWN BALD –** The highest mountain in Georgia, at 4,784 ft, rises in the heart of the Chattahoochee National Forest. Expect a dramatic vantage from which you can view four states—Tennessee, North Carolina, South Carolina, and Georgia. And sight is not the only sense that gets an aesthetic pick-me-up at Brasstown Bald: bushels of wildflowers in the spring and autumn give a boost to the nose. ⊠ *Off Rte. 180, 18 mi northwest of Helen via Rte. 17,* ☎ *706/896–2556, 706/745–6928.* ⊞ *Parking $3, shuttle to mountain from lot $2.* ☉ *Daily 10–6.*

Dining and Lodging

$$–$$$$ | ✗ **Hofbrauhaus Inn.** This beer hall, which shares its name with a famous counterpart in Munich, welcomes a convivial and lively bunch. The menu is saturated with hearty German food, including schnitzel and *bratkartoffeln* (fried potatoes); there are also plenty of options for other international fare, including Hungarian goulash, broiled African lobster tails, and *bistecca alla lupe* (char-grilled beef tenderloin with a creamy Parmesan sauce). ⊠ *Main St.,* ☎ *706/878–2248. AE, D, DC, MC, V.*

$–$$ | ✗ **Farmer's Market Café.** This cheerfully decorated eatery has hearty, reasonably priced American fare—seafood, sandwiches, salads, and vegetable plates. You won't go hungry soon after a visit here. ⊠ *63 Chattahoochee St.,* ☎ *706/878–3705. AE, D, DC, MC, V.*

$$$$ | ⌂ **Brasstown Valley Resort.** It's contemporary, upscale, and has lodge-style accommodations, plus a full line of sports activities: tennis, golf, hiking trails, and a fitness center. The rooms are comfortable and spacious, in an elegant but rustic style. Some have fireplaces and balconies overlooking the breathtaking valley. It's 28 mi northwest of Helen, just off U.S. 76 but surrounded by verdant woods and mountain vistas. ⊠ *6321 U.S. 76, Young Harris 30582,* ☎ *706/379–9900 or 800/201–3205,* FAX *706/379–4615,* WEB *www.brasstownvalley.com. 102 rooms, 32 cot-*

tages, 5 suites. Restaurant, bar, cable TV, 18-hole golf course, 4 tennis courts, pool, health club, hot tub, sauna, hiking, convention center. AE, D, DC, MC, V. BP.

$–$$ ⊞ **Fieldstone Inn.** Many of the beautifully appointed rooms in this massive lodge in the mountains are decorated with cherry-wood furniture and have a gorgeous view of Lake Chatuge. You can relax in the lobby before a towering fieldstone fireplace and admire the landscape from the floor-to-ceiling window that faces out across the lake. A nearby marina has boat rentals, including pontoons, paddleboats, sailboats, and kayaks. Sizable discounts are available in winter. It's 25 mi north of Helen. ⊠ *3499 U.S. 76, Hiawassi 30546,* ☎ *706/896–2262 or 800/ 545–3408,* FAX *706/896–4128,* WEB *www.fieldstoneinn.com. 66 rooms. Restaurant, cable TV, tennis court, pool, convention center. AE, D, DC, MC, V. BP.*

Shopping

Gift World of Helen (⊠ 8614 Main St., ☎ 706/878–2504) sells candles, ceramics, knives, and T-shirts, among other items. Check out **Festival of Arts and Crafts** (⊠ 8600 Main St., ☎ 706/878–1283) for its wood carvings and handcrafted dolls. **Jolly's Toys** (⊠ 8800 Main St., ☎ 706/878–2262) has wooden American and European toys. At **Kaiser Bill's II** (⊠ 8635 Main St., ☎ 706/878–1408) you'll find collectible beer steins and figurines.

Clayton

35 mi northeast of Helen via Rte. 356, Rte. 197, and U.S. 76; 106 mi northeast of Atlanta via I–85, I–985, and U.S. 23; 95 mi southwest of Asheville, NC, via I–40 and U.S. 23.

Clayton bills itself as the place "where spring spends the summer"— because of the characteristically mild temperatures during Georgia's otherwise sweltering summer months. An unassuming mountain town, Clayton is near spectacular **Tallulah Gorge State Park,** which at nearly 1,000 ft is the deepest canyon in the United States after the Grand Canyon and was a popular early 20th-century destination for Atlantans. The state of Georgia has designated more than 20 mi of the state park as walking and mountain-biking trails. There are also a 63-acre lake with a beach, a picnic shelter, and about 50 tent and RV sites. ⊠ *U.S. 441, Tallulah Falls,* ☎ *706/754–7970; 706/754–7979 for camping reservations,* WEB *www.ngeorgia.com/parks/tallulah.html.* ◻ *Parking $2.* ☉ *Daily 8–dusk.*

Clayton is rich in art galleries, flea markets, and antiques shops. The **Main Street Gallery** (⊠ 641 Main St., ☎ 706/782–2440), one of the state's best sources for folk art, carries works by regional artists, including Sarah Rakes, O. L. Samuels, Jay Schuette, and Rudy Bostick.

Dining and Lodging

$$$–$$$$ ✕⊞ **Glen-Ella Springs Country Inn.** This restored old hotel draws from
★ far and wide with its rustic charm, restful location, and fine food emphasizing regional specialties, such as trout pecan, pickled shrimp, and Lowcountry shrimp on grits. Rooms have no TVs but plenty of reading material, and they open onto common porches with rocking chairs. The splendid grounds invite hiking and exploring. The restaurant's cuisine has been showcased in many books, including *Great Cooking with Country Inn Chefs,* by Gail Greco. You have to BYOB. ⊠ *1789 Bear Gap Rd., Rte. 3, Box 3304, Clarkesville 30523 (15 mi south of Clayton),* ☎ *706/754–7295 or 877/456–7527,* FAX *706/754–1560,* WEB *www. glenella.com. 12 rooms, 4 suites. Restaurant, pool, hiking, meeting room. AE, MC, V. BP.*

$–$$$ ✕⊡ **Dillard House.** An inviting cluster of cottages and motel-style
★ rooms, this establishment sits on a plateau in the Little Tennessee
River valley. Some rooms and the glass-walled Dillard House Restau-
rant ($$) have vistas of the Blue Ridge Mountains. The restaurant serves
all-you-can-eat platters of Southern favorites such as country ham, fried
chicken, barbecue, corn on the cob, acorn squash, and cabbage casserole. Breakfast is a gut buster. The rooms are uniquely furnished; even
floor plans differ. Some have stone fireplaces and interior French doors,
others have window-seat alcoves and butler hutches, and many open
onto a large rocking-chair front porch. ⊠ *768 Franklin St., Box 10,
Dillard 30537 (7 mi north of Clayton),* ☎ *706/746–5348 or 800/541–
0671,* ℻ *706/746–3680,* ⓌⒺⒷ *www.dillardhouse.com. 75 rooms, 25
chalets, 4 cottages, 6 suites. Restaurant, cable TV, hot tub, some kitchens,
some refrigerators, tennis courts, stables. AE, D, DC, MC, V.*

New Echota State Historic Site

71 mi northwest of Atlanta via I–75 north to Rte. 225.

From 1825 to 1838 New Echota was the capital of the Cherokee Nation, whose constitution was patterned after that of the United States.
There was a council house, a printing office, a Supreme Court building, and the *Cherokee Phoenix,* a newspaper that utilized the Cherokee alphabet developed by Sequoyah. Some buildings have been entirely
reconstructed, and some originals have simply been restored. A museum details the site's history. ⊠ *Rte. 225, 1 mi east of I–75, near Calhoun,* ☎ *706/624–1321,* ⓌⒺⒷ *www.georgiastateparks.org.* 🎟 *$3.50.* ☻
Tues.–Sat. 9–5, Sun. 2–5:30.

About 15 mi north of New Echota, the beautifully restored two-story
brick **Chief Vann House,** with an intricately carved interior, was commissioned in 1805 by a leader of the Cherokee Nation, who hired
Moravian artisans to construct it. Of mixed Scottish and Cherokee parentage, Chief James Vann owned numerous slaves who worked on the construction of the house. Before he died, he became known as a rogue—he
killed his brother-in-law in a duel and shot his mother. ⊠ *Rte. 225 at
Rte. 52, Chatsworth,* ☎ *706/695–2598,* ⓌⒺⒷ *www.alltel.net/-vannhouse.*
🎟 *$2.50.* ☻ *Tues.–Sat. 9–5, Sun. 2–5:30.*

Dining and Lodging

$$ ✕ **La Scala.** Piero Barba from Capri, Italy, established this outpost of
Italian cooking in 1996. The menu is dominated by classic dishes: osso
buco, braciola, seafood, and pasta. The wine list, which Barba claims
is the largest in north Georgia, includes French, American, and Italian
wines. ⊠ *413 Broad St., Rome (30 mi southwest of Calhoun),* ☎ *706/
238–9000. AE, D, DC, MC, V. Closed Sun. No lunch.*

$–$$ ⊡ **Claremont House.** Jeff and Linda Williams's beautifully restored 1890s
Victorian inn has huge rooms furnished with period antiques. Break-
fast is sumptuous, with stuffed French toast and the like. ⊠ *906 E.
2nd Ave., Rome 30161 (30 mi southwest of Calhoun),* ☎ *706/291–
0900 or 800/254–4797,* ℻ *706/802–0551,* ⓌⒺⒷ *www.theclaremonthouse.
com. 4 rooms, 1 cottage. AE, D, MC, V. BP.*

Chickamauga and Chattanooga National Military Park

*110 mi northwest of Atlanta via I–75 and Rte. 2, 42 mi north of New
Echota State Historic Site via I–75, 8 mi south of Chattanooga, TN,
via U.S. 27.*

This site, established in 1890 as the nation's first military park, was
the scene of one of the Civil War's bloodiest battles (30,000 casualties), which ended in the Union capture of Chattanooga. The normally

thick cedar groves and foliage covering Chickamauga were supposedly so trampled that the area resembled an open field, and so shot up were the trees that a sweet cedar smell mingled with the blood of fallen soldiers. Monuments, battlements, and weapons adorn the road that traverses the 8,000-acre park, with markers explaining the action. An excellent visitor center has reproduction memorabilia, books, and a film on the battle. ☒ *U.S. 27, Fort Oglethorpe, 12 mi south of Chattanooga,* ☏ *706/866–9241,* WEB *www.nps.gov/chch.* ☒ *Free.* ☻ *Mid-Aug.–mid-June, daily 8–4:45; mid-June–mid-Aug., daily 8–5:45.*

Lodging

$$–$$$ 🏨 **Gordon-Lee Mansion.** To capture the feeling of the Civil War era, stay overnight at this antebellum mansion, which served as a field hospital during the battle. You stay in the log house, formerly Congressman Gordon Lee's office, and have the run of two bedrooms, a living room with fireplace, and a full kitchen, where you prepare your own breakfast. ☒ *217 Cove Rd., Chickamauga 30707,* ☏ *706/375–4728 or 800/487–4728, 800/487–4728,* FAX *706/375–9499,* WEB *www.fhc. org/gordon-lee. 4 rooms, 1 cottage. MC, V. BP.*

North Georgia A to Z

To research prices, get advice from other travelers, and book travel arrangements, visit www.fodors.com.

BUS TRAVEL

Greyhound Bus Lines serves Calhoun, Dalton, and Rome.

FARES AND SCHEDULES

➤ BUS INFORMATION: **Greyhound Bus Lines** (☏ 800/231–2222, WEB www. greyhound.com).

CAR TRAVEL

U.S. 19 runs north–south, passing through Dahlonega and up into the north Georgia mountains. U.S. 129 runs northwest from Athens, passing through Cleveland and subsequently merging with U.S. 19. Route 75 stems off U.S. 129 and goes through Helen and up into the mountains. U.S. 23/441 runs north through Clayton; U.S. 76 runs west from Clayton to Dalton, merging for a stretch with Route 5/515. Route 52 runs along the edge of the Blue Ridge Mountains. I–75 is the major artery in the northwesternmost part of the state and passes near the New Echota State Historic Site and the Chickamauga and Chattanooga National Military Park.

EMERGENCIES

➤ EMERGENCY SERVICES: **Ambulance, police** (☏ 911).
➤ HOSPITALS: **Laurelwood/Blairsville Hospital** (☒ 214 Hospital Circle, Blairsville, ☏ 706/745–8641).
➤ PHARMACIES: **CVS** (☒ 43 Hwy. 515, Blairsville, ☏ 706/745–9601; ☒ Hwy. 441, ☏ 706/782–2722).

LODGING

BED & BREAKFAST ONLINE HAS DETAILED CYBER-BROCHURES ON INNS IN ATLANTA AND SURROUNDING AREAS.
➤ RESERVATION INFORMATION: **Bed & Breakfast Online** (☒ Box 829, Madison, TN 37116, WEB www.bbonline.com/ga, ☏ 615/868–1946).

OUTDOORS AND SPORTS

FISHING

Upper Hi Fly Fishing and Outfitters offers personalized guided trout and fly-fishing trips in the southern Appalachian Mountains. It also operates a full-service fly-fishing shop with state-of-the-art equipment.

➤ CONTACTS: **Upper Hi Fly Fishing and Outfitters** (☎ 706/896–9075, WEB www.upper-hi-fly.com).

HIKING

Fort Mountain State Park has campgrounds amid prehistoric rock formations, plus hiking, mountain biking, horseback riding, miniature golf, fishing, boating, and swimming. It's 8 mi east of Chatsworth via Route 52.

A network of hiking trails—filled with ancient Indian carvings and historical markers—is dotted with cabins and camping accommodations run by **Trackrock Campground and Cabins**. It also has fishing and horseback riding. It's 9 mi east of Blairsville via Route 180.

➤ CONTACTS: **Fort Mountain State Park** (✉ 181 Fort Mountain Park Rd., Chatsworth 30705, ☎ 706/695–2621, WEB www.ngeorgia. com/parks/fort.html). **Trackrock Campground and Cabins** (✉ 4887 Trackrock Campground Rd., Blairsville 30512, ☎ 706/745–2420, WEB www.trackrock.com).

➤ TOURIST INFORMATION: **Alpine Helen–White County Convention and Visitors Bureau** (✉ Box 730, Helen 30545, ☎ 706/878–2181 or 800/858–8027, WEB www.helenga.org). **Blairsville/Union County Chamber of Commerce** (✉ 385 Blue Ridge Hwy., Blairsville 30512, ☎ 706/ 745–5789, WEB www.blairsvillechamber.com). **Clayton Chamber of Commerce** (✉ Box 702, 30525-0702, ☎ 706/782–4512, FAX 706/782– 4596, WEB www.claytoncham.org). **Dahlonega-Lumpkin Chamber of Commerce** (✉ 13 Park St. S, Dahlonega 30533, ☎ 706/864–3513 or 800/231–5543, FAX 706/864–7917, WEB www.dahlonega.org). **Helen Welcome Center** (✉ 726 Bruckenstrasse, Box 730, 30545, ☎ 706/878– 2181 or 800/858–8027, FAX 706/878–4032, WEB www.helenga.com).

SOUTHWEST GEORGIA

It's best to meander through southwest Georgia slowly—as deliberately as the drawl that drips sweetly off the lips of the locals who inhabit the many speck-on-the-map towns that pepper this region. Here travelers come to escape the rigors and daily grind of the state's more densely settled communities. You'll encounter few high-tech diversions, few cell phone–addled commuters, and few gripes about traffic jams and suburban sprawl. Many locals here are content to spend the afternoon fanning themselves on the front porches, rarely—if ever—locking the screen door behind them.

Within a day's drive of Atlanta you'll encounter the rolling agricultural landscapes of southwest Georgia—farming enterprises that have kept generations literally rooted to their hometowns. Peanuts, cotton, corn, tobacco, and other crops flourish throughout the countryside, usually punctuated by large groves of pecan trees.

Petite country hamlets beckon with their charming town squares, shaded glens, and elegant B&Bs. Towns that seem to be cut from the pages of the past attract antiques and flea-market aficionados. In southwest Georgia the inclination simply to relax is contagious—it can saturate you slowly but completely, like syrup on a stack of pancakes.

Pine Mountain

90 mi southwest of Atlanta via I-85, I-185, and U.S. 27.

Although Pine Mountain attracts a healthy pack of tourists every year, most are lured by the surrounding area's large-scale attractions and then are pleasantly surprised that the small-town burg has a folksy, inviting downtown square. Spend a bit of time here, shop browsing and chatting with the friendly locals.

☺ Just south of the village lies the main draw of this area: **Callaway Gardens** is a 14,000-acre family-style golf and tennis resort with elaborate gardens. This botanical wonderland was developed in the 1930s by a couple determined to breathe new life into the area's dormant cotton fields. The **Day Butterfly Center** has more than 1,000 varieties flying free. **Creek Lake** is well stocked with largemouth bass and bream. ⊠ *U.S. 27, Pine Mountain,* ☏ *706/663–2281 or 800/282–8181,* WEB *www.callawaygardens.com.* ☑ *$12; free to overnight guests.* ☉ *Mar.– Aug., daily 7–7; Sept.–Feb., daily 8–5.*

A few miles northwest of town, you can further commune with nature
☺ at the **Pine Mountain Wild Animal Safari.** Either drive yourself or ride a bus through a 500-acre animal preserve in which you won't believe you're still in Georgia. Camels, llamas, antelopes, and hundreds of other exotic animals traipse around freely, often coming close to vehicles. An added plus is the **Old McDonald's Farm,** a petting zoo with jovial monkeys and writhing-reptile pits. ⊠ *1300 Oak Grove Rd.,* ☏ *706/663– 8744 or 800/367–2751,* WEB *www.animalsafari.com.* ☑ *$12.95 summer, $11.95 spring and fall, $10.95 winter.* ☉ *Oct.–May, daily 10–5:30, June–Sept., daily 10–7:30.*

Dining and Lodging

$–$$ ✕ **McGuire's Family Restaurant.** This friendly, reasonably priced country kitchen serves breakfast anytime but doesn't stop there: the menu ranges broadly, with burgers, salads, chicken, and even an occasional quail entrée. And what would a quintessential Georgia dinner be without fried green tomatoes? Get yours here, hot and inexpensive. ⊠ *324 Main St.,* ☏ *706/663–2640. MC, V.*

$$–$$$ 🏨 **Callaway Gardens.** This sprawling resort dwarfs many nearby towns,
★ with lots of places to eat and shop and endless landscaped and wild grounds. Accommodations range from fairly basic motel-style guest rooms to fully furnished cottages and villas, all of them with lovely panoramic vistas and verdant garden settings. A 10-mi paved bike trail meanders through the property. There's great fishing in 13 stocked ponds, and the golf courses are famously impressive. Various meal and recreation packages are available. ⊠ *U.S. 27, Pine Mountain 31822,* ☏ *706/663– 2281 or 800/282–8181,* FAX *706/663–5068,* WEB *www.callawaygardens. com. 775 units. 5 restaurants, 2 bars, 2 seasonal cafés, 4 18-hole golf courses, 10 tennis courts, lake, health club, beach, fishing, bicycles, Ping-Pong, racquetball, volleyball, lounge, shops. AE, D, DC, MC, V.*

$$–$$$ 🏨 **Chipley Murrah House B&B.** Just 1 mi from Callaway Gardens and on the fringe of downtown Pine Mountain, this lavish inn occupies a high-style Queen Anne Victorian dating to 1895. A favorite perch in this period-decorated house is the wraparound porch, decked out with rockers, swings, and wicker chairs. Hardwood flooring, 12-ft ceilings, and decorative molding are among the beautifully preserved original details. There's also a fully furnished country cottage with three bedrooms. ⊠ *207 W. Harris St., 31822,* ☏ *706/663–9801 or 888/782–0797,* WEB *www.bbonline.com/ga/chipley. 4 rooms, 1 cottage. MC, V. BP.*

Shopping

In downtown Pine Mountain, check out the **Anne Tutt Gallery** (⊠ 709 Garden View Dr., ☏ 706/663–8032) for its selection of paintings, etchings, and designer jewelry. Don't miss **Now and Then Antiques** (⊠ 116 Main St., ☏ 706/663–2000), a former gas station–turned–curio shop of old local crafts, including antique pottery, finger puppets, and weavings. **Country Gardens** (⊠ 155 Main St., ☏ 706/663–7779) offers an enchanting collection of eclectic plants, gifts, and antiques.

Warm Springs

14 mi east of Pine Mountain via Rte. 18 and Rte. 194, 75 mi south of Atlanta via I–85 and Rte. 41.

The village of Warm Springs was the summer White House during the presidency of Franklin D. Roosevelt. After Roosevelt died here in 1945, Warm Springs became blighted, but in the '80s an influx of crafts and antiques shops revitalized it. At the south end of town, you can tour the **Little White House Historic Site,** the restored vacation home of President Roosevelt, who first visited Warm Springs in 1924 to take the therapeutic hot waters after he contracted polio. In 1932 he built what became known as the Little White House, a simple three-bedroom cottage. It contains his personal effects and looks much as it did the day he died here. The pools where Roosevelt once took his therapy are now open for tours. ⊠ *401 Little White House Rd.,* ☎ *706/655–5870.* ⊡ *$5.* ☉ *Daily 9–4:45.*

Lodging

$$ 🏠 **Magnolia Hall.** Painted green with taupe shutters, this handsome Victorian cottage about 15 mi south of both Pine Mountain and Warm Springs has gingerbread trim and a wraparound porch. Rooms are soundproof, and each has a thermostat. A terrific breakfast, with such dishes as stuffed French toast, bacon pie, and lemon biscuits, is served in the formal dining room. ⊠ *127 Barnes Mill Rd., Hamilton 31811,* ☎ *706/628–4566,* WEB *www.magnoliahallbb.com. 3 rooms, 2 suites. AE, MC, V. BP.*

Columbus

45 mi south of Warm Springs via U.S. 27 and Rte. 85, 105 mi south of Atlanta via I–85 and I–185, 90 mi east of Montgomery, AL, via I–85 and U.S. 280.

Touted as "Georgia's West Coast" because of its 12-mi Riverwalk along the Chattahoochee, Columbus—the state's third-largest city (population 185,000) sprouted from what was originally a prosperous mill town in 1827. Gracious antebellum and Victorian homes line the streets of downtown, along with character-rich shotgun shacks that once belonged to the mill's laborers.

This is the hometown of John Pemberton, the pharmacist who created Coca-Cola. The 1840 four-room **Pemberton House** is one of several buildings that constitute **Heritage Corner,** which you can visit via a guided walking tour given by the Historic Columbus Foundation, headquartered in an 1870 building. Other structures here include the one-room **log cabin** that's said to be the oldest extant structure in Muscogee County; the 1828 federal-style **Walker-Peters-Langdon House;** and the 1840s **Woodruff Farm House.** ⊠ *700 Broadway,* ☎ *706/322–3181.* ⊡ *$5 per person tour (2-person minimum).* ☉ *Tours weekdays at 11 and 2, weekends at 2.*

Military buffs and anybody else with an interest in the nation's Civil War past should make it a point to visit the **Port Columbus National Civil War Naval Museum,** which has been lauded for its interactive approach and high-tech exhibits. This is one of the nation's most innovative Civil War museums. You can walk the decks of partially reconstructed Civil War ships. The museum is heavily focused on the Confederate navy and its ultimate influence on the U.S. navy's subsequent development. ⊠ *1002 Victory Dr.,* ☎ *706/327–9798,* WEB *www.portcolumbus.org.* ⊡ *$4.50.* ☉ *Daily 9–5.*

The Riverwalk, a linear park that's ideal for jogging, strolling, biking, and rollerblading, is also the site of Columbus State University's **Coca-**

Cola Space Science Center, which houses a planetarium, an observatory, a replica of an Apollo space capsule, a space shuttle, and other space-related exhibits. ⊠ *701 Front Ave.,* ☎ *706/649-1470,* WEB *www. ccssc.org.* 🎫 *Free; planetarium show $4.* ⊙ *Tues.–Thurs. 10–4, Fri. 10–7, Sat. 1:30–7, Sun. 1:30–4.*

★ One of the city's most notable attractions, the current **Columbus Museum,** which opened in its current 86,000-square-ft location in 1989, is the state's second-largest art museum. Collections focus heavily on American art ranging from colonial portraiture to the Ashcan School to provocative contemporary works. Other exhibits concentrate on science and the history of the Chattahoochee Valley. ⊠ *1251 Wynnton Rd.,* ☎ *706/649-0713,* WEB *www.columbusmuseum.com.* 🎫 *Free.* ⊙ *Tues.–Wed. and Fri.–Sat. 10–5, Thurs. 10–9, Sun. 1–5. Closed Mon.*

Dining and Lodging

$–$$ ✕ **Olive Branch Cafe.** This dapper downtown eatery presents a menu heavily influenced by the islands of the Mediterranean. The lamb loin is a feast, and the fried–goat cheese Greek salad puts a distinctive spin on a traditional favorite. ⊠ *1032 Broadway,* ☎ *706/322-7410. AE, MC, V. Closed Sun.*

$ ✕ **Gabby's Diner.** If you're feeling nostalgic, take a dive back in time at this '50s diner with Formica counters and a hopping jukebox. Plates are piled high with good-time comfort food. Portions are enormous, from the breakfasts to the burgers to the concrete-thick malteds. Kids eat free on Wednesday. ⊠ *4641 Warm Springs Rd.,* ☎ *706/221-9031. No credit cards.*

$$–$$$ 🏨 **Columbus Hilton.** On the site of a vast 1860s complex of warehouses,
★ factories, mills, and a Confederate arsenal, this hotel is a key component of the Iron Works Convention Center, and it uses many of the original industrial materials. Millstones and conveyor belts decorate the lobby. Rooms are done in shades of eggplant and hunter green, and many overlook the Riverwalk park. With a terrific location and a reliable restaurant (Pemberton's) with a great Sunday brunch, the Hilton is a focal point of the city's downtown revival. ⊠ *800 Front Ave., 31901,* ☎ *706/324-1800 or 800/774-1500,* FAX *706/576-4413,* WEB *www. hilton.com. 175 rooms. 2 restaurants, bar, lounge, in-room data ports, cable TV, pool, laundry service, meeting rooms, free parking. AE, D, DC, MC, V.*

$–$$ 🏨 **Country Inn and Suites.** It's a reliable chain property that's ideal if you're staying more than a few days. The rooms and suites—decorated in a country style, with gingham-printed fabrics and grapevine wreaths on the walls—are spacious, and all have coffeemakers and other helpful amenities. ⊠ *1720 Fountain Ct., 31904,* ☎ *706/660-1880 or 800/ 456-4000,* FAX *706/243-3473,* WEB *www.countryinns.com. 49 rooms, 13 suites. Microwaves, refrigerators, pool, gym, free parking. AE, D, MC, V. CP.*

Plains

55 mi southeast of Columbus via U.S. 27 and U.S. 280.

The small farming town of Plains proudly bills itself as "the town that cultivated a president" because it is the home of former U.S. president Jimmy Carter, who was born here in 1924. Carter and his wife, Rosalynn (who was also born here), still live in a sprawling ranch house in Plains, and he still teaches Sunday school twice a month at the local **Maranatha Baptist Church** (⊠ 148 Rte. 45, ☎ 229/824-7896).

At the **Jimmy Carter National Historic Site** you can still see the late 1880s railroad depot that housed his 1976 presidential campaign headquarters, the 360-acre **Jimmy Carter Boyhood Farm** (currently being restored to its 1930s appearance), and the former **Plains High School,** in which Jimmy and Rosalynn were educated—it now contains a museum and visitor center. You can visit these places and tour the town either by picking up a self-guided tour book at the visitor center or renting an audio cassette. ⊠ *300 N. Bond St.,* ☎ *229/824–4104,* WEB *www.nps. gov/jica.* ⊡ *Free.* ⊙ *Daily 9–5.*

For a guided tour of this amiable and appealing community, contact **Plain Peanuts** (⊠ 616 Main St., ☎ 229/824–3462; ⊡ $5; ⊙ daily 9–5), which will squire you around in a van driven by a guide well versed in the art of country-spun gossip and tall tales. Sites range from the prominent to the mundane (such as the late, ex-first brother Billy Carter's dilapidated gas station).

Lodging

$ 🏠 **Plains Bed & Breakfast Inn.** Smack in the center of town, this graciously renovated B&B captures the dignity of the old South—while charging quite reasonable rates. Each of the four large rooms is decorated with turn-of-the-20th-century antiques. A grand veranda wraps around the facade of this Victorian mansion, which is crowned by a circular turret. Expect breakfast in the morning to be a traditional Southern gut-buster. ⊠ *100 Church St., 31780,* ☎ *229/824–7252. 4 rooms. V. BP.*

Americus

11 mi east of Plains via U.S. 280, 133 mi south of Atlanta via U.S. 19.

In this charming small-town hamlet, the past and present coexist pleasantly along the bustling streets of the downtown square, around which you'll find numerous shops. You'll also see the magnificent Windsor Hotel, a Victorian castle built in 1892 that—with its dazzling assemblage of turrets, towers, and verandas (not to mention its grand dining room)—is an important draw for tourists.

About 10 mi northeast of Americus via Route 49, you can visit a solemn reminder of the Civil War's tragic toll, the **Andersonville National Historic Site.** This infamous prisoner-of-war penitentiary is the nation's only POW museum. Inside you'll find photographs, artifacts, and high-tech exhibits detailing not just the plight of Civil War POWs, but also prison life and conditions affecting all of America's 800,000 prisoners of war since the Revolutionary War. Some 13,000 Union prisoners died—mostly from disease, neglect, and malnutrition—at Andersonville during its 14-month tenure at the tail of the war. At the conclusion of the Civil War, the Swiss-born commandant of Andersonville was tried, convicted, and hanged. Appropriately, the exterior of this 10,000-square-ft memorial of sorts looms forbiddingly over the rural countryside, with barred windows and jutting towers. ⊠ *496 Cemetery Rd., Andersonville,* ☎ *229/924–0343,* WEB *http://andersonville.areaparks.com/.* ⊡ *Free.* ⊙ *Daily 8:30–5.*

Dining and Lodging

$$ ✕🏠 **Windsor Hotel.** This jewel of a hotel garnered awards from the
★ National Trust for Historic Preservation. Built in 1892, it's a monument to Victorian architecture and remains one of the South's best showcases of American heritage. All rooms have 12-ft ceilings, and the circular Carter Presidential Suite is the entire floor of the hotel's tallest tower. On site is the Grand Dining Room ($$–$$$, no dinner Sunday), an elegant restaurant that serves a varied menu with a focus on Southern food, such as corn chowder, crab cakes, and pecan-crusted salmon. ⊠ *125 W. Lamar St., 31709,* ☎ *229/924–1555 or 888/297–9567,* FAX

229/928–0533, WEB *www.windsor-americus.com. 41 rooms, 12 suites. Restaurant, bar, fans. AE, D, MC, V.*

Shopping

Americus is known for its antiques and gift shops, a highlight being the **Americus Antique Mall** (✉ 201 W. Forsyth St., ☎ 229/924–6999), a collective of 23 different dealers. **Country Comforts** (✉ 701 S. Martin Luther King Jr. Blvd., ☎ 229/928–0077) sells handcrafted furniture, gift baskets, and Southern food products.

Southwest Georgia A to Z

To research prices, get advice from other travelers, and book travel arrangements, visit www.fodors.com.

BUS TRAVEL

Greyhound Bus Lines serves Americus and Columbus.
➤ BUS INFORMATION: **Greyhound Bus Lines** (☎ 800/231–2222, WEB www. greyhound.com).

CAR TRAVEL

A car is your best way to tour this part of Georgia; I–75 runs north–south through the eastern edge of the region and connects to several U.S. and state highways that traverse the region, and I–85 runs southwest through Columbus.

EMERGENCIES

➤ EMERGENCY SERVICES: **Ambulance, police** (☎ 911).
➤ HOSPITALS: **Columbus Doctors Hospital** (✉ 616 19th St., Columbus, ☎ 706/322–0753).

TAXIS

Yellow Cab in Columbus provides 24-hour taxi service.
➤ TAXI COMPANIES: **Yellow Cab** (☎ 706/322–1616).

VISITOR INFORMATION

➤ TOURIST INFORMATION: **Americus-Sumter Tourism Council** (✉ Windsor Hotel, 125 W. Lamar St., Box 275, Americus 31709, ☎ 229/928–6059 or 888/278–6837). **Columbus Convention and Visitors Bureau** (✉ 1000 Bay Ave., The Riverwalk, Box 2768, 31902, ☎ 706/322–3181 or 800/999–1613, WEB www.columbusga.com). **Warm Springs Welcome Center** (✉ 69 Broad St., Warm Springs 31830, ☎ 706/655–3322 or 800/327–1927, WEB www.warmspringsga.com).

GEORGIA A TO Z

To research prices, get advice from other travelers, and book travel arrangements, visit www.fodors.com.

AIRPORTS

Hartsfield Atlanta International Airport is 13 mi south of downtown. Numerous regional airports serve the state. For information on the state's local airports, *see* the A to Z coverage at the end of each regional section in this chapter.
➤ AIRPORT INFORMATION: **Hartsfield Atlanta International Airport** (✉ 6000 N. Terminal Pkwy., ☎ 404/530–6600, WEB www.atlanta-airport. com).

BIKE TRAVEL

With a membership of about 3,000, the Southern Bicycle League has promoted bicycling across Georgia and the South for more than 20 years. The Bicycle Ride Across Georgia (BRAG) is an annual event, and the

same organization holds numerous shorter bicycling events throughout the year. Advance application is required.

➤ CONTACTS: **Bicycle Ride Across Georgia** (☎ 770/921–6166, WEB
www.brag.org). **Southern Bicycle League** (✉ Box 870387, Stone Mountain 30087, ☎ 770/594–8350, WEB www.bikesbl.org).

BUS TRAVEL

Greyhound Bus Lines serves several dozen towns statewide.

➤ BUS INFORMATION: **Greyhound Bus Lines** (☎ 800/231–2222, WEB www.
greyhound.com).

CAR TRAVEL

Although Savannah and several of the state's most visited communities have highly walkable downtowns, a car is your most convenient
and practical way to tour the state. This is even true in most of Atlanta, a city where distances between attractions, restaurants, and hotels can be vast.

Georgia is traversed east and west by several interstate highways.
North and south are covered by I–75, running from northwest through
the center of the state to the Florida line; I–85 runs from the north-
eastern part of the state through the west to Alabama; I–95 runs along
the Georgia coast from South Carolina to Florida. I–85 and I–75 converge in Atlanta near its downtown; this nexus is called the Connector. Running east and west, I–20 stretches from Birmingham, Alabama,
to Augusta, Georgia, running through the center of downtown Atlanta
on its way. From Macon I–16 leads directly east to Savannah, where
it ends. Scenic routes include U.S. 76, a good highway running east–
west through the north Georgia mountains, and U.S. 441, running north–
south from the mountains to the Florida line. Along the way U.S. 441
links numerous charming small towns and is lined with barbecue joints
of worth. On the west side of the state, various pleasant small towns
are connected by U.S. 19, the north–south route of choice prior to development of the interstate and still a good option if I–75 comes to a
standstill, as it routinely does.

ROAD CONDITIONS

For road information call the Georgia Department of Transportation.

➤ CONTACTS: **Georgia Department of Transportation** (☎ 404/656–1267,
WEB www.dot.state.ga.us).

RULES OF THE ROAD

The speed limit on interstates is 55 mph in metropolitan areas and up
to 70 mph elsewhere. Right turns on red lights are permitted unless
indicated.

EMERGENCIES

➤ EMERGENCY SERVICES: **Ambulance, police** (☎ 911).

LODGING

FOR HOME STAYS BED & BREAKFAST ATLANTA REPRESENTS 80–100
HOMES AND CAN FIND LODGING IN CARRIAGE HOUSES,
APARTMENTS, AND B&B INNS.

➤ RESERVATION SERVICES: **Bed & Breakfast Atlanta** (✉ 1608 Briarcliff
Rd., Suite 5, Atlanta 30306, ☎ 404/875–0525 or 800/967–3224, FAX
404/875–8198).

OUTDOORS AND SPORTS

FISHING

The Georgia Department of Natural Resources, Game and Fish Division has free pamphlets covering Georgia's regulations, and has maps
detailing good fishing spots.

➤ CONTACTS: **Georgia Department of Natural Resources, Game and Fish Division** (✉ 2070 U.S. 278, Social Circle 30025, ☎ 770/918–6400, WEB www.state.ga.us).

TRAIN TRAVEL
Amtrak serves Atlanta and Savannah from major cities along the eastern seaboard, as well as New Orleans. Amtrak's Thru-Way bus service connects daily from Birmingham and Mobile, Alabama, to Atlanta's Brookwood Amtrak station. Another bus runs from Brookwood to Macon.

FARES AND SCHEDULES
➤ TRAIN INFORMATION: **Amtrak** (☎ 800/872–7245, WEB www.amtrak.com).

VISITOR INFORMATION
The Georgia Department of Industry, Trade, and Tourism operates visitor centers (most of them just off major interstate highways) in Augusta, Columbus, Kingsland, Lavonia, Plains, Ringgold, Savannah, Sylvania, Tallapoosa, Valdosta, and West Point. Housed under the Georgia Department of Natural Resources, Parks, Recreation & Historic Sites division has information on Georgia's parks.
➤ TOURIST INFORMATION: **Georgia Department of Industry, Trade, and Tourism** (✉ Box 1776, Atlanta 30301, ☎ 404/656–3590 or 800/847–4842, FAX 404/651–9063, WEB www.georgia.org). **Georgia Department of Natural Resources, Parks, Recreation & Historic Sites** (✉ 205 Butler St. SE, Suite 1352, Atlanta 30334, ☎ 404/656–3530; 800/864–7275 for reservations; 770/389–7275 for local reservations, WEB www.state.ga.us).

4 LOUISIANA

Louisiana is a state divided, both physically and philosophically. North Louisiana, with its rolling hills and piney woods, is strongly Southern in flavor and appeal. The flatter, marshy land in South Louisiana is Cajun Country, with sharp differences in food, music, and even language. Riverboats ply the mighty Mississippi, and antebellum homes line the wayside in both regions, but it's New Orleans, home of the famous Mardi Gras festivities, that garners the lion's share of attention, drawing most visitors to South Louisiana.

Updated by
Michaela
Morrissey

L OCALS GENERALLY DESCRIBE REGIONS of their states as "upstate,"
"to the south," and so on, but in Louisiana the land is clearly divided. There's a capitalized distinction: North Louisiana is Southern, and South Louisiana is not, and Louisianians never, ever, say
"northern" or "southern" Louisiana. The two regions are at least connected physically through I–49, which runs between Shreveport, the
unofficial capital of North Louisiana, and Lafayette, the so-called capital of French Louisiana, in the south.

North Louisiana was settled by English, Irish, and Scottish Protestants
who moved to the region in the early 19th century from the eastern
seaboard. In customs, culture, religion, and traits the region is very much
akin to Southern states such as Mississippi and Alabama. Louisiana's
Mason-Dixon line cuts through the state's midsection city of Alexandria, known as Alex and pronounced "Elleck" by most. North of
Alexandria are hills and pine forests, acres of hiking grounds, and fishing lakes. The terrain flattens out and becomes marshy to the south.

South Louisiana is a region completely different from any other part
of the country. New Orleans and its environs were settled by the
French in the early 18th century, and 22 parishes (the state's term for
counties) of South Louisiana were settled soon after by Cajuns. Cajuns are descendants of the French who colonized Acadia—present-
day Nova Scotia and New Brunswick, Canada. In the mid-1700s the
British expelled the Acadians, who resettled in the Louisiana Territory
and became known as Cajuns. The exception to French influence in
South Louisiana are the Feliciana parishes above Baton Rouge, which
were settled by the English.

French colonists in the New Orleans area took the term *Creole* from
the Spanish and Portuguese colonizers of the West Indies. *Criollo* designated a child born of full European parentage in the colonies, as opposed to a child of mixed race. Over time, Creole has come to define
anything indigenous to the New Orleans region, from architecture to
garlic.

In 1803 President Thomas Jefferson purchased not just New Orleans,
but the entire Louisiana Territory, from Napoléon Bonaparte. The territory encompassed all the land from the Alleghenies in the east to the
Rockies in the west. A veritable flood of settlers came rafting down
the Mississippi River from the Ohio Valley, adding yet more flavor to
the state's mix of nationalities.

South Louisiana's uniqueness has brought it most of the state's tourist
trade—the festivities of New Orleans's Mardi Gras pump millions of
dollars into the local economy. South Louisiana's success in luring tourists
has prompted Mardi Gras celebrations even in Protestant North
Louisiana. Outside New Orleans, in Cajun Country, you can ride a
pirogue (a small, flat-bottom boat) poled through a bayou, kick your
heels to fiddles, and eat at tables laden with crawfish, jambalaya, and
gumbo. The Great River Road between Baton Rouge and New Orleans
is decorated with stately antebellum homes, and frilly riverboats ply
the Mississippi. On a tour boat you can drift beneath lacy gray Spanish moss into mysterious cypress swamps and sloughs.

Pleasures and Pastimes

Biking

The Kisatchie National Forest, near Natchitoches, has miles of trails
through forest. In flat-as-a-pancake South Louisiana, the area around

Lafayette has more than 60 mi of marked trails. Some of the streets in New Orleans's French Quarter are blocked to all but bikers and pedestrians during the day. City Park and Audubon Park are great places for biking.

Dining

Louisiana is perhaps the only state in the country that has a distinctive regional cuisine. The famed French Creole cuisine cooked up in New Orleans kitchens has blended over the years with Cajun cuisine—born in the bayous and popularized by celebrity chef Paul Prudhomme—to produce what's known as South Louisiana Cooking. Cajun cooking, in particular, which usually means hot and spicy, has turned up on tables all over the world, but nobody does it like South Louisianians. Graced as the state is with waterways, Louisiana tables are also laden with seafood in every imaginable and innovative variety. Dress in restaurants is informal unless otherwise noted.

CATEGORY	COST*
$$$$	over $25
$$$	$17–$25
$$	$9–$16
$	under $9

per person, for a main course at dinner

Festivals

Hardly a day goes by in Louisiana without a festival of some sort, saluting everything from the tomato to petroleum. New Orleans is home to North America's biggest bash—Mardi Gras—but Lafayette celebrates the same holiday with a Cajun flair. The New Orleans Jazz and Heritage Festival is a world-class event, as is the Festival International de la Louisiane in Lafayette.

Lodging

Accommodations in Louisiana run from homey bed-and-breakfasts to chain motels, from luxury hotels to elegant antebellum mansions. Louisiana has well over 100 B&Bs; Cajun Country is loaded with charming ones, and Natchitoches alone has 16. Old and new blend in New Orleans, which also has many B&Bs in or near the city. Its French Quarter has a plethora of guest houses that emphasize old-world ambience in 19th-century town houses and carriage houses. As one of the nation's favorite convention cities, New Orleans has a Central Business District dominated by big and brassy high-rise, high-tech convention hotels.

CATEGORY	COST*
$$$$	over $200
$$$	$150–$200
$$	$100–$149
$	under $100

All prices are for a standard double room, excluding 12% tax.

Music

About a century ago, New Orleans gave birth to jazz, and the music has scarcely missed a beat since. It pours out of clubs along Bourbon Street in the French Quarter and floods the sightseeing riverboats on the Mississippi. North Louisiana favors country-and-western music, while in South Louisiana, feet fly to the intoxicating Cajun and zydeco rhythms.

Exploring Louisiana

South Louisiana encompasses all of the region south of Alexandria and extending east to the "instep" of this boot-shape state. Almost all of

Louisiana

ARKANSAS

Lake Claiborne

Bayou D Arbonne

165

167

133

20 Shreveport

Bossier City

Monroe

20

171

71

15

49

Red R.

84

165

Natchitoches

6

167

84

Ferriday

84

Catahoula Lake

15

Toledo Bend Reservoir

171

28

Red R.

Alexandria

TEXAS

1

De Ridder

71

1

190

New Roads

Sabine River

190 171

13

27

165

190

Eunice Opelousas

190

171

93 49 31

12

10

Vinton Sulphur

Lafayette

10

27

Lake Charles

342

Beaumont

14

Abbeville

90 31

Port Arthur

27

14

Erath

New Iberia

Lake Sabine

82 82 27

Lake Calcasieu

Grand Chenier

Grand Lake

White Lake

329

Franklin

Rockefeller Wildlife Refuge

82

Marsh Island

Gulf of Mexico

0   50 miles

0   75 km

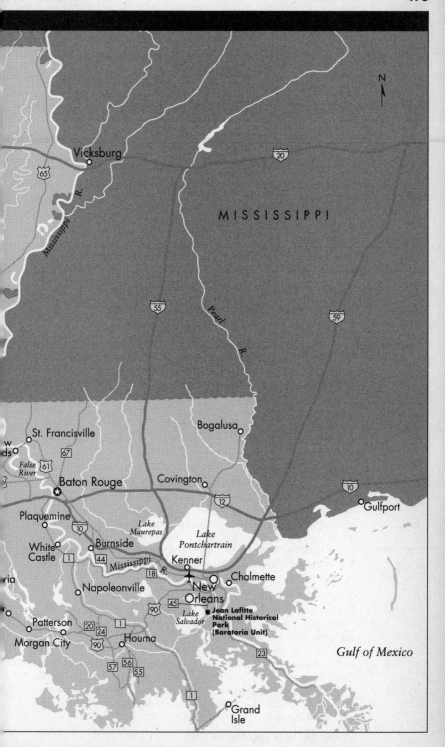

South Louisiana is considered Cajun Country, or French Louisiana, except for the region north of Baton Rouge. North of Alexandria hills start rolling, and the earth is red clay. By the time you reach Natchitoches, you're deep into North Louisiana, although the town also has rich Creole and Cajun textures. The state's main attraction, New Orleans, is in a class by itself, being characteristic of neither north nor south Louisiana. The city is a paradox in that it is both a major international port and an overgrown small town with an insouciant Caribbean vibe.

Great Itineraries

For a short visit of a few days, you'll want to focus on one area; for most visitors to Louisiana, this means New Orleans and, specifically, the French Quarter. If you have a few more days, you can get a taste of Plantation Country by touring restored plantations just 1½ hours west of the city.

With a week or more, you can explore key areas of the state outside New Orleans and Plantation Country. Lafayette, practically in the center of South Louisiana, is a good base from which to explore Cajun Country and is nearly as close to plantations as New Orleans. From here, you can also set out on direct routes west to Lake Charles and environs, or northwest to Natchitoches, the oldest permanent European settlement in the entire Louisiana Territory.

IF YOU HAVE 3 DAYS

Spend this time in ⊡ **New Orleans.** Many visitors never leave the French Quarter, even if they stay a week or more. One of the challenges of seeing New Orleans on a short visit is choosing among the city's vast number of outstanding restaurants. At least see the sights in and around Jackson Square, tour the Old Ursuline Convent, and stroll along Bourbon Street to hear the music pouring out of the jazz clubs. On your last day, spend a morning at the Aquarium of the Americas, and in the afternoon take the St. Charles Avenue streetcar to the Garden District and the Audubon Zoo.

IF YOU HAVE 5 DAYS

After a couple of days in ⊡ **New Orleans,** travel 80 mi northwest to ⊡ **Baton Rouge,** the capital of Louisiana, with its museums and sites that pertain to state lore. On your way, you can tour the River Road plantations that lie between the cities, particularly Nottoway, Madewood, and Laura. Baton Rouge is in the heart of the area called Plantation Country; drive north of the city to quaint little **St. Francisville,** where several of the restored estates are open for tours. Some of the plantations offer overnight accommodations.

IF YOU HAVE 10 DAYS

Get to know ⊡ **New Orleans** and ⊡ **Baton Rouge** for a few days, then take I–10 west out of Baton Rouge to spend at least a day in ⊡ **Lafayette,** whose many attractions focus on Cajun culture. Within a short drive south of Lafayette are colorful small towns and villages, such as **Erath** and **Abbeville,** that are typical of Cajun Country. Drive north to see the historic district in ⊡ **Natchitoches.** Although Natchitoches can be seen in a day and a half, it lies 142 mi north of Lafayette; en route Cane River Country has several sites that should be seen in a leisurely manner.

When to Tour Louisiana

The best times to visit Louisiana are October through December, and in the spring. During those times of the year temperatures and humidity are at bearable levels. Summers are scorchers throughout the state, with the mercury hovering above 90°F for much of June, July, August, and September. In South Louisiana, hurricane season runs from June through November, and the coastline is sometimes battered with high winds and heavy rain. An ideal time for a first visit to New Orleans is Spring Fiesta (the weekend following Easter), when the city is dressed in springtime finery and many of the handsome homes are open for tours. Mardi Gras (February or March) is not recommended for a first visit to New Orleans. All of the city is given over to raucous revelry, and its quiet charms are buried beneath the mighty hordes of merrymakers.

NEW ORLEANS

New Orleans's reputation as one of the country's favorite good-time towns has remained intact over the years, and the city is forever finding something to celebrate. World-famous Mardi Gras aside, new festivals crop up at the drop of a Panama hat. New Orleans party animals even celebrate each new addition to the main zoo.

The city's most famous party place is the French Quarter, bordered by Canal Street, Esplanade Avenue, North Rampart Street, and the Mississippi River. Also called the Vieux Carré (Old Square), the Quarter is the original colony, founded in 1718 by French Creoles. As you explore its famous restaurants, antiques shops, and jazz haunts, try to imagine a handful of determined early 18th-century settlers living in crude palmetto huts and battling swamps, floods, hurricanes, and yellow fever. Two cataclysmic fires in the late 18th century virtually leveled the town. The Old Ursuline Convent on Chartres Street is the only remaining original French colonial structure. Survival was a struggle for the Creoles, and the sobriquet "the City That Care Forgot" stems from a determination not only to live life but to celebrate it.

In the early 19th century, the American Sector was just upriver of the French Quarter. For that reason, street names change as you cross Canal Street from the French Quarter: Bourbon Street to Carondelet Street, Royal Street to St. Charles Avenue, and so on.

The nerve center of the nation's second-largest port and main parade route during Mardi Gras, the CBD (Central Business District) cuts a wide swath between Uptown and Downtown, with Canal Street the official dividing line. Bordered by Canal Street, the river, Howard Avenue, and Loyola Avenue, the CBD has the city's newest convention hotels along with ritzy shopping malls, old department stores, international trade agencies and consulates, fast-food chains, monuments, and the monumental Superdome.

Nestled in between St. Charles Avenue, Louisiana Avenue, Jackson Avenue, and Magazine Street, the Garden District is aptly named. The Americans who built their estates upriver surrounded their homes with lavish lawns, forgoing the Creoles' preference for secluded courtyards. Magazine Street is heaven on earth for shoppers. Joggers, golfers, tennis buffs, bicyclists, and horseback riders head for Audubon Park.

Directions in New Orleans are described with respect to the Father of Waters: the Mississippi River loops around the city, wreaking havoc with ordinary routes. New Orleanians, ever resourceful, refer instead to lakeside (toward Lake Pontchartrain), riverside (toward the Mississippi), upriver (also called Uptown), and downriver (Downtown).

Some words of caution are necessary: New Orleans is a high-crime city. The French Quarter and the Garden District can be very dangerous, even in broad daylight; walks at night can be particularly risky. Stay alert and streetwise, wherever and whenever you go—especially if you're carrying such obvious tourist accessories as cameras and opened maps.

Numbers in the text correspond to numbers in the margin and on the Downtown New Orleans map.

The French Quarter

The French Quarter is a carefully preserved historic district. It's also home to some 4,000 residents, some of the most famous French Creole restaurants, and many a jazz club. An eclectic crowd, which includes some of the world's best jazz musicians, ambles in and out of small two- and three-story frame, old-brick, and pastel-painted stucco buildings. Baskets of splashy subtropical plants dangle from the eaves of buildings with filigreed galleries, dollops of gingerbread, and dormer windows. Built flush with the banquettes (sidewalks), the houses, most of which date from the early to mid-19th century, front secluded courtyards awash with brilliant blossoms.

A Good Walk

A good place to start is **Jackson Square** ①, which has always been the heart and soul of the French Quarter. A flagstone pedestrian mall borders three sides of the square. As you face the statue, with St. Louis Cathedral behind you, the **New Orleans Welcome Center** ② is to your left, a few steps across the flagstones.

Turn right as you leave the visitor center to see the three historic buildings that sit on Chartres Street, facing the square. The white church in the middle is the late-18th-century **St. Louis Cathedral** ③. The two Spanish colonial buildings flanking the church are the **Cabildo** ④, on the left as you face the church, and the **Presbytère** ⑤, on the right. Alongside the church are Pirate's Alley and Père Antoine's Alley, cracked-flagstone passageways redolent of infamous plots and pirate intrigue—but, alas, the streets were laid long after Jean Lafitte and his Baratarian band had vanished. William Faulkner wrote his first novel, *A Soldier's Pay*, while living at 624 Pirate's Alley.

Lining Jackson Square, on St. Peter and St. Ann streets, the Pontalba Buildings are among the nation's oldest apartment buildings, built between 1849 and 1851. In the lower Pontalba (considered lower because it's downriver of the square) is the **1850 House** ⑥.

The promenade of **Washington Artillery Park** ⑦, opposite Jackson Square on Decatur Street, affords a splendid perspective of the square and the Mississippi River. On the Moon Walk promenade, across the tracks from the park, you can sit on a bench or stroll down the steps to the water's edge.

Washington Artillery Park is anchored on the upriver side by the Jackson Brewery and Millhouse, and downriver by the French Market. Jax Beer used to be made in the brewery, and the market is on the site of a late-17th-century Indian trading post. Both sites are now filled with boutiques and restaurants, with Planet Hollywood and Virgin Megastore hogging most of the brewery space. Two blocks toward Canal Street on Decatur Street is the Jackson Brewery Corporation's Marketplace, home of yet more restaurants and retail outlets.

On the same site for more than 100 years, Café du Monde at 800 Decatur Street is the upriver anchor for the French Market and is in one of its oldest buildings. Stretching from St. Ann Street downriver to Barracks Street, the market is alive with shops, outdoor cafés, and ice cream and candy stores. The downriver anchor of the French Market is the Old Farmers Market, where farmers from the countryside have been bringing their produce for more than 170 years, and where a Community Flea Market flourishes daily from dawn until dusk.

The area on the Esplanade Avenue fringe of the Quarter should be avoided at night, but you'll be safe during the day when you visit the jazz and Mardi Gras exhibits in the **Old U.S. Mint** ⑧. From the mint, walk up tree-lined Esplanade Avenue to Chartres Street and turn left to reach the **Old Ursuline Convent** ⑨, within a walled complex at the corner of Chartres and Ursulines streets; it was built in 1749. The Greek Revival house across the street from the Ursuline Convent is the **Beauregard-Keyes House** ⑩. From the house, turn right onto Ursulines Street, walk one block to Royal Street, and turn right again, where you'll find the **Gallier House** ⑪, built around 1857.

Turn right at the corner of Royal and St. Philip streets to see the 18th-century **Lafitte's Blacksmith Shop** ⑫, which now houses a neighborhood bar. Back at the intersection of Royal and St. Philip streets, look to the right at the **Cornstalk Fence** ⑬. Around the corner is the **New Orleans Historic Voodoo Museum** ⑭ on Dumaine Street. From the museum, turn right on Dumaine Street, and between Royal and Chartres streets is **Madame John's Legacy** ⑮, a West Indies–style raised cottage that is similar to those built by the early planters in this area.

Turn right after leaving Madame John's Legacy, walk down to Chartres Street, and make another right. Continue on Chartres Street through Jackson Square to St. Peter Street, turn right again, and walk one block up to Royal Street. Here you'll see the 19th-century **LaBranche Houses** ⑯. Directly across St. Peter Street from the LaBranche Houses is the four-story **First Skyscraper** ⑰, constructed between 1795 and 1811.

Next, walk up St. Peter Street, away from Jackson Square. About midway between Royal and Bourbon streets, behind weathered walls, is **Preservation Hall** ⑱, where old-time legends of traditional jazz hold forth nightly. Not much happens here during the day, but you can peer through the gate to see the carriageway and the courtyard beyond it. Return to Royal Street, turn right, and cross Toulouse Street to reach the old Merieult House, which contains the **Historic New Orleans Collection** ⑲.

Walk toward the Mississippi River on Toulouse Street and turn right to find the **New Orleans Pharmacy Museum** ⑳. On the same side of the street, at the corner of Chartres and St. Louis streets, is the bar **Napoleon House** ㉑, a longtime favorite haunt of artists and writers.

Wrench yourself from Napoleon House, walk away from the river, and cross Bourbon Street to reach the **Hermann-Grima House** ㉒, an American-style town-house museum dating from the early 19th century. After you leave the residence, walk less than a block and turn left on Dauphine Street. Turn right at Conti Street to the **Musée Conti Wax Museum** ㉓.

TIMING

This old historic district is only about 1 square mi, and it can be walked easily in a half day. But that would mean you'd miss peeking into the plethora of shops and knocking back a Dixie beer at Lafitte's Blacksmith Shop or a Pimm's Cup—a gin-based drink—at Napoleon House. Allow yourself at least a full day (you could spend a week here) to enjoy the Quarter's main attractions: the Cabildo and St. Louis Cathedral at Jackson Square, the Old Ursuline Convent, and Gallier House. April and October are ideal times for strolling around the neighborhood. Be prepared for crowds: the neighborhood is almost always full of visitors and/or conventioneers, except perhaps during the worst dog days of summer. Ambling is simply impossible during Mardi Gras, when the streets are packed.

180

Downtown New Orleans

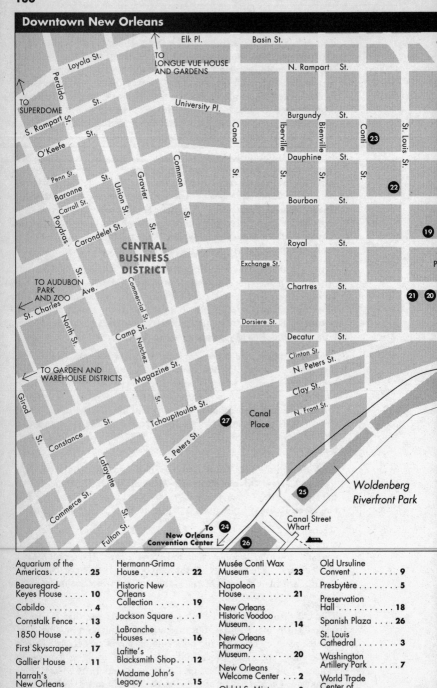

Elk Pl. · Basin St. · N. Rampart St. · TO LONGUE VUE HOUSE AND GARDENS · University Pl. · Loyola St. · Perdido St. · TO SUPERDOME · S. Rampart St. · O'Keefe · Penn St. · Baronne St. · Carroll St. · Poydras · Carondelet St. · Union St. · Gravier St. · Common St. · Canal St. · Burgundy St. · Iberville · Bienville · Dauphine St. · Bourbon St. · Conti St. · St. Louis St. · 23 · 22 · 19 · CENTRAL BUSINESS DISTRICT · TO AUDUBON PARK AND ZOO · St. Charles Ave. · North St. · Commercial St. · Camp St. · Natchez · Magazine St. · TO GARDEN AND WAREHOUSE DISTRICTS · Girod St. · Constance St. · Lafayette St. · Commerce St. · Fulton St. · Tchoupitoulas St. · S. Peters St. · 27 · Royal St. · Exchange St. · Chartres St. · Dorsiere St. · Decatur St. · Clinton St. · N. Peters St. · Clay St. · N. Front St. · Canal Place · 21 · 20 · P · 25 · Woldenberg Riverfront Park · Canal Street Wharf · To New Orleans Convention Center · 24 · 26

Aquarium of the Americas 25
Beauregard-Keyes House 10
Cabildo 4
Cornstalk Fence . . . 13
1850 House 6
First Skyscraper . . . 17
Gallier House 11
Harrah's New Orleans Casino 27

Hermann-Grima House 22
Historic New Orleans Collection 19
Jackson Square 1
LaBranche Houses 16
Lafitte's Blacksmith Shop . . . 12
Madame John's Legacy 15

Musée Conti Wax Museum 23
Napoleon House 21
New Orleans Historic Voodoo Museum 14
New Orleans Pharmacy Museum 20
New Orleans Welcome Center . . . 2
Old U.S. Mint 8

Old Ursuline Convent 9
Presbytère 5
Preservation Hall 18
Spanish Plaza 26
St. Louis Cathedral 3
Washington Artillery Park 7
World Trade Center of New Orleans (WTC) 24

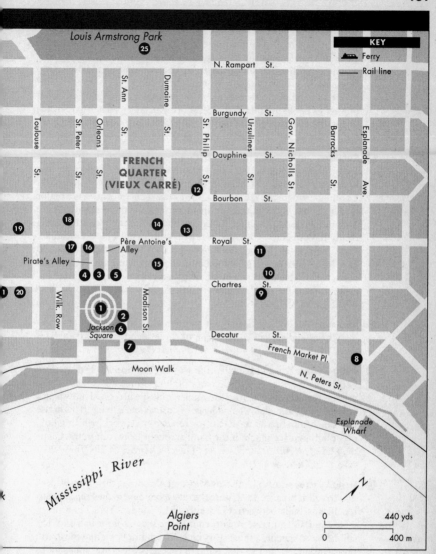

Louis Armstrong Park

25

N. Rampart St.

St. Ann St.

Dumaine St.

Toulouse St.

St. Peter St.

Orleans St.

Burgundy St.

Ursulines St.

St. Philip St.

Gov. Nicholls St.

Barracks St.

Esplanade Ave.

FRENCH QUARTER (VIEUX CARRÉ)

Dauphine St.

12

Bourbon St.

18

14

13

19

17 16

Père Antoine's Alley

Royal St.

11

Pirate's Alley

4 3 5

15

10

Chartres St.

9

1 20

Wilk. Row

Madison St.

1

2

Jackson Square

6

Decatur St.

French Market Pl.

7

8

Moon Walk

N. Peters St.

Esplanade Wharf

Mississippi River

Algiers Point

KEY

Ferry

Rail line

0   440 yds

0   400 m

Sights to See

⑩ Beauregard-Keyes House. For a brief period after the Civil War, this raised cottage with a Greek Revival portico was home to Confederate general Pierre Gustav Toutant Beauregard, the Creole New Orleanian who ordered the first shot fired at Fort Sumter. In the mid-1940s the house was bought by novelist Frances Parkinson Keyes (author of *Dinner at Antoine's*), whose office was in the former slave quarters. Some of Keyes's books are sold in the gift shop. The pretty French garden adjacent to the house is part of the tour. ⊠ *1113 Chartres St., French Quarter,* ☎ *504/523–7257.* 🕮 *$4.* ☼ *Mon.–Sat. 10–3; tours on the hr.*

④ Cabildo. This colonial building dating from 1799 was named for the Spanish governing council that met here. Transfer papers for the Louisiana Purchase of 1803 were signed on the second floor, in the Sala Capitular, and in 1825, Lafayette, the French general who was a major leader alongside Washington in the American Revolution, stayed here on a welcome-back tour of the United States. Among the artifacts is a death mask of Napoléon, who was a hero for many a New Orleanian. The Cabildo—along with the **Presbytère**, the **1850 House**, and the **Old U.S. Mint**—is a property of the Louisiana State Museum. A 20% discount is available when you purchase tickets to two or more LSM properties at the same time. ⊠ *Jackson Sq., French Quarter,* ☎ *504/568–6968.* 🕮 *$5.* ☼ *Tues.–Sun. 9–5.*

⑬ Cornstalk Fence. This heavy cast-iron fence, with its design of morning glories and ears of corn, is one of three such fences in the city; it dates from 1859. ⊠ *915 Royal St., French Quarter.*

⑥ 1850 House. You can see what life was like for upscale 19th-century Creole city dwellers on a guided tour of this restored apartment, which belongs to the Louisiana State Museum; it's filled with period furnishings, antique dolls, and plenty of evidence of cushy Creole living. This house was one of the first to have cast (or molded) ironwork, which would eventually replace much of the hand-wrought ironwork in the Quarter. ⊠ *523 St. Ann St., Jackson Sq., French Quarter,* ☎ *504/568–6968.* 🕮 *$3.* ☼ *Tues.–Sun. 10–5.*

⑰ First Skyscraper. Also known as Maison LeMonnier, this "skyscraper" was so called because it was once the tallest building in the French Quarter. It was built between 1795 and 1811 for Dr. Yves LeMonnier, whose initials can be seen worked into the second-floor balcony. The edifice was originally a three-story high-rise; rumor has it that the fourth floor was added later so that it might retain its towering name. Shops on the ground floor are open to the public. ⊠ *640 St. Peter St., French Quarter.*

⑪ Gallier House. Irishman James Gallagher Sr. changed his name to Gallier before moving to New Orleans in order to fit in with the Creoles. This handsome house was designed by his renowned architect son, James Gallagher Jr., around 1857; the architect lived here with his family. The house has early Louisiana and Victorian antique furnishings upholstered in rich brocades and velvets, living room chandeliers made of etched glass and brass, marble mantels, and elaborate ceiling medallions. There are also short films on architectural crafts and exhibits on 19th-century life. The residence was one of the settings used in the 1994 film *Interview with the Vampire*. ⊠ *1118–1132 Royal St., French Quarter,* ☎ *504/525–5661,* 🌐 *www.gnofn.org/~hggh.* 🕮 *$6; combination ticket with Hermann-Grima House is $10.* ☼ *Mon.–Sat. 10–4; tours 10:30–3:30 on ½ hr.*

㉒ Hermann-Grima House. William Brand designed this town house in 1831 for a wealthy merchant named Samuel Hermann, who later sold the house to attorney Felix Grima. It's one of the largest and best-preserved examples of American architecture in the Quarter. A guided tour takes in the first floor and the ancient rear kitchens, where Creole cooking demonstrations take place on Thursday from October through March. ✉ *820 St. Louis St., French Quarter*, ☎ *504/525–5661*, WEB *www.gnofn. org/~hggh.* 🖾 *$6; combination ticket with Gallier House is $10.* ⊙ *Mon.–Sat. 10–4; last tour at 3:30.*

⑲ Historic New Orleans Collection. One of the nation's largest private collections of documents, paintings, blueprints, and artifacts is contained in the 18th-century Merieult House, one of the few buildings to survive the fire of 1794. The ground-floor Williams Gallery, with changing exhibits relating to the city's past, is free to the public; other galleries can be seen on a guided tour. ✉ *533 Royal St., French Quarter*, ☎ *504/523–4662*, WEB *www.hnoc.org.* 🖾 *House tour $4, galleries tour $4.* ⊙ *Tues.–Sat. 10–4:45.*

★ ☾ **❶ Jackson Square.** Jackson Square, founded in 1718, was called Place d'Armes by the Creoles and was the center of all colonial life, home to parading militia, religious ceremonies, social gatherings, food vendors, entertainers, and pirates. Its sun-patterned landscaping was a popular design in the court of King Louis XIV, the Sun King. The square's focal point is a massive equestrian statue of General Andrew Jackson, hero of the 1815 Battle of New Orleans—in which he saved the city by defeating the British 5 mi downriver at Chalmette. Today the square remains a social hub. Pirate attire is not uncommon in the colorful crowd that flocks here.

The **Pontalba Buildings** that line either side of Jackson Square on St. Ann and St. Peter streets are among the oldest apartment houses in the country. Built between 1849 and 1851, they were constructed under the supervision of the baroness Micaela Pontalba, who occasionally lent the laborers a helping hand. ✉ *Bordered by Chartres, St. Ann, Decatur, and St. Peter Sts.*

⑯ LaBranche Houses. This complex of lovely town houses, built in the 1830s by widow LaBranche, fills the half block between Pirate's Alley, Royal, and St. Peter streets behind the **Cabildo** (☞ *above*). The one at 700 Royal Street (on the corner of Royal and St. Peter streets) is one of the most photographed edifices in the French Quarter. Its filigreed double balconies bedecked with flowering plants are cast iron with an oak-leaf-and-acorn motif. Cast iron such as this was introduced into New Orleans in about 1850, so the balconies would have been a later addition. All the houses are privately owned. There are shops and restaurants on the ground floor.

⑫ Lafitte's Blacksmith Shop. In the mid-19th century, notorious freebooters Jean and Pierre Lafitte are said to have operated a blacksmith shop in this tattered cottage, which served as a front for their slave trading, smuggling, and sundry nefarious deeds. The building dates to 1772. For many years, it has served as a popular neighborhood bar, especially favored by artists and writers, both famous and obscure. ✉ *941 Bourbon St., French Quarter*, ☎ *504/523–0066.*

⑮ Madame John's Legacy. The 19th-century writer George Washington Cable wrote often about New Orleans Creoles. He used several French Quarter homes as settings for his stories. This house is named for a character in his short story " 'Tite Poulette." The West Indies–style house was built in 1788 on the site of the birthplace of Renato Beluche, a Lafitte lieutenant who helped Andrew Jackson in the Battle of New Orleans. Owned by the Louisiana State Museum, the house, though unfurnished, contains photographs and exhibits that pertain to this structure and to 18th-century New Orleans. It played a role in the film *Interview with the Vampire*. ✉ *632 Dumaine St., French Quarter,* ☎ *504/568–6968.* ➳ *$3.* ⊗ *Tues.–Sun. 10–5.*

☾ ㉓ **Musée Conti Wax Museum.** For a great introduction to New Orleans history, be sure to visit New Orleans's answer to Madame Tussaud's. Each of the 100 colorful tableaux depicts an event in the city's history, beginning with the 1682 arrival of LaSalle. Among the Louisiana luminaries captured in wax are Andrew Jackson, Jean Lafitte, Marie Laveau, and former governor Edwin Edwards. ✉ *917 Conti St., French Quarter,* ☎ *504/525–2605,* WEB *www.get-waxed.com.* ➳ *$6.25.* ⊗ *Mon.–Sat. 10–5, Sun. noon–5.*

★ ㉑ **Napoleon House.** Arguably the most popular bar among New Orleanians, this is a wonderfully atmospheric place with peeling sepia walls and Napoleonic memorabilia. Napoléon never visited New Orleans, but he had many admirers here. Among them was Mayor Nicholas Girod, who formed a syndicate whose purpose was to rescue the Little Corporal from incarceration on St. Helena and bring him to this house to live in an apartment Girod had added for that purpose. Alas, Napoléon died before the rescue could take place. ✉ *500 Chartres St., French Quarter,* ☎ *504/524–9752,* WEB *www.napoleonhouse.com.* ⊗ *Mon.–Sat. 11 AM–1 AM, Sun. 11–7.*

⓮ **New Orleans Historic Voodoo Museum.** An only–in–New Orleans attraction, this is a dimly lighted place with a prominently featured portrait of 19th-century voodoo queen Marie Laveau, a voodoo altar, sundry potions, and information about voodoo as it is practiced today. ✉ *724 Dumaine St., French Quarter,* ☎ *504/523–7685,* WEB *www.voodoomuseum.com.* ➳ *$6.25.* ⊗ *Daily 10–8.*

⓴ **New Orleans Pharmacy Museum.** In 1823 Louis Dufilho, said to be the nation's first licensed pharmacist, had his pharmacy on the ground floor and lived upstairs. He grew medicinal herbs in the courtyard. This is a musty old place, full of ancient, mysterious medicinal items; there's also an Italian marble fountain used by 19th-century soda jerks. ✉ *514 Chartres St., French Quarter,* ☎ *504/565–8027,* WEB *www.pharmacymuseum.org.* ➳ *$2.* ⊗ *Tues.–Sun. 10–5.*

❷ **New Orleans Welcome Center.** The New Orleans Welcome Center should be one of your first stops for maps, brochures, and friendly advice about the city. The center shares space with an outlet of the Louisiana Office of Tourism, which offers information about attractions statewide. ✉ *529 St. Ann St., French Quarter,* ☎ *504/566–5068,* WEB *www.neworleanscvb.com.* ⊗ *Daily 9–5.*

❽ **Old U.S. Mint.** Built in 1835, the massive Greek Revival building was the first branch of the U.S. Mint, and it turned out money from 1838 until 1861. During the war Confederate coins were stamped here until the Confederate States of America went broke, and afterward the mint continued currency production until 1909. It's now a part of the Louisiana State Museum, with jazz and Mardi Gras exhibits. Among many other artifacts, the jazz exhibit displays the first horn used by native son Louis Armstrong and some of his famous white handkerchiefs. Glittering Carnival gowns, crowns, and scepters are among the colorful Mardi Gras exhibits. ✉ *400 Esplanade Ave., French Quarter,* ☎ *504/568–6968.* ➳ *$5.* ⊗ *Tues.–Sun. 9–5.*

★ ❾ **Old Ursuline Convent.** This handsome Greek Revival building is the oldest structure in the Lower Mississippi Valley and the only undisputed survivor of the late-18th-century fires. It was erected in 1749 by order of Louis XV, the second convent built on this site. The first Sisters of Ursula arrived in the colony in 1727, after surviving a torturous five-month voyage from France. The iron cross on the convent grounds came with the nuns from Rouen. The Ursulines stayed in another building until this one was completed; they occupied this convent from 1749 to 1824. The hand-hewn cypress spiral stairs inside are from the original convent. Guided tours of the complex include the lovely restored St. Mary's Church. ⊠ *1100 Chartres St., French Quarter,* ☎ *504/529–3040.* ▭ *$5.* ☉ *Tours Tues.–Fri. 10, 11, 1, 2, and 3; weekends 11:15, 1, and 2.*

★ ☾ ❺ **Presbytère.** This building was constructed in 1795 to house priests of the Catholic church but was never used for this purpose. Like the **Cabildo** (☞ *above*), it's also a museum, but here the entire structure is given over to a permanent, and dazzling, Mardi Gras exhibit. The exhibits trace the history of Mardi Gras around the world, showcase glittering costumes and crowns, and include kid-friendly interactive displays. The odd-shape structure in the arcade of the Presbytère is a Confederate submarine. ⊠ *Jackson Sq.,* ☎ *504/568–6968.* ▭ *Admission to each of the 4 state museums is $5, with a 20% discount on tickets to 2 or more museums purchased at the same time.* ☉ *Tues.–Sun. 9–5.*

★ ⓲ **Preservation Hall.** The Hall, as it is known locally, may be the best-known attraction in town. Preservation Hall Jazz Bands tour around the world as ambassadors for New Orleans, for traditional jazz, and for the sight itself (☞ Nightlife and the Arts, *below*). In the years prior to World War I, the city was full of places like this, but over time they disappeared. In the 1960s, Allen Jaffe—Pennsylvanian, tuba player, and jazz aficionado—opened the Hall, providing a place for musicians to play and tourists to throng. Jaffe was revered by musicians; upon his death in 1987, thousands came from all over the world to pay their last respects and to march in a traditional jazz funeral. ⊠ *726 St. Peter St., French Quarter,* ☎ *504/522–2841,* ⓦⓔⓑ *www.preservationhall. com.* ▭ *$5 cover.* ☉ *Daily 8 PM–midnight.*

❸ **St. Louis Cathedral.** Soaring above the earthly activity taking place right in its front yard, the small white church is a quiet reminder of the spiritual life of New Orleans residents. The first church on this site was built in 1724 and named for Louis IX, France's saint-king. The present church dates from 1794 and was restored and enlarged in 1849. It was elevated to the status of minor basilica in 1964, and in honor of Pope John Paul II's 1987 visit, the mall in front of the cathedral was christened Place Jean Paul Deux. ⊠ *Jackson Sq., on 700 block of Chartres St.,* ☎ *504/525–9585.* ☉ *Tours daily every ½ hr 9–5.*

❼ **Washington Artillery Park.** Named for the 141st Artillery, which has been mobilized for every war since 1845, when its commander was General Zachary Taylor, this small "park" is formed mostly of concrete. Ramps and steps lead from Decatur Street up to a promenade, where there are park benches, box trees, and a grand view of Jackson Square on one side and Old Man River on the other. Steps leading up to the promenade from Decatur Street form an amphitheater, with sundry jugglers and mimes entertaining on the sidewalk below. If you go down the steps on the river side of the park and cross the streetcar tracks, you'll reach Moon Walk. This promenade that stretches right along the Mississippi is lined with park benches, and stone steps lead down into the muddy water. Street musicians often play here. Beware the panhandlers: they can be verbally abusive and even violent at times. ⊠ *Decatur St. between St. Peter and St. Ann Sts.*

Foot of Canal

A walk around the foot of Canal Street in the Central Business District (CBD) takes in sights as varied as a trade center, an excellent aquarium, and a plaza anchored by a shopping mall.

A Good Walk

You can begin your tour at the Top of the Mart cocktail lounge on the 33rd floor of the city's **World Trade Center** ㉔. From the center, turn right, walk past the Canal Street Ferry landing, and cross Canal Street to reach the **Aquarium of the Americas** ㉕ in the 16-acre Woldenberg Riverfront Park.

To reach **Spanish Plaza** ㉖ behind the World Trade Center, backtrack across Canal Street to the ferry landing. Just to the right of the ferry landing is a large equestrian statue of Bernardo de Galvez, a governor of the Louisiana Territory during the Spanish colonial period. Behind the governor, a broad arch heralds Riverwalk. Spanish Plaza is across the tracks (watch out for the Riverfront Streetcar!), up the steps, and to the right.

The large Greek Revival–style building across from the World Trade Center is **Harrah's New Orleans Casino** ㉗.

TIMING

Allow at least a full morning or afternoon for a leisurely stroll around this riverfront area. You can easily devote two hours to the aquarium. The Riverwalk shopping mall at Spanish Plaza can take up a few more hours of your time.

Sights to See

★ ☺ ㉕ **Aquarium of the Americas.** In this major family attraction, more than 7,000 creatures swim in 60 separate displays representing four major environments—the Amazon River Basin, the Caribbean Reef, the Mississippi River, and the Gulf Coast. Another wing contains galleries and an IMAX movie theater. The 16-acre **Woldenberg Riverfront Park** around the aquarium is a tranquil spot with excellent views of the river. ⊠ *Foot of Canal St.,* ☎ *504/861–2538 aquarium; 504/581–4629 theater,* WEB *www.auduboninstitute.org.* 🎟 *Aquarium $13, IMAX $7.75; combination ticket $17.25.* ☉ *Aquarium Sun.–Thurs. 9:30–6, Fri.–Sat. 9:30–7; IMAX daily 10–8, shows on the hr.*

㉗ **Harrah's New Orleans Casino.** Louisiana's only land-based casino is this 100,000-square-ft facility with a slew of slots and gaming tables set in several New Orleans–themed "courts." The casino is open 24 hours, seven days a week, and also features nightly entertainment, daily parades, and whatever else it takes to keep the dice rolling. ⊠ *4 Canal St. (Canal St. at the Mississippi River), CBD,* ☎ *504/533–6000 or 877/277–4263,* WEB *www.harrahs.com/our_casinos/nor.*

OFF THE
BEATEN PATH

WAREHOUSE DISTRICT – This burgeoning part of the CBD, bordered roughly by Poydras Street, Baronne Street, Howard Avenue, and the Mississippi River, was long characterized by a plethora of mostly abandoned warehouses. It began to blossom in the 1970s with the opening of the **Contemporary Arts Center** (⊠ 900 Camp St., Warehouse District, ☎ 504/528–3800, WEB www.cacno.org), which has an art gallery and two theaters (admission is $3 for the gallery; theater tickets range from $10 to $20). The CAC is *the* trendsetter of the Warehouse District; its presence has spawned a host of gallery openings in the area. Julia Street, known as Gallery Row, is lined with top-of-the-line expressionist galleries, and during the October Art for Arts Sake festival, aficionados gallery-hop, ending up at the CAC for a gala featuring live music and much food and drink.

☺ The **Louisiana Children's Museum** (420 Julia St., Warehouse District, ☎ 504/523–1357, WEB www.lcm.org) is an excellent museum with a host of educational hands-on exhibits, including a market, a TV station, and a small port. You can reach the museum from Spanish Plaza (☞ *below*) by walking through Riverwalk and exiting at Julia Street. Admission is $5; the museum is open Tuesday to Saturday 9:30 to 4:30, Sunday noon to 4:30.

Inside a massive two-warehouse facility is the **National D-Day Museum** (✉ 925 Magazine St., Warehouse District, ☎ 504/527–6012, WEB www.ddaymuseum.org), the only museum dedicated to the 1944 D-Day invasion of Normandy and 18 other beach invasions during World War II. Exhibits include a replica of the Higgins boat troop-landing craft, which was made in New Orleans, and British Spitfire and American Avenger fighter planes. The Louisiana Memorial Pavilion building has a theater that plays war footage and documentaries. Admission is $6; the museum is open daily from 9 to 5.

The former landmark Howard Memorial Library on Lee Circle will open as the **Ogden Museum of Southern Art** (615 Howard Ave., Warehouse District, ☎ 504/539–9600, WEB www.ogdenmuseum.org) in early 2003. The cornerstone of its eclectic collection is the more than 500 works collected by local developer Robert Houston Ogden.

㉖ **Spanish Plaza.** A gift to the city from the Spanish government in the 1970s, this open expanse paved with mosaic tile stretches from behind the World Trade Center to the Mississippi River. The centerpiece of the plaza is a fountain emblazoned with Spanish coats of arms. Excursion boats for trips up the Mississippi take on passengers at the plaza, and there are often food vendors. The area is anchored downriver by the ferry landing and upriver by **Riverwalk,** a ½-mi-long shopping mall that stretches right along the river from the plaza to Julia Street in the Warehouse District. There are some 200 shops and restaurants, along with local specialty shops, such as Yvonne LaFleur and Louisiana Opal. *Riverwalk:* ✉ *Poydras St. at the river, CBD,* ☎ *504/522–1555.* ☺ *Mon.–Sat. 10–9, Sun. 11–7.*

㉔ **World Trade Center of New Orleans (WTC).** This skyscraper contains offices of foreign consulates and trade agencies. At press time, negotiations were under way to convert the first 18 floors into a hotel, possibly operated by Crowne Plaza. Slated to remain in its 33rd-floor perch, the venerable **Top of the Mart** (☎ 504/522–9795, ☺ weekdays 10 AM–midnight, Sat. 11 AM–1 AM, Sun. 2 PM–midnight) is a revolving cocktail lounge with grand vistas of the river and the city. ✉ *2 Canal St., CBD.*

The Garden District

The Americans who flocked to New Orleans after the 1803 Louisiana Purchase settled upriver of the French Quarter and built fine homes surrounded by luxuriant gardens. Many of the elegant Garden District homes were built during New Orleans's golden age, from 1830 until the Civil War. The easily walkable area is bounded by Jackson, Louisiana, and St. Charles avenues and Magazine Street. Its grand mansions are private homes and closed to the public, but they are worth seeing from the outside.

A Good Walk

Take a short streetcar ride from Canal Street to 4th Street (Stop 16) and walk toward the river one block to Prytania Street. At the corner of 4th and Prytania, Colonel Short's Villa (✉ 1448 4th St.) is a stunning Greek Revival–Italianate mansion. Walk down 4th Street to Coliseum Street, turn left, and go one block to 3rd Street. The Robinson

House (⊠ 1415 3rd St.) is a lovely white house, said to have been among the first in New Orleans to have indoor plumbing. Continue on Coliseum Street to 1st Street. The home of novelist Anne Rice and husband Stan (⊠ 1239 1st St.) is a handsome Greek Revival house, which the writer restored and used as the setting for her novel *The Witching Hour*. Like other Garden District mansions, it is not open to the public, but there are often fans hanging out on the sidewalk, hoping for an author sighting.

Walk toward St. Charles Avenue on 1st Street; at the corner of 1st and Prytania streets is Toby's Corner (⊠ 2340 Prytania St.), which is said to be the oldest house in the Garden District, dating from about 1838. Across the street from it, the Bradish Johnson House (⊠ 2343 Prytania St.), now the Louise McGehee School, was built in the late 1860s.

TIMING

Allow about an hour and a half to leisurely stroll around the Garden District. The walk suggested above is highly selective; the neighborhood is filled with stunning mansions, and you might want to allow extra time for picture taking.

OFF THE BEATEN PATH

AUDUBON PARK AND ZOO – To reach the Audubon Park and Zoo from the Garden District, board the St. Charles streetcar once again to head to Uptown. The 340-acre park rolls out across St. Charles Avenue from Tulane and Loyola universities. With its live oaks and lush tropical plants, Audubon Park was once part of the plantation of Etienne de Boré, the father of Louisiana's granulated-sugar industry. In addition to the 18-hole golf course, there is a 2-mi jogging track with 18 exercise stations along the way, a stable that offers guided trail rides, and 10 tennis courts.

The Friends of the Zoo operate a free shuttle that boards in front of Tulane every 15 to 20 minutes. A wooden walkway strings through the zoo, a miniature train rings around a part of it, and it can take an entire day to explore. More than 1,800 animals roam about in natural habitats. ⊠ *St. Charles Ave. (main entrance)*, ☎ *504/861–2537*, WEB *www. auduboninstitute.org.* ☜ *$9.* ☉ *Oct.–Mar., weekdays 9:30–5, weekends 9:30–6; Apr.–Sept., weekdays 9:30–5:30, weekends 9:30–6.*

Mid-City

This section of town stretches roughly lakeward from the French Quarter to City Park and from Esplanade Avenue to I–10. The early French Creole settlers made camp near Bayou St. John, which forms the eastern border of City Park. The sights here are spread out, and you'll need a car to get from one to the other.

A Good Drive

To reach the **Pitot House** from the French Quarter, drive straight out Esplanade Avenue. Just before the Esplanade Avenue Bridge, turn left on Moss Street. Bayou St. John will be on your right, the Pitot House on your left. To reach the **New Orleans Museum of Art,** backtrack to Esplanade Avenue, cross the Esplanade Avenue Bridge, and go to the right of the equestrian statue of General P. G. T. Beauregard. At this entrance to **City Park,** Lelong Avenue, a long oak-lined drive, leads to the museum's entrance at Collins-Diboll Circle. Behind the museum, a half circle to the right and over a bridge takes you to the park's Victory Avenue. The New Orleans Botanical Garden is on the right, and past the garden is the Storyland playground. Next door is the 1906 merry-go-round of Carousel Gardens, and farther on you'll see tennis courts on the left. Turn left at the end of the courts, and left again onto

Dreyfous Drive. The Casino building here (which doesn't have a casino) has a snack shop and rentals for pedal boats and canoes; fishing licenses are also issued here (you can't fish in the park without one). Turn left at the end of the road, then right onto Lelong Avenue and right again onto City Park Avenue. At I–10, City Park Avenue becomes Metairie Road. Continue on Metairie Road to the sign indicating **Longue Vue House and Gardens.**

TIMING

Plan to spend a minimum of two hours each at the New Orleans Museum of Art and Longue Vue House and Gardens. A tour of the Pitot House takes about an hour. As for City Park, you can do a drive-through in a half hour or so, but this is a place to return time and again, for golfing, tennis, fishing, canoeing, and riding the carousel.

Sights to See

City Park. With 1,500 luxuriant acres, this is one of the nation's largest urban parks. You can spend a great deal of time simply admiring the lagoons and majestic live oaks. But there is plenty to keep you busy if you are not an idler. There are four 18-hole golf courses, a double-deck driving range, 39 lighted courts in the Wisner Tennis Center, an ice-skating rink, baseball diamonds, stables, and the **New Orleans Botanical Garden** (☞ $3, ☉ Tues.–Sun. 10–4:30). The latter has a tropical conservatory, a water-lily pond, a formal rose garden, and azalea and camellia gardens. At the Casino concession building on Dreyfous Drive you can rent bikes, boats, and canoes—or just have a bite to eat. **Storyland** (☞ $1,50, ☉ daily 10–4:30), a children's playground, has puppet shows, talking storybooks, storybook exhibits, and storytelling. Next door, **Carousel Gardens** (☞ $1, rides $1 per ride or $8 unlimited rides, ☉ Wed.–Fri. 10–2:30, weekends 11–5:30) has the Last Carousel, a restored 1906 merry-go-round replete with wooden horses, zebras, and other exotic creatures. Unfortunately, City Park is not safe at night. ⊠ *Main entrance at Lelong Ave.,* ☏ *504/482–4888.*

★ **Longue Vue House and Gardens.** Right on the border between Orleans and Jefferson parishes, the elegant estate was patterned after the great country manor houses of England. Once a private home, it is now a museum of decorative arts, furnished with European and Oriental antiques. Eight acres of landscaped gardens surround the house. ⊠ *7 Bamboo Rd., Metairie,* ☏ *504/488–5488.* WEB *www.longuevue.com.* ☞ *$7.* ☉ *Mon.–Sat. 10–4:30, Sun. 1–5; last tour 45 mins before closing.*

OFF THE BEATEN PATH **LOUISIANA NATURE AND SCIENCE CENTER –** You can get a good in-town look at the surrounding swamps and bayous at this facility. There are nature trails, a children's discovery center, an interpretive center, and a planetarium. The center is in Joe W. Brown Memorial Park. To reach it from City Park, take I–10 east toward Slidell to Exit 244 (Read Boulevard) and turn right. At the third traffic light on Read Boulevard, turn left onto Nature Center Boulevard, which dead-ends at the facility. ⊠ *11000 Lake Forest Blvd., New Orleans East,* ☏ *504/246–5672.* ☞ *$4.75.* ☉ *Tues.–Fri. 9–5, Sat. 10–5, Sun. noon–5.*

New Orleans Museum of Art (NOMA). This white neoclassical building is large enough to exhibit virtually all of the museum's vast collections of 13th- to 18th-century Italian paintings, 20th-century European and American paintings and sculptures, Chinese jades, and the imperial treasures by Peter Carl Fabergé. ⊠ *City Park at 1 Collins-Diboll Circle, Mid-City,* ☏ *504/488–2631,* WEB *www.noma.org.* ☞ *$6.* ☉ *Tues.–Sun. 10–5.*

ANNE RICE'S NEW ORLEANS

THE ECCENTRIC CHARM and mystique of New Orleans have inspired many great fiction writers, but none has even approached the colossal commercial success enjoyed by Anne Rice—fans sporting vampire garb with pale makeup and black lipstick are just part of the scenery here. Two neighborhoods predominate in Rice's work: the French Quarter and the Garden District. Bear in mind that you need to be careful strolling through the French Quarter, even during the day; at night, cemetery visits or walks, which may have special appeal for Rice readers, can be particularly dangerous.

Start your French Quarter tour at **Gallier House** (✉ 1118–1132 Royal St., French Quarter, ☎ 504/525–5661), a restored mid-19th-century mansion. This residence is reputed to be the model for the home of the vampires Lestat, Louis, and Claudia, as described in *Interview with the Vampire, The Queen of the Damned,* and *The Tale of the Body Thief.* From Gallier House, turn left and walk two blocks along Royal Street to **Dumaine Street.** The house at 632 Dumaine Street, also known as Madame John's Legacy, appears in *Interview with the Vampire.* In Jackson Square, Lestat had his first encounter with Raglan James in *The Tale of the Body Thief,* and Lasher first appeared here in *The Witching Hour.*

The upper end of the French Quarter near Canal Street has several points of interest for Rice readers. Various characters in her books dine at **Galatoire's** (✉ 209 Bourbon St., French Quarter, ☎ 504/525–2021). In *The Witching Hour* Michael Curry and Rowan Mayfair grab a bite at **Desire Oyster Bar** (✉ 300 Bourbon St., French Quarter, ☎ 504/586–0300). The **St. Louis Hotel** (✉ 730 Bienville St., French Quarter, ☎ 504/581–7300) is possibly the influence for the "new Spanish hotel" featured in *Interview with the Vampire.* Just outside the French Quarter are the historic and labyrinthine **St. Louis Cemeteries #1 and #2** (✉ 400 Basin St., French Quarter, ☎ 504/482–5065 or 504/596–3050). St. Louis Cemetery #1 is mentioned in both *Interview with the Vampire* and *Queen of the Damned*; in the latter book it is the site of Louis's empty tomb. It's easy to get lost in the maze of aboveground graves; for this and other security reasons, it's well worth your while to take a guided tour.

In the Garden District, you can try to catch a glimpse of the writer herself at **Anne Rice's house,** the Greek Revival–Italianate mansion at 1239 1st Street. **Lafayette Cemetery #1** (✉ 1400 Washington Ave., Garden District, ☎ 504/588–9357) serves as the burial ground for the fictional Mayfairs in *The Witching Hour.* In *Interview with the Vampire,* Claudia requests a visit there to feed, and Lestat uses the graveyard as a hiding place for his valuables. Across the street from the cemetery is **Commander's Palace** (✉ 1403 Washington Ave., Garden District, ☎ 504/899–8221), the site of various Mayfair family dinners, especially after funerals.

Some outlying rural areas are also significant to Rice's novels. **Destrehan Plantation** (✉ 9999 River Rd. [LA 48], Destrehan, ☎ 504/764–9315 or 504/524–5522), a 1787 West Indies–style house, was one of the film locations in *Interview with the Vampire.* Seventy miles southwest of New Orleans near Napoleonville is **Madewood Plantation** (✉ 4250 Hwy. 308, Napoleonville, ☎ 800/375–7151), the prototype for the Mayfair family's country home, Fontrevault, in *The Witching Hour.*

Some 60 mi up and across the river near the town of Vacherie is **Oak Alley** (✉ 3645 Hwy. 18, Vacherie, ☎ 800/442–5539, WEB www.oakalleyplantation.com). This grand 1839 home was used as a film location in *Interview with the Vampire.* **Pitot House** (✉ 1440 Moss St., Bayou St. John, ☎ 504/482–0312), a late-18th-century West Indian cottage on Bayou St. John, inspired Louis's Pointe du Lac in *Interview with the Vampire.*

Pitot House. This charming West Indies–style house was built in the late 18th century and bought in 1810 by New Orleans mayor James Pitot as a country home. It is furnished with Louisiana and other American 19th-century antiques. ✉ *1440 Moss St., Bayou St. John,* ☎ *504/482–0312.* 🖾 *$5.* ⊙ *Wed.–Sat. 10–3; last tour at 2:15; sometimes closed Sat.*

Dining

By Gene
Bourg

A distinctive cooking style is as deeply embedded in New Orleans's psyche as its distinctive architecture and music. Each reflects in its own way an exuberance of spirit that has made the city a favorite destination of world travelers. Classifying the city's traditional cooking styles can be frustrating, however. The two major divisions of the cuisine—the urban Creole and the more rustic Acadian (or "Cajun")—often merge in a single dish. Mainstream southern Louisiana cooking is fraught with a network of subcuisines drawn from a polyglot of cultures.

Today's menus reflect nearly 300 years of ethnic overlap. The major influences came from France (both before and after the revolution of 1789), Africa, Spain, the region's Native Americans, the Caribbean, and, more recently, southern Italy, Germany, and the former Yugoslavia. During the 1980s, Asian chefs joined the culinary melting pot with brand-new treatments of seafood drawn from Louisiana's bountiful coastal wetlands and the Gulf of Mexico.

Despite the increasingly blurred lines separating all these styles, Creole and Cajun, the two mother cuisines, have some distinguishing characteristics. Creole cooking carries an urban gloss, whether it's a proletarian dish of semiliquid red beans atop steaming white rice or a supremely elegant sauce of wine and cream on delicate-flesh fish.

Cajun food, on the other hand, is decidedly more rough-hewn and rural. The first waves of Acadian settlers found their way to the Louisiana bayous and marshes in the last quarter of the 18th century. Most had already been farmers and fishermen in Canada and France. Lard was the tie that bound much of the Cajuns' early cooking. For the more sophisticated Creole cooks, it was butter and cream.

New Orleans's restaurants that specialize in local cuisines have been grouped into the following four categories:

Cajun-Inspired. Kitchens in these restaurants show direct and recognizable influences from the hearty and rustic cuisine of the southwest Louisiana Acadians. Seasonings are often more intense than in Creole cooking, and pork and game are prominent ingredients.

Contemporary Creole. The food usually includes some traditional Creole dishes, but there's more creativity. Local ingredients are used in novel ways, but the basic flavors adhere to the Creole standards of richness and depth. Trout with pecans and bread pudding soufflé are typical.

Creole with Soul. This food reflects both the robust style of Southern black cooks and the spicier aspects of early New Orleans cuisine.

Traditional Creole. These restaurants specialize in rather complex dishes that have been familiar to generations of New Orleans restaurant goers. Shrimp rémoulade, gumbo, trout meunière, and bread pudding are some examples.

The following terms appear frequently in the reviews and on menus:

Andouille (ahn-*dooey*). A mildly spiced Acadian sausage of lean pork, it often flavors gumbos, red beans and rice, and jambalayas.

Barbecue shrimp. The shrimp are not barbecued but baked in their shells in a blend of olive oil, butter, or margarine and usually seasoned with bay leaf, garlic, and other herbs and spices.

Béarnaise (bare-*nayz*). This sauce of egg yolk and butter with shallots, wine, vinegar, and seasonings is used on meats and fish.

Beignet (ben-*yay*). Although a beignet was originally a rectangular puff of fried dough sprinkled with powdered sugar, the term can also refer to fritters or crullers containing fish or seafood.

Bisque. A thick, heartily seasoned soup, bisque is most often made with crawfish, crab, or shrimp. Cream appears in the French versions.

Bouillabaisse (*booey*-yah-base). A Creole bouillabaisse is a stew of various fish and shellfish in a broth seasoned with saffron and often more assertive spices.

Boulette (*boo*-let). This is minced, chopped, or pureed meat or fish shaped into balls and fried.

Bread pudding. In the traditional version, stale French bread is soaked in a custard mix, combined with raisins, and baked, then served with a hot, sugary sauce flavored with whiskey or rum.

Café brûlot (broo-*loh*). Cinnamon, lemon, clove, orange, and sugar are steeped with strong coffee, then flambéed with brandy and served in special pedestaled cups.

Chicory coffee. The ground and roasted root of a European variety of chicory is added to ground coffee in varying proportions. It lends an added bitterness to the taste.

Dirty rice. In this cousin of jambalaya, bits of meat, such as giblets or sausage, and seasonings are added to white rice before cooking.

Étouffée (ay-too-*fay*). Literally, "smothered," the term is used most often for a thick stew of crawfish tails cooked in a roux-based liquid with crawfish, fat, garlic, and green seasonings.

Gumbo. From an African word for okra, it can refer to any number of stewlike soups made with seafood or meat and flavored with okra or ground sassafras (filé powder) and myriad other seasonings. Frequent main ingredients are combinations of shrimp, oysters, crab, chicken, andouille, duck, and turkey. A definitive gumbo is served over white rice.

Jambalaya (jam-buh-*lie*-uh). Rice is the indispensable ingredient in this relative of Spain's paella. The rice is cooked with a mix of diced meat and seafood in tomato and other seasonings. Shrimp and ham make frequent appearances in it, as do sausage, green pepper, and celery.

Meunière (muhn-*yehr*). This method of preparing fish or soft-shell crab entails dusting it with seasoned flour, sautéing it in brown butter, and using the butter with lemon juice as a sauce. Some restaurants add a dash of Worcestershire sauce.

Mirliton (merl-i-*tawn*). A pale green member of the squash family, a mirliton is usually identified as a vegetable pear. The standard preparation is to scrape the pulp from halved mirlitons, fill them with shrimp and seasoned bread crumbs, and bake them.

Muffuletta. The city's southern Italian grocers created this round-loaf sandwich traditionally filled with ham, salami, mozzarella, and a layer of chopped, marinated green olives. Muffulettas are sold whole and in halves or quarters.

Oysters Bienville (byen-*veel*). In this dish, oysters are lightly baked in their shells under a cream sauce flavored with bits of shrimp, mushroom, and green seasonings. Some chefs also use garlic or mustard.

Oysters en brochette (awn-bro-*shet*). Whole oysters and bits of bacon are dusted with seasoned flour, skewered, and deep-fried. Traditionally, they're served on toast with lemon and brown butter.

Oysters Rockefeller. This dish, baked oysters on the half shell in a sauce of pureed aromatic greens laced with anise liqueur, was created at Antoine's, which keeps its recipe a secret.

Panéed veal (pan-*aid*). Breaded veal cutlets are sautéed in butter.

Po'boy. A hefty sandwich, the po'boy is made with the local French bread and any number of fillings: roast beef, fried shrimp, oysters, ham, meatballs in tomato sauce, and cheese are common. A po'boy "dressed" contains lettuce, tomato, and mayonnaise or mustard.

Ravigote (rah-vee-*gote*). In Creole usage, this is a piquant mayonnaise, usually with capers, used to moisten cold lumps of blue crabmeat.

Rémoulade (ray-moo-*lahd*). The classic Creole rémoulade is a brick-red whipped mixture of olive oil with mustard, scallions, cayenne, lemon, paprika, and parsley. It's served on cold peeled shrimp or lumps of back-fin crabmeat.

Souffléed potatoes. These thin, hollow puffs of deep-fried potato are produced by two fryings at different temperatures.

Tasso (*tah*-so). Acadian cooks developed the recipe for this lean, intensely seasoned ham. It's used sparingly to flavor sauces and gumbos.

Reservations and What to Wear

You are strongly advised to make reservations and to book well in advance for weekends, particularly during holiday periods or conventions. Pricey restaurants adhere to a moderate dress code—jackets for men, and in some places, a tie. New Orleans is a conservative city; dining out is an honored ritual, and people are expected to dress the part. A man in faded jeans and sports coat may be turned away, and even if he isn't, he may not feel entirely welcome.

Louisiana Cuisine

CAJUN-INSPIRED

$$$$ ✕ **K-Paul's Louisiana Kitchen.** In this rustic French Quarter café, chef Paul Prudhomme started the blackening craze and added "Cajun" to America's culinary vocabulary. Two decades later, thousands still consider a visit to New Orleans partly wasted without a visit to K-Paul's for his inventive gumbos, fried crawfish tails, blackened tuna, roast duck with rice dressing, and sweet-potato–pecan pie. Prices are steep at dinner but moderate at lunch; servings are generous. ✉ *416 Chartres St., French Quarter,* ☎ *504/524–7394. AE, DC, MC, V. Closed Sun.*

$$$–$$$$ ✕ **Bayona.** "New World" is the label chef Susan Spicer applies to her cooking style, which results in such creations as turnovers filled with spicy crawfish tails; a bisque of corn, leeks, and chicken; or fresh salmon fillet in white-wine sauce with sauerkraut. These and other imaginative dishes are served in an early 19th-century Creole cottage. The chef supervised the renovation of the handsome building, now fairly glowing with flower arrangements, elegant photographs, and, in one small dining room, trompe l'oeil murals. ✉ *430 Dauphine St., French Quarter,* ☎ *504/525–4455. Reservations essential. AE, DC, MC, V. Closed Sun.*

$$$–$$$$ ✕ **Peristyle.** Some of the most creative cooking in New Orleans em-
★ anates from the kitchen of this smartly turned-out yet very approachable little restaurant on the French Quarter's edge. Chef Anne Kearney takes a thoroughly modern and personal approach to Continental cooking with a superb sauté of Gulf shrimp and fennel in a white-wine sauce, fork-tender lamb loin with a puree of garlicky white beans, and a whole, boned white trout filled with mussels, crab, and potatoes. ✉ *1041 Dumaine St., French Quarter,* ☎ *504/593–9535. Reservations essential. MC, V. Closed Sun., Mon. No lunch Tues.–Thurs. or Sat.*

$$$ ✕ **Bistro at Maison de Ville.** Small-scale chic has been the cachet of this sleekly intimate spot, a few steps from the bawdiness of Bourbon Street. Its fans certainly don't come in to stretch their limbs. Only inches separate the tables, with those along the full-length banquette close enough to become, in effect, a table for 20. But lustrous mahogany and soft light from elegant wall lamps work their magic. From the tiny kitchen come stylish, flavorful creations reflecting a modern approach to

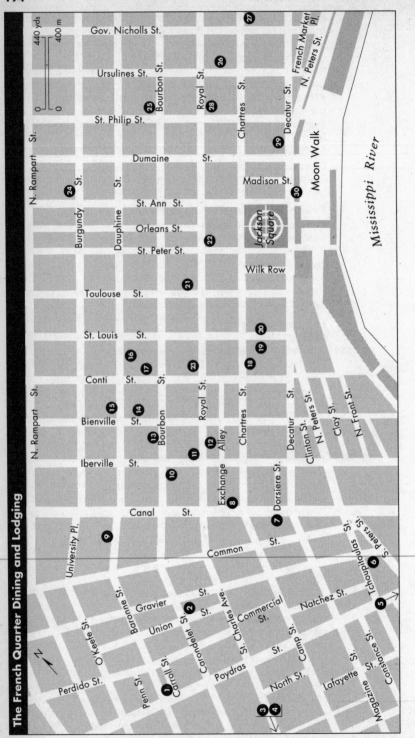

The French Quarter Dining and Lodging

Gov. Nicholls St.

Ursulines St.

St. Philip St.

Dumaine St.

St. Ann St.

Orleans St.

St. Peter St.

Toulouse St.

St. Louis St.

Conti St.

Bienville St.

Iberville St.

Canal St.

Common St.

Gravier St.

Union St.

Poydras St.

Perdido St.

North St.

Lafayette St.

Madison St.

Wilk Row

Jackson Square

Moon Walk

Mississippi River

French Market Pl.

N. Peters St.

Decatur St.

Chartres St.

Royal St.

Bourbon St.

Dauphine St.

Burgundy St.

N. Rampart St.

Exchange Alley

Dorsiere St.

Clinton St.

Clay St.

N. Front St.

University Pl.

O'Keefe St.

Baronne St.

Carondelet St.

St. Charles Ave.

Commercial St.

Camp St.

Natchez St.

Tchoupitoulas St.

S. Peters St.

Magazine St.

Constance St.

Carroll St.

Penn St.

440 yds
400 m

New Orleans Dining and Lodging

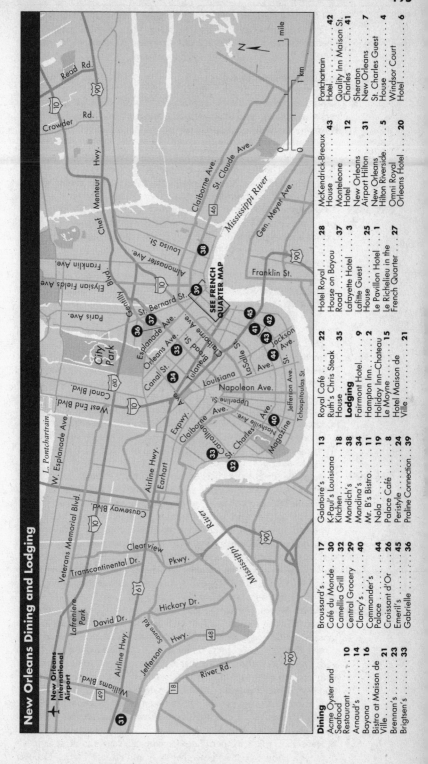

Dining

Acme Oyster and Seafood Restaurant	10
Arnaud's	14
Bayona	16
Bistro at Maison de Ville	21
Brennan's	23
Brigtsen's	33
Broussard's	17
Café du Monde	30
Camellia Grill	32
Central Grocery	29
Clancy's	40
Commander's Palace	44
Croissant d'Or	26
Emeril's	45
Gabrielle	36
Galatoire's	13
K-Paul's Louisiana Kitchen	18
Mandich's	38
Mandina's	34
Mr. B's Bistro	11
Nola	19
Palace Café	8
Peristyle	24
Praline Connection	39
Royal Café	22
Ruth's Chris Steak House	35

Lodging

Fairmont Hotel	9
Hampton Inn	2
Holiday Inn–Chateau Le Moyne	15
Hotel Maison de Ville	21
Hotel Royal	28
House on Bayou Road	37
Lafayette Hotel	3
Lafitte Guest House	25
Le Pavillon Hotel	1
Le Richelieu in the French Quarter	27
McKendrick-Breaux House	43
Monteleone Hotel	12
New Orleans Airport Hilton	31
New Orleans Hilton Riverside	5
Omni Royal Orleans Hotel	20
Pontchartrain Hotel	42
Quality Inn Maison St. Charles	41
Sheraton New Orleans	7
St. Charles Guest House	4
Windsor Court Hotel	6

Creole and American cooking—barbecue shrimp with New Orleans rice cakes, saffron-sage broth with quail ravioli, and grilled salmon with a pecan-flavored wild rice. ⊠ *733 Toulouse St., French Quarter,* ☎ *504/528–9206. AE, DC, MC, V. Closed Sun.*

CONTEMPORARY CREOLE

$$$–$$$$ ✕ **Brigtsen's.** Chef Frank Brigsten's fusion of Creole refinement and
★ Acadian earthiness reflects his years as a protégé of Paul Prudhomme. Everything is fresh and filled with deep and complex tastes. The cream-of-oysters-Rockefeller soup is a revelation. Rabbit and chicken dishes, usually presented in rich sauces and gravies, are full of robust flavor. Blackened steaks are definitive, and the roux-based gumbos are thick and intense. The fresh banana ice cream is worth every calorie. ⊠ *723 Dante St., Uptown,* ☎ *504/861–7610. Reservations essential. AE, MC, V. Closed Sun. and Mon.*

$$$–$$$$ ✕ **Commander's Palace.** No restaurant captures New Orleans's gas-
★ tronomic heritage and celebratory spirit as well as this one in a stately Garden District mansion. The upstairs Garden Room's glass walls have marvelous views of the giant oak trees on the patio below, and the other rooms promote conviviality with their bright pastels or delicate wall paintings. The menu's classics include poached oysters in a seasoned cream sauce with Oregon caviar; a spicy and meaty turtle soup; terrific crab cakes in an oyster sauce; and a wonderful sautéed trout coated with crunchy pecans. ⊠ *1403 Washington Ave., Garden District,* ☎ *504/899–8221. Reservations essential. Jacket required. AE, D, DC, MC, V.*

$$$–$$$$ ✕ **Emeril's.** The dining spaces are always jammed at celebrity chef Emeril Lagasse's big and bouncy flagship restaurant. A wood ceiling in an oversize basket-weave pattern muffles much of the clatter and chatter. In a far corner, the food bar is framed by a dramatic collection of glass-encased spices, legumes, and the like, exposing one of America's most luxurious restaurant kitchens. The ambitious menu gives equal emphasis to Creole and modern American cooking. ⊠ *800 Tchoupitoulas St., Warehouse District,* ☎ *504/528–9393. AE, D, DC, MC, V. Closed Sun. No lunch Sat.*

$$–$$$$ ✕ **Gabrielle.** Bright and energetic and about five minutes by taxi from
★ the French Quarter, Gabrielle is a hit, thanks to chef Greg Sonnier's marvelous interpretations of earthy, spicy southern Louisiana dishes. Some tables in the main dining room have little elbow room, but a small add-on room has its own homey atmosphere, complete with lace curtains and framed still-life prints. Regulars come for the spicy rabbit and veal sausages, buttery oysters gratinéed with artichoke and Parmesan, and a slew of excellent gumbos and étouffées. ⊠ *3201 Esplanade Ave., Mid-City,* ☎ *504/948–6233. Reservations essential. AE, D, DC, MC, V. Closed Sun. and Mon. No lunch.*

$$–$$$$ ✕ **Mr. B's Bistro.** The energy never seems to subside in this attractive
★ restaurant, with servers darting between the wood and glass screens that reduce the vastness of the dining room. The dependable contemporary Creole menu centers on meats and seafood from a grill fueled with aromatic woods. Pasta dishes, especially the pasta jambalaya with andouille sausage and shrimp, are fresh and creative. The traditional-style bread pudding with Irish whiskey sauce is excellent, too. Lunchtime finds most of the tables taken up by locals, who like the fixed-price menu. ⊠ *201 Royal St., French Quarter,* ☎ *504/523–2078. AE, D, DC, MC, V.*

$$$ ✕ **Nola.** Fans of chef Emeril Lagasse who can't get a table at Emeril's in the Warehouse District have this sassy and vibrant French Quarter restaurant as an alternative. Lagasse has not lowered his sights with Nola's menu. The kitchen stews *boudin* (blood sausage) with beer,

onions, cane syrup, and Creole mustard before ladling it all onto a sweet-potato crouton. Redfish is swathed in a horseradish-citrus crust before it's plank-roasted in a wood oven. At dessert time, try the coconut cream or apple-buttermilk pie. ⊠ *534 St. Louis St., French Quarter,* ☎ *504/522–6652. AE, D, DC, MC, V. No lunch Sun.*

$$$ ✕ **Palace Café.** Crafted from what used to be New Orleans's oldest
★ music store, the Palace is a convivial spot to try some of the more imaginative contemporary Creole dishes such as crab chops, rabbit ravioli in piquant sauce, grilled shrimp with fettuccine, and seafood Napoleon. Desserts, especially the white-chocolate bread pudding and Mississippi mud pie, are luscious. Drugstore-tile floors, stained-cherry booths, and soothing beige walls set the mood. The wraparound mezzanine is lined with a large, brightly colored wall painting populated by the city's famous musicians. ⊠ *605 Canal St., CBD,* ☎ *504/523–1661. Reservations essential. AE, DC, MC, V.*

$$–$$$ ✕ **Clancy's.** Understatement defines the mood at Clancy's. The decor
★ is neutral, with gray walls and a few ceiling fans above bentwood chairs and white linen cloths. The small bar is usually filled with regulars who know one another. Most of the dishes are imaginative treatments of New Orleans favorites. Some specialties, such as the fresh sautéed fish in cream sauce flavored with crawfish stock and herbs, are exceptional. Other signs of an inventive chef are the expertly fried oysters matched with warm Brie, the grilled chicken breast in lime butter, and a peppermint ice cream pie. ⊠ *6100 Annunciation St., Uptown,* ☎ *504/895–1111. AE, MC, V. Closed Sun. No lunch Mon. or Sat.*

$$–$$$ ✕ **Royal Café.** From the sidewalk at the corner of Royal and St. Peter streets you can almost hear the ceiling fans whirring overhead on the Royal Café's three tiers of iron-lace balconies, which overlook the bustling corner. In the busily, colorfully decorated downstairs room, the kitchen turns out dishes combining familiar New Orleans ingredients, such as fried eggplant sticks with a ladling of cream sauce; fried, cornmeal-crusted oysters with a peppery tartar sauce; oyster-and-artichoke soup; and pan-seared trout topped with crawfish. Reservations are accepted for the ground floor only. ⊠ *706 Royal St., French Quarter,* ☎ *504/528–9086. AE, D, DC, MC, V. Closed Sun.*

CREOLE WITH SOUL

$–$$ ✕ **Praline Connection.** Down-home cooking in the southern-Creole style is the forte of this rather quirky restaurant a couple of blocks from the French Quarter, with a branch in the Warehouse District. The fried or stewed chicken, smothered pork chops, barbecue ribs, and collard greens are definitively done. And the soulful filé gumbo, bread pudding, and sweet-potato pie are among the best in town. To all this add moderate prices, a congenial staff, and a neat-as-a-pin dining room, and the sum is a fine place to spend an hour or two. The adjacent sweet-shop holds such delights as sweet-potato cookies and Creole pralines. ⊠ *542 Frenchmen St., Faubourg Marigny,* ☎ *504/943–3934;* ⊠ *901 S. Peters St., Warehouse District,* ☎ *504/523–3973. Reservations not accepted. AE, D, DC, MC, V.*

TRADITIONAL CREOLE

$$$$ ✕ **Brennan's.** Lavish breakfasts of elaborate poached egg dishes are what first put Brennan's on the map. The best seats in this gorgeous 19th-century building include views of the courtyard and fountain. Eye-opening cocktails flow every morning, followed by the tasty poached eggs sandwiched between such things as hollandaise, creamed spinach, artichoke bottoms, Canadian bacon, and fried fish. Headliners at lunch or dinner include blue-ribbon, textbook versions of oysters Rockefeller and seafood gumbo, sautéed fish blanketed in crabmeat, good veal and beef dishes, and bananas Foster, a dessert that was created here. ✉ *417 Royal St., French Quarter,* ☎ *504/525–9711. Reservations essential. AE, D, DC, MC, V.*

$$$–$$$$ ✕ **Arnaud's.** In the main dining room, ornate etched glass reflects light from the charming old chandeliers while the late founder, Arnaud Cazenave, gazes from an oil portrait. When the main room fills up, the overflow spills into a labyrinth of plush banquet rooms and bars. The ambitious menu includes classic dishes as well as more contemporary ones. Always reliable are cold shrimp Arnaud, in a superb rémoulade, and creamy oyster stew, as well as the fish in crawfish sauce. Expect fairly hurried service on crowded nights, but rely on the reservations desk to perform efficiently. A jacket is required in the main dining room. ✉ *813 Bienville St., French Quarter,* ☎ *504/523–5433. Reservations essential. AE, D, DC, MC, V.*

$$$–$$$$ ✕ **Broussard's.** No French Quarter restaurant surpasses Broussard's for old-fashioned spectacle. It's a soft-edged, glittery mix of elaborate wall coverings, chandeliers, porcelain, and polished woods, with a manicured courtyard to boot. The menu contains respectable renditions of the fancier Creole standbys further upgraded with Continental touches. Fine entrées include shrimp in a sherry butter with basil and lemon and a veal chop moistened with two sauces. ✉ *819 Conti St., French Quarter,* ☎ *504/581–3866. AE, D, DC, MC, V. No lunch.*

$$–$$$$ ✕ **Galatoire's.** Galatoire's has always epitomized the old-style French-
★ Creole bistro. Many of the recipes date back to 1905. Fried oysters and bacon en brochette are worth every calorie, and the brick-red rémoulade sauce sets a high standard. The setting downstairs is a single, narrow dining room lit with glistening brass chandeliers, with bentwood chairs at the white-cloth tables adding to the timeless atmosphere. However, the din of the restaurant's regulars often fills the downstairs room, sometimes inhibiting conversation. Upstairs are dining rooms and a bar for those awaiting tables. ✉ *209 Bourbon St., French Quarter,* ☎ *504/525–2021. Jacket required. AE, DC, MC, V. Closed Mon.*

$$–$$$ ✕ **Mandich's.** This many-faceted favorite of locals resists categorizing.
★ It occupies a neat but unremarkable building in a blue-collar neighborhood. The decor—a mix of bright yellow paint, captain's chairs, and wood veneer—won't win prizes. The food ranges from straightforward, home-style dishes to ambitious trout and shellfish dishes. Fried oysters are swathed in a finely balanced butter sauce with garlic and parsley. Shrimp and andouille sausages trade flavors on the grill. The trout Mandich (breaded, broiled, and served with a butter, wine, and Worcestershire sauce) has become a classic of the genre, and more garlic boosts slices of buttery roasted potatoes. ✉ *3200 St. Claude Ave., Ninth Ward,* ☎ *504/947–9553. Reservations not accepted. MC, V. Closed Sun. and Mon. No lunch Sat., no dinner Tues.–Thurs.*

Back to Basics

DESSERT

$ ✕ **Croissant d'Or.** Locals compete with visitors for a table in this colorful, pristine pastry shop, which serves excellent and authentic French croissants, pies, tarts, and custards, as well as an imaginative selection of soups, salads, and sandwiches. Wash them down with real French breakfast coffee, cappuccino, or espresso. In good weather, the cheerful courtyard, with its quietly gurgling fountain, is the place to sit. A filling lunch can be had for less than $10. Hours are 7 to 5 daily. ✉ *617 Ursulines St., French Quarter,* ☎ *504/524–4663. MC, V.*

COFFEE SHOPS AND SANDWICHES

$–$$ ✕ **Camellia Grill.** Every diner should be as classy as Camellia Grill, a one-of-a-kind eatery that deserves its following. Locals vie until the early morning hours for one of the 29 stools at the gleaming counter. The hamburger is one of the best in town. Other blue-ribbon dishes are the chili, the fruit and meringue pies, and the garnished omelets. Everything's made on the premises and served by bow-tied, white-waistcoated waiters with the fastest feet in the business. ⊠ *626 S. Carrollton Ave., Uptown,* ☎ *504/866–9573. No credit cards.*

$–$$ ✕ **Central Grocery.** This old-fashioned Italian grocery store in the French Quarter produces authentic muffulettas, one of the gastronomic gifts of the city's Italian immigrants. Good enough to challenge the po'boy as the local sandwich champ, they're made by filling round loaves of seeded bread with ham, salami, mozzarella, and a salad of marinated green olives. Each sandwich, about 10 inches in diameter, is sold in quarters and halves. The grocery closes at 5:30 PM. ⊠ *923 Decatur St., French Quarter,* ☎ *504/523–1620. No credit cards.*

$ ✕ **Café du Monde.** For most visitors, no trip to New Orleans would
★ be complete without a cup of chicory-laced café au lait and a few sugar-dusted beignets in this venerable Creole institution. The tables are jammed at almost any hour with locals and tourists feasting on the views of Jackson Square. The magical time to go is just before dawn, when the bustle subsides and you can almost hear the birds in the crepe myrtles across the way. ⊠ *French Market, Decatur and St. Ann Sts., French Quarter,* ☎ *504/525–4544. No credit cards.*

SEAFOOD

$–$$ ✕ **Acme Oyster and Seafood Restaurant.** A rough-edge classic in every
★ way, this no-nonsense eatery at the entrance to the French Quarter is a prime source of cool and salty raw oysters on the half shell; great shrimp, oyster, and roast-beef po'boys; and state-of-the-art red beans and rice. Table service, once confined to the main dining room out front, is now provided in the rear room as well. Expect rather lengthy lines at the marble-top oyster bar. Crowds lighten in the late afternoon. ⊠ *724 Iberville St., French Quarter,* ☎ *504/522–5973. Reservations not accepted. AE, DC, MC, V.*

$–$$ ✕ **Mandina's.** The interior of this white clapboard corner building is a study in 1940s nostalgia, with its functional bar facing a roomful of laminated tables. Regulars—a cross section of the population—endure a 15-minute wait for a table under an old newspaper clipping or the latest artwork from a brewery. Butter, hearty seasonings, and tomato sauce are the staples. The shrimp rémoulade and old-fashioned gumbo are the logical appetizers. ⊠ *3800 Canal St., Mid-City,* ☎ *504/482–9179. Reservations not accepted. No credit cards.*

STEAK

$$$–$$$$ ✕ **Ruth's Chris Steak House.** Ruth's Chris is sacred to New Orleans steak lovers. The all-American menu fairly drips with butter, and the main draw is aged U.S. prime beef in he-man portions, charbroiled and served atop a sizzling, seasoned butter sauce. The hefty filet mignon is often taller than it is wide, and a monstrous porterhouse serves several. If the salads lack sparkle, the copious potato dishes are usually first-rate. Lighter entrées (chicken breast, veal, seafood) mollify the health conscious. The large and plush but unfussy dining rooms of the flagship Mid-City restaurant are lined in pale-wood paneling and understated landscape paintings. ⊠ *711 N. Broad St., Mid-City,* ☎ *504/486–0810;* ⊠ *3633 Veterans Blvd., Metairie,* ☎ *504/888–3600. Reservations essential. AE, D, DC, MC, V.*

Lodging

Updated by
Paul A.
Greenberg

Deciding where to stay in New Orleans is every bit as important as planning and managing the inevitable crowded itinerary. From elegant owner-operated bed-and-breakfast inns in centuries-old mansions to posh luxury hotels, the options are growing each year. For those who want to be in the center of tourist activity, the French Quarter is recommended. Within the blocks of the French Quarter you can choose from guest houses with as few as four or five rooms to elegant full-service hotels with rooftop pools and formal dining rooms. If the non-stop high activity is a bit much, consider the Faubourg Marigny, a historic urban wonderland where Creole cottages butt right up against one another and mix easily with cozy guest houses and inns. Still within walking distance from all major attractions, the Marigny is quieter and feels like the centuries-old neighborhood it is.

Because New Orleans increasingly draws honeymooners, international tourists, and large national conventions, it is essential to reserve well in advance—especially for events such as Mardi Gras or Jazz Fest. Expect considerably higher rates during these events and be prepared for a minimum three- to five-night stay; some properties may ask for full payment up front. Although summer was once the slow season in New Orleans with budget rates at even top properties, these days the city is busy year-round. Lower rates can often be found in outlying areas such as Westbank, New Orleans East, or Metairie.

French Quarter

If you're staying in a busy part of the Quarter, you may want to request a room away from the side of the building that faces the street. In larger hotels be sure to ask for a room with a balcony or view.

$$$$ ⊞ **Holiday Inn–Chateau Le Moyne.** This quiet hotel one block off Bour-
★ bon Street exudes old-world atmosphere and decor. Eight suites are in Creole cottages off a tropical courtyard; all rooms are furnished with antiques and reproductions and have coffeemakers, hair dryers, and irons and ironing boards. ✉ *301 Dauphine St., French Quarter 70112,* ☎ *504/581–1303 or 800/465–4329,* FAX *504/523–5709,* WEB *www.holiday-inn.com. 160 rooms, 11 suites. Restaurant, pool, lounge, parking (fee). AE, D, DC, MC, V.*

$$$$ ⊞ **Hotel Maison de Ville.** This small, romantic hotel lies in seclusion
★ amid the hustle and bustle of the French Quarter. Tapestry-covered chairs, a gas fire burning in the sitting room, and antiques-furnished rooms all contribute to a 19th-century atmosphere. Some rooms are in former slave quarters in the courtyard; others are on the upper floors of the main house. Breakfast is served with a rose on a silver tray, and port and sherry are available in the afternoon. Other meals can be taken at the intimate, adjacent Bistro. Those who seek a special hideaway will love the hotel's Audubon Cottages. ✉ *727 Toulouse St., French Quarter 70130,* ☎ *504/561–5858 or 800/634–1600,* FAX *504/528–9939,* WEB *www.maisondeville.com. 14 rooms, 2 suites, 7 cottages. Restaurant, minibars, pool, parking (fee); no children under 12. AE, D, DC, MC, V. CP.*

$$$$ ⊞ **Monteleone Hotel.** The grande dame of French Quarter hotels, with
★ its ornate baroque facade, liveried doormen, and shimmering lobby chandeliers, was built in 1886. It's the Quarter's oldest hotel, operated by the fourth generation of the Monteleone family. Rooms are extra-large and luxurious, with rich fabrics and a mix of four-poster beds, brass beds, and beds with traditional headboards. Junior suites are spacious, and sumptuous VIP suites come with extra pampering. The pool and exercise room are on the roof; the slowly revolving Carousel Bar (☞ Nightlife) in the lobby is a local landmark. Local chef Randy Buck prepares superb food in the Hunt Room Grill, one of the city's best-kept culinary secrets. ✉ *214 Royal St., French Quarter 70140,* ☎ *504/523–3341 or 800/535–9595,* FAX *504/528–1019,* WEB *www.hotelmonteleone.com. 598 rooms, 28 suites. 3 restaurants, pool, gym, bar, concierge, business services, meeting room. AE, D, DC, MC, V.*

$$$$ 🏨 **Omni Royal Orleans Hotel.** This elegant white-marble hotel, built in
★ 1960, is a replica of the grand St. Louis Hotel of the 1800s. Sconce-en-
hanced columns, gilt mirrors, fan windows, and three magnificent chandeliers blend to re-create the atmosphere of old New Orleans. Rooms
are well appointed with marble baths and marble-top dressers and tables; some have balconies. The rooftop pool has the best overhead view
of the French Quarter. ⊠ *621 St. Louis St., French Quarter 70140,* ☎
504/529–5333 or 800/843–6664, 𝖥𝖠𝖷 *504/529–7089,* 𝖶𝖤𝖡 *www.omnihotels.
com. 346 rooms, 16 suites. Restaurant, pool, gym, hair salon, 3 lounges,
business services, meeting room, parking (fee). AE, D, DC, MC, V.*

$$$–$$$$ 🏨 **Lafitte Guest House.** A four-story 1849 French-style manor house,
the Lafitte is meticulously restored, with rooms decorated with period
furnishings. Room 40 takes up the entire fourth floor and overlooks
French Quarter rooftops, and Room 5, the loft apartment, overlooks
the beautiful courtyard. Breakfast can be brought to your room, served
in the Victorian parlor, or enjoyed in the courtyard, and the owner serves
wine and hors d'oeuvres each evening. ⊠ *1003 Bourbon St., French
Quarter 70116,* ☎ *504/581–2678 or 800/331–7971,* 𝖥𝖠𝖷 *504/581–2677,*
𝖶𝖤𝖡 *www.lafitteguesthouse.com. 16 rooms, 2 suites. Cable TV, concierge,
free parking; no smoking. AE, D, DC, MC, V. CP.*

$–$$$ 🏨 **Le Richelieu in the French Quarter.** Close to the Old Ursuline Con-
★ vent and the French Market, Le Richelieu combines the friendly, per-
sonal charm of a small hotel with luxe touches (upscale toiletries, hair
dryers)—at a moderate rate. Some rooms have mirrored walls and large
walk-in closets, and all have brass ceiling fans, irons, and ironing
boards. Balcony rooms have the same rates as standard rooms. An intimate bar and café is off the courtyard, with tables on the terrace by
the pool. Many regular customers would never stay anywhere else. ⊠
1234 Chartres St., French Quarter 70116, ☎ *504/529–2492 or 800/
535–9653,* 𝖥𝖠𝖷 *504/524–8179,* 𝖶𝖤𝖡 *lerichelieuhotel.com. 69 rooms, 17
suites. Café, some kitchenettes, some refrigerators, pool, bar, concierge, free parking. AE, D, DC, MC, V.*

$–$$ 🏨 **Hotel Royal.** A pot of hot coffee and Persian cats greet you in the
lobby here. Many rooms in this circa 1830 home are pleasantly oversize; four have balconies overlooking Royal Street and a school playground, two have hot tubs, and each has a coffeemaker and a small
refrigerator. Distinctly modern amenities complement high ceilings
and antebellum furnishings. The complimentary Continental breakfast
comes from the nearby Croissant d'Or (☞ *Dining, French Quarter*).
⊠ *1006 Royal St., French Quarter 70116,* ☎ *504/524–3900 or 800/
776–3901,* 𝖥𝖠𝖷 *504/558–0566,* 𝖶𝖤𝖡 *www.melrosegroup.com. 30 rooms.
Parking (fee). AE, D, DC, MC, V. CP.*

CBD and Warehouse District

The CBD and Warehouse District will appeal to those who prefer accommodations in luxurious high-rise hotels or in one of the city's ever-
increasing collection of smaller boutique hotels. All the hotels listed
are within walking distance of the French Quarter, but shuttles, taxis,
buses, and the streetcar are readily available. If you're walking in the
CBD or Warehouse District after dark, it's wise to stay on populated
main streets. In the larger hotels, always ask for seasonal or package
rate availability. If you are traveling as part of a convention, ask for
the convention rate.

$$$$ 🏨 **Fairmont Hotel.** At this grand hotel built in 1893, the marble floor
★ and Victorian splendor of the massive, busy lobby evoke a more elegant and gracious era. Rooms have special touches such as down pillows, terry robes, upscale toiletries, and bathroom scales; suites have
fax machines. The lobby-level Sazerac Grill has an airy, cosmopolitan
feel. ⊠ *123 Baronne St., CBD 70140,* ☎ *504/529–7111 or 800/527–*

4727, FAX 504/529–4764, WEB *www.fairmontneworleans.com. 700 rooms, 85 suites. 3 restaurants, 2 tennis courts, pool, gym, hair salon, 2 bars, parking (fee). AE, D, DC, MC, V.*

$$$$ **Le Pavillon Hotel.** Magnificent chandeliers adorn the European-style
★ lobby of this historic hotel dating to 1907, and a handsome display of artwork lines the corridors. Another dramatic feature is the marble railing in the clubby Gallery Lounge, originally from the Grand Hotel in Paris. Guest rooms have high ceilings and identical traditional decor; suites are particularly luxurious. The elegant Crystal Room has a huge salad and pasta lunch buffet daily. ⊠ *833 Poydras St., CBD 70112,* ☎ *504/581–3111 or 800/535–9095,* FAX *504/522–5543,* WEB *www.lepavillon. com. 219 rooms, 7 suites. Restaurant, pool, gym, hot tub, bar, laundry service, parking (fee); no-smoking floor. AE, D, DC, MC, V.*

$$$$ **New Orleans Hilton Riverside.** This sprawling, multilevel complex is smack on the Mississippi with superb river views. Guest rooms have French provincial furnishings; the 180 rooms that share a concierge have fax machines. The health club is one of the best in the Gulf South, and there is an excellent business center. Pete Fountain's nightclub (☞ Nightlife, Music Venues, CBD and Warehouse District) is here, and the Riverfront streetcar stops out front. Adjacent to Riverwalk Shopping Center and Aquarium of the Americas, and directly across the street from Harrah's casino, the hotel has a resident golf pro and a four-hole putting green. ⊠ *Poydras St. at the Mississippi River, CBD 70140,* ☎ *504/561–0500 or 800/445–8667,* FAX *504/568–1721,* WEB *www.hilton. com. 1,600 rooms, 67 suites. 4 restaurants, putting green, 8 tennis courts, 2 pools, aerobics, hair salon, health club, outdoor hot tub, massage, sauna, racquetball, squash, 7 lounges, nightclub, business services, parking (fee); no-smoking floor. AE, D, DC, MC, V.*

$$$$ **Sheraton New Orleans.** The oversize atriumlike lobby of this hotel is usually bustling with conventioneers. A tropical atmosphere permeates the Pelican Bar, which presents jazz nightly and sells a fine assortment of cigars. Café Promenade encircles the second level. Executive rooms come with many special amenities, but even the regular guest rooms are spacious and well appointed. Expect top-quality service. The hotel is across Canal Street from one of the city's great downtown eateries, the Palace Café. ⊠ *500 Canal St., CBD 70130,* ☎ *504/525–2500 or 800/253–6156,* FAX *504/592–5615,* WEB *www.sheratonneworleans.com. 1,100 rooms, 72 suites. 3 restaurants, pool, health club, bar, lobby lounge, parking (fee); no-smoking rooms. AE, D, DC, MC, V.*

$$$$ **Windsor Court Hotel.** Exquisite, gracious, eminently civilized—these
★ words are frequently used to describe Windsor Court, but all fail to capture the wonderful quality of this hotel. From Le Salon's scrumptious afternoon tea, served daily in the lobby, to the unbelievably large rooms, this is one of *the* places to stay in New Orleans. Plush carpeting, canopy and four-poster beds, stocked wet bars, marble vanities, oversize mirrors, and dressing areas are just some of the touches. The Windsor's Grill Room is excellent, and the Polo Lounge has one of the best martini presentations to be found. ⊠ *300 Gravier St., CBD 70130,* ☎ *504/523–6000 or 800/262–2662,* FAX *504/596–4513,* WEB *www.windsorcourthotel. com. 58 rooms, 266 suites, 2 penthouses. 2 restaurants, in-room data ports, pool, health club, hot tub, sauna, steam room, lobby lounge, laundry service, parking (fee). AE, D, DC, MC, V.*

$$$–$$$$ **Lafayette Hotel.** This small brick building has housed the LaFayette
★ ever since it was built in 1916. Handsome millwork, brass fittings, and marble baths adorn the inn throughout. The lobby is tiny but chic, and guest rooms are spacious and sunny. Some rooms have four-poster beds; all have cushy easy chairs and ottomans. Shelves lined with books are a homey touch. Some rooms on the second floor have floor-length windows opening onto a balcony; a number overlook Lafayette Square.

✉ *600 St. Charles Ave., CBD 70130,* ☎ *504/524–4441 or 800/733–4754,* ⟨FAX⟩ *504/523–7327,* ⟨WEB⟩ *www.thelafayettehotel.com. 24 rooms, 20 suites. Restaurant, minibars, dry cleaning, laundry service, concierge, parking (fee); no-smoking rooms. AE, D, DC, MC, V.*

$$ 🏨 **Hampton Inn.** This moderately priced facility is among several office buildings that have been converted into hotels (the UNO Downtown Center has offices on the second and third floors). The lobby, with lavish furnishings and decor, is an oasis in the midst of a bustling business district. Rooms are large and comfortable, and all baths have hair dryers. Among the safety features are key-access elevators. Two blocks from Bourbon Street, the Hampton Inn is surrounded by great restaurants and tourist attractions. ✉ *226 Carondelet St., CBD 70130,* ☎ *504/529–9990 or 800/426–7866,* ⟨FAX⟩ *504/529–9996,* ⟨WEB⟩ *www.hamptoninn-suites.com. 186 rooms. Coffee shop, gym, concierge, parking (fee). AE, D, DC, MC, V. CP.*

Garden District/Uptown

These areas are ideal for those who prefer accommodations away from downtown. All the following are on or close to fashionable, mansion-lined St. Charles Avenue, where the streetcar runs (24 hours) to the CBD and the French Quarter in a mere 15–20 minutes. The trip can be longer at night owing to less-frequent service; a taxi is a better option if you are out late. Walking in this area after dark is not recommended.

$$$ 🏨 **Pontchartrain Hotel.** Maintaining the grand tradition is the hallmark
★ of this elegant, European-style hotel, which has reigned on St. Charles Avenue since 1927. Accommodations range from lavish, sun-filled suites to small pensione-type rooms with showers only (no bathtubs). The Pontchartrain has been the honeymoon hotel for such couples as Prince Aly Kahn and Rita Hayworth; suite names will tell you who else has passed through. Nowadays, though, more businesspeople than celebrities stay here. ✉ *2031 St. Charles Ave., Garden District 70140,* ☎ *504/524–0581 or 800/777–6193,* ⟨FAX⟩ *504/524–7828,* ⟨WEB⟩ *www.pontchartrainhotel.com. 84 rooms, 38 suites. 2 restaurants, piano bar, concierge, parking (fee). AE, D, DC, MC, V.*

$$–$$$ 🏨 **Quality Inn Maison St. Charles.** This is a lovely property in six his-
★ toric buildings that cluster around intimate courtyards. The porte cochere entrance has an attractive mural. A complimentary shuttle to the convention center and 24-hour security are among the amenities. ✉ *1319 St. Charles Ave., Garden District 70130,* ☎ *504/522–0187 or 800/831–1783,* ⟨FAX⟩ *504/528–9993,* ⟨WEB⟩ *www.qualityinn.com. 129 rooms, 16 suites. Pool, hot tub, bar, parking (fee); no-smoking rooms. AE, D, DC, MC, V.*

$$ 🏨 **McKendrick-Breaux House.** If you're looking for an alternative to the city's touristy quarters, this Greek Revival guest house in the Magazine Street antiques district is an excellent choice. In fact, the large rooms here, spread throughout the main house and a neighboring building, are one of the best values in the city. They have high ceilings, gorgeous wood floors, and fresh flowers; many have their own entrances on the property's garden courtyard. ✉ *1474 Magazine St., Garden District 70130,* ☎ *504/586–1700 or 888/570–1700,* ⟨FAX⟩ *504/522–7138,* ⟨WEB⟩ *www.mckendrick-breaux.com. 7 rooms. Free parking. AE, MC, V. CP.*

$–$$ 🏨 **St. Charles Guest House.** Simple and affordable, this European-style pension is in four buildings one block from St. Charles Avenue. Rooms in the A and B buildings are larger. The small "backpacker" rooms share a bath and do not have air-conditioning. A pleasant surprise is the large swimming pool and deck. Proprietors Dennis and Joanne Hilton will occasionally delight you with an impromptu crawfish boil or an introduction to New Orleans's red beans and rice. ✉ *1748 Prytania St., Garden District 70130,* ☎ *504/523–6556,* ⟨FAX⟩ *504/522–*

6340, WEB *www.stcharlesguesthouse.com. 36 rooms, 28 with bath. Pool. AE, MC, V. CP.*

Mid-City

$$–$$$$ 🏠 **House on Bayou Road.** This circa 1798 West Indies–style Creole plan-
★ tation home, set on 2 acres of lawns and gardens, has rooms filled with
Louisiana antiques, including handsome four-poster feather beds. Ac-
commodations are in the main house as well as in detached cottages.
The grand suite in the private cottage has a skylight over the bed, a
small kitchenette, bookshelves, and a whirlpool bath. A cooking school
is conducted on the premises. The house is in a remote setting, and walk-
ing in the area is not encouraged. ⊠ *2275 Bayou Rd., Bayou St. John
70119,* ☎ *504/945–0992, 504/949–7711, or 800/882–2968,* FAX *504/
945–0993,* WEB *www.houseonbayouroad.com. 4 rooms, 1 suite. Pool.
AE, DC. BP.*

Kenner/Airport

$–$$$ 🏠 **New Orleans Airport Hilton.** Directly across from the New Orleans
★ International Airport is this unexpectedly elegant hotel. The decor
throughout is superb, with muted pastel colors that coordinate well
with the soft pink Caribbean-style exterior. The handwoven area rugs
are from England. ⊠ *901 Airline Hwy., Kenner 70062,* ☎ *504/469–
5000 or 800/872–5914,* FAX *504/466–5473,* WEB *www.hiltonneworleans.
com. 317 rooms, 2 suites. Restaurant, putting green, tennis court,
pool, gym, bar, business services, airport shuttle, parking (fee). AE, D,
DC, MC, V.*

Nightlife and the Arts

Nightlife

New Orleans is a 24-hour town, meaning there are no legal closing
times; last call, especially on Bourbon Street, depends on how business
is. Your best bet is to phone ahead before tooling out to barhop at 2
AM. It is also smart to ask ahead about current credit-card policy,
cover, and minimum.

Gambit, the free weekly newspaper, has a complete listing of who's
doing what where. Things can change between press and performance
times, so if there's an artist you're especially eager to hear, it's wise to
call and confirm before turning up.

BARS

With imbibing a favorite local pastime, New Orleans is loaded, so to
speak, with good bars. The French Quarter has at least one on every
block; touristy Bourbon Street is lined with bars of every sort, from
oyster to topless. The University section, around Loyola and Tulane,
is also a great place for barhopping.

Definitely more a haunt for locals than for tourists, **The Abbey** (⊠ 1123
Decatur St., French Quarter, ☎ 504/523–7150) is cozy, funky, and brimming with character. On Saturday nights, a ragtime band takes the floor.
Bourbon Pub (⊠ 801 Bourbon St., French Quarter, ☎ 504/529–2107,
WEB www.bourbonpub.com) is a popular gay bar for young men.
Carousel Revolving Bar (⊠ 214 Royal St., French Quarter, ☎ 504/523–
3341), in the Monteleone Hotel, is a veritable institution. An authentic revolving carousel serves as a centerpiece, with the bar stools revolving around the service area. The convivial **Crescent City Brewhouse**
(⊠ 527 Decatur St., French Quarter, ☎ 504/522–0571) is known for
its extensive menu of micro- and specialty brews. The river view from
the second-floor balcony is worth a stop. The horseshoe-shape **El Mata-
dor** (⊠ 504 Esplanade Ave., French Quarter, ☎ 504/569–8361) is a
favorite perch among local and visiting musicians and film types and

the otherwise hip, day and night. In the Warehouse District, **Ernst Café** (✉ 600 S. Peters St., Warehouse District, ☎ 504/525–8544, WEB www. ernstcafe.net) is a friendly, atmospheric old bar.

One of the world's best-known bars and home of the Hurricane (a sweetly potent concoction of rum and fruit juices) is **Pat O'Brien's** (✉ 718 St. Peter St., French Quarter, ☎ 504/525–4823). There are three bars, including a lively piano bar and a large courtyard bar, and mobs of collegians and tourists line up to get in. Very lively, very loud, very late. The **Napoleon House** (✉ 500 Chartres St., French Quarter, ☎ 504/ 524–9752), with sepia walls, taped classical music, and Napoleonic memorabilia, is a favored local haunt. **Lafitte's Blacksmith Shop** (✉ 941 Bourbon St., French Quarter, ☎ 504/523–0066), in a tattered 18th-century cottage, has been a hangout for artists and writers for ages.

Sixties-era Vegas meets the Vieux Carré at **Shim Sham** (✉ 615 Toulouse St., French Quarter, ☎ 504/565–5400). Retro-theme acts, embracing every era from the '30s to the '80s, are a specialty: come on a Monday for the ever-popular punk 'n' porn night. Rattan furniture in the storefront window makes **The Spotted Cat** (✉ 623 Frenchmen St., Faubourg Marigny, ☎ 504/943–3887) a perfect perch for an afternoon libation. Solo acoustic performers sometimes take to the small raised area that passes for a stage. **St. Joe's** (✉ 5535 Magazine St., Uptown, ☎ 504/899–3744) bustles with energetic locals. Dry martinis are a favorite libation here; pool tables in back attract a dedicated crew. Lesbians have laid claim to the Thursday ladies' night at **Wit's Inn** (✉ 141 N. Carrollton Ave., Mid-City, ☎ 504/486–1600), a down-to-earth bar right in the center of Mid-City.

CASINOS

An imposing, land-based casino dominates the foot of New Orleans's famous Canal Street. Operated by Harrah's, the downtown casino joins three gambling riverboats; all are open 24 hours daily, and all have a lounge and/or grill and live music, plus slots, video poker, and gaming tables for roulette, craps, blackjack, and big six.

Harrah's New Orleans Casino (✉ 4 Canal St., CBD, ☎ 504/533–6000 or 877/277–4263), a 100,000-square-ft gambling den at the foot of Canal Street, is housed in a Greek Revival–style structure dressed to the nines in New Orleans–themed decor. You'll find the Mardi Gras Court, a Jazz Court, and a Smugglers Court, among its diversions, as well as plenty of music and daily parades replete with Mardi Gras revelers. Oh, and it also has 2,900 slots and 117 table games.

Belle of Orleans (✉ 1 Stars & Stripes Blvd., ☎ 504/248–3200 or 800/ 572–2559) is on Lake Pontchartrain adjacent to Lakefront Airport. **Boomtown Belle Casino** (✉ 4132 Peters Rd., on the Harvey Canal, Westbank, ☎ 504/366–7711 or 800/366–7711) has a Wild West theme. **Treasure Chest** (✉ 5050 Williams Blvd., Kenner, ☎ 504/443–8000 or 800/ 298–0711) is docked on Lake Pontchartrain, across from the Pontchartrain Center. It has a glitzy entertainment complex land-side.

DANCING

Two-stepping to a Cajun band is billed as the *"spécialité de la maison,"* but the **Maple Leaf Bar** moves with rock, R&B, reggae, and gospel as well. (Cajun nights are special.) ✉ *8316 Oak St., Uptown,* ☎ *504/ 866–9359.* 🎟 *$5 cover.* ⊙ *3 PM; closing time varies.*

This is New Orleans, so it shouldn't surprise you that even a bowling alley has live music. Locals flock to the **Mid-City Lanes Rock-N-Bowl** and its ground-level sibling, **Bowl Me Under**, to dance to homegrown bands. Admission varies, depending upon the bands. ✉ *4133 S. Car-*

rollton Ave., Mid-City, ☎ *504/482–3133.* ☒ *$10–$15.* ☉ *Rock-N-Bowl, Wed.–Sat. 9:30 PM–2:30 AM; bowling alley, daily noon–midnight.*

Jazz was born in New Orleans, and the music isn't always at night. Weekend jazz brunches are enormously popular and pop up all over town. But a stroll down Bourbon Street will give you a taste of the city's eclectic rhythms—Cajun, gutbucket, R&B, rock, ragtime—you name it, and you'll hear it almost around the clock.

Aboard the **Creole Queen** you'll cruise on the river with a Dixieland jazz band, and there's a buffet to boot. ☒ *Poydras St. Wharf,* ☎ *504/ 524–0814. Daytime cruise:* ☒ *$15.75.* ☉ *Daily 10:30 and 2. Dinner cruise:* ☒ *$45.* ☉ *Daily 8–10, boards 7–8.*

Donna's Bar & Grill is a great place to hear traditional jazz, R&B, and the city's young brass bands in an informal neighborhood setting. On Monday night, many of the city's musicians stop by after their regular gigs to sit in. ☒ *800 N. Rampart St., French Quarter,* ☎ *504/596– 6914.*

Named after jazz pioneer Buddy Bolden's signature tune and housed in art deco splendor, the **Funky Butt at Congo Square** is a top spot for contemporary jazz. Local talent and local connoisseurs are both found in plentiful supply here; Jason Marsalis, of the local musical dynasty, often plays here. ☒ *714 N. Rampart St., French Quarter,* ☎ *504/558–0872.*

There's live music five nights a week at the **Palm Court Jazz Café.** Traditional jazz is the rule, with blues thrown in on Wednesday. The fine Creole and international kitchen stays open until the music stops. ☒ *1204 Decatur St., French Quarter,* ☎ *504/525–0200.* ☒ *$5 cover to sit at tables, free at bar.* ☉ *7 PM–11 PM; live music Wed., Thurs., and Sun. at 8 PM, Fri.–Sat. at 7 PM. Closed Mon.–Tues.*

Pete Fountain's Club is a New Orleans legend with Pete's clarinet and his band, which plays in a plush 500-seat room on the third floor of the Hilton Hotel. This is Pete's home base, and the man's on the stand Tuesday, Wednesday, Friday, and Saturday when he's in town (he makes frequent appearances around the country, so it's wise to call ahead). ☒ *2 Poydras St., CBD,* ☎ *504/523–4374.* ☒ *$19 cover.* ☉ *Shows daily 10 PM–11:15 PM.*

★ Speaking of legends, the old-time jazz greats lay out the best traditional jazz in the world in a musty, funky hall that's short on comfort, long on talent. **Preservation Hall** is the place for traditional jazz. You may have to stand in line to get in (and it's often standing room only inside), but it will help if you get here about 7:30. ☒ *726 St. Peter St., French Quarter,* ☎ *504/522–2841,* WEB *www.preservationhall.com.* ☒ *$5 cover.* ☉ *Daily 8 PM–midnight.*

Rambling, rustic, and raucous **Snug Harbor** is where graybeards and undergrads get a big bang out of the likes of the Dirty Dozen, Charmaine Neville, the David Torkanowsky Trio, and Maria Muldaur. ☒ *626 Frenchmen St., Faubourg Marigny,* ☎ *504/949–0696.* ☒ *Weekdays $8–$10 cover, weekends $12–$15 cover.* ☉ *Daily 5 PM–2 AM; show times 8 PM and 11 PM.*

Vaughan's lights up on Thursdays for Kermit Ruffins's jazz sets. The neighborhood is not the safest, so a taxi is a necessity. ☒ *800 Lesseps St. at Dauphine St., Bywater,* ☎ *504/947–5562.*

If a popular band such as the Iguanas is playing, then it's strictly standing at **Café Brasil.** Tables line the sidewalk, though, and the music pours through the open doors. All kinds of music and people come to this bohemian hot spot, and it's also a popular place to show off costumes on Mardi Gras. ⊠ *2100 Chartres St., Faubourg Marigny,* ☎ *504/949–0851.*

Industrial-strength rock rolls out of the sound system at the **Hard Rock Cafe.** Hard Rock Hurricanes are dispensed at a guitar-shape bar, and the place is filled with rock-and-roll memorabilia. Hamburgers, salads, and steaks are served. There's no cover. ⊠ *440 N. Peters St., French Quarter,* ☎ *504/529–8617.* ◷ *Weekdays 11–11, weekends 11 AM–midnight.*

House of Blues is a $7 million music venue with an awesome sound system where local and nationally known artists perform. It is also home to a recording studio, restaurant, and shop. The cover and closing time vary, depending on the show. ⊠ *225 Decatur St., French Quarter,* ☎ *504/529–2624,* WEB *www.hob.com.* ◷ *Restaurant daily 11 AM–midnight; nightclub daily from 8 PM, sets begin 9:30 PM.*

Howlin' Wolf, in a former grain and cotton warehouse, is popular with locals. A grab bag of alternative rock, hip-hop, Latin music, and progressive country fills the schedule. Visiting musicians often hang out and may sit in. ⊠ *828 S. Peters St., Warehouse District,* ☎ *504/529–5844.*

The college crowd raises the rafters at **Jimmy's Music Club.** The music, by national as well as local groups, is rock, reggae, R&B, whatever. ⊠ *8200 Willow St., Uptown,* ☎ *504/861–8200.* ▱ *Cover $8–$15.* ◷ *Tues.–Sat. 9 PM, shows begin 9:30 PM; closing time varies.*

An absolute institution, the **Maple Leaf** hosts blues, zydeco, R&B, and more. The Rebirth Brass Band has held court here every Tuesday night for the past 15 years; the gig is an essential part of many locals' social routines. Although the club is only a few blocks from the Oak and Carrollton streetcar stop, it's best to take a cab. ⊠ *8316 Oak St., Uptown,* ☎ *504/866–9359.*

Fans of Jimmy Buffett flock to **Margaritaville Café,** where local funk and R&B acts perform, as occasionally does Buffett himself. The cover varies. ⊠ *1104 Decatur St., French Quarter,* ☎ *504/592–2565.* ◷ *Daily 11 AM, live band sets daily 2 PM, main stage weekend shows 10:30 PM; closing time varies.*

An institution, **Tipitina's** is a sort of microcosm of Jazzfest, featuring progressive jazz, reggae, ska, R&B, rock, blues—well, just about everything. It's funky, mellow, and loaded with laid-back locals. Tips also has a French Quarter branch, not far from the House of Blues. The **concert hot line** for both locations is ☎ *504/897–3943. 501 Napoleon Ave., Uptown,* ☎ *504/895–8477;* ⊠ *233 N. Peters St., French Quarter,* ☎ *504/566–7095. Cover* ▱ *$3–$25.* ◷ *Daily 5 PM; closing time varies.*

The Arts

Comprehensive listings of events can be found in the weekly newspaper *Gambit,* which is distributed free at newsstands, supermarkets, and bookstores. The Friday edition of the daily *Times-Picayune* carries a "Lagniappe" tabloid that lists weekend events. The monthly *New Orleans* magazine also has a "Calendar" section. Credit-card purchases of tickets for events at the Theatre for Performing Arts, the Saenger Performing Arts Center, the Orpheum Theater, and Kiefer UNO Lakefront Arena can be made through TicketMaster (☎ 504/522–5555, www.ticketmaster.com).

CONCERTS

Free **jazz concerts** are held on weekends during the day in Dutch Alley. Pick up a schedule at the French Market Visitor Center (⊠ French Market at Dumaine St., ☎ 504/596–3424). The **Louisiana Philharmonic**

Orchestra (☎ 504/523–6530) performs at the Orpheum Theatre (✉ 129 University Pl., CBD).

DANCE AND OPERA

The **New Orleans Ballet Association** (Office: ✉ 305 Baronne St., CBD, ☎ 504/522–0996, WEB www.nobadance.com) presents a superb season of classical and contemporary visiting troupes. The **New Orleans Opera Association** (Office: ✉ 305 Baronne St., CBD, ☎ 504/529–2278, WEB www.neworleansopera.org) produces a four-title season featuring talent from around the world. Both ballet and opera productions take place at the New Orleans Theatre for the Performing Arts in Armstrong Park, located across Rampart Street on the outer edge of the French Quarter.

THEATER

The avant-garde, the offbeat, and the satirical are among the theatrical offerings at **Contemporary Arts Center** (✉ 900 Camp St., Warehouse District, ☎ 504/523–1216, WEB www.cacno.org). At **Le Petit Théâtre du Vieux Carré** (✉ 616 St. Peter St., French Quarter, ☎ 504/522–9958) classics, contemporary drama, children's theater, and musicals are presented. Touring Broadway shows, dance companies, and top-name talent appear at the **Saenger Performing Arts Center** (✉ 143 N. Rampart St., CBD, ☎ 504/524–2490). The **Kiefer UNO Lakefront Arena** (✉ 6801 Franklin Ave., ☎ 504/286–7222) is a venue for major concerts.

Festivals

During the annual **Jazz and Heritage Festival,** held from the last weekend in April through the first weekend in May, musicians from all over the world pour in to mix it up with local talent. Called the Jazzfest by its devotees, this festival draws thousands of fans and internationally acclaimed musicians. The weekend venue is the infield of the Fair Grounds; the week in between sees music venues all over town filled to bursting. In addition to homegrown talent such as Wynton and Branford Marsalis, Harry Connick, Jr., Allen Toussaint, and the Neville Brothers, look for such luminaries as B. B. King, Al Green, and Ray Charles.

North America's biggest bash—**Mardi Gras**—takes place in February or March (the date depends on when Easter falls). Carnival season begins January 6 (Twelfth Night) and ends at midnight on Fat Tuesday, with the advent of Ash Wednesday and Lent. Mardi Gras means giant and fantastic floats rolling through downtown streets (though not in the French Quarter), eye-popping costumes, and the occasional exposed body parts. The last great push of the Carnival season is the weekend before Fat Tuesday (Mardi Gras Day), when parades roll day and night, and the city is given over to flat-out partying.

Outdoor Activities and Sports

Baseball

The **AAA New Orleans Zephyrs** (☎ 504/734–5155), a farm team of the Houston Astros, play ball at the 10,000-seat Zephyr Field (✉ 6000 Airline Hwy. [Hwy. 61], Metairie), near David Drive and Transcontinental Drive, in Jefferson Parish, a 15-minute drive west of New Orleans. The **University of New Orleans Privateers** take on their foes in Privateers Park at the school's Lakefront campus (☎ 504/286–7240). **Tulane Green Wave** teams play home games at the New Orleans Arena (✉ 1501 Girod St., adjacent to Superdome, CBD) and at the school's St. Charles Avenue campus (☎ 504/861–3661).

Basketball

The **Sugar Bowl Basketball Classic** (☎ 504/525–8573) is played in the Superdome the week preceding the annual football classic.

209

Biking

Rentals are available at **Bicycle Michael's** (⌧ 618 Frenchmen St.,
Faubourg Marigny, ☎ 504/945–9505) at $3.50 per hour and $12.50
per day. **French Quarter Bicycles** (⌧ 522 Dumaine St., French Quarter, ☎ 504/529–3136) has mountain bikes ($4.50 per hour, $14 and
up per day), baby strollers and baby carriages ($1 per hour, $4 per day),
and one wheelchair ($4.50 per hour, $14 per day) for rent.

Guided bike tours of Plantation Country and Cajun Country are available from **French Louisiana Bike Tours** (⌧ 3216 W. Esplanade Ave., PMB
302, Metairie 70002, ☎ 504/488–9844 or 800/346–7989). Prices
start at about $1,100 for a four-day tour that includes rental of a Can-
nondale hybrid (equipped with smooth tires, Avocet computer, back
rack, and handlebar pack), lodging, and meals.

Football

The **New Orleans Saints** (☎ 504/522–2600) play NFL games in the
Superdome. Home games of **Tulane University** (☎ 504/861–3661) are
played in the dome. The annual **Sugar Bowl Football Classic** (☎ 504/
525–8573) takes place in the dome on New Year's Day. In late November the **Bayou Classic** (☎ 504/587–3663) pits Southern University
against Grambling University. The Louisiana Superdome has hosted
the **Super Bowl** eight times, more than any other city, and undoubt-
edly will do so again.

Horseback Riding

Cascade Stables (⌧ 6500 Magazine St., Uptown, ☎ 504/891–2246)
has guided 45-minute trail rides, costing $20 per person, in Audubon
Park.

Ice Hockey

The New Orleans Brass (office: ⌧ 1201 St. Peter St., French Quarter,
☎ 504/522–7825) of the East Coast Ice Hockey League play home games
in the New Orleans Arena, the sports facility behind the Superdome.

Tennis

There are 39 courts in the **City Park Wisner Tennis Center** (⌧ 1 Dreyfous Ave., in City Park, Mid-City, ☎ 504/483–9383). **Audubon Park**
(☎ 504/895–1042) has 10 courts near Tchoupitoulas Street.

Shopping

Pralines, chicory coffee, Mardi Gras masks, vintage clothing, and jazz
records are usually hot tickets. The packaging of New Orleans food
to go is a growing trend.

Shopping Districts

New Orleans shops string along the Mississippi all the way from the
French Quarter to beyond Riverbend (at the Uptown bend in the
river). The **French Quarter** is the place to search for antiques shops,
art galleries, designer boutiques, bookstores, and all sorts of unique
shops in all sorts of edifices. Among **Canal Place**'s (⌧ 333 Canal St.,
CBD) lofty tenants you'll find Saks Fifth Avenue, Laura Ashley, Gucci,
Brooks Brothers, and the wares of New Orleans jewelry designer
Mignon Faget. **Riverwalk** (⌧ 1 Poydras St., CBD) is a long, tunnel-
like marketplace brightened by more than 200 splashy shops, restaurants, food courts, and huge windows overlooking the Mississippi. The
tony **New Orleans Centre,** between the Hyatt Regency Hotel and the
Superdome on Poydras Street, has more than 100 occupants, including Macy's and Lord & Taylor. Along 6 mi of **Magazine Street** are Victorian houses and small cottages filled with antiques and collectibles.
Stop at the New Orleans Welcome Center for a copy of the shopper's

guides published by the Magazine Street Merchants Association and the Royal Street Guild.

Turn-of-the-century Creole cottages cradle everything from toy shops to designer boutiques and delis in the **Riverbend** (⊠ Maple St. and Carrollton Ave., Uptown). Macy's and Mervyn's are among the 155 shops in Metairie's glittering three-level **Esplanade Mall** (⊠ 1401 W. Esplanade Ave., Kenner). The **Warehouse District** (⊠ bordered roughly by Girod St., Howard Ave., Camp St., and the river), particularly Julia Street, has become a major center for the visual arts, not unlike New York City's SoHo.

Specialty Stores

ANTIQUES

Shoulder to shoulder along **Royal Street** are some of the finest—and oldest—antiques stores in New Orleans. **Adler & Waldhorn** (⊠ 343 Royal St., French Quarter, ☎ 504/581–6379), the city's oldest antiques store, was established in 1881; specialties are English furniture, Victorian and Early American jewelry, and antique English porcelain and silver. **French Antique Shop** (⊠ 225 Royal St., French Quarter, ☎ 504/524–9861) has a large selection of European chandeliers and furniture, as well as some Creole and local designs. **Lucullus** (⊠ 610 Chartres St., French Quarter, ☎ 504/528–9620) carries fine Continental and English 17th- to 19th-century furniture, art, and cookware. **Moss Antiques** (⊠ 411 Royal St., French Quarter, ☎ 504/522–3981) has a large selection of antique and estate jewels, as well as fine French and English furnishings, paintings, and bric-a-brac. **Patout Antiques** (⊠ 920 Royal St., French Quarter, ☎ 504/522–0582) has high-quality antiques from Louisiana plantation houses. **Rothschild's Antiques** (⊠ 241 Royal St., French Quarter, ☎ 504/523–5816; ⊠ 321 Royal St., French Quarter, ☎ 504/523–2281) has a large collection of furniture, silver, jewelry, mantels, and clocks from the 18th through the 20th centuries. **Whisnant Galleries** (⊠ 222 Chartres St., French Quarter, ☎ 504/524–9766) has delightfully eclectic antique jewelry, African sculptures, clocks, and unusual pieces.

ART

Bergen Galleries (⊠ 730 Royal St., French Quarter, ☎ 504/523–7882) offers posters and collectibles by local artists. The **Black Art Collection** (⊠ 309 Chartres St., French Quarter, ☎ 504/529–3080) displays and sells works by local and national African-American artists. **Dyansen Gallery** (⊠ 433 Royal St., French Quarter, ☎ 504/523–2902) features the work of modern and contemporary artists. **Rodrigue Gallery** (⊠ 721 Royal St., French Quarter, ☎ 504/581–4244 or 800/899–4244) showcases artwork featuring the Blue Dog series of internationally acclaimed Cajun artist George Rodrigue. **Southern Expressions** (⊠ 521 St. Ann St., at Jackson Sq., French Quarter, ☎ 504/525–4530) shows the work of regional artists.

FLEA MARKET

Jazz is within earshot, and "junque" is at your fingertips at the **French Market Flea Market** (⊠ French Market Pl., French Quarter, ☎ 504/522–2621) daily from 7 to 7.

FOOD TO GO

Battistella's Sea Foods, Inc. (⊠ 910 Touro St., Ninth Ward, ☎ 504/949–2724) carries packaged seafood to go. The **New Orleans School of Cooking** (⊠ Jax Brewery, 620 Decatur St., French Quarter, ☎ 504/525–2665) stocks packaged red beans and rice, beignet mixes, Cajun spices, pecans, and other Louisiana specialties. **Louisiana Products** (⊠ 507 St. Ann St., on Jackson Sq., French Quarter, ☎ 504/524–7331) is another good source for Cajun and Creole foods and can ship anywhere in the country. **Foodies Kitchen** (✉ 720 Veterans Hwy., Metairie, ☎ 504/837–9695) is a Commander's Palace operation that has take-out foods, including a deli and bakery, as well as tables for those who prefer to eat in.

JAZZ RECORDS

Louisiana Music Factory (✉ 225 N. Peters St., French Quarter) has a good selection of regional vinyl, CDs, and tapes.

MASKS

Little Shop of Fantasy (✉ 523 Dumaine St., French Quarter, ☎ 504/529–4243, WEB www.littleshopoffantasy.com) specializes in feathered masks, though you can also get papier-mâché, leather, plaster, and cloth designs. For exotic handmade masks to decorate your face or your wall, visit **Rumors** (✉ 513 Royal St., French Quarter, ☎ 504/525–0292).

PRALINES

For the best pralines in town, try **Old Town Praline Shop** (✉ 627 Royal St., French Quarter, ☎ 504/525–1413).

Side Trip from New Orleans

Jean Lafitte National Historical Park

20 mi south of downtown.

Just 45 minutes by car from the French Quarter, you can sample Louisiana's exotic natural splendors in the park's 8,000-acre Barataria Unit. Paved walkways lace alongside bayous, over which hang frayed canopies of Spanish moss and in which alligators, snakes, and other critters slither. Park rangers conduct free walking tours daily, but you can also wander along the trails on your own. At the **Bayou Barn** (✉ intersection of Rtes. 31, 34, and 45, ☎ 504/689–2663 or 800/862–2968, FAX 504/689–4554, WEB www.nps.gov/jela) the intrepid can rent a canoe and paddle off alone; it's $7.50 per person for two hours. The less adventuresome can take a Bayou Barn guided tour (six-person minimum, $20 for two hours); and all can enjoy the fresh gumbo and jambalaya dished up by the friendly folks at the shop. To reach the park, take U.S. 90 over the Crescent City Connection (bridge) across the river and turn left on Route 45. ✉ *Just below Marrero on Lake Salvador (via U.S. 90, south of New Orleans, and Rte. 45),* ☎ *504/589–2330.*

New Orleans A to Z

AIR TRAVEL TO AND FROM NEW ORLEANS

CARRIERS

New Orleans is served by American, Continental, Delta, JetBlue, Northwest, Southwest, TWA, United, and US Airways (☞ Air Travel *in* Smart Travel Tips A to Z for telephone numbers), as well as by a number of foreign carriers.

AIRPORTS AND TRANSFERS

Louis Armstrong International Airport is 15 mi west of New Orleans. Locals sometimes still call it New Orleans International or Moissant Field, its two former names.

➤ AIRPORT INFORMATION: **Louis Armstrong International Airport** (✉ 900 Airline Dr., Kenner, ☎ 504/464–0831).

AIRPORT TRANSFERS

Buses operated by Louisiana Transit run every 22 minutes between the airport and Elk Place in the CBD. Hours of operation are 6 AM–6:20 PM; the last bus leaves the airport at 5:40 PM. The $1.50 trip downtown takes about an hour.

The Airport Shuttle leaves the airport every 5–10 minutes, 24 hours a day, for the 20- to 30-minute trip into town. Small vans drop passengers off at their hotels, so arrival time at your destination depends on the van's number of stops. The fare is $10 per person.

Taxi fare is a flat $21 for one or two passengers, $8 per additional person. The driver may offer three or four strangers together a rate comparable to the airport shuttle.

By car you can drive to New Orleans from Kenner via Airline Highway (U.S. 61) or I–10. Hertz, Avis, Budget, and other major car rental agencies have airport outlets (☞ Car Rental, *below*).
➤ Taxis and Shuttles: **Airport Shuttle** (☎ 504/522–3500 or 800/543–6332). **Louisiana Transit** (☎ 504/737–9611).

BIKE TRAVEL
The flat terrain of the French Quarter invites bikers, and Royal and Bourbon streets in the Quarter are closed off during the day to all but bikers and pedestrians. Many cyclists make the trek from the Quarter to City Park or Audubon Park, both good places for easy wheeling.

BOAT AND FERRY TRAVEL
The Canal Street Ferry will take you across the Mississippi from the Canal Street Wharf to Algiers Ferry Landing. The ride takes 25 minutes round-trip, and is free to pedestrians; motorists pay $1 for the return to Canal Street Wharf. The ferry is open daily 5:30 AM–9:30 PM.
➤ Boat and Ferry Information: **Canal Street Ferry** (☎ 504/364–8114).

BUS TRAVEL AROUND NEW ORLEANS
Buses require $1.25 exact change or a token (sold only in banks). Transfers are 10¢ extra—remember to ask for a slip. The Vieux Carré, a French Quarter shuttle operated by the Regional Transit Authority (RTA) runs weekdays from 5 AM to 7:30 PM. Other bus and streetcar service runs 24 hours a day, though wait times can be as long as an hour or more in the morning's earliest hours. Smoking, eating, and drinking are not permitted on RTA vehicles. Those who violate this rule can find themselves paying a hefty fine in Municipal Court, or worse, pulled off the bus and arrested.
➤ Bus Information: **RTA** (☎ 504/248–3900, 504/242–2600 automated information).

BUS TRAVEL TO AND FROM NEW ORLEANS
Greyhound operates out of Union Passenger Terminal (☞ Train Travel, *below*).
➤ Bus Information: **Greyhound** (✉ 1001 Loyola Ave., ☎ 800/231–2222, WEB www.greyhound.com).

CAR RENTAL
➤ Major Agencies: **Avis** (☎ 800/831–2847). **Budget** (☎ 800/527–0700). **Enterprise** (☎ 800/325–8007). **Hertz** (☎ 800/654–3131). **National** (☎ 800/227–7568).

CAR TRAVEL
I–10 runs from Florida through New Orleans and on to California. I–55 is the north–south route, connecting with I–12 west of Ponchatoula and with I–10 a touch west of New Orleans; I–59 runs northeast into Mississippi and Alabama; and I–49 slashes diagonally through the state's midsection, from Lafayette to Shreveport. U.S. 61, from the west, and U.S. 90, from the east, also run through New Orleans.

EMERGENCIES

All-night hospital emergency rooms include Tulane Medical Center, in the CBD near the French Quarter, and Touro Infirmary, near the Garden District.

➤ EMERGENCY SERVICES: **Ambulance, police** (☎ 911).

➤ HOSPITALS: **Touro Infirmary** (✉ 1401 Foucher St., Uptown, ☎ 504/897–8250). **Tulane Medical Center** (✉ 220 Lasalle St., CBD, ☎ 504/588–5711).

➤ 24-HOUR PHARMACIES: **Eckerd** (✉ 3400 Canal St., Mid-City, ☎ 504/488–6661). **Walgreens** (✉ 3057 Gentilly Blvd., Gentilly, ☎ 504/282–2621; ✉ 9999 Lake Forest Blvd., New Orleans East, ☎ 504/242–0981).

LODGING

BED AND BREAKFASTS

Bed & Breakfast, Inc.–Reservations Service has a variety of accommodations in all areas of New Orleans. Some are 19th-century historic homes. Guest cottages, rooms, and suites are also available. Prices range from $40 to $150. For more information, write or call Hazel Boyce. Credit cards are not accepted.

New Orleans Bed & Breakfast lists private homes, apartments, and condos among 300 properties. Prices range from $45 to $250. Call Sarah-Margaret Brown at the number below.

➤ RESERVATION SERVICES: **Bed & Breakfast, Inc.–Reservations Service** (Hazel Boyce: ✉ 1021 Moss St., Box 52257, 70152, ☎ 504/488–4640 or 800/729–4640, FAX 504/488–4639). **New Orleans Bed & Breakfast** (Sarah-Margaret Brown: ✉ Box 8163, 70182, ☎ 504/838–0071 or 504/838–0072, FAX 504/838–0140).

MEDIA

RADIO

AM: WWL 870, talk, news; WGSO 990, CNN radio; KGLA 1540, Spanish-language.

FM: WWNO 89.9, NPR, classical music, jazz; WWOZ 90.7, community radio, New Orleans jazz; WCKW 92.3, classic rock; WNOE 101.1, country music, news, weather.

TAXIS

Taxis are easy to find at all hours in tourist areas. Fares start at $2.10, plus 75¢ per additional passenger and $1 per mi or 40 seconds stopped in traffic. For trips to special events, such as a ride to the Fair Grounds during Jazzfest, cabs charge $3 per person or the meter rate, whichever is higher. Try United Cabs or Yellow-Checker Cabs.

➤ TAXI COMPANIES: **United Cabs** (☎ 504/522–9771). **Yellow-Checker Cabs** (☎ 504/525–3311).

TOURS

BOAT TOURS

The New Orleans Steamboat Company runs the mighty steamboat *Natchez,* which has two-hour cruises of the harbor during the day and two-hour dinner-jazz cruises in the evening. The harbor cruise is $15.75 (with lunch buffet $21.75), and departs daily at 11:30 and 2:30. The *Natchez* evening cruise is $25.50 ($45.50 with dinner) and sails daily 7–9, with boarding between 6 and 7.

The New Orleans Steamboat Company also runs the little *John James Audubon,* which cruises between the aquarium and the Audubon Zoo ($14.50 round-trip). Aside from the view of the city and the water lapping at the sides of the boats, kids (and some adults) love to watch the big stern wheel turning. The cruise departs daily at 10, noon, 2, and 4 from the aquarium, and at 11, 1, 3, and 5 from the zoo.

On the flatboats of Wagner's Honey Island Swamp Tours, steered by a professional wetland ecologist, you can tour one of the country's best-preserved river swamps ($20, $40 with hotel pickup).
➤ FEES AND SCHEDULES: **New Orleans Steamboat Company** (☎ 504/586–8777 or 800/233–2628). **Wagner's Honey Island Swamp Tours** (☎ 504/641–1769).

BUS TOURS

You can hop aboard an air-conditioned 45-passenger Gray Line bus for a two-hour tour of New Orleans's major sights ($22). Gray Line also offers several options of combined city/harbor/attractions tours. Tours by Isabelle uses air-conditioned 14-passenger vans for a multilingual and more intimate three-hour tool around town ($35).
➤ FEES AND SCHEDULES: **Gray Line** (☎ 504/587–0861). **Tours by Isabelle** (☎ 504/391–3544).

SPECIAL-INTEREST TOURS

Le 'Ob's Tours runs a daily African-American heritage/city tour ($35), as well as plantation, bayou, and Baton Rouge tours ($65–$80). Pat Bernard's Classic Tours is operated by a native New Orleanian who is in love with the city. Her chatty tours cover art, antiques, architecture, and history ($10). Save Our Cemeteries conducts lively guided tours of St. Louis Cemetery #1 ($12) and Lafayette Cemetery ($6). Statistics for the Superdome are staggering, and you can learn all about the huge facility during daily tours ($6). Tours by Isabelle takes you around town ($35), to plantations ($85–$95 with lunch included), and to the bayous for a visit with a Cajun alligator hunter ($55).
➤ FEES AND SCHEDULES: **Le 'Ob's Tours** (☎ 504/288–3478). **Pat Bernard's Classic Tours** (☎ 504/862–7849). **Save Our Cemeteries** (☎ 504/525–3377). **Superdome** (☎ 504/587–3810). **Tours by Isabelle** (☎ 504/391–3544).

WALKING TOURS

Classic Tours and Jean Lafitte National Park rangers both have Garden District walking tours. Heritage Tours conducts literary and historical walking tours of the French Quarter ($25). Voodoo haunts and such are covered by both Magic Walking Tours ($13) and the New Orleans Historic Voodoo Museum ($15).
➤ FEES AND SCHEDULES: **Classic Tours** (☎ 504/862–7849). **Heritage Tours** (☎ 504/949–9805). **Jean Lafitte National Park** (☎ 504/589–2636, WEB www.lsue.edu/acadgate/lafitte.htm). **Magic Walking Tours** (☎ 504/588–9693). **New Orleans Historic Voodoo Museum** (☎ 504/523–7685).

TRAIN TRAVEL

Amtrak trains pull into the CBD's Union Passenger Terminal. New Orleans is connected via rail to California, Chicago, Florida, New York, and points in between.
➤ TRAIN INFORMATION: **Amtrak** (☎ 800/872–7245). **Union Passenger Terminal** (✉ 1001 Loyola Ave., CBD, ☎ 504/528–1610).

TRANSPORTATION AROUND NEW ORLEANS

The St. Charles Streetcar, New Orleans's mobile Historic Landmark, clangs up St. Charles Avenue through the Garden District, past the Audubon Park and Zoo and other Uptown sights. The streetcar can be boarded in the CBD at Canal and Carondelet streets; the fare is $1.25. A round-trip self-guided sightseeing jaunt covers just over 13 mi and takes 90 minutes. The streetcar operates daily every five minutes from 7:30 AM to 6 PM, every 15–20 minutes from 6 PM to midnight, and hourly from midnight to 7 AM.

The Riverfront Streetcar follows the river between Esplanade Avenue and the Robin Street Wharf. It makes 10 stops, five above and five below Canal Street. The fare is $1.50, and it operates weekdays 6 AM–midnight; weekends 8 AM–midnight.

The Regional Transit Authority (RTA) has a 24-hour information service. One- and three-day visitor passes, available at hotels, cost $5 and $12, respectively, and allow unlimited travel on buses and streetcars.
➤ CONTACTS: **Regional Transit Authority** (☎ 504/248–3900). **Riverfront Streetcar** (☎ 504/248–3900). **St. Charles Streetcar** (☎ 504/248–3900).

VISITOR INFORMATION

If you want information in advance of your trip, write to the New Orleans Metropolitan Convention and Visitors Bureau. In the city, The Tourist Commission staffs a desk near the customs desk at New Orleans International Airport. Its main outlet is the Louisiana State Office of Tourism, which shares space with the city at the New Orleans Welcome Center; it's open daily 9–5.
➤ TOURIST INFORMATION: **New Orleans Metropolitan Convention and Visitors Bureau** (✉ 1520 Sugar Bowl Dr., New Orleans 70112, ☎ 504/566–5011 or 800/672–6124, FAX 504/566–5021, WEB www.neworleanscvb.com). **Tourist Commission** (✉ 529 St. Ann St., French Quarter, ☎ 504/566–5068).

BATON ROUGE AND PLANTATION COUNTRY

St. Francisville, Livonia, White Castle, Napoleonville

Baton Rouge, one of South Louisiana's major cities, is the state capital. Legend has it that in 1699 French explorers observed that a red stick planted in the ground on a high bluff overlooking the Mississippi served as a boundary between two Indian tribes. Sieur d'Iberville, leader of the expedition, noted *le baton rouge*—the red stick—in his journal, and voilà! Baton Rouge.

This is the city from which colorful, cunning Huey P. Long ruled the state; it is also the site of his assassination. Even today, more than half a century after Long's death, legends about the controversial governor and U.S. senator abound.

The parishes to the north of Baton Rouge are quiet and bucolic, with gently rolling hills, high bluffs, and historic districts. John James Audubon lived in West Feliciana Parish in 1821, tutoring local children and painting 80 of his famous bird studies. In both terrain and traits, this region is more akin to North Louisiana than to South Louisiana—which is to say, the area is very Southern.

The area designated Plantation Country begins with a reservoir of fine old homes north of Baton Rouge that cascades all the way down the Great River Road to New Orleans. After touring the state capital, we recommend taking LA 61 to the historic districts and plantations in the parishes north of Baton Rouge, overnighting in one of the plantation bed-and-breakfasts. From St. Francisville, take the ferry for $1 at the tip of town and start south on LA 1 to the antebellum gems that grace the Great River Road.

Numbers in the margin correspond to points of interest on the Baton Rouge and Plantation Country map.

Baton Rouge

28 *80 mi northwest of New Orleans via I-10.*

The **State Capitol Building** is a good place to start your tour; the Visitor Information Center in its lobby is loaded with maps and brochures. You can tour the first floor of the building, which includes the spot where Huey Long was shot in 1935. At 34 stories, this is America's tallest state capitol. An observation deck on the 27th floor affords a spectacular view of the Mississippi River and the city. ⊠ *State Capitol Dr., Capitol District,* ☎ *225/342–7317,* WEB *www.crt.state.la.us/crt/tourism/capitol/capitol. htm.* ☑ *Free.* ☉ *Daily 8–4:30; last tour at 4.*

Only one Revolutionary War battle was fought outside the 13 original colonies, and it was fought on the State Capitol grounds. One of the historic buildings, the **Old Arsenal Museum,** a restored heavy-duty structure dating from about 1838, is a terrific place for children. The museum has hands-on exhibits set up inside powder kegs, displays on Louisiana's Native American history, and a giant jigsaw puzzle comparing the grounds as they appear today to 1865. ⊠ *State Capitol grounds, Capitol District,* ☎ *225/342–0401.* ☑ *$1.* ☉ *Weekdays 9– 4, Sat. 10–4, Sun. 1–4.*

★ When the castlelike, Gothic Revival **Old State Capitol** was built in 1849, the structure was considered by some to be a masterpiece, by others a monstrosity. No one can deny that the restored building is colorful and dramatic. In the entrance hall a stunning purple, gold, and green spiral staircase winds toward a stained-glass atrium. The building now holds the **Louisiana Center for Political and Government History,** an education and research facility with audiovisual exhibits. In the House chamber a multimedia show plays every hour beginning at 10:15, with the last show at 4. ⊠ *100 North Blvd., at River Rd., Downtown,* ☎ *225/ 342–0500,* WEB *www.sec.state.la.us/museums/osc/osc/osc-index.htm.* ☑ *$4.* ☉ *Tues.–Sat. 10–4, Sun. noon–4.*

Across the street from the Old State Capitol is the **Louisiana Arts & Science Center Riverside Museum,** housed in a 1925 Illinois Central railroad station. There is a fine-arts museum with changing exhibits, an Egyptian tomb exhibit, restored trains from the 1890s to the 1950s, and a Discovery Depot with a children's art gallery and workshop. Once a month the museum presents a hands-on *Challenger* simulated space flight. Call for specific times. ⊠ *100 S. River Rd., Downtown,* ☎ *225/ 344–5272,* WEB *www.lascmuseum.org.* ☑ *$3; Sun. $1.* ☉ *Tues.–Fri. 10– 3, Sat. 10–4, Sun. 1–4.*

After an extensive two-year restoration that involved peeling multiple layers of paint off the walls to reveal original colors and handsome frieze work, the **Old Governor's Mansion** is again worth a visit. Built in 1930, during Huey Long's administration, the mansion has memorabilia that pertains to each governor who has served since the house was built—for example, in the Jimmy Davis room a saddle and cowboy hats are exhibited, and the Mike Foster room displays include wicker furniture used during his grandfather's administration. Each of the seven bathrooms is in a different, often vivid pastel (though some of the toilets are inexplicably missing). ⊠ *502 North Blvd., Downtown,* ☎ *225/ 343–3989,* WEB *www.cr.nps.gov/nr/travel/louisiana/ogov.htm.* ☑ *$4.* ☉ *Tues.–Fri. 10–4.*

The **Enchanted Mansion** is, indeed, an enchanting place. Included in its collection of more than 2,000 dolls are Shirley Temple dolls from the 1930s, antiques made between 1850 and 1925, a white-haired Mark Twain likeness, and an animated Huey Long making a stump speech.

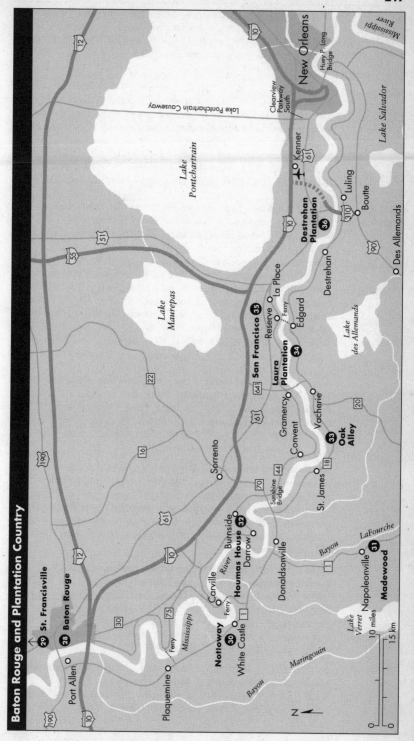

Baton Rouge and Plantation Country

The oldest doll is St. Michael the Archangel, which dates from 1750. Perched here and there are Animatronic clocks and animals, as well as talking dolls. ⊠ *190 Lee Dr., LSU Area,* ☎ *225/769–0005,* WEB *www.angelfire.com/la2/enchantedmansion/.* ⊡ *$4.50.* ☉ *Mon. and Wed.–Sat. 10–5, Sun. 1–4.*

★ The **USS Kidd,** a Fletcher-class destroyer, is a World War II survivor restored to its V-J Day configuration. A brochure details a self-guided tour that takes in more than 50 inner spaces of this ship and also the separate **Nautical History Museum.** Among its exhibits are articles from the 175 Fletcher-class ships that sailed for the United States, a collection of ship models, and a restored P-40 fighter plane hanging from the ceiling. ⊠ *305 S. River Rd. (Government St. at the levee), Downtown,* ☎ *225/342–1942,* WEB *www.usskidd.com.* ⊡ *$6.* ☉ *Daily 9–5.*

OFF THE BEATEN PATH — **ALLIGATOR BAYOU** – Eco-tours into a 900-acre backwater swampland are conducted aboard a 49-passenger covered barge, with lively commentary about the alligators, snakes, 250 species of birds, and giant cypress trees that abound here. Food, music, and Cajun and zydeco dance lessons are provided during regularly scheduled parties on a rustic pavilion; canoe rentals and nature walks are available. To reach Alligator Bayou from downtown Baton Rouge, take I–10 to Exit 166 at Highland Road and go east for half a block; turn right on Old Perkins Road and right again at LA Hwy 928. Immediately after crossing over I–10, turn right on Alligator Bayou Road. ⊠ *35019 Alligator Bayou Rd., South Baton Rouge,* ☎ *225/642–8297 or 888/379–2677,* WEB *www.alligatorbayou.com.* ⊡ *$15.* ☉ *Tours daily by appointment.*

About 1½ mi from the center of town, **Magnolia Mound Plantation** (circa 1791) is a raised cottage furnished with federal antiques and Louisiana artifacts. On Tuesday and Thursday, from October through May, cooking demonstrations are conducted in the outbuildings. ⊠ *2161 Nicholson Dr., LSU Area,* ☎ *225/343–4955,* WEB *www.magnoliamound.org.* ⊡ *$5.* ☉ *Tues.–Sat. 10–4, Sun. 1–4.*

Louisiana State University (LSU) was founded in Pineville in 1860. Its president was William Tecumseh Sherman, who resigned when war broke out; he made his famous march through Georgia four years later. The 200-acre campus has several museums as well as Indian burial mounds that are of particular interest to archaeology buffs. ⊠ *1 mi south of Magnolia Mound Plantation on Nicholson Dr.,* ☎ *225/388–3202,* WEB *www.lsu.edu.*

Spread over 5 acres of the 450-acre Burden Research Plantation, the LSU **Rural Life Museum** is an outdoor teaching and research facility. With three major areas—the Barn, the Working Plantation, and Folk Architecture—the compound's 20 or so rustic 19th-century structures represent the rural life of early Louisianians. The working plantation's several buildings include a gristmill, a blacksmith's shop, and several outbuildings. ⊠ *Essen La. off I–10,* ☎ *225/765–2437.* ⊡ *$5.* ☉ *Daily 8:30–5.*

Baton Rouge's other major institution of higher learning besides Louisiana State University is **Southern University.** Founded in 1880, Southern U is the nation's largest predominantly black university. ⊠ *About 5 mi north of town on U.S. 61,* ☎ *225/771–4500,* WEB *www.subr.edu.*

OFF THE BEATEN PATH — **PORT HUDSON STATE COMMEMORATIVE AREA** – This 650-acre park is the site of a fiercely fought Civil War battle that was the longest siege in American military history. There are high viewing towers, gun trenches, and, on the first Sunday of each month, small-arms demonstrations.

Seven miles of hiking trails wend peacefully throughout the park, 14 mi north of Baton Rouge on U.S. 61. ⊠ *756 W. Plains–Port Hudson Rd. (U.S. 61), Baker,* ☎ *225/654–3775.* ⊠ *$2.* ☉ *Wed.–Sun. 9–5.*

Dining and Lodging

$$–$$$$ ✕ **Drusilla's.** This rambling restaurant has large rooms decorated with murals and paintings of sea scenes and sea creatures, setting the mood for the food served here. Standout appetizers include escargot in mushroom caps, fried crab fingers, and oysters on the half shell. A Taste of Louisiana—a sampling of seafood gumbo, seafood eggplant casserole, shrimp au gratin, fried shrimp, fried catfish, french fries, and salad— is a good choice. There are several Cajun-fried sea critters and a lengthy list of broiled dishes. ⊠ *3482 Drusilla La. (Drusilla Shopping Center), South Baton Rouge,* ☎ *225/923–0896. AE, DC, MC, V.*

$$–$$$$ ✕ **Juban's.** An upscale bistro with a lush courtyard and walls adorned ★ with art, Juban's is a family-owned and -operated restaurant that proudly presents its specialty—Hallelujah Crabs, a delectable concoction of stuffed soft-shell crabs dressed in a Creole sauce. The sophisticated menu offers oysters Rockefeller and Bienville, and tempting main courses of seafood, beef, and veal dishes, as well as roasted duck, rabbit, and quail. Juban's own mango tea is delicious. The warm bread pudding is something to write home about. ⊠ *3739 Perkins Rd. (Acadiana Shopping Center), LSU Area,* ☎ *225/346–8422. AE, DC, MC, V. Closed Sun. No lunch Sat.*

$–$$ ✕ **Christina's.** Downtown businesspeople flock here for hearty, inexpensive breakfasts (two-fisted biscuits, pancakes, and the like) and lunches (spaghetti and meatballs is usually a special). In addition to plate lunches there are plenty of salads, sandwiches, and po'boys. The atmosphere couldn't be more casual, and the most expensive item is the rib eye for $7.95. ⊠ *320 St. Charles St., Downtown,* ☎ *225/336– 9512. AE, MC, V. Closed Sun. No dinner.*

$–$$ ✕ **Mamacita's.** Gussied up with splashy murals of Mexican scenes, bright hues of pink and green, and sombreros hanging here and there, Mamacita's is very popular with locals. A whole raft of combination platters, fajitas, burritos, tacos, and enchiladas are on the list, and portions are huge. Gringos can order "Less-Mex" items, such as mesquite-grilled burgers, grilled red snapper, and barbecued pork ribs. ⊠ *7524 Bluebonnet Blvd. (Bluebonnet Village), Bluebonnet,* ☎ *225/769–3850. AE, D, DC, MC, V.*

$–$$ ⊞ **Courtyard Baton Rouge Acadian Center.** Three miles from LSU, this three-story Marriott property has rooms in traditional decor complete with homey details such as a coffeemaker, a hair dryer, an iron and ironing board, and a desk with good lighting. Other amenities include phones with voice mail and data ports and a complimentary newspaper delivered to your door on weekdays. ⊠ *2421 S. Acadian Thruway, 70808,* ☎ *225/924–6400 or 800/321–2211,* FAX *225/923–3041. 149 rooms, 12 suites. Lounge, laundry facilities, business services. AE, D, DC, MC, V.*

$–$$ ⊞ **Embassy Suites.** This centrally located property has two-room suites, with peach-and-green decor, mahogany furniture, and a galley kitchen with microwave and coffeemaker. The complimentary full breakfast is cooked to order. ⊠ *4914 Constitution Ave., Downtown, 70808,* ☎ *225/924–6566 or 800/433–4600,* FAX *225/923–3712,* WEB *www.embassysuites.com. 224 suites. Restaurant, room service, indoor pool, sauna, steam room, bar, shop, laundry service, airport shuttle. AE, D, DC, MC, V.*

$–$$ ⊞ **Marriott Baton Rouge.** This high-rise hotel has somewhat formal rooms and public spaces with traditional furnishings. Of the six suites, two are split-level; the top two floors offer VIP perks such as Continental breakfast and afternoon hors d'oeuvres and cocktails. ✉ *5500 Hilton Ave., 70808,* ☎ *225/924–5000; 800/228–9290,* ℻ *225/926– 8152. 300 rooms, 6 suites. Restaurant, coffee shop, room service, 2 tennis courts, health club, sauna, lobby lounge, laundry service, concierge, business services, airport shuttle; no-smoking rooms. AE, D, DC, MC, V.*

Nightlife and the Arts

BARS AND NIGHTCLUBS

In an old movie house, the **Varsity Theatre** (✉ 3353 Highland Rd., LSU Area, ☎ 225/343–5267 or 225/383–7018) presents live shows, live music, and dancing. Pool tables along with blues, acoustic, and alternative bands attract a crowd to the **Caterie** (✉ Acadian Perkins Plaza, 3617 Perkins Rd., LSU Area, ☎ 225/383–4178). The popular **Chimes** (✉ 3357 Highland Rd., next to Varsity Theatre, LSU Area, ☎ 225/ 383–1754) has 40 draft beers; it draws businesspeople for lunch and happy hour, but after 10 PM the collegiates reign. **Gino's Restaurant** (✉ 4542 Bennington Ave., College Square, ☎ 225/927–7156) has a piano bar and occasionally a jazz trio. **Tabby's Blues Box & Heritage Hall** (✉ 244 Lafayette St., Downtown, ☎ 225/387–9715) is the home court for local blues legend Tabby Thomas and his pals. There's live jazz on weekends at **M's Fine & Mellow Cafe** (✉ 143 N. 3rd St., Downtown, ☎ 225/344–5368).

CAJUN CLUBS

Mulate's (✉ 8322 Bluebonnet Rd., Bluebonnet, ☎ 225/767–4794, ⓦⒺⒷ www.mulates.com), in Baton Rouge, is a chip off the famed old Breaux Bridge block.

CONCERTS

Touring Broadway shows and top-name stars are booked into the **Centroplex Theatre for the Performing Arts** (☎ 225/389–3030). Guest soloists perform frequently with the **Baton Rouge Symphony Orchestra** (✉ Centroplex Theatre for the Performing Arts, ☎ 225/387– 6166). LSU's annual **Festival of Contemporary Music** (☎ 225/388–5128), which takes place in February, is more than 40 years old.

COUNTRY AND WESTERN

The **Texas Club** (✉ 456 N. Donmoor Ave., Downtown, ☎ 225/928– 4655) is the hot spot for top-name country artists.

RIVERBOAT CASINOS

The **Casino Rouge** (☎ 800/447–6843) docks across from the capitol and is loaded up with games of chance and lively entertainment. The **Argosy Casino** (☎ 800/676–4847), formerly called the Belle of Baton Rouge, is a three-deck riverboat casino with all the games and entertainment you'd expect; it's berthed at Catfish Town, at the foot of South Boulevard.

THEATER

The **Swine Palace Theatre** (✉ LSU Theater on Dalrymple Dr., LSU campus, ☎ 225/388–5128) is an Equity theater whose director is the estimable Barry Kyle. The **Baton Rouge Little Theatre** (✉ 7155 Florida Blvd., Downtown, ☎ 225/924–6496) has been presenting musicals, comedies, and dramas for more than 40 years. **Cabaret Theatre** (✉ 3116 College Dr., LSU Area, ☎ 225/927–7529) presents productions by local groups.

Outdoor Activities and Sports

GOLF

Baton Rouge has two championship 18-hole, par-72 golf courses open to the public. **Santa Maria** (✉ 1930 Perkins Rd., LSU Area, ☎ 225/

752–9667) does not offer rentals. **Webb Park** (⊠ 1351 Country Club Dr., Southeast Baton Rouge, ☎ 225/383–4919), which is close to most hotels, rents clubs for $5.40.

SWIMMING

Blue Bayou Waterpark & Dixie Landin' Amusement Park, the state's largest water park, has a wave pool, a seven-story slide, and a lazy river. For the little ones there's a 7,000-square-ft pollywog pool. The amusement park includes roller coaster rides. There's also a seafood restaurant, a chicken restaurant, a pizzeria, and a fast-food facility. ⊠ *18142 Perkins Rd., off I–10, Baton Rouge,* ☎ *225/753–3333.* ☜ *$18.* ☉ *June–Labor Day, daily 10–6.*

TENNIS

You can lob and volley at the tennis courts of **City Park** (⊠ 1440 City Park Ave., Downtown, ☎ 225/344–4501). Newly constructed courts are found at **Highland Road Park** (⊠ Highland and Amiss Rd., Southeast Baton Rouge, ☎ 225/766–0247). Another venue for tennis aficionados is **Independence Park** (⊠ 549 Lobdell Ave., Mid-City, ☎ 225/923–1792).

St. Francisville

29 *25 mi north of Baton Rouge on U.S. 61.*

Described as a town 2 mi long and 2 yards wide, much of long, skinny St. Francisville is listed on the National Register of Historic Places. You'll find a number of bed-and-breakfasts here; call 225/635–3688 or check out www.stfrancisville.net for full listings.

Not to be confused with nearby Butler-Greenwood, **Greenwood Plantation** is a 1960s restoration of a grand 1830s Greek Revival mansion. It's a working plantation that produces hay and pecans, and raises cattle. Fully furnished with some of the original antiques and portraits, the house also has a widow's walk and a 70-ft hall with silver doorknobs and hinges. It has been the location for six movies, including *The North and The South.* ⊠ *LA 968, 3 mi. off LA 66,* ☎ *225/655–4475.* ☜ *$4.* ☉ *Mar.–Oct., daily 9–5; Nov.–Feb., daily 10–4.*

The Myrtles is noted for its 110-ft gallery with Wedgwood-blue cast-iron grillwork, a lovely setting for the weddings and receptions frequently held here. The house was built around 1796 and has elegant formal parlors with rich molding and faux-marble paneling. Friday- and Saturday-night mystery tours buttress the Myrtles' claim to the title America's Most Haunted House. The Carriage House Restaurant is a fine place for dinner. ⊠ *7747 U.S. 61, about 1 mi north of downtown St. Francisville on U.S. 61,* ☎ *225/635–6277.* ☜ *$8, mystery tours $10.* ☉ *Daily 9–5.*

Rosedown Plantation and Gardens, an opulent house that dates from 1835, is beautifully restored, and nestles in 28 acres of exquisite formal gardens. At this time, only tours of the mansion's exterior are offered. *12501 LA 10, just off U.S. 61,* ☎ *225/635–3332.* ☜ *$10.* ☉ *Mar.–Oct., daily 9–5; Nov.–Feb., daily 10–4.*

OFF THE
BEATEN PATH
AUDUBON STATE COMMEMORATIVE AREA – A few miles south of St. Francisville, off U.S. 61, you'll find the 100-acre park where John James Audubon did a major portion of his *Birds of America* studies. The three-story Oakley Plantation House on the grounds is where Audubon tutored the young Eliza Pirrie. ⊠ *LA 956,* ☎ *225/635–3739.* ☜ *Park and plantation $2.* ☉ *Daily 9–5.*

Lodging

$$
★ ⊞ **Butler Greenwood.** Shaded by live oaks draped with Spanish moss, Anne Butler's home—a two-story frame house with a wraparound veranda, dormers, and gables—was built in the early 1800s. A house tour, which includes such items as a 12-piece set of rosewood Victorian furniture, is part of an overnight stay. The B&B accommodations are in seven uniquely decorated cottages. Each has a TV, a hot tub, and a kitchen or kitchenette stocked with a coffeemaker, toaster oven, fresh juice, croissants, cereal, and fruit so you can prepare breakfast at your leisure. ⊠ 8345 U.S. 61, 70775, ☎ 225/635–6312, FAX 225/635–6370, WEB www. butlergreenwood.com. 7 cottages. Kitchenettes, pool. AE, MC, V.

Outdoor Activities and Sports

The Bluffs (⊠ LA 965, 6 mi east of U.S. 61, ☎ 225/634–5551) is an 18-hole, par-72 Arnold Palmer golf course. Reserve your tee time at least four days in advance. Club rentals are $20, golf carts are $12 per person, and greens fees are $60 ($70 from Friday through Sunday).

En Route Drive aboard the **ferry** ($1 per car) just outside St. Francisville for a breezy ride across the Mississippi. Pick up LA 1 in New Roads and head south. You'll be driving right alongside False River, which was an abandoned riverbed that became a lake. In contrast to the muddy Mississippi, False River is dark blue. This is an excellent fishing area, and you'll see long piers and fishing boats tied up all along the route.

White Castle

18 mi south of Baton Rouge on LA 1 on the east bank of the Mississippi.

30 White Castle is best known for **Nottoway,** the South's largest plantation home, built in 1859 by famed architect Henry Howard. Legend has it that the town, founded in 1885, was named for the plantation, which looked to residents like a magnificent castle. Others say the town was named for a grand plantation that no longer exists. The Greek Revival/Italianate mansion has 64 rooms filled with antiques and is noted for its white ballroom with original crystal chandeliers and hand-carved Corinthian columns. Some of the rooms are open for overnighters. Before you leave the lush grounds, walk across the road and go up on the levee for a splendid view of Old Man River. ⊠ 30970 LA 405, 2 mi north of White Castle, ☎ 225/346–8263, WEB www.nottoway.com. ⊡ $10. ☉ Daily 9–5.

OFF THE
BEATEN PATH

JOE'S "DREYFUS STORE." This restaurant ($$–$$$) 35 mi west of Baton Rouge is simply one of Louisiana's best. The rustic frame house contained the Dreyfus Store from 1920 until 1989; shelves along the wall are still lined with relics from its general-store days, and the restaurant still uses many of the store's original chairs and cabinets. The atmosphere is quite casual. The highly creative cuisine includes sherry-spiked turtle soup; bacon-wrapped, charbroiled quail; and a superb pork tenderloin, marinated, charbroiled, and served on a bed of braised red cabbage. ⊠ 2731 Maringouin Dr. (Rte. 77S), Livonia, ☎ 225/637–2625, WEB www.dreyfushouse.com. Reservations not accepted. No credit cards. Closed Mon. No dinner Sun.

Lodging

$$$–$$$$ ⊞ **Nottoway.** A massive Italianate mansion with elegant, antiques-filled rooms, this is reputed to be one of the most stunning B&Bs in the nation. Guests are welcomed with complimentary sherry upon arrival.

Your first breakfast of the day—of croissants, juice, and coffee—is served in your room; the second breakfast a short while later is a full feast in the Magnolia Room. ✉ *30970 LA 405, 2 mi north of White Castle, 70788,* ☎ *225/346–8263,* WEB *www.nottoway.com. 13 rooms. Dining room, lounge, room phones, room TVs, no-smoking rooms, pool. AE, D, MC, V.*

Donaldsonville

17 mi south of White Castle on LA 1.

In 1770 there was a settlement on this site called Fourche de Chitimacha. A town with the current name was founded in 1806; for a brief period in 1825 it was the state capital. A newspaper reporter at the time wrote that the capital was moved from New Orleans to Donaldsonville because the Crescent City was considered a "modern Sodom."

Dining

$$$–$$$$ ✕ **Lafitte's Landing at Bittersweet Plantation.** The Acadian cottage
★ that housed this stellar restaurant burned to the ground in 1998, and proprietor/chef John Folse—renowned the world over in culinary circles—immediately set about restoring his one-time residence in downtown Donaldsonville as the "new" Lafitte's Landing. Everything about the place is elegant, from the decor to the presentation of such Folse classics as Death by Gumbo, amberjack Magnolia Ridge (pan-seared and Jack Daniels–glazed) and sautéed fillet of trout on butternut beurre blanc topped with crawfish tails. There are two sumptuous suites for overnight guests. ✉ *404 Claiborne Ave.,* ☎ *225/473–1232. Reservations essential. Jacket required. D, MC, V.* ☺ *Closed Mon. No lunch Tues.–Sat.*

Napoleonville

16 mi southeast of Donaldsonville: take LA 70 and Spur 70 from Donaldsonville south to LA 308, and proceed southeast on LA 308 to Napoleonville.

Contrary to what many people think, Napoleonville was named not for the Little Corporal, but for a family of Napoleons who were early settlers. The town now has a population of just over 800.

★ ㉛ Henry Howard, of Nottoway fame, was also the architect for **Madewood** (☞ *below*), a magnificent 21-room Greek Revival mansion with double galleries and white columns. *A Woman Called Moses,* starring Cicely Tyson, was filmed in the house. Visitors can opt for tea with a tour, or lunch with a tour; reservations are not required for either. Madewood is open daily 10–5; admission is $8.

Lodging

$$$$ 🏨 **Madewood.** Expect gracious Southern hospitality in this antiques-filled Greek Revival mansion. What sets Madewood apart is its warmth as well as its elegance. As the weekend country home of the Marshall family, it exudes a comfortably lived-in ambience lacking at other plantation mansions. There are five rooms in the main mansion, and three suites in a cottage behind it. The room or suite rate includes not only a full breakfast but wine and cheeses in the parlor, followed by a candlelit Southern dinner in the stately dining room. ✉ *4250 LA 308, 2 mi south of Napoleonville, 70390,* ☎ *225/369–7151 or 800/375–7151,* WEB *www.madewood.com. 5 rooms, 3 suites. Dining room, no room phones, no room TVs, croquet, library, no kids under 10, no smoking. AE, D, MC, V.*

Burnside

20 mi northwest of Napoleonville: go 16 mi on LA 308 to Donald-sonville, then cross the Sunshine Bridge to LA 44 on the west bank and continue west for 4 mi.

The town is named for John Burnside who, in 1840, bought 20,000 acres of land and built Houmas House. On the east bank of the Mis-sissippi River, docents in antebellum garb guide you through **Houmas House,** a Greek Revival masterpiece famed for its three-story spiral stair-case. *Hush Hush, Sweet Charlotte,* with Bette Davis and Olivia de Hav-illand, was filmed here. ✉ *LA 942, ½ mi off LA 44,* ☎ *888/323–8314.* 🖭 *$8.* ⊙ *Feb.–Oct., daily 10–5; Nov.–Jan., daily 10–4.*

Vacherie

24 mi southeast of Burnside via the Sunshine Bridge and LA 18.

Although *vacherie* is a French word meaning pasturelands, this area was originally settled by Germans who came here shortly after the 1718 founding of New Orleans. Later inhabitants were Acadians.

Like many of its neighbors, the plantation **Oak Alley** is a movie star, having served as the setting for the Don Johnson/Cybill Shepherd TV remake of *The Long Hot Summer* and more recently for scenes in the Tom Cruise film *Interview with the Vampire*. The house dates from 1839, and the 28 gnarled and arching live oaks trees that give the house its name were planted in the early 1700s. There is a splendid view of those trees from the upper gallery. The plantation also has a restau-rant and overnight accommodations on the grounds. ✉ *3645 LA 18, 7½ mi upriver of Gramercy/Wallace Bridge,* ☎ *225/265–2151 or 800/442–5539,* 🌐 *www.oakalleyplantation.com.* 🖭 *$10.* ⊙ *Nov.–Feb., daily 9–5; Mar.–Oct., daily 9–5:30.*

Different from the dressed-up River Road mansions, **Laura Plantation** is an in-progress restoration of the main house and six slave cabins of a former sugar plantation. The $1.3 million project, scheduled for com-pletion in 2005, will include B&B accommodations. Opened for tours in 1994, it is named for the 1805 owner/manager Laura Locoul, and the restoration is based on historical documents that include 100 pages of her diary. The Br'er Rabbit stories are said to have first been told here by Senegalese slaves. ✉ *2247 Hwy. 18, Vacherie,* ☎ *225/265–7690,* 🌐 *www.lauraplantation.com.* 🖭 *$10.* ⊙ *Daily 9–5.*

Reserve

12 mi east of Vacherie on the west bank: from Vacherie, take LA 18 on the east bank 4 mi to the Veterans Memorial Bridge, cross the bridge to LA 44 on the west bank and go 5 mi east to Reserve.

Local lore has it that a 19th-century peddler who went from planta-tion to plantation selling trinkets and such was turned away from a particular home (not San Francisco) and vowed he'd "reserve" it for his own. The story (probably apocryphal) continues that the planta-tion was later sold at auction, and that the peddler purchased it for little more than a song.

San Francisco, completed in 1856, is an elaborate Steamboat Gothic house noted for its ornate millwork and ceiling frescoes. ✉ *LA 44 near Reserve,* ☎ *504/535–2341.* 🖭 *$8.* ⊙ *Daily 10–4:30.*

Destrehan

5 mi east of Reserve via LA 44 and LA 48 (the Great River Rd.), 23 mi from New Orleans via LA 48.

This town was named in the 18th century for one d'Estrehan des Tours, who was a royal treasurer when Louisiana was a French colony.

36 **Destrehan Plantation** is the oldest plantation left intact in the lower Mississippi Valley. The simple West Indies–style house, dating from 1787, is typical of the homes built by the earliest planters in the region. ⊠ *9999 River Rd.,* ☎ *504/764–9315 or 504/764–9345,* WEB *www. destrehanplantation.org.* ⌦ *$10.* ☉ *Daily 9–4.*

Baton Rouge and Plantation Country A to Z

AIR TRAVEL
Baton Rouge is served by American, Continental, Delta, and Northwest.

AIRPORTS
Baton Rouge Metropolitan Airport is 12 mi north of downtown.
➤ AIRPORT INFORMATION: **Baton Rouge Metropolitan Airport** (⊠ 9430 Jackie Cochran Dr., ☎ 225/355–0333).

BUS TRAVEL
Greyhound Southeast Lines has frequent daily service from New Orleans to Baton Rouge and surrounding towns.
➤ BUS INFORMATION: **Greyhound Southeast Lines** (☎ 800/231–2222).

CAR TRAVEL
I–10 and U.S. 190 run east–west through Baton Rouge. I–12 heads east, connecting with north–south I–55 and I–59. U.S. 61 leads from New Orleans to Baton Rouge and north. Ferries across the Mississippi cost $1 per car; most bridges are free.

LA 1 travels along False River, which is a blue oxbow lake created ages ago when the mischievous, muddy Mississippi changed its course. The route wanders past gracious homes and small lakeside houses.

EMERGENCIES
Dial 911 for assistance. Hospital emergency rooms are open 24 hours a day at Baton Rouge General Medical Center and Our Lady of the Lake Medical Center. Eckerd and Walgreens have 24-hour pharmacies.
➤ HOSPITALS: **Baton Rouge General Medical Center** (⊠ 3600 Florida Blvd., ☎ 225/387–7000). **Our Lady of the Lake Medical Center** (⊠ 5000 Hennessy Blvd., ☎ 225/765–6565).
➤ 24-HR PHARMACIES: **Eckerd** (⊠ 4530 S. Sherwood Forest Blvd., ☎ 225/291–0596). **Walgreens** (⊠ 4747 S. Sherwood Forest Blvd., ☎ 225/292–8975).

MEDIA
RADIO
AM: KBRH 1260, CNN news/talk; WIBR 1300, news/talk/sports.

FM: WBRH 90.3, jazz/alternative; WYNK 101.5, country.

TOURS
Tiger Taxi & Tours runs Baton Rouge city tours, tours of plantation country, and swamp tours. Rachel Hall's St. Francisville Tours conducts van tours of the Feliciana parishes north of Baton Rouge and of Cajun Country.

➤ FEES AND SCHEDULES: **Rachel Hall's St. Francisville Tours** (☎ 225/ 635–6283). **Tiger Taxi & Tours** (☎ 225/921–9199 or 225/635–4641).

VISITOR INFORMATION
➤ TOURIST INFORMATION: **Baton Rouge Area Convention and Visitors Bureau** (✉ 730 North Blvd., Box 4149, Baton Rouge 70804, ☎ 225/ 383–1825 or 800/527–6843). **Louisiana Visitor Information Center** (✉ Louisiana State Capitol Bldg., State Capitol Dr., Box 94291, Baton Rouge 70808-9291, ☎ 225/342–7317, FAX 225/342–8390, WEB www. louisianatravel.com). **West Feliciana Historical Society Information Center** (✉ 364 Ferdinand St., St. Francisville, ☎ 225/635–6330).

CAJUN COUNTRY
Lafayette, Abbeville, Lake Charles, Opelousas

French Louisiana has become famous in the rest of the country through its food (po'boys and blackened fish) and music (zydeco). Many people who live here are Cajuns, descendants of 17th-century French settlers who established a colony they called l'Acadie in the present-day Canadian provinces of Nova Scotia and New Brunswick. The Acadians—"Cajun" is a corruption of "Acadian"—were expelled by the British in the mid-18th century. Their exile was described by Henry Wadsworth Longfellow in his epic poem "Evangeline." They eventually found a home in South Louisiana, and there they have been since 1762, imbuing the region, the state, and the nation with their unique cuisine and culture. The flavor of the region is summed up in the Cajun phrase *Laissez les bons temps rouler!* (Let the good times roll).

U.S. 90 drops down from New Orleans into the marshlands of Houma, an area that abounds with campgrounds and charter freshwater and saltwater fishing boats. This route will take you through Morgan City, where the first Tarzan film was made; Franklin, an official Main Street USA town; and one of the state's Native American reservations. The rambling Bayou Teche (pronounced tesh) leads into St. Martinville in Evangeline Country, and next you'll head for Lafayette, which proudly calls itself, with some justification, the capital of French Louisiana. LA 14 is the scenic route to Lake Charles, which is fishing, camping, and bird-watching territory. Looping back toward Baton Rouge, you'll go through the area famed for the Courir de Mardi Gras, or Mardi Gras Run, during which masked and costumed horseback riders make a mad dash through the countryside. The trip ends near Baton Rouge on the Mississippi River.

While you're in Cajun Country, try to experience chank-a-chanking at a *fais do-do* (pronounced *fay* doh-doh). The little iron triangles in most Cajun bands make a rhythmic chank-a-chank sound, and most folks call dancing to the rhythm chank-a-chanking. As for fais do-do, that's the dance, or party, where you go to chank-a-chank. Fais do-dos crop up all over Cajun Country, sometimes in the town square, sometimes at somebody's house. There are also restaurants, dance halls, and lounges that regularly feature live Cajun music. The *Times of Acadiana* is a free newspaper that comes out every Wednesday and is available in hotels, restaurants, and shops. Check the "On the Town" section to see what's doing in the area.

Many restaurants and lounges regularly feature music for two-stepping, waltzing, and chank-a-chanking. Sunday afternoon is often devoted to dancing. Be sure to call to find out the schedule.

Numbers in the margin correspond to points of interest on the Cajun Country map.

Houma

37 *57 mi south of New Orleans on U.S. 90.*

Houma, in Terrebonne Parish, dates from 1795 and is in the heart of the old Hache Spanish Land Grant. The town is named for the Houmas Indians (the stressed first syllable of Houma sounds like "home"). Terrebonne Parish is a major center for shrimp and oyster fisheries, and the blessing of the shrimp fleets in Chauvin and Dulac is a colorful April event.

OFF THE BEATEN PATH
WILDLIFE GARDENS – The 1½-hr guided walking tour through this 30-acre park gives a real feel for swamp life. Creatures in the natural-habitat facility include bobcats, wild boar, turtles, peacocks, and a great-horned owl. There are twilight boat tours and a working alligator farm. Nature lovers can B&B in one of four rustic trapper's cabins. ✉ *14 mi west of Houma on U.S. 90 in Gibson,* ☎ *504/575–3676.* ✆ *$8, twilight boat tours $20.* ☉ *Grounds Tues.–Sat. 9–5; tours Sept.–May, Tues.–Sat. 10, 1, and 3:30; June–Aug., Tues.–Sat. 10 and 3:30.*

Morgan City

38 *37 mi northwest of Houma on U.S. 90.*

Morgan City, smack on the Atchafalaya River, struck it rich when the first oil-producing offshore well, Kerr-McGee Rig No. 16, was completed on November 14, 1947. Front Street runs alongside the 22-mi-long flood wall.

Atop the Great Wall, **Moonwalk** is a lookout with a great view of the Atchafalaya and displays depicting the history of the region. At the **Morgan City Information Center** you can see a video of the first Tarzan movie, which was filmed here in 1917. ✉ *725 Myrtle St.,* ☎ *504/384–3343.* ☉ *Daily 8–5.*

You can take a guided tour of 3½-acre **Swamp Gardens,** a heritage park that depicts the settlement of Atchafalaya Basin; displays include pirogues and other aspects of bayou life. ✉ *725 Myrtle St.,* ☎ *504/ 384–3343.* ✆ *$3.* ☉ *Tours Mon. 11, 1, 2, 3, and 4; Tues.–Sat. 10, 11, 1, 2, 3, and 4; Sun. 1, 2, 3, and 4.*

Franklin

39 *20 mi northwest of Morgan City on U.S. 90.*

If you're of a nostalgic bent, you'll love Franklin's **Main Street,** which was named an official Main Street USA by the National Trust for Historic Preservation. The street rolls out beneath an arcade of live oaks, and old-fashioned street lamps with NO HITCHING signs line the boulevard. Franklin is nestled along a bend in the bayou, and there is a splendid view of it from **Parc sur le Teche.** (To reach the park as you drive north through town, turn right on Willow Street by the courthouse square.)

For information about this pretty town and its environs, stop at the **St. Mary Parish Tourist Commission** (✉ 1600 Northwest Blvd., ☎ 337/828–2555).

A good way to travel to Franklin is via LA 182, which you pick up just outside Patterson. This is **Bayou Teche** country, and the state high-

228

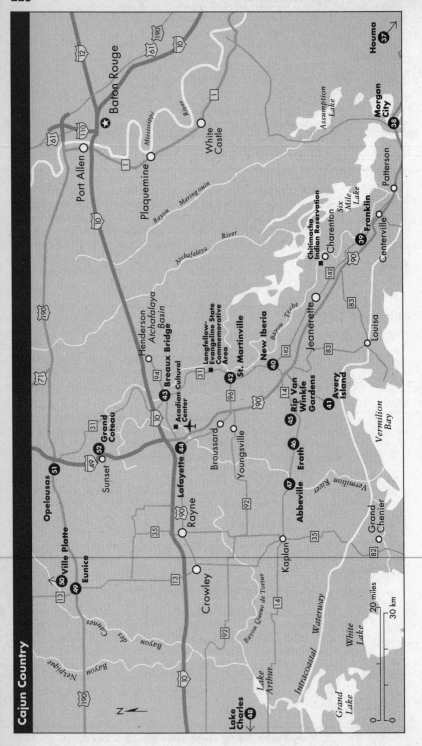

ways follow the writhing bayou along some stretches. *Teche* is a Native American word meaning snake. According to an ancient Indian legend, the death throes of a giant snake carved the bayou.

OFF THE
BEATEN PATH

CHITIMACHA INDIAN RESERVATION – For centuries the Chitimacha flourished along the shores of Bayou Atchafalaya. The tribe's main settlement was in Charenton, site of the present-day reservation. The tribe is famous for its weaving, and Chitimacha baskets as well as other small items are sold in the reservation's crafts shop. ⊠ *LA 326, Charenton, 3 mi north of Franklin,* ☎ *337/923-4830.* ☜ *Free.* ☉ *Daily 8–4:30.*

New Iberia

40 *25 mi northwest of Franklin via U.S. 90 or LA 182.*

New Iberia—the Queen City of the Teche—was founded in 1779 by Spanish settlers, who named the town after the Iberian Peninsula. The town is a blend of Spanish, French, and Acadian cultures.

On the bank of the bayou, in the shadows of moss-draped oaks, **Shadows-on-the-Teche,** built in 1834 for sugar planter David Weeks, is one of the South's best-known plantation homes. ⊠ *317 E. Main St.,* ☎ *337/369–6446.* ☜ *$8.* ☉ *Daily 9–4:30.*

☾ **City Park** is a 45-acre grassy playground across the Teche from Main Street, with tennis courts, playgrounds, baseball and softball fields, a fishing pond, boat ramps, and picnic shelters with barbecue facilities. ☜ *Free.* ☉ *Weekdays 8 AM–9 PM, Sat. 1–9, Sun. 1–5.*

Dining and Lodging

$$ ✕ **Café Lagniappe Too.** Just one block from Shadows-on-the-Teche is Elaine and Al Landry's charming, affordable restaurant. Elaine not only does the cooking, but also makes the huggable, oversize stuffed dolls with funny faces that perch here and there; Al creates the colorful paintings that hang on the walls. For lunch there are salads, soups, and sandwiches; the changing dinner menu might include medallions of veal, grilled quail, and trout meunière. ⊠ *204 E. Main St.,* ☎ *337/365–9419. AE, MC, V. Closed Sun. No lunch Sat.*

$–$$ ✕🏠 **leRosier.** Across the street from Shadows-on-the-Teche, set behind an antique rose garden, leRosier is a small family-run B&B whose dining room ($$–$$$) has won national acclaim. Chef Hallman Woods III has prepared his five-course crawfish degustation for the James Beard Foundation in New York. In addition to seafood there are specialties such as grilled marinated duck breast and rack of lamb. Rooms are quite small but are decorated with antiques or reproductions. ⊠ *314 E. Main St., 70560,* ☎ *337/367–5306 or 888/804–7673,* 𝐅𝐀𝐗 *337/365–1216,* 𝚆𝙴𝙱 *www.leRosier.com. 6 rooms. Restaurant. AE, MC, V.*

Avery Island

41 *7 mi southwest of New Iberia via LA 329.*

Avery Island (it's actually a salt dome) is the birthplace of Tabasco sauce, and descendants of Edmund McIlhenny continue making the spicy condiment he invented in the mid-1800s. Other attractions are the 200-acre **Jungle Gardens,** lush with tropical plants, and **Bird City,** a sanctuary with flurries of snow-white egrets. There's a 50¢ toll to enter Avery Island. ⊠ *Off LA 329,* ☎ *337/369–6243 Jungle Gardens; 337/373–6129 Tabasco factory,* 𝚆𝙴𝙱 *www.tabasco.com.* ☜ *Gardens and sanctuary $5.75; Tabasco factory free.* ☉ *Gardens daily 9–5; factory daily 9–4.*

St. Martinville

42 *10 mi north of New Iberia via LA 31.*

St. Martinville is awash with legends. Longfellow's poem "Evangeline" was based on the story of Emmeline Labiche and Louis Arceneaux, two young lovers separated for years during Canada's Acadian exile (St. Martinville was a major entry point for Acadian refugees). Louis arrived in the town first and waited years hoping to find Emmeline, but eventually despaired of ever seeing her again and became engaged to another woman. Emmeline finally did reach St. Martinville, and, the story is told, Louis saw her by chance as she stepped ashore. Pale with shock, he told her that he was betrothed to another, turned on his heel, and disappeared. Their last, unhappy meeting place was beneath the Evangeline Oak (⊠ Evangeline Blvd. at Bayou Teche). *The Romance of Evangeline* was filmed in St. Martinville in 1929. Dolores Del Rio starred as Evangeline and posed for the bronze statue that the cast and crew donated to the town. You can see the statue in the cemetery behind the church of St. Martin de Tours, near the grave of Emmeline Labiche. In the late 18th century, St. Martinville was known as Petit Paris because it was a major refuge for royalists who fled the French Revolution. Little Paris was the scene of many regal balls, soirees, and operas.

St. Martin de Tours, mother church of the Acadians, is one of the oldest Catholic churches (early 18th century) in the country. Inside there is a replica of the Lourdes Grotto and a baptismal font said to have been a gift from Louis XVI. ⊠ *123 S. Main St.,* ☎ *337/394–2233.* ▣ *$1.* ☉ *Daily 10–4.*

La Remise, the St. Martinville visitor center, is across the street from the Evangeline Oak Park, just behind the Church Square. ⊠ *127 New Market St.,* ☎ *337/394–2233.* ☉ *Daily 9–5.*

La Maison Duchamp is a Classic Revival structure built as a private home in 1876. Here you can see a bedroom furnished with period antiques and turn-of-the-century photographs of the town. Tours are conducted in French and English. ⊠ *Main St. at Evangeline Blvd.,* ☎ *337/394–2229.* ▣ *Free.* ☉ *Daily 9–3.*

Dining and Lodging

$ ✕▦ **La Place d'Evangeline.** This historic redbrick inn, once the Old Castillo Hotel, rests on the banks of the Bayou Teche and beneath the branches of the Evangeline Oak. Eighteenth-century royalists once held lavish balls and operas in what is now the high-ceilinged dining room ($$–$$$). Seafood is king here, with the likes of corn and crab bisque, red snapper (broiled, fried, stuffed, or blackened), and frogs' legs. Don't pass up the homemade bread. Overnighters sleep in large antiques-filled rooms, some with a lovely view of Bayou Teche; all have private baths, and a full breakfast is included. ⊠ *220 Evangeline Blvd., 70582,* ☎ *337/394–4010 or 800/621–3017,* ℻ *318/394–7983. 5 rooms. Restaurant. AE, MC, V.*

Breaux Bridge

43 *13 mi north of St. Martinville on LA 31.*

The little town of Breaux Bridge, which calls itself the Crawfish Capital of the World, is the home of the famous **Mulate's** restaurant. The **Crawfish Festival** (337/332–6655), held in May, draws upwards of 100,000 people.

Dining and Lodging

$$–$$$　✕ **Mulate's.** A roadhouse with flashing yellow lights outside and plas-
★　tic checkered cloths inside, Mulate's is an eatery, a dance hall, an age-
old family gathering spot, and a celebrity, having been featured on the
Today Show and *Good Morning, America,* among other programs. A
dressed-down crowd digs into the likes of stuffed crabs and the Super
Seafood Platters. There's live music at lunch and dinner. ⊠ *325 Mills
Ave.,* ☎ *800/634–9880; 800/422–2586 outside LA. AE, MC, V.*

Nightlife and the Arts

La Poussière (⊠ 1301 Grand Pointe Rd., Breaux Bridge, ☎ 337/332–
1721) is one of the oldest dance halls around, and regularly has live
Cajun music and dancing.

Lafayette

🅰 *9 mi west of Breaux Bridge on LA 94.*

Lafayette is a major center of Cajun lore and life, even if it does lack
the charm and rusticity of smaller, outlying villages. Its excellent restaurants and B&Bs make it a good jumping-off point for exploring the
region. In April the town hosts the Festival International de la Louisiane,
several days of music, food, and crafts, and in the fall Festival Acadiens takes the spotlight. Stop in at the **Lafayette Convention and Visitors Bureau** (⊠ Willow St. and Evangeline Thruway) and load up on
maps and brochures.

☉ The **Acadian Village,** a re-creation of an early 19th-century bayou settlement, has a general store, a blacksmith shop, a chapel, and houses.
In one of the houses, exhibits trace the life and works of native son
and internationally renowned artist George Rodrigue, creator of the
Blue Dog series. ⊠ *200 Greenleaf Rd. (LA 342),* ☎ *337/981–2364.*
⊠ *$6.* ☉ *Daily 10–5.*

The Louisiana Live Oak Society, founded in Lafayette more than 50
years ago, is on the grounds of the **Cathedral of St. John the Evange-
list,** a Romanesque church with Byzantine touches. A charter member
of that silent but leafy set of trees dominates the 900 block of St. John
Street. The **St. John Oak** is 400 years old and has a waistline of about
19 ft. ⊠ *914 St. John St.,* ☎ *337/276–4576.*

☉ The **Lafayette Natural History Museum** is a busy place, with workshops,
movies, concerts, and planetarium programs. It's also the venue for the
annual Louisiana Native & Contemporary Crafts Festival in September. ⊠ *637 Girard Park Dr.,* ☎ *337/291–5544.* ⊠ *Free.* ☉ *Mon. and
Wed.–Fri. 9–5, Tues. 9–9, weekends 1–5.*

☉ The natural history museum's sister facility is the **Acadiana Park Nature Station,** a three-story cypress-pole structure with an interpretive
center and discovery boxes to help children get acquainted with the
wildflowers, birds, and other things they'll see along a 3½-mi trail. ⊠
E. Alexandre St., ☎ *318/291–8448.* ⊠ *Free.* ☉ *Weekdays 9–5, weekends 11–3.*

The **Lafayette Art Gallery** gives visitors a close look at local arts and
crafts. ⊠ *412 Travis St.,* ☎ *337/269–0363.* ⊠ *Free.* ☉ *Tues.–Fri. noon–
5, Sat. by appointment.*

OFF THE　　**ACADIAN CULTURAL CENTER** – The center, a unit of the Jean Lafitte Na-
BEATEN PATH　tional Historical Park and Preserve, traces the history of the Acadians
　　　　　　　through numerous audiovisual exhibits of Cajun music, food, and folk-
　　　　　　　lore. ⊠ *501 Fisher Rd.,* ☎ *337/232–0789 or 337/232–0961.* ⊠
　　　　　　　Free. ☉ *Daily 8–5.*

Dining and Lodging

$$$-$$$$ ✕ **Café Vermilionville.** This 19th-century inn with crisp white napery, old-brick fireplaces, and a casual elegance serves French and Cajun cuisine. Among the specialties are pecan-crusted tilapia, Louisiana crab madness (crabmeat prepared au gratin or étoufféed), and snapper Anna (fillets of snapper sautéed in white wine and butter and laced with crawfish tails, mushrooms, and artichoke hearts). ⊠ *1304 W. Pinhook Rd.,* ☎ *337/237–0100. AE, D, DC, MC, V.*

$$-$$$ ✕ **Blue Dog Café.** In a little redbrick building with a snappy blue canopy, diners eat under the gaze of the wistful Blue Dog, paintings of which decorate the walls. Owned by world-renowned artist and native son George Rodrigue, the upscale eatery features renditions of honey-glazed duck breast and seafood wontons, plus staples such as gumbo, seafood platters, étouffées, and sweet potato–pecan pie. ⊠ *1211 W. Pinhook Rd.,* ☎ *337/237–0005. AE, DC, MC, V.*

$$-$$$ ✕ **Prejean's.** A local favorite, this cypress cottage has a cozy oyster bar, red-checkered cloths, live music nightly, and a jazz brunch on Sunday. Specialties include Prejean's Platter (seafood gumbo, fried shrimp, oysters, catfish, and seafood-stuffed bell peppers), as well as Cajun rack of elk, American buffalo au poivre, steak, and chicken. ⊠ *3480 U.S. 167N, next to Evangeline Downs,* ☎ *337/896–3247,* WEB *www.prejeans. com. AE, DC, MC, V.*

$ ✕ **Hub City Diner.** Quintessential diner fare—hearty breakfasts, chicken-fried steak with mashed potatoes and gravy, Mom's Famous Meat Loaf, plus milk shakes, malts, and sundaes—are served up in this '50s-style diner. You can eat in or take out. ⊠ *1412 S. College St.,* ☎ *337/235–5683. AE, MC, V.*

$ ▥ **Best Western Hotel Acadiana.** This centrally located hotel has standard rooms with marble-top dressers, mini-refrigerators, and wet bars. Rooms on the concierge floor have perks such as Continental breakfast, evening hors d'oeuvres, and turndown service. Even-numbered rooms face the pool. ⊠ *1801 W. Pinhook Rd., 70508,* ☎ *337/233–8120 or 800/826–8386,* FAX *337/234–9667,* WEB *www.bestwestern. com. 301 rooms, 3 suites. Restaurant, pool, 2 hot tubs, bar, airport shuttle. AE, D, DC, MC, V.*

$ ▥ **Holiday Inn Central–Holidome.** Built around an atrium that's banked with greenery, this modern motel has contemporary rooms and 17 acres with playgrounds, picnic areas, and tennis courts. Ask for a second-floor room to avoid the noise of the pool area. ⊠ *2032 N.E. Evangeline Thruway, 70509,* ☎ *337/233–6815 or 800/942–4868,* FAX *337/235–1954,* WEB *www.holidayinn.com. 244 rooms, 6 suites. Restaurant, 2 tennis courts, indoor pool, hot tub, sauna, lobby lounge, recreation rooms, airport shuttle. AE, D, DC, MC, V.*

Nightlife and the Arts

Randol's (⊠ 2320 Kaliste Saloom Rd., ☎ 337/981–7080) has hot dancing in a greenhouse setting. **Antler's** (⊠ 555 Jefferson St., ☎ 337/234–8877), in downtown Lafayette, is the city's oldest dance hall. It also has a lunchroom. Major concerts are held at the **Cajundome** (⊠ 444 Cajundome Blvd., ☎ 337/265–2100). Classical concerts and theater productions take place at **Heymann Performing Arts Center** (⊠ 1373 S. College Rd., ☎ 337/291–5540).

Outdoor Activities and Sports

BIKING

There are 60 mi of marked bike trails in Lafayette; flatlands and lush parks make for easy riding. Four-day to weeklong guided tours of Cajun Country ($500–$1200) are available through **French Louisiana Bike Tours** (⊠ 3216 W. Esplanade Ave., PMB 302, Metairie 70002, ☎ 504/488–

9844 or 800/346–7989, WEB www.flbt.com). Tours include the rental of a Cannondale hybrid bike, van support, lodging, and meals.

ICE HOCKEY

The **Ice Gators** (✉ 444 Cajundome Blvd., Lafayette, ☎ 337/265–2100, WEB www.icegators.com) of the East Coast Ice Hockey League play home games in the Cajundome.

Rip Van Winkle Gardens

🖑 ④⑤ *15 mi south of Lafayette via U.S. 90 and LA 675.*

The 20 acres of formal and informal gardens that make up Rip Van Winkle Gardens (formerly known as Live Oak Gardens) are part of a 5,000-acre tract that was purchased in the late 19th century by an American actor, Joseph Jefferson, who toured the country portraying Rip Van Winkle. On a hunting trip to South Louisiana, Jefferson fell in love with the area's groves of live oaks and lush countryside, and in 1870 he bought the land on which he built a winter home. His land came to be called **Jefferson Island.** The three-story **Jefferson house** is a comfortably opulent Southern Gothic home with Moorish touches. ✉ *5505 Rip Van Winkle Rd., off LA 14,* ☎ *337/365–3332.* 🖽 *House and gardens tour $9.* ☉ *Daily 9–5.*

Erath

④⑥ *24 mi south of Lafayette via U.S. 90 and LA 89.*

Erath's earliest settlers were Acadians who migrated across the state from St. James Parish, near New Orleans. Its name, however, comes from an enterprising Swiss immigrant. In 1860, August Erath (pronounced Eee-rat) came to New Orleans and worked as a bookkeeper in a brewery. Later, he opened his own brewery in New Iberia, as well as a hardware business and soda-and-seltzer-water factory. Erath purchased land in the center of the current town, and when the railroad was built through his property, the town was officially named in honor of him.

You can poke through all sorts of Acadiana at the **Acadian Museum.** The several rooms are filled to the rafters with memorabilia donated by local folks—everything from antique radios and butter churns to patchwork quilts and yellowed newspaper clippings. ✉ *203 S. Broadway,* ☎ *337/233–5832 or 337/937–5468.* 🖽 *Free, but donations welcome.* ☉ *Weekdays 1–4.*

Abbeville

④⑦ *5 mi west of Erath on LA 14.*

Abbeville is a charming town whose picturesque village square has a gazebo and moss-hung live oak trees. The vicinity of the square is the scene of the annual Giant Omelette Festival each November, when some 5,000 eggs go into the concoction. Pick up a self-guided walking tour brochure at the **Abbeville Main Street Program Office** in City Hall (✉ 101 N. State St., ☎ 337/898–4110). Many buildings in the 20-block Main Street district are on the National Register of Historic Places. **St. Mary Magdalen Catholic Church,** adjacent to the village square, is a fine Romanesque Revival building with stunning stained-glass windows.

On an earthy note, Abbeville is home to **Cajun Downs** (✉ on LA 338 off the LA 14 bypass, ☎ 337/893–8160 or 337/893–0421), a "bush" track cut smack through a cane field where all manner of critters race—horses, mules, maybe even pigs or chickens. The track is more than 100 years old and draws a Cajun Runyonesque crowd that cheers on the favorite with great enthusiasm. The track is open only on Sunday, when a half dozen or so races are run. Call first to see if the races are on; schedules tend to be pretty informal here.

OFF THE
BEATEN PATH **ROCKEFELLER WILDLIFE REFUGE –** Fifty-eight miles southwest of Abbeville via LA 82, you'll find an 84,000-acre tract where thousands of ducks, geese, gators, wading birds, otters, and others while away the winter months. ✉ *On LA 82 between villages of Little Pecan Island and Grand Chenier (information center),* ☎ *337/538–2165.* ✆ *Free.* ☉ *Refuge daily sunrise–sunset, information center daily 7–4.*

Lake Charles

④⑧ *74 mi west of Abbeville via LA 14, LA 13, and I–10.*

Lake Charles, the state's third-largest seaport, dates from the 1760s, when the first French settlers arrived. The first home was built by Charles Sallier on the shell beach by the lake, and the town was originally called Charlie's Lake. Today Lake Charles is a sprawling, not very attractive industrial town, whose wildly successful gambling riverboats (drawing in Texas money) have turned it into a boomtown. Nevertheless, the city has more than 50 mi of rivers, lakes, canals, and bayous, making it great for sailing, fishing, canoeing, shrimping, and crabbing.

🛈 **North Beach** is a white-sand beach on the north shore of the lake where you can loll in the sun, swim, or rent a Wave Runner during summer months. ✆ *$1 per vehicle June–Aug.; free other times.*

Twelve miles north of the city, **Sam Houston Jones State Park** is a 1,068-acre recreation area that beckons sports and nature enthusiasts. ✉ *LA 378,* ☎ *337/855–2665.* ✆ *$2 per vehicle.* ☉ *Daily 7 AM–8 PM.*

The **Imperial Calcasieu Museum,** on the site of Charles Sallier's home, has an extensive collection pertaining to Lake Charles and Calcasieu Parish. The museum includes a photograph of the house built by town founder Charles Sallier, an old-fashioned pharmacy, an Audubon collection, and a barbershop. Adjacent to the museum, the Artisans Gallery has paintings, woodwork, ceramics, and jewelry made by local craftspeople. ✉ *204 W. Sallier St., Lake Charles,* ☎ *318/439–3797.* ✆ *$2.* ☉ *Tues.–Fri. 10–5, weekends 1–5.*

🛈 The **Children's Museum** features interactive computers, a nature center, a TV station, a grocery store, and other hands-on exhibits as well as a toddlers' area. ✉ *925 Enterprise Blvd., Lake Charles,* ☎ *318/433–9420.* ✆ *$3.* ☉ *Tues.–Sat. 10–5.*

The **Mardi Gras Museum** is in the Central School Arts & Humanities Center, a restored schoolhouse that dates from 1912. The labyrinthine museum has a huge collection of costumes, headdresses, scepters, and glittering regalia, as well as photographs and exhibits—for example, on the art of costume making. New Orleans gets all the ink, but Carnival in Cajun Country is an event not to be sneezed at—the city boasts 33 krewes (carnival organizations). ✉ *809 Kirby St.,* ☎ *337/430–0043.* ✆ *$3.* ☉ *Tues.–Sat. 1–5.*

Dining and Lodging

$$$–$$$$ ✕ **Café Margaux.** Think candlelight, soft pinks, white linens, tuxedoed
★   waiters, and a 5,000-bottle mahogany wine cellar. Specialties include a marvelous lobster bisque, rack of lamb, good steaks, and roasted quail with raspberry demiglace. ✉ *765 Bayou Pines E,* ☎ *337/433–2902. Jacket and tie. AE, D, MC, V. Closed Sun.*

$-$$ ✕ **Steamboat Bill's.** In this busy, clattering country kitchen, you line up at the counter to place your order for fried, boiled, baked, or stuffed seafood platters. It couldn't be more casual. ⊠ *1004 Lakeshore Dr.,* ☎ *337/494–1070. AE, D, MC, V.*

$-$$ ⬒ **Isle of Capri Casino & Hotel.** This complex boasts two floating gaming palaces that alternate cruising, as well as a flourishing entertainment pavilion. Top-name entertainers appear in the Flamingo Bay Ballroom, which also features boxing matches. The modern six-story all-suites hotel has accommodations done in blond wood and pastels. ⊠ *101 Westlake Ave., Westlake 70669,* ☎ *337/430–2400 or 888/475–3847,* FAX *337/ 430–0963,* WEB *www.isleofcapri.com. 241 suites. 3 restaurants, deli, room service, pool, 2 bars, lobby lounge, 2 casinos, nightclub, video game room, airport shuttle; no-smoking rooms. AE, D, MC, V.*

$-$$ ⬒ **Players Island Casino Hotel.** An 8-acre tropical extravaganza set between the lake and the interstate, this hotel/casino complex has waterfalls, rockscapes, Animatronic tropical birds perched hither and yon, and activity aplenty. Gambling is done on two paddle wheelers, which alternate cruising on Lake Charles. At press time negotiations were under way for the Players to be purchased by Harrah's. ⊠ *507 N. Lakeshore Dr., 70601,* ☎ *337/437–1500 or 800/977–7529,* FAX *337/437–6010,* WEB *www.playersisland.com. 394 rooms, 6 suites. 5 restaurants, coffee shop, room service, pool, gym, 3 bars, lobby lounge, 2 casinos, video game room, airport shuttle; no-smoking rooms. AE, D, MC, V.*

Nightlife and the Arts

Major concerts are held at the **Lake Charles Civic Center** (⊠ 900 Lakeshore Dr., ☎ 337/491–1256). The **Lake Charles Little Theater** (⊠ 813 Enterprise Blvd., ☎ 337/433–7988) puts on a variety of plays and musicals.

CASINOS

Wildly successful since the day it opened, **Grand Casino Coushatta** (⊠ 20 mins north of I–10 on U.S. 165, ☎ 800/584–7263) is on the Coushatta Indian Reservation near Lake Charles. **Players Island Casino** (⊠ 507 N. Lakeshore Dr., Lake Charles, ☎ 800/977–7529), done up like a tropical island, has two riverboat casinos with 1,650 one-armed bandits, 100 table games, and 24-hour entertainment. The **Isle of Capri Casino & Entertainment Pavilion** (⊠ Exit 27 off I–10, ☎ 800/843–4753) operates two triple-decker paddle wheelers, open 24 hours, with table games and more than 900 slots.

Outdoor Activities and Sports

CANOEING

Paddling is almost a breeze on the easygoing **Whisky Chitto Creek,** near Oberlin. Canoes can be rented at **Arrowhead Canoe Rentals** (⊠ 11702 Hwy. 26, Oberlin, ☎ 337/639–2086 or 800/637–2086). Tours and rentals are also available at **White Sand Canoe Rental** (⊠ 11689 Hwy. 26, Oberlin, ☎ 800/621–9306).

GOLF

You can tee off at the 18-hole, par-72 **Pine Shadows Golf Center** (⊠ 750 Goodman Rd., Lake Charles, ☎ 337/433–8681). Greens fees are $10.50 weekdays, $14 weekends; club rentals are $4.50. The 18-hole, par-72 **Mallard Cove** (⊠ Chennault Airpark, Lake Charles, ☎ 337/491–1241) is popular with locals. Greens fees are $11.25 weekdays, $14.50 weekends; club rentals are $10, and golf carts are $8.30.

HIKING AND NATURE TRAILS

The Old Stagecoach Road, in **Sam Houston Jones State Park** (⊠ 12 mi north of Lake Charles on LA 378, ☎ 337/855–2665), is a favorite for hikers who want to explore the park and the various tributaries of the Calcasieu River.

En Route   The **Creole Nature Trail,** a 180-mi loop through exotic subtropical scenery, is one of only 14 rural roads in the country to be designated a National Scenic Byway by the Federal Highway Administration. Beginning on LA 27 in Sulphur, the state road dips south to the Gulf of Mexico on LA 82, and winds up LA 27 back to Lake Charles. Beautiful in the spring, this drive passes four wildlife refuges, including For information call the Southwest Louisiana Convention and Visitors Bureau (☎ 318/436–9588 or 800/456–7952).

Eunice

㊽ *66 mi northeast of Lake Charles via I–10 and LA 13.*

The tiny town of Eunice is home to the Cajun radio show **Rendez-Vous des Cajuns.** A live radio show, mostly in French, it has been described as a combination of the *Grand Ole Opry,* the *Louisiana Hayride,* and the *Prairie Home Companion.* ✉ *Liberty Theatre, Park Ave. at 2nd St.,* ☎ *337/457–7389.* 🎟 *$5.* 🕙 *Sat. 6 PM–8 PM.*

The **Eunice Museum** is in a former railroad depot and contains displays on Cajun culture, including Cajun music and Cajun Mardi Gras. ✉ *220 S. C. C. Duson Dr., Eunice,* ☎ *337/457–6540.* 🎟 *Free.* 🕙 *Tues.–Sat. 8–noon and 1–5.*

The **Prairie Acadian Cultural Center,** a large facility that's part of the Jean Lafitte National Historical Park, traces the history and culture of the Prairie Acadians, whose lore and mores differ from those of the Bayou Acadians around Lafayette. Food, crafts, and music demonstrations are held from time to time. ✉ *250 W. Park Ave., Eunice,* ☎ *337/457–8490 or 337/457–8499.* 🎟 *Free.* 🕙 *Daily 8–5.*

A number of places in Cajun Country make not just music but instruments, too. Among them is the **Savoy Music Center Accordion Factory,** its front half a music store, its back a Cajun accordion workshop. Proprietor Marc Savoy's factory turns out about five accordions a month and fills orders all the way from Alaska to New Zealand. On Saturday morning, accordions and other instruments tune up during jam sessions held in the shop. There's beer and two-stepping, and musicians from all over the area drop in. The Monday before Mardi Gras—Lundi Gras, as it's known in these parts—the center has a big blowout, with a bonfire, music, and dancing. ✉ *U.S. 190, 3 mi east of Eunice,* ☎ *337/457–9563.* 🎟 *Free.* 🕙 *Tues.–Fri. 9–5, Sat. 9–noon.*

Courir de Mardi Gras takes place the Sunday before Fat Tuesday (Mardi Gras Day). Le Capitain leads a band of masked and costumed horseback riders on a mad dash through the countryside, stopping at farmhouses along the way to shout, *"Voulez-vous recevoir cette bande de Mardi Gras* (Do you wish to receive the Mardi Gras band)?" The answer is always yes, and the group enlarges and continues, gathering food for the street festivals that wind things up. For information call the Lafayette Convention and Visitors Bureau (☎ 800/346–1958).

Ville Platte

㊿ *20 mi northeast of Eunice via LA 13 and LA 10.*

Ville Platte is home to the annual Cotton Festival, held in October, which features a medieval-style tournament with knights and jousting.

The **Louisiana State Arboretum** is a 600-acre facility with 2½ mi of nature trails leading past a variety of plants native to the state. ⊠ *8 mi north of Ville Platte,* ☎ *337/363–2503.* ☞ *Free.* ☉ *Dawn–dusk.*

En Route North of Eunice via LA 13 and I–49 lies Cheneyville. Here you'll find the perfect quiet getaway on 641 acres of a working, historic cotton plantation. **Loyd Hall Plantation** (⊠ 292 Lloyd Bridge Rd., 71325, ☎ 318/776–5641 or 800/240–8135, ℻ 318/776–5886, 🕸 www.louisianatravel.com/loyd_hall) has fully restored mid-1800s accommodations ($–$$) : a three-room cottage that once housed the commissary, two suites in the restored kitchens overlooking the pool, and one- or two-bedroom houses. All are furnished with a blend of antiques and modern comforts: woodburning fireplaces, four-poster or tester beds, porch rockers, air-conditioning, TVs, and full modern kitchens stocked with breakfast fixings.

Opelousas

🟡 *51 mi south of Cheneyville on I–49.*

Opelousas is the third-oldest town in the state—Poste de Opelousas was founded in 1720 by the French as a trading post. The town is named for the Appalousa Indians, who lived in the area centuries before the French and Spanish arrived. For a brief period during the Civil War, Opelousas served as the state capital. At the intersection of I–49 and U.S. 190, look for the **Opelousas Tourist Information Center** (☎ 337/948–6263), where you can get plenty of information; arrange for tours of historic homes; and see memorabilia pertaining to Jim Bowie, the Alamo hero who spent his early years in Opelousas. During the last full week in October, Opelousas stages the **Yambilee Festival,** a celebration of the superior local sweet potatoes.

The **Opelousas Museum and Interpretive Center** has among its eclectic exhibits a washbasin in which celebrity chef (and native son) Paul Prudhomme bathed as a babe, a Civil War Room, adorable dollhouses, and an old-time barbershop replete with antique accoutrements. ⊠ *329 N. Main St.,* ☎ *337/948–2589.* ☞ *Free.* ☉ *Tues.–Sat. 9–5.*

A tour through **Tony Chachere's** (⊠ 533 N. Lombard St., ☎ 800/551–9066, 🕸 www.cajunspice.com; ☞ free), a Creole seasoning factory, includes nose masks to filter the pepper that hangs in the air.

Dining

$ ✕ **Palace Café.** A down-home coffee shop on the town square run by the same family since 1927, this locals' favorite is famous for its homemade baklava. Among the eclectic specialties are cold fried-chicken salad, baked eggplant stuffed with Alaskan king crabmeat dressing, and Greek salad. Steaks, fried chicken, sandwiches, burgers, and seafood are also available. ⊠ *167 W. Landry St.,* ☎ *337/942–2142. Reservations not accepted. MC, V.*

Nightlife and the Arts

Slim's Y-Ki-Ki (⊠ LA 167, Washington Rd., ☎ 337/942–9980), a rural club, is one of the best zydeco dancing places in the state.

Grand Coteau

🟡 *10 mi south of Opelousas via I–49, exiting on LA 93.*

Virtually every structure in peaceful little Grand Coteau, a religious and educational center, is on the National Register of Historic Places. The **Church of St. Charles Borromeo** is a simple wooden structure with an ornate high baroque interior. There are 36 works of art inside, most of which were done by Erasmus Humbrecht, whose works can also be seen in St. Louis Cathedral in New Orleans. The church's unusual bell tower is one of the area's most photographed sights. ⊠ *174 Church St.,* ☎ *337/662–5279.* ⊡ *Tours $1 donation.* ☼ *Tours weekdays; you must call to make arrangements in advance.*

Established in 1821, the **Academy of the Sacred Heart** is the second-oldest institution of learning west of the Mississippi, remaining in operation through fire, epidemics, and war. The academy contains the **Shrine of St. John Berchmans,** in which the Miracle of Grand Coteau occurred. You'll hear all about the miracle on a guided tour. For tour information, call the Academy office. ⊠ *1821 Academy Rd.,* ☎ *337/662–5275.* ⊡ *$5.*

Chretien Point Plantation is noted not only for its grandeur but also for the role it played in *Gone With the Wind.* In the 1930s a photographer infatuated with the house took pictures of it and sent them to Hollywood. As a result, its staircase was the model for the one in Scarlett O'Hara's Tara. The house takes B&B guests, with rates ranging from $110 to $225 per night. ⊠ *About 4 mi from Sunset on the Bristol/Bosco Rd.,* ☎ *337/662–5876 or 800/880–7050,* ℻ *337/662–5876,* ᴡᴇʙ *www.louisianatravel.com/chretienpoint.* ⊡ *$6.50.* ☼ *Daily 10–5; last tour at 4.*

Cajun Country A to Z

AIR TRAVEL
Lafayette is served by American Eagle, Atlantic Southeast (a Delta connection), Continental, and Northwest Airlink. Lake Charles is served by American Eagle and Continental.

AIRPORTS
➤ Aɪʀᴘᴏʀᴛ Iɴꜰᴏʀᴍᴀᴛɪᴏɴ: **Lafayette Regional Airport** (⊠ 200 Terminal Dr., ☎ 337/266–4400). **Lake Charles Regional Airport** (⊠ 500 Airport Blvd., ☎ 337/477–6051).

BUS TRAVEL
Greyhound Southeast Lines has frequent daily departures from New Orleans to Franklin, Houma, Lafayette, Lake Charles, Morgan City, New Iberia, Opelousas, and Thibodaux.
➤ Bᴜs Iɴꜰᴏʀᴍᴀᴛɪᴏɴ: **Greyhound Southeast Lines** (☎ 800/231–2222, ᴡᴇʙ www.greyhound.com).

CAR TRAVEL
The fastest route from New Orleans through Cajun Country to Lafayette and Lake Charles is via I–10, which cuts coast to coast across the southern United States. However, if you have time, take the leisurely scenic drives for exploring.

LA 56 to LA 57 is a circular drive out of Houma, on which you can see shrimp and oyster boats docked along the bayous from May through December. Another circular drive is the Creole Nature Trail (LA 27) out of Lake Charles. LA 82 (Hug-the-Coast Highway) runs through the coastal marshes along the Gulf of Mexico.

EMERGENCIES
Dial 911 for assistance. Emergency rooms include the Medical Center of Southwest Louisiana and Lake Charles Area Medical Center. In Lafayette, Eckerd has a pharmacy that is open 24 hours. In Lake Charles, the Walgreens pharmacy is open all night.
➤ Hᴏsᴘɪᴛᴀʟs: **Lake Charles Area Medical Center** (⊠ 4200 Nelson Rd., Lake Charles, ☎ 337/474–6370). **Medical Center of Southwest Louisiana** (⊠ 2810 Ambassador Caffery Pkwy., Lafayette, ☎ 337/981–2949).

➤ 24-HOUR PHARMACIES: **Eckerd** (✉ 4406 Johnston St., Lafayette, ☎ 337/984–5220). **Walgreens** (✉ 300 18th St., Lake Charles, ☎ 337/433–4178).

MEDIA

RADIO

AM: KROF 960, French/Cajun; KPEL 1420, news/talk; KEUN 1490, country/news/sports.

FM: KYKZ 96.1, country; KTDY 99.9, adult contemporary; KROF 105.1, oldies.

OUTDOORS AND SPORTS

FISHING

Sportsman's Paradise is a charter-fishing facility 20 mi south of Houma, with eight boats available year-round. Salt, Inc. Charter Fishing Service offers fishing trips in the bays and barrier islands of lower Terrebonne Parish, as well as into the Gulf of Mexico.

In the far southwestern part of the state, Burgess Offshore, Inc. conducts offshore fishing trips. Hackberry Rod & Gun Club is a charter saltwater fishing service.
➤ CONTACTS: **Burgess Offshore, Inc.** (☎ 800/932–5077). **Hackberry Rod & Gun Club** (☎ 337/762–3391). **Salt, Inc. Charter Fishing Service** (✉ Coco Marina, LA 56 south of Houma, ☎ 504/594–6626 or 504/594–7581). **Sportsman's Paradise** (☎ 504/594–2414).

TOURS

Acadiana to Go gives guided tours of Acadiana, as well as the rest of Louisiana. Allons à Lafayette offers customized tours, with bilingual guides and itinerary planning for Lafayette and Cajun Country. Terrebonne Swamp & Marsh Tours is especially popular with kids. Annie Miller, who gets along great with gators, conducts daily swamp tours March 1 through November 1 out of Houma.

Coerte Voorhies, based in Lafayette, conducts tours into the 800,000-acre Atchafalaya Basin for photographers, ornithologists, and all nature lovers. Hammond's Flying Service has air tours, which soar out of Houma over the swamps, marshlands, and the Gulf of Mexico. McGee's Landing conducts pontoon-boat tours from the levee in Henderson into the Atchafalaya Basin. Airboat Tours skims through the remote swamps, bayous, and sloughs of Lake Fausse Pointe. Trips to fish, sightsee, or bird-watch can be arranged at Gator Guide Service.
➤ FEES AND SCHEDULES: **Acadiana to Go** (☎ 337/981–3918). **Airboat Tours** (☎ 337/229–4457). **Allons à Lafayette** (☎ 337/269–9607). **Coerte Voorhies** (☎ 337/233–7816). **Gator Guide Service** (✉ Box 9224, New Iberia, ☎ 337/365–6400). **Hammond's Flying Service** (☎ 504/876–0584). **McGee's Landing** (☎ 337/228–2384). **Terrebonne Swamp & Marsh Tours** (☎ 504/879–3934).

TRAIN TRAVEL

Amtrak serves Franklin, Schriever (12 mi from Houma), Lafayette, New Iberia, and Lake Charles.
➤ TRAIN INFORMATION: **Amtrak** (☎ 800/872–7245, WEB www.amtrak.com).

VISITOR INFORMATION

The Southwest Louisiana Convention and Visitors Bureau is open weekdays 8–5, weekends 9–3.
➤ TOURIST INFORMATION: **Iberia Parish Tourist Commission** (✉ 2690 Centre St., New Iberia 70560, ☎ 337/365–1540). **Lafayette Convention and Visitors Commission** (✉ 1400 N.W. Evangeline Thruway, 70505, ☎ 337/232–3808; 800/346–1958; 800/543–5340 in Canada,

FAX 318/232–0161, WEB www.lafayettetravel.com). **Southwest Louisiana Convention and Visitors Bureau** (⊠ 1205 N. Lakeshore Dr., Lake Charles 70601, ☎ 337/436–9588 or 800/456–7952, FAX 337/494–7952 WEB www.visitlakecharles.org).

NATCHITOCHES AND CANE RIVER COUNTRY

Natchitoches and environs have characteristics of both North and South Louisiana in terms of culture and cuisine. In this part of the state, barbecue is as popular as Cajun food, and country-and-western beats vie with zydeco for dancing feet. The terrain, however, is decidedly different. Here, the scent of pine trees pervades. Natchitoches is on the fringe of the Kisatchie National Forest, and although the area isn't exactly mountainous—the highest peak in all the state, the misnamed Driskill Mountain, farther north, soars to a dizzying 535 ft above sea level—it appears so after flat-as-a-pancake South Louisiana.

Natchitoches

264 mi northwest of New Orleans via I–10, U.S. 190, and I–49.

The earliest permanent European settlement in the Louisiana Purchase territory was not New Orleans but the little town of Natchitoches (pronounced Nak-a-tosh), which predates the Crescent City by four years. Nestled in rolling green hills and thick pine forests, Natchitoches has two other claims to fame. The town hosts a sparkling Christmas Festival of Lights, which was featured in the film *Steel Magnolias,* and it's the hometown of that film's screenwriter, Robert Harling. The friendly residents are happy to point out where Dolly Parton, Sally Field, Julia Roberts, and the other magnolias hung out during filming.

Front Street, which is lined with small, wrought-iron-faced buildings, lies alongside pretty Cane River Lake. The lake's sloping grass-green banks are shaded by giant live oak trees. The downtown area is part of a 33-block historic landmark district, which contains a number of homes open to the public.

Trolley tours, which focus on *Steel Magnolias* sites, are available through **Cane River Cruises** (☎ 318/352–2557).

The **Old Courthouse Museum,** in an 1896 Richardsonian Romanesque building that originally housed several Natchitoches Parish offices, is a facility of the Louisiana State Museum. Changing exhibits trace the history and culture of the region. ⊠ *Corner of 2nd and Church Sts.,* ☎ *318/357–2270.* 🔳 *$3.* ⊙ *Mon.–Sat. 9–5.*

Fort St. Jean Baptiste is a reconstruction of the outpost that stood near this site in 1716. The several replica buildings were constructed using 18th-century hardware, including hand-forged door latches and hinges. Structures include a church, powder magazine, and kitchen. ⊠ *Morrow and Jefferson Sts.,* ☎ *318/357–3101.* 🔳 *$2.* ⊙ *Daily 9–5.*

Natchitoches is on the fringe of the 100,000-acre **Kisatchie National Forest** (☎ 318/473–7160, WEB www.southernregion.fs.fed.us/kisatchie/). In addition to its hardwood and pine forests, it offers equestrian, hiking, and nature trails; picnic and camping sites; and splendid vistas.

Dining and Lodging

$$–$$$ ✕ **Landing.** This large, noisy bistro with white tablecloths is one of the
★   town's most popular restaurants. The extensive menu includes shrimp
           rémoulade, potato skins, and fried cheese sticks as starters. Pasta,

steak, chicken, and seafood entrées are prepared in a variety of ways. The spicy country-fried steak is distinctive; the garlic bread is superb, as is the bread pudding. ⊠ *530 Front St.,* ☎ *318/352–1579. AE, MC, V. Closed Mon.*

$–$$ ✕ **Lasyone's Meat Pie Kitchen.** Natchitoches is famed for its succulent meat pies, and the best place to sample them is this ultracasual country-kitchen café. Other offerings include meat, chicken, and seafood; for dessert, select from a display of Cane River cream pies. The kitchen closes at 7 PM. ⊠ *622 2nd St.,* ☎ *318/352–3353. Reservations not accepted. No credit cards. Closed Sun.*

$–$$ 🏠 **Jefferson House.** Jefferson House is a split-level frame structure in a serene setting. Guests occupy the entire first floor, which is decorated in a tasteful blend of traditional furnishings and East Asian objets d'art. A large, stately parlor has a high beamed ceiling, brick fireplace, and doors opening to a veranda with rocking chairs and a view of Cane River Lake. Bedrooms have quilted spreads and matching drapes; baths are large and modern. The downstairs room opens onto a patio that overlooks the lake. ⊠ *229 Jefferson St., 71457,* ☎ *318/352– 3957. 4 rooms. Dining room. MC, V.*

$–$$ 🏠 **Levy-East House.** This elegant B&B dates from 1838 and is one of Natchitoches's showplaces. Floors are heart pine, ceilings are 10½ ft, and much of the furniture is Victorian. Queen-size beds are wood-carved, with patchwork quilts and crocheted coverlets. Romantic taped music wafts into each guest room (and can be volume-controlled in each); armoires conceal TVs and phones. Guest baths have whirlpools. Amenities include sherry in each guest room, afternoon wine, and nightly turndown service with candy. Breakfast is served in a handsome formal dining room. The upstairs porch, with rocking chairs, overlooks Jefferson Street. ⊠ *358 Jefferson St., 71457,* ☎ *318/352–0662 or 800/840–0662. 4 rooms. Dining room; no kids, no smoking. AE, MC, V.*

$ 🏠 **Fleur-de-Lis.** The granddaddy of local B&Bs includes two houses: a 1903 rose-color Victorian and, next door, a 1920s craftsman-style guest house. The Victorian's guest rooms have four-poster, brass, or wicker beds. The guest house has a full kitchen and washer-dryer. Each house has a front porch with rocking chairs and swing and is decorated with family pictures and heirlooms. Baths in both houses are small but modern. There's a data port for laptops in the main house. Proprietors Tom and Harriette Palmer make guests feel right at home, with help from a friendly golden retriever named Ginger. Full breakfast is served family style in the dining room. ⊠ *336 2nd St., 71457,* ☎ *318/352–6621 or 800/489–6621. 8 rooms. Dining room. AE, MC, V.*

$ 🏠 **Ryders Inn.** Comfortable and predictable rooms are available in this erstwhile Holiday Inn on the outskirts of town. It offers a restaurant, outdoor pool, and cable TV. ⊠ *Hwy. 1 South Bypass, 71457,* ☎ *318/ 357–8281 or 888/252–8281,* FAX *318/352–9907. 143 rooms, 2 suites. Restaurant, bar, pool. AE, D, DC, MC, V.*

Nightlife and the Arts

The **Melrose Plantation Arts and Crafts Festival,** an annual event held the second weekend in June, showcases 135–150 regional craftspeople displaying their arts beneath the canopy of live oaks on the grounds of Melrose Plantation. There are also food booths galore featuring Natchitoches meat pies and oodles of homemade desserts. For information, call the Natchitoches Parish Tourist Commission at ☎ 318/ 352–8072 or 800/259–1714.

Cane River Country

South of Natchitoches is **Beau Fort Plantation,** constructed in the early 1800s of hand-hewn cypress and bousillage (an insulating material made of Spanish moss and mud). The handsome home, which is also a B&B, has an 84-ft gallery, and French doors line the front. The house is furnished with 19th-century Louisiana antiques and family heirlooms. ⊠ *Rte. 119, Bermuda, 11 mi south of Natchitoches,* ☎ *318/352–5340 or 318/352–9580.* ✆ *$5.* ☉ *Daily 1–4.*

The Cane River Lake drifts southward from Natchitoches, lined by tall trees, stately plantations, and humble cottages. Several plantation homes are open for tours. Eight miles south of Beau Fort Plantation, **Melrose Plantation** was the home of the late self-taught artist Clementine Hunter, who was known as the black Grandma Moses. The first owner of Melrose was a black freed slave who, with her family, began construction of the seven buildings in 1796. In this century, Melrose was the home of a patron of the arts whose guests included Erskine Caldwell, Lyle Saxon, and Alexander Woollcott. Particularly interesting is the African House, an unusual Congo-style structure, which has murals decorating the second floor. ⊠ *Rte. 119, Melrose,* ☎ *318/379–0055.* ✆ *$5.* ☉ *Daily noon–4.*

The still-working **Magnolia Plantation** is 6.2 mi south of Melrose. It is one of only two National Bicentennial farms west of the Mississippi River. The mansion's 27 rooms are furnished with an extensive collection of Louisiana and Southern Empire antiques. The outbuildings, which include brick cabins and a barn containing the only cotton press in the United States still in its original location, will become part of a projected Cane River Creole National Historical Park. Headquarters for the park will be a nearby Oakland Plantation, which at press time was undergoing a major restoration. ⊠ *Hwy. 119 near Derry, 22 mi south of Natchitoches,* ☎ *318/379–2221.* ✆ *$5.* ☉ *Daily 1–4 or by appointment.*

Handmade bricks, heart cypress, and wooden pegs were used to build the **Kate Chopin House,** which houses the **Bayou Folk Museum.** Completed in 1809, this raised cottage was the 1880s home of Kate Chopin, author of *The Awakening.* The museum contains photographs and memorabilia and a first edition of *Bayou Folk,* a collection of Chopin's short stories about Cane River Country. ⊠ *LA 491, 4 mi south of Magnolia Plantation in Cloutierville,* ☎ *318/379–2233.* ✆ *$5.* ☉ *Mon.–Sat. 9–5, Sun. 1–5.*

Natchitoches and Cane River Country A to Z

BUS TRAVEL
Natchitoches is served by Greyhound.
➤ Bus Information: **Greyhound** (☎ 800/231–2222).

CAR TRAVEL
Route 1 and I–49, which cut north–south through the state's midsection, bisect Natchitoches.

EMERGENCIES
➤ Contacts: **Ambulance, fire, police** (☎ 911). **Natchitoches Parish Hospital** (⊠ 501 Keyser, Natchitoches, ☎ 318/352–1200).

TOURS
Cane River Tours offers tours of Natchitoches by trolley, with the focus on sites featured in the film *Steel Magnolias.* Tours by Jan and Ducournau Square, Inc. both offer walking and driving tours of Natchitoches and the Cane River region.

➤ Fees and Schedules: **Cane River Tours** (☎ 318/352–2557). **Ducournau Square, Inc.** (☎ 318/352–5242). **Tours by Jan** (☎ 318/352–2324 or 318/352–3802, FAX 318/352–0666).

MEDIA

RADIO

KNWD 91.7, rock and alternative (FM).

VISITOR INFORMATION

The Natchitoches Parish Tourist Office provides information about the region, including self-guided walking/driving-tour brochures.

➤ Tourist Information: **Natchitoches Parish Tourist Office** (✉ 781 Front St., ☎ 318/352–8072 or 800/259–1714).

SHREVEPORT AND NORTHERN LOUISIANA

Although southern Louisiana dances to Cajun tunes and dines on Creole and Cajun fare, most of northern Louisiana has more in common with Mississippi, Georgia, and other Southern states; Shreveport's ties are largely to neighboring Texas. It's not for nothing that Louisiana is known as Sportsman's Paradise. The northern region of the state is laced with rivers and lakes, with ample places for camping and fishing.

Shreveport and Bossier City

Shreveport and Bossier City, joined by the Red River, constitute the largest metropolitan area in northern Louisiana. A cultural center, **Shreveport** has a symphony orchestra, resident opera and ballet companies, and excellent community-theater productions.

This area, like Lake Charles in the southwest corner of the state, is booming as a result of the riverboat casinos that operate on the Red River.

★ The prestigious **R. W. Norton Art Gallery** has superb European and American art, including the area's largest permanent collection of works by Frederic Remington and Charles M. Russell. ✉ *4747 Creswell Ave., Shreveport,* ☎ *318/865–4201.* ☜ *Free.* ⊙ *Tues.–Fri. 10–5, weekends 1–5.*

The **Louisiana State Exhibit Museum** has extensive displays and dioramas depicting the state's history, including a large collection of Native American artifacts from Poverty Point and other important excavations in Louisiana. ✉ *Fairgrounds, Shreveport,* ☎ *318/632–2020.* ☜ *$2.* ⊙ *Weekdays 9–4, Sat. noon–4.*

The **Ark-La-Tex Antique and Classic Vehicle Museum** traces automotive history in both classic and vintage models. ✉ *601 Spring St., Shreveport,* ☎ *318/222–0227.* ☜ *$4.* ⊙ *Mon.–Sat. 10–5, Sun. 1–5.*

The **Sci-Port Discovery Center** is a 67,000-square-ft science facility with hands-on interactive exhibits for all ages, as well as national traveling exhibitions and an IMAX theater. Admission is discounted the first Tuesday of each month. ✉ *820 Clyde Fant Pkwy., Shreveport,* ☎ *318/424–3466.* ☜ *$6 museum, $6 IMAX theater, $10 combination ticket.* ⊙ *Daily 10–6.*

The **American Rose Center,** headquarters of the American Rose Society, is a 118-acre piney-woods park with more than 20,000 rosebushes in more than 60 individual gardens. The place lights up like a Christmas tree during the Christmas in Roseland show, which runs from the day after Thanksgiving through New Year's Eve. ✉ *Jefferson-Paige Rd.,*

Shreveport, ☎ *318/938–5402.* 🖾 *$4.* ☉ *Apr.–Oct., weekdays 9–5, weekends 9–6; Christmas in Roseland, day after Thanksgiving–Dec. 30, daily 5:30–10* PM.

In Bossier City the **Eighth Air Force Museum** has World War II aircraft, dioramas, uniforms, and barracks of the Second Bomb Wing and the Eighth Air Force, which are headquartered at Barksdale Air Force Base. 🖾 *Barksdale Air Force Base,* ☎ *318/456–3067.* 🖾 *Free.* ☉ *Daily 9:30–4.*

The Shreveport-Bossier area has four **riverboat casinos** afloat on the Red River. All have a full complement of slot machines and table games, including roulette, blackjack, craps, baccarat, Caribbean stud, and big six; all have restaurants, and most have top-name entertainment as well. **Harrah's Casino, Shreveport** (🖾 Shreveport, ☎ 800/427–7247); **Isle of Capri Casino & Hotel** (🖾 Bossier City, ☎ 318/747–2400 or 800/221–4095); **Horseshoe Riverboat Casino & Hotel** (🖾 Bossier City, ☎ 800/895–0711); and **Casino Magic** (🖾 I–20, Exit 19B, ☎ 318/746–0711).

Louisiana Downs, one of the South's largest racetracks, has Thoroughbred racing from April through October. 🖾 *I–20, Bossier City,* ☎ *318/747–7223.*

South of Shreveport, the **Mansfield Battle Park** is the site of the last major Confederate victory of the Civil War. More than 30,000 men were involved in the bitter battle. The site contains monuments and an interpretive center with audiovisual displays. 🖾 *Rte. 2, 4 mi south of Mansfield,* ☎ *318/872–1474.* 🖾 *Free.* ☉ *Daily 9–5.*

Dining and Lodging

$$$$ ✕ **Monsieur Patou.** Expect crystal and candlelight at this small, prix-fixe, *très intime* restaurant. Classic French cuisine is represented by such dishes as roasted duck and medallion lamb with herb of Provence and sherry. Coats and ties are not required, but a meal like this does call for a little more than jeans and sneakers. 🖾 *855 Pierremont Rd.,* ☎ *318/868–9822. Reservations essential. AE, D, DC, MC, V.*

$$–$$$ ✕ **Jack Binion's Steakhouse.** Two-fisted steaks are served in this handsome, always busy restaurant of the Horseshoe Hotel, which is named for its founding father. 🖾 *711 Horseshoe Blvd, Bossier City,* ☎ *318/741–7870. Reservations essential. AE, D, DC, MC, V. No lunch.*

$–$$ ✕ **Glenwood Drug Co.** This lovely Victorian tearoom, serving shepherd's pie and delicious salads, is a popular lunch spot. It's in a historic drugstore that's now a small mall whose several vendors offer china, silver, linens, books, scented candles, and such. 🖾 *3310 Line Ave.,* ☎ *318/868–3651. AE, MC, V.*

$–$$ ✕ **Superior Bar & Grill.** Even with a reservation you may have to hang out in the bar to wait for a table, but the fine mesquite-grilled steaks and Mexican food served here are worth the wait. 🖾 *6123 Line Ave.,* ☎ *318/869–3243. AE, D, MC, V.*

$$ 🏨 **Horseshoe Hotel & Casino.** With a $204 million investment and a 26-story hotel, this facility is just plain huge. Blimp-size crystal chandeliers hang over the sleek lobby, which is adjacent to the casino. The hotel is all-suites with marble baths and many small luxuries; you'll even find a TV in the bathroom in the king-size–bed suites. The casino has nightly entertainment, and top-name headliners appear in the Riverdome. 🖾 *711 Horseshoe Blvd., Bossier City 71111,* ☎ *318/741–7870 or 800/895–0711,* FAX *318/741–7870,* WEB *www.horseshoe. com. 606 suites. 4 restaurants, in-room data ports, pool, hair salon, health club, lobby lounge, casino, nightclub. AE, D, DC, MC, V.*

$$ ⊡ **Isle of Capri Hotel & Casino.** The Isle features a tropical decor throughout, with indoor waterfalls and palm trees in the casino area. All accommodations are luxury suites, with whirlpool bath. ⊠ *3033 Hilton Dr., Bossier City 71111,* ☎ *318/747–2400 or 800/221–4095,* FAX *318/747–6822,* WEB *www.isleofcapricasino.com. 230 suites. 3 restaurants, room service, in-room data ports, pool, exercise equipment, lobby lounge, casino, nightclub, video game room, shop, baby-sitting. AE, D, DC, MC, V.*

$–$$ ⊡ **Sheraton Shreveport Hotel.** This luxury property is near the convention center, so it caters to a mostly business clientele. Every guest room has a wet bar, a refrigerator, three phones, and a modem line. ⊠ *1419 E. 70th St., 71105,* ☎ *318/797–9900 or 800/325–3535,* FAX *318/798–2923,* WEB *www.sheraton.com. 270 rooms. Restaurant, room service, in-room data ports, pool, health club, laundry service, business services, car rental. AE, D, DC, MC, V.*

Shreveport and Northern Louisiana A to Z

AIR TRAVEL
Shreveport is served by American Eagle, Continental Express, Delta, Northwest, TWA, and US Airways.

AIRPORTS
➤ AIRPORT INFORMATION: **Shreveport Regional Airport** (☎ 318/673–5370).

BUS TRAVEL
Greyhound/Trailways provides both interstate and intrastate bus service.
➤ BUS INFORMATION: **Greyhound/Trailways** (☎ 800/231–2222).

CAR TRAVEL
I–20 and U.S. 80 run east–west through the northern part of the state; Route 1 cuts diagonally from the northwest corner to the Gulf of Mexico; I–49 connects Shreveport with southern Louisiana. Other north–south routes are U.S. 171, 71, 165, and 167.

EMERGENCIES
All-night hospital emergency rooms include Christus Schumpert Bossier Healthplex in Bossier City and LSU Medical Center in Shreveport.
➤ CONTACTS: **Ambulance, police** (☎ 911). **Christus Schumpert Bossier Healthplex** (⊠ 2541 Viking Dr., ☎ 318/681–4500). **LSU Medical Center** (⊠ 1501 Kings Hwy., ☎ 318/675–6930).

MEDIA
RADIO
AM: KEEL 710, Talk.

FM: KITT, 93.7, country; KRUF 94.5, Top 40.

VISITOR INFORMATION
➤ TOURIST INFORMATION: **Shreveport-Bossier Convention & Tourist Bureau** (⊠ 629 Spring St., Shreveport 71166, ☎ 318/222–9391 or 800/551–8682, FAX 318/222–0056, WEB www.shreveport-bossier.com). **Visitor Centers** (⊠ Southpark Mall, Jewella Rd., Shreveport; ⊠ 100 John Wesley Blvd., Bossier City; ⊠ Pierre Bossier Mall, Airline Dr., Bossier City; ⊠ Mall St. Vincent, St. Vincent and Southern Aves., Shreveport, ☎ 318/227–9880).

LOUISIANA A TO Z

AIRPORTS
All major domestic carriers and a number of foreign carriers fly into
New Orleans International Airport, the state's largest airport. There
are regional airports served by commuter carriers in Baton Rouge,
Lafayette, Alexandria, Lake Charles, Shreveport, and Monroe.
➤ AIRPORT INFORMATION: **Alexandria** (☎ 318/449–4642). **Baton Rouge**
(☎ 504/357–4165). **Lafayette** (☎ 318/232–2808). **Lake Charles** (☎
318/477–6051). **Monroe** (☎ 318/329–2461). **New Orleans International Airport** (✉ 900 Airline Dr., Kenner, ☎ 504/464–0831). **Shreveport** (☎ 318/673–5370).

BUS TRAVEL
Greyhound/Trailways provides both interstate and intrastate bus service.
➤ BUS INFORMATION: **Greyhound/Trailways** (☎ 800/231–2222).

CAR TRAVEL
Major east–west arteries through the state are Interstate 20 (I–20), which
parallels U.S. 80 through North Louisiana, and Interstate 10 (I–10),
which goes coast to coast, cutting through downtown New Orleans
along the way. North–south routes include Interstate 49 (I–49), which
goes diagonally through the state from Lafayette in the south through
Shreveport and into Arkansas. Interstate 55 (I–55) comes south from
Chicago and connects with I–10 about 20 mi west of New Orleans.
LA Highway 1 is a scenic route, often over substandard roads, that
goes diagonally from Grand Isle on the Gulf of Mexico to the farthest
northwest tip of the state. The Official State Map, available from the
Louisiana Office of Tourism and visitor centers, has a mileage chart
as well as directories for each tourist area.

ROAD CONDITIONS
Call the 24-hour Highway Safety Hotline for information.
➤ CONTACTS: **24-hour Highway Safety Hotline** (☎ 800/259–4929 or
504/379–1541).

RULES OF THE ROAD
The speed limit on interstates is 70 mph. Right turns on red lights are
permitted unless otherwise indicated.

EMERGENCIES
For ambulance and fire emergencies statewide, call 911.

LODGING
BED AND BREAKFASTS
For a free illustrated brochure of statewide B&Bs, contact Louisiana
Bed & Breakfast.
➤ RESERVATION SERVICES: **Louisiana Bed & Breakfast** (✉ Box 4003,
Baton Rouge 70821-4003, ☎ 800/677–5597).

OUTDOORS AND SPORTS
FISHING
For information about licenses and lake maps, contact the Louisiana
Department of Wildlife & Fisheries.
➤ CONTACTS: **Louisiana Department of Wildlife & Fisheries** (✉ Box
98000, Baton Rouge 70898, ☎ 504/765–2800).

STATE PARKS
Detailed information about campsites and facilities in the state parks
can be obtained from the Louisiana Office of State Parks.

➤ CONTACTS: **Louisiana Office of State Parks** (✉ Box 44426, Baton Rouge 70804, ☎ 225/342–8111).

TAXES
SALES TAX

Louisiana is the first state to grant a sales tax rebate to foreign travelers. Look for shops, restaurants, and hotels that display the tax-free logo, then ask for a voucher for the tax, which varies from parish to parish, that's tacked onto most purchases. Present vouchers with your passport and airline ticket at the tax rebate office in New Orleans International Airport and receive up to $500 cash back. Rebates exceeding $500 will be mailed to your home address.

➤ TAX REFUNDS: **Tax rebate office** (☎ 504/568–5323).

TRAIN TRAVEL

Amtrak trains from Miami, New York, Chicago, Los Angeles, and points in between pull into New Orleans's Union Terminal in the Central Business District. Amtrak serves South Louisiana with stops in Schriever (between Thibodaux and Houma), New Iberia, Lafayette, and Lake Charles. There is one train that operates westbound on Monday, Wednesday, and Saturday, and an eastbound train Tuesday, Thursday, and Sunday.

➤ TRAIN INFORMATION: **Amtrak** (☎ 800/872–7245).

VISITOR INFORMATION

For a copy of the free "Louisiana Tour Guide" brochure, contact the Louisiana Office of Tourism.

➤ TOURIST INFORMATION: **Louisiana Office of Tourism** (✉ Box 94291, Baton Rouge 70804-9291, ☎ 225/342–8119 or 800/334–8626, FAX 225/342–8390, WEB www.louisianatravel.com).

5 MISSISSIPPI

Dotted with Civil War battlegrounds, Mississippi is a gold mine for history buffs and offers some of the best-preserved examples of antebellum architecture in the South. The Natchez Trace Parkway, strung with magnolia trees and hilltop vistas, cuts across the heart of Dixie, passing through Tupelo, Jackson, and antebellum Natchez. The mighty Mississippi forms the western border of the state, winding slowly through the Delta past the port towns of Greenville and Vicksburg. Along the Gulf Coast, the "Playground of the South" beckons with casinos, beaches, history, and cultural experiences.

A S YOU ENTER THE LUSH AND LOVELY Magnolia State, slow down, look around, and listen carefully so as not to miss a single one of the South's great treasures. Mississippi is, indeed, deep in the heart of Dixie, and Dixieland is steeped in legend and lore.

Updated by
Linda Peal
Herbst

Listen, and hear the soft, gentle drawl of an authentic Southern welcome. Stop in small towns, rich with historic houses and museums, busy with locals eager to regale you with slightly partisan tales of the Civil War. Sit quietly and catch snippets of the gossip that permeates the air of any eatery redolent with country cooking. Gossip and good food get on famously down South.

Mississippians eat, sleep, and breathe history—so much so that they subconsciously perpetuate the presence of ancestors. Dyed-in-the-wool Mississippians honor tradition, which manifests itself in everything from the meticulous upkeep of stately old homes—you can tour many of them during special pilgrimage times—to the painstaking preservation of colorful front-porch stories passed down from generation to generation.

If you're looking for something a bit more fast-paced, Mississippi now has more gaming space than any other place outside Las Vegas. In fact, the largest single business investment in the state's history—a $600 million casino/hotel project called Beau Rivage—opened its doors in Biloxi in 1999. In Mississippi the past still endures, but at least part of the state's future is in gaming.

Whatever you do in Mississippi, you'll probably encounter evidence of the state's rich artistic heritage in one form or another. You'll feel exalted reading William Faulkner's Nobel Prize address, you'll laugh at the characters in Eudora Welty's short stories, and you'll find pathos aplenty in Tennessee Williams's plays and thrills in John Grisham's bestsellers. Hear the Delta blues music of Robert Johnson and B. B. King, and roll to the rock of Tupelo native Elvis Presley. Mississippians all, they've contributed to a mystique no other state can touch.

Pleasures and Pastimes

Dining
Fresh Gulf seafood, particularly redfish, flounder, and speckled trout, stars in coast restaurants. Soft-shell crab is a coast specialty, and crab claws are a traditional appetizer. Coast locals are fond of quaffing Biloxi-born Barq's root beer with their seafood. In Tupelo, Jackson, and Natchez you can find everything from caviar to chitlins. Jackson has several elegant restaurants. Tupelo specializes in down-home cooking, but blue-plate dinners of fresh Mississippi vegetables are a widely available alternative. Southern breakfasts served in antebellum opulence are a Natchez trademark. All in all, good food and drink are required in the South; fancy surroundings aren't. Dress is casual unless otherwise noted.

CATEGORY	COST*
$$$$	over $26
$$$	$18–$26
$$	$10–$18
$	under $10

*per person for a main course at dinner, excluding drinks, service, and 8%–10% sales tax (depending on the area)

Gambling
Sip a cocktail, enjoy a show, or maybe even strike it rich at the splashy, Las Vegas–style casinos permanently docked along the waterfront in

Gulfport, Biloxi, and Bay St. Louis, on the Gulf Coast, or in the Delta's Tunica County. The casinos, built on huge barges that resemble land-based casinos more than actual boats, all have numerous bars, lounges, and restaurants and are open 24 hours a day, so night owls are never at a loss for a place to go.

Lodging

With the advent of dockside casinos, the Gulf Coast hotel business is booming. Reserve a couple of weeks ahead—as gambling aficionados say, "The coast is cookin'." National hotel and motel chains are found throughout the Natchez Trace region, though Jackson's historic mansions add variety. In Natchez, travelers will find plantation homes that open their doors in bed-and-breakfast courtesy.

CATEGORY	COST*
$$$$	over $150
$$$	$110–$150
$$	$70–$110
$	under $70

*All prices are for a standard double room, excluding 8%–9% tax (depending on the area).

Pilgrimage Tours

Mississippians love to show their Southern hospitality by opening their antebellum and Victorian homes to the public in the form of spring and fall pilgrimages. Annual or biannual pilgrimages take place on the coast, in Columbus, Holly Springs, Port Gibson, Natchez, and Vicksburg, with the Natchez tours the crown jewel. Dates change year to year, so call the visitor centers in the towns for details.

Exploring Mississippi

Mississippi is a state of contrasts. The Gulf Coast and the areas as far north as Vicksburg and Natchez have a decidedly New Orleans flavor, whereas the Delta—the rich area of farmland periodically delivered by Mississippi River floods—is more like Memphis: genteel, polite, but all business. A trip along the Natchez Trace, which stretches from Natchez northeast through Jackson and Tupelo, then on to Nashville, will carry you back to a time of settlers, outlaws, traveling preachers, and post riders. Holly Springs and Oxford are sophisticated courthouse towns in northern Mississippi that don't fit neatly under the Gulf Coast, Delta, or Natchez Trace banner. They exemplify yet another dimension of Mississippi's diversity.

Great Itineraries

How you tour Mississippi depends largely on whether you start at the top or the bottom. You can experience a section of the Natchez Trace whether you're in north, central, or south Mississippi, since it cuts diagonally through the state. Driving the entire Trace takes about seven hours, but you could spend seven days if you have the time. The same goes for the rest of Mississippi. You could drive from top to bottom in six hours, but your only memory might be of row after row of roadside pine trees. Instead, take at least three days to explore any one of Mississippi's areas, or span the state for a nine-day vacation.

IF YOU HAVE 3 DAYS
Casinos docked all along the Gulf Coast have kept the area from Ocean Springs to Bay St. Louis packed with tourists, but there are other activities besides gambling to keep you busy. Start your Gulf Coast tour in **Ocean Springs,** which is worth at least an afternoon with its Walter Anderson Museum of Art, Shearwater Pottery, and unique shops. Overnight in ☷ **Biloxi** and on Day 2 make an excursion to one of the

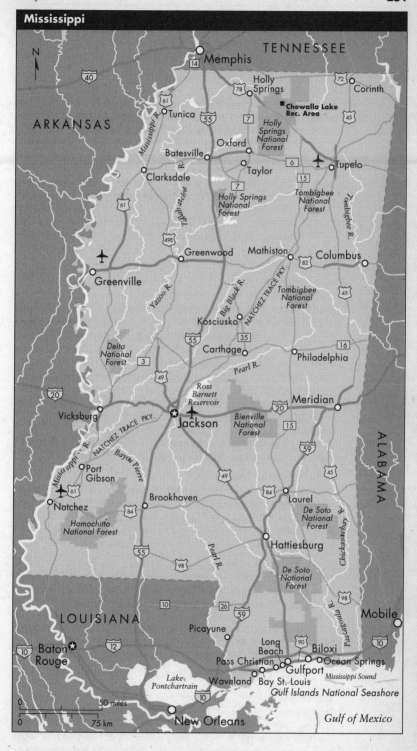

Mississippi

N

TENNESSEE

ARKANSAS

40

14 Memphis

61
55 Tunica

78 Holly
Springs

72

Corinth

■ Chewalla Lake
Rec. Area

7

45

Holly
Springs
National
Forest

Batesville

Oxford

6

Tupelo

Taylor

15

Tombigbee
National
Forest

Clarksdale

61

7

Holly Springs
National
Forest

49E

Greenwood

Mathiston

Columbus

82

45

Greenville

Yazoo R.

Big Black R.

Tombigbee
National
Forest

Kosciusko

NATCHEZ TRACE PKY.

Delta
National
Forest

55

35

16

Carthage

Philadelphia

3

Pearl R.

49

Ross
Barnett
Reservoir

20

Meridian

Vicksburg

NATCHEZ TRACE PKY.

Jackson

Bienville
National
Forest

15

59

Mississippi R.

Bayou Pierre

Port
Gibson

49

45

61

84

Laurel

Natchez

84

Brookhaven

De Soto
National
Forest

Homochitto
National
Forest

55

Hattiesburg

Chickasawhay R.

ALABAMA

98

Pearl R.

De Soto
National
Forest

10

26

Picayune

59

Pascagoula R.

98

Mobile

10

LOUISIANA

12

Long
Beach

90

Biloxi

Baton
Rouge

Pass Christian

Ocean Springs

10

Gulfport

Mississippi Sound

Lake
Pontchartrain

Waveland

Bay St. Louis

50 miles

Gulf Islands National Seashore

0

75 km

10

New Orleans

Gulf of Mexico

Tennessee
Tallahatchie R.
Tombigbee R.

barrier islands that separate the Gulf of Mexico from Mississippi Sound. On Day 3 head for ⊞ **Natchez,** where you might want to stay at one of the antebellum town's B&B establishments. Leave a full day for touring Natchez, more if you come during a pilgrimage time, when many of Natchez's lovely old homes are opened to visitors.

IF YOU HAVE 6 DAYS

Start out on the Gulf Coast, where you'll dine on some of the finest seafood in the nation. Overnight at either **Ocean Springs** or ⊞ **Biloxi.** On Day 2 head to ⊞ **Natchez,** worth at least an afternoon of exploration. On the third day enjoy a leisurely drive through **Port Gibson** to ⊞ **Jackson,** where you can spend your fourth day studying the city's notable architecture and admiring the regional and national artwork on display in its small museums. On the fifth day drive a long stretch of the Natchez Trace to ⊞ **Oxford,** where you can soak up the literary vibes set forth by such Southern heroes as William Faulkner, Eudora Welty, and Tennessee Williams. Visit Faulkner's Rowan Oak and the campus of the University of Mississippi, more commonly called Ole Miss, and the Eudora Welty Library in Jackson, where the region's rich literary history is felt most strongly.

IF YOU HAVE 9 DAYS

With nine days you'll have time to experience the Gulf Coast and a good portion of the Natchez Trace; see the itineraries above for suggested routes. Set aside the last three days to explore the Delta. Spend part of Day 7 in **Holly Springs,** which survived more than 50 raids during the Civil War. Though many of the town's historic homes are open to visitors only during pilgrimage time, their facades alone are worth seeing. Next morning, start toward ⊞ **Tunica County,** where you can try your luck at the slot machines and table games at any of several of the city's casino resorts. On your eighth day, head toward **Clarksdale,** home of the Delta Blues Museum. Stop for a hot tamale at Doe's in **Greenville** before continuing on to ⊞ **Vicksburg** at the south end of the Delta. Your ninth day can be spent touring Vicksburg's Civil War sights and cruising the Mississippi with Hydro-Jet Boat Tours.

When to Tour Mississippi

To be part of the action, hit the Gulf Coast's Mardi Gras celebrations in late January and February, Biloxi's Blessing of the Fleet in May, and Jackson's Jubilee! JAM, also in May. Fall brings historic house tours and antiques browsing in Natchez. The Mississippi Division of Tourism Development will gladly send you a travel planner.

Prepare for the weather—Mississippi's fairly fickle. Spring and fall are glorious, and lazy summer days call for cool drinks on a shady veranda. Now and then, a winter cold snap sends porch sitters scurrying inside. Locals say it's tolerable here year-round, but be prepared for a few mood swings.

THE GULF COAST

Ocean Springs, Biloxi, Gulfport

The Mississippi Gulf Coast extends for about 80 mi from Alabama to Louisiana. Although I–10 runs along the coast, it's better to drive U. S. 90 to experience the coast. Restaurants, bars, hotels, motels, and souvenir shops jostle for space along its busy four lanes, and the riverboat casinos permanently docked at the water's edge welcome anyone seeking a good time. But don't let the clamor of this neon strip hide the coast's quieter treasures: the ancient land, sculpted by wind and water, continually changing; serene beachfront houses set on green and shady lawns; the teeming wildlife of Mississippi Sound and its adjacent bayous and marshes; and the unspoiled natural beauty of the seven barrier islands that separate the Gulf of Mexico from Mississippi Sound.

On a clear day, if you have good eyesight or a good imagination, you can see these islands. Their names (from east to west) are Petit Bois (anglicized as "Petty Boy"), Horn, East and West Ship, and Cat. Two others, Round and Deer, lie within Mississippi Sound.

Three hundred years ago, France, England, and Spain ruled the area, according to their fortunes in international wars. Street names, family names, and traditions still reflect this colorful heritage. In the late 19th and early 20th centuries, the coast became a fashionable vacation spot for wealthy New Orleanians and Delta planters eager to escape yellow fever epidemics. Elegant hotels, imposing beachfront mansions, and smaller summer homes sprang up. Today the homes that have endured the vagaries of time and hurricanes stand along the beach—brave and beautiful survivors. Many of the homes along the coast are open for tours during pilgrimage time. The dates vary, so call the Mississippi Beach Convention and Visitors Bureau.

Today the coast's people are known to be easygoing and tolerant, artistic and hardy. Add the local love of fun, and you'll understand why Las Vegas–style gaming has been a major coastal to-do since its inception in 1992. Dockside gambling's floating barges recall the days of riverboat gambling once rampant along the mighty Mississippi. Casino vessels today, however, are permanently moored and connected to dockside hotels and open round the clock. Restaurants, waterfront cafés, and Southern hospitality are also in abundance.

Enjoy wondrous walks along the water, but take your cue from the locals and ignore any urge to swim. The Mississippi Sound is murky (at best). Instead, admire the stately live oaks and relax on the white sands. Go floundering and spear your supper. Above all, slow down. On the Mississippi Coast only the traffic on U.S. 90 moves quickly.

Ocean Springs

35 mi west of Mobile, 90 mi east of New Orleans.

To begin at the beginning, at least as far as Mississippi is concerned, start in Ocean Springs. Here, in 1699, the French commander Pierre LeMoyne Sieur d'Iberville established Fort Maurepas to shore up France's claim to the central part of North America. This first colony was temporary, but it's fondly remembered by Ocean Springs during its annual spring festival, which celebrates Iberville's landing. Magnificent oaks shade the sleepy town center, a pleasant area of small shops to explore on foot.

Walter Anderson (1903–65), an artist of genius and grand eccentricity, made his home in Ocean Springs. Drawings and watercolors, some not discovered until after his death, are on display at the **Walter Anderson Museum of Art**, built as an attachment to the **Old Community Center** where Anderson painted murals in 1951 (before it became the "Old" Community Center). The **Little Room** was extracted from Anderson's cottage home, loaded on a flatbed truck, and moved to the museum, with its murals intact. Anderson painted the intricate murals in the Old Community Center for a fee of $1; they are now appraised at $1 million. *Museum: ⊠ 510 Washington Ave., ☎ 228/872-3164. ▭ $5. ⊘ May–Sept., Mon.–Sat. 9:30–5, Sun. 12:30–5; Oct.–Apr., Mon.–Sat. 9:30–4:30, Sun. 12:30–4:30.*

The **Shearwater Pottery and Showroom** displays a wide selection of original Anderson family hand-thrown and hand-cast pottery. Potters demonstrate their craft in the Anderson family workshop; some pieces are for sale. ⊠ *102 Shearwater Dr.,* ☏ *228/875–7320.* 🎫 *Free.* ☉ *Showroom Mon.–Sat. 9–5:30, Sun. 1–5:30; workshop weekdays 9–noon, 1–4.*

A brochure from the Ocean Springs Chamber of Commerce will guide you on a driving tour of the **d'Iberville Trail,** shaded by moss-draped trees and bordered by weathered but lovely summer houses. The route, which begins at Ocean Springs's train station, winds through the area first explored 300 years ago by Pierre LeMoyne Sieur d'Iberville.

☺ The **Doll House** displays a collection of contemporary and antique dolls, stuffed animals, and dollhouses. ⊠ *1201 Bienville Blvd. (U.S. 90),* ☏ *228/872–3971.* 🎫 *$1 donation requested for YMCA Pet Shelter.* ☉ *Tues.–Sun. 1–5.*

★ **Gulf Islands National Seashore** (⊠ 3500 Park Rd., ☏ 228/875–9057), which includes Ship, Horn, and Petit Bois islands, has its headquarters on Ocean Springs's Davis Bayou. When the heat and humidity aren't overwhelming, have a picnic and explore the nature trails. Wilderness camping is available on Horn and Petit Bois islands, accessible by charter and private boat; call for a list of charter boat operators. Gulf Islands National Seashore has 50 campsites for trailers and RVs, with electrical hookups available.

Dining

$$–$$$$ ✕ **Germaine's.** Formerly Trilby's, this little house surrounded by live oaks has served many a great meal to its faithful clientele. It is reminiscent of New Orleans, with unadorned wooden floors, walls decked in local art for sale, fireplaces, and attentive service. Specialties include crabmeat au gratin, broiled trout served with mushrooms and sautéed crabmeat, and sautéed veal in a creamy port wine sauce. ⊠ *1203 Bienville Blvd., U.S. 90E,* ☏ *228/875–4426. AE, D, MC, V. Closed Mon. No dinner Sun.*

$$ ✕ **Jocelyn's Restaurant.** Jocelyn is formerly of Trilby's kitchen, now
★ Germaine's, and fans love her cooking just as much in this old frame house. This is as good as coast seafood gets. Specialties are fresh crabmeat fixed three or four ways. Trout, flounder, and, when available, snapper are subtly seasoned and served with garnishes as bright and original as modern art. Stuffed eggplant is another favorite. ⊠ *U.S. 90E, opposite SouthTrust Bank,* ☏ *228/875–1925. Reservations not accepted. No credit cards.*

$–$$ ✕ **Fisherman's Wharf.** A neighboring shrimp factory perfumes the parking lot here, but inside there are fresher air and views of oyster shuckers at work on the pier. You'll find soft-shell crab, gumbo, and oyster po'boys among the lunch specials; broiled catch of the day for dinner; and for dessert, the delicious Fisherman's Wharf pie, a top secret recipe that tastes a bit like a cross between a chess pie and a pecan pie (although there are no actual pecans in it). ⊠ *705 Bienville Blvd. (Hwy. 90),* ☏ *228/872–6111. Reservations not accepted. AE, D, DC, MC, V.*

Shopping

At **Ballard's Pewter** (⊠ 1110 Government St., Ocean Springs, ☏ 228/875–7550) you'll find necklaces and earrings made from sand dollars—or you can have the pewterer make a bespoke (custom-made) piece.

At **Realizations** (⊠ 1000 Washington Ave., in the old Train Depot, ☏ 228/875–0503) you can buy Walter Anderson prints and clothing printed with his unique designs.

Biloxi

2 mi west of Ocean Springs.

Biloxi (pronounced bi-*lux*-i) is the oldest continuous settlement on the Gulf Coast and the third-largest city in Mississippi. When Pierre LeMoyne Sieur d'Iberville met the Native Americans who called themselves Biloxi, or "first people," he gave their name to the area and to the bay. The French constructed Fort Louis here; it served as the capital of the Louisiana Territory from 1720 until 1722, when the capital was moved to New Orleans. Today casinos bring the city plenty of action. Biloxi also has a number of museums and a white-sand beach for more sedate pursuits.

The **J. L. Scott Marine Education Center and Aquarium** has 48 live exhibits and aquariums brimming with reptiles and several species of fish from the Gulf. The centerpiece is a spectacular 42,000-gallon tank. ✉ *115 Beach Blvd.,* ☎ *228/374–5550,* WEB *www.ims.usm.edu.* 🎟 *$4.* ☾ *Mon.–Sat. 9–4.*

Across U.S. 90 is **Point Cadet Plaza,** a waterfront complex that in the 1880s housed European immigrants who flocked to Biloxi to work in seafood canneries. Exhibits at the **Maritime & Seafood Industry Museum** (🎟 $3) depict the growth and development of the Gulf Coast seafood industry. Two re-created **schooners,** which dock at Point Cadet's marina, are available for short trips and charters; call for fees and schedules. ✉ *Point Cadet Plaza, Hwy. 90 and 1st St.,* ☎ *228/435–6320,* WEB *www.maritimemuseum.org.* ☾ *Mon.–Sat. 9–4:30.*

Biloxi's **Small Craft Harbor,** off U.S. 90 on the sound, feels like you're in a sleepy fishing village. Take the **Biloxi Shrimping Trip** aboard the *Sailfish* and experience 70 minutes as a shrimper as you pull the nets through the waters. ✉ *Hwy. 90 and Main St.,* ☎ *228/385–1182,* WEB *www.gcww.com/sailfish.* 🎟 *$11.* ☾ *Mar.–Nov. (call for schedule).*

Erected in 1848, the 48-ft-tall **Biloxi Lighthouse** is a landmark. During the Civil War, Union forces, operating from Ship Island, blockaded Mississippi Sound and cut Biloxi off from much-needed supplies. When the Yankees demanded that Biloxi submit or starve, they were told that the Union would have to "blockade the mullet" first. Ever since, mullet has been known as "Biloxi bacon" and honored with its own festival each October. The city defended itself with what appeared to be a formidable cannon array near the lighthouse but was actually only two cannons and many logs painted black. ✉ *U.S. 90 at Porter Ave.,* ☎ *228/435–6293.* 🎟 *$2.* ☾ *Mon.–Sat. 10 AM–11 AM (closing time varies depending on number of visitors; it's best to arrive right at opening).*

Mardi Gras is almost as grand a celebration in Biloxi as in nearby New Orleans, and the Krewe costumes are equally festive. Costumes and crowns are housed in the **Mardi Gras Museum** in the old Magnolia Hotel, an 1847 structure listed on the National Register of Historic Places. ✉ *119 Rue Magnolia,* ☎ *228/435–6245.* 🎟 *$2.* ☾ *Mon.–Sat. 11–4.*

★ **The Ohr/O'Keefe Museum of Art** houses a collection of intricate pottery crafted by the talented and eccentric Ohr, known as "the mad potter of Biloxi." To truly appreciate his great craftsmanship, take a few minutes to watch the film about his life. The center also exhibits the work of local artists. A new center, designed by architect Frank Gehry to house the museum, is due to open in 2004. ✉ *136 G. E. Ohr St.,* ☎ *228/374–5547,* WEB *www.georgeohr.org.* 🎟 *$6.* ☾ *Mon.–Sat. 9–6.*

Dining and Lodging

$$–$$$$ ✕ **Mary Mahoney's Old French House Restaurant.** Locals swear by it,
★   not only for the comfort of its old brick and age-darkened wood (the
        mansion Mary Mahoney's calls home dates to 1737) and for the mem-
        ory of Mary herself (who always went from table to table, chatting
        with customers), but also for the food. Start off with a bowl of rich,
        dark gumbo and move on to the lightly breaded panfried veal Anto-
        nio, topped with cheese sauce and plenty of fresh crabmeat for a main
        course. The bread pudding drenched in rum sauce is unforgettable. ⊠
        110 Rue Magnolia, ☏ *228/374–0163. AE, DC, MC, V. Closed Sun.*

$$ ✕ **Ole Biloxi Schooner.** Coast residents flock to this family-run restau-
        rant on Biloxi's serene back bay. It's tiny—little more than a shack—
        but the food is good, especially the gumbo and the po'boys, which come
        "dressed" and wrapped in paper. ⊠ *159 E. Howard,* ☏ *228/374–8071.*
        Reservations not accepted. No credit cards.

$–$$ ✕ **McElroy's Harbor House Restaurant.** Biloxi locals and real shrimpers
        eat hearty breakfasts, lunches, and dinners as fishing boats come and
        go and fisherfolk load and unload their nets just outside. Notable are
        the po'boys, oysters on the half shell, broiled stuffed flounder, and stuffed
        crabs. ⊠ *Biloxi Small Craft Harbor, 695 Beach Blvd.,* ☏ *228/435–*
        5001. Reservations not accepted. AE, D, DC, MC, V.

$$–$$$$ 🏨 **Beau Rivage.** The first grand Las Vegas–style hotel/casino on the Gulf
★   Coast, Mirage resorts pulled out all the stops when it built this impressive
        resort. In the lobby, majestic magnolia trees line the inside walkway that
        leads from the entrance to the mega-casino. The magnolia theme con-
        tinues to the spacious modern rooms where the Southern blooms dec-
        orate curtains and bedspreads. Among the eight restaurants on the
        property, Coral is the most spectacular, with floor-to-ceiling aquariums
        filled with schools of fish. For entertainment, there's the 72,000-square-
        ft casino with table games and slot machines. ⊠ *875 Beach Blvd.,* ☏
        228/386–7444 or 888/567–6667, 𝖥𝖠𝖷 *228/386–7446,* 🌐 *www.*
        beaurivageresort.com. 1,780 rooms. 12 restaurants, coffee shop, ice cream
        parlor, room service, pool, health club, hair salon, hot tub, spa, dock,
        bar, casino, shops; no-smoking floors. AE, D, DC, MC, V.

$$–$$$$ 🏨 **Palace Casino Resort.** The Palace has standard rooms that overlook
        Biloxi Bay and the Gulf of Mexico. The soaring atrium lobby has a
        25-foot skylight and a cascading fountain that marks the entrance to
        the casino. Outside, elegant cabanas ring the pool and are adjacent to
        a sand beach. ⊠ *158 Howard Ave., 39530,* ☏ *228/432–8888 or 800/*
        725–2239, 𝖥𝖠𝖷 *228/386–2300,* 🌐 *www.palacecasinoresort.com. 236*
        rooms, 11 suites. 4 restaurants, café, coffee shop, in-room data ports,
        golf privileges, 2 pools, gym, hair salon, outdoor hot tub, massage, sauna,
        spa, beach, volleyball, 2 bars, 2 lounges, casino, theater, video game
        room, shops, laundry service, concierge, concierge floor, airport shut-
        tle, free parking. AE, D, DC, MC, V.

$$–$$$ 🏨 **Grand Casino Biloxi Hotel and Bayview Resort & Spa.** These two
        Grand Casino properties are across the highway from each other on
        U.S. 90 and are connected by a climate-controlled, covered walkway.
        Together they offer 1,000 guest rooms and services including specialty
        shops, restaurants, a teen arcade, and a spa and salon. Both hotels have
        comfortable, bright and airy rooms. The 1,600-seat Biloxi Grand The-
        atre hosts live stage shows, and both properties are adjacent to the Grand
        Casino, with Las Vegas–style gambling. Hotel guests are shuttled to
        and from the property's Grand Bear golf course, an 18-hole champi-
        onship course designed by Jack Nicklaus. ⊠ *265 Beach Blvd., 39530,*
        ☏ *228/436–2946 or 800/354–2450,* 🌐 *www.grandcasinos.com.*
        1,000 rooms. 10 restaurants, 2 pools, gym, hair salon, spa, 5 bars, 2
        lounges, shops, children's programs (ages 6 wks–12 yrs), concierge, car
        rental, travel services, free parking. AE, D, DC, MC, V.

$$ ⊞ **Isle of Capri Casino Crowne Plaza Resort.** The Isle of Capri was the first gaming operation to open on the Gulf. Rooms are large, with ceiling fans; some have balconies with views of the Gulf. The casino, with slot machines, video poker, and table games, can be accessed through the mezzanine level. Weekends are usually packed here, so you might want to call ahead. ⊠ *151 Beach Blvd., 39530,* ☎ *228/435–5400 or 800/843–4753,* FAX *228/436–7834,* WEB *www.isleofcapricasino.com/ Biloxi/crowne. 370 rooms, 4 suites. 3 restaurants, pool, health club, casino, meeting rooms. AE, D, DC, MC, V.*

$–$$ ⊞ **Casino Magic Bay St. Louis.** This 14-story hotel has elegant rooms, all with a view of the Gulf of Mexico. The 18-hole, Arnold Palmer– designed Bridges Golf Resort provides challenging action for novices and low-handicappers alike. There are slot machines and table games in the casino, and the 24-hour entertainment complex showcases big-name talent. A 100-site RV park on the premises has barbecue grills. ⊠ *711 Casino Magic Dr., Bay St. Louis 39520,* ☎ *228/467–9257 or 800/562–4425,* FAX *228/466–2955,* WEB *www.casinomagic.com. 201 rooms. 4 restaurants, room service, cable TV with movies, pool, hot tub, spa, steam room, dock, 5 lounges, laundry facilities, meeting rooms. AE, D, DC, MC, V.*

$–$$ ⊞ **Casino Magic Biloxi.** This beachfront hotel is a sister property to Casino Magic hotel and casino in Bay St. Louis. It is adjacent to Las Vegas–style casino action and offers a host of amenities. Guests are shuttled to and from the 18-hole, Arnold Palmer–designed Bridges Golf Resort at the Bay St. Louis property. Players in the casino can wager on slot machines, blackjack, craps, roulette, and more. ⊠ *167 Beach Blvd., 39530,* ☎ *228/386–4000 or 800/562–4425,* WEB *www. casinomagic.com. 378 rooms. 4 restaurants, pool, spa, business services, meeting rooms. AE, D, DC, MC, V.*

En Route On U.S. 90 between Biloxi and Gulfport is **Beauvoir,** the antebellum beachfront mansion where Jefferson Davis spent the last 12 years of his life. It was here that the president of the Confederacy wrote his memoirs and his book *The Rise and Fall of the Confederate Government.* The serene, raised-cottage-style house, with its sweeping front stairs, is flanked by pavilions and set on a broad lawn shaded by ancient live oaks. A Confederate cemetery on the grounds includes the Tomb of the Unknown Soldier of the Confederacy. A presidential library holds materials about the era and about Davis. ⊠ *2244 Beach Blvd.,* ☎ *228/ 388–1313.* ⊟ *$7.50.* ☉ *Nov.–Feb., daily 9–4, Mar.–Oct., daily 9–5.*

Gulfport

12 mi west of Biloxi.

Many activities for children plus access to one of the Gulf's most historic islands makes Gulfport a nice stop for families. If you have time for only one activity on this part of the coast, make it a getaway to **Ship Island** on the passenger ferry from the **Gulfport Small Craft Harbor.** The ferry runs twice a day from March through October; the trip takes about 90 minutes. At Ship Island, a part of Gulf Islands National Seashore, a U.S. park ranger will guide you through **Fort Massachusetts,** built in 1859 and used by Union troops to blockade Mississippi Sound during the Civil War. The rangers will treat you to tales of the island's colorful past, including the story of the *filles aux casquettes—* young women sent by the French government as brides for the lonely early colonists. Each girl (*fille*) carried a small hope chest (*casquette*). Spend the day sunning, swimming in the clear green water, and beach-combing for treasures washed up by the surf. ⊠ *Ticket office at Gulfport Harbor in Joseph T. Jones Memorial Park, east of intersection of*

U.S. 49 and U.S. 90, ☎ *228/436–6010; 228/864–1014 after hrs for ferry schedule.* ☞ *Ferry $16.* ◷ *Ferry runs Mar.–Oct.*

☾ With its playground, bumper boats, and cars, and more than 100 arcade games, **Funtime USA** provides hours of entertainment for children of all ages. ✉ *U.S. 90 and Cowan Rd.,* ☎ *228/896–7315.* ☞ *Grounds free; 75¢–$3 for rides and games.* ◷ *June–Aug., daily 9 AM–midnight; Sept.–May, daily 9 AM–10 PM.*

☾ **Marine Life Oceanarium,** in the small craft harbor in the Joseph T. Jones Memorial Park, puts on shows with performing dolphins, sea lions, and macaws. ✉ *Joseph T. Jones Memorial Park, east of intersection of U.S. 49 and U.S. 90,* ☎ *228/863–0651.* ☞ *$13.75.* ◷ *Daily 9–6.*

Dining and Lodging

$$$–$$$$ ✕ **Vrazel's.** The interior of this charming brick building has a soothing intimacy about it, with soft lighting and dining nooks with large windows facing the beach or overlooking exquisite gardens. Choose from a substantial list of coastal water fare: red snapper, Gulf trout, flounder, and shrimp prepared every which way. When amberjack is the special, it's a sure hit. ✉ *3206 W. Beach Blvd. (U.S. 90), Gulfport,* ☎ *228/863–2229. AE, D, DC, MC, V. Closed Sun. No lunch Sat.*

$$–$$$ ✕ **Chappy's.** Special-occasion dining for coast residents often means a visit to this pleasant restaurant in Long Beach, just outside Gulfport. Specialties include rich gumbo, redfish panfried Cajun style, and barbecue shrimp. The fish, fresh from the Gulf, is cooked by chef Chappy himself. ✉ *624 E. Beach Blvd., Long Beach,* ☎ *228/865–9755. AE, D, DC, MC, V.*

$$–$$$ ✕ **The Chimneys.** After establishing itself at the Long Beach Harbor as a favorite lunch and dinner place for locals and visitors alike, the Chimneys relocated to Gulfport in a gracious antebellum home with a stunning view of the Gulf. The kitchen serves up trout dishes, shrimp prepared a variety of ways, and blackened stuffed fillet filled with a savory blend of crabmeat and shrimp. ✉ *1640 E. Beach Blvd., Gulfport,* ☎ *228/868–7020. AE, D, DC, MC, V. Closed Mon.*

$$–$$$$ ⊞ **Grand Casino Gulfport Hotel & Oasis Resort & Spa.** These two hotels are on either side of U.S. 49. They're connected by a covered, climate-controlled walkway. Although accommodations are in two separate buildings, the amenities and restaurants are easily accessible from both properties. Rooms are basic and comfortable; however, the ones at the Oasis have a slightly more laid-back, beachy feel. Kids Quest day care keeps the little ones entertained, and there's a shuttle to the property's Grand Bear golf course. You'll find that 24-hour casino action is never more than a few steps away. ✉ *U.S. 90 at U.S. 49, Gulfport,* ☎ *228/870–7777 or 800/354–2450,* 🕸 *www.grandcasinos. com. 1,000 rooms. 6 restaurants, coffee shop, room service, in-room data ports, 5 pools, gym, hair salon, spa, bar, children's programs (ages 6 wks–11 yrs), concierge, car rental. AE, D, DC, MC, V.*

Shopping

Prime Outlets of Gulfport (✉ Exit 34A off I–10, 1000 Factory Shops Blvd., ☎ 228/867–6100) has more than 80 famous-brand shops offering factory-outlet prices. The shops are connected by a covered walkway. A food court, tourist information booth, and playground are also on the premises.

En Route   The landscape grows increasingly broad, wild, and lovely west of Gulfport. From Long Beach through to Pass Christian, U.S. 90 bisects stretches of stately homes to the north and shimmering water to the south. Be sure to slow down in Long Beach to admire the Friendship Oak on the campus of the University of Southern Mississippi. Legend has it that those who stroll under the massive branches of the more than 500-year-old oak will remain forever friends.

Pass Christian

10 mi west of Gulfport.

Sailboat racing in the South began here, and consequently the second yacht club in the country was formed in this town (it still exists today)—Louisiana landowner Zachary Taylor was at the yacht club when he was persuaded to run for the presidency.

Twenty-six miles of man-made beach extend from Biloxi to Pass Christian. Toward the west the beaches become less commercialized and less crowded; Pass Christian's is the best of all. Tan, sail, jet-ski, or beachcomb, but *don't swim:* the waters are shallow and murky.

On Pass Christian's scenic drive, which runs parallel to U.S. 90, is some of the most admired real estate in the country. Most homes on the scenic drive are on the National Register of Historic Places, and you can tour many of them during the annual **Pass Christian Historical Society**'s home tour (☎ 228/452–0063).

OFF THE
BEATEN PATH
CROSBY ARBORETUM – Well worth a 30-mi detour northwest to the town of Picayune, the arboretum, with its 64-acre interpretive center, focuses on the ecosystems of the 16,000-square-mi Pearl River Drainage Basin of south Mississippi and Louisiana. ✉ *I–59, Exit 4 at Picayune, 370 Ridge Rd.,* ☎ *601/799–2311.* ☜ *$4.* ☉ *Wed.–Sun. 9–4:30.*

Shopping

Hillyer House (✉ 207 E. Scenic Dr., ☎ 601/452–4810) sells handmade jewelry, pottery, glass, and brass made by local and regional artists, plus packaged Southern delicacies.

Waveland

15 mi west of Pass Christian.

Travelers who think of Waveland as just a spot to get onto I–10 for New Orleans are missing one of the most accessible tourist information offices on the Gulf Coast, the **Hancock County Welcome Center** (✉ I–10 Exit 2, at Highway 607, ☎ 228/533–5554). Waveland also offers great camping and a pretty snazzy Mardi Gras parade.

Buccaneer State Park (✉ 1150 S. Beach Blvd., ☎ 228/467–3822) has an Olympic-size wave pool, open from Memorial Day through Labor Day (☉ daily 11–6:30; $9), that may lure you from the nature trail, the beach, and picnic sites. There are 129 campsites in a grove of live oaks streaming with moss. The park, open year-round, also has two tennis courts with lights, two basketball courts, and a seasonal camp store.

Dining

$$$–$$$$ ✕ **Armand's.** Chef Armand Jonte brings sophisticated cuisine to the coast in a small, intimate restaurant. The menu changes frequently to utilize the best fresh, local ingredients, but seafood always figures prominently, and Jonte's eggplant Eloise—a lightly breaded and fried slice of eggplant topped with shrimp, crab, and crawfish and drenched in decadent Choron sauce (a hollandaise/béarnaise mix)—is always available. ✉ *141 Hwy. 90,* ☎ *228/467–8255. MC, V.*

$ ✕ **Lil Ray's.** Though the appointments are limited to trestle tables and benches, this is a place to dream about when you're hungry for seafood platters and po'boys. A waitress, asked by a customer for a diet drink, said it best: "Mister, this ain't no diet place." ✉ *613 Hwy. 90,* ☎ *228/ 467–4566. Reservations not accepted. D, MC, V.*

The Gulf Coast A to Z

AIR TRAVEL

Gulfport-Biloxi Regional Airport is served by AirTran, American Eagle, ASA/The Delta Connection, Casino Airlink (scheduled charter service), Continental Express, and Northwest Airlink.

AIRPORTS

➤ AIRPORT INFORMATION: **Gulfport-Biloxi Regional Airport** (✉ Airport Rd. off Washington Ave., Gulfport, ☎ 228/863–5953).

BUS TRAVEL

Coast Area Transit provides coast-wide public transportation. Greyhound connects the coast with Jackson, New Orleans, and Mobile. Local service exists in Biloxi, Gulfport, and Bay St. Louis.

➤ BUS INFORMATION: **Coast Area Transit** (✉ 333 DeBuys Rd., Gulfport, ☎ 228/896–8080). **Greyhound** (✉ 166 Main St., Biloxi, ☎ 228/ 436–4335 or 800/231–2222; ✉ 2805 13th St., Gulfport, ☎ 228/863– 1022 or 800/231–2222; ✉ 512 Ulman Ave., Bay St. Louis, ☎ 228/ 467–4272 or 800/231–2222; WEB www.greyhound.com).

CAR TRAVEL

You can drive across the Gulf Coast in 1½ hours via I–10 and U.S. 90. From Gulfport, it takes just over an hour to reach New Orleans and less than three hours to get to Jackson via U.S. 49.

EMERGENCIES

Dial 911 or go to the emergency room at Gulf Coast Medical Center.
➤ CONTACTS: **Calvert-Gamble Pharmacy** (✉ 2561 Pass Rd., Biloxi, ☎ 228/338–1411). **Gulf Coast Medical Center** (✉ 180 DeBuys Rd., Biloxi, ☎ 228/388–6711). **K&B Drug Store** (✉ 292 Eisenhower Dr., Biloxi, ☎ 228/388–8500). **Sartin's Pharmacy** (✉ 4300 15th St., Gulfport, ☎ 228/864–3514).

MEDIA

RADIO
FM: WMJY 93.7, adult contemporary; KNN 99.1, country.

OUTDOORS AND SPORTS

FISHING
Charter boats for half-day, full-day, and overnight deep-sea fishing can be found at marinas and harbors all along the Gulf Coast. Prices start around $30 per person; group rates are usually available. The Mississippi Beach Convention and Visitors Bureau can recommend charter services. Unless you're on a chartered boat (where the captain's license will cover you), you'll need a fishing license. Three-day licenses are available in many bait shops and other stores along the harbor.

GOLF
The coast's climate allows for year-round golfing, and golf packages are offered by many coast hotels and motels. The Bridges Golf Resort has an 18-hole course (par 72) designed by Arnold Palmer. The course encompasses more than 17 lakes and 14 acres of wetlands. Golf carts come equipped with computers that give pro tips on how to play each hole. The resort is also the site of the Arnold Palmer Golf Academy. Grand Casino's lavish Grand Bear is a Jack Nicklaus–designed beauty that caters to resort guests only. The course (par 72) is on 650 acres that include natural wetland terrain, two rivers, and a man-made lake.

Diamondhead's Pine and Cardinal courses has two 18-hole courses (both par 72) that challenge even the pros. Wooded, gently rolling, and well kept, they are ringed by the large, elegant houses and condominiums of the Diamondhead resort community.

Beautifully landscaped Mississippi National Golf Club has fairways lined with whispering pines, tall oaks, magnolias, and dogwoods on an 18-hole course (par 72). Pine Island Golf Course was designed by Pete Dye, who created the tournament players' course in Jacksonville. This 18-hole course, with a par of 71, spans three islands, and its abundant wildlife, beautiful setting, and clubhouse will lessen the bite of any double bogeys. The Oaks Gulf Club, an 18-hole, par-72 championship course, has gotten rave reviews since its opening last year. It's the site of the annual Buy.Com Mississippi Gulf Coast Classic. Windance Country Club has an 18-hole, par-72 course ranked by *Golf Digest* among the top 100 in the United States; nonmembers can play here through hotel golf packages.

➤ CONTACTS: **The Bridges Golf Resort** (⊠ The Bridges at Casino Magic Resort, 711 Casino Magic Dr., Bay St. Louis, ☎ 228/466–4991 or 800/562–4425). **Diamondhead's Pine and Cardinal courses** (⊠ 7600 Country Club Circle, ☎ 228/255–3910). **Grand Bear** (⊠ North Harrison County, Grand Way, Gulfport, ☎ 228/604–7100). **Mississippi National Golf Club** (⊠ 900 Hickory Hill Dr., Gautier, ☎ 228/ 497–2372 or 800/477–4044). **Oaks Gulf Club** (⊠ 24384 Club House Dr., off Menge Ave., Pass Christian, ☎ 228/452–0909). **Pine Island Golf Course** (⊠ Gulf Park Estates, 2¼ mi east of Ocean Springs, 3 mi south of U.S. 90, ☎ 228/875–1674). **Windance Country Club** (⊠ 19385 Champion Circle, Gulfport, ☎ 228/832–4871).

TOURS

Celebrity Limousine and Tours Service charters bus tours of the coastal area and New Orleans. Magnolia Tours & Transportation custom-plans group tours in buses or vans.

➤ FEES AND SCHEDULES: **Celebrity Limousine and Tours Service** (⊠ 2421 South Shore Dr., Biloxi, ☎ 228/388–1384). **Magnolia Tours & Transportation** (⊠ 14035 Airport Rd., Gulfport 39503, ☎ 228/863–9005 or 800/642–4684).

VISITOR INFORMATION

Get a free *Attractions and Accommodations* guide to the Gulf Coast area at the Mississippi Gulf Coast Convention and Visitors Bureau, open weekdays from 8 to 5. Ocean Springs Chamber of Commerce, open from 8:30 to 5 weekdays, has racks of informational brochures on Ocean Springs and the Gulf Coast area.

➤ TOURIST INFORMATION: **Mississippi Gulf Coast Convention and Visitors Bureau** (☎ 228/896–6699 or 800/237–9493, WEB www.gulfcoast. org)). **Ocean Springs Chamber of Commerce** (⊠ 1000 Washington Ave., ☎ 228/875–4424, WEB www.oceanspringschamber.com).

THE NATCHEZ TRACE

Corinth, Tupelo, Jackson, Natchez

The flower-sprigged and forested Natchez Trace Parkway is a vast and verdant history lesson. This enchanted path between Nashville and Natchez is said to be about 8,000 years old. It follows the early trails worn by Choctaw and Chickasaw Native Americans, itinerant preachers, post riders, soldiers, and settlers. Landscaped by the National Park Service, the Trace winds through straight pines, haunting cypresses, peaceful vistas of reeds, and still waters with dense woodlands.

The Trace is almost 450 mi long, with 313 mi in Mississippi. The Mississippi segment of the Natchez Trace begins as you enter the state's northeast corner, between Iuka and Belmont. Mile markers are posted along the way to help drivers navigate. There are no billboards on the parkway, and commercial vehicles are forbidden to use it. Park rangers are serious about the 50 mph speed limit; you'll probably get acquainted with one if you drive any faster.

Numbers in the margin correspond to points of interest on the Natchez Trace map.

Corinth

❶ *90 mi southeast of Memphis.*

Settled just seven years before the Civil War as "Cross City" for its railroad junction, Corinth assumed military importance because of its Memphis and Charleston Railroad. In April 1862, after the bloody Battle of Shiloh, near Shiloh Church in Tennessee, 21 mi to the north, the Confederates retreated to Corinth and turned it into a vast medical center. In May 1862, the Confederates, under General P. G. T. Beauregard, were forced to withdraw farther. Their retreat involved the most ingenious hoax of the war: to fool the Union forces, campfires were lighted, dummy cannoneers were placed at fake cannons, empty trains were cheered as if they were carrying reinforcements, and buglers moved along the deserted works, playing taps. The ploy worked and was hailed as a triumph for Beauregard and a hollow victory for the Union forces who occupied the town. In October 1862, a Confederate attempt to recapture the town failed.

Markers and displays throughout town commemorate the Battles of Shiloh and Corinth. The **Northeast Mississippi Museum** displays Civil War artifacts and distributes a free self-guided–tour brochure to help you explore the town. ⌧ *4th St. at Washington St.,* ☎ *601/287–3120.* ⌦ *Free.* ☉ *Mar.–Oct., daily 10–5; Nov.–Feb., daily 10:30–4:30.*

J. P. Coleman State Park

❷ *13 mi north of Iuka off U.S. 25.*

With accommodations aplenty for overnighters, J. P. Coleman State Park (⌧ 613 County Rd. 321, Iuka 38852, ☎ 601/423–6515), open year-round, allows nature lovers ample time for exploring its various nature trails and playing in its waters. There are wooded campsites for tents and RVs, and 10 secluded cabins, some of them old and rustic, others from the 1970s with fireplaces and central air-conditioning and heat. Rooms at the balconied lodge overlook the shale beaches of serene Pickwick Lake. You can rent canoes and boats, fish, swim, and water-ski.

Jacinto

❸ *9 mi east of U.S. 45.*

Between Corinth and Tupelo on MS 356 is Jacinto, with its restored federal-style courthouse (1854). Nearby are a couple of pre-1870 buildings that are slowly being restored. Jacinto also has nature trails that lead to mineral springs, and a swinging bridge. For more information on Jacinto, call 601/286–8662.

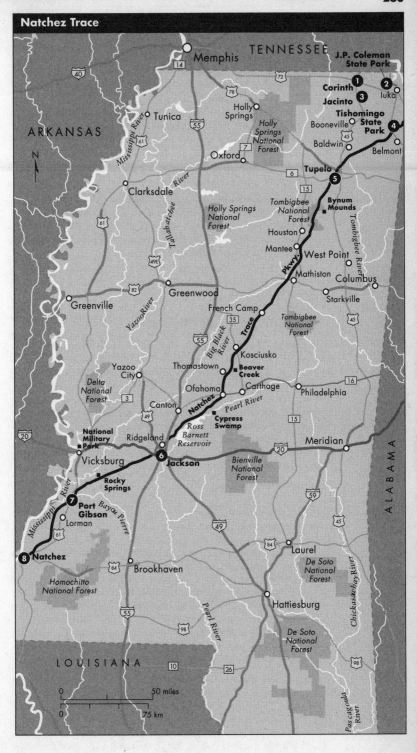

Natchez Trace

TENNESSEE

J.P. Coleman
State Park

Memphis

ARKANSAS

N

Tunica

Holly
Springs

Corinth

Jacinto

Iuka

Tishomingo
State
Park

Booneville

Oxford

Baldwin

Belmont

Holly
Springs
National
Forest

Clarksdale

Tupelo

Holly Springs
National
Forest

Tombigbee
National
Forest

Bynum
Mounds

Houston

West Point

Greenville

Greenwood

Mantee

Mathiston

Columbus

French Camp

Starkville

Yazoo
City

Thomastown

Kosciusko

Beaver
Creek

Tombigbee
National
Forest

Delta
National
Forest

Canton

Ofahoma

Carthage

Philadelphia

Natchez

Cypress
Swamp

National
Military
Park

Ridgeland

Ross
Barnett
Reservoir

Meridian

Vicksburg

Jackson

Bienville
National
Forest

Rocky
Springs

Port
Gibson

Lorman

Laurel

Natchez

Brookhaven

De Soto
National
Forest

Homochitto
National
Forest

Hattiesburg

De Soto
National
Forest

LOUISIANA

50 miles

75 km

Tishomingo State Park

❹ *15 mi south of Iuka.*

In the Appalachian foothills, Tishomingo State Park (✉ Natchez Trace MM 304, Box 880, Tishomingo 38873, ☎ 601/438–6914) has a unique terrain for Mississippi. If you're feeling peppy, 13 mi of nature trails wind through a canyon along steep hills by waterfalls, granite outcrops, and a swinging bridge; otherwise, take the winding roads through shady forests. Eight-mile canoe trips and float trips are offered from mid-March through October. Around Haynes Lake are primitive campsites and hookups. Rustic cabins are another option. Bring your own food. The park has an outdoor swimming pool open during warmer months; there's a $2 charge.

En Route The **Natchez Trace Parkway Visitor Center,** 6 mi north of Tupelo on the Trace, distributes the 4-ft *Official Map and Guide,* which has mile-by-mile information from Nashville to Natchez. The center also displays exhibits, some of which are geared toward kids, and shows a 12-minute film relating to the Parkway.

Tupelo

❺ *90 mi southeast of Memphis, 70 mi east of Oxford.*

The largest city in north Mississippi, Tupelo (named after the tupelo gum tree) was founded in 1859 and is a city of accomplishment—it's here, after all, that Elvis Presley was born in 1935. Progressive leaders have successfully lured business and industry to an area that only 30 years ago was predominantly agricultural. The arts flourish here, and the North Mississippi Medical Center is the largest hospital in rural America. Twice each year, in February and August, one of the largest furniture trade shows in the country is held at the Tupelo Furniture Market. The four-day events draw nearly 25,000 buyers and exhibitors from around the world; room reservations are almost impossible to get at those times. For outdoors lovers, Tupelo's scenic hill country provides beautiful places to camp, swim, fish, jog, and bike.

★ The **Elvis Presley Park and Museum** is anchored by the tiny, two-room shotgun-style house built by Presley's father, Vernon, for just $180. Elvis Aaron Presley was born here on January 8, 1935. The home has been restored and furnished much as it was when the Presleys lived in it. The house is now surrounded by Elvis Presley Park, land purchased with proceeds from Elvis's 1956 concert at the Mississippi-Alabama Fair. The park includes a swimming pool, tennis courts, a playground, a youth center with a gift shop (stocked with Elvis souvenirs), and the Elvis Presley Museum, which stores more than 3,000 pieces of Elvis memorabilia. The **Elvis Presley Memorial Chapel,** suggested by the singer in 1971 as a place for his fans to meditate, was dedicated in 1979, two years after Presley's death. ✉ *306 Elvis Presley Dr., off E. Main St.,* ☎ *662/841–1245.* 🌐 *Birthplace $2, museum $4.* ☼ *May–Sept., Mon.–Sat. 9–5:30, Sun. 1–5; Oct.–Apr., Mon.–Sat. 9–5, Sun. 1–5.*

The **Oren Dunn City Museum** displays Presley memorabilia along with other exhibits, including a turn-of-the-century Western Union office, a replica of a sorghum mill, a train depot and caboose, and an old-time country store. There are also space program–related displays, including space suits from the Apollo missions. ✉ *James J. Ballard Park, off MS 6W,* ☎ *662/841–6438.* 🌐 *$1.* ☼ *June–Aug., weekdays 8–4, Sept.–May, weekends 1–5.*

MISSISSIPPI MUSIC

IT MIGHT BE ENOUGH for most places to lay claim to a single musical genre—in this case, Mississippi Delta blues—but Mississippi went ahead and threw the King of Rock and Roll into the mix as well.

The musicians and storytellers who grew up in the Delta, a wedge-shaped piece of land lying in northern Mississippi between the Mississippi and Yazoo rivers, are typically credited with creating the blues around the turn of the 20th century. People such as Robert Johnson, Blind Lemon Jefferson, Son House, and Turner Johnson helped push what was then known as "devil's music" to the forefront of musical acceptability.

It's been said that the blues were created out of necessity in the rural areas of the Deep South, particularly on large plantations and in industries that required heavy manual labor. The blues reflected not only the social isolation and lack of formal training of its creators—much of the music was handed down orally one generation to the next—but also their ability to make do with the most basic of resources and survive under the most oppressive circumstances. The basic vocal material for the early blues came from hollers (improvised work songs) that were sung by workers in the fields and in other occupations requiring just plain hard toil. The moody song style endures today in song, speech, and music.

Locals say that if you find yourself in Mississippi and you're looking for a great juke joint, you might just check out the telephone poles. Over the years, they've proven to be a good informational source, since ads for the so-called chitlins circuit are often posted there.

Although the north end of the state upholds the tradition and culture of the blues, the bustling Mississippi Gulf Coast and Tunica County, with their numerous casinos, offer musical venues for other sounds. A random sampling of the na-

tion's entertainers who have played Tunica shows includes performers such as Loretta Lynn, Tanya Tucker, Johnny Cash, and the Platters. Drawing heavily from the nearby musical hotbed of New Orleans, the Gulf Coast casinos have presented everyone from Dr. John to the Neville Brothers to Irma Thomas.

If you have a few days and you're interested in musical roots, you might consider the following rough itinerary, which begins just over the state border in Tennessee. On Day 1 begin your Mississippi music heritage tour from Memphis—home of Beale Street and Graceland, Elvis Presley's mansion. Travel to Tupelo and tour the humble two-room house where the King was born. You can also see sites important to Elvis's early life—the school where he won his first talent contest singing "Old Shepp" and the hardware store where he bought his first guitar.

On Day 2 make your way to the Mississippi Delta and the area known as the Birthplace of the Blues. In Clarksdale visit the Delta Blues Museum with memorabilia of such music greats as Muddy Waters, Robert Johnson, and B. B. King. Take a ride down Highway 61 and see the famous crossroads where legend has it Johnson traded his soul for the unsurpassed talent that made him a star.

On Day 3 travel east across the state to Starkville, home of the **Templeton Music Museum** (✉ 46 Blackjack Rd., ☎ 601/325–8301), which has roller organs, player pianos, and music boxes from the ragtime era. Tours are by appointment. To the south is Meridian's Highland Park, home of the **Jimmie Rodgers Museum** (✉ Jimmie Rodgers Memorial Dr., ☎ 601/485–1808). This memorial to the father of country music includes Rodgers's original guitar and personal belongings.

Although the blues may be its past, the music of Mississippi is now as eclectic as the state itself.

The **Tupelo National Battlefield,** inside the city limits, commemorates the Civil War Battle of Tupelo with monuments and displays. In 1864 Union general A. J. Smith marched 14,000 troops against Nathan Bedford Forrest's forces near Tupelo. Smith's goal was to end the constant Confederate harassment of supply lines to Sherman's army and thereby secure the Union invasion of Atlanta. The battle, on July 14, 1864, was the last major battle in Mississippi and one of the bloodiest. ⊠ *W. Main St. (MS 6).* ☉ *Daily sunrise–sunset.*

Dining and Lodging

$$–$$$ ✕ **Harvey's.** It's a favorite in four cities, and here's why: Harvey's restaurants have based their reputation on consistency and quality in food and service. Try the prime rib, seafood, steak, or, for lighter fare, the chicken Alpine or great garden salad. Lots of plants and warm wood tones add to the appeal. ⊠ *424 S. Gloster St.,* ☎ *662/842–6763. AE, D, MC, V. Closed Sun.*

$$–$$$ ✕ **Jefferson Place.** Though this 19th-century house may look somewhat austere from the outside, red-check tablecloths and bric-a-brac brighten its interior. The place is popular with the college crowd; short orders and steaks are the specialties. ⊠ *823 Jefferson St.,* ☎ *662/844–8696. Reservations not accepted. AE, MC, V. Closed Sun.*

$$–$$$ ✕ **Vanelli's.** Family pictures and scenes of Greece adorn the walls at this comfortable restaurant. Lunch and dinner buffets include both Greek specialties and lighter fare. Vanelli's own bakery produces breads, strudels, and pastries. ⊠ *1302 N. Gloster St.,* ☎ *662/844–4410. AE, D, DC, MC, V.*

$–$$$ ▦ **Mockingbird Inn Bed & Breakfast.** Each of the seven rooms in this tiny inn is decorated with the theme of a different country. The Athens Room comes with Greek columns and statues and sheer flowing fabrics. One has a fireplace, and one has a whirlpool tub. In summer you can take refuge from the hot Mississippi sun under the inn's gazebo or on its porch swing. ⊠ *305 N. Gloster, 38801,* ☎ *662/841–0286,* FAX *662/840–4158. 7 rooms. AE, D, MC, V. BP.*

$–$$$ ▦ **Ramada Inn.** Near the Elvis Presley Park and Museum and the Natchez Trace Parkway Visitor Center, this modern hotel provides easy access to Tupelo's major areas of interest. Business travelers will appreciate the in-room modem lines. For families, there's a courtyard with a kiddie pool. Night owls can dance the night away in Bogart's Lounge every night except Sunday. ⊠ *854 N. Gloster, 38801,* ☎ *800/228–2828 or 662/844–4111,* ☎ FAX *662/844–4111. 230 rooms, 10 suites, 4 minisuites. Restaurant, in-room data ports, pool, spa, laundry service, meeting rooms. AE, D, DC, MC, V.*

$–$$ ▦ **Executive Inn.** Guest rooms in this large, contemporary hotel are plain and functional, but clean. ⊠ *1011 N. Gloster St., 38801,* ☎ *662/841–2222 or 800/533–3220,* FAX *601/844–7836. 116 rooms, 4 suites. Restaurant, indoor pool, hot tub, sauna, lounge. AE, DC, MC, V.*

$–$$ ▦ **Rex Plaza Suites.** Both short- and long-term stays can be arranged at this four-building hotel. Some of the suites have kitchens and washers and dryers. ⊠ *619 N. Gloster, 38804,* ☎ *662/840–8000 or 800/203–5917,* FAX *662/840–1116. 64 suites. Restaurant, cable TV, pool, gym, lounge, meeting rooms, free parking. AE, D, DC, MC, V.*

$ ▦ **Trace Inn.** On 15 acres near the Natchez Trace, this old motel accommodates the weary with neat rooms and friendly service. ⊠ *3400 W. Main St., 38801,* ☎ *662/842–5555,* FAX *662/844–3105. 134 rooms. Restaurant, pool, playground. AE, D, DC, MC, V.*

From Tupelo to Jackson

From Tupelo the trip to Jackson takes three hours if you don't stop. It can easily take an entire day, however, if you pause to read the brown wooden markers, explore nature trails, and admire the neat fields, trees, and wildflower meadows. If you have the time, don't miss Columbus and environs, an hour or so east of the parkway near the Alabama line. The parkway is incomplete from Mile Markers 101.5 to 87.0. Connecting routes are I–55, I–20, and I–220. To reach Jackson, follow I–55 south from the Trace.

Bynum Mounds (Mile Marker 232.4) are ceremonial hills that were constructed between 100 BC and AD 200 by prehistoric people. Exhibits describe their daily existence.

At **French Camp** (Mile Marker 180.7), where Frenchman Louis LeFleur established a stand in 1812, you can watch sorghum molasses being made on Saturday in late September and October. Native American and French artifacts are housed inside the authentic dogtrot-style cabin.

Cypress Swamp (Mile Marker 122.0), a pleasure today, was a treacherous, mosquito-infested morass for early travelers. A 20-minute self-guided nature walk takes you through the tree-canopied tupelo/bald cypress swamp.

The **Mississippi Crafts Center at Ridgeland** (Mile Marker 102.4) displays and sells high-quality crafts in a dogtrot log cabin. Members of the Craftsmen's Guild of Mississippi have created pewter and silver jewelry, pottery, handwoven and hand-screened clothing, whimsical wooden toys, highly prized Choctaw baskets, and other interesting items. The center sponsors free demonstrations (usually on weekends) of basket weaving, wood carving, pottery, and quilting. There are rest rooms and picnic tables on site. ⊠ *Natchez Trace at Ridgeland,* ☎ *662/856–7546,* WEB *www.misscraftsmensguild.org.* ⌑ *Free.* ☉ *Daily 9–5.*

OFF THE
BEATEN PATH

COLUMBUS – Forty-five miles east of the Natchez Trace on U.S. 82 is one of Mississippi's most undisturbed antebellum towns. This river city (on the Tombigbee) contains 100 pre–Civil War mansions—some of which are open to the public—and many historic sites. Columbus is called the town "where flowers healed a nation" because of a group of gracious women who, in 1866, placed flowers on the graves of both Confederate and Union soldiers in what is now called Friendship Cemetery. The gesture inspired the poem "The Blue and the Gray," written by Francis Miles Finch, and Columbus's Decoration Day at Friendship Cemetery is now observed as the nation's Memorial Day.

WAVERLY MANSION – This privately owned, restored showplace has been around since 1852. Outstanding antiques adorn each spacious room, and an antiques shop, Snow's Antiques, in on the premises. It's 10 mi northwest of Columbus off MS 50. ⊠ *1852 Waverly Mansion Road, West Point,* ☎ *662/494–1399.* ⌑ *$7.50.* ☉ *Daily 9–5.*

Jackson

❻ *180 mi southwest of Tupelo, 45 mi west of Vicksburg.*

At its spangled edges, Jackson has little to distinguish it, but the state capital becomes increasingly original toward its shady heart. The downtown area has many small museums and most of the city's notable architecture.

The city is named for Andrew Jackson, who was popular with Mississippians long before he became president. As Major General Jackson, he helped negotiate the Treaty of Doak's Stand, according to which the Choctaw ceded large chunks of Mississippi to the United

States on October 18, 1820. President Thomas Jefferson recommended that the town be laid out in a checkerboard pattern of alternating squares of buildings and parks. Peter A. Vandorn proposed the plan for Jackson and submitted a map for the new city in April 1822; today the Old Capitol, along with the Capitol Green on which it sits, is one of the few remaining examples of the scheme.

Jackson is also the county seat of Hinds County, named for another negotiator, Major General Thomas Hinds, an enterprising and daring hero of the Battle of New Orleans in the War of 1812.

The **Mississippi Agriculture and Forestry Museum** complex looks like an old farm marooned in the midst of expanding suburbs, but the city was actually here first. The 10 farm buildings were brought here to stand exactly as they once did in Jefferson Davis County, Mississippi. A crossroads town, similar to small Mississippi towns in the 1920s, has been assembled with a working blacksmith's shop and a cotton gin; meetings are held in the old Masonic Lodge, and weddings can be arranged at the 1897 Epiphany Episcopal Church building. The general store sells soft drinks, snacks, and souvenirs. A complete tour of the museum, which has fine exhibits on agriculture, forestry, and farm-related aviation, takes about 90 minutes. Also on the grounds is the **Jackson Visitor Information Center.** ⊠ *1150 Lakeland Dr., 39216,* ☎ *601/713–3365 or 800/844–8687.* 🖃 *$4.* ⊙ *Mon.–Sat. 9–5.*

The **Mississippi Sports Hall of Fame and Museum,** next to the Mississippi Agriculture and Forestry Museum off Lakeland Drive, honors Mississippi athletes past and present with interactive exhibits and films containing action-packed footage and interviews. It includes a high school exhibit and an Olympic exhibit, and showcases more than 200 sports figures. ⊠ *1152 Lakeland Drive, 39236-6021,* ☎ *601/982–8264 or 800/280–3263,* WEB *www.msfame.com.* 🖃 *$5.* ⊙ *Mon.–Sat. 10–4.*

The **Old Capitol,** flanked by the **War Memorial Building** (1940) to the north and the **Mississippi Archives Building** (1971) to the south, served as the state capitol from 1839 to 1903. Built between 1833 and 1838 with simple columns and elegant proportions, it's a tribute to Greek Revival architecture. The building was restored in 1959–61 to house the **State Historical Museum.** The Vandorn map, a blueprint of the city's original design, and other exhibits depicting Mississippi's history are on display in the museum. ⊠ *100 S. State St., Downtown,* ☎ *601/359–6920,* WEB *www.mdah.state.ms.us.* 🖃 *Free.* ⊙ *Weekdays 8–5, Sat. 9:30–4:30, Sun. 12:30–4:30.*

The **Jackson Zoological Park** uses more than 100 acres to re-create a natural habitat for about 500 animals. Children love the petting zoo, complete with hands-on exhibits, and the miniature train ride. ⊠ *2918 W. Capitol St., West Jackson,* ☎ *601/352–2580,* WEB *www.jacksonzoo. com.* 🖃 *$4.* ⊙ *Daily 9–5.*

Since its opening in 1847, **City Hall** (⊠ 219 S. President St., Downtown, ☎ 601/960–1035) has served continuously as Jackson's center of government. A Masonic Hall originally occupied the third floor of this stately white Greek Revival building. During the Civil War, City Hall was used as a hospital. Peek into the tiny city council chamber with its black-and-white floors. On the west side of the building is the formal Josh Halbert Garden, with a 1968 statue of Andrew Jackson.

Within the **Mississippi Arts Center** is the **Mississippi Museum of Art,** dedicated to preserving Mississippi's artistic heritage. With its impressive permanent collection of both regional and national paintings, plus changing exhibits and a sculpture garden, you may want to set aside a few hours to explore each and every corner. ✉ *201 E. Pascagoula St., Downtown,* ☎ *601/960–1515,* WEB *www.msmuseumofart.org.* 💲 *$3.* 🕐 *Tues.–Sat. 10–5.*

The **Russell C. Davis Planetarium** offers breathtaking science and nature adventures every day (except Monday). The planetarium's Mc-Nair Space Theater has a 60-ft domed screen (the largest in the mid-South), and a full complement of star, slide, special effect, and video shows. ✉ *201 E. Pascagoula St., Downtown,* ☎ *601/960–1550.* 💲 *$4.* 🕐 *Hrs vary; call ahead.*

The **U.S. Federal Courthouse,** constructed of concrete and sandstone, exemplifies the streamlined art deco style that was popular between the world wars, a time when many Jackson buildings were erected. This building was completed in 1934 and served as Jackson's post office and as a federal court building until 1988, when a new post office was built. The motifs of eagles, stars, and geometric designs on the exterior are repeated throughout the interior and on the freestanding light fixtures around the building. ✉ *245 E. Capitol St., Downtown.*

St. Andrew's Episcopal Cathedral is an important example of Gothic Revival architecture and is enhanced by fine stained-glass windows. ✉ *305 E. Capitol St., Downtown,* ☎ *601/354–1535,* WEB *www. standrewscathedral.org.* 🕐 *Weekdays 8:30–5.*

The **Mississippi Governor's Mansion** has been the official home of the state's first family since its completion in 1842. At that time, Jackson was a tiny city, and this grand Greek Revival dwelling was an optimistic statement. General Sherman presumably lived here in 1863. The mansion is one of only two executive residences to be designated a National Historic Landmark. Invest 30 minutes in the lively tours, strong on legend as well as fact. ✉ *300 E. Capitol St. Downtown,* ☎ *601/ 359–6421.* 💲 *Free.* 🕐 *Tours Tues.–Fri. 9:30–11:30.*

Smith Park is the only public square that remains from Thomas Jefferson's original plan for the city. The park was named after James Smith, a former Jacksonian (originally from Glasgow, Scotland), who donated $100 to fence and beautify the area. Eudora Welty used the park as the setting for her short story "The Winds." The park hosts frequent concerts, festivals, picnics, and art exhibits. ✉ *At center of Smith Park Historic District, Downtown.*

The **Cathedral of St. Peter the Apostle** (✉ 203 N. West St. Downtown), built between 1897 and 1900, is the third building of the congregation, which organized in 1846. Their first building was burned by Union troops in 1863, as were many others in the city. Their second building, now in the very center of the downtown area, at the site of the present rectory (✉ 123 N. West St., Downtown), was considered too remote from town. The cathedral is open to the public only for church services.

Mynelle Gardens is a 7-acre botanical showplace, with colorful paths surrounded by Southern flora and gentle streams. ✉ *4736 Clinton Blvd., Northwest Jackson,* ☎ *601/960–1894.* 💲 *$2.* 🕐 *Mon.–Sat. 9–5:15, Sun. noon–5:15.*

The two-story Second Empire–style **Galloway House** was completed in 1889. It was built for Methodist bishop Charles Galloway, a distinguished churchman of international renown. It is now in use as a law office. ✉ *304 N. Congress St., Downtown.*

The **New Capitol** sits in beaux arts splendor at the junction of Mississippi and North Congress streets, its dome surmounted by a gold-plated copper eagle with a 15-ft wingspan. Completed in 1903 at what was then the enormous cost of $1 million, the capitol underwent a $19 million renovation from 1979 to 1983. It was designed by the German architect Theodore C. Link, who was influenced by the design of the Capitol in Washington, D.C. Among the elaborate architectural details inside the building is a Tiffany window. ⊠ *400 High St., Downtown,* ☎ *601/359–3114.* ⌕ *Free.* ⊙ *Weekdays 8–5; guided tours weekdays at 9, 10, 11, 1:30, 2:30, and 3:30.*

Eudora Welty Library, the largest public library in Mississippi, is named for the city's famed short-story writer and novelist (*The Ponder Heart, Losing Battles, The Optimist's Daughter*). Opened in 1986, it houses a 42-ft-long circulation desk handcrafted in rosewood and maple by local craftsman Fletcher Cox. The Mississippi Writers' Room pays homage to the South's rich literary history with exhibits on Welty, as well as William Faulkner, Tennessee Williams, Margaret Walker Alexander, Ellen Douglas, and many others. ⊠ *300 N. State St., Downtown,* ☎ *601/968–5811.* ⊙ *Mon.–Thurs. 9–9, Fri.–Sat. 9–6, Sun. 1–5.*

On North State Street between College and Fortification streets stand a few **Victorian homes,** the survivors of the many large houses that lined this street in its heyday as Jackson's best address. The **Morris House** (⊠ 505 N. State St., Downtown) is a Classical Revival house built about 1900. The **Virden-Patton House** (⊠ 512 N. State St., Downtown), built about 1849, went undamaged through the Civil War, suggesting that Union officers may have used it as headquarters. The **Millsaps-Buie House** (⊠ 628 N. State St., Downtown), built in 1888, has been restored as a B&B inn. The **Garner Green House** (1910) has an imposing portico of Corinthian columns. This house was moved across the street from its original location and restored in 1988 as an office building. **Greenbrook Flowers** (⊠ 705 N. State St., Downtown), circa 1895–97, occupies the former St. Andrew's Episcopal rectory; it has been greatly altered. With the exception of the B&B, none of these homes is open to the public.

The **Manship House** was built about 1857 by Charles H. Manship, the Jackson mayor who surrendered the city to General William Tecumseh Sherman on July 16, 1863. The museum inside is a careful restoration of a small Gothic Revival cottage with wood graining painted by Manship himself. ⊠ *420 E. Fortification St. (enter parking area from Congress St.), Downtown,* ☎ *601/961–4724.* ⌕ *Free.* ⊙ *Tours Tues.–Fri. 9–4, Sat. 1–4.*

C. W. Welty and his wife, Chestina, built the house at **741 North Congress Street** in 1907. Their daughter, Eudora, was born in the master bedroom on the second floor in 1909. Welty used images of this house and neighborhood in many of her literary works, including *The Golden Apples*. It is now a law office.

The **Smith Robertson Museum and Cultural Center** has artifacts and exhibits depicting the history of black life in Mississippi. The building housed the first public school for black children in Jackson. ⊠ *528 Bloom St., Downtown,* ☎ *601/960–1457.* ⌕ *$1.* ⊙ *Weekdays 9–5, Sat. 9–noon, Sun. 2–5.*

Jackson's neat, tree-shaded neighborhoods are excellent for walking, jogging, or Sunday driving, especially the **Belhaven area** bounded by Riverside Drive, I–55, Fortification Street, and North State Street. **Carlisle, Poplar, Peachtree,** and **Fairview streets** are distinguished by fine homes.

OFF THE
BEATEN PATH

MUSEUM OF THE SOUTHERN JEWISH EXPERIENCE – The history of Southern Jewry is captured in an orientation video, exhibits of religious artifacts, and photographs of the rural South by Bill Aron. The museum preserves the fascinating history of communities that have seen many of their members move on to larger cities or to the North. Temple B'nai Israel in Natchez is a satellite of the museum; call about tours. The museum also sponsors multiday tours of Jewish sites in the region. Utica is a 40-minute drive southwest of Jackson. ⊠ *3863 Morrison Rd., Utica,* ☎ *601/362–6357,* WEB *www.msje.org.* ⊠ *Free, except for special exhibitions.* ☉ *Daily 10–5.*

Dining and Lodging

$$$–$$$$ ✕ **Nick's.** Seafood is the main fare at this elegant restaurant. Grilled blackfish with crabmeat is one of the many luncheon specials, although dinner brings out more elaborate seafood masterpieces. Soup or salad and vegetable du jour are included with the entrée. Desserts are wonderful, too, especially the white-chocolate mousse with raspberry sauce. ⊠ *1501 Lakeland Dr.,* ☎ *601/981–8017. AE, DC, MC, V. Closed Sun.*

$$–$$$$ ✕ **BRAVO!** This cheery, bustling restaurant is set in a shopping mall, but that doesn't diminish its impact. Traditional regional Italian cuisine—zesty pastas, wood-fired pizza, homemade breads, and antipasti—shares the menu with grilled meats topped with unique sauces, chutneys, and herb rubs. The menu changes frequently but is consistently good. ⊠ *244 Highland Village, South Plaza,* ☎ *601/982–8111. AE, D, DC, MC, V. Closed Mon.*

$$–$$$$ ✕ **Schimmel's.** Schimmel's specializes in prime meat and fresh Gulf seafood. Signature dishes include the veal chop, breadless crab cake, fried lobster tails, and an Asiago-crusted flounder, which nestles flounder under a layer of Italian cheese ⊠ *2615 N. State St.,* ☎ *601/981–7077. AE, D, MC, V.*

$$–$$$ ✕ **Primos.** Since 1964 this cozy and comfy eatery has pleased local palates. The main dining room recalls a French country inn, whereas the patio is pure American South. House specialties are fresh seafood and prime rib. ⊠ *4330 N. State St.,* ☎ *601/982–2064. AE, DC, MC, V. Closed Sun.*

$–$$ ✕ **Broad Street Baking Co. & Café.** You can enjoy breakfast, lunch, or dinner here, where some dozen different breads are baked fresh daily using European and old family recipes. Specialties include pizzas, sandwiches, pastries, and croissants. ⊠ *101 Banner Hall, I–55 at Northside Dr.,* ☎ *601/362–2900. MC, V. No dinner Sun.*

$–$$ ✕ **Gridley's.** Mexican-tile tables and floors enhance small, sunny dining areas. Gridley's is famous for its spicy barbecued pork and ribs served with all the trimmings—coleslaw, baked beans, and potatoes. ⊠ *1428 Old Square Rd.,* ☎ *601/362–8600. AE, D, MC, V.*

$$$–$$$$ 🏠 **Fairview Inn.** Listed on the National Register of Historic Places, this stately colonial Revival mansion is in Jackson's prestigious Belhaven section, conveniently situated near many of the major attractions yet secluded enough to suggest a country retreat. Period antiques fill the public rooms, and the guest rooms are decked out in chintz and Laura Ashley fabrics. Southern breakfast is included in the rate. ⊠ *734 Fairview St., 39202,* ☎ *601/948–3429 or 888/948–1908,* FAX *601/948–1203,* WEB *www.fairviewinn.com. 8 rooms. In-room data ports. AE, D, MC, V. BP.*

$$–$$$$ 🏠 **Edison Walthall Hotel.** The cornerstone and huge brass mailbox near the elevators are almost all that remain of the original Walthall Hotel, but the marble floors, gleaming brass, paneled library/writing room, and cozy bar almost fool you into thinking this is a restoration of a

19th-century home. Rooms are decorated with mahogany furniture. ⊠ *225 E. Capitol St., 39201,* ☎ *601/948–6161 or 800/932–6161,* FAX *601/948–0088,* WEB *www.edisonwalthall.com. 208 rooms, 6 suites. Restaurant, gym, hair salon, hot tub, bar, shop, airport shuttle. AE, D, DC, MC, V.*

$$–$$$$ ☑ **Millsaps-Buie House.** This Queen Anne–style home, with its corner
★ turret and tall-columned porch, was built in 1888 for Jackson financier and philanthropist Major Reuben Webster Millsaps, founder of Millsaps College. It is listed on the National Register of Historic Places. Its guest rooms are individually decorated with antiques. A full Southern breakfast is served in the Victorian dining room. ⊠ *628 N. State St., 39202,* ☎ *800/784–0221,* FAX *601/352–0221,* WEB *www. millsapsbuiehouse.com. 11 rooms. AE, DC, MC, V.*

$$ ☑ **Hilton Jackson.** Just off I–55N, this sleek and contemporary high-rise convention motel has good business facilities. Rooms are comfortable, with mahogany furniture. ⊠ *1001 County Line Rd., 39211,* ☎ *601/957–2800,* FAX *601/957–3191,* WEB *www.hilton-jackson.com. 300 rooms, 11 suites. 2 restaurants, in-room data ports, pool, gym, hair salon, 2 bars, shop, concierge floor, airport shuttle. AE, DC, MC, V.*

Nightlife and the Arts

Live rock and roll and rhythm and blues beckon a mix of young and old to the **Dock** (⊠ Main Harbor Marina at Ross Barnett Reservoir, ☎ 601/856–7765) from Thursday through Sunday. **Hal and Mal's** (⊠ 200 S. Commerce St., ☎ 601/948–0888) often has live music, and there's always plenty of room to dance. **Poet's** (⊠ 1855 Lakeland Dr., ☎ 601/982–9711) presents food, drink, and dance bands in an old-fashioned joint, with antiques, old signs, and a pressed-tin ceiling. **Rodeo's** (⊠ 6107 Ridgewood Rd., ☎ 601/957–9300) is an "in" spot, where live music and dancing attract big crowds.

Outdoor Activities and Sports

GOLF

Lefleur's Bluff Golf Course has nine holes (par 35) and a driving range. Tee time is required. ⊠ *1205 Lakeland Dr.,* ☎ *601/362–3885.* 🎫 *$8 weekdays, $10 weekends.*

Shopping

ANTIQUES

Bobbie King's (⊠ Woodland Hills Shopping Center, Old Canton Rd. at Duling Ave., ☎ 601/362–9803) specializes in new and heirloom textiles and exhibits them in lavish displays with one-of-a-kind accessories.

BOOKS

Books by Mississippi authors and about Mississippi are available from knowledgeable booksellers at **Lemuria** (⊠ 202 Banner Hall, 4465 I–55N, ☎ 601/366–7619). **Choctaw Books** (⊠ 926 North St., ☎ 601/352–7281) stocks first editions of Southern writers' works.

FLEA MARKET

If you're in the mood for a treasure hunt, the **Fairground Antique & Flea Market,** with 220 dealers, often harbors some fine pieces. ⊠ *900 High St.,* ☎ *601/353–5327.* ⊙ *Sat. 8–5, Sun. 10–5.*

GIFTS

The **Chimneyville Crafts Gallery** (⊠ 1150 Lakeland Dr., ☎ 601/981–2499) sells the work of members of the Craftsmen's Guild of Mississippi. Pottery, jewelry, woodwork, glasswork, quilts, and paper are among the offerings. The Craftsmen's Guild's objets d'art can also be found in the Mississippi Crafts Center at Ridgeland.

The **Everyday Gourmet** (✉ 2905 Old Canton Rd., ☎ 601/362–0723; ✉ 1625 County Line Rd., ☎ 601/977–9258) stocks local products, including pecan pie, bread, and biscuit mixes; muscadine jelly; jams and chutneys; cookbooks; fine ceramic tableware; and a complete selection of kitchenware and fine foods.

En Route Post riders stopped during the early 1800s at the Natchez Trace's **Rocky Springs** (Mile Marker 54.8). General Grant's army camped here on its march to Jackson and Vicksburg during the Civil War. Trails meander through the woods and up a steep hill to a tiny old cemetery and **Rocky Springs Methodist Church** (1837), where services are still held on Sunday.

At Mile Marker 41.5 is a portion of the **Old Trace,** a short section of the original Native American Trace of loess soil (easily eroded and compacted earth). You can park and walk along it for a short way.

Port Gibson

❼ *Mile Marker 39.2; 60 mi southwest of Jackson.*

This is the earliest still-existent town on the Trace, with a large concentration of antebellum homes. The aptly named **Church Street** is a shady main thoroughfare lined with houses of worship and stately homes. The **First Presbyterian Church,** erected in 1859, has a spire topped by a 10-ft hand pointing heavenward. Also on Church Street are **Gage House** (✉ 602 Church St.), circa 1830, with double galleries and a handsome brick dependency; **Temple Gemiluth Chassed** (✉ 706 Church St.), circa 1892, a synagogue with Moorish Byzantine architecture unique in Mississippi; **St. James Episcopal Church** (✉ 808 Church St.), circa 1897, a high Victorian Gothic structure designed by a Boston architect; **Port Gibson Methodist Church** (✉ 901 Church St.), built in 1860 and Romanesque Revival in style; the **Hughes Home** (✉ 907 Church St.), circa 1825, once owned by Henry Hughes, author of the first sociology textbook, and once the residence of poet Irvin Russell; and the Gothic **St. Joseph's Catholic Church** (✉ 909 Church St.), built in 1849, with a hand-carved Communion rail. The palatial mid-19th-century, 30-room mansion **Oak Square** is open for tours by appointment. The **Port Gibson Chamber of Commerce,** where you can get maps to local historic sites, is housed in a small 1805 home built by Port Gibson's founder, Samuel Gibson, and moved to this site in 1980.

Grand Gulf Military Monument, 7 mi northwest of Port Gibson, commemorates the town of Grand Gulf, site of an 1862 Civil War naval battle. The site is now a museum with an 1863 cannon, a collection of carriages, an 1820s dogtrot cabin, an old Catholic church, and a Spanish house from the 1790s. ✉ *North of Port Gibson off U.S. 61, Rte. 2,* ☎ *601/437–5911.* 🎫 *$2.* ☷ *Weekdays 8–5.*

Southwest of Port Gibson on MS 552 are the 23 vine-clad columns that are the romantic ruins of **Windsor,** a huge Greek Revival mansion built in 1861 that burned down in 1890. The remains of the largest plantation home ever built in Mississippi were featured in *Raintree County,* a late '50s film starring Elizabeth Taylor.

Lodging

$$–$$$ 🏨 **Oak Square.** Constructed circa 1850, this Greek Revival treasure, with its numerous outbuildings and lovely gardens, occupies an entire block on historic Church Street. It has comfortable rooms, each with a private bath. Full Southern breakfasts are included in the room rate. ✉ *1207 Church St., Port Gibson 39150,* ☎ *601/437–4350 or 800/729–0240,* 📠 *601/437–5768. 12 rooms. AE, D, MC, V.*

Shopping

Mississippi Cultural Crossroads (✉ 507 Market St., ☎ 601/437–8905) has an enviable collection of quilts on display and for sale.

Lorman and Environs

12 mi south of Port Gibson.

On U.S. 61 and 1 mi east of the Natchez Trace Parkway, the sleepy settlement of Lorman is worth a stop for its Old South charm. Handmade bonnets swing in the breeze on the porch of the **Old Country Store** (✉ 107 U.S. 61, Lorman, ☎ 601/437–3661), which was a plantation store built in 1875. You can buy souvenirs here, including handmade pewter, wooden toys, and antique dolls, and sample some down-home cooking at the restaurant. On weekends there's a flea market.

About 12 mi southwest of Lorman is the restored **Rodney Presbyterian Church.** The town of Rodney, once full of wealthy plantation owners and river merchants, became a ghost town when the Mississippi River shifted its course. Your visit to Rodney will be enhanced by reading Eudora Welty's powerful essay "Some Notes on River Country" and her short story "At the Landing."

Dining and Lodging

$ ✕ **Old Country Store.** Checkered tablecloths, wallpaper with magnolia borders, antiques, and watercolors depicting local scenes create a pleasant, old-fashioned interior. Home-cooked Southern fare, such as hearty po'boys, fried chicken, and collard greens, is made to order and generously portioned. Try the peach cobbler for dessert. ✉ *107 U.S. 61, Lorman,* ☎ *601/437–3661. MC, V.*

$$–$$$ 🏠 **Rosswood Plantation.** Once a cotton plantation, Rosswood is now a B&B and a Christmas tree farm. Rooms have canopied beds, Oriental rugs, and antique furnishings. Silver coins and jewels are reportedly buried somewhere on the grounds. The "hidden treasure" dates to the Civil War when residents, fearing that the Union army would confiscate their possessions, hid them in the ground instead. The nearby nature trails are perfect for an easy hike. ✉ *Hwy. 552E, Lorman 39096-9701,* ☎ *601/437–4215 or 800/533–5889,* 📠 *601/437–6888,* 🌐 *www.rosswood.net. 4 rooms. AE, D, MC, V.*

En Route   **Emerald Mound** (Natchez Trace Mile Marker 10.3) is the second-largest Native American mound in the country, covering almost 8 acres. It was built around 1300 for religious ceremonies practiced by ancestors of the Natchez Native Americans.

As you near Natchez, the Natchez Trace Parkway abruptly ends, putting you on U.S. 61. You'll pass through the little town of Washington, capital of the Mississippi Territory from 1802 to 1817. In 1802 **Jefferson College** (☎ 601/442–2901) was chartered as the territory's first educational institution; its historic buildings have been meticulously restored.

Natchez

★ ➑   *40 mi southwest of Port Gibson.*

Antebellum Natchez is named for the Natchez Native Americans who lived here and worshiped the sun in small villages before the French built Fort Rosalie in 1716. Later the city came under British rule (1763–79), and the district known today as **Natchez-Under-the-Hill** grew up at the Mississippi River landing beneath the bluff. The Spanish took control in 1779 and left their mark on the city by establishing straight streets that intersect at right angles atop the bluff. The United

States claimed Natchez by treaty, and the U.S. flag first flew over Natchez in March 1798. The city gave its name to the Natchez Trace and prospered as travelers heading for Nashville passed through with money in their pockets and a willingness to spend it on a good time.

Between 1819 and 1860, wealthy planters built stylish town houses and ringed the city with opulent plantation homes. Though Natchez survived the Civil War virtually unscathed, its economy suffered. Ironically, it was the city's decline that saved its architectural treasures— no one could afford to remodel or tear houses down. In 1932 the women of Natchez originated the idea of the pilgrimage, in which plantation families opened their homes for touring in hopes of raising money for preservation. The Natchez Pilgrimage is now held three times a year, in spring, fall, and around Christmas. During Pilgrimage, between 24 and 30 houses are open, and crowds flock to see them. Some houses are open year-round.

The following three **antebellum homes,** open daily from 9 to 5, are of particular note. All charge a $6 admission fee.

The 1857 **Stanton Hall** (⊠ 401 High St., ☎ 601/442–6282 or 800/647– 6742) is one of the most palatial and most photographed houses in America. Four giant fluted columns support double porticoes enclosed by delicate, lacy wrought-iron railings. This magnificent preservation project of the Pilgrimage Garden Club is furnished with Natchez antiques.

Rosalie (⊠ 100 Orleans St., ☎ 601/445–4555), circa 1823, established what's considered the quintessential Southern plantation house, with its white columns, hipped roof, and red bricks. Restored by the Natchez Garden Club, the house serves as the state home of the Daughters of the American Revolution. Furnishings purchased for the house in 1858 include a famous Belter parlor set.

Magnolia Hall (⊠ 215 S. Pearl St., ☎ 601/442–6672), circa 1858, was shelled by the Union gunboat *Essex* during the Civil War. A shell reportedly exploded in a soup tureen, scalding several diners at the table. The Greek Revival mansion has stucco walls and fluted columns topped with curving Ionic capitals. Note the plaster magnolia blossoms on the parlor ceiling. There is a costume museum on the second floor.

Natchez National Historical Park was established in 1988 to help preserve the city. Park headquarters are in **Fort Rosalie,** established in 1716 by French colonists. Currently, only one park property is open to the public: **Melrose,** circa 1845, a planter's estate that symbolizes the cotton era. A second property, the **William Johnson House,** circa 1841, is undergoing extensive renovation and at press time could be viewed only from the outside. When completed, the home will be a museum dedicated to African-American history. *Park headquarters:* ⊠ *210 State St.,* ☎ *601/442–7047. Melrose:* ⊠ *1 Melrose-Montebello Pkwy.,* ☎ *601/446–5790.* ⚊ *$6.* ☉ *Daily 8:30–5. Tours on the hr.*

Longwood, circa 1860–61, is the largest octagonal house in the United States. Under construction during the Civil War, it was never completed. Preserved in its unfinished state, Longwood is now a museum for the Pilgrimage Garden Club and a National Historic Landmark. ⊠ *140 Lower Woodville Rd.,* ☎ *601/442–5193.* ⚊ *$6.* ☉ *Daily 9–5, except during pilgrimages, which take place in spring and fall. Call ahead to confirm hrs.*

Natchez in Historic Photographs offers a pictorial history of the city in the late 19th and early 20th centuries through the photography of Henry and Earl Norman. Several hundred prints made from the original glass negatives portray everything from river scenes to street scenes, leaving little to imagine about life in early Natchez. ✉ *117 S. Pearl St., 2nd floor,* ☎ *601/442–4741.* 🎟 *Suggested donation $3.* ⏲ *Mon.–Sat. 10–5, Sun. 1–5.*

Grand Village of the Natchez Indians. This archaeological park and museum depict the culture of the Natchez Native Americans, which reached its zenith in the 1500s. ✉ *400 Jefferson Davis Blvd.,* ☎ *601/446–6502.* 🎟 *Free.* ⏲ *Mon.–Sat. 9–5, Sun. 1:30–5.*

Dining and Lodging

$$–$$$ ✕ **Pearl Street Pasta.** Visit the intimate Pearl Street Pasta for a taste of Italy in the Mississippi heartland. The fresh pasta dishes include pasta primavera, and breast of chicken with *tasso* (spiced ham), onions, and mushrooms over angel-hair pasta. ✉ *105 S. Pearl St.,* ☎ *601/442–9284. AE, D, DC, MC, V.*

$–$$ ✕ **Carriage House Restaurant.** On the grounds of Stanton Hall (☞ Natchez, *above*), the Carriage House serves up fried chicken, baked ham, and its famous mouthwatering miniature biscuits. The restaurant has a delightful Victorian-parlor interior. ✉ *401 High St.,* ☎ *601/445–5151. AE, MC, V. No dinner except during Pilgrimage wks.*

$–$$ ✕ **Cock of the Walk.** In a marvelous old train depot overlooking the Mississippi River, this famous original of a regional franchise specializes in fried catfish fillets, fried dill pickles, hush puppies, mustard greens, and coleslaw. Blackened or grilled catfish and chicken are also offered. ✉ *200 N. Broadway, on bluff,* ☎ *601/446–8920. AE, D, DC, MC, V. No lunch.*

$ ✕ **The Pig Out Inn Barbeque.** The menu at this funky, and extremely casual, place includes delectable chopped or sliced pork, beef, turkey, chicken, or hot sausage all topped by a crave-inducing barbecue sauce. Top it all off with a slice of the homemade pecan or sweet potato pie and you'll truly know what it means to "pig out." ✉ *116 S. Canal St.,* ☎ *601/442–8050. AE, D, DC, MC, V. Closed Sun.*

$$$–$$$$ 🏨 **The Briars Inn.** Once the home of Varina Howell, the wife of Jefferson Davis, the Briars sits on a promontory overlooking the Mississippi River. The 19 acres of landscaped grounds are a perfect place for peaceful strolling, and the inn's rooms are beautifully decorated with period furnishings imparting a gracious plantation feel. A Southern breakfast is served in the dining room. ✉ *31 Irving La. (behind Ramada Hilltop), 39121,* ☎ *601/446–9654 or 800/634–1818,* FAX *601/445–6037. 14 rooms. Dining room. AE, D, MC, V.*

$$$–$$$$ 🏨 **The Burn.** Noted for its semispiral staircase, this elegant 1836 Greek Revival mansion is so lovely that its owners also offer private tours. The guest rooms are quiet and comfortable and furnished throughout with antiques. The Burn's verdant surroundings lend it the atmosphere of a country home, despite its size. Seated plantation breakfasts are included in the room rate. ✉ *712 N. Union St., 39120,* ☎ *601/442–1344 or 800/654–8859,* FAX *601/445–0606. 7 rooms. Pool. AE, D, MC, V.*

$$–$$$ 🏨 **Dunleith.** Stately, colonnaded Dunleith is a popular Natchez B&B with elegant, plantation-style rooms furnished with four-poster beds and antiques. Guests are served lemonade upon arrival. The breakfast room is a former poultry house with old brick walls. Beautiful gardens enhance the grounds. ✉ *84 Homochitto St., 39120,* ☎ *601/446–8500 or 800/433–2445. 11 rooms. No children under 18. MC, V.*

$$ 🏨 **The Guest House Historic Inn.** A renovated home built in 1840, this cozy inn is in the heart of Natchez, on Antique Row. Its rooms are decorated with antiques and reproductions, like a small European hotel. ✉ *201 N. Pearl St., 39120,* ☎ *601/442–1054,* FAX *601/442–1374. 17 rooms. Meeting room. AE, D, DC, MC, V. CP.*

Nightlife and the Arts

King's Tavern (⊠ 619 Jefferson St., ☎ 601/446–8845) is in the oldest house in the Natchez Territory (1789). The lounge is rustic and inviting, especially if you're an "Old Natchez" aficionado. The **Under-the-Hill Saloon** (⊠ 25 Silver St., ☎ 601/446–8023) has live entertainment—from blues to folk—on weekends in one of the few original buildings left in Natchez-Under-the-Hill.

Natchez Trace A to Z

AIR TRAVEL

Golden Triangle Regional Airport is served by American Eagle, Atlantic Southeast Airlines, and Northwest Airlink, with connections nationwide through Memphis and Atlanta.

American Eagle, Continental Express, Delta, and Northwest Airlink make nonstop daily flights from Jackson to Dallas, Atlanta, and New Orleans, with direct service available nationally. Tupelo Municipal Airport is served by Northwest Airlink and American Eagle.

AIRPORTS

Jackson International Airport is 10 minutes from downtown. Tupelo Municipal Airport is 5 miles west of Tupelo.

➤ AIRPORT INFORMATION: **Golden Triangle Regional Airport** (⊠ U.S. 82, 10 mi west of Columbus, ☎ 601/327–4422). **Jackson International Airport** (⊠ east of Jackson off I–20, ☎ 601/939–5631). **Tupelo Municipal Airport** (⊠ 631 Jackson Extended, ☎ 601/841–6570).

BUS TRAVEL

Greyhound offers daily service to Columbus, Corinth, Jackson, Natchez, Philadelphia, Port Gibson, and Tupelo.

➤ BUS INFORMATION: **Greyhound** (☎ 800/231–2222, WEB www.greyhound.com; ⊠ 904 Main St., Columbus, ☎ 601/328–4732; ⊠ 204 U.S. 72E, Corinth, ☎ 601/287–1466; ⊠ 201 S. Jefferson St., Jackson, ☎ 601/353–6342; ⊠ 103 Lower Woodville Rd., Natchez, ☎ 601/445–5291; ⊠ West Side Finance and Insurance Bldg., 270B W. Beacon St., Philadelphia, ☎ 601/656–2851; ⊠ 17 Church St., Port Gibson, ☎ 601/431–5751; ⊠ 201 Commerce St., Tupelo, ☎ 601/842–4557).

CAR TRAVEL

A car is the only way to tour the Natchez Trace properly, though you can reach major cities by plane and by bus. Corinth is at the intersection of U.S. 72 and U.S. 45, and Tupelo is 5 mi south of the Natchez Trace Parkway at the intersection of U.S. 45 and U.S. 78.

The Natchez Trace Parkway breaks at Jackson; pick up either I–55 or I–20, which run through the city. Jackson is accessed by U.S. 49 and U.S. 51. Natchez, at the beginning of the Natchez Trace Parkway, is served by U.S. 61.

EMERGENCIES

In towns and cities dial 911 for police or ambulance. For help on the Natchez Trace Parkway, dial 0 and ask for the nearest park ranger. Seek medical help at North Mississippi Regional Medical Center, Mississippi Baptist Medical Center, and Jefferson Davis Hospital.

Eckerd and Super D Drugs have 24-hour pharmacies.

➤ CONTACTS: **Eckerd** (⊠ Deville Plaza, I–55, E. Frontage Rd., Jackson, ☎ 601/956–5143). **Jefferson Davis Hospital** (⊠ 54 Sgt. Prentiss Dr., Natchez, ☎ 601/442–2871). **Mississippi Baptist Medical Center** (⊠ 1225 N. State St., Jackson, ☎ 601/968–1776). **North Mississippi Regional Medical Center** (⊠ 830 S. Gloster St., Tupelo, ☎ 601/841–

3000). **Super D Drugs** (⊠ 327 Meadowbrook, Meadowbrook Shopping Center, Jackson, ☎ 601/366–1449).

LODGING
BED AND BREAKFASTS
Natchez Pilgrimage Tours can answer questions and handle reservations for B&Bs.

MEDIA
RADIO
AM: WKTS 95.5, country; WTUP 1490, all-sports talk.

FM: WQNZ 95.1, country; WTRC 97.3, adult contemporary/news/sports; WJMI 99.7, urban contemporary.

TOURS
Jackson Tour & Travel, one of the South's premier tour operators, arranges independent departures to the state's prime attractions; Natchez and New Orleans are popular destinations.

Natchez Pilgrimage Tours takes groups of 20 or more to tour about a dozen antebellum homes year-round. Carriage rides through downtown Natchez are also available.

➤ FEES AND SCHEDULES: **Jackson Tour & Travel** (⊠ 1801 Crane Ridge Dr., Jackson 39216, ☎ 601/981–8415 or 800/873–8572). **Natchez Pilgrimage Tours** (⊠ 200 State St., Natchez 39121, ☎ 601/446–6631 or 800/647–6742).

VISITOR INFORMATION
The Alliance in Corinth is open weekdays 8–5; Metro Jackson Convention and Visitors Bureau is open weekdays 8:30–5. The Natchez Trace Parkway Visitor Center and the Natchez Convention & Visitors Bureau are both open weekdays 8–5. Natchez Pilgrimage Tours is open weekdays 8:30–5:30. The Port Gibson Chamber of Commerce is open weekdays 8–4, Saturday 9–4, Sunday noon–4, and the Tupelo Convention and Visitors Bureau is open weekdays 8–5, Saturday 9–5, Sunday 1–5.

➤ TOURIST INFORMATION: **Alliance** (⊠ 810 Tate St., Corinth 38834, ☎ 601/287–5269 or 800/748–9048). **Metro Jackson Convention and Visitors Bureau** (⊠ Box 1450, Jackson 39215, ☎ 601/960–1891 or 800/354–7695). **Natchez Trace Parkway Visitor Center** (⊠ 2680 Natchez Trace Pkwy. [MM 266], Tupelo 38801, ☎ 601/680–4025 or 800/305–7417). **Natchez Convention & Visitors Bureau** (⊠ 640 S. Canal, Natchez 39120, ☎ 601/446–6345 or 800/647–6724). **Natchez Pilgrimage Tours** (tickets for tours and activities: ⊠ Canal St. at State St., Box 347, Natchez 39120, ☎ 601/446–6631 or 800/647–6742). **Port Gibson Chamber of Commerce** (⊠ Box 491, Port Gibson 39150, ☎ 601/437–4351). **Tupelo Convention and Visitors Bureau** (⊠ 399 E. Main St., Box 47, Tupelo 38802, ☎ 601/841–6521 or 800/533–0611).

HOLLY SPRINGS AND OXFORD

Holly Springs and Oxford, just east of I–55 in northern Mississippi, are sophisticated versions of the Mississippi small town; both are courthouse towns incorporated in 1837. They have historic architecture, arts and crafts, literary associations, and those unhurried pleasures of Southern life that remain constant from generation to generation—entertaining conversation, good food, and nostalgic walks at twilight.

Holly Springs

40 mi southeast of Memphis.

Holly Springs arose from a crossroads of old Native American trails originally called Spring Hollow. Chickasaw and travelers stopped to rest here and bathe in medicinal spring waters sheltered by holly trees. Settlers came from the Carolinas, Virginia, and Georgia in the 1830s, and Holly Springs became an educational, business, and cultural center as the newly arrived planters began to rake in profits. Cotton barons built palatial mansions and handsome commercial buildings. Today Holly Springs has more than 200 structures (61 of which are antebellum homes) listed on the National Register of Historic Places.

At least 50 raids befell Holly Springs during the Civil War. The worst took place in December 1862, when the Confederate army, under General Earl Van Dorn, destroyed $1 million worth of Union supplies intended to aid General Grant in his march against Vicksburg. Bent on reprisals against the city, Grant ordered General Benjamin Harrison Grierson to burn it to the ground. That's when a clever Holly Springs matron, Maria Mason, invited General Grierson into her home to chat. They discovered that they shared a love of music and that they had studied piano under the same teacher; so instead of destroying Holly Springs, Grierson enjoyed its hospitality at a series of afternoon gatherings and piano concerts.

Montrose (1858), which serves as headquarters for the Holly Springs Garden Club, has an elegant spiral staircase, elaborate cornices, and plaster ceiling medallions. The grounds have been designated a state arboretum. Tours are by appointment with the Holly Springs Chamber of Commerce. ✉ *307 E. Salem Ave.,* ☎ *662/252–2943.* ◻ *$5.*

Rust College (✉ N. Memphis St., ☎ 662/252–4661), founded in 1866, contains **Oak View** (circa 1860), one of the oldest buildings in the area. Metropolitan Opera star Leontyne Price, a native of Laurel, Mississippi, gave a brief concert in 1966 that raised money to build the library named for her. It houses the extensive memorabilia of civil rights leader Roy Wilkins. The **Yellow Fever House** (✉ 104 E. Gholson Ave.), built in 1836, was Holly Springs' first brick building. It was used as a hospital during the 1878 yellow fever epidemic. **Hill Crest Cemetery** (✉ 380 S. Maury St.) contains the graves of 13 Confederate generals. Many of the iron fences surrounding the graves were made locally before the Civil War.

The **Kate Freeman Clark Art Gallery** is dedicated solely to the work of Holly Springs resident Kate Freeman Clark, who was trained as a painter in New York City during the 1890s. Clark completed more than 1,000 works, including landscapes and portraits. She returned to Holly Springs in the 1920s and never painted again. Many of her friends did not know of her talent until her paintings were discovered after her death. In her will she left funds to establish a museum. ✉ *292 E. College Ave.,* ☎ *662/252–4211.* ◻ *$2.* ☉ *By appointment.*

Many of Holly Springs' **historic homes** are open only during Spring Pilgrimage (the third weekend in April), but their exteriors alone are quite spectacular. On Salem Avenue, you'll find **Cedarhurst** and **Airliewood,** brick houses constructed in the Gothic style popularized in the 1850s by Andrew Jackson Downing. General Grant used Airliewood as his headquarters during his occupation of Holly Springs.

Dining

$ ✕ **Phillips Grocery.** The building housing Phillips was constructed in 1882 as a saloon for railroad workers. Today it's decorated with antiques and crafts and serves big, old-fashioned hamburgers. ⊠ *541A Van Dorn St., across from old depot,* ☎ *662/252–4671. Reservations not accepted. No credit cards. Closed Sun. No dinner.*

Outdoor Activities and Sports

Holly Springs' **Chewalla Lake and Recreation Area** is part of Holly Springs National Forest and has nature trails, picnic areas, swimming, boating, camping, and fishing (license required). ⊠ *MS 4 to Higdon Rd., then turn east; 7 mi to entrance. Information:* ⊠ *National Forests Mississippi, 100 W. Capitol St., Suite 1141, Jackson 39269,* ☎ *601/ 965–4391.*

Oxford

60 mi southeast of Memphis, 50 mi east of Tupelo.

Oxford and Lafayette County were immortalized as the Jefferson and Yoknapatawpha County of the novels of Oxford native William Faulkner, but even if you're not a Faulkner fan, this is a great place to experience small-town living. You won't be bored: the characters who fascinated Faulkner still live here, and the University of Mississippi keeps things lively.

Faulkner received the 1949 Nobel Prize, and his readers will enjoy exploring the town that inspired *The Hamlet, The Town,* and *The Mansion.* "I discovered that my own little postage stamp of native soil was worth writing about, and that I would never live long enough to exhaust it," said Faulkner. "I created a cosmos of my own."

Many people who knew the eccentric "Mr. Bill" still live in Oxford and are willing to share stories about him. You may encounter them around **Courthouse Square,** a National Historic Landmark in the center of town. At the center of the square is the white-sandstone **Lafayette** (pronounced luh-*fay*-it) **County Courthouse** named for the French Revolutionary War hero the Marquis de Lafayette. The courthouse was rebuilt in 1873 after Union troops burned it down; on its south side is a monument to Confederate soldiers, donated by the Faulkner family. The courtroom on the second floor is original.

University Avenue, which runs from South Lamar Boulevard just south of the Courthouse Square to the University of Mississippi, is one of the state's most beautiful sights when the trees flame orange and gold in the fall or when the dogwoods blossom in the spring.

The **University Museums** display the brightly colored paintings of local artist Theora Hamblett. Hamblett gained international fame for her works depicting dreams and visions, Mississippi landscapes, and scenes from her childhood. Here, too, is a collection of Greek and Roman antiquities and what may perhaps be the country's quirkiest exhibit— a collection of fully dressed fleas. The museum's cultural center hosts regional and national art shows year-round. ⊠ *University Ave. at 5th St.,* ☎ *662/232–7073.* 🎟 *Free.* ☉ *Tues.–Sat. 10–4:30, Sun. 1–4.*

The state's beloved Ole Miss, or the **University of Mississippi,** opened in 1848 with 80 students. The **Grove,** the tree-shaded heart of the campus, is almost as important a meeting place as Courthouse Square. (Supposedly, it was here that Faulkner, just fired from his position as postmaster for writing novels on the job, said, "Never again will I be at the beck and call of every son of a bitch who's got two cents to buy a stamp.") Walking through the Grove on home football weekends, when a large portion of the state's population is in attendance, is great for people-watching. Contact the school's **public relations department** (☎ 662/232–7236) for information about university plays, lectures, sporting events, and special events.

The **Center for the Study of Southern Culture** (☎ 662/232–5993) is housed in antebellum Barnard Observatory, facing the Grove. The center has exhibits on Southern music, folklore, and literature and has the world's largest blues archives (40,000 records). Its annual Faulkner seminar attracts scholars from around the world, and its Oxford Conference for the Book, held each April, draws book lovers from all across the United States. The center's remarkable *Encyclopedia of Southern Culture* is on sale here.

The **Mississippi Room** (☎ 662/232–5855) in the John Davis Williams Library contains both a permanent exhibit on Faulkner, including his Nobel Prize medal, and first editions of other Mississippi authors, such as Eudora Welty, Richard Wright, and Barry Hannah.

★ **Rowan Oak** was William Faulkner's home from 1930 until his death in 1962. Although this is one of Mississippi's most famous attractions, there are no signs to direct you and only an unobtrusive historic marker at the site. The house and its surrounding 32 acres are as serene and private as they were when Faulkner lived and wrote here. Built about 1848 by Colonel Robert Sheegog, the two-story, white-frame house with square columns represents the primitive Greek Revival style of architecture common to many Mississippi antebellum homes. After the Civil War it fell into disrepair, but in 1930 it was purchased by Faulkner and his bride of one year, Estelle Oldham Franklin.

The house was both a sanctuary and a financial burden to the author; it is now a National Historic Landmark owned by the University of Mississippi. Faulkner made improvements and additions to the house, including a brick wall to shield him from curious strangers. After winning the Nobel Prize, he added the study where his bed, typewriter, desk, and other personal items—such as his sunglasses, a Colgate shave-stick refill, an ink bottle, and a can of dog repellent—still evoke his presence. Faulkner wrote an outline for his novel *The Fable* on the walls of the study, which is reputed to be the most photographed room in the state. The days of the week are neatly printed over the head and length of the bed, and to the right of the door leading into the room is the notation TOMORROW. ⌧ *Old Taylor Rd.,* ☎ *662/234–3284.* FAX *601/232–5371.* 🎟 *Free.* ☉ *Tues.–Sat. 10–noon and 2–4, Sun. 2–4.*

Faulkner's funeral was held at Rowan Oak, and he was buried in the family plot in **St. Peter's Cemetery,** at Jefferson and North 16th streets, beside his relatives. Also buried here is Caroline Barr, "Mammy Callie," Faulkner's childhood nurse. The tomb of the author's brother, Dean Faulkner, who was killed in an airplane crash, bears the same epitaph as the one Faulkner had given to John Sartoris in the novel *Pylon.*

OFF THE BEATEN PATH

COLLEGE HILL PRESBYTERIAN CHURCH – William Faulkner was married at this little church 8 mi northwest of Oxford on College Hill Road on June 20, 1929. The original pews are intact, and it's believed that Sherman stabled horses here during his occupation of College Hill in 1862. Behind the church is one of north Mississippi's oldest cemeteries.

TAYLOR – From Oxford take Old Taylor Road 9 mi (about 15 minutes by car) to the town of Taylor. Downtown Taylor comprises three buildings—two grocery stores and a potter's shop. The old **Taylor Grocery** (☎ 662/236–1716) has a restaurant in back where catfish and trimmin's are served Thursday through Sunday nights. In sculptor William Beckwith's studio you can see his statue of Temple Drake, the character who waited for the train in Taylor in Faulkner's novel *Sanctuary*. Small as it is, Taylor is achieving cult status; it's proper to brag about coming here.

Dining and Lodging

$$$–$$$$ ✕ **City Grocery.** What was once a grocery store is now a trendy bistro
★ on Oxford's historic Courthouse Square. The chef's innovative menu is more suggestive of New Orleans than north Mississippi. A signature dish is the shrimp and grits, and the bananas Foster bread pudding is a showstopper. ⊠ *1118 Van Buren Ave.,* ☎ *662/232–8080. AE, MC, V. Closed Sun.*

$–$$ ✕ **Ajax Diner.** Upscale down-home cooking in a lively atmosphere is what you'll get at this Southern version of a diner. Specialties include chicken and dumplings, sweet potato casserole, and po'boys. ⊠ *118 Courthouse Sq.,* ☎ *662/232–8880. AE, D, MC, V. Closed Sun.*

$–$$ ✕ **Downtown Grill.** With its comfortable plaid chairs and dark walls, the Grill's bar could be a club in Oxford, England. But then there's the light and airy balcony overlooking the square—pure Oxford, Mississippi. Downstairs in the restaurant, specialties include seafood gumbo, Mississippi catfish either grilled or Lafitte (topped with shrimp, julienned ham, and a savory cream sauce), and rich desserts. ⊠ *110 Courthouse Sq.,* ☎ *662/234–2659. AE, D, MC, V. Closed Sun.*

$ ✕ **Bottletree Bakery.** This is the closest to crusty European-style bread that you'll find in Mississippi and perhaps in all of the South. If that isn't reason enough to stop in, check out the saucer-size cinnamon rolls. The bakery serves breakfast and lunch as well as pastries and specialty coffees. ⊠ *923 Van Buren Ave.,* ☎ *662/236–5000. MC, V. Closed Mon.*

$$–$$$ ▥ **Puddin' Place.** Near the Ole Miss campus, this Victorian house has a wonderful back porch with swings and rockers. The two suites—each with sitting room, separate bedroom, and private bath—are thoughtfully furnished with antiques. The downstairs suite has its own washer and dryer as well as two working fireplaces; the upstairs suite has four working fireplaces—including one in the bathroom. A Southern breakfast is included in the room rate. ⊠ *1008 University Ave., 38655,* ☎ *662/234–1250,* ℻ *662/236–4285. 2 suites. No credit cards.*

$$ ▥ **The Oliver-Britt House.** Each comfortable, pleasant room has its own bath and color TV in this restored Greek Revival built about 1900 and run as a casual B&B. The location, midway between the university and Courthouse Square, is convenient. A Southern breakfast is included in the room rate. ⊠ *512 Van Buren Ave., 38655,* ☎ *662/234–8043,* ℻ *662/281–8065. 5 rooms. AE, DC, MC, V.*

$–$$ ▥ **Alumni Center Hotel.** The modern rooms bring a fresh look to a unique location on the Ole Miss campus. All rooms are done in rich, dark colors. ⊠ *Alumni Dr., University of Mississippi, 38677,* ☎ *662/234–2331. 96 rooms. Snack bar, pool, 6 meeting rooms. MC, V.*

$–$$ ▥ **Downtown Inn.** These functional rooms have no surprises. The restaurant, however, can do a remarkably good breakfast. ⊠ *400 N. Lamar, 38655,* ☎ *662/234–3031,* ℻ *662/234–2834. 123 rooms, 2 suites. Restaurant, pool, lounge. AE, DC, MC, V.*

Nightlife and the Arts

The **Faulkner and Yoknapatawpha Conference,** held the first week in August, includes lectures by Faulkner scholars and field trips to the sites of the fictional Yoknapatawpha County. The annual **Oxford Conference for the Book** has an emphasis on Southern authors.

Proud Larry's (⊠ 211 S. Lamar Blvd., ☎ 662/236–0050) regularly schedules regional bands playing blues, folk, funk, jazz, and rock.

Outdoor Activities and Sports

Oxford's **Avent Park** (⊠ Park Dr., the continuation of Bramlett Blvd., which runs north of E. Jackson Ave.) has tennis courts, a playground, picnic areas, and a jogging trail.

Holly Springs and Oxford A to Z

BUS TRAVEL
Greyhound has a station in Holly Springs.
➤ BUS INFORMATION: **Greyhound** (⊠ 490 Craft St., Holly Springs, ☎ 662/252–1353 or 800/231–2222, WEB www.greyhound.com).

CAR TRAVEL
A 30-minute drive from Memphis, Holly Springs is in north Mississippi near the Tennessee state line on U.S. 78 and MS 4, MS 7, and MS 311.

EMERGENCIES
In Holly Springs, dial 0 for assistance. In Oxford, dial 911. Medical help is available at Baptist Memorial North Mississippi Hospital.
➤ CONTACTS: **Baptist Memorial North Mississippi Hospital** (⊠ Off I–55; take Batesville exit, 1 mi south of Oxford Sq. on S. Lamar Ave., Oxford, ☎ 662/232–8100).

MEDIA
RADIO
AM: WSUH 1420, news/talk.

FM: WOXD 95.5, oldies; WWMS 97.5, contemporary and country.

VISITOR INFORMATION
Holly Springs Chamber of Commerce is open weekdays 9–5. Oxford Information Center and the Oxford Tourism Council are both open daily 9–5. Oxford-Lafayette County Chamber of Commerce is open weekdays 8:30–4.
➤ TOURIST INFORMATION: **Holly Springs Chamber of Commerce** (⊠ 154 S. Memphis St., ☎ 662/252–2943). **Oxford Information Center** (⊠ Cottage next to city hall, ☎ 662/232–2419). **Oxford Tourism Council** (⊠ 111 Courthouse Sq., Box 965, 38655, ☎ 662/234–4680 or 800/758–9177, WEB www.oxfordms.net). **Oxford-Lafayette County Chamber of Commerce** (⊠ 299 W. Jackson Ave., ☎ 662/234–4651, WEB www.oxfordms.com).

THE DELTA

"The Delta begins in the lobby of the Peabody Hotel in Memphis and ends on Catfish Row in Vicksburg," said Greenville journalist David Cohn. In between is a vast agricultural plain created by the Mississippi River. If life should give you only one day in the Delta, use it to cruise down U.S. 61 and the Great River Road (MS 1) from Memphis to Vicksburg. Gamble your way through Tunica. Time it right for lunch in Clarksdale, Merigold, or Boyle and for dinner at Doe's in Greenville. Then on a Saturday night you'll be able to pick up public radio's *Highway 61*, which will be playing the blues about the time you glimpse the first kudzu near Vicksburg.

Numbers in the margin correspond to points of interest on the Mississippi Delta map.

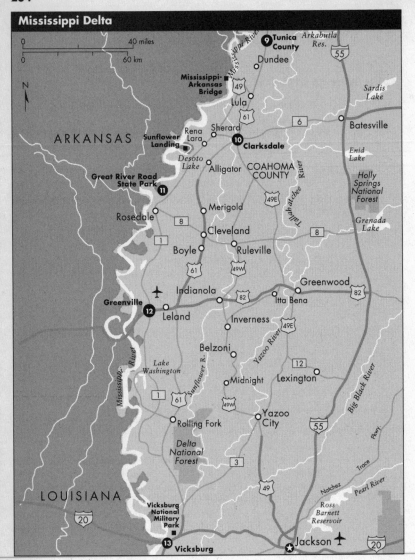

Mississippi Delta

0 — 40 miles
0 — 60 km

N

9 Tunica County
Dundee
Arkabutla Res.
Mississippi River
55
Sardis Lake
Mississippi-Arkansas Bridge
49
Lula
61
Sherard
Rena Lara
6
Batesville
ARKANSAS
Sunflower Landing
10 Clarksdale
Enid Lake
Desoto Lake
Alligator
COAHOMA COUNTY
Holly Springs National Forest
Great River Road State Park
11
49E
Tallahatchie River
Grenada Lake
Merigold
Rosedale
8
Cleveland
8
1
Boyle
Ruleville
61
49W
Greenwood
82
Indianola
82
Leland
Greenville **12**
Itta Bena
49E
Inverness
Yazoo River
Belzoni
Lake Washington
12
Lexington
Mississippi River
Sunflower R.
Midnight
1
61
49W
Yazoo City
55
Big Black River
Rolling Fork
55
Delta National Forest
3
Trace Pkwy
49
LOUISIANA
Vicksburg National Military Park
Natchez Trace
Ross Barnett Reservoir
Pearl River
20
13 Vicksburg
Jackson
20

Tunica County

9 *30 mi south of Memphis off U.S. 61.*

This region is a gambler's paradise. Las Vegas–style casinos have sprung up all along the otherwise empty and somewhat barren strip of Delta highway. The view of these garish entertainment and hotel complexes emerging from the cotton fields is quite surreal, but step inside and you'll never know you're not in Vegas or Atlantic City.

There are more than 7,000 hotel rooms in the area, and ten casinos fill the sky: Bally's Saloon, Fitzgeralds Casino & Hotel, the Gold Strike Casino Resort, Hollywood Casino & Hotel, Harrah's Tunica Casino & Hotel, Grand Casino Tunica, Horseshoe Casino and Hotel, Sam's Town Hotel & Gambling Hall, the Sheraton Casino Hotel, and the Isle of Capri Hotel and Casino. The three listed below are the best of the field. If you're not interested in gambling, you can still take advantage of good entertainment at the hotels—everything from comedy acts to blues and country music.

Lodging

$$–$$$$ 🏨 **Horseshoe Casino and Hotel.** One of the casino resorts that have forever changed the North Mississippi Delta skyline, the Horseshoe pays homage to the blues. You can stay in either the modern, 14-story, all-suites hotel tower or in rooms above the casino. Players at the Horseshoe Casino can indulge in 100% Las Vegas–style action: roulette, poker, slot machines, and more. The Bluesville complex includes the Blues & Legends Hall of Fame Museum, dedicated to the blues heritage of the Delta, and the Bluesville Showcase Nightclub, which stages live music. ⊠ *1021 Casino Center Dr., Robinsonville 38664,* ☎ *662/ 357–5500 or 800/363–7666,* FAX *662/357–5600,* WEB *www. horseshoecasino.com. 194 rooms, 311 suites. 4 restaurants, pool, gym, massage, sauna, meeting room. AE, D, DC, MC, V.*

$–$$ 🏨 **Sam's Town Hotel and Gambling Hall.** An Old West theme pervades this mammoth hotel-casino just south of the Memphis International Airport. Rooms and suites are adjacent to the casino, which contains more than 1,500 slot machines, 60 table games, and live poker and keno. Past performers at the resort's River Palace Arena have included Bill Cosby, Wynonna Judd, and Wayne Newton. Riverbend Links is the adjacent 18-hole championship golf course. Sam's five restaurants, including 24-hour Smokey Joe's, serve everything from juicy Angus steaks to spicy barbecue. ⊠ *1477 Casino Strip Blvd., Robinsonville 38664,* ☎ *800/456–0711,* FAX *662/363–0746,* WEB *www.samstowntunica.com. 850 rooms, 44 suites. 5 restaurants, golf, pool, gym, lounge, 7 meeting rooms. AE, D, DC, MC, V.*

$ 🏨 **The Hollywood Casino and Hotel.** Movie memorabilia is everywhere at this full-service casino/hotel, including the model of the *Titanic* used in making the blockbuster film and the motorcycle driven by Peter Fonda in *Easy Rider.* Rooms are basic but spacious, with amenities such as coffeemakers and extras such as video games. The Hollywood also has its own 72-space RV park with full hookups. Downstairs at the casino you can choose from more than 1,300 slot machines and video poker stations plus 44 table games. ⊠ *1150 Casino Strip Blvd., Robinsonville 38664,* ☎ *662/357–7700 or 800/871–0711,* FAX *662/357– 7895,* WEB *www.hollywoodcasino.com. 506 rooms, 26 suites. 6 restaurants, pool, gym, meeting room. AE, D, DC, MC, V.*

En Route   At Rena Lara, turn west to **Sunflower Landing** on Desoto Lake. Near here, in May 1541, Hernando DeSoto "discovered" the Mississippi River.

At the town of Rich, swing west on U.S. 49 for a spectacular view of the Mississippi River from the **Mississippi–Arkansas Bridge.** Continue south on MS 1 to skirt serene Moon Lake and Friars Point. The levee parallels MS 1 for most of the southbound trip; park and climb up for a look at the Father of Waters.

Clarksdale

🔟   *60 mi southwest of Memphis.*

As a child, author Tennessee Williams spent time in Clarksdale, visiting his grandfather, the rector of St. George's Episcopal Church. (In Williams's *Cat on a Hot Tin Roof,* Brick was running high hurdles at nearby Friars Point when he broke his leg.)

The **Delta Blues Museum** is a testament to the important role played by Clarksdale and Coahoma County in the history of the blues. Exhibits and programs trace the influence of the blues on rock, jazz, and pop music through videotapes, slides, records, and books. The museum is housed in the restored Illinois Central Freight Train Depot. ✉ *1 Blues Alley*, ☎ 662/627–6820, WEB *www.deltabluesmuseum.org*. ✉ *$6, under 18, $4.* ☉ *Mon.–Sat. 9–5.*

Dining

$–$$ ✕ **Rest Haven.** The Delta's large Lebanese community influences the food, which is considered regional fare. Among the favorites are *kibbe* (seasoned lean ground lamb with cracked wheat), spinach and meat pies, and cabbage rolls. Daily plate-lunch specials include chicken and dumplings, and red beans and sausage over rice. ✉ *419 State St. (Hwy. 61)*, ☎ 662/624–8601. *No credit cards. Closed Sun.*

En Route   The McCartys of **Merigold** are famous throughout the state for their pale stoneware. Their shop showcases their pottery and handcrafted jewelry; in the spring and summer you may get a peek at their gardens. Around the corner from the shop is an eatery called the Gallery, where a choice of two entrées is offered for lunch. ✉ *Corner Goff and St. Mary Sts.*, ☎ 662/748–2293. ☉ *Feb.–Dec., Tues.–Sat. 10–4.*

Cleveland

30 mi southwest of Clarksdale.

Home to 15,000 residents plus the students at Delta State University, Cleveland is said to have inspired the music of W. C. Handy (1873–1958), who was among the first to write down the blues. It's a small town that has an outstanding restaurant, KC's.

Dining

$$$$ ✕ **KC's Restaurant.** A hidden treasure in the heart of the Delta, this funky restaurant could hold its own anywhere. The eclectic, sophisticated menu changes every two weeks and has French, Italian, Asian, and Southwestern influences. Count on seeing wild game, fresh fish, free-range meats, and organic vegetables. There's a walk-in wine cellar (with a table for those who like to dine among the bottles) that offers evidence of the restaurant's amazing wine list. ✉ *U.S. 61N at 1st St.*, ☎ 662/843–5301. *AE, MC, V. No lunch Sat. No dinner Sun.*

Rosedale

18 mi west of Cleveland.

This pastoral town on MS 8 offers sweeping views of the Mississippi River and an 800-acre park with the state's largest campground inside ⑪ the levee. The **Great River Road State Park,** on the bluffs of the Mississippi River, has a 75-ft-high overlook tower. A boat ramp, both developed and primitive campsites, canoeing and tubing, fishing, nature trails, and picnic shelters are also available. ✉ *Off MS 1, Box 292, 38769*, ☎ 662/759–6762. ☉ *Daily 8–5.*

Greenville

⑫ *35 mi southwest of Cleveland.*

Greenville, the seat of Washington County, is named for Revolutionary War hero General Nathaniel Greene, a close friend of George Washington. The city's history has been dominated by the Mississippi River. The river created the rich soil in which cotton flourished, and Greenville was—and is—the port used by the massive Delta plantations to ship their bales to market. During the Civil War battle for Vicksburg, Union troops burned Greenville to the ground. The citizens rebuilt the town only to suffer a yellow fever epidemic in 1877. Then, in 1890, the city experienced disastrous flooding; levees finally solved the problem after the great flood of 1927. At the turn of the 20th century Greenville developed into a major river port.

Greenville probably has produced more writers than any other city of its size in the country, including William Alexander Percy (*Lanterns on the Levee*), his nephew Walker Percy (*The Last Gentleman, The Moviegoer*), Ellen Douglas (*A Family's Affair, The Magic Carpet*), Hodding Carter (Pulitzer Prize–winning crusading journalist), Shelby Foote (*The Civil War, Love in a Dry Season*), and Hodding Carter III (television news commentator and journalist). The best reason to visit Greenville, however, is to eat at Doe's.

The **Birthplace of the Frog Exhibit,** in Leland, on the outskirts of Greenville, is a tribute to the late Muppet creator Jim Henson and a must for Kermit fans. In the same building as the Leland Chamber of Commerce, the exhibit includes Henson family memorabilia, videos of Henson's first attempts at kiddie TV, three original Muppets on loan, and more. Henson was born in Greenville but grew up in Leland. ⌧ *MS 82 at S. Deer Creek Dr. E,* ☎ *662/686–2687.* 🎟 *Free.* ☉ *Weekdays 10–4, tours on weekends by appointment.*

Dining

$$$–$$$$ ✕ **Doe's.** Visually as uninspiring as any restaurant you'll find—Formica-top tables, mismatched chairs, mismatched cutlery, mismatched plates—Doe's isn't known for its ambience. But when you see that huge steak hanging off your plate, you'll know why this place is famous. Hot tamales and the house salad dressing (olive oil, lemon juice, garlic) are specialties. ⌧ *502 Nelson St.,* ☎ *662/334–3315. MC, V. No lunch.*

OFF THE
BEATEN PATH

FLOREWOOD RIVER PLANTATION STATE PARK – It's worth straying from the Delta path to visit this living-history park 2 mi west of Greenwood on Highway 82. Near Greenwood, it's an exact copy of an 1850s working plantation, complete with reenactments in the school, blacksmith shop, plantation store, and more. ⌧ *Box 680, Greenwood 38930,* ☎ *662/455–3821.* 🎟 *$3.50.* ☉ *Tues.–Sat. 9–noon and 1–5, Sun. 1–5.*

MAMA'S DREAM WORLD – In Belzoni, 35 mi southeast of Greenville, Mama's Dream World contains pictures embroidered by the late Ethel Wright Mohamed, who took up needlework in her sixties to record her life in the Delta with her storekeeper husband and eight children. Some of Mrs. Mohamed's work is in the Smithsonian's permanent collection. The gallery is in the Mohamed family home. ⌧ *307 Central St.,* ☎ *662/247–1433.* 🎟 *$2.* ☉ *By appointment.*

Vicksburg

⓭   *75 mi south of Greenville, 35 mi west of Jackson.*

Vicksburg began as a mission founded by the Reverend Newitt Vick in 1814. He chose a spot high on the bluffs above a bend in the Mississippi River, a location that would have important consequences for the young city during the Civil War.

In June 1862 the Union had control of the Mississippi River, with the exception of Vicksburg, which was in Confederate hands. Ulysses S. Grant's men doggedly slogged through canals and bayous in five futile attempts to capture the city, which was called the Gibraltar of the Confederacy because of its impregnable natural defenses. Then, in a series of raids and battles, Grant laid waste the area between Vicksburg and Jackson to the east and Port Gibson to the south, before returning to Vicksburg. His attacks were repulsed once again; he then laid siege to the city for 47 days as its residents, hiding in caves, slowly starved. On July 4, 1863, the city surrendered, giving the Union control of the river and a critical victory.

★ **Vicksburg National Military Park,** which nearly surrounds Vicksburg, keeps the city's past close to today's constituents. The park comprises 1,800 acres of fortifications and earthworks lined with monuments and markers tracing battle positions. A guided tour is a good investment, should time and money ($20 for two hours) permit. The self-guided driving tour is well marked, however, and a cassette tape may be rented for $4.50. About 7 mi into the park is the USS *Cairo,* a Union gunboat raised from the Yazoo River and restored. Civil War artifacts recovered from the *Cairo* are on display at the adjacent USS *Cairo* Museum. ☒ *3201 Clay St.,* ☎ *601/636–0583 for main switchboard; 601/636–2199 for USS Cairo;* WEB *www.nps.gov.* ☞ *$4 per car.* ☉ *National Military Park grounds fall–spring, daily 7–5; summer, daily 7–8; USS Cairo fall–spring, daily 8:30–5; summer, daily 9:30–6.*

The Vanishing Glory is a 15-projector, multimedia show portraying the sights and sounds of Vicksburg under siege. ☒ *717 Clay St.,* ☎ *601/634–1863.* ☞ *$5.* ☉ *Mon.–Sat. 9–5, Sun. 1–5.*

Vicksburg's **historic homes** may have cannonballs imbedded in their walls, but they have been beautifully restored. Visit **Cedar Grove** (☒ 2200 Oak St.), now a beautiful B&B. Built in 1840, the house's Greek Revival style is complemented by French empire gasoliers, Bohemian Glass doors, towering gold leaf mirrors and exquisite clocks and paintings. A canon ball from Civil War days is still lodged in the parlor wall, and the house is surrounded by five acres of lush gardens. The **Martha Vick House** (☒ 1300 Grove St.) was built by the daughter of the founder of Vicksburg, Newitt Vick.

One-hour **Hydro-Jet Boat tours** depart from Vicksburg for those longing for a Mississippi River adventure. ☒ *Box 506, 39181,* ☎ *601/638–5443 or 800/521–4363.* ☞ *$16.* ☉ *Mar.–Nov., daily at 10, 2, and 5.*

In 1894 Coca-Cola was bottled at the **Biedenharn Candy Company,** which is now a Coke museum. The history of one of the world's favorite soft drinks is documented through Coca-Cola advertisements and memorabilia. There's also an old-fashioned soda fountain on site. ☒ *1107 Washington St.,* ☎ *601/638–6514.* ☞ *$2.25.* ☉ *Mon.–Sat. 9–5, Sun. 1:30–4:30.*

Dining and Lodging

$$–$$$ ✕ **Jacque's Café in the Park.** A popular spot with a varied menu, Jacque's has juicy steaks, veal, fresh seafood, and Cajun and Italian dishes to choose from. ☒ *4137 I–20 Frontage Rd. (in Park Inn International),* ☎ *601/638–5811. AE, DC, MC, V. No lunch.*

$ ✕ **Walnut Hills.** If you're yearning for authentic regional cooking, this restaurant is a must. Don't miss the outstanding fried chicken, served with fresh snap beans or purple-hull peas, and the blackberry cobbler. ☒ *1214 Adams St., at Clay St.,* ☎ *601/638–4910. Reservations essential. AE, DC, MC, V. Closed Sat. No lunch weekdays.*

$$–$$$$ 🛏 **Cedar Grove.** An entire city block is consumed by this 1840s man-
★ sion and its grounds. All rooms are furnished with period antiques and Civil War artifacts, the most impressive of which is the Union cannonball still lodged in the parlor wall. You can hear nearby river traffic at night from the otherwise quiet, gaslighted grounds, and survey the watery scene during the day from the rooftop veranda. A house tour and hearty Southern breakfast are included. ☒ *2200 Oak St., 39180,* ☎ *601/636–1000 or 800/862–1300,* FAX *601/634–6126. 35 rooms. Restaurant, tennis court, pool, bicycles, croquet, piano bar. AE, D, DC, MC, V.*

$$–$$$$
★   🏠 **Duff Green Mansion.** Used as a hospital during the Civil War, this mansion has been standing since 1856. Each guest room is decorated with antiques, including half-tester beds. A large, Southern-style breakfast and a tour of the home are included in the price. ⊠ *1114 1st East St., 39180,* ☎ *601/636–6968 or 800/992–0037. 4 rooms, 2 suites. Pool. AE, D, MC, V.*

$$–$$$
🏠 **Belle of the Bends.** Built in 1876 by Mississippi State senator Murray F. Smith and his wife, Kate, Belle of the Bends is a classic example of Victorian Italianate architecture. It is decorated throughout with antiques, Oriental rugs, and memorabilia of the steamboats that plied the waters of the Mississippi River in the 1880s and early 1900s. A plantation-style breakfast and house tour are included in the room rate, as is a tour of nearby **Cedar Grove.** The only downside is the nearby railroad line. ⊠ *508 Klein St., 39180,* ☎ *601/634–0737 or 800/844–2308,* WEB *www.belleofthebends.com. 4 rooms. AE, MC, V.*

Nightlife and the Arts

Beechwood Restaurant & Lounge (⊠ 4449 Hwy. 80E, ☎ 601/636–3761) has nightly country-and-western bands and a spacious bar area.

Shopping

Climb up into the **Attic Gallery** (⊠ 1101 Washington St., Vicksburg, ☎ 601/638–9221) to see regional art and fine crafts chosen with a discriminating eye—it's a Southern rival to New York galleries, and represents some of Mississippi's finest artists, displayed with a funky flair.

Delta A to Z

AIRPORTS

The Greenville Municipal Airport is served by Northwest Airlink.
➤ AIRPORT INFORMATION: **Greenville Municipal Airport** (⊠ Air Base Rd., ☎ 662/334–3121).

BUS TRAVEL

Greyhound stops in Belzoni, Clarksdale, Cleveland, Columbus, Greenville, and Vicksburg.
➤ BUS INFORMATION: **Greyhound** (☎ 800/231–2222, WEB www.greyhound.com; ⊠ West Side Grocery, 711 Francis St., Belzoni, ☎ 662/247–2150; ⊠ 1604 State St., Clarksdale, ☎ 662/627–7893; ⊠ U.S. 61N, Cleveland, ☎ 662/843–5113; ⊠ 904 Main St., Columbus, ☎ 601/328–4732; ⊠ 1849 U.S. 82E, Greenville, ☎ 662/335–2633; ⊠ 1295 S. Frontage Rd., Vicksburg, ☎ 601/638–8389).

CAR TRAVEL

U.S. 61 runs from Memphis through the Delta to Vicksburg and Natchez and to Baton Rouge, Louisiana. The Great River Road (MS 1) parallels U.S. 61 and the river through part of this route.

EMERGENCIES

Dial 911 for police and ambulance. Seek medical help at Delta Regional Medical Center and at Vicksburg Medical Center.
➤ CONTACTS: **Delta Regional Medical Center** (⊠ 1400 E. Union St., Greenville, ☎ 662/378–3783). **Vicksburg Medical Center** (⊠ 1111 N. Frontage Rd., Vicksburg, ☎ 601/636–2611).

MEDIA

RADIO
FM: WBBV 101.1, country; WAID 106.5, urban contemporary.

VISITOR INFORMATION

➤ TOURIST INFORMATION: **Clarksdale-Coahoma County Chamber of Commerce** (⊠ 1540 De Soto Ave., Box 160, Clarksdale 38614, ☎ 662/627–7337, WEB www.clarksdale.com). **Cleveland-Bolivar County Chamber of Commerce** (⊠ 600 3rd St., Box 490, Cleveland 38732, ☎ 662/843–2712). **Greenville-Washington County CVB** (⊠ 410 Washington Ave., Greenville 38701, ☎ 662/334–2711 or 800/467–3582, WEB www.thedelta.org). **Greenwood Convention & Visitors Bureau** (⊠ 1902 Le Flore Ave., Box 739, Greenwood 38935-0739, ☎ 662/453–9197 or 800/748–9064, WEB www.gcvb.com). **Mississippi Welcome Center** (⊠ 4210 Washington St., Vicksburg 39180, ☎ 601/638–4269, WEB www.visitmississippi.org). **Vicksburg Convention & Visitors Bureau** (⊠ Clay St. and Old Hwy. 27, Box 110, Vicksburg 39181, ☎ 601/636–9421 or 800/221–3536, WEB www.vicksburgcvb.org). **Washington County Welcome Center** (⊠ U.S. 82 at Reed Rd., Box 6022, Greenville 38701, ☎ 662/332–2378).

MISSISSIPPI A TO Z

AIRPORTS

Most visitors use Jackson International Airport or Memphis International Airport.

➤ AIRPORT INFORMATION: **Jackson International Airport** (⊠ east of Jackson, off I–20, ☎ 601/939–5631). **Memphis International Airport** (⊠ 2491 Winchester Rd., ☎ 901/922–8000).

BUS TRAVEL

Greyhound serves most major cities in Mississippi. Coast Area Transit provides a coast wide public transportation system.

➤ BUS INFORMATION: **Coast Area Transit** (⊠ 333 DeBuys Rd., Gulfport, ☎ 228/896–8080). **Greyhound** (☎ 800/231–2222, WEB www.greyhound.com).

CAR TRAVEL

The state's main north–south artery is I–55. I–20 crosses the state east–west from Meridian through Jackson to Vicksburg. I–10 crosses the Gulf Coast, and I–59 links Meridian with Picayune.

RULES OF THE ROAD

The speed limit on Mississippi interstate highways is 70 mph unless otherwise posted. The speed limit on the Natchez Trace Parkway is 50 mph. There's one service station on the Parkway, at Mile Marker 193.1. Right turns on red lights are permitted throughout the state unless otherwise indicated. Crash helmets approved by the American Association of Motor Vehicle Administrators are required for motorcycle riders. Drivers and front-seat passengers in any vehicle designed to carry 10 riders or fewer must wear seat belts. A new "click-it or ticket" program by the state's law enforcement agencies helps ensure seat belt compliance. Children under four years of age must be in an approved child passenger restraint device.

EMERGENCIES

In towns and cities, dial 911 for police or ambulance. Cellular calls to the Highway Patrol are free by dialing HP (47).

TRAIN TRAVEL

Amtrak serves Batesville, Biloxi, Brookhaven, Canton, Durant, Grenada, Gulfport, Hattiesburg, Hazlehurst, Jackson, Laurel, McComb, Meridian, Pascagoula, Picayune, and Winona.

➤ TRAIN INFORMATION: **Amtrak** (☎ 800/872–7245, WEB www.amtrak. com).

VISITOR INFORMATION

The Mississippi Division of Tourism will send you a travel planner.

➤ TOURIST INFORMATION: **Mississippi Division of Tourism** (✉ Box 1705, Ocean Springs 39566, ☎ 601/359–3297 or 800/927–6378, WEB www. visitmississippi.org).

6 NORTH CAROLINA

Indulge yourself in the historical sites and natural wonders of North Carolina, from Old Salem in Winston-Salem, where the 1700s spring to life today, to the Great Smoky and Blue Ridge mountains. On the Cape Hatteras and Cape Lookout national seashores, lighthouses stand as they have for 200 years, and unspoiled beaches stretch for miles. You'll find sophisticated shopping and dining in Charlotte; first-class golf in the Sandhills; and high technology, health care, and culture within the Triangle, a shape traced by Raleigh, Durham, and Chapel Hill.

By Lisa H. Towle

Updated by Rob Fleming

THE FIRST STANZA OF NORTH CAROLINA'S OFFICIAL toast reads: "Here's to the land of the longleaf pine/ The summer land where the sun doth shine/ Where the weak grow strong and the strong grow great/ Here's to 'Down Home,' the Old North State!" Sure, it's hyperbolic, but it's catchy and rhythmic. It also speaks to a deeper truth: as much as geography, people have shaped the state's landscape over the years. In a moving tribute that was both videotaped and printed, the late Charles Kuralt, television journalist, author, and inveterate traveler, noted that North Carolina—his "state of grace"—has been the home of Whistler's mother, Billy Graham, Michael Jordan, Chief Manteo, and three U.S. presidents.

In 1524 the explorer Giovanni da Verrazano landed on what is now North Carolina's shore and wrote in his log that it was ". . . as pleasant and delectable [a land] to behold as is possible to imagine." Sixty years later the New World's first English-speaking settlers found their way to the state's eastern edge, which is bordered by 300 mi of beaches, islands, and inlets. Hernando de Soto searched for gold in the western part of the state, an area bounded by two ranges of the southern Appalachians, the Blue Ridge Mountains and the Great Smoky Mountains. In 1540 he and his band of Spanish explorers met the centuries-long residents of the area, the Cherokee, at the ancient village of Guasili, close by what is today the town of Murphy. Several centuries later, in 1799, the first gold rush in the United States got its start in the heartland, the Piedmont—near Concord, to be exact—when young Conrad Reed discovered a 17-pound nugget that would eventually be identified as gold. And although North Carolina was the last state to secede during the Civil War, the state provided more troops and supplies to the Confederacy than any other Southern state and suffered the most casualties.

Thanks to efforts of the state and many determined citizens, this history and more has been carefully preserved. A lot of it can be found along 1,500 mi of roads designated by the state's Department of Transportation as Scenic Byways. Thirty-one such byways (all marked with signs) crisscross the state. The soul of North Carolina can be glimpsed on these meandering routes. Here the views can quickly shift from panoramic to intimate, and the jasmine and galax, azaleas and rhododendrons, magnolias and dogwoods, and soft Spanish moss grow undisturbed.

Unlike many other states, North Carolina does not have one city that stands head and shoulders above all others. Rather, because of a confluence of circumstance, custom, and capitalistic acuity, a number of centers of business, art, and education have grown up throughout the state. Citizens, from African-American to Quaker, are proud of their contributions to North Carolina's development and protective of the areas and unique cultures from which they sprang. Indeed, some have described the Old North State as a collection of fiercely independent city-states reminiscent of those in ancient Greece or 19th-century Italy. Taken as a whole, North Carolina is now more urban and suburban than rural. You won't find gritty, noisy, oversize cities here, though. Instead, the pace is a bit slower. Manners and smiles still count, and canopies of hardwoods and pine trees characterize cities and countryside alike.

Thanks to its temperate climate, world-class schools, and one of the most dynamic economies in the nation, North Carolina attracts residents in record numbers. These new inhabitants have come from

North Carolina

KENTUCKY

APPALACHIAN MTS.

VIRG

TENNESSEE

Blue Ridge Parkway

75

81

Jefferson
221

Sparta

Reidsvi

52

Valle Crucis
Boone

Winston-Salem

G

40

Blowing Rock

421

Knoxville

40

Hot
Springs

40

Pisgah
National
Forest

Banner Elk

77

High
Point

Weaverville

23
19

Penland

Lenoir

16

Asheville

321

40

Hickory

Statesville

220

Great Smoky
Mts. Nat'l
Park

441

Black Mtn.

85

Cherokee

Waynesville

280

26

Concord

Uwharrie
National
Forest

Bryson City

Chimney Rock

321

Dillsboro

Hendersonville

Saluda

Gastonia

Locust

Nantahala
National
Forest

Franklin

Flat Rock

74

Charlotte

Pine

Brevard
Lake
Toxaway

74

385

77

85

SOUTH CAROLINA

26

20

GEORGIA

Columbia

20

around the world and around the country, and their myriad artistic, cultural, culinary, spiritual, and academic influences have been unmistakable. Ultimately, however, what newcomers find to be one of North Carolina's great appeals is its timelessness. In 1749 Peter Jefferson, the father of Thomas Jefferson, and his group of surveyors discovered a river in western North Carolina. Because they believed it to be a large, undiscovered branch of the Mississippi River, the surveyors dubbed it the New River. Later, archaeologists determined that it is actually the oldest river in the United States and the second oldest in the world, after the Nile. Today, amid majestic scenery, its two forks continue to flow.

Pleasures and Pastimes

Beaches

From the thin band of barrier islands known as the Outer Banks, along the northern coastline, to the area around Wilmington and the Cape Fear Coast to the South Brunswick Islands, near the South Carolina border, North Carolina's beaches are a year-round destination. You can visit national seashores or wildlife refuges, go surfing, diving, fishing, hiking, bird-watching, hang gliding—or just watch the waves. North Carolinians are proud that the nation's first national seashore, Cape Hatteras, is in their state, as is Roanoke Island, where the country's first European settlers landed more than 400 years ago.

Dining

In North Carolina's cities, risotto and dim sum have become as common as grits and corn bread. Ethnic specialties of all kinds are available, as well as contemporary American cuisine. The Sandhills, too, have a number of sophisticated restaurants. But you can find plenty of good old-fashioned Southern cooking, including Southern-fried chicken, Brunswick stew, ham, vegetables, biscuits, and fruit cobblers. Chopped or sliced pork barbecue is still a big item.

By far the best fare around the Outer Banks is fresh seafood. Raw bars serve oysters and clams on the half shell, and seafood houses offer fresh crabs (soft-shells in season, which is early in the summer) and whatever local fish—tuna, wahoo, mahimahi—have been hauled in that day. Cuisine in the Wilmington and Morehead City areas is strong on seafood, whether it's shrimp, Atlantic blue crab, or king mackerel, but pork barbecue and international cuisines are also options.

From Cherokee County to Asheville the dining choices are many: upscale restaurants, middle-of-the-road country fare, and fast-food eateries. Fresh mountain trout and such game meats as pheasant and venison are regional specialties.

Unless otherwise noted, neat, casual wear (including golf wear in the Sandhills) is acceptable throughout North Carolina.

CATEGORY	COST*
$$$$	over $25
$$$	$17–$25
$$	$10–$17
$	under $10

*per person for a main course at dinner

Historic Places

You'll find plenty of ways to get out of the fast lane and onto the back roads that lead to places where history is kept alive. Whether it's the site of a key battle in the Revolutionary War or the largest troop surrender of the Civil War, a Quaker settlement, or studios where artisans carry on a 200-year-old tradition in pottery, North Carolina cherishes its past. Places to visit are as varied as the site of man's first flight and the architectural legacies of America's industrial barons.

Lodging

In North Carolina's cities you'll find everything from economy motels to convention hotels to bed-and-breakfasts in lovely historic districts. Most major chains are represented, and some hotels offer great weekend packages. A few warnings, though: during the twice-a-year furniture market in High Point, when 75,000 people descend on the city, empty hotel rooms and rental cars are almost impossible to find. May is graduation time for all of the Triangle's colleges and universities. Hotels and restaurants are booked, in some cases, years in advance.

Most lodging options in the Sandhills are in the luxury resort category, with full amenities and services. Many of the prices quoted are for golf packages. However, there are some chain motels in Southern Pines and Aberdeen, as well as B&Bs in the area.

Motels and hotels are clustered up and down the Outer Banks, with rental properties in all the towns that dot the Cape Hatteras National Seashore. If you're going to Wilmington and the Cape Fear Coast, and New Bern and the Central (or Crystal) Coast, you can choose from chains, condos, and resorts overlooking water, whether it's a river or the ocean. There are also in-town guest houses. Lodging options in the western mountains range from posh resorts to mountain cabins, country inns, and economy chain motels. When you're planning your trip, always ask about special packages and possible off-season rates.

CATEGORY	COST*
$$$$	over $175
$$$	$125–$175
$$	$75–$125
$	under $75

All prices are for a standard double room, excluding 6%–12% tax (depending on county).

Outdoor Activities

North Carolina's unique geological and biological resources give outdoor enthusiasts lots of options. There are hundreds of choices if you want to rough it, from primitive camping to family camping. Hikers and backpackers come here for the trails—from one-day hikes to week-long trips. Quite a few stables offer rental horses, and some have llama treks. Hard-core mountain bikers can ride a 27-mi loop through the Great Smoky Mountains National Park. Local outfitters regularly conduct white-water rafting trips. The state has eight ski resorts, and if you like height but not snow, there's hang gliding across the dunes at Nags Head.

Exploring North Carolina

Charlotte, the state's largest city, is known as a center of high finance in the South, and prides itself on its cosmopolitan flair. The cities of the Triad (Greensboro, Winston-Salem, and High Point), in the upper Piedmont, showcase the legacies of some of the state's founding families. The Triangle (Raleigh, Durham, and Chapel Hill), in the central Piedmont, is the hub of higher education, scientific research, and state-sponsored cultural resources. The Sandhills, on the Coastal Plain, is a favorite among antiques lovers and is recognized worldwide as a major golfing destination. On the Outer Banks comes solitude in the form of miles of pristine shore. Boating, scuba diving, and fishing are the main pastimes in Morehead City and the Central Coast, whereas history is alive in genteel New Bern. Wilmington and the Cape Fear Coast aren't just resort vacation spots—they're a thriving business and cultural center for the southeastern portion of North Carolina. In the western mountains, which are anchored by the city of Asheville, you'll find everything from hiking trails and Southern crafts to boot-scoot music and Brahms.

Great Itineraries

North Carolina is a large state, and touring it comfortably from end to end could easily take two weeks, although you could whiz through in a week. Many people focus each trip on one region: mountains, Piedmont, or Coastal Plain. A week could be spent in each of these, but there are many worthwhile trips of shorter duration.

IF YOU HAVE 3 DAYS

Start your tour of the Outer Banks from its north end, coming in on U.S. 158. Drive north on Route 12 your first morning there to spend time in **Corolla,** visiting the Currituck Beach Lighthouse. After lunch head south through **Kitty Hawk, Kill Devil Hills,** and **Nags Head,** with a stop at the Wright Brothers National Memorial. Spend the first night (and the next) on ☒ **Roanoke Island,** where you'll take the second day to visit historical locations and the North Carolina Aquarium. On Day 3 leave Roanoke and spend the day along the **Cape Hatteras National Seashore,** visiting sights on **Hatteras Island** in the morning and ☒ **Ocracoke Island** in the afternoon.

IF YOU HAVE 5 DAYS

☒ **Asheville** is the logical starting point for a tour of the North Carolina mountains. It will take the full first day to cover the Biltmore Estate and neighboring village. Day 2 should be devoted to the attractions south of Asheville, including **Chimney Rock** and the Carl Sandburg Home National Historical Site, in **Flat Rock.** Another day back in Asheville will allow you to visit the remaining area attractions, including Pack Place. On the fourth morning begin your journey up the **Blue Ridge Parkway,** lingering at the many scenic stopping points along the way, and arrive in the ☒ **Boone** area for the night. Day 5 will be occupied with High Country activities, including a visit to the Tweetsie Railroad, in **Blowing Rock.**

IF YOU HAVE 7 DAYS

With a full week at your disposal you can do a whirlwind tour from one end of North Carolina to the other. Start your journey by touring the Biltmore Estate in ☒ **Asheville.** Next head for ☒ **Charlotte;** be sure to visit Discovery Place and the Mint Museum of Craft & Design during your day here. The Triad and the historical attractions of Old Salem are the focus of the third day; overnight in ☒ **Winston-Salem.** The next two days will allow time for a taste of the Triangle, including the Duke University campus and Sarah Duke Gardens, in **Durham;** the Morehead Planetarium and Franklin Street shopping, in **Chapel Hill;** and the museums and capital area of ☒ **Raleigh.** Your sixth day should be spent in the Sandhills area enjoying antiques shops and the world-class golf in ☒ **Pinehurst.** Wind up your visit in ☒ **Wilmington,** where you can visit the historic downtown and USS *North Carolina* Battleship Memorial, or just head for the nearby beaches.

When to Tour North Carolina

North Carolina particularly shines in the spring (April and May) and fall (September and October), when the weather is temperate and the trees and flowers burst with color. At these times you'll avoid the peak tourist season. Summer trips are best spent in the mountains or at the coastal beaches, where temperatures are significantly cooler. In winter many mountain attractions close just as the ski resorts open for the season.

CHARLOTTE

Although Charlotte dates from Revolutionary War times (it is named for King George III's wife, Queen Charlotte), its Uptown is distinctively New South, with gleaming skyscrapers and broad streets. Uptown encompasses all of downtown Charlotte, a center of government, commerce, and culture. It also has some fashionable historic neighborhoods that are noted for their architecture and their winding, tree-shaded streets. Public art—such as the sculptures at the four corners of Trade and Tryon streets—is increasingly displayed in the city. Erected at Independence Square, the sculptures symbolize Charlotte's beginnings: a gold miner (commerce), a mill worker (the city's textile heritage), an African-American railroad builder (transportation), and a mother holding her baby aloft (the future). Residents of the Queen City take enormous pride in their city being not only the largest city in the Carolinas but also the second-largest banking center in the nation.

Heavy development has created some typical urban problems. Outdated road systems in this metropolis make traffic a nightmare during rush hour, and virtually all the city's restaurants are packed on weekends. But the locals' Southern courtesy is contagious, and people still love the laid-back pleasures of jogging, picnicking, and sunning in Freedom Park.

You'll be able to walk around Uptown and the Fourth Ward, and buses are adequate for getting around within the city limits. Cars, however, remain the best bet for touring.

Numbers in the text correspond to numbers in the margin and on the Charlotte map.

Uptown Charlotte

Uptown Charlotte is ideal for walking. The city was laid out in four wards around Independence Square, at Trade and Tryon streets. The Square, as it is known, is the center of the Uptown area.

A Good Walk

Stop first at **INFO! Charlotte** (⊠ 330 S. Tryon St., Uptown, ☎ 704/331–2700) for information on a self-guided walking tour of the Fourth Ward and a historic tour of Uptown, as well as maps and brochures. Take a stroll north on Tryon Street and enjoy this revitalized area, noting the outdoor sculptures on the plazas and the creative architecture of some of the newer buildings, including the **Bank of America Corporate Center** ①.

Walk two blocks west on Trade Street to the **First Presbyterian Church** and begin exploring the **Fourth Ward** ②, Charlotte's "old" city. Next head south to North Tryon Street just above 6th Street, where you will find the science and technology museum **Discovery Place** ③, a leading attraction. Finish your walk at the **Mint Museum of Craft & Design** ④, which showcases North Carolina's rich crafts tradition.

TIMING

You can spend a pleasant half day to a day touring these areas. Allow an hour to browse through the Bank of America Corporate Center and Founders Hall. You can tour the Fourth Ward in an hour or so. The bulk of your time will be spent in Discovery Place, which can occupy

Charlotte

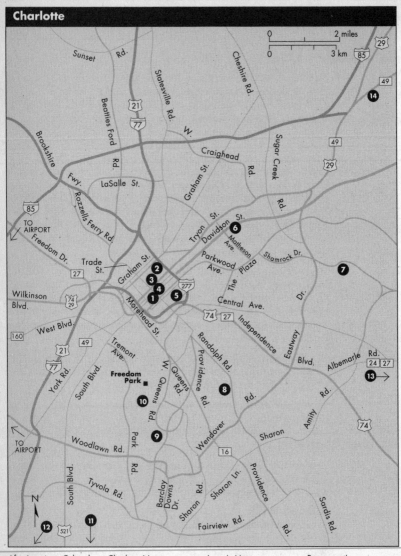

Sunset Rd.
Statesville Rd.
Cheshire Rd.
Brookshire Fwy.
Beatties Ford Rd.
21
77
W.
Craighead
Sugar Creek Rd.
49
29
85
29
14
49
LaSalle St.
Rozzells Ferry Rd.
Graham St.
Tryon St.
Davidson St.
Matheson Ave.
Shamrock Dr.
6
85
TO AIRPORT
Freedom Dr.
Trade St.
27
Graham St.
Parkwood Ave.
The Plaza
7
Wilkinson Blvd.
74
29
2
3
4
1
5
277
Central Ave.
Dr.
Morehead St.
74
27
Independence
Eastway
West Blvd.
160
Randolph Rd.
Blvd.
Albemarle Rd.
24
27
21
77
49
Tremont Ave.
York Rd.
South Blvd.
Freedom Park
W. Queens Rd.
Queens Rd.
Providence Rd.
8
13
TO AIRPORT
10
Rd.
Amity Rd.
74
Woodlawn Rd.
Park Rd.
9
Wendover
Sharon Rd.
South Blvd.
Tyvola Rd.
Barclay Downs Dr.
Sharon Rd.
Sharon Ln.
Providence Rd.
Sardis Rd.
N
16
12
11
521
Fairview Rd.
Rd.

0   2 miles
0   3 km

Afro-American Cultural Center. 5	Charlotte Nature Museum 10	Lowe's Motor Speedway 14	Paramount's Carowinds. 12
Bank of America Corporate Center 1	Discovery Place 3	Mint Museum of Art . . 8	Reed Gold Mine State Historic Site 13
Charlotte Museum of History and Hezekiah Alexander Homesite . . 7	Fourth Ward 2	Mint Museum of Craft & Design 4	Wing Haven Gardens and Bird Sanctuary . . . 9
	James K. Polk Memorial. 11	North Davidson Arts District (NoDA) . . 6	

as much of the day as you wish. You can avoid the workday bustle by visiting on the weekend, but note Discovery Place's Sunday hours.

Sights to See

❶ Bank of America Corporate Center. This 60-story structure with a crownlike top designed by Cesar Pelli is one of the city's most striking buildings. Its main attractions are three monumental frescoes by Ben Long, whose themes are making/building, chaos/creativity, and planning/knowledge. Also in the tower are the **North Carolina Blumenthal Performing Arts Center** and the restaurants, shops, and exhibition space of **Founders Hall.** ⊠ *100 N. Tryon St., Uptown.*

★ ☺ **❸ Discovery Place.** At Charlotte's premier attraction, the wonderful hands-on **Science Museum** is a priority; also allow at least two hours for the **aquariums,** the three-story **rain forest,** the **Omnimax theater,** and **Kelly Space Voyager Planetarium,** the largest in the United States. A ham radio room, a puppet theater, and a 10-ft model of an eyeball that you can walk through are other highlights. Check the schedule for special exhibits. ⊠ *301 N. Tryon St., Uptown,* ☎ *704/372–6261 or 800/935–0553,* WEB *www.discoveryplace.org.* ☞ *$7.50 for 1 area, plus $3 for any additional area visited.* ☉ *Sept.–May, weekdays 9–5, Sat. 9–6, Sun. 1–6; June–Aug., Mon.–Sat. 9–6, Sun. 1–6.*

❷ Fourth Ward. Charlotte's popular old neighborhood began as a political subsection created for electoral purposes in the mid-1800s. The architecture and sensibility of this quiet, homespun neighborhood provide a feeling for life in a less hectic time. A brochure available at INFO! Charlotte includes 18 historic places of interest. Be sure to stop by **Old Settlers Cemetery,** behind the **First Presbyterian Church** (⊠ 200 W. Trade St., Uptown, ☎ 704/332–5123), which contains tombstones that date from the 1700s. The Gothic Revival church, which takes up a city block and faces West Trade Street, reflects the prosperity of the early settlers and their descendants. **Fourth Ward Park** is an oasis in the middle of the city. **Alexander Michael's** (⊠ 401 W. 9th St., Uptown/Fourth Ward, ☎ 704/332–6789) is a warm and worn neighborhood bar. **Poplar Street Books** is housed in the Victorian Young-Morrison House (⊠ 226 W. 10th St., Uptown). U.S. president William Taft spent the night in the **McNinch House** (⊠ 511 N. Church St., Uptown), now a restaurant, when he visited Charlotte in 1909. **Spirit Square** (⊠ 345 N. College St., Uptown), in a former church, includes galleries, a performing arts center, and classrooms that used to be the sanctuary for the First Baptist Church. The **public library** (⊠ 310 N. Tryon St., Uptown), which contains a mural reproducing a Romare Bearden painting, is open weekdays 9–9, Saturday 9–6, and Sunday 2–6.

❹ Mint Museum of Craft & Design. A sister to the Mint Museum of Art, the museum is in what used to be an upscale women's clothing store. The gallery alone is 16,000 square ft. Add on the permanent collections of ceramics, glass, fiber, metal, and wood, and you have one of the country's major crafts museums. You can use your receipt from the crafts museum to enter the Mint Museum of Art free on the same day. ⊠ *220 N. Tryon St., Uptown,* ☎ *704/337–2000,* WEB *www.mintmuseum.org.* ☞ *$6.* ☉ *Tues.–Sat. 10–5, Sun. noon–5.*

Greater Charlotte

Beyond Uptown and farther afield lie many of Charlotte's most interesting sights, from gardens to museums. You can reach the ones listed below by car or by city bus; for visits elsewhere a car is essential.

A Good Tour

From Uptown follow 7th Street east and turn north on North Myers Street to visit the galleries of the **Afro-American Cultural Center** ⑤. Backtrack to North Davidson Street, turn right, and continue for just over 2 mi to Matheson Avenue, the start of the **North Davidson Arts District (NoDa)** ⑥. This revived main street of a former mill village—now with a collection of singular galleries, bars, coffeehouses, shops, and artist's residences—extends north to 36th Street. Travel east on 36th Street less than a mile to the Plaza, turn right, and go south to Shamrock Drive and turn left toward the **Charlotte Museum of History and Hezekiah Alexander Homesite** ⑦, where you can see the county's oldest building. Return west on Eastway Drive and follow it south until it becomes Wendover Road. Continue 1⅔ mi to Randolph Road and then turn right to reach the **Mint Museum of Art** ⑧, a wide-ranging collection in a former mint. The next stop, **Wing Haven Gardens and Bird Sanctuary** ⑨, is in Myers Park, a handsome neighborhood. More experience with nature can be found at the **Charlotte Nature Museum** ⑩, next to Freedom Park.

TIMING

Within a few miles of each other, these sites can easily be covered on foot over two days.

Sights to See

⑤ **Afro-American Cultural Center.** In a historic former church, this center, with its galleries and theater, is a showcase for art, music, drama, and dance. ⊠ *401 N. Myers St., Uptown,* ☎ *704/374-1565,* WEB *www.aacc-charlotte.org.* ☞ *Free.* ☉ *Tues.–Sat. 10–6, Sun. 1–5.*

☺ ⑩ **Charlotte Nature Museum.** Although affiliated with Discovery Place, the museum is in the southeast section of the city. You'll find a butterfly pavilion, live animals, nature trails, Indian relics, a puppet theater, and hands-on exhibits just for children. ⊠ *1658 Sterling Ave. (next to Freedom Park), Uptown,* ☎ *704/372-0471,* WEB *www.discoveryplace.org.* ☞ *$4.* ☉ *Weekdays 9–5, Sat. 10–5, Sun. 1–5.*

⑦ **Charlotte Museum of History and Hezekiah Alexander Homesite.** The stone house, built in 1774, is the oldest dwelling in the county. Alexander and his wife, Mary, reared 10 children in this house and farmed the land. Seasonal events commemorate the early days. Permanent and rotating exhibits in the museum span 300 years of southern Piedmont history. ⊠ *3500 Shamrock Dr., East Charlotte/Merchandise Mart,* ☎ *704/568-1774,* WEB *www.charlottemuseum.org.* ☞ *Museum and homesite $6; free Sun.* ☉ *Tues.–Sat. 10–5, Sun. 1–5; tours by costumed docents weekdays 1:15 and 3:15.*

★ ⑧ **Mint Museum of Art.** Built in 1836 as a U.S. Mint, this building has served as a home for art since 1936. Among the holdings in its impressive permanent collections are American and European paintings, furniture, and decorative arts; African, pre-Columbian, and Spanish colonial art; porcelain and pottery; and regional crafts and historic costumes. On the day you visit this museum your receipt will entitle you to free admission to downtown's Mint Museum of Craft & Design. ⊠ *2730 Randolph Rd., East Charlotte/Merchandise Mart,* ☎ *704/337-2000,* WEB *www.mintmuseum.org.* ☞ *$6.* ☉ *Tues. 10–10, Wed.–Sat. 10–5, Sun. noon–5.*

⑥ **North Davidson Arts District (NoDa).** Historic NoDa is as funky as Uptown is elegant. Creative energy flows through the reclaimed textile mill and mill houses, cottages, and commercial spaces of this north Charlotte neighborhood where you'll find both the kooky and the conformist—artists, musicians, and dancers; street vendors; and restaurateurs—sharing space. The heart of this architecturally significant district is the **Neighborhood Theatre** (✉ 511 E. 36th St., North Davidson Arts District, ☎ 704/358–9298), a converted movie house that seats 300 and presents all manner of performance art. **Center of the Earth** (✉ 3204 N. Davidson St., North Davidson Arts District, ☎ 704/375–5756) and **Blue Pony Gallery and Press** (✉ 3202-A N. Davidson St., North Davidson Arts District, ☎ 704/334–9390) are representative of the contemporary art galleries that have made a home here. Adding to the spice of this compact enclave are several notable restaurants and working-class bars. **Fat City** (✉ 3127 N. Davidson St., North Davidson Arts District, ☎ 704/343–0242) serves deli food and mixed drinks, and attracts an eclectic clientele. **Pat's/23 Studio** (✉ 3203 N. Davidson St., North Davidson Arts District, ☎ 704/358–0539) offers food, beverage, poetry, and comedy. To truly experience NoDa, attend a nighttime Gallery Crawl, held the first and third Fridays of every month. The crawls, which run officially from 6 to 9:30, have gained a regional reputation for their informal and entertaining nature.

❾ Wing Haven Gardens and Bird Sanctuary. In Myers Park, one of Charlotte's loveliest neighborhoods, 4 acres of formal gardens and wild woodlands developed by the Clarkson family house more than 135 species of birds. ✉ *248 Ridgewood Ave., South Park,* ☎ *704/331–0664,* WEB *www.winghavengardens.com.* ✇ *Free.* ☉ *Sun. 2–5, Tues. 3–5, Wed. 10–noon, or by appointment.*

Other Area Attractions

Historic sites, a speedway, and a theme park provide plenty to explore beyond the city.

⓫ James K. Polk Memorial. A state historic site south of Charlotte marks the humble 1795 birthplace and childhood home of the 11th president. Guided tours of the log cabins (replicas of the originals) are available. ✉ *308 S. Polk St., Pineville,* ☎ *704/889–7145.* ✇ *Free.* ☉ *Apr.–Oct., Mon.–Sat. 9–5, Sun. 1–5; Nov.–Mar., Tues.–Sat. 10–4, Sun. 1–4.*

⓮ Lowe's Motor Speedway. Learn all about NASCAR racing, one of the nation's fastest-growing sports, at this state-of-the-art, 167,000-seat facility; browse through the gift shop; or even take a "hot laps" (160 mph) lesson at the track through the **Richard Petty Driving Experience** (☎ 704/455–9443) or **Fast Track Driving School** (☎ 704/455–1700). Classes are given year-round, though intermittently. ✉ *5555 Concord Pkwy. S, University/Speedway Concord, northeast of Charlotte,* ☎ *704/455–3200 or 800/455–3267,* WEB *www.lowesmotorspeedway.com.* ✇ *$10–$60; prices vary.* ☉ *Racing season runs Apr.–Nov.*

⓬ Paramount's Carowinds. A 100-acre amusement park on the South Carolina state line has rides and attractions based on films. Costumed movie characters and actors greet visitors, and the Palladium offers musical concerts with star entertainers. Rides include the heart-stopping Drop Zone. ✉ *14523 Carowinds Blvd., South Charlotte/Pineville,* ☎ *704/588–2600 or 800/888–4386,* WEB *www.carowinds.com.* ✇ *$40.* ☉ *Late Mar.–May and mid-Aug.–early Oct., weekends; June–mid-Aug., daily. Park usually opens around 10; closing hrs vary.*

⓭ Reed Gold Mine State Historic Site. This area, east of Charlotte in Cabarrus County, is where America's first documented gold rush began, following Conrad Reed's discovery of a 17-pound nugget in 1799. Forty-minute guided underground tours of the gold mine are available, as well as seasonal gold panning, walking trails, and a stamp mill. ✉ *9621 Reed Mine Rd., north of Rte. 24/27, Locust, follow signs beyond town,* ☎ *704/721–4653.* ✇ *Free; gold panning $2 per pan.* ☉ *Apr.–*

Oct., Mon.–Sat. 9–5, Sun. 1–5; Nov.–Mar., Tues.–Sat. 10–4, Sun. 1– 4; call for tour schedules.

Dining

$$$$ ✕ **Étienne's Townhouse.** Chef-owner Étienne Jaulin and his wife, Amanda, serve exquisitely prepared American cuisine with a French twist. The restaurant has a country-club-elegant style—with crown molding and white linen. The menu shifts frequently as Jaulin encourages sous chefs to go to the market and "come back with something fun." The end result may be thousand-layer salmon terrine or roasted Dover sole with a sweet pea vanilla sauce. ⊠ *1011 Providence Rd., South Park,* ☎ *704/335–1546. AE, D, DC, MC, V. No dinner Sun.*

$$–$$$ ✕ **Campania.** Warmth is the byword for this restaurant in a country-club community. The walls are golden and textured, there is richly toned wood and lots of candlelight, and the music is genuine Italian, from opera to contemporary. The food, too, is about as authentic as it gets outside southern Italy. The *gamberoni mergellina* (shrimp sautéed in garlic butter and herbs) is sublime. Another option is linguine *posillipo,* which pairs clams with red or white sauce; the veal chops are also popular. ⊠ *6414 Rea Rd., South Park,* ☎ *704/541–8505. AE, D, MC, V. No dinner Sun.*

$$–$$$ ✕ **Latorre's.** The emphasis at this downtown retreat is on the heat, color, and tastes of Latin America. Art splashed with vibrant shades of mango, lemon, and salmon complement exposed-brick walls and hardwood floors. Live salsa and merengue music is sometimes offered. It's the perfect backdrop for the likes of orange-and-cumin-encrusted salmon over black-bean rice cakes and tender grilled *chimichurri* (a piquant Argentinian herb sauce) flank steak served with tortillas and three salsas. ⊠ *118 W. 5th St., Uptown,* ☎ *704/377–4448,* WEB *www.lattores. net. AE, MC, V. Closed Sun.*

$$–$$$ ✕ **Providence Café.** The signature purple awnings and trendy furnishings lend atmosphere to the original of this lively spot. The menu may be comfortably predictable—with chicken, beef, seafood, and pasta options—but the focaccia baked daily on the premises stands out. It's a great place for Sunday brunch, and on Wednesday evening there's live jazz. ⊠ *110 Perrin Pl., South Park,* ☎ *704/376–2008;* ⊠ *15205 John Jay Delaney Dr., South Park,* ☎ *704/540–2244;* ⊠ *8708 J. W. Clay Blvd., University/Speedway,* ☎ *704/549–0050. AE, D, DC, MC, V.*

$–$$ ✕ **Landmark Diner.** This spacious and informal place in the Eastland Mall neighborhood is a cut above most other inexpensive restaurants, and it's open until 3 AM on weeknights and 24 hours on weekends. The chocolate cream pie and chef's salad with grilled chicken are must-tries. ⊠ *4429 Central Ave., East Charlotte/Merchandise Mart,* ☎ *704/532–1153. Reservations not accepted. AE, DC, MC, V.*

$–$$ ✕ **Thai House.** Fiery pleasures await you here if you're an adventurous diner. Sample from a selection of vegetarian, seafood, and classic Thai dishes—the food has proved so popular here that the owners opened two more branches. The *satays* (skewers of meat, fish, or poultry with peanut sauce) are mild enough for any taste buds, and you can order many dishes as spicy or mild as you wish. ⊠ *3210 N. Sharon Amity Rd., East Charlotte/Merchandise Mart,* ☎ *704/532–6868;* ⊠ *Tower Plaza Shopping Center, 8652 Pineville-Matthews Rd., No. 1000, South Charlotte/Pineville,* ☎ *704/542–6300;* ⊠ *4918 Central Ave., East Charlotte/Merchandise Mart,* ☎ *704/535–6716. AE, D, DC, MC, V.*

$–$$ ✕ **300 East.** The gentrified, leafy Dilworth neighborhood in which this
★ casual spot resides doesn't lack for older, refurbished houses. Even so, 300 East makes its mark, and not just because of its brightly hued signage, private dining nooks and crannies, and open-air patio. The bold

menu—Thai pork tenderloin with banana-mango salsa and saffron rice, for instance, or penne with duck and lobster—attracts a hip and eclectic bunch. Here, people-watching is as much fun as eating. ⊠ *300 East Blvd., South Park,* ☎ *704/332–6507. AE, D, DC, MC, V. Closed Wed.*

$ ✕ **College Place Restaurant.** Expect simple down-home cooking—and plenty of it. Come for breakfast or lunch (7–3), and know that you'll have to work hard to spend more than $5. Breakfasts in particular are big and include any combination of eggs, pancakes, grits, bacon, and sausage, among other items. Lunch has lots of vegetable choices (12), meats, homemade corn bread, and cobblers. This cafeteria and grill is close to the convention center. ⊠ *300 S. College St., Uptown,* ☎ *704/ 343–9268. No credit cards. Closed weekends. No dinner.*

Lodging

Hotels and Motels

$$$ 🏨 **Adam's Mark.** This is the city's largest convention hotel, within walking distance of the convention center. The expansive main lobby, with its woodwork and shades of green and gray, feels a bit clubby. Guest rooms are done in blues and plums. Bravo!—its popular signature restaurant, which serves northern Italian cuisine—is known for its singing waiters. ⊠ *555 S. McDowell St., Uptown 28204,* ☎ *704/372– 4100 or 800/444–2326,* 🅵🅰🆇 *704/348–4646,* 🆆🅴🅱 *www.adamsmark.com. 631 rooms, 21 suites. Restaurant, indoor-outdoor pool, health club, sauna, racquetball, bar, dry cleaning, laundry service, concierge, business services, meeting room, airport shuttle, free parking. AE, D, DC, MC, V.*

$$$ 🏨 **The Park.** Executives, entertainers, sports stars, and heads of state
★ appreciate the privacy and pampering as well as the parklike setting of this hotel on a former estate in the southeast corner of the city. Antique furnishings, polished marble, and art grace the public areas, and the hotel owns more than 20 paintings by French artist Yolanda Ardisonne. Guest rooms, with lush fabrics, seem more like a home than a hotel. ⊠ *2200 Rexford Rd., South Park 28211,* ☎ *704/364–8220 or 800/334– 0331,* 🅵🅰🆇 *704/365–4712,* 🆆🅴🅱 *www.theparkhotel.com. 187 rooms, 7 suites. Restaurant, minibars, 18-hole golf course, 9-hole putting green, pool, health club, massage, spa, piano bar, business services, meeting room, airport shuttle, free parking. AE, D, DC, MC, V.*

$$ 🏨 **Hyatt Charlotte at SouthPark.** The focal point of the four-story atrium is a Mexican water fountain surrounded by 25-ft olive trees. Scalini, the restaurant, serves northern Italian cuisine; the Club piano bar is a favorite. The hotel, with contemporary rooms, lies within walking distance of the upscale South Park Mall. ⊠ *5501 Carnegie Blvd., South Park 28209-3462,* ☎ *704/554–1234 or 800/233–1234,* 🅵🅰🆇 *704/ 554–8319,* 🆆🅴🅱 *www.hyatt.com. 258 rooms, 4 suites. Restaurant, indoor pool, health club, hot tub, sauna, piano bar, business services, airport shuttle. AE, D, DC, MC, V.*

$ 🏨 **Bradley Motel.** Clean and functional is what you get with this motel, which has been family-owned and -operated since 1959. Popular with families and NASCAR fans, the Bradley, near the airport and the coliseum, fills up on race weekends. The rooms are large, with full ceramic baths. There's a Mexican restaurant adjacent. ⊠ *4200 S. I–85 Service Rd., Airport/Coliseum 28214,* ☎ *704/392–3206,* 🅵🅰🆇 *704/392– 5040. 21 rooms. AE, D, MC, V.*

$ 🏨 **Comfort Inn–Lake Norman.** This economy motel, north of Charlotte on I–77 near Lake Norman and Davidson College, offers basic guest rooms with coffeemakers; some come with whirlpool baths. Jogging trails are nearby. ⊠ *20740 Torrence Chapel Rd., North Charlotte/Lake Norman, Cornelius 28031,* ☎ *704/892–3500 or 800/848–9751,* 🅵🅰🆇 *704/892–6473,* 🆆🅴🅱 *www.choicehotels.com. 84 rooms, 6 suites. Some* *in-room VCRs, some microwaves, pool, business services, meeting room. AE, D, DC, MC, V. CP.*

$ ⊞ **Sterling Inn.** This economy option has an upscale sensibility. Rooms are large and tastefully decorated. The inn is near several restaurants. Every room of this motel, which is close by Queens College as well as I–77 and I–85, has oversize beds and coffeemakers. ⊠ *242 E. Wood-lawn Rd., Airport/Coliseum 28217,* ☎ *704/525–5454,* FAX *704/525–5637. 100 rooms. Refrigerators, health club, laundry service, airport shuttle, meeting room, free parking. AE, D, DC, MC, V. CP.*

Bed-and-Breakfasts

$$$–$$$$ ⊞ **Morehead Inn.** Although it's now a commercial venture catering to corporate clients, this grand colonial revival B&B in the Dilworth neigh-borhood was once a private estate and still has all the comforts of a beau-tiful home. ⊠ *1122 E. Morehead St., South Park 28204,* ☎ *704/376–3357 or 888/667–3432,* FAX *704/335–1110,* WEB *www.moreheadinn. com. 8 rooms, 2 suites, 1 2-bedroom apartment. In-room VCRs, meet-ing room. AE, DC, MC, V. CP.*

$$$ ⊞ **Inn Uptown.** This 1891 brick château on the edge of the historic Fourth Ward neighborhood is popular because of its proximity to Up-town businesses and attractions. Many rooms have fireplaces. Most fun is the Tower Room, with its spiral staircase leading to a tower with a whirlpool bath and skyline view. ⊠ *129 N. Poplar St., Uptown 28202,* ☎ *704/342–2800 or 800/959–1990,* FAX *704/342–2222,* WEB *www. innuptown.com. 6 rooms. Business services. AE, D, DC, MC, V. BP.*

$$–$$$ ⊞ **Homeplace.** This spotless early 20th-century Victorian gem in a res-★ idential neighborhood has a wraparound porch, fireplaces, and 10-ft ceilings and is full of antiques and memorabilia. Rooms, with four-poster beds, are country Victorian in style. The no-smoking inn is best for adults and older children. ⊠ *5901 Sardis Rd., South Park 28270,* ☎ *704/365–1936,* FAX *704/366–2729,* WEB *www.bbonline.com/nc/homeplace/. 2 rooms, 1 suite. AE, MC, V. BP.*

Nightlife and the Arts

The Arts

The key venue for performing arts is the **North Carolina Blumenthal Performing Arts Center,** or PAC (⊠ 130 N. Tryon St., Uptown, ☎ 704/372–1000). It houses several resident companies, including the Char-lotte Symphony Orchestra, North Carolina Dance Theatre, Charlotte Repertory Theatre, and Opera Carolina. PAC also presents national tours of Broadway musicals. The **Spirit Square Center for the Arts & Education** (⊠ 345 N. College St., Uptown, ☎ 704/372–7469) is an in-terdisciplinary arts center with classes, exhibits, and national acts, such as Wynton Marsalis and Jerry Jeff Walker.

Verizon Wireless Amphitheater (⊠ 707 Pavilion Blvd., University/Speed-way, ☎ 704/549–1292) spotlights big-name concerts (Tom Petty, Reba McEntire, *NSYNC) from spring through fall. The **Paladium Am-phitheater,** at Paramount's Carowinds (⊠ 14523 Carowinds Blvd., South Charlotte/Pineville, ☎ 704/588–2600 or 800/888–4386), presents stars in concert from midspring through midfall.

Nightlife

Comedy Zone (⊠ 516 N. College St., Uptown, ☎ 704/348–4242) show-cases live comedy nightly Tuesday through Saturday. The **Double Door Inn** (⊠ 218 E. Independence Blvd., Uptown, ☎ 704/376–1446; no credit cards) is a staple of the national blues circuit and offers live music nightly. Eric Clapton, Junior Walker, and Stevie Ray Vaughn are among the legends who've played this laid-back venue. **Ri Ra** (⊠ 208 N. Tryon

St., Uptown, ☎ 704/333–5554), Gaelic for "uproar" or "a lot of fun," is filled with Irish food, ale, and, on Sunday night, live traditional Irish music. Other musical styles are presented Thursday through Saturday. Snazzy **Swing 1000** (✉ 1000 Central Ave., Uptown, ☎ 704/334–4443) jumps with 1940s supper club atmosphere and a seven-piece house orchestra, which plays nightly.

Outdoor Activities and Sports

Participant Sports

CAMPING

Near Charlotte, campsites, fishing, and live animal exhibits can be found at **McDowell Park and Nature Reserve** (✉ 15222 York Rd., South Charlotte/Pineville, ☎ 704/588–5224). Next to the theme park, **Paramount's Carowinds** (✉ 14523 Carowinds Blvd., off I–77, South Charlotte/Pineville, ☎ 704/588–2600 or 800/888–4386), you can pitch a tent or park a mobile home right next to roller coasters. **Lake Norman State Park** (✉ Rte. 2, North Charlotte/Lake Norman Troutman, ☎ 704/528–6350) is ideal for hiking and water sports.

CANOEING

Inlets on Lake Norman and Lake Wylie are ideal for canoeing, as are some spots of the Catawba River. The Pee Dee River east of Charlotte and the New River in the mountains offer other options.

FISHING

You'll find good fishing in Charlotte's neighboring lakes and streams. A mandatory state license can be bought at local bait-and-tackle shops or over the phone (with a credit card) from the **North Carolina Wildlife Commission** (☎ 919/662–4370).

GOLF

There are more than 50 golf courses within a 40-mi drive of Uptown Charlotte. **Highland Creek Golf Club** (✉ 7001 Highland Creek Pkwy., University/Speedway, ☎ 704/875–9000), an 18-hole, par-72 course with a driving range, is considered by some to be the best public course in Charlotte. **Larkhaven Golf Club** (✉ 4801 Camp Stewart Rd., East Charlotte/Merchandise Mart, ☎ 704/545–4653) is a championship 18-hole, par-72 course with clubhouse and pro shop. **Paradise Valley Golf Center** (✉ 9309 N. Tryon St., University/Speedway, ☎ 704/548–1808) has an 18-hole, all-par-3 course. The driving range is a half mile down the street (✉ 9615 N. Tryon St., University/Speedway, ☎ 704/548–8114). **Woodbridge Golf Links** (✉ 922 New Camp Creek Church Rd., Kings Mountain, ☎ 704/482–0353), an attractive par-72 course, has 18 holes and a driving range.

TENNIS

Tennis courts are available in several Charlotte city parks, including Freedom, Hornet's Nest, Park Road, and Veterans. For details call the **Charlotte Park and Recreation Department** (☎ 704/336–3854).

Spectator Sports

AUTO RACING

NASCAR races, such as the Coca-Cola 600 and UAW/GM 500, draw huge crowds at the **Lowe's Motor Speedway** (✉ 5555 Concord Pkwy. S, Concord, northeast of Charlotte, ☎ 704/455–3200).

BASEBALL

The AAA minor league **Charlotte Knights,** an affiliate of the Chicago White Sox, play from April through August at Knights Castle (✉ 2280 Deerfield Dr., at I–77 and Gold Hill Rd., Exit 88, South Charlotte/Pineville, ☎ 704/357–8071 or 803/548–8050).

FOOTBALL

The National Football League's **Carolina Panthers** play from August through December in the 73,000-seat Ericsson Stadium (⊠ 800 S. Mint St., Airport/Coliseum, ☎ 704/358–7800).

Shopping

Charlotte is the largest retail center in the Carolinas. The majority of stores are in suburban malls, and villages and towns in outlying areas have regional specialties.

Shopping Malls

Carolina Place Mall (⊠ 11025 Carolina Place Pkwy., off I–277 at Pineville, South Charlotte/Pineville, ☎ 704/543–9300) is the only Charlotte shopping center with five anchors and interstate access. Ask for a visitor discount card at the customer service center. **SouthPark Mall** (⊠ 4400 Sharon Rd., South Park, ☎ 704/364–4411 or 888/364–4411), in the most affluent section of the city, offers high-end stores, including Tiffany & Co., Montblanc, Coach, Eddie Bauer, and Godiva Chocolatier. A concierge provides executive services, gift wrap, and delivery.

The **Outlet Marketplace** (⊠ off I–77, Fort Mill, SC, 18 mi south of Charlotte, ☎ 704/377–8630) carries well-known brands at a discount.

Specialty Stores

ANTIQUES

Waxhaw, Pineville, and Matthews are the best places to find antiques. Waxhaw sponsors an annual antiques fair each February. You can find a good selection of antiques and collectibles at the sprawling **Metrolina Expo** (⊠ off I–77 at 7100 N. Statesville Rd., North Charlotte/Lake Norman, ☎ 704/596–4643 or 800/824–3770) on the first and third weekends of the month.

BOOKS

You'll find a good selection of contemporary fiction, classics, and children's books at **Little Professor Book Center** (⊠ Park Road Shopping Center, 4139 Park Rd., South Park, ☎ 704/525–9239; ⊠ Jetton Village, 19910 N. Cove Rd., North Charlotte/Lake Norman, Cornelius, ☎ 704/896–7323).

FOOD AND PLANTS

The **Charlotte Regional Farmers Market** (⊠ 1801 Yorkmount Rd., Airport/Coliseum, ☎ 704/357–1269) sells produce, fish, plants, and crafts.

Charlotte A to Z

To research prices, get advice from other travelers, and book travel arrangements, visit www.fodors.com.

AIRPORTS AND TRANSFERS

Charlotte-Douglas International Airport is west of the city off I–85. Most major airlines serve the facility.

➤ AIRPORT INFORMATION: **Charlotte-Douglas International Airport** (⊠ 5501 Josh Birmingham Blvd., Airport/Coliseum, ☎ 704/359–4013, WEB www.charlotteairport.com).

AIRPORT TRANSFER

Taxis charge a set fee to designated zones. From the airport to most destinations the cost is $15–$20 ($2 each additional person). Airport vans are approximately $8 per person to Uptown. By car take the Billy Graham Parkway, then Wilkinson Boulevard (U.S. 74) east to I–277, which leads to the heart of Uptown.

BUS TRAVEL TO AND FROM CHARLOTTE

Greyhound/Carolina Trailways serves the Charlotte area.

➤ BUS INFORMATION: **Greyhound/Carolina Trailways** (✉ 601 W. Trade St., Uptown, ☎ 704/372–0456 or 800/231–2222, WEB www.greyhound. com).

BUS TRAVEL WITHIN CHARLOTTE

Center City Circuit operates free shuttle service on four routes throughout Uptown beginning at 7 and 7:30. Look for the UPTOWN CIRCUIT street signs. Charlotte Transit provides public transportation throughout the city. Fares are $1 for local rides and $1.40 for express service within Charlotte.

FARES AND SCHEDULES

➤ BUS INFORMATION: **Center City Circuit** (☎ 704/332–2227). **Charlotte Transit** (☎ 704/336–3366).

CAR TRAVEL

Charlotte is a transportation hub; I–77 comes in from Columbia, South Carolina, to the south, and then continues north to Virginia, intersecting I–40 on the way. I–85 arrives from Greenville, South Carolina, to the southwest, and then goes northeast to meet I–40 between Winston-Salem and the Triangle. From the Triangle I–85 continues northeast and merges with I–95 in Petersburg, Virginia.

EMERGENCIES

➤ EMERGENCY SERVICES: **Ambulance, police** (☎ 911).

➤ HOSPITALS: **Carolinas Medical Center** (✉ 1001 Blythe Blvd., South Park, ☎ 704/355–2000). **Presbyterian Hospital** (✉ 200 Hawthorne La., East Charlotte/Merchandise Mart, ☎ 704/384–2273). **University Hospital** (✉ 8800 N. Tryon St., University/Speedway, ☎ 704/548–6000).

➤ LATE-NIGHT PHARMACIES: **Eekerd Drugs** (✉ Park Road Shopping Center, South Park, ☎ 704/523–3031; ✉ 3740 E. Independence Blvd., East Charlotte/Merchandise Mart, ☎ 704/536–3600).

TAXIS

Crown Cab and Yellow Cab have taxis and airport vans. University Towncar caters to business travelers. You won't pay more for the company's flat rate than you would for a cab ride.

➤ TAXI COMPANIES: **Crown Cab** (☎ 704/334–6666). **Yellow Cab** (☎ 704/332–6161). **University Towncar** (☎ 704/553–2424 or 888/553–2424).

TOURS

BOAT TOURS

The *Catawba Queen* paddle wheeler gives dinner cruises and tours on Lake Norman. Reservations are essential.

➤ FEES AND SCHEDULES: *Catawba Queen* (✉ Rte. 150, Exit 36, North Charlotte/Lake Norman, Mooresville, ☎ 704/663–2628).

TRAIN TRAVEL

Amtrak offers daily service from Charlotte to Washington, D.C., Atlanta, and points beyond, and there's daily service to cities in the Triangle.

➤ TRAIN INFORMATION: **Amtrak** (✉ 1914 N. Tryon St., Uptown, ☎ 704/376–4416 or 800/872–7245, WEB www.amtrak.com).

VISITOR INFORMATION

➤ TOURIST INFORMATION: **INFO! Charlotte** (✉ 330 S. Tryon St., Uptown, ☎ 704/331–2700 or 800/231–4636, WEB www.charlottecvb. org).

THE TRIAD

Greensboro, Winston-Salem, High Point

North Carolinians group six urban centers in the Piedmont into two threesomes: the Triad and the Triangle. Although this shorthand is a verbal convenience, it's also testament that the whole can be greater than the sum of the parts. Make no mistake, however. Although they share geography and the major arteries of the region and claim rich histories as well as institutions of higher learning, the Triad's leading cities have very distinct personalities. Greensboro, to the east, bustles as a center of commerce. Smaller Winston-Salem, to the west, will catch you by surprise with its eclectic arts scene. High Point, to the south, has managed to fuse the simplicity of Quaker forebears with its role as a world-class furniture market.

Greensboro

96 mi northeast of Charlotte, 26 mi east of Winston-Salem, 58 mi west of Durham.

With 200,000 citizens, Greensboro is the largest population center in the Triad, and thanks to spacious convention facilities, it's an increasingly popular destination for business travelers. Yet this city, named in honor of General Nathanael Greene, a Revolutionary War hero, takes pride in its role in American history and has taken great pains to preserve and showcase the sights of past eras.

With the exception of Old Greensborough and the downtown historic district, however, walking is not a comfortable sightseeing option. To tour the grand historic homes, glimpse monuments to famous native sons and daughters—Dolley Madison, Edward R. Murrow, O. Henry—or visit one of the many recreation areas, you'll need a car.

Guilford Courthouse National Military Park, the nation's first Revolutionary War park, has monuments, military memorabilia, and more than 200 acres with wooded hiking trails. It memorializes one of the earliest events in the city's history and a pivotal moment in the life of the colonies. On March 15, 1781, the Battle of Guilford Courthouse so weakened British troops that they surrendered seven months later at Yorktown. Today many families use the 3 mi of foot trails. ✉ *2332 New Garden Rd., Northwest Metro,* ☎ *336/288–1776.* ⬚ *Free.* ☉ *Daily 8:30–5.*

Tannenbaum Park, a hands-on history experience near Guilford Courthouse National Military Park, draws you into the life of early settlers. With advance notice costumed reenactors will escort you through exhibits at the **Colonial Heritage Center,** in the visitor center. The restored **1778 Hoskins House** (tours by appointment) and a blacksmith shop and barn are on the property. The park has one of the most outstanding collections of original colonial settlement maps in the country. ✉ *2200 New Garden Rd., Northwest Metro,* ☎ *336/545–5315.* ⬚ *Free.* ☉ *Tues.–Sat. 9–5, Sun. 1–5.*

Roam through a dinosaur gallery, learn about gems and minerals, and see the lemurs, snakes, and amphibians at the **Natural Science Center of Greensboro.** There are also a planetarium and a petting zoo. ✉ *4301 Lawndale Dr., adjacent to Country Park, Northwest Metro,* ☎ *336/288–3769.* ⬚ *Science Center $6, planetarium $1; prices subject to change for special exhibits and events.* ☉ *Science Center Mon.–Sat. 9–5, Sun. 12:30–5; zoo Mon.–Sat. 10–4:30, Sun. 12:30–4:30.*

The **Greensboro Historical Museum,** in a Romanesque 1892 church, has exhibits about native son O. Henry and native daughter Dolley Madison, as well as one about the Woolworth sit-in, which launched the civil rights movement struggle to desegregate Southern eating establishments. Behind the museum are the graves of several Revolutionary War soldiers. ✉ *130 Summit Ave., Downtown,* ☎ *336/373–2043,* WEB *www.greensborohistory.org.* ⊟ *Free.* ☉ *Tues.–Sat. 10–5, Sun. 2–5.*

☾ **Greensboro Cultural Center at Festival Park,** an architectural showplace, houses 25 visual and performing arts organizations, five art galleries, rehearsal halls, a sculpture garden, a restaurant with outdoor café-style seating, and an outdoor amphitheater. **ArtQuest,** developed by educators and artists, is North Carolina's only permanent interactive children's art gallery. ✉ *200 N. Davie St., Downtown,* ☎ *336/373–2712.* ⊟ *Free; ArtQuest $3.* ☉ *Weekdays 8 AM–10 PM, Sat. 9–5, Sun. 2–5.*

☾ Exhibits and activities at the **Greensboro Children's Museum** are designed for children under 12. They can tour an airplane cockpit with an interactive screen, dig for buried treasure, or wrap themselves in a gigantic bubble. ✉ *220 N. Church St., Downtown,* ☎ *336/574–2898,* WEB *www.gcmuseum.com.* ⊟ *$5.* ☉ *Early Sept.–late May, Tues.–Sat. 9–5, Sun. 1–5; late May–early Sept., Mon.–Sat. 9–5, Sun. 1–5.*

Elm Street, with its turn-of-the-20th-century architecture, is the heart of **Old Greensborough** (✉ 100 block of N. Elm St. to 600 block of S. Elm St., with portions of several other streets, Downtown), which is listed on the National Register of Historic Places. Stop by the offices of **Downtown Greensboro, Inc.** (✉ 122 N. Elm St., Downtown, ☎ 336/ 379–0060) to collect your shopping guide and self-guided tour map.

In Old Greensborough, the elegant **Blandwood Mansion,** home of former governor John Motley Morehead, is considered the prototype of the Italian villa architecture that swept the country during the mid-19th century. Designed by noted architect Alexander Jackson Davis, the house still contains many of its original furnishings. ✉ *447 W. Washington St., Downtown,* ☎ *336/272–5003,* WEB *www.blandwood.org.* ⊟ *$5.* ☉ *Tues.–Sat. 11–2, Sun. 2–5.*

The **Weatherspoon Art Museum,** on the campus of the University of North Carolina–Greensboro, consists of six galleries and a sculpture courtyard. It is nationally recognized both for its permanent collection, which includes lithographs and bronzes by Henri Matisse, and for its changing exhibitions of 20th-century American art. ✉ *Tate and Spring Garden Sts., University,* ☎ *336/334–5770,* WEB *www.uncg.edu/wag/.* ⊟ *Free.* ☉ *Tues. and Thurs.–Fri. 10–5, Wed. 10–8, weekends 1–5.*

Dining and Lodging

$$$$ ✕ **Paisley Pineapple.** The dining is formal in this romantic Old Greensborough restaurant in a restored 1920s building. The fare on the extensive menu—rack of lamb, grilled veal tenderloin, and Black Angus beef—tends toward the hearty. On the lighter side are the soups (try the berry bisque if it's available) and fish such as Atlantic salmon poached in court bouillon. Upstairs, there's a bar with sofas and background music. ✉ *345 S. Elm St., Downtown,* ☎ *336/279–8488. AE, MC, V. Closed Sun. and Mon.*

$$$–$$$$ ✕ **Gate City Chop House.** This place has a lock on the upscale, everything-is-bigger-here steak house concept in the Triad. The look is masculine and clubby, and portions are geared for large appetites. Beef is the star, but there's plenty of good to say about other menu items, such as seafood (try the shrimp bisque) and salads. The wine list is respectable. ✉ *106 S. Holden Rd., West Metro,* ☎ *336/294–9977. AE, D, DC, MC, V. Closed Sun.*

$$-$$$ ✗ **Noble's Restaurant.** Murals of the Italian countryside adorn some walls, and from the upstairs seating area you can see the wood-burning tile oven and the slowly turning spit that turns out Tuscan-inspired cuisine. The menu changes regularly, but a typical entrée is grilled rack of lamb with polenta cake, sautéed spinach, oyster mushroom, and artichoke with a lamb jus. The piano bar on the lower level is a nice place to end the evening—a jazz trio plays Wednesday through Saturday. ⊠ *172 Battleground Ave., Northwest Metro,* ☎ *336/333–9833. AE, D, MC, V.*

$$ ✗ **Casaldi's Cafe.** Light gray-green is the predominant color in this sleek little trattoria—the motif appears in the tile floors and the marble countertops, providing a powerful lure to sample the myriad pasta dishes. Especially popular are the spinach-and-walnut ravioli and the bow-tie pasta with chicken and mushrooms. ⊠ *1310 Westover Terr., Northwest Metro,* ☎ *336/379–8191. Reservations not accepted. D, MC, V. Closed Sun.*

$$$$ 🏨 **O. Henry Hotel.** Named for the renowned author, this is one of the newest and grandest establishments in the city. The furnishings evoke the arts and crafts style, with lots of wood, tapestries, and upholstery in warm tones. Particularly nice touches are the oversize rooms, tile bathrooms with standing shower stalls and separate tubs, and bed coverlets that are laundered daily. A complimentary breakfast buffet is served in a sunny pavilion overlooking a small garden. ⊠ *624 Green Valley Rd., Northwest Metro 27408,* ☎ *336/854–2000 or 800/965–8259,* FAX *336/854–2223,* WEB *www.o.henryhotel.com. 121 rooms, 10 suites. Restaurant, room service, in-room safes, refrigerator, pool, exercise room, laundry service, business services, meeting room, airport shuttle. AE, D, DC, MC, V. BP.*

$$$ 🏨 **Greenwood Bed and Breakfast.** Eclectic antiques, art, and various other collections fill this 1905 craftsman-style home in historic Fisher Park. Owners Bob (a former New Orleans chef) and Dolly (a decorator) Guertin serve a full breakfast at the time of your choosing. Café au lait, French bread, eggs Benedict, and crêpes suzette come with freshly squeezed orange juice and fruit. Desserts are set out in the evening. This no-smoking B&B is best for older children. ⊠ *205 N. Park Dr., Downtown 27401,* ☎ *336/274–6350 or 877/374–7067,* WEB *www.greenwoodbb.com,* FAX *336/274–9943. 5 rooms. Pool, meeting room. AE, D, DC, MC, V. BP.*

$$-$$$ 🏨 **Sheraton Greensboro Hotel at Four Seasons/Joseph S. Koury Convention Center.** Business travelers are the mainstay here, at the state's largest hotel, which is adjacent to the convention center. Accommodations are a notch above standard, and the hotel and its nearby sister property, the **Park Lane Hotel** (☎ 336/294–4565), are convenient to major thoroughfares and the Four Seasons Town Centre, a three-story regional mall. ⊠ *3121 High Point Rd., West Metro 27407,* ☎ *336/292–9161 or 800/242–6556,* FAX *336/292–1407,* WEB *www.sheratongreensboro. com. 1,016 rooms, 78 suites. 5 restaurants, room service, pool, wading pool, health club, sauna, racquetball, 4 bars, nightclub, business services, convention center, meeting rooms, airport shuttle, kennel. AE, D, DC, MC, V.*

$-$$ 🏨 **Biltmore Greensboro Hotel.** In the heart of the central business district, the Biltmore has an old-world but slightly faded feel, with 16-ft ceilings, a cage elevator, and a lobby area with walnut-paneled walls and a fireplace. Some guest rooms have Victorian or Victorian-style furniture and electric candle sconces. ⊠ *111 W. Washington St., Downtown 27401,* ☎ *336/272–3474 or 800/332–0303,* FAX *336/275–2523,* WEB *www.biltmorehotelgreensboro.com. 25 rooms, 4 suites. Minibars,* *refrigerator, business services, meeting room, airport shuttle. AE, D, DC, MC, V. CP.*

Nightlife and the Arts

The **Broach Theatre** (⌧ 520 S. Elm St., Downtown, ☎ 336/378–9300) has professional adult (February–December) and children's (September–May) theater in the Old Greensborough historic district. The **Carolina Theatre** (⌧ 310 S. Greene St., Downtown, ☎ 336/333–2605), a restored vaudeville venue, serves as one of the city's principal performing arts centers, showcasing dance, concerts, films, and plays.

The vast **Greensboro Coliseum Complex** (⌧ 1921 W. Lee St., West Metro, ☎ 336/373–7474) hosts arts and entertainment events throughout the year, as well as professional, college, and amateur sports. The **Greensboro Symphony** (☎ 336/333–7490) and the **Greensboro Opera Company** (☎ 336/273–9472) perform at the Greensboro Coliseum Complex.

The **Eastern Music Festival** (⌧ 200 N. Davie St., Downtown, ☎ 336/333–7450 or 877/833–6753), whose alumni include Wynton Marsalis, brings six weeks of classical music concerts to Greensboro in summer.

Outdoor Activities and Sports

CAMPING

You can rent a cabin or bring a tent to the **Greensboro KOA** (⌧ 2300 Montreal Ave., Southeast Metro, ☎ 336/274–4143 or 800/562–4143). **Hagan-Stone Park** (⌧ 5920 Hagan-Stone Rd., Southeast Metro, ☎ 336/674–0472) is a wildlife reserve with hiking, water sports, and other activities available.

GOLF

Golfers can choose from among 27 public courses and four driving ranges. **Bryan Park and Golf Club** (⌧ 6275 Bryan Park Rd., Browns Summit, ☎ 336/375–2200) is a highly regarded 18-hole, par-72 course 6 mi north of Greensboro. The **Grandover Resort/Grandover Golf Club** (⌧ One Thousand Club Rd., South Metro, ☎ 336/294–1800 or 800/472–6301) has two 18-hole, par-72 courses. The **Greensboro National Golf Club** (⌧ 330 Niblick Dr., Summerfield, ☎ 336/342–1113), 15 minutes north of Greensboro, is an 18-hole, par-72 course.

The PGA's (Professional Golfers' Association) **Greater Greensboro Chrysler Classic** is held each April at the Forest Oaks Country Club (⌧ U.S. 421S, Southeast Metro, ☎ 336/379–1570).

HIKING

The **Bog Garden** (⌧ on Hobbs Rd. and Starmount Farms Dr., Northwest Metro, ☎ 336/373–2199) has an elevated wooden walkway through a swampy area with more than 8,000 individually labeled trees, shrubs, ferns, and wildflowers. There are walking trails and an exercise course at the 120-acre **Oka T. Hester Park** (⌧ 910 Ailanthus St., South Metro, ☎ 336/373–2937).

TENNIS

Greensboro Jaycee Park (⌧ Forest Lawn Dr. off Pisgah Church Rd., adjacent to Country Park, North Metro, ☎ 336/545–5342) has sports facilities, including a tennis center with 13 championship soft courts.

Shopping

OUTLET CENTERS

More than 75 stores and services constitute the **Burlington Manufacturers Outlet Center** (⌧ off I-85, Exit 145, Burlington, ☎ 336/227–2872), which makes the area off I-85 near here—about 25 mi east of Greensboro—a trove for bargain hunters.

SPECIALTY STORES

Replacements, Ltd. (⊠ I–85/I–40 at Mt. Hope Church Rd., Exit 132, Metro East, ☎ 800/737–5223), the world's largest retailer of discontinued and active china, crystal, flatware, and collectibles, stocks nearly 6 million pieces of inventory and 125,000 patterns. The cavernous showroom is open 8 AM–9 PM daily, and free tours are given.

Side Trips from Greensboro

CHARLOTTE HAWKINS BROWN MEMORIAL STATE HISTORIC SITE.
10 mi east of Greensboro.

On the site of the Palmer Institute, the memorial honors the African-American woman who founded the school in 1902. Before closing in 1971, this accredited preparatory school for African-Americans was recognized as one of the country's best and had expanded to more than 350 acres of land. There are a visitor center and a gift shop. ⊠ *6136 Burlington Rd., Sedalia, off I–85, Exit 135,* ☎ *336/449–4846,* WEB *www. chbfoundation.org.* ☞ *Free.* ☉ *Oct.–Apr., Tues.–Fri. 10–4, Sun. 1–4; May–Sept., Mon.–Sat. 9–5, Sun. 1–5.*

CHINQUA-PENN PLANTATION
★ *25 mi north of Greensboro.*

The **Chinqua-Penn Plantation,** a National Register of Historic Places English-country mansion, was built by tobacco and utility magnate Jeff Penn and his wife, Betsy, in 1925. The Penns, world travelers, filled the 27-room house with an eclectic collection of artifacts representing 30 countries. The 22-acre estate also has a 1-mi walking trail, Chinese pagoda, a three-story clock tower, greenhouses, and formal gardens—even a cemetery for all the Penns' beloved dogs. ⊠ *2138 Wentworth St., Reidsville,* ☎ *336/349–4576 or 800/948–0947,* WEB *www.chinquapenn.com.* ☞ *$13.* ☉ *Mar.–Dec., Tues.–Sat. 9–5, Sun. noon–5.*

Winston-Salem

81 mi north of Charlotte, 26 mi west of Greensboro.

Winston-Salem residents' donations to the arts are among the highest per capita in the nation: the city bills itself as the City of the Arts, and its museums show the benefits of this support. The North Carolina School of the Arts commands international attention. Salem College, the oldest women's college in the country, is here, as is Wake Forest University, where writer Maya Angelou teaches. Old Salem, a restored 18th-century Moravian town within the city, has been a popular attraction since the early 1950s.

Staff at the **Winston-Salem Visitor Center** (⊠ 601 N. Cherry St., Downtown, ☎ 336/777–3796 or 800/331–7018) will assist with directions and help you make dining and lodging reservations.

Founded in 1766 as a Moravian congregation town and backcountry
★ trading center, **Old Salem** has become one of the nation's most authentic and well-documented colonial sites. At this living history museum with more than 80 restored and original buildings, costumed interpreters recreate household activities and trades common in Salem in the late 18th and early 19th centuries. You can participate in African-American programs that include a stop by St. Philip's Church, the state's oldest-standing African-American church. Old Salem has many museum shops, the Old Salem Furniture & Accessories Shop, the 1816 Salem Tavern restaurant, and the Winkler Bakery (don't pass up the Moravian sugar cake). The village is a few blocks from downtown Winston-Salem and near Business I–40 (take the Old Salem/Salem College exit). ⊠ *600 S. Main St., Old Salem,* ☎ *336/721–7300 or 888/653–7253,* WEB *www.oldsalem.*

org. ☜ *$15; combination ticket with Museum of Early Southern Decorative Arts $20.* ☉ *Mon.–Sat. 9–5, Sun. 12:30–5.*

★ The **Museum of Early Southern Decorative Arts (MESDA),** on the southern edge of Old Salem, is the only museum dedicated to exhibiting and researching the regional decorative arts of the early South. Twenty-four intricately detailed period rooms and seven galleries showcase the furniture, painting, ceramics, and metalware made and used regionally through 1820. The bookstore carries current and hard-to-find books on Southern decorative arts, culture, and history. ✉ *924 S. Main St., Old Salem,* ☎ *336/721–7360 or 888/653–7253,* WEB *www.mesda.org.* ☜ *$10; combination ticket with Old Salem $20.* ☉ *Mon.–Sat. 9:30–5, Sun. 1:30–5.*

☯ The **SciWorks** complex includes a 120-seat planetarium, a 15-acre Environmental Park, and 45,000 square ft of interactive or hands-on exhibits, including the *Coastal Encounters* wet lab. ✉ *400 W. Hanes Mill Rd., North Metro,* ☎ *336/767–6730.* ☜ *Museum $7, the Works (planetarium, park, and museum) $8.* ☉ *Mon.–Sat. 10–5.*

You can take a guided tour through the exhibits on tobacco growing and auctioning at **R. J. Reynolds Whitaker Park,** view historical memorabilia related to the tobacco industry, and visit the gift shop. Tours of the factory floor are no longer offered, however. ✉ *1100 Reynolds Blvd., East Metro,* ☎ *336/741–5718.* ☜ *Free.* ☉ *Weekdays 8–6.*

☯ **Historic Bethabara Park,** set in a wooded 175-acre wildlife preserve, is the site of the first Moravian settlement (1753) in North Carolina. Bethabara—meaning "house of passage"—was to be temporary until the town of Salem was established. You can tour restored buildings such as the 1788 congregation house, explore the foundations of the town, or browse the colonial and medicinal gardens. Children love the reconstructed fort from the French and Indian War. Brochures for self-guided walking tour available year-round at the visitor center. ✉ *2147 Bethabara Rd., University,* ☎ *336/924–8191,* WEB *www.bethabarapark. org.* ☜ *$1.* ☉ *Exhibit buildings Apr.–Nov., weekdays 9:30–4:30, weekends 1:30–4:30; guided tours Apr.–Nov. or by appointment.*

The **Museum of Anthropology** has exhibits of peoples and cultures of the Americas, Asia, Africa, and Oceania. The museum shop holds special sales in May and December. ✉ *1834 Wake Forest Rd., Wake Forest Reynolda Campus University,* ☎ *336/758–5282.* ☜ *Free.* ☉ *Tues.–Sat. 10–4:30.*

Reynolda House Museum of American Art, formerly the home of tobacco magnate Richard Joshua Reynolds and his wife, Katherine, is filled with American paintings, prints, and sculptures by such artists as Thomas Eakins, Frederic Church, and Georgia O'Keeffe. There's also a costume collection, as well as vintage clothing and toys used by the Reynolds children. The museum is next to **Reynolda Village,** a collection of shops, restaurants, and gardens that fill the estate's original outer buildings. ✉ *2250 Reynolda Rd., University,* ☎ *336/725–5325,* WEB *www.reynoldahouse.org.* ☜ *$6.* ☉ *Tues.–Sat. 9:30–4:30, Sun. 1:30–4:30.*

Exhibits at the **Southeastern Center for Contemporary Art (SECCA),** near Reynolda House, showcase regional arts and crafts and works by nationally known artists. The Centershop sells many one-of-a-kind pieces. ✉ *750 Marguerite Dr., University,* ☎ *336/725–1904,* WEB *www.secca. org.* ☜ *$3.* ☉ *Tues.–Sat. 10–5, Sun. 2–5.*

Just 10 minutes south of the city, on land once claimed for Queen Elizabeth by Sir Walter Raleigh, is **Tanglewood Park.** The home of the late

William and Kate Reynolds is now open to the public; in addition to golfing, boating, hiking, fishing, horseback riding, and swimming, it puts on a holiday lights festival, the largest such display in the Southeast. The **Tanglewood Festival of Lights** runs from mid-November to January every year. ⊠ *U.S. 158 off I–40, South Metro, Clemmons,* ☎ *336/778–6300,* WEB *www.tanglewoodpark.org.* 🖾 *$2 per car; separate fees for each activity.* ⊘ *Daily dawn–dusk.*

Dining and Lodging

$$$–$$$$ ✕ **Noble's Grille.** French and Mediterranean flavors are key to the menu, which changes nightly. Typical entrées, grilled or roasted over the omnipresent oak-and-hickory fire, might include Roquefort risotto–stuffed Portobello mushroom with roasted polenta and veal sweetbreads with garlic-mashed potatoes. The dining room, with tall windows and track lighting, has a view of the grill. ⊠ *380 Knollwood St., Metro West,* ☎ *336/777–8477,* WEB *www.noblesrestaurants.com. AE, DC, MC, V.*

$$$ ✕ **Opie's Southbound Grille.** Although housed in a building erected in 1913 as the headquarters for Southbound Railway, this place is anything but old-fashioned. A new menu each week brings surprises, from grilled steak with fried sweet potatoes to grilled ostrich topped with honeyed onions and spicy cantaloupe chutney. ⊠ *300 S. Liberty St., Downtown,* ☎ *336/723–0322. AE, MC, V. Closed Sun.–Mon. No lunch Sat.*

$$–$$$ ✕ **Leon's Café.** This quiet, well-kept eatery in a renovated building near Old Salem serves some of the tastiest food in town—fresh seafood, grilled duck with a berry cognac sauce, and other specialties. Stained-glass windows, artwork, and an open-air patio create an eye-pleasing experience. ⊠ *924 S. Marshall St., Old Salem,* ☎ *336/725–9593. AE, D, MC, V. No lunch.*

$$–$$$ ✕ **Old Salem Tavern Dining Room.** The costumed staff happily details the varied lunch and dinner menus, from which you might order traditional Moravian chicken pie or the bratwurst platter. You can also opt for something more innovative, such as fillet of beef with brandied green peppercorns. In the warm months drinks are served under the arbor, and outdoor seating draws diners to the covered back porch. ⊠ *736 S. Main St., Old Salem,* ☎ *336/748–8585. AE, D, MC, V.*

$$–$$$ ✕ **The Vineyards.** The innovative seasonal menu, with such dishes as grilled swordfish on a bed of black-eyed-pea salsa, and stuffed eggplant, keeps people coming back to this Reynolda Village restaurant, a participant in the Heart Healthy Dining Program (sponsored by Wake Forest University's Baptist Medical Center). The homemade bread pudding is considered the best in town. There's live music Thursday through Saturday. ⊠ *120 Reynolda Village Rd., University,* ☎ *336/748–0269. AE, MC, V. Closed Sun. No lunch.*

$$$–$$$$ 🏨 **Adam's Mark Winston Plaza Hotel.** Centrally located off I–40, the hotel occupies two towers connected by a climate-controlled skywalk. The East Tower has a traditional look, although the West Tower is a bit sleeker and more contemporary. The Cherry Street Bar, with its smoothly tailored living-room, is a great place to relax. ⊠ *425 N. Cherry St., Downtown 27101,* ☎ *336/725–3500 or 800/444–2326,* FAX *336/ 721–2240,* WEB *www.adamsmark.com/winstonsalem. 603 rooms, 26 suites. Restaurant, room service, indoor pool, health club, sauna, steam room, 2 bars, dry cleaning, laundry service, business services, meeting room, parking (fee). AE, D, DC, MC, V.*

$$$ 🏨 **Brookstown Inn.** Handmade quilts, two-person tubs, and wine and cheese and freshly baked cookies in the lobby are just a few of the amenities at this inn. The rooms, with their rafters, high ceilings, and brick walls, retain the character of the 1837 textile mill this building once housed. ⊠ *200 Brookstown Ave., Old Salem 27101,* ☎ *336/725–1120 or 800/845–4262,* FAX *336/773–0147,* WEB *www.brookstowninn.com.*

40 rooms, 31 suites. Exercise room, business services, meeting room. AE, DC, MC, V. CP.

$$–$$$ ⊡ **Henry F. Shaffner House.** Accessible to downtown and Old Salem, this B&B is a favorite with business travelers and honeymooning couples. The rooms in the restored English Tudor house are meticulously furnished in 19th-century Victorian elegance. Rates include afternoon tea and evening wine and cheese. ⊠ *150 S. Marshall St., Old Salem 27101,* ☎ *336/777–0052 or 800/952–2256,* FAX *336/777–1188. 6 rooms, 3 suites. Restaurant, business services, meeting room. AE, MC, V. BP, CP.*

$$ ⊡ **Tanglewood Manor House Bed & Breakfast.** The former home of a branch of the Reynolds family includes 10 rooms in the antiques-filled manor house, 18 rooms in a more contemporary motel behind the house, and four cottages on Mallard Lake in Tanglewood Park. Those staying in the motel can purchase the Continental breakfast served in the manor house. Admissions to the park and swimming pool are included; a fishing license is extra. Greens fees at park courses are discounted. ⊠ *U.S. 158 off I–40, South Metro, Clemmons 27012,* ☎ *336/778–6300,* FAX *336/778–6379,* WEB *www.tanglewoodpark.org. 28 rooms, 4 cottages, guest house. Picnic area, driving range, 2 18-hole golf courses, pool, wading pool, fishing, horseback riding, playground, meeting room. AE, DC, MC, V. CP.*

$–$$ ⊡ **Comfort Inn–Cloverdale,** Off I–40 Business near downtown and Old Salem, this hotel is near the business and nightlife nexus of Winston-Salem. ⊠ *110 Miller St., Downtown 27103,* ☎ *336/721–0220 or 800/228–5150,* FAX *336/723–2117,* WEB *www.choicehotels.com. 122 rooms. Microwaves, refrigerators, pool, exercise room, sauna, laundry service, meeting room. AE, D, DC, MC, V. CP.*

Nightlife and the Arts

THE ARTS

Many North Carolina School of the Arts musical and dramatic performances are held at the **Stevens Center** (⊠ 405 W. 4th St., Downtown, ☎ 336/721–1945), a restored 1929 movie palace downtown and part of the NCSA campus. The Broadway Preview Series stages first-run productions, featuring big-name actors, before they move on to Broadway engagements. Every two years the North Carolina Black Repertory Company hosts the **National Black Theatre Festival** (⊠ 610 Coliseum Dr., University, ☎ 336/723–2266). This weeklong showcase of African-American talent attracts tens of thousands of people, including a who's who of celebrities. The *New York Times* has hailed this event as "one of the most historic and culturally significant in the history of black theatre and American theatre in general." The festival usually held during the summer.

NIGHTLIFE

Burke Street Pub (⊠ 1110 Burke St., West Metro, ☎ 336/750–0097) is an Irish-style pub with music, dancing, games, and sports TV. In the Adam's Mark Winston Plaza, the **Cherry Street Bar** (⊠ 425 N. Cherry St., Downtown, ☎ 336/725–3500) has cozy chairs and a smart style. **Lucky 32** (⊠ 109 S. Stratford Rd., University, ☎ 336/777–0032), a fine bar adjoining a restaurant, caters to a professional crowd.

Outdoor Activities and Sports

BASKETBALL

Winston-Salem's Atlantic Coast Conference entry is the Wake Forest University **Demon Deacons** (☎ 336/758–3322 or 888/758–3322).

GOLF

Tanglewood Park Golf Club (⊠ Rte. 158, Clemmons, ☎ 336/778–6320) has two fine 18-hole, par-72 courses, the Reynolds Course and the

Championship Course, where the Vantage Championship is played each year. The **Reynolds Park Golf Course** (⊠ 2931 Reynolds Park Rd., East Metro, ☎ 336/650–7660) has 18 holes with a view of the city skyline and a par 71.

Shopping

SHOPPING DISTRICTS AND MALLS

The **Art District,** at 6th and Trade streets (just behind the Winston-Salem Visitor Center), has several galleries and arts-and-crafts shops. **Reynolda Village** is near the Reynolda House Museum of American Art. **Stratford Place,** a collection of upscale shops, restaurants, and cafés, is off I–40 Business in the Five Points area, where Country Club, Miller Road, and 1st Street converge.

CRAFTS

All items at the **Piedmont Craftsmen's Shop and Gallery** (⊠ 1204 Reynolda Rd., University, ☎ 336/725–1516) are juried. An annual fair is held in November. **erl Originals** (⊠ 3069 Trenwest Dr., West Metro, ☎ 336/760–4373), near I–40 and Hanes Mall, has 8,000 square ft of gallery space and represents more than 300 artists.

High Point

76 mi northeast of Charlotte, 20 mi southwest of Greensboro.

Originally settled by Quakers in the 1700s, High Point was incorporated in 1859. Its name is derived from its former position as the highest point on the railroad between Goldsboro and Charlotte. It's also the childhood home of legendary jazz saxophonist John Coltrane. But today when people think of High Point, they think of furniture, for it is where the twice-a-year (April and October) International Home Furnishings Market, the largest wholesale furniture market in the world (not open to the public), takes place. Tens of thousands of buyers and others associated with the trade "go to market" and in the process lend a sophistication to this warm and hospitable city. More than 70 retail outlets here offer furniture and home accessories at bargain prices.

The **High Point Museum/Historical Park,** focusing on Piedmont history and Quaker heritage, includes the 1786 Haley House and a mid-1700s blacksmith shop and weaving house. Exhibits highlight furniture, pottery, communication, transportation, and military artifacts. Tours of the buildings are available weekends and are conducted by costumed staff. The park also serves as base camp for the Guilford Militia Living Historians. ⊠ *1859 E. Lexington Ave.,* ☎ *336/885–6859.* ☜ *Free.* ☉ *Museum Tues.–Sat. 10–4:30, Sun. 1–4:30; park buildings Sat. 10–4, Sun. 1–4.*

The **Furniture Discovery Center,** in a renovated fabric warehouse downtown, simulates the furniture design and manufacturing process. It has a Furniture Hall of Fame and an extensive miniature collection exhibited in room displays. ⊠ *101 W. Green Dr.,* ☎ *336/887–3876,* WEB *www. furniturediscovery.org.* ☜ *$5; combination ticket with Angela Peterson Doll and Miniature Museum $8.50.* ☉ *Apr.–Oct., weekdays 10– 5, Sat. 9–5, Sun. 1–5; Nov.–Mar., Tues.–Fri. 10–5, Sat. 9–5, Sun. 1–5.*

The **Angela Peterson Doll and Miniature Museum** houses the collection begun by one woman and now including more than 2,000 dolls, costumes, miniatures, and dollhouses. ⊠ *101 W. Green Dr.,* ☎ *336/ 885–3655.* ☜ *$4; combination ticket with Furniture Discovery Center $8.50.* ☉ *Apr.–Oct., weekdays 10–4:30, Sat. 9–4:30, Sun. 1–4:30; Nov.–Mar., Tues.–Sat. 10–4:30, Sun. 1–4:30.*

MENDENHALL PLANTATION – A few miles northwest of High Point is this well-preserved example of 19th-century Quaker domestic architecture. The Mendenhalls opposed slavery, and here you'll find one of the few surviving false-bottom wagons, used to help slaves escape to freedom on the Underground Railroad. ⊠ *603 W. Main St., Jamestown,* ☎ *336/454–3819.* ☞ *$2.* ☼ *Mid-Apr.–Nov., Tue.–Fri. 11–2, Sat. 1–4, Sun. 2–4.*

Dining and Lodging

$$$ ✕ **Act I.** This easygoing respite from the fast-paced world is tucked in a commercial area of town, its three dining areas—atrium, lounge, and gallery—hung attractively with local art. Appealing, too, are the daily specials, which have included roasted duck in peach sauce and honey-mango shrimp. ⊠ *130 E. Parris Ave.,* ☎ *336/869–5614,* WEB *www. act1highpoint.com. AE, MC, V. No lunch Sat.*

$$–$$$ ✕ **J. Basul Noble's.** Locals hold this place in high esteem, and it's easy to see why. It's architecturally dramatic, with 10-ft pillars, a pyramid-shape glass ceiling, and a river-rock wall. The menu covers all the bases—fish, veal, pork, game, beef, and lamb. You could make a meal out of the fine breads (baked daily on the premises) and desserts. There's live jazz Thursday through Saturday. ⊠ *101 S. Main St.,* ☎ *336/889–3354,* WEB *www.noblesrestaurants.com. AE, DC, MC, V.*

$$–$$$ 🏨 **Radisson Hotel High Point.** The central location makes the Radisson a favorite with people coming to town for weekend shopping trips. Guest rooms are standard, but each suite is outfitted with furniture from the different manufacturers represented in the area. ⊠ *135 S. Main St., 27260,* ☎ *336/889–8888,* FAX *336/885–2737,* WEB *www.radisson.com/highpoint. 239 rooms, 13 suites. Restaurant, indoor pool, gym, bar, business services, meeting room, airport shuttle, parking (fee). AE, D, DC, MC, V.*

$$ 🏨 **Toad Alley Bed & Bagel.** This three-story 1924 house, in a quiet neighborhood 1 mi north of downtown, is fronted by a wide wraparound porch. Rooms are distinguished by 9-ft ceilings and individual decorating schemes—in one there's a dramatic custom-designed four-poster bed. You can relax while sipping wine by the fireplace or on the front porch swing. ⊠ *1001 Johnson St., 27262,* ☎ *336/889–8349,* FAX *336/886–6646,* WEB *www.toadalley.com. 6 rooms. In-room VCRs. MC, V. BP.*

Nightlife and the Arts

Headquartered in High Point is the **North Carolina Shakespeare Festival.** The professional troupe performs from August through October and in December at the **High Point Theatre** (⊠ 1014 Mill St., ☎ 336/841–2273, WEB www.ncshakes.org).

Outdoor Activities and Sports

GOLF

There are six public golf courses in High Point: three have 18 holes, and three have 9. Pete Dye designed the notable par-72 course at **Oak Hollow** (⊠ 3400 N. Centennial St., ☎ 336/883–3260).

HIKING

The 376-acre **Piedmont Environmental Center** (⊠ 1220 Penny Rd., ☎ 336/883–8531, WEB www.piedmontenvironmental.com) has 11 mi of hiking trails adjacent to City Lake Park, with recreational activities and a nature preserve. There's also access to a 6-mi greenway trail.

TENNIS

In Oak Hollow Lake Park, the **Reitzel Tennis Center** (⊠ 3401 N. Centennial St., ☎ 336/883–3493) has 12 outdoor and 4 indoor courts. Reservations are a must.

Shopping

There are more than 70 retail furniture stores in and around High Point. The 36 stores in the **Atrium Furniture Mall** (✉ 430 S. Main St., ☎ 336/882–5599) carry items by more than 700 manufacturers of furniture and home accessories.

Art shows rotate through the three exhibition spaces of **Theatre Art Galleries** (✉ 220 E. Commerce Ave., ☎ 336/887–3415), open weekdays noon–5 and weekends by appointment but closed during market weeks in April and October.

The Triad A to Z

To research prices, get advice from other travelers, and book travel arrangements, visit www.fodors.com.

AIRPORTS

Just west of Greensboro, the Piedmont Triad International Airport is off Route 68 north from I–40; it's served by American, ATA, Continental, Delta, Eastwind, Northwest, United, and US Airways.

Taxi service to and from the airport is provided by Airport Express and other tour, charter, limousine, and cab services, including the Golden Eagle Cab Company and Piedmont Executive Transportation. ➤ AIRPORT INFORMATION: **Airport Express** (☎ 800/934–8779). **Golden Eagle Cab Company** (☎ 336/724–6481). **Piedmont Executive Transportation** (☎ 336/723–2179). **Piedmont Triad International Airport** (✉ 6451 Bryan Blvd., Greensboro, ☎ 336/665–5666, WEB www.ptia.org).

BUS TRAVEL

Greyhound/Carolina Trailways serves Burlington, Greensboro, High Point, Lexington, and Winston-Salem.
➤ BUS INFORMATION: **Greyhound/Carolina Trailways** (☎ 800/231–2222, WEB www.greyhound.com).

CAR TRAVEL

Greensboro and Winston-Salem are on I–40, which runs east–west through North Carolina. From the east I–40 and I–85 combine coming into the Triad, but in Greensboro, I–85 splits off to go southwest to Charlotte. High Point is off a business bypass of I–85 southwest of Greensboro.

TOURS

Carolina Treasures and Tours offers a look at historic Winston-Salem.
➤ CONTACTS: **Carolina Treasures and Tours** (✉ 1031 Burke St., ☎ 336/631–9144).

TRAIN TRAVEL

Amtrak serves Greensboro and High Point.
➤ TRAIN INFORMATION: **Amtrak** (☎ 800/872–7245, WEB www.amtrak.com).

VISITOR INFORMATION

➤ TOURIST INFORMATION: **Greensboro Area Convention and Visitors Bureau** (✉ 317 S. Greene St., 27401, ☎ 336/274–2282 or 800/344–2282, WEB www.greensboro.org). **High Point Convention and Visitors Bureau** (✉ 300 S. Main St., 27260, ☎ 336/884–5255 or 800/720–5255, WEB www.highpoint.org). **Winston-Salem Convention and Visitors Bureau** (✉ Box 1409, 27102, ☎ 336/728–4200 or 800/331–7018; visitor center, ✉ 601 N. Cherry St., ☎ 336/777–3796, WEB www.wscvb.com).

THE TRIANGLE

Raleigh, Durham, Chapel Hill

The cities of Raleigh, Durham, and Chapel Hill make up the Triangle, with Raleigh to the east, Durham to the north, Chapel Hill to the west, and, in the center, Research Triangle Park—a renowned complex of corporations and public and private research facilities set in 6,800 acres of lake-dotted pineland that attracts scientists, academicians, and businesspeople from all over the world. Throughout the Triangle, an area that's been characterized as "trees, tees, and PhDs," politics and basketball are always hot topics. The NCAA basketball championship has traded hands among the area's three major universities.

Raleigh

143 mi northeast of Charlotte, 104 mi east of Winston-Salem.

Raleigh is Old South and New South, down-home and upscale, all in one. Named for Sir Walter Raleigh (who established the first English colony on the coast in 1585), it's the state capital and the biggest of the three cities. Many of the state's largest and best museums are here, as are North Carolina State University and six other universities and colleges.

Numbers in the text correspond to numbers in the margin and on the Downtown Raleigh map.

A Good Walk

Downtown the streets are laid out in an orderly grid with the state capitol as the hub. Most downtown Raleigh attractions are state government buildings, historic buildings, and museums and are free to the public. Begin with a walk through **Oakwood Historic District** ⑮. Next, stroll by the **executive mansion** ⑯, the home of governors since 1891.

Follow Jones Street west past Wilmington Street to visit the **State Legislative Building** ⑰. Cross Jones Street to Bicentennial Plaza, flanked by the **North Carolina Museum of Natural Sciences** ⑱, to the west, and the **North Carolina Museum of History** ⑲, to the east. Continue south across Edenton Street to Capitol Square and the **state capitol** ⑳.

Starting just south of the capitol across Morgan Street and continuing for four blocks is the **Fayetteville Street Mall** ㉑, a pedestrians-only walkway. From the mall walk two blocks east on Hargett Street to **Exploris** ㉒, a children's museum. One block south is the **City Market** ㉓, a revitalized area between Blount and Person streets. Just south of the market are the studios and galleries of **Artspace** ㉔, at the corner of Blount and Davie streets.

TIMING

You'll need several hours just to hit the sights of this walk and even more time if you're the kind of person who tends to get hooked on museums.

Sights to See

㉔ **Artspace.** Adjacent to the Moore Square art district, Artspace is a private, nonprofit visual arts center offering open studios, exhibits, and galleries. The gift shop showcases the work of the resident artists, who are happy to talk to you about their work. ✉ *201 E. Davie St., Downtown,* ☎ *919/821-2787,* WEB *www.artspace.citysearch.com.* ☜ *Free.* ☉ *Tues.–Sat. 10–6.*

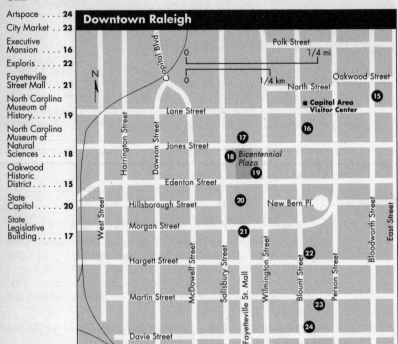

Downtown Raleigh

㉓ City Market. This revitalized area with cobblestone streets has specialty shops, art galleries, restaurants, a comedy club, and a small farmers' market. The free Entertainment Trolley shuttles between the market and other downtown restaurant and nightlife locations from 6:40 PM to 12:40 AM Thursday through Saturday. ☒ *Martin St. and Moore Sq., Downtown,* ☎ *919/828–4555,* WEB *www.citymarket.citysearch.com.* ☉ *Stores Mon.–Sat. 10–5:30, restaurants Mon.–Sat. 7 AM–1 AM, Sun. 11:30–10.*

㉖ Executive Mansion. The mansion is a brick early 20th-century Queen Anne cottage–style structure with gingerbread trim and manicured lawns. Tour hours vary; check with the Capital Area Visitor Center. ☒ *200 N. Blount St., Downtown,* ☎ *919/733–3456.* ☒ *Free.*

㉒ Exploris. This 84,000-square-ft architectural showplace (the marble wall is a dazzler) is a learning center that stands apart from most other children's museums. It emphasizes a global perspective, as opposed to specific health and natural science topics. Exhibits explore language, culture, geography, trade, and communications. ☒ *201 E. Hargett St., Downtown,* ☎ *919/834–4040,* WEB *www.exploris.org.* ☒ *$7.* ☉ *Mon.–Sat. 9–5, Sun. noon–5.*

㉑ Fayetteville Street Mall. Extending from the state capitol to the Raleigh Civic and Convention Center, this pedestrian walkway provides entrance to a number of high-rise office buildings. The shops and restaurants in the area cater to the weekday business crowd.

㉙ North Carolina Museum of History. Founded in 1898, the museum is now in a state-of-the-art facility on Bicentennial Plaza. It uses artifacts, audiovisual programs, and interactive exhibits to bring the state's history to life. Exhibits include the *N.C. Sports Hall of Fame; N.C. Folklife;* and *Militaria, Politics, and Society.* ☒ *5 E. Edenton St., Downtown,*

☎ 919/715–0200, 〚WEB〛 *http://nchistory.dcr.state.nc.us/musuems.* 🖂 *Free.* ⊙ *Tues.–Sat. 9–5, Sun. noon–5.*

★ ☾ ⑱ **North Carolina Museum of Natural Sciences.** At 200,000 square ft, this museum is the largest of its kind in the Southeast. It has permanent exhibits and dioramas that celebrate the incredible diversity of species in the state's three regions—coast, piedmont, and mountains. There are enough animals and insects—including butterflies, hummingbirds, snakes, and a two-toed sloth—to qualify as a small zoo. One signature exhibit contains rare whale skeletons. The pièce de résistance, however, is the *Terror of the South* exhibit, featuring the dinosaur skeleton of "Acro," a giant carnivore that lived in the South 110 million years ago. ⊠ *11 W. Jones St., Downtown,* ☎ *919/733–7450 or 877/462–8724,* 〚WEB〛 *www. naturalsciences.org.* 🖂 *Free.* ⊙ *Mon.–Sat. 9–5, Sun. noon–5.*

⑮ **Oakwood Historic District.** Many fine examples of Victorian architecture can be seen in this tree-shaded neighborhood. Self-guided walking tours of the area, which encompasses 20 blocks bordered by Person, Edenton, Franklin, and Watauga/Linden streets, are available at the **Capital Area Visitor Center.** Adjacent to historic Oakwood is **Oakwood Cemetery** (⊠ 701 Oakwood Ave., Downtown, ☎ 919/832–6077). Established in 1869, it is the resting place of 2,800 Confederate soldiers, Civil War generals, governors, and numerous U.S. senators. Free maps are available at the cemetery office.

⑳ **State Capitol.** A beautifully preserved example of Greek Revival architecture from 1840, the capitol once housed all the functions of state government. Today it's part museum, part executive offices. The capitol contains, under the domed rotunda, a copy of Antonio Canova's statue of George Washington depicted as a Roman general with tunic, tight-fitting body armor, and a short cape. ⊠ *Capitol Sq. (1 E. Edenton St.), Downtown,* ☎ *919/733–4994,* 〚WEB〛 *www.ah.dcr.state.nc.us/ sections/capitol.* 🖂 *Free.* ⊙ *Weekdays 8–5, Sat. 10–4, Sun. 1–4.*

⑰ **State Legislative Building.** One block north of the state capitol, this complex hums with lawmakers and lobbyists when the legislature is in session. It's fun to watch from the gallery. A free guided tour is also available through the **Capital Area Visitor Center.** ⊠ *Salisbury and Jones Sts., Downtown,* ☎ *919/733–7928,* 〚WEB〛 *www.ncga.state.nc.us.* 🖂 *Free.* ⊙ *Weekdays 8–5, Sat. 9–5, Sun. 1–5.*

Other Area Attractions

The city is spread out, so a car is almost a necessity for museums and parks beyond downtown.

OFF THE
BEATEN PATH
AVA GARDNER MUSEUM – This museum in the hometown of the legendary beauty and movie star has an extensive collection of memorabilia that trace her life from childhood on the farm to Hollywood glory days. It's about 30 mi east of Raleigh in downtown Smithfield. ⊠ *325 E. Market St., Smithfield,* ☎ *919/934–5830,* 〚WEB〛 *www.avagardner.org.* 🖂 *$4.* ⊙ *Mon.–Sat. 9–5, Sun. 2–5.*

Joel Lane Museum House. The oldest dwelling in Raleigh was the home of the "father of Raleigh" and dates from the 1760s. Joel Lane sold the state the property on which the capital city grew. Costumed docents tell the story and show the restored house and beautiful period gardens. ⊠ *720 W. Hargett St., at St. Mary's St., Downtown,* ☎ *919/833–3431.* 🖂 *$3.* ⊙ *Mar.–mid-Dec., Tues.–Fri. 10–2, Sat. 1–4.*

Mordecai Historic Park. You can see the Mordecai family's plantation home and other structures, including the house where President Andrew Johnson was born, in 1808. One-hour guided tours are given on the half hour. You can also board a trolley for a narrated 45-minute tour of historic Raleigh (March–December, Saturday noon–3; $5). ⊠ *1 Mimosa St., at Wake Forest Rd., University,* ☎ *919/834-4844.* 🖃 *$4.* ☉ *Weekdays 10–4.*

★ **North Carolina Museum of Art.** On the west side of Raleigh, the NCMA houses 5,000 years of artistic heritage, including one of the nation's largest collections of Jewish ceremonial art. Other exhibits range from ancient Egyptian times to the present, from the Old World to the New. The museum hosts touring exhibitions of works by such artists as Caravaggio and Rodin. The glass-wall **Museum Café** looks out on an outdoor performance center–cum–sculpture that when viewed from above spells the words PICTURE THIS. ⊠ *2110 Blue Ridge Rd., Northwest/Airport,* ☎ *919/839-6262; 919/833-3548 for restaurant,* WEB *www. ncartmuseum.org.* 🖃 *Free.* ☉ *Tues.–Thurs. and Sat. 9–5, Fri. 9–9, Sun. 11–6; tours Tues.–Sun. 1:30.*

☾ **Pullen Park.** In summer crowds come to picnic and ride the 1911 Dentzel carousel, the train, and paddleboats. You can swim here in a large public indoor aquatic center or outdoor pool, play tennis, explore an arts-and-crafts center, or, if the timing is right, see a play at the Theater in the Park. ⊠ *520 Ashe Ave., near North Carolina State University, University,* ☎ *919/831-6468 or 919/831-6640,* WEB *www.raleigh-nc. org/parks&rec/pullenpark.htm.* 🖃 *Fees vary.* ☉ *Apr.–Oct., daily 10 AM–dusk; Mar. and Nov., Fri.–Sat. 10–5, Sun. 1–5; summer hrs vary.*

Dining and Lodging

$$$$ ✕ **Second Empire.** Wood paneling, crown molding and high ceilings,
★ floral arrangements, muted lighting, and well-spaced tables make for a calming and elegant dining experience. The menu, which changes monthly, has a regional flavor; the food is best described as art on a plate, intricately styled so that colors, textures, and tastes fuse. For an entrée you might get roasted mahimahi, paired with collard greens, butternut squash, and garlic cream. A wood-and-brass tavern on the lower level has a simpler and less expensive menu. ⊠ *300 Hillsborough St., Downtown,* ☎ *919/829-3663. AE, MC, V. Closed Sun. No lunch.*

$$$–$$$$ ✕ **Angus Barn.** A huge rustic barn houses a Raleigh tradition that is justifiably famous. The astonishing wine and beer list is 35 pages long. The restaurant is known for its steaks, baby-back ribs, prime rib, and fresh seafood and for its clubby Wild Turkey Lounge. Desserts are amazing. Reservations aren't accepted for Saturday dinner. ⊠ *U.S. 70W (Glenwood Ave.) near Aviation Pkwy., Northwest/Airport,* ☎ *919/781-2444,* WEB *www.angusbarn.com. AE, D, DC, MC, V. No lunch.*

$$–$$$ ✕ **Greenshields Brewery & Pub.** You can sip beer and ale brewed on the premises with your soup, salad, sandwich, or such entrées as fish-and-chips, shepherd's pie, and steak in this English-style pub. Oak paneling and working fireplaces enhance the mood. There are also an open-air patio, and live music on Saturday night. ⊠ *214 E. Martin St., City Market, Downtown,* ☎ *919/829-0214,* WEB *www.greenshields. com. AE, D, MC, V.*

$$–$$$ ✕ **Irregardless Café.** The blond wood, brightly hued contemporary art, sunlighted dining areas, and well-spaced tables all underscore one theme: relaxation. The seasonal menu, although offering some meat-based dishes, emphasizes vegetarian items. Salads are amply portioned, and the breads, soups, and yogurts are homemade. There are live music every night, dancing on Saturday evening, and brunch on Sunday. The restaurant is midway between North Carolina State University and downtown. ⊠ *901 W. Morgan St., University,* ☎ *919/833-8898. AE, D, DC, MC, V. No lunch Sat., no dinner Sun.*

$$–$$$ ✕ **Margaux's.** Eclectic is the key word for the cuisine at this intimate, dimly lighted north Raleigh fixture, where a massive stone fireplace warms the room. A blackboard lists the diverse specials, such as red-chili fettuccine with goat cheese, lamb with coconut curry sauce, or grilled shrimp and crawfish tostada with roasted corn, black beans, and salsa *verde*. ✉ *8111 Creedmoor Rd., Brennan Station Shopping Center, North Hills,* ☎ *919/846–9846. DC, MC, V.*

$$–$$$ ✕ **Tony's Bourbon Street Oyster Bar.** The mood here—already festive with red walls, feather masks, and street lamps from New Orleans—jumps up a notch with live music Friday and Saturday. Cajun and creole dishes, such as gumbo, jambalaya, and crawfish étouffée, are served in the large white-linen dining room or the large stainless-steel oyster bar. Cary, near the entrance to Research Triangle Park, is 25 minutes west of downtown Raleigh. ✉ *107 Edinburgh Dr., MacGregor Village Shopping Center, Cary,* ☎ *919/462–6226. AE, D, DC, MC, V. Closed Sun. No lunch.*

$ ✕ **Big Ed's City Market Restaurant.** A must for breakfast or lunch, Big Ed's is filled with antique farm implements and the owner's political memorabilia, including pictures of presidential candidates who have stopped at this landmark. Every Saturday morning a Dixieland band plays. Come here for down-home cookin' and make sure you indulge in the biscuits. ✉ *220 Wolfe St., City Market, Downtown,* ☎ *919/836–9909. Reservations not accepted. No credit cards. Closed Sun. No dinner.*

$$$–$$$$ ⌂ **Raleigh Marriott Crabtree Valley.** Fresh floral arrangements adorn the elegantly decorated public rooms of one of the city's most luxurious hotels. Standard rooms have soft colors, Asian floral prints, and dark cherry-wood furnishings. You can dine at the Crabtree Grill and at Quinn's, a lounge where light fare and drinks are served daily. ✉ *4500 Marriott Dr., U.S. 70 near Crabtree Valley Mall, University 27612,* ☎ *919/781–7000 or 800/228–9290,* ℻ *919/781–3059,* ⓦⓔⓑ *www.marriotthotels.com/RDUNC. 375 rooms, 4 suites. Restaurant, lounge, indoor-outdoor pool, health club, hot tub, bar, laundry facilities, laundry service, concierge, business services, meeting room, airport shuttle. AE, D, DC, MC, V.*

$$–$$$ ⌂ **Hampton Inn & Suites.** In the southwest corner of Cary, right over the Raleigh line, this hotel is just minutes from Raleigh's Entertainment & Sports Arena, the State Fairgrounds, and North Carolina State University. Rooms are typical of the chain; you'll need a car to get to restaurants. ✉ *111 Hampton Woods La., Cary 27607,* ☎ *919/233–1798 or 800/426–7866,* ℻ *919/854–1166,* ⓦⓔⓑ *www.hampton-inn.com. 126 rooms. Kitchenettes, refrigerators, pool, exercise room, baby-sitting, laundry service, business services, meeting room. AE, D, DC, MC, V.*

$$–$$$ ⌂ **William Thomas House.** A stately but not stuffy Victorian home is a B&B on the edge of downtown Raleigh a few blocks from the governor's mansion. Rooms, named for family members, are traditionally and elegantly decorated and have oversize windows and 12-ft ceilings. The richly hued common rooms are filled with heirlooms, including a grand piano from 1863, and antique china. ✉ *530 N. Blount St., Downtown 27604,* ☎ *919/755–9400 or 800/653–3466,* ℻ *919/755–3966,* ⓦⓔⓑ *www.williamthomashouse.com. 4 rooms. Fans, refrigerators, library. AE, D, DC, MC, V. BP.*

$$ ⌂ **North Raleigh Hilton.** This is a favorite spot for corporate meetings. The standard rooms are done in mauve and green, with traditional furniture and prints. You can dine in Lofton's restaurant and listen to the piano afterward in the lobby bar. Bowties is a popular nightspot for dancing. ✉ *3415 Wake Forest Rd., North Hills 27609,* ☎ *919/872–2323 or 800/445–8667,* ℻ *919/876–0890,* ⓦⓔⓑ *www.hilton.com. 331 rooms, 7 suites. Restaurant, room service, indoor pool, exercise room,*

*2 bars, nightclub, business services, meeting room, airport shuttle.
AE, D, DC, MC, V.*

$$ 🖭 **Ramada Inn Crabtree.** Pluses at this comfortable chain property are
landscaped grounds large enough for a stroll and rooms done in muted
autumnal colors. This may be the friendliest motel in town. It's also
where football and basketball teams like to stay when they're here for
a game, as evidenced by the sports memorabilia in the Brass Bell
Lounge. ⊠ *3920 Arrow Dr., U.S. 70 and Beltline/I–440, North Hills
27612,* ☎ *919/782–7525 or 800/441–4712,* FAX *919/781–0435,* WEB
*www.ramada.com. 157 rooms, 17 suites. Restaurant, room service, in-
door pool, exercise room, bar, laundry service, business services, meet-
ing room, airport shuttle. AE, D, DC, MC, V. CP.*

Nightlife and the Arts

THE ARTS

The **BTI Center for the Performing Arts** (⊠ 1 E. South St., Downtown)
is a multivenue complex that includes a 1,700-seat concert hall, 2,300-
seat auditorium, 600-seat theater for opera, and 170-seat venue for live
theater: **Memorial Auditorium** (☎ 919/831–6061) is home base for
the North Carolina Theatre, which stages productions that have been
on Broadway and off-Broadway. **Meymandi Concert Hall** (☎ 919/733–
2750) hosts the North Carolina Symphony. **Fletcher Opera Theater** (☎
919/831–6011) provides a showcase for the nationally acclaimed Car-
olina Ballet and productions of the Opera Company of North Carolina.
And the **Kennedy Theater** (☎ 919/831–6011) stages shows of smaller,
sometimes alternative theater groups.

The **North Carolina State University Arts Programs** (☎ 919/515–1100)
include the Center Stage series, host to professional touring produc-
tions and world-class artists. All arts program performances are open
to the public.

Alltel Pavilion at Walnut Creek (⊠ 3801 Rock Quarry Rd., Southeast
Metro, ☎ 919/831–6666), known as "the Creek," accommodates
20,000. Headliners appear spring through midfall and cover the mu-
sical spectrum. This is the most attended amphitheater on the East Coast.

NIGHTLIFE

The **Berkeley Café** (⊠ 217 W. Martin St., Downtown, ☎ 919/821–
0777) is one of the hottest gathering places in the Triangle for live music:
rock and roll, R&B, and blues. **Bowties** (⊠ North Raleigh Hilton, 3415
Wake Forest Rd., University, ☎ 919/878–4917) is a popular after-hours
spot for dancing. **Cappers** (⊠ 4216 Six Forks Rd., North Hills, ☎ 919/
787–8963), a restaurant and tavern, is also *the* spot for jazz and blues.
Charlie Goodnight's Comedy Club (⊠ 861 W. Morgan St., University,
☎ 919/828–5233) combines dinner with a night of laughs. Alumni in-
clude Jay Leno, Jerry Seinfeld, and Elaine Boosler. **Tir na nog** (⊠ 218
S. Blount St., Downtown, ☎ 919/833–7795) has Irish entertainers and
Murphy's Irish Amber, Guinness, and even whiskey on tap. In the ware-
house district is the **Warehouse Restaurant and Entertainment Center**
(⊠ 427 S. Dawson St., Downtown, ☎ 919/836–9966), with a huge
dance floor and game room.

Outdoor Activities and Sports

BASKETBALL

Raleigh's Atlantic Coast Conference entry is the North Carolina State
University **Wolfpack** (☎ 919/515–2106 or 800/310–7225).

BIKING

Raleigh has 40 mi of greenways for biking or walking, and maps are
available through the **Raleigh Division of Transportation** (☎ 919/890–
3285).

CAMPING

Try the **North Carolina State Fairgrounds** (⊠ 1025 Blue Ridge Rd., ☎ 919/821–7400) if you have an RV, as it's RVs only. The 5,439-acre **William B. Umstead State Park** (⊠ 8801 Glenwood Ave., ☎ 919/571–4170) is between Raleigh and Durham. **Clemmons State Forest** (⊠ 2411 Old Garner Rd., ☎ 919/553–5651) is near Clayton. **Jordan Lake** (⊠ 280 State Park Rd., ☎ 919/362–0586) is between Apex and Pittsboro.

FISHING

Jordan Lake, a 13,900-acre reservoir in Apex, is a favorite fishing spot. Others are Lake Wheeler, in Raleigh, and the Falls Lake State Recreation Area, in Wake Forest.

GOLF

There are 20 golf courses, either public or semiprivate, within a half-hour drive of downtown Raleigh. **Cheviot Hills Golf Course** (⊠ 7301 Capital Blvd., North Hills, ☎ 919/850–9983) is a par-71, 18-hole championship course. **Devil's Ridge Golf Club** (⊠ 5107 Links Land Dr., Holly Springs, ☎ 919/557–6100), about 15 mi from Raleigh, is a challenging par-72, 18-hole course with large, rolling greens. **Lochmere Golf Club** (⊠ 2511 Kildaire Farm Rd., Cary, ☎ 919/851–0611) provides a friendly environment, good value, and a challenge with 18 holes at par 71. A 30-minute drive from Raleigh is the **Neuse Golf Club** (⊠ 918 Birkdale Dr., Clayton, ☎ 919/550–0550), an attractive par-72, 18-hole course on the banks of the Neuse River.

HOCKEY

The NHL's **Carolina Hurricanes** play in the 21,000-seat **Raleigh Entertainment & Sports Arena** (⊠ 1400 Edwards Mill Rd., Northwest/Airport, ☎ 919/467–7825 or 888/645–8491).

JOGGING

Runners frequent Shelley Lake, the track at North Carolina State University, and the **Capital Area Greenway** system (☎ 919/831–6833 for a map).

Shopping

SHOPPING MALLS AND OUTLET CENTERS

Cameron Village Shopping Center (⊠ 1900 Cameron St., Downtown), Raleigh's first shopping center contains specialty shops and boutiques and restaurants. **Prime Outlets** (⊠ Exit 284 off I–40, Airport Blvd., Northwest/Airport, Morrisville, between Raleigh and Durham, ☎ 919/380–8700) is decidedly un-mall-like with its wooden floors and greenery. The area's only factory outlet center has more than 40 stores, including Off Fifth (Saks Fifth Avenue) and Geoffrey Beene.

ART AND ANTIQUES

City Market is a revitalized downtown shopping area with shops and art galleries. At **Artspace** (⊠ 201 E. Davie St., Downtown, ☎ 919/821–2787, WEB www.artspace.citysearch.com) you can visit artists' studios and purchase their works. The merchandise changes daily at **Carolina Antique Mall** (⊠ 1900 Cameron St., ☎ 919/833–8227), in Cameron Village, where 75 dealers stock the floor.

FOOD

Open year-round, the 60-acre **State Farmers' Market** (⊠ 1201 Agriculture St., Lake Wheeler Rd. and I–40, Southwest Metro, ☎ 919/733–7417 for market; 919/833–7973 for restaurants) includes a garden center, a seafood restaurant, and a down-home restaurant. **Wellspring Grocery** (⊠ 3540 Wade Ave., University, ☎ 919/828–5805) has outstanding produce, fresh-baked breads, health foods, and specialty items, as well as a place to sit and eat your purchases.

Durham

23 mi northwest of Raleigh on I–40 and Rte. 147 (Durham Fwy.).

Durham has three of North Carolina's 22 National Historic Landmarks and long ago shed its tobacco-town image. It is now known as the City of Medicine for the medical and research centers at Duke University, one of the top schools in the nation. With more than 20,000 employees, Duke is not only the largest employer in Durham but also one of the largest in the state. Warehouses and mills around the city have been converted to chic shops, offices, and condos.

Numbers in the text correspond to numbers in the margin and on the Durham map.

A Good Drive

Durham has some areas appropriate for a good walk, such as Duke University's campus. However, it's best to drive. Start your tour 1½ mi south of downtown, exiting the Durham Freeway (Route 147) at Fayetteville Street, along which you will find the **North Carolina Central University Art Museum** ㉕ and the **Hayti Heritage Center** ㉖.

The next stop is about 3 mi away. Return to the Durham Freeway and continue northwest to the exit at Chapel Hill Street. Follow Chapel Hill west into the West Campus of **Duke University,** which includes the **Duke Chapel** ㉗ and the **Sarah P. Duke Gardens** ㉘. Return to Chapel Hill Street and take it past the Durham Freeway to Duke Street and turn left. Head north toward downtown, stopping at **Brightleaf Square** ㉙. From here it's a short drive to the **North Carolina Museum of Life and Science** ㉚. Continue north to reach the **Duke Homestead** ㉛. And conclude your tour at **West Point on the Eno** ㉜.

TIMING

You should allow 1–1½ days to explore these Durham highlights; select a number of sights that interest you if you have only a day.

Sights to See

㉙ **Brightleaf Square.** Named for the kind of tobacco once manufactured here, Brightleaf Square, with its flowering courtyard, striking turn-of-the-century architecture, upscale shops, and funky restaurants, is the shining star of a downtown revitalization effort. It anchors a larger arts and entertainment district, which includes the Carolina Theatre and Durham Bulls Athletic Park. ⊠ *905 W. Main St., Duke University,* ☎ *919/682–9229,* WEB *www.brightleaf.citysearch.com.*

★ ㉗ **Duke Chapel.** A Gothic-style gem built in the early 1930s, the chapel is the centerpiece of the campus. Modeled after Canterbury Cathedral, it has 77 stained-glass windows and a 210-ft bell tower. ⊠ *Chapel Dr., West Campus, Duke University,* ☎ *919/684–2572,* WEB *www.chapel. duke.edu.* ☉ *Daily 8 AM–9 PM.*

㉛ **Duke Homestead.** The Duke family empire began here in the 1860s with tobacco, and it is now a National Historic Landmark. You can tour the small wood-frame factories, pack house, and curing barn; guides demonstrate early manufacturing processes. The visitor center exhibits early tobacco advertising. ⊠ *2828 Duke Homestead Rd., Downtown,* ☎ *919/477–5498.* ⊡ *Free.* ☉ *Apr.–Oct., Mon.–Sat. 9–5, Sun. 1–5; Nov.–Mar., Tues.–Sat. 10–4, Sun. 1–4.*

Duke University. A stroll along the wide tree-lined streets of this campus is a lovely way to spend a few hours. In all, the university encompasses 525 acres in the heart of Durham. The East Campus, off Broad Street, has Georgian architecture and the **Duke University Museum of Art** (⊠ Buchanan Blvd. at Trinity Ave., Duke University, ☎ 919/684–

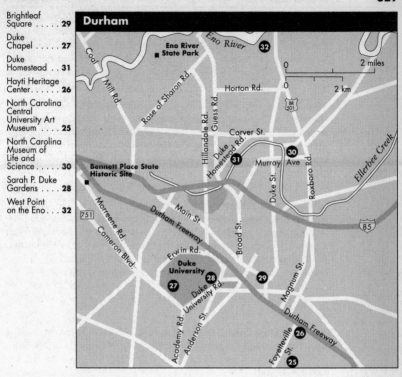

Durham

5135, WEB www.duke.edu), a showcase for pre-Columbian, African, Russian, European medieval, and Renaissance art. A mile or so away is the West Campus, dominated by the **Duke Chapel,** on Chapel Drive, and late-Gothic-style buildings. The sprawling medical school is on Erwin Road. A bus system and bike paths connect the campuses.

26 Hayti Heritage Center. One of Durham's oldest ecclesiastical structures, St. Joseph's A.M.E. Church, houses this center for African-American art and culture. In addition to exhibitions of traditional and contemporary art by local, regional, and national artists, the center hosts special events such as the Black Diaspora Film Festival. ⊠ *804 Old Fayetteville St., Downtown,* ☎ *919/683–1709 or 800/845–9835,* WEB *www.hayti.org.* ☞ *Free; fees for special events vary.* ☉ *Weekdays 9–7:30, Sat. 9–3, Sun. hrs vary.*

25 North Carolina Central University Art Museum. African-American art is showcased at the nation's first publicly supported liberal arts college for African-Americans. Besides the permanent collection, known for its 19th-century masterpieces, you can see works by students and local artists. ⊠ *1801 Fayetteville St., South/NCCU University,* ☎ *919/560–6211,* WEB *www.nccu.edu/artmuseum.* ☞ *Free.* ☉ *Tues.–Fri. 9–5, Sun. 2–5.*

30 North Carolina Museum of Life and Science. Here you can create a tornado, encounter dinosaurs on the prehistoric trail, view NASA artifacts, and ride a train through a wildlife sanctuary. The nature center has such native North Carolina animals as flying squirrels. The three-story **Magic Wings Butterfly House** has a tropical butterfly conservatory and includes the Insectarium, where you can see and hear live insects under high magnification and amplification. ⊠ *433 Murray Ave., off I–85, Downtown,* ☎ *919/220–5429,* WEB *www.ncmls.citysearch.com.* ☞ *Museum $8, train ride $1.50.* ☉ *Mon.–Sat. 10–5, Sun. noon–5.*

★ ㉘ **Sarah P. Duke Gardens.** These 55 acres, complete with a wisteria-draped gazebo and a Japanese garden with a lily pond teeming with fat goldfish, have more than 5 mi of pathways through formal plantings and woodlands. ☒ *Main entrance on Anderson St., West Campus, Duke University,* ☎ *919/684–8861,* ᴡᴇʙ *www.hr.duke.edu/dukegardens.* ☒ *Free.* ☉ *Daily 8–dusk.*

㉜ **West Point on the Eno.** Included in a city park on the banks of the Eno River are a 19th-century blacksmith shop, an 1880s home, and a restored mill dating from 1778. It's the site of an annual three-day folklife festival surrounding the Fourth of July; musicians, artists, and craftspeople come from around the region. ☒ *5101 N. Roxboro Rd. (U.S. 501N), North Metro,* ☎ *919/471–1623.* ☒ *Free.* ☉ *Mar.–Dec., daily 8–sunset; historic bldgs. weekends only 1–5.*

Other Area Attractions

Bennett Place State Historic Site. In this farmhouse, in April 1865, Confederate general Joseph E. Johnston surrendered to U.S. general William T. Sherman, 17 days after Lee's surrender to Grant at Appomattox. The two generals then set forth the terms for a "permanent peace" between the South and the North. Historical reenactments are held annually. ☒ *4409 Bennett Memorial Rd., 10 mi from downtown,* ☎ *919/ 383–4345.* ☒ *Free.* ☉ *Apr.–Oct., Mon.–Sat. 9–5, Sun. 1–5; Nov.–Mar., Tues.–Sat. 9–5, Sun. 1–5.*

Eno River State Park. The park's 2,733 acres include hiking trails, a picnic area, rough camping, and Class II rapids (after a heavy rain). ☒ *6101 Cole Mill Rd., North Metro,* ☎ *919/383–1686.* ☒ *Free.* ☉ *Daily 8–sunset.*

Dining and Lodging

$$$$ × **Magnolia Grill.** This bistro is consistently one of the area's finest,
★ most innovative places to dine. The food is as eye-catching as the art on the walls. On the daily menu you may find grilled jumbo sea scallops on spicy black beans with blood-orange-and-onion marmalade or grilled hickory-smoked pork tenderloin in a sun-dried cherry sauce. ☒ *1002 9th St., Downtown,* ☎ *919/286–3609. MC, V. Closed Sun.–Mon. No lunch.*

$$–$$$ × **Café Parizäde.** Soft lighting, white tablecloths, and an enclosed courtyard are among the inviting aspects of this Erwin Square bistro. One particularly fine appetizer is fried calamari with jalapeño-tomato salsa; popular entrées include fettuccine with fresh salmon and black-pepper dill cream, sesame pasta with scallops, and roast duck with fresh vegetables. ☒ *2200 W. Main St., Downtown,* ☎ *919/286–9712. AE, D, DC, MC, V. No lunch weekends.*

$$–$$$ × **George's Garage.** In the heart of happening 9th Street, George's is the latest success for well-known Triangle restaurateur Giorgios Bakatsias, and it defies pigeonholing. It's part nouvelle restaurant, part market, part bar (sushi and drinks), and part bakery—all in a cavernous, pumped-up room. Fresh fish and Mediterranean fare are specialties, but there are also grilled chicken, pork, lamb, and beef. Live entertainment and dancing make this a popular after-hours hangout. ☒ *737 9th St., Downtown,* ☎ *919/286–1431. AE, D, DC, MC, V.*

$$–$$$ × **Pop's.** The roof is rough tin and the sculptures wrought-iron and steel industrial, and one latticework wall is covered in silk flowers and vines. Like the New South–Old South style, the menu mixes contemporary Italian and down-home cuisine. You can get a grilled pork chop with polenta or *fritto misto* calamari (batter-fried squid) and other seafood. Arrive early; it fills up quickly. ☒ *810 W. Peabody St., Downtown,* ☎ *919/956–7677. MC, V. No lunch weekends.*

$$$$ ✕⊡ **Washington Duke Inn & Golf Club.** On the campus of Duke Uni-
★   versity, this luxurious hotel overlooks a Robert Trent Jones golf course.
Rooms evoke the feeling of an English country inn, with floral bedspreads
and creamy striped wall coverings. On display in the public rooms are
memorabilia belonging to the Duke family, for whom the hotel and university are named. At the quietly sophisticated Fairview restaurant
($$$–$$$$), you can start with Moroccan–spiced lamb sausage or
chestnut soup with rosemary cream and then move on to entrées such
as breast of Muscovy duck with mashed white beans, roasted garlic,
and sweet-and-sour cranberry sauce. ⊠ *3001 Cameron Blvd., Duke Uni-
versity 27706,* ☎ *919/490–0999 or 800/443–3853,* ℻ *919/688–0105,*
WEB *www.washingtondukeinn.com. 164 rooms, 7 suites. Restaurant, room
service, driving range, 18-hole golf course, putting green, 12 tennis courts,
pool, health club, bar, business services, laundry service, concierge,
meeting room, airport shuttle. AE, D, DC, MC, V.*

$$–$$$$ ⊡ **Arrowhead Inn.** Brick chimneys and tall Doric columns distinguish
this B&B inn in an 18th-century white-clapboard farmhouse. It's a few
miles outside Durham and has a cozy style, with antiques, heritage plants,
fireplaces, and a log cabin in the garden. ⊠ *106 Mason Rd., North
Metro 27712,* ☎ *919/477–8430 or 800/528–2207,* ℻ *919/471–9538,*
WEB *www.arrowheadinn.com. 9 rooms, 2 suites. Picnic area, business
services. AE, D, DC, MC, V. BP.*

$$–$$$ ⊡ **Blooming Garden Inn.** Truly a bright spot in the Holloway Historic
District, this B&B is painted yellow outside. Inside, the inn explodes with
color and warmth, thanks to exuberant hosts Dolly and Frank Pokrass.
Breakfast might be walnut crepes with ricotta cheese and warm raspberry sauce. A sister B&B, the Victorian Holly House, across the street,
accommodates extended stays. ⊠ *513 Holloway St., Downtown 27701,*
☎ *919/687–0801 or 888/687–0801,* ℻ *919/688–1401,* WEB *www.
bloominggardeninn.com. 4 rooms, 2 suites. AE, D, DC, MC, V. BP.*

$$–$$$ ⊡ **Durham Marriott at the Civic Center.** Several fountains run through
the lobby entrance of this nine-floor hotel, which has reasonable rates
given the excellent location in the downtown art-and-entertainment district, atop the Durham Civic Center. Rooms are spacious and well appointed. Guests can use a health club one block away. ⊠ *201 Foster
St., Downtown 27701,* ☎ *919/768–6000,* ℻ *919/768–6037,* WEB
*www.marriotthotels.com. 185 rooms, 2 suites. Restaurant, room ser-
vice, in-room safes, bar, exercise room, dry cleaning, laundry service,
concierge floor, business services, free parking. AE, D, DC, MC, V.*

Nightlife and the Arts

THE ARTS

The 1926 beaux arts **Carolina Theatre** (⊠ 309 W. Morgan St., Downtown, ☎ 919/560–3030) hosts film festivals, orchestras, and operas,
as well as the International Jazz Festival (March) and the Doubletake
Documentary Film Festival (May). Most of the performances at the
internationally known **American Dance Festival,** held annually in June
and July, take place at the **Page Auditorium** and **Reynolds Theater** (⊠
West Campus, Duke University, ☎ 919/684–4444). The old **Durham
Athletic Park** (⊠ 428 Morris St., Downtown) and **St. Joseph's Church**
(⊠ 804 Old Fayetteville St., Downtown), at the Hayti Heritage Center, are the venues for the two-day Bull Durham Blues Festival (☎ 800/
845–9835), presented early each September.

NIGHTLIFE

The **Edge** (⊠ 108 Morris St., Downtown, ☎ 919/667–1012) is a multilevel dance club with the feel of a slick renovated warehouse. There's
something for every taste: live music, a DJ, game rooms, even karaoke.

Outdoor Activities and Sports

BASEBALL

The **Durham Bulls,** a tradition since 1902, were immortalized in the hit movie *Bull Durham*. The AAA team, an affiliate of the Tampa Bay Devil Rays, plays at a 10,000-seat stadium near Downtown (⊠ 409 Blackwell St., North Metro, ☎ 919/687–6500).

BASKETBALL

Durham's Atlantic Coast Conference team is Duke's **Blue Devils,** which plays its home games at Cameron Indoor Stadium (⊠ Duke University, ☎ 919/681–2583 or 800/672–2583).

GOLF

Durham has four 18-hole public golf courses. **Duke University** (⊠ Cameron Blvd. and Science Dr., ☎ 919/681–2288) has a Robert Trent Jones course that is par 72. **Hillandale Golf Course** (⊠ Hillandale Rd., Duke University, ☎ 919/286–4211) has a par-71 George Cobb course.

TENNIS

The city's **Parks and Recreation Department** (☎ 919/560–4355) has information on the city's 72 public tennis courts.

Shopping

SHOPPING DISTRICTS AND MALLS

Durham's **9th Street** has funky shops and restaurants. **Brightleaf Square** (⊠ 905 W. Main St., Downtown, ☎ 919/682–9229) is an upscale shopping-entertainment complex housed in old tobacco warehouses downtown.

CRAFTS

One World Market (⊠ 1918 Perry St., Duke University, ☎ 919/286–2457) carries unique, affordable gifts. One goal of the store is to provide increased self-employment for low-income crafters from around the world.

FOOD

Fowler's Gourmet (⊠ 112 S. Duke St., Downtown, ☎ 919/683–2555) stocks everything from exotic spices to wines, fresh seafood, and European chocolates. Customized gift baskets are shipped all over the country. **Wellspring Grocery** (⊠ 621 Broad St., Downtown, ☎ 919/286–0765) has outstanding fresh produce, soups, salads, and sandwiches prepared daily.

Chapel Hill

12 mi southwest of Durham on U.S. 15/501, 28 mi northwest of Raleigh.

Chapel Hill may be the smallest city in the Triangle, but its reputation as a seat of learning—and of liberalism—looms large. The home of the nation's first state university, the 208-year-old University of North Carolina (UNC), Chapel Hill retains the feel of a quiet, tree-shaded village while crowded with students and retirees.

Morehead Planetarium, where the original Apollo astronauts and many since have trained, is one of the largest in the country. You can learn about the constellations and take in laser-light shows. ⊠ *250 E. Franklin St., University,* ☎ *919/962–1236; 919/549–6863 show information,* WEB *www.morehead.unc.edu.* ☞ *$4.50.* ☉ *Mon. 12:30–5, Tues.–Fri. and Sun. 12:30–5 and 7–9:45, Sat. 10–5 and 7–9:45; call ahead for show times.*

★ **Franklin Street,** in the heart of downtown Chapel Hill, is lined with bicycle shops, bookstores, clothing stores, restaurants and coffee shops, and a movie theater.

Franklin Street runs along the northern edge of the **University of North Carolina** campus, which is filled with oak-shaded courtyards and stately old buildings. The **Louis Round Wilson Library** (✉ South St., University, ☎ 919/962–0114) houses the largest single collection of state literature in the nation. Its **North Carolina Collection Gallery** (☎ 919/962–1172) has exhibits of rare books, photos, and oil portraits. Several historic rooms highlight topics in the state's history, such as the Walter Raleigh Room. The university's **Ackland Art Museum** (✉ Columbia and Franklin Sts., University, ☎ 919/406–9837) showcases some of the Southeast's strongest collections of art from India and of Western art, as well as old-master paintings and sculptures. Of special interest is North Carolina folk art.

The **ArtsCenter** (✉ 300G E. Main St., Carrboro, ☎ 919/929–2787, WEB www.carrboro.com/artscenter.html) has exhibits, offers classes of all kinds for children, and hosts dance, theater, and music events.

The **North Carolina Botanical Garden,** south of downtown via U.S. 15/501 Bypass, has the largest collection of native plants in the Southeast. Nature trails wind through a 300-acre Piedmont forest; the herb garden and carnivorous plant collection are impressive. ✉ *Old Mason Farm Rd., South Metro,* ☎ *919/962–0522,* WEB *www.unc.edu/depts/ncbg.* 🎟 *Free.* ☉ *Apr.–Oct., weekdays 8–5, Sat. 10–6, Sun. 1–6; Nov.–Mar., weekdays 8–5, Sat. 9–5, Sun. 1–5.*

Dining and Lodging

$$–$$$ ✕ **Aurora.** Vaulted ceilings, skylights, and vivid hues of blue, lavender, mauve, and yellow help create a stylish and lively dining experience. The menu of northern Italian cuisine may include succulent sea scallops and shiitake mushrooms in rosemary and white wine, fresh chive pasta stuffed with four cheeses and tossed with walnut sauce, or veal with apples. ✉ *1350 Raleigh Rd. (Rte. 54 Bypass), Metro East,* ☎ *919/942–2400,* WEB *www.aurorarestaurant.com. AE, MC, V. No lunch.*

$$–$$$ ✕ **Crook's Corner.** This small, often noisy restaurant is an exemplar of Southern chic. The menu changes often, and highlights such regional specialties as snapper with mint, pecans, and oranges, as well as hot-pepper jelly, crab gumbo, and buttermilk pie. A wall of bamboo and a waterfall fountain make the patio a delightful alfresco experience. Look for the pink pig atop the building. ✉ *610 W. Franklin St., Downtown,* ☎ *919/929–7643. AE, D, DC, MC, V. No lunch.*

$$–$$$ ✕ **Pyewacket Restaurant.** What began as a hole-in-the-wall vegetarian restaurant in 1977 has become one of Chapel Hill's most popular eateries. Now with sleeker, larger digs and courtyard dining, Pyewacket has expanded its repertoire. Entrées range from Indonesian curried shrimp to spinach lasagna. ✉ *431 W. Franklin St., Downtown,* ☎ *919/929–0297,* WEB *www.pyewacketrestaurant.com. AE, D, DC, MC, V. Closed Sun. No lunch.*

$–$$ ✕ **Mama Dip's Country Kitchen.** Mildred Edna Cotton Council (a.k.a. Mama Dip) is just about as well known in this town as another tall, gregarious Chapel Hillian, Michael Jordan. That's because she and her restaurant, which serves authentic home-style Southern meals in a roomy but simple setting, have been on the scene since the early '60s. Everything from chicken and dumplings, ribs, and country ham to fish, beef, salads, a mess of fresh vegetables, and melt-in-your-mouth buttermilk biscuits appear on the lengthy menu. ✉ *408 W. Rosemary St., Downtown,* ☎ *919/942–5837. MC, V.*

$$$$ ✕🏨 **Fearrington House.** A member of the prestigious Relais & Châteaux ★ group, this country inn is on a 200-year-old farm that has been remade into a residential community resembling a country village. The village mascots, the "Oreo cows" (black on the ends, snow white in the mid-

dle), roam the pasture at the entrance. The inn's modern guest rooms, overlooking a courtyard, gardens, and pasture, are furnished with antiques, English pine, and oversize tubs. The restaurant serves dressed-up regional food, such as collard-pecan-pesto-stuffed chicken breast with Hoop cheddar grits. Dinner is prix fixe. ⊠ *2000 Fearrington Village Center, 8 mi south of Chapel Hill on U.S. 15/501, Pittsboro 27312,* ☎ *919/542–2121,* FAX *919/542–4202,* WEB *www.fearringtonhouse.com. 29 rooms, 2 suites. 2 restaurants, 2 tennis courts, pool, croquet, business services, meeting room. AE, MC, V. BP.*

$$$$ ✕🏨 **Siena Hotel.** Sam and Susan Longiotti's love for Siena, Italy, has carried over to their posh European-style hotel. The lobby and rooms have imported carved-wood furniture, along with fabrics and artwork that conjure the Italian Renaissance. The public areas are filled with plush furniture grouped for conversation. Tuscan cuisine is the hallmark of Il Palio Ristorante ($$$). You won't be hurried here, which is a good thing because it takes a while just to get through the antipasto while you anticipate entrées such as *filetto di branzino* (black grouper filled with greens and wrapped with prosciutto, in a saffron broth). ⊠ *1505 E. Franklin St., North Metro 27514,* ☎ *919/929–4000 or 800/223–7379,* FAX *919/968–8527,* WEB *www.sienahotel.com. 68 rooms, 12 suites. Restaurant, picnic area, room service, bar, laundry service, concierge, business services, meeting room, airport shuttle. AE, DC, MC, V. BP.*

$$$–$$$$ 🏨 **Sheraton Chapel Hill.** The look of the guest rooms here differs a bit from other area hotels, as they're done in a modern, Scandinavian style, with fitted bedding and sleek furniture, including work desks. The marble lobby has a clean, spare look as well. Almost all the rooms offer a view of pine-dotted grounds. This property, with its outdoor garden, is conveniently located on U.S. 15/501 at the far edge of the University of North Carolina campus; it's easily accessible from Durham and Raleigh. ⊠ *1 Europa Dr., University 27514,* ☎ *919/968–4900 or 800/325–3535,* FAX *919/929–8170,* WEB *www.sheratonchapelhill.com. 168 rooms, 4 suites. Restaurant, room service, outdoor pool, exercise room, 2 bars, business services, meeting rooms, airport shuttle. AE, D, DC, MC, V.*

Nightlife and the Arts

THE ARTS

The **Dean E. Smith Center** (⊠ Skipper Bowles Dr., on the UNC campus, University, ☎ 919/962–7777) is the place not only for UNC men's basketball games but for special events and concerts. **Playmakers Repertory Company** (⊠ Country Club Dr., on the UNC campus, University, ☎ 919/962–7529), a nonprofit professional theater, performs six plays annually (September–May) at the Paul Green Theatre.

NIGHTLIFE

The Chapel Hill area is the place to hear live rock and alternative bands. **Cat's Cradle** (⊠ 300 E. Main St., Carrboro, ☎ 919/967–9053) is smoky and dark and presents entertainment nightly. The **West End Wine Bar** (⊠ 450 W. Franklin St., Downtown, ☎ 919/967–7599) attracts professionals and postgraduates with its comprehensive wine list (more than 80 vintages by the glass) and urbane sensibility.

Outdoor Activities and Sports

BASKETBALL

The University of North Carolina's **Tarheels** (☎ 919/962–2296 or 800/722–4335) are Chapel Hill's Atlantic Coast Conference team.

GOLF

There are three public golf courses in Orange County; Chapel Hill has one of them: **Finley Golf Course** (⊠ Finley Golf Course Rd., off Rte. 54 on the UNC campus, University, ☎ 919/962–2349) is a championship par-72, 18-hole course with a driving range and putting green.

TENNIS

There are 21 public courts in Chapel Hill. For information call the **Chapel Hill Parks and Recreation Department** (☎ 919/968–2784).

Shopping

SHOPPING DISTRICTS AND MALLS

Minutes from downtown, the lively **Eastgate Shopping Center** (⊠ between E. Franklin St. and U.S. 15/501, North Metro) sells everything from antiques to wine. **Fearrington Village,** a planned community 8 mi south of Chapel Hill on U.S. 15/501 in Pittsboro, has upscale shops selling art, garden items, handmade jewelry, and more. **Franklin Street** in Chapel Hill has a wonderful collection of shops, including bookstores, art galleries, crafts shops, and clothing stores.

BOOKS

At **McIntyre's Fine Books and Bookends** (⊠ Fearrington Village, U.S. 15/501, Pittsboro, ☎ 919/542–3030), an independent operation, you can read by the fire in one of the cozy rooms. It has extensive collections of travel and gardening books.

FOOD

A Southern Season (⊠ Eastgate Shopping Center, North Metro, ☎ 919/929–9466 or 800/253–3663) stocks a dazzling variety of cookware, books, wine, and treats, including barbecue sauces, peanuts, and hams. The adjoining Weathervane Café has indoor and alfresco dining.

The Triangle A to Z

To research prices, get advice from other travelers, and book travel arrangements, visit www.fodors.com.

AIRPORTS

The Raleigh-Durham International Airport, off I–40 between the two cities, is served by most major airlines. It takes about 20 minutes to get to any of the three cities from the airport.

➤ AIRPORT INFORMATION: **Raleigh-Durham International Airport** (⊠ 1600 Terminal Blvd., Morrisville, ☎ 919/840–2123, WEB www.rdu.com).

BUS TRAVEL

Greyhound/Carolina Trailways serves Raleigh, Durham, and Chapel Hill.

➤ BUS INFORMATION: **Greyhound/Carolina Trailways** (☎ 800/231–2222, WEB www.greyhound.com).

CAR TRAVEL

U.S. 1, which runs north–south through the Triangle and the Sandhills, also links to I–85 going northeast. U.S. 64, which makes an east–west traverse across the Triangle, continues eastward all the way to the Outer Banks. I–95 runs northeast–southwest to the east of the Triangle and the Sandhills, crossing U.S. 64 and I–40 from Virginia to South Carolina.

EMERGENCIES

For minor emergencies go to one of the many urgent-care centers in Raleigh, Cary, Durham, and Chapel Hill. Eckerd Drug Store and the Wal-Mart pharmacy are open 24 hours. Eckerd Drugs is open 8 AM–midnight weekdays and 9 AM–11 PM weekends.

➤ EMERGENCY SERVICES: **Ambulance, police** (☎ 911).

➤ 24-HOUR AND LATE-NIGHT PHARMACIES: **Eckerd Drug Store** (⊠ Lake Boone Shopping Center, Wycliff Rd., Raleigh, ☎ 919/781–4070). **Eckerd Drugs** (⊠ 3527 Hillsborough Rd., Durham, ☎ 919/383–5591). **Wal-Mart pharmacy** (⊠ 6600 Glenwood Ave., Raleigh, ☎ 919/783–9693).

TAXIS

More than 25 taxi companies serve the Triangle; fares are calculated by the mile.

➤ TAXI COMPANIES: **City Taxi** (✉ Raleigh, ☎ 919/832–1489). **National Cab** (✉ Raleigh-Durham Airport, ☎ 919/469–1333). **Orange Cab** (✉ Durham, ☎ 919/682–6111).

TOURS

The Capital Area Visitor Center in Raleigh offers maps, brochures, and free guided and self-guided tours of government buildings; it's open weekdays 8–5, Saturday 10–4, and Sunday 1–4.

The Historic Chapel Hill/UNC Trolley Tour is given Wednesday 2–3, mid-April to mid-November. Departure is from the Horace Williams House, and the fare is $5; call for reservations.

➤ FEES AND SCHEDULES: **Capital Area Visitor Center** (✉ 301 N. Blount St., 27611, ☎ 919/733–3456). **Historic Chapel Hill/UNC Trolley Tour** (✉ Horace Williams House, 610 E. Rosemary St., ☎ 919/942–7818).

TRAIN TRAVEL

Amtrak serves Raleigh, Durham, and Cary; the *Carolinian* has one daily train northbound and one southbound; and the in-state *Piedmont* connects nine cities between Raleigh and Charlotte each day.

➤ TRAIN INFORMATION: **Amtrak** (☎ 800/872–7245, WEB www.amtrak. com).

TRANSPORTATION AROUND THE TRIANGLE

Capital Area Transit is Raleigh's public transport system. Fares are 75¢. Chapel Hill Transit, at 75¢ a ride, takes you around the city. Durham Area Transit Authority is Durham's intracity bus system. Fares are 75¢. The Triangle Transit Authority, which links downtown Raleigh with Cary, Research Triangle Park, Durham, and Chapel Hill, runs weekdays except major holidays. Rates start at $1.

➤ CONTACTS: **Capital Area Transit** (☎ 919/833–5701, WEB www. raleigh-nc.org/transit). **Chapel Hill Transit** (☎ 919/968–2769). **Durham Area Transit Authority** (☎ 919/683–3282). **Triangle Transit Authority** (☎ 919/549–9999).

VISITOR INFORMATION

The Durham Bullhorn provides 24-hour recorded information on events and activities.

➤ TOURIST INFORMATION: **Chapel Hill/Orange County Visitors Bureau** (✉ 501 W. Franklin St., Suite 104, Chapel Hill 27516, ☎ 919/968–2060 or 888/968–2060, WEB www.chocvb.org). **Downtown Chapel Hill Welcome Center** (✉ Old Post Office Building, 179 E. Franklin St., ☎ 919/929–9700). **Durham Convention and Visitors Bureau** (✉ 101 E. Morgan St., 27701, ☎ 919/687–0288 or 800/446–8604, WEB www. dcvb.durham.nc.us). **Durham Bullhorn** (☎ 919/688–2855 or 800/ 772–2855). **Greater Raleigh Convention and Visitors Bureau** (✉ Bank of America Bldg., 421 Fayetteville Street Mall, Suite 1505, 27601, ☎ 919/834–5900 or 800/849–8499, WEB www.raleighcvb.org).

THE SANDHILLS

Southern Pines, Pinehurst

Because of their sandy soil—they were once Atlantic beaches—the Sandhills weren't of much use to early farmers, most of whom switched to lumbering and making turpentine for a livelihood. Since the turn of the 20th century, however, this area with its gently undulating hills has proved ideal for golf and tennis. Promoters call it "the golf capital of the world"; the Tufts Archives honors the sport and the founding of Pinehurst. First-class resorts are centered on the 40 championship golf courses, including the famed Pinehurst Number 2, which have hosted PGA tournaments. Public tennis courts can be found in many communities, and the area has also long been popular with horse owners.

The Highland Scots who settled the area left a rich heritage perpetuated through festivals and gatherings. In colonial times English potters were attracted to the rich clay deposits in the soil, and today their descendants and others turn out beautiful wares sold in more than 40 local shops.

Southern Pines

104 mi east of Charlotte, 71 mi southwest of Raleigh.

Southern Pines, the center of the Sandhills, is a good place to start your visit to the area.

Sandhills Horticultural Gardens has a wetland area that can be observed from elevated boardwalks. It's part of a 32-acre series of gardens showcasing roses, fruits and vegetables, herbs, conifers, hollies, a formal English garden, pools, and a waterfall. ⊠ *2200 Airport Rd., Sandhills Community College campus,* ☎ *910/695–3882 or 800/338–3944,* WEB *www.sandhills.cc.nc.us/lsg/hort.html.* ☜ *Free.* ☽ *Daily sunrise–sunset.*

The **Shaw House,** the oldest structure in town (circa 1820), serves as headquarters for the Moore County Historical Association. It and two other restored historic houses on the property, all of which date to 1700, depict the lives of early settlers. ⊠ *S.W. Broad St. and Morganton Rd.,* ☎ *910/692–2051.* ☜ *$2, suggested donation.* ☽ *Apr.–Dec., Wed.–Sun. 1–4.*

Weymouth Center, former home of author and publisher James Boyd, hosts numerous concerts and lectures. Boyd, who died in 1944, was visited by many well-known writers; his home served as a cultural center for the area. The North Carolina Literary Hall of Fame is on the 24-acre property, as is a writer-in-residence program, which has hosted more than 600 writers. ⊠ *555 E. Connecticut Ave.,* ☎ *910/692–6261,* WEB *www.weymouthcenter.org.* ☜ *Free.* ☽ *Weekdays 10–2; call ahead to arrange tours.*

Weymouth Woods Sandhills Nature Preserve, on the eastern outskirts of town, is a 571-acre wildlife preserve with 4 mi of hiking trails, a beaver pond, and a naturalist on staff. ⊠ *1024 N. Fort Bragg Rd., off U.S. 1,* ☎ *910/692–2167,* WEB *www.ils.unc.edu/parkproject/visit/wewo/home.html.* ☜ *Free.* ☽ *Apr.–Oct., daily 9–7; Nov.–Mar., daily 9–6.*

OFF THE BEATEN PATH **CAMERON –** Cameron, which hasn't changed much since the 19th century, is the place to shop for antiques. Approximately 60 antiques dealers operate out of several stores. The town itself, off U.S. 1, has been declared a historic district. Most shops are open Tuesday through Saturday 10–5, Sunday 1–5; call the historic district office (☎ 910/245–7001) for information. The town is 12 mi north of Southern Pines.

Dining and Lodging

$$$–$$$$ ✕ **Lob Steer Inn.** Salad and dessert bars complement generous broiled seafood and prime rib dinners at this casual, dimly lighted steak house. ⊠ *U.S. 1,* ☎ *910/692–3503. Reservations essential. AE, DC, MC, V. No lunch.*

$ ✕ **Sweet Basil.** This cozy corner café is run by a family whose considerable restaurant expertise shows in the service and the cooking: lots of homemade breads, hefty loaded sandwiches, and lush salads are offered. Special treats are the soups—especially the ginger-carrot and flavorful red-pepper varieties—and decadent desserts. Arrive early to avoid the lunch rush. ⊠ *134 Broad St.,* ☎ *910/693–1487. MC, V. Closed Sun. No dinner.*

$$$$ ⌂ **Pine Needles Lodge and Golf Club.** One of the bonuses of staying at this informal lodge is the chance to meet Peggy Kirk Bell, a champion golfer and golf instructor. She built the resort with her late husband and continues to help run it. The club has even hosted the U.S. Women's Open. The rooms are done in a rustic chalet style; many have exposed beams. ⊠ *1005 Midland Rd., Box 88, 28387,* ☎ *910/692–7111 or 800/ 747–7272,* FAX *910/692–5349,* WEB *www.pineneedles-midpines.com. 71 rooms. Dining room, snack bar, driving range, 18-hole golf course, putting green, 2 tennis courts, pool, bicycles, bar, business services, meeting room, airport shuttle. AE, MC, V. FAP.*

$$$ ⌂ **Mid Pines Inn and Golf Club.** This resort community includes a Georgian-style clubhouse and a golf course designed by Donald Ross that has been the site of numerous tournaments. The spacious rooms in the 1921 inn are Wedgwood blue, with American antiques or good copies. Jackets are required in the dining room. ⊠ *1010 Midland Rd., 28387,* ☎ *910/692–2114 or 800/323–2114,* FAX *910/692–4615,* WEB *www. pineneedles-midpines.com. 112 rooms, 5 houses, 7 villas. Dining room, snack bar, 18-hole golf course, putting green, 4 tennis courts, pool, gym, bar, recreation room, business services, meeting room, airport shuttle. AE, D, DC, MC, V. FAP.*

Outdoor Activities and Sports

There are many excellent 18-hole golf courses here. **Club at Longleaf** (⊠ 2001 Midland Rd., ☎ 910/692–6100 or 800/889–5323) was built on a former horse farm. The front nine of the par-71 course plays through posts, rails, and turns of the old racetrack. **Mid Pines Golf Club** (⊠ 1010 Midland Rd., ☎ 910/692–2114 or 800/323–2114) is a golf getaway with a Donald Ross–designed par-72 course. **Pine Needles Resort** (⊠ 1005 Midland Rd., ☎ 910/692–7111 or 800/747–7272) has a Donald Ross–designed par-71 course complemented by practice facilities, grass tennis courts, and an outdoor swimming pool. **Talamore at Pinehurst** (⊠ 1595 Midland Rd., ☎ 910/692–5884 or 800/552–6292), with its unusual llama caddies, is a par-71 course designed by Rees Jones.

Shopping

Country Bookshop (⊠ 140 N.W. Broad St., ☎ 910/692–3211), in the historic downtown district, often has regional authors do readings and signings. The store stocks a lot of everything, including children's books and classical and jazz CDs.

Pinehurst

6 mi west of Southern Pines.

Pinehurst, a New England–style village with quiet, shaded streets and immaculately kept cottages, was laid out in the late 1800s in a wagon-wheel design by landscape genius Frederick Law Olmsted. Annie Oakley lived here for a number of years and headed the gun club. Today it attracts sports enthusiasts, retirees, and tourists.

Tufts Archives recounts the founding of Pinehurst in the letters, pictures, and news clippings, dating from 1895, of James Walker Tufts, who served as president of the United States Golf Association. Golf memorabilia are on display. ⊠ *Given Memorial Library, 150 Cherokee Rd.,* ☎ *910/ 295–6022 or 910/295–3642.* ☞ *Free.* ☉ *Weekdays 9:30–5, Sat. 9:30– 12:30.*

Dining and Lodging

$ ✕ **Pinehurst Playhouse Restaurant.** This casual eatery in the shop-filled Theater Building is in the heart of the village. It's *the* place to meet for soups and sandwiches. ✉ *W. Village Green,* ☎ *910/295–8873. Reservations not accepted. No credit cards. Closed Sun. No dinner.*

$$$$ ✕🖭 **The Carolina.** The Carolina is the centerpiece of the Pinehurst Com-
★ pany Resorts, which includes the Holly Inn, the Manor Inn, and villas and condos. This stately hotel, in operation since 1901, has never lost the charm that founder James Tufts intended it to have. Civilized decorum rules in the spacious public rooms, on the rocker-lined wide verandas, and amid the gardens. Guest rooms are elegantly traditional. You can tee off on one of eight signature golf courses. Two blocks away, the 45-room Manor Inn, with its bar and grill, has the feel of a B&B. Manor Inn guests have access to all the resort facilities, including the very formal Carolina Dining Room. The esoteric menu changes daily. ✉ *1 Carolina Vista Dr., Box 4000, 28374,* ☎ *910/295–6811 or 800/ 487–4653,* FAX *910/295–8503,* WEB *www.pinehurst.com. 338 rooms, 130 condos. 2 restaurants, room service, 8 18-hole golf courses, 24 tennis courts, 5 pools, health club, massage, windsurfing, boating, fishing, bicycles, croquet, bar, children's programs, concierge, business services, meeting room. AE, D, DC, MC, V.*

$$$$ ✕🖭 **Holly Inn.** This historic hotel, affiliated with the Pinehurst Resort, was the first in the village. Molding, lighting, and plumbing fixtures, based on research from local archives, recall the 1890s, the decade of its opening. Luxuries include silk hangers; embroidered robes; and afternoon sandwiches, cookies, and iced tea. A two-night stay is required. The menu at 1895, the bistro-style restaurant, changes seasonally. Inventive dinner entrées may include pinecone-smoked free-range chicken with truffles, tarragon-scented roast tenderloin of veal, and Carolina blue-crab hash. Jackets are requested at the restaurant. ✉ *Cherokee Rd., 28374,* ☎ *910/295–6811 or 800/487–4653,* FAX *910/295–8503,* WEB *www.pinehurst.com. 78 rooms, 7 suites. Restaurant, room service, golf privileges, pool, croquet, bar, library, concierge, business services, meeting room. AE, DC, MC, V. MAP.*

$$$ ✕🖭 **Magnolia Inn.** This turn-of-the-20th-century inn, once just a hangout for golfing buddies, is tastefully decorated with unusual antiques. Most guest rooms are in the Victorian style with wicker and brass beds; bathrooms have original fixtures such as claw-foot tubs. The inn's dining rooms ($$$–$$$$), with their dusty-rose wallpaper and fireplaces, are cozy. The regional menu includes Magnolia duck–breast and leg of duck with a pear, sweet potato, and wild cherry glaze. There's also an English-style pub. ✉ *Magnolia and Chinquapin Rds., Box 818, 28370,* ☎ *910/295–6900 or 800/526–5562,* FAX *910/215–0858,* WEB *www.themagnoliainn.com. 11 rooms. Dining room, golf privileges, pool, business services. AE, MC, V. BP.*

$$$–$$$$ 🖭 **Pine Crest Inn.** Chintz and mahogany fill the rooms of this slightly faded gem once owned by golfing great Donald Ross. The chefs whip up meals reminiscent of Sunday supper: homemade soups, fresh fish dishes, and the house special, stuffed pork chops. Mr. B's Bar is the liveliest nightspot in town. Guests have golf and tennis privileges at local clubs. ✉ *Dogwood Rd., Box 879, 28370,* ☎ *910/295–6121 or 800/371–2545,* FAX *910/295–4880,* WEB *www.pinecrestinnpinehurst. com. 40 rooms. Dining room, bar. AE, D, DC, MC, V. MAP.*

Outdoor Activities and Sports

GOLF

Pinehurst Resort and Country Club (✉ 1 Carolina Vista Dr., ☎ 910/ 295–6811 or 800/487–4653) has eight courses designed by such masters as Donald Ross, including the famed par-72 Number 2.

The par-71 **Pit Golf Links** (⌗ Rte. 5, ☎ 910/944–1600 or 800/574–4653) was designed by Dan Maples and sculpted from a 230-acre sand quarry.

Riding instruction and carriage rides are available by appointment at **Pinehurst Stables** (⌗ Rte. 5, ☎ 910/295–8456).

The **Lawn and Tennis Club of North Carolina** (⌗ 1 Merrywood, ☎ 910/692–7270) has seven courts and a swimming pool. **Pinehurst Resort and Country Club** (⌗ Carolina Vista Dr., ☎ 910/295–8556) is considered one of the best facilities in the country and has clay courts.

Aberdeen

5 mi southeast of Pinehurst, 5 mi southwest of Southern Pines.

Aberdeen, a small town of Scottish ancestry, has a beautifully restored early 20th-century train station and plenty of shops with antiques and collectibles. The **Bethesda Presbyterian Church,** on Bethesda Road east of town, was founded in 1790. The present wooden structure, which is used for weddings, funerals, and reunions, was built in the 1860s and still has preserved its slave gallery as well as exterior bullet holes from a Civil War battle. The cemetery, where many early settlers are buried, is always open.

Malcolm Blue Farm, one of the few remaining examples of the 19th-century Scottish homes that dotted the area, has farm buildings and an old gristmill. A September festival recalls life here in the 1800s. The farm and museum are part of the North Carolina Civil War Theme Trail. ⌗ *Bethesda Rd.,* ☎ *910/944–7558; 910/944–9483 for museum.* ⌗ *Free.* ☉ *Wed.–Sat. 1–4.*

OFF THE BEATEN PATH

FORT BRAGG/POPE AIR FORCE BASE – This army–air force duo outside Fayetteville, 45 mi east of Aberdeen via Route 211 and U.S. 401, is one of the world's largest military complexes. Pope hosts an open house and air show annually (☎ 910/394–4183). Bragg, the biggest army post east of the Mississippi, is open year-round, and self-guided tours are available. The welcome center (☎ 910/907–2026, WEB www.bragg.army.mil), at the corner of Randolph and Knox streets on Fort Bragg, has maps indicating public access areas. Free sites include the 82nd Airborne Division War Memorial Museum (☎ 910/432–3443), which tells the story of this unit, famous from World War I through Desert Storm. ⌗ *Off Rte. 24 or the All American Freeway. Some sites closed Mon.*

AIRBORNE AND SPECIAL OPERATIONS MUSEUM – The Army's newest museum tells the story of the fabled airborne and special-ops units through film and video, interactive displays, walk-through dioramas, and rare artifacts. The $22.5 million facility is in downtown Fayetteville. ⌗ *100 Bragg Blvd.,* ☎ *910/483–3003,* WEB *www.asomf.org.* ⌗ *Museum free; Vistascope Theater $3; motion simulator $3. Tues.–Sat. 10–5, Sun. noon–5.*

Lodging

$–$$ **Inn at Bryant House.** One block east of U.S. 1, this charming downtown B&B, built in 1913, is a home away from home. All rooms are individually decorated; some have canopy beds. The inn has golf packages and arranges tennis and horseback riding. ⌗ *214 N. Poplar St.,*

28315, ☎ 910/944–3300 or 800/453–4019, FAX 910/944–8898, WEB
*www.innatbryanthouse.com. 9 rooms, 7 with bath. Picnic area, busi-
ness services. AE, D, MC, V. CP.*

Outdoor Activities and Sports

Legacy Golf Links (✉ U.S. 15/501, ☎ 910/944–8825 or 800/344–8825)
has the first American course designed by Jack Nicklaus II (par 72).

Seagrove

35 mi northwest of Pinehurst via Rte. 211 and U.S. 220.

★ Potters, some of whom are carrying on traditions that have been in
their families for generations and others who are newer to the art, hand-
craft mugs, bowls, pitchers, platters, vases, and clay "face jugs" in the
Seagrove area. More than 90 potteries are scattered along and off Route
705 and U.S. 220. Some of the work of local artisans is exhibited in
national museums, including the Smithsonian. Most shops are open
Tuesday through Saturday 10–5.

★ The **North Carolina Pottery Center,** a museum and educational facility, has exhibitions of pottery from around the state and maps locat-
ing the various studios around the area. ✉ *250 East Ave.,* ☎ *336/873–
8430,* WEB *www.ncpotterycenter.com.* ☉ *Tues.–Sat. 10–4.*

Asheboro

13 mi north of Seagrove, 23 mi south of Greensboro on U.S. 64.

Asheboro, the seat of Randolph County, sits in the Uwharrie National
Forest, a haven for hikers, bikers, horseback riders, and fisherfolk. This
part of the southern Piedmont is a lovely place to view scenery and
visit crafts shops.

★ ☾ The **North Carolina Zoological Park,** a 1,500-acre home for more than
1,100 animals and 60,000 exotic and tropical plants, was the first zoo
in the country designed from the get-go as a natural habitat facility.
The park includes the 300-acre African Pavilion, an aviary, a gorilla
habitat, a Sonoran Desert habitat, and a 200-acre North American habitat with polar bears and sea lions. You can take a tram between areas.
✉ *4401 Zoo Pkwy.,* ☎ *336/879–7000 or 800/488–0444,* WEB *www.
nczoo.org.* ▧ *$10, including tram ride.* ☉ *Apr.–Oct., daily 9–5; Nov.–
Mar., daily 9–4.*

The Sandhills A to Z

*To research prices, get advice from other travelers, and book travel ar-
rangements, visit www.fodors.com.*

AIR TRAVEL
CARRIERS
US Airways Express serves the Moore County Airport with connec-
tions from the Charlotte, Raleigh, and Piedmont Triad airports.
➤ AIRLINES AND CONTACTS: **Moore County Airport** (✉ Rte. 22, South-
ern Pines, ☎ 910/692–3212). **US Airways Express** (☎ 800/428–4322).

CAR TRAVEL
U.S. 1 runs north–south through the Sandhills and is the recommended
route from the Raleigh-Durham area, a distance of about 70 mi.

EMERGENCIES

Moore Regional Hospital is an acute-care facility with an emergency room.

➤ EMERGENCY SERVICES: **Ambulance, fire, police** (☎ 911).

➤ HOSPITALS: **Moore Regional Hospital** (⊠ 155 Memorial Dr., Pinehurst, ☎ 910/215–1000).

TRAIN TRAVEL

Both southbound and northbound Amtrak trains, one daily in each direction, stop in Southern Pines.

➤ TRAIN INFORMATION: **Amtrak** (☎ 800/872–7245, WEB www.amtrak. com).

VISITOR INFORMATION

Pinehurst Area Convention and Visitors Bureau serves the Pinehurst, Southern Pines, and Aberdeen areas. For details on local events call the events hot line. Moore County Parks and Recreation Department can provide recreation information.

➤ TOURIST INFORMATION: **Events Hot Line** (☎ 910/692–1600). **Moore County Parks and Recreation Department** (☎ 910/947–2504, WEB www.co.moore.nc.us). **Pinehurst Area Convention and Visitors Bureau** (⊠ 1480 U.S. 15/501, Box 2270, Southern Pines 28388, ☎ 910/692–3330 or 800/346–5362, WEB www.homeofgolf.com).

THE OUTER BANKS

Cape Hatteras, Cape Lookout

North Carolina's Outer Banks, a series of barrier islands in the Atlantic Ocean, stretch from the Virginia state line south to Cape Lookout. Throughout history these waters have been the nemesis of shipping, gaining them the nickname the Graveyard of the Atlantic; the network of lighthouses and lifesaving stations draws lots of curious travelers, and the many submerged wrecks attract scuba divers. The islands' coves and inlets offered privacy to pirates—the notorious Blackbeard lived and died here.

For many years the Outer Banks remained isolated, with only a few families, which made their living by fishing. Times may have changed, but fishing still prevails as the industry of note here: about 40 million pounds of fish are caught here annually—a $27 million industry. Flounder and crab alone account for half the industry; other fish and seafood include bluefish, dolphin, mussels, clams, mackerel, marlin, shark, tuna, and shrimp. Many locals still use crab pots and process their catches in their backyards, and it's not unusual to see a fisherman arrive at a restaurant with a fresh catch and ask the chef to cook it up.

Today the islands, linked by bridges and ferries, have become popular destinations for vacationers. Much of the area is included in the Cape Hatteras and Cape Lookout national seashores. The largest towns are Kitty Hawk, Kill Devil Hills, Nags Head, and Manteo. Vacation rentals are popular—there are about 12,000 weekly rental cottages available on the Outer Banks. Rates run about $800–$1000 a week in summer.

On the inland side of the Outer Banks is the historic Albemarle region, a remote area of small villages and towns surrounding Albemarle Sound. Edenton was the colonial capital for a while, and many of its early structures are preserved.

You can tour the Outer Banks from the south end by taking a car ferry to Ocracoke Island or, as in the following route, from the north end. Driving the 120-mi stretch of Route 12 from Corolla to Ocracoke can be managed in a day, but be sure to allow plenty of time in summer to wait for the ferry connecting the islands and for exploring the undeveloped beaches, historic lifesaving stations, and charming beach communities stretched along the national seashores. Rentals are available throughout the area, with the highest concentration of accommodations between Kill Devil Hills and Nags Head. Mile markers (MM) indicate addresses for sites where there aren't many buildings. Be aware that during major storms and hurricanes the roads and bridges become clogged with traffic following the blue-and-white evacuation signs.

Numbers in the margin correspond to points of interest on the Outer Banks map.

Corolla, Duck, and Kitty Hawk

Kitty Hawk: 87 mi south of Norfolk, VA, via U.S. 17 and U.S. 158; 215 mi east of Raleigh via U.S. 64 and Rte. 12. Duck: 7 mi north of Kitty Hawk. Corolla: 19 mi north of Duck.

The small settlements of Corolla and Duck are largely seasonal residential enclaves full of summer rental condominiums. Upscale **Duck** has lots of restaurants and shopping outlets. The **Currituck Beach Lighthouse** (☉ Easter to Thanksgiving, daily 10–5), in **Corolla,** is the northernmost lighthouse on the Outer Banks. Weather permitting, you can climb to the top. Drive slowly in Corolla; wild ponies wander free here and always have the right of way. **Kitty Hawk,** with a few thousand permanent residents, is among the quieter of the beach communities, with fewer rental accommodations.

OFF THE
BEATEN PATH

ELIZABETH CITY – This city's historic district has the largest number of pre–Civil War commercial buildings in the state. The **Museum of the Albemarle** (✉ 1116 U.S. 17, ☎ 252/335–1453, WEB www.albemarle-nc.com/moa; ✆ free; ☉ Tues.–Sat. 9–5, Sun. 2–5), an affiliate of the North Carolina Museum of History, has displays on local history. Elizabeth City is 50 mi northwest of Kitty Hawk on the Albemarle Sound.

MERCHANTS MILLPOND STATE PARK – A 200-year-old man-made millpond and an ancient swamp form one of the state's rarest ecosystems. Cypress and gum trees hung with Spanish moss reach out of the still, dark waters, which are ideal for canoeing. Fishing, hiking, and camping are also available. The park is 80 mi northwest of Kitty Hawk, on the mainland. ✉ 71 U.S. 158, Gatesville, ☎ 252/357–1191. ✆ Free. ☉ June–Aug., daily 8 AM–9 PM; Sept. and Apr.–May, daily 8–8; Oct. and Mar., daily 8–7; Nov.–Feb., daily 8–6.

Dining and Lodging

$$$ ✕ **Blue Point Bar & Grill.** The upscale spot with an enclosed porch overlooking Currituck Sound is as busy as a diner and as boldly colored—with a red, black, and chrome interior—but you won't find burgers, fries, or blue-plate specials here. Both the service and the menu, which stresses "Southern coastal cuisine," such as a seasonal seafood stew with saffron, citrus, tomatoes, and grilled roasted-garlic crostini, is decidedly uptown. Sunday brunch is served. ✉ 1240 Duck Rd., Duck, ☎ 252/261–8090. *Reservations essential. AE, D, MC, V. No lunch.*

$$$$ ✕☷ **The Sanderling Inn.** This inn on a remote beach 5 mi north of Duck is a fine place to be pampered. Recreation choices include tennis, swimming, and nature walks through the Pine Island Sanctuary. Although it has all the contemporary conveniences, the resort has the won-

The Outer Banks

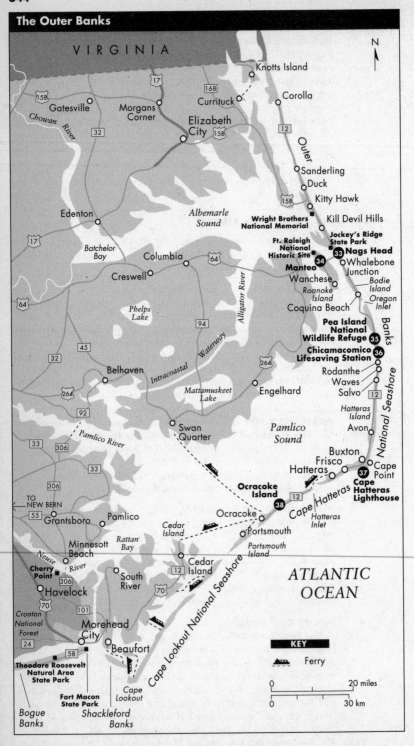

N

VIRGINIA

Knotts Island

Corolla

Currituck

17

168

Gatesville

158

Morgans Corner

Elizabeth City

158

Chowan River

32

Sanderling

Duck

Kitty Hawk

Outer

12

158

Edenton

Albemarle Sound

Kill Devil Hills

Wright Brothers National Memorial

Jockey's Ridge State Park

17

Batchelor Bay

Columbia

64

Ft. Raleigh National Historic Site

Manteo

33

Nags Head

34

Whalebone Junction

Creswell

Wanchese

Bodie Island

Roanoke Island

Phelps Lake

Alligator River

Coquina Beach

Oregon Inlet

94

Pea Island National Wildlife Refuge

35

Banks

45

32

Intracoastal Waterway

Chicamacomico Lifesaving Station

36

264

Belhaven

Mattamuskeet Lake

Engelhard

Rodanthe

Waves

Salvo

264

92

12

33

306

Pamlico River

Swan Quarter

Pamlico Sound

Hatteras Island

Avon

National Seashore

33

Buxton

306

Frisco

Cape Point

TO NEW BERN

55

Grantsboro

Pamlico

Hatteras

37

Cape Hatteras Lighthouse

Ocracoke Island

Minnesott Beach

Neuse River

Rattan Bay

Cedar Island

Ocracoke

38

Cape Hatteras

Hatteras Inlet

Cherry Point

Portsmouth

12

306

Havelock

South River

Cedar Island

Portsmouth Island

ATLANTIC OCEAN

70

101

12

70

Croatan National Forest

Morehead City

Cape Lookout National Seashore

KEY

24

58

Beaufort

Ferry

Theodore Roosevelt Natural Area State Park

Fort Macon State Park

Cape Lookout

0   20 miles

Bogue Banks

Shackleford Banks

0   30 km

derfully stately, mellow look of old Nags Head. With ceiling fans, wicker, and neutral tones, the rooms feel casual and summery. The Sanderling restaurant ($$$–$$$$; dinner reservations essential) occupies a renovated lifesaving station. On the seasonal menu you may find crab cakes, roast duckling, or fricassee of shrimp. The newer restaurant, the Left Bank ($$$; dinner only; reservations essential; jacket required) serves fine American food with a French influence. ⊠ *1461 Duck Rd., Sanderling 27949,* ☎ *252/261–4111 or 800/701–4111,* FAX *252/261–1638,* WEB *www.sanderlinginn.com. 88 rooms, 29 efficiencies. 2 restaurants, room service, minibars, golf privileges, 2 tennis courts, pool, health club, hot tub, spa, fishing, bicycles, hiking, racquetball, squash, bar, library, shop, meeting room. AE, D, MC, V. CP.*

$$$–$$$$ ⌑ **Advice 5¢.** The name may be quirky, but this contemporary B&B in Duck's North Beach area is very serious about guest care. Just a short walk from downtown shops and restaurants, Advice 5¢ also offers the use of the tennis courts and swimming pool at Sea Pines, a nearby property. Beds in each room are dressed with crisp, colorful linens. All rooms have private decks, ceiling fans, and baths stocked with thick cotton towels. ⊠ *111 Scarborough La., 27949,* ☎ *252/255–1050 or 800/238–4235,* WEB *www.advice5.com. 4 rooms, 1 suite. MC, V. Closed Dec.–Feb. CP.*

Outdoor Activities and Sports
Sea Scape Golf Course (⊠ 300 Eckner St., MM 2.5, Kitty Hawk, ☎ 252/261–2158) is a par-72 links course set amid the dunes.

Nags Head

③③ *4 mi south of Kill Devil Hills.*

Nags Head got its name because Outer Bankers hoping for shipwrecks would tie lanterns around the heads of their horses to lure merchant ships onto the shoals, thus profiting from the cargo that washed ashore (or which they brought ashore when they pirateered the boats). This is a somewhat commercialized and congested area, but, on the upside, you are convenient to plenty of restaurants, motels, hotels, and shops. Vacation rentals are a big industry here; older homes have wraparound porches, and most can house an entire family (or two).

Nags Head has 11 mi of **beach** with 33 public access areas, all with parking and some with rest rooms and showers. One point of interest is mile marker 11.5, the first North Carolina Historic Shipwreck Site. The USS *Huron* lies in 20 ft of water off the Nags Head Pier.

Coquina Beach (⊠ off Rte. 12, 8 mi south of U.S. 158), in the **Cape Hatteras National Seashore,** is considered the loveliest beach in the Outer Banks according to locals. The wide-beamed ribs of the shipwreck *Laura Barnes* rest in the dunes here. Free parking, showers, and picnic shelters are available.

♺ **Jockey's Ridge State Park** has 400 acres that encompass the tallest sand dune in the East (about 88 ft), although it has lost some 22 ft since the 1930s thanks to the million visitors a year who carry sand away on their persons. The climb to the top is a challenge; nevertheless, it's a popular spot for hang gliding, kite flying, and sand boarding. You can also explore an estuary and several trails through the park. In summer join the free Sunset on the Ridge program: watch the sun disappear while you sit on the dunes and learn about their local legends and history. ⊠ *U.S. 158 Bypass, MM 12,* ☎ *252/441–7132.* ☎ *Free.* ☉ *Daily 8–sunset.*

The **Tanger Outlet Center,** an outlet mall, includes 2-dozen stores, from designer clothes and shoes to casual attire, books, and sun glasses.

FIRST IN FLIGHT

DECEMBER 17, 1903, was a cold and windy day on the Outer Banks, but Wilbur and Orville Wright took little notice. The slightly built brothers from Ohio were undertaking an excellent adventure. With Orville at the controls, Wilbur running alongside, and the men of the nearby Lifesaving Service stations acting as ground crew, the fragile *Wright Flyer* lifted off from the dunes of Kill Devil Hills and flew 120 ft in 12 seconds.

John Daniels, an Outer Banker, photographed the instant the world forever changed: a heavier-than-air machine was used to achieve controlled, sustained flight with a pilot aboard. To prove that they were not accidental aviators, the Wrights made three more powered flights that day. Wilbur took his turn, flying 195 ft in a little over 15 seconds. Finally, it was Wilbur's chance again. In a 59-second period he took the first airplane 852 ft.

In fact, everything about the start of modern aeronautical science was very intentional. Wilbur and Orville began experimenting in 1899 with their first kite and achieved their goals in 1905,

when they built a truly practical airplane. What happened in between, with their work in Kill Devil Hills, helped them solve the problems of mechanical flight, lift, propulsion, and control that had vexed scientists for hundreds of years.

It was the ideal combination of wind and sand and privacy that brought Wilbur and Orville to the then-remote corner of North Carolina. There they were welcomed and provided food and assistance. In 2003 the state will celebrate the Year of the Centennial of Flight, which will culminate in a special series of events at the Outer Banks and the Wright Brothers National Memorial. April 6, 2003, is the grand opening of the **Aviation World's Fair**, at Kill Devil Hills (☎ 252/441–4434). Activities during the year will include aerial tours of the memorial, parades, rallies, a kite festival, an antique airplane exhibit, and history programs and exhibits. From December 13 to 17, 2003, a celebration with aviation flyovers and aircraft-related events is planned. See the official Web site for information on all events (www.celebrate100.org).

— By Lisa H. Towle

✉ *U.S. 158 Bypass, MM 16,* ☎ *252/441–5634.* ☉ *Mar.–Dec., Mon.–Sat. 9–9, Sun. 11–6; Jan.–Feb., call for hrs.*

Dining and Lodging

$$$–$$$$ ✗ **Windmill Point.** The menu changes here, but you can always count on the signature seafood trio: diners may choose any combination of three fish. The preparation is at the whim of the chef: lightly poached or grilled, and topped with roasted red pepper and capers, or shredded cucumber and dill, or a pineapple salsa. The restaurant has stunning views of the sound at sunset, eye-catching memorabilia from the luxury liner SS *United States,* and, yes, a real windmill. It's a reproduction of the German-style windmills used in the area a century ago. ✉ *U.S. 158 Bypass, MM 16.5,* ☎ *252/441–1535. AE, D, DC, MC, V.*

$$–$$$$ ✗ **Owens' Restaurant.** In an old Nags Head–style clapboard cottage, this old-fashioned dining spot has been in the same family since 1946. Stick with the seafood or chops, at which they excel. Pecan-encrusted sea scallops are plump, tender, and intensely delicious. Also popular are Margarita sea scallops, coconut shrimp with an orange creole sauce, and filet mignon topped with lump crabmeat and asparagus béarnaise sauce. Seafood gumbo is studded with crawfish, Andouille sausage, and Tasso ham. Service is attentive and the wine list hefty. The 16-layer lemon and chocolate cakes are delicious. The brass-and-glass Station Keeper's Lounge has entertainment. ✉ *U.S. 158, MM 17,* ☎ *252/441–7309. Reservations not accepted. AE, D, DC, MC, V. Closed Jan.–Feb. No lunch.*

$$–$$$ ✗ **Pier House Restaurant.** A sign above the entrance reads THE HAPPIEST PEOPLE IN THE WORLD PASS THROUGH THIS DOOR—no kidding, especially if you count the decidedly spectacular view over the ocean, the friendly service, and the tremendous selection of fresh seafood. This seasonal restaurant is literally *on* the crooked, rickety Nags Head Fishing Pier, which juts into the ocean, and while you're waiting for your food, you can stroll down and watch ruddy fishermen haul up their catch. It's open from 7 AM until 9 PM. At breakfast and lunch ($) you can get anything from seafood omelets to crab cakes to burgers and grilled-cheese sandwiches. ✉ *U.S. 158, MM 12,* ☎ *252/441–4200. Reservations not accepted. AE, D, MC, V. Closed Thanksgiving–Easter. No dinner Oct.–Easter.*

$$–$$$ ✗ **RV's.** If fiery red sunsets, spicy marinated tuna, sweet scallops, or peanut butter pie mean anything to you, head immediately to this busy place on the Causeway between Nags Head and Roanoke Island. It's where locals come to eat, drink, and take in serene views of Roanoke Sound. Both lunch and dinner are served. Seafood choices range from clam chowder to barbecued shrimp to piquant crab cakes and tuna. You can also get steak, ribs, and chicken. Portions are huge. There are a little pier outside and an attached indoor-outdoor gazebo where you can get a drink. The marvelous turtle cake is a dieter's nightmare, with chocolate, pecans, and caramel. ✉ *Nags Head Manteo Causeway, MM 16.5,* ☎ *252/441–4963. Reservations not accepted. MC, V. Closed Dec.–Jan.*

$ ✗ **Sam & Omie's.** This charming, no nonsense little niche, named after two fishermen who were father and son, is the oldest restaurant in the Outer Banks. Fishing illustrations hang on the walls, and Merle Haggard plays in the background. It's open daily 7–7 and serves every imaginable kind of seafood, plus other items. The chef has been serving she-crab soup for 22 years, and it's easy to see why locals love it. Also, try the fine marinated tuna steak, Cajun tuna bites, or frothy crab–asparagus soup. Diehard fans claim that Sam & Omie's serves the best oysters on the beach. Dress is beach-casual. ☒ *U.S. 158, MM 16.5,* ☎ *252/441–7366. Reservations not accepted. D, MC, V.*

$$$–$$$$ 🏨 **First Colony Inn.** You'll get great ocean views from the verandas that
★ encircle this historic three-story B&B. Two rooms have wet bars, kitch-
enettes, and whirlpool baths; others have four-poster or canopy beds,
handcrafted armoires, and English antiques. All rooms offer extras, such
as heated towel bars. The entire property is no-smoking. ☒ *6720 S.
Virginia Dare Trail, 27959,* ☎ *252/441–2343 or 800/368–9390,* FAX
252/441–9234, WEB *www.firstcolonyinn.com. 26 rooms. Picnic area,
microwaves, refrigerators, pool, beach, croquet, library, business ser-
vices. AE, D, MC, V. CP.*

Outdoor Activities and Sports

GOLF
Nags Head Golf Links (☒ 5615 S. Seachase Dr., MM 15, ☎ 252/441–
8074 or 800/851–9404) has a par-71, 18-hole course with ocean views.

HANG GLIDING
Kitty Hawk Kites (☒ U.S. 158, MM 13, ☎ 800/334–4777, WEB www.
kittyhawk.com) offers lessons and gear. It's the oldest (and biggest) hang-
gliding school on the East Coast.

Roanoke Island

10 mi southwest of Nags Head.

On a hot July day in 1587, 117 men, women, and children left their
boat and set foot on Roanoke Island to make the first permanent En-
glish settlement in the New World. Three years later they disappeared
without a trace, leaving a mystery that continues to intrigue histori-
ans. Today Roanoke Island is a sleepy, well-kept place; much of the
12-mi-long island remains wild. In summer Roanoke and its two vil-
lages—picturesque Manteo and Wanchese—come alive. You get to the
34 island by taking U.S. 64/264 from the U.S. 158 Bypass. **Manteo** has
some sights related to the island's history, as well as an aquarium.

A history, educational, and cultural arts complex opposite the waterfront
in Manteo, **Roanoke Island Festival Park** includes the *Elizabeth II* State
Historic Site. Costumed interpreters conduct tours of the 69-ft ship, a
re-creation of a 16th-century vessel, except when it is on educational voy-
ages in the off-season (call ahead). The complex also has an interactive
museum, a fossil pit, plays, concerts, arts-and-crafts exhibitions, and spe-
cial programs. ☒ *Downtown Manteo,* ☎ *252/475–1500; 252/475–
1506 for 24-hr event hot line,* WEB *www.roanokeisland.com.* 💲 *$8.* ⊙
Mar. and Nov.–Dec., daily 10–5; Apr.–Oct., daily 9–7.

Clustered together on the outskirts of Manteo are the lush **Elizabethan
Gardens,** a re-creation of a 16th-century English garden, established
as a memorial to the first English colonists. They contain antique stat-
uary, wildflowers, rose gardens, and a sunken garden and are impec-
cably maintained by the Garden Club of North Carolina. ☒ *1411 U.
S. 64/264, 3 mi north of downtown Manteo,* ☎ *252/473–3234,* WEB
www.outerbanks.com/elizabethangardens. 💲 *$5.* ⊙ *Mid-Sept.–May,
daily 9–5; June–early Sept., daily 9–8.*

Fort Raleigh National Historic Site is a restoration of the original 1585
earthworks that mark the beginning of English colonial history in
America. Be sure to see the orientation film and then take a guided tour
of the fort. A nature trail leads to an outlook over Roanoke Sound.
Native American and Civil War history is also preserved here. ☒ *Off
U.S. 64/264, 3 mi north of Manteo,* ☎ *252/473–5772,* WEB *www.nps.
gov/fora.* 💲 *Free.* ⊙ *Daily 9–5; extended hrs in summer.*

☺ The **Lost Colony,** begun in 1937, is the country's first and longest-running outdoor drama. Staged at the Waterside Amphitheatre, it reenacts the story of the first colonists, who settled here in 1587 and then disappeared. ⊠ *1409 U.S. 64/264,* ☎ *252/473–3414 or 800/488–5012,* WEB *www.thelostcolony.org.* ☎ *$16 (reservations essential).* ☾ *Performances June–Aug., Sun.–Fri. at 8:30 PM.*

☺ **Manteo Booksellers** stocks an admirable collection of books oriented to local attractions, cuisine, history, nature, and fiction. Local authors are featured, and author readings are frequent. It's easy to get captivated and browse here for a long time. The children's section is quite large, and the staff is helpful and friendly. ⊠ *105 Sir Walter Raleigh St., Downtown Manteo,* ☎ *252/473–1221,* WEB *www.manteobooksellers.com.* ☾ *Summer, weekdays 10–8, weekends 10–6; fall–spring, daily 10–6.*

☺ The **North Carolina Aquarium at Roanoke Island,** overlooking Croatan Sound, occupies 68,000 square ft. There are touch tanks and a shoreline boardwalk with observation decks. *The Graveyard of the Atlantic* is the centerpiece exhibit. It is a 285,000-gallon ocean tank containing the re-created remains of the USS *Monitor,* sunken off Hatteras Island. The aquarium hosts a slew of workshops and field trips, from feeding fishes to learning about medicinal aquatic plants to kids' workshops. ⊠ *374 Airport Rd., off U.S. 64,* ☎ *252/473–3493 for aquarium; 252/473–3494 for educational programs,* WEB *www.aquariums.state.nc.us.* ☎ *$4.* ☾ *Daily 9–5.*

OFF THE BEATEN PATH | **EDENTON –** Rich with history, North Carolina's first permanent settlement and the colony's first capital is a placid, immensely scenic place on the north side of the Albemarle Sound (65 mi west of Manteo). Originally incorporated in 1715 with the name the Towne on Queen Anne's Creek, the spot was renamed Edenton seven years later in honor of Governor Charles Eden. A fine collection of 18th-century buildings has been well maintained. Stop by the visitor center (⊠ 108 N. Broad St., ☎ 252/482–2637) to hear tales about the colonists, such as the women of the Edenton Tea Party, who fought for liberty. An inexpensive pamphlet serves as a guide on a 1½-mi walking tour. Guided tours of the historic district are available—and are recommended.

Dining and Lodging

$$–$$$ ✕ **Weeping Radish Brewery and Restaurant.** This Bavarian-style restaurant and microbrewery is known for its German cuisine and the annual Oktoberfest weekend held after Labor Day, which showcases German and blues bands. Brewery tours are offered free of charge on request. The beer is superb. There's also a gift shop. ⊠ *U.S. 64, Manteo,* ☎ *252/473–1157,* WEB *www.weepingradish.com. D, MC, V.*

$–$$ ✕ **Full Moon Café.** Come at lunch or dinner to this wonderfully cheerful bistro near the waterfront, with high ceilings, bright blue walls, and red-and-green-flowered tablecloths. The herbed hummus with roasted pita is fantastic, as are the crab cakes. Light eaters beware: even the Waldorf salad comes with a million pecans and apples. Expect lots of cheese on any dish that includes it. Choices include salads, veggie wraps, quesadillas, Cuban-style enchiladas, Lowcountry shrimp and grits, burgers of all kinds, and a dozen innovative and hearty sandwiches. The café also serves specialty cocktails and maintains a thoughtful wine list. ⊠ *306 Queen Elizabeth Ave., Manteo,* ☎ *252/473–6666. AE, D, DC, MC, V. No dinner Sun.*

$ ✕ **Magnolia Grille.** Freddy and Pam Ortega, cheerful New York transplants, run this new and immensely popular lunch and dinner spot on Manteo's downtown waterfront. Choose anything from lean, char-grilled chili cheeseburgers to deli sandwiches, quesadillas, salads, and hearty chicken dishes. Quirkier options include spicy shrimp jammers (battered, filled with jalapeño cheese, and fried) or the specials, such as fried oyster sandwiches or burgers topped with crabmeat. The place is hopping, even at breakfast; lunch gets the overflow from nearby Festival Park. Do like the locals do: get takeout and savor your sandwich by the waterfront. Or come for a stack of pancakes at breakfast; the restaurant opens daily at 7 AM. ⊠ *408 Queen Elizabeth St., Manteo, ☎ 252/475–9877. AE, D, MC, V. No dinner Sun.–Mon.*

$$$–$$$$ ✕⌂ **Tranquil House Inn.** This charming 19th-century-style waterfront inn is only a few steps from shops, restaurants, and the Roanoke Island Festival Park. The mood of the individually decorated rooms is cozy: handmade comforters, Oriental rugs, and hardwood floors. Complimentary wine and cheese are served in the evening. The popular restaurant, 1587 ($$$), is known for its chop-house-style cuts and other inventive entrées: char-grilled duck breast with black mission fig and dried cherry spiked Bordelaise and the cornmeal-crusted Rockfish fillet. ⊠ *405 Queen Elizabeth Ave., Box 2045, Manteo 27954, ☎ 252/473–1404 or 800/458–7069, FAX 252/473–1526, WEB www.1587.com. 25 rooms. Restaurant, bicycles, business services, meeting room. AE, D, MC, V. Closed Dec.–Jan. CP.*

$–$$ ⌂ **Scarborough Inn.** Off Manteo's main road, within walking distance of popular shops and restaurants and about 3 mi from the beach, the two-story Scarborough is modeled after a turn-of-the-20th-century inn. Each spacious room is decorated differently and includes family heirlooms as well as modern conveniences such as coffeemakers. Outside on the wraparound porch of each room are benches and rocking chairs. ⊠ *524 U.S. 64/264, Manteo 27954, ☎ 252/473–3979, WEB www.scarborough-inn.com. 12 rooms. Microwaves, room service, refrigerators, bicycles. AE, D, DC, MC, V. CP.*

Cape Hatteras National Seashore

Extends 70 mi south of Nags Head.

★ **Cape Hatteras National Seashore** has more than 70 mi of unspoiled beaches stretching from south Nags Head to Ocracoke Inlet across three narrow islands: Bodie, Hatteras, and Ocracoke. The islands are linked by Route 12 and the Hatteras Inlet ferry. This coastal area is ideal for swimming, surfing, windsurfing, diving, boating, and other water activities. It's easy to find your own slice of beach as you drive south down Route 12, but park only in designated areas. If you want to swim, beware of strong tides and currents—there are no lifeguard stations. Fishing piers are in Rodanthe, Avon, and Frisco.

Hatteras Island

15 mi south of Nags Head.

The Herbert C. Bonner Bridge arches for 3 mi over Oregon Inlet and carries traffic to Hatteras Island, known as the "blue marlin capital of the world." The island, a 33-mi-long ribbon of sand, juts out into the Atlantic Ocean; at its most distant point (Cape Hatteras), Hatteras is 25 mi from the mainland. About 85% of the island belongs to Cape Hatteras National Seashore, and the remainder is privately owned in seven small, quaint villages strung along Route 12, the island's fragile lifeline to points north.

🟢 **Pea Island National Wildlife Refuge** is made up of more than 5,000 acres of marsh. This birder's delight, with observation platforms and spotting scopes, is on the Atlantic flyway: more than 265 species are sighted regularly, including endangered peregrine falcons and piping plovers. Route 12 travels through marsh areas, and you can hike or drive, depending on the terrain. A visitor center, 5 mi south of Oregon Inlet on Route 12, has an informational display. Remember to douse yourself in bug spray, especially in the spring. ⊠ *Pea Island Refuge Headquarters, Rte. 12,* ☎ *252/473–1131.* ☞ *Free.* ☉ *May–Sept., daily 9–4; Oct.–Apr., Thurs.–Sun. 9–4.*

36 In the village of Rodanthe, the restored 1911 **Chicamacomico Lifesaving Station** has a museum that tells the story of the 24 stations that once lined the Outer Banks. These were the precursors to today's Coast Guard. Living-history reenactments are performed June through August. ⊠ *Off Rte. 12,* ☎ *252/987–1552,* WEB *www.chicamacomico. org.* ☞ *Free.* ☉ *Apr.–Oct., Tues.–Sat. 9–5.*

37 **Cape Hatteras Lighthouse,** about 30 mi south of Rodanthe, is a beacon to ships offshore. It was the first lighthouse built in the region, after being authorized by Congress in 1794 to help prevent shipwrecks. At 208 ft it is the tallest brick lighthouse in the world, and it's painted with distinctive black-and-white spirals. Endangered by the sea, in 1999 the lighthouse was actually picked up and moved slightly inland to its present location. In summer the principal keeper's quarters are open for viewing. Offshore lie the remains of the USS *Monitor,* a Confederate ironclad ship that sank in 1862. ⊠ *Hatteras Island Visitor Center, off Rte. 12 near Buxton,* ☎ *252/995–4474,* WEB *www.nps.gov/caha.* ☞ *Free.* ☉ *Visitor center daily 9–5; climbing Apr.–mid-Oct., daily 10–2; summer, daily 10–6.*

Dining

$$–$$$ ✕ **Tides.** Just south of the entrance for the Cape Hatteras Lighthouse, this place is popular for its good service, well-prepared food, and homey manner. In addition to offering the usual seafood, the menu has chicken and ham. It's also a popular breakfast spot. ⊠ *Rte. 12, Buxton,* ☎ *252/995–5988. MC, V. Closed Dec.–early Apr. No lunch.*

Ocracoke Island

38 *Southwest of Hatteras Island.*

Much of Ocracoke Island is part of Cape Hatteras National Seashore. A free ferry that leaves every hour during the day will take you from Hatteras to the island in 40 minutes; other ferries leave from the mainland. Ocracoke was cut off from the world for a long time, but now the island is somewhat of a refuge for people seeking peace and quiet. A village of shops, motels, and restaurants is around Silver Lake Harbor, where the pirate Blackbeard met his death in 1718. The **Ocracoke Lighthouse,** the oldest operating lighthouse in North Carolina—it can be seen from 14 mi out at sea—is unfortunately not open for climbing but is a photographer's dream. The **Ocracoke Island Visitor Center** (⊠ Ocracoke Village, south end of Rte. 12 on Silver Lake, ☎ 252/928–4531), run by the National Park Service, provides plenty of useful information.

Ocracoke Island **beaches** are among the least populated and most beautiful on the Cape Hatteras National Seashore. Four public access areas have parking as well as off-road vehicle access. At the **Ocracoke Pony Pen** (⊠ Rte. 12, 6 mi southwest of the Hatteras-Ocracoke ferry landing), you can observe from a platform what some believe are the direct descendants of Spanish mustangs that once roamed wild on the island.

Dining and Lodging

$$ ✕▥ **Island Inn and Dining Room.** The inn, built as a private lodge back in 1901, shows its age a bit but is full of Outer Banks character. The rooms in the modern wing are good for families. The large rooms in the Crow's Nest, on the third floor, have the most architectural interest—they have cathedral ceilings and look out over the island. The restaurant ($–$$) is known for its oyster omelet, crab cakes, and hush puppies. This is a no-smoking property. ✉ *Lighthouse Rd. and Rte. 12, Box 9, 27960,* ☎ *252/928–4351; 877/456–3466 for inn; 252/928–7821 for dining room;* FAX *252/928–4352,* WEB *www.ocracokeislandinn. com. 35 rooms, 4 villas. Restaurant, cable TV, pool, lobby lounge, airport shuttle. AE, MC, V.*

Cape Lookout National Seashore

Southwest of Ocracoke Island via Cedar Island.

★ **Cape Lookout National Seashore** extends for 55 mi from Portsmouth Island to Shackleford Banks and includes 28,400 acres of uninhabited land and marsh. The remote, sandy islands are linked to the mainland by private ferries. Ferry service is available from Harkers Island to the Cape Lookout Light area, from Davis to Shingle Point, from the Atlantic to an area north of Drum Inlet, and from Ocracoke to Portsmouth Village. Portsmouth, a deserted village that was inhabited from 1753 until the early 1970s, is being restored and is open to the public from April to early November. To the south, wild ponies roam Shackleford Banks. Four-wheel-drive vehicles are allowed on the beach, and primitive camping is available.

The Outer Banks A to Z

To research prices, get advice from other travelers, and book travel arrangements, visit www.fodors.com.

AIR TRAVEL

CARRIERS

Outer Banks Airways provides charter service between the Dare County Regional Airport and major cities along the East Coast, as does Flightline Aviation, which flies into the First Flight depot, at the Wright Memorial in Kill Devil Hill.

➤ AIRLINES AND CONTACTS: **Outer Banks Airways** (☎ 252/441–7677). **Flightline Aviation** (☎ 800/916–3226).

AIRPORTS

The closest commercial airports are Raleigh-Durham, a five-hour drive, and, in Virginia, Norfolk International, a 1½-hour drive.

➤ AIRPORT INFORMATION: **Dare County Regional Airport** (✉ 410 Airport Rd., Manteo, ☎ 252/473–2600, WEB www.fly2mqi.com). **Norfolk International** (✉ 2200 Norview Ave., ☎ 757/857–3351, WEB www. norfolkairport.com).

BOAT AND FERRY TRAVEL

Seagoing folks travel the Intracoastal Waterway through the Outer Banks and the Albemarle region. Boats may dock at nearly 150 marinas, including Elizabeth City, Manteo Waterfront Docks, and National Park Service Silver Lake Marina, in Ocracoke.

For information about the state-run ferry system and its schedules and costs, call the North Carolina Department of Transportation's ferry information line. From Ocracoke there are car ferries to Cedar Island and Swan Quarter on the mainland. You need a reservation for the ferry.

FARES AND SCHEDULES
➤ BOAT AND FERRY INFORMATION: **Elizabeth City** (☎ 252/338–2886). **Manteo Waterfront Docks** (☎ 252/473–3320). **National Park Service**

Silver Lake Marina (☎ 252/928–5111). **North Carolina Department of Transportation Ferry Information** (☎ 800/293–3779).

CAR TRAVEL

U.S. 158 links the Outer Banks with U.S. 17 leading to Norfolk, Virginia, and other places north. Route 12 goes north toward Corolla and south toward Ocracoke.

EMERGENCIES

Dial 911 for emergencies on Oregon Inlet, Roanoke Island, Hatteras Island, and Ocracoke Island. The Healtheast/Outer Banks Medical Center is open 24 hours a day. Beach Medical Care provides help around the clock. The Outer Banks Hospital, which opened in spring 2002 in Nags Head, is open daily and has 24-hour emergency care. For Coast Guard assistance call the number listed below. A CVS Pharmacy is open weekdays 8:30 AM–9 PM, Sat. 8:30–6, and Sun. 10–6.

➤ DOCTORS AND DENTISTS: **Beach Medical Care** (✉ 5200 N. Croatan Hwy., MM 1.5, Kitty Hawk, ☎ 252/261–4187). **Healtheast/Outer Banks Medical Center** (✉ 2808 S. Croatan Hwy., Nags Head, ☎ 252/441–7111).**Outer Banks Hospital** (✉ 4800 S. Croatan Hwy., Nags Head, ☎ 252/449–4500).

➤ EMERGENCY SERVICES: **Ambulance, police** (☎ 911). **Coast Guard** (☎ 252/995–6411).

➤ PHARMACIES: **CVS** (✉ 1101 S. Croatan Hwy., Kill Devil Hill, ☎ 252/441–3633).

LODGING

CAMPING

Camping is permitted in four designated areas along the Cape Hatteras National Seashore. These campgrounds can serve tents, trailers, and motor homes. All camping at Cape Lookout National Seashore is in the primitive style and is allowed from mid-April through mid-October. Be sure to take extralong tent stakes for sand, and don't forget insect repellent. All sites are available on a first-come, first-served basis, except Ocracoke, where reservations are accepted. For information about private campgrounds contact the Dare County Tourist Bureau.

➤ CONTACTS: **Cape Hatteras National Seashore** (✉ 1401 National Park Dr., Manteo 27954, ☎ 252/473–2111, WEB www.nps.gov/caha). **Cape Lookout National Seashore** (✉ 131 Charles St., Harkers Island 28531, ☎ 252/728–2250). **Dare County Tourist Bureau** (☎ 252/473–2138 or 800/446–6262).

OUTDOORS AND SPORTS

FISHING

Fishing, whether surf casting or deep-sea, is wonderful here. You don't need a license for saltwater fishing. You can board a charter boat or head your own craft out of Oregon Inlet Fishing Center or Pirates Cove Yacht Club and Marina in Manteo. For fishing regulations, call the North Carolina Division of Marine Fisheries.

➤ CONTACTS: **North Carolina Division of Marine Fisheries** (☎ 252/726–7021). **Oregon Inlet Fishing Center** (☎ 252/441–6301 or 800/272–5199). **Pirates Cove Yacht Club and Marina** (☎ 252/473–3906 or 800/367–4728).

KAYAKING

Carolina Outdoors, part of Kitty Hawk Kites, operates sea-kayaking Ecotours along the banks of the villages Duck and Manteo (in the latter's downtown area) and through wildlife refuges, islands, and even a maritime forest. It also rents kayaks. Kitty Hawk Sports (a different company altogether, opposite Jockeys Ridge) rents kayaks to the public and offers surf-kayaking lessons and ecotours.

➤ CONTACTS: **Carolina Outdoors** (☎ 252/334–4777; 252/441–4124 for reservations, WEB www.kittyhawk.com). **Kitty Hawk Sports** (✉ U. S. 158, MM 13, Nags Head, ☎ 252/441–6800, WEB www.khsports.com).

SCUBA DIVING

About 2,000 shipwrecks have occurred off the coast of the Outer Banks—which means scuba-diving options are virtually unlimited. The USS *Monitor* is off-limits, however. The USS *Huron* Historic Shipwreck Preserve, which lies offshore between mile markers 11 and 12, is a popular diving site. Full-service dive shops include the Outer Banks Dive Center.

➤ CONTACTS: **Outer Banks Dive Center** (✉ 3917 S. Croatan Hwy., Nags Head, ☎ 252/449–8349, WEB www.obxdive.com).

WATER SPORTS

Surfing and windsurfing are excellent on the Outer Banks, and parasailing and kite surfing have become increasingly popular. For lessons and rentals contact Kitty Hawk Watersports, the oldest water-sports outfitter in the area, offering sailing, windsurfing, parasailing, jet skiing, kite boarding, and kayaking. (It also has a retail store, Kitty Hawk Sports, at mile marker 12 on U.S. 158.) Bert's Surf Shop rents surfboards, offers private lessons, and runs 3- and 5-day surf school programs; it also has a retail shop.

➤ CONTACTS: **Kitty Hawk Water Sports** (✉ U.S. 158, MM 16.5, Nags Head, ☎ 252/441–2756, WEB www.khsports.com). **Bert's Surf Shop** (✉ U.S. 158, MM 11, Nags Head, ☎ 252/441–1939).

TAXIS

Beach Cabs, based in Nags Head, offers 24-hour service from Norfolk to Ocracoke and towns in between; a ride to the Norfolk airport will run you about $140. Coastal Cab serves the Outer Banks—from the southern shores down to Nags Head—and charges you $135 to get to the airport. Coastal Limo, which serves the entire 100 mi stretch of the Outer Banks, is quite a bargain: $68 for one or two people from Nags Head, Kill Devil Hills, or Kitty Hawk to the Norfolk airport. If you're farther south or are going to the airport at odd hours, the price increases, depending on what you need. The Outer Banks Limousine Service, headquartered in Kill Devil Hills, serves the entire area and Norfolk International Airport and runs around the clock; getting to the airport costs about $125 from Nags Head, though fees vary depending on where you are and when you're going.

➤ TAXI COMPANIES: **Beach Cabs** (☎ 252/441–2500 or 800/441–2503). **Coastal Cab** (☎ 252/449–8787). **Coastal Limo** (☎ 252/441–2262). **Outer Banks Limousine Service** (☎ 252/261–3133 or 800/828–5466).

TOURS

Historic Albemarle Tour, Inc., runs guided tours of Edenton and publishes a brochure on self-guided tour of the Albemarle region.

Kitty Hawk AeroTours leaves from the First Flight Airstrip or from Manteo for Kitty Hawk, Corolla, Cape Hatteras, Ocracoke, Portsmouth Island, and other areas along the Outer Banks. Tours take place March through Labor Day.

➤ FEES AND SCHEDULES: **Historic Albemarle Tour, Inc.** (✉ 1 Harding Sq., Washington, ☎ 252/974–2950 or 800/734–1117, WEB www.historicalbemarletour.com). **Kitty Hawk AeroTours** (✉ behind Wright Brothers Monument, U.S. 158, MM 8, Kill Devil Hills, ☎ 252/441–4460).

TRAIN TRAVEL

Amtrak is available to Norfolk, Virginia, about 75 mi to the north, but it does not serve the Outer Banks.

➤ TRAIN INFORMATION: **Amtrak** (☎ 800/872–7245, WEB www.amtrak. com).

VISITOR INFORMATION

Dare County Tourist Bureau operates three information centers. The Aycock Brown Welcome Center is open daily 9–5:30 and offers extensive resources, including photos, maps, and ferry schedules. The smaller Hatteras Island Welcome Center is right before Bodie Island. This center is open from Memorial Day to October 1, daily 9–5, and on weekends in April, May, and November. The Outer Banks Welcome Center on Roanoke Island, in Manteo, opened in 2002 and is open daily 9–5. It's a state-of-the-art center with touch screens—you can pick up a phone, push a number, and be connected to an accommodation instantly.

The National Park Service's group headquarters, at the Fort Raleigh National Historic Site in Manteo, has a 24-hour general information line about Cape Hatteras National Seashore, or you can write the superintendent at the address listed below.

The National Park Service, Cape Lookout National Seashore, has information about visiting Cape Lookout.

➤ VISITOR INFORMATION: **Aycock Brown Welcome Center** (✉ U.S. 158, MM 1.25, Kitty Hawk 27949, ☎ 252/261–4644). **Dare County Tourist Bureau** (✉ 704 S. U.S. 64/264, Box 399, Manteo 27954, ☎ 252/473–2138 or 800/446–6262, WEB www.outerbanks.org). **Hatteras Island Welcome Center** (☎ no phone). **National Park Service, Cape Lookout National Seashore** (✉ 131 Charles St., Harkers Island 28531, ☎ 252/728–2250, WEB www.nps.gov/calo). **National Park Service's Group Headquarters** (✉ 1401 National Park Dr., Manteo, ☎ 252/473–2111 for 24-hr general information, WEB www.nps.gov/fora). **National Park Service's superintendent** (✉ Rte. 1, Box 675, Manteo 27954). **Outer Banks Welcome Center on Roanoke Island** (✉ 1 Visitors Center Circle, Manteo 27954, ☎ 877/298–4373).

NEW BERN AND THE CENTRAL COAST

Craven County—where you'll find New Bern, a good chunk of the 157,000-acre Croatan National Forest, and Cherry Point, the world's largest Marine Corps air station—is by turns genteel and historic, modern and commercialized, rural and wild. Golfers, boaters, and a growing number of retirees find the area a haven.

Neighboring Carteret County, with nearly 80 mi of ocean coastline, is known as the Central, or Crystal, Coast. It is composed of the south-facing beaches along the barrier island Bogue Banks (Atlantic Beach, Pine Knoll Shores, Indian Beach, Salter Path, and Emerald Isle), three mainland townships (Morehead City, Beaufort, and Newport), and a series of small, unincorporated "down-east" communities traversed by a portion of U.S. 70 that's been designated a Scenic Byway.

New Bern

112 mi southeast of Raleigh.

The pace is quiet and slow in New Bern, the second-oldest town in North Carolina. Settled in 1710 by Swiss and German colonists and named for Bern, Switzerland, the city has a heraldic Swiss black bear symbol that is everywhere. New Bern, the state capital from the period of English rule until immediately after the revolution, is where North Carolina's first newspaper was printed and Pepsi-Cola was invented. History is taken seriously here; it has more than 150 sites included in the National Register of Historic Places.

Sailors and sun seekers will enjoy the area, as the Neuse and Trent rivers are perfect for such activities as waterskiing and crabbing. The historic downtown area is filled with shops, many of them selling antiques. As in much of North Carolina, golf is a favorite New Bern pastime.

The reconstructed **Tryon Palace,** an elegant Georgian building, was the colonial capital and the home of Royal Governor William Tryon during the 1770s. It was rebuilt according to architectural drawings of the original palace and furnished with English and American antiques according to Governor Tryon's inventory. An audiovisual orientation will prepare you for a tour of the house led by costumed guides. In summer actors deliver monologues detailing a day in the life of everyday citizens and the governor. Tours of the 18th-century formal gardens are self-guided. The stately **John Wright Stanly House** (circa 1783), the **Dixon-Stevenson House** (circa 1826), and the **New Bern Academy** (circa 1809) are within or near the 13-acre Tryon Palace complex. ⊠ *610 Pollock St.,* ☎ *252/514–4900.* ▣ *Self-guided tours $8; tours of garden, kitchen office, and stables $7; tour of all bldgs. and gardens $15.* ☉ *Late May–early Sept., Mon.–Sat. 9–7, Sun. 1–7; early Sept.–late May, Mon.–Sat. 9–5, Sun. 1–5.*

Dining and Lodging

$$–$$$ ✕ **The Chelsea.** This two-story restored 1912 structure, originally the second drugstore of the pharmacist who invented Pepsi-Cola, retains some fine architectural details, such as its tin ceiling. It's a magnet for weekenders, who look forward to selecting from sandwiches (wrapped, pita, and burgers), large salads, and entrées such as shrimp and grits. The bar is well stocked, and Pepsi, of course, is the nonalcoholic drink of choice. ⊠ *335 Middle St.,* ☎ *252/637–5469,* WEB *www.thechelsea. com. AE, D, DC, MC, V.*

$$–$$$ ✕ **The Flame.** The considerate staff at this dark, woodsy steak house, with furnishings vaguely reminiscent of the Victorian era, helps make dinners special. Steak, lobster, grilled shrimp, and teriyaki chicken are all good bets. Sunday brunch is popular. ⊠ *2303 Neuse Blvd.,* ☎ *252/ 633–0262. AE, D, DC, MC, V. No dinner Sun. No lunch Mon.–Sat.*

$ ✕ **Pollock Street Deli.** Good-size crowds gather in the tiny rooms of an authentic colonial house in the historic district and its sidewalk tables for classic deli treats or Sunday brunch. Service can be leisurely. ⊠ *208 Pollock St.,* ☎ *252/637–2480. AE, MC, V. No dinner Sun.*

$$$ ▥ **Sheraton New Bern Hotel and Marina.** At the confluence of the Neuse and Trent rivers, this Sheraton—with marina facilities—is actually two properties in one. A hotel has guest rooms overlooking the Trent River, and rooms at the inn have either waterfront or city views. ⊠ *100 Middle St., 28560,* ☎ *252/638–3585 or 888/625–5144,* FAX *252/638– 8112,* WEB *www.newbernsheraton.com. 150 rooms, 22 suites. Restaurant, room service, pool, marina, exercise room, 2 bars, concierge, business services, meeting room, airport shuttle. AE, D, DC, MC, V.*

$$ ▥ **Bridge Pointe Hotel & Marina.** On the Trent River, just across the bridge from the historic section of New Bern, this property has standard rooms with above-average views of the rivers that circle the eastern side of the city. The grounds also include a small lake, on which a few ducks reside. Next door is a steak house. ⊠ *101 Howell Rd., 28562,* ☎ *252/636–3637 or 877/283–7713,* FAX *252/637–5028,* WEB *www. bridgepointehotel.com. 116 rooms. Restaurant, pool, marina, lounge, laundry service, meeting rooms. AE, D, DC, MC, V.*

$$ ★ **⊞ Harmony House Inn.** This historic B&B has a fascinating past. At one point, two brothers sawed the house in half, creating double hallways and stairs and a dividing wall. Today the only external hint of the dual identity is the double front doors. You sleep in spacious rooms that lodged Yankee soldiers during the Civil War. Rooms are furnished with a mix of antiques and reproductions. Complimentary white and dessert wines are served in the evening. ⊠ *215 Pollock St., 28560,* ☎ *252/636–3810 or 800/636–3113,* 𝔽𝔸𝕏 *252/636–3810,* 𝕎𝔼𝔹 *www.harmonyhouseinn. com. 10 rooms. Dining room, business services, airport shuttle. AE, D, MC, V. BP.*

Morehead City

35 mi southeast of New Bern.

Morehead City is a fishing and boating center across Bogue Sound from the barrier island Bogue Banks. Popular family beaches on the island are **Atlantic Beach** and **Emerald Isle.** Among the more developed areas are these beach towns, as well as Pine Knoll Shores.

The **North Carolina Aquarium at Pine Knoll Shores,** in a maritime forest on Bogue Banks, has a 2,000-gallon salt-marsh tank with live alligators, a loggerhead turtle nursery, and a shipwreck exhibit. ⊠ *Salter Path Rd., MM 7, Atlantic Beach,* ☎ *252/247–4004,* 𝕎𝔼𝔹 *www. aquariums.state.nc.us.* ⌨ *$3.* ☉ *Daily 9–5.*

Dining and Lodging

$$–$$$ ✕ **Bistro by the Sea.** Although the stonework and stucco exterior hint at the Mediterranean style within, the cuisine defies any particular theme. Beef, chicken, and seafood all share space on the menu—favorites include stir-fry chicken with rice and wontons; and *capellini* tossed with pesto, fresh scallops, and vegetables. Vegetables are always garden fresh, and the service is consistently friendly. There are also a piano bar and cigar lounge. ⊠ *4301 Arendell St.,* ☎ *252/247–2777. MC, V. Closed Sun.–Mon. in Jan. No lunch.*

$$–$$$ ✕ **Sanitary Fish Market & Restaurant.** In 1938, when the Sanitary was founded, many fish houses were ill kept. The owners wanted to signal that theirs was different. Clean, simple, and generous are bywords at this waterfront place where diners sit on wooden benches. It can get noisy (the restaurant seats 600), but people from around the world gush about the food. ⊠ *501 Evans St.,* ☎ *252/247–3111,* 𝕎𝔼𝔹 *www. sanitaryfishmarket.com. D, MC, V. Closed Dec.–Jan.*

$$ **⊞ Best Western Buccaneer.** The inn sits beside the Morehead Plaza shopping center, a 10-minute drive from Atlantic Beach. Rooms are attractive and comfortable. ⊠ *2806 Arendell St., 28557,* ☎ *252/726–3115 or 800/682–4982,* 𝔽𝔸𝕏 *252/726–3864,* 𝕎𝔼𝔹 *www.bestwestern.com. 91 rooms. Restaurant, refrigerators, pool, bar, exercise room, business services, meeting room. AE, D, DC, MC, V. BP.*

$$ **⊞ Windjammer Inn.** If you're focused on one thing—easy access to the ocean—this is the place for you. What you get here is straightforward—a comfortable oversize room with a private balcony and ocean view. The five-story, glass-enclosed elevator sets the inn apart from typical beach lodging. There's a two-night minimum stay on summer weekends. ⊠ *Salter Path Rd. in Pine Knoll Shores, Atlantic Beach 28512,* ☎ *252/247–7123 or 800/233–6466,* 𝔽𝔸𝕏 *252/247–0133,* 𝕎𝔼𝔹 *www.windjammerinn.com. 46 rooms. Refrigerators, pool. AE, D, MC, V.*

Beaufort

3 mi east of Morehead City.

Beaufort, a small seaport with a bustling boardwalk, brims with charm. The third-oldest town in North Carolina, it was named for Henry Somerset, duke of Beaufort. Boat rides of all types are available for a fee at the town docks on Taylor's Creek.

The **Beaufort Historic Site,** in the center of town, consists of restored buildings dating from 1767 to 1859, including the **Carteret County Courthouse** and the **Apothecary Shop and Doctor's Office.**Don't miss the **Old Burying Grounds** (1731). Here Otway Burns, a privateer in the War of 1812, is buried under his ship's cannon; a nine-year-old girl who died at sea is buried in a rum keg; and an English soldier saluting the king is buried upright in his grave. Tours on an English-style double-decker bus and guided walking tours depart from the visitor center. ✉ *130 Turner St.,* ☎ *252/728–5225,* WEB *www.historicbeaufort. com.* ⌕ *Bus tour $6, bus and walking tour $10.* ☾ *Visitor center Easter– Oct., Mon.–Sat. 9:30–5, Sun. 1:30–4; Nov.–Easter, Mon.–Sat. 10–4, Sun. 1:30–4.*

Beaufort's **North Carolina Maritime Museum** documents the state's seafaring history and includes an exhibit about the infamous pirate Blackbeard and the discovery of his flagship near Beaufort Inlet. The museum includes the **Watercrafts Center,** across the street, which gives boatbuilding classes. Its education staff also provides year-round programs, including trips to the marsh and barrier islands. ✉ *315 Front St.,* ☎ *252/728–7317.* ⌕ *Free.* ☾ *Museum weekdays 9–5, Sat. 10–5, Sun. 1–5; watercrafts center Tues.–Fri. 9–5, Sat. 10–5, Sun. 1–5.*

Dining and Lodging

$$–$$$ ✕ **Clawson's 1905 Restaurant and Pub.** Housed in what was a general store in the early 1900s and stuffed with memorabilia, Clawson's serves hearty food such as ribs, steaks, pasta, and local seafood. It gets very crowded in summer, so arrive early for both lunch and dinner. The coffee bar, Fishtowne Java, opens at 7 AM. ✉ *425 Front St.,* ☎ *252/ 728–2133,* WEB *www.clawsonsrestaurant.com. D, MC, V. Closed Sun., Sept.–Apr.*

$$–$$$ ⌂ **The Cedars by the Sea.** Two side-by-side homes (circa 1768 and 1851) and a private cottage make up this romantic B&B in the historic district. All rooms are individually and elegantly decorated and reflect an eye for detail. They combine contemporary and antique furnishings from world travels, and many have fireplaces, four-poster beds, and original art. There's a small wine bar. The gardens are a favorite spot for wedding receptions. ✉ *305 Front St., 28516,* ☎ *252/728–7036 or 800/ 732–7036,* FAX *252/728–1685,* WEB *www.cedarsinn.com. 10 rooms. Dining room. AE, D, MC, V. BP.*

New Bern and the Central Coast A to Z

To research prices, get advice from other travelers, and book travel arrangements, visit www.fodors.com.

AIR TRAVEL
CARRIERS

➤ AIRLINES AND CONTACTS: **Midway** (☎ 800/446–1392, WEB www. midwayair.com). **US Airways Express** (☎ 800/428–4322, WEB www. usair.com).

AIRPORTS
US Airways Express and Midway fly into Craven County Regional Airport, where charter service and car rentals are available.
➤ AIRPORT INFORMATION: **Craven County Regional Airport** (✉ U.S. 70, New Bern, ☎ 252/638–8591).

BOAT AND FERRY TRAVEL
The Intracoastal Waterway provides access to many Central Coast destinations, including Beaufort, Morehead City, and Emerald Isle. Beaufort has plentiful anchorage and more than 35 marinas, including the Beaufort Town Docks and the Morehead City Yacht Basin.

New Bern can be reached via the Neuse River from Pamlico Sound. Several marinas are available here, including the Sheraton Grand Marina. You can dock for the day (but not overnight) at the public docks of Union Point Park.

For information about the state-run ferry system, call the North Carolina Department of Transportation's ferry information line.

FARES AND SCHEDULES
➤ BOAT AND FERRY INFORMATION: **Beaufort Town Docks** (☎ 252/728–2053). **Ferry information line** (☎ 800/293–3779). **Morehead City Yacht Basin** (☎ 252/726–6862). **Sheraton Grand Marina** (☎ 252/638–3585). **Union Point Park** (☎ 252/636–4060).

BUS TRAVEL
Greyhound/Carolina Trailways serves Morehead City and New Bern.
➤ BUS INFORMATION: **Greyhound/Carolina Trailways** (☎ 800/231–2222, WEB www.greyhound.com).

CAR TRAVEL
U.S. 70 connects New Bern, Morehead City, and Beaufort with points to the west, including Raleigh and I–95. East of Beaufort, U.S. 70 connects to Route 12, which continues on the Outer Banks via ferry. U.S. 17 leads north from New Bern toward the Albemarle region and south to Wilmington.

EMERGENCIES
For emergencies contact Carteret General Hospital, in Morehead City, or Craven Regional Medical Center, in New Bern.
➤ EMERGENCY SERVICES: **Ambulance, police** (☎ 911). **Coast Guard assistance** (☎ 252/247–4598).
➤ HOSPITALS: **Carteret General Hospital** (✉ 3500 Arendell St., ☎ 252/247–1616). **Craven Regional Medical Center** (✉ 2300 Neuse Blvd., ☎ 252/633–8111).

OUTDOORS AND SPORTS
BEACHES
Route 58 passes through all of the beach communities on the Bogue Banks, and locations are noted by mile markers (MM). Points of public access along the shoreline are marked by orange-and-blue signs. Lifeguards monitor some of the beaches. You can fish, swim, picnic, and hike at Fort Macon State Park, outside Morehead City.
➤ CONTACTS: **Fort Macon State Park** (☎ 252/726–3775).

FISHING
The Atlantic Beach King Mackerel Tournament (☎ 252/247–2334) is held on the Crystal Coast in September, and one of the largest and oldest sportfishing contests, the Big Rock Blue Marlin Tournament, is held in various locations each June. Fishing piers are found mostly on Bogue

Banks and are closed during the winter. Dozens of charter boats operate year-round. In New Bern bass-fishing tournaments are popular.

GOLF

Golf courses are abundant, and locals prefer to play in the spring and fall months, when it's cooler. For a list of courses and help with reservations, contact the Crystal Coast Regional Golf Association. Two notable courses are the par-72, 18-hole course at Carolina Pines Golf and Country Club, off Route 70, between New Bern and Havelock, and the par-72, 18-hole course designed by Rees Jones at the semiprivate Emerald Golf Club, on the Route 70 Bypass.

➤ CONTACTS: **Carolina Pines Golf and Country Club** (✉ 390 Carolina Pines Blvd., ☎ 252/444–1000). **Crystal Coast Regional Golf Association** (✉ 801 Arendell St., Box 1193, Morehead City 28557, ☎ 888/991–7529). **Emerald Golf Club** (✉ 5000 Clubhouse Dr., ☎ 252/633–4440).

SCUBA DIVING

Morehead City is considered one of North America's top scuba-diving destinations by many. Two popular wreck sites are the *Schurz,* sunk in World War I, and the *Papoose,* a World War II tanker inhabited by docile sand sharks. The Olympus Dive Center has five dive boats and offers full- and half-day charters, equipment rental, and lessons.

➤ CONTACTS: **Olympus Dive Center** (✉ 713 Shephard St., Morehead City, ☎ 252/726–9432, WEB www.olympusdiving.com).

TAXI

A-1 Yellow Cab Co. serves Atlantic Beach, Beaufort, Morehead City, and the airport. Cherry Cab operates in the New Bern area.

➤ TAXI COMPANIES: **A-1 Yellow Cab Co.** (☎ 252/240–2700). **Cherry Cab** (☎ 252/447–3101).

VISITOR INFORMATION

The Carteret County Tourism Development Bureau operates two visitor centers, one in Morehead City and one on Route 58 just north of the Cameron Langston Bridge to Emerald Isle.

➤ TOURIST INFORMATION: **Carteret County Tourism Development Bureau** (✉ 3409 Arendell St., Morehead City 28557, ☎ 800/786–6962; ✉ 263 Rte. 58, Swansboro 28584, ☎ 252/393–3100, WEB www.sunnync.com). **Craven County Convention and Visitors Bureau** (✉ 314 S. Front St., New Bern 28560, ☎ 252/637–9400 or 800/437–5767, WEB www.visitnewbern.com).

WILMINGTON AND THE CAPE FEAR COAST

The Wilmington/Cape Fear Coast area, between the Cape Fear River and the Atlantic Ocean near the south end of the North Carolina coast, is simultaneously a beach resort and a shipping and trading center. Artists, golfers, history buffs, naturalists, and shoppers will all find something of interest here. The old seaport town of Wilmington has much to celebrate these days, including a once-decayed downtown that has been transformed with upscale places to shop and dine. On the surrounding Cape Fear Coast, you can tour old plantation houses and azalea gardens, study sea life at the state aquarium, or bask in the sun at nearby beaches.

Wilmington

130 mi south of Raleigh.

The city's long history, including its part in the American Revolution and its role as the main port of the Confederacy, is revealed in sights downtown and in the surrounding area. Chandler's Wharf, the Cotton Exchange, and Water Street Market are old buildings now used as shopping and entertainment centers. *Henrietta II*, a paddle wheeler similar to those that plied the waters of the Cape Fear River, has been put into service as a tourist vessel. Wilmington, also a college town, has special annual events such as the Azalea Festival, North Carolina Jazz Festival, Christmas candlelight tours, and fishing tournaments.

At the **USS *North Carolina* Battleship Memorial** you can tour a ship that participated in every major naval offensive in the Pacific during World War II. The self-guided tour takes about two hours, and a 10-minute film is shown throughout the day. Narrated tours on cassette can be rented. Warning: a climb down into the ship's interior is not for the claustrophobic. The ship can be reached by car or by taking the river taxi from Riverfront Park, Memorial Day through Labor Day, at a cost of $2 per person. ⊠ *Junction of U.S. 74/76 and U.S. 17 and 421, west bank of Cape Fear River, Downtown,* ☎ *910/251–5797,* WEB *www. battleshipnc.com.* ☜ *$8.* ⊙ *Mid-May–mid-Sept., daily 8–8; mid-Sept.– mid-May, daily 8–5.*

The **Cotton Exchange,** a shopping-dining complex, is in a rambling restored cotton warehouse on the Cape Fear River in an area that has flourished as a trading center since pre–Civil War days. ⊠ *321 N. Front St., Downtown,* ☎ *910/343–9896,* WEB *www.shopcottonexchange. com.*

The **Cape Fear Museum** traces the natural, cultural, and social history of the lower Cape Fear region from its beginnings to the present. One exhibit follows the youth of one of Wilmington's most famous native sons, basketball superstar Michael Jordan. ⊠ *814 Market St., Downtown,* ☎ *910/341–7413.* ☜ *$5.* ⊙ *Early Sept.–late May, Tues.–Sat. 9–5, Sun. 1–5; late May–early Sept., daily 9–5.*

Built in 1770 on the foundations of a jail, the **Burgwin-Wright Museum House** is a fine restoration of a colonial gentleman's town house and includes seven distinct period gardens. Open-hearth cooking demonstrations are presented one Saturday each month (call ahead). In April 1781 General Cornwallis used the house as his headquarters. ⊠ *224 Market St., Downtown,* ☎ *910/762–0570.* ☜ *$5.* ⊙ *Tues.–Sat. 10–4.*

St. John's Museum of Art is known for its originals by Mary Cassatt, as well as for its works by North Carolina artists. Up to a dozen temporary exhibitions annually highlight art from many different parts of the world. The museum is housed in three buildings, including the 1804 Masonic Lodge Building, the oldest such lodge in the state. There is also a sculpture garden. ⊠ *114 Orange St., Downtown,* ☎ *910/763– 0281,* WEB *www.stjohnsmuseum.com.* ☜ *$3.* ⊙ *Tues.–Sat. 10–5, Sun. noon–4.*

The **Zebulon Latimer House,** built in 1852 in the Italianate style, is a reminder of opulent antebellum living. The Lower Cape Fear Historical Society is based here; it offers guided walking tours of the downtown historic district that depart from the house on Wednesday and Saturday mornings at 10. ⊠ *126 S. 3rd St., Downtown,* ☎ *910/762– 0492,* WEB *http://latimer.wilmington.org.* ☜ *$6.* ⊙ *Weekdays 10–4, weekends noon–5.*

Chandler's Wharf (⊠ 225 S. Water St., Downtown), on the Cape Fear River, contains shops and some seafood restaurants, such as Elijah's. It's a great place to conclude a tour of downtown Wilmington.

Greenfield Park offers picnic spots, bike paths, nature trails, and canoe and paddleboat rentals on a 150-acre lake bordered by cypress trees laden with Spanish moss. In April the park is ablaze with azaleas. ⊠ *S. 3rd St. (U.S. 421), 1 mi south of downtown, South Metro,* ☎ *910/ 341–7852.* ☞ *Free.* ☉ *Daily.*

At **Poplar Grove Historic Plantation,** an 1850 Greek Revival manor house 9 mi northeast of downtown, you can tour the manor house and outbuildings, see crafts demonstrations, shop in the country store, and pet the farm animals. ⊠ *10200 U.S. 17, North Metro,* ☎ *910/686–9989,* WEB *www.poplargrove.com.* ☞ *Guided tours $7.* ☉ *Feb.–Dec., Mon.– Sat. 9–5, Sun. noon–5.*

The **New Hanover County Arboretum** has 33 exhibits, including magnolia and patio gardens, 100 varieties of shade-loving camellias, a salt-spray garden, and a children's garden with a maze. ⊠ *6206 Oleander Dr., Midtown,* ☎ *910/452–6393.* ☞ *Free.* ☉ *Daily sunrise–sunset.*

OFF THE   **MOORE'S CREEK NATIONAL BATTLEFIELD** – Military history buffs will ap-
BEATEN PATH   preciate this site, where American patriots defeated the Loyalists in 1776. The 85-acre park is also a wildlife habitat. ⊠ *200 Moores Creek Rd., Currie, 20 mi northwest of Wilmington on Rte. 210,* ☎ *910/283– 5591,* WEB *www.nps.gov/mocr.* ☞ *Free.* ☉ *Daily 8–5.*

Dining and Lodging

$$–$$$ ✗ **Pilot House.** This Chandler's Wharf restaurant is known for its seafood, pastas, fresh vegetables, and Carolina seafood bisque. You can dine indoors at tables with linen tablecloths secured by vases of fresh flowers or outdoors overlooking the Cape Fear River. Sunday brunch, which starts at 11:30, is popular. ⊠ *2 Ann St., Downtown,* ☎ *910/ 343–0200,* WEB *www.pilothouserest.com. AE, D, DC, MC, V.*

$$–$$$ ✗ **Water Street Restaurant and Sidewalk Café.** A restored two-story brick waterfront warehouse dating from 1835 holds an outdoor café and restaurant that serves up Greek, Mexican, and Middle Eastern dishes, as well as salads, pitas, burgers, and pasta. Seafood chowder is made daily on the premises. ⊠ *5 Water St., Downtown,* ☎ *910/343–0042. AE, MC, V.*

$–$$ ✗ **K-38 Baja Grill.** K-38 refers to the popular surfers' side road in Baja, Mexico, that leads to ideal waves—and the menu heavily references Baja culinary traditions. You won't find Americanized Mexican fare here; instead, sample tricolor corn tortillas with shrimp, scallops, and crab with cheese and roasted garlic cream, and chicken breast baked with artichokes, sun-dried tomatoes, green-chili pesto, and goat cheese cream. Rice, grilled vegetables, and fresh fruit accompany many dishes. ⊠ *5410 Oleander Dr., Midtown,* ☎ *910/395–6040,* WEB *www.k38baja. com. AE, D, MC, V.*

$$$–$$$$ ▥ **The Wilmingtonian.** Many clients at this historic garden-laced complex are businesspeople and members of the entertainment industry. Former commercial buildings, an antebellum home, and a convent have been meticulously transformed into luxurious suites, each in a different theme—classic movies, nautical heritage, country French, and so on. Many rooms have gas fireplaces and large whirlpool tubs. It's best for older children. ⊠ *101 S. 2nd St., Downtown 28401,* ☎ *910/343– 1800 or 800/525–0909,* FAX *910/251–1149,* WEB *www.thewilmingtonian. com. 40 suites. Room service, in-room VCRs, library, laundry service, business services, meeting room. AE, D, DC, MC, V. CP.*

$$$ ⊞ **Hilton-Riverside.** Overlooking the Cape Fear River on one side and the city on the other, the spacious Hilton is one of the most convenient places to stay in town. The lobby is plush; guest rooms are traditional, with dark woods and autumn colors. Rollicking parties are held poolside on summer weekends. ⊠ *301 N. Water St., Downtown 28401,* ☎ *910/763–5900 or 800/445–8667,* FAX *910/763–0038,* WEB *www. wilmingtonhilton.com. 263 rooms, 11 suites. Restaurant, pool, exercise room, dock, bar, concierge floor, business services, meeting room, airport shuttle. AE, D, DC, MC, V.*

$$ ⊞ **Catherine's Inn.** This two-story Italianate home, built in 1883 in what is now a historic district overlooking the Cape Fear River, is a B&B with hardwood floors, a sunken garden, four-poster and canopy beds, and phones in each room. Many items were collected by the innkeepers over the years. Coffee is delivered to your door every morning. This is the only inn in the area with a direct river view. ⊠ *410 S. Front St., Downtown 28401,* ☎ *910/251–0863 or 800/476–0723,* FAX *910/772–9550,* WEB *www.catherinesinn.com. 5 rooms. Dining room, library. MC, V. BP.*

$$ ⊞ **Hampton Inn.** This moderately priced chain motel is only 3 mi from downtown and 6 mi from Wrightsville Beach. Perks include in-room movies and free local calls. ⊠ *5107 Market St., Midtown 28403,* ☎ *910/395–5045 or 800/426–7866,* FAX *910/799–1974,* WEB *www.hampton-inn. com. 118 rooms. Pool, exercise room, laundry service, business services, meeting room. AE, D, DC, MC, V. CP.*

Nightlife and the Arts

THE ARTS

The city has its own symphony orchestra, oratorio society, civic ballet, and concert association; and the North Carolina Symphony makes four appearances here each year. The annual **North Carolina Jazz Festival,** held in February, and the **Cape Fear Blues Festival,** in July, draw crowds. **Thalian Hall Center for the Performing Arts** (⊠ 310 Chestnut St., Downtown, ☎ 910/343–3664 or 800/523–2820), an opera house built between 1855 and 1858 and restored to its former grandeur, hosts more than 250 theater, dance, and musical performances each year. Theatrical productions are staged by the Thalian Association, Opera House Productions, and Tapestry Players.

NIGHTLIFE

Alleigh's (⊠ 4925 New Centre Dr., Midtown, ☎ 910/793–0999) suits many tastes, with a restaurant and five entertainment areas, including a game room, sports bar, and jazz/blues club. **Charley Brownz** (⊠ 21 S. Front St., Downtown, ☎ 910/245–9499) has nightly musical entertainment that ranges from reggae and rock to karaoke and DJ dance music.

Outdoor Activities and Sports

There are approximately 40 public-access golf courses in the Greater Wilmington area. **Beau Rivage Resort Golf Club** (⊠ 649 Rivage Promenade, South Metro, ☎ 910/392–9022 or 800/628–7080) is a par-72 course in a natural links setting. The **Cape Golf & Racquet Club** (⊠ 535 The Cape Blvd., Carolina Beach, ☎ 910/799–3110) is a par-72 resort course with 24 lakes and ponds and a driving range.

South Brunswick County, about 30–40 mi from Wilmington on the coast, has lots of wonderful golfing, especially the areas around Calabash, Sunset Beach, and Ocean Isle. **Lockwood Folly Golf Links** (⊠ 100 Club House Dr., Holden Beach, ☎ 910/842–5666 or 877/562–9663) is a semiprivate highly rated par-72 resort course. **Marsh Harbour Golf Links** (⊠ Rte. 179, Calabash, ☎ 910/579–3161 or 800/552–2660) has a highly rated par-71 course, offering views of marsh and marina activity. The par-70 **Oyster Bay Golf Links** (⊠ Rte. 179, Sunset Beach, ☎ 910/579–

3528 or 800/552–2660) is known for its oyster-shell hazards and gator sightings. **Sea Trail Resort** (✉ 211 Clubhouse Rd., Sunset Beach, ☎ 910/579–4350 or 800/624–6601) has three courses designed by Dan Maples, Rees Jones, and Willard Byrd, all of which are par 72.

Wrightsville Beach

12 mi east of Wilmington.

Wrightsville Beach is a small, quiet island community that's very family oriented. It has a number of fine restaurants, and beaches good for swimming, boating, and surfing.

Dining and Lodging

$$–$$$ ✕ **Oceanic Restaurant and Grill.** Thanks to three floors of seating, you'll have a panoramic view of the Atlantic for miles around—a great backdrop for the fresh seafood, steaks, and chicken. Dinner on the pier at sunset is a treat. ✉ *703 S. Lumina St.,* ☎ *910/256–5551. AE, MC, V.*

$$$$ ✕🏨 **Blockade Runner Resort Hotel and Conference Center.** This oceanside complex is widely known for its Ocean Terrace Restaurant and supervised summer children's programs. Guest rooms, done in bright colors, overlook either the Intracoastal Waterway or, for a higher price, the ocean. Service can be uneven, especially at the height of the season, but the hotel's beachfront location and guaranteed parking keep them coming back. Spa privileges are another plus. The Ocean Terrace ($$– $$$, reservations essential) attracts crowds with its weekend buffets and jazz brunch on Sunday. Two-night minimum spring through fall weekends. ✉ *275 Waynick Blvd., 28480,* ☎ *910/256–2251 or 800/541–1161,* FAX *910/256–5502,* WEB *www.blockade-runner.com. 147 rooms, 3 suites. Restaurant, refrigerators, indoor-outdoor pool, health club, beach, boating, parasailing, bicycles, volleyball, bar, children's programs, business services, meeting room, airport shuttle. AE, D, DC, MC, V.*

Kure Beach

17 mi south of Wilmington.

Kure Beach is a resort community that's a bit livelier than Wrightsville Beach as it's next to Carolina Beach, which has amusement parks and a boardwalk with bars. Historic site Fort Fisher and the North Carolina Aquarium (closed for renovations until at least mid-2002) provide further interest. In some places twisted live oaks still grow behind the dunes. The community has miles of beaches; public access points are marked by orange-and-blue signs.

Fort Fisher State Historic Site marks the largest and one of the most important earthworks fortifications in the South during the Civil War. A reconstructed battery and Civil War relics and artifacts from sunken blockade-runners are on site. The fort is part of the **Fort Fisher Recreation Area**, with 4 mi of undeveloped beach. ✉ *U.S. 421,* ☎ *910/458–5538.* 🎫 *Free.* ⊙ *Apr.–Oct., Mon.–Sat. 9–5, Sun. 1–5; Nov.–Mar., Tues.–Sat. 10–4, Sun. 1–4.*

Dining and Lodging

$$–$$$ ✕ **Big Daddy's.** You can't miss this place—the huge sign outside sits next to the only stoplight in town. Inside the enormity continues: three dining areas seat nearly 500 people. And the menu is substantial, with more than 40 items. Although some chicken, steak, and prime rib are thrown in for good measure, seafood stars. It comes prepared almost any way you could want it, and portions are large. ✉ *202 K Ave.,* ☎ *910/458–8622. AE, D, MC, V. Closed late Nov.–Feb.*

$$$ ⚏ **Docksider Inn.** The nautical theme is no surprise given that this hotel is just yards from the beach. The inn is furnished in light-color beach-type furniture. Owners Kip and Maureen Darling have another property a block away on Atlantic Avenue. The five contemporary luxury suites of Darlings by the Sea are for adults only. Each has an expansive ocean view, custom drapes, bed skirting, and cabinetry. There are whirlpools for two and wet bars. ⊠ *202 Fort Fisher Blvd. (U.S. 421), 28449,* ☎ *910/458–4200 or 800/383–8111,* FAX *910/458–6468,* WEB *www.docksiderinn.com. 34 rooms. Pool, beach. AE, D, MC, V.*

Southport

30 mi south of Wilmington.

This small town, which sits quietly at the mouth of the Cape Fear River, is listed on the National Register of Historic Places. An increasingly desirable retirement spot, Southport retains its village charm and character. Stately and distinctive homes, antiques stores, gift shops, and restaurants line streets that veer to accommodate ancient oak trees. The town, portrayed in Robert Ruark's novel *The Old Man and the Boy,* is ideal for walking; it's also popular with moviemakers—*Crimes of the Heart* was filmed here.

If you're approaching the town from Fort Fisher and Route 421, the **Southport–Fort Fisher Ferry,** a state-operated car ferry, provides a river ride between Old Federal Point at the tip of the spit and the mainland. The Old Baldy Lighthouse, on Bald Head Island, is seen en route. It's best to arrive 30 minutes prior to ferry departure, as it's first come, first served. ☎ *910/458–3329 or 800/293–3779.* 🖃 *$3 per car.* ☉ *Ferries run mid-Mar.–mid-Nov., daily every 45 mins 6:15 AM–9:15 PM; mid-Nov.–mid-Mar., daily every 1½ hrs 6:15 AM–4:45 PM.*

Lodging

$$–$$$ ⚏ **Bald Head Island Resort.** Reached by ferry from Southport, this private, self-contained, carless community complete with grocery store and restaurants has bleached-wood villas and shingle cottages. You can explore the semitropical island on foot, by bicycle, or in a golf cart. Pastimes are doing all manner of warm-weather outdoor activities, climbing to the top of the lighthouse, watching the loggerhead turtles, and taking a guided tour through the maritime forest. Accommodations include fully equipped rental condos, villas, cottages, and B&Bs; a two-night minimum stay is required. The ferry (☎ 910/457–5003) costs $15 per person round-trip and runs on the hour, 8–6 (except noon on weekdays), from Southport. Advance reservations are necessary for both the ferry and resort. ⊠ *Bald Head Island 28461,* ☎ *910/457–5000 or 800/432–7368,* FAX *910/457–9232,* WEB *www.baldheadisland.com. 195 condos, villas, and cottages; 25 rooms in 2 B&Bs. 5 restaurants, 18-hole golf course, 4 tennis courts, pool, boating, fishing, croquet, babysitting, concierge, business services. AE, DC, MC, V.*

Outdoor Activities and Sports

For golf the par-72 **Gauntlet at St. James Plantation** (⊠ Rte. 211, ☎ 910/253–3008 or 800/247–4806) lives up to its reputation as a challenging course.

Winnabow

12 mi north of Southport, 18 mi south of Wilmington.

Winnabow is more of a crossroads than a town to visit; the draws here are gardens and a historic site, both off Route 133 near the Cape Fear River. The house at **Orton Plantation Gardens** is not open to the public, but the 20 acres of beautiful, comprehensive gardens are great for strolling. The former rice plantation holds magnolias, ancient oaks, and all kinds of ornamental plants; the grounds are a refuge for waterfowl. Some or all of 35 movies have been made here. ⊠ *9149 Orton Rd. SE, off Rte. 133,* ☎ *910/371–6851,* WEB *www.ortongardens.com.* ☎ *$8.* ☉ *Mar.–Aug., daily 8–6; Sept.–Nov., daily 10–5.*

At **Brunswick Town State Historic Site** you can explore the excavations of a colonial town; see Fort Anderson, a Civil War earthworks fort; and have a picnic. Special events include reenactments of Civil War encampments. ⊠ *8884 St. Phillips Rd., off Rte. 133,* ☎ *910/371–6613.* ☎ *Free.* ☉ *Apr.–Oct., Mon.–Sat. 9–5, Sun. 1–5; Nov.–Mar., Tues.–Sat. 10–4, Sun. 1–4.*

Wilmington and the Cape Fear Coast A to Z

To research prices, get advice from other travelers, and book travel arrangements, visit www.fodors.com.

AIR TRAVEL

US Airways, Atlantic Southeast Airlines, and Midway serve the Wilmington International Airport.

➤ AIRPORT INFORMATION: **Wilmington International Airport** (⊠ 1740 Airport Blvd., ☎ 910/341–4125, WEB www.flyilm.com).

BOAT AND FERRY TRAVEL

A state-run car ferry connects Fort Fisher with Southport on the coast.

FARES AND SCHEDULES

➤ BOAT AND FERRY INFORMATION: **Southport–Fort Fisher Ferry** (☎ 800/ 293–3779.)

BUS TRAVEL

Greyhound/Carolina Trailways serves the Union Bus terminal.

➤ BUS INFORMATION: **Greyhound/Carolina Trailways** (☎ 800/231–2222, WEB www.greyhound.com).

EMERGENCIES

For emergency medical attention contact the Cape Fear Memorial Hospital or the New Hanover Regional Medical Center, a trauma center.

➤ EMERGENCY SERVICES: **Ambulance, police** (☎ 911). **Coast Guard** (☎ 910/343–4881).

➤ HOSPITALS: **Cape Fear Memorial Hospital** (⊠ 5301 Wrightsville Ave., ☎ 910/452–8100). **New Hanover Regional Medical Center** (⊠ 2131 S. 17th St., ☎ 910/343–7000).

OUTDOORS AND SPORTS

BEACHES

Three beaches—Wrightsville, Carolina, and Kure—are within a short drive of Wilmington, and miles and miles of sand stretch northward to the Outer Banks and southward to South Carolina. The beaches offer activities from fishing to sunbathing to scuba diving, and the towns here have a choice of accommodations. Approximately 100 points of public access along the shoreline are marked by orange-and-blue signs. Some of the smaller beaches have lifeguards on duty, and many are accessible to people with disabilities. Some fishing piers are open to the public. Camping, fishing, swimming, and picnicking are permitted at Carolina Beach State Park.

➤ CONTACTS: **Carolina Beach State Park** (☎ 910/458–8206; 910/458–7770 for marina).

BOATING

A number of hotels provide docking facilities for guests. The Wilmington area has public marinas at Carolina Beach State Park and Wrightsville Beach. Public boat access is also offered at Atlantic Marina, Masonboro Boat Yard and Marina, Seapath Transient Dock, and Wrightsville Gulf Terminal.

➤ CONTACTS: **Carolina Beach State Park** (☎ 910/458–7770). **Wrightsville Beach** (☎ 910/256–6666).

FISHING

There's surf fishing on the piers that dot the coast, and charter boats are available for off-shore fishing. Four major tournaments, all offering substantial prize money, are held each year—the Cape Fear Marlin Tournament, the Wrightsville Beach King Mackerel Tournament, the East Coast Open King Mackerel Tournament, and the U.S. Open King Mackerel Tournament.

SCUBA DIVING

Wrecks such as the World War II tanker *John D. Gill* make for exciting scuba diving off the coast. Aquatic Safaris rents equipment and leads trips.

➤ CONTACTS: **Aquatic Safaris** (✉ 5751–4 Oleander Dr., Wilmington, ☎ 910/392–4386).

SURFING

Surfing and board sailing are popular at area beaches, and rentals are available at shops in Wilmington, Wrightsville Beach, and Carolina Beach.

TOURS

From April through December Cape Fear Riverboats, Inc., runs cruises aboard a stern-wheel riverboat, the *Henrietta III,* that departs from Riverfront Park. The cost is $18–$33. Cape Fear Tours gives walking and driving tours of the Wilmington Historic District, the mansions, and the beaches. Individual tours are $20 per hour.

➤ FEES AND SCHEDULES: **Cape Fear Tours** (✉ 8112 Sidbury Rd., Wilmington, ☎ 910/686–7744). **Cape Fear Riverboats, Inc.** (✉ docked at Hilton in downtown Wilmington, ☎ 910/343–1611 or 800/676–0162).

VISITOR INFORMATION

➤ TOURIST INFORMATION: **Cape Fear Coast Convention and Visitors Bureau** (✉ 24 N. 3rd St., Wilmington 28401, ☎ 910/341–4030 or 800/222–4757, WEB www.cape-fear.nc.us). **South Brunswick Islands Chamber of Commerce** (✉ 4948 Main St., Box 1380, Shalotte 28459, ☎ 910/754–6644 or 800/426–6644, WEB www.ncbrunswick.com).

THE MOUNTAINS

Cherokee, Asheville, and the High Country

The majestic peaks, meadows, and valleys of the Appalachian, Blue Ridge, and Smoky mountains characterize the western corner of the state, which is divided into three distinct regions: the southern mountains, with the Cherokee reservation; the northern mountains, known as the High Country (Blowing Rock, Boone, Banner Elk); and the central mountains, anchored by Asheville, for decades a retreat for the wealthy and famous. National parks, national forests, handmade-crafts centers, and the Blue Ridge Parkway are the area's main draws, providing prime shopping, skiing, hiking, bicycling, camping, fishing, canoeing, or just taking in the views.

At the southern terminus of the Blue Ridge Parkway and the North Carolina entrance to the Great Smoky Mountains lies the homeland of the Eastern Band of the Cherokee Indians. Through a combination of museums, dramas, assorted outdoor attractions, and the showing of everyday living, the Cherokee attempt to explain what's precious in their Land of the Blue Mist.

The biggest city in the mountains, Asheville has a lovely landscape, a choice of hotels and restaurants, and a thriving arts community. The city's revitalized downtown has good shopping, galleries, museums, restaurants, and nightlife.

Picture-book towns such as Boone, Blowing Rock, and Banner Elk have boomed in the 30 years since the introduction of snowmaking equipment. Luxury resorts now dot the valleys and mountaintops, and you can take advantage of the many crafts shops, music festivals, and theater offerings. The passing of each season is a visual event here, and autumn is the star.

Cherokee

165 mi west of Charlotte, 50 mi west of Asheville.

The 56,000-acre Cherokee reservation is known as the Qualla Boundary, and the town of Cherokee is its capital. Truth be told, there are two Cherokees. There's the Cherokee with the sometimes tacky pop culture, designed to appeal to the masses of tourists, many of whom are visiting the nearby Great Smoky Mountains National Park. But there's another Cherokee that explores the rich heritage of the tribe's Eastern Band. Although now relatively small in number—tribal enrollment is 12,500—these Cherokee and their ancestors have been responsible for keeping alive the Cherokee culture. They are the descendants of those who hid in the Great Smoky Mountains to avoid becoming part of the Trail of Tears, the forced removal of the Cherokee Nation to Oklahoma in the 19th century. They are survivors, extremely attached to the hiking, swimming, trout fishing, and natural beauty of their ancestral homeland.

The **Museum of the Cherokee Indian,** with displays and artifacts that cover 12,000 years, is one of the best Native American museums in the United States. Computer-generated images, lasers, specialty lighting, and sound effects help re-create events in the history of the Cherokee: for example, you'll see children stop to play a butter bean game while adults shiver along the snowy Trail of Tears. The museum has an art gallery, a gift shop, and an outdoor living exhibit of Cherokee life in the 15th century. ⊠ *U.S. 441 at Drama Rd.,* ☎ *828/497–3481,* WEB *www.cherokeemuseum.org.* ⊠ *$8.* ☉ *June–Aug., Mon.–Sat. 9–8, Sun. 9–5; Sept.–May, daily 9–5.*

The **Qualla Arts and Crafts Mutual,** across the street from the Museum of the Cherokee Indian, is a cooperative that displays and sells items created by 300 Cherokee craftspeople. The store also has a large section of baskets, masks, and wood carvings. ⊠ *U.S. 441 at Drama Rd.,* ☎ *828/497–3103.* ☉ *June–Aug., daily 8–8; Sept.–Oct., daily 8–6; Nov.–May, daily 8–4:30.*

At the historically accurate, re-created **Oconaluftee Indian Village,** guides in native costumes will lead you through a village of 225 years ago while others demonstrate traditional skills such as weaving, pottery, canoe construction, and hunting techniques. ⊠ *U.S. 441 at Drama Rd.,* ☎ *828/497–2315,* WEB *www.dnet.net/~cheratt.* ⊠ *$12.* ☉ *May 15–Oct. 25, daily 9:30–5.*

Every mountain county has significant deposits of gems and minerals, and at the **Smoky Mountain Gold and Ruby Mine,** on the Qualla Boundary, you can search for gems such as aquamarines. Children love panning precisely because it can be wet and messy. Here they're guaranteed a find. Gem ore can be purchased, too: gold ore costs $5 per bag. ⊠ *U.S. 441N,* ☎ *828/497–6574.* ⌧ *$4–$10, depending on the gems.* ☉ *Mar.–Nov., daily 10–6.*

Dining and Lodging

$$–$$$ ✕ **Nantahala Village Restaurant.** This roomy rock-and-cedar restaurant with front-porch rocking chairs is about 10 mi southwest of Cherokee and is a local favorite. The food isn't fancy, but the choices—trout, chicken, country ham, and even some vegetarian options—are good and filling. Sunday brunch has some surprises, including *huevos rancheros* (tortilla with fried eggs and salsa) and eggs Benedict. ⊠ *9400 U.S. 19W, Bryson City,* ☎ *828/488–9616 or 800/438–1507. MC, V. Closed late Nov.–early Mar.*

$$$ ✕🏨 **Hemlock Inn.** Even if you're not a guest at the inn, which is built on a small mountain that overlooks three valleys, you can make a reservation for dinner ($$) Monday through Saturday and for lunch on Sunday. The fixed-price all-you-can-eat meals are prepared with regional foods, including locally grown fruits and vegetables and mountain honey. Each cozy room is decorated with antiques and crafts. ⊠ *Galbraith Creek Rd., 1 mi north of U.S. 19, Bryson City 28713,* ☎ *828/488– 2885,* FAX *828/488–8985,* WEB *www.innbrook.com/hemlock/. 29 rooms. Restaurant, recreation room. D, MC, V. Closed Nov.–mid-Apr. MAP.*

$$ 🏨 **Holiday Inn Cherokee.** Guest rooms are standard chain fare, but the staff at this well-equipped, full-service facility is very friendly. The Chestnut Tree restaurant has dinner buffets that are veritable groaning boards, and the native crafts shop, the Hunting Ground, with works by local artists, is a nice touch. ⊠ *U.S. 19, 28719,* ☎ *828/497–9181 or 800/465–4329,* FAX *828/497–5973,* WEB *www.hicherokee.com. 150 rooms, 4 suites. Restaurant, indoor pool, wading pool, sauna, recreation room, shop, playground, business services, meeting room. AE, D, DC, MC, V.*

Nightlife and the Arts

THE ARTS

Unto These Hills Outdoor Drama (⊠ Mountainside Theater on Drama Rd., off U.S. 441N, ☎ 828/497–2111, WEB www.untothesehills.com) is a colorful and well-staged history of the Cherokee from the time of Spanish explorer Hernando de Soto's visit in 1540 to the infamous Trail of Tears. It runs from mid-June to mid-August and starts at $14.

NIGHTLIFE

The 175,000-square-ft **Harrah's Cherokee Casino** (⊠ U.S. 19 off U.S. 441, ☎ 828/497–7777) has action 24 hours a day. Its 2,700 gaming machines, including video poker, video blackjack, and video craps, make it the largest casino within a 500-mi radius. The complex also has a 1,500-seat concert hall, three restaurants, and a child-care area. The casino is alcohol-free.

Outdoor Activities and Sports

FISHING

There are 30 mi of regularly stocked trout streams on the **Cherokee Indian Reservation.** To fish in tribal water, you need a tribal fishing permit, available at nearly two dozen reservation businesses. The $7 permit is valid for one day and has a creel limit of 100. For information call ☎ 828/497–5201 or 800/438–1601.

In the downtown area you can cross the Oconaluftee River on a foot-bridge to **Oconaluftee Islands Park & Trail** (✉ across from Cherokee Elementary School on U.S. 441) and walk a trail around the perimeter of the Island Park, which also has picnic facilities. The flat 1½-mi **Oconaluftee River Trail** begins at the Great Smoky Mountains National Park entrance sign on U.S. 441 (near the entrance to the Blue Ridge Parkway) and ends at the Mountain Farm Museum–Park Visitor Center. A five-minute hike from the Mingo Falls Campground area (✉ Big Cove Rd. about 4 mi north of Acquoni Rd.) will reward you with a view of the 200-ft-high **Mingo Falls.**

Great Smoky Mountains National Park

3 mi north of Cherokee.

★ Natural assets and proximity to several metro areas help make the **Great Smoky Mountains National Park** the most visited national park in the United States. No mountains in the world are older, and no place on Earth can claim such biological diversity: more than 1,600 types of wild-flowers and more than 140 species of trees flourish in this wildlife sanctuary. The Appalachian Trail runs along the crest of the mountains through the park, the largest protected land area east of the Rocky Mountains. Within its 800 square mi (276,000 acres lie in North Carolina, 244,000 in Tennessee) are 800 mi of trails, more than 600 mi of trout streams, and some 200,000 acres of virgin forest.

The Smokies are so named because of the frequently occurring smoke-like blue mist that hovers in the air and can get so dense as to obscure mountaintops. In actuality, the "smoke" occurs when vegetation releases water vapor and natural oils produced by plants into the air. Along the twists and turns of the Blue Ridge Parkway are scores of scenic overlooks, and many byways lead to areas that grip the imagination.

U.S. 441 is the only road that passes all the way through the park. Fishing permits and visitor information are available at ranger stations at the north and south entrances. Depending on your location, the **Oconaluftee Visitors Center** (☎ 828/497–1900) is the terminus of the Blue Ridge Parkway or its starting point. Adjacent to the visitor center, at mile marker 469.1, is **Mountain Farm Museum**, a re-created pioneer homestead. ✉ *107 Park Headquarters Rd., Gatlinburg, TN 37738,* ☎ *423/436–5615,* WEB *www.nps.gov/grsm.* ✆ *Free.*

Dillsboro

13 mi southeast of Cherokee on U.S. 441.

The tiny town of Dillsboro, in Jackson County, has a big reputation for good shopping, particularly if you favor folk art and crafts. The popular train rides of the **Great Smoky Mountains Railway** include six regular excursions and six special trips on diesel-electric or steam locomotives. Open-sided cars or cabooses are ideal for picture taking as the mountain scenery glides by. There's a train museum, too. ✉ *119 Front St.,* ☎ *828/586–8811 or 800/872–4681,* WEB *www.gsmr.com.* ✆ *$28–$74; some rides include a meal.* ⊙ *Mar.–Dec., call for schedule.*

Franklin

32 mi south of Cherokee on U.S. 441.

Franklin, the Macon County seat, lies at the convergence of U.S. 441, U.S. 64, and Route 28. In the 1500s Hernando de Soto came in search of gold and overlooked the wealth of gemstones for which this area is so famous. A dozen gem mines and nearly as many gem stores are nearby.

The **Scottish Tartans Museum** has the official registry of all publicly known tartans and is the only American extension of the Scottish Tartans Society. Scottish heritage can be traced in the research library. ⊠ *86 E. Main St.,* ☎ *828/524–7472,* WEB *www.scottishtartans.org.* ☜ *$1.* ☉ *Mon.–Sat. 10–5.*

Waynesville

17 mi east of Cherokee on U.S. 19.

This is where the Blue Ridge Parkway meets the Great Smokies. Pretty, arty Waynesville is the seat of Haywood County. About 40% of the county is occupied by the Great Smoky Mountains National Park, Pisgah National Forest, and the Harmon Den Wildlife Refuge.

The **Museum of North Carolina Handicrafts,** in the Shelton House (circa 1875), has a comprehensive exhibit of 19th-century heritage crafts as well as a working pioneer village and railroad memorabilia. ⊠ *307 Shelton St.,* ☎ *828/452–1551.* ☜ *$4.* ☉ *May–Oct., Tues.–Fri. 10–4.*

Cold Mountain, the vivid best-seller by Charles Frazier, has made a destination out of the real **Cold Mountain.** About 15 mi from Waynesville in the Shining Rock Wilderness Area of Pisgah National Forest, the 6,030-ft rise had stood in relative anonymity. But with the success of Frazier's book, people want to see the region that Inman and Ada, the book's Civil War–era protagonists, called home.

There are different ways to experience Cold Mountain. For a view of the splendid mass—or at least of the surrounding area—stop at any of a number of overlooks off the Blue Ridge Parkway. Try the Cold Mountain Parking Overlook, just past mile marker 411.9; the Wagon Road Gap parking area, at mile marker 412.2; or the Waterrock Knob Interpretative Station, at mile marker 451.2. You can climb the mountain, but beware, as the hike to the summit is rather strenuous. No campfires are allowed in Shining Rock, so you'll need a stove if you wish to cook. Inform the ranger station (☎ 828/877–3350) if you plan to hike or camp.

Lodging

$$$$ ⌂ **The Swag.** This exquisite, rustic inn sits high atop the Cataloochee Divide overlooking a swag—a deep depression in otherwise high ground. Its 250 wooded acres share a border with Great Smoky Mountains National Park and have access to hiking trails. Guest rooms and cabins were assembled from six authentic log structures transported here. All have rough wooden walls, exposed beams, and wooden floors and are furnished with early American crafts. A two-night minimum stay is required. ⊠ *2300 Swag Rd., 28786,* ☎ *828/926–0430 or 800/789–7672,* FAX *828/926–2036,* WEB *www.theswag.com. 16 rooms, 3 cabins. Dining room, pond, massage, sauna, badminton, croquet, racquetball, library, business services. AE, D, MC, V. Closed Nov.–Mar. FAP.*

Asheville

50 mi east of Cherokee, 115 mi west of Charlotte.

The largest and most cosmopolitan city in the mountains, Asheville has been rated America's favorite place to live among cities of its size. It has scenic beauty, a good airport and road system, a moderate four-season climate, and a thriving arts community. Banjo pickers are as revered as violinists, and mountain folks mix with city slickers. Experience the renaissance of the city's downtown, a pedestrian-friendly place with upscale shopping, art galleries, museums, restaurants, and nightlife.

Downtown Asheville is noted for its eclectic architecture. The **Battery Park Hotel** (1924) is neo-Georgian; the **Flatiron Building** (1924) is neo-classical; the **Basilica of St. Lawrence** (1912) is Spanish baroque; **Pack Place,** formerly known as Old Pack Library (1925), is in the Italian Renaissance style; the **S&W Cafeteria** (1929) is art deco. The city has the largest collection of art deco buildings in the Southeast after Miami.

The 92,000-square-ft **Pack Place Education, Arts & Science Center,** in downtown Asheville, houses the **Asheville Art Museum, Colburn Gem & Mineral Museum, Health Adventure,** and **Diana Wortham Theatre.** The **YMI Cultural Center,** also maintained by Pack Place, is across the street. ✉ 2 *S. Pack Sq., Downtown,* ☎ *828/257–4500,* WEB *www.packplace.org.* 🎫 *$6 for art museum, $4 each for other museums, $14 combination ticket.* ⊙ *June–Oct., Tues.–Sat. 10–5, Sun. 1–5; Nov.–May, Tues.–Sat. 10–5.*

Asheville's most famous son, novelist Thomas Wolfe, grew up in a 29-room Queen Anne–style home that his mother ran as a boarding-house. The home, a state historic site, burned as a result of arson. It is closed while undergoing restoration. However, the visitor center at the **Thomas Wolfe Memorial** remains open, showing a video about Wolfe and displaying photographs and other memorabilia related to his career. Some items salvaged from the house are also here. Guided tours of the house's exterior and heirloom gardens are given. ✉ *52 Market St., Downtown,* ☎ *828/253–8304.* 🎫 *$1.* ⊙ *Apr.–Oct., Mon.–Sat. 9–5, Sun. 1–5; Nov.–Mar., Tues.–Sat. 10–4, Sun. 1–4.*

★   The astonishing **Biltmore Estate,** which faces Biltmore Village, was built in the 1890s as the private home of George Vanderbilt. This 250-room French Renaissance château is America's largest private residence (some of Vanderbilt's descendants still live on the grounds but open the bulk of the home and grounds to visitors). Richard Morris Hunt designed it, and Frederick Law Olmsted landscaped the original 125,000-acre estate (now 8,000 acres). It took 1,000 men five years to complete the gargantuan project. On view are the priceless antiques and art collected by the Vanderbilts, along with 75 acres of gardens and formally landscaped grounds. You can also see the state-of-the-art winery and take Christmas candlelight tours of the house. Allow a full day to tour the house and grounds. ✉ *Exit 50 off I–40, South Metro,* ☎ *828/255–1700 or 800/624–1575,* WEB *www.biltmore.com.* 🎫 *$34; prices for special events vary.* ⊙ *Jan.–Mar., daily 9–5; Apr.–Dec., daily 8:30–5.*

The **North Carolina Arboretum,** 426 acres that were part of the original Biltmore Estate, completes Frederick Law Olmsted's dream of creating a world-class arboretum in the western part of the state. Highlights include southern Appalachian flora in stunning settings, including the Blue Ridge Quilt Garden, with bedding plants arranged in patterns reminiscent of Appalachian quilts. There is also the formal Stream Garden, which capitalizes on the Bent Creek trout stream that runs through the grounds. An extensive network of trails is available for walking or mountain biking. ✉ *100 Frederick Law Olmsted Way, 10 mi southwest of downtown Asheville, adjacent to Blue Ridge Pkwy. (near I–26 and I–40), South Metro,* ☎ *828/665–2492,* WEB *www.ncarboretum. org.* 🎫 *Free; call for group tour fees.* ⊙ *Visitor education center Mon.–Sat. 9–5, Sun. noon–5; gardens and grounds daily 8 AM–7 PM.*

OFF THE
BEATEN PATH

PENLAND SCHOOL OF CRAFTS – This world-famous institution about 45 mi northeast of Asheville on a remote mountaintop is the oldest and largest school for high-quality mixed-media arts and crafts in North America. It has classes in book and paper making, glassblowing, ceramics, textile arts, and other media. A gallery, open mid-April–early December, displays works (some are for sale; call to check hours and winter closing). Classes aren't open to the public, but you can call about a free campus tour. ⊠ *Penland Rd. off U.S. 19/23, Penland,* ☎ *828/765-2359 for school; 828/765-6211 for gallery and campus tours,* WEB *www.penland.org.*

Dining and Lodging

$$–$$$ ✕ **Café on the Square.** The local business crowd frequents this elegant and airy restaurant during lunch, but theatergoers favor it for dinner. All entrées are served with the Café salad and homemade bread. The menu's pasta dishes are particularly creative: for example, cracked-pepper fettuccine with scallops and shrimp in a white bean, tomato, and basil ragout. There's also patio dining. ⊠ *1 Biltmore Ave., Downtown,* ☎ *828/251-5565. AE, D, MC, V. Closed Sun. Nov.–May.*

$$–$$$ ✕ **The Market Place.** Clean lines, neutral colors, and brushed steel mobiles create a sophisticated style. The food offers refreshing twists on ingredients indigenous to the mountains (game and trout) and the South in general. Possible entrées are smoked trout and green-apple salad, or tenderloin of pork with a sweet-potato timbale. Iron gates open onto an exterior courtyard and dining patio. ⊠ *20 Wall St., Downtown,* ☎ *828/252-4162,* WEB *www.marketplace-restaurant.com. AE, MC, V. Closed Sun. No lunch.*

$$–$$$ ✕ **Vincenzo's.** There are two distinct halves of this pastel-hue *ristorante,* a casual trattoria downstairs and a more formal dining room upstairs. The trattoria serves an abbreviated version of the full northern Italian menu. Specialties include fillet of beef in a Gorgonzola cream sauce topped with pine nuts and caramelized shallots and chicken breast with prosciutto, sautéed spinach, and mushrooms in a sage-sherry cream sauce, served over fettuccine. The wine list is extensive. Smoking is allowed in the bistro, where you can find live music nightly. ⊠ *10 N. Market St., Downtown,* ☎ *828/254-4699. AE, D, DC, MC, V. No lunch.*

$$–$$$ ✕ **West Side Grill.** This '50s-style diner has a little bit of everything, including daily blue-plate specials, from "Mile-High" meat loaf to Southern-fried catfish. Vegetarians have a number of choices, including the focaccia veggie melt and the blackened garden burger. ⊠ *1190 Patton Ave., West Metro,* ☎ *828/252-9605. Reservations not accepted. AE, D, MC, V.*

$–$$ ✕ **Laughing Seed Café.** You'll get more than brown rice and beans at this vegetarian eatery. The extensive menu ranges from fruit drinks to sandwiches and pizzas to dinner specialties influenced by the flavors of India, China, and Morocco. Fruits and vegetables come from local organic farms during the growing season. Breads are baked daily on premises. There's outdoor dining. ⊠ *40 Wall St., Downtown,* ☎ *828/252-3445,* WEB *www.laughingseed.com. AE, D, MC, V. Closed Tues.*

$–$$ ✕ **Salsa.** In a diminutive space with a slightly retro-hippy look, you'll find spicy and highly creative Mexican and Caribbean fare in huge portions. Fire-roasted pepper tacos, black bean and goat cheese tacos, and plantains stuffed with herbs, meat, and vegetables are among the recommended entrées. Delicious desserts include caramelized mango. ⊠ *6 Patton Ave., Downtown,* ☎ *828/252-9805. AE, D, MC, V. Closed Sun.*

$$$$ ✕🏨 **Grove Park Inn Resort.** With its children's activities, special week-
★ end packages, and views of the Blue Ridge Mountains, this is Asheville's premier resort. Since the resort's opening in 1913, Henry Ford, Thomas

Edison, and Michael Jordan have stayed here. The inn is furnished with oak antiques in the arts and crafts style. Although largely underground so as not to inhibit views, it has abundant light thanks to the inspired use of skylights and natural stone. Fireplace lounges, waterfalls, plunge pools, and a juice bar complete the experience. The restaurants offer plenty of choices: for example, Horizons specializes in game dishes from ostrich to boar; you can also order free-range chicken. ⊠ *290 Macon Ave., North Metro 28804,* ☎ *828/252–2711 or 800/438–5800;* ℻ *828/253–7053 for guests; 828/252–6102 reservations,* WEB *www.groveparkinn.com. 498 rooms, 12 suites. 4 restaurants, 18-hole golf course, putting green, 9 tennis courts, indoor pool, health club, hot tub, spa, shops, 3 bars, nightclub, playground, laundry service, concierge, business services, meeting room. AE, D, DC, MC, V.*

$$$$ ✕🖫 **Inn on Biltmore Estate.** Many people who have in the past come
★ here to see this mansion have longed to lodge here overnight. In 2001 their wishes were granted when this posh ridge-top property opened. The hotel mimics the look of the Biltmore house with natural stone and copper. French manor houses inspired the interior, where windows offer mountain views. Nice touches include carriage rides around the estate and afternoon tea in the library. The dining room ($$$–$$$$) is bookended by large windows and a massive fireplace. Menus deftly blend local and international ingredients; dinner might begin with herbed goat cheese and then move on to pheasant with country ham. ⊠ *Biltmore Estate, Exit 50 off I–40, South Metro,* ☎ *800/922–0084,* ℻ *828/225–1629,* WEB *www.biltmore.com/inn. 131 rooms, 72 suites. Restaurant, room service, golf privileges, pool, health club, hot tub, mountain bikes, hiking, horseback riding, bar, library, shops, concierge, meeting rooms. AE, D, DC, MC, V.*

$$$$ ✕🖫 **Richmond Hill Inn.** Once a private residence, this elegant Victorian
★ mansion is on the National Register of Historic Places. Many rooms in the mansion are furnished with canopy beds, Victorian sofas, and other antiques, whereas the more modern cottages have contemporary pine poster beds. Gabrielle's is known for its innovative cuisine, cherry-wood paneling, and three-tier chandelier. Reservations are necessary here but not at the Arbor Grille, in a glass-enclosed sun porch. Gabrielle's is only open to the public for dinner and Sunday brunch; jacket and tie are required. ⊠ *87 Richmond Hill Dr., North Metro 28806,* ☎ *828/252–7313 or 888/742–4536,* ℻ *828/252–8726,* WEB *www.richmondhillinn.com. 24 rooms, 3 suites, 9 cottages. 2 restaurants, croquet, library, business services, meeting room. AE, MC, V. BP.*

$$$–$$$$ ✕🖫 **Haywood Park Hotel.** The lobby of this art deco downtown hotel, once a department store, has golden oak woodwork accented with gleaming brass. The suites are spacious, with baths done in Spanish marble. The hotel's elegant restaurant, 23 Page, has an oft-changing French-influenced menu. An entrée might be a grilled lamb chop with radicchio and artichoke mousse. There's live music every Friday evening during the summer. Adjoining the property is a shopping galleria. ⊠ *1 Battery Park Ave., Downtown 28801,* ☎ *828/252–2522 or 800/228–2522,* ℻ *828/253–0481,* WEB *www.haywoodpark.com. 33 suites. Restaurant, room service, exercise room, sauna, bar, shops, laundry service, concierge, business services, meeting room. AE, D, DC, MC, V. CP.*

$$$–$$$$ 🖫 **Cedar Crest Victorian Inn.** Biltmore craftspeople constructed this beautiful cottage, with its lead-glass front door and corbeled brick fireplaces, as a private residence in 1891. The lovingly restored guest rooms are furnished with period antiques. You are treated to afternoon tea, evening coffee or chocolate and to a breakfast of fruit, pastry, and coffee. It's best for older children. ⊠ *674 Biltmore Ave., South Metro 28803,* ☎ *828/252–1389 or 800/252–0310,* ℻ *828/252–7667,* WEB *www.*

cedarcrestvictorianinn.com. 9 rooms, 2 cottage suites. Croquet, business services. AE, D, DC, MC, V.

$$–$$$ 🏨 **Comfort Inn.** This chain hotel, off I–240 near the River Ridge Outlet Mall, has a fireplace in a large sitting area. Most guest rooms are standard fare, but suites have private balconies and dinette areas. A walking trail surrounds the property. Pets are allowed. ⊠ *800 Fairview Rd., South Metro 28803,* ☎ *828/298–9141,* FAX *828/298–6629,* WEB *www.choicehotels.com. 149 rooms, 28 suites. Pool, kitchenettes, exercise room, playground, business services, meeting room. AE, D, DC, MC, V. CP.*

$$ 🏨 **Hampton Inn–Biltmore Square.** You can relax beside the fire in the lobby at this motel off I–26 that's 5 mi southwest of downtown. Some guest rooms have whirlpool baths. Cookies and coffee are served every evening. ⊠ *1 Rocky Ridge Rd., South Metro 28806,* ☎ *828/667–2022 or 800/426–7866,* FAX *828/665–9680,* WEB *www.hampton-inn.com. 121 rooms. Indoor pool, exercise room, sauna, dry cleaning, laundry service, business services, meeting room, airport shuttle. AE, D, DC, MC, V. CP.*

$–$$ 🏨 **Mountaineer Inn.** A fixture along Tunnel Road, this family-owned inn is ever popular with families and others who care less about fanciness than they do about affordable, comfortable surroundings. A newer addition contains larger rooms. ⊠ *155 Tunnel Rd., Downtown 28805,* ☎ *828/254–5331 or 800/255–4080,* FAX *828/254–5331. 79 rooms. Pool, business services, meeting room. AE, D, MC, V. CP.*

Outdoor Activities and Sports

GOLF

Colony Lake Lure Golf Resort (⊠ 201 Blvd. of the Mountains, Lake Lure, ☎ 828/625–2888 or 800/260–1040), 25 mi from Asheville, has two 18-hole, par-72 courses known for their beauty. **Etowah Valley Country Club and Golf Lodge** (⊠ U.S. 64, Etowah, ☎ 828/891–7141 or 800/451–8174), about 20 mi from Asheville, has three very different (one par-72, two par-73) 18-hole courses with good package deals. **Grove Park Inn Resort** (⊠ 290 Macon Ave., North Metro, ☎ 828/252–2711 or 800/438–5800) has a beautiful par-71 course.

HORSEBACK RIDING

Trail rides are offered by stables throughout the region between April and November, including **Pisgah View Ranch** (⊠ Rte. 1, Candler, ☎ 828/667–9100), where you can gallop through the wooded mountainside. **Cataloochee Ranch** (⊠ 119 Ranch Rd. [Rte. 1], Maggie Valley, ☎ 828/926–1401 or 800/868–1401) allows riders to explore the property's mile-high vistas on horseback.

LLAMA TREKS

One-day and overnight hikes with llamas carrying your pack through local forests are arranged by **Windsong Llama Treks, Ltd.** (⊠ 120 Ferguson Ridge Rd., Clyde, ☎ 828/627–6111). **Avalon Llama Trek** (⊠ 310 Wilson Cove Rd., Swannanoa, ☎ 828/298–5637) leads trips on the lush trails of the Pisgah National Forest.

SKIING

In addition to having outstanding skiing, **Cataloochee Resort** (⊠ Rte. 1, Maggie Valley, ☎ 828/926–0285 or 800/768–0285) hosts lots of different activities for the whole family. **Fairfield-Sapphire Valley** (⊠ 4000 U.S. 64W, Sapphire Valley, ☎ 828/743–3441 or 800/533–8268) offers basic skiing despite minimal snowfall. **Wolf Laurel** (⊠ Rte. 3, Mars Hill, ☎ 828/689–4111) has night skiing and excellent snowmaking capabilities.

ARTS AND CRAFTS IN THE MOUNTAINS

A CENTURY AGO, AS YOUNG GEORGE VANDERBILT prepared to build a retreat in then-bucolic Asheville, he and an architect traveled the French countryside looking for designs that could be incorporated into the home he was going to model after a 16th-century Loire Valley château. Craftspeople labored long to create the Biltmore Mansion, including its unlikely gargoyles and grotesques.

The message is this: when it comes to arts and crafts in western North Carolina, expect the unexpected. (Note: if a place mentioned here isn't described elsewhere in the chapter, an address or telephone number is given.) There's so much more going on than first meets the eye. And that's the fun of it: the hunt. Sometimes handmade treasures are found out in the open: more than 85 crafts fairs are held annually throughout the rural 21-county region. At the **Balsam Mountain Inn** (⊠ off Rte. 23/74, Balsam, ☎ 828/456–9498), just off the Blue Ridge Parkway near Waynesville, the work of a number of artisans is tastefully showcased year-round.

More than 4,000 people here earn part or all of their living from crafts, and many of them can be found "around the bend" and in homes tucked back in forested hollows. They patiently coax form from clay and wood and metal, and they are usually happy to talk about what they do—so explore. Interesting roads that are off the map can lead to workshops. If hours are posted, however, it's best to respect them.

In the beginning it was practical function, not notions of folk art, behind all the quilting, weaving, woodworking, and pottery making. But by the late 19th-century missionaries, social workers, and women of means—Frances Goodrich and Edith Vanderbilt among them—began to recognize that the things of day-to-day life contained artistry and thus economic salvation for a beautiful but isolated and impoverished area.

Today utility and aesthetics have melded. From furnaces in the northwest counties of Mitchell and Yancey come gobs of hot liquid shaped by hand into art glass prized by collectors and dealers worldwide. Many glassblowers have perfected their métier at the prestigious Penland School of Crafts, whose courses include printmaking, wood, surface design, metals, drawing, clay, and fibers. The work of students and graduates, much of it contemporary, is on display in area galleries, including Penland's own extensive gallery shop.

In the tiny village of Crossnore, in southern Avery County, a rock cottage houses the **Crossnore School's Weaving Room** (⊠ U.S. 221, ☎ 828/733–4660). Favored here are patterns used by the early settlers of the Appalachians; however, in a nod to modernity the ladies spin with easy-care rayon and synthetics as well as with cotton, wool, and linen.

On the Cherokee Reservation, in the shadow of the Smoky Mountains, elders pass on to children the secrets of finger weaving, wood carving, and mask and beaded jewelry making. Their work, intricate and colorful and found in shops such as **Medicine Man Crafts** (⊠ U.S. 441, ☎ 828/497–2202) in downtown Cherokee, is ageless, a connective thread to a time that predates the United States by thousands of years.

Shopping

Biltmore Village (⊠ Hendersonville Rd., South Metro, ☎ 828/274–5570), on the Biltmore Estate, is a cluster of specialty shops, restaurants, galleries, and hotels in a decidedly early 20th-century-English-hamlet style. You'll find everything from children's books to music, antiques, and wearable art.

Grovewood Gallery at the Homespun Shops (⊠ 111 Grovewood Rd., North Metro, ☎ 828/253–7651, WEB www.grovewood.com), adjacent to the Grove Park Inn and established by Mrs. George Vanderbilt, sells furniture and contemporary and traditionally crafted woven goods made on the premises.

Side Trips from Asheville

Within 40 mi of Asheville are towns with parks and historic sites. Some are resort destinations in themselves.

BREVARD
40 mi southwest of Asheville on Rte. 280.

Plenty of nearby waterfalls and the **Brevard Music Center** (☎ 828/884–2011, WEB www.brevardmusic.org), which has a seven-week music festival each summer, are draws in this resort town. Nearby Pisgah National Forest has the **Cradle of Forestry in America National Historic Site** (⊠ 1001 Pisgah Hwy., ☎ 828/884–5823, WEB www.cradleofforestry.com).

☺ At **Sliding Rock** in summer you can skid 60 ft on a natural water slide. Wear old jeans and tennis shoes and bring a towel. ⊠ *Pisgah National Forest, north of Brevard, off U.S. 276,* ☎ *828/877–3265.* 🎟 *Free.* ☉ *Late May–early Sept., daily 10–5:30.*

CHIMNEY ROCK
25 mi southeast of Asheville on U.S. 64/74A.

This town is deep in the Blue Ridge Mountains. At privately owned **Chimney Rock Park** an elevator travels through a 26-story shaft of rock for a staggering view of Hickory Nut Gorge and the surrounding mountains. Trails, open year-round, lead to 400-ft Hickory Nut Falls, where *The Last of the Mohicans* was filmed. The Old Rock Café can prepare picnics to go. ⊠ *U.S. 64/74A,* ☎ *828/625–9611 or 800/277–9611,* WEB *www.chimneyrockpark.com.* 🎟 *$12.* ☉ *Daily 8:30–4:30.*

FLAT ROCK
21 mi southwest of Chimney Rock, 25 mi south of Asheville via I–26.

Flat Rock has been a summer resort since the mid-19th century. The
★ **Carl Sandburg Home National Historic Site** is the spot to which the poet and Lincoln biographer Carl Sandburg moved with his wife, Lillian, in 1945. Guided tours of their house, Connemara, where Sandburg's papers still lie scattered on his desk, are given by the National Park Service. In summer *The World of Carl Sandburg* and *Rootabaga Stories* are presented at the amphitheater. ⊠ *1928 Little River Rd.,* ☎ *828/693–4178,* WEB *www.nps.gov/carl.* 🎟 *$3.* ☉ *Daily 9–5.*

The **Flat Rock Playhouse** (⊠ 2661 Greenville Hwy., ☎ 828/693–0731, WEB www.flatrockplayhouse.org) has a high reputation for summer stock theater. The season runs from May to mid-December.

SALUDA
30 mi southeast of Asheville.

At the top of the steepest railroad grade east of the Rockies, this salubrious town along the tracks is strung with antiques and crafts shops in 19th-century brick buildings. The surrounding area has apple orchards, woods, and waterfalls.

18 mi north of Asheville via U.S. 23/19.

This town's state historic site, the **Zebulon B. Vance Birthplace,** has a reconstructed two-story log cabin and several outbuildings. This is where Vance, governor of North Carolina during the Civil War and later a U.S. senator, grew up. Crafts and chores typical of his period are often demonstrated. Picnic facilities are available. An entrance to the Blue Ridge Parkway is nearby. ⊠ *911 Reems Creek Rd. (Rte. 1103),* ☎ *828/ 645-6706.* 🎦 *Free.* ☉ *Apr.–Oct., Mon.–Sat. 9–5, Sun. 1–5; Nov.–Mar., Tues.–Sat. 10–4, Sun. 1–4.*

Lake Toxaway

40 mi southwest of Asheville.

A century ago a group called the Lake Toxaway Company created a 640-acre lake in the high mountains between Brevard and Cashiers. Nearby, a grand 500-room hotel built with the finest materials, providing the most modern conveniences, and serving European cuisine attracted many of the country's elite. That hotel is long gone, but the scenic area, which some still call "America's Switzerland," has a number of fine resorts and some of the priciest real estate in the North Carolina mountains.

Those who love nature, even if it's just looking at it, will enjoy being in this mountain wilderness. And for those to whom shopping is a sport, a number of upscale stores—many specializing in antiques and regional arts and crafts—can be found.

Lodging

$$$$ 🏨 **Earthshine Mountain Lodge.** You can have as much solitude or adventure as you want at this spacious cedar log cabin with stone fireplaces. The lodge, which sits on 70 acres midway between Brevard and Cashiers on a ridge that adjoins the Pisgah National Forest, offers horseback riding, hiking, fishing, and even an opportunity to gather berries, feed the goats, pan for gems, take guided trail rides, or master some Cherokee skills. In the evening people gather around an open fire to sing songs, square dance, or exchange stories. A minimum stay of two nights is required. ⊠ *Golden Rd., off Silversteen Rd. off U.S. 64, Box 216C, 28747,* ☎ *828/862–4207,* WEB *www.earthshinemtnlodge.com. 10 rooms. Dining room, fishing, hiking, horseback riding, baby-sitting, children's programs, meeting room. D, MC, V. FAP.*

$$$$ 🏨 **Greystone Inn.** In 1915 Savannah resident Lucy Molz built a second home in Lake Toxaway. Today the six-level Swiss-style mansion is an inn listed on the National Register of Historic Places. Guest rooms have antiques or period reproductions, and suites that border the lake of this mountain resort are modern. Rates include breakfast and dinner, afternoon tea and cake, and cocktails. The inn is open weekends only January through March. ⊠ *Greystone La., 28747,* ☎ *828/966–4700; 800/ 824–5766 outside NC,* FAX *828/862–5689,* WEB *www.greystoneinn.com. 33 rooms. Dining room, in-room VCRs, golf privileges, putting green, 5 tennis courts, pool, lake, massage, spa, dock, waterskiing, fishing, children's programs, business services. AE, MC, V. MAP.*

Hot Springs

30 mi northwest of Asheville via U.S. 23/19 and U.S. 25/70 past Marshall.

This picturesque village is a way station for hikers on the Appalachian Trail. The **Hot Springs Spa**'s mineral springs maintain a natural 100°F temperature year-round and since the turn of the 20th century have provided relief for those suffering various ailments, including rheumatism and pelvic troubles. Massage therapy is also available. ✉ *315 Bridge St.,* ☎ *828/622–7676 or 800/462–0933,* WEB *www.hotspringsspa-nc. com.* 🖙 *$10–$30 per hr, depending on time of day and number of people in tub.* ☉ *Feb.–Nov., daily 9 AM–11 PM; Dec.–Jan., hrs vary, call in advance.*

Dining and Lodging

$ ✕▥ **Bridge Street Café & Inn.** This renovated storefront, circa 1922, is right on the Appalachian Trail and overlooks Spring Creek. Upstairs are simply decorated rooms and two baths filled with antiques. One bathroom has a claw-foot tub. The café ($–$$$) downstairs has a wood-fired oven and grill from which emerge delicious pizzas. There's also a Sunday brunch. ✉ *Bridge St., Box 502, 28743,* ☎ *828/622–0002,* FAX *828/622–7282,* WEB *www.main.nc.us/bridgecafe/. 4 rooms without bath. Restaurant. AE, D, MC, V. Closed Nov.–mid-Mar.*

Blue Ridge Parkway

Entrance 2 mi east of Asheville, off I–40.

★ The beautiful **Blue Ridge Parkway** (✉ Superintendent, Blue Ridge Pkwy., 199 Hemphill Knob Rd., Asheville 28803, ☎ 828/298–0398, WEB www.nps.gov/blri) gently winds through mountains and meadows and crosses mountain streams for more than 469 mi on its way from Cherokee, North Carolina, to Waynesboro, Virginia. This is the most scenic route from Asheville to Boone and Blowing Rock. The parkway is generally open year-round but often closes during inclement weather. Maps and information are available at visitor centers along the high-way. Mile markers (MMs) identify points of interest and indicate the distance from the parkway's starting point in Virginia.

The **Folk Art Center** sells authentic mountain crafts made by members of the Southern Highland Craft Guild. ✉ *Blue Ridge Pkwy., MM 382,* ☎ *828/298–7928.* ☉ *Jan.–Mar., daily 9–5; Apr.–Dec., daily 9–6.*

☖ You can tour an underground mine or dig for gems of your own at **Emerald Village.** ✉ *McKinney Mine Rd. at Blue Ridge Pkwy., MM 334, Little Switzerland,* ☎ *828/765–6463 or 877/389–4653,* WEB *www. emeraldvillage.com.* 🖙 *Mine $4, plus cost of gem bucket chosen ($3–$100).* ☉ *June–early Sept., daily 9–6; May and early Sept.–Oct., daily 9–5.*

Linville Caverns are the only caverns in the Carolinas. The caverns go 2,000 ft beneath Humpback Mountain and have a year-round temperature of 51°F. North of Asheville, exit the parkway at mile marker 317.4 and turn left onto U.S. 221. ✉ *U.S. 221 between Linville and Marion,* ☎ *828/756–4171,* WEB *www.linvillecaverns.com.* 🖙 *$5.* ☉ *June–early Sept., daily 9–6; Apr.–May and early Sept.–Oct., daily 9–5; Nov. and Mar., daily 9–4:30; Dec.–Feb., weekends 9–4:30.*

From the **Linville Falls Visitor Center** (✉ Rte. 1, Spruce Pine, ☎ 828/ 765–1045), at mile marker 316.3, a half-mile hike leads to one of North Carolina's most photographed waterfalls. The easy trail winds through evergreens and rhododendrons to overlooks with views of the series of cascades tumbling into Linville Gorge. There are also a campground and a picnic area.

Just off the parkway at mile marker 305, **Grandfather Mountain** soars to 6,000 ft and is famous for its Mile-High Swinging Bridge, a 228-ft-long bridge that sways over a 1,000-ft drop into the Linville Valley. The **Natural History Museum** has exhibits on native minerals, flora and fauna, and pioneer life. The annual **Singing on the Mountain,** in

June, is an opportunity to hear old-time gospel music and preaching, and the **Highland Games** in July bring together Scottish clans from all over North America for athletic events and Highland dancing. ⊠ *Blue Ridge Pkwy. and U.S. 221, Linville,* ☎ *828/733–4337 or 800/468–7325,* WEB *www.grandfather.com.* 🕾 *$12.* ⊙ *Apr.–mid-Nov., daily 8–dusk; mid-Nov.–Mar., daily 8–5, weather permitting.*

Green spaces along the parkway include **Julian Price Park** (MM 295–MM 298.1), which has hiking, canoeing on a mountain lake, trout fishing, and camping. The **Moses H. Cone Park** (MM 292.7–MM 295) has a turn-of-the-20th-century manor house that's now the **Parkway Craft Center.** The center sells fine work by area craftspeople.

Dining and Lodging

$$$$ ✕🏠 **Eseeola Lodge and Restaurant.** Rebuilt in 1936 after a fire, this
★ lakeside lodge, best described as dressed-up rustic, sits 3,800 ft above sea level and is one sure way to beat summer's heat. Golf is a passion here, but the diversions are many. All rooms overlook the manicured grounds and gardens. Rich chestnut paneling and stonework grace the public areas. Entrées at the restaurant may include free-range chicken and rainbow trout; jacket and tie are required at dinner. ⊠ *175 Linville Ave., off U.S. 221, Linville 28646,* ☎ *828/733–4311 or 800/742–6717,* FAX *828/733–3227,* WEB *www.eseeola.com. 19 rooms, 5 suites, 1 cottage. Restaurant, 18-hole golf course, putting green, 8 tennis courts, pool, exercise room, boating, fishing, hiking, croquet, bar, children's programs, playground, business services. MC, V. Closed late Oct.–mid-May. MAP.*

Outdoor Activities and Sports

HIKING

More than 100 trails lead off the Blue Ridge Parkway, from easy strolls to strenuous hikes. For more information on parkway trails, contact the Blue Ridge Parkway. Another good source is *Walking the Blue Ridge: A Guide to the Trails of the Blue Ridge Parkway,* by Leonard Adkins, available at most parkway visitor center gift shops. The **Bluff Mountain Trail,** at Doughton Park (MM 238.5), is a moderately strenuous 7½-mi trail winding through forests, pastures, and valleys, and along the mountainside. Moses H. Cone Park's (MM 292.7) **Figure 8 Trail** is an easy and beautiful trail that the Cone family designed for their morning walks. The half-mile loop winds through a tunnel of rhododendrons and a hardwood forest. Those who tackle the half-mile, strenuous **Waterrock Knob Trail** (MM 451.2), near the south end of the parkway, will be rewarded with spectacular views from the 6,400-ft-high Waterrock Knob summit.

ROCK CLIMBING

One of the most challenging climbs in the country is the **Linville Gorge** (MM 317), often called "the Grand Canyon of North Carolina." Permits are available from the district forest ranger's office in Nebo (☎ 828/652–2144) or from the Linville Falls Texaco station on U.S. 221.

SKIING

Moses H. Cone Park (☎ 828/295–7591) is known for its cross-country skiing trails. On the Blue Ridge Parkway, **Roan Mountain** (☎ 615/772–3303), open daily during the winter, is famous for its deep powder. Tours and equipment are available from **High Country Ski Shop** (☎ 828/733–2008), in Pineola on U.S. 221.

Blowing Rock

86 mi northeast of Asheville, 93 mi west of Winston-Salem.

Blowing Rock, a draw for mountain visitors since the 1880s, has retained the flavor of a quiet village. About 1,000 people are permanent residents, but the population swells each summer. To ensure that the town would remain rural, the community banded together to prohibit large hotels and motels. Blowing Rock is the inspiration for the small town in resident Jan Karon's novels about country life in the fictional town of Mitford. To get here from the Blue Ridge Parkway, take U.S. 221/321 to just north of the entrance to Moses H. Cone Park.

The **Blowing Rock** looms 4,000 ft over the Johns River Gorge. If you throw your hat over the sheer precipice, it may come back to you, should the wind gods be playful. The story goes that a Cherokee man and a Chickasaw maiden fell in love. Torn between his tribe and his love, he jumped from the cliff, but she prayed to the Great Spirit, and he was blown safely back to her. ⊠ *Off U.S. 321,* ☎ *828/295-7111,* WEB *www.blowingrock.org.* 🎫 *$4.* ☉ *June–Oct., Sun.–Thurs. 8:30–7, Fri.–Sat. 8:30–8; Nov.–Dec. and Mar.–May, daily 9–5; Jan.–Feb., weekends 8–5.*

⊙ The **Tweetsie Railroad** is a popular Wild West theme park built into the side of a mountain and centered on a steam locomotive beset by robbers. A petting zoo, carnival amusements, gem panning, shows, and concessions are also here. Several of the attractions are at the top of the mountain and can be reached by foot or ski lift. ⊠ *U.S. 321/221, off Blue Ridge Pkwy., MM 291,* ☎ *828/264-9061 or 800/526-5740,* WEB *www.tweetsie-railroad.com.* 🎫 *$23.* ☉ *Early May and mid-Aug.–Oct., Fri.–Sun. 9–6; mid-May–mid-Aug., daily 9–6.*

Lodging

$$$–$$$$ 🏨 **Chetola Resort.** This small gem, named for the Cherokee word meaning "haven of rest," grew out of an early 20th-century stone-and-wood lodge. The original building now houses the resort's restaurant and meeting rooms and is adjacent to the 1988 lodge. Many guest rooms in the lodge have private balconies facing either the mountains, the lake, or both. Condominiums are spread among the hills. The property adjoins Moses H. Cone Park, with hiking trails and riding facilities. ⊠ *N. Main St., Box 17, 28605,* ☎ *828/295-5500 or 800/243-8652,* FAX *828/295-5529,* WEB *www.chetola.com. 37 rooms, 5 suites, 62 condominiums. 2 restaurants, minibars, 5 tennis courts, indoor pool, health club, hot tub, massage, boating, fishing, bicycles, racquetball, piano bar, playground, business services, meeting room. AE, D, MC, V.*

$$$–$$$$ 🏨 **Inn at Ragged Gardens.** With a grand stone staircase in the entry hall, colorful gardens, richly toned chestnut paneling, and the chestnut bark siding found on many older homes in the High Country, it's no wonder that this manor-style house in the heart of Blowing Rock gets rave reviews. You'll definitely appreciate the attention to detail: the European and American antiques blended with contemporary art and the all-hours butler's pantry. All rooms have fireplaces, and some have private balconies. It's best for older children. A two-night minimum is required on weekends. ⊠ *203 Sunset Dr., 28605,* ☎ *828/295-9703,* WEB *www.ragged-gardens.com. 6 rooms, 6 suites. Dining room, some hot tubs, meeting room. MC, V. BP.*

$$$ 🏨 **Maple Lodge Bed & Breakfast.** Blowing Rock's oldest continuously operating B&B is just off Main Street. Built in 1946, the inn has a wonderful garden, pine paneling in the foyer and twin parlors, and pine ceilings and woodwork throughout. Some rooms are small, but most can hold a queen-size bed and antique dresser, table, and chair com-

fortably. The full breakfast, served in an enclosed porch, includes delicious homemade breads and muffins. There's a two-night minimum many weekends. ⊠ *152 Sunset Dr., 28605,* ☎ *828/295–3331,* 𝖥𝖠𝖷 *828/295–9986,* 𝖶𝖤𝖡 *www.maplelodge.net. 10 rooms, 1 suite. Dining room. AE, D, MC, V. BP.*

$–$$ 🏨 **Alpine Village Inn.** This motel in the heart of Blowing Rock harks back to a simpler time. Rooms are neat and attractive in a homey way. Owners Rudy and Lynn Cutrera have decorated them with antiques, quilts, even flowers on holidays. Room refrigerators are available, and morning coffee is served. ⊠ *297 Sunset Dr., 28605,* ☎ *828/295–7206,* 𝖶𝖤𝖡 *www.alpine-village-inn.com. 15 rooms. AE, D, MC, V.*

Outdoor Activities and Sports
HORSEBACK RIDING
Blowing Rock Stables (⊠ U.S. 221, ☎ 828/295–7847) runs trail rides.

SKIING
There's downhill skiing at **Appalachian Ski Mountain** (⊠ 940 Ski Mountain Rd., ☎ 828/295–7828 or 800/322–2373).

Shopping
Bolick Pottery (⊠ Rte. 8 off U.S. 321, Lenoir, ☎ 828/295–3862), 3 mi southeast of Blowing Rock, sells mountain crafts and pottery hand-crafted by Glenn and Lula Bolick, fifth-generation potters.

Boone

8 mi north of Blowing Rock.

Boone, named for frontiersman Daniel Boone, is a city of several thousand residents at the convergence of three major highways—U.S. 321, U.S. 421, and Route 105. You'll find mountain crafts in stores and at crafts fairs here. **Mast General Store,** at the Old Boone Mercantile (⊠ 630 W. King St., ☎ 828/262–0000), is a classic general store.

Horn in the West, a project of the Southern Appalachian Historical Association, is an outdoor drama that traces the story of the lives of Daniel Boone and other pioneers, as well as the Cherokee, during the American Revolution. ⊠ *Amphitheater off U.S. 321,* ☎ *828/264–2120.* 🎫 *$12.* ☾ *Performances mid-June–mid-Aug., Tues.–Sun. at 8 PM.*

The **Appalachian Cultural Museum** at Appalachian State University examines the lives of Native Americans and African-Americans in the High Country, showcases the successes of such mountain residents as stock-car racer Junior Johnson and country singers Lula Belle and Scotty Wiseman, and exhibits a vast collection of antique quilts, fiddles, and handcrafted furniture. ⊠ *University Hall Dr., near Greene's Motel, U.S. 321,* ☎ *828/262–3117,* 𝖶𝖤𝖡 *www.museum.appstate.edu.* 🎫 *$4.* ☾ *Tues.–Sat. 10–5, Sun. 1–5.*

OFF THE
BEATEN PATH

BLUE RIDGE MOUNTAIN FRESCOES – In the 1970s North Carolina artist Ben Long and his students painted four luminous big-as-life frescoes in two churches about 45 mi northeast of Boone, in Ashe County, past Blue Ridge Parkway mile marker 258.6. *The Last Supper* is in the Glendale Springs Holy Trinity Church; the others, including *Mary, Great with Child,* are in St. Mary's Episcopal Church at Beaver Creek near West Jefferson. Signs from the parkway lead to the churches. ☎ 336/982–3076. 🎫 *Free.* ☾ *Freely accessible. Guide service available by prior arrangement.*

Dining and Lodging

$$ ✕ **Dan'l Boone Inn Restaurant.** Very near Appalachian State University, in a former hospital surrounded by a picket fence and flowers, Dan'l

Boone offers old-fashioned food served family style. Warning: the portions of fried chicken, country-style steak, mashed potatoes, scrambled eggs, bacon, and breads (to name a few) are extremely generous. (You can't get breakfast on weekdays.) A gift shop sells food items, among other things. ⊠ *130 Hardin St.,* ☎ *828/264–8657,* WEB *www. danlbooneinn.com. No credit cards. No lunch weekdays, Nov.–late May.*

$$$$ 🏨 **Hound Ears Lodge and Club.** This alpine inn, overlooking Grandfather Mountain and a lush golf course, offers amenities such as a swimming pool secluded in a natural grotto and comfortable, well-kept rooms dressed in Waverly print fabrics. From April through October the room rate for special packages includes breakfast and dinner. The dining area is open only to guests and members; reservations are required, as are a jacket and tie for dinner. ⊠ *328 Shulls Mill Rd., off Rte. 105, 6 mi from Boone, Box 188, 28605,* ☎ *828/963–4321,* FAX *828/963– 8030,* WEB *www.houndears.com. 29 rooms. Dining room, 18-hole golf course, 6 tennis courts, pool, fishing, business services, meeting room. AE, MC, V.*

$$$–$$$$ 🏨 **Lovill House Inn.** This restored two-story country farmhouse built in 1875 occupies 11 wooded acres at the western edge of Boone. On the grounds are a picnic area, gardens, and a stream with a waterfall. Some rooms have antique iron bedsteads or sleigh beds, and fireplaces. Every evening the owners host a beer and wine social hour. Kids 12 and up are welcome. ⊠ *404 Old Bristol Rd., 28607,* ☎ *828/264–4204 or 800/849–9466,* WEB *www.lovillhouseinn.com. 6 rooms. Dining room. MC, V. Closed Mar. BP.*

$–$$ 🏨 **Smoketree Lodge.** Views of Grandfather Mountain and an in-house art gallery that shows the work of local artists are the highlights of this mountain inn near the ski slopes. All rooms are fully equipped and have a kitchenette; use of the laundry facilities is free. ⊠ *11914 Rte. 105, Box 3407, 28607,* ☎ *828/963–6505 or 800/422–1880,* FAX *828/963– 7815,* WEB *www.smoketreelodge.com. 46 rooms. Room service, indoor pool, exercise room, hot tub, recreation room. AE, D, MC, V.*

Outdoor Activities and Sports

CANOEING AND WHITE-WATER RAFTING

Near Boone and Blowing Rock, the New River, a federally designated Wild and Scenic River (Classes I and II rapids) provides excitement for canoeists and rafters, as do the Watauga River, Wilson Creek, and the Toe River. One outfitter is **Wahoo's Adventures** (☎ 828/262–5774 or 800/444–7238, WEB www.wahoosadventures.com).

GOLF

Western North Carolina has many challenging courses. **Boone Golf Club** (⊠ Fairway Dr., ☎ 828/264–8760) is a good par-71 course for the whole family. **Hound Ears Club** (⊠ Rte. 105, ☎ 828/963–4312) has a par-72 18-hole course with great mountain views. **Linville Golf Club** (⊠ Linville, ☎ 828/733–4363), 17 mi from Boone, has a par-72 Donald Ross course.

Valle Crucis

5 mi south of Boone.

This tiny mountain town has the state's first rural historic district; vintage stores line the downtown streets. Everything from ribbons and overalls to yard art and cookware is sold in the **Mast General Store** (⊠ Rte. 194, ☎ 828/963–6511, WEB www.mastgeneralstore.com). Built in 1882, the store has plank floors worn to a soft sheen and an active old-timey post office. You can take a shopping break by sipping bottled soda pop while sitting in a rocking chair on the store's back porch.

Dining and Lodging

$$$–$$$$ ✕☉ **Mast Farm Inn.** You can turn back the clock and still enjoy modern amenities at this charming pastoral inn, built in the 1800s and now on the National Register of Historic Places. Rooms are in the farmhouse or in log outbuildings. The restaurant uses locally and organically grown vegetables to enhance its innovative uptown menu. Organic gardening demonstrations are held in the inn's gardens. ✉ *2543 Broadstone Rd., Box 704, 28691,* ☎ *828/963–5857,* FAX *828/963–6404 or 888/963–5857,* WEB *www.mastfarminn.com. 9 rooms, 6 cottages. Restaurant. MC, V. BP.*

Banner Elk

6 mi southwest of Valle Crucis, 11 mi southwest of Boone.

Banner Elk is a popular ski resort town surrounded by the lofty peaks of Grandfather, Hanging Rock, Beech, and Sugar mountains.

Dining and Lodging

$$$–$$$$ ✕ **Jackalope's View.** The outside is brought indoors at this restaurant, at Archer's Inn, whose plentiful and oversize picture windows upstairs and down look out over the countryside (there's also a dining deck on the lower level). Jackalope classics include Jamaican jerk shrimp over linguine and Wiener schnitzel. The chef also prepares weekly specials, such as duck confit with a raspberry glaze over matchstick vegetables and potatoes. In the summer season there's live music on weekends. ✉ *2489 Beech Mountain Pkwy.,* ☎ *828/898–9004. D, MC, V. Closed Mon.*

$$–$$$ ☉ **The Inns of Beech Mountain.** As these two Appalachian Mountain resorts—the Beech Alpen Inn and the Top of Beech Inn—are in eastern America's highest town, they overlook the slopes of the Blue Ridge Mountains. The staff is friendly at these country inns, and some rooms have fireplaces and balconies. The restaurant at Beech Alpen is open for dinner only. ✉ *700 Beech Mountain Pkwy., 28604,* ☎ *828/387–2252,* WEB *www.beechalpen.com. 48 rooms. Restaurant. AE, D, MC, V. CP.*

Outdoor Activities and Sports

CANOEING AND WHITE-WATER RAFTING

Edge of the World Outfitters (✉ Rte. 184, ☎ 828/898–9550 or 800/789–3343) offers white-water rafting, rappelling, canoeing, and snowboarding lessons in the Banner Elk area.

HORSEBACK RIDING

Banner Elk Riding Stables (✉ Rte. 184, ☎ 828/898–5424) runs trail rides.

SKIING

At 5,506 ft above sea level, **Ski Beech** (✉ Rte. 184, Beech Mountain, ☎ 828/387–2011 or 800/438–2093) is the highest resort in the eastern United States. One of the larger resorts in the area, **Sugar Mountain** (✉ off Rte. 184, Banner Elk, ☎ 828/898–4521 or 800/784–2768) has an equipment shop and lessons and tubing for the kids. A higher-end resort, **Hawksnest Golf and Ski Resort** (✉ 1800 Skyland Dr., Seven Devils, ☎ 828/963–6561 or 800/822–4295) has full snowmaking capability and challenging slopes. For **ski conditions** call ☎ 800/962–2322.

The Mountains A to Z

To research prices, get advice from other travelers, and book travel arrangements, visit www.fodors.com.

AIR TRAVEL

CARRIERS

➤ AIRLINES AND CONTACTS: **US Airways Express** (☎ 800/428–4322, WEB www.usair.com).

AIRPORTS

Asheville Regional Airport is served by Midway Connections, Atlantic Southeast Airlines, ComAir, and US Airways. US Airways Express serves the Hickory Airport, about 40 mi from Blowing Rock.

➤ AIRPORT INFORMATION: **Asheville Regional Airport** (✉ 708 Airport Rd., Fletcher, ☎ 828/684–2226, WEB www.ashevilleregionalairport. com). **Hickory Airport** (✉ U.S. 321, ☎ 828/323–7408).

BUS TRAVEL

Greyhound/Carolina Trailways serves Asheville.

➤ BUS INFORMATION: **Greyhound/Carolina Trailways** (☎ 800/231–2222, WEB www.greyhound.com).

CAR TRAVEL

I–40 runs east and west through Asheville. I–26 runs from Charleston, South Carolina, to Asheville. I–240 forms a perimeter around the city. U.S. 23–19A is a major north and west route. The Blue Ridge Parkway runs northeast from Great Smoky Mountains National Park to Shenandoah National Park in Virginia, passing Cherokee, Asheville, and the High Country. U.S. 221 runs north to the Virginia border through Blowing Rock and Boone and intersects I–40 at Marion. U.S. 321 intersects I–40 at Hickory and heads to Blowing Rock and Boone.

EMERGENCIES

Dial 911 for police and ambulance service everywhere but the Cherokee Reservation, where the police and the EMS can be reached at the numbers listed below.

➤ DOCTORS AND DENTISTS: **Mission St. Joseph's** (✉ 509 Biltmore Ave., Asheville, ☎ 828/213–1111). **Watauga Medical Center** (✉ 336 Deerfield Rd., Boone, ☎ 828/262–4100).

➤ EMERGENCY SERVICES: **Ambulance, police** (☎ 911). **Cherokee Reservation Police and EMS** (☎ 828/497–4131 for police; 828/497–6402 for EMS).

➤ HOSPITALS: **Blowing Rock Hospital** (✉ 416 Chestnut Dr., Blowing Rock, ☎ 828/295–3136). **Cannon Memorial Hospital** (✉ 805 Shawneehaw Ave., Banner Elk, ☎ 828/898–5111).

LODGING

CAMPING

You can camp at the five developed, or "frontcountry," campgrounds in the North Carolina part of Great Smoky Mountains National Park; one of these, Smokemont, accepts reservations through the National Park Service Reservation Service. The remaining four campgrounds— Balsam Mountain, Big Creek, Cataloochee, and Deep Creek—are first come, first served only. All frontcountry camping in the park is primitive by design.

➤ CONTACTS: **Great Smoky Mountains National Park Headquarters** (✉ 107 Park Headquarters Rd., Gatlinburg, TN 37738, ☎ 865/436– 1230; 865/436–1231 for inquiries about backcountry camping, WEB www. gsmnp.com). **National Park Service Reservation Service** (☎ 800/365– 2267).

OUTDOORS AND SPORTS

CANOEING AND RAFTING

For canoeing and white-water rafting in the Asheville area, the Chattooga, Nolichucky, French Broad, Nantahala, Ocoee, and Green rivers offer Class I–V rapids. One of the largest area outfitters is Nantahala Outdoor Center.

➤ CONTACTS: **Nantahala Outdoor Center** (✉ 13077 U.S. 19W, Bryson City, ☎ 828/488–2175 or 800/232–7238, WEB ww.noc.com).

GOLF

Western North Carolina offers many challenging golf courses. For a complete listing of public courses in Asheville, Black Mountain, Brevard, Hendersonville, Lake Lure, Old Fort, and Waynesville, contact the Asheville Convention and Visitors Bureau.

HIKING

Anyone into serious hiking can explore the Appalachian Trail, which runs along the crest of the Appalachian Mountains at the North Carolina–Tennessee border. It can be picked up at several points, including the Newfound Gap parking area in the Great Smoky Mountains National Park and Grandfather Mountain, where you can get trail maps.
➤ CONTACTS: **Grandfather Mountain** (☎ 828/733–4337). **Great Smoky Mountains National Park** (☎ 615/436–5615).

VISITOR INFORMATION

In Asheville, the Asheville Convention and Visitors Bureau will answer questions and provide maps. The Cherokee Visitors Center provides information on the reservation. North Carolina High Country Host is a complete information center for the High Country counties of Watauga, Ashe, and Avery. Smoky Mountain Host of North Carolina has information about the state's seven westernmost counties.
➤ TOURIST INFORMATION: **Asheville Convention and Visitors Bureau** (✉ 151 Haywood St., Box 1010, 28802, ☎ 828/258–6102 or 800/257–1300, WEB www.ashevillechamber.org). **Cherokee Visitors Center** (✉ U.S. 441 Business, ☎ 828/497–9195 or 800/438–1601, WEB www.cherokee-nc.com). **North Carolina High Country Host** (✉ 1701 Blowing Rock Rd., Boone 28607, ☎ 828/264–1299 or 800/438–7500, WEB www.visitboonenc.com). **Smoky Mountain Host of NC** (✉ 4437 Georgia Rd., Franklin 28734, ☎ 828/369–9606 or 800/432–4678, WEB www.visitsmokies.org).

NORTH CAROLINA A TO Z

To research prices, get advice from other travelers, and book travel arrangements, visit www.fodors.com.

AIR TRAVEL

AIRPORTS

Among the major airports in the state are Charlotte-Douglas International Airport, the Piedmont Triad International Airport, and the Raleigh-Durham International Airport.
➤ AIRPORT INFORMATION: **Charlotte-Douglas International Airport** (✉ 5501 Josh Birmingham Blvd., ☎ 704/359–4013). **Piedmont Triad International Airport** (✉ 6451 Bryan Blvd., Greensboro, ☎ 336/665–5666). **Raleigh-Durham International Airport** (✉ 1600 Terminal Blvd., Morrisville, ☎ 919/840–2123).

BIKE TRAVEL

North Carolina has more than 5,000 mi of mapped and signed bicycle routes, many on scenic country roads. For maps and information contact the Division of Bicycle and Pedestrian Transportation.
➤ BIKE MAPS: **Division of Bicycle and Pedestrian Transportation** (✉ Box 25201, Raleigh 27611, ☎ 919/733–2804).

BOAT AND FERRY TRAVEL

Ferries connect coastal communities. Routes and schedules are printed on the official North Carolina State Transportation Map and are available by phone from the Department of Transportation.

➤ BOAT AND FERRY INFORMATION: **Department of Transportation** (☎ 800/293–3779).

BUS TRAVEL

Greyhound/Carolina Trailways links the cities of North Carolina with major cities in the southeastern United States and links cities and towns throughout the state.
➤ BUS INFORMATION: **Greyhound/Carolina Trailways** (☎ 800/231–2222, WEB www.greyhound.com).

CAR TRAVEL

I–40 traverses the state from Asheville, in the west, to Wilmington, in the east. I–85 passes through the Triangle, the Triad, and Charlotte as it crosses from northeast to southwest. I–77 passes through the western part of the state from Virginia through Charlotte to South Carolina, and I–95 carries north–south traffic in the eastern part of the state.
➤ CONTACTS: **North Carolina Department of Transportation** (✉ Public Affairs Division, Box 25201, Raleigh 27611, ☎ 919/733–7600; 800/ 847–4862 outside NC). **Scenic Byways information** (☎ 919/733– 2920).

The speed limit on interstates varies; it's generally 65 or 70 mph. Right turns on red are permitted unless otherwise indicated.

EMERGENCIES

In almost all cities and towns dial 911 for police or ambulance in an emergency. Most hospital emergency rooms are open 24 hours a day. Smaller ones are often connected by air evacuation systems to major trauma centers.
➤ EMERGENCY SERVICES: **Ambulance, police** (☎ 911).

OUTDOORS AND SPORTS

A mandatory state license can be bought at local bait and tackle shops or over the phone (with a credit card) from the North Carolina Wildlife Commission. The cost for nonresidents is as follows: one day, $10; three days, $15; and a one-year pass $30.
➤ CONTACTS: **North Carolina Wildlife Commission** (☎ 919/715– 4091).

TRAIN TRAVEL

Amtrak offers daily service from major cities on the eastern seaboard to the state's main population centers, including Charlotte, Greensboro, Raleigh, Cary, Durham, and Southern Pines; Amtrak also offers daily service between a number of cities and towns within the state.
➤ TRAIN INFORMATION: **Amtrak** (☎ 800/872–7245, WEB www.amtrak. com).

VISITOR INFORMATION

The North Carolina Division of Tourism, Film and Sports Development has information packets and an information line. Operators will answer questions about everything from beaches to snow conditions.
➤ TOURIST INFORMATION: **North Carolina Division of Tourism, Film and Sports Development** (✉ 301 N. Wilmington St., Raleigh 27601, ☎ 919/733–4171 or 800/847–4862, FAX 919/733–8582).

7 SOUTH CAROLINA

South Carolina's scenic Lowcountry shoreline is punctuated by the historic yet vibrant port city of Charleston, known for its elegant homes and fine museums. The recreational resorts of Myrtle Beach and Hilton Head anchor each end of the coast. Columbia, the state capital, is in the fertile interior of the state, which stretches toward the Blue Ridge Mountains. Also to the west are the rolling fields of Thoroughbred Country. Upcountry South Carolina, at the northwestern tip of the state, has incredible mountain scenery and white-water rafting.

Updated by
Mary Sue
Lawrence

FROM ITS LOWCOUNTRY SHORELINE, with wide sand beaches, spacious bays, and forests of palmettos and moss-draped live oaks, South Carolina extends into an undulating interior region rich with fertile farmlands, then reaches toward the Blue Ridge Mountains, whose foothills are studded with scenic lakes, forests, and wilderness hideaways. What this smallest of Southern states lacks in land area it makes up for in diversity and enthusiasm. People here like to celebrate. Every month of the year there's a local festival that turns on regional pride, feting critters such as jumping frogs, edibles such as peaches and watermelons, or rarefied delicacies such as okra and chitterlings. South Carolina owes much of its growth to the tourism industry, which brings in billions of dollars and millions of people annually.

The historic port city of Charleston, although beautifully preserved, is not a museum city. Many of its treasured double-galleried antebellum homes are authentically furnished house museums, but just as many are homes for Charlestonians and newcomers. Residents air their quilts over piazzas, walk their dogs down cobblestone streets, and tend their famous gardens in much the same way their ancestors did 300 years ago. Locals bravely rebounded from Hurricane Hugo, which hit in 1989, to painstakingly rebuild and renovate, making the city seem as gleaming and fresh as it must have been during the 18th century. Renovation continues to expand to the far reaches of the downtown historic district, extending across the Cooper River Bridge and out of the town of Mount Pleasant into Awendaw and McClellanville. Culturally vibrant, Charleston nurtures theater, dance, music, and visual arts, showcased each spring during the internationally acclaimed Spoleto Festival USA.

Myrtle Beach is the glitzy jewel of the Grand Strand, a 60-mi stretch of wide white-sand beaches and recreational activities, especially golf, a top attraction throughout the state. South from Myrtle Beach to Georgetown, it's almost one continuous community. Georgetown itself is enjoying a healthy tourism trade, offering a small-town respite smack-dab between the urbane sophistication of Charleston and the amusement-park excitement of Myrtle Beach.

To the south, tasteful, low-key Hilton Head—divided into several self-contained resorts—also offers beautiful beaches and wonderful golf and tennis. A toll expressway handles traffic to the resort areas. Sun City, a large, newly developed retirement community, is attracting scores of fiftysomethings to the area.

Nearby is the port city of Beaufort, with lovely streets dotted with preserved 18th-century homes. A stopover popular with New York–to–Florida commuters, it's also the favorite of early retirees in search of small-town life and great deals on real estate; many have converted its historic houses into bed-and-breakfasts.

Columbia, the state capital, is a busy and historic city blessed by three rushing rivers. Besides museums and a good minor-league baseball team, the city has one of the country's top zoos and a riverside botanical garden. The presence of the University of South Carolina, with a student body of 40,000, means that nightlife and cheap and cheerful restaurants are plentiful. Nearby lakes and state parks provide abundant outdoor recreation and first-rate fishing, and the Congaree Swamp National Monument has the oldest and largest trees east of the Mississippi.

Thoroughbred Country, centered on the town of Aiken, is a peaceful area of rolling pastures where top racehorses are trained. In this part of the state, charming, old-fashioned towns such as Abbeville and Cheraw draw more and more interest for their history, abundant outdoor activities, sleepy main streets, and friendly residents.

Upcountry South Carolina, at the northwestern tip, is less visited than the rest of the state but repays time spent here with dramatic mountain scenery, excellent hiking, and challenging white-water rafting. Greenville has seen a dramatic growth spurt in the last few years. Downtown Greenville is changing rapidly; trendy cafés, shops, and boutiques, plus a newfound cultural diversity, are vivifying the city.

Pleasures and Pastimes

Beaches
South Carolina's mild climate makes the surf enjoyable from April through October. The beaches are expanses of white sand—some serene and secluded, others bustling and lined with high-rises. You can choose the high-voltage action at busy Myrtle Beach or the more low-key scene on the resort island of Hilton Head, or just stroll the sands at Huntington Beach State Park.

Dining
South Carolinians love to cook and share good food, from dishes marinated in tradition to the creatively contemporary. Lowcountry specialties include she-crab soup, stuffed oysters, and infinite variations on pecan pie. Seafood—often the fresh catch of the day—is likely to be traditionally prepared on the Grand Strand and gussied up on Hilton Head. Elsewhere in the state, try barbecue and look for various cuisines, from cosmopolitan to country cookery. And don't write off grits until you've tasted them laced with cheese and cream, topped with *tasso* (spiced ham) gravy, or folded into a veal or quail entrée.

CATEGORY	COST*
$$$$	over $25
$$$	$17–$25
$$	$10–$17
$	under $10

per person for a main course at dinner

Gardens
Gardening devotees can and do build vacations around South Carolina gardens, where camellias, azaleas, other flowering shrubs, and blooming trees abound. Along the coast are some of the nation's most famous, including Middleton Place, with the oldest landscaped garden in America; Cypress Gardens, where cypress trees tower in dark waters with azaleas on the banks; and Brookgreen Gardens, with a superb outdoor sculpture collection set amid giant oaks and colorful flowers. Inland, remarkable gardens planted with roses, irises, or mountain laurel make some small towns a worthwhile side trip. Along the way you can see peach orchards in bloom in spring.

Lodging
From predictable but dependable chains to luxurious resort hotels and quaint B&Bs, accommodations are available for every budget. Reservations are a must, especially on the coast, and prices do vary with the seasons—in fact, winter rates in Charleston and along the coast can be a pleasant surprise.

CATEGORY	CHARLESTON, HILTON HEAD, MYRTLE BEACH, AND THE COAST*	OTHER AREAS*
$$$$	over $200	over $150
$$$	$150–$200	$110–$150
$$	$100–$150	$75–$110
$	under $100	under $75

All prices are for a standard double room, excluding 7% tax.

Outdoor Activities

On South Carolina's many rivers and lakes you can indulge in boating, fly- and deep-water fishing, kayaking, sailboarding, sailing, tubing, and, in the Upcountry, white-water rafting. Canoeing is popular on waters near Columbia. Anglers frequently break records with hauls of largemouth bass, stripers, crappie, and catfish caught in Lakes Marion and Moultrie. The first passages of the Palmetto Trail—a hiking, mountain-biking, and horseback-riding trail that will eventually wind 400 mi across the state—are open: the High Hills of Santee Passage, the Lake Moultrie Passage, and the Swamp Fox Passage, in Francis Marion National Forest. Golfing, of course, reigns supreme practically year-round; the state has more than 380 courses.

Exploring South Carolina

South Carolina has three regions—its 200-mi coastline, its interior heart, and its hilly north country. Charleston and points south are the Lowcountry, distinguished by aristocratic elegance and an accent unlike any other in the South. Because Hilton Head Island, in the southern part of the state, has become world renowned as a posh resort, it is treated separately here, along with the coastal towns near it. Natives consider the upper coasts part of what they call the Pee Dee (after the Pee Dee River), but the world knows Myrtle Beach and its environs by their more famous other name—the Grand Strand. It refers to the sandy strip of beaches more than 60 mi long.

The Heartland, including the Midlands core of the state, is an eclectic collection of towns and the capital city, Columbia. It also includes Thoroughbred Country, lush pasture for Triple Crown contenders. The Upcountry, noted for mountain scenery, is in the northwest.

Great Itineraries

To enjoy South Carolina to the fullest, you need a week or more to savor the coast and visit briefly inland. But you can have a memorable experience, however fleeting, by choosing sights that strike your fancy and promising yourself to return another time for more. The Lowcountry and Charleston are priorities; every traveler to South Carolina should visit that historic city—and most want to. With a bit more time you can travel north from there to the Grand Strand or south to Hilton Head or west into the Heartland.

IF YOU HAVE 1 DAY

Spend the day in the historic district in ▣ **Charleston.** Take a carriage ride through it for a look at some of the city's most elegant homes. Then browse through the shops in the Old City Market area, where most of the carriage tours begin and end. After that, walk south along East Bay Street or any of the side streets on your way to a couple of the area's museums.

IF YOU HAVE 2–3 DAYS

▣ **Charleston** has so many charms—a rich antebellum and Civil War history, plantations and historic homes, beaches, golf, and superb restaurants—that you could spend a week here. Expand your itinerary on Day 2 by adding more sights within the historic district, by browsing along

25
11
Landrum
26
Kings Mtn.
Nat'l. Mil. Park
Table Rock
State Park
14
Gaffney
Oconee
State Park
Salem
Keowee Toxaway
State Park
85
Spartanburg
Rock Hill
76
Sumter
National
Forest
11
Lake
Keowee
Greenville
9
123
Clemson
Pendleton
385
176
72
Chester
Hartwell
Lake
29
Sumter
National
Forest
321
Wate
Lak
85
Anderson
Clinton
121
77
28
Lake
Greenwood
Newberry
26
Abbeville
Greenwood
Ninety Six
Lake
Murray
Columb
72
28
121
378
Sumter
National
Forest
25
Saluda
Congaree
Swamp
National
Monument
S
Hickory Knob
State Park
McCormick
Clarks
Hill
Lake
Trenton
20
Aiken
Montmorenci
321
78
321
20
Augusta
Bamberg
GEORGIA
Ulmers
301
Walter
Savannah R.
Yemassee
Statesboro
95
16
Bea
17
278
170
Savannah
Hilton Hea

NORTH CAROLINA

Charlotte

Fayetteville

Monroe

74

Rockingham

601

95

Pageland

Cheraw

Bennettsville

Lumberton

601

Sandhills
State Forest

9

521

74

Whiteville

Wateree
Lake

52

Darlington

41

701

1

Camden

Florence

Marion

76

Calabash

Boykin

20

501

701

9

umbia

Sumter

Woods Bay
State Park

378

Conway

Atlantic
Beach

Poinsett
State Park

261

15

95

Lake City

Windy Hill
Beach

North
Myrtle
Beach

521

Surfside
Beach

Myrtle
Beach

Manchester
State Forest

601

52

41

Murrells
Inlet

Litchfield
Beach

17

Orangeburg

301

Lake
Marion

Black R.

521

St. Stephen

Santee R.

Andrews

Pawleys
Island

Georgetown

Lake
Moultrie

45

78

26

Moncks
Corner

17

Hampton Plantation
State Park

Edisto R.

Francis Marion
National Forest

McClellanville

21

52

Cypress
Gardens

41

17/701

Cape Romain
National Wildlife
Refuge

Summerville

61

526

Mount
Pleasant

ATLANTIC
OCEAN

alterboro

ALT
17

Middleton
Place

Isle of Palms

Sullivans Is.

17

Osborn

Charleston

James Is.

ee

174

Folly Is.

Johns Is.

St. Helena
Island

Edisto
Island

Kiawah Is.

Seabrook Is.

Beaufort

21

Hunting Island
State Park

N

170

Hunting
Island

278

Parris
Island

Fripp Is.

Bluffton

Head

Daufuskie
Is.

0   100 miles

0   150 km

King Street, and by including the Charleston Museum and other nearby museums. On the afternoon of Day 2 or Day 3, you could visit Mount Pleasant, with access to Fort Sumter National Monument, nice beaches, and Boone Hall Plantation to the north. Or you could head west of the Ashley River to visit Charles Towne Landing State Park and Magnolia Plantation and Gardens.

IF YOU HAVE 5–6 DAYS
On Day 4 take a leisurely exit from Charleston along Route 61 and see **Drayton Hall** and **Middleton Place** as you make your way inland for a quick visit to ▥ **Columbia,** with its State House, historic university campus, and zoo and botanical garden. Another choice is to take U.S. 17 north toward the beaches of the **Grand Strand,** where you can stay in busy ▥ **Myrtle Beach** or the more quiet ▥ **Pawleys Island,** or south toward ▥ **Beaufort** or ▥ **Hilton Head Island.** There are beautiful gardens, stately plantations, and fine museums in both directions.

IF YOU HAVE 10 DAYS
Follow the itineraries above and then extend your time in ▥ **Columbia.** Take a canoe ride on the scenic Saluda River or down the Congaree River, and visit Congaree Swamp National Monument. Take a day trip to historic, horsey **Camden** or **Aiken** to get the flavor of other Heartland towns. On Day 8 head to the Upcountry for magnificent scenery. You can explore ▥ **Greenville,** perhaps driving north to the Cherokee Foothills Scenic Highway or to Kings Mountain National Military Park. You might head west and raft on the Chattooga River and spend your last day in ▥ **Pendleton,** with its historic district and proximity to Clemson and the South Carolina State Botanical Garden.

When to Tour South Carolina
South Carolina is loveliest in spring, when azaleas, dogwood, and other flowering bushes and trees are in bloom, but flowers brighten every season—even winter, when pansies and camellias thrive. Between mid-March and mid-April you can catch tours of private mansions in Charleston, and the city is alive with Spoleto events in May and June. Beaufort holds its Water Festival in mid-July. For price breaks on the coast, consider visiting in the off-season, October through February, but remember that some restaurants and a few attractions close around that time, and the water may be cool.

CHARLESTON

At first glimpse Charleston resembles an 18th-century etching come to life. Its low-profile skyline is punctuated with the spires and steeples of 181 churches, representing 25 denominations—the reason that Charleston, known for religious freedom during its formation, is called the Holy City. Parts of the city appear frozen in time; block after block of old downtown structures have been preserved and restored for residential and commercial use, and some brick and cobblestone streets remain. Charleston has survived three centuries of epidemics, earthquakes, fires, and hurricanes, and it is today one of the South's loveliest and best-preserved cities. It is not a museum, however: throughout the year festivals add excitement and sophistication.

Besides the historic district (which we've divided, for ease of exploration, into two parts: the area north of Broad Street, and the Battery and area south of Broad Street), a visit to the city can easily include nearby towns, plantations and outstanding gardens, and historic sites, whether in Mount Pleasant or the area west of the Ashley River.

North of Broad

To really appreciate Charleston, you must walk its streets. The downtown historic district, roughly bounded by Calhoun Street to the north, the Cooper River to the east, the Battery to the south, and Legare Street to the west, is large, with 2,000 historic homes and buildings on the southeastern tip of the Charleston peninsula. In a fairly compact area you'll find churches, museums, and lovely views at every turn.

The area north of Broad Street has some of the finest historic homes and neighborhoods in the city, including the Mazyck/Wraggborough neighborhood, where you'll find the Aiken-Rhett House. Large tracts of land made this area ideal for urban plantations during the early 1800s. Although there are a number of prerevolutionary buildings here (including the Old Powder Magazine, the oldest public building in Charleston), in general, the farther north you travel on the peninsula, the newer the development. Still, because the peninsula was built-out by the early 1900s, North of Broad is rich with historic buildings from the 19th century and can be lovely—especially since most tourists are busy conquering the waterfront area.

Numbers in the text correspond to numbers in the margin and on the Charleston map.

A Good Walk

Before you begin touring, drop by the **visitor information center** ① on Meeting Street for an overview of the city, a map, and tickets for shuttle services if you want to give your feet a break. Start across the street at the **Charleston Museum** ②, with its large decorative arts collection; then turn right on Ann Street and follow it to Elizabeth Street to the palatial **Aiken-Rhett House** ③. After touring the house, head south down Elizabeth Street and turn right on John Street for the **Joseph Manigault Mansion** ④, another impressive house museum dating to the early 1800s. Continue on John Street to reach the **American Military Museum** ⑤. Return to Meeting Street and walk south toward Calhoun Street, passing the **Old Citadel Building** ⑥, converted into an Embassy Suites. Take a left on Calhoun Street; a half block down on your left is the **Emanuel African Methodist Episcopal Church** ⑦, where slave rebellion leader Denmark Vesey was a member. From here you may want to use the shuttle bus DASH to give your feet a rest, or cross the street to Marion Square Mall for a drink and a break.

Retrace your steps on Calhoun Street (passing the Francis Marion Hotel, in the 1920s the highest building in the Carolinas) and continue two blocks west to St. Phillips Street, where you turn left to end up in the midst of the romantic campus of the **College of Charleston** ⑩, the oldest municipal college in the country. Enter through one of the gated openings on St. Phillips Street for a stroll under the many moss-draped trees. Then head east to King Street, Charleston's main shopping thoroughfare, and turn right; turn left on Hasell Street to see **Kahal Kadosh Beth Elohim Reform Temple** ⑪, a Greek Revival building. Across the street is **St. Mary's Catholic Church** ⑫. Keep walking down Hasell Street and turn right on Meeting Street. Two blocks to the south are **Market Hall** ⑭ and the bustling **Old City Market** ⑮. Now is a good time for a carriage tour, many of which leave from here. Across Meeting Street is the classy **Charleston Place** ⑬, with its graceful hotel and cluster of shops. You can browse from one end to the other, exiting on King Street.

Cross the street and walk a block down Market Street, turning left on quiet Archdale Street to wander through **St. John's Lutheran Church** ⑯ and the peaceful graveyard of the **Unitarian Church** ⑰. Turn left on Queen

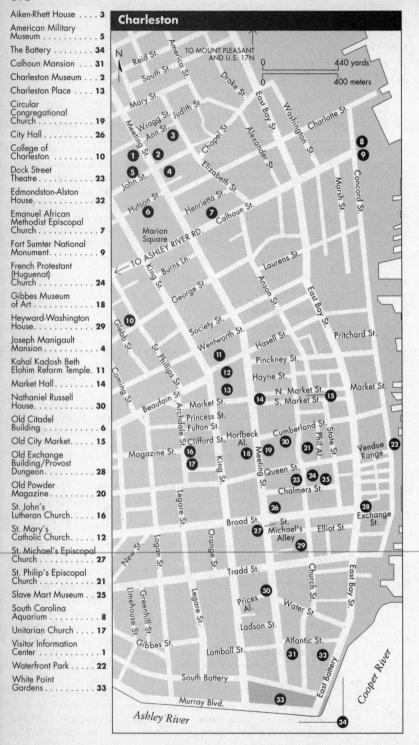

Street at the bottom of Archdale and walk two blocks to Meeting Street, where you turn left for the **Gibbes Museum of Art** ⑱, with its spectacular stained-glass dome. Across the street is the **Circular Congregational Church** ⑲. Behind it, on Cumberland Street, is the **Old Powder Magazine** ⑳. To the left as you face the building, you'll catch a glimpse of the steeple of **St. Philip's Episcopal Church** ㉑, famous in the city's skyline; it's around the corner on Church Street.

Cross over to picturesque Church Street to the **French Protestant (Huguenot) Church** ㉔ and the **Dock Street Theatre** ㉓, across the street. You might detour east here, down Queen Street and along Vendue Range to **Waterfront Park** ㉒, to relax in a bench swing overlooking beautiful river views, dramatic fountains, and a fishing pier.

TIMING

Set aside from two to four hours for this walk, depending on your pace. Most of the house-museum tours last about 40 minutes, so you might choose the two or three that interest you most. Charleston rickshaws (bicycle-powered two-seaters), which can take you anywhere downtown for $6, can ease the trip back.

Sights to See

③ Aiken-Rhett House. This stately 1819 mansion, with its original wallpaper, paint colors, and some of its furnishings, was the headquarters of Confederate general P. G. T. Beauregard during his 1864 Civil War defense of Charleston. The house, kitchen, slave quarters, and work yard are maintained much as they were when the original occupants lived here, making this one of the most complete examples of African-American urban life of the period. ⊠ 48 Elizabeth St., Upper King, ☎ 843/723–1159, WEB www.historiccharleston.org. ☞ $7; combination ticket with Nathaniel Russell House $12. ☉ Mon.–Sat. 10–5, Sun. 2–5.

⑤ American Military Museum. The museum displays hundreds of uniforms and artifacts from all branches of service, beginning with the Revolutionary War. Its collections also include antique toy soldiers, war toys, miniatures, and weaponry. ⊠ 44 John St., Upper King, ☎ 843/723–9620. ☞ $5. ☉ Mon.–Sat. 10–6, Sun. 1–6.

★ ② Charleston Museum. Founded in 1773, the country's oldest city museum is in a contemporary complex. The 500,000 items in the collection—in addition to Charleston silver, fashions, toys, snuffboxes, and the like—include objects relating to natural history, archaeology, and ornithology. Its South Carolina decorative arts holdings are extraordinary. The Discover Me Room, designed just for children, has computers and other hands-on exhibits. Two historic homes—the **Joseph Manigault Mansion** and the **Heyward-Washington House**—are owned and managed by the museum. ⊠ 360 Meeting St., Upper King, ☎ 843/722–2996, WEB www.charlestonmuseum.com. ☞ $8; museum and houses $18; 2 of the 3 sights $12. ☉ Mon.–Sat. 9–5, Sun. 1–5.

⑬ Charleston Place. The city's only world-class hotel, this Orient-Express property is flanked by a complex of upscale boutiques and specialty shops. Peek into the lobby or have cocktails or tea in the intimate Lobby Lounge. Entrances for the garage and reception area are on Hasell Street between Meeting and King streets. ⊠ 130 Market St., Market area, ☎ 843/722–4900.

⑲ Circular Congregational Church. The corners of this unusual Romanesque church were rounded off, they say, so the devil would have no place to hide. Simple but pretty, it has a beamed, vaulted ceiling. ⊠ 150 Meeting St., Market area, ☎ 843/577–6400. ☉ Call for tour schedule.

⑩ College of Charleston. The lovely, tree-shaded campus of this college, founded in 1770, has a graceful main building, the Randolph House (1828), designed by Philadelphia architect William Strickland. It's a romantic backdrop for the Cistern, often used as a grassy stage for concerts and other activities. Within the college, centered at the corner of George and St. Phillips streets in what was once a school for freed slaves, is the **Avery Research Center for African-American History and Culture,** which traces the heritage of Lowcountry African-Americans. Civil Rights activist Cleveland Seller's personal letters, telegrams, newspaper clippings, and other papers—one of the best series of manuscript collections documenting the Civil Rights movement—is here. ⊠ *Avery Research Center, 125 Bull St., College of Charleston Campus,* ☎ *843/953–7609,* WEB *www.cofc.edu/INSERT TILDEaveryrsc.* ⬚ *Free.* ☉ *Mon.–Sat. noon–5, mornings by appointment.*

㉓ Dock Street Theatre. Built on the site of one of the nation's first playhouses, the building combines the reconstructed early Georgian playhouse and the preserved Old Planter's Hotel (circa 1809). The theater, which offers fascinating backstage views, welcomes visitors except when technical work for a show is under way. ⊠ *135 Church St., Market area,* ☎ *843/720–3968.* ⬚ *Free tours; call ahead for ticket prices and performance times.* ☉ *Weekdays 10–4.*

❼ Emanuel African Methodist Episcopal Church. Home of the South's oldest A.M.E. congregation, the church had its beginnings in 1818. It was closed in 1822 when authorities learned that Denmark Vesey had used the sanctuary to plan his slave insurrection, but the church reopened in 1865 at the present site. ⊠ *110 Calhoun St., Upper King,* ☎ *843/722–2561.* ☉ *Daily 9–4.*

㉔ French Protestant (Huguenot) Church. This church is the only one in the country still using the original Huguenot liturgy, which can be heard in a special service held each spring. ⊠ *110 Church St., Market area,* ☎ *843/722–4385.* ☉ *Weekdays 10–12:30 and 2–4.*

⑱ Gibbes Museum of Art. The collections of American art include notable 18th- and 19th-century portraits of Carolinians and an outstanding group of more than 400 miniature portraits. Don't miss the miniature rooms—intricately detailed with fabrics and furnishings and nicely displayed in shadowboxes inset in dark-paneled walls—or the Tiffany-style stained-glass dome in the rotunda. ⊠ *135 Meeting St., Market area,* ☎ *843/722–2706,* WEB *www.gibbes.com.* ⬚ *$5.* ☉ *Tues.–Sat. 10–5, Sun.–Mon. 1–5.*

NEED A BREAK? Just across the street from the Gibbes Museum, **Joseph's** (⊠ 129 Meeting St., Market area, ☎ 843/958–8500) serves a great Southern breakfast, lovely lunch, and super Sunday brunch in its courtyard garden.

❹ Joseph Manigault Mansion. A National Historic Landmark and an outstanding example of neoclassical architecture, this home was designed by Charleston architect Gabriel Manigault in 1803 and is noted for its carved-wood mantels and elaborate plasterwork. Some furnishings are British and French, but most are Charleston antiques; some rare tricolor Wedgwood pieces are noteworthy. ⊠ *350 Meeting St., Upper King,* ☎ *843/723–2926,* WEB *www.charlestonmuseum.com.* ⬚ *$7; museum and houses $18; 2 of the 3 sights $12.* ☉ *Mon.–Sat. 10–5, Sun. 1–5.*

⑪ Kahal Kadosh Beth Elohim Reform Temple. Considered one of the nation's finest examples of Greek Revival architecture, this temple was built in 1840 to replace an earlier one—the birthplace of American reform Judaism in 1824—that was destroyed by fire. ⊠ *86 Hasell St., Market area,* ☎ *843/723–1090,* WEB *www.kkbe.org.* ☉ *Weekdays 10–noon.*

⑭ Market Hall. Built in 1841 and modeled after the Temple of Nike in Athens, this imposing landmark, now open after a five-year renovation, includes the **Confederate Museum,** where the Daughters of the Confederacy preserve and display flags, uniforms, swords, and other Civil War memorabilia. ⊠ *188 Meeting St., Market area,* ☎ *843/723–1541,* ☞ *$5.* ☉ *Mon–Sat. 10–4, Sun. 1–4.*

⑥ Old Citadel Building. Built in 1822 to house state troops and arms, this fortresslike building—now the Embassy Suites Historic Charleston—faces Marion Square. This is where the Carolina Military College—the Citadel—had its start. (The Citadel is now on the Ashley River.) ⊠ *Upper King.*

☕ ⑮ Old City Market. A series of low sheds that once housed produce and fish markets, this area is often called the Slave Market, although Charlestonians dispute that slaves ever were sold there. It now has restaurants, shops, gimcracks and gewgaws for children, vegetable-and-fruit vendors, and local "basket ladies" weaving and selling sweet-grass, pine-straw, and palmetto-leaf baskets—a craft passed down through generations from their West African ancestors. ⊠ *Market St. between Meeting and E. Bay Sts., Market area.* ☉ *Daily 9–sunset, hrs may vary.*

⑳ Old Powder Magazine. This structure was built in 1713 and used during the Revolutionary War. It is now a museum with costumes, armor, and other artifacts from 18th-century Charleston, plus a fascinating audiovisual tour. ⊠ *79 Cumberland St., Market area,* ☎ *843/805–6730,* WEB *www.historiccharleston.org.* ☞ *Free.* ☉ *Apr.–Oct., Mon.–Sat. 10–5, Sun. 2–5.*

⑯ St. John's Lutheran Church. This Greek Revival church was built in 1817 for a congregation that was established in 1742. Notice the fine craftsmanship in the delicate wrought-iron gates and fence. Musicians may be interested in the 1823 Thomas Hall organ case. ⊠ *5 Clifford St., Market area,* ☎ *843/723–2426,* WEB *www.stjohns-lutheran.org.* ☉ *Weekdays 9:30–3:30.*

⑫ St. Mary's Catholic Church. Established in 1839, this pretty white-pillared church is the earliest Roman Catholic church in the Carolinas and Georgia. Beautiful stained glass, wall paintings, and an enchanting cemetery tucked between stone walls are highlights. ⊠ *89 Hasell St., Market area,* ☎ *843/722–7696.* ☉ *By appointment.*

㉑ St. Philip's Episcopal Church. The graceful late-Georgian church is the second on its site; the congregation's first building burned down in 1838. You find the burial places of Charlestonians in the graveyard on the church side of the street; "foreigners" (including John C. Calhoun, who was from the faraway location of Abbeville, South Carolina) lie in the graveyard on the other side. ⊠ *146 Church St., Market area,* ☎ *843/722–7734.* ☉ *By appointment.*

㉕ Slave Mart Museum. Here—at a spot where slaves were once bought and sold—exhibits highlight the African-American experience in Charleston, from slavery to emancipation and reconstruction, and, finally, to the civil rights movement. ⊠ *6 Chalmers St., Market area.* ☉ *Mon.–Sat. 9–5.*

⑰ Unitarian Church. Completed in 1787, this church was remodeled in the mid-19th century using plans inspired by the Chapel of Henry VII in Westminster Abbey. The Gothic fan-tracery ceiling was added during that renovation. An entrance to the church grounds is on 161½–163 King Street. The secluded and romantically overgrown graveyard invites contemplation. ⊠ *8 Archdale St., Market area,* ☎ *843/723–4617 weekdays 8:30–2:30.* ⊙ *Sept.–May, 11 AM service.*

❶ **Visitor Information Center.** The center gives a fine introduction to the city and sells tickets for shuttle services. Garage parking is $1 per hour; the first hour is free if you purchase a $2 shuttle pass. Take time to see *Forever Charleston,* an insightful 20-minute film. For $32.95 you can also buy a Charleston Heritage Passport, good for admission at Gibbes Museum of Art, Nathaniel Russell House, Edmondston-Alston House, Aiken-Rhett House, Drayton Hall, and Middleton Place. ⊠ *375 Meeting St., Upper King,* ☎ *843/853–8000 or 800/868–8118.* WEB *www.charlestoncvb.com.* 🎞 *Film $2.50.* ⊙ *Mar.–Oct., daily 8:30–5:30; Nov.–Feb., daily 8:30–5; shows daily 9–5 on the ½ hr.*

㉒ **Waterfront Park.** A sprinkle from the park's interactive fountain will refresh you on hot summer days. Here you'll also find swings, a fishing pier, picnic tables, and gardens overlooking Charleston Harbor. It's at the foot of Vendue Range, along the east side of Charleston Harbor. *Market area,* ☎ *843/724–7321.* 🎞 *Free.* ⊙ *Daily 6 AM–midnight.*

NEED A BREAK?	With a great view of the harbor and Waterfront Park, the **Rooftop Lounge at Vendue Inn** (⊠ 19 Vendue Range, Market area, ☎ 843/577–7970 or 800/845–7900) serves drinks and appetizers alfresco.

The Battery and South of Broad

Along the Battery, on the point of a narrow peninsula bounded by the Ashley and Cooper rivers, handsome mansions surrounded by gardens face the harbor. Their distinctive look is reminiscent of the West Indies: before coming to the Carolinas in the late 17th century, many early British colonists had first settled on Barbados and other Caribbean isles, where they'd built houses with high ceilings and broad piazzas at each level to catch the sea breezes. In Charleston they adapted these designs. One type—narrow two- to four-story "single houses" built at right angles to the street—emerged partly because buildings were taxed according to the length of their frontage.

Heavily residential, the area south of Broad Street has many beautiful private homes, almost all of which have a plaque with a short written description of the home's history. You might get a peek at tucked-away English-style gardens, too. An open gate in Charleston once signified that all were welcome to venture inside for a closer look at the owner's garden. Open gates are rare today, but keep an eye out, as you never know when you'll get lucky.

Numbers in the text correspond to numbers in the margin and on the Charleston map.

A Good Walk

Start at the top of Broad Street at the **Old Exchange Building/Provost Dungeon** ㉘, which held prisoners during the American Revolution. Two blocks down Broad Street are the Four Corners of Law, including **City Hall** ㉖, with some historical displays and portraits, and **St. Michael's Episcopal Church** ㉗, the city's oldest surviving church. In the famously affluent South of Broad neighborhood are several of the city's lavish house museums. The **Heyward-Washington House** ㉙ is a block south of Broad Street on Church Street. Next to it is picturesque Cabbage

ANTEBELLUM CHARLESTON: THE GOLDEN YEARS

CHARLESTON, CALLED CHARLES TOWNE until the British left in 1783, boomed with the plantation economy in the years before the Civil War. South Carolina's rice, indigo, and cotton crops produced an extraordinary concentration of wealth, enriching a few hundred plantation owners, merchants, and shippers. Rice was the most profitable export in large part because the enormous labor necessary to grow the rice was supplied by slaves. Cotton, too, was a huge moneymaker; by the outbreak of the Civil War, in 1861, cotton accounted for 57% of the nation's exports.

From Charleston's beginnings the planter aristocracy set out to entertain itself in style, seeking a social and cultural lifestyle to match its financial success. By the mid-17th century the city had a thriving musical community. The first playhouse, the original Dock Street Theatre, was open for business. There were dances and concerts; the town attracted some of the most important performers in colonial America. During the 1770s there were more than 23 singing and dancing masters teaching in the city, which also had a reputation for turning out the Colonies' best Shakespearean productions.

The city was known for its talented goldsmiths, silversmiths, gunsmiths, tobacconists, brewers, and cabinetmakers, and was one of the best shopping towns in North America. Immigrants and others seeking religious freedom poured into Charleston. More than 200 private residences were built during this boom. Although Charleston had half the population of New York during the early 1770s, its annual export trade exceeded the tonnage that passed through New York's port.

Until the Civil War Charleston's fortunes continued to grow. The city's native sons played a huge part in the forming of the new national government; four Charlestonians signed the U.S. Constitution. Writers and artists filled the city. Charlestonian Robert Mills, who designed the Washington Monument, also designed many buildings in Charleston. George Washington toured Charleston in 1791, staying in many of the city's now-historic homes.

Charleston thrived as the social and cultural center of planter families. The social season, from late January to March, was defined by balls, dinners, masquerades, concerts, plays, and horse races. The elite and their slaves moved from the plantations to their Charleston residences, embellished with silk curtains, Dutch linens, French china, English silver, and lavish ornamental gardens. They commissioned famous portrait artists and European craftsmen and gave extravagant dinners where guests were served by black slaves. Lowcountry gentlemen joined private clubs and favored foxhunts, races, and gambling. Lowcountry sons traveled to England for their education. By the 1840s construction pervaded the city: City Hall was under renovation, the Battery was being made into a city park, and such buildings as the four-story Charleston Hotel had become part of the emerging cityscape. By 1850 the city's population had grown to nearly 43,000.

When the Union-held Fort Sumter was bombarded on April 11, 1861, signaling the beginning of the Civil War, Charlestonians celebrated. But the merriment, along with the years of splendor and luxury, was soon over; the collapse of slavery ended the plantation system, sending much of the state's economy into depression.

Row, the inspiration for Catfish Row in *Porgy and Bess*. The **Nathaniel Russell House** ㉚ and the **Calhoun Mansion** ㉛ are about two blocks apart on Meeting Street. Around the corner is the **Edmondston-Alston House** ㉜, overlooking Charleston's famous **Battery** ㉞ and Charleston Harbor. A park bench in the shade of **White Point Gardens** ㉝, so named because of the bleached whiteness of oyster shells left here by Native Americans, is a splendid spot for a rest. From here go north along the Cooper River by shuttle, car, or rickshaw to the **South Carolina Aquarium** ⑧. Next door, at the Fort Sumter Visitor Education Center, at Liberty Square, you can catch the ferry for a harbor ride to **Fort Sumter National Monument** ⑨.

TIMING

Plan to spend from two to four hours doing this walk, depending on your pace and which buildings you visit. A trip to the aquarium can add two or so hours, as will a trip to Fort Sumter; you may wish to split the trip into two half-days.

Sights to See

㉞ **The Battery.** This sea wall and promenade has sweeping views of Charleston Harbor. ⊠ *Murray Blvd., South of Broad.*

㉛ **Calhoun Mansion.** Opulent by Charleston standards, this is a no-holds-barred example of Victorian taste. Built in 1876, this 24,000-square-ft mansion is full of ornate plasterwork and fine wood moldings and has a 75-ft dome ceiling. ⊠ *16 Meeting St., South of Broad,* ☎ *843/ 722–8205.* ≅ *$15.* ☉ *Feb.–Dec., Wed.–Sun. 10–4.*

㉖ **City Hall.** The intersection of Meeting and Broad streets is known as the Four Corners of Law, representing the laws of nation, state, city, and church. On the northeast corner is the graceful City Hall, dating from 1801. The second-floor council chambers has historical displays and portraits, including John Trumbull's 1791 satirical portrait of George Washington and Samuel F. B. Morse's likeness of James Monroe. ⊠ *80 Broad St., South of Broad,* ☎ *843/577–6970 or 843/724– 3799.* ≅ *Free.* ☉ *Weekdays 10–5.*

OFF THE BEATEN PATH **COLONIAL LAKE –** Joggers, walkers, and folks looking for a tranquil city spot flock to this small man-made lake circled by a wide sidewalk, trees, and benches. In the late 19th century Colonial Common, as it was called at the time, was a popular gathering place for Victorian Charleston. Today it is surrounded by stately Victorian buildings. ⊠ *Ashley and Rutledge Aves. to the east and west, Broad and Beaufain Sts. to the north and south, South of Broad,* ☎ *843/724–7327.*

㉜ **Edmondston-Alston House.** With commanding views of Charleston Harbor, this imposing home was built in 1825 in late-federal style and transformed into a Greek Revival structure during the 1840s. It is tastefully furnished with antiques, portraits, Piranesi prints, silver, and fine china. ⊠ *21 E. Battery, South of Broad,* ☎ *843/722–7171,* WEB *www. middletonplace.org.* ≅ *$8; combination ticket with Middleton Place $27.* ☉ *Tues.–Sat. 10–4:30, Sun.–Mon. 1:30–4:30.*

★ ♻ ⑨ **Fort Sumter National Monument.** It was here, on a man-made island in Charleston Harbor, that Confederate forces fired the first shot of the Civil War, on April 12, 1861. After a 34-hour bombardment Union forces surrendered and Confederate troops occupied Sumter, which became a symbol of Southern resistance. The Confederacy held the fort, despite almost continual bombardment, for nearly four years, and when it was finally evacuated, it was a heap of rubble. Today National Park Service rangers conduct free guided tours of the restored structure, which includes a free **museum** (☎ 843/883–3123) with historical displays. The fort is accessible only by boat; ferries depart from Patriots Point or the **Fort Sumter Visitor Center at Liberty Square**, next to the South Carolina Aquarium, which contains exhibits on the introduction of the war. ✉ *340 Concord St., Upper King,* ☎ *843/727–4739 for visitor center; 843/881–7337 or 800/789–3678 for Fort Sumter Tours Inc.,* WEB *www.nps.gov/fosu.* ✍ *Museum free, ferry fare $11.* ⊙ *Tours Apr.–early Sept., 9:30, noon, 2:30, and 4; early Sept.–Mar., 9:30, noon, and 2:30.*

㉙ Heyward-Washington House. Built in 1772 by rice king Daniel Heyward, this home was the backdrop for DuBose Heyward's book *Porgy*, which was the basis for the beloved folk opera *Porgy and Bess*. The neighborhood, known as Cabbage Row, is central to Charleston's African-American history. President George Washington stayed in the house during his 1791 visit. It is full of fine period furnishings by such local craftsmen as Thomas Elfe, and its restored 18th-century kitchen is the only one in Charleston open to visitors. ✉ *87 Church St., South of Broad,* ☎ *843/722–0354,* WEB *www.charlestonmuseum.com.* ✍ *$8; museum and houses $18; 2 of 3 sights $12.* ⊙ *Mon.–Sat. 10–5, Sun. 1–5.*

★ ㉚ Nathaniel Russell House. One of the nation's finest examples of Adam-style architecture, the Nathaniel Russell House was built in 1808. The interior is distinguished by its ornate detailing, its lavish period furnishings, and the "flying" circular staircase that spirals three stories with no apparent support. ✉ *51 Meeting St., South of Broad,* ☎ *843/724–8481,* WEB *www.historiccharleston.org.* ✍ *$7, combination ticket with Aiken-Rhett House $12.* ⊙ *Mon.–Sat. 10–5, Sun. 2–5.*

☺ ㉘ Old Exchange Building/Provost Dungeon. Originally a customs house, this building was used by the British to house prisoners during the Revolutionary War. Today a tableau of lifelike mannequins recalls this era. ✉ *122 E. Bay St., South of Broad,* ☎ *843/727–2165,* WEB *www. oldexchange.com.* ✍ *$6.* ⊙ *Daily 9–5.*

㉗ St. Michael's Episcopal Church. Modeled after London's St. Martin-in-the-Fields and completed in 1761, this is Charleston's oldest surviving church. Its steeple clock and bells were imported from England in 1764. ✉ *14 St. Michael's Alley, South of Broad,* ☎ *843/723–0603,* WEB *www.stmichaelschurch.net.* ⊙ *Weekdays 9–5, Sat. 9–noon.*

| NEED A BREAK? | On your way down Broad Street toward Church Street, duck into the dark-paneled, tin-ceiling **Blind Tiger Pub** (✉ 38 Broad St., South of Broad, ☎ 843/577–0088) for a drink or beer on the patio out back, or a meal from the Four Corners Cafe next door. |

★ ☺ ⑧ South Carolina Aquarium. The 322,000-gallon Great Ocean Tank has the tallest aquarium window in North America. Exhibits display more than 10,000 living organisms, representing more than 500 species. You travel through the five major regions of the Southeast Appalachian Watershed as found in South Carolina: the Blue Ridge Mountains, the Piedmont, the coastal plain, the coast, and the ocean. The little ones can pet stingrays at one touch tank and horseshoe crabs and conchs at another. ✉ *3250 Concord St., Upper King,* ☎ *843/720–1990 or 800/722–6455,* WEB *www.scaquarium.org.* ✍ *$14.* ⊙ *July–Aug., daily 9–7; Mar.–June and Sept.–Oct., daily 9–5; Nov.–Feb., daily 10–5.*

☺ ㉝ White Point Gardens. Pirates once hung from gallows here; now this park, with a gazebo, Charleston benches, and views of the harbor and Fort Sumter, is the number one marriage site in the city. Children love to climb on the cannon and cannonball replicas. ✉ *Murray Blvd. and E. Battery, South of Broad,* ☎ *843/724–7327.* ⊙ *Weekdays 9–5, Sat. 9–noon.*

Mount Pleasant and Vicinity

East of Charleston across the Cooper River Bridge, via U.S. 17N, is the town of Mount Pleasant, named not for a mountain or a hill but for a plantation in England from which some of the area's settlers hailed. In its Old Village neighborhood are antebellum homes and a sleepy, old-time town center that has a drugstore with an old-fashioned soda fountain. Along Shem Creek, where the local fishing fleet brings in the daily catch, are several seafood restaurants. Other attractions in the area are museums, plantations, and, farther north, the Cape Romain National Wildlife Refuge.

A Good Tour

There's enough adventure here to stretch over a number of days, especially if you're a war history buff. On the first day you might drive to **Patriots Point,** veering right from the Cooper River Bridge onto Coleman Boulevard in the direction of Sullivan's Island and the Isle of Palms. Later, continue along Coleman Boulevard and, just after crossing the boat-lined docks and restaurants at Shem Creek, turn right at Whilden Street for a drive through the Old Village. Returning to Coleman Boulevard, you'll pass the Common, a cluster of shops on your left. Stop here for the **Museum on the Common,** featuring the *Hurricane Hugo Revisited* exhibit. Follow the signs to **Fort Moultrie.** Spend the rest of the day relaxing on the beach or bicycling through Sullivan's Island, a residential community of early 20th-century beach houses, or the Isle of Palms, which has a pavilion and more abundant parking.

On another day, drive out U.S. 17N 8 mi to **Boone Hall Plantation** and its famous Avenue of Oaks, stopping at nearby **Charles Pinckney National Historic Site,** with interpretations of African-American life on the plantation. Bring a picnic and rent bikes at **Palmetto Islands County Park,** across Boone Hall Creek from the plantation; you'll need a swimsuit for Splash Island, a mini–water park. Another option is a ferry ride and visit to Bull Island, part of the **Cape Romain National Wildlife Refuge,** one of the nation's most pristine wildlife areas. The Sewee Visitor & Environmental Education Center (on U.S. 17, 35 mi north of Charleston) has information and exhibits on the refuge as well as live birds of prey, red wolves, and trails.

TIMING

You need three days to see all the attractions here; if you have one day or less, choose a few based on your interests.

Sights to See

★ **Boone Hall Plantation.** This plantation is approached along one of the South's most majestic avenues of oaks, which was the model for the grounds of Tara in *Gone With the Wind.* You can tour the first floor of the classic columned mansion, which was built in 1935, incorporating woodwork and flooring from the original house. The primary attraction is the grounds, with formal azalea and camellia gardens, as well as the original slave quarters—the only "slave street" still intact in the Southeast—and the cotton-gin house used in the made-for-television movies *North and South* and *Queen.* ✉ *1235 Long Point Rd., off U.S. 17N, Mount Pleasant/East Cooper,* ☎ *843/884–4371.* 🖾 *$12.50.* ☉ *Apr.–early Sept., Mon.–Sat. 8:30–6:30, Sun. 1–5; early Sept.–Mar., Mon.–Sat. 9–5, Sun. 1–4.*

NEED A BREAK?   Driving north of Mount Pleasant along U.S. 17, you'll see **basket ladies** at roadside stands. If you have the heart to bargain, you *may* be able to purchase the baskets at somewhat lower prices than in Charleston. But remember that you are buying a nearly lost art, and sweet grass is no longer plentiful in the wild.

Cape Romain National Wildlife Refuge. A grouping of barrier islands and salt marshes, this 60,000-acre refuge is one of the most outstanding in the country. At the **Sewee Visitor & Environmental Education Center** you can view exhibits about the refuge and arrange to take a ferry to Bull Island for a day visit. The island is a nearly untouched wilderness; the beach here, strewn with bleached driftwood, is nicknamed Bone Beach. ⊠ *5821 U.S. 17N, Awendaw,* ☎ *843/928–3368.* 🎟 *Free.* ☉ *Daily 9–5.*

Charles Pinckney National Historic Site. Across the street from Boone Hall, this is the only protected remnant of the country estate of Charles Pinckney, drafter and signer of the Constitution. A self-guided tour explores many fascinating interpretations of African-American life, including the plantation owner–slave relationship. You can also tour an 1820s tidewater cottage. ⊠ *1254 Long Point Rd., off U.S. 17N, Mount Pleasant/East Cooper,* ☎ *843/881–5516,* ℻ *843/881–7070,* 🕸 *www.nps.gov/chpi.* 🎟 *Free.* ☉ *Daily 9–5.*

☾ **Fort Moultrie.** Here Colonel William Moultrie's South Carolinians repelled a British assault in one of the first Patriot victories of the Revolutionary War. Completed in 1809, this is the third fort on this site at **Sullivan's Island,** which you'll reach on Route 703 off U.S. 17N (8 mi southeast of Charleston). A 20-minute film tells the history of the fort. ⊠ *W. Middle St., Mount Pleasant/East Cooper Sullivan's Island,* ☎ *843/883–3123.* 🎟 *$2.* ☉ *Daily 9–5.*

☾ **Museum on the Common.** This small museum has an outdoor maritime museum and a Hurricane Hugo exhibit prepared by the South Carolina State Museum; it shows the 1989 storm damage through video and photos. ⊠ *217 Lucas St., Mount Pleasant/East Cooper, Shem Creek Village, Mount Pleasant,* ☎ *843/849–9000.* 🎟 *Free.* ☉ *Mon.–Sat. 10–4.*

☾ **Palmetto Islands County Park.** You'll find a Big Toy playground, 2-acre pond, paved trails, an observation tower, marsh boardwalks, and a "water island" at this park across Boone Hall Creek from Boone Hall Plantation. Bicycles and paddleboats can be rented in season. ⊠ *Long Point Rd. (½ mi past Boone Hall Plantation), Mount Pleasant/East Cooper,* ☎ *843/884–0832.* 🎟 *$2.* ☉ *Apr. and Sept.–Oct., daily 9–6; May–Aug., daily 9–7; Nov.–Feb., daily 10–5; Mar., daily 10–6.*

★ ☾ **Patriots Point.** Tours are available on all vessels here at the world's largest naval and maritime museum, now houses the Medal of Honor Society. Berthed here are the aircraft carrier USS *Yorktown,* the World War II submarine USS *Clamagore,* the destroyer USS *Laffey,* the nuclear merchant ship *Savannah,* and the Coast Guard cutter *Ingham,* responsible for sinking a U-boat during World War II. The film *The Fighting Lady* is shown regularly aboard the *Yorktown,* and there is a Vietnam exhibit. ⊠ *Foot of Cooper River Bridge, Mount Pleasant/East Cooper,* ☎ *843/884–2727,* 🕸 *www.state.sc.us/patpt.* 🎟 *$11.* ☉ *Early Sept.–Mar., daily 9–6:30; Apr.–early Sept., daily 9–7:30.*

West of the Ashley River

A Good Tour

The sights covered here are each a few miles apart along Ashley River Road, Route 61, which begins a few miles northwest of downtown Charleston over the Ashley River Bridge. Still, you'll need time to see them all. One day you could spend a few hours exploring **Charles Towne Landing State Park,** veering off Route 61 onto Old Towne Road (Route 171); then finish your day at **Middleton Gardens.** Another day you might tour the majestic simplicity of **Drayton Hall** before continuing on to **Magnolia Plantation and Gardens** and all their splendor.

TIMING

Nature and garden enthusiasts can easily spend a full day at Magnolia Gardens, Middleton Gardens, or Charles Towne Landing State Park, so budget your time accordingly. Spring is a peak time for the gardens, although they are lovely throughout the year.

Sights to See

★ ♻ **Charles Towne Landing State Park.** Commemorating the site of the original 1670 Charleston settlement, this park on Route 171 has a reconstructed village and fortifications, English park gardens with bicycle trails and walkways, and a replica 17th-century vessel moored in the creek. In the animal park native species roam freely—among them alligators, bison, pumas, bears, and wolves. Bicycle and kayak rentals and cassette and tram tours are available. The park has begun a $5 million renovation that includes a comprehensive archaeological dig and a new visitor center–museum. ⊠ *1500 Old Towne Rd., West Ashley,* ☎ *843/852–4200,* WEB *www.southcarolinaparks.com.* ⌨ *$5.* ☉ *Late May–early Sept., daily 9–6; early Sept.–late May, daily 9–5.*

★ **Drayton Hall.** Considered the nation's finest example of unspoiled Georgian-Palladian architecture, this mansion is the only plantation house on the Ashley River to have survived the Civil War. A National Historic Landmark, built between 1738 and 1742, it is an invaluable lesson in history as well as in architecture. Drayton Hall has been left unfurnished to highlight the original plaster moldings, opulent hand-carved woodwork, and other ornamental details. Connections, an African-American focus presentation offered before the tour, is fascinating. You will learn about the conditions under which slaves were brought from Africa and can view copies of documents recording the buying and selling of local plantation slaves. ⊠ *3380 Ashley River Rd., 13 mi north of Charleston, West Ashley,* ☎ *843/766–0188,* WEB *www.draytonhall.org.* ⌨ *$12.* ☉ *Guided tours Mar.–Oct., daily 10–4; Nov.–Feb., daily 10–3.*

♻ **Magnolia Plantation and Gardens.** The 50-acre informal garden, begun in 1685, has a huge collection of azaleas and camellias. A tram will take you for an overall tour with three stops. You can canoe through the 125-acre Waterfowl Refuge, explore the 30-acre **Audubon Swamp Garden** along boardwalks and bridges, or walk or bicycle more than 500 acres of wildlife trails. Tours of the manor house, built during Reconstruction, depict plantation life. The grounds also hold a petting zoo and a miniature-horse ranch. ⊠ *3550 Ashley River Rd., just north of Drayton Hall, West Ashley,* ☎ *843/571–1266 or 800/367–3517,* WEB *www.magnoliaplantation.com.* ⌨ *$12; house tour $7 extra; nature tram $6 extra; nature boat tour $5 extra; swamp garden $6; canoe and bike rentals.* ☉ *Daily 8–5:30.*

★ ♻ **Middleton Place.** The nation's oldest landscaped gardens, dating from 1741, are magnificently ablaze with camellias, magnolias, azaleas, roses, and flowers of all seasons planted in floral *allées* and terraced lawns and around ornamental lakes. Much of the mansion was destroyed during the Civil War, but the south wing has been restored and houses impressive collections of silver, furniture, paintings, and historic documents. In the stable yard craftspeople use authentic tools and equipment to demonstrate spinning, blacksmithing, and other domestic skills from the plantation era. Farm animals, peacocks, and other creatures roam freely. The Middleton Place restaurant serves Lowcountry specialties for lunch daily; a gift shop carries local arts, crafts, and souvenirs. Also on the grounds is a modern Danish-style inn (access to the gardens is included in the room price) with floor-to-ceiling windows dramatizing views of the Ashley River; here you can sign up for kayaking and biking tours. ⊠ *Ashley River Rd. (4 mi north of Magnolia Plantation), West Ashley,* ☎ *843/556–6020 or 800/782–3608,* WEB *www.middletonplace.org.* 🖘 *$15; house tours $8 extra.* ☉ *Daily 9–5; house tours Tues.–Sun. 10–4:30, Mon. 1:30–4:30.*

OFF THE
BEATEN PATH

AMERICAN CLASSIC TEA PLANTATION – On a small rural island about 20 mi southwest of Charleston on Route 700 is the country's only commercial tea plantation. Tours run from May through October and cover tea history, harvesting, and production and include a discussion with the plantation's official tea taster. The tour ends with tea and cookies.. ⊠ 6617 Maybank Hwy., Wadmalaw Island, ☎ 800/443–5987. 🖘 Free. ☉ May–Oct., 1st Sat. each month 10–1:30.

🕙 **ANGEL OAK –** This magnificent live oak has a massive canopy that creates 17,000 square ft of shade. Long a favorite with local children because of its bending branches that slope gently, armlike to the ground, Angel Oak is believed to be more than 1,400 years old. It's about 12 mi southwest of Charleston off Route 700. ⊠ 3688 Angel Oak Rd., Johns Island, ☎ 843/559–3496. 🖘 Free. ☉ Daily 9–4:45.

🕙 **CAW CAW INTERPRETIVE CENTER –** Once part of a 1700s rice plantation, this 650-acre cypress swamp park has 8 mi of historical and interpretive trails that include a 1,200-ft marsh boardwalk, informative and well-executed exhibits on rice cultivation, Gullah storytelling, and African-American music and craft demonstrations, and an in-depth documentation of the vital role slaves played in the rice fields. It's about 15 mi west of Charleston on U.S. 17. ⊠ 5200 Savannah Hwy., Ravenel, ☎ 843/889–8898, WEB www.ccprc.com/cawcaw.htm. 🖘 $4. ☉ Nov.–Feb., Tues.–Sun. 9–5; Mar.–Apr. and Sept.–Oct., Tues.–Sun. 9–6; May–Aug., Tues.–Sun. 8–7.

Dining

She-crab soup, sautéed shrimp and grits, variations on pecan pie, and other Lowcountry specialties are served all over the Charleston area— as are creative contemporary dishes crafted by local chefs. Outstanding eateries, from seafood houses to elegant French restaurants, make Charleston a favorite for gastronomes. Trendy Mount Pleasant, across the East Cooper Bridge, has a number of good restaurants.

Contemporary

$$$–$$$$ ✕ **Circa 1886.** If you've got an occasion for champagne cocktails and foie gras, celebrate at this formal, conducive-to-conversation dining room in a carriage house behind the Wentworth Mansion. Grilled antelope loin with sweet-potato spoon bread and chocolate Bailey's Irish cream soufflé are the signature dishes. ⊠ *149 Wentworth St., Market area,* ☎ *843/853–7828. AE, D, DC, MC, V. No lunch.*

$$$–$$$$ ✕ **McCrady's.** This elegant restaurant, in a 1778 tavern, has locals rav-
★ ing over its potato gnocchi, tuna tartare, grouper with a creamy leek sauce and truffle oil, herb-marinated rack of lamb with mint drizzle, and bitter-chocolate bread pudding. The dining room is elegant and somewhat formal; the long bar has cozy booths. ⊠ *2 Unity Alley, Market area,* ☎ *843/577–0025. AE, MC, V. No lunch.*

$$$-$$$$ ✕ **Peninsula Grill.** Surrounded by walls covered in olive-green velvet,
  ★   black-iron chandeliers, and 18th-century-style portraits, diners at this
             busy spot in the Planters Inn can feast on such delights as lobster cit-
             ron, rabbit loin wrapped in veal bacon with tapenade linguine and mus-
             tard vinaigrette, and New Zealand benne-seed-encrusted rack of lamb
             with wild mushroom potatoes and coconut-mint pesto. ✉ *112 N.
             Market St., Market area,* ☎ *843/723–0700. AE, D, DC, MC, V. No
             lunch. Jackets essential.*

   $$$ ✕ **Cypress.** From the owners of Magnolias and Blossom Cafe comes
             this sleek restaurant in a renovated 1834 brick-wall building, now very
             groovy with rust-color leather booths, a ceiling with circular lights that
             change color, and an entire "wine wall" of 4,000 bottles under glass.
             Here you'll find not only wonderful vino, but also a fabulous arugula
             salad with apples, Gorgonzola and pecans; green tea-smoked duck; and
             hickory-grilled fillet with a house-made Boursin cheese and Madeira
             sauce. If you've forgotten the jacket, dine upstairs. ✉ *167 E. Bay St.,
             Market area,* ☎ *843/727–0111. AE, D, DC, MC, V. No lunch.*

    $$ ✕ **Sermet's Corner.** Colorful, bold artwork by chef Sermet Aslan dec-
             orates the walls of this lively eatery. The Mediterranean-influenced menu
             has *panini* (grilled Italian sandwiches), seafood, and flavorful pastas.
             The poached pear salad and lavender pork are favorites. ✉ *276 King
             St., Market area,* ☎ *843/853–7775. AE, MC, V.*

French

  $$$$ ✕ **Robert's of Charleston.** A classically trained singer and chef, Robert
             offers a special experience: four rich, generously portioned courses (scal-
             lop mousse with lobster sauce, duckling with grilled vegetables, roast
             tenderloin with bordelaise sauce, and dessert) with lovely wines, im-
             peccable service, and the best of Broadway tunes in a warm, intimate
             dining room. ✉ *182 E. Bay St., Market area,* ☎ *843/577–7565. MC,
             V. Closed Sun.–Wed. No lunch.*

$$-$$$ ✕ **39 Rue de Jean Bar Cafe.** In classy, traditionally French style—
             gleaming wood, white-papered tables, and booths—the trendy set
             dines late (until 1 AM, except Sunday) on wonderful mussels, steak frites,
             scallops St. Jacques, and even sushi. It's noisy and happening, but there's
             a quiet back room. ✉ *39 John St., Upper King,* ☎ *843/722–8881. AE,
             D, DC, MC, V. No lunch weekends.*

  $-$$ ✕ **Gaulart and Maliclet Café.** This casual, chic eatery serves Continental
             dishes—breads and pastries, soups, salads, sandwiches, and specials
             such as seafood Normandy and chicken sesame. ✉ *98 Broad St.,
             South of Broad,* ☎ *843/577–9797. AE, D, MC, V. Closed Sun. No din-
             ner Mon.*

Italian

$$$-$$$$ ✕ **Fulton Five.** There are just 15 tables in this romantic restaurant on
             a side road off King Street. The chartreuse walls and antique brass ac-
             cents provide the perfect environment for savoring northern Italian spe-
             cialties, such as risotto, lemon sherbet with Campari, and antipasto
             Spoleto (mozzarella and prosciutto wrapped in a romaine lettuce leaf
             and drizzled with olive oil and diced tomatoes). ✉ *5 Fulton St., Mar-
             ket area,* ☎ *843/853–5555. AE, DC, MC, V. Closed Sun. and late Aug.–
             1st wk Sept. No lunch.*

$$-$$$ ✕ **Il Cortile del Re.** Great wines, hearty soups and pastas, and lovely
             cheeses and breads make it feel just like Tuscany here. Tucked off King
             Street behind a women's clothing shop, this hard-to-find spot has a cozy
             back room and a romantic courtyard with a crumbling brick wall. ✉
             193 King St., Market area, ☎ *843/853–1888. AE, DC, MC, V. Closed
             Sun.–Mon. No lunch Thurs.–Sat.*

Charleston Dining and Lodging

Lowcountry

\$\$–\$\$\$\$ ✕ **Slightly North of Broad.** This high-ceiling former warehouse with
★ brick-and-stucco walls has several seats looking directly into the exposed kitchen (great for single diners). Chef Frank Lee's inventive
dishes include grilled barbecued tuna with fried oysters and sautéed
squab with coriander. You can order most items as either a small plate
or a main course. The extensive wine list is moderately priced. A sister restaurant, **Slightly Up the Creek** (⊠ 130 Mill St., Mt. Pleasant, ☎
843/884–5005; no lunch; brunch only on Sun.), at Shem Creek in Mount
Pleasant, has waterfront views and more seafood dishes. ⊠ *192 E. Bay
St., Market area,* ☎ *843/723–3424. Reservations not accepted for
lunch. AE, D, DC, MC, V. No lunch weekends.*

\$\$–\$\$\$ ✕ **Carolina's.** This lively, casual bistro, styled in black and white, with
terra-cotta tiles and 1920s French posters, has long been a favorite.
Fans return for the "appeteasers" such as Crowder pea cakes (made
with Crowder peas, spices, egg, and bread crumbs) and fried calamari,
plus smoked baby-back ribs and pasta with crawfish and tasso. Dinner entrées are selections from the grill, including pork tenderloin with
Jamaican seasoning and salmon with cilantro, ginger, and lime butter.
⊠ *10 Exchange St., South of Broad,* ☎ *843/724–3800. Reservations
essential. D, MC, V. No lunch.*

Lowcountry/Southern

\$\$\$–\$\$\$\$ ✕ **Anson.** After an afternoon of strolling through the Old City Mar-
ket, you can walk up Anson Street to this softly lighted, gilt-trimmed
dining room. Framed by about a dozen French windows, Anson's has
elegant booths anchored by marble-top tables. New South specialties
include shrimp and grits, fried corn-bread oysters, and barbecued
grouper. The she-crab soup is some of the best around. ⊠ *12 Anson
St., Market area,* ☎ *843/577–0551. AE, D, DC, MC, V. No lunch.*

\$\$\$–\$\$\$\$ ✕ **Charleston Grill.** Its clubby chairs and dark paneling create a com-
★ fortably elegant venue for chef Bob Waggoner's famously fabulous new
South cuisine. Dishes include lump crab cake over yellow tomato
coulis, venison tenderloin with caramelized mushrooms and truffle potatoes, zucchini blossoms stuffed with lobster mousse, and beef medallions over garlic grits. Many nights there's live jazz. ⊠ *224 King St.,
Charleston Place Hotel, Market area,* ☎ *843/577–4522. AE, D, DC,
MC, V.*

\$\$\$–\$\$\$\$ ✕ **High Cotton.** Feast on spit-roasted and grilled meats and fish in this
elegant and airy, brick-walled eatery studded with palm trees. Weeknight
specials are great deals; at the popular bar there is live jazz. The chocolate soufflé with blackberry sauce and the praline soufflé are fabulous.
⊠ *199 E. Bay St., Market area,* ☎ *843/724–3815. AE, D, DC, MC,
V. No lunch weekdays.*

\$\$\$–\$\$\$\$ ✕ **Magnolias.** Locals love this popular place, in an 1823 warehouse,
★ with a magnolia theme evident in its vivid paintings, etched glass,
wrought iron, and candlesticks. The uptown down-South cuisine shines
with its specialties: egg roll stuffed with chicken and collard greens with
a spicy mustard sauce and sweet pepper purée. Equally innovative appetizers include seared yellow-grits cakes with tasso gravy, yellow corn
relish, and sautéed greens. You may also want to try the **Blossom Café**
(⊠ 171 E. Bay St., Market area, ☎ 843/722–9200), owned by the same
people but with a more Continental menu, including pizzas cooked in
a wood-burning oven, pastas, and fish. ⊠ *185 E. Bay St., Market area,*
☎ *843/577–7771. Reservations essential. AE, DC, MC, V.*

\$\$–\$\$\$ ✕ **Elliott's on the Square.** Come to this bright and cheerful restaurant
if you have a hankering for Southern Sunday-dinner-style entrées for
lunch and dinner, including black-eyed pea cakes, fried chicken, barbecued salmon over grits, and butter pound cake. The food may be

down-home, but the service is not. ⊠ *387 King St., Francis Marion Hotel, Upper King,* ☎ *843/724–8888. AE, D, DC, MC, V.*

$$–$$$ ✕ **J. Bistro.** Funky steel cutouts liven up the outside and inside walls, and the lighting is whimsical—hanging low over tables lined up against a banquette. A varied list of appetizers and small plates makes this a great place to graze. Choose from such innovations as steamed lobster wontons, grouper with a champagne-crabmeat cream sauce, and pecan-crusted catfish over grits. The lamb chops are superb. It's about 7 to 10 mi from town. ⊠ *819 Coleman Blvd., Mount Pleasant/East Cooper,* ☎ *843/971–7778. Reservations essential. AE, MC, V.* ◷ *Closed Mon. No dinner Sun. No lunch.*

$–$$$ ✕ **Hominy Grill.** Locals lunch and brunch at this breezy café-style restaurant. Although a bit off the beaten path (a few blocks east of King Street), it's worth a special trip. The young chef's Southern upbringing is evident in everything from the vegetable plate (collards, squash casserole, black-eyed pea cakes with guacamole, and mushroom hominy) to the pimento cheese sandwich and the turkey club with homemade french fries. The avocado and *wehani* rice (a clay-colored, aromatic variety of brown rice) salad with grilled vegetables is a refreshing don't-miss in summer. Leave room for the excellent buttermilk pie or bread pudding. ⊠ *207 Rutledge Ave., Upper King,* ☎ *843/937–0930. AE, MC, V. No dinner Sun.*

$–$$$ ✕ **Sticky Fingers.** Specializing in ribs six ways (Memphis style wet and dry, Texas style wet and dry, Carolina sweet, and Tennessee whiskey) and barbecue, this family-friendly restaurant has locations downtown and in Mount Pleasant and Summerville. Tuesday night is children's night, with supervised games and cartoons in a playroom. ⊠ *235 Meeting St., Market area,* ☎ *843/853–7427 or 800/671–5966;* ⊠ *341 Johnnie Dodds Blvd., Mount Pleasant/East Cooper,* ☎ *843/856–9840;* ⊠ *1200 N. Main St., Summerville,* ☎ *843/875–7969. AE, DC, MC, V.*

$–$$ ✕ **Alice's Fine Foods.** The food Southerners crave is here in its origi-
★ nal, beloved form: baked or fried chicken, ribs, fried fish, and other entrées come with a choice of three home-cooked vegetables and side dishes, including green beans, collard greens, red rice, macaroni-and-cheese pie, okra and tomatoes, lima beans, rice and gravy, yams, and squash. The tone here is very casual, and the buffet is cafeteria-style. ⊠ *468–470 King St., Upper King,* ☎ *843/853–9366. MC, V.*

$–$$ ✕ **Boulevard Diner.** There are no frills at this simple diner with booths and a counter and booths where the service is friendly and attentive, and the food is quite decent. Among the winners are: the daily variety of homemade veggies, the fried eggplant-and-blue-cheese sandwich, and the Cajun meatloaf and chili. ⊠ *409 W. Coleman Blvd., Mount Pleasant/East Cooper,* ☎ *843/216–2611. MC, V.* ◷ *Closed Sun.*

Middle Eastern

$ ✕ **Doe's Pita Plus.** This is a favorite spot, at lunch in particular, among locals working downtown. Among the best-sellers: pitas stuffed with chicken salad, Greek salad, or avocado salad, pita chips, hummus, meat pies, tabbouleh. There's a simple grouping of small tables and chairs, as well as some outdoor seating. ⊠ *334 E. Bay St., Market area,* ☎ *843/577–3179. AE. No dinner weekends.*

Seafood

$$–$$$ ✕ **Boathouse Restaurant.** Large portions of fresh seafood at reason-
★ able prices make both locations of the Boathouse Restaurant wildly popular. The crab dip, fish specials, and lightly battered fried shrimp and oysters are irresistible. Entrées come with nice helpings of mashed potatoes, grits, collard greens, or blue-cheese coleslaw. The original Isle of Palms location is right on the water. ⊠ *101 Palm Blvd., Isle of Palms,*

☎ *843/886–8000;* ✉ *14 Chapel St., Upper King,* ☎ *843/577–7171.*
Reservations essential. AE, DC, MC, V.

$$–$$$ ✕ **The Wreck.** Dockside and full of wacky character, this spot serves
up such traditional dishes as boiled peanuts, fried shrimp, shrimp
pilaf, deviled crab, and oyster platters. They weren't kidding with the
name—expect a shabby, candlelighted screened-in porch and small dining area. Nonetheless, it has a kind of seaside-joint charm. ✉ *106 Had-
drell St., Mount Pleasant/East Cooper,* ☎ *843/884–0052. Reservations
not accepted. No credit cards.*

Lodging

Rates tend to be highest during the spring and fall (except at resort
areas, when summer is high season) and during special events, including the Spring Festival of Houses and Spoleto—when reservations
are essential.

Hotels and Motels

$$$$ 🏨 **Best Western King Charles Inn.** This inn in the historic district is a
cut above the typical chain, with a welcoming lobby and sitting area
and spacious rooms furnished with 18th-century period reproductions. ✉ *237 Meeting St., Market area 29401,* ☎ *843/723–7451 or
800/528–1234,* 𝖥𝖠𝖷 *843/723–2041,* 𝖶𝖤𝖡 *www.kingcharlesinn.com. 91
rooms. Restaurant, in-room data ports, pool, free parking. AE, D, DC,
MC, V.*

$$$$ 🏨 **Charleston Place.** This Orient-Express property, a graceful low-rise
★ structure in the historic district, is surrounded by upscale boutiques
and specialty shops. The lobby has a magnificent handblown Venetian-
glass chandelier, an Italian marble floor, and antiques from Sotheby's.
Rooms are furnished with period reproductions, linen sheets and robes,
and fax machines. Overall, this hotel is simply world class. ✉ *130 Market St., Market area 29401,* ☎ *843/722–4900 or 800/611–5545,* 𝖥𝖠𝖷
843/724–7215, 𝖶𝖤𝖡 *www.charlestonplacehotel.com. 400 rooms, 40
suites. 2 restaurants, minibars, 2 tennis courts, indoor pool, hot tub,
health club, spa, bar, lobby lounge, concierge, concierge floor, business
services, meeting rooms. AE, D, DC, MC, V.*

$$$–$$$$ 🏨 **Embassy Suites Historic Charleston.** The courtyard of the Old Citadel
military school where cadets once marched is now a skylighted atrium
with stone floors, armchairs, palm trees, and a fountain. The restored
brick walls of the breakfast room and some guest rooms in this con-
temporary hotel contain original gun ports, reminders that the 1822
building was originally a fortification. Teak and mahogany furniture,
safari motifs, and sisal carpeting recall the British colonial era. Break-
fast and evening refreshments are complimentary. ✉ *341 Meeting St.,
Upper King 29403,* ☎ *843/723–6900 or 800/362–2779,* 𝖥𝖠𝖷 *843/723–
6938,* 𝖶𝖤𝖡 *www.embassysuites.com. 153 suites. Restaurant, room ser-
vice, some in-room hot tubs, outdoor hot tubs, microwaves, refriger-
ators, pool, gym, lounge, shop, meeting rooms, business services. AE,
D, DC, MC, V. BP.*

$$$–$$$$ 🏨 **Hampton Inn–Historic District.** This downtown chain has hardwood
★ floors and a fireplace in the elegant lobby, guest rooms with period re-
productions, and a courtyard garden. It's also conveniently near a
DASH shuttle stop. ✉ *345 Meeting St., Upper King 29403,* ☎ *843/
723–4000 or 800/426–7866,* 𝖥𝖠𝖷 *843/722–3725,* 𝖶𝖤𝖡 *www.hamptoninn.
com. 166 rooms, 5 suites. Some refrigerators, some microwaves, pool,
meeting rooms. AE, D, DC, MC, V. CP.*

$$$–$$$$ 🏨 **HarborView Inn.** Overlooking the harbor and Waterfront Park,
this inn is close to most downtown attractions. Calming earth tones
and rattan are abundant; high ceilings, four-poster beds, and sea-grass
rugs complete the Lowcountry look. Some of the rooms are in a for-

mer 19th-century shipping warehouse with exposed brick walls; some have fireplaces and whirlpool tubs. Afternoon wine and cheese as well as evening cookies are included. ⊠ *2 Vendue Range, Market area 29401,* ☎ *843/853–8439 or 888/853–8439,* FAX *843/853–4034,* WEB *www.charlestownmanagement.com/hvi. 51 rooms, 1 suite. Some in-room hot tubs, in-room data ports, concierge, business services. AE, D, DC, MC, V. CP.*

$$$–$$$$ ⊞ **Mills House Hotel.** Antique furnishings and period furnishings give this luxurious Holiday Inn property plenty of charm. It's a reconstruction of an old hostelry on its original site in the historic district, and although rooms are small and a bit standard, the hotel has a lounge with live entertainment and a nice dining room. ⊠ *115 Meeting St., Market area 29401,* ☎ *843/577–2400 or 800/874–9600,* FAX *843/722–0623,* WEB *www.millshouse.com. 199 rooms, 16 suites. Pool, restaurant, room service, bar, lounge, concierge, concierge floor, business services, meeting rooms, parking (fee). AE, D, DC, MC, V.*

$$–$$$$ ⊞ **Doubletree Guest Suites Historic Charleston.** Across from the City Market, this hotel has a restored entrance portico from an 1874 bank, a refurbished 1866 firehouse, and three lush gardens. The spacious suites, all decorated with 18th-century reproductions and canopy beds, have wet bars with microwave ovens and refrigerators. ⊠ *181 Church St., Market area 29401,* ☎ *843/577–2644 or 877/408–8733,* FAX *843/577–2697,* WEB *www.doubletree.com. 182 suites. Gym, lounge, business services, meeting room. AE, D, DC, MC, V.*

$$$ ⊞ **Meeting Street Inn.** Built in 1874, this salmon-color former tavern in the historic district overlooks a lovely courtyard with fountains and gardens. Spacious rooms have hardwood floors, high ceilings, and reproduction furniture including four-poster rice beds. ⊠ *173 Meeting St., Market area 29401,* ☎ *843/723–1882 or 800/842–8022,* FAX *843/577–0851,* WEB *www.meetingstreetinn.com. 54 rooms. Some refrigerators, outdoor hot tub, bar. AE, D, DC, MC, V. CP.*

$$–$$$ ⊞ **Holiday Inn Charleston/Mount Pleasant.** Just over the Cooper River Bridge, the Holiday Inn is a 10-minute drive from the downtown historic district. Everything has been gracefully done: big banana trees in the lobby, brass lamps, crystal chandeliers, contemporary furniture. ⊠ *250 U.S. 17, Mount Pleasant/East Cooper 29464,* ☎ *843/884–6000 or 800/290–4004,* FAX *843/881–1786,* WEB *www.holidayinn-mtpleasant.com. 158 rooms. Restaurant, some refrigerators and microwaves, pool, gym, sauna, lounge, meeting room. AE, D, DC, MC, V.*

$$–$$$ ⊞ **Westin Francis Marion Hotel.** Built in 1924 as the largest hotel in the Carolinas, the Francis Marion is now a Westin property. However, it has retained its big-band and tea-dance glamour with its windowed ballrooms, wrought-iron railings, columns, high ceilings, crown moldings, decorative plasterwork, and views of Marion Square and the harbor. Excellent Southern cuisine can be had at Elliott's on the Square. ⊠ *387 King St., Upper King 29403,* ☎ *843/722–0600 or 888/625–5144,* FAX *843/723–4633,* WEB *www.westinfm.com. 160 rooms, 66 suites. Restaurant, coffee shop, in-room data ports, gym, lounge, Internet, concierge, business services, meeting rooms, parking (fee). AE, D, DC, MC, V.*

$$ ⊞ **Holiday Inn Historic District.** Although this hotel changed hands and went through a major renovation, it still draws loyal repeat visitors because of its free parking and location—a block from the Gaillard Municipal Auditorium and within walking distance of many must-see spots. Rooms are motel modern. ⊠ *125 Calhoun St., Upper King 29401,* ☎ *843/805–7900 or 877/805–7900,* FAX *843/805–7700,* WEB *www.charlestonhotel.com. 126 rooms. Restaurant, in-room data ports, pool, bar, concierge, concierge floor, Internet, business services, meeting rooms, parking. AE, D, DC, MC, V.*

$-$$ ◫ **Hampton Inn Charleston–North.** This upscale Hampton Inn, just off Ashley Phosphate Rd., has a grand marble lobby, a solarium overlooking the pool, crown moldings, and Lowcountry-style furniture. The mostly business clientele rates it tops for service and design. ⊠ *7424 Northside Dr., North Charleston 29420,* ☎ *843/820–2030 or 877/870–2030,* FAX *843/820–2010,* WEB *www.hamptoninncharleston.com. 102 rooms. In-room data ports, some hot tubs, some kitchens, in-room VCRs, pool, gym, business services, laundry service, meeting room. AE, D, DC, MC, V.*

$ ◫ **Red Roof Inn.** At the foot of the Cooper River Bridge in Mt. Pleasant, about 10 minutes from historic Charleston, this chain motel is clean and well lighted. Some rooms have work areas. ⊠ *301 Johnnie Dodds Blvd., Mount Pleasant/East Cooper 29403,* ☎ *843/884–1411 or 800/843–7663,* FAX *843/884–1411,* WEB *www.redroof.com. 124 rooms. Pool, some refrigerators, some microwaves. AE, D, DC, MC, V.*

Inns and Guest Houses

$$$$ ✕◫ **Wentworth Mansion.** This spectacular brick mansion, built around 1886 as a private home, is now a luxury inn. Hand-carved marble fireplaces, rich woodwork, chandeliers, 14-foot ceilings, and Second Empire reproductions create a sense of elegance in the spacious guest rooms. Breakfast buffet, evening wine and cheese, sherry, and turndown service are included. Rooms have king-size beds and CD players; most have gas fireplaces and some have daybeds. Circa 1886, in the former carriage house, serves inventive food and is the perfect spot for a special occasion. ⊠ *149 Wentworth St., College of Charleston 29403,* ☎ *843/853–1886 or 888/466–1886,* FAX *843/723–8634,* WEB *www. wentworthmansion.com. 21 rooms. Restaurant, hot tubs, lounge, free parking. AE, D, DC, MC, V. BP.*

$$$$ ◫ **John Rutledge House Inn.** This 1763 house, built by John Rutledge, ★ one of the framers of the U.S. Constitution, is one of Charleston's most luxurious inns. The ornate ironwork, original woodwork, plaster moldings, parquet floors, marble fireplaces, and 14-ft ceilings are impressive. A lovely afternoon tea including wine is served in the ballroom, and a Continental breakfast is served—on the patio, if you prefer sitting outside. Newspapers are delivered to your room. Some guest rooms have fireplaces. There are also two charming period carriage houses that you can stay in. ⊠ *116 Broad St., South of Broad 29401,* ☎ *843/723–7999 or 800/476–9741,* FAX *843/720–2615,* WEB *www.charminginns.com. 11 rooms in mansion, 4 in each of 2 carriage houses. Some hot tubs, refrigerators, business services. AE, D, DC, MC, V. CP.*

$$$$ ◫ **Planters Inn.** High-ceiling rooms and suites are beautifully appointed with opulent furnishings, including mahogany four-poster beds and marble baths. Twenty-one rooms have a piazza overlooking the garden courtyard. The inn's Peninsula Grill is wonderful. ⊠ *112 N. Market St., Market area 29401,* ☎ *843/722–2345 or 800/845–7082,* FAX *843/577–2125,* WEB *www.plantersinn.com. 56 rooms, 6 suites. Restaurant, some hot tubs, room service, concierge, business services; no-smoking floors. AE, D, DC, MC, V.*

$$$-$$$$ ◫ **Ansonborough Inn.** Formerly a stationer's warehouse dating from the early 1900s, this spacious all-suites inn is furnished in period reproductions. It offers hair dryers, irons, a morning newspaper, message service, wine reception, and rooftop terrace, but it's best known for its friendly staff. ⊠ *21 Hasell St., Market area 29401,* ☎ *843/723–1655 or 800/522–2073,* FAX *843/527–6888,* WEB *www.ansonboroughinn. com. 37 suites. Bar, meeting room. AE, MC, V. CP.*

$$$-$$$$ ◫ **Hayne House.** One block from the Battery, in Charleston's prestigious South of Broad neighborhood, the Hayne house was built in 1755.

It has old furnishings but a fresh, light spirit. Rooms have federal antiques and other heirlooms from the proprietors' families. Two of the guest rooms are in the main house; the other four are in the kitchen house, with its narrow stairway, colonial brickwork, and chimney. ✉ *30 King St., South of Broad 29401,* ☎ *843/577–2633,* FAX *843/577–5906,* WEB *www.haynehouse.com. 4 rooms, 2 suites. MC, V. CP.*

$$$–$$$$ ⊞ **Phoebe Pember House.** Built in 1807, the mansion has a separate carriage house, which has two guest rooms upstairs and a living room, dining room, kitchenette, and garden downstairs. Colors and fabrics are cheerful yet refined; artwork is by Charleston artists. The inn is off a busy street, but the piazza is cocooned by a walled garden overlooking Charleston's port. A nearby studio offers yoga classes and workshops. ✉ *26 Society St., Market area 29401,* ☎ *843/722–4186,* FAX *843/722–0557,* WEB *www.phoebepemberhouse.com. 6 rooms. Massage, free parking; no smoking. AE, MC, V. CP.*

$$$–$$$$ ⊞ **Two Meeting Street.** As pretty as a wedding cake and just as romantic,
★   this early 20th-century inn on the Battery has two suites with working fireplaces and balconies. In the public spaces there are Tiffany windows, carved English oak paneling, and a chandelier from the former Czechoslovakia. Expect to be treated to afternoon high tea and a Continental breakfast. ✉ *2 Meeting St., South of Broad 29401,* ☎ *843/723–7322,* WEB *www.twomeetingstreet.com. 7 rooms, 2 suites. No credit cards. CP.*

$$$ ⊞ **Cannonboro Inn and Ashley Inn.** Two of the most elegant inns in town, these B&B neighbors on the edge of the historic district near the Medical University of South Carolina have luxurious rooms, tastefully decorated in period furnishings. Expect to be treated to a full English breakfast on a piazza overlooking the Charleston gardens. Use of the bicycles and afternoon refreshments are included. ✉ *Cannonboro: 184 Ashley Ave., Medical University of South Carolina 29403,* ☎ *843/723–8572,* FAX *843/723–8007,* WEB *www.charleston-sc-inns.com. 6 rooms. Bicycles, business services, free parking. MC, V. BP.* ✉ *Ashley: 201 Ashley Ave., Medical University of South Carolina 29403,* ☎ *843/723–1848,* FAX *843/579–9080. 6 rooms, 1 suite. Bicycles, business services, free parking. AE, D, MC, V. BP.*

$$$ ⊞ **Vendue Inn.** This elegant yet friendly inn is close to the harbor and Waterfront Park (though its views are now obstructed by a condo building). Guest rooms have four-poster beds, cozy seating areas, and large bathrooms. A full buffet breakfast, afternoon wine and cheese, and evening milk and cookies are complimentary. The inn's rooftop terrace bar has sweeping harbor views. ✉ *19 Vendue Range, Market area 29401,* ☎ *843/577–7970 or 800/845–7900,* WEB *www.vendueinn. com. 31 rooms, 35 suites. Restaurant, in-room data ports, bicycles, bar, business services, meeting room. AE, D, DC, MC, V. BP.*

$$–$$$ ⊞ **1837 Bed and Breakfast and Tea Room.** Although not as fancy as some of the B&Bs in town, this inn has an extremely hospitable staff; you'll get a sense of what it's really like to live in one of Charleston's beloved homes. Restored and operated by two artists-teachers, the home and carriage house have rooms filled with antiques, including romantic canopied beds. The delicious breakfast includes homemade breads and hot entrées such as sausage pie or ham frittatas. ✉ *126 Wentworth St., Market area 29401,* ☎ *843/723–7166 or 877/723–1837,* FAX *843/722–7179,* WEB *www.1837bb.com. 8 rooms, 1 suite. AE, D, MC, V. BP.*

$$–$$$ ⊞ **Elliott House Inn.** Listen to the chimes of St. Michael's Episcopal Church as you sip wine in the courtyard of this lovely old inn in the heart of the historic district. You can then retreat to a cozy room with period furniture, including canopied four-posters and Oriental carpets. ✉ *78 Queen St., Market area 29401,* ☎ *843/723–1855 or 800/729–*

1855, FAX *843/722–1567,* WEB *www.elliotthouseinn.com. 24 rooms. Hot tub, bicycles. AE, D, MC, V. CP.*

$$–$$$ 🏨 **Guilds Inn.** An easygoing elegance characterizes this place in Mount Pleasant's historic and scenic Old Village, a residential area with a pharmacy whose soda fountain will take you back in time. The National Historic Register property has hardwood floors, traditional Lowcountry furnishings, and a mix of antiques and reproductions. Rooms have whirlpool tubs. Although the self-serve morning pastries are grocery store–bought, the laid-back management is part of the unstuffy charm of this inn. ✉ *101 Pitt St., Mount Pleasant/East Cooper 29464,* ☎ *843/881–0510 or 800/569–4038,* FAX *843/884–5020,* WEB *www. guildsinn.com. 5 rooms, 1 suite. AE, D, MC, V. CP.*

Resort Islands

On the semitropical islands dotting the South Carolina coast near Charleston you'll find several sumptuous resorts that offer lots of different packages. Peak season rates (during spring and summer vacations) range from $140 to $300 per day, double occupancy for stays up to five nights; rates drop for weekly stays and during off-season.

$$$$ 🏨 **Wild Dunes.** This 1,600-acre resort on the Isle of Palms has one- to six-bedroom villas and homes for rent, plus the plantation-style Boardwalk Inn. Rental locations range from oceanfront to courtside to marsh side. The inn is just off the beach, in a relaxing boardwalk cluster of villas and shops; guest rooms have balconies and overlook the ocean. Nearby is a yacht harbor on the Intracoastal Waterway. You have a long list of recreational options here. ✉ *Palm Blvd. at 41st Ave., Isle of Palms (Box 20575, Charleston 29413),* ☎ *843/886–6000 or 888/845–8926,* FAX *843/886–2916,* WEB *www.wilddunes.com. 430 units, 93 rooms. 2 restaurants, pizzeria, snack bar, ice cream parlor, fans, some in-room hot tubs, 2 18-hole golf courses, 17 tennis courts, 4 pools, indoor pool, wading pool, health club, boating, fishing, bicycles, volleyball, lounge, video game room, children's programs (ages 3–12), concierge, meeting rooms, airport shuttle. AE, D, DC, MC, V.*

$$$–$$$$ 🏨 **Kiawah Island Resort.** Choose from newly renovated inn rooms and completely equipped one- to five-bedroom villas and private homes in two luxurious resort villages on 10,000 wooded acres. There are 10 mi of fine broad beaches and plenty of recreational opportunities. Dining options are many and varied. ✉ *12 Kiawah Beach Dr., Kiawah Island 29455,* ☎ *843/768–2121 or 800/654–2924,* FAX *843/768–6099,* WEB *www.kiawahresort.com. 150 rooms, 430 villas and private homes. 8 restaurants, 5 18-hole golf courses, 28 tennis courts, pro shop, 5 pools, wading pool, boating, fishing, bicycles, lounges, shops, children's programs (ages 3–12). AE, D, DC, MC, V.*

$$$–$$$$ 🏨 **Seabrook Island Resort.** About 200 completely equipped one- to six-bedroom villas, cottages, and beach houses occupy this property (the number varies according to how many homeowners sign up for the rental program). The resort is noted for its secluded wooded areas and abundance of wildlife—look for bobcats and white-tailed deer. The Beach Club and Island House, open to guests, are centers for dining and leisure activities. Bohicket Marina Village, the hub of activity around the island, offers restaurants as well as pizza and sub shops, plus opportunities for scuba diving, deep-sea- and inshore-fishing charters, and small-boat rentals. ✉ *1002 Landfall Way, Seabrook Island 29455,* ☎ *843/768–1000 or 800/845–2475,* FAX *843/768–3096,* WEB *www. seabrookresort.com. 200 units. 3 restaurants, 2 18-hole golf courses, 13 tennis courts, 2 pools, wading pool, boating, parasailing, fishing, bicycles, horseback riding, children's programs. AE, D, DC, MC, V.*

Nightlife and the Arts

The Arts

CONCERTS

The **Charleston Concert Association** (☎ 843/722–7667) has information on visiting performing arts groups including symphonies, ballets, and operas. The **Charleston Symphony Orchestra** (843/723–7528) presents MasterWorks Series, Downtown Pops, Family Series, and an annual holiday concert at Gaillard Municipal Auditorium (⌧ 77 Calhoun St., Upper King, ☎ 843/577–4500). The orchestra also performs the Sotille Chamber Series at the Sotille Theater (⌧ 44 George St., Market area, ☎ 843/953–6340) and the Light and Lively Pops at Charleston Southern University (⌧ U.S. 78, ☎ 843/953–6340). The College of Charleston has a free **Monday Night Recital Series** (☎ 843/953–8228).

DANCE

Anonymity Dance Company (☎ 843/886–6104), a modern dance troupe, performs throughout the city. The **Charleston Ballet Theatre** (⌧ 477 King St., Upper King, ☎ 843/723–7334) performs everything from classical to contemporary dance at locations around the city. The **Robert Ivey Ballet Company** (☎ 843/556–1343), a semiprofessional company that includes College of Charleston students, gives a fall and spring program of jazz, classical, and modern dance at the Sotille Theater (⌧ 44 George St., Market area, ☎ 843/953–6340).

FESTIVALS

The **Fall Candlelight Tours of Homes and Gardens** (☎ 843/722–4630), sponsored by the Preservation Society of Charleston in September and October, offers an inside look at Charleston's private buildings and gardens.

During the **Festival of Houses and Gardens** (☎ 843/724–8484), held during March and April each year, more than 100 private homes, gardens, and historic churches are open to the public for tours sponsored by the Historic Charleston Foundation. There are also symphony galas in stately drawing rooms, plantation oyster roasts, and candlelight tours.

The **MOJA Arts Festival** (☎ 843/724–7305), which takes place during the last week of September and first week of October, celebrates the rich heritage of the African continent and Caribbean influences on African-American culture. It includes theater, dance, and music performances; art shows; films; lectures; and tours of the historic district.

Piccolo Spoleto Festival (☎ 843/724–7305) is the spirited companion festival of Spoleto Festival USA, showcasing the best in local and regional talent from every artistic discipline. There are about 300 events—from jazz performances to puppet shows—held at 60 sites in 17 days from mid-May through early June, and most performances are free.

The **Southeastern Wildlife Exposition** (☎ 843/723–1748 or 800/221–5273), in mid-February, is one of Charleston's biggest annual events. You'll find art by renowned wildlife artists, live animal demonstrations, and a chili cook-off.

Spoleto Festival USA (☎ 843/722–2764), founded by the composer Gian Carlo Menotti in 1977, has become a world-famous celebration of the arts. For two weeks, from late May to early June, opera, dance, theater, symphonic and chamber music, jazz, and the visual arts are showcased in concert halls, theaters, parks, churches, streets, and gardens throughout the city.

FILM

The **American Theater** (⌧ 446 King St., Upper King, ☎ 843/722–3456), a renovated theater from the 1940s, shows current movies in a table-

and-chairs setting with pizza, burgers, finger foods, beer, and wine. Upstairs there's a virtual reality game center. IMAX fans should check out the **IMAX Theater** (⊠ 360 Concord St., Upper King, ☎ 843/725–4629) next to the South Carolina Aquarium.

THEATER

Several groups, including the Footlight Players and Charleston Stage Company, perform at the **Dock Street Theatre** (⊠ 135 Church St., Market area, ☎ 843/723–5648). **Pluff Mud Productions** puts on comedies at the Isle of Palms's Windjammer (⊠ 1000 Ocean Blvd., Mount Pleasant/East Cooper, ☎ 843/886–8596). The Footlight Players regularly perform at the **Footlight Players Theatre** (⊠ 20 Queen St., Market area, ☎ 843/722–4487). Performances by the College of Charleston's theater department and guest theatrical groups are presented during the school year at the **Simons Center for the Arts** (⊠ 54 St. Phillips St., Market area, ☎ 843/953–5604).

Nightlife

DANCING AND MUSIC

Cumberland's (⊠ 26 Cumberland St., Market area, ☎ 843/577–9469) has live blues, rock, reggae, and bluegrass; the place is also known for buffalo wings and cheap beer. There's live music and dancing at the **City Bar** (⊠ 5 Faber St., Market area, ☎ 843/577–7383) each weekend. The **Mills House Hotel** (⊠ 115 Meeting St., Market area, ☎ 843/577–2400), favored by an elegant, mature crowd, has a lively bar. Most evenings **Momma's Blues Palace** (⊠ 46 John St., Upper King, ☎ 843/853–2221) has live music starting at 10 PM. The cavernous **Music Farm** (⊠ 32 Ann St., Upper King, ☎ 843/853–3276), in a renovated train station, showcases live national and local alternative bands. There are dancing and funky '70s music at **Trio Club** (⊠ 139 Calhoun St., Upper King, ☎ 843/965–5333) Wednesday through Saturday. The **Windjammer** (⊠ 1000 Ocean Blvd., Mount Pleasant/East Cooper, ☎ 843/886–8596), on the Isle of Palms, is an oceanfront spot with live rock. Nearby on Sullivan's Island, **Bert's Bar** (⊠ 2209 Middle St., Mount Pleasant/East Cooper, ☎ 843/883–3924), a true beach-bum neighborhood joint, has live music on weekends and a great all-you-can-eat fish fry on Friday night from 6 to 9.

DINNER CRUISES

For an evening of dining and dancing, climb aboard the luxury yacht *Spirit of Carolina* (☎ 843/722–2628). Reservations are essential; there are no cruises Sunday and Monday. Breakfast, brunch, deli, and hot luncheons are prepared on board the *Charlestowne Princess* (☎ 843/722–1112), which also offers its Harborlites Dinner with live entertainment and dancing while cruising the harbor and rivers.

HOTEL AND JAZZ BARS

The **Best Friend Lounge** (⊠ 115 Meeting St., Market area, ☎ 843/577–2400), in the Mills House Hotel, has a guitarist playing light tunes most nights. The elegant **Charleston Grill** (⊠ 224 King St., Market area, ☎ 843/577–4522), in Charleston Place, offers live jazz nightly. In the **Lobby Lounge** (⊠ 130 Market St., Market area, ☎ 843/722–4900), on Charleston Place, afternoon high tea, cocktails, and appetizers are accompanied by piano. At **Mistral Restaurant** (⊠ 99 S. Market St., Market area, ☎ 843/722–5709) there's a regular four-piece jazz band on weekends. **Mitchell's** (⊠ 102 N. Market St., Market area, ☎ 843/722–0732) has nightly acts, from jazz pianists to Latin dance bands.

LOUNGES AND BARS/BREWERIES

Charlie's Little Bar (⊠ 141 E. Bay St., Market area, ☎ 843/723–6242), above Saracen Restaurant, is intimate, cozy, and popular with young professionals. **Club Habana** (⊠ 177 Meeting St., Market area, ☎ 843/

853–5900) is a chic wood-paneled martini bar (open late) with a cigar shop downstairs. **Southend Brewery** (⊠ 161 E. Bay St., Market area, ☎ 843/853–4677) has a lively bar with beer brewed on the premises; the food is good, especially the soups. You'll find authentic Irish music at **Tommy Condon's Irish Pub & Restaurant** (⊠ 160 Church St., Market area, ☎ 843/577–3818). **Vickery's Bar & Grill** (⊠ 139 Calhoun St., Market area, ☎ 843/723–1558) is a festive nightspot with a spacious outdoor patio and good late-night food. There's another equally popular location in Mount Pleasant (⊠ 1205 Shrimp Boat La., Mount Pleasant/East Cooper, ☎ 843/849–6770).

Outdoor Activities and Sports

Beaches

The Charleston area's mild climate generally is conducive to swimming from April through October. This is definitely not a "swingles" area; all public and private beaches are family oriented, providing a choice of water sports, sunbathing, shelling, fishing, or quiet moonlight strolling. The **Charleston County Parks and Recreation Commission** (☎ 843/762–2172) operates several public beach facilities.

Beachwalker Park, on the west end of Kiawah Island (which is otherwise a private resort), has 300 ft of beach frontage, seasonal lifeguard service, rest rooms, outdoor showers, a picnic area, snack bar, and a 150-car parking lot. ⊠ *Beachwalker Dr., Kiawah Island,* ☎ *843/768–2395.* ⊠ *$5 per car (up to 8 passengers).* ☉ *June–Aug., daily 10–7; May and Sept., daily 10–6; Apr. and Oct., weekends 10–6.*

Folly Beach County Park, 12 mi south of Charleston via U.S. 17 and Route 171 (Folly Road), has 4,000 ft of ocean frontage and 2,000 ft of river frontage. Lifeguards are on duty seasonally. Facilities include dressing areas, outdoor showers, rest rooms, and picnicking areas; beach chair, raft, and umbrella rentals; and parking. ⊠ *1100 W. Ashley Ave., Folly Island,* ☎ *843/588–2426.* ⊠ *$5 per car (up to 8 passengers).* ☉ *May–Aug., daily 9–7; Apr. and Sept.–Oct., daily 10–6; Nov.–Mar., daily 10–5.*

Isle of Palms County Park is on the Isle of Palms at the foot of the Isle of Palms connector. Lifeguards are on duty seasonally along a 600-ft section of the beach. Facilities include dressing areas, outdoor showers, rest rooms, picnicking areas, beach chair and raft rentals, and a 350-vehicle parking lot. ⊠ *1 14th Ave., Isle of Palms, Mount Pleasant/East Cooper,* ☎ *843/886–3863.* ⊠ *$5 per car (up to 8 passengers).* ☉ *May–Aug., daily 9–7; Apr. and Sept.–Oct., daily 10–6; Nov.–Mar., daily 10–5.*

Participant Sports

BIKING

The historic district is ideal for bicycling as long as you stay off the main, busy roads; many city parks have biking trails. Palmetto Islands County Park also has trails. Bikes can be rented at the **Bicycle Shoppe** (⊠ 280 Meeting St., Market area, ☎ 843/722–8168; also Kiawah Island, ☎ 843/768–9122). **Island Bike and Surf Shop** (⊠ Kiawah Island, ☎ 843/768–1158) rents bikes, surfboards, and Rollerblades. You'll get a better deal at **Alligator Bike** (⊠ 1823 Paulette Dr., Johns Island, ☎ 843/559–8200), which serves Kiawah and Seabrook islands. **Sea Island Cycle** (⊠ 4053 Rhett Ave., North Charleston, ☎ 843/747–2453) serves all the local islands.

GOLF

One of the most appealing aspects of golfing in the Charleston area is the relaxing pace. With fewer golfers playing the courses than in destinations that are primarily golf oriented, players find choice starting times and an unhurried environment. Nonguests may play on a space-available basis at private island resorts, such as Kiawah Island, Seabrook Island, and Wild Dunes. Top public courses in the area are 18-hole, par-72 courses. For a listing of area golf packages, contact **Charleston Golf Inc.** (☎ 800/774–4444).

The prestigious Pete Dye–designed **Ocean Course at Kiawah Island Resort** (✉ 1000 Ocean Course Dr., Kiawah Island, ☎ 843/768–7272) is an 18-hole, par-72 course that was the site of the 1991 Ryder Cup. The Championship **Kiawah courses,** all 18-hole and par 72, are the Gary Player–designed Marsh Point; Osprey Point, by Tom Fazio; and Turtle Point, a Jack Nicklaus layout (for all three: ✉ 12 Kiawah Beach Dr.). **Seabrook Island Resort,** a secluded hideaway on Johns Island, offers two more 18-hole, par-72 championship courses: Crooked Oaks, by Robert Trent Jones Sr., and Ocean Winds, designed by William Byrd (for both: ✉ Seabrook Island Rd., ☎ 843/768–2529). **Wild Dunes Resort,** on the Isle of Palms, has two 18-hole, par-72 Tom Fazio designs: the Links (✉ 10001 Back Bay Dr., Mount Pleasant/East Cooper, ☎ 843/886–2180) and Harbor Course (✉ 5881 Palmetto Dr., Mount Pleasant/East Cooper, ☎ 843/886–2301).

Charleston Municipal (✉ 2110 Maybank Hwy., James Island, ☎ 843/795–6517) is a public, walker-friendly course. **Charleston National Country Club** (✉ 1360 National Dr., Mount Pleasant/East Cooper, ☎ 843/884–7799) is well maintained and tends to be quiet on weekdays. The **Dunes West Golf Club** (✉ 3535 Wando Plantation Way, Mount Pleasant/East Cooper, ☎ 843/856–9000) has great marshland views and lots of modulation on the greens. **Links at Stono Ferry** (✉ 5365 Forest Oaks Dr., Hollywood, ☎ 843/763–1817) is a popular public course with great rates. **Oak Point Golf Course** (✉ 4255 Bohicket Rd., Johns Island, ☎ 843/768–7431) has water on 16 holes, narrow fairways, and lots of chances to spot wildlife. **Patriots Point** (✉ 1 Patriots Point Rd., Mount Pleasant/East Cooper, ☎ 843/881–0042) has a partly covered driving range and spectacular harbor views. **Shadowmoss Golf Club** (✉ 20 Dunvegan Dr., West Ashley, ☎ 843/556–8251) is a well-marked, forgiving course with one of the best finishing holes in the area.

HORSEBACK RIDING

M & M Farms (✉ Mount Pleasant/East Cooper, ☎ 843/336–4886), in the National Forest Equestrian Center of Francis Marion Forest, offers guided trail tours. **Seabrook Island Equestrian Center** (✉ Seabrook Island, ☎ 843/768–7541) is open to the public and offers trail rides on the beach and through maritime forests and has pony rides for the kids.

SCUBA DIVING

The **Cooper River Underwater Heritage Diving Trail** is more than 2 mi long and consists of six submerged sites, including ships that date to the Revolutionary War. Contact the **East Coast Dive Connection** (✉ 206B E. 5th North St., Hwy. 78, Summerville, ☎ 843/821–0001) for lessons, rentals, and information. **Charleston Scuba** (✉ 335 Savannah Hwy., West Ashley, ☎ 843/763–3483) for maps, rentals, and excursion information.

TENNIS

You can play for free at neighborhood courts, including several across the street from Colonial Lake and at the Isle of Palms Recreation Center on the Isle of Palms. Courts are open to the public at **Kiawah Island** (☎ 843/768–2121). **Shadowmoss Plantation** (☎ 843/556–8251) has public courts available. **Wild Dunes** (☎ 843/886–6000) is a swanky resort with nice courts and a full tennis shop. **Maybank Tennis Center** (✉ 1880 Houghton Dr., James Island, ☎ 843/406–8814) has lights on its six courts. **Charleston Tennis Center** (✉ 19 Farmfield Ave., West Ashley, ☎ 843/724–7402) is a city facility with lots of courts and locker rooms. The Family Circle Cup takes place at the **Town Center Park on Daniel Island** (☎ 843/534–2400), a 32-acre tennis and recreational park with a racquet club and 17 public tennis courts.

Shopping

Shopping Districts

The Market is a complex of specialty shops and restaurants. Vendors sell beaded jewelry, hats, clothing, T-shirts, antique silver, and more in the open-air flea market called **Old City Market** (✉ E. Bay and Market Sts., Market area). You'll find locally made sweet-grass baskets here—and can even watch as they're crafted. **Rainbow Market** (✉ 40 N. Market St., Market area) occupies two interconnected mid-19th-century buildings (don't miss the filled-to-the-hilt **Good Scents** in Rainbow Market, known for its perfume oils and lotions). **Shops at Charleston Place** (✉ 130 Market St., Market area) has Gucci, Cache, Limited Express, and Brookstone. **King Street** has some of Charleston's oldest and finest shops, including **Croghan's Jewel Box** (✉ 308 King St., Market area, ☎ 843/723–3594), **Saks Fifth Avenue** (✉ 211 King St., Market area, ☎ 843/853–9888), and the chichi **Christian Michi** (✉ 220 King St., Market area, ☎ 843/723–0575), which carries elegant women's clothes, makeup, and housewares. From May until September a festive **farmers' market** takes place Saturday mornings at Marion Square.

Antiques

King Street is the center for antiques shopping. **Birlant & Co.** (✉ 191 King St., Market area, ☎ 843/722–3842) presents fine 18th- and 19th-century English antiques, as well as the famous Charleston Battery bench, a small wood-slat bench with cast-iron sides. **Period Antiques** (✉ 194 King St., Market area, ☎ 843/723–2724) has 18th- and 19th-century pieces. **Petterson Antiques** (✉ 201 King St., Market area, ☎ 843/723–5714) offers curious objets d'art, books, furniture, porcelain, and glass. **Livingston & Sons Antiques,** dealers in 18th- and 19th-century English and Continental furniture, clocks, and bric-a-brac, has a large shop west of the Ashley River (✉ 2137 Savannah Hwy., West Ashley, ☎ 843/556–6162) and a smaller one on King Street (✉ 163 King St., Market area, ☎ 843/723–9697).

On James Island, a 10-minute drive from downtown, **Carolopolis Antiques** (✉ 2000 Wappoo Dr., ☎ 843/795–7724) has good bargains on country pieces, many of which are bought by downtown stores. On U.S. 17 in Mount Pleasant, **Hungryneck Mall** (✉ 401 Johnnie Dodds Blvd., Mount Pleaant/East Cooper, ☎ 843/849–1744) has more than 60 dealers hawking sterling silver, oak and mahogany furnishings, linens, and Civil War memorabilia. In Mount Pleasant, **Page's Thieves Market** (✉ 1460 Ben Sawyer Blvd., Mount Pleasant/East Cooper, ☎ 843/884–9672) has furniture, glassware, and "junque."

Art and Crafts Galleries

The **Birds I View Gallery** (✉ 119A Church St., Market area, ☎ 843/723–1276) sells bird paintings and prints by Anne Worsham Richardson. **Charleston Crafts** (✉ 87 Hasell St., Market area, ☎ 843/723–2938) has a fine selection of pottery, quilts, weavings, sculptures, and jewelry fashioned mostly by local artists. The **Pink House Gallery** (✉ 17 Chalmers St., Market area, ☎ 843/723–3608), in the oldest stone house in the city, has prints and paintings of traditional Charleston scenes by local artists. Be sure to go all the way to the third floor to get a look at the small, 17th-century living quarters. Prints of Elizabeth O'Neill Verner's pastels and etchings are on sale at **Elizabeth O'Neill Verner Studio & Gallery** (⊠ 38 Tradd St., South of Broad, ☎ 843/722–4246). The **Marty Whaley Adams Gallery** (⊠ 2 Queen St., Market area, ☎ 843/853–8512) has original vivid watercolors and monotypes, plus prints and posters by this Charleston artist. At **Nina Liu and Friends** (⊠ 24 State St., Market area, ☎ 843/722–2724), you'll find contemporary art objects including handblown glass, pottery, jewelry, and photographs. Famous for his Lowcountry beach scenes, local watercolorist Steven Jordan displays his best at **Steven Jordan Gallery** (⊠ 463 Coleman Blvd., Mount Pleasant/East Cooper, ☎ 843/881–1644).

Books

Atlantic Books (⊠ 191 E. Bay St., Market area, ☎ 843/723–7654; ⊠ 310 King St., Upper King, ☎ 843/723–4751), in two downtown locations, has historic, rare, and out-of-print books. The **Preservation Society of Charleston** (⊠ King and Queen Sts., Market area, ☎ 843/722–4630) carries books and tapes of historic and local interest, sweetgrass baskets, prints, and posters.

Gifts

Charleston's and London's own **Ben Silver** (⊠ 149 King St., Market area, ☎ 843/577–4556), premier purveyor of blazer buttons, has more than 800 designs, including college and British regimental motifs. He also sells British neckties, embroidered polo shirts, and blazers. **Blink** (⊠ 62B Queen St., Market area, ☎ 843/577–5688) has regionally and locally produced paintings, photos, pottery, jewelry, and garden art. **Charleston Collections** (⊠ Straw Market, Kiawah Island Resort, Johns Island, ☎ 843/768–7487; ⊠ 625 Skylark Dr., West Ashley, ☎ 843/556–8911) has Charleston chimes, Rainbow Row prints, Charleston rice spoons and rice steamers, and more. **East Bay Gallery** (⊠ 280 W. Coleman Blvd., Mount Pleasant/East Cooper, ☎ 843/216–8010) has jewelry, chess sets, chimes, and ceramics by local artists. The **Sugar Plantation** (⊠ 48 N. Market St., Market area, ☎ 843/853–3924) has melt-in-your mouth pralines, fudge, Charleston chews, and benne-seed wafers. You can find Charleston foods, including benne-seed wafers, pepper jelly, she-crab soup, and pickled okra, at area **Piggly Wiggly** grocery stores (two locations: ⊠ 1501 U.S. 17N, Mount Pleasant/East Cooper, ☎ 843/881–7921; ⊠ IOP Connector, Mount Pleasant/East Cooper, ☎ 843/881–8939).

Period Reproductions

Historic Charleston Reproductions (⊠ 105 Broad St., South of Broad, ☎ 843/723–8292) has superb replicas of Charleston furniture and accessories, all authorized by the Historic Charleston Foundation. Royalties from sales contribute to restoration projects. At the **Old Charleston Joggling Board Co.** (⊠ 652 King St., Upper King, ☎ 843/723–4331), these Lowcountry oddities (on which people bounce) can be purchased.

Side Trips from Charleston

Gardens, parks, and the charming town of Summerville are good reasons to travel a bit farther afield for day trips.

Moncks Corner

30 mi north of Charleston on U.S. 52.

This town is a gateway to a number of attractions in Santee Cooper Country. Named for the two rivers that form a 171,000-acre basin, the area brims with outdoor pleasures centered on the basin and nearby Lakes Marion and Moultrie.

Cypress Gardens, a swamp garden created from what was once the freshwater reserve of the vast Dean Hall rice plantation, is about 24 mi north of Charleston via U.S. 52, between Goose Creek and Moncks Corner. You can explore the inky waters by boat or walk along paths lined with moss-draped cypress trees, azaleas, camellias, daffodils, wisteria, and dogwood. ⊠ *3030 Cypress Gardens Rd.,* ☎ *843/553-0515.* ☜ *$7.* ☉ *Daily 9–5.*

Mepkin Abbey, overlooking the Cooper River, is an active Trappist monastery and former plantation home of Henry Laurens and, later, of publisher Henry Luce. You can tour the gardens and abbey, take a look at the egg-farming business, or even stay here on a long retreat—these one- to six-night stays are open to anybody willing to observe the rules of the abbey (including married couples); reservations are required, and donations greatly appreciated. ⊠ *Dr. Evans Rd. (about 8 mi southeast of Moncks Corner via Rte. 402),* ☎ *843/761-8509,* WEB *www.mepkinabbey.org.* ☜ *Free.* ☉ *Daily 9–4:30.*

☺ On the banks of the Old Santee Canal is the **Old Santee Canal Park.** You can explore on foot or take a canoe. The park includes a 19th-century plantation house; the Berkeley Museum, focusing on cultural and natural history; and an interpretive center. ⊠ *Rembert C. Dennis Blvd.,* ☎ *843/899-5200,* WEB *www.oldsanteecanalpark.org.* ☜ *$3.* ☉ *Sept.–May, daily 9–5; June–Aug., daily 9–6.*

Francis Marion National Forest consists of 250,000 acres of swamps, vast oaks and pines, and little lakes thought to have been formed by falling meteors. It's a good place for picnicking, camping, boating, and swimming. At the park's **Rembert Dennis Wildlife Center** (⊠ off U.S. 52 in Bonneau, just north of Moncks Corner, ☎ 843/825-3387) deer, wild turkey, and striped bass are reared and studied. ⊠ *U.S. 52 (35 mi north of Charleston),* ☎ *843/336-3248.* ☜ *Free.* ☉ *Daily 9–5.*

LODGING

$$$–$$$$ 🏨 **Rice Hope Plantation.** A former rice plantation in Moncks Corner overlooking the Cooper River, this inn is on 11 acres of live oaks and gardens designed by landscape architect Loutrell Briggs. The house has six working fireplaces and antiques and reproductions. Guest rooms have four-poster beds, comfortable seating, and private baths; the suite has a porch overlooking the river. ⊠ *206 Rice Hope Dr., 29461,* ☎ *843/761-4832 or 800/569-4038,* FAX *843/884-5020,* WEB *www.ricehope. com. 4 rooms, 1 suite. Tennis court, boating, fishing, basketball; no smoking. AE, MC, V. CP.*

OUTDOOR ACTIVITIES AND SPORTS

Two good fishing spots are **Lakes Marion** and **Moultrie,** both full of bream, striped bass, catfish, and large- and smallmouth bass. For information about fishing, contact **Santee Cooper Counties Promotion Commission** (⊠ Drawer 40, Santee 29142, ☎ 843/854-2131; 800/227-8510 outside SC).

Summerville
25 mi northwest of Charleston via I–26 (Exit 199) to Rte. 165.

Built by wealthy planters, this picturesque town has lots of lovely of Victorian buildings, many of which are listed on the National Register of Historic Places. Colorful gardens of camellias, azaleas, and wisteria abound, and many streets curve around tall pines, as a local ordinance prohibits cutting them down. This is a good place for antiquing. To get oriented, stop by the **Greater Summerville/Dorchester County Chamber of Commerce and Visitor Center** (⊠ 402 N. Main St., Box 670, 29484, ☎ 843/873-2931).

$$$$ ✕⊞ **Woodlands Inn.** People drive from Charleston for superb meals
★   ($$$$) at this luxury inn, part of the prestigious Relais & Châteaux
group. A four-course menu and a five-course menu with wine are
available at the restaurant. Delicate sauces and subtle touches are key
in entrées—Angus beef with a Barolo wine reduction, potato-encrusted
crab cakes, and Asian-spiced lobster. Although the inn, built in 1906
as a winter home, backs up to a suburb, it's a first-rate getaway, with
such niceties as fireplaces, whirlpool or claw-foot tubs, and heated towel
racks. Rates include a split of champagne at arrival and afternoon tea.
⊠ *125 Parsons Rd., 29483,* ☎ *843/875–2600 or 800/774–9999,* FAX
843/875–2603, WEB *www.woodlandsinn.com. 15 rooms, 4 suites.
Restaurant, 2 tennis courts, pool, bicycles, croquet, lounge. AE, D, DC,
MC, V.*

Charleston A to Z

*To research prices, get advice from other travelers, and book travel ar-
rangements, visit www.fodors.com.*

AIRPORTS AND TRANSFERS
Charleston International Airport on I–26, 12 mi west of downtown,
is served by Continental, Comair, Delta, Midway Express, United Ex-
press, Northwest, TWA, and US Airways.
➤ AIRPORT INFORMATION: **Charleston International Airport** (⊠ 5500
International Blvd., North Charleston, ☎ 843/767–1100).

Several shuttle and cab companies service the airport. It costs about
$18–$22 to travel downtown by taxi; to Mount Pleasant, $23–$35.
Fares are approximately $1.65 per mile. Airport Ground Transporta-
tion arranges shuttles, which cost $10 per person to the downtown area.
Some hotels provide shuttle service.
➤ TAXIS AND SHUTTLES: **Thurman's Limo** (☎ 843/607–2912). **Absolute Charleston** (☎ 843/817–4044). **Harvie's Taxi Limo Service** (☎
843/709–4276). **Lee's Limousine** (☎ 843/797–0041). **Airport Ground
Transportation** (☎ 843/767–1100).

BOAT AND FERRY TRAVEL
Boaters on the Intracoastal Waterway may dock at Ashley Marina and
City Marina, in Charleston Harbor, or at Wild Dunes Yacht Harbor,
on the Isle of Palms.

CHARTS is the only full-service water taxi providing transportation
to and from Patriots Point naval and maritime museum. It also offers
harbor cruises.

➤ BOAT AND FERRY INFORMATION: **Ashley Marina** (⊠ Lockwood Blvd.,
Medical University of South Carolina, ☎ 843/722–1996). **CHARTS**
(⊠ 196A Concord St., North of Calhoun, ☎ 843/853–4700). **City Marina** (⊠ Lockwood Blvd., Medical University of South Carolina, ☎
843/723–5098). **Wild Dunes Yacht Harbor** (☎ 843/886–5100).

BUS TRAVEL TO AND FROM CHARLESTON
Greyhound serves Charleston and Moncks Corner.
➤ BUS INFORMATION: **Greyhound** (☎ 800/231–2222).

BUS TRAVEL WITHIN CHARLESTON
Charleston Area Regional Transit Authority (CARTA) runs buses on
routes that cover most of Charleston from 5:35 AM until 10 PM, until
1 AM in and to North Charleston. The cost is $1 (free transfers). DASH

(Downtown Area Shuttle) trolley-style buses provide fast service in the main downtown areas. A single fare is $1; $3 is the cost of an all-day pass.

FARES AND SCHEDULES
➤ BUS INFORMATION: **CARTA** (☎ 843/724–7420).

CAR TRAVEL
I–26 traverses the state from northwest to southeast and terminates at Charleston. U.S. 17, the coast road, passes through Charleston. I–526, also called the Mark Clark Expressway, runs primarily east–west, connecting the West Ashley area to Mount Pleasant.

EMERGENCIES
The emergency rooms are open all night at Charleston Memorial Hospital, MUSC Hospital, and Roper Hospital all have 24-hour emergency rooms.
➤ EMERGENCY SERVICES: **Ambulance, police** (☎ 911).
➤ HOSPITALS: **Charleston Memorial Hospital** (✉ 326 Calhoun St., Upper King, ☎ 843/577–0600). **MUSC Hospital** (✉ 169 Ashley Ave., Upper King, ☎ 843/792–3826). **Roper Hospital** (✉ 316 Calhoun St., Upper King, ☎ 843/724–2000).
➤ LATE-NIGHT PHARMACIES: **Eckerds** (✉ Calhoun St. and Rutledge Ave., Upper King, ☎ 843/805–6022).

LODGING
APARTMENT AND HOUSE RENTALS
Rates tend to increase and reservations are essential during both the Spring Festival of Houses and Spoleto. For historic home rentals in Charleston, contact Charleston Carriage Houses–Oceanfront Realty. For condo and house rentals on Kiawah Island, Sullivan's Island, and the Isle of Palms—some with private pools and tennis courts—try Great Beach Vacations.
➤ LOCAL AGENTS: **Great Beach Vacations** (✉ 1517 Palm Blvd., Isle of Palms 29451, ☎ 843/886–9704). **Charleston Carriage Houses–Oceanfront Realty** (✉ Box 6151, Hilton Head 29938, ☎ 843/785–8161).

BED-AND-BREAKFASTS
To find rooms in homes, cottages, and carriage houses, try Historic Charleston Bed and Breakfast. Southern Hospitality B&B Reservations handles rooms in homes and carriage houses.
➤ RESERVATION SERVICES: **Historic Charleston Bed and Breakfast** (✉ 60 Broad St., South of Broad, Charleston 29401, ☎ 843/722–6606). **Southern Hospitality B&B Reservations** (✉ 110 Amelia Dr., Lexington 29072, ☎ 843/356–6238 or 800/374–7422).

TAXIS
Fares within the city average $3–$4 per trip. Companies include Safety Cab, Checker Cab, and Yellow Cab.

Charleston Rickshaw Company has two-adult pedicabs that will take you anywhere in the historic district for about $6–$12.
➤ TAXI COMPANIES: **Charleston Rickshaw Company** (✉ 21 George St., Market area, ☎ 843/723–5685). **Checker Taxi** (☎ 843/747–9200). **Safety Cab** (☎ 843/722–4066). **Yellow Cab** (☎ 843/577–6565).

TOURS
BOAT TOURS
Charleston Harbor Tour and Princess Gray Line Harbor Tours ply the harbor. Fort Sumter Tours includes a stop at Fort Sumter and also offers Starlight dinner cruises aboard a luxury yacht.

➤ FEES AND SCHEDULES: **Charleston Harbor Tour** (☎ 843/722–1691). **Fort Sumter Tours** (☎ 843/722–1691, 843/881–7337, or 800/789–3678). **Princess Gray Line Harbor Tours** (☎ 843/722–1112 or 800/344–4483).

BUS TOURS

Adventure Sightseeing and the Colonial Coach and Trolley Company do motor-coach tours of the historic district. Gray Line has tours of the historic district plus seasonal trips to gardens and plantations. Doin' the Charleston, a van tour, combines its narration with audiovisuals and makes a stop at the Battery.

➤ FEES AND SCHEDULES: **Adventure Sightseeing** (☎ 843/762–0088 or 800/722–5394). **Colonial Coach and Trolley Company** (☎ 843/795–3000). **Doin' the Charleston** (☎ 843/763–1233 or 800/647–4487). **Gray Line** (☎ 843/722–4444).

CARRIAGE TOURS

Lowcountry Carriage Co., Old South Carriage Company, and Palmetto Carriage Tours run horse- and mule-drawn carriage tours of the historic district, some conducted by guides in Confederate uniforms, that each last about one hour. We highly recommend carriage tours if you want a great overview of Charleston. They have a set itinerary and cover one of four zones in the historic district; once the carriages have picked up passengers the drivers draw from a lottery to decide which zone each carriage will cover. Go before 5 PM so you'll get to see the residential section.

➤ FEES AND SCHEDULES: **Lowcountry Carriage Co.** (☎ 843/577–0042). **Old South Carriage Company** (☎ 843/723–9712). **Palmetto Carriage Tours** (☎ 843/723–8145).

ECOTOURS

Barrior Island Ecotours, at the Isle of Palms Marina, offers three-hour pontoon-boat tours to a barrier island, sunset tours, crabbing and fishing expeditions, and even a day camp for kids. Coastal Expeditions Kayak Tours offers half-day and full-day naturalist-led kayak tours down historic rivers. You can also rent kayaks. Cap'n Richard's ACE Basin Nature Tour takes you into the ACE (for Ashepoo, Cumbahee, and Edisto rivers) Basin—a managed wilderness that includes 350,000 acres of wetlands—for a river tour as well as a land tour of a private plantation.

➤ FEES AND SCHEDULES: **Barrior Island Ecotours** (☎ 843/886–5000). **Cap'n Richard's ACE Basin Nature Tour** (☎ 843/766–9664). **Coastal Expeditions Kayak Tours** (☎ 843/884–7684).

SPECIAL-INTEREST TOURS

Flying High over Charleston provides aerial tours. Chai Y'All shares stories and sites of Jewish interest. Gullah Tours is expert in local African-American culture. Sweetgrass Tours focuses on African-American influences on Charleston architecture, history, and culture.

➤ FEES AND SCHEDULES: **Chai Y'All** (☎ 843/556–0664). **Flying High over Charleston** (☎ 843/569–6148). **Gullah Tours** (☎ 843/763–7551). **Sweetgrass Tours** (☎ 843/556–0664 for groups).

PRIVATE GUIDES

To hire a private guide, contact Associated Guides of Historic Charleston; Charleston's Finest Historic Tours, which offers tours of the city and plantations; or Janice Kahn, who has been doing individualized guiding for more than 25 years.

➤ CONTACTS: **Associated Guides of Historic Charleston** (☎ 843/724–6419). **Charleston's Finest Historic Tours** (☎ 843/577–3311). **Janice Kahn** (☎ 843/556–0664).

WALKING TOURS

Walking tours are given by Charleston Strolls; Charleston Tea Party Walking Tour, whose walks include tea in a private garden; On the Market Tours; and the Original Charleston Walks. For a spookier view of the city, take the Ghosts of Charleston walking tour. The same guides also celebrate the city in the Story of Charleston walking tour.

➤ FEES AND SCHEDULES: **Charleston Strolls** (☎ 843/766–2080). **Charleston Tea Party Walking Tour** (☎ 843/577–5896 or 843/722–1779). **Ghosts of Charleston** (☎ 843/723–1670 or 800/854–1670). **On the Market Tours** (☎ 843/853–8687). **Original Charleston Walks** (☎ 843/577–3800 or 800/729–3420).

TRAIN TRAVEL

➤ TRAIN INFORMATION: **Amtrak** (✉ 4565 Gaynor Ave., North Charleston, ☎ 843/744–8264 or 800/872–7245).

VISITOR INFORMATION

You can pick up a schedule of events at the visitor center or at area hotels, inns, and restaurants. Also see "Tips for Tourists" each Saturday in the *Post & Courier.* The Charleston Area Convention and Visitors Bureau has information on the city and also on Kiawah Island, Seabrook Island, Mount Pleasant, North Charleston, Edisto Island, Summerville, and the Isle of Palms. The Historic Charleston Foundation and the Preservation Society of Charleston have information on house tours.

➤ TOURIST INFORMATION: **Charleston Area Convention and Visitors Bureau** (✉ Box 975, Charleston 29402, ☎ 843/853–8000 or 800/868–8118, WEB www.charlestoncvb.com). **Historic Charleston Foundation** (✉ Box 1120, Charleston 29402, ☎ 843/723–1623). **Preservation Society of Charleston** (✉ Box 521, Charleston 29402, ☎ 843/722–4630). **Visitor Center** (✉ 375 Meeting St., Upper King).

MYRTLE BEACH AND THE GRAND STRAND

The lively, family-oriented Grand Strand, a booming resort area along the South Carolina coast, is one of the eastern seaboard's megavacation centers. Myrtle Beach alone accounts for about 40% of the state's tourism revenue. The main attraction, of course, is the broad, beckoning beach—60 mi of white sand, stretching from the North Carolina border south to Georgetown, with Myrtle Beach as the hub. All along the Strand you can enjoy shell hunting, fishing, swimming, sunbathing, sailing, surfing, jogging, or just strolling on the beach. Here you'll find more than 100 championship golf courses, designed by Arnold Palmer, Robert Trent Jones, Jack Nicklaus, and Tom and George Fazio, among others; excellent seafood restaurants; giant shopping malls and factory outlets; amusement parks, water slides, and arcades; a dozen shipwrecks for divers to explore; fine fishing; campgrounds, most of which are on the beach; plus antique-car and wax museums, the world's largest outdoor sculpture garden, an antique pipe organ and merry-go-round, and a museum dedicated entirely to rice. The Strand has also emerged as a major center for country music, with an expanding number of theaters.

Myrtle Beach—whose population of 26,000 explodes to about 450,000 in summer—is the center of activity on the Grand Strand. It is here that you'll find the amusement parks and other children's activities that make the area so popular with families, as well as most of the nightlife that keeps parents and teenagers alike happy. On the North Strand are Little River, with a thriving fishing and charter industry, and the several communities that make up North Myrtle Beach. On the South Strand the family retreats of Surfside Beach and Garden City offer more summer homes and condominiums. Farther south are towns as alluring to visit as are the sights along the way: Murrells Inlet, once a pirates' haven and now a scenic fishing village and port; and Pawleys Island, one of the East Coast's oldest resorts, which prides itself on being "arrogantly shabby." Historic Georgetown forms the southern tip.

Myrtle Beach

94 mi northeast of Charleston via U.S. 17, 138 mi east of Columbia via U.S. 76 to U.S. 378 to U.S. 501.

Myrtle Beach, with its high-rises and hyperdevelopment, is a swirl of seaside activity. To capture its flavor, start at the Myrtle Beach Pavilion Amusement Park and wind your way north on Ocean Boulevard. Here's where you'll find an eclectic assortment of gift and novelty shops, a wax museum, and a museum of oddities. Turn east when it suits your fancy and make your way back on the beach amid children building sand castles and kids-at-heart flying kites.

Dozens of colorful streetlight displays around major intersections add yet a few more volts of energy to the already pulsating scene, and at Christmas Myrtle Beach stages one of the largest, most colorful light shows in the South.

☺ **Myrtle Beach Pavilion Amusement Park** has thrill and children's rides, the Carolinas' largest flume, a wooden roller coaster, video games, a teen nightclub, specialty shops, antique cars, and sidewalk cafés. ⊠ *9th Ave. N and Ocean Blvd., the Strip,* ☎ *843/448–6456,* WEB *www. mbpavilion.com.* ☞ *Fees for individual attractions; 1-day pass for unlimited access to most rides $22.* ☉ *Mid-Mar.–May and mid-Aug.–Sept., weekdays 6 PM–10 PM, Sat. 1–10, Sun. 1–8; June–mid-Aug., daily 1 PM–midnight, operating hrs can vary, so call ahead.*

Ripley's Haunted Adventure. Convincing vampires and other costumed characters will taunt and entice you to come inside this fun, creepy haunted house. ⊠ *915 N. Ocean Blvd., the Strip,* ☎ *843/448–2261.* ☞ *$10.* ☉ *Late Feb.–May and Sept.–mid-Oct., daily 9 AM–11 PM; June–Aug., daily 9 AM–2 AM.*

☺ **Hawaiian Rumble** is the crown jewel of Myrtle Beach, the minigolf capital of the world. The course, the site of several championship tournaments, has a smoking mountain that erupts with fire and rumbles at timed intervals. ⊠ *3210 33rd Ave. S, at U.S. 17, North Myrtle Beach,* ☎ *843/458–2585.* ☞ *$8 all day (9–5), $6 per round after 5 PM.* ☉ *Mar.–Dec., daily 9 AM–midnight.*

★ ☺ **Alligator Adventure** has exciting interactive reptile shows, including an alligator-feeding demonstration. The boardwalks go through marshes and swamps on the 15-acre property, where you'll see wildlife of the wetlands, including the only known collection of the rare white albino alligator; the gavial, an exotic crocodilian from Asia; giant Galápagos tortoises; and all manner of other reptiles, including boas, pythons, and anacondas. Unusual plants and exotic birds also thrive here. ⊠ *U.S. 17 at Barefoot Landing, North Myrtle Beach,* ☎ *843/361–0789,* FAX *843/361–0742,* WEB *www.alligatoradventure.com.* ☞ *$12.95.* ☉ *Daily 10–9.*

☺ **Myrtle Beach Grand Prix Family Thrill Park** is auto-mania heaven with Formula 1 race cars, go-carts, bumper boats, mini-go-carts, and bumper boats, plus a kids' park for children ages 3 and up with mini-go-carts, kids' cars, and mini–bumper boats. New is a log flume and music express ride. ✉ *3201 U.S. 17, North Myrtle Beach,* ☎ *843/272–7770;* ✉ *Windy Hill, 3900 U.S. 17S, North End,* ☎ *843/272–7770,* WEB *www. mbgrandprix.com.* ✍ *$29.95 unlimited rides or individual rides $3–$5 each.* ☼ *Mar.–Oct., daily 3–midnight.*

At **NASCAR Speedpark** you can drive on seven different NASCAR-replica tracks; the 26-acre facility also has racing memorabilia, an arcade, and miniature golf. ✉ *U.S. 17 Bypass and 21st Ave. N, at Broadway at the Beach, Central Myrtle Beach,* ☎ *843/918–8725,* WEB *www. nascarspeedpark.com.* ✍ *$21.95 unlimited day pass or $5 each ride.* ☼ *Mar.–Oct., weekdays 5* PM*–midnight, weekends noon–midnight; hrs vary, so call to confirm.*

The **Butterfly Pavilion** has a fully enclosed glass butterfly conservatory where you can walk among 2,000 native North American and tropical butterflies. The Nature Zone Discovery Center has 22 animal exhibits including those featuring exotic frogs, insects, and a working beehive; in the Lorikeet Aviary you're surrounded by and can hand-feed colorful lorikeets. ✉ *1185 Celebrity Circle, at Broadway at the Beach, Central Myrtle Beach,* ☎ *843/839–4444 or 877/280–2751,* WEB *www.butterflypavilion.com.* ✍ *$12.95.* ☼ *Jan.–early Mar., daily 9–6; early Mar.–late Mar., daily 9–8; Apr.–May, daily 9* AM*–10* PM*; June–early Sept., daily 9* AM*–11* PM*; early Sept.–Dec., daily 9–9.*

The **Ripley's Aquarium** has an underwater tunnel exhibit longer than a football field and exotic marine creatures from poisonous lionfish to moray eels and an octopus. Children can examine horseshoe crabs and eels in touch tanks. ✉ *9th Ave. N and U.S. 17N Bypass, at Broadway at the Beach, Central Myrtle Beach,* ☎ *843/916–0888 or 800/734–8888,* WEB *www.ripleysaquarium.com.* ✍ *$14.95.* ☼ *Sun.–Thurs. 9–9, Fri.–Sat. 9* AM*–10* PM*; closing time varies.*

South of Myrtle Beach about 9 mi, **Wild Water** provides splashy family fun for all ages in 25 water-oriented rides and activities. ✉ *910 U. S. 17S, Surfside Beach,* ☎ *843/238–3787,* WEB *www.wild-water.com.* ✍ *$20, $13 after 3* PM*.* ☼ *Late May–early Sept., daily 10–7.*

Myrtle Waves is a huge water park. ✉ *Hwy. 17 Bypass and 19th Ave. N, South End,* ☎ *843/448–1026 or 800/524–9283,* WEB *www. myrtlewaves.com.* ✍ *$22 for full day, $13.95 for ½ day.* ☼ *Late May–early Sept., daily 10–6.*

Dining and Lodging

MYRTLE BEACH

$$$–$$$$ ✗ **Collectors Cafe.** A successful restaurant, art gallery, and coffeehouse ★ rolled into one, this unpretentious arty spot has bright, funky paintings and tile work covering its walls and tabletops. You can shop for a painting while enjoying black-bean cakes, grilled tuna, or pan-sautéed scallop cakes. ✉ *7726 N. Kings Hwy., North Myrtle Beach,* ☎ *843/449–9370. AE, D, DC, MC, V. Closed Sun. No lunch.*

$$–$$$ ✗ **Sea Captain's House.** At this picturesque restaurant with a nautical theme, the best seats are in the windowed porch room, which overlooks the ocean. The fireplace in the wood-paneled dining room inside is warmly welcoming on cool off-season evenings. Menu highlights include Lowcountry crab casserole and avocado-seafood salad. The breads and desserts are baked on the premises. ✉ *3000 N. Ocean Blvd., the Strip,* ☎ *843/448–8082. AE, D, MC, V.*

$–$$ ✗ **Villa Katrina's Underground Cantina.** Head downstairs into a fun, tavernlike space for Mexican fare of the elegant variety, including flaming coffees and desserts. Chicken-and-spinach burritos and tacos are a specialty. ✉ *821 Main St., the Strip,* ☎ *843/946–6216. No credit cards. Closed Sun.*

$–$$ ✕ **Vintage House Café.** Locals dine here on beef tips, smoked chicken ravioli, and homemade bananas Foster cheesecake. The style hints of Granny's house: entrées are served on an assortment of vintage china; old sideboards, pitchers, and lace doilies are among the accents. ⊠ *1210 N. Kings Hwy., the Strip,* ☎ *843/626–3918. AE, D, DC, MC, V. Closed Sun. No dinner Mon.*

$ ✕ **Croissants Bakery & Café.** The lunch crowd loves this spot, which has an on-site bakery. Black-and-white tile floors, café tables, checked tablecloths, and glass pastry cases filled with sweets create an appetizing feel to the place. Try the chicken or broccoli salads, a Reuben sandwich, the pasta specials, a Monte Cristo sandwich, and the peanut butter cheesecake. ⊠ *504A 27th Ave. N, the Strip,* ☎ *843/448–2253. D, MC, V. Closed Sun. No dinner.*

$$ ✕🏨 **Sea Island Inn.** In the quiet residential end of Myrtle Beach, this inn has oceanfront rooms with comfortable standard furnishings plus several social areas. Breakfast and dinner are served in the elegant oceanfront dining room. ⊠ *6000 N. Ocean Blvd., North End 29577,* ☎ *843/449–6406 or 800/548–0767,* FAX *843/449–4102,* WEB *www.seaislandinn.com. 113 rooms, 1 suite, 1 penthouse. Restaurant, 2 pools, Ping-Pong, children's programs. AE, D, MC, V. MAP.*

$$$–$$$$ 🏨 **Kingston Plantation.** The Grand Strand's most luxurious property,
★   the 20-story glass-sheathed tower is part of a complex of shops, restaurants, hotels, and one- to three-bedroom condominiums in 145 acres of ocean-side woodlands. An Embassy Suites property, the hotel has guest rooms with bleached-wood furnishings and a whimsical theme; all have kitchenettes. ⊠ *9800 Lake Dr., North End 29572,* ☎ *843/449–0006 or 800/876–0010,* FAX *843/497–1110,* WEB *www.kingstonplantation.com. 255 suites, 510 villas and condos. 2 restaurants, tennis court, indoor pool, aerobics, health club, sauna, racquetball, lounge. AE, D, DC, MC, V.*

$$$ 🏨 **Hampton Inn and Suites Oceanfront.** This property combines the classic reliability of this respected midpriced range with the joys of a beach resort. Rooms have balconies and a cheerful style; all rooms have ocean views, and there's a lazy river—a pool with a moving current— that carries swimmers along its course. ⊠ *1803 S. Ocean Blvd, South End 29577,* ☎ *843/946–6400 or 877/946–6400,* FAX *843/236–9415,* WEB *www.hamptoninnoceanfront.com. 80 rooms, 36 suites. Microwaves, refrigerators, 2 indoor pools, 2 outdoor pools, gym, hot tub, business services, meeting rooms. AE, D, DC, MC, V. CP.*

$$–$$$ 🏨 **Breakers Resort Hotel.** The rooms in this tall oceanfront hotel (within walking distance of the Pavilion) are airy and spacious, with contemporary furnishings. Most have kitchenettes and Murphy beds; the new Paradise Tower (next door to the original tower) has one-, two- and three-bedroom suites, a lazy river, and a pirate-ship facade that kids can swim in and around. ⊠ *2006 N. Ocean Blvd., Box 485, 29578,* ☎ *843/444–4444 or 800/845–0688,* FAX *843/626–5001,* WEB *www.breakers.com. 204 rooms, 186 suites. 2 restaurants, room service, refrigerators, 2 pools, indoor-outdoor pool, gym, outdoor hot tubs, saunas, lounge, video game room, children's programs, laundry service. AE, D, DC, MC, V.*

$$–$$$ 🏨 **Holiday Inn Oceanfront.** This oceanfront inn is right in the heart of the action. The spacious rooms are done in cool sea tones. After beach basking you can prolong the mood in the inn's spacious, plant-bedecked indoor recreation center. ⊠ *415 S. Ocean Blvd., the Strip 29577,* ☎ *843/448–4481 or 800/845–0313,* FAX *843/448–0086,* WEB *www.basshotels.com. 306 rooms. 2 restaurants, snack bar, indoor pool, hot tub, sauna, lounge, recreation room. AE, D, DC, MC, V.*

$$–$$$ ⊞ **Sheraton Myrtle Beach Resort.** All rooms and suites have a fresh, contemporary look. Oceanfront Lounge, highlighted by tropical colors and rattan furnishings, is a lively evening gathering spot. There are a lazy river (artificial stream) and an arcade nearby. ⊠ *2701 S. Ocean Blvd., South End 29577,* ☎ *843/448–2518 or 800/992–1055,* FAX *843/449–1879,* WEB *www.sheratonresort.com. 211 rooms, 8 suites. Restaurant, indoor pool, health club. AE, D, DC, MC, V.*

$$ ⊞ **Chesterfield Inn.** A remnant from the past, this oceanfront brick inn, hidden beneath the towers of Myrtle Beach's glitzier hotels, has been in operation for more than a half century. The rooms in the original building are plain and a bit worn, but many people prefer them to those in the newer wing. The highlight here is the family-style meals, served on white tablecloths in the seafront dining room. ⊠ *700 N. Ocean Blvd., the Strip 29578,* ☎ *843/448–3177,* FAX *843/626–4736,* WEB *www. chesterfieldinnmb.com. 63 rooms. Restaurant, some kitchenettes, pool, shuffleboard. AE, D, DC, MC, V. MAP.*

$$ ⊞ **Landmark Resort Hotel.** This high-rise oceanfront resort hotel has artificial "lazy rivers" indoors and out. Rooms are colorfully decorated in a Caribbean motif. All have balconies and refrigerators; some have kitchenettes. ⊠ *1501 S. Ocean Blvd., South End 29577,* ☎ *843/448–9441 or 800/845–0658,* FAX *843/448–6701,* WEB *www.landmarkresort. com. 313 rooms, 257 suites. Restaurant, snack bar, 2 pools, 2 indoor pools, wading pool, gym, sauna, hot tubs, pub, video game room, laundry facilities, airport shuttle; no-smoking rooms. AE, D, DC, MC, V.*

$ ⊞ **Days Inn at Waccamaw.** Relax by the pool or in the gazebo after a day of shopping at the nearby Waccamaw Pottery and Factory Shoppes. The theaters of the Fantasy Harbor complex are also close at hand. Rooms here are clean and functional and filled with contemporary furnishings. ⊠ *3650 U.S. 501, Waccamaw Pottery area 29577,* ☎ *843/236–1950 or 800/325–2525,* FAX *843/236–9415,* WEB *www.daysinn.com. 157 rooms. Pool, hot tub. AE, D, DC, MC, V.*

$ ⊞ **Driftwood on the Oceanfront.** Under the same ownership for more than 65 years, the Driftwood is popular with families. Some rooms are on the oceanfront, and all are decorated in sea, sky, or earth tones. ⊠ *1600 N. Ocean Blvd., Box 275, 29578,* ☎ *843/448–1544 or 800/942–3456,* FAX *843/448–2917,* WEB *www.driftwoodlodge.com. 90 rooms. Microwaves, refrigerators, 2 pools, gym, shuffleboard, laundry facilities. AE, D, MC, V.*

$ ⊞ **Serendipity Inn.** This cozy Spanish villa-style inn is about 300 yards from the beach. Though the layout is much like a hotel, each guest room is decorated in a different way. There's also a colorful pool area dotted with hanging flowers and a trickling fountain. A breakfast of homemade coffee cake, hardboiled eggs, yogurt, cereal, and fruit is served in the white-wicker Garden Room. ⊠ *407 71st Ave. N, North End 29572,* ☎ *843/449–5268 or 800/762–3229,* WEB *www.serendipityinn. com. 12 rooms, 1 suite. Refrigerators, some kitchenettes, pool, outdoor hot tub, Ping-Pong, shuffleboard; no room phones. MC, V.*

NORTH MYRTLE BEACH

Dinner cruises are a popular dining option here. The cruise ship **Hurricane** and yachts of the Hurricane pleasure fleet (☎ 843/249–3571) depart from Vereen's Marina (⊠ U.S. 17N and 11th Ave., North Myrtle Beach). The **Barefoot Princess** (☎ 843/272–7743 or 800/685–6601), a replica of a side-wheel riverboat, offers dinner, sunset, and sightseeing cruises along the Intracoastal Waterway from Barefoot Landing (⊠ 4898 U.S. 17S, North Myrtle Beach).

$$–$$$$ ✕ **Greg Norman's Australian Grille.** Overlooking the Intracoastal Waterway, this large restaurant in Barefoot Landing has leather booths, hand-painted walls, an extensive wine list, and a classy bar area.

There's an extensive choice of grilled meats, and much of the menu has an Asian flair; try the lobster dumplings, miso-marinated sea bass, or habanero-rubbed tenderloin. ⊠ *4930 U.S. 17S, North Myrtle Beach,* ☎ *843/361–0000. Reservations essential. AE, D, MC, V.*

$$$ ⛳ **Barefoot Resort and Golf.** This golf resort—which when complete (in 2005) will total 500-plus condos—includes one- to- four-bedroom units along fairways as well as in the 118-unit North Tower, which overlooks the Intracoastal Waterway. There are a man-made sandy beach and a waterfront pool. When fully completed, there will be meeting spaces, restaurants, shops, and a water taxi to transport you to Barefoot Landing. ⊠ *Harborpoint Blvd., North Myrtle Beach (mail: 4980 Barefoot Resort Bridge Rd., North Myrtle Beach 29577),* ☎ *866/ 888–6606,* WEB *www.bfresort.com. 118 condos. Pool, 4 18-hole golf courses, spa. AE, D, DC, MC, V.*

Nightlife and the Arts

CLUBS AND LOUNGES

Clubs offer varying fare, including beach music, the Grand Strand's unique '50s-style sound. Some clubs and resorts have sophisticated live entertainment in summer. Some hotels and resorts also have piano bars or lounges with easy-listening music.

South Carolina's only Hard Rock Cafe, Planet Hollywood, and NASCAR Cafe are just a few of the hot spots in **Broadway at the Beach** (⊠ U.S. 17 Bypass between 21st and 29th Aves. N, the Strip, ☎ 843/ 444–3200), which also has shopping. You can dance the shag (the state dance) at **Duck's** (⊠ 229 Main St., North Myrtle Beach, ☎ 843/249– 3858). **Gypsy's** (⊠ 501 8th Ave. N, the Strip, ☎ 843/916–2244) is great for late-night blues music and has a nice wine selection. **Sandals** (⊠ 500 Shore Dr., North Myrtle Beach, ☎ 843/449–6461) is an intimate lounge with live entertainment. The shag is popular at **Studebaker's** (⊠ 2000 N. Kings Hwy., the Strip, ☎ 843/448–9747 or 843/626–3855).

FILM

The **IMAX Discovery Theater** at Broadway at the Beach (⊠ U.S. 17 Bypass between 21st and 29th Aves. N, the Strip, ☎ 843/448–4629) shows educational films on a six-story-high screen.

MUSIC AND LIVE SHOWS

Live acts, and country-and-western shows in particular, are a big draw at the Grand Strand. Music lovers have many family-oriented shows to choose from. The 2,250-seat **Alabama Theater** (⊠ Barefoot Landing, 4750 U.S. 17, North Myrtle Beach, ☎ 843/272–1111) has a regular variety show with a wonderful patriotic closing; the theater also hosts different guest music and comedy artists during the year. **Carolina Opry** (⊠ 82nd Ave. N, North End, ☎ 843/238–8888 or 800/843–6779) is a family-oriented variety show featuring country, light rock, show tunes, and gospel music. At **Dolly Parton's Dixie Stampede** (⊠ 8901B U.S. 17 Business, next door to Carolina Opry, North End, ☎ 843/497– 9700 or 800/843–6779), you can dine and enjoy a rousing horse-based show. **Legends in Concert** (⊠ 301 U.S. 17 Business, Surfside Beach, ☎ 843/238–7827 or 800/843–6779) has high-energy shows by impersonators of Little Richard, Elvis, Cher, and the Blues Brothers. The elegant **Palace Theater** (⊠ Broadway at the Beach, U.S. 17 Bypass between 21st and 29th Aves. N, the Strip, ☎ 843/448–0588 or 800/905– 4228) hosts performances by the likes of Aretha Franklin, Kenny Rogers, and the Radio City Rockettes.

The **Fantasy Harbor** complex (⊠ Rte. 51, across from Waccamaw Factory Shoppes, Waccamaw Pottery area) includes several theaters: the 2,000-seat **Crook and Chase Theater** (☎ 843/236–8500 or 800/681–

5209), the **Savoy** (☎ 843/236–2200 or 800/681–5209), **Medieval Times Dinner & Tournament** (☎ 843/236–8080 or 800/436–4386), and the 2,000-seat **Forum Theater** (☎ 843/236–8500).

The **House of Blues** (✉ 4640 U.S. 17S, North Myrtle Beach, ☎ 843/ 272–3000 for tickets), adjacent to Barefoot Landing, showcases big names and up-and-coming talent in blues, rock, jazz, country, and R&B on stages in its Southern-style restaurant and patio as well as in its 2,000-seat concert hall. The gospel brunch is a great deal.

PERFORMING ARTS

Theater productions, concerts, art exhibits, and other cultural events are regularly offered at the **Myrtle Beach Convention Center** (✉ Oak and 21st Ave. N, the Strip, ☎ 843/448–7166).

Outdoor Activities and Sports

BEACHES

All the region's beaches are family oriented, and most are public. The widest expanses are in North Myrtle Beach, where at low tide the sand stretches as far as 650 ft from the dunes to the water. Those who wish to combine their sunning with enjoying nightlife and amusement-park attractions can enjoy it all at Myrtle Beach, the Strand's longtime hub. Vacationers seeking a quieter day in the sun head for the South Strand communities of Surfside Beach and Garden City.

Besides ocean swimming, **Myrtle Beach State Park** has surf fishing, a nature trail, and a pool; there's camping, too, but book in advance. ✉ *U.S. 17, 3 mi south of Myrtle Beach, Surfside Beach, ☎ 843/238–5325.* ☜ *$2 (age 17 and older).*

FISHING

The Gulf Stream makes fishing usually good from early spring through December. Anglers can fish from 10 piers and jetties for amberjack, sea trout, and king mackerel. Surfcasters may snare bluefish, whiting, flounder, pompano, and channel bass. In the South Strand, salt marshes, inlets, and tidal creeks yield flounder, blues, croakers, spots, shrimp, clams, oysters, and blue crabs. The annual **Grand Strand Fishing Rodeo** (☎ 843/626–7444 Apr.–Oct.) hosts a fish-of-the-month contest, with prizes for the largest catch of a designated species.

GOLF

Many of the Grand Strand's nearly 100 courses are championship layouts; most are public. **Tee Times Central** (☎ 843/347–4653 or 800/344–5590) books tee times for eight courses, including 18-hole, par-72 **Long Bay** (✉ 350 Foxtail Dr., Longs, ☎ 843/399–2222); 18-hole, par-72 **Myrtle Beach National Golf Club** (✉ 4900 National Dr., Waccamaw Pottery area, ☎ 843/448–2308); and 9-hole, par-36 **Waterway Hills** (✉ U.S. 17N, North Myrtle Beach, ☎ 843/449–6488). A popular course in Myrtle Beach is the 18-hole, par-72 **Arcadian Shores Golf Club** (✉ 701 Hilton Rd., North End, ☎ 843/449–5217). In North Myrtle Beach you'll find the three 18-hole, par-72 courses of the **Legends** (✉ U.S. 501, North Myrtle Beach, ☎ 843/236–9318). The 18-hole, par-72 **Bay Tree Golf Plantation** (✉ Rte. 9, North Myrtle Beach, ☎ 843/249–1487 or 800/845–6191) has varying degrees of difficulty on its silver, gold and green courses. Nine holes of the **Grande Dunes Golf Course** (✉ U.S. 17N, North End 1000 Grande Dunes Blvd., ☎ 888/ 886–8877) play along the Intracoastal waterway; the course also has elevated vistas. **Heather Glen Golf Links** (✉ U.S. 17N, Little River, ☎ 843/249–9000) is a links-style course with lots of pot-bunkers and pretty water holes. **Robbers Roost Golf Club** (✉ 1400 U.S. 17N, North Myrtle Beach, ☎ 843/249–1471 or 800/352–2384) has wide fairways and lots of holes with water. Near Surfside Beach is the 18-hole, par-72 **Black-**

moor **Golf Club** (⊠ Rte. 707, Murrells Inlet, ☎ 843/650–5555), one of the country's top women-friendly courses. In Cherry Grove Beach you'll find the much-touted 18-hole, par-72 **Tidewater** (⊠ 4901 Little River Neck Rd., North Myrtle Beach, ☎ 800/446–5363), one of just two courses in the area that offer ocean views.

SCUBA DIVING

In summer, many warm-water tropical fish travel to the area from the Gulf Stream. Off the coast of Little River, near the North Carolina border, rock and coral ledges teem with coral, sea fans, sponges, reef fish, anemones, urchins, and crabs. Several outlying shipwrecks are flush with schools of spadefish, amberjack, grouper, and barracuda. Instruction and equipment rentals, as well as an indoor dive tank, are available from **New Horizons Dive and Travel,** in the Sports Corner shopping center (⊠ 515 Hwy. 501, Suite A, the Strip, ☎ 843/839–1932).

TENNIS

There are more than 200 courts on the Grand Strand. Facilities include hotel and resort courts, as well as free municipal courts in Myrtle Beach, North Myrtle Beach, and Surfside Beach. **Prestwick Tennis and Swim Club** (☎ 843/828–1000) offers court time, rental equipment, and instruction. **Grande Dunes Tennis** (☎ 843/449–4486) is a full fitness facility with 10 Har-Tru courts, two of which are lighted; the club also offers private and group lessons.

WATER SPORTS

Surfboards, Hobie Cats, Jet Skis, Windsurfers, and sailboats are available for rent at **Downwind Sails** (⊠ Ocean Blvd. at 29th Ave. S, South End, ☎ 843/448–7245). **Myrtle Beach Yacht Club** (⊠ 720 Hwy. 17, Coquina Harbor, Little River, ☎ 843/249–5376) rents water-sports equipment.

Shopping

DISCOUNT OUTLETS

The **Factory Shoppes** (⊠ U.S. 501, Waccamaw Pottery area, ☎ 843/236–6152) is a large outlet center with Gap, Nike, Polo, and Off 5th (a division of Saks Fifth Avenue). In North Myrtle Beach head for the **Myrtle Beach Factory Stores** (⊠ U.S. 501 and Waccamaw Pines Dr., Waccamaw Pottery area, ☎ 843/903–1614) for Brooks Brothers, Donna Karan, Banana Republic, and Eddie Bauer. **Tanger Outlet** (⊠ 10785 Kings Rd., Waccamaw Pottery area, ☎ 843/449–0491) has 75 factory outlet stores, including Polo and Old Navy. At **Waccamaw Pottery and Linen** (⊠ U.S. 501 at the Waterway, Waccamaw Pottery area, ☎ 843/236–1100) more than 3 mi of shelves in several buildings are stocked with china, glassware, brass, pewter, and other items, and about 50 factory outlets sell clothing, furniture, books, jewelry, and more.

MALLS

Barefoot Landing in North Myrtle Beach (⊠ 4898 S. Kings Hwy., North Myrtle Beach, ☎ 843/272–8349), built over marshland and water, has scores of shops and restaurants, plus rides—including a thrill ride called the Accelorator.

Murrells Inlet

15 mi south of Myrtle Beach on U.S. 17.

Murrells Inlet, a fishing village with some popular seafood restaurants, is a perfect place to rent a fishing boat or join an excursion. A notable garden and state park provide other diversions from the beach.

★ **Brookgreen Gardens,** begun in 1931 by railroad magnate–philanthropist Archer Huntington and his wife, Anna (herself a sculptor), displays more than 500 sculptures by such artists as Frederic Remington and Daniel Chester French. The works are set amid beautifully landscaped grounds, with avenues of live oaks, reflecting pools, and more than 2,000 plant species. Also on the site are a wildlife park, an aviary, a cypress swamp, nature trails, and an education center. Summer nights sculptures are illuminated. ⊠ *West of U.S. 17, 3 mi south of Murrells Inlet,* ☎ *843/237–4218 or 800/849–1931,* WEB *www.brookgreen.org.* ☒ *$12.* ☉ *Oct.–May, daily 9:30–5; June–Sept., Wed.–Fri. 9:30–9:30, Sat.–Tues. 9:30–5.*

Huntington Beach State Park, the 2,500-acre former estate of Archer and Anna Huntington, lies east of U.S. 17, across from the couple's Brookgreen Gardens. The park's focal point is **Atalaya** (circa 1933), their Moorish-style 30-room home, open to visitors in season. In addition to the splendid beach, there are nature trails, fishing, an interpretive center, and an education center with fresh- and saltwater aquariums and a loggerhead sea turtle nesting habitat. There are also picnic areas, a playground, concessions, and a campground. ⊠ *East of U.S. 17, 3 mi south of Murrells Inlet,* ☎ *843/237–4440,* WEB *www.southcarolinaparks.com.* ☒ *$4.* ☉ *Nov.–mid-Mar., daily 6–6; mid-Mar.–Oct., daily 6 AM–10 PM.*

Nightlife and the Arts

THE ARTS

In the fall the **Atalaya Arts Festival** (☎ 843/237–4440), at Huntington Beach State Park, is a big draw.

NIGHTLIFE

Drunken Jack's (⊠ U.S. Business 17, ☎ 843/651–2044 or 843/651–3232), overlooking the docks, has been a popular restaurant for 23 years. It has a lounge, waterfront deck, and working crab traps to occupy young diners.

Outdoor Activities and Sports

Capt. Dick's (⊠ U.S. Business 17, ☎ 843/651–3676) runs half- and full-day fishing and sightseeing trips.

Pawleys Island

10 mi south of Murrells Inlet via U.S. 17.

About 4 mi long and ½ mi wide, this island, referred to as "arrogantly shabby" by locals, began as a resort before the Civil War, when wealthy planters and their families summered here. It's mostly made up of weathered old summer cottages nestled in groves of oleander and oak trees. You can watch the famous Pawleys Island hammocks being made and bicycle around admiring the beach houses, many dating to the early 1800s. Golf and tennis are nearby.

Dining and Lodging

$$$–$$$$ ✕ **Frank's.** Seasonal ingredients make this a local favorite. In a former 1930s grocery store with wood floors, framed French posters, and cozy fireside seating, diners indulge in large portions of fish, seafood, beef, and lamb cooked over an oak-burning grill. The roasted asparagus with prosciutto in phyllo and the pork tenderloin with shiitake mushrooms and a Dijon cream sauce are two highlights. Behind Frank's is the casual (but still pricey) Outback at Frank's, specializing in rotisserie chicken, salads, and lighter fare. ⊠ *10434 Ocean Hwy. (U.S. 17),* ☎ *843/237–3030. Reservations essential. D, MC, V. Closed Sun.*

$$–$$$ ✕ **Pawleys Island Tavern.** This little eatery has terrific crab cakes, hickory-smoked barbecue, roasted chicken, and pizza (they deliver). Summer weekend nights tiki torches outside blaze and live music rocks the place. ⊠ *The Island Shops, U.S. 17,* ☎ *843/237–8465. AE, MC, V.*

$ ✕ **Landolphi's.** This Italian pastry shop and deli, fourth generation owned, has excellent coffee, hearty hoagies, pizzas, homemade sorbet, and delicious and authentic pastries, including cannoli and *pasticciotti* (a rich pastry). ⊠ *9305 Ocean Hwy.,* ☎ *843/237–7900. AE, MC, V. Closed Sun. No dinner Mon.–Thurs.*

$$$$ ✕🏨 **Litchfield Plantation.** Period furnishings adorn four spacious suites of this impeccably restored 1750 rice-plantation manor house–turned–country inn. Use of a beach-house club a short drive away is part of the package, as is a full breakfast at the elegant Carriage House Club ($$–$$$); guests also have golf privileges at eight nearby courses. The resort is approximately 2 mi south of Brookgreen Gardens on U.S. 17 (turn right at the Litchfield Country Club entrance and follow the signs). ⊠ *River Rd., Box 290, 29585,* ☎ *843/237–9121 or 800/869–1410,* FAX *843/237–8558,* WEB *www.litchfieldplantation.com. 38 rooms, 4 suites, 10 2- and 3-bedroom cottages. Restaurant, 2 tennis courts, pool, library, concierge. AE, D, DC, MC, V. BP.*

$$$–$$$$ 🏨 **Sea View Inn.** A "barefoot paradise," Sea View is a no-frills beach-side boardinghouse with long porches. Rooms, with views of the ocean or marsh, have half baths; showers are down the hall and outside. Three meals, served family style—with grits, gumbo, crab salad, pecan pie, and oyster pie—make this an unbeatable deal. There is a 2-night minimum during May and September and a 1-wk minimum from June through August. ⊠ *Myrtle Ave., 29585,* ☎ *843/237–4253,* FAX *843/237–7909,* WEB *www.seaviewinn.net. 20 rooms. Dining room. No credit cards. Closed Nov.–Mar. FAP.*

$$–$$$ 🏨 **Litchfield Beach and Golf Resort.** Rentals from one-bedroom condos to four-bedroom villas are available at this 4,500-acre resort, which runs along both sides of U.S. 17. The almost 2-mi stretch of ocean-front accommodations ranges from condos to the 160-room Litchfield Inn, which has standard motel rooms; other units overlook fairways or lakes and are within a 10-minute walk to the beach. The 120-unit Bridgewater, with its oceanfront pool, lazy river (an artificial, moving, river-shaped pool that carries swimmers along its course) and clubhouse, is popular with families. Most suites are decorated in pastel tones and light woods. ⊠ *U.S. 17, 2 mi north of Pawleys Island (Drawer 320, 29585),* ☎ *843/237–3000 or 800/845–1897,* FAX *843/237–4282,* WEB *www.litchfieldbeach.com. 140 rooms, 216 suites, 200 condominiums, cottages, and villas. 2 restaurants, 9 18-hole golf courses, 26 tennis courts, 2 indoor pools, 18 pools, health club, bicycles, children's programs. AE, D, DC, MC, V.*

$ 🏨 **The Inn at Pawleys.** You'll find that excellent golf packages are available at this well-maintained inn (however, the 18-hole course next door is not affiliated with the hotel). Outfitted with motel-modern furnishings, the rooms are spacious, bright, and airy. ⊠ *U.S. 17S, Box 2217, 29585,* ☎ *843/237–4261 or 800/272–6232,* FAX *843/237–9703,* WEB *www.ramada.com. 100 rooms. Café, pool, lounge. AE, D, DC, MC, V.*

Outdoor Activities and Sports

GOLF

The **Litchfield Beach and Golf Resort** (⊠ U.S. 17S, Litchfield Beach, ☎ 843/237–3000 or 800/845–1897) is a popular 18-hole course. **Pawleys Plantation Golf & Country Club** (⊠ U.S. 17S, Pawleys Island, ☎ 843/237–8497 or 800/367–9959) is a Jack Nicklaus–signature course; several holes play along saltwater marshes. **Tee Times Central** (☎ 843/347–4653 or 800/344–5590) books tee times—though you can also call courses directly to book time. **Litchfield Country Club** (⊠ U.S. 17S, Pawleys Island, ☎ 843/237–3411) is a mature, old-style course with tight fairways and moss-laden oaks. The newly renovated **River Club** (⊠ U.S. 17S, Pawleys Island, ☎ 843/626–9069) has water on 14 of its holes. **Willbrook** (⊠ U.S. 17S, Pawleys Island, ☎ 843/247–4900) is on a former rice plantation and winds past historical markers, a slave cemetery, and a tobacco shack.

TENNIS

You can get court time, rental equipment, and instruction at **Litchfield Country Club** (☎ 843/237–3411).

Shopping

The **Hammock Shops at Pawleys Island** (⊠ 10880 Ocean Hwy., ☎ 843/237–8448) is a complex of two dozen boutiques, gift shops, and restaurants built with old beams, timber, and ballast brick. Outside the Original Hammock Shop, in the Hammock Weavers' Pavilion, craftspeople demonstrate the 19th-century art of weaving the famous cotton-rope Pawleys Island hammocks. Also look for jewelry, toys, antiques, and designer fashions.

Georgetown

13 mi south of Pawleys Island via U.S. 17.

Founded on Winyah Bay in 1729, Georgetown became the center of America's colonial rice empire. A rich plantation culture developed on a scale comparable to Charleston's, and the historic district, which can be walked in a couple of hours, is among the prettiest in the state. Today oceangoing vessels still come to Georgetown's busy port, and the **Harborwalk,** the restored waterfront, hums with activity.

The graceful market and meeting building in the heart of Georgetown, topped by an 1842 clock and tower, has been converted into the **Rice Museum,** with maps, tools, and dioramas. At the museum's Prevost Gallery next door, you can buy glass, local pearls, African dolls, and art. ⊠ *Front and Screven Sts.,* ☎ *843/546–7423.* ⊒ *$5; combination ticket for Rice Museum, Harold Kaminski House, and tour of Georgetown $13.50.* ۞ *Mon.–Sat. 9:30–4:30.*

Prince George Winyah Episcopal Church (named after King George II) still serves the parish established in 1721. It was built in 1737 with bricks brought from England. ⊠ *Broad and Highmarket Sts., Georgetown,* ☎ *843/546–4358.* ⊒ *Donation suggested.* ۞ *Mar.–Oct., weekdays 11:30–4:30.*

Overlooking the Sampit River from a bluff is the **Harold Kaminski House** (circa 1769). It's especially notable for its collections of regional antiques and furnishings, its Chippendale and Duncan Phyfe furniture, Royal Doulton vases, and silver. ⊠ *1003 Front St.,* ☎ *843/546–7706.* ⊒ *$4; combination ticket for Rice Museum, Harold Kaminski House, and tour of Georgetown $13.50.* ۞ *Mon.–Sat. 10–5, Sun. 1–4.*

Hobcaw Barony Visitors Center is at the entrance of Hobcaw Barony, on the vast estate of the late Bernard M. Baruch; Franklin D. Roosevelt and Winston Churchill came here to confer with him. A small interpretive center has exhibits on coastal history and ecology, with special emphasis on the Baruch family. There are aquariums, touch tanks, and video presentations; you can also tour the 17,500-acre wildlife refuge. ⊠ *On U.S. 17, 2 mi north of Georgetown,* ☎ *843/546–4623,* WEB *www. hobcawbarony.com.* ⊒ *Visitors center free, tours $15.* ۞ *Weekdays 10–5; reservations necessary.*

Hopsewee Plantation, surrounded by moss-draped live oaks, magnolias, and tree-size camellias, overlooks the North Santee River. The circa-1740 mansion has a fine Georgian staircase and hand-carved Adam lighted-candle moldings. ⊠ *U.S. 17, 12 mi south of Georgetown,* ☎ *843/546–7891 or 800/648–0478,* WEB *www.hopsewee.com.* ⊒ *Man-*

sion $8; grounds $5 per car; parking fees apply toward tour, if taken. ☉ Mansion Mar.–Nov., Tues.–Fri. 10–4; Dec.–Feb., by appointment (if you come across a tour group already on the grounds, you can join them). Grounds, including nature trail, daily dawn–dusk.

Hampton Plantation State Historic Site preserves the home of Archibald Rutledge, poet laureate of South Carolina for 39 years until his death in 1973. The 18th-century plantation house is a fine example of a Lowcountry mansion. The exterior has been restored; cutaway sections in the finely crafted interior show the changes made through the centuries. The grounds are landscaped, and there are picnic areas. ⊠ Off U.S. 17, at edge of Francis Marion National Forest, 16 mi south of Georgetown, ☎ 843/546–9361. 🏛 Mansion $2, grounds free. ☉ Mansion June–Aug., daily 11–4; Sept.–May, Thurs.–Mon. 11–4. Grounds Thurs.–Mon. 9–6.

Dining and Lodging

$$$–$$$$ ✕ **Rice Paddy.** Locals flock in for vegetable soup, garden-fresh salads,
★   and sandwiches at lunch, when this Lowcountry restaurant tends to get crowded. Dinner in the Victorian building is more relaxed; options might include broiled seafood, crab cakes, or quail with ham-and-cream grits. ⊠ 732 Front St., ☎ 843/546–2021. AE, D, MC, V. Closed Sun.

$$–$$$ ✕ **River Room.** This restaurant on the Sampit River specializes in char-grilled fish, Cajun fried oysters, seafood pastas, and steaks. For lunch you can have shrimp and grits or your choice of sandwiches and salads. The dining room has river views from most tables. It's especially romantic at night, when the oil lamps and brass fixtures cast a warm glow on the dark wood and brick interior of the early 20th-century building. ⊠ 801 Front St., ☎ 843/527–4110. Reservations not accepted. AE, MC, V. Closed Sun.

$$ ✕ **Kudzu Bakery.** Indulge in some of the best desserts in town: deep-dish pecan pie and red velvet cake. There's also fresh bread, deli items, and jams and jellies. Sit at the counter if you want a quick bite. ⊠ 714 Front St., ☎ 843/546–1847. MC, V. Closed Sun. No dinner.

$ ✕ **Thomas Cafe.** There's great fried chicken, homemade biscuits, and pie here at this dinerlike lunch counter with stools, booths, and café tables, in a 1920s storefront building. ⊠ 714 Front St., ☎ 843/546–7776. MC, V. Closed Sun. No dinner.

$$$$ 🏠 **Lodge at Lofton Landing.** To stay here you must rent this entire lodge, a modern facility overlooking the marshland of Cape Romain National Wildlife Refuge. It has a furnished kitchen, a wraparound porch, and a dock for fishing and crabbing, and it sleeps eight. ⊠ 8889 U.S. 17 (about 22 mi south of Georgetown), McClellanville 29458, ☎ 843/720–7332, FAX 843/856–8468. 1 lodge with 3 rooms. Boating, fishing. AE, D, DC, MC, V.

$$ 🏠 **Laurel Hill Plantation.** This B&B overlooks the marsh close to the Intracoastal Waterway, near the quaint shrimping village of McClellanville. It's furnished with country antiques and folk art. Here relaxation is key: you can read in the hammock, go fishing or crabbing, take a boat ride, or watch the birds. ⊠ 8913 U.S. 17N (22 mi south of Georgetown), Box 190, McClellanville 29458, ☎ 843/887–3708 or 888/887–3708. 4 rooms. Fishing. AE, D, DC, MC, V. BP.

$$ 🏠 **Mansfield Plantation.** As you drive up the unpaved road to the 760-acre plantation, past former slave quarters and under a canopy of moss-draped oaks, you'll sense what a plantation must have looked like 200 years ago. You can stay in one of three historic redbrick outbuildings—the old kitchen, the former schoolhouse, and the 1930s guest house—that overlook the Black River. Rooms have hardwood pine floors, reproduction period antiques, four-poster rice beds, and wood-burn-

ing fireplaces. Children and pets are welcome, and you can roam freely on the plantation grounds. ⊠ *U.S. 701N (Rte. 8, Box 590), 29440,* ☎ *843/546–6961 or 800/355–3223,* 𝐅𝐀𝐗 *843/546–5235,* 𝐖𝐄𝐁 *www.bbonline.com/sc/mansfield. 8 rooms. In-room VCRs, boating, fishing, bicycles. No credit cards. BP.*

$$ 🖫 **1790 House.** Built in the center of town after the revolution, at the peak of Georgetown's rice culture, this lovely restored white Georgian house with a wraparound porch contains 18th- and 19th-century Asian and European pieces brought by new owners, who've also added bathrobes, turndown service, and whirlpools. Besides a (very) full breakfast, you can also expect evening refreshments. Guest rooms downstairs in the former slave quarters have exposed brick walls. ⊠ *630 Highmarket St., 29440,* ☎ *843/546–4821 or 800/890–7432,* 𝐖𝐄𝐁 *www.1790house.com. 4 rooms, 1 suite, 1 cottage. Bicycles. AE, D, MC, V. BP.*

Outdoor Activities and Sports

BOATING

The **tall ships** *Jolly Roger & Carolina Rover* (⊠ 735 Front St., ☎ 843/546–8822 or 800/705–9063) are docked at the Harborwalk at the foot of Broad Street. Kids will love the two-hour sailing adventure aboard the *Jolly Roger* along the Intracoastal Waterway, with Captain Kidd in period dress telling pirate tales. Three-hour ecotours on the *Carolina Rover* include a visit to a historic lighthouse.

CANOEING AND KAYAKING

Black River Expeditions (⊠ 21 Garden Ave., U.S. 701, ☎ 843/546–4840) offers naturalist-guided canoe and kayak day and evening (including moonlight) tours of the tidelands of Georgetown. They also do rentals and sales.

GOLF

The city of Georgetown's premier course is the nearby 18-hole, par-73 **Wedgefield Plantation** (⊠ 129 Club House La., off U.S. 701, ☎ 843/448–2124 or 843/546–8587). The 18-hole, par-70 **Winyah Bay Golf Club** (☎ 877/527–7765) is a popular option.

TARGET SHOOTING

At the **Back Woods Quail Club** (⊠ Rte. 51 at Rte. 41, ☎ 843/546–1466), there are target shooting, gun rentals, a skeet shooting center, and quail hunting.

Myrtle Beach and the Grand Strand A to Z

To research prices, get advice from other travelers, and book travel arrangements, visit www.fodors.com.

AIRPORTS

The Myrtle Beach International Airport is served by Air Canada, Air-Tran, Continental, COMAIR, Delta's regional carrier Atlantic Southeast, Spirit, Vanguard, and US Airways.

➤ AIRPORT INFORMATION: **Myrtle Beach International Airport** (⊠ 1100 Jetport Rd., ☎ 843/448–1580).

BOAT AND FERRY TRAVEL

Boaters traveling the Intracoastal Waterway may dock at Hague Marina, Harbor Gate, and Marlin Quay.

➤ BOAT AND FERRY INFORMATION: **Hague Marina** (⊠ Myrtle Beach, ☎ 843/293–2141). **Harbor Gate** (⊠ North Myrtle Beach, ☎ 843/249–8888). **Marlin Quay** (⊠ Murrells Inlet, ☎ 843/651–4444).

BUS TRAVEL

Greyhound Bus Lines serves Myrtle Beach, Georgetown, and Mc-Clellanville.

➤ Bus Information: **Greyhound Bus Lines** (☎ 800/231–2222).

CAR TRAVEL

Midway between New York and Miami, the Grand Strand isn't connected directly by any interstate highways but is within an hour's drive of I–95, I–20, I–26, and I–40. U.S. 17 is the major north–south coastal route through the Strand.

EMERGENCIES

Both the Grand Strand Regional Medical Center and Georgetown Memorial Hospital have emergency rooms open 24 hours a day. The Grand Strand Regional Medical Center also has the only pharmacy in the area open all night.

➤ Emergency Services: **Ambulance, fire, police** (☎ 911).

➤ Hospitals: **Georgetown Memorial Hospital** (✉ 606 Black River Rd., Georgetown, ☎ 843/527–7000). **Grand Strand Regional Medical Center** (✉ 809 82nd Pkwy., off U.S. 17, Myrtle Beach, ☎ 843/692–1000).

➤ 24-Hour Pharmacies: **Grand Strand Regional Medical Center Pharmacy** (✉ 809 82nd Pkwy., off U.S. 17, Myrtle Beach, ☎ 843/692–1000).

LODGING

With more than 60,000 rooms available along the Grand Strand, it's seldom difficult to find a place to stay, and discounting is rampant. Package deals are offered year-round, the most attractive of them between Labor Day and spring break. You can choose among cottages, villas, condominiums, and hotel-style high-rise units.

APARTMENT AND VILLA RENTALS

For the free directory *Where to Stay and Play,* call the Myrtle Beach Area Convention Bureau. For Pawleys Island and Litchfield Beach, try Pawleys Island Realty.

➤ Local Agents: **Myrtle Beach Area Convention Bureau** (☎ 843/448–1629 or 800/356–3016). **Pawleys Island Realty** (☎ 843/237–4257 or 800/937–7352).

OUTDOOR ACTIVITIES AND SPORTS

GOLF

Spring and fall, when off-season rates are offered, are the busiest times for golf, and there are many packages available in the area; call Golf Holiday. Tee Times Central books tee times at a number of area courses.

➤ Contacts: **Golf Holiday** (☎ 843/448–5942 or 800/845–4653). **Tee Times Central** (☎ 843/347–4653 or 800/344–5590).

TAXIS

Taxi service in Myrtle Beach is provided by Coastal Cab Service.

➤ Taxi Companies: **Coastal Cab Service** (☎ 843/448–4444).

TOURS

Through Georgetown County Chamber of Commerce and Information Center, you can arrange to tour historic areas March through October by tram, by 1840 horse-drawn carriage, or by boat. You can also pick up free driving- and walking-tour maps. Georgetown Tour Company offers tram tours of the historic district, the Ghostbusting Tour, and the afternoon Tea 'n' Tour. It also offers tram tours of the historic district on the hour, departing from the chamber of commerce Monday through Saturday. For an insider's view hire Georgetown native Miss Nell to take you on one of Miss Nell's "Real South" Tours. Pal-

metto Tour & Travel and Leisure Time Unlimited/Gray Line, both in
Myrtle Beach, offer tour packages and guide services.

➤ FEES AND SCHEDULES: **Georgetown County Chamber of Commerce
and Information Center** (☎ 843/546–8436 or 800/777–7705). **Georgetown Tour Company** (☎ 843/546–6827). **Leisure Time Unlimited/Gray
Line** (☎ 843/448–9483). **Miss Nell's "Real South" Tours** (☎ 843/546–
3975). **Palmetto Tour & Travel** (☎ 843/626–2660).

TRAIN TRAVEL

Amtrak service for the Grand Strand is available through a terminal
in Florence. Buses connect with Amtrak there for the 65-mi drive to
Myrtle Beach.

➤ TRAIN INFORMATION: **Amtrak** (☎ 800/872–7245).

VISITOR INFORMATION

➤ TOURIST INFORMATION: **Georgetown County Chamber of Commerce
and Information Center** (✉ 1001 Front St., Box 1776, Georgetown
29442, ☎ 843/546–8436, WEB www.georgetownsc.com). **Myrtle Beach
Area Chamber of Commerce and Information Center** (✉ 1200 N. Oak
St., Box 2115, Myrtle Beach 29578, ☎ 843/626–7444 or 800/356–3016,
WEB www.myrtlebeachlive.com). **Pawleys Island Chamber of Commerce**
(✉ U.S. 17, Box 569, Pawleys Island 29585, ☎ 843/237–1921).

HILTON HEAD AND BEYOND

Anchoring the southern tip of South Carolina's coastline is Hilton Head
Island, named after English sea captain William Hilton, who claimed
the 42 square mi for England in 1663. It was settled by planters in the
1700s and flourished until the Civil War. Thereafter, the economy de-
clined and the island languished until Charles E. Fraser, a visionary South
Carolina attorney, began developing the Sea Pines resort in 1956.
Other developments followed, and today Hilton Head's casual pace,
broad beaches, myriad activities, and genteel good life make it one of
the East Coast's most popular vacation getaways.

Beaufort, some 40 mi north of Hilton Head, is a graceful antebellum
town with a compact historic district preserving lavish 18th- and 19th-
century homes from an era of immense prosperity, based on silky-tex-
tured Sea Island cotton. The *beau* in Beaufort is pronounced as in
"beautiful," and Beaufort certainly is. Southeast, on the ocean, lies Fripp
Island, a self-contained resort with controlled access. And midway between Beaufort and Charleston is Edisto (pronounced *ed*-is-toh) Island,
settled in 1690, also once notable for its Sea Island cotton. Some of its
elaborate mansions have been restored; others are in disrepair.

Hilton Head Island

*108 mi southwest of Charleston via U.S. 17, 164 mi southeast of
Columbia via I–26, I–95, and U.S. 278.*

Lined by towering pines, palmetto trees, and wind-sculpted live oaks,
Hilton Head's 12 mi of beaches are a major attraction, and the semitropical barrier island also has oak and pine woodlands and meandering
lagoons. Choice stretches are occupied by various resorts, called "plantations," among them Sea Pines, Shipyard, Palmetto Dunes, and Port
Royal. In these areas accommodations range from rental villas and lavish private houses to luxury hotels. The resorts are also private residential communities, although many have public restaurants, marinas,
shopping areas, and recreational facilities. All are secured, and cannot
be toured unless arrangements are made at the visitor office near the
main gate of each plantation. A 5¾-mi Cross Island Parkway toll

bridge ($1) makes it easy to bypass traffic and reach the south end of the island, where most of the resort areas and hotels are.

Hilton Head prides itself on its strict regulations that keep "light pollution" to a minimum; but the lack of neon and streetlights also makes it difficult to find your way at night, so be sure to get good directions.

Audubon-Newhall Preserve, in the south of the island, is 50 acres of pristine forest, where you'll find native plant life identified and tagged. There are trails, a self-guided tour, and seasonal plant walks. ⊠ *Palmetto Bay Rd., South End,* ☎ *843/785–5775.* ✉ *Free.* ☉ *Daily dawn-dusk.*

Sea Pines Forest Preserve is a 605-acre public wilderness tract on Sea Pines Plantation with walking trails, a well-stocked fishing pond, a waterfowl pond, and a 3,400-year-old Indian shell ring. Both guided and self-guided tours are available. ⊠ *Southwest tip of island, accessible via U.S. 278, South End,* ☎ *843/363–1872.* ✉ *Sea Pines Plantation $5 per car for nonguests, includes access to preserve.* ☉ *Daily dawn-dusk; closed during MCI Heritage golf tournament in Apr.*

The **Coastal Discovery Museum** has a permanent collection depicting Native American life and hosts changing exhibits. The museum also sponsors historical and natural history tours of Native American sites, forts, and plantations as well as kayak trips, turtle watches, cruises, birding, and visits to wildlife preserves. ⊠ *100 William Hilton Pkwy., North End,* ☎ *843/689–6767.* ✉ *Free.* ☉ *Mon.–Sat. 9–5, Sun. 10–4.*

At the **James M. Waddell Jr. Mariculture Research & Development Center,** 3 mi west of Hilton Head Island, you may tour the 24 ponds and the research building to see how methods of raising seafood commercially are studied. ⊠ *Sawmill Creek Rd. near U.S. 278 at Rte. 46,* ☎ *843/837–3795.* ✉ *Free.* ☉ *Tours weekdays at 10 AM and by appointment.*

OFF THE BEATEN PATH

DAUFUSKIE ISLAND – From Hilton Head you can go by boat to nearby Daufuskie Island, the setting for Pat Conroy's novel *The Water Is Wide,* which was made into the movie *Conrack.* The Daufuskie Island Club & Resort—with an oceanfront inn, cottages, golf courses, tennis, pools, water sports, and several restaurants—is a wonderful getaway (☎ 843/341–4820 or 800/648–6778). Amidst increasing development on the island, a few descendants of former slaves live on small farms among remnants of churches, homes, and schools—reminders of antebellum times. Excursions to Daufuskie are run out of Hilton Head by **Adventure Cruises** (⊠ Shelter Cove Marina, Mid-Island, ☎ 843/785–4558), **Calibogue Cruises** (⊠ 164B Palmetto Bay Rd., Mid-Island, ☎ 843/785–8242), and **Vagabond Cruises** (⊠ Harbour Town Marina, South End, ☎ 843/842–4155).

BLUFFTON – Tucked away from the bustle of Hilton Head's resorts, charming Bluffton village has several historic homes and churches, a growing artists' colony, and oak-lined streets dripping with moss. There are several great little shops around here, including **Eggs'n'tricities** (⊠ 71 Calhoun St., Bluffton, ☎ 843/757–3446), with fun and funky gifts, clothes, and even home accessories, and **Red Stripe Gallery** (⊠ 69 Calhoun St., Bluffton, ☎ 843/757–2318), with pottery, ironwork, and outdoor art. You could grab delicious picnic food from **Vino & Vitto** (☎ 843/815–7777) and head to the boat dock at the end of Pritchard Street or the boat landing at Brighton Beach for great views. From Hilton Head backtrack about 6 mi up U.S. 278, then make a left on Route 46.

Dining

$$$–$$$$ ✕ **Old Fort Pub.** Tucked away on a quiet site overlooking the sweeping marshlands of the Intracoastal Waterway and beside the Civil War ruins of Fort Mitchell, this romantic restaurant specializes in such dishes as grilled scallops, duck confit, crab cakes, and fresh fish. The views are almost panoramic, the wine list extensive, and there's outdoor seating plus a third-floor porch for toasting the sunset. Sunday brunch is also a good bet. ⊠ *65 Skull Creek Dr., North End,* ☎ *843/ 681–2386. AE, D, DC, MC, V. No lunch.*

$$–$$$ ✕ **Brick Oven Café.** Velvet drapes, chandeliers, booths, and '40s lounge-style entertainment—on top of good, reasonably priced food served late—make this the trendy place to be. There's a nice wine selection. ⊠ *Park Plaza, South End,* ☎ *843/686–2233. Reservations essential. AE, D, DC, MC, V. No lunch.*

$$–$$$ ✕ **Juleps.** In this dimly lit terrace-style restaurant, Southern ingredients—grits, cured ham, fresh fish, and peach preserves—add sparkle to the menu. The mint juleps are incredible; try the magnolia salad with hearts of palm, apples, pecans, and mint vinaigrette; the barbecued duck with cornmeal pancake; or the quail stuffed with andouille and greens. ⊠ *14 Greenwood Dr., the Galley of Shops, South End,* ☎ *843/842– 5857. AE, D, MC, V. No lunch.*

$–$$ ✕ **Kenny B's French Quarter Cafe.** Surrounded by Mardi Gras memorabilia, Kenny serves jambalaya, po'boys, muffalettas, and gumbo against a wall mural of Bourbon Street. A local favorite, this café—in a strip mall—is open from morning until 9 PM; at the Sunday buffet brunch you can get chicory coffee, beignets, and Cajun omelettes. ⊠ *70 Pope Ave., BiLo Circle, Mid-island,* ☎ *843/785–3315. AE, D, MC, V. Closed Mon.*

$–$$ ✕ **Mi Tierra.** At this friendly Mexican restaurant (easy to miss, in a rather run-down strip mall), freshness is the key to such tasty fare as ceviche fish tacos. Next door, **Baja Tacos**—run by the same people—is a simple taco stand with counter service, café tables, and a condiments bar with fresh, fresh salsas and relishes. ⊠ *160 Fairfield Sq., North End,* ☎ *843/342–3409. MC, V.*

$–$$ ✕ **Upper Crust.** Dine on great pizza with creative combinations at this traditional family-friendly eatery with booths and café tables. There's also a bar; sodas come with a long noodle "straw." ⊠ *Moss Creek Shopping Center, U.S. 278, Bluffton,* ☎ *843/837–5111. AE, DC, MC, V. No lunch Sun.*

Lodging

Sea Pines, the oldest and best known of Hilton Head's resort developments, or plantations, occupies 4,500 thickly wooded acres with three golf courses, a fine beach, tennis clubs, stables, and shopping plazas. The focus of Sea Pines is **Harbour Town,** built around the charming marina, which has shops, restaurants, some condominiums, and the landmark Hilton Head Lighthouse. Accommodations are in luxurious houses and villas facing the ocean or the golf courses.

The **Crowne Plaza Resort** is the oceanfront centerpiece of **Shipyard Plantation,** which also has villa condominiums, three 9-hole golf courses, a tennis club, and a small beach club. **Palmetto Dunes Resort** has the oceanfront Hilton Head Marriott Beach & Golf Resort, Hilton Resort, and other accommodations, along with the renowned Rod Laver Tennis Center, a good stretch of beach, three golf courses, and several oceanfront rental villa complexes. At **Port Royal Plantation** there's the posh Westin Resort, which is on the beach and has three golf courses and a tennis club.

Hilton Head Central Reservations (☎ 843/785–9050 or 800/845–7018, FAX 843/686–3255, WEB www.vacationcompany.com) represents almost every hotel, motel, and rental agency on the island. Other options are available through the **Hilton Head Condo Hotline** (☎ 843/785–2939), which handles condo accommodations for all of Hilton Head. **Hilton Head Reservations and Golf Line** (☎ 843/444–4772) books both hotels and tee time. **Island Rentals** (☎ 800/845–6134, WEB www.irhhi.com) offers oceanfront, ocean-oriented, and golf-oriented home, condo and villa rentals, as well as a concierge service.

$$$$ 🏨 **Crowne Plaza Resort.** This oceanfront resort glimmers with brass railings and accents, and shiny wood floors and trim. Decorated in a nautical theme and set in a luxuriant garden, the Crowne Plaza has access to all the amenities of Shipyard Plantation. ✉ *130 Shipyard Dr., Mid-Island 29928,* ☎ *843/842–2400 or 800/334–1881,* FAX *843/785–8463,* WEB *www.crowneplazaresort.com. 331 rooms, 9 suites. 2 restaurants, snack bar, room service, 3 18-hole golf courses, indoor pool, 2 pools, hot tub, outdoor hot tub, health club, biking, racquetball, lounge, children's programs (ages 3–12), business services, meeting room. AE, D, DC, MC, V.*

$$$$ 🏨 **Disney's Hilton Head Island Resort.** The villas here have fully fur-
★   nished dining, living, and sleeping areas. The smallest is a studio villa, and the largest has three bedrooms, four baths, and sleeping accommodations for 12; all have marsh or marina views. The villas are decorated in cheerful colors and have porches with rocking chairs and picnic tables—it all gives off the rusticity of Adirondack cabins. The resort offers golf, tennis, and romance packages, beach shuttle service, and a fishing pier. The resort's 13,000-square-ft cabana has a fireplace in the living room, a heated pool, an adult lounge, and a video game room. ✉ *22 Harbourside La., Mid-Island 29928,* ☎ *843/341–4100 or 800/453–4911,* FAX *843/341–4130,* WEB *www.disney.com/vacation. 102 units. Snack bar, kitchens, fans, some in-room hot tubs, golf privileges, 2 pools, gym, outdoor hot tub, dock, boating, marina, fishing, bicycles, billiards, horseshoes, Ping-Pong, shuffleboard, recreation room, video game room, children's programs, playground, laundry service. AE, MC, V.*

$$$$ 🏨 **Hilton Oceanfront Resort.** There's a Caribbean sensibility to this five-story resort hotel, located mid-island. The grounds are beautifully landscaped, and the spacious rooms, all ocean side, are spacious and decorated with contemporary wood furniture and warm colors. ✉ *23 Ocean La., Box 6165, 29938,* ☎ *843/842–8000 or 800/845–8001,* FAX *843/842–4988,* WEB *www.hiltonheadhilton.com. 303 rooms, 20 suites. 2 restaurants, kitchenettes, 3 18-hole golf courses, 2 pools, health club, hot tub, sauna, boating, fishing, bicycles, Ping-Pong, volleyball, lounge, children's programs. AE, D, DC, MC, V.*

$$$$ 🏨 **Holiday Inn Oceanfront Resort.** A handsome high-rise motor hotel, this property is on one of the busiest stretches of beach on the island—at the south end, within walking distance of shops and restaurants. The rooms are spacious and furnished in a contemporary style; golf and tennis packages are available. The outdoor Tiki Hut lounge, a poolside bar, is hugely popular. ✉ *S. Forest Beach Dr., Box 5728, 29938,* ☎ *843/785–5126 or 800/423–9897,* FAX *843/785–6678,* WEB *www.hihiltonhead.com. 201 rooms. Restaurant, snack bar, pool, wading pool, bicycles, volleyball, gym, lounge, children's programs (ages 3–12), meeting rooms; no-smoking rooms. AE, D, DC, MC, V.*

$$$$ 🏨 **Main Street Inn.** The outside of this inn looks like an Italianate villa, with gardens, shuttered French doors, and iron railings. Luxury abounds inside, too, in the antique furnishings and the heart-pine floors covered in Turkish and sisal rugs. Guest rooms have velvet and silk bro-

cade linens, feather duvets, and porcelain and brass sinks. The European breakfast includes imported meats, cheeses, quiches, breads, and pastries. ⊠ *2200 Main St., North End 29926,* ☎ *843/681–3001 or 800/471–3001,* FAX *843/681–5541,* WEB *www.mainstreetinn.com. 34 rooms. Pool, hot tub, bar. AE, MC, V. BP.*

$$$–$$$$ 🏨 **Hilton Head Marriott Beach & Golf Resort.** After a complete renovation and flag change, this new property opened in 2002. All guest rooms have private balconies, desk areas, contemporary cherry furniture with sunny yellow and green floral fabrics, and down comforters. ⊠ *One Hotel Circle, South End 29928,* ☎ *843/686–8400,* FAX *843/686–8450,* WEB *www.marriotthiltonhead.com. 452 rooms, 31 suites. Restaurant, café, pizzeria, room service, some kitchens, some minibars, driving range, 3 18-hole golf courses, putting green, 26 tennis courts, outdoor pool, indoor pool, beach, biking, hot tubs, outdoor hot tubs, gym, piano bar, bar, shop, baby-sitting, children's programs (ages 3–12), concierge, business services, meeting rooms. AE, D, DC, MC, V.*

$$$ 🏨 **Westin Resort, Hilton Head Island.** One of the area's most luxuri-
★ ous properties, the horseshoe-shape Westin sprawls on lushly landscaped oceanfront (and it's on the island's quietest, least inhabited stretch). The hotel guest rooms, most with ocean views, have crown molding and, because of the down pillows, rich colors, and comfortable wicker and contemporary furniture, it manages to seem somewhat residential. All rooms have seating areas and desks. The resort also includes 100 two- and three-bedroom villas, each with a kitchen, VCR, and washer-dryer. ⊠ *2 Grass Lawn Ave., North End 29928,* ☎ *843/681–4000 or 800/228–3000,* FAX *843/681–1087,* WEB *www.westin.com. 412 rooms, 29 suites. 3 restaurants, in-room data ports, driving range, 3 18-hole golf courses, 16 tennis courts, pro shop, indoor pool, pool, wading pool, health club, outdoor hot tub, beach, bicycles, Ping-Pong, lounges, children's programs (ages 4–12), concierge, concierge floor, business services, meeting rooms. AE, D, DC, MC, V.*

$$ 🏨 **Hampton Inn.** A short drive from the public beaches, this inn is clean, nicely landscaped, and sheltered from the noise and traffic, making it popular with business and leisure travelers alike. Rooms have one king or two double beds; some double rooms have refrigerators and microwaves; some king rooms have sleeper sofas. A friendly staff keeps customers coming back year after year. ⊠ *1 Dillon Rd., Mid-Island 29926,* ☎ *843/681–7900,* FAX *843/681–4330,* WEB *www.hampton-inn.com. 124 rooms. Some microwaves, some refrigerators, pool. AE, D, DC, MC, V.*

$ 🏨 **Best Western Inn.** Just a five-minute walk from the beach, this is a front-runner in the budget category; rooms are smallish but clean, with standard furnishings. ⊠ *40 Waterside Dr., South End 29928,* ☎ *843/842–8888,* FAX *843/842–5948,* WEB *www.bestwestern.com. 91 rooms. Pool. AE, D, DC, MC, V.*

$ 🏨 **Red Roof Inn.** This two-story inn is popular with families. Clean and functional rooms are just a short drive from the public beaches. ⊠ *5 Regency Pkwy., Mid-Island 29928,* ☎ *843/686–6808 or 800/843–7663,* FAX *843/842–3352,* WEB *www.redroof.com. 111 rooms. In-room data ports, refrigerators, pool. AE, D, DC, MC, V.*

Nightlife and the Arts

THE ARTS

The **Self Family Arts Center** (⊠ Shelter Cove La., Mid-Island, ☎ 843/686–3945) has details on Hilton Head arts events; it includes an art gallery, a theater, and a theater program for youth. In warm weather free **outdoor concerts** are held at Harbour Town and Shelter Cove. Concerts, plays, films, art shows, sporting events, food fairs, and mini-tournaments make up Hilton Head's **SpringFest** (☎ 843/686–4944 or

800/424–3387), which runs for the month of March. The Winter Carnival and Winefest are held each year.

Bars, like everything else in Hilton Head, are often in strip malls. Try the **Blue Nite** (⊠ 4 Target Rd., South End, ☎ 843/842–6683) for live music. **Hilton Head Brewing Co.** (⊠ Hilton Head Plaza, South End, ☎ 843/785–2739) has late-night disco every Wednesday. The **Lodge** (⊠ Hilton Head Plaza, South End, ☎ 843/842–8966) has pool tables and roaring fires in the stone fireplaces. **Moneypenny's** (⊠ Palmetto Bay Rd., Village Exchange, South End, ☎ 843/785–7878) is a cozy spot with acoustic music. **Monkey Business** (⊠ Park Plaza, South End, ☎ 843/686–3545) is a dance club popular with young professionals. During the summer Monday and Tuesday are teen nights. **Salty Dog Cafe** (⊠ South Beach Marina, Sea Pines, South End, ☎ 843/671–2233) has a great dockside happy hour, ice cream shop for kids, and live music.

The **Pelican Poolside** (☎ 843/681–4000), an oceanfront lounge at the Westin Resort, offers informal entertainment every night but Sunday. **Regatta** (⊠ 23 Ocean La., Mid-Island, ☎ 843/842–8000), a sophisticated oceanfront nightspot in the Hilton Resort, has live beach and jazz music nightly. **Tiki Hut** (⊠ S. Forest Beach Dr., South End, ☎ 843/785–5126), a locally popular beachside bar at the Holiday Inn Oceanfront Resort, has live music during the high season.

Outdoor Activities and Sports

Although the resort beaches are reserved for guests and residents, there are four public entrances to Hilton Head's 12 mi of ocean beach. Two of the main parking and changing areas are at Coligny Circle, near the Holiday Inn, and on Folly Field Road off U.S. 278. Signs along U.S. 278 point the way to Bradley and Singleton beaches, where parking space is limited.

There are pathways in several areas of Hilton Head (many in the resorts), and pedaling is popular along the firmly packed beach. Bicycles can be rented at most hotels and resorts. You can also rent bicycles from the **Hilton Head Bicycle Company** (⊠ 11B Archer Rd., South End, ☎ 843/686–6888). **South Beach Cycles** (⊠ Sea Pines Plantation, South End, ☎ 843/671–2453) rents bikes, helmets, tandems, and adult tricycles. **Outside Hilton Head** (⊠ South Beach Marina, South End, ☎ 843/671–2643 or 800/686–6996; ⊠ Shelter Cove Plaza, Mid-Island, ☎ 843/686–6996 or 800/686–6996) rents bikes and Rollerblades.

Outside Hilton Head (⊠ South Beach Marina, South End, ☎ 843/671–2643 or 800/686–6996; ⊠ Shelter Cove Plaza, Mid-Island, ☎ 843/686–6996 or 800/686–6996) is an ecologically sensitive company that rents canoes and kayaks; it also has nature tours.

On Hilton Head you can pick oysters, dig for clams, or cast for shrimp; supplies are available at the **Shelter Cove Marina,** at Palmetto Dunes (☎ 843/842–7001). Local marinas offer inshore and deep-sea fishing charters. Each year a billfishing tournament and two king mackerel tournaments attract anglers.

Many of Hilton Head's nearly 30 championship courses are open to the public. The **Island West Golf Course** (⊠ U.S. 278, 8 mi before bridge to Hilton Head, ☎ 843/689–6660) is an 18-hole course. **Old South Golf**

Links (⊠ U.S. 278, Bluffton, ☎ 843/785–5353) has scenic holes with marshland and intracoastal waterway views. **Palmetto Dunes** (⊠ Ocean La., Mid-Island, ☎ 843/785–1138) includes two 18-hole courses, including an Arthur Hills course with an old lighthouse (and lots of alligator sightings). **Port Royal** (⊠ Grass Lawn Ave., North End, ☎ 843/689–5600) has three 18-hole courses, all on Bermuda grass. **Ocean Course at Sea Pines** (⊠ 100 North Sea Pines Dr., South End, ☎ 843/842–8484) is a championship course with narrow fairways and water on all but four holes. **Harbour Town Golf Links at Sea Pines** (⊠ 11 Lighthouse La., South End, ☎ 843/671–2448 or 800/955–8337) hosts the MCI Heritage Classic every spring.

HORSEBACK RIDING

Many trails wind through woods and nature preserves. **Lawton Stables** (⊠ Sea Pines Plantation, South End, ☎ 843/671–2586) also offers pony rides and lessons. At **Sea Horse Farms** (⊠ 34 Mitchellville Rd., North End, ☎ 843/681–7746) you can ride on the beach on ponies or horses. **Old South** (⊠ Fording Island Rd., Bluffton, ☎ 843/842–7433) offers riding. Rates are generally per person by the hour. **Rose Hill Plantation** (⊠ 1 Equestrian Way, Bluffton, ☎ 843/757–3082) welcomes experienced riders only.

SUMMER CAMP

On Hilton Head Island all major hotels offer summer youth activities; some have full-scale youth programs. The **Island Recreation Center** runs a summer camp that visiting youngsters can join. ⊠ *Hilton Head Island Recreation Association, Wilborn Rd., Box 22593, North End, Hilton Head Island 29925,* ☎ *843/681–7273.* ☉ *Camp mid-June–late Aug., weekdays.*

TENNIS

There are more than 300 courts on Hilton Head. **Port Royal** (⊠ 15 Wimbledon Ct., North End, ☎ 843/686–8803) has 16 courts, including two grass. **Sea Pines Racquet Club** (⊠ 32 Greenwood Dr., South End, ☎ 843/842–8484) has 23 courts, instructional programs and a pro shop. **Shipyard** (⊠ Shipyard Dr. next to Crowne Plaza Resort, Mid-Island, ☎ 843/686–8804) has clay courts and hard courts, a few of which are lighted. **Palmetto Dunes** (⊠ 6 Trent Jones La., Mid-Island, ☎ 843/785–1151) welcomes guests. **Van der Meer Tennis Center** (⊠ 19 deAllyon Rd., Shipyard Plantation, Mid-Island, ☎ 843/785–8388) is highly rated and is recognized for tennis instruction; 4 of its 28 courts are covered.

Shopping

MALLS AND OUTLETS

Hilton Head Factory Stores 1 & 2 (⊠ U.S. 278 at island gateway, Bluffton, ☎ 843/837–4339 or 888/746–7333) has more than 80 clothing and housewares outlets, including J. Crew, Gap, Brooks Brothers, Harry & David, and Coach. The **Mall at Shelter Cove** (⊠ U.S. 278, ½ mi north of Palmetto Dunes Resort, Mid-Island, ☎ 843/686–3090) has 55 shops and four restaurants. **Shoppes on the Parkway** (⊠ U.S. 278, 1 mi south of Palmetto Dunes Resort, Mid-Island, ☎ 843/686–6233) comprises 30 outlets, including Dansk, Gorham, and Van Heusen.

ART GALLERIES

The **Red Piano Art Gallery** (⊠ 220 Cordillo Pkwy., Mid-Island, ☎ 843/785–2318) showcases 19th- and 20th-century works by regional and national contemporary artists.

BOOKS

Authors Bookstore (⊠ The Village at Wexford, Mid-Island) carries a good selection of books on local history and culture.

JEWELRY

The **Bird's Nest** (⊠ Coligny Plaza, South End, ☎ 843/785–3737) sells locally made shell and sand-dollar jewelry, plus island-theme charms. The **Goldsmith Shop** (⊠ 3 Lagoon Rd., Mid-Island, ☎ 843/785–2538) carries classic jewelry and island charms.

NATURE

The **Audubon Nature Store** (⊠ The Village at Wexford, Mid-Island, ☎ 843/785–4311) has items with a nature theme. The **Hammock Store** (⊠ The Plaza at Shelter Cove, Mid-Island, ☎ 843/686–6996 or 800/ 686–6996) sells Pawleys Island hammocks, swings, and other items that have an emphasis on nature and gardening.

Beaufort

38 mi north of Hilton Head via U.S. 278 and Rte. 170, 70 mi southwest of Charleston via U.S. 17 and U.S. 21.

Charming homes and churches from Beaufort's prosperous antebellum days as a cotton center grace this historic town on Port Royal Island. Although it is unusual for the private homes in the historic district of Old Point to be open to visitors, some may be included in the annual Fall House Tour, in mid-October, and the Spring Tour of Homes and Gardens, in April or May. The **Greater Beaufort Chamber of Commerce** (☎ 843/524–3163) can provide more information about house-tour schedules. The Gullah Festival, which takes place Memorial Day weekend, celebrates Lowcountry and West African culture.

The **John Mark Verdier House Museum,** built about 1790 in the federal style, has been restored and furnished as it would have been between 1790 and the visit of Lafayette in 1825. It was the headquarters for Union forces during the Civil War. ⊠ *801 Bay St., Historic Downtown,* ☎ *843/524–6334.* ☜ *$4.* ☉ *Mon.–Sat. 10–4:30.*

Built in 1795 and remodeled in 1852, the Gothic-style arsenal that was the home of the Beaufort Volunteer Artillery now houses the **Beaufort Museum,** with prehistoric relics, native pottery, and Revolutionary War and Civil War exhibits. ⊠ *713 Craven St., Historic Downtown,* ☎ *843/525–7077.* ☜ *$2.* ☉ *Mon.–Tues. and Thurs.–Sat. 10–5.*

St. Helena's Episcopal Church (1724) was turned into a hospital during the Civil War, and gravestones were brought inside to serve as operating tables. ⊠ *501 Church St., Historic Downtown,* ☎ *843/522–1712.* ☉ *Mon.–Sat. 10–4.*

Henry C. Chambers Waterfront Park, off Bay Street in historic Beaufort, is a great place to survey the scene. Barbra Streisand filmed *Prince of Tides* here. Its seven landscaped acres along the Beaufort River, part of the Intracoastal Waterway, include a seawall promenade, a crafts market, gardens, and a marina. Some events of the popular mid-July Beaufort Water Festival, as well as a seasonal farmers' market, take place here.

At **Parris Island,** 10 mi south of Beaufort via Route 802, you can observe U.S. Marine Corps recruit training and either take a guided tour or drive through the base on your own. There's a replica of the Iwo Jima flag-raising monument on the base.

The **Parris Island Museum** exhibits uniforms, photographs, and weapons chronicling military history since 1562, when the French Huguenots built a fort on St. Helena. ☎ *843/525–2951.* ☜ *Free.* ☉ *Fri.–Wed. 10–4:30, Thurs. 10–7.*

St. Helena Island, 9 mi southeast of Beaufort via U.S. 21, is the site of the **Penn Center Historic District** and **York W. Bailey Museum.** Penn Center, established in the middle of the Civil War as the South's first school for freed slaves, today provides community services and has cottages for rent. The **York W. Bailey Museum** (formerly a clinic) has displays reflecting the heritage of Sea Island blacks. These islands are where Gullah, a musical language that combines English and African languages, developed. ⊠ *Land's End Rd., St. Helena Island,* ☎ *843/838–2432.* ⊡ *Donation suggested.* ☼ *Tues.–Fri. 11–4 and by appointment.*

OFF THE
BEATEN PATH

HUNTING ISLAND STATE PARK – This secluded domain of beach, nature trails, and varied fishing has about 3 mi of public beaches—some of it dramatically yet beautifully eroding. The 1,120-ft fishing pier is among the longest on the East Coast. You can climb the 181 steps of the 140-ft **Hunting Island Lighthouse** (built in 1859 and abandoned in 1933) for sweeping views. The park is 18 mi southeast of Beaufort via U.S. 21; write for cabin and camping reservations. ⊠ *1775 Sea Island Pkwy., St. Helena 29920,* ☎ *843/838–2011.* ⊡ *$2 per person Mar.–Oct., free rest of year; 50¢ to climb lighthouse.* ☼ *Lighthouse daily 10–5. Gates close at sunset.*

Dining and Lodging

$$$–$$$$ ✕ **Bistro 205.** This well-lit spot, with a comfortable counter bar and indoor courtyard motif, is popular with the lunch crowd. Try the rack of lamb, beef fillet with Brie quesadilla, coriander-encrusted pork, or macadamia-dusted mahimahi. ⊠ *205 West St., Historic Downtown,* ☎ *843/524–4994. AE, D, MC, V. No lunch Sun. and Mon.*

$$–$$$ ✕ **11th Street Dockside.** The succulent fried oysters, shrimp, and fish here are some of the best around. Other seafood specialties are the steamed seafood pot and, by request only, Frogmore stew (with shrimp, potatoes, sausage, and corn). It's all served in a classic wharf-side environment—you can eat in a screened porch (if you prefer), and you'll get water views from nearly every table. ⊠ *11th St. W, Port Royal,* ☎ *843/524–7433. AE, D, DC, MC, V. No lunch.*

$$–$$$ ✕ **Emily's.** Long, narrow, and wood-paneled, Emily's is a lively restaurant and tapas bar that serves until 11 PM. The crowds linger over tapas including chicken spring rolls, lamb chops, and crab wontons. This is definitely *not* a no-smoking haven. ⊠ *906 Port Republic St., Historic Downtown,* ☎ *843/522–1866. AE, MC, V. Closed Sun. No lunch.*

$–$$ ✕ **Shrimp Shack.** On the way to Hunting Island, stop here, as locals have for 20 years—for shrimp burgers, sweet-potato fries, and sweet tea. On weekends dinner is served only until 7 PM. ⊠ *1929 Sea Island Pkwy., St. Helena,* ☎ *843/838–2962. AE, D, DC, MC, V. Closed Sun. No dinner Mon.–Thurs.*

$$–$$$ ✕⌂ **Beaufort Inn and Restaurant.** This peach-color 1897 Victorian inn, with its many gables and porches, has a superb restaurant ($$$–$$$$) with two mahogany-paneled dining rooms, porch dining, and a wine bar. Among the classy seafood dishes are crispy flounder with yucca chips and sashimi tuna in peanut sauce. Guest rooms are decorated with period reproductions, tasteful fabrics, and comfortable chairs. All have pine floors; several have fireplaces and four-poster beds. ⊠ *809 Port Republic St., Historic Downtown 29902,* ☎ *843/521–9000,* Ⅸ *843/ 521–9500,* ⅷⅢ *www.beaufortinn.com. 15 rooms. Restaurant. AE, D, MC, V. BP.*

$$$–$$$$ ⌂ **Rhett House Inn.** This storybook inn (circa 1820) in the heart of the ★ historic district is filled with art and antiques and abounds in little luxuries—down pillows and duvets, cotton linens, a CD player in each room, and fresh flowers. Breakfast, afternoon tea, evening hors d'oeu-

THE WORLD OF GULLAH

I N THE LOWCOUNTRY, Gullah refers to several things: language, people, and a culture. Gullah (the word itself is believed to be a version of Angola), an English-based dialect rooted in African languages, is the unique language of the African-Americans of the Sea Islands of South Carolina and Georgia. More than 300 years old, this rhythmic language has survived, in part, because of the geographic isolation of the people who speak it; most locally born African-Americans of the area can understand, if not speak, Gullah.

Descended from thousands of slaves who were imported by planters in the Carolinas during the 18th century, the Gullah people have maintained not only their dialect but also their heritage. Much of Gullah culture traces back to the African rice-coast culture and survives today in the art forms and skills, including sweet-grass basket making, of Sea Islanders. During the colonial period, when rice was king, Africans from the West African rice kingdoms drew high premiums as slaves. Those with basket-making skills were extremely valuable because baskets were needed for agricultural and household use. Still made by hand, sweet-grass baskets are intricate coils of a marsh grass called sweet grass. Highly prized by residents and visitors alike, the baskets are named for the sweet, haylike aroma of the sweet grass. Other Gullah art forms can be seen in hand-carved bateaus and gourds and in hand-tied nets used to catch shrimp in local creeks and rivers.

Nowhere is Gullah culture more evident than in the foods of the region. Rice appears at nearly every meal—Africans taught planters how to grow rice and how to cook and serve it as well. Like many African dishes, Lowcountry dishes use okra, peanuts, benne (the African word for sesame seeds), field peas, and hot peppers. Gullah food reflects the bounty of the islands: shrimp, crabs, oysters, fish, and such vegetables as greens, tomatoes, and corn. Watermelons, indigenous to West Africa, are grown all over the Lowcountry.

Many dishes are prepared in one pot, similar to the stew-pot cooking of West Africa. Frogmore stew calls for cooking shrimp, potatoes, sausage, and corn together in one large pot. Hoppin' John—a one-pot mixture of rice and field peas traditionally served on New Year's Day—is similar to rice and pigeon peas, a mainstay in West Africa.

The practices of plantation owners unknowingly helped the Gullah culture survive: from praise houses—one-room houses of worship where Christianity was introduced to keep slaves from running away—came plantation melodies. These songs live on in performances by groups including the Hallelujah Singers, Sea Island Singers, Mt. Zion Spiritual Singers, and Ron and Natalie Daise, all of whom perform regularly in Charleston and Beaufort.

The Penn Center, on St. Helena Island near Beaufort, is the unofficial Gullah headquarters, preserving the culture and developing opportunities for Gullahs. Until 1927 or so St. Helena felt little influence from the outside world. Blacks retained the land, their language, and their unique culture. Many still go shrimping with hand-tied nets, harvest oysters, and grow their own vegetables. Nearby on Daufuskie Island, as well as on Edisto, Wadmalaw, and Johns islands near Charleston, Gullah communities can still be found, although development continues to encroach. A number of companies can help visitors you this world.

A famous Gullah proverb says: *If oonuh ent kno weh oonuh dah gwine, oonuh should kno weh oonuh come f'um.* Translation: If you don't know where you're going, you should know where you come from.

vres, and dessert are included in the rate. Visiting celebrities have included Barbra Streisand, Jeff Bridges, and Dennis Quaid. The remodeled house across the street has eight rooms, each of which has a gas fireplace, a whirlpool bath, a private entrance, and a porch. ⊠ *1009 Craven St., Historic Downtown 29902,* ☎ *843/524–9030,* FAX *843/524–1310,* WEB *www.rhetthouseinn.com. 16 rooms, 1 suite. Bicycles. AE, MC, V. BP.*

$$$ ⊡ **Cuthbert House Inn.** Overlooking the bay, this pillared 1790 home has original federal fireplaces and crown and rope molding. The owners have filled it with 18th- and 19th-century heirlooms; rooms are elegant yet comfortable, with Oriental rugs on pine floors, commanding beds, quilts, and books. ⊠ *1203 Bay St., Historic Downtown 29902,* ☎ *843/521–1315 or 800/327–9275,* FAX *843/521–1314,* WEB *www.cuthberthouseinn.com. 7 rooms, 1 suite. Bicycles. AE, D, MC, V. BP.*

$$–$$$ ⊡ **Craven Street Inn.** This double-piazza 1870 inn is decorated in clean, Pottery Barn–style, with olive and neutral tones, hand-crafted cabinets, wreaths, and baskets. Spacious guest rooms in the main house have pine floors, high ceilings, and fireplaces; those in the 1920s garden house are small but cozy and comfortable. Breakfast might be stuffed French toast or a ham-and-cheese omelet with homemade crumpets. ⊠ *1103 Craven St., Historic Downtown 29902,* ☎ *843/522–1668 or 888/522–0250,* FAX *843/522–9975,* WEB *www.cravenstreetinn.com. 7 rooms, 2 suites. AE, D, MC, V. BP.*

$$–$$$ ⊡ **Fripp Island Resort.** This highly exclusive resort encompasses the entire island; access is limited to guests only. Two- and three-bedroom villas and homes are contemporary in style. The island is 19 mi south of Beaufort via U.S. 21, just beyond Hunting Island State Park. There's a pavilion with shops, restaurants, and a marina. During peak season a 4-night minimum is required; off-peak there is a 2-night minimum. ⊠ *1 Tarpon Blvd., Fripp Island 29920,* ☎ *843/838–3535 or 800/845–4100,* FAX *843/838–9079,* WEB *www.frippislandresort.com. 240 units. 5 restaurants, 2 18-hole golf courses, 10 tennis courts, 4 pools, boating, bicycles, children's programs. AE, D, DC, MC, V.*

$$ ⊡ **Best Western Sea Island Inn.** At this well-maintained but standard inn in the downtown historic district, rooms are basic. The inn is centrally located, however, and within walking distance of shops, restaurants, and the waterfront area. ⊠ *1015 Bay St., Box 532, Historic Downtown 29902,* ☎ *843/522–2090 or 800/528–1234,* FAX *843/521–4858,* WEB *www.sea-island-inn.com. 43 rooms. Refrigerators, pool, gym. AE, D, DC, MC, V. CP.*

$ ⊡ **Howard Johnson.** This clean and cheerfully staffed hotel sits on the edge of the marsh a few miles from the historic district. Rooms are spacious and have desks; many have views of the river and marsh. ⊠ *3651 Trask Pkwy. (U.S. 21), Outskirts 29902,* ☎ *843/524–6020 or 800/528–1234,* FAX *843/521–4858. 63 rooms. Microwaves, refrigerators, pool. AE, D, DC, MC, V. CP.*

Nightlife and the Arts

Plum's (⊠ 904½ Bay St., Historic Downtown, ☎ 843/525–1946) is good for a late drink and has live bands during the weekend.

Outdoor Activities and Sports

BIKING

Beaufort is great for bicycling. Rentals are available from **Lowcountry Bicycles** (⊠ 904 Port Republic St., Historic Downtown, ☎ 843/524–9585).

GOLF

Most golf courses are about a 10- to 20-minute drive from Beaufort. Try the 27 holes designed by Tom Fazio at **Callawassie Island Club** (⊠

Rte. 170, Callawassie Island, ☎ 800/221–8431). The 18-hole **Cat Island Golf Club** (✉ 8 Waveland Ave., Port Royal, ☎ 843/524–0300) is challenging and beautiful. **Dataw Island** has two 18-hole, par-72 courses (✉ Dataw Club Rd., 6 mi east of Beaufort off U.S. 21, Dataw Island, ☎ 843/838–8250).

Shopping

ART GALLERIES

On canvas and sculpture as well as on bits of tin roofing, rugs, frames, and furniture, the colorful, whimsical designs of Suzanne and Eric Longo decorate their **Longo Gallery** (✉ 407 Carteret St., Historic Downtown; 103 Charles St., Historic Downtown; ☎ 843/522–8933 for both). The **Rhett Gallery** (✉ 901 Bay St., Historic Downtown, ☎ 843/524–3339) sells Lowcountry art by members of the Rhett family and antique maps and prints, including Audubons. On nearby St. Helena Island, the **Red Piano Too Art Gallery** (✉ 853 Sea Island Pkwy., St. Helena Island, ☎ 843/838–2241), in a huge old wooden building, is filled with quirky Southern and folk art, beads, and pottery.

GIFTS

Browse for gifts—handcrafted jewelry, candles, purses, hats, perfume, wall clocks—at **Out of Hand** (✉ 915 Greene, Historic Downtown, ☎ 843/522–8525). Art supplies and classes are also offered. **Juxtaposition** (✉ 720 Bay St., Historic Downtown, ☎ 843/521–1415) has beaded bags, copper-roof birdhouses, beautiful cards, potpourri, and more. Just outside Beaufort, in the charming little town of Walterboro, the **SC Artisans Center** (✉ 334 Wichmann St., Walterboro, ☎ 843/549–0011) carries the works of more than 200 South Carolina artists, with pottery, glass, folk art, furniture, quilts and metalwork for sale. Most Saturdays there are craft demonstrations.

JEWELRY

The **Craftseller** (✉ 818 Bay St., Historic Downtown, ☎ 843/525–6104) displays jewelry and other items by Southern craftspeople.

En Route   The ruins of **Sheldon Church,** built in 1753, make an interesting stop if you're driving from Beaufort to Edisto Island. The church was burned in 1779 and again in 1865. Only the brick walls and columns remain beside the old cemetery. The place is lovely—it's dripping with moss—and has become a favorite spot for people to get married. Get here from Beaufort on U.S. 21; it's about 1 mi west of Gardens Corner.

Edisto Island

62 mi northeast of Beaufort via U.S. 17 and Rte. 174, 44 mi southwest of Charleston via U.S. 17 and Rte. 174.

On this rural island, magnificent stands of age-old oaks festooned with Spanish moss border quiet streams and side roads; wild turkeys may still be spotted on open grasslands and amid palmetto palms. Many of the island's inhabitants are descendants of former slaves. **Edisto Beach State Park** has 3 mi of beach with excellent shelling, housekeeping cabins by the marsh, and campsites by the ocean (although severe erosion is limiting availability). Luxury resort development has begun to envelop the edges of the park. For camping reservations call ☎ 843/869–2156 or 843/869–3396.

Dining and Lodging

$$$ ✕ **Old Post Office.** Try the fussed-over pork chop or the blue-crab-and-
★   asparagus pie, served with the house salad, vegetables, and fresh-baked bread. The house specialty at this restaurant on Store Creek is

shrimp and grits and, well, *anything* with grits, rumored to be the best around these parts. ⊠ *1442 Rte. 174,* ☎ *843/869–2339. MC, V. Closed Sun. Closed Mon. Oct.–May. No lunch.*

$$ 🏨 **Fairfield Ocean Ridge Resort.** Although not on the beach, most accommodations are a short walk away from it, and combine resort amenities with a get-away-from-it-all environment. Well-furnished one- to five-bedroom villas and homes tastefully decorated in contemporary style are available. A trolley transports you to the resort's beach shelter. ⊠ *1 King Cotton Rd., Box 27, 29438,* ☎ *843/869–2561 or 800/ 845–8500,* FAX *843/869–2384,* WEB *www.efairfield.com. 100 units. Restaurant, 18-hole golf course, miniature golf, 4 tennis courts, pool, wading pool, beach, boating, fishing, hiking, lounge. AE, D, MC, V.*

Hilton Head and Beyond A to Z

To research prices, get advice from other travelers, and book travel arrangements, visit www.fodors.com.

AIRPORTS

Hilton Head Island Airport is served by US Airways Express and Midway. Most travelers use the Savannah International Airport, about an hour from Hilton Head, which is served by AirTran, ComAir, Continental Express, Delta, and US Airways.

➤ AIRPORT INFORMATION: **Hilton Head Island Airport** (☎ 843/681–6386). **Savannah International Airport** (⊠ 400 Airways Ave., ☎ 912/ 964–0514).

BOAT AND FERRY TRAVEL

Hilton Head is accessible via the Intracoastal Waterway, with docking available at Harbour Town Marina, Schilling Boathouse, and Shelter Cove Marina.

➤ BOAT AND FERRY INFORMATION: **Harbour Town Marina** (☎ 843/671–2704). **Schilling Boathouse** (☎ 843/681–2628). **Shelter Cove Marina** (☎ 843/842–7001).

CAR TRAVEL

Hilton Head Island is 40 mi east of I–95 (Exit 28 off I–95S, Exit 5 off I–95N). If you're heading to the south end of the island, your best bet to save time and avoid traffic is to take the Toll Expressway ($1 each way). Beaufort is 25 mi east of I–95, on U.S. 21.

EMERGENCIES

Emergency medical service is available at the Hilton Head Medical Center and Clinics. CVS is open until 9 PM.

➤ EMERGENCY SERVICES: **Ambulance, fire, police** (☎ 911).

➤ HOSPITALS: **Hilton Head Medical Center and Clinics** (⊠ Hospital Center Blvd., ☎ 843/681–6122).

➤ LATE-NIGHT PHARMACIES: **CVS** (⊠ 95 Matthews Dr., Hilton Head, ☎ 843/681–8363).

TAXIS

Lowcountry Taxi and Limousine Service and Yellow Cab provide service in Hilton Head. Other options include At Your Service and Lowcountry Adventures. In Beaufort Point Tours and Yellow Cab provide service.

➤ TAXI COMPANIES: **At Your Service** (☎ 843/837–3783). **Greyline Lowcountry Adventures** (☎ 843/681–8212). **Lowcountry Taxi and Limousine Service** (☎ 843/681–8294). **Point Tours** (☎ 843/522–3576). **Yellow Cab** (☎ 843/686–6666 in Hilton Head; 843/522–1121 in Beaufort).

TOURS

Hilton Head's Adventure Cruises offers dinner, sightseeing, and murder-mystery cruises. Several companies, including Harbour Town Charters in Hilton Head, run dolphin sightseeing and environmental trips. Lowcountry Adventures offers tours of Hilton Head, Beaufort, and Charleston.

Carolina Buggy Tours will show you Beaufort's historic district. Carriage Tours of Beaufort has tours of the historic district by horse-drawn carriage. Gullah 'n' Geechie Mahn Tours provides tours of Beaufort and sea islands such as St. Helena, which focus on the traditions of African-American culture. Costumed guides sing and act out history during walking tours by the Spirit of Old Beaufort tour group. Call the Greater Beaufort Chamber of Commerce to find out about self-guided walking or driving tours of Beaufort.

➤ FEES AND SCHEDULES: **Adventure Cruises** (☏ 843/785–4558). **Carolina Buggy Tours** (☏ 843/525–1300). **Carriage Tours of Beaufort** (☏ 843/221–1651). **Greater Beaufort Chamber of Commerce** (☏ 843/524–3163). **Gullah 'n' Geechie Mahn Tours** (☏ 843/838–7516). **Harbour Town Charters** (☏ 843/363–2628). **Lowcountry Adventures** (☏ 843/681–8212). **Spirit of Old Beaufort** (☏ 843/525–0459).

VISITOR INFORMATION

For information on Edisto, call the Edisto Island Chamber of Commerce. The Greater Beaufort Chamber of Commerce has information about Beaufort and the surrounding area. Two Hilton Head welcome centers, run by a private real-estate firm, are on U.S. 278 next to the bridge to Hilton Head and at 6 Lagoon Road, at the island's south end. The centers provide visitor information and also attempt to entice you into purchasing real estate. In Hilton Head your best bet is to stop by the Welcome Center and Museum of Hilton Head.

➤ TOURIST INFORMATION: **Edisto Island Chamber of Commerce** (✉ 430 Rte. 174, Box 206, Edisto Island 29438, ☏ 843/869–3867 or 888/333–2781, WEB www.edistochamber.com). **Greater Beaufort Chamber of Commerce** (✉ 1006 Bay St., Box 910, Beaufort 29901, ☏ 843/524–3163, WEB www.beaufortsc.org). **Welcome Center and Museum of Hilton Head** (✉ 100 William Hilton Pkwy., 29938, ☏ 800/523–3373, WEB www.hiltonheadisland.org).

COLUMBIA AND THE HEARTLAND

Camden, Cheraw, Sumter, Aiken, Greenwood

South Carolina's Heartland, between the coastal Lowcountry and the mountains, is a varied region of swamps and flowing rivers, fertile farmland, and vast forests of pines and hardwoods. Lakes Murray, Marion, and Moultrie have wonderful fishing, and the many state parks are popular for hiking, swimming, and camping. At the center of the region is the state capital, Columbia, an engaging contemporary city superimposed on cherished historic remnants. It has restored mansions, several museums, a university, lots of restaurants, a lively arts scene, and a fine zoo and botanical garden.

In Aiken, the center of South Carolina's Thoroughbred Country, such champions as Sea Hero and Pleasant Colony were trained. The beautiful landscape is studded with the fine mansions of wealthy Northerners such as the Vanderbilts and Whitneys. Throughout the region, such towns as Ninety Six, Sumter, and Camden preserve and interpret the past, with historic re-creations, exhibits, and restorations. Several public gardens provide islands of color during most of the year.

Columbia

112 mi northwest of Charleston via I–26, 101 mi southeast of Greenville via I–395 to I–26.

In 1786 South Carolina's capital was moved from Charleston to Columbia, in the center of the state along the banks of the Congaree River. One of the nation's first planned cities, Columbia has streets that are among the widest in America—because it was then thought that stagnant air in narrow streets fostered the spread of malaria. The city soon grew into a center of political, commercial, cultural, and social activity, but in early 1865 General William Tecumseh Sherman invaded South Carolina and incinerated two-thirds of Columbia. A few homes and public buildings were spared—as was the First Baptist Church, where secession was declared, because a janitor directed Sherman's troops to a Methodist church when asked directions. Today the city is a sprawling blend of modern office blocks, suburban neighborhoods, and the occasional antebellum home. Here, too, is the expansive main campus of the University of South Carolina, including the historic and scenic Horseshoe.

The **Columbia Museum of Art** contains art from the Kress Foundation Collection of Renaissance and baroque treasures, sculpture, decorative arts, including art glass, and European and American paintings, including a Monet and a Botticelli; there are also changing exhibitions. Kids love this place, especially when they get to see mummies; if you have children with you, the guides will often tailor the tour to them. ⊠ *Main and Hampton Sts., Main St. Area,* ☎ *803/799–2810.* ⊡ *$4.* ⊘ *Tues. and Thurs.–Sat. 10–5, Wed. 10–9, Sun. 1–5.*

Stop by the **Museum Shop** of the Historic Columbia Foundation in the Robert Mills House (⊠ 1616 Blanding St., Main St. Area, ☎ 803/252–1770), in the historic district, to get a map and buy tickets to tour four Columbia houses: the Hampton-Preston Mansion, the Robert Mills House, the Mann-Simons Cottage, and the Woodrow Wilson Boyhood Home. ⊡ *Each house $4.* ⊘ *All houses Tues.–Sat. 10:15–3:15, Sun. 1:15–4:15.*

The **Hampton-Preston Mansion** (⊠ 1615 Blanding St., Main St. Area, ☎ 803/252–1770), dating from 1818, is filled with lavish furnishings collected by three generations of two influential families.

The classic, columned 1823 **Robert Mills House** (⊠ 1616 Blanding St., Main St. Area, ☎ 803/252–1770) was named for its architect, who later designed the Washington Monument. It has opulent Regency furniture, marble mantels, and spacious grounds.

The **Mann-Simons Cottage** (⊠ 1403 Richland St., Main St. Area, ☎ 803/252–1770) was the home of Celia Mann, one of only 200 free African-Americans in Columbia in the mid-1800s.

The **Woodrow Wilson Boyhood Home** (⊠ 1705 Hampton St., Main St. Area, ☎ 803/252–1770) displays the gaslights, arched doorways, and ornate furnishings of the Victorian period.

The **Fort Jackson Museum,** on the grounds of a U.S. army training center, displays heavy equipment from the two world wars and has exhibits on the history of the fort from 1917 to the present. ⊠ *Bldg. 4442, Jackson Blvd.,* ☎ *803/751–7419.* ⊡ *Free.* ⊘ *Tues.–Fri. 10–4, Sat. 1–4.*

Exhibits at the **South Carolina State Museum,** in a refurbished textile mill, interpret the state's natural history, archaeology, historical development, and technological and artistic accomplishments. One exhibit portrays noted black astronauts (dedicated to South Carolina native

Dr. Ronald McNair, who died on the *Challenger*); one focuses on the Confederate submarine the *Hunley;* and another focuses on the cotton industry and slavery. An iron gate made for the museum by Phillip Simmons, the "dean of Charleston blacksmiths," is on display, as is the surfboard that biochemist Kary Mullis was riding when he heard he'd won the Nobel Prize. In the Stringer Discovery Center, an interactive display, children can check out microorganisms under a microscope and climb trees to observe the animals that live in the branches. ✉ *301 Gervais St., Vista,* ☎ *803/898–4921.* ➤ *$4.* ☉ *Mon.–Sat. 10–5, Sun. 1–5.*

South Carolina's capitol, the **State House,** started in 1855 and completed in 1950, is made of native blue granite in the Italian Renaissance style. Six bronze stars on the western wall mark direct hits by Sherman's cannons. The interior is richly appointed with brass, marble, mahogany, and artwork. ✉ *Main and Gervais Sts., Main St. Area,* ☎ *803/734–9818.* ➤ *Free.* ☉ *Weekdays 9–5, Sat. 10–5, 1st Sun. of month 1–5.*

☾ Make sure it's dark out when you drive by **Tunnelvision,** an optical illusion painted on the wall of the Federal Land Bank Building by local artist Blue Sky. Next to it is Sky's bigger-than-life silver "busted" **Fire Hydrant,** a working fountain. ✉ *Taylor and Marion Sts., Main St. Area.*

A highlight of the sprawling **University of South Carolina** is its original campus—the scenic, tree-lined **Horseshoe**—dating to 1801. Researchers explore the special collections on state history and genealogy at the **South Caroliniana Library** (✉ Sumter St., USC Campus, ☎ 803/777–3131), established in 1840. Here, too, is the **McKissick Museum** (✉ Sumter St., USC Campus, ☎ 803/777–7251), with geology and gemstone exhibits and a fine display of silver.

☾ **Riverfront Park and Historic Columbia Canal,** where the Broad and Saluda rivers form the Congaree River, was created around the city's original waterworks and hydroelectric plant. Interpretive markers describe the area's plant and animal life and tell the history of the buildings. ✉ *312 Laurel St., Vista,* ☎ *803/733–8613.* ➤ *Free.* ☉ *Daily dawn–dusk.*

★ ☾ **Riverbanks Zoological Park and Botanical Garden** contains more than 2,000 animals and birds, some endangered, in natural habitats. Walk along pathways and through landscaped gardens to see sea lions, polar bears, Siberian tigers, and black rhinos. Koalas are the latest addition. The South American primate collection has won international acclaim, and the park is noted for its success in breeding endangered and fragile species. The Aquarium/Reptile Complex has South Carolina, desert, tropical, and marine specimens. At the Bird Pavilion you can view birds and wildlife under a safarilike tent. You can ride the carousel and also take a tram over the Saluda River to the 70-acre botanical gardens on the west bank. (A new entrance in West Columbia, off Highway 378, takes you directly to the botanical gardens.) A forested section with walking trails travels past historic ruins and spectacular views of the river. ✉ *I–126 and U.S. 76 at Greystone Riverbanks exit, West Columbia,* ☎ *803/779–8717,* ⓦⓔⓑ *www.riverbanks.org.* ➤ *$76.25.* ☉ *Apr.–Oct., weekdays 9–4, weekends 9–5; Nov.–Mar., daily 9–4.*

Dining and Lodging

$$$ ✕ **Motor Supply Co. Bistro.** This elegant but casual bistro-style eatery has wooden tables, dim lighting, and an outdoor patio (with heat lamps in cold months). You can choose from such entrées as seared grouper with tomato basil relish, pork chops with Gorgonzola sauce, or spinach and walnut stuffed mushrooms over pasta. On Sunday there's a bountiful brunch. ✉ *920 Gervais St., Vista,* ☎ *803/256–6687. AE, DC, MC, V. Closed Mon.*

$$–$$$ ✕ **California Dreaming.** This airy, greenery-bedecked space is the renovated old Union train station. The only drawback is an echo that's noticeable when it's crowded. Specialties include prime rib, barbecued baby-back ribs, Mexican dishes, and homemade pasta. ✉ *401 S. Main St., USC Campus,* ☎ *803/254–6767. AE, MC, V.*

$$–$$$ ✕ **Mangia! Mangia!** Earth tones, hammered copper, and mosaic tiles
★ transform an early 20th-century building into an elegant place to dine. Window-side tables have a view of the Columbia skyline across the Congaree River; there's a lively outdoor patio, too, with heaters for chilly nights. Try the mussels steamed in a garlicky wine sauce, followed by wild-mushroom pizza baked in the wood-burning oven. The Tuscan-influenced menu also includes lamb shank roasted in red wine with herbs. The entire restaurant, except for the bar, is no-smoking. ✉ *100 State St., West Columbia,* ☎ *803/791–3443. AE, D, DC, MC, V. Closed Sun.*

$$ ✕ **Blue Marlin.** With polished wood, lines of booths, and an oceanic mural over the bar, this restaurant speaks of bygone years—fitting for an eatery that was once a train station. Seafood and pasta dishes include talapia with shrimp and crabmeat sauce, lobster ravioli, and a basic lobster or fish fillet—all mains are served with steaming collard greens and grits. Fruit cobblers come topped with liqueur-laced whipped cream. It's great for late lunches or early dinners because it opens at 11 and stops serving around 10 PM. ✉ *1200 Lincoln St., Vista,* ☎ *803/ 799–3838. Reservations not accepted. AE, D, DC, MC, V.*

$–$$ ✕ **Maurice Gourmet Barbecue–Piggie Park.** One of the South's best-known barbecue chefs, Maurice Bessinger has a fervent national following for his mustard-sauce-based, pit-cooked ham barbecue. Fans also love the chicken, ribs, hash over rice, and thick-battered onion rings. ✉ *1600 Charleston Hwy., Cayce,* ☎ *803/796–0220;* ✉ *800 Elmwood Ave., Main St. Area,* ☎ *803/256–4377;* ✉ *1141 Lake Murray Blvd., Irmo,* ☎ *803/732–5555. Reservations not accepted. AE, D, MC, V.*

$ ✕ **The Gourmet Shop.** This French-style café, styled in black and white, with mirrors and French art prints, has long been serving wonderful coffee, sandwiches, and salads, including a super chicken salad, potato salad, and tomato, feta, and basil salad. Next door, the shop sells food to go (great for picnics), wine, and fancy food items. ✉ *724 Saluda Ave., Five Points,* ☎ *803/799–9463. AE, MC, V. No dinner Sun.*

$$$–$$$$ ⊞ **Embassy Suites Hotel Columbia–Greystone.** In the spacious seven-story atrium lobby with skylights, fountains, pool, and live plants, you can enjoy full breakfasts and evening cocktails. All rooms are suites with sleeper sofas. The staff, which caters mainly to a business clientele, works hard to please. ✉ *200 Stoneridge Dr., St. Andrews 29210,* ☎ *803/252–8700 or 800/362–2779,* ℻ *803/256–8749,* WEB *www. embassysuites.com. 214 suites. Restaurant, microwaves, refrigerators, indoor pool, hot tub, gym, lounge, recreation room, business services, meeting rooms. AE, D, DC, MC, V. BP.*

$$–$$$$ ⊞ **Adam's Mark.** This upscale downtown hotel is near state offices and the University of South Carolina. It has leather armchairs, suspended lights, and brass accents in public areas. Guest rooms are contemporary, with armoires and desks. ✉ *1200 Hampton St., Five Points 29201,* ☎ *803/771–7000 or 800/444–2326,* ℻ *803/254–8307,* WEB *www.adamsmark.com. 296 rooms, 4 suites. Restaurant, indoor pool, health club, hot tub, lounge, sports bar, business services. AE, D, DC, MC, V.*

$$–$$$$ ⊞ **Hampton Inn Downtown Historic District.** This classy chain is conveniently located within walking distance of restaurants and nightlife in the Vista. The hotel's staff offers attentive service, and rooms have comfortable, though standard, furnishings, including desks and blonde-

color wood furniture. ⊠ *822 Gervais St., Vista 29201,* ☎ *803/231–2000,* 🅵🅰🆇 *803/231–2868,* 🆆🅴🅱 *www.hamptoninncolumbia.com. 102 rooms. Some microwaves and refrigerators, some hot tubs. AE, D, DC, MC, V. BP.*

$$$ 🏨 **Claussen's Inn.** It's a small hotel in a converted bakery warehouse in the attractive Five Points area, and near lively nightlife and specialty shops. The open, airy lobby has a Mexican-tile floor; the rooms are arranged around the lobby. The eight loft suites have downstairs sitting rooms, period reproductions, spiral staircases, and four-poster beds. Some of the rooms have modern metallic furniture; generally rooms have floral or print fabrics and desk areas. ⊠ *2003 Greene St., Five Points 29205,* ☎ *803/765–0440 or 800/622–3382,* 🅵🅰🆇 *803/799–7924. 21 rooms, 8 suites. Hot tub, meeting room. AE, D, MC, V. CP.*

$ 🏨 **La Quinta Motor Inn.** At this three-story inn on a quiet street near the zoo, the rooms are spacious and well lighted, with very large working areas. ⊠ *1335 Garner La., St. Andrews 29210,* ☎ *803/798–9590 or 800/531–5900,* 🅵🅰🆇 *803/731–5574,* 🆆🅴🅱 *www.laquinta.com. 120 rooms. Pool. AE, D, DC, MC, V.*

$ 🏨 **Riverside Inn.** Close to the University of South Carolina's Williams-Brice Stadium, this inn has comfortable rooms and a cheerful staff. Locally owned, the Riverside is a favorite with state senators and legislators who stay here during legislative sessions. Rooms were upgraded in 2002 to include new carpet, mattresses, and bedspreads. The Continental breakfast includes breads, fruit, yogurt, grits, and oatmeal. ⊠ *111 Knox Abbott Dr., West Columbia 29033,* ☎ *803/939–4688,* 🅵🅰🆇 *803/926–5547,* 🆆🅴🅱 *www.riversideinn.com. 64 rooms. Putting green, pool. AE, D, DC, MC, V. CP.*

Nightlife and the Arts

THE ARTS

The **Columbia Music Festival Association** (☎ 803/771–6303) will provide information by phone about events of the Choral Society, the opera, Opera Guild, Dance Theatre, Brass Band, Caroliers, and Cabaret Company. The **Koger Center for the Arts** (⊠ Assembly St., USC Campus, ☎ 803/777–7500) presents national and international theater, ballet, and musical groups, as well as individual performers. Call the **South Carolina Philharmonic** (☎ 803/254–7445) for information about scheduled concerts of the Philharmonic, chamber orchestra, and youth orchestra.

The **Town Theatre** (⊠ 1012 Sumter St., USC Campus, ☎ 803/799–2510), founded in 1919, stages six plays a year from September to late May, plus a special summer show. The **Workshop Theatre of South Carolina** (⊠ 1136 Bull St., USC Campus, ☎ 803/799–4876) produces a number of plays.

NIGHTLIFE

In the hopping Vista neighborhood, the **Art Bar** (⊠ 1211 Park St., Vista, ☎ 803/254–4792) is funky, with splash-painted walls, lighted lunch boxes, and dancing to world music. At **Billy G's** (⊠ 828 Gervais Rd., Vista, ☎ 803/806–8870) you'll find live bands. **Willy's Restaurant & Grill** (⊠ 1200B Lincoln St., Vista, ☎ 803/799–3111), in a former train station waiting room, has live music and an outdoor patio. In Five Points, **Goatfeathers** (⊠ 2017 Devine St., Five Points, ☎ 803/256–3325 or 803/256–8133) is a bohemian spot that's popular with university and law-school students, and it also appeals to late-night coffee and dessert seekers.

Outdoor Activities and Sports

BASEBALL

The **Capital City Bombers** (☎ 803/256–4110), a Class-A affiliate of the New York Mets, play from mid-April through August at **Capital City Stadium** (⊠ 301 S. Assembly St., USC Campus) downtown.

CANOEING AND KAYAKING

Self-guided canoe trails traverse an alluvial floodplain bordered by high bluffs at the 22,200-acre, **Congaree Swamp National Monument** (⊠ 20 mi southeast of Columbia, off Rte. 48, Old Bluff Rd., Hopkins, ☎ 803/776–4396). The beautifully eerie water and trees here, including many old-growth bottomland hardwoods (the oldest and largest trees east of the Mississippi River) are full of wildlife. The Saluda River near Columbia offers challenging Class III and Class IV rapids for kayaking and canoeing. Guided river and swamp canoeing excursions can be arranged, as can canoe rentals, from **Adventure Carolina** (⊠ 1107 State St., Cayce, ☎ 803/796–4505), which is just outside Columbia. You can rent canoes or take a guide river or swamp expedition through the **River Runner Outdoor Center** (⊠ 905 Gervais St., Vista Columbia, ☎ 803/771–0353). Canoe and kayak rentals are available at **Saluda Shoals Park** (⊠ 5605 Bush River Rd., Irmo, ☎ 803/772–1228).

GOLF

Sedgewood (⊠ Sumter Hwy., Hopkins, ☎ 803/776–2177), with 18 holes at par 72, is among the many fine area courses. Call the booking company **Golf Vacations of Columbia** (☎ 888/501–0954) for tee times.

HIKING

Congaree Swamp National Monument (⊠ 20 mi southeast of Columbia, off Rte. 48, Old Bluff Rd., Hopkins, ☎ 803/776–4396) has 22 mi of trails for hikers and nature lovers and a ¾-mi boardwalk for people with disabilities. Guided nature walks leave Saturday at 1:30.

Shopping

ANTIQUES AND FLEA MARKETS

Many of Columbia's antiques outlets, boutique shops, and restaurants are in the ever-growing **Congaree Vista** around Huger and Gervais streets, between the state house and the river. A number of intriguing shops and cafés are in **Five Points,** around Blossom at Harden streets. There are antiques shops across the river on Meeting and State streets in **West Columbia.** The **Old Mill Antique Mall** (⊠ 310 State St., West Columbia, ☎ 803/796–4229) has items from many dealers, including furniture, glassware, jewelry, and books.

FARMERS' MARKET

The **State Farmers' Market** (⊠ Bluff Rd., USC Campus, ☎ 803/737–4664) is one of the 10 largest in the country. Fresh vegetables, along with flowers, plants, seafood, and more, are sold weekdays 6 AM–9 PM and Sunday 1–6.

Camden

32 mi northeast of Columbia via I–20.

Charming Camden, a town with a horsey history and grand Southern colonial homes, has never paved its fanciest roads for the sake of the hooves of the horses that regularly trot over them. The Carolina Cup and Colonial Cup are run here; in addition to the horse races, you'll see champagne tailgate parties with elegant crystal and china.

Camden is South Carolina's oldest inland town, dating from 1732. British general Lord Cornwallis established a garrison here during the Revolutionary War and burned most of Camden before evacuating it. A center of textile trade from the late 19th century through the 1940s, Camden attracted Northerners escaping the cold winters; DuPont is one of Camden's major employers. Because General Sherman spared the town during the Civil War, most of its antebellum homes still stand.

The **Bonds Conway House** was built by the first black man in Camden to buy his freedom. The circa-1812 home has the fine details of a skilled craftsman, including wonderful woodwork and heart-pine floors. ✉ *811 Fair St.,* ☎ *803/425–1123.* ☞ *Free.* ☾ *Thurs. 1–5 or by appointment.*

Ⓒ The **Historic Camden Revolutionary War Site** re-creates and interprets historical structures of 18th- and early 19th-century Camden, with an emphasis on the British occupation of 1780. Several structures dot the site, including the 1789 **Craven House** and the **Blacksmith Shed.** The **Kershaw House,** a reconstruction of the circa-1770 home of Camden's founder, Joseph Kershaw, also served as Cornwallis's headquarters; it's furnished with period pieces. A nature trail, fortifications, powder magazine, picnic area, and crafts shop are also here. ✉ *U.S. 521, 1½ mi north of I-20,* ☎ *803/432–9841,* 🌐 *www.historic-camden.org.* ☞ *$5; admission to grounds and trail free.* ☾ *Tues.–Sat. 10–5, Sun. 1–5; call for guided tours.*

OFF THE
BEATEN PATH

HISTORIC BOYKIN – This 19th-century agricultural community, on the National Register of Historic Places, was once centered around the now restored and working grist mill. You can visit the mill; buy freshly ground grits or cornmeal from the Boykin Mill General Store, which has floor-to-ceiling shelves; step inside a restored 1740 slave house (Broom Place) and see brooms being handmade on late-19th-century equipment; and visit the 1820s Swift Creek Baptist Church. The Mill Pond Restaurant occupies two historic buildings. ✉ *Rtes. 261 and 28 (10 mi south of Camden via U.S. 521),* ☎ *803/424–4731.* ☞ *Free.* ☾ *Broom Place weekdays 10–5, Sat. 10:30–2; general store Mon.–Sat. 7–6; church and mill open by appointment.*

Dining and Lodging

$$$–$$$$ ✕ **Mill Pond Restaurant.** In a pair of historic buildings overlooking a
★ sprawling millpond, this restaurant, about a 10-minute drive south of Camden in Boykin, specializes in Mediterranean-influenced dishes. You can dine alfresco, close enough to see pond wildlife, on the spicy, perfectly fried Cajun oysters, bacon-wrapped scallops, or crab cakes with shrimp tartar sauce. The more casual side of the restaurant has a vintage saloon-style bar. ✉ *84 Boykin Mill Rd., Boykin,* ☎ *803/425–8825. MC, V. Closed Sun.–Mon. No lunch.*

$$ ✕ **The Pearl.** Chances are Ms. Pearl has put out her sign and is serving her famous collards, pork chops, catfish, fried chicken, and banana pudding, but you'll have to call or drop by to be sure. A meat-and-two (lunch) or -three (dinner) comes with salad and beverage. Each room has a theme: for example, the Pearl Room has framed pearl necklaces on the wall. ✉ *707 DeKalb St.,* ☎ *803/713–8009. AE, MC, V.*

$–$$ ✕ **Lucy's Food & Spirits.** You can sit at the immense wooden bar or at café tables in this high-ceilinged, brick-walled turn-of-the-20th-century building. Veal, pork, quail, and lamb are specialties; don't miss the sweet-potato chips, the pear and endive salad, or, for lunch, the curried-chicken salad. ✉ *1034 Broad St.,* ☎ *803/432–9096. AE, D, MC, V. Closed Mon.–Sun. No lunch Tues.*

$$ ✕🏠 **Greenleaf Inn of Camden.** You won't find a nicer or better-value
★ lodging in the region. This property, in Camden's historic district, consists of the main inn, with four rooms on the second floor above the inn's restaurant; a nearby house, circa 1805, with seven rooms; and a 1930s bungalow, which is good for families. The grander rooms in the inn are spacious and have classic Victorian furniture; rooms in the other house are smaller but more private. All baths are modern. High ceilings, elaborately tiled fireplaces, and patio dining set the tone for

an elegant yet casual meal in the restaurant ($–$$$; no lunch). Try the wonderful eggplant Parmesan, crispy whole flounder, or seafood lasagna. ⊠ *1308 Broad St., 29020,* ☎ *803/425–1806 or 800/437–5874,* FAX *803/425–5853,* WEB *www.greenleafinncamden.com. 10 rooms, 2 suites, 1 bungalow. Restaurant. AE, D, MC, V. BP.*

$ 🏨 **Colony Inn.** A short drive from the historic district, this well-maintained hotel is popular with business travelers. Because of the friendly staff, clean rooms, and the great location, the inn is always busy. ⊠ *2020 W. DeKalb St. (U.S. 1), 29020,* ☎ *803/432–5508 or 800/356–9801,* FAX *803/432–0920. 71 rooms. Restaurant, pool. AE, DC, MC, V.*

Nightlife and the Arts

The **Paddock Restaurant & Pub** (⊠ 514 Rutledge St., ☎ 803/432–3222) has music and dancing weekends. The prolific **Fine Arts Center of Kershaw County** (⊠ 810 Lyttleton St., ☎ 803/425–7676) sponsors many events, including a blues festival, music and theater performances, and art shows.

Shopping

Real European butter is key to the divine cheese sticks at the **Mulberry Market Bake Shop** (⊠ 536 E. DeKalb St., ☎ 803/424–8401); also sample almond Danishes, lemon bars, and macaroons. It's a delightful culinary asset in a small town.

Camden is known for its antiques shopping, with several shops and multidealer malls along Broad Street, including the **Camden Antique Mall** (⊠ 830 Broad St., ☎ 803/432–0818), with furniture, sterling, glassware, and reproduction pieces in some 30 stalls. The **Granary** (⊠ 830 Broad St., ☎ 803/432–8811) specializes in English and American items and has whimsical garden furniture.

Nearby, **Charles Dixon Antiques & Auction Co.** (⊠ 818 Broad St., ☎ 803/432–3676) has distinctive architectural pieces. At **Springdale Antiques** (⊠ 951 Broad St., ☎ 803/432–0312), the proprietor always provides great history on his items.

Outdoor Activities and Sports

EQUESTRIAN EVENTS

Camden puts on two steeplechase events at the **Springdale Race Course** (⊠ 200 Knights Hill Rd., ☎ 803/432–6513): the Carolina Cup, in late March or early April; and the Colonial Cup, in November. You're likely to see Thoroughbreds working out most mornings October through April; also on site, the **National Steeplechase Museum** (☎ 803/432–6513, WEB www.carolina-cup.org; 🎟 free; ◷ Sept.–Apr., daily 10–5; May–Aug., by appointment) shows off National Steeplechase artifacts and horse memorabilia.

Polo matches are held annually in May at **Camden Polo Field** (⊠ Polo La., ☎ 803/425–7676).

GOLF

White Pines Golf Club (⊠ 615 Mary La., ☎ 803/432–7442) is an 18-hole, par-72 course.

Cheraw

55 mi northeast of Camden via U.S. 1.

The small and historic town of Cheraw, named for the Native American tribe that once thrived in this region, is worth visiting to see its well-preserved 213-acre historic district, anchored by the town green, which dates to the original 1768 village plan. The district encompasses more than 50 antebellum public buildings and homes, including Victorian, classical revival, federal, upcountry farmhouse, and colonial styles, plus some mill buildings. The **Greater Cheraw Chamber of Commerce** (⊠ 221 Market St., ☏ 843/537–8425 or 888/537–0014) distributes brochures that delineate self-guided tours.

Notable buildings on the **town green** include the **Cheraw Town Hall,** built in 1858, which has massive columns and now contains city offices. Brokers once bought and sold cotton in **Market Hall,** which dates to 1837.

The small brick **Lyceum,** which dates to 1820, has served as a chancery court and as headquarters for both Confederate and Union quartermasters. Now a small museum with Indian artifacts and local historical relics, it includes engaging artifacts on the late jazz musician Dizzy Gillespie, who hailed from Cheraw. ⊠ *220 Market St.,* ☏ *843/537–8425.* 🎫 *Free.* ⊙ *Obtain key from chamber of commerce, weekdays 9–5, or call for appointment.*

The **Old St. David's Episcopal Church** dates to the early 1770s and was the last Anglican church built in South Carolina under King George III. Inside you can view simple box pews and gaze out the windows toward graceful magnolias; outside in the graveyard, soldiers from every American war have been buried. Both the Americans and the British used Old St. David's as quarters during the revolution; both the Confederate and the Union armies used it as a hospital during the Civil War. The acoustics are splendid. ⊠ *91 Church St.,* ☏ *843/537–8425.* 🎫 *Free.* ⊙ *Obtain key from chamber of commerce, weekdays 9–5, or call for appointment.*

Dining and Lodging

$ ✗ **Country Kitchen.** This no-frills lunch place—a short drive from the historic district—serves all-you-can-eat home-cooked fried chicken, macaroni and cheese, squash, corn bread, peach pie, vegetable soup, and other delights. Every Friday there's fried fish. ⊠ *908 Chesterfield Hwy. (Rte. 9),* ☏ *843/537–3662. AE, MC, V. Closed Sat. No dinner.*

$ ✗ **El-Sherif's House of Pizza.** Expect great pizza, fair prices, and tasty chicken salad at this casual spot in the former soda fountain of an early 20th-century hotel, right behind Town Hall. ⊠ *217 2nd St.,* ☏ *843/921–0066. AE, MC, V. Closed Sun.*

$ 🏨 **501 Kershaw and Spears Guest House.** Accommodations at this inn consist of four rooms in the Spears Guest House (a 1940s cottage with an enchanting front porch) and one in the owner's 1845 federal-style home across the street. Although on the small side, rooms have antique and reproduction furnishings. You have access to a fully equipped kitchen and a gas grill. Breakfast is self-serve: the refrigerator is stocked with juice and packaged foods. ⊠ *501 Kershaw St., 29520,* ☏ *843/537–7733 or 888/424–3729,* 🅵🅰🆇 *843/537–0302,* 🆆🅴🅱 *www.bbonline.com/sc/kershaw. 5 rooms. AE, D, DC, MC, V. CP.*

Shopping

A few miles west at the **Chesterfield Outlet** (⊠ Rte. 9, Chesterfield, ☏ 843/623–7474), you'll find knit polo shirts embroidered with the state palmetto tree logo, made of local cotton grown and spun here in Chesterfield County.

Outdoor Activities and Sports

Cheraw State Park, about 4 mi south of Cheraw off U.S. 52, contains a terrific golf course. Also within the park's 6,000 acres are the Turkey Oak Trail and the scenic Boardwalk Trail, the latter jutting into the lake for awesome views (pack lunch and a swimsuit because this trail leads to a lovely picnic area and a small beach with lifeguards). There's a cypress swamp that's ideal for canoeing (canoes and paddleboat rentals are available), and great fishing, too. Overnighters can consider eight log cabins built by the Civilian Conservation Corps in the 1930s that are fully furnished, quaint, and comfortable. ⊠ *100 State Park Rd.,* ☎ *843/537–2215 or 800/868–9630.* ⚏ *Free.* ☉ *Daily 7–7.*

Golf

The championship Tom Jackson–designed 18-hole course at **Cheraw State Park** (⊠ 100 State Park Rd., ☎ 843/537–2215 or 800/868–9630) has been rated by *Golf Digest* as one of the best buys in the nation (ask about the $50 per person deal that includes overnight cabin accommodations, greens fees, and a cart). The course takes in beautiful pine forest and lake views. Right by the state park, **Cheraw Country Club** (⊠ 1601 Cash Rd., ☎ 843/537–3412) has a short but heavily bunkered 18-hole course that's nice for beginners because it's unintimidating and unhurried.

Sumter

70 mi south of Cheraw via U.S. 52 to U.S. 15, 30 mi southeast of Camden on U.S. 521, 44 mi east of Columbia on U.S. 378/76.

Sumter—named for the Revolutionary War hero and statesman General Thomas Sumter—was settled about 1740 as the center of a cultivated plantation district. Today it houses varied industries, lumbering, agricultural marketing, and nearby Shaw Air Force Base.

The **Sumter County Museum** (headquarters of the Sumter County Historical Society), in a lovely 1845 Victorian Gothic house, exhibits fine period furnishings, Oriental carpets, vintage carriages, dolls, and various memorabilia. Behind the museum is an 1800s re-created "old South" village with live reenactments. ⊠ *122 N. Washington St.,* ☎ *803/775–0908.* ⚏ *Free.* ☉ *Tues.–Sat. 10–5, Sun. 2–5.*

The **Sumter Opera House,** built in 1892, has a clock tower and a stunning art deco interior, including detailed plasterwork and an intricate, hand-painted stage area. Theater, film, and music performances are held here. ⊠ *21 N. Main St.,* ☎ *803/436–2581.* ⚏ *Free.* ☉ *Tours by appointment weekdays 8:30–5.*

Swan Lake Iris Gardens is like Eden when its thousands of irises are in bloom. All eight known species of swans—including the *coscoroba,* whooper, trumpeter, and black Australian varieties—paddle leisurely about the 45-acre lake. The 150-acre park also includes walking trails, picnic areas, tennis courts, a playground, and concessions. ⊠ *W. Liberty St.,* ☎ *803/775–1231.* ⚏ *Free.* ☉ *Daily 8–sunset.*

Lodging

$$ ⬚ **Magnolia House.** In Sumter's historic district, this four-column Greek Revival structure is a pleasing alternative to the region's generic chain properties. Antiques, many of which are French, furnish the rooms; there are also stained-glass windows, inlaid oak floors, and five fireplaces. ⊠ *230 Church St., 29150,* ☎ *803/775–6694 or 888/666–0296,* WEB *www.bbonline.com/sc/magnolia. 3 rooms, 1 suite. AE, D, MC, V. BP.*

$–$$ ⬚ **Holiday Inn.** This well-maintained motor inn is 4 mi west of town, near Shaw Air Force Base. Simple, clean rooms are as you would expect from this chain. ⊠ *2390 Broad St. Ext., 29150,* ☎ *803/469–9001 or 800/465–4329,* FAX *803/469–7001,* WEB *www.basshotels.com. 124 rooms. Café, pool, gym. AE, D, DC, MC, V.*

Outdoor Activities and Sports

About 20 mi east of Sumter, a mysterious canoe trail leads into a remote swampy depression at **Woods Bay State Park** (⊠ east on U.S. 378, then north on U.S. 301, ☎ 803/659–4445), where rentals are available for $3 per hour or $10 for a full day. About 20 mi southwest of Sumter, **Poinsett State Park** (⊠ west on U.S. 378, then south on Route 261, ☎ 803/494–8177) is part of the state-wide Palmetto Trail and offers great hiking.

GOLF

Inveterate duffers appreciate the affordable, unhurried golfing at several nearby 18-hole courses, including **Lakewood Links** (⊠ 3600 Greenview Pkwy., ☎ 803/481–5700). You can walk the par 71 course at **Pocalla Springs** (⊠ 1700 U.S. 15S, ☎ 803/481–8322). **Crystal Lakes Golf Course** (⊠ 1305 Clara Louise Kellogg Dr., ☎ 803/775–1902) offers nine holes.

Aiken

100 mi southwest of Sumter via U.S. 378/76 to I–20 to U.S. 1, 56 mi southwest of Columbia via I–20 to U.S. 1.

Aiken, in Thoroughbred Country, first earned its fame in the 1890s, when wealthy Northerners wintering here built stately mansions and entertained one another with lavish parties, horse shows, and hunts. Many of the mansions—some with up to 60 rooms—remain as a testament to this era of opulence. The town is still a center for all kinds of outdoor activity, including the equestrian events of the Triple Crown, as well as tennis and golf.

The area's horse farms have produced many national champions, which are commemorated at the **Aiken Thoroughbred Hall of Fame** with exhibitions of horse-related decorations, paintings, and sculptures, plus racing silks and trophies. The Hall of Fame is on the grounds of the 14-acre **Hopeland Gardens,** with winding paths, quiet terraces, and reflecting pools. There's a Touch and Scent Trail with Braille plaques. Open-air free concerts and plays are presented on Monday evening May through August. ⊠ *Dupree Pl. and Whiskey Rd.,* ☎ *803/642–7630.* ☜ *Free.* ☉ *Museum Oct.–May, Tues.–Sun. 2–5; grounds daily dawn–dusk.*

The **Aiken County Historical Museum,** in one wing of an 1860 estate, is devoted to early regional culture. It has Native American artifacts, firearms, an authentically furnished 1808 log cabin, a schoolhouse, and a miniature circus display. ⊠ *433 Newberry St. SW,* ☎ *803/642–2015.* ☜ *Donations suggested.* ☉ *Tues.–Fri. 9:30–4:30, weekends 2–5.*

Aiken surrounds the serene and wild **Hitchcock Woods** (⊠ enter from junction of Clark Rd. and Whitney Dr., Berrie Rd., and Dibble Rd.), 2,000 acres of Southern forest with hiking trails and bridal paths. Listed on the National Register of Historic Places and three times the size of New York's Central Park, it's the largest urban forest in the country.

The renovated 1951 **Monetta Drive-In** (⊠ US 1, Monetta, ☎ 803/685–7949) plays past and present favorites every weekend and some weekdays.

Stop for a wine tasting at **Montmorenci Vineyards** (⊠ U.S. 78, 2½ mi east of Aiken, ☎ 803/649–4870, ☉ Wed.–Sat. 10–6). Montmorenci wines are made from French-American hybrid grapes, many typical of the Southeast, and include rosés, blushes, whites, and reds.

Dining and Lodging

$$–$$$ ✕ **Malia's.** Locals love this busy lunch and dinner spot, with dim lighting and dark fabrics that convey a cool, classy style. You can sample creative international cuisine, including lamb soup with curry, veal with shiitake mushrooms and brandy demiglace, or the baked ham, Brie, and Portobello mushroom sandwich. ⊠ *120 Laurens St.,* ☎ *803/643–3086. D, MC, V. No lunch weekends, No dinner Sun.–Tues.*

$$ ✕ **Linda's Bistro.** In an open and clean bistro-style environment, chef Linda Rooney elevates traditional favorites, turning out mushroom-Gruyère tarts, risotto with roasted mushrooms and Asiago, steak *frites,* and rum–coconut cream bread pudding. Main courses come with a salad, a vegetable, and potatoes. ⊠ *210 The Alley,* ☎ *803/648–4853. AE, D, DC, MC, V. Closed Sun.–Mon. No lunch.*

$ ✕ **Track Kitchen.** The who's who of Aiken's horsey set can be found here most mornings, feasting on the heavy and hearty cooking of Carol and Pockets Curtis. The small dining room is unpretentious, with walls of mint-green cinder block and simple Formica counters. ⊠ *420 Mead Ave.,* ☎ *803/641–9628. No credit cards. No dinner.*

$$$$ ⊞ **The Willcox.** Winston Churchill, Franklin D. Roosevelt, and the Astors have slept at this elegant inn, built in the grand style in the late 19th century and now newly renovated. The lobby is graced with massive stone fireplaces, rosewood woodwork, heart-pine floors, Oriental rugs, and antiques. Most rooms are well-proportioned suites with high four-poster beds, soaking tubs, and fireplaces. Some of the special details include bedside lavender linen spray and CD players. ⊠ *100 Colleton Ave., 29801,* ☎ *803/648–1898 or 877/648–2200,* ʆᴬˣ *803/643–0971,* ᵂᴱᴮ *www.thewillcox.com. 7 rooms, 15 suites. Dining room, room service, gym, spa, lobby lounge. AE, D, DC, MC, V. CP.*

$ ⊞ **Briar Patch.** You can learn plenty about both the Old and New South
★ from the knowledgeable innkeepers of this terrific B&B, which was formerly tack rooms in Aiken's stable district. You get two choices— either the frilly room with French provincial furniture or the less dramatic one with pine antiques and a weather vane. ⊠ *544 Magnolia La. SE, 29801,* ☎ *803/649–2010,* ᵂᴱᴮ *www.bbonline.com/sc/briar. 2 rooms. Tennis court. No credit cards. CP.*

Outdoor Activities and Sports

EQUESTRIAN EVENTS

In Aiken **polo matches** are played at Whitney Field (☎ 803/648–7874) on Sunday afternoon September through November and March through July. Three weekends in late March and early April are set aside for the famed **Triple Crown** (☎ 803/641–1111)—Thoroughbred trials of promising yearlings, a steeplechase, and harness races by young horses making their debut.

GOLF

Aiken Golf Club (⊠ 555 Highland Park Ave., ☎ 803/649–6029) is one of the many fine 18-hole, par-70 courses in the area. The **River Golf Club** (⊠ 307 Riverside Blvd., North Augusta, ☎ 803/202–0110), just outside Aiken, is adjacent to the Savannah River.

Greenwood

60 mi northwest of Aiken via Rte. 19 to U.S. 25, 75 mi west of Columbia via U.S. 378 to U.S. 178.

Founded by Irish settlers in 1802, Greenwood received its name from the site's gently rolling landscape and dense forests. Andrew Johnson, the 17th U.S. president, operated a tailor shop at Courthouse Square before migrating to East Tennessee. Anglers, swimmers, and boaters head for nearby Lake Greenwood's 200-mi shore. Two sections of Sumter National Forest are nearby.

The **museum** has more than 7,000 items in eclectic displays: Native American artifacts, natural history and geology exhibits, and a replicated village street, including a one-room school and a general store. ⊠ *106 Main St.,* ☎ *864/229–7093.* ☞ *$2.* ☉ *Wed.–Sun. 10–5.*

The **Gardens of Park Seed Co.,** one of the nation's largest seed supply houses, maintains colorful experimental gardens and greenhouses 6 mi north on U.S. 178 at Hodges. The flower beds are especially vivid June 15 through July, and seeds and bulbs are for sale in the company store. The **South Carolina Festival of Flowers**—with a performing-artists contest, a beauty pageant, private house and garden tours, and live entertainment—is held at Park's headquarters annually at the end of June. ⊠ *On Rte. 254, 7 mi north of town,* ☎ *864/941–4213 or 800/845–3369.* ☞ *Free.* ☉ *Gardens daily dawn–dusk; store Mon.–Sat. 9–5.*

Lodging

$$ 🆃 **Inn on the Square.** This inn, renovated in 2001, was fashioned out of a warehouse in the heart of town. New carpet, drapes, and linens brighten spacious guest rooms furnished with reproduction 18th-century antiques, four-poster beds, and writing desks. Also note thoughtful touches such as turndown service and complimentary morning newspapers. ⊠ *104 Court St., 29648,* ☎ *864/223–4488 or 800/231–9109,* 𝖥𝖠𝖷 *864/223-7067,* 𝖶𝖤𝖡 *www.innonthesquare.com. 48 rooms. Restaurant, pool, lounge. AE, D, DC, MC, V.*

Ninety Six

10 mi east of Greenwood on Rte. 248.

The town of Ninety Six, on an old Native American trade route, is so named for being 96 mi from the Cherokee village of Keowee in the Blue Ridge Mountains—the distance a young Cherokee maiden, Cateechee, is supposed to have ridden to warn her English lover of a threatened Native American massacre. The **Ninety Six National Historic Site** commemorates two Revolutionary War battles. The visitor center's museum has descriptive displays, and there are remnants of the old village, a reconstructed French and Indian War stockade, and revolutionary-era fortifications. ⊠ *Rte. 248,* ☎ *864/543–4068,* 𝖶𝖤𝖡 *www. nps.gov/nisi.* ☞ *Free.* ☉ *Daily 8–5.*

Abbeville

14 mi west of Greenwood on Rte. 72.

★ **Abbeville** may well be one of inland South Carolina's most satisfying although lesser-known small towns. An appealing historic district includes the old business district, early churches, and residential areas. What was called the "Southern cause" by supporters of the Confederacy was born and died here, where the first organized secession meeting was held and where, on May 2, 1865, Confederate president Jefferson Davis officially disbanded the defeated armies of the South in the last meeting of his war council. The Confederate council met at the 1830 **Burt-Stark House.** ⊠ *306 N. Main St.,* ☎ *864/459–4297 or 864/459–2181.* ☞ *$3.* ☉ *Sept.–May, Fri.–Sat. 1–5 or by appointment; June–Aug., Tues.–Sat. 1–5 or by appointment.*

An 1850s jail houses the **Abbeville County Museum,** which contains area memorabilia. It's adjacent to the 1837 log-cabin home of Marie Cromer Siegler, founder of the 4-H clubs, and to an educational garden. ⊠ *Poplar and Cherry Sts.,* ☎ *864/459–4600.* ☞ *Free.* ⊙ *Wed. and Sun. 3–5 or by appointment.*

The **Abbeville Opera House** (⊠ Town Sq., ☎ 864/459–2157) faces the historic town square. Built in 1908, it has been renovated to reflect the grandeur of the days when lavish road shows and stellar entertainers were center stage here. Current productions range from contemporary light comedies to local renderings of Broadway musicals. Call about tours.

OFF THE BEATEN PATH	**HICKORY KNOB STATE RESORT PARK –** This park on the shore of Strom Thurmond Lake, about 20 mi south of Abbeville, has everything for a complete vacation: fishing, waterskiing, sailing, motorboating, a swimming pool, a tackle shop, nature trails, an 18-hole championship golf course, a pro shop, tennis courts, and a skeet/archery range. A 1770s log cabin, a 78-room motel ($), nine duplex lakeside cottages, campgrounds, and a restaurant round out Hickory Knob's offerings. You're also near a stretch of the **Savannah River Scenic Highway,** which follows the Savannah River along the Georgia border, winding 100 mi and past three lakes. ⊠ *Rte. 1, Box 199B (off Rte. 33, just north of U.S. 378), McCormick 29835,* ☎ *864/391–2450 or 800/491–1764.* ☞ *Free; fees for some activities.* ⊙ *Office daily 7 AM–11 PM.*

Dining and Lodging

$–$$ ✕ **Village Grille.** Locals come to this high-ceiling room with
★ pomegranate-color walls and antique mirrors for the herb rotisserie chicken. Other choices are the ribs, homemade pastas, and cordial-laced desserts. The feeling here is trendy yet easygoing; the staff bend over backward to please. ⊠ *114 Trinity St.,* ☎ *864/459–2500. AE, D, MC, V. Closed Sun.–Mon.*

$ ✕ **Yoder's Dutch Kitchen.** You'll find authentic Pennsylvania Dutch home cooking in this unassuming redbrick building. There are a lunch buffet and an evening smorgasbord with fried chicken, stuffed cabbage, Dutch meat loaf, breaded veal Parmesan, and plenty of vegetables. Shoofly pie, Dutch bread, and apple butter can be purchased to go. ⊠ *Rte. 72 (east of downtown),* ☎ *864/459–5556. No credit cards. Closed Sun.–Tues. No dinner Wed.*

$$ 🏨 **Belmont Inn.** Built in the early 1900s, this restored Spanish-style structure is a popular overnight stop with opera house visitors. Guest rooms are spacious, with high ceilings and pine floors. Theater-and-dining package plans are available. ⊠ *104 E. Pickens St., 29620,* ☎ *864/459–9625 or 877/459–8118,* 🌐 *www.belmontinn.net. 25 rooms. Restaurant, lounge, business services, meeting rooms. AE, D, DC, MC, V. CP.*

Nightlife and the Arts

The **Abbeville Opera House** (⊠ Town Sq., ☎ 864/459–2157) stages high-caliber productions in an early 20th-century setting.

Shopping

Abbeville's **Town Square** is lined with attractive gift and specialty shops in restored historic buildings dating from the late 1800s.

Columbia and the Heartland A to Z

To research prices, get advice from other travelers, and book travel arrangements, visit www.fodors.com.

AIRPORTS

Columbia Metropolitan Airport, 10 mi west of downtown, is served by ASA/Delta, ComAir, Continental, Delta, United Express, and US Airways/Express.

➤ Airport Information: **Columbia Metropolitan Airport** (✉ 3000 Aviation Way, ☎ 803/822–5000).

BUS TRAVEL

The Columbia Trolley runs a midday route weekdays 11:20–2:30 along Main Street and around the Congaree Vista; fare is 25¢; there's also evening service Sunday–Thursday 5:30–11, which also covers Five Points and Devine Street.

Greyhound serves Aiken, Camden, Columbia, Greenwood, and Sumter.
➤ Bus Information: **Columbia Trolley** (☎ 803/748–3019). **Greyhound** (☎ 800/231–2222).

CAR TRAVEL

I–77 leads into Columbia from the north, I–26 runs through north–south, and I–20 east–west.

EMERGENCIES

Emergency room services are available at Richland Memorial Hospital. Kroger Sav-on has a pharmacy open 24 hours; other regional locations are open until 9.
➤ Emergency Services: **Ambulance, fire, police** (☎ 911).
➤ Hospitals: **Richland Memorial Hospital** (✉ 5 Richland Medical Park, Columbia, ☎ 803/434–7000).
➤ 24-Hour Pharmacies: **Kroger Sav-On** (✉ 7467 Woodrow St., Irmo, ☎ 803/732–0426).

OUTDOORS AND SPORTS

FISHING

For fishing, Lakes Marion and Moultrie attract anglers after bream, crappie, catfish, and several kinds of bass. Supplies, camps, guides, rentals, and accommodations abound. For information contact Santee Cooper Counties Promotion Commission & Visitors Center.
➤ Contacts: **Santee Cooper Counties Promotion Commission & Visitors Center** (✉ 9302 Old Hwy. 6, Drawer 40, Santee 29142, ☎ 803/854–2131; 800/227–8510 outside SC, WEB www.santeecoopercountry.org).

HIKING

For information on hiking trails in the Francis Marion National Forest and the Sumter National Forest, contact the National Forest Service.
➤ Contacts: **National Forest Service** (✉ 4931 Broad River Rd., Columbia 29210-4021, ☎ 803/561–4000).

LAKES

The 41-mi-long Lake Murray, just 15 mi west of Columbia via I–26 (Irmo exit), has swimming, boating, picnicking, and superb fishing. There are many marinas and campgrounds in the area. For information contact the Capital City/Lake Murray Country Visitors Center.
➤ Contacts: **Capital City/Lake Murray Country Visitors Center** (✉ 2184 N. Lake Dr., Irmo 29063, ☎ 803/781–5940 or 866/785–3935, WEB www.scjewel.com).

TAXIS

Companies providing service in Columbia include AAATaxi and Airport Shuttle Service, Blue Ribbon, and Checker-Yellow. Gamecock Cab Co. offers citywide service as well as service to other cities statewide. It's about $15–$17 from the airport to downtown Columbia.
➤ Taxi Companies: **AAATaxi and Airport Shuttle Service** (☎ 803/796–3626). **Blue Ribbon** (☎ 803/754–8163). **Checker-Yellow** (☎ 803/799–3311). **Gamecock Cab Co.** (☎ 803/796–7700).

TOURS

The Aiken Chamber of Commerce runs a 90-minute tour of the historic district ($6) and will customize tours to suit individual interests. In Sumter the charismatic former mayor "Bubba" McElveen gives walking, bus, and auto tours of the area. In Camden, Camden Carriage Company takes you on a tour on a horse-drawn carriage through Camden's loveliest neighborhood and down unpaved roads. Customized excursions of Camden are available from Greenleaf Tours. Richland County Historic Preservation Commission runs guided tours of Columbia and rents out historic properties.

➤ FEES AND SCHEDULES: **"Bubba" McElveen** (☎ 803/775–2851). **Camden Carriage Company** (☎ 803/425–5737). **Greenleaf Tours** (contact Louise Burns, ☎ 803/432–1515). **Richland County Historic Preservation Commission** (☎ 803/252–1770).

TRAIN TRAVEL

Amtrak makes stops at Camden, Columbia, Denmark, Florence, and Kingstree in the Heartland.

➤ TRAIN INFORMATION: **Amtrak** (☎ 800/872–7245).

VISITOR INFORMATION

➤ TOURIST INFORMATION: **Columbia Metropolitan Convention and Visitors Bureau** (✉ Box 15, 29202; visitor center: ✉ 1012 Gervais St., ☎ 803/254–0479 or 800/264–4884, WEB www.columbiasc.net). **Capital City/Lake Murray Country Visitors Center** (✉ 2184 N. Lake Dr., Irmo 29063, ☎ 803/781–5940 or 866/785–3935, WEB www.scjewel. com). **Greater Abbeville Chamber of Commerce** (✉ 104 Pickens St., Abbeville 29620, ☎ 864/459–4600, WEB www.emeraldis.com/abbeville). **Greater Aiken Chamber of Commerce** (✉ 121 Richland Ave. E, Box 892, Aiken 29802, ☎ 803/641–1111, WEB www.chamber.aiken.net). **Greater Cheraw Chamber of Commerce** (✉ 221 Market St., 29520, ☎ 843/537–8425 or 888/537–0014, WEB www.cheraw.com). **Kershaw County Chamber of Commerce** (✉ 724 S. Broad St., Box 605, Camden 29020, ☎ 803/432–2525 or 800/968–4037, WEB www.camden-sc. org). **Ninety Six Chamber of Commerce** (✉ 112 N. Cambridge St., Box 8, 29666, ☎ 864/543–2900). **Greater Sumter Convention & Visitors Bureau** (✉ 32 E. Calhoun St., Sumter 29150, ☎ 803/436–2640 or 800/ 688–4748, WEB www.sumter.sc.us).

THE UPCOUNTRY

The Upcountry, in the northwest corner of the state, has long been a favorite for family vacations because of its temperate climate and natural beauty. The abundant lakes and waterfalls and several state parks (including Caesar's Head, Keowee-Toxaway, Oconee, Table Rock, and the Chattooga National Wild and Scenic River) provide all manner of recreational activities. Beautiful anytime, the 130-mi Cherokee Foothills Scenic Highway (Route 11), which goes through the Blue Ridge Mountains, is especially delightful in spring (when the peach trees are in bloom) and autumn.

Greenville is growing fast and attracting lots of industry, much of it textile-related, in keeping with the area's history. Clemson, home of Clemson University and the "Orange Wave," is pretty much a university town. Pendleton, just a few miles away, has one of the nation's largest historic districts. With its village green, surrounded by shops and restaurants, it's a lovely step back in time. The comfortable communities of Spartanburg and Anderson are beginning to rejuvenate their downtown areas.

Greenville

100 mi northwest of Columbia via I–26 and I–385.

Known for its textile and other manufacturing plants, Greenville has many tree-lined streets and a revitalized turn-of-the-20th-century downtown. It also claims a number of attractions, including a zoo, and nearby state parks, such as Caesar's Head and Table Rock. Here you'll also find Bob Jones University, which has a gallery of religious art and antiquities.

The renowned international collection of religious art at **Bob Jones University Art Gallery and Museum** includes works by Botticelli, Rembrandt, Rubens, and Titian. ⊠ *Bob Jones University, 1700 Wade Hampton Blvd.,* ☎ *864/242–5100.* ⊡ *$5, free Sun.* ☉ *Tues.–Sun. 2–5.*

Housed in an innovative modern building, the **Greenville County Museum of Art** displays American works dating from the colonial era. Exhibited are works by Paul Jenkins, Jamie Wyeth, Jasper Johns, and noted Southern artists. ⊠ *420 College St.,* ☎ *864/271–7570.* ⊡ *Free.* ☉ *Tues.–Sat. 10–5, Sun. 1–5.*

Dining and Lodging

$$–$$$ ✕ **Johann's.** In a high-ceilinged, spacious structure inside the West End Market (a former mill building), Johann's makes appealing use of the building's industrial history, with exposed brick walls and large windows upstairs. Sample crepes, salmon steak, honey-glazed duck, sea bass, and pastas. Sunday brunch is a big to-do. ⊠ *1 Augusta St.,* ☎ *864/235–2774. MC, V. Closed Mon. No lunch Sat.*

$–$$ ✕ **Stax's Omega Diner.** This contemporary diner with booths and a half-circle counter with stools serves everything from bacon and eggs and burgers to souvlaki, Greek-style chicken, and shrimp and grits. It's all good, and it's open almost around-the-clock. ⊠ *72 Orchard Park Dr.,* ☎ *864/297–6639. AE, DC, MC, V.*

$$$ ✕🏨 **Phoenix–Greenville's Inn.** Plantation shutters, gardens, and four-poster beds create the residential feel of a Southern inn; the service is excellent. Ask for a room overlooking the courtyard pool area. Palms Restaurant ($$–$$$$), one of Greenville's best, serves sophisticated dishes—grilled peach salad with strawberry-basil vinaigrette, and grouper with risotto cake and shrimp vermouth sauce. ⊠ *246 N. Pleasantburg Dr., 29607,* ☎ *800/257–3529,* ☎ FAX *864/233–4651,* WEB *www.phoenixgreenvillesinn.com. 181 rooms, 3 suites. Restaurant, pool, lounge, piano bar, pub, business services, meeting room, airport shuttle. AE, D, DC, MC, V. BP.*

$$–$$$ 🏨 **Westin Poinsett Hotel.** After sitting dormant for many years, this historic 12-story hotel, dating to 1925, opened to an enthusiastic and supportive community. The large guest rooms have down comforters, marble baths, and high ceilings. All public spaces are back in their original opulence, including ornate plaster details and mosaic tile work. ⊠ *120 S. Main St., 29601,* ☎ *864/421–9700,* FAX *864/421–9719. 181 rooms, 9 suites. Restaurant, coffee shop, health club, lounge, concierge. AE, D, DC, MC, V.*

Nightlife and the Arts

The **Peace Center for the Arts** (⊠ 101 W. Broad St., ☎ 864/467–3030), which sits along the Reedy River, presents star performers, touring Broadway shows, dance companies, chamber music, and local groups.

Outdoor Activities and Sports

GOLF

South Carolinians sometimes prefer Upcountry courses to those on the coast, as they're less crowded and enjoy a slightly cooler climate. The area's rolling hills provide challenging courses. **Links O'Tryon** (✉ 11250 New Cut Rd., Campobello, ☎ 864/468–4995) is an Upcountry 18-hole course. **Rock at Jocassee** (✉ 171 Sliding Rock Rd., Pickens, ☎ 864/878–2030) is a mountain course with many water hazards; its signature hole has a waterfall view.

Spartanburg

31 mi east of Greenville via I–85.

Spartanburg once produced the state's largest peach crop. Lovely country drives in the area meander through peach orchards, which delight with fragrant, papery blossoms each spring and juicy treats at roadside stands each summer. Although it's still part of the state's largest peach-producing area, today the town is better known as an international business center. So many foreign corporations have plants here that some local attractions provide brochures in German, French, and Spanish. In Spartanburg county 20 German (including a BMW plant), Swiss, and Austrian companies are visible from I–85. The town's early 20th-century downtown is slowly being revitalized with trendy shops and cafés. The NFL's Carolina Panthers train here each summer; their practice sessions at Wofford College (☎ 704/358–7000) are free and open to the public.

The **BMW Zentrum** plant, the company's only one in North America, exhibits BMW engineering in the auto, motorcycle, and aviation industries. On display is the Z3 James Bond drove in the film *Golden Eye,* classics dating to the 1910s, and BMWs painted by artists including Warhol and Lichtenstein. The Virtual Factory Tour, about the making of the BMW Z3 roadster, takes you down the factory line. ✉ *Rte. 101S, Exit 60 off I–85 (18 mi west of Spartanburg), Greer,* ☎ *864/989–5297 or 888/868–7269.* ⊡ *Free; plant tours $5.* ☉ *Tues.–Sat. 9:30–5:30; plant tours by appointment.*

More than 10,000 plants make **Hatcher Gardens** a refuge for birds and wildlife. It also has walking trails and ponds. ✉ *Reidville Rd.,* ☎ *864/ 574-7724.* ⊡ *Free.* ☉ *Daily dawn–dusk.*

Dining and Lodging

$$–$$$ ✕ **Abby's Grill.** A classy eatery downtown, Abby's has a lounge and live piano most evenings. High ceilings make the dining room open and airy. The menu changes nightly to include such items as smoked salmon *bruschetta,* panfried flounder, grilled salmon with lemon-caper sauce, and roasted pork loin with red-wine mushroom sauce. ✉ *149 W. Main St.,* ☎ *864/583–4660. AE, DC, MC, V. Closed Sun.*

$ ✕ **Beacon Drive-In.** This Spartanburg institution—and some of its staff—have been around for 50 years. They'll serve you curbside, but the action is inside at the counter. Locals come for the Beacon burgers (hamburgers with all the fixin's), onion rings, hot dogs, fried fish sandwiches, and sundaes. ✉ *255 Reidville Rd.,* ☎ *864/585-9387. AE, DC, MC, V. Closed Sun.*

$$ ⊡ **Brookwood Inn.** You'll find comfort and simple style here, as well as clean rooms and a welcoming staff. It's at I–26 and I–85, on the west side of town. ✉ *4930 College Dr., 29301,* ☎ *864/576–6080 or 800/426–7866,* 𝖥𝖠𝖷 *864/587–8901,* 𝖶𝖤𝖡 *www.hamptoninn.com. 112 rooms. Pool, business services, meeting room. AE, D, DC, MC, V. CP.*

$$ ⊡ **Inn at Merridun.** This antebellum 1855 home in Union, about 27 mi south of Spartanburg, has country style and cozy floral rooms. Rates include full breakfast and evening dessert. Afternoon tea, picnic lunches, and dinners are available. ✉ *100 Merridun Pl., off U.S. 176, Union 29379,* ☎ *864/427–7052 or 888/892–6020,* 𝖥𝖠𝖷 *864/429–0373,* 𝖶𝖤𝖡 *www.merridun.com. 5 rooms. Dining room. AE, D, MC, V. BP.*

$$ 🏠 **Red Horse Inn.** You'll travel through pretty countryside to get to this inn, near several state parks and the North Carolina border. Victorian-style cottages with porches and hand-painted murals are scattered on the inn's 190 acres, about 25 mi north of Greenville and near the charming Upcountry village of Landrum. Each cottage has a sitting area, fireplace, and board games; some have lofts and whirlpools. In each cottage's small kitchen you'll find a nice basket of breakfast items. ⊠ *4930 College Dr., Landrum 29301,* ☎ *864/895–4968,* FAX *864/587–8901,* WEB *www.bedandbreakfast.com. 9 cottages. AE, D, DC, MC, V. BP.*

Shopping

The more than 90 outlets at the **Prime Outlets of Gaffney** include the Gap, Nike, Levi's, and Donna Karan. The playground will keep older kids busy while you shop. ⊠ *I–85, Exit 90, Gaffney,* ☎ *864/902–9900 for information center.*

Pendleton

30 mi southwest of Greenville via U.S. 123.

Charming Pendleton, a few miles from Clemson University, has a historic district and interesting architecture. The Farmers Hall, built in 1826, was originally built to be a courthouse. The Square, a district of restaurants and shops, faces the Village Green.

Ⓒ   The **South Carolina State Botanical Garden,** on the Clemson University campus in nearby Clemson, holds more than 2,000 varieties of plants on more than 270 acres, including wildflower, fern, and bog gardens, as well as nature trails. The **Fran Hanson Discovery Center** has information on regional history and cultural heritage, and a hands-on learning station on natural history, a microscope with a big-screen monitor, and a talking animated raccoon. ⊠ *102 Garden Trail,* ☎ *864/656–3405,* WEB *www.clemson.edu/scbg.* 🎟 *Free.* ☉ *Daily dawn–dusk.*

Kings Mountain National Military and State Park

70 mi northeast of Greenville via I–85.

A Revolutionary War battle considered an important turning point was fought here on October 7, 1780. Colonial Tories commanded by British major Patrick Ferguson were soundly defeated by ragtag patriot forces from the southern Appalachians. Visitor center exhibits, dioramas, and an orientation film describe the action. A paved self-guided trail leads through the battlefield. ⊠ *20 mi northeast of Gaffney, SC, off I–85 (exit 2) via a marked side road in NC,* ☎ *864/936–7921,* WEB *www. southcarolinaparks.com.* 🎟 *Free.* ☉ *Early Sept.–late May, daily 9–5; late May–early Sept., daily 9–6.*

The 6,000-acre **Kings Mountain State Park** (☎ *864/222–3209*), adjacent to the national military park, has camping, swimming, fishing, boating, and nature and hiking trails.

Upcountry A to Z

To research prices, get advice from other travelers, and book travel arrangements, visit www.fodors.com.

AIRPORTS

Greenville-Spartanburg Airport, off I–85 between the two cities, is served by US Airways, Delta ComAir, United Express, Northwest, American Eagle, and Continental.

➤ AIRPORT INFORMATION: **Greenville-Spartanburg Airport** (⊠ 2000 G. S.P. Dr., ☎ 864/867–7426).

BUS TRAVEL

Greyhound serves Greenville and Spartanburg.

➤ BUS INFORMATION: **Greyhound** (☎ 800/231–2222).

CAR TRAVEL

I–85 provides access to Greenville, Spartanburg, Pendleton, and Anderson. I–26 runs from Charleston through Columbia to the Upcountry, connecting with I–385 into Greenville.

EMERGENCIES

➤ EMERGENCY SERVICES: **Ambulance, police** (☎ 911).

OUTDOORS AND SPORTS

CANOEING AND RAFTING

The Chattooga National Wild and Scenic River, on the border of South Carolina and Georgia, is excellent for guided rafting, canoeing, and kayaking trips. Contact Nantahala Outdoor Center, Southeastern Expeditions, or Wildwater Ltd.

➤ CONTACTS: **Nantahala Outdoor Center** (☎ 864/647–9014 or 800/232–7238). **Southeastern Expeditions** (☎ 800/868–7238). **Wildwater Ltd.** (☎ 864/647–9587 or 800/451–9972).

STATE PARKS

Devils Fork State Park, on Lake Jocassee, has luxurious villas and facilities.

➤ CONTACTS: **Devils Fork State Park** (✉ 161 Holcombe Circle, Salem 29676, ☎ 864/944–2639).

TRAIN TRAVEL

Amtrak stops in Greenville and Spartanburg.

➤ TRAIN INFORMATION: **Amtrak** (☎ 800/872–7245).

VISITOR INFORMATION

➤ TOURIST INFORMATION: **Discover Upcountry Carolina Association** (✉ Box 3116, Greenville 29602, ☎ 864/233–2690 or 800/849–4766, WEB www.the upcountry.com). **Greater Greenville Convention and Visitors Bureau** (✉ 206 S. Main St., Box 10527, 29603, ☎ 864/421–0000 or 800/351–7180, WEB www.greatergreenville.com). **Spartanburg Convention and Visitors Bureau** (✉ 298 Magnolia St., 29306, ☎ 864/594–5050 or 800/374–8326, WEB www.spartanburgsc.org).

SOUTH CAROLINA A TO Z

To research prices, get advice from other travelers, and book travel arrangements, visit www.fodors.com.

AIR TRAVEL

CARRIERS

South Carolina is served by Air Canada, AirTran, American Eagle, ASA, ComAir, Continental, Delta, Midway, Northwest, Spirit, United Express, US Airways, and Vanguard.

AIRPORTS

Major airports are Charleston International Airport; Columbia Metropolitan Airport; Greenville-Spartanburg Airport; Hilton Head Island Airport, served by US Airways Express; Myrtle Beach International Airport; and Savannah International Airport, about an hour's drive from Hilton Head.

➤ AIRPORT INFORMATION: **Charleston International Airport** (✉ 5500 International Blvd., ☎ 843/767–1100). **Columbia Metropolitan Airport** (✉ 3000 Aviation Way, ☎ 803/822–5000). **Greenville-Spartanburg Airport (✉ 2000 G.S.P. Dr., ☎ 864/867–7426). **Hilton Head Island Airport** (☎ 843/681–6386). **Myrtle Beach International Airport** (✉ 1100 Jetport Rd., ☎ 843/448–1589). **Savannah International Airport** (✉ 400 Airways Ave., ☎ 912/964–0514).

BUS TRAVEL

Greyhound serves many towns and cities throughout South Carolina and links several cities and towns throughout South Carolina.

➤ BUS INFORMATION: **Greyhound** (☎ 800/231–2222).

CAR TRAVEL

Many interstates lead into South Carolina from its neighbors Georgia and North Carolina. From western North Carolina I–26 runs southeast through Greenville, Columbia, and Charleston; from central North Carolina I–77 leads south into Columbia and I–85 leads southwest into Greenville; and from eastern North Carolina I–95 leads southwest through Florence, intersecting with I–20 and I–26. From Atlanta, Georgia, I–85 runs northeast into Greenville, and I–20 leads east via Augusta into Columbia; from southern Georgia I–95 leads northeast into the state. U.S. 17, a north–south coastal route, runs along the coastal edge of the entire state.

RULES OF THE ROAD

The speed limit on interstates can run as high as 70 mph but is lower in congested areas. You can turn right at a red light unless otherwise noted by street signs. If it's raining and you have your windshield wipers on, you must have your headlights on, too.

EMERGENCIES

➤ CONTACTS: **Ambulance, fire, police** (☎ 911).

LODGING

BED-AND-BREAKFASTS

Contact the South Carolina Bed and Breakfast Association for a current state directory of member B&Bs. For a complete list of B&Bs contact the South Carolina Division of Tourism and ask for the pamphlet *Bed & Breakfasts of South Carolina*.

➤ RESERVATION SERVICES: **South Carolina Bed and Breakfast Association** (✉ Box 1275, Sumter 29150-1275, ☎ 888/599–1234, WEB www.southcarolinabedandbreakfast.com).

TOURS

Lowcountry Adventures offers tours of Hilton Head, Beaufort, and Charleston. For information about other specific tours contact the South Carolina Division of Tourism.

➤ FEES AND SCHEDULES: **Lowcountry Adventures** (☎ 843/681–8212).

TRAIN TRAVEL

Amtrak stops in Charleston, Camden, Columbia, Denmark, Florence, Greenville, Kingstree, and Yemassee (near Beaufort). Amtrak provides service to these cities along an East Coast route that runs from Boston to Miami.

➤ TRAIN INFORMATION: **Amtrak** (☎ 800/872–7245).

TRANSPORTATION AROUND SOUTH CAROLINA

A car is easily the best way to get around South Carolina; however, if you're spending most of your time in Charleston, you can get by fairly easily either on foot or using public transportation. In virtually every other city you need a car to get to and from attractions, accommodations, and restaurants.

VISITOR INFORMATION

➤ TOURIST INFORMATION: **South Carolina Department of Parks, Recreation, and Tourism** (⊠ 1205 Pendleton St., Suite 106, Columbia 29201, ☎ 803/734–0122 or 800/872–3505, WEB www.travelsc.com). **Tourist welcome centers** (⊠ U.S. 17, near Little River; I–95, near Dillon, Santee and Lake Marion, and Hardeeville; I–77, near Fort Mill; I–85, near Blacksburg and Fair Play; I–26, near Landrum; I–20, at North Augusta; and U.S. 301, near Allendale).

8 TENNESSEE

Tennessee's dominating characteristics are its music—the blues developed in Memphis; rock and roll was born and came into popularity with the rise of Elvis Presley; country music claims Nashville as its capital—and its scenic geographical borders, the Great Smoky Mountains on the east and the Mississippi River on the west. Here, too, are forests, fields, and streams for the nature lover, outlet malls for the die-hard shopper, and activities and entertainment for the whole family.

MOUNTAINS AND MUSIC—these gifts Tennessee was given in abundance and shares generously with millions of visitors each year.

Updated by
Martha L.
Rodríguez
Rivera

Memphis, home of the blues, rises out of the flat, cotton-kissed southwest corner of the state, on the banks of the Mississippi River. Beale Street, in the core of its downtown, nurtured some of the finest talents of the genre, from blues artists W. C. Handy and B. B. King to rockers Elvis Presley and Jerry Lee Lewis. Today, with live music in Handy Park, Beale Street again reverberates with the moody sounds that made it legendary.

Nashville, Tennessee's largest city, retains its title as the country-music capital of the world. Music City, USA, as it is known, is also the state's capital. Here, in the heart of Tennessee's green, gently rolling hills, country music is king. The recording studios on Music Row are thriving, and the Grand Ole Opry continues to pack its auditorium. The long-running radio-show extravaganza has launched many a singer's and picker's career and is a major attraction for visitors.

As for mountains, they don't come any more beautiful than the Great Smokies—site of the nation's most-visited national park and part of the Appalachian chain; they're in East Tennessee and are shared with North Carolina. Covered with a dense carpet of wildflowers in spring and ablaze with foliage in autumn, the Smokies—named for the mantle of blue haze that so often blankets them—are a joy to hike or drive through. Spend some time in the little mountain towns and villages dotting the hollows to experience homegrown bluegrass music and traditional cooking, along with the natural warmth of the people.

Pleasures and Pastimes

Dining

If you expect Tennessee dining to be all corn bread, turnip greens, and grits, you're in for a staggering surprise. Two decades ago Memphis had little more than various neighborhood "home cooking" restaurants, several chop-suey houses, a handful of spaghetti-and-lasagna spots, and numerous establishments serving pork barbecue. Today, in addition to a number of restaurants offering imaginative American cuisine, Memphis claims many competent international dining rooms. As in other cities around the country, hotel dining has improved greatly.

Memphis's top culinary attraction, however, remains barbecue, and a visit to one of the 70-odd barbecue restaurants is a must. True fanciers should schedule their visit around the World Championship Barbecue Cooking Contest, held during the annual Memphis in May International Festival. This cook-off draws more than 400 teams from around the world for its three-day run.

Nashville dining patrons are often casually dressed and prone to linger over meals. The city's mix of politics, country music, conventions, sports, and business means deal making at every meal, lending prosperity and longevity to some of its best restaurants. Such tenure translates into high-quality dining. Nashville's restaurant scene has benefited from an influx of different ethnic groups as well as transplants from both coasts. Nowadays it is a healthy mix of contemporary, ethnic, and experimental eateries, as well as classic Southern favorites.

East Tennessee mountain cooks have long been noted for preparing fresh ingredients many different ways. Corn remains the old standby, used in the making of grits, luscious muffins, corn bread, and savory

Tennessee

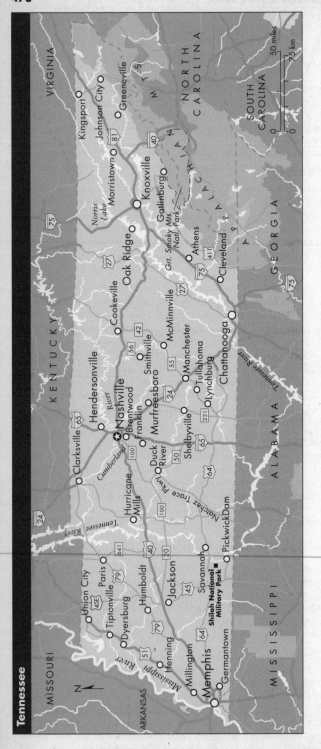

spoon bread. Barbecued ribs, thick pork chops, and generous slices of country ham with red-eye gravy rank as local favorites. Freshwater fish, such as varieties of trout, walleye, crappie, muskie, and catfish, will also be found in varied and delicious preparations (but remember to save room for home-baked pies and cobblers).

CATEGORY	COST*
$$$$	over $30
$$$	$20–$30
$$	$10–$20
$	under $10

per person for a main course at dinner, excluding service, and 8%–10% sales tax (depending on the area)

Lodging

Memphis hotels are especially busy in the spring, when the Memphis in May International Festival and June's Carnival Memphis are in progress; in mid-August, when pilgrims observe Elvis Presley's death; between Christmas and New Year's during the Axa/Equitable Liberty Bowl Football Classic; and in early January, when the faithful celebrate Elvis's birth. Another busy time is early November, when the city of Memphis hosts the Holy Convocation of God in Christ, a huge convention that virtually fills the city. Be sure to reserve well in advance during those times.

With more than 125 hotels and motels, Nashville has an impressive selection of accommodations in all price categories and levels of luxury. Although some establishments increase rates slightly during the peak summer travel season, especially Fan Fair week in mid-June, most maintain the same rates year-round. Some downtown luxury hotels offer lower rates on weekends, when the legislators have gone home.

Tennessee has 19 state parks with overnight accommodations ranging from rustic cabins to beautiful chalets. Prices vary, with a low of $45 a night for a cabin and a high of $140 a night for a three-bedroom chalet. Call 888/867–2757 for information and reservations.

CATEGORY	COST*
$$$$	over $160
$$$	$110–$160
$$	$70–$110
$	under $70

All prices are for a standard double room, excluding 10%–11¾% tax.

Music

Music is everywhere in Tennessee. The blues and rock flood Beale Street in Memphis, whereas country is king on Nashville's Music Row, at the Grand Ole Opry, and in the District. Then there's Dollywood and an assortment of top-notch nightspots across the state that ensure Grammy Award–winning talent and rising stars without all the hype.

Outdoor Activities and Sports

Tennesseans take advantage of the state's generally mild climate and spend a lot of time outdoors. Many fish, hike, or swim at the many state parks. Others prefer to enjoy a picnic or cool off under waterfalls or in caves. And Tennesseans like to cheer for their favorite teams. The NFL's Tennessee Titans make their home at Adelphia Stadium on the banks of the Cumberland River in Nashville. The National Hockey League also has a Nashville franchise, the Nashville Predators, who play in the Gaylord Entertainment Center (formerly Nashville Arena). Both Memphis and Nashville have AAA baseball teams. Professional sports were slow to reach Tennessee, but fans have been demonstrating their love of football for decades, filling the University of Tennessee's Neyland Stadium in Knoxville to overflowing.

Exploring Tennessee

Tennessee spans more than 500 mi west to east but only about 115 mi north to south. Geographically, the state can be divided into West Tennessee, from the Mississippi River to the Tennessee River near Camden; Middle Tennessee, from the Tennessee River to the Cumberland Plateau at Crossville; and East Tennessee, to the Great Smoky Mountains and the border with North Carolina. All three sections are anchored by major cities with a wealth of cultural and historical attractions and first-rate lodging establishments.

Great Itineraries

Exploring Tennessee will require some time on the road. Fortunately, hopping on and off I–40, which crosses the state from east to west, will get you most places you want to go. Plan to spend at least two days to see the high points of any of Tennessee's major cities: Memphis, Nashville, Knoxville, or Chattanooga. Much of what's interesting about Tennessee is outside the major cities, however, so if you get to Memphis, for instance, allow some time for side trips.

IF YOU HAVE 3 DAYS

Explore 🔟 **Memphis,** home to Elvis Presley's Graceland. Be sure to see the morning or afternoon march of ducks to or from the Peabody Hotel's lobby fountain. Listen to the blues on Beale Street and don't miss the barbecue. Study the history of the great Mississippi River at Mud Island and the history of music at the Memphis Music Hall of Fame. Take a day to make a side trip from Memphis, perhaps to the Casey Jones Museum in **Jackson,** to the northeast, or east to **Shiloh National Military Park** if you're a Civil War buff. Either of these could easily be visited on the way from Memphis to Nashville.

IF YOU HAVE 6 DAYS

After a few days in 🔟 **Memphis,** visit 🔟 **Nashville** and its surrounding area. Take in some country music at the Grand Ole Opry, or view the works of Georgia O'Keeffe, Picasso, and Renoir at Fisk University's Van Vechten Art Gallery. Combine Nashville's Music Row and the District and fill a day seeing the sights and museums such as the Country Music Hall of Fame, and do some shopping. At night, hear some live music, watch the stars come out at restaurants downtown, or take in a Broadway show at the Tennessee Performing Arts Center. Make time to venture to historic **Franklin** or to **Lynchburg** to see the home of Jack Daniel's sippin' whiskey. Try to work in a brief visit to 🔟 **Chattanooga,** a spruced-up, midsize city on the move.

IF YOU HAVE 9 DAYS

Start at one end of the state and head for the other, hitting the highlights. There's a lot to see and do after 🔟 **Memphis** and 🔟 **Nashville.** 🔟 **Chattanooga** has emerged as a fine family destination with its first-rate aquarium, IMAX theater, and fun museums, coupled with Civil War sites. Devote at least one full day here. Northeast of Chattanooga, **Great Smoky Mountains National Park** is spectacular; either its gateway, 🔟 **Gatlinburg,** or nearby 🔟 **Pigeon Forge,** a shopping and entertainment complex with outlet malls, Dollywood, and theaters, is good for an overnight stay. Combine the three, trying a day of hiking and nature watching and then a day of shopping, sightseeing, and entertainment.

When to Tour Tennessee

Although spring and fall are the most popular times to tour Tennessee, there is something going on all year. The Smokies and East Tennessee are especially beautiful but crowded during the fall color change. University of Tennessee home football games in Knoxville draw crowds exceeding 100,000, which means a lot of road congestion. Temperatures stay mild until late June, when humidity begins to pick up. Late July and August heat can make outdoor activities trying.

MEMPHIS

Memphis was founded in 1819, but long before that, the Mississippi River, on whose banks it was built, exerted a powerful influence on the area. Both the river and the people who first appreciated it are celebrated in Memphis today. The Native American river culture that existed here from the 11th through the 15th centuries is documented in archaeological excavations, reconstructions, and exhibits at the Chucalissa Archaeological Museum. The river itself is celebrated with a museum dedicated to its history—part of Mud Island, a unique park on an island in the river.

The other significant influence on the city has been the music that has flowed through it. W. C. Handy moved from Alabama to Memphis in 1902–03, drawn by the long-thriving music scene, and it was here that he produced most of the blues songs that made him famous. However, economic decline in the mid-20th century brought the city to its knees, and the unrest after the assassination in 1968 of Dr. Martin Luther King Jr. at the Lorraine Motel, just south of Beale, dealt a near-fatal blow. Today, thanks to public improvements and an economy built around such distribution giants as Federal Express, Memphis has been brought back to life, and Beale Street has numerous clubs and restaurants, as it did in its heyday.

When you mention Memphis, one name springs to most minds: Elvis, the undisputed king of rock and roll. Although he was actually born across the state line in Tupelo, Mississippi, Elvis put Memphis on the map, recording his first hits here in what came to be known as Sun Studio. His legacy burns bright at Graceland, the estate where he lived, died, and rests in peace. Each year hundreds of thousands of fans make the pilgrimage to pay homage to the man and his music. Elvis International Tribute Week, held each August at Graceland, has grown to match the myth.

Downtown Memphis

Numbers in the text correspond to numbers in the margin and on the Downtown Memphis map.

Old and new mingle as Memphis progresses with its riverfront development and urban renewal. Peabody Place, a collection of offices, shops, restaurants, and apartments, is a new development in the area surrounding the historic Peabody Hotel at 2nd Street and Union Avenue. For travelers who want to tour the area without parking worries, the downtown trolley system runs a north–south route down Main Street, connecting major attractions. A loop adjacent to Riverside Drive completes the 5-mi circle.

A Good Walk and Drive

Pick up a map of the city at the **Tennessee Welcome Center** ① on Riverside Drive, where free parking is available. Take the Main Street trolley south to South Main Street to **Peabody Place** ③ to visit the **Center for Southern Folklore** ②, where the region's colorful past is chronicled in poignant exhibits. Continue south on foot to Beale Street and sneak a peek at the stately **Orpheum Theatre** ④; walk east to **A. Schwab Dry**

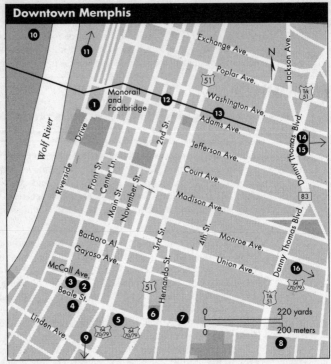

Downtown Memphis

Goods Store ⑤, a most unusual emporium. A few blocks east on Beale is **Handy Park** ⑥, where the father of the blues is immortalized. You can learn all about him at the nearby **W. C. Handy Memphis Home and Museum** ⑦. Walk farther east on Beale to the **Hunt-Phelan Home** ⑧. Head for the south end of downtown (take the Main Street trolley five blocks) to tour the **National Civil Rights Museum** ⑨, on the site where Dr. Martin Luther King Jr. was assassinated in 1968.

Take the Main Street trolley north to Adams Avenue and walk west to the **Mud Island** ⑩ Monorail to catch a ride over to the Mississippi River Park and Museum. When you come back, the **Pyramid** ⑪ is several blocks away from Mud Island parking and can be visited by trolley. Afterward, pick up your car and drive east on Adams, first to the **Fire Museum of Memphis** ⑫, then on to the Victorian Village Historic District for tours of the **Magevney** ⑬, **Mallory Neely** ⑭, and **Woodruff-Fontaine** ⑮ houses. On the way out of downtown, stop at **Sun Studio** ⑯ for a dose of Memphis music history.

TIMING

Spend the morning in the Beale Street Historic District &del;and work in lunch while you're there. The rest of downtown Memphis will take more than a day to cover, so depending on your schedule, you may want to pick and choose. Most of these attractions are closed Monday; the National Civil Rights Museum is closed Tuesday.

Sights to See

⑤ **A. Schwab Dry Goods Store.** Step into the past at this highly eccentric shop where unusual odds and ends such as voodoo potions stock the shelves, along with souvenirs and clothes. It's served many a customer, including Elvis, since it was founded in 1876. ⊠ *163 Beale St., Beale Street Historic District*, ☎ *901/523–9782.* ☉ *Mon.–Sat. 9–5.*

★ ❷ **Center for Southern Folklore.** These must-see exhibits on the people, music, food, crafts, and traditions of the South, particularly of the Mississippi Delta region, pay tribute to one of America's most flavorful cultural identities. Perhaps more than any other Memphis institution, the center has its finger on the pulse of local culture, and a visit here is both edifying and entertaining. There is space for exhibitions; a restaurant with Southern food such as barbecue, greens, and corn bread; a bar and performance area; and videos about Memphis and Beale Street. Concerts daily at noon (free) and on weekend evenings ($5 donation) feature blues, gospel, jazz, rockabilly, and folk music. Each year the center sponsors one of Memphis's finest music festivals, the three-day **Memphis Music Heritage Festival,** held Labor Day weekend. Tours of local interest are available (by reservation only). The gift shop carries regional folk art and handiwork, plus cassettes, videos, and books pertaining to the South. ⊠ *119 S. Main St., Downtown,* ☎ *901/525–3655,* WEB *www.southernfolklore.com.* ☞ *$2.* ☉ *Sun.–Wed. 11–7, Thurs.–Sat. 11–11.*

☾ ⓬ **Fire Museum of Memphis.** In Fire Engine House No. 1, a restored 1910 building, curiosity seekers of all ages can learn about the history of firefighting from the 19th-century bucket brigades to the present in an educational environment designed to increase fire safety awareness. An interactive center comes equipped with video games that teach safety tips and a fire truck that can be climbed. In the Fire Room, the *Fire Show* uses visual and sound effects to simulate an actual fire. ⊠ *118 Adams Ave., Downtown,* ☎ *901/320–5650,* WEB *www.firemuseum. com.* ☞ *$5.* ☉ *Mon.–Sat. 9–5.*

❻ **Handy Park.** The park holds a statue of W. C. Handy clutching his famed trumpet. In the core of the Beale Street Historic District, Handy Park is a prime venue for outdoor entertainment, including festivals and impromptu jam sessions. ⊠ *Between 3rd and 4th Sts., Downtown.*

❽ **Hunt-Phelan Home.** This restored antebellum home was originally designed by Robert Mills. Ulysses S. Grant began the initial plans for the Battle of Vicksburg in the library, which contains an impressive collection of first-edition books. A rare 1874 rosewood piano from Steinway and Sons is another house treasure. At press time it was unclear whether the house would remain open for public tours; call ahead. ⊠ *533 Beale St.,* ☎ *901/344–3166 or 800/350–9009.* ☞ *$10.*

⓭ **Magevney House.** This charming white-clapboard cottage, built in the 1830s, is one of Memphis's oldest dwellings. It's furnished with some of the original possessions of Eugene Magevney, a pioneer schoolteacher and ardent Catholic. The city's first Catholic church service was held in this house, and Magevney later helped build the church next door. ⊠ *198 Adams Ave., Downtown,* ☎ *901/526–4464,* WEB *www.memphismuseums.org.* ☞ *Free.* ☉ *Mar.–Dec., Tues.–Fri. 10–2, Sat. 10–4..*

⓮ **Mallory Neely House.** Original family furnishings fill this 25-room Italianate Victorian. Note the hand-carved cornices and frescoed ceilings on the first floor, and the stained-glass panels in the double front doors. ⊠ *652 Adams Ave., Victorian Village,* ☎ *901/523–1484,* WEB *www.memphismuseums.org.* ☞ *$5.* ☉ *Mar.–Dec., Tues.–Sat. 10–4, Sun. 1–4, last tour at 3:30.*

☾ ❿ **Mud Island.** Accessible by monorail or pedestrian walkway, this 52-acre park on an island explores Memphis's intimate relationship with the Mississippi. At the **Mississippi River Museum,** galleries bring the history of the Mississippi to life with exhibits ranging from scale-model boats to life-size, animated river characters (Mark Twain spins his tales anew here) and the Theater of River Disasters. The most extraordinary exhibit is outside: **River Walk,** a five-block-long scale model of the Mississippi, which replicates its every twist, turn, and sandbar from Cairo, Illinois, to New Orleans, ending in a huge swimming pool bordered by a man-made, sandy beach. Also here are shops, restaurants serving regional foods, and a 5,400-seat amphitheater. The famed World War II B-17 bomber *Memphis Belle,* the first plane of its kind to complete 25 missions without casualties, is housed in an open pavilion topped by a gleaming white dome. Plans to move the plane off Mud Island have been discussed, so call ahead if it's of particular interest to you. ⊠ *125 North Front St. (footbridge and monorail), Downtown,* ☎ *901/576–6595 or 800/507–6507,* WEB *www.mudisland.com.* 🎟 *$8 for all attractions.* ☉ *Apr.–May and Sept.–Oct., Tues.–Sun. 10–5; June–Aug., daily 10–8; closed Nov.–Mar.*

❾ National Civil Rights Museum. The Lorraine Motel, where Dr. Martin Luther King Jr. was assassinated on April 4, 1968, has been transformed into a museum that documents the struggle of African-Americans and the civil rights movement. A Montgomery, Alabama, bus, like the one in which Rosa Parks refused to give up her seat, sparking an uprising against segregation; scenes of lunch-counter sit-ins; and audiovisual displays are among the exhibits. ⊠ *450 Mulberry St., Downtown,* ☎ *901/ 521–9699,* WEB *www.civilrightsmuseum.org.* 🎟 *$8.50; free Mon. 3–5.* ☉ *Wed.–Mon. 9–5.*

❹ Orpheum Theatre. This former vaudeville palace and movie theater, opened in 1928, has been refurbished as a center for the performing arts. Step inside to admire its crystal chandeliers, gilt decorations, and ornate tapestries. The theater hosts touring Broadway shows as well as performances by Opera Memphis and Ballet Memphis. At the Friday-night film series, moviegoers sink into the red-velvet seats to aim their gaze either on classics of the silver screen or on silent serial films accompanied by an organist. ⊠ *203 S. Main St., Downtown,* ☎ *901/ 525–3000,* WEB *www.orpheum-memphis.com.*

❸ Peabody Place. This retail and entertainment center between Front and Main streets near Beale includes apartments, shops, banks, bars, restaurants, entertainment venues, galleries, a 21-screen movie complex, an IMAX theater, and more. The Center for Southern Folklore makes its home here, as does the **Peabody Place Museum & Gallery** (☎ 901/523–2787; 🎟 $5; ☉ Tues.–Fri. 10–5:30, weekends noon–5), which has Chinese art from the Manchu dynasty. Gallery visitors enter through a round moon gate, and displays include 6-ft-tall cloisonné foo dogs, which stood watch over the Forbidden City. **Jillian's** entertainment complex has a sports-video café, seven bars, 12 billiard tables, private party and banquet rooms, a bowling alley, a dance club, and more than 200 electronic simulation games. ⊠ *119 Main St., Downtown,* ☎ *901/821–7500.* ☉ *Hrs vary.*

⓫ Pyramid Arena. One of Memphis's downtown landmarks, the Pyramid, a gleaming, stainless-steel structure and the third-largest pyramid in the world, is at Front and Auction, six blocks north of Adams Avenue. This 32-story, 22,000-seat arena, covering the equivalent of six football fields, is home to the University of Memphis Tigers basketball team and a venue for concerts and other events. Guided tours are available. The **WONDERS: Memphis International Cultural Series** brings blockbuster art exhibitions to the Pyramid for five months out of the year (☎ 901/576–1231 for details). ⊠ *1 Auction St., at Front St., Downtown,* ☎ *901/521–9675,* WEB *www.pyramidarena.com.* ☉ *Tours daily at noon, 1, and 2 but subject to change because of event schedules.*

Slavehaven/Burkle Estate Museum. This pre–Civil War era house was a stop on the Underground Railroad. A German immigrant built the modest middle-class home circa 1850, when Memphis was a slave trade center. Displays of ads, auctions, and artifacts depict the history of slavery, and secret cellars and trapdoors reveal the escape route of runaway slaves; the basement sheltered the runaways for weeks at a time. Heritage Tours operates the museum and provides guided tours. ⊠ *826 N. 2nd St., Downtown,* ☎ *901/527–3427,* WEB *www.memphistravel. com.* ⊡ *$6.* ⊙ *Mon.–Sat. 10–4; closed Mon. and Tues. Nov.–Mar.*

⑯ Sun Studio. Sun Studio is still housed in the original, albeit modest, building into which Elvis himself wandered one day and recorded two songs—one in honor of his beloved mother—for producer Sam Phillips. Pictures of Elvis and other well-loved musicians, from B. B. King to Jerry Lee Lewis to Roy Orbison, adorn the walls, and their hits play in the background during tours. At night, recording sessions crank up once again, with artists hoping to make it as big as their predecessors did. Upstairs there's a small gift shop with well-chosen paraphernalia (guitar picks, drinking glasses) and a hall-of-fame gallery. ⊠ *706 Union Ave., Downtown,* ☎ *901/521–0664,* WEB *www.sunstudio.com.* ⊡ *$8.50.* ⊙ *Daily 10–6, tours every hr on the ½ hr, last tour at 5:30.*

NEED A BREAK?	At the **Sun Studio Cafe** (⊠ 706 Union Ave., Downtown, ☎ 901/521–0664, WEB www.vgg.com), part of the Sun Studio building, eat like a king (of rock and roll, that is) or just look at the memorabilia. It was called Taylor's when Elvis ate here, and in his honor, the menu includes some of his favorite snacks, such as a fried peanut-butter-and-banana sandwich. Burgers are around $5.

❶ Tennessee Welcome Center and Memphis Visitors Center. The center is a good place to stock up on free maps, brochures, and other literature about Memphis and the Beale Street Historic District. ⊠ *119 N. Riverside Dr., Midtown,* ☎ *901/543–5333,* WEB *www.memphistravel.com.*

Victorian Village Historic District. This downtown district comprises some 25 blocks on Adams between Front and Manassas. Here, 18 houses ranging from neoclassical to Gothic Revival in style have been restored to their appearance in the days when cotton was king. Most are privately owned, but the **Magevney House,** the **Mallory Neely House,** and the **Woodruff-Fontaine House** are open to the public.

❼ W. C. Handy Memphis Home and Museum. Handy, who wrote some of his most famous blues pieces in this small wood-frame house, is recalled here through photographs, sheet music, and memorabilia. Visitors get an inside look at the humble beginnings of the "Father of the Blues," who lived in this basic two-room house with his wife and six children. ⊠ *352 Beale St., Beale Street Historic District,* ☎ *901/522–1556.* ⊡ *$2.* ⊙ *Apr.–Sept., Sat. 10–5; Oct.–Mar., Tues.–Sat. 11–4.*

⑮ Woodruff-Fontaine House. This exquisite three-story French Victorian mansion was built in 1870 and has a grand drawing room graced with original parquet floors and large mirrors. Antique furnishings include Aubusson carpets, marble mantels, and a Venetian crystal chandelier. The formal garden still has its gingerbread playhouse, now the museum shop. ⊠ *680 Adams Ave., Victorian Village,* ☎ *901/526–1469.* ⊡ *$5.* ⊙ *Mon. and Wed.–Sat. 10–4, Sun. 1–4.*

Greater Memphis

Numbers in the text correspond to numbers in the margin and on the Greater Memphis map.

Graceland is the reason many visitors come to Memphis, but there are plenty of museums in the sprawling area outside downtown that range in appeal from the simply visual to the historical.

A Good Drive

The **National Ornamental Metal Museum** ⑰ is tricky to find (many a visitor has taken an unplanned detour to the first I–55 exit in Arkansas), but worth it. Loop south to **Chucalissa Archaeological Museum** ⑱, where the Native American culture of the mid-South is preserved. Continue east to **Graceland** ⑲, the must-see stop. After Elvis's Jungle Room, you can relax at **Dixon Gallery and Gardens** ⑳ in East Memphis on Park Avenue. Take Park Avenue west to Goodlett Street, then proceed north to Central Avenue. Turn left (west) on Central, and you'll be headed toward the imposing **Memphis Pink Palace Museum and Mansion and Sharpe Planetarium** ㉑. If you have kids in tow, head several blocks west on Central to the **Children's Museum of Memphis** ㉒. From there, continue west on Central to Airways Boulevard, turn right (north), then left (west) onto Poplar Avenue, where Overton Park houses the **Memphis Brooks Museum of Art** ㉓ and the **Memphis Zoo** ㉔. Continue east down Poplar to Goodlett, take a right, then a left on Southern, and another right on Cherry, to visit the **Memphis Botanic Garden** ㉕.

TIMING

It would take several days to explore everything on the driving tour. Better to narrow down the choices according to your interests. Graceland is usually packed, and you'll probably have to wait in line for any of the tours. It's least crowded early in the morning, so try to arrive as it opens. Allot about an hour and a half for the house tour and at least two more hours for the rest of the Graceland attractions.

Sights to See

☝ ㉒ **Children's Museum of Memphis.** At Memphis's only children's museum, youngsters can touch, climb, and explore their way through a child-size city, including a food mart, recycling center, skyscraper, and house. An airplane displayed out front makes a favorite exploring ground. Seasonal events, such as an October pumpkin patch, weekend celebrations such as themed scavenger hunt parties, and interactive exhibits—about tools, castles, nature, and other topics—provide further fun and education. ✉ 2525 Central Ave., Midtown, ☎ 901/458–2678, WEB www.cmom.com. ☎ $7. ◷ Tues.–Sat. 9–5, Sun. noon–5.

⑱ **Chucalissa Archaeological Museum.** About 10 mi southwest of downtown, this museum immortalizes a river culture that existed from AD 1000 to 1500. The 4-acre reconstruction is operated by the University of Memphis, and on-site archaeological excavations are often conducted in summer. In the museum, prehistoric tools, pottery, and weapons and a free 15-minute slide presentation describing Chucalissa life and culture provide clues to that world. Outside, skilled Choctaw craftspeople sell jewelry, weapons, and pottery. An annual August powwow is a highlight. ✉ 1987 Indian Village Dr., Whitehaven, ☎ 901/785–3160, WEB http://cas.memphis.edu/chucalissa. ☎ $5. ◷ Apr.–Oct., Tues.–Sat. 9–5, Sun. 1–4:40; Nov.–Mar., Tues.–Sat. 9–5.

⑳ **Dixon Gallery and Gardens.** Its 17 acres of formal and informal gardens and woodlands make Dixon Gallery and Gardens a bucolic enclave near the heart of the city. The Georgian-style estate and its superb art collections once belonged to the late Margaret and Hugo Dixon, philanthropists and cultural leaders. French and American impressionist paintings, British portraiture and landscapes, and the Stout Collection of 18th-century German porcelain are on display. In special exhibitions impressionism reigns supreme, with previous high-

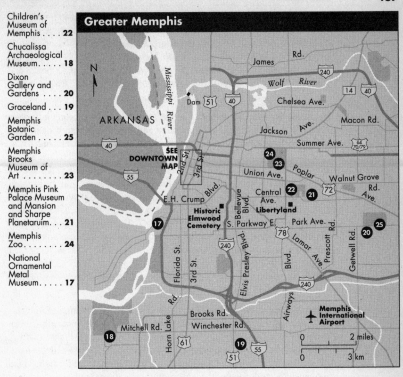

lights having included works by Raoul Dufy and Paul Gauguin. In the gardens, designed in the style of English parks, regional plants flourish. The two-acre Woodland Garden, a cutting garden, the Stout Camellia House conservatory, and ample statuary contribute to the oasis. At the summer outdoor film series, the back lawn fills with picnickers and fireflies. Other garden entertainment includes jazz performances, symphonies, and more. ⊠ *4339 Park Ave., East Memphis,* ☎ *901/761-5250,* WEB *www.dixon.org.* ▣ *$5.* ⊘ *Tues.–Sat. 10–5, Sun. 1–5.*

★ ⓳ **Graceland.** The tour of the colonial-style mansion once owned by Elvis Presley reveals the spoils of stardom—from gold records to glittering show costumes—and a circuit of the grounds (shuttle service is available) leads to Meditation Garden, where Elvis is buried. Separate tours are available for additional fees. Among them is the **Elvis Presley Automobile Museum,** where a continuously run film montage of Elvis on the road is shown drive-in style as viewers sit in seats pulled from 1957 Chevys. Elvis's jet, the *Lisa Marie* (named for his daughter), complete with 24-karat gold-plated seat-belt buckles and a queen-size bed covered in light blue ultrasuede, stars in the **Airplanes Tour.** **Sincerely Elvis** is a small museum with personal items such as home movies, photos, and clothes. There are several restaurants and, of course, shops on the premises, along with a post office—few can resist the lure of a Graceland date stamp. ⊠ *3764 Elvis Presley Blvd. (off I-55), 12 mi southeast of downtown, South Haven,* ☎ *901/332-3322; 800/238-2000 outside TN,* WEB *www.elvis.com.* ▣ *Home tour $16, all attractions $25, parking $2.* ⊘ *Mon.–Sat. 9–5, Sun. 10–4. Hrs may vary with season.*

Historic Elmwood Cemetery. Founded in 1852, the county's oldest active cemetery is where 70,000 local ancestors are buried—politicians, tycoons, "bosses," madams, Rebel soldiers, martyred nuns, and other notables. A stroll through its 80 landscaped acres, studded with Victorian statues and monuments, is educational and fascinating. Audiocassettes, CDs, and walking maps are available at the Victorian gate cottage. ✉ *824 S. Dudley St., South Memphis,* ☎ *901/774–3212,* WEB *www.elmwoodcemetery.org.* 🎟 *Free; audiocassette or CD rental $5; walking map $5.* ⊙ *Cottage open weekdays 8–4:30, Sat. 8–noon; cemetery grounds open daily 8–4:30.*

㉕ Memphis Botanic Garden. Across the street from the Dixon Gallery lie these 96 landscaped acres of outdoor gardens. A profusion of themes include Southern staples such as dogwoods, azaleas, irises, and roses, as well as wildflowers, herbs, perennials, daylilies, and cacti, and sculpture. All trails lead to the Japanese Garden of Tranquility, the crown jewel of the gardens, where a red bridge arcs over a pond and its audience of begging goldfish. In the Goldsmith Civic Garden Center special exhibits feature porcelain, art, and various horticultural shows such as bonsai, orchids, succulents, and roses. The botanic garden is part of East Memphis's main park—the **Audubon**—which includes a golf course, tennis courts, and walking trails. ✉ *750 Cherry Rd., East Memphis,* ☎ *901/685–1566,* WEB *www.memphisbotanicgarden.com.* 🎟 *$4; free on Tues. after 12:30.* ⊙ *Nov.–Feb., Mon.–Sat. 9–4:30; Mar.–Oct., Mon.–Sat. 9–6, Sun. 11–6.*

㉓ Memphis Brooks Museum of Art. The collections of this museum in Overton Park span eight centuries and contain 7,000 pieces, including a notable collection of Italian Renaissance works, English portraiture, impressionist and American modernist paintings, decorative arts, prints, photographs, and one of the nation's largest displays of Doughty bird figurines. A popular exhibit upstairs gives a global survey of ancient art from Greece and the Mediterranean, the Americas, and Africa. Film buffs flock to the **Brooks Film Series** on Wednesday evening and Sunday afternoon for cinema classics and foreign films; the schedule varies, so call for details. ✉ *1934 Poplar Ave., Overton Park,* ☎ *901/722–3500,* WEB *www.brooksmuseum.org.* 🎟 *$6; free on Wed. Fees vary for major exhibits.* ⊙ *Tues.–Fri. 10–4, Sat. 10–5, Sun. 11:30–5; first Wed. of month 10–8.*

NEED A BREAK?

At the **Brushmark Restaurant** (☎ 901/544–6200, WEB www.brooksmuseum.org), an elegant but casual eatery on the Memphis Brooks Museum of Art's first floor, art lovers can rest their feet while enjoying lunch, wine, and serene views of Overton Park. It's open Tuesday–Sunday 11:30–2:30.

㉑ Memphis Pink Palace Museum and Mansion and Sharpe Planetarium. Clarence Saunders, founder of the Piggly Wiggly self-service stores that are the predecessors of today's supermarkets, built this rambling pink-marble mansion in the 1920s. Exhibits are eclectic, including natural and cultural history displays, a hand-carved miniature three-ring circus, and a replica of the original Piggly Wiggly. The Sharpe Planetarium explores the most current cosmic discoveries. The museum also has the Union Planters IMAX Theater. ✉ *3050 Central Ave., Midtown,* ☎ *901/320–6320,* WEB *www.memphismuseums.org.* 🎟 *Planetarium $3.50, museum $6, IMAX theater $6.* ⊙ *Mon.–Thurs. 9–4, Fri.–Sat. 9–9, Sun. noon–6.*

㉔ Memphis Zoo. One of the South's most notable zoos has more than 400 species living on 70 well-kept wooded acres in Overton Park. State-of-the-art exhibits feature larger, more natural habitats such as *Cat Country, Dragon's Lair, Primate Canyon, Madagascar, Animals of the Night,* a natural African veldt setting for larger creatures, a large reptile facility, and an animal-contact area. The zoo also has several eateries, shops, fountains, a farm discovery center, and a library. In summer, **Zoo Nights** offer family entertainment with live music and performances. ✉ *2000 Prentiss Place, Overton Park,* ☎ *901/276–9453,* WEB *www. memphiszoo.org.* 🎫 *$9.50, parking $2.* ☉ *Mar.–late Oct., daily 9–6 (last admission 5); late Oct.–Feb., daily 9–5 (last admission 4:30).*

⓱ National Ornamental Metal Museum. The nation's only museum preserving the art and the craft of metalworking—from wrought iron to gold—overlooks the Mississippi River. The museum has a working blacksmith shop, and organizes changing exhibitions and metalworking demonstrations. The grounds hug the bluffs south of downtown and, with their vistas of river and skyline, have become a favorite spot for outdoor blues concerts, such as **Blues on the Bluffs,** held each September. ✉ *374 Metal Museum Dr. (via I–55N, last exit before bridge), Downtown,* ☎ *901/774–6380,* WEB *www.metalmuseum.org.* 🎫 *$4.* ☉ *Tues.–Sat. 10–5, Sun. noon–5.*

Dining

American

$$–$$$ ✕ **Folk's Folly Prime Steak House.** Folk's is a Memphis favorite for one simple reason: the juiciest sizzling-hot steaks in town. "Steak house" is a bit misleading, though—this restaurant resembles a suburban home, with a lounge and five separate dining rooms, plus eight private rooms for small parties. The generous vegetable side dishes, such as stuffed baked potatoes and asparagus, are reliably fresh, and heaping portions of seafood and whole lobster are always available. It's in East Memphis, near some of the city's nicest residential areas. ✉ *551 S. Mendenhall St., East Memphis,* ☎ *901/762–8200,* WEB *www.folksfolly. com. AE, MC, V. No lunch.*

$$ ✕ **Café Society.** This sidewalk café in Midtown brings imagination and fresh choices to its lunch and dinner menu. Outdoor tables, across the street from a small park, are popular with the happy-hour crowd. Expect to find bacon-wrapped shrimp with horseradish sauce, and grilled salmon with sesame- and poppy-seed crust and shrimp Biscayne sauce. The best dessert is the crème brûlée. ✉ *212 N. Evergreen St., Midtown,* ☎ *901/722–2177. AE, MC, V. No lunch weekends.*

$–$$ ✕ **Blues City Café.** This downtown diner specializes in huge steaks and ribs, hamburgers, and hot tamales. ✉ *138 Beale St., Beale Street Historic District,* ☎ *901/526–3637. AE, MC, V.*

Barbecue

$$ ✕ **Charlie Vergos' Rendezvous.** Charlie Vergos, who has been in busi-
★ ness since 1948, has become something of a Memphis ambassador of barbecued ribs: not only does his downtown basement restaurant draw thousands of tourists each year, but he also ships his ribs by air express all over the country. The walls are filled with memorabilia, from old newspaper cartoons to Essolene gas signs, but what really packs in the crowds are the delicious barbecued pork ribs. ✉ *52 S. 2nd St., Downtown,* ☎ *901/523–2746,* WEB *www.hogsfly.com. Reservations not accepted. AE, MC, V.* ☉ *Closed Sun.–Mon.*

$–$$ ✕ **Corky's Bar-B-Q.** Expect to wait in line at this no-frills East Memphis barbecue joint, a leader in sending ribs to loyal fans by air-express service. One taste of the ribs or pork platter explains why. Letters from customers and articles on Corky's cover the walls. ✉ *5259 Poplar Ave., East Memphis,* ☎ *901/685–9744. Reservations not accepted. AE, D, DC, MC, V.*

$ ✕ **Interstate Bar-B-Q.** The Neely family has barbecue sauce running through its veins, and it all started here. Jim Neely's nephews have opened

Dining

Lodging

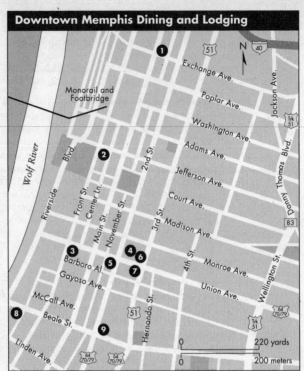

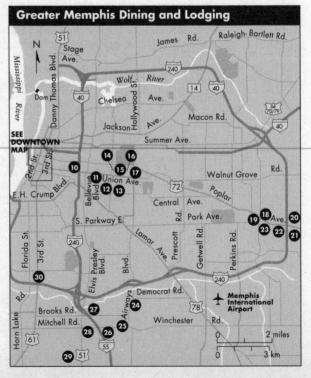

their own places around town, but they all learned their secrets at this restaurant. The long list of barbecue includes barbecued spaghetti, pork sandwiches, beef ribs and links, and Polish and smoked sausage. Save room for the homemade pecan pie. ✉ 2265 S. 3rd St., South Memphis, ☎ 901/775–2304. Reservations not accepted. AE, MC, V.

Continental

$$–$$$ ✕ **Paulette's.** This Overton Square restaurant, which served bistro-style cooking before it became popular in Memphis, has retained its vitality for more than two decades. A crisp, fresh house salad and airy popovers with strawberry butter help pack in the crowds for their signature Sunday brunch, along with lunch and dinner. Entrées include several crepe dishes, along with grilled salmon, swordfish, chicken, baked scallops, and brochettes of shrimp or beef. The hot chocolate dessert crepes are sinful. On weekends a pianist plays requests ranging from Gershwin to Beale Street blues. ✉ 2110 Madison Ave., Overton Square, ☎ 901/726–5128. AE, MC, V.

Eclectic

$$–$$$ ✕ **Automatic Slim's Tonga Club.** This hip restaurant is downtown across from the Peabody Hotel. The split-level dining room is usually crowded. Southwestern and Caribbean fare are served in thick, spicy sauces; signature dishes include deep-fried red snapper with tomato and jalapeño relish and Jamaican jerk duck. ✉ 83 S. 2nd St., Downtown, ☎ 901/525–7948. AE, DC, MC, V. Closed Sun. No lunch Sat.

$$–$$$ ✕ **Tsunami.** In a city where the finer restaurants consistently look to Europe for inspiration, chef Ben Smith's exciting Asian-American–Pacific Rim cuisine adds new vistas to the landscape. His ever-changing menu might include sea bass on black Thai rice one month, and sake-steamed mussels in a fiery Thai red curry sauce the next. ✉ 928 S. Cooper St., Cooper-Young District, ☎ 901/274–2556, WEB www.tsunamimemphis. com. AE, MC, V. Closed Sun. No lunch.

French

$$$–$$$$ ✕ **Chez Philippe.** The interior here is wonderfully lavish, with high ceil-
★ ings, faux-marble columns, and huge murals depicting a masked ball. And the service is impeccable. But most important, the cuisine—among Memphis's most innovative and sophisticated—lives up to its regal surroundings. The menu ranges from delicate terrines to lamb tenderloin in puff pastry to hot soufflés. ✉ Peabody Hotel, 149 Union Ave., Downtown, ☎ 901/529–4188. Reservations essential. AE, DC, MC, V. Closed Sun.–Mon. No lunch.

$$$–$$$$ ✕ **Erling Jensen.** The chef characterizes his cuisine as French with
★ global influences, but to put it simply, his rack of lamb is the best in town, and the orange roughy and veal tenderloin aren't bad either. ✉ 1044 S. Yates St., off Poplar, East Memphis, ☎ 901/763–3700. Reservations essential. AE, D, DC, MC, V. No lunch.

$$$ ✕ **La Tourelle.** This quiet, turn-of-the-century bungalow with fine lace
★ curtains and wooden floors is reminiscent of a small country restaurant in France. The interior is as charming as the cuisine is acclaimed, and many of the city's finest chefs have worked here. The menu varies, but each night there's a special lobster creation as well as a game dish. The five-course prix-fixe tasting menu is a good bet. ✉ 2146 Monroe Ave., near Overton Sq., Midtown, ☎ 901/726–5771. Reservations essential. MC, V. Closed Mon. No lunch Tues.–Sat.

$$ ✕ **Owen Brennan's Restaurant.** This New Orleans–style eatery in an upscale Memphis shopping center specializes in those fine Cajun and Creole dishes that usually require a jaunt to the French Quarter. Favorite dishes include blackened chicken or seafood gumbo. The lavish Sunday brunch is attended religiously, and easy banter, champagne, and

jazz flow freely. Best of all, an outdoor patio under towering shade trees offers a cool respite from Memphis's sizzling summer sun. ✉ *6150 Poplar Ave., East Memphis,* ☎ *901/761–0990. AE, DC, MC, V.*

Mexican

$–$$ ✕ **Cafe Olé.** If Mexican with a healthy twist sounds intriguing, this popular Midtown hangout is for you. Specialties—cooked without the heavy animal fats used in most Mexican fare—include spinach enchiladas and chili *rellenos.* The exposed brick walls are decorated with Mexican paintings and ceremonial masks. ✉ *959 S. Cooper St., Cooper Young District,* ☎ *901/274–1504. AE, D, DC, MC, V.*

Seafood

$$–$$$ ✕ **Landry's Seafood House.** This riverfront restaurant, one of Memphis's busiest, seats more than 300, but the wait can still be more than an hour. Patio dining is especially refreshing—if you can get a table. The fare—seafood, steaks, and Cajun—is simple but consistently good. Among the better offerings are shrimp in a brown-butter sauce, flounder stuffed with shrimp and crabmeat, and fried oysters and shrimp. ✉ *263 Wagner Pl., Beale Street Historic District,* ☎ *901/526–1966. Reservations not accepted. AE, MC, V.*

Southern

$ ✕ **The Cupboard.** Owner Charles Cavallo knows fresh produce, and his cooks turn out masterful "meat-and-three" plates. Lucky is the soul who visits when both macaroni and cheese and fried green tomatoes are on the menu. ✉ *1400 Union Ave., Midtown,* ☎ *901/276–8015. AE, D, MC, V.*

$ ✕ **Gus's Fried Chicken.** Gus's serves only one item, and serves it better than anyone else in town (and, according to many, better than any place in the country). The kitchen dominates the stripped down interior of this small restaurant, practically hidden on a downtown street. ✉ *310 S. Front St., Downtown,* ☎ *901/527–4877. AE, DC, MC, V.*

Lodging

$$$$ 🏨 **Peabody Hotel.** This 14-story Italian Renaissance Revival hostelry ★ has been a city landmark since 1925. The lobby preserves its original stained-glass skylights and ornate travertine marble fountain—home to the hotel's famed resident ducks, who waddle down each morning from their penthouse apartment and parade across a red carpet to the stirring sounds of Sousa's "King Cotton March." The small, simply furnished but comfortable rooms are in complete contrast to the grandeur of the hotel's common areas. ✉ *149 Union Ave., 38103,* ☎ *901/529–4000 or 800/732–2639,* 📠 *901/529–3600,* 🌐 *www.peabodymemphis.com. 468 rooms, 15 suites. 4 restaurants, in-room data ports, indoor pool, health club, bar, business services. AE, DC, MC, V.*

$$$$ 🏨 **Radisson Hotel.** Across the street from the Peabody is this downtown hotel with its own lobby fountain and waterfall. Glass-walled elevators whisk guests to rooms around a 10-story atrium. The guest rooms have modern furniture. ✉ *185 Union Ave., 38103,* ☎ *901/528–1800,* 📠 *901/526–3226,* 🌐 *www.radisson.com. 280 rooms. Restaurant, in-room data ports, cable TV, pool. AE, D, DC, MC, V.*

$$–$$$$ 🏨 **Elvis Presley's Heartbreak Hotel.** It had to happen sooner or later—a Memphis hotel named for the King and owned and operated by Elvis Presley Enterprises, Inc. Across from Graceland, the '50s-themed hotel has a profusion of leopard prints and gold as well as a heart-shape swimming pool. Guest rooms come with kitchenettes. Themed suites are more than 1,000 square ft and reflect aspects of Presley's career. ✉ *3677 Elvis Presley Blvd., 38116,* ☎ *901/332–1000,* 📠 *901/332–2107,* 🌐

www.heartbreakhotel.net. 124 guest rooms, 4 suites. Kitchenettes, pool, health club, lounge, meeting rooms. AE, DC, MC, V.

$$$ 🏨 **Adam's Mark Hotel.** This luxury property, a 27-story circular glass tower, is in the flourishing eastern suburbs of Memphis near I–240. From your glass-walled aerie, you'll have sweeping vistas of Memphis and its outskirts. On weekend nights the lounge comes alive with highly regarded visiting jazz performers and other musicians. ✉ *939 Ridge Lake Blvd., 38120,* ☎ *901/684–6664 or 800/444–2326,* FAX *901/ 762–7411,* WEB *www.adamsmark.com. 408 rooms, 5 suites. Restaurant, in-room data ports, room TVs with movies and video games, pool, health club, lounge. AE, D, DC, MC, V.*

$$$ 🏨 **French Quarter Suites Hotel.** With its mellow rose-brick exterior and
★ classic architectural lines, this pleasant Overton Square hostelry is reminiscent of an older, New Orleans–style inn. All the one-bedroom suites have living rooms and whirlpool baths that accommodate two, and some are balconied. ✉ *2144 Madison Ave., 38104,* ☎ *901/728–4000 or 800/ 843–0353,* FAX *901/278–1262,* WEB *www.memphisfrenchquarter.com. 104 suites. Restaurant, in-room hot tubs, refrigerators, cable TV, pool, gym, meeting rooms. AE, DC, MC, V.*

$$$ 🏨 **Holiday Inn Select East.** Close to the bustling Poplar/Ridgeway office complex, this sleek 10-story hotel is popular with business travelers. The rooms are comfortable, but the hotel's main draw is its proximity to the I–240 loop, which provides easy access to the whole city. ✉ *5795 Poplar Ave., 38119,* ☎ *800/465–4329,* FAX *901/682–7881,* WEB *www.holiday-inn.com. 243 rooms. Restaurant, in-room data ports, cable TV, pool, gym, laundry facilities, meeting rooms. AE, D, DC, MC, V.*

$$$ 🏨 **Memphis Marriott Downtown.** Adjacent to the downtown Convention Center, the sleek high-rise (18 floors) has ample work space and lighting in the spacious guest rooms. The lobby lounge, a tasteful, greenery-filled retreat, is a pleasant spot to relax and listen to music from the grand piano. ✉ *250 N. Main St., 38103,* ☎ *901/527–7300,* FAX *901/526–1561,* WEB *www.marriotthotels.com. 404 rooms, 8 suites. Restaurant, in-room data ports, cable TV, indoor pool, health club, hot tub, sauna, concierge floor, meeting rooms. AE, D, DC, MC, V.*

$$–$$$ 🏨 **Days Inn Graceland.** Proximity to Graceland is this modest hotel's
★ claim to fame, and it makes the most of that with a guitar-shape swimming pool and free Elvis movies 'round the clock. ✉ *3839 Elvis Presley Blvd., 38116,* ☎ *901/346–5500,* FAX *901/345–7452,* WEB *www.the. daysinn.com. 60 rooms. Pool. AE, DC, MC, V.*

$$ 🏨 **Hampton Inn Airport.** This member of the economy-priced chain that
★ spun off from Holiday Inn has a pleasing contemporary design. Spacious, well-lighted rooms have Scandinavian-style teakwood furnishings. ✉ *2979 Millbranch Rd., 38116,* ☎ *901/396–2200 or 800/426– 7866,* FAX *901/396–7034. 128 rooms. In-room data ports, cable TV, pool; no-smoking rooms. AE, DC, MC, V.*

$$ 🏨 **Sleep Inn at Court Square.** This chain hotel is conveniently located near two highways and within walking distance of Mud Island and the Pyramid; Beale Street is a 15-minute walk or a quick trolley ride away (there's a stop right out back). Extras include a free Continental breakfast, free parking, and free local phone calls. Business rooms have a desk, fax, data port, and VCR. ✉ *40 N. Front St., 38103,* ☎ *901/522– 9700,* FAX *901/522–9710. 124 rooms. In-room data ports, cable TV, gym, laundry service, business services. AE, D, MC, V.*

$ 🏨 **Best Value Inn.** This four-story motor lodge near Graceland has spacious, modern rooms. ✉ *3222 Airways Blvd., 38116,* ☎ *901/332–3800 or 800/221–2222,* FAX *901/345–8118,* WEB *www.bestvalueinn.com. 118 rooms. Restaurant, cable TV, pool, gym, laundry facilities. DC, MC, V. CP.*

$ ☎ **La Quinta Inn–Medical Center.** This two-story inn is convenient to midtown with its restaurants and shops, and has spacious rooms. ⊠ *42 S. Camilla St., 38104,* ☎ *901/526–1050,* FAX *901/525–3219,* WEB *www. laquinta.com. 130 rooms. In-room data ports, pool, laundry facilities, some pets allowed. AE, D, DC, MC, V. CP.*

$ ☎ **Quality Inn.** All units here have private patios or balconies; many have refrigerators and microwave ovens, and four have kitchens. There's a coin laundry on site. ⊠ *1541 Sycamore View, 38134,* ☎ *901/ 388–1300,* FAX *901/388–1300,* WEB *www.qualityinn.com. 96 rooms. Pool. AE, D, DC, MC, V. CP.*

$ ⚠ **Memphis Graceland RV Park and Campground.** This campground with tent and RV sites as well as cabins is only a few yards from Graceland's entrance. ⊠ *3691 Elvis Presley Blvd., 38116,* ☎ *901/396– 7125 or 866/571–9236,* WEB *www.koa.com. 72 campsites, 4 cabins. Pool, playground, laundry facilities. D, MC, V.*

Nightlife and the Arts

For a complete listing of weekly events, check the "Playbook" section in the Friday *Memphis Commercial Appeal* or the *Memphis Flyer,* distributed free at newsstands around the city. The Tennessee Welcome Center will also provide an up-to-date rundown of events.

The Arts

CONCERTS, DANCE, AND OPERA

The **Orpheum Theatre** (⊠ 203 S. Main St., Downtown, ☎ 901/525– 3000, WEB www.orpheum-memphis.com) is the scene of performances by **Ballet Memphis** (☎ 901/323–1947, WEB www.balletmemphis.org), which features professional dancers and celebrity guest artists, and **Opera Memphis** (☎ 901/678–2706 for tickets) during fall, winter, and spring. Touring Broadway musicals are also staged here; past performances have included *Cats, Chicago,* and *Phantom of the Opera.*

The **Germantown Performing Arts Centre** (⊠ 1801 Exeter Rd., Germantown, 22 mi. east of downtown Memphis, ☎ 901/751–7500), celebrated for its acoustics, brings in world-class music, dance, theater and opera. Itzhak Perlman, Yo-Yo Ma, Mikhail Baryshnikov, and Ray Charles have all performed here.

The 2,100-seat **Cannon Center for the Performing Arts** (⊠ 255 N. Main St., Downtown, ☎ 901/576–1200), includes a large auditorium and an outdoor plaza.

The **Memphis Symphony Orchestra** (⊠ 3100 Walnut Grove Rd., Downtown, ☎ 901/324–3627) is an 80-piece symphony that hosts worldrenowned soloists in a classical masterworks series and a pops series. The symphony holds concerts at Cannon Center for Performing Arts, outdoor concerts at Dixon Gallery and Gardens, and on the riverfront at the Sunset Symphony during Memphis in May.

THEATER

Playhouse on the Square (⊠ 51 S. Cooper St., Midtown, ☎ 901/726– 4656, WEB www.playhouseonthesquare.org), open September through July, has the city's only professional repertory company. A professional acting group performs at **Circuit Playhouse** (⊠ 1705 Poplar Ave., Midtown, ☎ 901/726–4656). At **Ewing's Children's Theatre** (⊠ 2635 Avery Ave., Midtown, ☎ 901/452–3968), performances are directed, designed, and acted entirely by children under the guidance of the Ewing Children's Theatre. **Theatre Memphis** (⊠ 630 Perkins Extended, East Memphis, ☎ 901/682–8323) is one of the best regarded community theaters in the United States. At the University of Memphis, **Univer-**

sity Theatre (⊠ 3745 Central Ave., ☎ 901/678–2523) provides a venue for drama students and visiting performers.

Festivals

The **Memphis in May International Festival** (☎ 901/525–4611, WEB www. memphisinmay.org) salutes the cuisine, crafts, and other cultural offerings of a different country each year over four consecutive weekends. This festival—Memphis's largest—galvanizes the city each year with its **Beale Street Music Fest** and **World Championship Barbecue Cooking Contest.** Music Fest brings in many music greats, from Bob Dylan to Bobby Bland to Delta gospel artists. The month culminates with the **Sunset Symphony,** where picnickers watch the Memphis Symphony Orchestra perform Southern classics such as *Ole Man River* on the bluffs.

The **Africa in April Cultural Awareness Festival** (☎ 901/947–2133) is an annual downtown festival that celebrates the African diaspora with music, food, fashion, and workshops. **Arts in the Park** (⊠ Robert Church Park, Midtown, ☎ 901/761–1278, WEB www.memphisartsfestival. org) was named Tennessee's number-one fine-arts festival by the Harris List. Held for four days each October in the Memphis Botanic Garden, the festival includes arts booths, music, dance, theater, and lots of children's activities. Sponsored by the Center for Southern Folklore, the **Memphis Music and Heritage Festival** (☎ 901/525–3655, WEB www. southernfolklore.com) in late August showcases many kinds of music at Main Street Mall and Peabody Place. As with all activities sponsored by the Center for Southern Folklore, this festival is a great opportunity for discovering Delta talent.

Nightlife

DOWNTOWN

A handful of areas make for good stepping out downtown. **Beale Street,** however touristy, tops the list, with more venues per square foot than any other place in town.

Alfred's on Beale (⊠ 197 Beale St., Beale Street Historic District, ☎ 901/525–3711, WEB www.alfreds-on-beale.com), one of the city's hottest dance clubs, also serves great food. Rock bands perform from Wednesday through Saturday, and a DJ—sometimes the legendary George Klein, Elvis's best man—spins popular dance tunes during the week. For quality blues, **B. B. King's Blues Club** (⊠ 143 Beale St., Beale Street Historic District, ☎ 901/524–5464, WEB www.bbkingsclub.com) sets the standard among Memphis's high-profile clubs, with infrequent appearances from the legendary blues artist for whom the club is named. You're more likely to see local legends such as Ruby Wilson than King. The food focuses on Southern specialties, naturally. The place can be packed; it's a favorite among locals and visitors alike.

Elvis Presley's Memphis (⊠ 126 Beale St., Beale Street Historic District, ☎ 901/527–6900) has live bands Tuesday through Sunday. The menu—with Elvis's favorites, such as fried peanut-butter-and-banana sandwiches—speaks for itself. Even for those who aren't die-hard fans of the King, this venue is worth a trip for the kitsch. It has lots of red velvet, a retail counter hawking Elvis souvenirs, Vegas showroom-style booths, an ornate chandelier, and a large screen behind the stage. Upstairs, guests can play pool at Elvis's personal billiard table. The live bands—usually rockabilly or gospel—put on a fun show. Of particular interest is the Sunday Gospel Brunch, from 11 to 3.

At the **New Daisy Theatre** (⊠ 330 Beale St., Beale Street Historic District, ☎ 901/525–8981, WEB www.newdaisy.com)—the 900-seat venue where B. B. King got his start—blues, jazz, and (predominantly) rock

496

IF BEALE STREET COULD TALK . . .

HAILED AS THE BIRTHPLACE OF THE BLUES, the Delta's most famous street rises from the bluffs of Ole Man River and meanders for miles into Memphis's flat downtown. Among its brightly lighted bar fronts and barren lots lies a history of race and music, prosperity and decline, and, ultimately, renewal. Today's Beale is a chaotic, sometimes seamy mix of tourism and authenticity; a place where Old Beale's notorious bawdiness and prosperity have been reinvented in restored facades.

In the 1840s Beale Street was a thriving suburb, home to scores of Irish and Italian immigrants and at least 300 free African-Americans. During the Civil War Ulysses S. Grant came to town and, with his keen eye for Southern properties, chose the Hunt-Phelan home as his headquarters and mapped out his Vicksburg campaign from Beale.

Bloodshed and disease marred the street during Reconstruction. When an African-American boy was accused of killing an Irish boy, mob riots and fires ravaged the street for days. In the 1870s the entire city was besieged—and eventually bankrupted—by cholera and yellow fever epidemics. African-Americans, with a higher degree of immunity to these diseases, were able to remain in the Beale area and helped rebuild the community.

Soon Beale became "Main Street" for Southern African-American life, with dentists, clothiers, dry goods and grocery stores, saloons, furniture stores, restaurants, loan offices, newspaper offices, photography studios, pawn shops, and tailors. The South's first black millionaire, Robert Church, known as the "Boss of Beale Street," owned land, stores, several saloons, and more. In 1905 he founded Memphis's first African-American bank, the Solvent Savings Bank and Trust, at 392 Beale.

Next door, at 391 Beale, he built a 6-acre park and concert hall, where peacocks roamed and children played among the planted trees; "Church's Park" became a social center.

Onto this street at the turn of the century stepped the young W. C. Handy, credited with writing the first blues song here, in 1909: "The Memphis Blues." Beale was a natural destination, home, during the Civil War era, to the Young Man's Brass Band, the first all-black musical group. During Reconstruction several bands rose to prominence here, playing violins and banjos, without written scores, in the honky-tonks and juke joints. The Handy era was the street's heyday, when many distinguished musicians got their start, such as Muddy Waters, Furry Lewis, Albert King, Alberta Hunter, Bobby "Blue" Bland, Memphis Minnie McCoy, and Riley "Blues Boy" King, who became known as B. B. King.

After the depression took its toll, the bustling neighborhood fell into decline, and in the late 1960s a ghostly version of Beale was named to the National Register of Historic Places. In the 1980s community and government revitalization efforts breathed life into the deserted blocks, and soon clubs, theaters, shops, and restaurants returned to the area, leading to today's somewhat self-conscious entertainment district and tourist playground.

Despite the tourism, Beale remains an excellent place to pay respects, catch a show, people-watch, and chow down. Venues such as the New Daisy Theatre and B. B. King's Blues Club and festivals such as the Memphis Music Heritage Festival and Handy Awards Music Festival keep the history alive and continue to give Beale Street something worth talking about.

bands perform. As an old stage theater turned music hall, the New Daisy has excellent acoustics. It's a great place to see musicians such as Bob Dylan and Herbie Hancock up close. Professional boxing is held once a month.

The **Rum Boogie Cafe** (✉ 182 Beale St., Beale Street Historic District, ☎ 901/528–0150, WEB www.rumboogie.com) stages live blues nightly, accompanied by Cajun cuisine and barbecue. There are live jam sessions with local blues artists.

Big-name entertainers and musical groups ranging from Harry Connick Jr. to Widespread Panic appear at the **Mud Island Amphitheatre** (☎ 901/576–7222) from April through October. With its backdrop of the downtown skyline, this outdoor theater is scenic, but on a breeze-less summer night the heat is not for the faint of heart.

Among the offerings at the **Orpheum Theatre** (✉ 203 S. Main St., Downtown, ☎ 901/525–3000, WEB www.orpheum-memphis.com) are easy-listening and jazz concerts, traveling Broadway shows, comedians, and a much-loved summer film series.

The historic **Pinch District,** north of downtown between North Front and North 3rd streets, was a working-class neighborhood back in the 1920s and '30s, but now is famous for delis, bars, and restaurants. The Main Street Trolley travels into the heart of the Pinch District. The **North End** (✉ 346 N. Main St., Pinch District, ☎ 901/527–3663) is a popular bar and restaurant that hosts bands. **High Point Pinch** (✉ 111 Jackson Ave., Pinch District, ☎ 901/525–4444) has live music and is a good spot for lunch, near the Main Street Trolley. The 32-story **Pyramid Arena** (✉ 1 Auction St., at Front St., Downtown, ☎ 901/521–9675) hosts big-name country, rock, and R&B artists who draw large crowds.

OFF THE BEATEN PATH — The atmospheric blocks surrounding **South Main,** though often eerily quiet, house a handful of Memphis's most authentic clubs. **Earnestine & Hazel's** (✉ 531 S. Main St., ☎ 901/523–9754), an old-time juke joint, is cherished for its greasy-spoon cheeseburgers, jukebox, and occasional live blues and dancing. **Marmalade's Restaurant and Lounge** (✉ 153 Calhoun St., ☎ 901/522–8800) serves up soul food along with occasional live performances by local jazz, blues, and R&B artists. **Raiford's** (✉ 115 Vance Ave., ☎ 901/525–9210) has become a Memphis institution, attracting patrons from all walks of life to its DJ-driven dance floor.

MIDTOWN

Among Midtown's nightlife offerings, **Overton Square** is the best known. With its concentration of theaters, restaurants, and bars within a few blocks, amblers are sure to stumble onto something lively. Wine lovers can enjoy a glass from the city's largest wine list at **Le Chardonnay Wine Bar** (✉ 2105 Overton Sq., Midtown, ☎ 901/725–1375). At **Bayou Bar & Grill** (✉ 2100 Overton Sq. Ln., Midtown, ☎ 901/278–8626) Cajun specialties and lots of beer are served on an outdoor patio.

Another Midtown destination, the **Cooper-Young District,** can be found, appropriately, at the crossroads of Cooper Street and Young Avenue, several blocks down from Overton Square. Cooper-Young has a neighborhood feel, where the locals gather to meet and greet. **Cafe Olé** (✉ 959 S. Cooper St., Midtown, ☎ 901/274–1504) is a lively Mexican restaurant with an outdoor patio. **Young Avenue Deli** (✉ 2119 Young Ave., Midtown, ☎ 901/278–0034, WEB www.youngavenuedeli.com) has one of the city's largest beer selections and some of the best french fries in the country.

Huey's (✉ 1927 Madison Ave., Midtown, ☎ 901/726–4372) is famous
locally for its burgers, live music on Sunday afternoon, and live blues
or jazz on Sunday night. Year-round, the **Mid-South Coliseum** (✉ 996
Early Maxwell Blvd., Midtown, ☎ 901/274–3982) draws its share of
country and rock musicians, plus the occasional tractor pull or wrestling
event. The unpretentious **P & H** (✉ 1532 Madison Ave., Midtown),
which stands for the Poor & Hungry, is one of the best places in town
for local color on weekend nights. The live music ranges from classical to rock to blues to jazz and then some, and the burgers are delectable.

Outdoor Activities and Sports

Auto Racing

The 600-acre **Memphis Motorsports Park** hosts weekly dirt-track and drag
racing, including three separate NASCAR events every season. Occasionally, amateurs can race their own cars on the track. ✉ *5500 Taylor
Forge Rd., Millington,* ☎ *901/358–7223,* WEB *www.memphismotorsports.
com.* ✍ *Prices vary.* ☺ *Mar.–Nov.*

Baseball

The **Memphis Redbirds,** a St. Louis Cardinals AAA farm team and Memphis's highest-profile professional sports team, play at AutoZone Park
(✉ 175 Toyota Plaza, Downtown, ☎ 901/721–6050, WEB www.
memphisredbirds.com).

Boating, Biking, and Hiking

Get back to nature at **Meeman-Shelby Forest State Park,** a 12,500-acre
tract bordering the Mississippi with boat rentals, hiking, and biking.
✉ *10 mi north of Memphis, off U.S. 51,* ☎ *901/876–5215,* WEB *www.
state.tn.us.* ✍ *$3 per car.* ☺ *Daily 7 AM–10 PM.*

There are hiking trails and horseback riding at the 4,500-acre **Shelby
Farms** (☎ 901/382–0235). The **Lichterman Nature Center** (☎ 901/767–
7322) offers 65 acres of wildlife in East Memphis, along with three
miles of trails alongside a lake. ✍ *$6.* ☺ *Mon.–Thurs. 9–4, Fri.–Sat.
9–5, and Sun. 12–5.*

Football

Conference USA's top college team plays in the **AXA/Equitable Liberty
Bowl** (☎ 901/274–4600) between Christmas and New Year's at Liberty Bowl Memorial Stadium (✉ 335 S. Hollywood, Midtown) at the
Mid-South Fairgrounds complex. The stadium also hosts the University of Memphis Tigers and other football teams. Every September fans
flock from all over the South for the **Southern Heritage Classic** (☎ 901/
398–6655), when Tennessee State University takes on Jackson State
University at the Liberty Bowl the second Saturday of the month.
Weekend festivities surrounding the event include receptions, luncheons, concerts, parties, a golf tournament, and a fashion show.

Golf

In June the Tournament Players Club at Southwind Country Club (✉
3325 Club, at Southwind, ☎ 901/748–0330) hosts the **FedEx St. Jude
Classic,** featuring top pros.

If you prefer playing to watching, the **Memphis Park Commission** (☎
901/385–4326) operates two 9-hole and five 18-hole public golf
courses; some good choices are **Galloway** (✉ 3815 Walnut Grove Rd.,
East Memphis, ☎ 901/685–7805), 18 holes, par 71; and T. O. Fuller
State Park (✉ 1500 Mitchell Rd. W, ☎ 901/543–7771), 18 holes,
par 72.

Hockey

The **Memphis RiverKings** (☎ 901/323–5525), a minor-league club, play from November through March at the Mid-South Coliseum, in the Mid-South Fairgrounds complex.

Tennis

The **Memphis Park Commission** (☎ 901/325–5966) operates nine facilities that offer tennis lessons, tournaments, and league play. **Leftwich** (✉ 4145 Southern Ave., East Memphis, ☎ 901/685–7907), **Wolbrecht Tennis Center** (✉ 1645 Ridgeway Rd., Hickory Mill, ☎ 901/767–2889), and **Whitehaven** (✉ 1500 Finley Rd., Whitehaven, ☎ 901/332–0546) have indoor courts.

Shopping

More than a dozen shopping centers and malls are scattered about Memphis. The **Mid America Mall,** on Main Street between Beale and Poplar streets, is one of the nation's longest pedestrian malls—better known for its trolley rides and people-watching than for shopping. Two antiques districts bracket Mid America Mall: **South Main,** on Main Street between Beale and Calhoun streets; and the **Pinch District,** just north of downtown between Front and 3rd streets, also known for its bars and restaurants. For more local color, midtown's **Cooper-Young District,** at the intersection of Cooper Street and Young Avenue, offers a handful of funky shops, vintage clothing stores, and cafés. **Overton Square** (✉ 24 S. Cooper St., Midtown, ☎ 901/278–6300) in midtown—a three-block shopping, restaurant, and entertainment complex in vintage buildings and newer structures—has upscale boutiques and specialty shops. **Oak Court Mall** (✉ 4465 Poplar Ave., East Memphis, ☎ 901/682–8928), in the busy Poplar/Perkins area of East Memphis, has 70 specialty stores and two department stores. At **Wolfchase Galleria** (✉ 2760 N. Germantown Pkwy., at U.S. 64, about 18 mi east of downtown Memphis, Cordoba, ☎ 901/381–2769), the four anchor stores are Goldsmith's, Dillard's, Sears, and JCPenney. A large carousel attracts scores of children, and there is a multiplex cinema.

Belz Factory Outlet Mall (✉ 3536 Canada Rd., Exit 20 off I–40, 20 mi east of downtown Memphis, Lakeland, ☎ 901/386–3180) has 50 stores, from Bugle Boy to Van Heusen.

A. Schwab Dry Goods Store (✉ 163 Beale St., Beale Street Historic District, ☎ 901/523–9782) is an old-fashioned store whose motto is "If you can't find it at A. Schwab's, you're better off without it!" Elvis shopped here, and you can, too—for top hats, spats, tambourines, bow ties, dresses to size 60, and men's trousers to size 74. **Davis-Kidd Booksellers** (✉ 387 Perkins Extended, East Memphis, ☎ 901/683–9801) is a Tennessee-based chain with an expansive collection of titles as well as in-store cafés. The **Woman's Exchange** (✉ 88 Racine St., Midtown, ☎ 901/327–5681) specializes in children's wear and handcrafted items. There's a tearoom for weekday luncheons.

Side Trips from Memphis

The flatness of the northern tip of the Mississippi Delta is a sharp contrast to East Tennessee's mountains. Cotton and soybeans thrive in the rich dirt of West Tennessee, particularly around Henning, the hometown of Alex Haley, author of *Roots.* Those who love the great outdoors will want to make the two-hour trip north to Tiptonville's Reelfoot Lake, and points east of Memphis, such as Jackson and Shiloh National Military Park, will suit the Civil War buff.

Henning
50 mi north of Memphis.

The quiet, historic byways north of Memphis seem light-years away from the busy river city. Driving northward along U.S. 51 through the fertile Mississippi River bottomlands brings you into the heart of King Cotton's domain. Less than an hour from Memphis is Henning, a friendly little town remarkably untouched by its world acclaim as the boyhood home and burial place of Alex Haley, Pulitzer Prize–winning author of *Roots*. The **Alex Haley House Museum,** the only state-owned historic site in West Tennessee, displays family portraits, mementos, and furnishings. ⌧ *200 Church St.,* ☎ *731/738–2240.* ⌫ *$2.50.* ◷ *Tues.–Sat. 10–5, Sun. 1–5.*

Tiptonville
105 mi north of Memphis.

Anglers and outdoors lovers of any sort are drawn to Tiptonville, in Tennessee's northwest corner, for its nearby bird and game refuge and spellbinding flora and fauna. The **Reelfoot Area Chamber of Commerce** (☎ 731/253–8144, WEB www.reelfootareachamber.com) can answer questions about dining and lodging.

Tiptonville's **Reelfoot Lake** gains a peculiar and mysterious beauty from a romantic scattering of cypress trees and charred stumps. The 13,000-acre lake was formed between 1811 and 1812, when the New Madrid earthquakes caused the Mississippi River to flood into the sinking land where a luxuriant forest once stood. From late November through mid-March the lake is a major sanctuary for American bald eagles. The quiet lake provides good fishing year-round for bass, crappie, trout, bream, and catfish. The Tennessee Department of Conservation conducts eagle-spotting tours at **Reelfoot Lake State Park Vistors Center** (☎ 731/253–9652, WEB www.reelfootlakeoutdoors.com).

Jackson
85 mi east of Memphis.

Jackson, site of several Civil War battles, was also a major railroad hub. It was home to John Luther "Casey" Jones, who was immortalized in the "Ballad of Casey Jones." The famed engineer became a hero by staying aboard his locomotive in a vain attempt to stop his engine from plowing into another train. For more information on Jackson, call the **Jackson/Madison County Convention & Visitors Bureau** (⌧ 314 E. Main St., Jackson 38301, ☎ 731/425–8333 or 800/498–4748, WEB www.jacksontncvb.com), open weekdays 8:30–4:30.

↻ In **Casey Jones Village,** the Casey Jones Home and Railroad Museum (☎ 731/668–1223, WEB www.caseyjones.com) contains a diverse assortment of railroad memorabilia. On the grounds is a replica of Old No. 382, Casey's steam engine. The **Casey Jones Village Old Country Store,** also in the village, has a restaurant, an 1890s-style ice cream parlor, and gift, souvenir, confectionery, and antiques shops. ⌧ *At U.S. 45 Bypass.* ⌫ *Museum $4.* ◷ *Jan.–Feb., daily 9–5; Mar.–Dec., daily 8 AM–9 PM.*

Savannah
110 mi east of Memphis on TN 57E.

Scenic Savannah, on the bluff of the Tennessee River, is a small, quiet town that exemplifies the charm and grace of Southern life. The historic **Cherry Mansion** (⌧ 101 Main St.), built in 1830, served as General Grant's headquarters during the Battle of Shiloh. The house is privately owned, but visitors are allowed to walk around the grounds and take pictures.

The **Tennessee River Museum** has exhibits on the Civil War, the river, and fossils from 65 million years ago, when this area was underwater. ✉ *507 Main St.,* ☎ *731/925–2364.* ✆ *$2.* ⊙ *Weekdays 9–5, Sat. 10–5, Sun. 1–5.*

Shiloh National Military Park

100 mi east of Memphis, 165 mi southwest of Nashville.

Site of one of the Civil War's grimmest and most pivotal battles, Shiloh National Military Park is the resting place of almost 4,000 soldiers, many unidentified, in the national cemetery. A self-guided auto tour (about 2½ hours) leads you past markers explaining monuments and battle sites. The visitor center runs a 25-minute film explaining the battle's strategy and has a display of Civil War artifacts. To get to Shiloh from Memphis, head east from Memphis on U.S. 64, then 10 mi south on TN 22. ✉ *TN 22, Shiloh,* ☎ *731/689–5275,* WEB *www.nps.gov.* ✆ *$5.* ⊙ *Visitor center daily 8–5.*

Pickwick Dam

110 mi southeast of Memphis.

Named after the eponymous character in Charles Dickens's *Pickwick Papers,* Pickwick Dam is considered by locals to be the playground of southwestern Tennessee's Hardin County.

Pickwick Landing State Resort Park (✉ TN 57, ☎ 731/689–3135 or 800/250–8615, WEB www.state.tn.us) has a resort inn, a restaurant, playgrounds, swimming beaches, picnic areas, campsites, and a par-72, 18-hole golf course.

Memphis A to Z

AIRPORTS AND TRANSFERS
Memphis International Airport is 9 mi south of downtown.
➤ AIRPORT INFORMATION: **Memphis International Airport** (✉ 2491 Winchester Rd., Whitehaven, ☎ 901/922–8000, WEB www.mscaa.com).

AIRPORT TRANSFER
The taxi fare from the airport to downtown Memphis is about $20; try the Yellow Cab car service. By car, take the I-240 to downtown.
➤ TAXIS AND SHUTTLES: **Yellow Cab** (☎ 901/577–7700, WEB www.tlpa.org).

BOAT AND FERRY TRAVEL
The paddle-wheel steamers of the Delta Queen Steamboat Company stop at Memphis and Nashville. The *Delta Queen,* the *Mississippi Queen,* and the *American Queen* travel between St. Louis and New Orleans.
➤ BOAT AND FERRY INFORMATION: **Delta Queen Steamboat Company** (✉ Robin St. Wharf, New Orleans, LA 70130, ☎ 800/543–1949).

BUS TRAVEL AROUND MEMPHIS
Memphis Area Transit Authority buses cover the city and immediate suburbs; they run weekdays 4:30 AM–11:15 PM, Saturday 5 AM–6:15 PM, Sunday 9–6:15. The fare is $1.15, transfers 10¢. There is short-hop service on designated buses between Front, 3rd, and Exchange streets from 9 to 3 and between downtown and the Medical Center complex from 7 to 6. The fare is 35¢.
➤ BUS INFORMATION: **Memphis Area Transit Authority** (☎ 901/274–6282, WEB www.matatransit.com).

BUS TRAVEL TO AND FROM MEMPHIS
Greyhound offers service throughout the region.

➤ Bus Information: **Greyhound** (☎ 800/231–2222, WEB www. greyhound.com).

CAR TRAVEL

From Memphis, which is encircled by I–240, I–55 leads north to St. Louis and south to Jackson, Mississippi; I–40, east to Nashville and Knoxville.

EMERGENCIES

Near-downtown hospitals with 24-hour emergency service in Memphis are the Baptist Memorial Hospital Medical Center and Methodist Health Care University Hospital.

➤ Emergency Services: **Ambulance, police** (☎ 911).

➤ Hospitals: **Baptist Memorial Hospital Memphis** (✉ 6019 Walnut Grove Road, East Memphis, ☎ 901/227–2727, WEB www.palmettohealth. org). **Methodist Health Care University Hospital** (✉ 1265 Union Ave., Midtown, ☎ 901/726–7000, WEB www.methodisthealth.org).

➤ 24-hour Pharmacies: **Walgreens** (✉ 1863 Union St., Midtown, ☎ 901/272–1141).

LODGING
BED AND BREAKFASTS

➤ Reservation Services: **Bed & Breakfast in Memphis Reservation Service** (✉ Box 111141, Memphis 38111-1141, ☎ 901/327–6129, FAX 901/ 458–1003).

MEDIA
RADIO

AM: WMC 79, news and talk.

FM: WHRK 97, rhythm and blues; WEGR 103, adult contemporary and easy listening.

TAXIS

The fare in Memphis is $2.90 for the first mile, $1.40 for each additional mile. There are stands at the airport and bus station. To order a taxi, call Checker Cab.

➤ Taxi Companies: **Checker Cab** (☎ 901/577–7777).

TOURS
BOAT TOURS

Memphis Queen Line Riverboats has 1½-hour sightseeing and two-hour dinner cruises. Sightseeing cruises run daily throughout the year, and dinner cruises run March through November from Wednesday through Sunday. Blues City Tours offers riverboat rides.

➤ Fees and Schedules: **Blues City Tours** (☎ 901/522–9229). **Memphis Queen Line Riverboats** (☎ 901/527–5694 or 800/221–6197, WEB www.memphisqueen.com).

BUS TOURS

Blues City Tours offers motor-coach tours to Memphis sites, including Graceland, Mud Island, and Beale Street, plus nightly tours that include dinner and a show. Gray Line/Stardust operates day and night motor-coach tours to downtown and greater Memphis.

➤ Fees and Schedules: **Gray Line/Stardust** (☎ 901/346–8687).

SPECIAL-INTEREST TOURS

The Center for Southern Folklore gives tours of Beale Street, a farm on the Delta, and prominent areas of musical interest. Carriage Tours of Memphis offers horse-drawn carriage rides. Heritage Tours explores the area's rich African-American cultural heritage. Unique Tours has three-day, two-night tours of Graceland, the National Civil Rights Museum, Mud Island, and other attractions.

➤ FEES AND SCHEDULES: **Carriage Tours of Memphis** (☏ 901/527–7542). **Center for Southern Folklore** (119 S. Main St., Downtown, ☏ 901/525–3655, WEB www.southernfolklore.com). **Heritage Tours** (☏ 901/527–3427). **Unique Tours** (☏ 901/527–8876 or 800/235–1984).

TRAIN TRAVEL

Amtrak operates the *City of New Orleans,* which stops in Memphis on the trip between New Orleans and Chicago.

➤ TRAIN INFORMATION: **Amtrak** (✉ 545 S. Main St., Downtown, ☏ 901/526–0052 or 800/872–7245, WEB www.amtrak.com).

TRANSPORTATION AROUND MEMPHIS

The Memphis Area Transit Authority operates the 2½-mi Main Street Trolley, fare 50¢ (25¢ during weekday lunch hours), in downtown Memphis. The Riverfront Loop extension, adjacent to Riverside Drive, connects with the Main Street Trolley.

VISITOR INFORMATION

Tennessee Welcome Center is open 24 hours a day, seven days a week and is staffed daily from 9 to 6. Memphis Convention & Visitors Bureau is open weekdays 8:30–5.

➤ TOURIST INFORMATION: **Memphis Convention & Visitors Bureau** (✉ 47 Union Ave., 38103, ☏ 901/543–5300 or 800/873–6282, WEB www.memphistravel.com). **Tennessee Welcome Center** (✉ 119 N. Riverside Dr., 38103, ☏ 901/543–5333).

NASHVILLE

Heralded as Music City, USA, and the country-music capital of the world, Tennessee's fast-growing capital city also shines as a leading center of higher education, appropriately known as the Athens of the South. Both labels fit. Nashville has prospered from them both, emerging as one of the South's most vibrant cities in the process. The Gaylor Entertainment Center (formerly Nashville Arena), a 20,000-seat facility that spans three blocks at 5th and Broadway, opened in 1996. A successful drive to land both a National Football League and a National Hockey League franchise, coupled with a population gain that has pushed Nashville ahead of Memphis, has put Nashville into the major leagues of American cities.

Nashville's *Grand Ole Opry* radio program, which began as station WSM's *Barn Dance* in 1925 and thrived throughout the Great Depression right into today's MTV years, established the town as a music center. The Opry performs most of the year in a sleek $15 million Opry House and moves back to its old home in Ryman Auditorium from November through January. The constant infusion of new talent attracts more fans every year. The Opry is still as gleeful and down-home informal as it was when ticket holders with handheld fans to combat the sweltering heat used to jam into the old Ryman. Bolstering Nashville's reputation as a music town are dozens of clubs, performance stages (including the revitalized Ryman), and television tapings open to the public, as well as memorials to many country-music stars. The District, the downtown area along 2nd Avenue and historic Broadway, has emerged as another destination for tourists and locals alike, with restaurants, specialty shopping, and entertainment options. And, of course, legendary Music Row continues to beckon aspiring singers, musicians, and songwriters with stars in their eyes and lyrics tucked in their back pockets.

Much of Nashville's role as a cultural leader, enhanced by the presence of the Tennessee Performing Arts Center that opened in 1985, is derived from the presence of 16 colleges and universities, two medical schools, two law schools, and six graduate business schools. Several, including Vanderbilt University, have national or international reputations, and many have private art galleries. As ancient Athens was the "School of Hellas," so Nashville, where a full-size replica of the Parthenon graces Centennial Park, fills this role in the contemporary South. The historic sites throughout the city—such as the Hermitage, Belle Meade Plantation, and Travellers' Rest—add another dimension.

The Cumberland River horizontally bisects Nashville's central city. Numbered avenues, running north–south, are west of and parallel to the river; numbered streets are east of the river and parallel to it.

Downtown Nashville

Numbers in the text correspond to numbers in the margin and on the Downtown Nashville map.

Downtown Nashville has much to offer in the way of history, music, entertainment, dining, and specialty shopping. A walk through this compact area is a good way to take it all in.

A Good Walk

Begin at **Bicentennial Mall** ㉖, an outdoor history park, and the farmers' market. Walk around James Robertson Parkway and turn left on Charlotte Avenue to visit the Greek Revival **State Capitol** ㉗. Across the avenue are the **War Memorial Auditorium** ㉘, the **Tennessee State Museum** ㉙, and the **Tennessee Performing Arts Center** ㉚.

Walk down 5th Avenue to **Downtown Presbyterian Church** ㉛ on Church Street and then go three blocks east to 2nd Avenue and the **District** ㉜, a good spot for lunch, dinner, or dancing. Nearby, toward the river, is a re-creation of historic **Fort Nashborough** ㉝. South on 1st Avenue is **Riverfront Park** ㉞, a fine place for resting before proceeding two blocks west to **Hatch Show Print** ㉟, a longtime poster print shop on Broadway, and on to the **Ryman Auditorium and Museum** ㊱, on 5th Avenue between Broadway and Commerce Street. Continue along 5th Avenue to the **Country Music Hall of Fame** ㊲ between Demonbreun and Franklin. End up at the **Frist Center for Visual Arts** ㊳ with its three art galleries and café, by taking a left on Demonbreun and walking to 10th Avenue South.

TIMING

Allow at least a day, depending on how long you tend to linger and whether you shop for souvenirs. Most of these attractions offer self-guided tours, so you can set your own pace. Keep in mind that the Tennessee State Museum is closed Monday.

Sights to See

㉖ **Bicentennial Mall.** This 19-acre outdoor history park, complete with a 200-ft granite map of Tennessee and the Walk of Counties, was built in 1996 in honor of the state's 200th birthday. The highlight of the park is a 2,000-seat amphitheater where community bands and children's shows are often staged. Staff at the welcome center can answer questions. The adjacent **farmers' market** (✉ 900 8th Ave. N, Downtown) contains 208 open-air stalls and a food court with local restaurants (most of which are open for lunch but not dinner). ✉ *598 James Robertson Pkwy., Downtown,* ☎ *615/741–5800.* ☉ *Daily 7 AM–10 PM.*

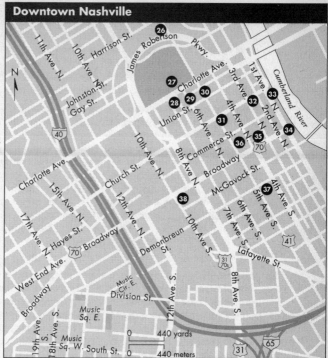

★ **37** **Country Music Hall of Fame and Museum.** Costumes, instruments, films, and photos immortalize well-loved country music stars from Roy Acuff to Patsy Cline to Vince Gill. The museum's huge, modern building across from the Gaylord Entertainment Center has state-of-the-art interactive displays, as well as daily live performances in its conservatory. ⊠ *222 Fifth Ave. S, Downtown,* ☎ *615/416-2001,* WEB *www. countrymusichalloffame.com.* ⚞ *$14.95.* ☉ *Daily 10–6.*

32 **The District.** Thanks to an extensive preservation program begun in the early 1980s, this 16-square-block area between Church Street and Broadway is packed with handsomely restored 19th-century redbrick warehouses and storefronts. On Thursday, June through September, an after-work street party, Dancin' in the District, assembles with live music ranging from jazz to alternative rock. Revelers flock to The Wildhorse Saloon, a huge country music dance hall, plus the popular restaurants and clubs.

31 **Downtown Presbyterian Church.** This Egyptian Revival tabernacle (circa 1851) was designed by noted Philadelphia architect William Strickland. It's a National Historic Landmark. Docents are available weekdays 10–2. Other times, ring the buzzer for admittance. ⊠ *Corner of 5th Ave. and Church St., Downtown.*

33 **Fort Nashborough.** High on limestone bluffs along the river, a crude log fort, whose original was built in 1779 to protect and shelter early settlers, overlooks Nashville. This painstaking re-creation, built in 1962, serves as a monument to courageous city founders. In five log cabins, costumed interpreters evoke the indomitable spirit of the American age of settlement. ⊠ *170 1st Ave. N, Downtown,* ☎ *615/862–8400.* ⚞ *Free.* ☉ *Daily 9–5.*

🕐 ③⑧ **Frist Center for Visual Arts.** This museum occupies the 1930s-era former Nashville Post Office, maintaining its original art deco exterior. It puts on changing national and international traveling shows in its three art galleries; recent exhibitions have ranged from medieval Europe to contemporary abstract art. ✉ *919 Broadway, Downtown,* ☎ *615/244–3340,* WEB *www.fristcenter.org.* 🎫 *$6.50.* ☉ *Mon.–Sat. 10–5:30, Sun. 1–5.*

Gibson Bluegrass Showcase. The Opry Mills complex is the setting for this bluegrass extravaganza, which provides an inside look at the music that gave country its roots. The Showcase is an all-in-one museum, performance venue, production facility, and retail center. From a sight-and-sound history of bluegrass to on-site crafting of bluegrass instruments such as the Dobro (a kind of acoustic guitar) and banjo, it explores the music to its fullest. The Video Cafe is open daily for lunch and has live music on Saturdays. Special events at the Showcase include bluegrass, country, and gospel artists. Allow at least 45 minutes for a visit. ✉ *161 Opryland Mills Dr., Opry Mills,* ☎ *615/871–4500 or 615/514–2200,* WEB *www.gibsonshowcase.com.* 🎫 *Museum and store free.* ☉ *Mon.–Sat. 10–9:30, Sun. 11–8.*

③⑤ **Hatch Show Print.** One of the nation's oldest letter-press poster print shops, Hatch Show Print has been in business since 1879 and has printed posters for vaudeville shows, circuses, sporting events, and, most notably, Grand Ole Opry stars. The store now makes posters and prints for contemporary artists and events. There's no formal tour, but this place is a slice of history that you can explore on your own. Hatch Show is owned by the Country Music Hall of Fame and Museum. ✉ *316 Broadway, Music Row,* ☎ *615/256–2805.* ☉ *Fri. 9:30–5:30, Sat. 10:30–5:30.*

③④ **Riverfront Park.** Though considerably smaller, the Cumberland River has been as important to Nashville as the Mississippi has been to Memphis. This welcoming green enclave on its banks has an expansive view of the busy barge traffic on the muddy river. The park serves as a popular venue for free summer concerts, block parties, and picnics, as well as a docking spot for riverboat excursions. It is also the home of the Tennessee Fox Trot Carousel. ✉ *100 1st Ave. N, Downtown.*

③⑥ **Ryman Auditorium and Museum.** A country-music shrine, the Ryman Auditorium and Museum was home to the Grand Ole Opry from 1943 to 1974. The auditorium seats 2,000 for live performances of classical, jazz, pop, gospel, and, of course, country. The museum displays photographs and memorabilia of past Ryman Auditorium performances that provide a history of both the facility and country music. ✉ *116 5th Ave. N, between Broadway and Commerce St., Downtown,* ☎ *615/254–1445; 615/889–6611 for tickets,* WEB *www.ryman.com.* 🎫 *Tours $8.* ☉ *Daily 9–4; call for show schedules and ticket prices.*

②⑦ **State Capitol.** The state capitol was designed by noted Philadelphia architect William Strickland (1788–1854), who was so impressed with his Greek Revival creation that he requested—and received—entombment behind one of the building's walls. On the grounds—guarded by statues of such Tennessee heroes as Andrew Jackson—are buried the 11th U.S. president, James K. Polk, and his wife. ✉ *Charlotte Ave. between 6th and 7th Aves.,* ☎ *615/741–1621.* 🎫 *Free.* ☉ *Tours weekdays 8–4.*

★ 🕐 **Tennessee Fox Trot Carousel.** A new attraction at Riverfront Park, the carousel is a unique tribute to the state's culture and history. Nashville native and internationally renowned artist Red Grooms designed 37 riding figures for the carousel, from Andrew Jackson and Davy Crockett to Kitty Wells, Chet Atkins, and other country greats. There's even a figure for the spooky folk legend, the Bell Witch. ⊠ *Riverfront Park, 100 1st Ave. N, Downtown.* ⌨ *$2.* ⊘ *Daily 8:30–5:30.*

㉚ Tennessee Performing Arts Center. Part of the state capitol complex, TPAC, as it's known, comprises Jackson Hall, Johnson Hall, and Polk Theater—named for the three U.S. presidents Tennessee has produced. **TPAC Friends** (☎ 615/298–3877) offers backstage tours of the center by appointment. ⊠ *505 Deaderick St., Downtown,* ☎ *615/255–9600,* WEB *www.tpac.org.* ⌨ *Free.* ⊘ *Tues.–Sat. 10–5, Sun. 1–5.*

㉙ Tennessee State Museum. More than 6,000 artifacts and rotating art and history exhibits trace the state's history from the days of Native American settlement through the Civil War and into the 20th century. ⊠ *505 Deaderick St., Downtown,* ☎ *615/741–2692,* WEB *www.csmisfun.com.* ⌨ *Free.* ⊘ *Tues.–Sat. 10–4, Sun. 1–4.*

㉘ War Memorial Auditorium. Inside this 1,900-seat venue for meetings, concerts, and theater is a military museum honoring the state's World War I dead. ⊠ *Corner of 7th and Union Sts., Downtown,* ☎ *615/741–2692.* ⌨ *Free.* ⊘ *Tues.–Sat. 10–4. Closed Sun. and Mon.*

OFF THE
BEATEN PATH

CARL VAN VECHTEN GALLERY – Alfred Stieglitz rewarded Fisk University's progressive arts program with a bequest from his collection of 20th-century paintings and his own superb photographs. Stieglitz's wife, Georgia O'Keeffe, helped install the collection, which holds some of her own paintings as well as works by Picasso and Renoir. The gallery also exhibits African sculpture. ⊠ *Fisk University at 18th Ave. N and Jackson St.,* ☎ *615/329–8720.* ⌨ *Donation suggested.* ⊘ *Tues.–Fri. 10–5, weekends 1–5.*

AARON DOUGLAS GALLERY – Also at Fisk University, on the library's third floor, this gallery shows African-American art, including paintings, drawings, sculpture, watercolors, and prints. Artists on display include William H. Johnson, Aaron Douglas, James Lesesne Wells, Malvin Gray Johnson, and Henry Ossawa Tanner. In addition, you'll find African art and pastel portraits by Winold Reiss on the first floor and Gregory Ridley's abstract paintings and copper repoussé on the second floor. ⊠ *Fisk University at 18th Ave. N, University Library and Jackson St.,* ☎ *615/329–8720.* ⌨ *Free.* ⊘ *Tues.–Fri. 11–4, weekends 1–4.*

Greater Nashville

To get a more complete feeling for the city, you'll want to explore the area beyond downtown. Among the offerings are historic plantations, museums covering everything from toys to science, and some great places for kids, including the Nashville Zoo—not to mention the Grand Ole Opry.

The complex includes the 200-store Opry Mills shopping complex, Cumberland Landing (a riverside eating and entertainment venue), and the Grand Ole Opry.

Numbers in the text correspond to numbers in the margin and on the Greater Nashville map.

A Good Drive

Nashville's attractions are like spokes on a wagon wheel, so expect to spend a lot of time in the car. The **Grand Ole Opry** ㊴ is a good first stop, northeast of downtown off Briley Parkway. Next door the **Opryland Hotel** ㊵ is worth a look. From the hotel you might choose to pur-

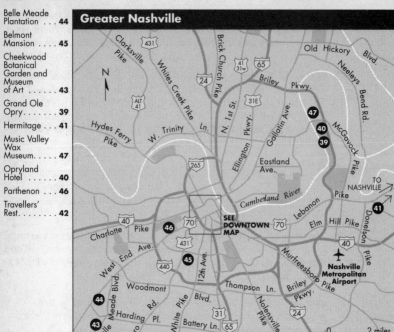

Greater Nashville

sue the attractions in a clockwise fashion, starting at Donelson Pike with Andrew Jackson's home, the **Hermitage** ㊶, and continuing along Harding Place to **Travellers' Rest** ㊷ (a house built by one of Jackson's friends), the **Cheekwood Botanical Garden and Museum of Art** ㊸, and the lovely Greek Revival **Belle Meade Plantation** ㊹. The Italianate **Belmont Mansion** ㊺ is off Hillsboro Road and is near the **Parthenon** ㊻, a copy of the Greek original, on West End Avenue. The **Music Valley Wax Museum** ㊼ is a good place to wind up the tour.

TIMING

Allow at least a day and a half to two days to tour these attractions. The guided tours at the homes can be more time consuming than self-guided attractions.

Sights to See

★ ㊹ **Belle Meade Plantation.** Known as the "queen of the Tennessee plantations," this stunning Greek Revival house is recognizable by the Civil War bullet holes in its columns. Guides in period costumes lead you through the mansion, furnished in a pre–Civil War Victorian style, and the carriage house with its antique carriages. The mansion is the centerpiece of a 5,300-acre estate that was one of the nation's first and finest Thoroughbred breeding farms. It's also the site of the famous Iroquois, the oldest amateur steeplechase in America, a society event now run each May in nearby Percy Warner Park. A Victorian carriage museum with an impressive collection continues the equine theme. The two-story **visitor center**, modeled after a traditional Southern paddock, includes **Martha's at the Plantation**, a fine restaurant on the second floor. ⊠ *5025 Harding Rd., Belle Meade*, ☎ *615/356-0501*, WEB *www.bellemeadeplantation.com.* ⊡ *$10.* ⊘ *Mon.–Sat. 9–5, Sun. 11–5.*

45 **Belmont Mansion.** This 1850s Italianate villa was the home of Adelicia Acklen, Nashville's answer to Scarlett O'Hara, who married "once for money, once for love, and once for the hell of it." On Belmont College's campus, it's a gem right down to its sweeping staircase designed for grand entrances and cast-iron gazebos perfect for romance. ✉ *1900 Belmont Blvd., Belmont,* ☎ *615/460–5459,* WEB *www.belmont. edu.* 🎟 *$7.* ☉ *June–Aug., Mon.–Sat. 10–4, Sun. 1–5; Sept.–May, Tues.–Sat. 10–4.*

43 **Cheekwood Botanical Garden and Museum of Art.** No visit to Nashville is complete without a trip to these 55 beautiful acres, which include the Botanical Garden, the mile-long Woodland Sculpture Trail, and the Pineapple Room restaurant. Among the displays are color, seasonal, water, and Japanese gardens, as well as herb, wildflower, and perennial gardens. Cheekwood, a Georgian-style mansion built in the late 1920s, was once the private residence of the Cheek family of Maxwell House Coffee fame. The permanent exhibition at the museum is American art to 1945, whereas the *Temporary Contemporary Series* showcases the work of local and regional artists. ✉ *1200 Forrest Park Dr., Belle Meade,* ☎ *615/356–8000,* WEB *www.cheekwood.org.* 🎟 *$10.* ☉ *Tues.–Sat. 9:30–4:30, Sun. 11–4:30.*

🖐 **Cumberland Science Museum and Sudekum Planetarium.** Children are invited to look, touch, smell, climb, and listen through interactive exhibits unveiling natural wonders. A 2,800-square-ft Adventure Tower with interactive displays and live science demonstrations and animal shows add to the educational mix. The 40-ft-high planetarium has daily shows. ✉ *800 Fort Negley Blvd., East Nashville,* ☎ *615/862–5160,* WEB *www.csmisfun.com.* 🎟 *$7.95.* ☉ *Tues.–Sat. 10–5, Sun. 12:30–5:30.*

★ **39** **Grand Ole Opry.** This enormously popular radio show, performed in the Grand Ole Opry House, has been bringing America country music for more than 70 years. You can see superstars, legends, and up-and-coming stars on this stage. The Opry seats about 4,400 people and is broadcast live on WSM AM 650 every Friday and Saturday night at 6:30 and 9:30; buy tickets well in advance, particularly during Fan Fair week in June. Opry shows move to their historic home, the Ryman Auditorium in downtown Nashville, between November and February, while a Christmas show featuring the Radio City Rockettes plays at the Grand Ole Opry. ✉ *2804 Opryland Dr., Opryland,* ☎ *615/889–6611 for ticket information,* WEB *www.opry.com.* 🎟 *$20.50–$22.50 for weekend lineups, $27.50 for special shows.*

★ **41** **Hermitage.** The life and times of Andrew Jackson, who was known as Old Hickory, are reflected with great care at this house and museum. Jackson built the mansion on 600 acres for his wife, Rachel, for whose honor he fought and won a duel. Both are buried in the family graveyard. The **Andrew Jackson Center,** a 28,000-square-ft museum, visitor center, and education center, contains many Jackson artifacts. Guides take you through the mansion, furnished with many original pieces. An 18-minute film, *Old Hickory,* provides further background on the seventh president. Note the guitar-shape driveway designed to honor the "bluegrass state." By the 1840s more than 140 African-American slaves lived and worked on the Hermitage Plantation, and archeological digs have uncovered the remains of many slave dwellings—**yard cabins, Alfred's cabin, and field quarters.** Across the road from the plantation stands the **Tulip Grove Mansion,** built by Mrs. Jackson's nephew, and the **Hermitage Church,** fondly known as "Rachel's church." ✉ *4580 Rachel's La., Hermitage,* ☎ *615/889–2941,* WEB *www.thehermitage.com; about 12 mi east of Nashville (I–40E to Old Hickory Blvd. exit).* 🎟 *$10.* ☉ *Daily 9–5.*

47 **Music Valley Wax Museum.** The lure of lifelike wax figures is as strong as ever, and certainly Nashville's country music stars make ripe material. Here fans can stroll among 54 of country music's brightest all dressed in actual costumes. A walk down the Sidewalk of the Stars yields the rewards of 280 entertainers' footprints, handprints, and signatures pressed in concrete. ⊠ *2515 McGavock Pike, Opryland,* ☎ *615/883–3612.* ⊡ *$3.50.* ◷ *Memorial Day–Labor Day, daily 9–9; Labor Day–Memorial Day, daily 9–5.*

Nashville Shores. This sunny water theme park is a good place to exhaust the kids and have some fun while you're at it. The park, alongside Percy Priest Lake, offers a smorgasbord of outdoor entertainment, including the seven largest water slides in Tennessee, giant lily-pad hops, sand dunes, dinosaur fossils, beaches, pools, miniature golf, boat and jet-ski rentals, and picnic areas. The *Nashville Shoreliner* offers cruises. ⊠ *4001 Bell Rd., Hermitage,* ☎ *615/889–7050,* WEB *www.nashvilleshores. com.* ⊡ *$17.95; half price after 3 weekdays.* ◷ *May–Sept., Sun.–Fri. 10–7, Sat. 10–8.*

Nashville Toy Museum. The crowd-pleasing museum and train store houses one of America's most prestigious model train collections, with trains operating on enormous layouts. This attraction in the Grand Ole Opry area also has toy soldiers from around the world, a collection of vintage German teddy bears, giant ship models, early planes, farm tractors, dollhouses, and antique china dolls. The collections span 150 years and transport even the most curmudgeonly adults back to the joys of childhood. **Peterson's Train Store** is a hub for train enthusiasts and collectors, offering hundreds of new and vintage models, as well as opportunities for trade, repairs, and shoptalk. ⊠ *2613 McGavock Pike, Grand Ole Opry,* ☎ *615/391–3516.* ⊡ *$3.50.* ◷ *Daily 10–5.*

Nashville Zoo at Grassmere. More than 600 exotic animals are on display in naturalistic environments, including clouded leopards, lions, white tigers, ring-tailed lemurs, giraffes, and red pandas. The *Unseen New World* exhibit has red-eyed tree frogs, rhino iguanas, leaf-nosed bats, and about 75 other species of reptiles, amphibians, insects, mammals, and birds, many of which have never before been exhibited in Nashville. At the **Jungle Gym Playground,** children can enjoy 66,000 square ft of play area, including a pond, cargo netting, slides, and climbers. The **Grassmere Historic Home and Farm** brings to life an 1880s-era working farm, with a barn, barnyard, livestock, hands-on demonstrations, and period gardens illustrating a typical variety of uses—culinary, medicinal, and decorative. The Italianate-style home, built in 1810, is the second-oldest residence in Davidson County open to the public. ⊠ *3777 Nolensville Rd., 5 mi south of downtown, Nolensville,* ☎ *615/833–1534,* WEB *www.nashvillezoo.org.* ⊡ *$6, parking $2.* ◷ *Apr.–Oct., daily 9–6; Nov.–Mar., daily 9–4.*

40 **Opryland Hotel.** Famous for its imaginative public spaces and displays of artwork, the Opryland Hotel is a Nashville highlight. Three indoor garden areas covering acres of space are crowned by sparkling glass roofs. The newest is the Delta, which spreads over 4½ acres and has a river running through it. The hotel and convention center have numerous lounges with free music, as well as restaurants; parking is $6. ⊠ *2800 Opryland Dr.,* ☎ *615/889–1000,* WEB *www.opryhotel.com.*

★ **46** **Parthenon.** An exact copy of the Athenian original, Nashville's Parthenon was constructed to commemorate Tennessee's 1897 centennial. Across the street from Vanderbilt University's campus, in Centennial Park, it's a magnificent sight, perched on a gentle green slope beside a duck pond. Inside are the Cowan Collection, with 63 works of art by American artists, traveling exhibits, and such exquisite statuary as the 42-ft *Athena Parthenos*, the tallest indoor sculpture in the Western world. ⊠ *West End and 25th Aves., Centennial Park,* ☎ *615/862–8431,* WEB *www.parthenon-mpa.com.* ☑ *$3.50.* ☉ *Oct.–Mar., Tues.–Sat. 9–4:30; Apr.–Sept., Tues.–Sat. 9–4:30, Sun. 12:30–4:30.*

㊷ Travellers' Rest. Following the fortunes of pioneer landowner and judge John Overton—the law partner, mentor, campaign manager, and lifelong friend of Andrew Jackson, whose own home is nearby—this early 19th-century clapboard home metamorphosed from a 1799 four-room cottage to a 12-room mansion with federal-influenced and Greek Revival additions. The mansion's interior has been restored to its mid-19th-century state with period furnishings. Also on the grounds are a restored smokehouse, kitchen house, and formal gardens. Travellers' Rest is off I–65S at the first of two Harding Place exits. ⊠ *636 Farrell Pkwy., Oak Mills,* ☎ *615/832–2962,* WEB *www.travellersrestplantation. org.* ☑ *$8.* ☉ *Tues.–Sat. 10–4, Sun. 1–4.*

☙ Wave Country. A mile from the Grand Ole Opry and a great place for a cooldown if you're visiting in the summer, Wave Country has a large wave pool and a three-flume water slide. ⊠ *2320 Two Rivers Pkwy., off Briley Pkwy.,* ☎ *615/885–1052.* ☑ *$6.* ☉ *Memorial Day–Labor Day, daily 10–5.*

Dining

American

$$$$ ✕ **Belle Meade Brasserie.** The menu is a symphony of best-loved recipes from all over the United States—an appetizer of corn fritters and pepper jelly, double pork chops with Thai barbecue sauce, oven-roasted grouper, and crawfish étouffée. Desserts are just as compelling, including a knockout Russian raspberry gratin. ⊠ *106 Harding Place, Belle Meade,* ☎ *615/356–5450. AE, DC, MC, V. Closed Sun. No lunch.*

$$$$ ✕ **Capitol Grille and Oak Bar.** This charming restaurant in down-
★ town's historic Westin Hermitage Hotel serves cuisine with a regional flair, such as sautéed grouper accompanied by garlic whipped potatoes. Another top pick is the filet mignon with a Portobello mushroom demiglace (a rich brown sauce). The Capitol Grille is consistently ranked as one of Nashville's top restaurants by local food reviewers. ⊠ *231 6th Ave. N, Downtown,* ☎ *615/345–7116. AE, DC, MC, V.*

$$–$$$ ✕ **The Bound'ry.** One of the most popular restaurants in Nashville, the Bound'ry is known for its creative menu, with different main courses every day. The lobster BLT pizza probably is as good an indication as any of the spirit that moves the kitchen staff. A street-front patio gives diners a chance to see and be seen; on Wednesday evenings from July through September, the Bound'ry sponsors outdoor rock, jazz, and blues bands in a nearby lot. ⊠ *911 20th Ave. S Midtown,* ☎ *615/321–3043. AE, D, DC, MC, V.*

$$–$$$ ✕ **F. Scott's.** Contemporary American bistro cuisine is served in this Green Hills spot, which has both the comfort of a neighborhood eatery and the sophistication of an upscale restaurant. The art deco–style dining room is a warm mocha color. Popular dishes on the seasonal menu are oven-roasted veal tenderloin with a tomato, artichoke, potato, and bacon ragout and braised lamb shank with rosemary tomato broth; lobster with ginger butter, sugar snap peas, and sticky rice is a summer choice. The wine list is extensive. There's live jazz nightly in the bar. ⊠ *2210 Crestmoor Rd., Green Hills,* ☎ *615/269–5861. AE, D, DC, MC, V. No lunch.*

$$–$$$ ✕ **Mad Platter.** This local favorite in historic Germantown Nashville blends traditional cooking with California cuisine, using ingredients

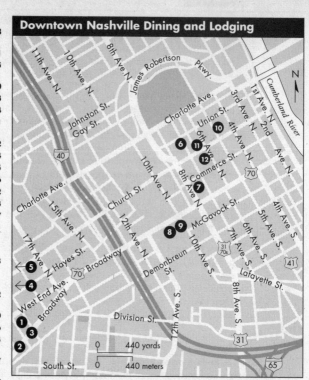

Downtown Nashville Dining and Lodging

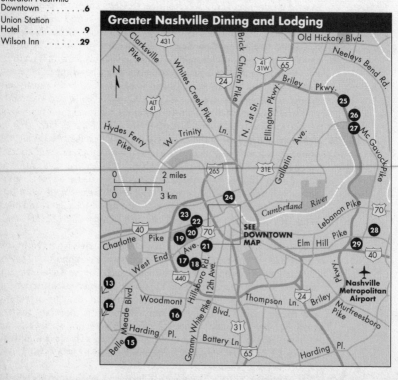

Greater Nashville Dining and Lodging

from the nearby farmers' market. The baked salmon with red grapes and feta cheese, rack of lamb, and bananas Foster are favorites here. It's a popular spot for power lunches by day. ⊠ *1239 6th Ave. N, Germantown,* ☎ *615/242–2563. Reservations essential. AE, D, DC, MC, V. No lunch Sat.–Mon.*

$$–$$$ ✗ **Nick and Rudy's.** A menu of American and European continental fare backs up the classic steakhouse staples at Nick and Rudy's. Go beyond steak and try the lobster bisque. The piano bar, which has live music from Tuesday through Saturday, adds to the romance. ⊠ *204 21st Ave. S, Midtown,* ☎ *615/329–8994,* WEB *www.nickandrudys. com. AE, D, DC, MC, V. Closed Sun.*

$$–$$$ ✗ **Sunset Grill.** Seafood, pastas, steaks, and vegetarian specials high-
★ light the menu of this modern restaurant that displays the work of local artist Paul Harmon. A good entrée choice is voodoo pasta with andouille sausage, chicken, and shrimp in a roasted pepper sauce served with jalapeño-flavored fettuccine. Seventy wines are served by the glass. A tip: food prices are slashed by 50% after 10 PM (midnight on weekends) until closing at 1:30 AM. ⊠ *2001A Belcourt Ave., Hillsboro Village,* ☎ *615/386–3663. AE, D, DC, MC, V. No lunch weekends.*

Continental

$$$$ ✗ **Arthur's.** This restaurant is in the stylishly renovated Union Station, where an upscale hotel has taken the place of the train terminal. The seven-course meals are dazzling, or if you prefer, à la carte is also available. The menu changes daily, but specialties include rainbow trout, duck, and lamb. Save room for dessert: the bananas Foster is especially good. The lush, romantic interior has lace curtains, velveteen-upholstered chairs, white linen, and fine silver service. ⊠ *Union Station, 1001 Broadway, Downtown,* ☎ *615/255–1494. AE, DC, MC, V. No lunch.*

$$$–$$$$ ✗ **Wild Boar.** Superb contemporary French cuisine is presented in an
★ elegant setting that resembles a European hunting lodge. On the menu are Maine lobster, Canadian elk steak, and seared guinea hen. The 15,000-bottle wine cellar gives the Wild Boar one of the top wine lists in the world, and 25 wines are available by the glass. ⊠ *2014 Broadway, Midtown,* ☎ *615/329–1313. AE, D, DC, MC, V. Closed Sun.– Mon. No lunch Sat.*

Italian

$$–$$$$ ✗ **Mario's Ristorante Italiano.** Owner Mario Ferrari and his restaurant are a Nashville institution, consistently drawing political figures and celebrities for northern Italian food served in elegant surroundings. The seafood and veal—such as the saltimbocca, veal medallions with mozzarella, prosciutto, mushrooms, and fresh sage—are delicious. ⊠ *2005 Broadway, Midtown,* ☎ *615/327–3232. Reservations essential. Jacket and tie. AE, D, DC, MC, V. Closed Sun.*

Mediterranean

$$$–$$$$ ✗ **Zola.** From the romantic interior to the adventurous menu, this restaurant re-creates a Mediterranean journey. A 27-ft mural graces the main dining room, and gauzy fabric billows in the Tent Room. Specialties include grandma Zola's paella, pistacho-crushed salmon, and herb-crusted filet mignon. ⊠ *3001 West End Ave., Vanderbilt,* ☎ *615/320– 7778. AE, D, DC, MC, V.*

Southern

$–$$ ✗ **Loveless.** This is an experience in true down-home Southern cook-
★ ing. Don't come for the decor—decidedly lax, with red-and-white-check tablecloths—but rather for the featherlight homemade biscuits and preserves, country ham and red-eye gravy, and fried chicken. ⊠ *8400 Hwy. 100, Pasquo Community,* ☎ *615/646–9700. MC, V.*

$ ✕ **Pancake Pantry.** This Nashville institution is the place to go for breakfast. It's a favorite haunt of celebrities such as Garth Brooks and Alan Jackson and also popular with local politicos. Breakfast is the biggie, with 20 kinds of pancakes and homemade syrups, but there are soups and sandwiches for lunch. Expect to wait in line for breakfast on the weekends. ⊠ *1796 21st Ave. S, Hillsboro Village,* ☎ *615/383–9333. Reservations not accepted. AE, D, DC, MC, V. No dinner.*

$ ✕ **Swett's Restaurant.** A family-owned restaurant in business since 1954, Swett's offers some of the best meat-and-three meals in Nashville. Turnip greens, green beans, pork chops, fried chicken, and real mashed potatoes are all temptations. *2725 Clifton Ave., Northwest Nashville,* ☎ *615/329–4418. MC, V.*

Lodging

$$$$ ⊡ **Loew's Vanderbilt Plaza Hotel.** Celebrities and business travelers grav-
★   itate to this quiet European-style luxury hotel known for top-notch service. Musicians play nightly in the piano bar, and there's a cigar bar. Gracious guest rooms, some with skyline views, have dark cherry furniture. Plaza suites are individually decorated, and the club-level rooms have baths and extra phone and fax lines. ⊠ *2100 West End Ave., 37203,* ☎ *615/320–1700 or 800/235–6397,* FAX *615/320–5019,* WEB *www. loewshotels.com. 327 rooms, 13 suites. 2 restaurants, room service, cable TV, health club, piano bar, laundry service. AE, DC, MC, V.*

$$$$ ⊡ **Opryland Hotel.** This massive hostelry is one of the 25 largest in the
★   world. In addition to nearly 3,000 rooms, the hotel has an indoor river, a 110-ft-wide waterfall, and an amphitheater under a 4-acre glass dome. Harp music is played nightly at the revolving bar at the Cascades, another skylighted interior space with streams, waterfalls, and a half-acre lake. Rooms, which are fairly standard in size, have a Victorian floral design in beige and rose tones; request one overlooking the gardens. The 18-hole golf course was designed by Larry Nelson. ⊠ *2800 Opryland Dr., 37214,* ☎ *615/889–1000,* FAX *615/871–7741,* WEB *www.oprylandhotel. com. 2,883 rooms, 200 suites. 5 restaurants, pool, wading pool, gym, convention center. AE, D, DC, MC, V.*

$$–$$$$ ⊡ **Sheraton Nashville Downtown.** Downtown, near the state capitol building, this 28-story tower has a vast, skylighted atrium lobby awash with greenery and overseen by glassed-in elevators. Rooms are spacious with contemporary designs, and have great views of the growing Nashville skyline. The hotel is topped by the Pinnacle, Nashville's only revolving rooftop restaurant. ⊠ *623 Union St., 37219,* ☎ *615/ 259–2000 or 800/447–9825,* FAX *615/742–6057,* WEB *www.sheraton. com. 473 rooms, 14 suites. 2 restaurants, coffee shop, cable TV, lounge, no-smoking rooms. AE, D, DC, MC, V.*

$$–$$$$ ⊡ **Union Station Hotel.** This Victorian-era hotel in a convenient downtown location was reincarnated from a bustling train station. Late-19th-century opulence is evoked in the 65-ft barrel-vaulted ceiling, gold-leaf mirrors, and Tiffany stained glass. Rooms are handsomely appointed, and extra luxury awaits Heritage Club Level members, who receive turndown service, shoe shines, Continental breakfast, and cocktails. ⊠ *1001 Broadway, 37203,* ☎ *615/726–1001 or 800/996–3426,* FAX *615/248–3554,* WEB *www.wyndham.com. 124 rooms, 13 suites. Restaurant, room service, in-room data ports, cable TV with movies. AE, D, DC, MC, V.*

$$$ ⊡ **Hermitage Hotel.** Called the last of Nashville's grand hotels, this historic downtown building sits across from the capitol and the Tennessee Performing Arts Center. Built in 1910, the beaux-arts-style hotel once served as headquarters for both suffragist and antisuffragist groups in the 1920s. The elegant lobby soars three stories tall toward stained-glass ceilings. The suites have living rooms with work desks and wet

bars. ⊠ *231 6th Ave. N, 37219,* ☎ *615/244–3121 or 888/888–9414,* FAX *615/254–6909,* WEB *www.thehermitagehotel.com. 123 rooms. Restaurant, cable TV, meeting rooms. AE, D, DC, MC, V.*

$$$ 🏨 **Radisson Opryland.** This contemporary-style, low-rise motor inn is across the street from the Opryland Hotel. ⊠ *2401 Music Valley Dr., 37214,* ☎ *615/889–0800,* FAX *615/883–1230,* WEB *www.radisson.com. 03 rooms. Restaurant, cable TV, indoor pool, gym, hot tub, sauna, lounge, meeting rooms. AE, DC, MC, V.*

$$$ 🏨 **Renaissance Nashville Hotel.** This luxurious, modern high-rise hotel adjoins the Nashville Convention Center. Spacious rooms are furnished with period reproductions. Executive Club concierge floors offer extra privacy and personal services. ⊠ *611 Commerce St., 37203,* ☎ *615/255–8400,* FAX *615/255–8202,* WEB *www.renaissancehotels. com. 649 rooms, 24 suites. Restaurant, coffee shop, cable TV with movies, indoor pool, hot tub, health club, sauna, lounge, laundry service, concierge floors. AE, DC, MC, V.*

$$ 🏨 **Courtyard by Marriott–Airport.** This handsome low-rise motor inn with a sunny, gardenlike courtyard offers some amenities you'd expect in higher-price hotels: spacious rooms, king-size beds, oversize work desks, and hot-water dispensers for in-room coffee. ⊠ *2508 Elm Hill Pike, 37214,* ☎ *615/883–9500 or 800/321–2211,* FAX *615/883–0172,* WEB *www.nashville.realhotels.com. 133 rooms, 12 suites. Restaurant, hot tub, lounge; no-smoking rooms. AE, D, DC, MC, V.*

$$ 🏨 **Hampton Inn Vanderbilt.** Near the Vanderbilt University campus and Music Row, this six-story inn is clean and contemporary and especially popular with visiting music executives and musicians. Rooms are spacious. A multipurpose hospitality suite has a conference table, chairs, and an audiovisual unit for meetings, making this a popular corporate choice. ⊠ *1919 West End Ave., 37203,* ☎ *615/329–1144 or 800/426– 7866,* FAX *615/320–7112,* WEB *www.hamptoninnnashville.com. 171 rooms. Pool, gym, meeting room. AE, D, DC, MC, V.*

$ 🏨 **Wilson Inn.** Three miles from the Grand Ole Opry, and just two from Nashville's airport, this five-story hotel has spacious, comfortably furnished guest rooms. Many rooms have kitchens or microwave ovens. ⊠ *600 Ermac Dr. (Elm Hill Pike exit from Briley Pkwy.), 37214,* ☎ *615/ 889–4466 or 800/333–9457,* FAX *615/889–0484,* WEB *www.wilsonhotels. com. 110 rooms. No-smoking rooms. AE, D, DC, MC, V. CP.*

$ 🛆 **Opryland KOA.** This 27-acre campground is unique among KOAs, in that local performers put on country music shows here from April through November. Its proximity to Opryland makes it a favorite destination for families. The campground is 11 mi from downtown. Rates vary with the season. ⊠ *2626 Music Valley Dr., 37214,* ☎ *615/889– 0282 or 800/KOA–7789. 423 campsites, 27 cabins. 1 pool, 1 indoor pool, playground, laundry facilities. AE, D, MC, V.*

Nightlife and the Arts

For a listing of weekly events, consult the **Nashville Visitor Center** (☎ 615/259–4747) or the local newspapers. **TicketMaster** (☎ 615/255–9600) has information on events at various Nashville venues.

The Arts

Nashville has emerged as an arts center, with a full schedule of concerts and other performances; the city also has fine galleries for the visual arts.

LIVE TAPINGS
Anyone wanting to be part of an audience for a live taping of a television show can attend the regular free taping of the *Crook & Chase* show (⊠ 1525 McGavock St., ☎ 615/256–7700) on weekdays at Jim

Owens Studios, between Music Row and downtown. At the cable television network **CMT: Country Music Television** (✉ 2161 Opryland Dr., Opry Mills, ☎ 615/831–0338) opportunities abound to see shows in production, and to participate in live audiences for such shows as CMT Most Wanted Live.

MUSIC AND DANCE
The Nashville Symphony Orchestra's classical and pops series and concerts by visiting performers are staged at **Andrew Jackson Hall** (TicketMaster, ☎ 615/255–9600), part of the Tennessee Performing Arts Center. Chamber concerts, touring Broadway shows, and local theatrical performances take place at the Tennessee Performing Arts Center's **Polk Theater** (☎ 615/255–9600). Rock and country events are held at the **Gaylord Entertainment Center** (✉ 501 Broadway, Downtown, ☎ 615/770–2000). The **AmSouth Amphitheatre** (✉ 3839 Murfreesboro Rd., Murfreesboro, ☎ 615/641–5800) is the site of rock, pop, country, and jazz concerts, musicals, and special events; it also hosts some performances of the Nashville Symphony.

The **Nashville Ballet** (☎ 615/297–2966) performs works at the Tennessee Performing Arts Center, and is accompanied by the Nashville Symphony Orchestra. Vanderbilt University stages music, dance, and drama productions (many free) at its **Blair School of Music** (✉ 2400 Blakemore Ave., ☎ 615/322–7651).

THEATER
The **Nashville Children's Theatre** (✉ 724 2nd Ave. S, Downtown, ☎ 615/254–9103) is home to a professional children's theater troupe that performs September through May. At **Chaffin's Barn** (✉ 8204 Hwy. 100, Belleview, ☎ 615/646–9977 or 800/282–2276) Nashville's first professional theater offers Southern buffet-style eating and Broadway plays year-round in two theaters. **Circle Players** (✉ 505 Deaderick St., Downtown, ☎ 615/254–0113), in operation for more than 50 seasons, is Nashville's oldest volunteer-run theater. The community troupe presents six shows a year at the Tennessee Performing Arts Center (TPAC), from September through April. The **Tennessee Repertory Theatre** is the state's largest professional theater company, staging four productions a year at the Tennessee Performing Arts Center (TPAC) (✉ 505 Deaderick St., Downtown, ☎ 615/244–4878), from September through May. For more experimental fare, the **Darkhorse Theater** (✉ 4610 Charlotte Ave., South Nashville, ☎ 615/297–7113) puts on original works and alternative theater and dance.

Nightlife
BARS
Big River Grille & Brewery Works (✉ 111 Broadway, Downtown, ☎ 615/251–4677) is one of Nashville's hottest brew pubs. The Nashville start-up **Boscos Nashville Brewing Company** (✉ 1805 21st Ave. S, Hillsboro Village, ☎ 615/385–0050), in the heart of Hillsboro Village, serves Famous Flaming Stone Beer, a steinbier, or stone beer, brewed using hot granite (a method beloved among beer connoisseurs for the slightly caramel tone and taste it produces in the brew). Every weekday a cellar man taps the real ale keg, and pub food is cooked in wood-fired ovens. Nashville's version of the **Hard Rock Cafe** (✉ 100 Broadway, Downtown, ☎ 615/742–9900) is great for burgers.

COUNTRY MUSIC
Grammy Award–winning talent and Music City's up-and-coming stars often try out their latest material at **Bluebird Cafe** (✉ 4104 Hillsboro Rd., Green Hills, ☎ 615/383–1461). **Douglas Corner Cafe** (✉ 2106A 8th Ave. S, Downtown, ☎ 615/298–1688) is well known for every-

thing from blues to country. The **Grand Ole Opry** (✉ 2804 Opryland Dr., Opryland, ☎ 615/889–6611, WEB www.opry.com) is the site of country performances on Friday and Saturday evenings. **Nashville Nightlife Dinner Theater** (✉ 2620 Music Valley Dr., Opryland, ☎ 615/885–5201 or 800/308–5779) presents a 1½-hour country music show accompanied by all the trimmings of a full Southern country buffet. **Robert's Western World** (✉ 416 Broadway, Downtown, ☎ 615/244–9552) was originally a clothing store; cowboy boots adorn the walls, but today country music is what you come for. The **Texas Troubadour Theatre** (✉ 2416 Music Valley Dr., Opryland, ☎ 615/889–2474) presents a country music lover's dream come true—a free midnight jam featuring Opry acts and country music newcomers alike. Audiences can attend the live broadcast of the **Ernest Tubb Midnite Jamboree** each Saturday night. The **Cowboy Church** features artists singing hymns every Sunday at 10 AM. Opry star Mike snyder records his show on Sundays at 7 PM. For a honky-tonk joint with all day/all night music, hit **Tootsie's Orchid Lounge** (✉ 422 Broadway, Downtown, ☎ 615/726–0463). Boot-scoot over to the **Wildhorse Saloon** (✉ 120 2nd Ave. N, Downtown, ☎ 615/251–1000), with its 3,300-ft dance floor and seating for 1,600.

JAZZ, BLUEGRASS, ROCK, AND VARIETY

Bluegrass lovers flock to the **Bluegrass Inn** (✉ 418 Broadway, Downtown, ☎ 615/726–2799) for live performances by Hillbilly All Stars and others.

Big-name pop and rock artists can be found at **Exit/In** (✉ 2208 Elliston Pl., Elliston Place, ☎ 615/321–4400). Past performers have included Jerry Lee Lewis, Chuck Mangione, Steve Martin, and the Allman Brothers. **Caffe Milano** (✉ 176 3rd Ave, N, Downtown, ☎ 255–0073) presents fine food along with some of Nashville's best musicians. For the cigar and martini set, the **Havana Lounge** (✉ 154 2nd Ave., Downtown, ☎ 615/313–7665) is a popular spot, especially on evenings featuring top DJs. For alternative rock, try **Indienet Record Shop** (✉ 1707 Church St., Downtown, ☎ 615/321–0882). At this record store/club, rock bands such as Braid, Anti-Flag, and Fury 66 perform. No alcohol or smoking is allowed.

Festivals

Dancin' in the District (☎ 615/256–2073) is a huge, free street party held downtown every Thursday night from May through August; hours are 5–10.

The **International Country Music Fan Fair,** held by the Grand Ole Opry and the Country Music Association during the second week in June at the **Tennessee State Fairgrounds** (✉ I-65 South, Wedgewood Avenue exit 81, ☎ 615/862–8980) is country music's premier event. Many tour companies offer packages, but plan ahead: tickets sell out months in advance.

Outdoor Activities and Sports

Participant Sports

BOATING AND FISHING

You'll find boat rentals at lovely **J. Percy Priest Lake** (✉ 11 mi east of Nashville, off I-40, ☎ 615/889–1975). Boats can be rented from **Nashville Shores** (✉ 4001 Bell Rd., Hermitage, ☎ 615/889–9070).

GOLF

Public courses open year-round include the 18-hole, par-72 **Harpeth Hills** (✉ 2424 Old Hickory Blvd., Belle Meade, ☎ 615/862–8493). In northern Nashville is the 18-hole, par-72 **Rhodes Golf Course** (✉ 1901

Ed Temple Blvd., North Nashville, ☎ 615/862–8463). Two 18-hole, par-72 links are at the **Hermitage Golf Course** (⊠ 3939 Old Hickory Blvd., Old Hickory City, ☎ 615/847–4001). Hermitage is the site each April of the LPGA Sara Lee Classic.

JOGGING

Centennial Park, the Vanderbilt University running track, J. Percy Priest Lake, and Percy Warner Park are great for jogging. The Music City Marathon takes place in late April. The 1,000-member running club **Nashville Striders** (☎ 615/331–0111) can recommend choice running spots and will provide information on many summer races.

Spectactor Sports

AUTO RACING

NASCAR Winston Racing Series weekly stock-car racing takes place March through September at **Nashville Speedway USA** (⊠ Tennessee State Fairgrounds, ☎ 615/726–1818).

BASEBALL

The **Nashville Sounds,** a AAA affiliate of the Pittsburgh Pirates, play home games from mid-April through mid-September at **Hershel Greer Stadium** (☎ 615/242–4371).

FOOTBALL

Nashville's **Adelphia Coliseum** (⊠ 1 Titans Way, ☎ 615/565–4000 or 888/313–8326) is home to the NFL's **Tennessee Titans.** The 67,000-seat natural-grass stadium sits on the banks of the Cumberland River across from Downtown Nashville.

The **Nashville Kats,** a professional indoor football franchise, bring the excitement of the 50-yard indoor war to the Gaylord Entertainment Center (⊠ 501 Broadway, Downtown, ☎ 615/254–5287).

HOCKEY

The National Hockey League franchise team, the **Nashville Predators,** plays at the Gaylord Entertainment Center (⊠ 501 Broadway, Downtown, ☎ 615/770–2000).

HORSE SHOW

For 10 days from late August to early September, Shelbyville, 50 mi southeast of Nashville, holds the **Tennessee Walking Horse National Celebration** (⊠ Box 1010, 37160, ☎ 931/684–5915), the world's greatest walking-horse show.

Shopping

Antiques

Browse for distinctive 18th- and 19th-century English antiques and objets d'art at **Tennessee Antique Mall** (654 Wedgewood Ave., ☎ 615/259–4077). Just outside of Nashville is the **Goodlettsville Antique Mall** (⊠ 213 N. Main St., Goodlettsville, Fairgrounds, ☎ 615/859–7002). In Andrew Jackson's old stomping grounds, the **Hermitage Antique Mall** (⊠ 4144-B Lebanon Rd., Hermitage, ☎ 615/883–5789) offers miles of antiques. The shops along **8th Avenue South** in Nashville make a good browsing ground.

Arts and Crafts

Cumberland Gallery (⊠ 4107 Hillsboro Circle, Green Hills, ☎ 615/297–0296) sells the works of major regional artists. **The Arts Company** (⊠ 215 5th Ave. N, Downtown, ☎ 615/254–2040) carries photography, painting, sculpture, outsider art, and unexpected fun art.

The annual **Tennessee Crafts Fair** (☎ 615/385–1904), a juried crafts festival held on the grounds of the Parthenon in early May, is a great source for Tennessee crafts. There are works by 165 contemporary and traditional crafts artists, as well as demonstrations and children's activities.

Books

Bibliophiles appreciate the three-story **Davis-Kidd Booksellers and Cafe** (✉ Grace's Plaza, 4007 Hillsboro Rd., Green Hills, ☎ 615/385–2645), open late on weekends. Curl up in a chair with a glass of wine and the latest best-sellers.

Flea Market

From treasures to just plain "junque"—the **Nashville Flea Market** (✉ Tennessee State Fairgrounds: Wedgewood and Rains Aves., ☎ 615/862–5016; ◷ Fri. noon–5, Sat. 7–6, Sun. 7–4) has it all. Usually, 1,000 traders, craftspeople, and antiques dealers ply their wares the fourth weekend of every month except December (when it's the third weekend of the month).

Music

Country music fans can find the best of country tapes and CDs at **Ernest Tubb Record Shops** (✉ 2416 Music Valley Dr., Music Valley, ☎ 615/889–2474; ✉ 417 Broadway, Downtown, ☎ 615/255–7503). The **Great Escape** (✉ 1925 Broadway, Midtown, ☎ 615/327–0646; ✉ 111 Gallatin Rd. N, Madison, ☎ 615/865–8052) has great used records of all kinds.

Shopping Centers

Opry Mills (✉ 2802 Opryland Dr., Opryland) consists of more than a million square ft of stores, restaurants, and entertainment spots. In addition to mall perennials such as Bass, Barnes & Noble, and movie theaters, this supercomplex also houses the **Gibson Bluegrass Showcase**, a simulated racecar speedway, and an IMAX theater, among others. The **Bellevue Center Mall** (✉ 7620 Hwy. 70S, off Bellevue exit of I–40W, Bellevue, ☎ 615/646–8690) has more than 125 stores. The **Mall at Green Hills** (✉ Hillsboro and Abbott Martin Rds., Green Hills, ☎ 615/298–5478), about 15 minutes from Music Row, has specialty stores such as Brookstone, Williams-Sonoma, Laura Ashley, and Brooks Brothers, plus a Dillard's department store. **100 Oaks** (✉ I–65 South to Exit 79, Armory Dr. to Powell, South Nashville, ☎ 615/383–6002) is one of Nashville's more upscale factory outlets. Twenty-five miles east of Nashville, the **Prime Outlets of Lebanon** (✉ I–40 at Highway 231, Lebanon, ☎ 615/444–0433) is a favorite of locals looking for deals on Brooks Brothers, Ralph Lauren, Nike, and more.

Side Trips from Nashville

The middle Tennessee area surrounding Nashville is a pocket of gently rolling Cumberland Mountain foothills and bluegrass meadows. It is one of the state's richest farming areas. Such small towns as Lynchburg and Franklin, the latter of which historian Shelby Foote calls one of the nation's top Civil War sites, offer wonderful antiques shops and crafts boutiques.

The **Tennessee Antebellum Trail** (☎ 800/381–1865 for a map and admission prices), which has more than 54 historic sites, plantations, and Civil War battlefields, is a 90-mi loop tour that begins in Nashville and continues through historic Maury and Williamson counties. Nine sites are open to the public daily.

Loretta Lynn's Ranch

65 mi west of Nashville.

Loretta Lynn's Ranch encompasses the entire village of Hurricane Mills. The singer's personal museum is here, and you can take tours of the first floor of the coal miner's daughter's stately antebellum home, of a simulated coal mine, and of a re-creation of her simple childhood home. Camping, canoeing, paddleboats, trout fishing, and swimming are among the many recreational activities available here. ⊠ *44 Hurricane Mills Rd., Hurricane Mills,* ☎ *931/296–7700.* ☞ *Tour $10, museum $10, camping $17–$22 per night for 2 people.* ☉ *Apr.–Oct.*

Franklin
18 mi south of Nashville.

The town of Franklin rivals Natchez, Mississippi, in charm and Civil War history. A self-guided walking tour begins at the town square and covers several antebellum homes plus the meticulously restored downtown business district, which has more than 50 shops, including several antiques shops and art galleries. The **Carnton Plantation,** where some of the Civil War's bloodiest battles were fought, and **Confederate Cemetery** are nearby. Also in the area is the entrance to the **Natchez Trace Parkway** (off I–40), which wends its way through gorgeous scenery in three states. For more information on Franklin and its attractions, contact **Williamson County / Franklin Chamber of Commerce** (⊠ City Hall, Franklin 37065, ☎ 615/794–1225, WEB www.williamsoncvb.org).

Lynchburg
75 mi southeast of Nashville.

Lynchburg has been depicted worldwide in ads for its best-known product: whiskey. The quaint town is home to the **Jack Daniel's Distillery,** the oldest registered distillery in the country, where you can observe every step of the art of making sour-mash whiskey. ⊠ *On TN 55,* ☎ *931/759–4221,* WEB *www.jackdaniels.com.* ☞ *Free.* ☉ *Guided tours daily 9–4:30.*

DINING

$ ✕ **Miss Mary Bobo's Boarding House.** Diners flock to this two-story 1867 white-frame house with a white picket fence to feast family style at tables laden with fried chicken, roast beef, fried catfish, stuffed vegetables, and sliced tomatoes, along with corn on the cob, homemade biscuits, corn bread, pecan pie, lemon icebox pie, fruit cobblers, and strawberry shortcake. There's only one meal served Monday–Friday, at 1; Saturday has two seatings, at 11 and 1. ⊠ *Main St., ½ block from Public Sq.,* ☎ *931/759–7394. Reservations essential. No credit cards.*

Nashville A to Z

AIRPORTS AND TRANSFERS
Nashville International Airport, approximately 12 mi east of downtown, is served by most major airlines.
➤ AIRPORT INFORMATION: **Nashville International Airport** (⊠ 1 Terminal Dr., ☎ 615/275–1600, WEB www.nashintl.com).

AIRPORT TRANSFER
Shuttle service downtown costs $8–$10 per person. A cab costs about $20 plus tip. To reach downtown by car, take I–40W.
➤ TAXIS AND SHUTTLES: **Gray Line Shuttle Service** (☎ 615/275–1180).

BUS TRAVEL AROUND NASHVILLE
Metropolitan Transit Authority (MTA) buses serve the entire county; the fare is $1.75 (exact change), and they run 4 AM–11:15 PM.
➤ BUS INFORMATION: **Metropolitan Transit Authority** (☎ 615/862–5950, WEB www.nashvillemta.org).

BUS TRAVEL TO AND FROM NASHVILLE

➤ Bus Information: **Greyhound** (✉ 200 8th Ave. S, at McGavock St., Nashville, ☎ 800/231–2222, WEB www.greyhound.com).

CAR TRAVEL

From Nashville I–65 leads north into Kentucky and south into Alabama, and I–24 leads northwest into Kentucky and Illinois and southeast into Chattanooga and Georgia. I–40 traverses the state east–west, connecting Knoxville with Nashville and Memphis. I–440 connects I–40, I–65, and I–24, and helps circumvent clogged major arteries during Nashville's rush hour. I–840, which will skirt Nashville's north side and connect I–40 with I–24N and I–65N, is under construction.

EMERGENCIES

Emergency rooms are open all night at centrally located Baptist Hospital and Vanderbilt University Medical Center.

➤ Emergency Services: **Ambulance, police** (☎ 911).

➤ Hospitals: **Baptist Hospital** (✉ 2000 Church St., West End, ☎ 615/284–5555, WEB www.baptisthospital.com). **Vanderbilt University Medical Center** (✉ 1211 22nd Ave. S, Vanderbilt, ☎ 615/322–7311, WEB www.mc.vanderbilt.edu).

➤ 24-hour Pharmacy: **Kroger Pharmacy** (✉ 4560 Harding Pike, Belle Meade, ☎ 615/297–2279).

MEDIA

RADIO

AM: WLAC 1510, news and talk.

FM: WPLN 90.3, classical and jazz; WSM 95, country; WSIX 97.9, country.

TAXIS

Try Allied Taxi, Music City Taxi, or Madison Rivergate Taxi.

➤ Taxi Companies: **Allied Taxi** (☎ 615/244–7433). **Madison Rivergate Taxi** (☎ 615/865–4100). **Music City Taxi** (☎ 615/262–0451).

TOURS

BOAT TOURS

The *General Jackson,* Opryland's four-deck paddle wheeler, has several two-hour cruises along the Cumberland River daily, including lunch and dinner cruises, with a music review in the Victorian Theater. Opryland's other boat is the *Music City Queen,* a 350-passenger paddle-wheel excursion boat on which there is a sightseeing lunch cruise every Tuesday.

➤ Fees and Schedules: **Gaylord Opryland** (☎ 615/871–6100).

BUS TOURS

Gray Line and Grand Ole Opry Tours have tours that include drives past stars' homes and visits to the Grand Ole Opry, Music Row, and the District. Johnny Walker Tours has three-hour sightseeing tours and special concert tours.

➤ Fees and Schedules: **Grand Ole Opry Tours** (☎ 615/889–9490, WEB www.gaylordopryland.com). **Gray Line** (☎ 800/251–1864, WEB www.graylinenashville.com). **Johnny Walker Tours** (☎ 615/834–8585 or 800/722–1524, WEB www.johnnywalkertours.com).

TRANSPORTATION AROUND NASHVILLE

Nashville Trolley Co., fare $1 (exact change), runs regularly scheduled trolleys through downtown and along Music Row during summer months. All-day trolley tokens are sold at the visitor information center for $3.

➤ Contacts: **Nashville Trolley Co.** (☎ 615/862–5950).

VISITOR INFORMATION

The Visitor Information Center is loaded with information and has staffers who know Nashville.

➤ TOURIST INFORMATION: **Nashville Visitor Center** (✉ Arena Tower at 5th Ave. and Broadway, ☎ 615/259–4747, WEB www.nashvillecvb. com).

EAST TENNESSEE

East Tennessee combines wholesome vacation ingredients much in the way a skilled mountain cook creates a sumptuous down-home feast, with bounty from forests, fields, ice-cold streams, and the family farm. From the misty heights of the Great Smoky Mountains to the Holston, French Broad, Nolichucky, and Tennessee rivers, this exquisitely beautiful part of the state beckons with a cornucopia of scenic grandeur and recreational possibilities from hiking to white-water rafting. The highest and most rugged elevations are in the Great Smoky Mountains National Park, a cool and scenic retreat for those seeking relief from the humidity of summer.

Numbers in the margin correspond to points of interest on the East Tennessee map.

Oak Ridge

162 mi east of Nashville.

The famous Atomic City was established secretly during World War II. Some of the original installations here include the **Oak Ridge National Laboratory,** still involved in programs of nuclear fission and magnetic fusion energy; the **Graphite Reactor,** 10 mi southwest, now a National Historic Landmark with a display area open to the public; and the **K-25 Visitors Overlook,** for views of the **Oak Ridge Gaseous Diffusion Plant,** where uranium is enriched for use in nuclear reactors.

The **American Museum of Science and Energy** focuses on uses of nuclear, solar, and geothermal energy, mainly for peaceful purposes. Exhibits include hands-on experiments, demonstrations, and computer games. A slide show furnishes valuable background on Oak Ridge and the museum. ✉ *300 S. Tulane Ave.,* ☎ *865/576–3200,* WEB *www. amse.org.* ⊡ *$3.* ☉ *Tues.–Sun. 9–5.*

Outdoor Activities and Sports

South Hills Golf Club (✉ 795 Tuskegee Dr., ☎ 865/483–5747) has an 18-hole, par-72 golf course open to the public.

Knoxville

48   *25 mi southeast of Oak Ridge.*

In 1786 patriot general James White and a few pioneer settlers built a fort beside the Tennessee River. A few years later, territorial governor William Blount selected White's fort as capital of the newly formed Territory of the United States South of the River Ohio and renamed the settlement Knoxville after his longtime friend, Secretary of War Henry Knox. It flourished from its beginning and became the state capital when Tennessee was admitted to the Union in 1796.

Throughout the 20th century, and into the 21st, Knoxville has been synonymous with energy: the headquarters of the Tennessee Valley Authority (TVA), with its hydroelectric dams and impounded recreational lakes, is here, and during World War II, atomic energy was secretly developed at nearby Oak Ridge. Today the University of Tennessee adds

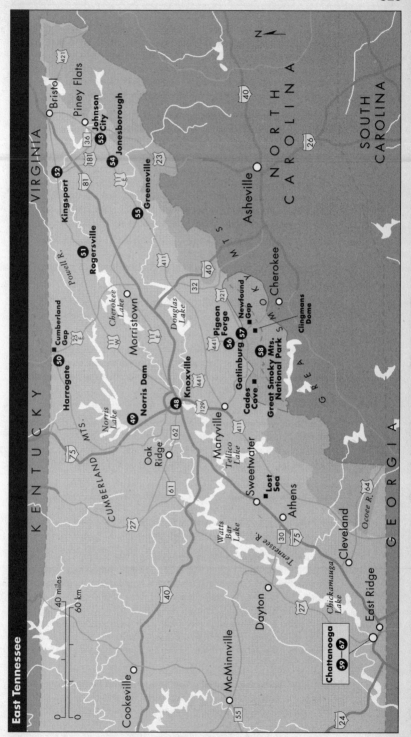

East Tennessee

VIRGINIA

KENTUCKY

NORTH CAROLINA

SOUTH CAROLINA

GEORGIA

Bristol

Piney Flats

Johnson City

Jonesborough

Kingsport

Rogersville

Greeneville

Asheville

Cumberland Gap

Harrogate

Morristown

Cherokee Lake

Douglas Lake

Norris Dam

Norris Lake

Knoxville

Pigeon Forge

Gatlinburg

Cades Cove

Great Smoky Mts. National Park

Newfound Gap

Cherokee

Clingmans Dome

GREAT SMOKY MTS.

Oak Ridge

Maryville

Tellico Lake

Sweetwater

Lost Sea

Athens

Cleveland

Watts Bar Lake

Tennessee R.

Ocoee R.

Chickamauga Lake

East Ridge

Dayton

McMinnville

Cookeville

Chattanooga

Powell R.

CUMBERLAND MTS.

N

40 miles

60 km

421

36

181

81

E

23

40

26

25

E

111

411

32

40

321

441

129

411

62

75

61

27

30

75

64

27

40

55

24

43

49

50

51

52

53

54

55

56

57

58

59 — 67

its own energy—both intellectual and cultural—to this dynamic city, and a riverfront development, Volunteer Landing, is alive with shops, restaurants, and residential space. The city's motto is "Where Nature and Technology Meet." Knoxville is surrounded by Oak Ridge National Laboratory and three national parks—Great Smoky Mountains National Park, Cumberland Gap National Historic Park, and Big South Fork National River and Recreation Area.

At the **Governor William Blount Mansion,** a modest white-frame structure dating from 1792, the governor and his associates planned the admission of Tennessee as the 16th state in the Union. The home is furnished with original and period antiques, along with memorabilia of Blount's checkered career. A **visitor center** adjacent to the 1818 **Craighead-Jackson House** presents an introductory slide program, museum exhibits, and a glass collection. ⊠ *200 W. Hill Ave.,* ☎ *865/525–2375,* WEB *www.blountmansion.org.* ⊡ *$4.95.* ☉ *Apr.–Dec., Mon.–Sat. 9:30–5; Jan.–Mar., weekdays 9:30–5; last tour at 4.*

Different eras of Knoxville history are celebrated at **James White Fort,** a series of seven log cabins with authentic furnishings and pioneer artifacts. ⊠ *205 E. Hill Ave.,* ☎ *865/525–6514,* ☉ *Mon.–Fri. 9:30–4.30, Sat. 9.30–3.30.* ⊡ *$5.*

John Sevier Historical Site (⊠ 1220 John Sevier Hwy., ☎ 865/573–5508) houses Marble Springs, the summer home of John Sevier, Tennessee's first governor.

The **Armstrong-Lockett House,** an elegant farm mansion dating from 1834, showcases American and British furniture, silver, and ornate appointments, along with terraces and fountains in Italianate gardens. ⊠ *2728 Kingston Pike,* ☎ *865/637–3163.* ☉ *Tues.–Sat. 10–4, Sun. 1–4.* ⊡ *$5.*

The **Mabry-Hazen House** served as headquarters for both Confederate and Union forces during the Civil War. It was built by prominent Knoxvillian Joseph A. Mabry Jr. in 1858 and is now on the National Historic Register. ⊠ *1711 Dandridge Ave.,* ☎ *865/522–8661.* ⊡ *$5.* ☉ *Tues.–Fri. 10–5, Sat. 10–2.*

The **McClung Museum,** on the University of Tennessee campus, has diverse collections in anthropology, natural history, geology, science, and fine arts. ⊠ *1327 Circle Park Dr.,* ☎ *865/974–2144,* WEB *http://mcclungmuseum.utk.edu.* ⊡ *Free.* ☉ *Mon.–Sat. 9–5, Sun. 1–5.*

The **Knoxville Museum of Art** is housed in a handsome 53,000–square-ft structure at World's Fair Park. Designed by renowned museum architect Edward Larrabee Barnes, the four-level concrete-and-steel building is faced in Tennessee pink marble. The museum includes four exhibition galleries, an exploratory gallery for children, a great hall, an auditorium, a museum store, and outdoor sculpture and educational program gardens. ⊠ *1050 World's Fair Park Dr.,* ☎ *865/525–6101,* WEB *www.knoxart.org.* ⊡ *$3.* ☉ *Tues.–Thurs. and Sat. 10–5, Fri. 10–9, Sun. noon–5.*

☙ The **East Tennessee Discovery Center and Akima Planetarium** contain pioneer tools and clothes, mounted animals, and fresh- and saltwater aquariums. Children love the hands-on and audiovisual exhibits. ⊠ *516 Beaman St., in Chilhowee Park,* ☎ *865/594–1480.* ⊡ *$3.* ☉ *Weekdays 9–5, Sat. 10–5; no admissions after 4; planetarium show times vary.*

☙ You can spend a full day at the **Knoxville Zoological Park,** famous for breeding large-cat species and African elephants. Among the 1,100 animals are rare red pandas, wild creatures native to the African plains, polar bears, seals, and penguins. The working miniature steam train, elephant rides, and petting zoo will keep kids occupied for hours. Gorilla Valley, Cheetah Savanna, and Chimpanzee Ridge are among the best exhibits. ⊠ *In Chilhowee Park on Rutledge Pike S, 4½ mi east of I–40 Exit 392,* ☎ *865/637–5331,* WEB *www.knoxville-zoo.org.* ☒ *$8.* ☉ *Memorial Day–Labor Day, daily 9:30–6; Labor Day–Memorial Day, daily 10–4:30.*

Volunteer Landing, a festive development of shops, restaurants, houses, and a park along the Tennessee River, is being finished in phases. The **Gateway Regional Visitor Center** (⊠ 900 Volunteer Landing Lane, ☎ 865/971–4440 or 800/727–8045, WEB www.volunteermarina.com) offers an overview of the region. The mile-long development includes such restaurants as Calhoun's on the River and Regas Riverside Tavern.

Near Volunteer Landing, the **Women's Basketball Hall of Fame** is the first Hall of Fame devoted exclusively to women's sports. Exhibits include a collection of 23 jerseys from the WNBA's inaugural all-star game, a modern locker room where you can listen to halftime talks by some of the country's top coaches, along with three practice courts where you can work on your dribble or try on historic uniforms. ⊠ *700 Hall of Fame Dr.,* ☎ *865/633–9000,* WEB *www.wbhof.com.* ☒ *$7.95.* ☉ *Mon.–Sat. 10–7, Sun. 1–6.*

Dining and Lodging

$$–$$$ ✕ **Copper Cellar/Cumberland Grill.** A favorite of the college crowd and young professionals, the original downstairs Copper Cellar is intimate, with friendly service. Upstairs, the Cumberland Grill serves aged Colorado beef, fresh seafood, salads, sandwiches, and desserts. There is a children's menu and a lavish Sunday brunch. ⊠ *1807 Cumberland Ave., across from University of Tennessee campus,* ☎ *865/673–3411,* WEB *www.coppercellar.com. AE, D, DC, MC, V.*

$$–$$$ ✕ **Regas Restaurant.** This cozy Knoxville classic, with fireplaces and
★ original art, has been around for more than 75 years. The specialty, prime rib, is baked very slowly all day, then sliced to order and served with creamy horseradish sauce. ⊠ *318 N. Gay St.,* ☎ *865/637–9805. AE, D, DC, MC, V. No lunch Sat.*

$–$$ ✕ **Calhoun's on the River.** Delicious barbecued ribs are served riverside at this sprawling rib house across the street from the site of one of Knoxville's original hot spots, the long-gone Chisholm's Tavern of pioneer days. Calhoun's ribs are famous throughout the South. ⊠ *400 Neyland Dr.,* ☎ *865/673–3399. Reservations not accepted. AE, D, DC, MC, V.*

$–$$$ 🏨 **Hyatt Regency Knoxville.** This is a handsome, contemporary adap-
★ tation of an Aztec pyramid atop a hill overlooking the Tennessee River, the city, and mountainous hinterlands. The eight-story skylighted atrium lobby blends modern furnishings and art in Meso-American motifs with abundant flora and colorful accessories. Rooms, in light woods and pastels, have either windows or balconies that open to fresh breezes. ⊠ *500 Hill Ave. SE, Box 88, 37915,* ☎ *865/637–1193 or 800/ 233–1234,* FAX *865/522–5911,* WEB *www.hyatt.com. 384 rooms, 25 suites. Restaurant, coffee shop, pool, gym, volleyball, sports bar. AE, D, DC, MC, V.*

$ 🏨 **La Quinta Motor Inn.** The rooms here are spacious and well lighted, with convenient working areas. ⊠ *258 N. Peters Rd., 37923,* ☎ *865/ 690–9777 or 800/531–5900,* FAX *865/531–8304,* WEB *www.laquinta.com. 130 rooms. Pool. AE, D, DC, MC, V.*

Outdoor Activities and Sports

Whittle Springs Municipal Golf Course (⊠ 3113 Valley View Dr., ☎ 865/525–1022) is an 18-hole, par-70 golf course open to the public.

Nightlife and the Arts

The **Knoxville Opera Company** (☎ 865/524–0795) sponsors New York Metropolitan Opera competitions each year, along with two locally produced operatic performances. The **Knoxville Symphony Orchestra** (☎ 865/523–1178) presents nearly 200 concerts a year, often with esteemed guest artists. The Knoxville Opera Company and the Knoxville Symphony Orchestra both perform at the **Bijou Theater Center** (✉ 803 S. Gay St., ☎ 865/522–0832), which also stages seasonal ballet and plays.

The Old City, on the north side of downtown, is the site of Knoxville's most varied nightlife, with restaurants and clubs sharing space with industries that have been in the warehouse district for decades. Among the nightspots to check out is **Patrick Sullivan's** (✉ 100 N. Central Ave., ☎ 865/637–4255) for saloon shenanigans. The piano lounge at the **Orangery Restaurant** (✉ The Orangery, 5412 Kingston Pike, ☎ 865/588–2964) is the place to go for a more "old-world" experience.

Norris

25 mi northwest of Knoxville.

Scenic U.S. 441 leads to Norris, a delightful planned town built in 1933 as a workers' community during construction of the Tennessee Valley Authority's first dam. The **Norris Dam,** which spans the Clinch River and impounds a 72-mi-long lake, has a visitor lobby and two overlooks. Some of the best views, though, are from Norris Dam State Resort Park, which has cabins and campsites.

Norris's prime attraction is the **Museum of Appalachia,** where about 35 log structures—among them a molasses mill powered by mules—have been restored to reflect the hardscrabble life of the early mountaineers. More than 250,000 period furnishings and implements are in the buildings, and there is a working farm. Musicians play mountain music daily from April to December. ✉ *2819 Andersonville Hwy.,* ☎ *865/494–7680,* WEB *www.thesmokies.com.* ☎ *$10.* ☉ *Daily 8–5; open later in summer.*

Outdoor Activities and Sports

At Norris Lake, there's seasonal angling for striped bass, walleye, white bass, and muskie, as well as boat launch ramps (but no rentals) at **Norris Dam State Resort Park** (✉ 125 Village Green Circle, Lake City, ☎ 865/426–7461, WEB www.state.tn.us). Largemouth and white bass swim in Cherokee, Douglas, and Fort Loudon lakes. Trout lovers do best at Tellico-Chilhowee Lakes, especially at night in April and May. Fly-fishing is popular in the Smokies' many streams.

Harrogate

50 *50 mi northeast of Norris.*

Harrogate, by the Virginia border, is home to **Lincoln Memorial University.** Founded in 1897, the school celebrates the Great Emancipator's principles and philosophies. The **Abraham Lincoln Library and Museum** contains one of the world's largest collections of Lincolniana. ✉ *On Lincoln Memorial University campus, on U.S. 25E,* ☎ *423/869–6235.* ☎ *$3.* ☉ *Weekdays 9–4, Sat. 11–4, Sun. 1–4.*

Rogersville

51 *45 mi southeast of Harrogate.*

Along U.S. 11W, Rogersville is a little hideaway East Tennessee town established in 1786. All of downtown is on the National Register of Historic Places, and it has both the oldest courthouse and oldest inn in the state. A walking-tour brochure, available throughout town, points out the various sites of interest.

Kingsport

52 *30 mi northeast of Rogersville.*

Founded in 1761, Kingsport is along U.S. 11 W, surrounded by hills, meadows, and woodlands. At **Exchange Place, Gaines-Preston Farm,** a restored pioneer homestead, craftspeople demonstrate their skills in commodious log houses. Their handmade quilts, baskets, wood carvings, ceramics, and stuffed dolls are sold in nearby shops. ⊠ *4812 Orebank Rd.,* ☎ *423/288–6071.* ✍ *Free.* ⊙ *May–Oct., Thurs.–Fri. 10–2, weekends 2–4:30.*

Outdoor Activities and Sports

The 18-hole, par-72 **Warrior's Path State Park Golf Course** (⊠ 1687 Fall Creek Rd., ☎ 423/323–4990) is open to the public.

Johnson City

53 *22 mi southeast of Kingsport.*

Reached via U.S. 23, Johnson City is an important center for agriculture, manufacturing, and education—**Washington College,** the oldest institution of higher education in the state, and **East Tennessee State University,** with more than 9,000 students are both here. At **Tipton-Haynes Historic Site,** the 19th-century main house, outbuildings, horse barn, and law office have been painstakingly restored. ⊠ *2620 S. Roan St., off I–181 Exit 31, 1 mi south via University Pkwy. and S. Roan St.,* ☎ *423/926–3631,* ⸬WEB *www.tipton-haynes.org.* ✍ *$4.* ⊙ *Apr.–Nov., Mon.–Sat. 10–4; Dec.–Mar., Mon.–Fri. 10–4.*

OFF THE
BEATEN PATH

ROCKY MOUNT MUSEUM – This two-story log mansion, completed in 1772, was Governor William Blount's territorial capitol from 1790 until he moved to Knoxville two years later. Faithful restoration and careful selection of authentic furnishings testify eloquently to the simple pioneer lifestyle. The entire farmstead is presented as living history, and you get to see the kitchen, slave quarters, blacksmith shop, and even a flax house where there are often weaving demonstrations. ⊠ *4 mi northeast of Johnson City on U.S. 11E at Piney Flats, 200 Hyder Hill Rd.,* ☎ *423/538–7396 or 888/538–1791,* FAX *423/538–1086.* ✍ *$6.* ⊙ *Mon.–Sat. 10–3.*

Jonesborough

54 *10 mi southwest of Johnson City.*

The state's oldest town beckons visitors to admire a trio of antebellum churches, lovely vintage houses, brick and wooden fretwork shops, and the courthouse, all dating from the late 1700s. The Pangeaea World Music Festival brings international musicians to Jonesborough at the beginning of May. During October's famous National Storytelling Festival, professional and amateur storytellers from throughout the world come for a weekend to spin their tales. At the **Visitor Center and History Museum** (⊠ 117 Boone St., ☎ 423/753–1010, WEB http://jonesborough.tricon.net), a video slide show and a monthly art exhibit present aspects of the town's history.

Greeneville

55 *25 mi southwest of Jonesborough.*

In 1826 a young Andrew Johnson (later 17th president of the United States) settled in Greeneville, which was founded in 1783. After his arduous trek over the mountains from North Carolina, Johnson opened a tailor shop and married. The **Andrew Johnson National Historic Site** preserves his primitive tailor shop, the homestead where he lived from 1851 until his death in 1875, and his hilltop grave site, marked by an elaborate monument. Displays in the visitor center include notes he made at his impeachment trial. ☒ *Depot and College Sts.,* ☎ *423/638–3551,* WEB *www.nps.gov.* ☒ *Homestead $2.* ☉ *Daily 9–5.*

Pigeon Forge

56 *25 mi southeast of Knoxville.*

Pigeon Forge, home of mountain native Dolly Parton's namesake theme park, Dollywood, has exploded with enough heavy-duty outlet shopping and kids' entertainment (from indoor skydiving simulators to laser tag) to keep families busy for a few days. But the intentionally cornpone image can become wearing, and it fails to reflect the quiet folksiness of the Appalachian communities scattered throughout these parts. Pigeon Forge has more than 200 outlet specialty stores, crafts shops, country hoedown emporiums, and kid-friendly attractions that line the main thoroughfare for several miles.

A favorite with families is **Carbo's Smoky Mountain Police Museum,** housing police memorabilia such as badges, guns, and the car in which legendary West Tennessee sheriff Buford Pusser was killed in a traffic accident. ☒ *3311 Pkwy.,* ☎ *865/453–1358.* ☒ *$6.95.* ☉ *Apr., weekends 10–5; May, Fri.–Wed. 10–5; June–Aug., daily 10–5; Sept.–Oct., Fri.–Wed. 10–5.*

The 1830s-era **Old Mill,** beside the Little Pigeon River, still grinds corn, wheat, and rye on water-powered stone wheels. A 20-minute tour explains the process. Flour, meal, grits, and buckwheat are for sale. ☒ *160 Old Mill Ave.,* ☎ *865/453–4628,* WEB *www.old-mill.com.* ☒ *$3.* ☉ *Mon.–Sat. 8:30–6:30, Sun. 10–6.*

★ **Dollywood,** singer Dolly Parton's popular theme park, embodies the country superstar's own flamboyance—plenty of Hollywood flash mixed with simple country charm that you either love or hate. This endeavor brings to life the folklore, fun, food, and music of the Great Smokies, which inspired many of Parton's early songs. In a re-created 1880 mountain village, scores of talented and friendly craftspeople demonstrate their artistry. Museum exhibits trace Parton's rise to stardom from her backwoods upbringing. There are many amusement rides (including Daredevil Falls, a waterfall ride), but music, of course, is the park's underpinning: live shows are performed on the park's seven stages, and several times per season, Dolly shows up for a surprise appearance. The gala Harvest Celebration, held from October to early November, includes the Smokies' only outdoor crafts festival as well as the Southern Gospel Jubilee. Smoky Mountain Christmas is the star attraction from mid-November through December. When hunger strikes, try Aunt Granny's Restaurant for down-home mountain cookery. ☒ *1020 Dollywood La.,* ☎ *865/428–9488 or 800/365–5996,* WEB *www.dollywood.com.* ☒ *$34.25; free next day on tickets purchased after 3.* ☉ *Mid-Apr.–Oct., daily 9–6; extended hrs mid-June–mid-Aug. Closed Tues. and Thurs. in May and Sept., Thurs. in Oct.; call for varying hrs Nov.–Dec.*

Ogle's Water Park. This family park has a giant wave pool, a kiddie play area, and 10 water slides. ☒ *2530 Pkwy., Pigeon Forge,* ☎ *865/453–8741,* WEB *www.oglesproperties.com.* ☒ *$21.* ☉ *May, weekends 10–6; June–Labor Day, daily 10–7.*

Dining and Lodging

$-$$ ✕ **Apple Tree Inn Restaurant.** A traditional East Tennessee menu is of-
★ fered here, including fried chicken and spoon bread, a regal soufflé of
cornmeal, flour, eggs, buttermilk, and seasonings, served hot from the
baking dish. Order family style or individually in this very relaxed dining room. ⊠ *3215 Pkwy.,* ☎ *865/453–4961. AE, MC, V. Closed Dec.–
Feb.*

$$ ⊡ **Hampton Inn & Suites.** Conveniently located near shopping, restau-
rants, and theaters, this chain property has double rooms as well as
one- and two-bedroom suites with kitchens. ⊠ *2025 Pkwy.,* ☎ *865/
428–1600 or 800/310–8082,* ℻ *865/429–3347. 101 rooms, 26 suites.
Pool, outdoor hot tub, gym, laundry facilities. AE, D, DC, MC, V. CP.*

$$ ⊡ **Holiday Inn.** This inn is in the middle of the action. Its vast Holidome
Indoor Recreation Center has activities for everyone in the family. Rooms
are spacious and include refrigerators, irons, and coffeemakers. ⊠ *3230
Pkwy., 37863,* ☎ *865/428–2700 or 800/782–3119,* ℻ *865/428–2700,*
ⱲⒺⒷ *www.sixcontinentshotels.com. 204 rooms, 4 suites. Restaurant, in-
door pool, health club, hot tub, sauna. AE, D, DC, MC, V.*

$-$$ ⊡ **Best Western Plaza Inn.** Convenient to shops, restaurants, and at-
tractions, the Best Western is a best bet for families. Rooms are spacious and well furnished, and all have refrigerators; some overlook
mountain scenery, others an indoor swimming pool. ⊠ *3755 Pkwy.,
Box 626, 37868,* ☎ *865/453–5538 or 800/232–5656,* ℻ *865/453–
2619. 198 rooms, 2 suites. 2 pools, 1 indoor pool, wading pool, hot
tub, sauna, recreation room. AE, D, DC, MC, V. CP.*

$-$$ ⊡ **Grand Resort Hotel and Convention Center.** This centrally located
five-story inn has some ultramodern rooms with water beds and fireplaces. A few rooms even have large whirlpool tubs. ⊠ *3171 Pkwy.,
37863,* ☎ *865/453–1000 or 800/362–1188,* ℻ *865/453–0056,* ⱲⒺⒷ
*www.grandresorthotel.com. 415 rooms, 12 suites. Restaurant, pool,
hot tub. AE, D, DC, MC, V.*

Nightlife and the Arts

Pigeon Forge has a host of theaters. From March through October, hearty
chicken-and–pork loin dinners are accompanied by a colorful, West-
ern-theme musical show and rodeo at **Dixie Stampede** (⊠ 3849 Pkwy.,
☎ 865/453–4400 or 800/356–1676).

The **Comedy Barn** (⊠ 2775 Pkwy., ☎ 865/428–5222) presents a family variety show. The **Country Tonight Theater** (⊠ 129 Showplace Blvd.,
☎ 865/453–2003) has foot-stompin' country music and a magic show
mid-March through December. The **Louise Mandrell Theater** (⊠ 2046
Pkwy., ☎ 865/453–6263), open April through December, is a high-
energy show starring Mandrell, who sings, dances, and plays many instruments.

Shopping

Every imaginable outlet store can be found somewhere in the maze of
outlet centers at the heart of Pigeon Forge. Three major outlet malls
are the indoor **Belz Factory Outlet Mall** (⊠ 2655 Teaster La., ☎ 865/
453–3503), the **Pigeon Forge Factory Outlet Mall** (⊠ 2850 Pkwy., ☎
865/428–2828), and the **Tanger Factory Outlet Center** (⊠ 161 East Wears
Valley Rd., ☎ 865/428–7002). The **Tanger Outlet Center at Five Oaks**
(⊠ 1645 Pkwy., ☎ 865/453–1053) is in Sevierville, a few miles north
of Pigeon Forge.

For mountain crafts, stop at **Old Mill Village** (⊠ off Parkway, turn left
at traffic light No. 7, next to Patriot Park), whose shops include **Pigeon Forge Pottery** (☎ 865/453–3883) and **Waynehouse Artcrafts** (☎
865/453–6798).

Gatlinburg

57 *8 mi southeast of Pigeon Forge.*

Gateway city to Great Smoky Mountains National Park, Gatlinburg, popular with honeymooners and families, has steadily expanded from a remote little town with a sprinkling of hotels, chalets, and mountain crafts shops to the sprawling network of minigolf courses and home-made-candy "shoppes" it is today. During the summer, the town is clogged with visitors, complete with the annoyances of traffic jams and packed restaurants. Nevertheless, Gatlinburg is Tennessee's premier mountain resort town and is set in the narrow valley of the Little Pigeon River—actually a turbulent mountain stream.

With more than 400 specialty shops, Gatlinburg is also a browsing heaven. You can visit the local trout farms around the town. The **Gatlinburg Sky Lift** (⊠ ☎ 865/436–4307), via which you can reach the top of Crockett Mountain, makes a fun outing for the family. There is a **Guinness World Record Museum** (631 Parkway, ☎ 865/436–9100), which includes the "Batmobile" from the 1960s TV series and original Beatles memorabilia. The **Ober Gatlinburg Tramway** (☎ 865/436–5423) leads to a mountaintop amusement park, ski center, and shopping mall/crafts market. **Arrowmont School of Arts & Crafts** (⊠ 556 Pkwy., ☎ 865/436–5860) is a nationally known visual arts complex. Gatlinburg also hosts numerous festivals, the longest of which is the Smoky Mountain Lights, which runs from November through February, when the town is decorated with more than 2 million lights.

Dining and Lodging

$$–$$$ ✕ **Smoky Mountain Trout House.** Of the 15 distinctive trout preparations to choose from at this cozy restaurant, an old favorite is trout Eisenhower: panfried, with cornmeal breading and served with bacon-and-butter sauce. Prime rib, country ham, and grilled chicken are also on the menu. ⊠ *410 Pkwy.,* ☎ *865/436–5416. Reservations not accepted. AE, DC, MC, V. No lunch.*

$$ ✕ **Heidelberg Restaurant.** German, Swiss, and American dishes are served at this restaurant. There's German entertainment nightly. ⊠ *605 Airport Road,* ☎ *865/430–3094. AE, D, DC, MC, V.*

$–$$ ✕ **Burning Bush Restaurant.** Reproduction antique furnishings and accessories evoke a colonial style. Broiled Tennessee quail and beef Rossini—an 8-ounce fillet served on an English muffin with Madeira sauce—are house specialties. Bountiful breakfasts are also offered. ⊠ ★ *1151 Pkwy.,* ☎ *865/436–4669. AE, D, MC, V.*

$ ✕ **Pancake Pantry.** This restaurant, with its century-old brick, polished-oak paneling, rustic copper accessories, and spacious windows, is a family favorite. Austrian apple-walnut pancakes covered with apple cider compote, black walnuts, apple slices, sweet spices, powdered sugar, and whipped cream are a house specialty. Other selections include omelets, sandwiches, and fresh salads. Box lunches are available for mountain picnics. ⊠ *628 Pkwy.,* ☎ *865/436–4724. Reservations not accepted. No credit cards. No dinner.*

$$$ ✕🖬 **Buckhorn Inn.** This small inn owned and operated by the Young ★ family is set on 40 acres of remote woodlands about 5 mi outside Gatlinburg. Guests—including seclusion-seeking diplomats, government officials, and celebrities—have been coming here for more than 40 years. The views of Mt. LeConte and the Great Smokies are spectacular, and the Great Smoky Arts and Crafts Community is nearby. The interior has wicker rockers, paintings by local artists, a huge stone fireplace, and French doors that open onto a large stone porch. All rooms are spacious, and some have king-size beds. Full breakfasts are included

in the rate. A four-course dinner, with such items as home-baked breads, creamed soups, marinated beef tenderloin, and fruit tortes, is available to guests and nonguests, by reservation only. ✉ *Off U.S. 321, 2140 Tudor Mountain Rd., 37738,* ☎ *865/436–4668,* WEB *www. buckhorninn.com. 9 rooms, 7cottages, 1 2-bedroom house. Fishing, hiking. D, MC, V.*

$$–$$$ 🏨 **Park Vista Resort Hotel.** Set on a mountain ledge, this large hotel has modern, lavishly decorated public areas and spacious, elegant guest rooms, each with a balcony overlooking colorful gardens, the town of Gatlinburg, the Little Pigeon River, and the mountains beyond. Nonetheless, this white, semicircular contemporary tower is a jarring sight in the Great Smoky Mountains. ✉ *705 Cherokee Orchard Rd., 37738,* ☎ *865/436–9211 or 800/421–7275,* FAX *865/436–5141,* WEB *www.parkvista.com. 306 rooms, 6 suites. Restaurant, 2 indoor pools, wading pool, hot tub, sauna, lounge, sports bar, meeting rooms. AE, DC, MC, V.*

$–$$$ 🏨 **Holiday Inn Sunspree Resort.** This complex offers kids and adults
★ plenty to do and also has family programs. All rooms have a refrigerator and coffeemaker, and there is a general store. The hotel is two blocks from the convention center. ✉ *520 Historic Nature Trail, 37738,* ☎ *865/436–9201 or 800/465–4329,* FAX *865/436–7974,* WEB *www. sixcontinentshotels.com. 400 rooms. 2 restaurants, 1 outdoor pool, 1 indoor pool, hot tub, sauna, nightclub, meeting rooms. AE, D, DC, MC, V.*

$$ 🏨 **Best Western Twin Islands Motel.** In the center of Gatlinburg, beside the surging Little Pigeon River, this motel is notable for its contemporary architectural style. All rooms have balconies overlooking the river. Kitchenette units are also available. ✉ *539 Pkwy., 37738,* ☎ *865/436–5121 or 800/223–9299,* FAX *865/436–6208. 97 rooms, 10 suites. Restaurant, pool, fishing, playground. AE, DC, MC, V.*

$ 🏨 **Rainbow Motel.** This small, neat, well-maintained lodging is a pleasant choice for budget-minded vacationers. ✉ *390 E. Pkwy. (3 blocks east of U.S. 441), Box 1397, 37738,* ☎ *865/436–5887 or 800/422–8922,* WEB *www.rainbowmotelandrentals.com. 41 rooms, 1 efficiency, 2 two-bedroom units. Pool. D, MC, V.*

Nightlife and the Arts

Sweet Fanny Adams Theatre and Music Hall (✉ 461 Pkwy., ☎ 877/ 388–5484 or 865/436–4039, WEB www.sweetfannyadamstheatre.com) stages original musical comedies, Gay '90s revues, and old-fashioned sing-alongs. Reservations are advised.

Outdoor Activities and Sports

Bent Creek Golf Resort (✉ 3919 E. Pkwy., ☎ 865/436–3947) has an 18-hole, par-72 course that is open to the public.

Shopping

The mountain towns of East Tennessee are known for Appalachian folk crafts, especially wood carvings, cornhusk dolls, pottery, dulcimers, and beautiful handmade quilts. The **Great Smoky Arts and Crafts Community** is a collection of 80 shops and craftspeople's studios along 8 mi of rambling country road. Begun in 1937, the community includes workers in leather, pottery, weaving, hand-wrought pewter, stained glass, quilt making, hand carving, marquetry, and more. Everything sold here is made on the premises by the community members. Also here are two restaurants and the popular Wild Plum Tearoom. ✉ *Off U.S. 321, 3 mi east of Gatlinburg,* ☎ *865/671–3600,* WEB *www.smokymtnarts-crafts. com. For more information:* ✉ *Box 807, Gatlinburg 37738.*

Great Smoky Mountains National Park

★ ⑤⑧ *45 mi from Knoxville.*

At Great Smoky Mountains National Park, the southern Appalachians reach their ultimate grandeur as 16 peaks soar more than 6,000 ft. Fall brings an unparalleled fiesta of colors to these mountains, and in the early springtime wild azaleas and rhododendrons lace the mountainsides with delicate pinks, lavenders, and whites. No wonder hikers, campers, and boaters flock to what the National Park Service says is America's most heavily visited national park, whose 800 acres are divided almost equally between Tennessee and North Carolina.

From Gatlinburg, the northern gateway to the park, drive south along the scenic Newfound Gap Road (U.S. 441) to the Sugarlands Visitor Center at park headquarters, which has informative films, exhibits, maps, and brochures about the park. Driving along on the Newfound Gap Road, be sure to stop often at scenic overlooks, perhaps taking time to explore one or more of the nature trails that lead off from many of them. The road ascends to **Newfound Gap** on the Tennessee–North Carolina border, a haunting viewpoint. From here, a 7-mi spur road leads to **Clingmans Dome**—at 6,643 ft, the highest point in Tennessee—where you can walk up a spiral pathway to an observation tower for panoramic views of the Smokies. Autumn is the favorite season for the spectacular foliage.

The isolated mountain valley of **Cades Cove,** at the junction of U.S. 321 and TN 73, has preserved 19th-century farmhouses, barns, churches, and an old gristmill that make it one of the region's most worthwhile attractions. Drive through on the 11-mi loop road (which can be very busy in season) or, better yet, walk the grounds to get a sense of the area and its history. From spring through fall, special park ranger programs and demonstrations describe the pioneer agriculture, crafts, and folkways in the Cove. At the old gristmill—open from April 5 through October, daily 9:30–5—you can take a tour and purchase stone-ground cornmeal. For a deep-forest drive, take Parson Branch Road, a quiet, one-way trek out of the park to U.S. 129. The Foothills Parkway will get you back into the park. ⊠ *107 Park Headquarters Rd., Gatlinburg 37738,* ☎ *865/436–1200,* 🌐 *www.nps.gov.* 🎫 *Free.*

Outdoor Activities and Sports

HIKING

An unusually elevated and scenic portion of the **Appalachian Trail** runs along high ridges in the Great Smoky Mountains National Park. The trail can be easily reached at Newfound Gap from U.S. 441.

HORSEBACK RIDING

Smoky Mountain Stables (⊠ U.S. 321 North, ☎ 865/436–5634) arranges guided horseback riding in Great Smoky Mountains National Park from March through November.

RAFTING

Rafting in the Smokies (☎ 865/436–5008 or 800/776–7238) offers guided white-water raft trips from March through October.

En Route   Driving between Great Smoky Mountains National Park and Chattanooga along U.S. 321, U.S. 411, or TN 68 will give travelers a chance to visit the **Lost Sea,** outside Sweetwater, where you can explore a 41½-acre underground lake by glass-bottom boat. ⊠ *TN 68, 140 Lost Sea Rd.,* ☎ *865/337–6616.* 🎫 *$9.* ⊙ *Nov.–Feb., daily 9–5; Mar.–Apr., daily 9–6; May–June and Aug., daily 9–7; July, daily 9–8; Sept.–Oct., daily 9–6.*

East Tennessee A to Z

AIRPORTS

Knoxville Airport is 12 mi from downtown.

➤ AIRPORT INFORMATION: **Knoxville Airport** (⊠ 2055 Alcoa Pkwy., ☎ 865/970–2773, WEB www.tys.org).

BUS TRAVEL

Greyhound has a station in Knoxville.

➤ BUS INFORMATION: **Greyhound** (100 East Magnolia Ave., ☎ 865/522–5144, 800/231–2222, WEB www.greyhound.com).

CAR TRAVEL

I–75 runs north–south from Kentucky through Knoxville, then to Chattanooga, where it enters Georgia. I–81 enters East Tennessee from Virginia at Bristol and continues southwest until it ends at the junction with I–40 northeast of Knoxville. I–40 enters from North Carolina, traces a northwesterly course to Knoxville, then heads west. U. S. 11 joins Chattanooga with Knoxville.

EMERGENCIES

Medical assistance is available in Knoxville at Baptist Hospital. The Kroger Pharmacy in Knoxville is open 24 hours.

➤ CONTACTS: **Ambulance, police** (☎ 911). **Baptist Hospital** (⊠ 137 Blount Ave., ☎ 865/632–5011). **Kroger Pharmacy** (⊠ 4409 C. C. Chapman Hwy., ☎ 865/573–9906).

LODGING

APARTMENT AND VILLA RENTALS

For reservations at hotels, motels, chalets, and condominiums throughout the Great Smoky Mountains area, contact Smoky Mountain Accommodations Reservation Service.

➤ LOCAL AGENTS: **Smoky Mountain Accommodations Reservation Service** (⊠ Box 947, Gatlinburg 37738, ☎ 865/436–6943 or 800/231–2230).

MEDIA

RADIO

FM: WDEF 92.3, contemporary easy listening; WMLB 97.5, adult contemporary; WUSY 101.7, country; WMYU 102.1, oldies; WIVK 107.7, country.

TOURS

Self-guided-tour maps and brochures are available at many local visitor information centers. In Pigeon Forge, Smoky Mountain Tours offers guided tours through East Tennessee back roads, the Smoky Mountains, and to major East Tennessee sites. The Smoky Mountain Adventure Guide Service offers custom guided trips for fishing, hiking, boating, camping, and other outdoor fun in the Smokies and along the Appalachian Trail.

A boat ride on the *Star of Knoxville* offers views of an especially scenic portion of the Tennessee River. Sightseeing excursions as well as lunch and dinner cruises are scheduled daily April through December.

➤ FEES AND SCHEDULES: **Smoky Mountain Tour Connection** (☎ 800/882–1061). **Steve Ellis Tour and Receptive/Smoky Mountain Show tickets** (☎ 800/953–7469). *Star of Knoxville* (⊠ Neyland Dr., Knoxville, ☎ 865/522–4630).

VISITOR INFORMATION

The Knoxville Area Convention and Visitors Bureau is open daily 8:30–5; the Northeast Tennessee Tourism Association is open weekdays 8–5. Pigeon Forge Chamber of Commerce is open weekdays 8–5, Saturday 8–8, and the Rogersville Chamber of Commerce is open weekdays 9–4.

➤ TOURIST INFORMATION: **Gatlinburg Chamber of Commerece** (✉ Box 527, Gatlinburg 37738, ☎ 800/822–1998, WEB www.gatlinburg-tennessee.com). **Gateway Regional Visitor Center** (✉ 900 Volunteer Landing La., Knoxville 37915, ☎ 865/971–4440 or 800/727–8045, WEB www.knoxville.org). **Pigeon Forge Chamber of Commerce** (✉ Box 1278, Pigeon Forge 37863, ☎ 865/453–5700 or 800/221–9858, WEB www.pigeonforgechamber.com). **Rogersville Hawkinsville County Chamber of Commerce** (✉ 415 S. Depot, Rogersville 37857, ☎ 423/272–2186, WEB www.rogersville.net).

CHATTANOOGA

Chattanooga is an up-and-coming river and railroad town with an intriguing past. In less than 20 years, Chattanooga has transformed itself from a polluted city struggling to clean up its outmoded industries to a bright, revitalized community that's a model for any small city looking to reinvent itself. Chattanooga's Tennessee Aquarium, the world's largest freshwater aquarium, is a must-see.

Back in 1969, Chattanooga ranked among the nation's worst in air pollution. Since the mid-1980s, civic pride and unity, as well as an $850 million downtown revitalization effort, have continued to transform the ragged downtown area into a vibrant community. A rich Civil War history, a verdant mountainous countryside, and the presence of such unabashedly old-fashioned, but popular, tourist attractions as Rock City Gardens and Ruby Falls laid the promising foundation for the city's comeback. New specialty museums, a restored carousel and interactive play fountain in Coolidge Park, and expanded shopping have added further appeal, particularly for families.

Downtown Chattanooga

Numbers in the text correspond to numbers in the margin and on the Chattanooga map.

The city's revitalized downtown, still a work in progress, has museums and shopping, in addition to an attractive riverfront walk. A good place to start exploring is the Chattanooga Visitors Center, next to the Tennessee Aquarium, at 2 Broad Street. It has brochures for sights and self-guided walking tours of historic districts, as well as combination tickets to many attractions.

A Good Tour

The riverfront **Tennessee Aquarium** (59), in **Ross's Landing Park and Plaza,** and the **Creative Discovery Museum** (60), two blocks south on Chestnut Street, are both ideal for children. You can take the Riverwalk or drive to the Bluff View Art District, near the **Hunter Museum of Art** (61) and the **Houston Museum of Decorative Art.** Retracing your steps on the Riverwalk, the **Walnut Street Bridge** (62) offers a chance to sit and rest or to walk and cycle above the Tennessee River. Back downtown, you can take a free electric bus shuttle south to the former train station, now part of a hotel called the **Chattanooga Choo-Choo** (63), and to **Warehouse Row,** which is full of designer outlet stores.

TIMING

You could easily spend a day downtown visiting the Tennessee Aquarium (worth several hours), IMAX theater, Creative Discovery Museum, and other museums. There is time ticketing for the aquarium, and you can make reservations for the IMAX.

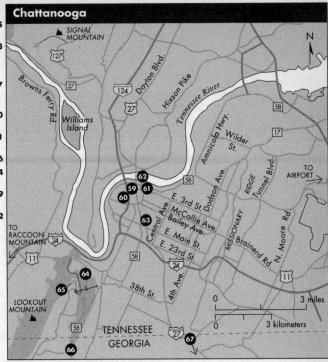

Sights to See

63 Chattanooga Choo-Choo. Chattanooga's turn-of-the-century terminal station, immortalized in song by Glen Miller in the 1940s, is now a Holiday Inn, but it's still one of the area's best-loved attractions. Stop by if only to see the elegant lobby under the original 85-ft freestanding dome, which appears much as it did before trains stopped chugging into the terminal in 1970. Though the dining room has a sense of grandeur about it, the food is standard. Save your appetite and explore the area around the renovated train cars (now used for lodging), the hotel's gardens, and a model railroad. ⊠ *1400 Market St.,* ☎ *423/ 266–5000,* WEB *www.choochoo.com.*

60 Creative Discovery Museum. Abundant, inventive hands-on activities and displays in four exhibit areas—an artist's studio, a musician's workshop, an inventor's studio, and a field scientist's lab—bring out the kid in visitors of all ages. In the artist's studio, for example, kids learn about and try printmaking, painting (including portraiture), and sculpture. The Little Yellow House play space has activities for children from 18 months to four years old. ⊠ *321 Chestnut St., 37402,* ☎ *423/756–2738,* WEB *www.cdmfun.org.* ⊶ *$7.95; parking $5.* ☾ *Memorial Day–Labor Day, daily 10–6; Labor Day–May, Tues.–Sat. 10–5, Sun. noon–5.*

OFF THE
BEATEN PATH

FRAZIER AVENUE ARTS DISTRICT – Across the river (you can walk over the Walnut Street Bridge) from downtown is this tourist and local hot spot, with restaurants, galleries, the Chattanooga Theatre Center, and shopping. A popular stop is the Mudpie Coffeehouse and Newsstand. It's about a half mile from the Tennessee Aquarium.

61 Hunter Museum of Art. Housed partially in a restored Classical Revival mansion, the riverside Hunter Museum, in the Bluff View Art District, houses an eclectic collection of mostly American paintings (from early portraits and Hudson River School works to impressionist paintings and abstract pieces by artists such as Helen Frankenthaler), photography, and sculpture. There's also a sculpture garden. ⊠ *10 Bluff View,* ☎ *423/267–0968,* WEB *www.huntermuseum.org.* 🎟 *$5.* ☉ *Tues.– Sat. 10–4:30, Sun. 1–4:30.*

Houston Museum of Decorative Art. This small Victorian home, in the Bluff View Art District, is packed literally to the rafters with mainly American decorative arts collected by the eccentric Anna Safley Houston (who eventually owned 15,000 pitchers). The emphasis is on antique art glass and American pressed glass; also of note are the pieces of blue Staffordshire and English lusterware china. ⊠ *201 High St.,* ☎ *423/267–7176,* WEB *www.chattanooga.net.* 🎟 *$6.* ☉ *Mon.–Sat. 9:30–4, Sun. noon–4.*

☾ **International Towing and Recovery Museum.** The first tow truck was created in Chattanooga, and this beguiling collection of shiny vehicles from the past and present grab the attention of adults as well as kids. ⊠ *401 Broad St., Downtown,* ☎ *423/267–3132,* WEB *www. internationaltowingmuseum.org.* 🎟 *$4.* ☉ *Weekdays 10–4:30, weekends 11–5.*

Ross's Landing Park and Plaza. This area includes the **Tennessee Aquarium** and **Tennessee Aquarium 3-D IMAX Theater.** World-class architects, artists, and landscape designers have provided an open-air retrospective of Chattanooga's long history as the starting point for the infamous Trail of Tears, the forced march of the Cherokee tribe from their home territories; the site of key Civil War battles; and a major railroad town. The Chattanooga Visitors Center is also here.

★ ☾ ➎➒ **Tennessee Aquarium.** Chattanooga *is* river country, and the world's largest freshwater facility of its kind, a 130,000-square-ft monument to the Tennessee River, tells the story. This aquarium displays the inhabitants behind glass in a spectacular 60-ft canyon with two living forests and 22 tanks. Five main areas, including explorations of the Tennessee River from its origin in the Appalachian highlands to midstream and on to the Mississippi Delta, contain habitats and tanks. In the Discovery Hall visitors can reach out and touch various species of aquatic life from throughout the region. *Seahorses: Beyond Imagination* is the current changing exhibit, featuring hands-on activities and many seahorse species. Designed by the Cambridge Seven Associates, who created Baltimore's National Aquarium, the aquarium's contemporary riverside structure, crowned with four glass rooftop pyramids, is a distinctive element in the city's low, sprawling skyline. A separate building holds the Tennessee Aquarium IMAX 3-D Theater. ⊠ *1 Broad St., Downtown,* ☎ *800/262–0695,* WEB *www.tnaqua.org.* 🎟 *$12.95; $17 for joint ticket with IMAX 3-D theater.* ☉ *Daily 10– 6, until 8 on summer weekends.*

☾ **Tennessee Aquarium IMAX 3-D Theater.** The six-story-high screen, 3-D cameras, and special technology give viewers the feeling of being part of the movie. Educational films explore topics such as outer space, dolphins, and other wildlife. An environmental learning lab is part of the theater. ⊠ *201 Chestnut St., Downtown,* ☎ *800/262–0695,* WEB *www. tnaqua.org.* 🎟 *$7.25; $16.25 for joint ticket with Tennessee Aquarium.* ☉ *Sun.–Thurs. 11–6, Fri.–Sat. 11–9.*

➏➋ **Walnut Street Bridge.** The Tennessee Riverwalk promenade connects Ross's Landing Park and Plaza to the Walnut Street Bridge, the longest pedestrian bridge in the world. Built in 1891 and listed in the National Register of Historic Places, this 2,370-ft truss bridge spans the Tennessee River and has lovely views of the city and surrounding mountains. The bridge is popular for strolling and also as a site for special events and festivals.

Greater Chattanooga

Numbers in the text correspond to numbers in the margin and on the Chattanooga map.

Beyond downtown are a number of the area's longtime attractions, including some musts for Civil War buffs.

A Good Drive

A number of Chattanooga's attractions are clustered near **Lookout Mountain,** where most of the terrain isn't ideal for walking. Drive instead, taking Broad Street from downtown to **Ruby Falls** ㉔. From there, it's a short hop to the **Incline Railway** and **Point Park,** which is close to the **Battles for Chattanooga Museum** ㉕. Cross the Tennessee state line into Georgia for some old-fashioned fun at **Rock City Gardens** ㉖ and a history lesson at **Chickamauga and Chattanooga National Military Park** ㉗.

TIMING

A good day of sightseeing could be devoted to Lookout Mountain, whether your focus is family fun in places such as Rock City and Ruby Falls or historical highlights such as Chickamauga/Chattanooga National Military Park.

Sights to See

㉕ **Battles for Chattanooga Museum.** Music, narration, and lights on an electric-map rendering of critical battles help you visualize key events in Chattanooga's Civil War history. There are also small displays of war artifacts and a good bookstore. The museum is near the entrance to **Point Park** on Lookout Mountain. ⊠ *1110 E. Brow Rd., Lookout Mountain Fort Oglethorpe,* ☎ *423/821–2812,* WEB *www. battlesforchattanooga.com.* ⊡ *$5.95.* ⊙ *June–Labor Day, daily 9:30– 6; Labor Day–May, daily 10–5.*

★ ㉗ **Chickamauga and Chattanooga National Military Park.** The 1863 battles for Chattanooga were some of the most violent ever fought—and they were a major turning point in the Civil War. The Union hoped to gain control of the area and the city, a rail center and a gateway to the Confederacy, but was defeated at nearby Chickamauga by General Bragg. Southern troops surrounded Union ones in Chattanooga before generals Thomas and Grant launched assaults that led to Union control of most of the state. In 1864, General Sherman started from Chattanooga on his march to Atlanta and the sea. At this battlefield, apart from taking advantage of hiking and driving trails past monuments and acres of scenic beauty, you can explore a gun museum, check the bookstore, and watch a multimedia presentation about the battles. ⊠ *U.S. 27, Fort Oglethorpe, GA,* ☎ *706/866–9241,* WEB *www.nps.gov.* ⊡ *Free; $4 for movie.* ⊙ *Daily 8–4:45.*

OFF THE
BEATEN PATH

DAYTON – A 36-mi drive north along U.S. 27 from Chattanooga, this small town was the site of the famous Scopes "Monkey Trial" in 1925. The room where the trial took place has been preserved at the **Rhea County Courthouse.** A small museum has displays about the trial. ⊠ *1475 Market St.,* ☎ *423/775–7801.* ⊡ *Free.* ⊙ *Mon.–Fri. 8–4:30.*

Incline Railway. The steepest passenger railway in the world, at a grade of 72.7 degrees, the Incline Railway seems to defy gravity as its tracks cut a swath straight up Lookout Mountain. The view is spectacular.

✉ *827 E. Brow Rd., Lookout Mountain,* ☎ *423/821–4224,* WEB *http://ngeorgia.com.* ❐ *$9.* ☉ *Labor Day–Memorial Day, daily 8:30 AM–9 PM; trains run every 15–20 mins.*

★ **Lookout Mountain.** Chattanooga's poshest homes sit atop Lookout Mountain, which extends into Georgia. Plan to visit Point Park and Rock City Gardens. Though Lookout Mountain can be reached by car, the Incline Railway is a thrilling alternative.

Point Park. Part of Chickamauga/Chattanooga National Military Park, this breezy, wooded promontory atop Lookout Mountain has sweeping views of the outlying region. Markers remind you of the Union soldiers who scrambled up the craggy mountainside in a mad effort to escape the relentless showers of Confederate bullets during the 1863 "Battle Above the Clouds," part of the eventual Union victory. A visitor center has information; from June through August, rangers give tours and talks on the site. ✉ *E. Brow Rd.,* ☎ *423/821–7786,* WEB *http://ngeorgia.com.* ❐ *$3.* ☉ *Visitor center daily 8–4:45.*

Reflection Riding. You can drive or walk through this lovely botanical garden near Lookout Mountain. Native American and Civil War history are part of the landscape, too. ✉ *400 Garden Rd.,* ☎ *423/821–9582,* WEB *www.chattanooga.net.* ❐ *$6 per car.* ☉ *Mon.–Sat. 9–5, Sun. 1–5.*

②⑞ **Rock City Gardens.** At one time more than 900 barns throughout the Southeast were emblazoned with the words SEE ROCK CITY. Only a few remain, but visitors still come here for such simple pleasures as walking a swinging bridge. This craggy tribute to fairy tales and geology, just over the state line in Georgia, began in 1932 as a network of paths through rock formations with such names as Fat Man's Squeeze. The project grew, as exhibits depicting the tales of Mother Goose and Little Red Riding Hood were added. Walt Disney even consulted with Rock City's founders before designing his own magical kingdom. The garden's position atop Lookout Mountain provides views for hundreds of miles (a sign shows directions to seven states). Winter holiday displays of lights are popular. ✉ *1400 Patten Rd., Lookout Mountain, GA,* ☎ *706/820–2531,* WEB *www.seerockcity.com.* ❐ *$11.95.* ☉ *Summer, daily 8:30–8; fall–spring, daily 8:30–5.*

②⑜ **Ruby Falls.** There are two elements here: aboveground are a restaurant, souvenir shops, lookout tower, and children's playground, all contained within one castlelike structure. Inside, an elevator whisks groups of visitors several hundred feet below to a natural cave. A ½-mi path leads past formations such as stalagmites and stalactites to the deepest and highest underground waterfall (145 ft) in America. ✉ *1720 Lookout Mountain Scenic Hwy.,* ☎ *423/821–2544,* WEB *www.rubyfalls. com.* ❐ *$11.50.* ☉ *Memorial Day–Labor Day, daily 8 AM–9 PM; Sept.–Oct. and Apr.–May, daily 8–8; Nov.–Mar., daily 8–6.*

⎈ **Tennessee Valley Railroad.** Ride the rails of the largest historic railroad still operating in the South aboard a steam locomotive or diesel trains dating from World War II. There's also a train museum on the premises. ✉ *4119 Cromwell Rd.,* ☎ *423/894–8028,* WEB *www.tvrail.com.* ❐ *$11.50.* ☉ *May–Labor Day, Mon.–Sat. 10–5, Sun. noon–5; Apr. and Sept.–Nov., Sat. 10–5.*

Dining

$$–$$$ ✕ **Southside Grill.** This handsome downtown restaurant in a former meatpacking plant reinterprets the food of the region with a gourmet touch. Hardwood floors offset the dark paneled walls, which are hung with fine art. Smoked salmon on a crispy grits cake and grilled rib eye with crawfish cakes and chilled leek soup are just two possible choices on the seasonally changing menu. ⊠ *1400 Cowart St., Downtown,* ☎ *423/266–9211,* WEB *www.southsidegrill.com. AE, D, MC, V.*

$$ ✕ **212 Market.** This restaurant near the Tennessee Aquarium serves
★   New American cuisine, with an emphasis on healthful fare. Try the grilled salmon, or the Taylor River enchilada with fresh spinach, black beans, cheeses, and salsa. The cavernous, contemporary dining room is bright and unpretentious. ⊠ *212 Market St., Downtown,* ☎ *423/265–1212,* WEB *www.212market.com. AE, D, DC, MC, V.*

$–$$ ✕ **Big River Grille & Brewing Works.** You can watch the brewing process through a soaring glass wall beside the bar of this restored trolley warehouse, handsomely designed with high ceilings, exposed brick walls, and hardwood floors. Order the sampler for a taste of this microbrewery's four different concoctions. The sandwiches and salads are generous and tasty. ⊠ *222 Broad St., Downtown,* ☎ *423/267–2739. Reservations not accepted. AE, D, DC, MC, V.*

$–$$ ✕ **Town & Country.** This Chattanooga fixture, which has offered great food and service for 40 years, is across the bridge from the aquarium. The menu combines Southern cuisine with beef, chicken, prime rib, and seafood entrées. The setting is casual and prices are reasonable. *110 N. Market St., North Shore,* ☎ *423/267–8544. AE, D, DC, MC, V.*

Lodging

$$–$$$$ ⊞ **Bluff View Inn.** Painstakingly restored and tastefully decorated with
★   18th-century English antiques and art, this colonial revival mansion was built in 1928 on a bluff overlooking the river. The River Gallery Sculpture Garden is beside the inn, near the Riverwalk, and the Tennessee Aquarium is within walking distance. There are also rooms in two other early 20th-century mansions; a complimentary breakfast is made to order. The inn is part of the Bluff View Art District area of shops and restaurants. ⊠ *412 E. 2nd St., 37403,* ☎ *423/265–5033 or 800/725–8338,* FAX *423/265–5944,* WEB *www.tennessee-inns.com. 13 rooms, 3 suites. 3 restaurants, café. D, MC, V.*

$$$ ⊞ **Chattanooga Choo-Choo Holiday Inn.** This hotel incorporates the landmark 1905 Southern Railway terminal, one of the first to be salvaged in the South. It's been renewed with restaurants, lounges, shops, exhibits, well-groomed gardens, and an operating trolley on 30 acres. Trains are parked on the tracks. Besides standard rooms in three buildings, the hotel has Victorian parlor cars—replete with the brocade and red upholstery of the period—converted to overnight berths. ⊠ *1400 Market St., 37402,* ☎ *423/266–5000 or 800/872–2529,* FAX *423/265–4635,* WEB *www. choochoo.com. 303 rooms, 10 suites, 48 railcars. 5 restaurants, 3 tennis courts, 2 pools, 1 indoor pool, hot tub, lounge. AE, D, DC, MC, V.*

$$–$$$ ⊞ **Chattanooga Clarion Hotel.** The Clarion has a convenient downtown location only two blocks from the Tennessee Aquarium and other downtown attractions. Popular among business travelers, the simply furnished rooms have coffeemakers and irons and ironing boards. ⊠ *407 Chestnut St.,,* ☎ *423/756–5150 or 800/252–7466,* FAX *423/265–8708,* WEB *www.chattanoogaclarion.com. 203 rooms, 2 suites. 2 restaurants, data ports, pool, gym. AE, D, DC, MC, V.*

$$–$$$ ⊞ **Marriott at the Convention Center.** This 16-floor downtown convention hotel is the town's largest. Rooms are spacious, and those on the higher floors have a great view of either the Tennessee River or Lookout Mountain. Adjacent to the city's convention center, this hotel is the choice of many business travelers, but families will appreciate its health club. ⊠ *2 Carter Plaza, 37402,* ☎ *423/756–0002 or 800/841–1674,* FAX *423/266–2254,* WEB *www.marriotthotels.com. 342 rooms, 2*

suites. 2 restaurants, 1 outdoor pool, 1 indoor pool, health club, lounge, laundry service. AE, D, DC, MC, V.

$$–$$$ 🏨 **Read House Hotel & Suites** The Georgian-style Read House dates from the 1920s and has been restored to the original grandeur that drew heads of state to lodge here in its heyday. The lobby has a large archway, stately columns, and polished walnut panels. Mailboxes from the days when guests stayed for months still neatly line one passageway. Guest rooms in the main hotel continue the Georgian motif; rooms in the annex are more contemporary. ⊠ *827 Broad St., 37402,* ☎ *423/266–4121 or 800/333–3333,* FAX *423/267–6447,* WEB *www.readhouse.com. 140 rooms, 100 suites. Restaurant, coffee shop, dining room, pool, hot tub, sauna, lounge. AE, DC, MC, V.*

$–$$ 🏨 **Days Inn Rivergate.** A half block from the Chattanooga Trade and Convention Center, this hotel is very convenient to downtown. Rooms are the chain's standard fare. ⊠ *901 Carter St., 37402,* ☎ *423/266–7331 or 800/329–7466,* FAX *423/266–9457,* WEB *www.daysinn.com. 140 rooms. Pool, meeting rooms. AE, D, DC, MC, V.*

$ 🏨 **Econo Lodge East Ridge.** Rooms here are spacious with contemporary furnishings. ⊠ *1417 St. Thomas St., 37412,* ☎ *423/894–1417 or 800/446–6900,* FAX *423/242–1257,* WEB *www.econolodge.com. 89 rooms. Pool. AE, D, DC, MC, V.*

Nightlife and the Arts

The Arts

The **Memorial Auditorium** (⊠ 399 McCallie Ave., Downtown, ☎ 423/757–5042) is a venue for concerts and operas. Throughout the summer free concerts from blues to Celtic play on **Miller Plaza** (⊠ 850 Market St., Downtown, ☎ 423/265–0771). The **Chattanooga Theatre Center** (⊠ 400 River St., North Chattanooga, ☎ 423/267–8534) stages 20 productions a year.

A city highlight, the mid-June **Riverbend Festival** (☎ 423/265–4112, 🎫 $30 at the gate, $23 at the outlet stores) brings live rock, country, blues, jazz, and folk music to five stages over nine days and nights. The single admission is good for all the 100 or so acts.

Nightlife

The **Southside Jazz Junction and Tapas Restaurant** (⊠ 114 W. Main St., Downtown, ☎ 423/267–9003) tempts both the ear and the taste buds with live jazz performances Wednesday through Saturday along with delectable hors d'oeuvres, part of a full menu. Every Friday night between 8 and 11, the free **Mountain Opry** (⊠ Walden Ridge Civic Center, Fairmount Rd., Chattanooga) showcases traditional bluegrass and mountain music.

Outdoor Activities and Sports

Canoeing and Rafting

The Ocoee River site of international kayaking competitions has powerful Class III and IV rapids. **Outdoor Adventure Rafting** (☎ 800/627–7636) can take you for a ride on the Ocoee. The Sequatchie River, gentler than the Ocoee, is suitable for year-round floating; try **Canoe the Sequatchie** (☎ 423/949–4400), April through October, for equipment. **Hiwassee Outfitters** (☎ 423/338–8115), in Reliance, open from mid-March to early November, has kayaks and rafts for beginners and intermediates; the nearby Hiwassee has occasional rapids.

Golf

Six miles south of the city in Georgia, the 18-hole, par-72 **Windstone Golf Club** (⊠ 9230 Windstone Dr., Ringgold, ☎ 423/894–1231) is one of the area's best courses. It's a daily fee course within the private Windstone community.

Hang Gliding

At **Lookout Mountain Flight Park and Training Center** (✉ 7201 Scenic Hwy., Rising Fawn, GA, ☎ 706/398–3541 or 800/688–5637, WEB www.hanglide.com), you can soar solo or tandem (with an instructor); lessons and packages are available.

Shopping

Hamilton Place (✉ 2100 Hamilton Place Blvd., North Chattanooga, ☎ 423/894–7177) is one of Tennessee's largest malls, with five department stores, more than 200 other stores, 30 eateries, and 17 theaters. An outlet center, **Warehouse Row** (✉ 12th and Market Sts., Downtown, ☎ 423/267–1111) yields some of the region's best (and most chic) buys. More than 30 upscale shops—such as Tommy Hilfiger, Polo/Ralph Lauren, Coach, and Corbin—are in several attractive, restored redbrick railroad warehouses downtown.

River Gallery (✉ 400 E. 2nd St., ☎ 423/267–7353), in the Bluff View Art District, carries lovely crafts, from pottery to wood and metal pieces, as well as paintings and sculpture.

Chattanooga A to Z

AIR TRAVEL
Chattanooga is served by ASA, ComAir, Delta, Northwest Airlink, United Express, and US Airways.

AIRPORTS
Chattanooga Metropolitan Airport is 8 mi east of downtown.
➤ AIRPORT INFORMATION: **Chattanooga Metropolitan Airport** (✉ 1001 Airport Rd., ☎ 423/855–2200, WEB www.chattairport.com).

BUS TRAVEL TO AND FROM CHATTANOOGA
➤ BUS INFORMATION: **Greyhound** (✉ 960 Airport Road, ☎ 423/892–1277 or 800/231–2222, WEB www.greyhound.com).

CAR TRAVEL
I–75 runs north–south from Kentucky through Chattanooga and on to Georgia. U.S. 11 joins Chattanooga with Knoxville.

EMERGENCIES
Medical assistance is available at Erlanger Medical Center. The pharmacy at Eckerd is open Monday–Saturday, 8 AM–10 PM, and Sunday noon–10.
➤ CONTACTS: **Ambulance, police** (☎ 911). **Eckerd** (✉ 3569 Brainerd Rd., Downtown, ☎ 423/629–7323). **Erlanger Health System** (✉ 975 E. 3rd St., Downtown, ☎ 423/778–7000, WEB www.erlanger.org).

MEDIA
RADIO
AM: WGOW 1050, news and talk.

FM: WGOW 102.3, news and talk; WOGT 107.9, oldies.

TRANSPORTATION AROUND CHATTANOOGA
Carta, a free downtown shuttle on electric buses, runs between the Chattanooga Choo-Choo Hotel and the Tennessee Aquarium.
➤ CONTACTS: **Carta** (☎ 423/629–1473, WEB www.carta-bus.org).

VISITOR INFORMATION

The visitor center at the Chattanooga Area Convention and Visitors Bureau is open daily 8:30–5:30.

➤ TOURIST INFORMATION: **Chattanooga Area Convention and Visitors Bureau** (✉ 2 Broad St., 37402, ☎ 423/756–8687 or 800/322–3344, WEB www.chattanooga.net/cvb/).

TENNESSEE A TO Z

To research prices, get advice from other travelers, and book travel arrangements, visit www.fodors.com.

AIRPORTS

For information about flying to and from Tennessee, please see city and regional A to Z sections.

BUS TRAVEL

Greyhound links most cities in Tennessee.

➤ BUS INFORMATION: **Greyhound** (☎ 800/231–2222, WEB www.greyhound.com).

CAR TRAVEL

The state's main east–west artery is I–40. I–55 runs north–south in West Tennessee. In Middle Tennessee, I–65 and I–24 cross in Nashville. I–75 links Chattanooga to Knoxville in East Tennessee. I–81 runs from just east of Knoxville through upper East Tennessee.

RULES OF THE ROAD

The speed limit on interstate highways ranges from 65 to 70 mph, as indicated, unless otherwise posted. Right turns on red lights are allowed unless a sign indicates otherwise. Scenic highways within Tennessee are marked by a mockingbird sign above the sign giving the route number.

EMERGENCIES

In towns and cities, dial 911 for police or ambulance. Cellular calls to the Highway Patrol are free by dialing *THP (*847).

➤ CONTACTS: **Ambulance, police** (☎ 911).

LODGING

BED AND BREAKFASTS

➤ RESERVATION SERVICES: **Tennessee Bed & Breakfast Innkeepers' Association** (✉ Box 120428, Nashville 37212, ☎ 800/820–8144, WEB www.tennessee-inns.com).

VISITOR INFORMATION

To request brochures, call the toll-free number listed below. For other information, contact the Tennessee Department of Tourist Development.

➤ TOURIST INFORMATION: **Tennessee Travel Guide** (☎ 800/836–6200). **Tennessee Department of Tourist Development** (✉ 320 6th Ave. N, 5th floor, Nashville 37243, ☎ 615/741–2159, WEB www.state.tn.us/tourdev).

INDEX

Icons and Symbols

★ Our special recommendations

✕ Restaurant

🏠 Lodging establishment

✕🏠 Lodging establishment whose restaurant warrants a special trip

🦆 Good for kids (rubber duck)

☞ Sends you to another section of the guide for more information

✉ Address

☎ Telephone number

🕐 Opening and closing times

💷 Admission prices

Numbers in white and black circles ③ ❸ that appear on the maps, in the margins, and within the tours correspond to one another.

A

A. Schwab Dry Goods Store, 482
Aaron Douglas Gallery, 507
Abbeville, LA, 233–234
Abbeville, SC, 466–467
Abbeville County Museum, 466–467
Abbeville Main Street Program Office, 233
Abbeville Opera House, 467
Aberdeen, NC, 340–341
Abraham Lincoln Library and Museum, 526
Academy of the Sacred Heart, 238
Acadian Cultural Center, 231
Acadian Museum, 233
Acadian Village, 231
Acadiana Park Nature Station, 231
Ackland Art Museum, 333
African-American Trail, 10
African American Panoramic Experience (APEX), 78
Afro-American Cultural Center, 302
Aiken, SC, 464–465
Aiken County Historical Museum, 464
Aiken-Rhett House, 397
Aiken Thoroughbred Hall of Fame, 464
Air Travel, x–xii
Airborne and Special Operations Museum, 340

Airliewood (historic house), 279
Airports, xii
Alabama, 4–5, 12–62
Alabama Constitution Village, 28
Alabama Department of Archives and History, 39
Alabama Jazz Hall of Fame, 19
Alabama Museum, 33
Alabama Music Hall of Fame and Museum, 30
Alabama *Princess* (riverboat), 33
Alabama Sports Hall of Fame Museum, 17
Alabama Writers' Symposium, 46
Alex Haley House Museum, 500
Alligator Adventure, 428
Alligator Bayou, 218
American Classic Tea Plantation, 407
American Military Museum, 397
American Museum of Science and Energy, 522
American Rose Center, 243–244
Americus, GA, 167–168
Amicalola Falls, 158
Andersonville National Historic Site, 167
Andrew Jackson Center, 509
Andrew Johnson National Historic Site, 528
Andrew Low House, 115
Angel Oak, 407
Angela Peterson Doll and Miniature Museum, 318
Apothecary Shop and Doctor's Office, 358
Appalachian Cultural Museum, 382
Aquarium of the Americas, 186
Ark-La-Tex Antique and Classic Vehicle Museum, 243
Arlington Antebellum Home and Gardens, 19
Armstrong House, 120
Armstrong-Lockett House, 524
Arrowmont School of Arts and Crafts, 530
Arts and crafts in the North Carolina mountains, 376
ArtQuest (gallery), 311
ArtsCenter (gallery), 333
Artspace (studios), 321
Asheboro, NC, 341
Asheville, NC, 371–375, 378

Atlanta Botanical Garden, 80
Atlanta Cyclorama & Civil War Museum, 72
Atlanta Daily World Building, 78
Atlanta Fulton Public Library, 72, 78
Atlanta History Center, 84
Atlanta International Museum of Art and Design, 72
Atlanta Journal-Constitution, 72–73
Atlanta Life Insurance Company, 75, 78
Atlanta Market Center, 75
Atlanta Marriott Marquis, 75
ATMs, xxvii
Auburn Avenue Research Library on African-American Culture and History, 78
Audubon Park and Zoo, 188
Audubon-Newhall Preserve, 442
Audubon State Commemorative Area, 221
Audubon Swamp Garden, 406
Augusta, GA, 148, 154–155
Ava Gardner Museum, 323
Ave Maria Grotto, 26
Avery Island, LA, 229
Avery Research Center for African-American History and Culture, 398

B

Bacchanalia (Atlanta, GA) ✕, 7
Bank of America Building, 73
Bank of America Corporate Center, 301
Bank of America Plaza Tower, 80
Banner Elk, NC, 384
Baptist Student Center, 78
The Battery, 402
Battles for Chattanooga Museum, 537
Battleship Memorial Park, 51
Bayou Folk Museum, 242
Bayou Teche, 227, 229
Beach Institute African-American Cultural Center, 115
Beale Street (Memphis, TN), 9, 496
Beau Fort Plantation, 241–242
Beaufort, NC, 358
Beaufort, SC, 448–449, 451–452
Beaufort Historical Site, 358
Beaufort Museum, 448